Law Among Nations

GERHARD VON GLAHN

Professor of Political Science, University of Minnesota–Duluth

LAW
Among Nations

AN INTRODUCTION TO

Public International Law

SECOND EDITION

THE MACMILLAN COMPANY

COLLIER-MACMILLAN LIMITED · LONDON

Library of Congress catalog card number: 79-93184

THE MACMILLAN COMPANY
866 THIRD AVENUE, NEW YORK, NEW YORK 10022
COLLIER-MACMILLAN CANADA, LTD., TORONTO, ONTARIO

Printed in the United States of America

TO
Dorothy, Peter, and *Karen*

PREFACE TO SECOND EDITION

THE second edition has been brought up to date with regard to both events and cases. Internal rearrangements have resulted in the amalgamation of several previous chapters in order to bring together related materials. A new chapter on the individual, to the extent that he may be viewed as a subject of the law, has been added in order to include recent developments in the sphere of human rights. Although some peripheral material in connection with the settlement of disputes and with neutrality has been eliminated, the coverage of the sanctions of international law has been expanded, in response to the request of several readers; the Suggested Readings have also been expanded in several chapters.

In preparing this new edition I have benefited greatly from numerous valuable suggestions of colleagues (particularly members of the Department of Law, U.S. Air Force Academy) and students. Their advice and help is gratefully acknowledged.

GERHARD VON GLAHN

Duluth, Minnesota

PREFACE TO FIRST EDITION

TRADITIONAL texts in international law have fallen into one of three basic categories: (1) commentaries, heavily weighted with historical background material, (2) casebooks, and (3) combinations of cases and extensive editorial notes.

The writer has long felt a need for a text adapted specifically for the typical undergraduate course in international law: an upper-level offering commonly limited to one semester or two quarters in length. He believes that the bulk of the students enrolled in such a course do not intend to enter law schools, government service, or the employment of an international agency after the completion of undergraduate training. Such students may be assumed to take a course in international law because it forms a part of the required curriculum for majors in political science or because of their personal interest in a rather fascinating and timely subject.

If the foregoing assumptions are correct, then available texts, regardless of excellence, do not really satisfy the needs of the student clientele, for those texts are, on the whole, too extensive in their treatment of the subject considering the time available in the typical course. They also require, in the instance of commentaries, a casebook to accompany the text. Such collections are, again, extremely comprehensive in scope, expensive, and appear to be designed primarily for use in law schools or on the graduate level of instruction.

These considerations led to the writing of a relatively brief text on international law, using the traditional approach to the subject but incorporating in the actual text, whenever called for as illustrative materials, abstracts of classic and modern cases. The volume thus obviates the use of a casebook and stands as a self-contained unit. Admittedly, an obvious disadvantage of this unique feature is that students miss the complete wording of the judges in some of the great classic cases. Nothing would prevent the instructor, on the other hand, from assigning selected cases as outside reading and for practice in briefing. Most of the chapters are followed by lists of suggested readings in order to make possible the adaptation of the text for use in a course running for a full academic year.

In view of the notorious inability of undergraduates to read foreign languages with any degree of fluency, the references in both footnotes and suggested readings have been deliberately restricted to sources in the English language. This has meant the sacrifice of a very large number of valuable contributions to international law by foreign scholars but has resulted in references usable by students. The omission of this portion of the scholarly "apparatus" has also kept the volume within manageable limits. Most references have been restricted intentionally to sources likely to be found in the library of a college offering courses in international law; if lacking, they could be added at modest cost. The inclusion of numerous references to legal journals was prompted by the fact that the legal profession has created central reference libraries in many urban centers; such facilities may be available to students by special arrangement.

The inclusion or omission of subject matter is the responsibility of the writer. Dictated by his own experience in teaching international law courses, the selection of topics and the extent of their coverage also reflect his views as to the importance of each of them. Thus, since the text is intended to present a realistic picture of what the law is and not what it ought to be, relatively extensive treatment has been accorded the law of war.

The use of force has not been eliminated from the world scene and when states or international agencies have recourse to force, the rules of the law designed for such purposes still find application. Despite the eloquence of the writings of many men of good will, methods for the peaceful settlement of international disputes have been, and are likely to be, abandoned in favor of war. Neutrality, pronounced dead on many occasions by learned jurists, has shown a perhaps not too surprising ability to survive in the practice of nations. And assertions of the present or rapidly approaching existence of a world law must as yet be regarded as utopian.

It may well be that at some future time men will utilize their reason more fully and bring into being a peaceful world under the rule of law. For the time being, however, realism dictates the regrettable assumption that the scourge of war is with us and will be so for a long time. Hence the rules governing the use of force must be studied by the generations which will be affected most profoundly by recourse to forcible settlements of disputes. Condensation of the law of war and neutrality into a chapter, or total omission of such disagreeable topics, would be an inexcusable and unrealistic approach to the totality of international law.

The title of this volume has been chosen with care: the principles and rules embodied in what is termed international law represent, not law above nations or supranational law, but rather law *among* nations, *jus inter gentes*. Jurists may smile at such a concept since to them law must stand above its subjects. This is not true, however, in the case of general international law which at present is only a weak and developing form of law. It applies to a relatively unorganized community and lacks specialized agencies dedicated to its enforcement. Nevertheless it represents the best that a chaotic community composed of sovereign states has been able to evolve to date. And whenever the often elaborate particular law of such international agencies as the United Nations fails to be applied to relations among states, recourse is had to the general law based on custom and on general law-making treaties in order to regulate such relations.

GERHARD VON GLAHN

Duluth

CONTENTS

ABBREVIATIONS   XV

I. THE LAW OF NATIONS

CHAPTER
1. The Nature of International Law   3
2. Sources of International Law   10
3. Relation Between International Law and Municipal Law   23
4. Development of Law Among Nations   34
5. Sanctions of International Law   52

II. SUBJECTS OF INTERNATIONAL LAW

6. The Community of Nations   61
7. Recognition of States and of Governments   90
8. Loss of International Personality (State Extinction; State
     Succession)   117
9. Rights and Privileges of International Persons   123
10. Duties of States   162

III. THE LAW AND THE INDIVIDUAL

11. Individuals Under the Law   187
12. Jurisdiction Over Persons   198
13. Responsibilities of States for the Protection of Resident Aliens 222
14. Extradition   250

IV. TERRITORIAL QUESTIONS

15. Title to Territory   273
16. Land Boundaries   302

CHAPTER

17. The Maritime Border   309

18. The High Seas   322

19. Jurisdiction Over Vessels   345

20. Jurisdiction Over the National Air and Outer Space   360

V. INTERNATIONAL TRANSACTIONS

21. Agents of International Intercourse   375

22. International Agreements   420

23. Peaceful Settlement of Disputes   455

24. Coercive Self-help Short of War   494

VI. WAR

25. Legal Nature of War Today   517

26. Laws of War   541

27. Modern War: Commencement, Effects, Termination   559

28. Laws of War on Land and in the Air   582

29. Laws of War at Sea   604

30. Neutrality   621

31. Belligerent Occupation   663

32. Crimes Under International Law   692

VII. CONCLUSION

33. The Present Status of International Law   723

TABLE OF CASES   729

INDEX   739

ABBREVIATIONS

Certain sources utilized frequently throughout this volume are cited in abbreviated form as follows:

BOOKS

Brierly.   J. L. Brierly. *The Law of Nations* (6th ed., by Sir Humphrey Waldock). London: Oxford University Press, 1963.

Briggs.   Herbert W. Briggs, ed. *The Law of Nations: Cases, Documents, and Notes*, 2nd ed. New York: Appleton-Century-Crofts, 1952.

Bishop.   William W. Bishop, Jr. *International Law: Cases and Materials*, 2nd ed. Boston: Little, Brown & Co., 1962.

Cheng.   Bin Cheng. *General Principles of Law as Applied by International Courts and Tribunals*. London: Stevens & Sons, Ltd., 1953.

Claude.   Inis L. Claude, Jr. *Swords into Plowshares: The Problems and Progress of International Organizations* (3rd ed., rev.). New York: Random House, 1964.

Corbett.   Percy E. Corbett. *Law and Society in the Relations of States*. New York: Harcourt, Brace & World, 1951.

Fenwick.   Charles G. Fenwick. *International Law*, 4th ed. New York: Appleton-Century-Crofts, 1965.

Gould.   Wesley L. Gould. *An Introduction to International Law*. New York: Harper & Row, 1957.

Hackworth.   Green H. Hackworth. *Digest of International Law*. (8 Vols.) Washington: U.S. Government Printing Office, 1940–1944.

Higgins-Colombos.   C. John Colombos. *The International Law of the Sea* (3rd rev. ed. of A. Pearce Higgins and C. John Colombos, *The International Law of the Sea*). London and New York: Longmans, Green & Co., 1954.

Hudson.	Manley O. Hudson. *Cases and Other Materials on International Law*, 3rd ed. St. Paul: West Publishing Co., 1951.
Hyde.	Charles Cheney Hyde. *International Law Chiefly as Interpreted and Applied by the United States*, 2nd ed. (3 Vols.) Boston: Little, Brown & Co., 1945.
Jacobini.	H. B. Jacobini. *International Law—A Text*, Rev. ed., Homewood, Ill.: Dorsey Press, 1968.
Jessup.	Philip C. Jessup. *A Modern Law of Nations: An Introduction*. New York: The Macmillan Company, 1949.
Kaplan-Katzenbach.	Morton A. Kaplan and Nicholas deB. Katzenbach. *The Political Foundations of International Law*. New York: John Wiley & Sons, 1961.
Land Warfare.	Department of the Army. *The Law of Land Warfare* (FM. 27–10). Washington, D.C.: U.S. Government Printing Office, July, 1956.
Lauterpacht's *Oppenheim*	L. F. L. Oppenheim. *International Law: A Treatise*. Vol. I, *Peace* (8th ed., by Hersch Lauterpacht). London and New York: Longmans, Green & Co., 1955; Vol. II, *Disputes, War and Neutrality* (7th ed., by Hersch Lauterpacht). London and New York: Longmans, Green & Co., 1952.
Lipsky.	George A. Lipsky, ed. *Law and Politics in the World Community*. Berkeley: University of California Press, 1953.
Manual.	Max Sørensen, ed. *Manual of Public International Law*. New York: St. Martin's Press, 1968.
Moore.	John Bassett Moore. *A Digest of International Law*. (8 vols.) Washington: U.S. Government Printing Office, 1906.
Nussbaum.	Arthur Nussbaum. *A Concise History of the Law of Nations*, rev. ed. New York: The Macmillan Company, 1954.
Plischke.	Elmer Plischke, ed. *Systems of Integrating the International Community*. Princeton, N.J.: D. Van Nostrand Co., 1964.
Reiff.	Henry Reiff. *The United States and the Treaty Law of the Sea*. Minneapolis: University of Minnesota Press, 1959.

Stone.
: Julius Stone. *Legal Controls of International Conflict: A Treatise on the Dynamics of Disputes and War-Law* (2nd impr., rev. with Supplement, 1953–1958). London: Stevens & Sons, Ltd., 1959.

Svarlien.
: Oscar Svarlien. *An Introduction to the Law of Nations.* New York: McGraw-Hill Book Co., 1955.

Tung.
: William M. Tung. *International Law in an Organizing World.* New York: Thomas Y. Crowell, 1968.

von Glahn.
: Gerhard von Glahn. *The Occupation of Enemy Territory: A Commentary on the Law and Practice of Belligerent Occupation.* Minneapolis: University of Minnesota Press, 1957.

Whiteman.
: Marjorie M. Whiteman. *Digest of International Law.* Washington: U.S. Government Printing Office, 1963–1969.

PERIODICALS, ETC.

A.J.I.L.
: *American Journal of International Law*

A.P.S.R.
: *American Political Science Review*

B.Y.I.L.
: *British Year Book of International Law*

I.C.J. Reports.
: International Court of Justice, *Reports of Judgments, Advisory Opinions and Orders* (1947–   )

P.C.I.J.
: Permanent Court of International Justice:

Ser. A
: *Judgments and Orders* (1922–1930)

Ser. B.
: *Advisory Opinions* (1922–1930)

Ser. A/B.
: *Judgments, Orders, and Advisory Opinions* (1931–1940)

Proceedings.
: *Proceedings of the American Society of International Law*

T.G.S.
: *Transactions of the Grotius Society* [London]

Tijdschrift.
: *Nederlands Tijdschrift voor Internationaal Recht*

U. S.
: *United States Reports* (Supreme Court of the United States). Cases before 1875 are cited by the name of the reporter:

Dallas (1787–1800)   Howard (1843–1860)
Cranch (1801–1815)   Black (1861–1862)
Wheaton (1816–1827)   Wallace (1863–1874)
Peters (1828–1842)

PART I
The Law of Nations

I

The Nature of International Law

DEFINITION *of International Law.* International law is a body of principles, customs, and rules that are recognized as effectively binding obligations by sovereign states and other international persons in their mutual relations.

This definition of the subject corresponds closely to the current opinion of most writers on international law but represents by no means the only acceptable definition. Few areas of knowledge have been defined as often and in as many different ways as' has international law. As Jessup has pointed out, an old and possibly apocryphal Chinese proverb is said to counsel, "One should always have in the background of one's mind a multiplicity of definitions covering the subject at hand in order to prevent oneself from accepting the most obvious." [1] In the spirit of that advice, the following definitions are offered:

The Law of Nations, or International Law, may be defined as the body of rules and principles of action which are binding upon civilized states in their relations with one another. [2]

International law consists in certain rules of conduct which modern civilized states regard as being binding on them in their relations with one another with a force comparable in nature and degree to that binding the conscientious person to obey the law of his country, and which they also regard as being enforceable by appropriate means in case of infringement. [3]

The Law of Nations is the science of the rights which exist between Nations or States, and of the obligations corresponding to these rights. [4]

International law consists of a body of rules governing the relations between states. [5]

On the other hand, the definition given by Abba Eban, then the Israeli ambassador to the United States, on Edward Murrow's television program

[1] Jessup, p. 4 (Full references to this and other works cited subsequently by author only may be found in the list of abbreviations, p. xv.

[2] Brierly, p. 1.

[3] W. E. Hall, *A Treatise on International Law*, 8th ed., A. Pearce Higgins, ed. (New York: Oxford University Press, 1924), p. 1.

[4] E. de Vattel, *Le Droit des Gens*, Charles G. Fenwick, trans. (Washington, D.C.: Government Printing Office, 1916 [1758]).

[5] Hackworth, Vol. I, p. 1. See also the extensive documented coverage in Whiteman, Vol. II, pp. 35-50.

"Person to Person" on September 20, 1957, corresponds to a widespread popular belief concerning the nature of the law: "International law is the law which the wicked do not obey and which the righteous do not enforce."

In part this difference of opinion about the very nature of the law has been caused by events or philosophies in the century in which a given definition was composed; in part it was the theory of law cherished by a given writer that dictated the nature of his definition; and, again, it may have been the relative importance placed by an author on the sources of the law that influenced the wording of his definition. Early writers, for instance, commonly emphasized natural law as the primary source of international law, which more recently custom and law-making treaties have been considered to be the more important sources of the law.

It should be realized even at this early point that the scope, and hence the subjects, of international law, created by states, are determined by those same states. The definition given in the opening paragraph may, therefore, quite possibly be changed in the future to accommodate additional categories of subjects, such as individuals. Many modern writers do, in fact, include individuals among the subjects of the law, although they usually are forced to admit that, generally speaking, practice does not yet support their theoretical contention. The variations found currently among definitions of international law can also be explained logically by the fact that the law itself is in a state of transition. It may therefore be anticipated that the somewhat conservative definition adopted for this volume may be outdated by the developments of the next few decades.[6]

THE INDIVIDUAL IN RELATION
TO INTERNATIONAL LAW

Position of the Individual. The position of individuals in relation to international law may be stated as follows: They are subjects of the law as far as their conduct is regulated *directly* by treaties or by international organizations, provided the latter themselves possess the status of international legal persons. The rules obligating individuals stipulate *individual* sanctions or punishments, whereas interstate, or international, rules of the law call for *collective* sanctions aimed at the group united in the form of a state or, possibly, at an international agency considered to be such a group unit. It is, therefore, possible to conceive of limited numbers of individuals as being true subjects of international law at the present time.

Object Status of the Individual. The idea that rules of international law

---

[6] Cf. the unusual definition of Marek St. Korowicz: "International law is the body of legal rules which govern mutual relations of sovereign States, and also the situations of other legal persons and of individuals which are not subject to the internal law of any particular State."—*Introduction to International Law* (The Hague: Martinus Nijhoff, 1959), p. 390.

can be applied directly to individuals without the intervention of their own state is not a new one at all but can be traced through the entire modern history of the law.[7] Traditionally, states and certain international organizations have been regarded as the true subjects of international law, that is, as legal "persons to whom the law attributes rights and duties directly and not through the medium of states."[8] Individuals, on the other hand, have been viewed as objects of the law.

There can be no question today that the classic limitation of true subjects of the law to sovereign states, recently expanded to include certain international persons in the form of organizations, is being challenged from a variety of directions to include also individuals. Although most of the claims to success in this endeavor have been overly optimistic and often grossly exaggerated, the fact remains that a slow movement in the direction of the inclusion of the individual as a subject of the law of nations is well under way. The consequences of this development cannot be fully perceived at this stage, and only time will show whether the move, if it succeeds measurably, will be as beneficial as its proponents claim. (See Chapter 11 for developments in transforming the individual into a subject of international law.)

DUALISM VERSUS MONISM

Views of the Dualists. Legal theorists are still sharply divided in their views as to the distinction between international law and domestic (national, municipal) law. This disagreement goes beyond mere academic speculation, because the attitudes of governments and their courts reflect in most instances the prevalent major philosophies in question. The so-called dualists hold that the two systems of law are essentially different from each other.[9] The argument in support of their contention runs somewhat as follows. In the first place, the sources of the two systems differ: domestic law is derived from customs grown up in the territory of a state and from legislative enactments deriving from the latter's lawmaking authorities; international law is derived primarily from customs grown up in a community of states and from law-making treaties concluded between independent legal persons called states. In the second place, international law regulates, basically, relations between members of that community of states, as well as between them and other international entities; whereas

---

[7] See the heavily documented study by Korowicz, "The Problem of the International Personality of Individuals," 50 *A.J.I.L.* (1956); pp. 533–562, at pp. 534–539, as well as the historical analysis by Peter P. Remec, *The Position of the Individual in International Law According to Grotius and Vattel* (The Hague: Martinus Nijhoff, 1960).

[8] Korowicz, *op. cit.* (n. 7), p. 535; see also Chapter 6.

[9] See the works of such writers as Strupp, Triepel, Anzilotti, and particularly Lauterpacht's *Oppenheim*, Vol. I, pp. 37–38.

domestic law governs relations between individuals within a given state and also between them and their government. Lastly, in the present international order among whose members we must look for the application of international law, there exists no superior central authority comparable to a national government, no authority able to secure obedience to its commands, whereas in any given state the individual citizen is subject to the police powers of his government in the enforcement of domestic law.

Views of the Monists. The opposing school of legal thought, commonly referred to as the "monists," affirms, on the other hand, that there is no real difference between international and domestic law, that they really represent two manifestations of one and the same conception of law.[10] It maintains that there exists a single legal order in which all norms (principles, rules) exist in the form of a hierarchy in which, according to such writers as Max Wenzel and Albert Lorn, domestic law occupies the higher rank. Kelsen and his major followers, on the other hand, have asserted with much vigor that international law merited the higher position and thus could be held to limit national sovereignty; that, indeed, national governments derived their lawful authority from international law. Georges Scelle must be regarded as the leading exponent of the last-mentioned, somewhat extreme, view.

The monist approach ignores the fact that normally it is the national unit, the state, which consents to the application of the rules of international law, permits such rules to apply to itself, and thus, in some degree, transfers to international law such authority as it does possess. The monist school also holds that, fundamentally, individual persons are regulated by the law, irrespective of labels. It contends that in both spheres law is basically a command binding upon its subjects regardless of their wishes. It believes that international law determines the limits of both personal and territorial jurisdiction on the part of states.

An appraisal of the ideas advanced by these two legal schools in terms of actual developments in international life and in international law would show that the clear-cut separation posited by the dualist approach does not conform completely to actual experience. On the other hand, that same experience would appear to this writer to confound monist claims as stated up to now. It can be said that international law does set limits to the power exercised by a state, but that power cannot be held to be a delegation of international law. States are, in practice, quite opposed to an acceptance of the idea that their authority was conceded to them by some outside agency or legal order. It would be very difficult to prove that any such concession or delegation had been effected in actuality when the states of the world themselves are the creators of the rules of international

---

[10] See the writings of von Verdross, Kunz, Scelle, Wright, and Hans Kelsen. For one of the most concise explanations of Kelsen's key concepts, see Leo Gross, "States as Organs of International Law and the Problem of Autointerpretation," in Lipsky, pp. 59ff.

law. That law cannot regulate any part of national activity until and unless domestic law, that is to say, the national sovereignties, have yielded that particular area or sphere of activity to regulation by international law.

The whole argument points up a basic weakness in the monist view: it neglects to consider the fact that in international law the consent of the units subject to that law is required before the law can be applied to them. True, the "consent of the governed" forms a part of the theory of democracy and is expressed in practice in most instances through representation and not through direct and personal assent. The international body of law, however, requires effective, personal, and provable consent of the affected international entity through any of a considerable variety of procedures. An American citizen is bound by an Amendment to his Constitution, enacted by Congress and ratified by state legislatures or state constitutional conventions, even though he, as an individual, might be bitterly opposed to the provisions of the Amendment. A state is bound only by such rules of international law as it accepts, barring certain exceptions to be noted later.

A reasonable interpretation of the entire issue would appear to be that international law is derived from domestic law through the openly or tacitly expressed will of the states recognizing the obligatory character of a rule of international law.

Is international law really law? An answer to that question depends on one's definition. If one contends, as did the English writer John Austin in the nineteenth century, that there must exist not only adequate and well-defined rules but also fully developed institutions and, above all, an "enforcer" of sanctions or punishments, then international law is not law proper. The correct view, however, is that international law should be regarded as true but imperfect law. The institutional apparatus for its development as well as for its enforcement are inadequate and incomplete as yet.

The validity of the accepted rules of international law is not affected, of course, by the absence of universally shared standards and values in a heterogeneous congeries of sovereign states nor by the limitation on the scope of that law imposed by the unwillingness of those same states to subordinate their vital interests to an international legal order. The danger exists, quite obviously, that the present trend toward the creation of regional (or particular) law may continue until all legal rules governing the actions of states across the borders of the various systems will have disappeared. Such an atomistic division of the law, however, is not anticipated even by the most critical analysts of the international situation. Within the preceding limits, there *exists* a community of nations whose international relations in nonvital spheres are subject to the application of principles and rules which are accepted as obligatory by the states out of whose needs the law grew through custom and treaty.

It is true, on the other hand, that although dependence on legal settlement of many controversies continues among Western states, such legal basis for the resolution of disagreements between the nations of the Communist portion of the world as well as between the new Asian and African nations, on the one hand, and the Western states, on the other, is, to some extent at least, lacking. A degree of regionalism rather than universalism may possibly be the order of the day for the time being.

This conclusion is founded not only on a suspected fear of losing a case but even more on a belief voiced on occasion by African and Asian commentators of standing: that large portions of the "universal" rules of international law are foreign to their own non-European culture, tradition, or legal system. They assert that such rules and principles are based, in essence, on Western legal thought and political history and are thereby tainted with Christian, imperialistic, capitalistic, exploitive aspects. They maintain that such rules can at best form part of a general customary Western law but not of universal international law, hence should not be regarded as binding the new African and Asian states.

The justification of such beliefs is the argument that any system of law, domestic or international, must derive its validity from consensus, and that no law will prevail over the *mores*, customs, and beliefs of a people or of a group of peoples. Without such consensus, the approval of the law will be lacking: the rule may be "on the books" but will remain a dead letter.

The views outlined above are not shared by all observers, of course. Thus the distinguished British jurist C. Wilfred Jenks insisted with great vigor that the non-Western legal systems afford sufficient common ground with the Western system to "give us elements of an effective universal system of international law." [11] To assert, however, that all rules of general customary international law must possess automatic applicability (the traditional view) or do possess such applicability may be conducive to more harm than good. It obscures rather than reveals the existence of diverse legal systems and distracts attention from the urgent need to locate divisive issues and to find possible methods for their resolution.

The contemporary applicability of the rules of international law might be viewed realistically as divided into two related and partially overlapping spheres: certain rules have been accepted generally or universally and represent general law in effect on a worldwide scale; other rules have been accepted and are applied only within given groups of states (Jessup called these "selective communities"), that is, they represent particular law, adopted by some grouping of nations linked by a common philosophy of law as applied to their mutual relations.

[11] C. W. Jenks, *The Common Law of Mankind* (New York: Praeger, 1958), p. 169; see also the excellent analyses of the problem by R. P. Anand, "Rôle of the 'New' Asian-African Countries in the Present International Legal Order," 56 *A.J.I.L.* (1962), pp. 383–406, and by J. J. G. Syatauw, *Some Newly Established Asian States and the Development of International Law* (The Hague: Martinus Nijhoff, 1961).

If we proceed under the assumption that there exists a world community of limited scope, then an analysis of its composition is essential to an understanding of the valid rules of international law and to the discovery of which aspects of international relations are capable of being placed under a rule of law and which are not. The members of the community represent the group which created international law and which delimited the domain within which the members were willing to settle disputes through legal procedures. Unless a state is somehow forced into agreeing to settle questions of major interest on a legal basis, it will restrict as much as possible the number and scope of the problems subject to legal adjustment. It has been asserted that there are no conceivable international problems that could not be handled on a legal basis if the members of the community wished to do so. But because most of these members attempt to draw a relatively sharp distinction between "legal" and "political" (nonjusticiable) problems, the latter ones being normally regarded as the more fundamental problems, the rules of the law apply only to legal questions and the rest will be settled by diplomacy, by war, and sometimes by time.

SUGGESTED READINGS

NATURE OF THE LAW IN GENERAL

Brierly, pp. 1–7, 41–49; Gould, pp. 1–30; Kaplan-Katzenbach, pp. 19–29; Lauterpacht's *Oppenheim*, Vol. I, pp. 15–23.

THE INDIVIDUAL AND INTERNATIONAL LAW

Bishop, pp. 270–283; George Manner, "The Object Theory of the Individual in International Law," 46 *A.J.I.L.* (1952), pp. 428–449.

2

Sources of International Law

A COMMON difficulty experienced by both students and judges has been the determination or location of the specific rule of international law that would apply to a given dispute between two countries. If a law code were found on an international scale, the problem would at most be minimal: a clear-cut listing of all existing rules, exceptions to rules, and variations in national interpretations would enable an inquirer to locate with relative ease the relevant article or paragraph applicable to the case at hand. Unfortunately no such code exists as yet, despite numerous private attempts, often of great value, to compile codes of law on specific subjects within the general sphere and despite the commendable efforts, frequently crowned with success, of the International Law Commission of the United Nations.

How, then, are the rules of international law determined or, more to the point at this stage of the coverage of the subject, what are the sources of international law rules and principles? General agreement appears to have been reached, and has been embodied clearly in Article 38 of the Statute of the International Court of Justice, that there are three major sources of international law, as well as two subsidiary means for the determination of the rules of that law. It is to these sources and to these means that one has to turn to verify the existence and the meaning of the rules of the law of nations.

MEANS FOR DETERMINING RULES OF LAW

Article 38 of the Statute directs the International Court of Justice to apply: (1) international conventions, whether general or particular, establishing rules expressly recognized by the contesting states; (2) international custom, as evidence of a general practice accepted as law; (3) the general principles of law recognized by civilized nations; and (4) subject to the provisions of Article 59, judicial decisions and the teachings of the most highly qualified publicists (writers) of various nations as subsidiary means for the determination of rules of law. These sources need to be examined as to their nature and characteristics.

INTERNATIONAL TREATIES

In contrast to commentaries of a hundred years ago, *treaties* are now generally accepted as a major (and by some as *the* major) source of international law. One must beware, however, of taking such a statement too literally. Obviously the bulk of the thousands of treaties concluded among nations does not create one single general rule of international law. A commercial treaty between Guatemala and France, a military alliance between the Soviet Union and Bulgaria, an extradition or consular treaty between the United States and Ceylon cannot create any rule of conduct for the community of nations. At best such instruments are declaratory of existing rules.

Law-making Treaty. There is only one special type of treaty that can be regarded as a source of international law: the so-called law-making treaty, concluded between a number of countries acting in their joint interest, intended to create a new rule, and adhered to later by other states, either through formal action in accordance with the provisions of the treaty or by tacit acquiescence in and observance of the new rule. A law-making treaty, then, is an instrument through which a substantial number of states declare their understanding of what a particular rule of law is, by which new general rules for the future conduct of the ratifying or adhering states are laid down, by which some existing customary or convention rule of law is abolished or modified, or by which some new international agency is created. It is this kind of treaty through which conventional international law is created.

In view of the sovereign nature of the modern state, such a treaty will be obligatory originally only on such states as signed and ratified it. If the initial number of ratifying states is small, the treaty does not create a new rule of general international law but, at best, only a rule of particular or regional application. As acquiescence in the new rule or formal ratification of it by additional states increase and as finally the overwhelming majority of all states accepts the new rule, a new principle or a new interpretation of an old rule has become a part of general international law. States which specifically refuse to acquiesce in the new rule or which refuse to ratify the treaty or to adhere to it are, of course, not normally bound by the rule, principle, or interpretation in question.[1]

The procedure just outlined may be compared to national legislation on an international scale, but the comparison is quite obviously imperfect, for the majority rule normally characteristic of the democratic process of law-making is lacking. And a law-making treaty does not apply to

---

[1] See Whiteman, Vol. I, pp. 70–74; Josef L. Kunz, "Revolutionary Creation of Norms of International Law," 41 *A.J.I.L.* (1947), pp. 119–126, at p. 124; for a contrary view relative to Art. 2(6) of the Charter, see Hans Kelsen, "Sanctions in International Law Under the Charter of the UN," 31 *Iowa Law Review* (1946), pp. 499–543, and his "Membership in the United Nations," 46 *Columbia Law Review* (1946), pp. 391–411.

those who do not grant their consent to the new rule, whereas domestic legislation applies to all subjects of the state in question. It would also appear that one goes too far when one compares the states of the community of nations with legislators on the domestic scene, particularly in view of the presently existing standards of behavior of some of those states on the international scene.

The past 150 years have seen the conclusion of a great number of true law-making treaties. Among the outstanding instruments of this type have been the agreement concluded at the Congress of Vienna (diplomatic ranks), the Declaration of Paris of 1856 (privateering, rights of neutrals in naval war), the Geneva Red Cross Convention of 1864, the Universal Postal Union Convention of 1874, the Convention for the Suppression of the African Slave Traffic of 1890, the various Hague Conventions of 1899 and 1907, the Covenant of the League of Nations, the Charter of the United Nations, the Geneva Conventions of 1949 (regulation of certain aspects of war, including prisoners of war and belligerent occupation), and the recent agreements, discussed in subsequent chapters, on the Law of the Sea, at Geneva in 1958, and the 1961 Vienna Convention on Diplomatic Privileges and Immunities.[2]

Classification of Law-making Treaties. Law-making treaties may be divided into a number of categories on the basis of content and intent. Some of these instruments merely transform existing customary law or legal rules laid down by some judicial agencies into the equivalent of statutory legislation. The Final Act of the Congress of Vienna (1815, Arts. 108, 117, 118) belongs in this grouping, with its codification of rules governing freedom of navigation on international rivers and of the classification of diplomatic representatives.

Other law-making treaties interpret existing customary or conventional rules without necessarily adding new principles to the body of the law. And finally, and most promisingly, a number of law-making treaties create new principles of law by international agreement, as in the case of the Convention on International Civil Aviation (1944), the International Opium Convention (1912), and the Convention concerning the International Circulation of Motor Vehicles (1909).

Many law-making treaties combine two or all of these functions: the Hague Conventions on the Laws and Customs of War of 1907 and the four Geneva Conventions of 1949 supply excellent examples of such multipurpose instruments.

Even though a law-making treaty may not achieve virtually universal acceptance and may be restricted in its applicability to a small number of states, it may nevertheless represent a source of international law: but, in

---

[2] Consult also the very valuable monographic study by the International Law Commission, "Historical Survey of Development of International Law and Its Codification by International Conferences," 41 *A.J.I.L.* (October, 1947), Supp., pp. 29–147.

such a case, of what is called particular law or, in some instances where a geographic basis exists for it, of regional international law, binding only the relatively few states involved and not setting up a rule of general law. Thus the Latin American states and Spain recognize a right of asylum for political offenders in their respective embassies or legations, as well as on their public vessels; the majority of the rest of the states do not recognize such a right.

Resolutions and Declarations. A special problem has been posed for some time now by the resolutions and declarations adopted by certain inter-American conferences. Because no ratification is required, the resolutions and declarations in question do not correspond to treaties in the orthodox sense. On the other hand, Latin American states have regarded these resolutions as creating binding legal obligations. If such an interpretation can be shown to have been accepted by the participating states through their subsequent actions, then it has to be admitted that, in the instances in question, regional law has been created. Thus far little investigation has been undertaken in this field; it must be suspected, however, that a rather considerable volume of regional (or particular) law has been created, in the course of time, by this method.

Closely related to the foregoing topic is the question of the legal significance to be attributed to the declarations and resolutions adopted by the General Assembly.[3]

From a traditional point of view, such declarations and resolutions, lacking the characteristics of a treaty, must be denied any obligatory force, hence cannot be termed law-making. On the other hand, there appears to be developing a slight but discernible trend from consent to consensus as a basis of legal obligations binding states.[4]

This trend reflects the provisions of Article 13 (1a) of the UN Charter which state that the General Assembly shall initiate studies and make recommendations for the purpose of "encouraging the progressive development of international law and its codification."

General Assembly declarations, if they assert principles observed by the community of nations as legally binding, in fact reformulate legal norms for UN member states and, on occasion, interpret the meaning

---

[3] See, *inter alia*, Obed Y. Asamoah, *The Legal Significance of the Declarations of the General Assembly of the United Nations* (The Hague: Martinus Nijhoff, 1966); Whiteman, Vol. I, pp. 68–70; Gabriella R. Lande, "The Changing Effectiveness of Assembly Resolutions," *Proceedings* (1964), pp. 162–173; Sir Kenneth Bailey, "Making International Law in the United Nations," *ibid.* (1967), pp. 233–239; Krzysztof Skubiszewski, "The General Assembly of the United Nations and its Power to Influence National Action," *ibid.* (1964), pp. 153–170; and also Hungdah Chin and R. R. Edwards, "Communist China's Attitude Toward the United Nations: A Legal Analysis," 62 *A.J.I.L.* (1968), pp. 20–50, especially pp. 28–33.

[4] See the persuasive argument favoring this trend in Richard A. Falk, "On the Quasi-Legislative Competence of the General Assembly," 60 *A.J.I.L.* (1966), pp. 782–791.

of such norms, as viewed by the assenting states. The same would be true of Assembly recommendations under the conditions described.[5]

Beyond this point, however, both declarations and resolutions can be held to possess only quasilegislative authority and normally would require member ratification of a subsequent draft convention based on the initial declaration or resolution. (See Chapter 11 for reference to the Universal Declaration of Human Rights.)

In essence, then, General Assembly declarations and resolutions lay down standards of state behavior and, if endorsed positively through ratification of relevant conventions (and, if need be, through passage of domestic implementing legislation), represent the initial *phase* in the creation of new rules of international law.

Naturally, if a given resolution, approved by an overwhelming majority of the members of the General Assembly, is then accepted *in practice* by those members as representing a binding international legal obligation, a new rule of customary international law must be accepted as having come into being. In that instance, only those members that had voted against the resolution in question or that had indicated soon afterward that they would not be bound by the new principle involved, would be exempt from the application of the new legal obligation.

Consensus, then, as expressed in the General Assembly, may represent nothing more than a hopeful exhortation, or it may turn out to have been the first phase in the creation of a new rule of conventional law, or it may be seen as the first phase in the rapid evolution of a new principle of international customary law.

Regrettably, the General Assembly itself does not always acknowledge the limits of its legislative powers and has tended all too often to use phraseology appearing to claim a definite authority to make new rules of law.[6]

INTERNATIONAL CUSTOM

Custom represents a second source of international law. In contrast to the normal meaning of the term, that is, the description of a habit—a legal custom represents a usage with a definite obligation attached to it. In other words, failure to follow a legal custom entails the possibility of punishment, of sanctions, of retaliation; it involves, therefore, state responsibility toward other nations.

The presence of customary international law is evident from the existence of an extensive body of detailed rules which comprised the bulk

[5] See Rosalyn Higgins, "Law, Politics and the United Nations," pp. 1–10 in *The Development of International Law Through the Political Organs of the United Nations* (London: Oxford University Press, 1963).

[6] For instance, see the wording used in such resolutions as A/RES/2160 (XXI), A/RES/2184 (XXI), A/RES/2189 (XXI), and A/RES/2202 (XXI), all concerned with the question of colonialism.

of accepted general international law until shortly after the end of the nineteenth century. Into this sphere of the law fall most of the rules governing such diverse areas as jurisdiction over territory, freedom of the high seas, the privileges and immunities of states, and the rights of aliens.

Origin of Rules. Some of the rules in question originated through the practices of a small number of states—practices that were adopted by others because of the usefulness involved, until at last general acceptance resulted in new rules of law entailing definite obligations. In other instances a custom resulted from the existence of a single powerful nation in some part of the Western world which imposed its will on its neighbors in relation to some matter; eventually, other countries accepted that policy or practice without challenge or protest, and when the number of assenting states reached nearly universal proportions, a new rule of law had been created. It should be remembered, however, that mere usage without the concurrent existence of a legal obligation does not represent a rule of law but merely what is termed "comity" among nations, that is, usages based essentially on expediency or courtesy and not yet possessed of an obligatory character.

Proof of Existence of a True Rule. Obviously, serious differences could arise about the exact point at which a habitual act (usage) by certain states was transformed into a rule of customary law. No single authority has ever been accepted as to the point of change. In other words, the question is: How often, and by how many different states, does a habitual act have to be performed, or be accepted without protest, in order to achieve the status of a principle or rule of law entailing a legal obligation?

The task of determination devolves upon both national and international tribunals, and as yet no settled rule has been evolved. At times little quarreling could ensue because sufficient factual data could be presented to prove the existence of a true rule of customary international law; on other occasions the action in question has been duplicated so seldom that the existence of a rule could be questioned effectively. One of the better illustrations of the evolution of a set of concepts from rudimentary and habitual beginnings to the status of a legal principle was supplied in the decision in the well-known case of *The Scotia:*

THE SCOTIA

United States, Supreme Court, 1872
14 Wall. (81 U.S.) 170

FACTS

Appeal from Circuit Court, Southern District of New York, in a case of collision between the American sailing vessel *Berkshire* and the British steamer *Scotia,* by which the *Berkshire* was lost.

The owners of the *Berkshire* sued in the District Court to recover their losses, claiming that the collision occurred through the fault of the *Scotia.*

The Court ruled against the plaintiffs, holding that courts of admiralty were required to take judicial notice of the existence of British orders-in-council promulgating regulations for preventing collisions at sea and of the fact that so many maritime states had accepted those regulations as to create a general rule and usage of the sea. By the regulations in question and in accordance with an Act of Congress of 1864, the *Berkshire* was bound to show only colored lights; having failed to do so, no remedy could be obtained for the loss of the vessel. When the case was appealed to the Circuit Court, the decree of the District Court was affirmed.

It appears that the *Berkshire* did not display any colored lights at all but only a white light, at the bow, fastened about four feet above deck level. The *Scotia*, acting in accordance with the regulations mentioned, mistook the white light for the masthead light of a steamer, assuming in consequence that the presumed steamer was some distance away. Subsequently the two vessels collided, the *Scotia* obeying at all times the steering and sailing regulations required under the rules of the sea.

ISSUE *

What was the law prevailing at the place and time of the collision?

DECISION

The law prevailing was the law of the sea, which was violated by the *Berkshire*. Decree of lower court affirmed.

REASONING

(1) In 1863 the British government issued orders-in-council prescribing rules and regulations for the display of lights and for movements of both sailing vessels and steamers. Before the end of 1864, nearly all [34] maritime nations had adopted the same regulations respecting lights.

(2) No single nation can change the law of the sea, which rests on the common consent of civilized communities. It possesses force because it has been generally accepted as a rule of conduct. But when navigation rules originally laid down by two countries [Great Britain, later the United States] are accepted as obligatory rules by more than thirty of the principal maritime nations, those rules have become a part of the law of the sea, a usage has been changed into a legal custom, and the rules in question were the law at the place and at the time the collision occurred. "This is not giving to the statutes of any nation extra-territorial effect. It is not treating them as general maritime laws, but it is recognition of the historical fact that by common consent of mankind, these rules have been acquiesced in as of general obligation. Of that fact we think we may take judicial notice. Foreign municipal law must indeed be proved as facts, but it is not so with the law of nations."

Evidence for Existence of a Rule. Unlike law-making treaties, which are easily available for study and reference, the evidence for the existence of customary law is scattered and at times extremely difficult to locate. Published diplomatic correspondence often contains clues to the existence of legal custom; instructions to diplomats, consuls, military and naval officers of high rank, and similar documents may point out the accepted

---

* Several minor issues have been omitted for purposes of emphasizing the main issue of the case.

customary rules; decisions of domestic courts, referring to habitual practices become legal custom, frequently indicate the existence of such custom; and opinions of certain legal officers, especially in Great Britain and in the United States, have been found to be of great value in locating rules of customary international law.

Weaknesses of Customary Law. The development and growth of customary international law has clearly shown up some of the inadequacies of this particular source of the law and has led, in more recent times, to the substitution of treaties as the major source of international law. Custom, almost by definition, represents a slow process; in some instances a given usage did not become a general and legally obligatory custom until several hundred years had passed. Some writers have charged with some justice that in numerous cases a customary rule, when finally arriving at that exalted position, was quite outdated and archaic. In other words, the slow growth of a usage into a customary rule of law did not allow the law to keep up to date with changing aspects of the very international relations that were to be governed and regulated by the rule. As a result states, recognizing the inadequacy of a customary rule, fell into the habit of violating it because of that inadequacy.

A second weakness of custom as a source of international law results from the fact that as a usage develops into legal custom, any country objecting to the usage may state its objections and refuse to follow the example of others who assent to the practice in question. When the usage changes into a legal custom at a later date, the objecting nation is not bound by the new rule. On the other hand, it is understood quite generally that when a *new* state comes into being and is admitted into the community of nations, it is bound by all rules of international law originating in custom.

Replacement of Rules. A new law-making treaty overrides an earlier conflicting rule of customary law and, in fact, has often been drawn up for the specific purpose of achieving the end of a customary rule. But if a custom has been so generally accepted that its provisions could be said to be ingrained in national behavior, a subsequent and contrary rule of conventional law may be found to be unenforceable.

It should be mentioned that when a law-making treaty modifies or replaces a rule of customary international law, the changes in question affect, of course, only the states which are parties to the agreement. In their relations with other states, such parties would still be bound by the rule of customary law.

Recent Status of Customary Law. More recently, customary international law has been challenged increasingly by Asian, African, Latin American, and certain totalitarian states when the homogeneous values commonly claimed for the Western state system based on Europe began to be applied to communities not necessarily sharing all of those values; when, in other words, the attempt was made to expand the rule of customary law to that of a universal law applicable to diverse legal orders. A striking example of the unwillingness to accept traditional Western values or judgments based on them may be found in the opposition encountered in many countries to subject themselves to a so-called minimum standard of justice with regard to the treatment of resident aliens. The problem posed by the attempted extension of Western legal values to non-Western communities is indeed a most formidable one, for in essence the attempt requires an integration or at least the achievement of a consensus of general principle and practice of such varied systems as are represented by Western law, Islamic law, Hindu law, Jewish law, African legal systems, as well as Soviet law and its variations in the satellite states and in Communist China.

GENERAL PRINCIPLES OF LAW

General principles of law (or, better, of justice) form the third major source of international law.[7] The meaning of "general principles of law recognized by civilized nations" has been the subject of extensive discussion. Two major opinions prevail: one holds that the phrase embraces such general principles of domestic jurisprudence, particularly of private law, as can be applied to international relations. Such principles might include the concept that both sides in a dispute should have a fair hearing, that no one should sit in judgment on his own case, and so on. The other view asserts that the phrase refers to general principles of justice closely linked to natural law as interpreted during recent centuries in the Western world, that is, the transformation of broad universal principles of a law applicable to all of mankind into specific rules of international law.[8] It must be assumed, however, that from a legal point of view the law of nature represents at best a vague and ill-defined source of international law.[9] Most modern writers appear to regard general principles of law as a secondary source of international law, little used in practice but helpful on occasion. A close examination of most of the rules claimed

[7] Consult Whiteman, Vol. I, pp. 75–90.

[8] One of the most persuasive modern defenses of this view is found in Cheng, pp. 1–26. See also Wolfgang Friedmann, "The Uses of 'General Principles' in the Development of International Law," 57 *A.J.I.L.* (1963), pp. 279–299, and consult Whiteman, Vol. I, pp. 5–8, 21–26, and particularly pp. 90–94.

[9] See the valuable discussion in Josef L. Kunz, "Natural-Law Thinking in the Modern Science of International Law," 55 *A.J.I.L.* (1961), pp. 951–958. It should be mentioned here that the present writer does not share the belief of some of his colleagues that international law constitutes a science. The law of nations represents an area of state practice, a subject for study, research, and teaching; to refer to it as a science, except by an unwarranted stretching of the meaning of that term, reflects the common modern tendency to reject, or at least to look down on, anything not labeled a science or scientific. The fact that international law represents a set of rules and principles, some of which possess truly universal applicability, does not equate the law with physics or with mathematics, even when students of international law make use, within permissible or possible limits, of what may be called the scientific method.

to have originated in natural law or in general principles of justice indicates clearly that the dividing line between the source in question and custom (or, initially, usage) is scarcely discernible. This conclusion becomes even more evident when one delves into the history of the concept of natural law and into its origins in the Greco-Roman period from *practices* found to be existing on an almost universal scale in the Mediterranean world.

The major difficulty encountered in an attempt to accept general principles of law, that is, morality and justice, as a source of international law is the fact that morality and justice are quite subjective concepts in the eyes of many persons. Justice, which is indeed only a part of morality, can be defined in many ways, such as "to each his own." But what does such a definition mean from a legal point of view, when conceptions of justice vary from country to country and, indeed, even within any given country?

Law and justice do not necessarily coincide but, on the other hand, every law, domestic or international, represents someone's idea of what is just, whether that someone is a group of legislators, an absolute monarch, or an assortment of presumably independent national governments or states.

In any case, certain rules of international law can be traced unquestionably to "general principles of law," but the number of such examples is quite small. They would include, among others, such principles as that a state may bring a claim if one of its citizens has been injured by an act done by another state in violation of international law, and that a claim of denial of justice to a private individual cannot be heard by an international tribunal before all local remedies available in the injuring state have been exhausted by that individual.

Summing up the preceding discussion, it appears that, as yet, many international lawyers as well as statesmen harbor serious doubts as to the validity of the claim that "general principles" represent a definite and usable source of international law. Dissent from this view has occurred, it must be admitted, with increasing frequency in recent decades, notably in the writings of Jessup, Jenks, and particularly of Rudolph B. Schlesinger of Cornell University.[10]

JUDICIAL DECISIONS

Decisions of courts and tribunals, when applying international law, form at most an indirect and subsidiary source of international law. Decisions of domestic courts do not even bind their own governments in their international relations; yet a given decision reflects not only the interpretation of other courts as to the existence or meaning of a rule of

---

[10] See Schlesinger, "Research on the General Principles of Law Recognized by Civilized Nations," 51 *A.J.I.L.* (1957), pp. 734–753.

international law, but also indicates what that rule is held to mean in the country in question at the time the decision is drafted. This view was expressed eloquently by Chief Justice Marshall in the case of *Thirty Hogsheads of Sugar* v. *Boyle*[11] when he said:

The law of nations is the great source from which we derive those rules . . . which are recognized by all civilized and commercial states throughout Europe and America. This law is in part unwritten, and in part conventional. To ascertain that which is unwritten, we resort to the great principles of reason and justice: but, as these principles will be differently understood by different nations under different circumstances, we consider them as being, in some degree, fixed and rendered stable by a series of judicial decisions. The decisions of the Courts of every country, so far as they are founded upon a law common to every country, will be received not as authority, but with respect. The decisions of the Courts of every country show how the law of nations, in the given case, is understood in that country, and will be considered in adopting the rule which is to prevail in this.

As precedents and recorded decisions multiply over the years, a vast and instructive body of opinion is put on record for inspection and study; courts tend to attach weight to those precedents and to the opinions laid down by other courts, domestic and foreign.

On the other hand, the decisions of international tribunals have begun to play an increasingly important part in determining the existence and meaning of rules of law. The very nature of an international tribunal such as the International Court of Justice (a group of carefully chosen, able, and impartial legal authorities representing many different legal backgrounds and systems), with its presumed advantage over a national court conceivably influenced by nationalistic or political considerations or by a common legal philosophy, tends to elevate the decisions and advisory opinions of such a body above mere domestic court decisions.[12] Hence increasing respect has been paid to the decisions of international tribunals.

It should be kept in mind that the more often a rule involved in a decision happens to be in line with the basic structure of the regional or general legal system affected, the more likely will it be accepted, respected, and followed by the legal persons in that system. Furthermore, the decisions of an international tribunal may sometimes be highly effective in changing the law or abolishing a rule if the latter corresponds no longer to the needs of the community of nations. Thus the decisions of international courts and arbitral awards handed down by international tribunals may serve to interpret a rule, apply a rule, or eliminate an obsolete rule.

[11] United States, Supreme Court, 1815, 9 Cranch 191.
[12] See also Whiteman, Vol. I, pp. 94–97.

WRITINGS OF PUBLICISTS

The writings of publicists, that is, the works of text writers and other private commentators, represent a definitely subsidiary source of international law; they serve today primarily as a means for determining varying interpretations of the law.[13] No text writer creates international law, regardless of his professional eminence. At most a really outstanding writer may state what the law is in his own time and may speculate on future developments.[14] He thus may voice his considered opinion as to how the law might be improved on a given point. To the extent that his government may adopt suggestions and utilize them in the development of a usage or by incorporating them in a law-making treaty concluded with a number of other states, the writer may be regarded as an indirect source of international law.

The position of the private writer in his relation to international law was different several hundred years ago; since then, it has declined drastically as the relative importance of judicial decisions, customary rules of law, and now conventional law has mounted steadily. In past centuries, however, the work of the publicist was of profound importance. The writings of Grotius, Gentilis, de Vattel, and other "greats" in the history of the law played a vital part in the growth of international law, primarily as evidence submitted by authorities to show what the rules were in their time, and not as true sources of new rules.[15]

SUGGESTED READINGS

SOURCES OF THE LAW, GENERAL

Brierly, pp. 56–68; Wolfgang Friedmann, "The Uses of 'General Principles' in the Development of International Law," *A.J.I.L.*, 57 (1963), pp. 279–299, and his *The Changing Structure of International Law* (New York: Columbia University Press, 1964); Ignaz Seidl-Hohenveldern, "General Principles of Law as Applied by the Conciliation Commissions Established Under the Peace Treaty with Italy of 1947," 53 *A.J.I.L.* (1959), pp. 853–873; Gould, pp. 136–144; Kaplan-Katzenbach, pp. 231–264; Lauterpacht's *Oppenheim*, Vol. I, pp. 24–35; Felix E. Oppenheim, "The Natural Law Thesis: Affirmation or De-

---

[13] See the excerpt from the decision of the Supreme Court of the United States in *Hilton* v. *Guyot* (159 U.S. 113), cited in the abstract of the *Paquette Habana* case, Chapter 3.

[14] The most striking modern example of the influence of a publicist on the development of new rules of law has been the work of Raphaël Lemkin who, through his volume on *Axis Rule in Occupied Europe* (1944) and numerous scholarly articles contributed materially to the framing and widespread ratification of the Convention on Genocide by member states of the United Nations. The term *genocide* was coined by Lemkin.

[15] Consult Whiteman, Vol. I, pp. 97–98.

nial," 51 *A.P.S.R.* (1957), pp. 41–53, as well as comments and rebuttals on same, *ibid.*, pp. 54–66; Kathryn B. Doherty, "Rhetoric and Reality: A Study of Contemporary Official Egyptian Attitudes toward the International Legal Order," 62 *A.J.I.L.* (1968), pp. 335–364; A. A. D'Amato, "The Concept of Special Custom in International Law," *ibid.*, 63 (1969), pp. 211–223; R. P. Anand, "Attitudes of the Asian-African States toward Certain Problems of International Law," 15 *International and Comparative Law Quarterly* (1966), pp. 55–75; and Clive Parry, *Sources and Evidences of International Law* (Dobbs Ferry, N.Y.: Oceana Publications, 1965).

Cases

Cayuga Indians Claim (*Great Britain* v. *United States*) (Claims Arbitration under the Agreement of August 18, 1910) 1926.

Free Zones of Upper Savoy and the District of Gex Case, P.C.I.J., 1937, Ser. A/B, No. 70.

Jurisdiction of the Courts of Danzig, Advisory Opinion, P.C.I.J., 1928, Ser. B, No. 15.

New Jersey v. *Delaware*, United States, Supreme Court, 1934, 291 U.S. 361.

United States v. *The Schooner La Jeune Eugénie, Rabaud and Labatut, Claimants*, United States, Circuit Court, 1st Circuit, 1822, 2 Mason 409.

3

Relation Between International Law and Municipal Law

IN VIEW of the philosophical disagreements concerning the relationship existing between international law and domestic or municipal law, it may be well to inquire into the actual practice of states as regards this subject.

Anglo-American legal opinion has accepted for a long time the idea that international law is part of the "law of the land" and is enforced, accordingly, by domestic authorities. Insofar as Great Britain is concerned, this position was laid down clearly in a classic case:

WEST RAND CENTRAL GOLD MINING CO., LTD., v. THE KING [1]

Great Britain, King's Bench Div., 1905 (1905) 2 K.B. 391

FACTS

The company was a British concern operating a gold mine in the Transvaal. In October, 1899, a quantity of gold valued at £3,804 was seized from the company by officials of and by order of the South African Republic. The company claimed that under the laws of the Republic the government had to return either the seized gold or its value to the owners. Neither action was taken, however, since the South African Republic was conquered in the war which started in October, 1899, and became a part of the British Empire under the terms of a proclamation dated September 1, 1900. The company sought to recover the gold or its value from the British government by a petition of right, arguing that the Government had

---

[1] This case has been abstracted at length because it touches on a number of important legal principles.

succeeded to all duties, rights, property, and obligations of the defunct South African Republic by virtue of the conquest and annexation of that Republic.

ISSUES

(1) Whether under international law the sovereign of a conquering state is liable for the obligations of a conquered state;

(2) Whether international law forms part of the law of Great Britain;

(3) Whether the rights and obligations which were binding on the conquered state had to be protected and could be enforced by the domestic courts of the conquering state.

DECISION

Judgment for the Crown.

As to issue (1): The sovereign of a conquering state is free to decide which obligations of a conquered state are to be accepted as a liability of the conquering state.

As to issue (2): Only such parts of international law as have either been accepted by Great Britain or as have been so widely accepted that it could not be supposed that any civilized state would repudiate them, form a part of the law of England.

As to issue (3): Domestic courts of a conquering state cannot exercise jurisdiction over matters which fall properly under the jurisdiction of the government and which are determinable by treaty or by act of state; rights claimed under such matters cannot be enforced by domestic courts of the conquering state.

REASONING

(1) Passages from various writers on international law were cited in support of issue No. 1 but in many instances their pronouncements must be regarded as their views as to what ought to be, from an ethical standpoint, rather than the statement of a rule or practice so universally approved as to constitute law among independent nations.

The proposition that a conquering state should assume, under international law, the obligations of a conquered country cannot be sustained. When making peace, the sovereign of the conquering state is entirely free to state to what extent he is willing to adopt as his own the obligations in question. If the conquering state, by proclamation or otherwise, has promised something that is not consistent with the repudiation of some particular obligations, then good faith should prevent repudiation. But silence on the part of the conquering state cannot be accepted as confirmation and adoption of all liabilities of the conquered state.

(2) It is true that whatever has received the common consent of civilized nations must have received the consent of Great Britain, and that to which the latter had assented along with other nations in general could properly be called international law. As such it will be acknowledged and applied by British courts when legitimate occasion arises for those courts to decide questions to which doctrines of international law are relevant. But any doctrine so invoked must be one really accepted as binding between nations, and the international law sought to be applied must, like anything else, be proved by satisfactory evidence. The latter must show, either that the particular proposition put forward has been recognized and acted on by England, or that it is of such a nature, and has been so widely and generally accepted, that it can hardly be supposed

that any civilized state would repudiate it. The mere opinions of jurists, however eminent or learned, that it ought to be so recognized, are not in themselves sufficient. They must have received the express sanction of international agreement or have gradually grown to be a part of international law by their frequent practical recognition in dealings between various nations.

"The expression 'the law of nations forms part of the law of England,' ought not to be construed so as to include as part of the law of England opinions of textwriters upon a question as to which there is no evidence that Great Britain has ever assented, and *a fortiori* if they are contrary to the principles of her laws as declared by her Courts."

(3) The obligations of conquering with regard to private property, particularly land as to which the title was perfected before conquest, are entirely different from obligations arising out of personal contracts. Cession of territory does not mean the confiscation of private property of individuals. The question of the adoption by the conquering state of contractual obligations of the conquered state toward individuals is an entirely different matter.

More recently, Lord Atkin stated in connection with *Chung Chi Cheung* v. *The King* (1939, A.C. 160) that

The Courts acknowledge the existence of a body of rules which nations accept among themselves. On any judicial issue they seek to ascertain what the relevant rule is, and, having found it, they will treat it as incorporated into the domestic law, so far as it is not inconsistent with rules enacted by statutes or finally declared by their tribunals.

The reader will have noted that the opinions handed down in the preceding cases refer to rules of *customary* international law that have either been accepted generally or have been agreed to specifically by the country in question. *Treaties* affecting private property rights or which require in their implementation a change or modification of common law or of a statute must be agreed to through the medium of an enabling act passed by a legislative body such as Parliament. If enabling legislation were not required, it would be possible for the Crown to legislate for the people of England without obtaining the consent of the legislative branch of the government. At the same time, English courts have held repeatedly that international law is part of the common law, and the latter must always yield to statutory law. Thus the courts are bound by an Act of Parliament even though that Act may conflict with a rule of international law. In certain doubtful cases, especially in prize cases, it is presumed, however, that Parliament did not intend to overrule a principle of international law.

The binding force of statutory enactments, as far as British courts are concerned, has been laid down most forcefully in a very well-known case:

MORTENSEN v. PETERS

*Great Britain, High Court of Justiciary of Scotland,
1906
(1906) 8 S.C., 5th Series, 99, 14 Scot. L.T. 227*

FACTS

Appeal from decision of a sheriff who had imposed a fine of £50, with the alternative of fifteen days in prison.

Mortensen, a Danish citizen resident in England and master of a trawler registered in Norway, had been charged with violating the Sea Fisheries Act and Herring Fisheries (Scotland) Act by "otter-trawling" in the Moray Firth at a distance of more than three marine miles from the nearest land. The statutes in question, and a By-Law enacted by the Fishery Board in 1892, forbade the fishing method in question in the Firth, that body of water having a mouth of approximately seventy-five miles across from point to point.[2] Mortensen appealed, arguing that the statutes and by-law applied only to British subjects or to persons within British territory and that the place in question, that is, the location where the alleged violation of law had taken place, was outside of British territory under international law and hence not subject to the statutes and by-law.

Peters, the Procurator-Fiscal of the Court, argued in reply that the terms of the statutes and by-law were universal and that even if international law were applied, the offense had been committed in British waters and that even if the Firth were not altogether part of British territory for all purposes, the British government was fully entitled to undertake protective measures as regards fishing in those waters.[3]

ISSUES

(1) Whether a British statute applied not only to British subjects but also to all other persons within British territory;

(2) Whether the waters of the Moray Firth outside the three-mile limit were British territorial waters and hence subject to British jurisdiction;

(3) Whether domestic courts were bound by a statute contravening a rule of international law.

DECISION

The Court ruled unanimously in the affirmative on all three issues and upheld the conviction of Mortensen.

REASONING

(1) The wording of the legislation in question, that is, the use of such

---

[2] Normally the territorial sea of a given state extends three marine miles from the low-tide mark; hence a body of water fronting on the ocean and having a width at the mouth of seventy-five miles would include a goodly portion of waters terminable "high seas," not subject to the jurisdiction of the coastal state. See Chapter 17 for a detailed discussion of the subject of territorial waters.

[3] It should be pointed out that the Norwegian registration of Mortensen's vessel by its British owners represented a common subterfuge adopted at that time by British operators of fishing vessels, apparently in order to avoid compliance with the protective legislation which, it was believed, did not apply to ships flying a foreign flag and plying their trade beyond the three-mile limit.

expressions as "it shall not be lawful," "every person who . . . ," and so on, clearly indicated that the legislature intended, for the purpose on hand, to have the statutes apply against all persons, regardless of nationality. The whole purpose of the legislation would have been defeated if only British fishermen had been controlled and all others would have been free to use any method of fishing in the area.

(2) There were many instances on record where a given nation legislated for waters beyond a three-mile limit and land-locked or land-embraced by that nation and where the validity of such legislation had been upheld by the courts.

(3) "There is no such thing as a standard of international law extraneous to the domestic law of a kingdom, to which appeal may be made. International law, so far as this Court is concerned, is the body of doctrine regarding the international rights and duties of States which has been adopted and made part of the law of Scotland. . . . It may probably be conceded that there is always a certain presumption against the Legislature of a country asserting or assuming the existence of a territorial jurisdiction going clearly beyond limits established by the common consent of nations—that is to say, by international law. Such assertion or assumption is of course not impossible. . . . A Legislature may quite conceivably, by oversight or even design, exceed what an international tribunal (if such existed) might hold to be its international rights. Still, there is always a presumption against its intending to do so. . . . In this Court we have nothing to do with the question of whether the Legislature has or has not done what foreign powers may consider a usurpation in a question with

them. Neither are we a tribunal sitting to decide whether an Act of the Legislature is *ultra vires* [in excess of authority conferred by law and hence invalid] as in contravention of generally acknowledged principles of international law. For us an Act of Parliament duly passed by Lords and Commons and assented to by the King, is supreme, and we are bound to give effect to its terms."

POSTSCRIPT

Following the decision in *Mortensen* v. *Peters*, several foreign masters of trawlers registered in Norway were arrested and convicted in Scotland for the same offense in the same place; they were released, however, following a series of protests by the Norwegian Government. This leniency appears to have been based on a tacit agreement between Great Britain and Norway to the effect that the latter's trawlers would be restrained from fishing in the Moray Firth. Norway issued a warning to all trawlers registered under its flag that no further diplomatic protection would be extended if charges of illegal fishing in the Firth were lodged against them; it also amended its own regulations so as to make it more difficult to register foreign vessels in Norway.

The British Foreign Office in turn admitted through Mr. Walter Runciman in the House of Commons in 1907 that the Fisheries Acts as interpreted in the Mortensen case were "in conflict with international law." Consequently no further attempts were made to arrest and punish masters of foreign trawlers operating in waters adjacent to British territorial waters, but instead Parliament enacted a statute prohibiting the landing and selling in Great Britain of any fish caught by prohibited methods in the prohibited areas in question.

It has long been a practice of English courts to inquire of the executive branch of their government as to facts and other information relating to matters in the executive sphere, and to accept information supplied without taking evidence in the normal manner. Thus an English court, in attempting to find out whether a given body constituted the recognized government of state X or whether state Y represented an independent political entity, with consequent rights and privileges accruing to its head of state, would send an inquiry to the Secretary of State for Foreign Affairs (or, in certain cases, to the Colonial Office) and would accept his statement on the issue at hand without further judicial inquiry. In such cases responsibility for making certain that the decision of the court is in agreement with international law is shifted from the judicial to the executive branch. American courts normally pursue a similar course of action, addressing their inquiry to the Department of State.

Both English and American courts are limited in their ability to apply principles of international law to a given case when a so-called act of state has taken place. For example, when an alien has been injured through an act authorized (then or later) by the government, no remedy for the injury can be found in the courts but only through action on the diplomatic level, initiated by the alien's own government at its discretion.

In the United States the concept that international law is the "law of the land" has been adopted even more forcefully than in Great Britain. A long list of cases decided by the Supreme Court has firmly established the doctrine.[4] According to American practice, all generally accepted principles of international law, or at least such as have received the assent of the United States, and all international conventions ratified by the United States are binding on American courts, even if they conflict with earlier Acts of Congress. Thus, generally speaking, *customary* and *conventional* rules of international law override earlier domestic legislation, *provided* they do not violate express prohibitions contained in the Constitution of the United States or, in the case of conventional rules, require implementation through legislation which has not yet been forthcoming. It has to be assumed, of course, that a treaty, properly signed and ratified, is in accordance with the Constitution; otherwise bad faith would have been manifested in the act of ratification.

The separate members of a federal state are automatically bound by the principles of international law, customary or conventional, to which their federal government has assented or by which it is obligated. Existing constitutional or statutory provisions of such member states contravening the principles binding the federal authorities are null and void as far as domestic effect is concerned. These concepts have been illustrated in a striking manner in the basic American case of *Missouri v. Holland:*

---

[4] Such as *The Nereide*, 1815, 9 Cranch 388; *United States* v. *Smith*, 1820, 5 Wheaton 153; *The Scotia*, 1871, 14 Wallace 170; and *The Paquette Habana*, 1900, 175 U.S. 677; see also Bishop, pp. 71–75, for an excellent historical summary of American practice.

STATE OF MISSOURI v. HOLLAND, U.S. GAME WARDEN

United States, Supreme Court, 1920
252 U.S. 416

FACTS

Bill in equity brought by the State of Missouri to prevent a game warden of the United States from attempting to enforce the Migratory Bird Treaty Act of July 3, 1918, and the Regulations made under that act by the Secretary of Agriculture.

Congress had passed an act which sought to regulate the hunting of migratory birds by providing closed seasons and other forms of protection. That act had been held by a U.S. District Court to contravene the provisions of the Constitution as an invasion of the reserved powers of the states (*United States* v. *Shauver*, 214 F. 154; *United States* v. *McCullagh*, 221 F. 288).

On December 8, 1916, the President proclaimed a treaty between the United States and Great Britain which recited the value of migratory birds, described their annual migrations through parts of Canada and the United States, and provided for specific closed seasons and other forms of protection for migratory birds. Both countries agreed that they would make, or submit to their lawmaking bodies, proposals to carry out the provisions of the treaty. In implementation of the agreement, Congress passed the Migratory Bird Treaty Act of 1918, authorizing, among other provisions, the Secretary of Agriculture to issue regulations compatible with the terms of the treaty. These regulations were issued in July and October of 1918. When Holland, a United States Game Warden, attempted to enforce the federal regulations, the State of Missouri brought a bill in equity to prevent such enforcement.

ISSUE

Whether the treaty and statute were void as an interference with the rights reserved to the States under the Constitution.

DECISION

The Court upheld both the treaty and the statute.

REASONING

(1) By Article 2, section 2, of the Constitution, the power to make treaties is delegated specifically to the federal government.

(2) By Article 6 of the Constitution, treaties made under the authority of the United States, along with the Constitution and laws of the United States made in pursuance thereof, are declared to be the supreme law of the land.

(3) If the treaty is valid, then the statute implementing the treaty is valid also.

(4) The treaty in question does not contravene any prohibitive words to be found in the Constitution.

(5) Wild birds are not in the possession of anyone, but possession is the beginning of ownership. Migratory birds travel from State to State, hence the whole foundation of any States' rights is the relatively momentary presence of birds in their boundaries.

(6) Valid treaties are binding within the territorial limits of the States as they are elsewhere throughout the United States. While the bulk

of private relations usually fall under the control of the States, a treaty may override the power of the latter.

(7) A national interest of the first magnitude is involved. The States cannot be relied upon to protect that interest, hence the Federal Government has the right to act, in the absence of prohibitory wording in the Constitution.

On the other hand, if statutory legislation is enacted subsequent to assent to customary or conventional international law, and conflicts with the latter, then American courts are bound by the later (federal) legislation. In doubtful cases there exists a strong presumption that Congress did not intend to override international law: ". . . the laws of the United States ought not, if it be avoidable, so be construed as to infract the common principles and usages of nations. . . ." [5] and ". . . An Act of Congress ought never to be construed to violate the law of nations, if any other possible construction remains, and, consequently, can never be construed to violate neutral rights, or to affect neutral commerce further than is warranted by the law of nations as understood in this country." [6]

It is rather doubtful whether the invalidation of legislation or administrative acts in violation of international treaties preceding the statute or act would be preferable to the present practice of protesting the alleged violation on the diplomatic level. Actual American practice warrants the assertion that no treaty will be considered as abrogated or modified by subsequent legislation unless Congress clearly indicated such an intent in the statute itself.[7] If such intent were shown, the courts would be bound by the statute and the United States would be responsible to other nations for any violations of the treaty and of international law.

Contrariwise, when a state has failed to adopt, by treaty, legislation, or other public act, a policy contrary to a rule of international law previously assented to by that state, then the courts under the latter's jurisdiction are bound to accept, or at least to take judicial notice of, that rule. This principle has been elucidated most clearly by the Supreme Court of the United States in a classic decision:

THE PAQUETTE HABANA; THE LOLA

Supreme Court of the United States, 1900
175 U.S. 677

FACTS

Two appeals from decrees at the U.S. District Court, Southern District of Florida, condemning two fishing vessels and their cargoes as prizes of war.

Each vessel, operating out of Havana, was regularly engaged in Cuban coastal waters, sailed under the Spanish flag, and was owned by a Spanish subject of Cuban birth, living in Havana. The cargo, when the vessels

---

[5] *Talbot* v. *Seeman*, 1801, 1 Cranch 1.

[6] *Murray* v. *The Charming Betsey*, 1804, 2 Cranch 64.

[7] See *Cook* v. *United States*, 1939, 288 U.S. 102, for a detailed analysis of the question on the part of the Supreme Court.

were seized, consisted of fresh fish. Apparently neither captain had any knowledge until the vessels were captured, that a state of war existed between Spain and the United States or that a blockade of Spanish ports had been proclaimed by the United States.

Both vessels were brought to Key West and condemned in the U.S. District Court, with a decree of sale of both vessels and cargoes.

ISSUE

Whether unarmed coastal fishing vessels of one belligerent are subject to capture by vessels of another belligerent.

DECISION

(1) Unarmed coastal fishing vessels are exempt from seizure by a belligerent.

(2) Decree of District Court reversed, proceeds of the sale of vessels and cargoes to be restored to the claimants, with damages and costs.

REASONING

(1) By an ancient usage among civilized nations, beginning centuries ago and "gradually ripening into a rule of international law," coastal fishing vessels pursuing their vocation have been recognized as exempt, with their cargoes and crews, from capture. This usage can be traced by means of documents back as far as 1403 A.D. in England. Subsequent evidence indicates that France and other countries followed the same usage. Eminent writers on international law have indicated through the past few centuries that the usage became general in scope.

(2) The United States recognized the immunity of coastal fishing vessels as far back as the Mexican War of 1846.

(3) In more recent times, numerous states issued specific orders to naval commanders concerning fishing vessels, recognizing their exemption from seizure unless military operations should make it necessary.

(4) "International law is part of our law, and must be ascertained and administered by courts of justice of appropriate jurisdiction, as often as questions of right depending upon it are duly presented for their determination. For this purpose, where there is no treaty and no controlling executive or legislative act or judicial decision, resort must be had to the customs and usages of civilized nations; and, as evidence of these, to the works of jurists and commentators, who by years of labor, research, and experience, have made themselves peculiarly well acquainted with the subjects of which they treat. Such works are resorted to by judicial tribunals, not for the speculations of their authors concerning what the law ought to be, but for trustworthy evidence of what the law really is. . . ." [*Hilton v. Guyot*, 159 U.S. 113]

(5) ". . . at the present day, by the general consent of the civilized nations of the world, and independently of any express treaty or other public act, it is an established rule of international law, founded on considerations of humanity to a poor and industrious order of men, and of the mutual convenience of belligerent States, that coast fishing vessels, with their implements and supplies, cargoes and crews, unarmed and honestly pursuing their peaceful calling of catching and bringing in fresh fish, are exempt from capture as prize of war."

(6) "This rule of international law is one which prize courts, administering the law of nations, are bound to take judicial notice of, and to give effect to, in the absence of any treaty or other public act of their own government in relation to the matter."

It should be noted that the rule discussed in the preceding decision is no longer generally observed by leading maritime powers in time of war, even though it was affirmed as late as 1907 in Hague Convention No. XI. The establishment of tight blockades of enemy coasts during both World Wars with the avowed intention of cutting off all food supplies from the enemy state, together with repeated clear evidence that ostensible fishing vessels have acted as the eyes and ears of their naval forces, led to the issue of administrative regulations by virtually all naval powers which had the "public act" character required to set aside the effective application of the rule laid down in the case of *The Paquette Habana*.

Whenever a law-making treaty can only be made effective or operative domestically through the passage of implementing legislation or perhaps even through the appropriation of funds, each ratifying state is under an obligation to take the appropriate domestic steps to implement the agreement. A similar obligation can be said to exist in the case of customary rules of law when such achieve obligatory status but require domestic implementation.

The general concept of the "incorporation" of international law into the "law of the land," found originally only in the Anglo-Saxon countries, has spread in modern times into many other parts of the world. Courts of numerous countries (Belgium, France, and Switzerland, to name but a few) have sustained the doctrine, and a growing number of states have incorporated the principle in their constitutions.

It should be mentioned that the "assent" of states which has been mentioned repeatedly, should not be overestimated in connection with the doctrine of incorporation. The practice of states indicates quite clearly that *express* assent, particularly in the form of legislation or executive acknowledgment, is quite commonly lacking. Customarily accepted rules and principles of international law, as distinct from conventional law arising out of specific law-making treaties, must be regarded as part of the "law of the land" and do not require express assent in order to become such a part. Interestingly enough, the constitution of the Netherlands provides specifically for an absolute supremacy of treaties over domestic law, but does not apply this principle to the rules of customary international law.

SUGGESTED READINGS

THE INTERNATIONAL/MUNICIPAL RELATIONSHIP
IN GENERAL

Whiteman, Vol. I, pp. 103–116; Richard A. Falk, *The Role of Domestic Courts in the International Legal Order* (Syracuse, N.Y.: Syracuse University Press, 1964); David R. Deener, "International Law Provisions in Post-World War II Constitutions," 36 *Cornell Law Quarterly* (1951), pp. 505–533; Lauterpacht's *Oppenheim*, Vol. I, pp. 35–47; Daniel P. O'Connell, "The Relationship Between

International Law and Municipal Law," 48 *Georgetown Law Journal* (1960), pp. 431–485; H. F. van Panhuys, "The Netherlands Constitution and International Law," 58 *A.J.I.L.* (1964), pp. 88–108; Ignaz Seidl-Hohenveldern, "Transformation or Adoption of International Law into Municipal Law," 12 *International and Comparative Law Quarterly* (1963), pp. 88–124; Edward Dumbault, "John Marshall and Treaty Law," 50 *A.J.I.L.* (1956), pp. 69–81; Josef L. Kunz, "International Law by Analogy," *ibid.*, 45 (1951), pp. 329–335; and Edward D. Dickinson, "The Law of Nations as Part of the National Law of the United States," 101 *University of Pennsylvania Law Review* (1953), pp. 793–833.

Cases

Certain German Interests in Polish Upper Silesia, P.C.I.J., 1926, Ser. A, No. 7.
Exchange of Greek and Turkish Populations, Advisory Opinion, P.C.I.J., 1925, Ser. B, No. 10.
The Greco-Bulgarian 'Communities,' Advisory Opinion, P.C.I.J., 1930, Ser. B, No. 17.
Treatment of Polish Nationals in Danzig, Advisory Opinion, P.C.I.J., 1932, Ser. B, No. 44.

4

Development of Law Among Nations

EARLY DEVELOPMENT OF INTERNATIONAL LAW

PRE-GREEK *Civilization.* International law as we know it today is a product of Western civilization. Its true existence covers only the past 300 to 500 years, but its roots extend into the distant past. Some authors have attempted to link the modern law with customs and usages encountered in pre-Greek civilizations, but it now appears that our present law cannot claim such an impressive genealogy. It is perfectly true that even the earliest documents describing relations between states contain evidence of rules and procedures found in modern international law. For instance, a treaty concluded in the very dawn of recorded history, about 3100 B.C., between the rulers of two Mesopotamian communities (Lagash and Umma) provided for the settlement of a boundary dispute through arbitration, with solemn oaths for the observance of the agreement. A thousand years later a multitude of recorded treaties deal with subjects such as the creation of vassal states, alliances, boundary settlements, extradition, and similar modern questions. Any examination of Hebrew, Assyrian, Babylonian, Hindu, and early Chinese records in the fields of warfare and diplomacy reveals many customs and usages which are still part of the practices of modern states.[1]

The facts mentioned should not lead one to assume, however, that the modern law can be traced back directly to those early civilizations. In the world of antiquity, our own concept of a community of nations was utterly lacking. Each country had its own language, laws, morality, and religion. The interests of each unit were purely local, not "international." Although it was true that relations with neighboring countries could not be avoided, with wars being waged, ambassadors being sent, with international trade developing on a modest or at times an impressive scale, and with arbitration of disputes a well-established method, nevertheless the consciousness of a community of mankind—fundamental to the creation of a true system of international law—was absent, except among some of the Greek philosophers.

---

[1] See Nussbaum, pp. 1–5; Lauterpacht's *Oppenheim,* Vol. I, pp. 72–74; and the excellent study by F. M. Russell, *Theories of International Relations* (New York: Appleton-Century-Crofts, 1936), Chapters 1–4.

Greek Civilization. Even the civilization of the Greeks, great though its achievements were in many spheres, did not contribute much to the development of modern international law. There did exist common bonds of race, culture, language, and religion, as well as a distinct feeling of enmity toward all non-Greeks (the "barbarians"), but, on the other hand, the well-known passion of the Greeks for local independence appears to have outweighed the common links among the Greek city-states and their numerous colonies around the shores of the Mediterranean. Relations between Greek states were based on a feeling of kinship and on convenience, rather than upon the concept of the oneness of mankind or of a community of states. True, new customs sprang up among the Greeks, many of which are again found in modern practice. But it should be remembered that similarities of Greek practices to modern rules of law were just that—accidental similarities and little more. Modern practice cannot be traced, at least on a basis of true international law, to the customs of the Greeks.

Development of Roman Law. In contrast to the Greek civilization, ancient Rome contributed immensely to the development of Western law as such and, indirectly, to the subsequent appearance of international law. In view of the fact that many of the older texts attributed the origin of the modern law to the Romans and even applied the term *international law* to the *jus gentium* of Rome, it will be necessary to examine just what relevant developments did occur in the Roman state as far as law was concerned.

The original law of the community, applying only to Roman citizens, the *jus civile*, represented an archaic remnant from the days when Rome comprised seven hills inhabited by a primitive agricultural community. When the settlement expanded, contacts with foreigners inaugurated increasing difficulties in the administration of justice in view of the absence of any law applicable to them.

Hence the status of foreigners was recognized as early as 242 B.C. by the creation of a special official, the *praetor peregrinus,* who appointed judges to settle disputes arising between Romans and aliens or between aliens alone.

The body of rules which developed under the institution of the *praetor peregrinus* dealt with a large variety of subjects, such as verbal contracts, partnership agreements, loans, rights of owners over slaves, and so on. This whole group of rules became known as the *jus gentium,* far more liberal in outlook and operation than the old *jus civile,* which still applied to controversies between Roman citizens.

In the course of time, dissatisfaction with the narrow limitations of the older law grew until, in the imperial age, the rules of the *jus gentium* were gradually absorbed in the *jus civile,* in effect supplanted much of the earlier law, and became the basis of domestic law for Romans and aliens alike. However, it should be emphasized that the *jus gentium* (later

synonymous with the *jus civile*) had nothing to do with a "law of nations," or international law, as it is known today. The *jus gentium* as
practiced in Rome was Roman domestic law, a body of rules that regulated the conduct and transactions of individuals, not of states.

Roman legal writers defined the two kinds of law in another manner,
far removed from the market place and from the jurisdiction of the
praetor peregrinus: in philosophical discussions of the law, they characterized as *jus civile* the law which each country created for itself,
whereas *jus gentium* referred to a body of law established among all men
by reason and observed by all countries, that is, the common elements
of the legal systems of all civilized states.

It was this second interpretation of the *jus gentium* which was preserved among legal thinkers of the Middle Ages, with increasing emphasis
on the existence of a universal law applicable to all states. On the other
hand, that medieval period lacked the conditions under which a system
akin to modern international law could exist. Despite the presence of such
unifying forces as the Church and the Holy Roman Empire, medieval
society was torn by recurring conflicts between these two entities as well
as by constant strife among lesser political units, so that the period re-
sembled our own in the lack of a real sense of community.

Still later, in the seventeenth century, the term *jus gentium* became
specialized in its meaning and referred to the principles assumed to prevail
in the relations between independent states, was translated as "law of
nations" (*droit des gens*) by Vattel in 1758, and became "international
law" through its use in that form by the Englishman Jeremy Bentham in
1780. Bentham followed the Latin title of an earlier work by Richard
Zouche (1650), who had written about *juris inter gentes.*

The development of modern international law and the derivation of its
name was complicated further by the existence of the concept of the law
of nature (*jus naturale*), adopted about 150 B.C. by Roman philosophers
from Greek Stoic thinkers. The law of nature, later termed *natural law*,
was believed to have been implanted in men by nature, to comprehend
unchangeable and exact justice, universal in scope, self-evident to any
individual exercising his "right reason," or the moral faculty with which
he was endowed. Various Roman legal sources identified this law of
nature with the philosophical interpretation of the *jus gentium*, even
though differences were readily admitted.

The decline and fall of the Western Empire was followed by a period
of instability, even anarchy at times, which we call the Dark Ages, an
era in history singularly unfavorable to the observance of a presumed
universal law. To be sure, as various barbarian kingdoms were established on the soil of the vanished empire. Roman law was preserved to
an astonishing extent. A dual system of law was frequently observed:
barbarian law governing the new ruling minority, Roman law governing the remaining "native" majority. As time went on, the two systems

intermingled and in most instances evolved into a new synthesis, called Frankish law, Neustrian law, Burgundian law, and so on. These new legal systems combined desirable elements of barbarian (Teutonic) law with bulky remnants of Roman civil law and may be envisioned as crude forebears of modern national legal systems.

Contrary to a widespread belief, the medieval period did contain, however, some of the seeds of the future international law as well as of our modern sovereign nations. First and foremost among integrating factors was the Catholic Church. At first the important element was the existence of a single religion, increasingly centralized administratively, developing a common law (canon law) for its members, irrespective of race, nationality, or location. Ecclesiastical law, as it evolved during the medieval period, influenced many areas considered today to lie within the sphere of international law: the conclusion of treaties and their observance, authority over territory, the right of conquest with the sanction of the Church, papal activity in arbitration and the general emphasis in canon law on arbitration as a desirable method for the settlement of disputes, and above all regulations concerning many facets of warfare.[2] Few chapters in Western intellectual history are more fascinating than the repeated attempts on the part of the Church to eliminate private war entirely and to mitigate the evils of legitimate international conflict.

Beginning of International Law. The germination of the seeds of international law traditionally took place in the sixteenth century, even though the decentralization of the *res publica christiana* of Europe, the true beginning of the law, came somewhat earlier. The rise of Protestantism not only destroyed the traditional unity of Christendom but made papal arbitration of secular disputes unacceptable to Protestant rulers. From an overall point of view, the outstanding event of the entire century was the emergence of the national state—first in the shapes of England, France, and Spain. A growing number of writers began to treat of national and international questions, and a goodly proportion of those related directly to the sphere of international law.

The remainder of this chapter will summarize briefly a few of the outstanding writers of this and the succeeding centuries. Limitations of space prevent the inclusion of many authors famous in the history of international law, such as Pierino Belli and Balthasar Ayala on the laws of war; Samuel Rachel on positive law; Martin Huebner and the Abbé Galliani on the laws of neutrality; Christian Wolff, the great teacher of Vattel; and Georg von Martens on the natural rights of states and on certain aspects of positive law.[3]

---

[2] See Lauterpacht's *Oppenheim*, Vol. I, pp. 77–83, and Nussbaum, pp. 17–44.

[3] Fortunately for the serious student, virtually all the classics in international law are available in the famous *Classics of International Law* (Washington: U.S. Government Printing Office, n.d.). Summaries of the most important writers are found in

WRITERS OF THE LAW

Francisco de Vitoria (1480–1546). Vitoria was a well-known Dominican professor of theology at the Spanish University of Salamanca. Two of his works, *De Indis* and *The Law of War Made by the Spaniards on the Barbarians* (1532), related particularly to international law. Vitoria placed great emphasis on the question of what exactly made a war a just one and examined in great detail the bases of Spanish authority in the Americas, particularly as far as relations between Indians and Spaniards were concerned.

Certain claims supporting warfare and conquest in the Americas were upheld by him with a wealth of theological reasoning. It is in this section of his works that many fascinating speculations are encountered. He held that the Spaniards enjoyed certain rights under natural law and the *jus gentium,* including the right to travel and to carry on trade with the natives—provided they did not injure the latter. If those rights were denied to visitors, then the latter had been injured and a resulting war waged against the Indian populations in question represent a just war.

Such speculations quite naturally led Vitoria to investigate the rules of war themselves.

Vitoria's discussion of the rules of warfare reflected, almost by necessity, the barbarism and cruelty of his own age, yet the general tone of his remarks was humane and well in advance of the thinking and the practices of his time. In fact, many of his ideas concerning military conduct in time of war anticipated the principles crystallized much later in such codes as the relevant Hague Conventions of 1899 and 1907, although it is of course not possible to show a definite link tying them to Victoria's writings. It could even be asserted that the modern theory of human rights represents a development of principles first laid down by Vitoria.

Francisco Suárez (1548–1617). Another early Spanish writer on the subject of international law was Francisco Suárez, professor of theology at the university of Coïmbra.[4] In his famous *Treatise on Laws and God as Legislator* (1612) he held that the *jus gentium* was different in kind from natural law, was in fact a body of law applying between independent states rather than one common to all states, and furthermore represented a body of rules voluntarily instituted by men. Although countries were independent, Suárez argued, they were never wholly relieved of some interrelationship existing among them, were in some measure dependent on one another, and therefore required a body of rules to govern their relations. It is thus with Suárez that one first encounters the modern

---

Nussbaum, in Lauterpacht's *Oppenheim,* Vol. I, pp. 85–95, and in Svarlien, pp. 71–79; much material on selected writers such as Vitoria and Grotius may also be found in standard histories of Western political thought, particularly in the writings of Dunning.

[4] Nussbaum, pp. 80–91.

concept of a society or community of sovereign states, tied together by a body of law applying to their mutual relations. *Jus gentium* was considered by him to be an intermediary system of law, lying between natural law and civil (domestic) law. He differentiated, however, quite clearly between the two usages of the term *jus gentium:* he showed that it could mean the common elements of different legal systems as well as the principles and rules to be observed in the relations between independent states; to him, the latter meaning was the more correct and important one.

Albericus Gentilis (1552–1608). In the founding of modern international law, Gentilis was the third of the outstanding forerunners of Hugo Grotius.[5] An Italian Protestant refugee from religious persecution, Gentilis came to England in 1580 and received an appointment to Oxford University in the following year. In 1585 he published an important treatise on law, the *Three Books on Embassies.* After a brief period spent in Germany, he returned to England and became Regius Professor of Civil Law at Oxford. In 1598 he published his major work, *Three Books on the Law of War.*

The importance of Gentilis in the development of international law rests on his quite remarkable ability to divorce that law from theology. Although he never fully achieved the separation—and it could not have been expected of him in his age—Gentilis did succeed in seceding, most of the time, from the scholastic tradition characteristic of his predecessors and contemporaries in the legal field. Much of his documentation was based on civil law and on the writings of historians rather than on the Scriptures and the Church Fathers.

In his *Pleas of a Spanish Advocate,* published posthumously in 1613, Gentilis wrote primarily on matters connected with maritime law, such as freedom of the seas, sovereignty over coastal waters, privateering, and piracy. In this work he relied almost exclusively on legal writings for supporting evidence; no other kind of documentation appeared to be wholly satisfactory to him and as a result the work presented an exceedingly modern outlook and approach.

Huigh Cornets de Groot (1583–1645). Better known as Hugo Grotius, de Groot is generally accepted as the father of international law.[6] His interest in the subject developed through an unusual and important case. In the course of the war against Spain, a fleet of the Dutch East India Company captured, in 1601, a Portuguese vessel. The ship was brought,

[5] See Nussbaum, pp. 94–101; also the translations of Gentilis' two major works: the *Hispanicae Advocationis Libri Duo,* Latin text with English trans. by F. Abbott (New York, 1921), and the *De Jure Belli Libri Tres,* Latin text with English translation by J. C. Rolfe (Washington, D.C.: U.S. Government Printing Office, 1933).

[6] See Nussbaum, pp. 102–114, and Lauterpacht's *Oppenheim,* Vol. I, pp. 91–94. Grotius' two major works are available in English: *The Law of War and Peace,* F. W. Kelsey *et al.,* trans. (London, 1925), and *The Freedom of the Seas,* R. Van D. Magoffin, trans. (New York, 1916).

with its cargo, to Holland and sold as a prize of war, Portugal then being under Spanish domination. Oddly enough, some stockholders in the Company objected to the highly profitable transaction, claiming that Christians should not wage war, certainly not upon one another. The Company retained Grotius, requesting an opinion on the objections raised, and the young lawyer fulfilled his assignment by writing an essay, *Commentary on the Law of Prize and Booty (De Jure Praedae Commentarius)*, in 1604–5. The bulk of this work remained in manuscript form and was discovered only in 1864; the twelfth chapter, however, was revised and published in 1609 under the title *The Freedom of the Seas (Mare Liberum)*, an illuminating study of the doctrine of the freedom of the seas.[7]

He wrote his greatest work, the *Three Books on the Law of War and Peace (De Jure Belli ac Pacis Libri Tres*, 1625), the first systematic treatment of positive international law, in France. Despite its title, the work dealt only incidentally with the law of peace, and its bulk was concentrated, as in the case of most of his predecessors, on war. Nevertheless the portions of the book dealing with peace (Book II, Chapters 1–19), filled with elaborate rules of national conduct based on the Scriptures, ancient history, and the classics, represented a unique contribution to the law and, in addition, a decided innovation in works on the subject.

With respect to the laws of warfare, Grotius leaned heavily in the direction of the scholastic writers, with frequent citations, particularly from the works of Vitoria. In discussing the nature of the traditional *jus gentium*, however, Grotius went to considerable lengths to explain that it represented, in his opinion, law both human (that is, not divine in origin) and volitional, a body of rules deliberately created by human beings to serve human needs. In other words, the rules governing relations between states were to Grotius not just customs, or perhaps derivations obtained through the use of "right reason," but rules created independently by human will.

Grotius believed that there were customary rules governing the behavior of states as well as rules which he thought to be the outcome or results of the law of nature. He consistently referred to the first group as the *jus gentium* or *jus voluntarium* and to the latter group of rules as the *jus naturale* (later called natural law of nations). Unfortunately he vacillated between the two kinds of law and apparently was unable to draw a clear-cut distinction between them.

The customary or voluntary law appears to have been viewed by Grotius as relatively unimportant and the bulk of his writing was con-

---

[7] The complete work was made available in English for the first time in 1950 as the final number of the *Classics of International Law* (2 vols., London). The *Commentary* is characterized by an unusual emphasis on the rights of the individual under natural law, an emphasis said to be unequaled again in the literature of international law until very recent years. A good summary may be found in *Current History*, October, 1951, pp. 225–226.

centrated on the natural law aspects of his subject. It was this distinction between a natural law of nations, as developed by him, and the customary or voluntary law, expounded by Zouche, which was the direct cause of the rise of three separate schools of legal philosophy in the seventeenth and eighteenth centuries: the Naturalists, the Positivists, and the Grotians. The Naturalists, led by Samuel Pufendorf, denied that any positive law of nations originated from custom or treaties; they maintained, with Thomas Hobbes, that international law was merely a part of the law of nature.

The Positivists, in turn, opposed the followers of Pufendorf in believing that a positive law of nations had its true origin in custom and treaties, hence in the consent of states, and that this law was far more important than any natural law of nations. Some of the writers of this school went so far as to deny the very existence of a law of nature. The leading positivist was the famous Dutch jurist Cornelius van Bynkershoek.

The Grotians held to a middle position in the controversy, asserting that Grotius himself had drawn tenable distinctions between natural and voluntary law. They differed from the founder in insisting that both kinds of law possessed equal importance. Most of the leading legal writers of the period were Grotians, but few of them, with the exception of Emmerich de Vattel, attained an international reputation.

Virtually all forerunners of Grotius had limited their learned discussions of war, both just and unjust, to the beginning of a conflict. Grotius opened a vast new area for speculation and debate when he included in his work a detailed discussion of the conduct of military operations and of the legal consequences and considerations involved. With insight, tolerance, and an eloquent use of examples borrowed from the past he urged moderation in warfare, discussed the status and fate of hostages, the destruction of property, the problem of the religious beliefs of defeated peoples, and a host of other questions ignored or evaded by his predecessors. He did not believe that this particular portion of the *Law of War and Peace* represented a collection of legally binding principles: he saw his discussion of the conduct of hostilities as a form of personal advice to statesmen and military commanders. It is a tribute to the essential goodness of human nature that even his early readers and critics regarded this section of the work as one of the most admirable contributions made by Grotius.

The writings of Grotius also contributed much new and original thought on a great number of specific topics, particularly those of neutrality, freedom of the seas, treaties, and diplomatic practice. Neutrality did exist in fact, though much hampered, in his own time, but his was the first analysis of the legal status, rights, privileges, and duties of a neutral state. Considering the time in which his contribution was composed, it is not strange, of course, that belligerents received far more favorable treatment at his hands than did neutral nations. As far as the high seas were concerned, Grotius was the first writer to proclaim in unmistakable terms the concept of the freedom of the world's oceans and to attack with energy and vast learning the monopolistic claims of his own era to navigation and fishing privileges.

Treaties appeared in his books as distinct from normal contracts and, furthermore, as binding, in general, on the successors of a ruler who had been an original party to the agreement in question. Grotius, as could be expected, upheld good faith and the sanctity of international pacts but apparently could not bring himself to deny the old claim that a treaty was null and void when conditions prevailing at the time of its conclusion had changed subsequently. So he compromised, accepted the voidance of a treaty specifically made in contemplation of a continuation of existing conditions, and finally went so far as to admit that if a state found further observance of an agreement "too grave and unbearable," it would be freed of its obligation.

The most important contribution made by Grotius to the laws and rules of diplomacy was his explicit statement of the notion of diplomatic extraterritoriality, that is, of the "fiction" that a diplomat was to be considered immune from the jurisdiction of his host state. In the elaboration of this concept, Grotius went into considerable detail about privileges and immunities of diplomatic agents.

Richard Zouche (1590–1660). For many years a successor of Gentilis at Oxford and also for a time a judge of the Admiralty Court, Zouche must be considered (even though briefly) in view of his profound influence on the development of international law.[8] In 1650, he published a heavy tome oddly styled *Explanation of the Jus Fetiale and of the Questions Concerning It (Juris et Judicii Fecialis, sive Juris inter Gentes et Quaestionum de Eodem Explicatio).* This represented the sixth and final volume in a series of texts written by Zouche for the use of his students. The main title was traceable to the author's reluctance to make use of the obvious term *jus gentium* for international law. Apparently suspecting correctly that most of his readers would not recognize any reference to the fetial law of ancient Rome, Zouche inserted *jus inter gentes* (law among nations) as a kind of subtitle.

Zouche is important because his treatise represents the first systematic and comprehensive treatment of the entire subject of international law, elevating, in contrast to Grotius, the law of peace to a position of equality with the law of war. More important from the historical point of view, Zouche must be regarded as the true founder of the positivist school of law, that is, of those writers who maintain that the actual practice of states, based on consent (assent, agreement), constitutes the true source of international law.

His work, despite many weaknesses and the inclusion of numerous

[8] The text of Zouche's work is available in an English translation by James T. Brierly (Washington, D.C.: U.S. Government Printing Office, 1911).

topics not considered today to lie within the scope of international law, is usually represented as marking the dividing point between the old reliance on natural law and the new emphasis on manmade rules for the conduct of international relations.

Samuel Pufendorf (1632–1694). Pufendorf was the world's first professor of international law. On the other hand, scholars still disagree, in a surprisingly voluminous literature, as to whether he contributed much or little to the growth of the law, beyond being the founder of the so-called naturalist school of legal philosophy.

He developed a new system of jurisprudence of his own which he eventually published in 1660 under the title *Two Books on the Elements of Universal Jurisprudence.* The work attracted considerable attention and in consequence of his new fame, Pufendorf was appointed to a newly created professorship of natural and international law at the University of Heidelberg. In 1670 he went to Sweden to teach at the University of Lund; there he wrote and published a second major work, *Eight Books on the Law of Nature and of Nations* (1672).[9] The rest of his life was devoted to historical studies, first at Stockholm, later at Berlin.

The *Elements* summarized Pufendorf's essential contributions to international law. Admitting his indebtedness to both Grotius and Thomas Hobbes, he apparently stood midway between their rather divergent views and attempted to reconcile them. He denied the importance and binding force of custom and treaties, refusing to accept them as true sources of the law. In common with most thinkers of his age, Pufendorf implicitly believed in the existence of a state of nature antedating the historical state and held that in this prepolitical situation a law of nature was binding on all men. Only this law, rather than the consent of states, could establish legally binding principles and hence had to be regarded as the sole source of international law. His concept of the law of nature embraced those standards of behavior which experience and reason (the latter growing out of both experience and instruction) showed men, as they grew in knowledge, to be essential for their own good and for the good of the human society of which they formed a part in accordance with the design of nature.

Thus Pufendorf's natural law could be defined as the product of reason and experience in society. He maintained in consequence that international law was merely a part of natural law and that peace was more in harmony with that natural law than was true of war.

Cornelius van Bynkershoek (1673–1743). A celebrated Dutch jurist, member and, from 1724 to his death, president of the Supreme Court of Holland, Zeeland, and West Friesland, Bynkershoek was the leading exponent of the positivist school. While he never wrote a comprehensive

[9] Both works are available in English; the *Elements,* F. G. Moore, trans. (New York: Oxford University Press, 1927); the *Eight Books,* C. H. and W. A. Oldfather, trans. (New York: Oxford University Press, 1931).

treatise on the law of nations, he dealt with specific parts of the subject in a number of well-known works, notably the early *Dominion of the Seas* (1702), *Jurisdiction over Ambassadors* (1721), and his major work, *Questions of Public Law* (1737).[10]

He maintained that the basis of international law was to be found only in the common consent of nations, expressed in turn either through custom or through treaties. The source of the law was in reason, in the use of common sense in finding the best and most just solution to a particular problem. Bynkershoek believed that such reason could find support in treaties and in widely established precedents (customs). Unlike most of his contemporaries, he rejected recourse to ancient history as a source of acceptable illustrations and concentrated on the recent and current practice of states.

Most of Bynkershoek's contributions to the development of the law were in the sphere of the rules governing neutrality, with emphasis on a neutral duty to abstain from showing any preference to a belligerent, on blockade, on prize law, and on the subject of treaties in general. One famous tenet of the Dutch jurist has become beloved by all historians of international law: he held that control of territorial waters off a national coast extended only as far as cannon could carry. This principle, almost universally accepted shortly after its formulation, became the basis of the three-mile limit of territorial waters when the range of coastal artillery remained fixed, for an appreciable period of time during the late eighteenth century, at about one marine league (about three miles).

Emmerich de Vattel (1714–1767). A leading early proponent of the Grotian school of legal philosophy, Vattel was a native of Switzerland. During most of his adult life he served in a diplomatic capacity, later as a privy councillor in charge of foreign affairs, under the Elector of Saxony. His major work, *International Law: or, Principles of Natural Law Applied to the Conduct and Affairs of Nations and of Sovereigns* (1758), designed as a practical manual for statesmen, became the standard European reference work in international law and is cited even today on rare occasions.[11] It can be maintained seriously that despite the vital contributions of Grotius, no single writer has exercised as much direct and lasting influence on the men engaged in the conduct of international affairs in the legal sphere, at least until very modern times, as did Vattel. And this appears to have been true despite the well-known fact that Vattel was the father of the doctrine of the equality of states, "a misleading deduction from unsound premises," [12] with a consistent and exagger-

---

[10] English versions of the three works are available: the *Dominion*, R. Van D. Magoffin, trans. (New York, 1923); the *Jurisdiction over Ambassadors*, G. J. Laing, trans. (New York: Oxford University Press, 1939); the *Questions*, T. Frank, trans. (New York: Oxford University Press, 1930).

[11] The work was translated into English by Charles G. Fenwick (Washington, D.C.: U.S. Government Printing Office, 1916).

[12] Brierly, p. 37.

ated emphasis on the sovereign independence of states found throughout the work.

Vattel's writings, almost forgotten now except in France, have been criticized severely by modern legal historians. Most of the adverse comments have centered on his deliberate lowering of the importance attributed to natural law compared with that accorded to voluntary law while at the same time lacking any convincing explanation of the pertinent question, Why should states feel obliged to observe a voluntary law of nations? Failure to supply an adequate basis for obedience trapped Vattel into unfortunate contradictions and exceptions to dogmatic statements.[13]

Nevertheless, despite theoretical weaknesses, Vattel's work went through edition after edition and was a best seller among legal commentaries for many decades. It was a particular favorite in the United States and as late as 1887 was cited in decisions of the Supreme Court of the United States.

Johann Jakob Moser (1701–1785). With Bynkershoek, Moser shares the claim to be one of the fathers of the positivist school, not because he originated the positivist approach but because the most vigorous attacks on the older metaphysical approach to international law are to be found in his writings. His major work, the *Essay on the Newest European International Law* (eight volumes, 1777–1780), contained a biting criticism of the natural law school, based primarily on Moser's contention that the leading defenders of that law could not agree on its fundamental principles and that the princes of this world paid no attention to such a "law."

Instead, Moser founded the principles of international law on treaties as the basic source, followed by far more numerous customs that had attained legally binding character and constituted his second source of the law. His approach soon became the fashionable view among most publicists of the nineteenth and twentieth centuries and has even been enshrined, as we have seen, in Article 38 of the Statute of the International Court of Justice.

PROGRESS OF INTERNATIONAL LAW SINCE 1800

International law has progressed greatly since the days of the classical writers. As Oppenheim pointed out,[14] three factors proved to be of particular importance: the willingness of most states, after the Congress of Vienna, to submit to the rules of the law; the conclusion of numerous law-making treaties during the past 150 years (the latest important ones being the four Geneva Conventions of 1949 and the various conventions on the law of the sea signed at Geneva in 1958); and the rise of the posi-

---

[13] Corbett, pp. 29–32, supplied some illuminating examples of such flaws in Vattel's reasoning.

[14] Lauterpacht's *Oppenheim*, Vol. I, pp. 106–107.

tivist school to a position of predominance in legal thought.[15] By the end of the nineteenth century, most authorities on international law conceded only the will of nations to be the source of the law, a view typical of a period in which the absolute sovereignty of states was affirmed with conviction by virtually every statesman and publicist.

The growth of positivist thought had taken place concurrently with the decline of natural law doctrines and with the increasingly powerful intrusion of political factors in international relations. As nationalism prompted state after state to engage in power politics of the crassest sort, the concept of an international law based primarily on moral foundations, on principle, retreated and in its place was substituted the criterion of effectiveness, of "is" over "ought." Many positivists did not deny the existence of an order superior to man-made law but denied emphatically that such an order bore any kind of relationship to legal rules prevailing in relations among states.

Since the end of World War I, a change in outlook has been clearly in evidence and the trend of juristic thinking has veered away to some extent from a rigid adherence to the traditional positivist philosophy. Many leading publicists admit today that when no rule based on actual state practice exists, reference can and should be made to principles of justice and to general principles of law. It therefore has been claimed by some that pure positivism is being replaced by an approach very much akin to that adopted by the old Grotian school of legal philosophy.

It cannot be denied that the positivists carried the attempt to reduce international law to a system too far when seen from the point of view of reality. By exaggerating the validity of principles claimed to be valid and by separating many of those same principles from the political sphere in which they were held to operate, reality was sacrificed and the law as stated proved to be quite inadequate to meet the demands of international political behavior. On the other hand, it can scarcely be doubted that moral principles and ethics play only a relatively minor part in the bulk of modern international relations and that such parts of international law as are observed in the regular practices of nations rest essentially on custom and treaties. Hence the basic element of positivism, the exclusion of everything not traceable directly to explicit or implied agreements among states, appears to possess considerable validity, provided that it is related to actual observance and is not expanded into an all-inclusive and static system.

International law, when viewed from this position, can be analyzed and explained in realistic terms and can be shown to grow and expand in scope even in this age of power politics. At the same time, a modified positivist

---

[15] See the valuable study by John P. Humphrey, "On the Foundations of International Law," 39 *A.J.I.L.* (1945), pp. 231–243; Roberto Ago, "Positive Law and International Law," *ibid.*, 51 (1957), pp. 691–733; and Gould, pp. 69–86, as well as Whiteman, Vol. I, pp. 9–19.

approach along the preceding lines may show the weaknesses of approaches such as that taken by the neopositivist school founded by Hans Kelsen. The latter tried to separate completely the world of actuality and a world of legal norms. Such a divorce of principles supposedly establishing the conduct of states from the political aspirations and political methods utilized by states in their individualistic struggle for survival and for power must be condemned as an extremely unrealistic and scarcely fruitful enterprise, except when viewed as a contribution to pure legal philosophy. It cannot be said to contribute much to the knowledge of students desiring to learn about the operative rules of the law of nations, for, as Machiavelli argued with great insight in *The Prince* (Chapter XV), "how we live is so different from how we ought to live that he who studies what ought to be done rather than what is done will learn the way to his downfall rather than to his preservation."

Kelsen's school of thought (the Vienna School) attempted to create a "pure science of law" by drawing clear-cut distinctions between natural law and positive law. The latter was viewed as a rule that had to be obeyed because certain acts were lawful since they were done under the authority of the constitution. This basic principle (norm) enabled one, so it was claimed, to determine accurately what were the rules of law in force in contrast to those that "ought to be" in force. In the sphere of international law, the basic assumption was that custom possessed the creative force to make obligatory rules of law. Later came treaties, drawing their own obligatory binding power from the customary law principle *pacta sunt servanda* (treaties must be observed). Still later came rules issued by international agencies, such as the World Court, in turn created by treaty.[16]

Other monists, such as A. von Verdross (and Josef L. Kunz in the United States), espoused the doctrine of the primacy of international law, asserting that only that primacy could be taken as the basis of a unified and unitary legal system.[17]

In contrast, a number of modern writers have emphasized the social aspects involved in the formulation of legal principles. Such theorists as Hugo Krabbe and Leon Duguit have held that law (at any level) develops naturally from the social organization and problems of society.[18] In other words, these so-called Social Naturalists believed that regardless of the "justness" of legal principles, the latter stemmed as logical consequences

[16] See Hans Kelsen, *General Theory of Law and State* (Cambridge, Mass.: Harvard University Press, 1945) and his *Principles of International Law* (New York: Holt, Rinehart & Winston, 1952), especially the latter work at pp. 403–447 (a second edition, revised and edited by Robert W. Tucker, appeared in 1966).

[17] See particularly J. L. Kunz, "On the Theoretical Basis of the Law of Nations," 10 *T.G.S.* (1924), pp. 115–142.

[18] See Hugo Krabbe, *The Modern Idea of the State* (New York: Appleton-Century-Crofts, 1922), at pp. 83–90; Leon Duguit, "Objective Law," 20 *Columbia Law Review* (1920), pp. 817–831; *ibid.*, 21 (1921), pp. 17–34, 126–143, and 242–256.

from certain causal actions or events.[19] Sovereignty as such therefore could not be viewed as the cause of law, but instead social solidarity and the problem of actual societies were to be taken as the causative factors.

Beginning in 1933, Judge A. Alvarez advocated a reconstruction of international law based on a "psychology of peoples" concept, an approach more recently emphasized by F. S. C. Northrup in his "philosophical-sociological theory." [20]

The approach adopted in this volume reflects a modified positivist and dualist point of view, with emphasis on rules of law accepted in the actual conduct of international relations and based on customs and treaties as the basic sources of the law. It must not be forgotten, however, that just as the theories underlying the nature of the law change, so do the principles and rules which comprise that law. International law is, and has been for some decades, in a definite state of transition. New principles have been added by such treaties as the Charter of the United Nations, the Genocide Convention, the four Geneva Conventions of 1949; new interpretations of accepted rules have been supplied by international tribunals; and a vast amount of research and attempts at codification has been and is being undertaken by private and public bodies.[21]

Many rules generally accepted only thirty or so years ago are being challenged by an increasing number of states, particularly by the Communist states of Europe and Asia.[22] Limitations of space do not permit a detailed analysis of the development of a separate Soviet theory of international law, a theory which, too, is in a state of flux, particularly since the death of Stalin.

It should be noted that the keystone of Soviet legal thought is the doctrine of national sovereignty, with particular emphasis on nonintervention in the internal affairs of other states, in this case, of course, in the affairs of the Soviet Union. This emphasis may strike Western observers as incongruous, in view of the actual foreign policies of the U.S.S.R., but it is typical of a society claiming to be revolutionary. Nonintervention would quite obviously be based on a double standard as long as the missionary zeal for world improvement dominated the Soviet outlook on foreign affairs. Mutuality would then depend entirely on the current foreign policy of the revolutionary society which, at all times, would insist that no intervention should be applied to it.

In the period following World War II, Soviet writers have tended to emphasize a tripartite division in international law: one body of rules is

[19] See also Jacobini, at p. 29.

[20] F. S. C. Northrup, "Contemporary Jurisprudence and International Law," 61 *Yale Law Journal* (1952), pp. 623–654; see Stone, pp. lii–liii, for a critique of Northrup's concepts.

[21] See the monographic study by the International Commission (n. 2, Chapter 2, *supra*).

[22] See Josef L. Kunz, "Pluralism of Legal and Value Systems and International Law," 49 *A.J.I.L.* (1955), pp. 370–376.

said to apply to relations between "socialist" (that is, Communist) states; another body of rules is held to apply between non-Communist (that is, "bourgeois") states; and a third group of rules and principles is said to govern relationships between socialists and bourgeois nations. The last of these groupings is the one which appears to be heavily influenced by the twin concepts of consent and absolute sovereignty. Thus, in the belief that the U.S.S.R. is by definition in the right, it has been asserted that a war would be nonannexationist and of a liberating nature if it had "for its purpose either the defense of a nation against external aggression [a most unobjectionable point of view, of course] and the attempt at enslaving her, or the liberation of the people from capitalist slavery, or the emancipation of colonies and dependent territories from the imperialist yoke." [23]

Contrary to popular belief, the Soviet Union has observed routinely most of the rules of customary international law as well as the nonpolitical (technical) agreements concluded with other states and with public international organizations. Russian acceptance and observance of international law finds its obvious basis in expediency dictated by the need for coexistence with non-Communist states as well as by the obvious fact that selected interests of Communist and non-Communist states do coincide. On the other hand, international law has also been utilized extensively and frequently for the promotion of the political and ideological aims of the Soviet state. Propaganda campaigns in the uncommitted nations as well as in Latin America have centered repeatedly on slogans based on ideas culled from the principles of international law, primarily on component parts of sovereignty, such as self-determination, nonintervention, equality, and so on.

The key concept developed by Soviet legal experts is a sort of "natural law," based on the Marxist-Leninist "laws" of historical development. This new "law" allegedly occupies a place higher than positive international law. Its main current source, according to the Soviet analysis, is to be found in the Charter of the United Nations, and that source is to be applied as a "criterion" of the validity of the rules of positive international law. This approach permits Soviet analysts to select treaties (or rules of customary law) and to hold them void as being contrary to the superior Marxist-Leninist "natural law." [24] The latter normally is styled, propagandistically, "socialist international law" or "modern international law."

[23] W. W. Kulski, "Present Trends in Soviet International Law," *Proceedings* (1953), pp. 59–75, at pp. 61 ff.

[24] See the lucid and authoritative analysis in Bernard A. Ramundo, *Peaceful Coexistence: International Law in the Building of Communism* (Baltimore: The Johns Hopkins Press, 1967), as well as the brief but heavily documented study by John B. Quigley, Jr., "The New Soviet Approach to International Law," 7 *Harvard International Law Club Journal* (Winter, 1965), pp. 1–32; and consult Whiteman, Vol. I, pp. 29–32. See also the Brezhnev Doctrine, p. 167 below.

In essence, the Soviet lawyers and government are willing to recognize such parts of international law as can be utilized to facilitate the execution of the "stated tasks" of the Soviet Union, while rejecting those which conflict with, or hinder, those purposes. Hence the Soviet state has been selective in its use of international law, denying the applicability of a given treaty or rule, despite the fact that Soviet authorities pay lip-service to the principle of *pacta sunt servanda* and to the importance of customary law. It follows naturally that if all states adopted this Soviet attitude, all international law would lose any element of meaning.

In view of the changes and challenges observable in the international law of our day, it should be remembered that the rules and principles outlined in the following chapters are not at all static in nature. In a number of instances a given customary or conventional rule will clearly appear to be outdated or at best inadequate—the greater portion of the law of war comes to mind as the most striking example. In other instances an obvious gap will show itself in the legal regulation of some well-known part of interstate activity—economic international relations in both peace and war may serve as an illustration. Again, wholly new areas of possible international action have appeared or are likely to appear soon, for which no rules have yet been developed, except on an academic basis by analogy to various existing rules applying to a sphere which may or may not correspond closely to the new area of intercourse. This appears to be particularly true for the area of national space programs which, almost by definition, may impinge on what may be claimed as natural preserves or legal rights of other nations engaged in similar activities. It can only be hoped that time, reason, and goodwill may join in creating an expanded and current body of rules generally accepted as obligatory by the states of the world for the sake of expediency, justice, and peace.

SUGGESTED READINGS

DEVELOPMENT OF THE LAW, GENERAL

Brierly, pp. 25–40, 51–56; Corbett, pp. 21–52; Gould, pp. 31–100; Paul Guggenheim, "What Is Positive International Law?" in Lipsky, pp. 15–30; Kaplan-Katzenbach, pp. 56–80; Stone, pp. 26–49; Kurt Wilk, "International Law and Global Ideological Conflict: Reflections on the Universality of International Law," 45 *A.J.I.L.* (1951), pp. 648–670; Philip C. Jessup, "Diversity and Uniformity in the Law of Nations," *ibid.*, 58 (1964), pp. 341–358; and Anthony A. D'Amato, "The Neo-Positivist Concept of International Law," *ibid.*, 59 (1965), pp. 321–324.

CODIFICATION OF INTERNATIONAL LAW

Whiteman, Vol. I, pp. 131–220; Herbert W. Briggs, *The International Law Commission* (Ithaca, N.Y.: Cornell University Press, 1965); Hersch Lauterpacht, "Codification and Development of International Law," 49 *A.J.I.L.*

(1955), pp. 16–43; Eugeniusz Wyzner, "Selected Problems of the U.N. Program for the Codification and Progressive Development of International Law," *Proceedings* (1962), pp. 90–99; Ernest L. Kerley, "United Nations Contribution to Developing International Law," *ibid.*, pp. 99–105; Edwin C. Hoyt, "The Contribution of the International Law Commission," *ibid.* (1965), pp. 2–8; Luke T. Lee, "The International Law Commission Re-Examined," 59 *A.J.I.L.* (1965), pp. 545–569.

SOVIET ATTITUDES

Consult the excellent and readable summary in Gould, pp. 86–100, which includes copious bibliographical notes for further research. See also John N. Hazard, "Soviet Socialism as a Public Order System," *Proceedings* (1959), pp. 30–41; Oliver J. Lissitzin, "Western and Soviet Perspectives on International Law," *ibid.*, pp. 21–30, and the valuable discussion of those papers, *ibid.*, pp. 41–48. Other informative studies of the subject include Jan F. Triska and R. M. Slussar, "Treaties and Other Sources of Order in International Relations: The Soviet View," 52 *A.J.I.L.* (1958), pp. 699–726, and their more extensive study, *The Theory, Law and Policy of Soviet Treaties* (Stanford, Calif.: Stanford University Press, 1962); the heavily documented study by Edward McWhinney, " 'Peaceful Co-Existence' and Soviet-Western International Law," 56 *A.J.I.L.* (1962), pp. 951–970; the commentary and numerous bibliographical suggestions in Arthur Larson, *Design for Research in International Law* (Durham, N.C.: World Rule of Law Center, Duke University School of Law, 1961), pp. 85–91; Hans W. Baade, ed., *The Soviet Impact on International Law* (Dobbs Ferry, N.Y.: Oceana Publications, 1966); Edward McWhinney, *"Peaceful Coexistence" and Soviet-Western International Law* (Leyden: A. W. Sythoff, 1964) and his *Law, Foreign Policy, and the East-West Détente* (Toronto: University of Toronto Press, 1964)—both works influenced by the author's somewhat unorthodox concepts—his ideas are condensed in his "Changing International Law Method and Objectives in the Era of the Soviet-Western Détente," 59 *A.J.L.L.* (1965), pp. 1–14; George Ginsburgs, "A Case Study of the Soviet Use of International Law: Eastern Poland in 1939," *ibid.*, 52 (1958), pp. 69–84; Evgeny N. Nasinovsky, "The Impact of Fifty Years of Soviet Theory and Practice on International Law," *Proceedings* (1968), pp. 189–196; George Ginsburgs, "The View from Without," *ibid.*, pp. 196–203; A. V. Freeman, "Some Aspects of Soviet Influence on International Law," 62 *A.J.I.L.* (1968), pp. 710–722; J. B. Quigley, Jr., "The New Soviet Approach to International Law," *Harvard International Law Club Jl.*, (Winter, 1965), pp. 1–32.

CHINESE ATTITUDES

Hungdah Chiu, "Communist China's Attitude toward International Law," 60 *A.J.I.L.* (1966), pp. 245–267; Jerome A. Cohen, "Chinese Attitudes toward International Law—and Our Own," *Proceedings* (1967), pp. 108–116; Hungdah Chiu, assisted by R. R. Edwards, "Communist China's Attitude Toward the United Nations: A Legal Analysis," 62 *A.J.I.L.* (1968), pp. 20–50: see in particular notes 31 and 32, pp. 29–30.

5

Sanctions of International Law

I N STRIKING contrast to domestic law, no effective institutional machinery has as yet been developed for the application and enforcement of international law. Existing judicial agencies, including the International Court of Justice, are bypassed more frequently than they are utilized, and even those agencies cannot be regarded as true "enforcers" of the law. International law does not possess the equivalent of a hierarchy of tribunals under which a case by appeal can move from lower to higher levels. And there is no effective authority for the enforcement of decisions or awards handed down by the available courts and tribunals.

This state of affairs raised the important question of why nations consistently abide by the rules of international law, with only occasional violations considering the total number of cases in which the rules are obeyed on a day-to-day basis.

PROBLEMS OF OBEDIENCE TO INTERNATIONAL LAW

Motivation for Obedience. Much of the discussion of this question of obedience centered traditionally on the unproved assumption that the only real motivation involved was fear of the use of force by some superior. Because no such superior exists in the international sphere—barring the use of, say, United Nations forces in overwhelming strength or direct unilateral action by one of the superpowers—the assumption cannot be conceded validity. Assuredly, fear of "punishment" may on occasion play a part in bringing about a willingness, expressed by word or deed, to abide by the rules of the law. But other and more important causative factors appear to play a part.

As Brierly pointed out,[1] the ultimate reason for the binding force of any kind of law is that man, whether he is an individual or whether he is joined with others in a state, is compelled as a reasonable being to believe that order rather than chaos is the governing principle of his world.

Enlightened Self-interest. Among factors of a nonlegal nature that play a part in the maintenance of legal norms may be mentioned, as one of

[1] Brierly, p. 56.

primary importance, what could be called enlightened self-interest: the attitude that the risk of losing a decision through the application of the law might well be offset by the advantages accruing to one and all from living in a world society in which quarrels and disputes would be settled peacefully under the same set of rules of law. The process of give-and-take applied in the international sphere as it does domestically: those who profit most from living in an order regulated by law can, in the long run, expect to be able to maintain that order only by themselves making concessions, large and small, to make the order acceptable and tolerable to the members profiting least from it. At the same time, both those who profit most from the order and those who profit the least have a definite responsibility for seeing to it that the changes and concessions are achieved in an orderly manner and not through eruptions of violence. Such attitudes reflect the basic concept involved in every code of morality, as well as in every organized community, that the good of the whole may require sacrifice of a bit of the good of each part. The more this fundamental and obvious fact is realized and acted on by the community of states, the closer it will approach to the realization of a world ruled by law.

World Public Opinion. Other factors undoubtedly playing a part in promoting obedience to the rules of international law are world public opinion, already finding expression on occasion in such a forum as the General Assembly of the United Nations; the reactions, in the traditional sense, of statesmen and of peoples on a global scale; and the well-known concept of the "habit of law," the habitual acceptance of law by the individual elevated to the international (state) level.

Social Approval and Costs. In addition, a very real motivation for obedience is encompassed by the desire for social approval, found not only in individuals but also in their grouping called the state. There is also the material factor of costs: the relative burdens to a state posed by the alternatives of using force to achieve goals and of making use of legal processes to redress grievances and to achieve aims.

Expediency. There is also the extremely important factor of expediency (linked, really, quite closely to the self-interest mentioned previously): the usually undeniable advantages in pursuing international policies along established and accepted channels contrasted with the disadvantages in pursuing headstrong tactics ruthlessly and against the will, and possibly the military strength, of others, with consequent irritations, aggravations, and lack of future cooperation on the part of other states. Any government contemplating a violation of the law must consider the possible reactions of other states. Equally important, law-abiding behavior may possess definite advantages for a state: a reputation for principled behavior must be regarded, at least by most states, as an asset and as a guarantee of dependability and reliability in the eyes of other states.[2]

[2] Kaplan-Katzenbach, p. 343.

METHODS OF ENFORCING THE LAW

Two Kinds of Compliance. Any discussion of the enforcement of compliance with international law has to deal with two rather distinct concepts: violation of the rules of law themselves and failure to carry out arbitral awards or judicial decisions. The latter topic is covered subsequently. (See Chapter 23.) Here we are concerned primarily with the enforcement of the law itself.

Compliance might be brought about in a variety of ways, of which the pressure of a presumed "world public opinion" must be held to be the least effective. Although frequent reference is made to such an opinion whenever a crisis develops or the peace of the world is threatened, the fact appears to be that, except on most rare occasions, the alleged violator of international law pays little attention to world opinion.

A major and as yet unsolved problem centers on the shortness of the world's memory: unless immediate steps (political, economic, military) are taken to return the "delinquent" to observance of the rules of law, world opinion will tend to forget about the violation of the rules in a short while.

Diplomatic Protests. The traditional method of preserving the integrity of the law has been the lodgment of protests by injured or offended states against acts deemed to be violations of existing law. Such protests would commonly be coupled with demands that the wrong done be righted in an appropriate manner. Although minor violations of the law might be corrected in consequence of such protests (if only for the sake of expediency and of continued good relations), major intentional violations of the law would in most instances remain unaffected by the lodgment of diplomatic protests.

Other Modes of Legal Enforcement. If disagreement about claimed violations of international law persisted, a variety of devices could be called into play in order to secure compliance with the rules of the law: mediation by a third party, reference to a commission of inquiry or of conciliation, and so on. (See Chapter 23 concerning details of these methods for the settlement of disputes.)

Next, or alternatively, reference to an arbitration tribunal or to an international court could be attempted in order to effect compliance with the law. Arbitration could be effected only if the violator of the law agreed to such a settlement procedure. Adjudication might be found, on occasion, to be a poor way of securing compliance, in view of the weakness of current international judicial institutions, a weakness caused by the very nature of a decentralized international community.[3]

Again, compliance with international law might be secured through

---

[3] See Richard A. Falk, "On Identifying and Solving the Problem of Compliance with International Law," *Proceedings* (1964), pp. 1–9, especially p. 2.

reference to, and subsequent action by, a universal or regional international agency: to the Security Council or the General Assembly of the United Nations, or to the various regional agencies such as the Organization of American States. Such reference would initially secure extensive publicity for the alleged failure to comply with the rules of the law, and possibly public condemnation of the delinquent state. It might, more importantly, lead to the imposition of a variety of sanctions against the offending state.

Finally, national efforts could be made to bring about compliance with the rules of the law, through acts toward that effect on the part of the executive, legislative, and judicial branches of the complaining state.[4]

Sanctions. Failure to achieve compliance with international law through the normal methods for peaceful settlement of disputes could bring into being the imposition of sanctions. Political considerations would intrude even more than normally at this stage, for only such sanctions would likely be attempted as would be not only technically feasible but also politically possible and advisable: boycotts, embargoes, reprisals, and pacific blockades, adopted by an individual state, a group of states, or collectively at the behest of a universal or regional agency.[5]

The threat of sanctions, of punishment for violations of the rules of the law, has been shifted increasingly from the use of outright force to non-military techniques. Among these can be listed the rupture of diplomatic and possibly of consular relations; economic sanctions, ranging from selective reductions to total stoppage of trade; travel limitations; financial restrictions on the flow of currencies; and elimination of transportation (land, sea, air) to and from the state against which sanctions are established. In addition, the offending state may be suspended or even expelled from membership in an international agency and thus be deprived of benefits accruing from such membership as well as of the ability to vote on policies and decisions. Several agencies of the United Nations may constitutionally revoke aid or membership as an enforcement measure. A member of the United Nations organization itself, once enforcement action has begun by the Security Council under Article 5 of the Charter, may be suspended from membership, and a member which has persistently violated the principles of the Charter may be expelled by the General Assembly on recommendation of the Security Council (Article 6 of Charter).

The Security Council itself may have recourse to enforcement measures, including sanctions, under Articles 10, 39, 41, 42, 45, and 94(2) of the Charter. Thus, concerned over the failure of previous UN measures to bring an end to the secession of Southern Rhodesia, the Council

[4] Consult John G. Laylin, "Holding Invalid Acts Contrary to International Law—A Force Toward Compliance," *ibid.* (1964), pp. 33–39.

[5] Consult Chapter 24 for details on these techniques; see also Josef L. Kunz, "Sanctions in International Law," 54 *A.J.I.L.* (1960), pp. 324–347.

adopted unanimously, on May 29, 1968, a series of economic sanctions against Rhodesia.[6]

Economic sanctions have been shown to be relatively ineffective, for they have tended to unify public opinion in the sanctioned state while, concurrently, their application has tended to divide the international community. And once such coercive measures have been employed, it has become obvious to all parties that previous reliance on criticism and public opinion failed to achieve compliance with the law.[7] In fact, the record of attempted economic sanctions shows few successful applications. (See also Chapter 24.)

The Use of Force. Finally, the ultimate sanction of military force could be employed to secure compliance with international law. In view of current attitudes concerning war, a true and legal sanction could now be imposed by the United Nations by means of a collective military effort. Because such a contingency is remote, however, unilateral or multilateral military efforts might conceivably be launched, with or without approval by the Security Council or the General Assembly. The legal standing of such an action would be clouded, to say the least, in view of the rather precise provisions of the UN Charter and of the obligations assumed thereunder by the members of the United Nations.

Violations of the Laws of War. Insofar as the special area of the laws of war is concerned, compliance with existing customary or conventional rules might be enforced through the employment of four tools: publicity given by the offended party to the violations of law claimed; fear of the prosecution of guilty individuals at all levels by the offended party as war criminals (see Chapter 32); reprisals adopted by the offended party; and possibly payment of damages or reparations by the state guilty of violations, under the terms of Hague Convention IV of 1899.[8]

Another form of sanction for violations of international law is represented on occasion by individual or collective intervention in the internal affairs of a given state by other states or even by an international organization. This subject is discussed elsewhere, but can be stated to involve some very delicate interpretations of international law if the intervention is to remain lawful as a tool and sanction in the cause of law and not of aggrandizement.

Summary. Summarizing what has been said, common consent appears to be the primary reason for obedience to the law: the states of the world have agreed to be bound by generally accepted rules for the conduct of

---

[6] Text in 62 *A.J.I.L.* (1968), pp. 965–969; consult also Whiteman, Vol. 13, pp. 733–749.

[7] See the excellent treatment of economic sanctions in Rita F. and Howard J. Taubenfeld, "The 'Economic Weapon': The League and the United Nations," *Proceedings* (1964), pp. 183–205.

[8] Consult R. R. Baxter, "Forces for Compliance with the Law of War," *Proceedings* (1964), pp. 81–89.

their international relations. Once such agreement had been reached, it became a matter of reciprocal interest for states to maintain the accepted rules, particularly in view of the reciprocal need of predictability of state behavior in the areas of activity covered by the accepted rules.

However, and this fact has caused much distress to overly optimistic defenders of the law, the principles of international law appear to have been normally observed by states because they do not, as yet, make very stringent demands on those states and do not generally affect what are considered to be "vital national interests" in the opinions of those states. Basically, therefore, obedience to the law has fallen into line with Jessup's view that "international law reflects and records those accommodations which over centuries states have found it to their interest to make." [9] Self-interest, enlightened or not, appears to have been the basic reason for compliance, and all other factors mentioned must be assigned a secondary or lesser rôle. Consent to the law, and self-limitation in abiding by that consent, still represent the essential sanctions of the rules of international law.

SUGGESTED READINGS

THE SANCTIONS OF THE LAW, GENERAL

Whiteman, Vol. I, pp. 58–66; E. K. Nantwi, *The Enforcement of International Judicial Decisions and Arbitral Awards in Public International Law* (Leyden: A. W. Sijthoff, 1966); Hans Kelsen, "Sanctions in International Law under the Charter of the United Nations," 31 *Iowa Law Review* (1946), pp. 499–543; Wolfgang Friedmann, "National Sovereignty, International Cooperation, and the Reality of International Law," 10 *UCLA Law Review* (1963), pp. 739–753; Saul Mendlovitz, " 'Unrealistic' Compliance Goals," *Proceedings* (1964), pp. 9–23; Julius Stone, "Realistic Compliance Goals," *ibid.*, pp. 24–31; Gerald G. Fitzmaurice, "The Foundations of the Authority of International Law," 19 *Modern Law Review* (1956), pp. 1–13; Arthur L. Goodhart, "The Rule of Law and Absolute Sovereignty," 106 *University of Pennsylvania Law Review* (1958), pp. 943–963; Kaplan-Katzenbach, pp. 30–55; and Lauterpacht's *Oppenheim*, Vol. I, pp. 15–19.

[9] Philip C. Jessup, "International Law in 1953 A.D.," *Proceedings* (1953), pp. 8–15, at p. 10.

PART II
Subjects of International Law

6

The Community of Nations

THE existence and application of a system of law relating to all civilized states presupposes the actuality of a system of common values and attitudes, a sense of community, or in other words, that vague concept called the "community," or "family," of nations. This idea had been implanted firmly in the European tradition by the time international law assumed its modern form, even though no formal machinery existed then through which the community could operate in the legal or political sphere.

REALITY OF THE COMMUNITY CONCEPT

The concept of a community of mankind is one of the oldest heritages in Western civilization. Its origins can be traced back to the Stoic philosophers of antiquity and to such conceptions as the brotherhood of man, the social nature of man, and man's membership in a worldwide community ruled by right reason (natural law). Such beliefs, transmitted through the centuries by philosophers such as Cicero and Seneca, by Roman jurists, and by the Christian Church, received new vigor during the Renaissance when legal theorists faced the problem of a politically divided Europe.

Renaissance thought, well-expressed by Suárez and other scholars, held that man's nature, his need and desire for mutual help, could not be fulfilled in individual states but involved humanity as a whole in one great society. And that society, just like its component political parts, needed a body of law to regulate and order the relations between those parts. This conception of a world society ruled by a universal and obligatory law has dominated the thinking of most subsequent writers in the field and has not been questioned seriously until recently. Evidences of its existence have been couched in terms of international organizations, starting with the first technical groupings of the nineteenth century and ending with the founding and subsequent operations of the United Nations. Yet the argument failed because those public (state-created) agencies did not actually represent proofs of the existence of a community of nations. That concept constituted but an assertion with which the recitation of the growth of international organization and cooperation begins.

On the other hand, there has been a general assumption that there did exist a worldwide community composed of states and that these units possessed rights as well as moral obligations. The fact is that there does exist such a community for the simple reason that people talk, write, and within limits behave as if there were a community. It would, of course, be illusionary to assume that this essentially hypothetical community possesses the coherence and unity of communities of more limited scope, such as the state and lesser associations of men. As writers have pointed out on numerous occasions, the community of states fails to achieve normal standards of coherence because equality among its members is not achieved except "before the law" and, more importantly, the basic principle that the good of the whole is more weighty, more vital, than the good of any part is not accepted by the community of states—at least not yet.

Furthermore, the community of states lacks, especially in our age, a sense of solidarity, a spirit of community, with the concurrent willingness of the individual members to regulate their daily international conduct in a manner conforming to the demands of the common good of a universal society or family of nations.[1]

It must be concluded that an international community represents as yet a potential order, not an operating system. The world will lack a true legal community of mankind as long as there is a lack of legal and effective control of the use of force, as long as there has not been drawn a generally accepted and binding distinction between legal and illegal use of force, as long as no system of peaceful change has replaced self-help, and as long as no effective and obligatory collective action against any and all aggressors has been developed. In the meantime, Jeremy Bentham's comment appears still appropriate: "The community is a fictitious body, composed of the individual persons who are considered as constituting, as it were, its members. The interest of the community, then, is what? The sum of the interests of the several members who compose it" (Jeremy Bentham, *The Principles of Morals and Legislation*, I, 1789).

Until a perfected community has evolved, each state will reserve to itself the defense of its sovereignty against the application of a legal rule concerned with interests deemed to be vital by the state in question and defined as such by that state. The assertion that modern problems are transnational and must be given transnational solutions is not generally true, is too sweeping in its scope, is too optimistic, and most definitely is premature when viewed in terms of the real world of states. Today only a relatively limited number of categories of state interests are open to the

---

[1] See the stimulating discussion of this point in Kurt Wilk, "International Law and Global Ideological Conflict: Reflections on the Universality of International Law," 45 *A.J.I.L.* (1951), pp. 648–670, as well as the elaborate discussion of the breakdown of universalism in Myres S. McDougal and Harold D. Lasswell, "The Identification and Appraisal of Diverse Systems of Public Order," 53 *A.J.I.L.* (1959), pp. 1–29.

application of international law, and, repeating a portion of a quotation given earlier, that law "reflects and records those accommodations which over centuries states have found it to their interest to make." [2]

DEVELOPMENT OF THE COMMUNITY

A state may exist for a long time, functioning as an operative political community, without being a "state" in the *legal* sense. Transformation into the legal personality known as a state only comes about through the admission of the entity in question into the community of nations as a recognized member. Numerous communities possessing territory, citizens, a government, and all other appurtenances commonly associated with the concept of a state were not "persons" in international law until admitted to the community.

Beginning of the Community of Nations. The end of the Thirty Years' War (1648) is generally held to mark the true beginning of the community of nations itself: the European states participating in the peace settlements at Münster and Osnabrück may be said to have constituted the charter members of the community. The latter remained limited in the number of its members, even though occasional accessions were recorded. But until 1856 only Christian nations could join the group of states subject to the rules of international law. And, from a geographic point of view, legal writers were concerned until the beginning of the nineteenth century about the *Droit des Gens de l'Europe* (the law of the nations of Europe), referring to all other states as *pays hors chrétienté* (countries outside of Christianity). By the terms of Article 7 of the Treaty of Paris, the Ottoman Empire was admitted "to participate in the public law and system of Europe." [3] Soon the various Balkan states followed suit and by the end of the nineteenth century such non-European and non-Christian countries as Persia, Siam, China, and Japan had been admitted to the community, even though certain restrictions in the form of extraterritorial privileges were exacted from them. The current century witnessed a great expansion in the membership of the community until today more than one hundred states form its components. As yet there is no closing of the gates in sight, since a number of colonial areas still look forward to political independence and to admission into the family of nations.

Legal Status of the Community. The legal status of the community has been the subject of much dispute among jurists. Beginning originally as a concept primarily moral in nature, the community achieved increasingly positive status. Newly admitted members were, and still are, bound at once and without choice by all generally accepted rules of customary interna-

---

[2] Philip C. Jessup, "International Law in 1953 A.D.," *Proceedings* (1952), p. 10.
[3] Hugh M. Wood, "The Treaty of Paris and Turkey's Status in International Law," 37 *A.J.I.L.* (1943), pp. 262–274.

tional law; they were expected to adhere, in general, at their early convenience to the major law-making treaties in force. Their position was stated clearly by Secretary of State Daniel Webster as early as 1842:

Every nation, on being received, at her own request, into the circles of civilized governments, must understand that she not only attains rights of sovereignty and the dignity of national character, but that she binds herself also to the strict and faithful observance of all those principles, laws, and usages which have obtained currency among civilized states, and which have for their object the mitigation of the miseries of war.[4]

Problems Posed by International Organizations. Several problems were posed for the community of nations by the creation first of the League of Nations and later of the United Nations. The basic concept of the League was a universal body, even though its initial membership was limited in number and though specific provision for withdrawal from the organization was inserted in the Covenant. Despite the fact that numerous countries were neither original nor subsequent members of the League, admission of countries hitherto not regarded as full or qualified members of the family of nations was generally accepted by all other countries as evidence of admission into that family. On the other hand, lack of membership in the League did not prevent a state from continuing as a member of the family of nations or would have prevented it from becoming a member of that family. As far as the United Nations Organization is concerned, with a present membership of more than 100 states, including all major powers (considering "China" to be representing both parts of that divided country), a number of states, such as Switzerland, Liechtenstein, Monaco, Western Samoa, and others, are not members of the Organization yet must be regarded as full or limited members of the family of nations. ("Germany" is not a member of the United Nations; the Federal Republic of Germany has, however, joined certain specialized agencies of the United Nations, as well as numerous regional international organizations in Europe.) On the other hand, two formal members of the United Nations, the Ukraine and the Byelorussian Republic, are not generally acknowledged to be independent states in the legal sense or in practice; they were admitted, even though they are merely components of the Soviet Union, in deference to manifestations of power politics at the San Francisco Conference in 1945. Thus membership in a comprehensive international organization does not necessarily equate with membership in the family of nations, nor is the reverse true.

MEMBERS OF THE COMMUNITY OF NATIONS

Who are the members of the community of nations? States, by definition, alone are eligible for such membership. Although certain international

[4] Moore, Vol. I, p. 10.

agencies, such as the European Coal and Steel Community and the United Nations, possess juridical personality through the treaties creating them, they are not "persons" in the meaning of being members of the family of nations.

FULLY SOVEREIGN AND INDEPENDENT STATES

In order to be a legal person, a state must own to certain characteristics. It must, first of all, occupy a fixed territory over which it exercises exclusive jurisdiction. Within this territory, stability of organization and administration must prevail and the entity must be able to fulfill its international duties and obligations.

Population represents an obvious second characteristic of a state, for without it no government would be possible. An uninhabited island would represent territory but could not be a state without a population being present.

Operation of a government forms a third characteristic of a state, for without it there could be no assurance of internal stability and of the ability to fulfill international obligations.

The presence of all three factors listed would not, however, necessarily guarantee the existence of a state in the legal sense. Puerto Rico, for instance, has territory, a government, and a population, yet Puerto Rico is not a state in the international law meaning of the term, is not a "person" subject to that law. It lacks the final and decisive requirement to be met by a state: independence. Unless a group of people possessing territory and governmental institutions also possess independence, that is the ability to regulate its internal affairs without outside interference or control, that group cannot properly claim to be a state and cannot normally become a member of the community of nations. This necessary ingredient, independence, must be as absolute as the modern legal order of the world permits it to be: even nominal subordination to an outside governmental authority must be absent.

Statehood, furthermore, involves the possession of certain other characteristics—Gould called them "physical capacities,"[5] namely the ability to send and to receive diplomatic agents, the capacity of its agents to conclude treaties in the name of the state, and the ability to apply to international tribunals in the event that grievances exist against other states. In addition, a state must assume responsibility for actions taken by any of its members acting as agents or in some other official capacity. Obviously, no community can commit a wrong except as individual members of that community commit a wrong. This means that the state ought to be responsible for all individual actions undertaken in connection with the operation or functioning of the state. Normally, if an individual transgresses against the domestic law of a given state, even though acting nominally on behalf of that state, no responsibility attaches to the latter

[5] Gould, p. 184.

unless it had directed the action to be undertaken or subsequently approves, ratifies, or otherwise endorses it.

In short, if a given entity possesses territory, population, a government operating effectively within the territory, independence from outside control and specific international capacities, then a state in the true legal sense of the term exists. Once admitted, such a state would constitute a full-fledged member of the family, or community, of states. Thus the United States, the United Kingdom, France, the Soviet Union, Denmark, Turkey, and scores of other countries are full members of the community. They are true international persons and represent in every way what are called subjects of international law.

UNIONS OF SOVEREIGN STATES

In addition to these *individual* independent states, historical development has caused the appearance of what are commonly termed *composite international persons*. Such an entity comes into being when two independent states are linked in such a manner that they act internationally as a single unit. Two varieties of such composite units exist today: real unions and federal states. On the other hand, so-called personal unions and confederations are not international persons, except as far as their individual components are concerned.

Personal Unions. A personal union exists when two sovereign states are joined through the fact that they possess the same monarch. Examples would be the union of Great Britain and Hanover from 1714 to 1837, that of the Netherlands and Luxembourg from 1815 to 1890, that of Belgium and the Congo Free State from 1885 to 1908, and, since 1931, each of the members of the British Commonwealth of Nations in its relation to Great Britain (union through Queen Elizabeth II at the present time: she is, concurrently, Queen of Canada and Queen of England, for example).[6] In every instance each state remained a separate and distinct person in the eyes of international law. Theoretically, the members of such a personal union could even wage war against one another, unlikely as such a possibility would be. If, as has happened, the members of the union are represented in a given foreign capital by one and the same individual, that agent is the envoy of both states at the same time but not of the personal union itself.

Confederations. Confederations are encountered when a number of independent states are linked by treaty in a union with central governmental organs of its own, invested with specified powers over the member states but not over the citizens of those states. Such a confederation normally is not an international person: each of its member states remains a separate

[6] A discussion of the intriguing development of the British Dominions from colonial status to independence exceeds the limits of this work. Interested readers are referred to the succinct account in Bishop, pp. 229–232 and to the sources cited there, as well as to Lauterpacht's *Oppenheim*, Vol. I, pp. 198–212.

subject of international law.[7] It may conclude treaties with other countries (provided such agreements do not prejudice the interests of the confederation as a whole), maintain its own diplomatic representation abroad, and act in virtually all respects as an independent nation. History has demonstrated repeatedly that this form of organization has not proved very satisfactory, and in every modern instance a different structural form has replaced the original confederation—usually the federal form. The most prominent recent confederations have included that of the Netherlands from 1580 to 1795, the United States from 1778 to 1787, the German Confederation from 1815 to 1866, Switzerland from 1291 to 1798 and again from 1815 to 1848, and the short-lived Confederation of the Rhine from 1806 to 1813. The most recent, and briefest of all, was the Republic of Central America, a confederation embracing El Salvador, Nicaragua, and Honduras from 1895 to 1898.

Real Unions. A real union, on the other hand, comes into existence when two independent states are linked by treaty under the same ruler and henceforth act internationally as a single unit.[8] A real union therefore is by no means a single state but a union of two separate states acting as a single composite international person. Normally, under the treaty or constitution linking the components, they cannot wage war against each other or separately against a foreign state; they might conclude separate treaties of commerce or of extradition, to cite two examples, but it would always be the union which would conclude the agreement on behalf of the individual members, because the latter no longer possess the status of international persons. Modern history has seen several real unions: Austria-Hungary between 1867 and 1918, Denmark and Iceland from 1918 to 1944,[9] and the Swedish-Norwegian union from 1814 to 1905, dissolved by the Treaty of Karlstad. The members of a real union represent, without question, potential individual international persons and normally achieve that status as soon as the real union is liquidated.

The union of Egypt and Syria into the single entity termed the United Arab Republic, proclaimed by the heads of the two states on February 1, 1958, did not represent a real union but rather a merger of two sovereign entities into a single unitary state.[10]

Federal States. A federal state is a permanent union of several previously independent states, with governmental organs of its own and power over its member states as well as over the citizens of the latter. A federal state is a real state, from the point of view of international law, primarily by virtue of the extensive authority exercised by the central government over the citizens of the separate member states.[11] It is the federal state which

---

[7] See Whiteman, Vol. I, pp. 426–429.
[8] *Ibid.*, pp. 476–544.
[9] *Ibid.*, pp. 366–368.
[10] *Ibid.*, pp. 422–424.
[11] *Ibid.*, pp. 380–417.

alone is competent to declare war, make peace, and conclude international political or military agreements; none of the member states can participate in any of these activities and none of them can be considered to be an international person in the true meaning of that term. Domestic constitutional provisions may, on occasion, permit limited international activity to members of a federal state, as was the case under the German constitution of 1871 and has been recently with Canada.[12] Such privileges in the international sphere must, however be regarded as abnormal; by all standards applied to international persons, individual members of a federal union are not persons under international law, are not members of the community of nations.

Most federal states provide in relevant constitutional documents for complete and exclusive assumption of foreign relations by the federal central authority. This is particularly true in the case of the United States and those federal states whose constitutions were modeled on the American pattern. The striking exceptions to the general rule are the already mentioned Soviet republics of the Ukraine and Byelorussia. Neither entity can claim to be a state in the true sense, even though both enjoy the status of voting members in the United Nations and "participated" in the making of the Satellite and Italian peace treaties in 1947.

Leaving aside the category of qualified full members of the community, full sovereignty is generally held to be a necessary condition of statehood and of international personality. For example, Count 30 of the indictment charging the defendants before the Tokyo War Crimes Tribunal with waging aggressive war against the Commonwealth of the Philippines was set aside by the Tribunal, which pointed out that from a legal point of view the Philippines had to be regarded as a part of the United States prior to the achievement of independence and that the aggressive war in question had been waged against the United States, not against a nonsovereign entity styled the Commonwealth of the Philippines.

QUALIFIED FULL MEMBERS

In addition to fully independent and sovereign states, the community of nations includes a number of categories of states which have been termed "qualified full members": neutralized states and states admitted to the community under conditions.

Neutralized States. A neutralized state differs from a neutral state in that the status of permanent neutrality (except for the obvious right of self-defense in the case of direct attack) is imposed on the neutralized state by a group of outside powers, while a neutral state adopts its status on a voluntary basis at the outset of a conflict between other countries. A neutralized state normally is also forced to agree not to enter into an alliance

[12] See Gerald F. FitzGerald, "Educational and Cultural Agreements and Ententes: France, Canada, and Quebec—Birth of a New Treaty-Making Technique for Federal States?" 60 *A.J.I.L.* (1966), pp. 529–537.

requiring its participation in any future conflict. The powers requiring its neutrality in turn obligate themselves to respect that status, such a guarantee being given either severally or jointly and severally. The number of neutralized states has never been very large: Switzerland (since 1815); Belgium (1831 and 1839); Luxembourg (1867); the Ionian Islands (1863–64); the Congo (1885); Austria (1955 to date); and Laos (1962 to date). Both World Wars saw violations of guarantees extended to neutralized states and it is doubtful whether any members of the community of nations can be considered to remain in this category except for Austria, Laos, and Switzerland. An interesting sidelight cast on the neutralized status of Switzerland was its admission into the League of Nations without being required to accept the obligations imposed on other members by Article 16 of the Covenant. On the demise of the League, Switzerland decided not to become a member of the United Nations but does "participate" in the operation of the International Court of Justice. However, it appears that since 1966 the Swiss government has become interested in eventual membership in the United Nations. On June 17, 1967, it announced that a preliminary study was to be undertaken of the advisability and implications of an application for UN membership. It should be noted that even in the event of such action, Switzerland proposed to retain her neutralized status.[13]

The neutralization of the small South Asian kingdom of Laos was accomplished by a fourteen-nation conference held in Geneva in July, 1962. The final Declaration and Protocol, both dated July 23, 1962, marked the emergence of a neutralized state in an obvious attempt to prevent a further degeneration of an already explosive military and political situation in South Asia.[14]

Numerous writers have maintained that a neutralized state is not an international person equal in standing to fully sovereign states, because the right to go to war has been asserted traditionally as one of the characteristics of an independent state and because a neutralized state has been deprived of the free exercise of this right, except in direct self-defense. The present writer does not share this attitude and feels that a neutralized state is as sovereign as most other states. But because of the widespread belief that something of vital importance has been taken away through neutralization, this group of states usually is placed in the category of "qualified full members" of the community of nations.

[13] *The New York Times,* June 18, 1967, p. 14.

[14] On neutralized entities in general, consult Cyril E. Black et al., *Neutralization and World Politics* (Princeton, N.J.: Princeton University Press, 1968), as well as Whiteman, Vol. I, pp. 342–345. On Switzerland, see Whiteman, Vol. I, p. 345; on Austria, *ibid.,* pp. 348–355; on Laos, *ibid.,* pp. 355–357, as well as John J. Czyzak and C. F. Salans, "The International Conference on the Settlement of the Laotian Question and the Geneva Agreements of 1962," 57 *A.J.I.L.* (1963), pp. 300–317. The texts of the Geneva Agreements and related documents may be found in 47 *Department of State Bulletin* (1962), pp. 259 ff., or in *The New York Times,* July 22, 1962.

States Admitted Under Conditions. A second grouping commonly encountered in this category comprises countries which were admitted into the community of nations under specific conditions, that is, under a formal engagement to adhere to certain rules or to fulfill certain promises imposed by the other members as a kind of price of admission. The theory behind this arrangement was that admission under conditions represented in no way a reflection on the sovereignty of the country in question, because the obligations assumed were embodied in the texts of formal treaties, entered into freely, and normally did not differ materially from the standards of conduct generally expected to be observed by a civilized community. Yet in view of the fact that internal authority was circumscribed to a certain extent by the terms imposed on the new member of the community, it appears reasonable to include the states in question in the same category as neutralized states.

The conditions imposed varied, of course, from case to case. When Montenegro was admitted into the community in 1878, special obligations regarding religious and racial toleration, maintenance of fortifications, and freedom of transit across the country were imposed by the Congress of Berlin. Similar conditions accompanied the admissions of Bulgaria, Serbia, and Romania. When the new states of Poland, Czechoslovakia, and Jugoslavia were admitted in 1919, special conditions concerning the treatment of various minority groups were imposed. Ethiopia was admitted on condition that slavery would be abolished in territories under its jurisdiction.

One of the most recent examples of both neutralization and admission under conditions was supplied by Austria after World War II. A treaty signed at Vienna on May 15, 1955, between the Soviet Union, the United Kingdom, France, and the United States, on the one hand, and Austria, on the other, re-established an independent Austrian state.[15] The document contained a long list of conditions imposed by the four major powers (particularly Articles 4, 6–8, 10–19, and portions of Articles 22, 23–26, 29, 31–32), involving, among other matters, a prohibition on political or economic union with Germany, the granting of equal human rights, elections by secret ballot, restrictions concerning persons serving in the Austrian armed forces, prohibition of selected categories of weapons, denial of the right to utilize aircraft of German or Japanese design or assembly, and so on.

It is interesting to note that, with the exception of the Austrian example, virtually every instance of admission under conditions was followed within a relatively short time by a unilateral cancellation of the conditions by the new member of the community of nations. No serious efforts were made by the other members to enforce the conditions imposed by them, even though some of the violations committed assumed quite startling proportions. In other cases, mere lip service was rendered to the promises made

[15] Full text in 49 *A.J.I.L.* (1955), Supp., pp. 162–191. Consult also Robert E. Clute, *The International Legal Status of Austria 1938–1955* (The Hague: Martinus Nijhoff, 1962).

and the new member continued to act internally as it had done prior to admission into the community. It thus appears that the practice of laying down conditions for admissions has achieved little beyond calling attention, on a quite temporary basis, to what might be termed a substandard situation in a given country.

Divided States. A peculiar phenomenon in the post-1945 world has been the emergence of several states divided into two entities, each equipped with an operative government: Germany (Federal Republic and Democratic Republic), Korea (North and South), Vietnam (North and South), and China (Chinese People's Republic and the Republic of China on Taiwan). These divisions reflect the bipolar orientation of current world politics, and each instance in question has been the focal point of a rich, controversial, and growing body of literature.

The legal status of the German subdivisions, both during Allied occupation and subsequently, represents one of the more confusing aspects of the legal scene since 1945.[16] And solution to the questions posed was not made easier when the government of the German Democratic Republic applied in March, 1966, for membership in the United Nations, recommending at the same time that the Federal Republic of Germany be admitted as well.[17] Neither entity was able to secure admission, however, despite strong support for the application of the GDR on the part of the Soviet Union, backed by seven other Communist members. The Federal Republic, which has had an observer at the United Nations since 1952, stated that it would not seek membership as long as Germany remained divided. Following the GDR application, the West German Vice Chancellor stated that the "Soviet Zone of Germany" was disqualified from UN membership on both legal and moral grounds.[18]

The community of nations has accepted the Federal Republic of Germany as a legal person and as a member of the community, through formal recognition, exchange of diplomatic and consular agents, and conclusion of numerous treaties. As far as the German Democratic Republic is concerned, even though it has been recognized by a number of states, some doubts must be maintained concerning its true independence. As late as December 30, 1961, Walter Ulbricht, First Secretary of the Communist Party and Chairman of the (GDR) Council of State, admitted in an article in *Pravda* (Moscow) that the existence of his government depended on the continuing presence of Russian forces in his state.[19]

---

[16] See, *inter alia*, von Glahn, pp. 273–290, for details preceding the contractual agreements of 1952; Gould, pp. 186–187; Whiteman, Vol. I, pp. 325–332, 911–916, 969–983, and *ibid.*, Vol. II, pp. 787–799; Roland Stanger, *West Berlin: the Legal Context* (Columbus: Ohio State University Press, 1965); and Wilhelm G. Grewe, "Other Legal Aspects of the Berlin Crisis," 56 *A.J.I.L.* (1962), pp. 510–513.

[17] See UN Doc. S/7192, March 10, 1966, and 14 *The Bulletin* (Bonn) (March 8, 1966), p. 2.

[18] See 14 *The Bulletin* (Bonn) (March 22, 1966), p. 2.

[19] Grewe, *op. cit.*, p. 511.

The government of South Korea was recognized by the bulk of the then membership of the United Nations as the only legal government of all of Korea, and by 1968 had been recognized by over seventy states.[20] The North Korean government, on the other hand, has been recognized only by members of the socialist bloc.

Divided China represents a subject so enmeshed in legal and political controversy that no attempt can be made in a general text to treat such an enormous topic.[21] Similarly, the complexities surrounding the legal status of the two Vietnamese governments defy brief coverage. It can be maintained, however, that, regardless of the provisions of the 1954 Geneva Accords, two operative governments evolved in Vietnam, each possessing the normal attributes of sovereignty and each, by now, recognized by a substantial number of states. Both must be regarded as members of the community of nations.[22]

THE CITY OF THE VATICAN

The list of undoubted members of the community of nations would not be complete if the State of the City of the Vatican were not added to fully sovereign and to qualified full members.[23] Most of the questions that had plagued relations between the Holy See and the government of Italy since the extinction of the Papal States in 1870 were resolved by the Lateran Treaty of 1929. That agreement recognized the State of the City of the Vatican as a sovereign and independent state, possessed of all the rights and privileges attached to that status, including diplomatic representation.

The new state agreed to surrender alleged fugitives from justice to Italy without requiring the usual formal request for such action, and Italy in turn assumed responsibility for criminal jurisdiction over all offenses committed on the territory of the Vatican state. Most unusual, however, was the unilateral declaration issued by the Vatican, stating that the new entity wished to remain aloof from the worldly rivalries of other states, except when parties to a dispute would call unanimously on the Vatican to assist in arriving at a peaceful solution to their problems. That declaration is the

---

[20] Consult Whiteman, Vol. I, pp. 320–325 on Korea.

[21] See the concise treatment by Frank P. Morello, *The International Legal Status of Formosa* (The Hague: Martinus Nijhoff, 1966), as well as the materials cited in Chapter 7.

[22] See, *inter alia*, the collection of opposing views as well as of key documents and policy statements in Richard A. Falk, ed., *The Vietnam War and International Law* [Sponsored by the American Society of International Law] (Princeton, N.J.: Princeton University Press, 1968), and also Marvin E. Gettleman, ed., *Vietnam: History, Documents, and Opinions on a Major World Crisis* (Greenwich, Conn.: Fawcett Publications, 1965).

[23] See H. F. Cumbo, "The Holy See and International Law," 2 *International Law Quarterly* (1948–49), pp. 603–620, as well as Lauterpacht's *Oppenheim*, Vol. I, pp. 250–255, and Whiteman, Vol. I, pp. 587–593.

reason for the unique position occupied by the City of the Vatican in the community of nations. It is true that as the ideological conflict between communism and the free world deepened in intensity and extent, the Vatican state has taken an active part in that struggle. But insofar as the "normal" rivalries of states for territory, power, and military advantages have been concerned, the Vatican observed its self-imposed abstention.

There cannot be any doubt that the Lateran Treaty and the subsequent recognition extended to the Vatican state by many countries admitted a new member into the community of nations. Today some fifty countries maintain diplomatic representatives at the Vatican, proof of the wide acceptance of the new member.

The problem of fitting the State of the City of the Vatican into accepted categories of states has never been resolved quite satisfactorily. In many respects the Vatican state corresponds to the definition of a free city, while in others it resembles the components of that group of "limited" members of the community of nations called "dwarf" states. This latter statement is based on the minuscule territory of the Vatican: 108.7 acres.

On the other hand, the Vatican state possesses worldwide interests and carries on many activities on a global basis; it is a member of at least one major international organization (the Universal Postal Union). All in all, the state represents a unique type of member of the community of nations and is, therefore, normally listed separately from the other categories of full and qualified members.

LIMITED MEMBERS AND BORDERLINE CASES

Depending on the writer consulted, listings of the membership of the community of nations have included a number of categories of states of which some could claim a somewhat limited type of membership. During the nineteenth century most of these entities were referred to as "semi-sovereign states," whereas in our own time the term *dependent state* has found favor. Neither appellation appears to be very satisfactory. The present writer prefers the term *limited members* for such few of the following categories as possess any real claim to some form of membership in the community of nations.

Vassal States. Vassal states were political units which enjoyed a considerable degree of internal autonomy but were dependent, with regard to their foreign relations, on the head of a *suzerain* state, a head to which they paid homage, whom they regarded as their overlord in the feudal, medieval sense. This relationship, varying in detail from case to case and also from time to time, approached in modern times what might be called constitutional links. Owing to the great differences existing among the various vassal states in their relations with their suzerain, no definite rules could be worked out concerning the exact position enjoyed by vassal states in the community of nations.

If, on the other hand, the suzerain state permitted its vassal to engage in limited relations of its own with other countries, then the vassal state could be said to enjoy at least limited or partial membership in the community. Such was the position of certain vassals of the Ottoman Empire during portions of the nineteenth century: Moldavia and Wallachia (the major components of modern Romania) from 1829 to 1878; Serbia during the same period; the island of Crete from 1878 to 1913; and Bulgaria from 1878 to 1908. Egypt occupied a position of vassalage relative to Turkey for a time, definitely from 1840 to 1883, and on a somewhat dubious legal and practical basis from the latter year until 1914.

Protectorates. The modern concept of a protectorate came into existence when a weaker state surrendered itself into the protection of a stronger state in such a manner as to transfer to the latter the management of its external affairs, including both diplomatic representation and defense.[24] This process was normally accomplished by means of a formal treaty which, in addition, usually provided for control of the military forces of the protectorate by the protecting nation. The degree of internal self-government left to the protectorate varied from case to case. Once a protectorate had been established, the protected state had to be considered as having lost its full sovereignty and normally ceased to function as a member of the community of states.

The heads of state of protectorates continued to enjoy normal immunities in the courts of the protecting state and, by comity, in many other states. This privileged status was demonstrated clearly in the following case:

COURT OF APPEAL
MIGHELL v. *SULTAN OF JOHORE*

Great Britain, Queen's Bench Division
(1894) 1 Q.B. 149

FACTS

The Sultan of Johore, visiting in England, used the pseudonym of Albert Baker. He became acquainted with the plaintiff and promised to marry her. When he failed to keep that promise, she sued him for breach of promise, and he in turn pleaded that English courts had no jurisdiction since he was an independent sovereign ruler who had not waived his privilege of immunity. The Court of First Instance upheld the Sultan and the case came to the Court of Appeal at the request of the plaintiff.

The Court inquired at the Colonial Office as to the legal status of the Sultan of Johore and received a reply stating that the Sultan was an independent sovereign ruler.

ISSUES

(1) Whether the letter sent on behalf of the Secretary of State for Colonies was sufficient proof of the status of the Sultan of Johore.

(2) Whether the Sultan was im-

---

[24] See Whiteman, Vol. I, pp. 431–453, 492–509, on the Indian Princely States.

mune from the jurisdiction of British courts.

DECISION

Judgment for the defendant; appeal dismissed.

As to Issue No. 1: Certification by a Minister of the Crown as to the status of the Sultan of Johore was sufficient and decisive, insofar as British courts were concerned.

As to Issue No. 2: In view of the facts brought out in the letter from the Colonial Office, the Sultan of Johore had to be regarded in British courts as an independent sovereign ruler and hence as immune from the jurisdiction of those courts.

REASONING

(1) Certification of the status of a foreign sovereign by means of an official communication from an advisor of the British sovereign binds English courts and is to be accepted as conclusive as far as those courts are concerned. [A similar situation would prevail if an American court were to inquire about such a matter of the Department of State; the court would accept the "certificate" of the Department as conclusive.]

(2) The relationship existing between Great Britain and the Sultanate of Johore was based on a treaty of protection by which the Sultan was to enjoy the protection of Great Britain, engaging, on his part, not to enter into treaties with any foreign states. In the opinion of the Court, "the agreement by the Sultan not to enter into treaties with other Power does not seem . . . to be an abnegation of his right to enter into such treaties, but only a condition upon which the protection stipulated for is to be given. If the Sultan disregards it, the consequences may be the loss of that protection, or possibly other difficulties with this country; but I do not think that there is anything in the treaty which qualifies or disproves the statement in the letter that the Sultan of Johore is an independent sovereign."

The protectorate itself, not constituting an integral part of the protecting state, was not bound to enter a conflict in which its protector engaged, and treaties concluded by the latter did not bind a protectorate unless such was specified in the instrument.[25]

Today the relative weakening of most of the surviving protecting states, coupled with an insistent demand on the part of eager though administratively inexperienced nationalist elements in various protectorates, promises an early resumption or achievement of full independent status by existing protected entities.

Administered Provinces. The term *administered provinces* has been applied to the relatively few instances in which territory nominally under the sovereignty of one state has been actually administered by another state. In name such foreign control has been based on the assent of the nominal sovereign: examples commonly cited for administered provinces are Bosnia and Herzegovina, officially parts of the Ottoman Empire but

[25] See *The Ionian Ships, Great Britain*, Admiralty Prize Court, 1855, 2 Spinks 212, for a striking illustrative case.

under Austro-Hungarian control from 1878 to 1908, and the island of Cyprus, then a part of the Ottoman domain yet administered by Great Britain from 1878 until annexation by the administrator following the outbreak of war between Turkey and Great Britain in 1914. No evidence has yet been submitted by any of the writers claiming some sort of international status for administered provinces that these entities possessed any degree of independence or autonomy or that they participated in any manner in international relations. Hence such territories never could or did form a part of the community of nations.

Free Cities. Strategic considerations, economic resources desired by two countries, and boundary disputes of various kinds, induced in part by nationalistic sentiments or historical tradition, produced in the twentieth century the paradoxical reappearance of the medieval concept of the independent city-state in the form of free cities and free territories. This development must be viewed as an anachronism, since the realities of the power politics dominating international relations obviated the likelihood of an extended or effective life for such archaic political units.

The city of Danzig, on the shores of the Baltic, was transferred by Articles 100–108 of the Treaty of Versailles from German sovereignty to that of the Allied and Associated Powers, which thereupon established the community as a "free city" under the protection of the newly created League of Nations. The city possessed a considerable degree of internal autonomy, despite the existence of a High Commissioner representing the League. Foreign affairs were lodged in the hands of Poland, the latter also being officially responsible for the protection of Danzig citizens abroad.

After falling under the influence of the local National Socialist Party in 1936, Danzig was formally annexed to Germany in 1939. Its final fate was decided at the Potsdam Conference of 1945, when the territory was included in the portion of East Prussia detached from Germany and transferred to Poland.

Failure to achieve a satisfactory settlement of a boundary dispute dividing Jugoslavia and Italy at the end of World War II led to the creation of the "Free Territory of Trieste" under the terms of the Allied peace treaty with Italy in 1947.[26] The area was to have its independence and territorial integrity guaranteed by the Security Council of the United Nations, with a rather elaborate form of local government scheduled to come into being under the terms of a Permanent Statute.

When the permanent members of the Security Council could not agree on the future of Trieste, particularly after the so-called Zone B of the area had been virtually annexed to Jugoslavia, whose troops had occupied that portion of the "state," a Memorandum of Understanding was negotiated between Italy and Jugoslavia in October, 1954. After that document was

[26] See Allied and Associated Powers and Italy, *Treaty of Peace*, February 10, 1947, in 42 *A.J.I.L.* (1948), Supp., pp. 47–143, at pp. 109–121 for Annexes VIII-X, for texts dealing with the Free Port of Trieste.

approved by the United States, the Soviet Union, and Great Britain, the city of Trieste itself as well as the area known as Zone A (86 square miles, inhabited by 310,000 people) was brought under Italian sovereignty, and Zone B (199 square miles, with 75,000 inhabitants) was formally annexed to Jugoslavia.

There is little or no evidence available to show that the Free Territory of Trieste ever really assumed international personality during its existence.

Dwarf States. Four small countries in Europe are commonly joined in the category of dwarf states: Liechtenstein, Monaco, San Marino, and Andorra. They represent curious legacies of the past, anachronistic survivals from conditions prevailing in the seventeenth century, strangely out of place in a world of superpowers, nuclear weapons, and space satellites. Until recently none of the four little countries could be said to participate to any real extent in the international relations of the world, but in the past decade or so Liechtenstein, Monaco, and to some extent San Marino have emerged from their relative seclusion, have sent capable and active delegates to a number of international conferences, and have signed and ratified a surprisingly large number of conventions, thus demonstrating their right to be called, at the very least, limited members of the community of nations.

It does not appear that Andorra is a member of the community of nations, nor can it be classified as an independent state.[27]

The existence of extremely small and thinly populated political entities, such as the Maldive Islands, Nauru, Western Samoa, and so on, poses few political problems as yet, but it has complicated the membership problem of the United Nations. The issue of these "ministates," more of which are expected to come into being, has led to a warning, in 1967, by the Secretary-General that a line will have to be drawn somewhere before most of these entities attempt to join the United Nations.[28] But nothing has been done thus far about the matter. Western Samoa elected not to join the organization but created an arrangement under which the former colonial power, New Zealand, will represent Samoan interests in the United Nations, leaving Western Samoa free to join specialized agencies of the UN whenever such may appear desirable. The Republic of Nauru, independent since January 31, 1968, is expected, at the time of writing, to seek a similar working agreement with Australia. However, the prospect of many additional small member states in the UN still persists. The obvious solution—barring ministates—has been deemed to be politically undesirable. Hence hopes have been expressed by various UN delegations that small political

[27] Cf. Bishop, p. 240, however, who lists Andorra as a member of the community of nations and contrast this with Whiteman, Vol. I, pp. 277–280. See Walter S. G. Kohn, "The Sovereignty of Liechtenstein," 61 *A.J.I.L.* (1967), pp. 547–557, for an analysis of the current legal status of the principality.

[28] *The New York Times*, December 24, 1967, p. 22; May 29, 1966, p. 53; and April 13, 1969, p. 27.

units in the Caribbean and elsewhere would be granted self-government in the form of groupings under an arrangement (with the present colonial or protecting power) which would permit them to opt for group independence at a later date.[29]

Condominiums. A territory jointly governed by two or more states is called a condominium. Modern history has produced a surprisingly large number of such entities,[30] three of which are still in existence today. The best-known of all was the Anglo-Egyptian Sudan, under the joint control of Egypt and Great Britain between 1889 and 1956, in which latter year the Sudan emerged as an independent state. The international Régime of the Tangier Zone was abolished by treaty on October 29, 1956, and the Zone was integrated into Morocco.

In the Southwest Pacific, the island group of the New Hebrides has been under joint Anglo-French administration since 1887. Under the Condominium Treaty of 1906, effective on April 1, 1908, the native population was placed under two Resident Commissioners, one British, the other French. The two officials control the ordinary governmental functions of posts, constabulary, and commerce. Australia has recently joined in the administration of the islands. An advisory council, designed to improve supervision of the indigenous population, was added to the governmental structure in 1958.[31]

Europe contains a condominium (two, if Andorra were to be classified as such an entity), tiny in size but unique from a political point of view: the Île des Faisans. This small island is located near the mouth of the Bidassoa River, which forms the common frontier between Spain and France for a distance of seven miles to the Bay of Biscay. Under treaties concluded in 1856 and 1901, the two countries police the island in turn for periods of six months; individuals committing offenses in the condominium are subject to their respective national authorities.

The third of the existing condominiums consists of the two small Pacific islands of Enderbury and Canton, since 1939 under the joint control of Great Britain and the United States, an arrangement which was to end after a period of fifty years. These two desolate specks on the map became

[29] See also Jacques G. Rapoport, "The Participation of Ministates in International Affairs," *Proceedings* (1968), pp. 155–163, and Roger Fisher, "The Participation of Microstates in International Affairs," *ibid.*, pp. 164–170, as well as the commentary on these items, *ibid.*, pp. 177–188.

[30] Schleswig-Holstein (Prussia and Austria, 1864–1866); Samoa (Great Britain-U.S.A.-Germany, 1889–1900); the New Hebrides (Great Britain-France, 1906 to date); the Anglo-Egyptian Sudan (Great Britain-Egypt, 1889–1956); Tangier (Great Britain-France-Spain-Portugal-Belgium-the Netherlands-Italy, 1923–1956); Albania (International Commission, 1913–1914); the Saar (International Commission under the League of Nations, 1919–1934); Leticia (International Commission under the League, 1933–1934); Memel (Allied Conference of Ambassadors, 1919–1923); the Île des Faisans (France-Spain, 1856 to date); and the tiny islands of Enderbury and Canton (Great Britain-U.S.A., 1939 to date).

[31] See Whiteman, Vol. I, pp. 280–282, for background materials.

important only with the realization of trans-Pacific air routes and it was this factor which caused them to be placed in the condominium category.

Condominiums are not members of the community of nations: they play no active part in international relations, have no governments of their own, and do not possess any vestige of national sovereignty.

Mandates; Trust Territories. Article 22 of the Covenant of the League of Nations established a system of "mandates" whereby a form of international supervision was created for certain colonies and territories formerly under German or Turkish sovereignty. The areas in question had been detached from their legal owners in consequence of the defeat of the Central Powers in World War I, but this action had not been followed by annexation in view of wartime promises to refrain from seeking territorial aggrandizement or to grant full independence to certain Turkish territories. The basic concept underlying the mandate system was that the well-being and development of the areas in question constituted a trust of civilized nations and that these territories should be placed under the tutelage of advanced states, subject to the supervision of the League of Nations on whose behalf they were to be administered.[32]

In view of the fact that the areas under mandate had arrived at greatly varying stages of development, three separate groupings were devised. The A mandates consisted of former subdivisions of the Ottoman Empire, all deemed to have reached a stage of development at which independence could soon be granted. These areas were provisionally recognized as states, subject to a temporary system of administrative control and assistance by a Mandatory Power possessed of limited authority within its assigned territory. All of the Class A mandates have achieved independence by now.

The Class B mandates consisted of all but one of the former German colonies in Africa. Unlike the Class A mandates, the territories in this second group did not possess any degree of international personality. They were administered separately from neighboring colonies of the Mandatory Power, subject to restrictions and regulations embodied in the terms of the mandate instrument.

The third group, styled Class C mandates, comprised the former German South-West Africa and all former German colonies in the Pacific. These territories, because of the smallness of their populations, their remoteness from the centers of civilization, or their relative backwardness, were administered under the laws of the Mandatory Power as integral portions of its own territories, subject to protective safeguards for the indigenous population, again embodied in the terms of the mandate agreement. All former Class B mandates are now independent or have been joined to other African entities; several former Class C mandates have also achieved independence in recent years.

All Class B and Class C mandates, with the exception of South-West

[32] On the mandate system as a whole, see Lauterpacht's *Oppenheim*, Vol. I, pp. 192–202, and especially Whiteman, Vol. I, pp. 598–731.

Africa, were placed under the trusteeship system of the United Nations through bilateral agreements concluded between that organization and the former Mandatory Powers. The United States was substituted for Japan as trustee for the former German colonies in the Pacific north of the equator. In addition, the former Italian colony of Somaliland was transformed into a trust territory and Italy, though not a member of the United Nations, was appointed as trustee.

When the mandate system was abolished on the demise of the League of Nations and was replaced by the trusteeship system of the United Nations, South Africa refused to enter into a trusteeship agreement regarding its administration of South-West Africa. It is reasonable to presume that this refusal was based on the assumption that if legal title to the territory could be acquired by the Union, perhaps by action of the General Assembly, the protective safeguards embodied in the mandate instrument could be set aside and the government of the Union could then proceed to institute the same racist policies against the colored population of South-West Africa as were then being introduced against the colored population of the Union itself. When the issue of the status of the mandated territory was brought in 1949 before the International Court of Justice, the tribunal held in an advisory opinion that the extinction of the League of Nations did not affect in any manner the mandated area or its administration and that the General Assembly and the International Court of Justice had assumed the functions of the League and of its judicial organ as far as mandates were concerned.[33] At the same time, however, it was made clear by the Court that the Union of South Africa (now styled the Republic of South Africa) was under no legal obligation to accept a new trusteeship agreement for South-West Africa, but was still bound by its obligations as outlined in Article 22 of the League Covenant and by its mandate agreement.[34]

The next major development in the long dispute concerning legal control over South-West Africa came on March 16, 1961, when the General Assembly censured South Africa, by a vote of 74–0, with nine abstentions, for repeatedly ignoring United Nations resolutions aimed at the eventual achievement of independence by South-West Africa. The vote of censure followed South Africa's decision to withdraw from the British Commonwealth because of criticism of its "white supremacy" policies.

The resolution in the General Assembly called on all United Nations

---

[33] *International Status of South-West Africa* (Advisory Opinion), *I.C.J. Reports, 1950,* p. 128, digested in 44 *A.J.I.L.* (1950), pp. 757–770. A subsequent Advisory Opinion on the *Admissibility of Hearings of Petitioners by the Committee on South-West Africa, I.C.J. Reports, 1956,* p. 23, digested in 50 *A.J.I.L.* (1956), pp. 954–959, declared that the United Nations Committee on South-West Africa (etsablished by the General Assembly on November 28, 1953) could grant oral hearings to petitioners on matters relating to the territory in question.

[34] See Francis B. Sayre, "Legal Problems Arising from the United Nations Trusteeship System," 42 *A.J.I.L.* (1948), pp. 263–298, at pp. 272–273 on this important point.

members closely associated with South Africa to bring pressure on that country to change its policies in the mandated territory. It charged South Africa with holding a referendum in October, 1960, aimed at assimilating the territory but limiting the vote to the European population of 66,000 out of approximately 540,000 inhabitants. And the resolution stated the obvious: that South African conduct in the mandated territory constituted a "challenge to the authority of the United Nations." A 1959 resolution of the General Assembly's Fourth Committee, approved by the parent body, recommended that individual members initiate action against South Africa in the International Court of Justice. This suggestion was carried out by Ethiopia and Liberia, and in December, 1962, the Court held that it had jurisdiction.[35]

The case represented the longest and most voluminous one heard by the International Court of Justice: sixteen volumes of written pleadings and almost 300 hours of oral sessions were involved.

On May 19, 1965, the applicant states accepted as true all averments of fact in South Africa's written pleadings. This meant, in effect, that on the applicants' part the sole contention was that South Africa had acted contrary to an international norm and/or standard of nondiscrimination or nonseparation of racial groupings.

The Court handed down its second judgment, on the validity as distinguished from the admissibility, of the claims, on July 18, 1966.[36] The Court rejected the plaintiffs' claim, on the grounds that "the Applicants cannot be considered to have established any legal right or interest appertaining to them in the subject-matter of the present claims, and that, accordingly, the Court must decline to give effect to them." Hence, the Court majority of eight held that it was unnecessary to give a ruling on the merits of the case, even though the Court had had to consider the substance of the dispute in order to reach its decision on the validity of the claims.

The 1966 judgment dismissing the claims of the applicant states produced a great volume of criticism, including a 129-page dissent by the United States judge Philip C. Jessup.[37] The latter pointed out the extraordinary change in the Court's views: in three previous Advisory Opinions and in its judgment of 1962, the Court had never deviated from its conclusion that the Mandate survived the dissolution of the League of Nations

---

[35] *South-West Africa Cases (Ethiopia* v. *South Africa; Liberia* v. *South Africa), Preliminary Objections. I.C.J. Reports, 1962*, p. 319, digested by William Bishop, Jr., in 57 *A.J.I.L.* (1963), pp. 640–659.

[36] *South-West Africa Cases (Ethiopia* v. *South Africa; Liberia* v. *South Africa), Second Phase. I.C.J. Reports, 1966*, p. 6; digested and excerpted in 61 *A.J.I.L.* (1967), pp. 116–210, by William Bishop, Jr. Consult also the searching analysis of Milton Katz, *The Relevance of International Adjudication* (Cambridge, Mass.: Harvard University Press, 1968), pp. 69–103.

[37] See excerpts in Bishop's digest, at pp. 162–206.

and that South-West Africa was still a territory subject to the Mandate. By its 1966 judgment, however, the Court had, in effect, decided that the applicants had no standing to ask the Court even for a declaration that the territory was still subject to the Mandate.

Adjudication having failed, the thirty-six African members of the United Nations proceeded to political action by means of a termination of the mandate over South-West Africa and transfer of legal control to the General Assembly as the relevant organ of the United Nations.

On October 27, 1966, the General Assembly, by Resolution 2145 (XXI), ended the mandate and asserted that henceforth South-West Africa constituted a direct responsibility of the United Nations.[38]

In accordance with the terms of the resolution (which was the seventy-fourth measure passed in the General Assembly on the question of South-West Africa), the President of the Assembly then designated the members of an *Ad Hoc* Committee for South-West Africa, consisting of fourteen states' representatives. The committee was to recommend practical means by which the territory could be administered in a manner that would enable ultimate independence to be achieved. The government of South Africa indicated at once that it would not honor the terms of the General Assembly resolution.

The *Ad Hoc* Committee reported, as instructed, to a special session of the General Assembly held from April 21 to May 23, 1967. It submitted three proposals to the parent body: an African plan for a complete assumption of control over South-West Africa by the United Nations by June, 1968; a Latin American plan for the establishment of a United Nations administration for the former mandate; and a Western proposal for discussions with the Republic of South Africa based on the provisions of Resolution 2145 (XXI). On May 19, 1967, the General Assembly decided by a vote of 85 to 2, with thirty abstentions, to create an eleven-member council which was to assume control over the territory from South Africa.[39]

From a UN constitutional point of view, the procedure adopted in the General Assembly for the termination of the South-West Africa mandate must lead to the conclusion that Resolution 2145 (XXI) did not legally achieve its intended aims, because a General Resolution is not a legally binding decision under the Charter.[40] Assuming that South African control over South-West Africa constituted a "threat to the peace," action by the Security Council under Article 41, after invocation of Article 39 of the Charter, could bring about a revocation of the mandate that would be legally binding under the terms of Article 25. Preferably, however, a legal

[38] Text reprinted in 61 *A.J.I.L.* (1967), pp. 649–651.

[39] Resolution 2248 (S–V); consult also the detailed study by John Dugard, "The Revocation of the Mandate for South West Africa," 62 *A.J.I.L.* (1968), pp. 78–97, and Whiteman, Vol. 13, pp. 756–768.

[40] See Dugard, *op. cit.*, p. 95, on this paradoxical situation.

termination of the mandate should have been carried out through a General Assembly resolution following a relevant Security Council recommendation.[41]

By the fall of 1967, no United Nations control over South-West Africa had been achieved. On September 12 of that year, the UN "Special Committee on the Situation with Regard to the Implementation of the Granting of Independence to Colonial Countries and Peoples," in condemning certain arrests made in South-West Africa, referred to the area as "the international Territory of South West Africa," despite the physical absence of an international administration.[42] The international status of the territory was reasserted in a related resolution, condemning illegal application of the "Terrorism Act" to South-West Africa, by the General Assembly on December 16, 1967.[43] On that day, too, the Assembly adopted another resolution, 2325 (XXII), confirming its earlier decisions on the termination of the mandate and the assumption of control by the United Nations, calling on the government of South Africa to withdraw militarily and administratively from the former mandate, urging all member states to take effective economic measures against South Africa to bring about such withdrawal, and maintaining the South-West African item on the General Assembly agenda.

The Assembly also accepted, on December 16, 1967, without a vote a proposal of the Secretary-General to extend the existing interim arrangement of an appointed Acting UN Commissioner for South-West Africa. The Legal Counsel of the United Nations was, therefore, continued in this office until such time as the General Assembly, on the nomination of the Secretary-General, would appoint a Commissioner.

The Security Council entered fully into the South-West African dispute by its Resolution 245 of January 25, 1968. "Noting" the pertinent General Assembly resolutions and condemning the refusal of South Africa to comply with Assembly Resolution 2324 (XXII) relative to the trial of certain indigenous inhabitants of the territory, the Security Council invited all member states to "exert their influence" in order to induce South African compliance.[44]

On March 14, 1968, the Security Council, by Resolution 246 (1968), reaffirmed its previous stand on the question of the former mandate and censored the South African government for its "flagrant defiance of Security Council resolution 245 (1968) as well as of the authority of the United Nations . . ." and urged all member states to cooperate with the

---

[41] *Ibid.*, pp. 96–97.

[42] See text of the committee resolution in 62 *A.J.I.L.* (1968), p. 161, and the relevant statement by the U.S. member of the committee, *ibid.*, pp. 161–162.

[43] Res. 2324 (XXII), reprinted in 62 *A.J.I.L.* (1968), p. 488; see also the statement by U.S. ambassador Goldberg, *ibid.*, pp. 488–493, as well as B. C. Denny's statement, *ibid.*, 63 (1969), pp. 320–324.

[44] Text in 62 *A.J.I.L.* (1968), pp. 759–760.

Security Council in all ways possible to bring about compliance with the terms of this and previous relevant resolutions.[45]

This was the inconclusive situation, as respected South-West Africa, at the time of writing.

Trust territories under the United Nations do not possess any international personality. The trustee represents the trust territory as far as any possible international relations are involved and at the same time assumes any possible international duties and obligations on behalf of the territory.

The indigenous inhabitants of the remaining trust territories (and this was true in the former B and C mandates also) do not possess a distinct nationality of their own.[46]

Under the provisions of Articles 82 and 83 of the Charter of the United Nations, specific parts or all of a given trust territory could be designated as a strategic trust territory. If this was done in any trusteeship agreement, supervision of the administration of the affected area was transferred from the Trusteeship Council to the Security Council. Thus far only one trustee has taken advantage of this arrangement: the trust territory administered by the United States has been classified as a strategic territory. The basic difference between the two types is that in a strategic trust area the administering state may close off certain areas to visits, for security reasons.

Only two trust territories exist at the time of writing: the Australian one of New Guinea and the American one of the Pacific Islands (Micronesia).

Belligerent Communities and Insurgents. Certain communities, seeking to achieve independence from a parent country or to secure control of the entire state for a rebel government, lack statehood yet occupy, after the initiation of hostilities, territory extensive enough to remove the conflict from the characteristics of a purely local uprising. Frequently the hostile actions in question impinge on the interests of other countries and it becomes desirable to have the laws of war apply to the situation described.

When this point is reached in the development of a rebellion, other states may grant to the community a limited measure of international personality by recognizing a status of belligerency, by terming the group a belligerent community.[47] Obviously, the rebellious community cannot obtain its lim-

---

[45] Text reprinted in 62 *A.J.I.L.* (1968), pp. 764–765.

[46] See Resolution of the Council of the League of Nations, 24th Session, in *Official Journal*, VI/23, pp. 567–568, 604; consult also the decision in *Rex* v. *Ketter*, Great Britain, Court of Criminal Appeal, 1939, 55 Times Law Reports, p. 449, digested in 34 *A.J.I.L.* (1940), p. 529–532; and see Lauterpacht's *Oppenheim*, Vol. I, pp. 225–226. See, on the other hand, the decision in *Rex* v. *Jacobus Christian*, South African Law Reports, 1924, Appellate Division 101, in which the Court held that an inhabitant of the mandated territory of South-West Africa could be tried and convicted of treason against the Union of South Africa; for text of this decision, see *B.Y '.L.* (1924), pp. 211–219.

[47] See Whiteman, Vol. I, pp. 930–946, for illustrative examples.

ited standing by its own desire or proclamation. Recognition of a status of belligerency on the part of other states is necessary for the legal creation of that status. Such recognition takes place frequently through express proclamation to the effect that a given community is recognized as a belligerent community. Regardless of the method adopted, however, the fact that belligerency has been acknowledged requires treatment of the community as a state engaged in war and, on the other hand, imposes on that community responsibility for all violations of the laws of war and for the treatment of foreign property and alien persons. Normally the warships of the belligerent community are treated as belligerent warships and are granted the right of visit and search. On the other hand, again, the community lacks the right to send or to receive diplomatic agents, to join international organizations, and to benefit in a normal manner from multilateral conventions concerned with peacetime international relations and activities of states.

If the lawful government recognizes the rebels as a belligerent community, a foreign state is free to grant or withhold the same recognition. If it withholds it, then it has to refrain from assisting the rebel group, but is free to grant or withhold aid to the lawful government. In fact, unless the foreign state wishes to enter the conflict, it will withhold, after its recognition of belligerency, all aid to both sides in the conflict under way.

If the lawful government does not recognize the rebels as a belligerent community, a foreign state is free to grant or to withhold such recognition. If it fails to recognize a state of belligerency, the foreign state must abstain from all assistance to the rebels but is free to assist the lawful government. If the foreign state does grant recognition of belligerency, it must refrain from assisting either belligerent unless it wishes to enter the conflict.

If the rebel group has been recognized by a foreign state as the *de facto* government of the entire state in which the civil war is going on, then the foreign state must abstain from all assistance to the lawful (*de jure*) government of the state at war, being free, at the same time, to give or deny such aid to the belligerent community. If the foreign state grants aid to the *de facto* government recognized by it, and that *de facto* regime is defeated in the war, then the lawful government may hold the foreign state responsible for an act of unjustifiable aggression and of premature recognition.

In essence, then, the principles of customary international law impose an obligation of neutrality on a foreign state when the belligerency of a rebel group has been recognized, unless the foreign state desires, as a matter of policy, to cast its lot with one side or the other: in other words, enter the war. On the other hand, recognition of a rebel group during a civil war as a *de jure* government represents a violation of international law by the recognizing state.

Recognition of belligerency is not synonymous with recognition as a state; the belligerent community is still legally an integral part of the state against whose government it is conducting hostilities. Statehood in the legal sense can be acquired by the community only if and when it succeeds in its enterprise, either by achieving independence or by replacing the lawful government of its state by its own chosen representatives. Until such success is recorded, the belligerent community possesses only limited aspects, temporary in nature, of an international personality and must therefore be regarded as a temporary and limited member of the community of nations.

By contrast, a rebellion which has not yet achieved the standing of a belligerent community is said to be a state of "insurgency," a condition described as intermediate between internal tranquillity and civil war. Recognition of insurgency is to be viewed primarily as a domestic matter by other states, because it normally entails the issuing of a proclamation calling public attention to the existence of an insurgent group in a foreign country and cautioning the public to exercise due caution as regards travel, business relations, and other dealings with and in the area in question. Such a proclamation of a state of insurgency does not correspond to recognition of a belligerent community and does not create rights under international law for the rebellious group involved. Third states are not bound to be neutral toward the insurgents, may resist with armed force an attempt by armed ships of such a group to stop foreign vessels for purposes of visit and search, and normally will not grant any special rights to such insurgent vessels beyond refraining from treating them as pirate ships. An insurgent group again represents a transitory phase in an unstable political situation: either the rebels are subdued quickly by the lawful government of their country or they develop their activities to the point where they gain stature as a belligerent community, with rights and obligations accruing from recognition of such status on the part of foreign countries.[48]

International Organizations. Public international organizations,[49] that is to say, agencies established for state purposes by states, possess in many instances a definite international personality, with powers of negotiation, of concluding binding international agreements, of appearing as plaintiffs or defendants before international tribunals, and, recently, of being able to claim immunity from legal process for defined categories of their officials in the same manner as is true for accredited representatives of members of the community of nations. A number of these organizations must be regarded as international persons, notably the United Nations. (See Chapter 9.)

[48] See *De Republiek Maluku Selatan* v. *De Rechtspersson Nieuw-Guinea*, Netherlands, High Court of Justice for New Guinea, 1952, reported in 49 *A.J.I.L.* (1954), p. 511.

[49] Space does not permit an analysis of the structures and operations of the League of Nations and the United Nations. While numerous aspects of both entities are discussed at various points in this volume, an extended treatment of the two world organizations belongs properly in a text dealing specifically with the subject of international organization.

The legal character of the League of Nations was the subject of much scholarly disagreement. Most jurists held that the agency did possess a minimum of corporate capacity: it supervised the administration of mandated territories; it concluded certain agreements with its host state, Switzerland; it administered its own properties; and it concluded contracts as a corporate body. Beyond these minimal aspects of international personality, the League's proponents could not show convincing evidence that the organization was much more than an international union with limited objectives.

The position of the United Nations Organization has been wholly different since the very inception of that agency: it possesses a definite international personality, even though it is not a state and therefore should perhaps not be included as yet in the membership of the community of nations as long as the latter title is in use.

By deliberate intention, identified as an effort to avoid real or fancied defects in the League Covenant, numerous articles in the Charter (Articles 24, 26, 41, 42, and 104) specifically outline the legal powers as well as the responsibilities of the United Nations and, incidentally, spell out clearly its status as an international person. Again it should be pointed out that the Organization is not a state or a superstate and that its rights and obligations are not identical in all respects with those assigned to a state. But the United Nations possesses legal personality and is a subject of international law. (See also Chapters 9 and 21.)

The International Court of Justice, in its Advisory Opinion of April 11, 1949, on *Reparation for Injuries Suffered in the Service of the United Nations*,[50] held that the Organization "is a subject of international law and capable of possessing international rights and duties, and that it has capacity to maintain its rights by bringing international claims." The Court observed also that "throughout its history, the development of international law has been influenced by the requirements of international life, and the progressive increase in the collective activities of States has already given rise to instances of action upon the international plane by certain entities which are not States." It held that "fifty States, representing the vast majority of the members of the international community, had the power, in conformity with international law, to bring into being an entity possessing objective international personality, and not personality recognized by them alone, together with capacity to bring international claims." Finally, the Court observed with considerable insight that "the subjects of law in any legal system are not necessarily identical in their nature or in the extent of their rights, and their nature depends upon the needs of the community."

The European Economic Community, a supranational agency capable of making regulations binding its member states as well as industrial con-

---

[50] *I.C.J. Reports, 1949*, p. 174.

cerns operating within its functional sphere, represents another excellent example of an international agency possessed of the status of an international person.

The powers conferred on some of these organizations can no longer be said to be merely powers or rights of the separate member states, and thus it was but logical to grant legal status as subjects of international law to the agencies exercising those powers. On the other hand, no international organization can yet be called a member of the community of nations, because membership is as yet limited to sovereign states.

Status of Tribes. Indian tribes in North America and other tribes elsewhere were at one time held to be equivalent to international persons by a few writers. States, on the other hand, usually denied such status to tribes, and agreements made with them were subsequently (and often quite unfairly) denied the character of binding treaties, regardless of the nomenclature applied to the original agreement at the time of its conclusion. Tribes, therefore, do not constitute members of the community of nations.

SUGGESTED READINGS

THE COMMUNITY IN GENERAL

Brierly, pp. 126–137; Gould, pp. 144–152, 183–212; Hyde, Vol. I, pp. 21–146; Richard W. Van Wagenen, "The Concept of the Community and the Future of the United Nations," 19 *International Organization* (Summer, 1965), pp. 812–827.

SPECIAL PROBLEMS

Briggs, pp. 78–80 [Acquisition of Statehood by Indonesia]; John J. Czyzak and Carl F. Salans, "The International Conference on the Settlement of the Laotian Question and the Geneva Agreements of 1962," 57 *A.J.I.L.* (1963), pp. 300–317; Méir Ydit, *Internationalised Territories: From the "Free City of Cracow" to the "Free City of Berlin"* (Leyden: A. W. Sythoff, 1961); Angelo P. Sereni, "The Status of Croatia under International Law," 35 *A.P.S.R.* (1941), pp. 1144–1151; René Lemarchant, "The Limits of Self-Determination: The Case of the Katanga Secession," *ibid.*, 56 (1962), pp. 404–416; Clyde Eagleton, "The Case of Hyderabad before the Security Council," 44 *A.J.I.L.* (1950), pp. 277–302; Whiteman, Vol. I, pp. 544–582, on the unique structure and internal relationships of the French Community; H. E. Richardson, *A Short History of Tibet* (New York: E. P. Dutton, 1962); Tsepon W. D. Shakabpa, *Tibet: A Political History* (New Haven: Yale University Press, 1967); Tieh-tseng Li, "The Legal Position of Tibet," 50 *A.J.I.L.* (1956), pp. 394–404; C. H. Alexandrowicz–Alexander, "The Legal Position of Tibet," *ibid.*, 48 (1954), pp. 265–274; Hungdah Chiu and R. R. Edwards, "Communist China's Attitude Toward the United Nations: A Legal Analysis," *ibid.*, 62 (1968), pp. 20–50, at p. 31, including n. 33 and n. 34; and the U.S. denial of China's claim to sovereignty over Tibet, as stated by Francis W. Tully, a press officer in the

Department of State, on September 11, 1959, and reported the following day in all major American newspapers.

THE TRUSTEESHIP SYSTEM

Whiteman, Vol. I, pp. 731–911 and *ibid.*, Vol. 13, pp. 679–699; Claude, pp. 318–343 (an excellent and thoughtful brief treatment); Donald Sleeper, "Trusteeship Compared with Mandate," 49 *Michigan Law Review* (1951), pp. 1199–1210; Clifford N. Smith, "America and the Pacific Islands," 2 *American Perspective* (1948), pp. 243–253; Willard Price, *America's Paradise Lost* (New York: John Day, 1966); E. J. Kahn, Jr., "Micronesia I: The American Period," 42 *New Yorker* (June 11, 1966), pp. 42–111 *passim*, and his "Micronesia II: From U to Kapingamarangi," *ibid.*, 42 (June 18, 1966), pp. 42–109 *passim;* 90 *Time* (November 3, 1967), pp. 36–37; and *The New York Times*, June 4, 1967, p. 15; July 30, 1967, p. 6-E; and November 5, 1967, p. 11.

SOUTH-WEST AFRICA

Whiteman, Vol. I, pp. 706–731; E. J. Kahn, Jr., "The International Court's Advisory Opinion on the International Status of South-West Africa," 4 *International Law Quarterly* (1951), pp. 78–99; his "South Africa: II—South West," 43 *New Yorker* (February 3, 1968), pp. 32–74 *passim;* Faye Carroll, *South West Africa and the United Nations* (Lexington: University of Kentucky Press, 1967).

Cases

The Helena, Great Britain, High Court of Admiralty, 1801, 4 Ch. Rob. 3.
The Indonesian Case, Security Council of the U.N., July 31–August 1, 1947, in 3 *United Nations Bulletin* (1947), pp. 215–225.
Nationality Decrees Issued in Tunis and Morocco, Advisory Opinion, P.C.I.J., 1923, Ser. B, No. 4.
Principality of Monaco v. *Mississippi*, United States, Supreme Court, 1933, 291 U.S. 643 and 292 U.S. 313.
Statham v. *Statham and Gaekwar of Baroda*, Great Britain, Probate, Divorce and Admiralty Division, 1911, [1912] Probate 62.
Case Concerning the Northern Cameroons (Cameroons v. *United Kingdom), Preliminary Objections* (Majority Opinion), *I.C.J. Reports, 1963*, p. 15, excerpted by William Bishop, Jr., in 58 *A.J.I.L.* (1964), pp. 448–505.

7
Recognition of States and of Governments

RECOGNITION OF STATES

THE TERM *recognition* means "a formal acknowledgment or declaration by the government of an existing state that it intends to attach certain customary legal consequences to an existing set of facts which, in its view, justify it (and other states) in doing so." [1] Normally recognition possesses a more specialized meaning in international law, relating to the acknowledgment of the existence of a new state or of a new government in an existing foreign state, coupled with an expression of willingness on the part of the recognizing state to enter into relations with the recognized entity or government. Recognition is also used with reference to belligerent communities or insurgent groups (see Chapter 6), in connection with the validity of title to territory (for example, recognition of conquest) and, lastly, to the commission of acts by governments (see Chapter 9, under Acts of State).

A state comes into existence when the community involved acquires the characteristics associated with the concept of a state: a defined territory, an operating and effective government, and independence from outside control. Because all these aspects of statehood involve ascertainable facts, the dating of the beginning of a new state is merely a question of fact and not of law. The new state exists, regardless of whether it has been recognized by other states, when it has met the factual requirements of statehood. Or, as stated in Article 3 of the Inter-American Convention on Rights and Duties of States (Montevideo, December 26, 1933),

The political existence of the State is independent of recognition by the other States. Even before recognition the State has the right to defend its integrity and independence, to provide for its conservation and prosperity, and consequently to organize itself as it sees fit, to legislate upon its interests, administer its services, and to define the jurisdiction and competence of its courts. . . .

The other states must answer, each for itself, the question of whether a new entity has come into being, but only in order to enter into relations with the new unit. This is what recognition of a new state means.

[1] Kaplan-Katzenbach, p. 109.

Despite much reasoned argument to the effect that the recognition of new states (and of new governments) is a legal matter, the majority of writers as well as the practice of states indicate that it is, rather, a political act with legal consequences. This is demonstrated convincingly by the dependence of national courts on executive recognition policy. On the other hand, definite and important legal effects result from the political act, tinged, in addition, with economic and sometimes moral overtones.

LEGAL SIGNIFICANCE OF RECOGNITION

Constitutive Theory. Much legalistic controversy has centered on the effect of recognition on the recognized state. According to one theory, it has "constitutive" effect: "A state is, and becomes, an International Person through recognition only and exclusively." [2] In other words, international personality is held to be conferred only through recognition by the community in question. [3] Such a view is related quite openly to an extreme positivist approach, for if consent is posited as the major source of international law, then it would be quite simple to assert that international personality can be obtained only through the consent of existing legal persons by the performance of an act constituting recognition. Logically, however, this premise is not altogether correct, for if the "rights" and duties of a new state are based on its own will as a state, they cannot be derived from the will of other states.

In this connection we must return once more to the concept of the community of nations. It was asserted formerly that that community admitted new members (states) through recognition. But many communities were states in every sense of the word long before they were "admitted" to the community—China, Turkey, Siam, and Russia represent excellent examples. It can thus be maintained that recognition is not essential to statehood.

Declarative Theory. The second theory about the legal significance of recognition holds that the latter represents a "declaratory" act, that recognition is at most a formal admission of already existing facts. This view has been endorsed on many occasions by international conventions, arbitral decisions, and even by the International Court of Justice. There does exist a qualification concerning the declarative theory: since states are free to deny or to grant access to their courts, recognition of a state is constitutive with respect to those domestic courts, and not every community claiming to be a state has the capacity to appear before permanent international tribunals.

[2] Lauterpacht's *Oppenheim*, Vol. I, p. 125 [the late Sir Hersch Lauterpacht was the original formulator of the constitutive theory]; see also Corbett, pp. 62–63.

[3] The constitutive theory has been presented with great vigor in Hans Kelsen, "Recognition in International Law: Theoretical Observations," 35 *A.J.I.L.* (1941), pp. 605–617. It represents, however, a minority view among writers; see, *inter alia*, H. W. Briggs, "Recognition of States: Some Reflections on Doctrine and Practice," 43 *A.J.I.L.* (1949), pp. 113–121, and Whiteman, Vol. II, pp. 17–26.

In summary, the basic function of recognition ought to be the acknowledgment as fact of something that has been uncertain up to then, namely the possession of statehood by some community. When such recognition is granted, it indicates the willingness of the recognizing state to accept the consequences of its act and to enter into normal relations with the recognized state A *duty* to recognize new states cannot be demonstrated convincingly, despite many ingenious attempts to do so.[4]

RECOGNITION AND NONRECOGNITION OF STATES

Forms of Recognition. Recognition is said to be *express*, or *explicit*, when a formal statement is issued by a recognizing state. It is *implied*, or *tacit*, when a state enters into official relation with a new state by sending a diplomatic representative to it, acknowledges or salutes its flag, communicates officially with its chief of state, concludes an agreement with it, or otherwise, by deed, takes note of its existence as a state.

The establishment of the new state of Israel on May 14, 1948, was followed within a few hours on May 15 by a statement from President Harry S Truman which read:

This government has been informed that a Jewish state has been proclaimed in Palestine, and recognition has been requested by the provisional government thereof. The United States Government recognizes the provisional government as the *de facto* authority of the new state of Israel.

That statement represented explicit recognition both of the new state and of its government. To have recognized the state alone would have represented a manifest absurdity.

The reasons involved in the decision to recognize a new state vary of course from case to case. Commercial interests, such as the possibility of receiving the grant of a concession or even a monopoly, have played a part. Other factors of importance may include the number of states that have already extended recognition, domestic political repercussions, the possibility of enlisting the new state as a military ally, humanitarian motives, and so on. The reader must be cautioned, however, that any detailed analysis of recognition policies followed by the United States since World War II would show that the criteria which in the past were utilized in the determination of the recognition of new states have virtually disappeared.

Nonrecognition of Statehood. Most writers agree that nonrecognition of an existing state represents a rather ineffectual political measure. The disadvantages resulting from nonrecognition are numerous, including the

---

[4] See, for instance, Hersch Lauterpacht, *Recognition in International Law*, pp. 5–6, 12–33, 73–78, 409–410. For a denial of the existence of the duty, see particularly Josef L. Kunz, "Critical Remarks on Lauterpacht's "Recognition in International Law," 44 *A.J.I.L.* (1950), pp. 713–719; and Quincy Wright, "Some Thoughts on Recognition," 44 *A.J.I.L.* (1950), pp. 548–559.

fact that legitimate interests of one's citizens cannot be protected adequately in the unrecognized state. The latter cannot have access to the courts of the state refusing recognition, but on the other hand is also immune from suit in those same courts. The nonrecognized state may, however, be prevented from joining international organizations or general conventions.

In one instance, that of Manchuria, an unparalleled case of what might be termed "collective nonrecognition" of an entity took place. On February 24, 1933, the Assembly of the League of Nations adopted a resolution stating that the members of the organization would not recognize the new state of Manchuria *de facto* or *de jure*. The League then created an Advisory Committee to advise its members on any measures to be taken by them as a result of their joint decision not to recognize the new state.

On the whole, nonrecognition appears to pose more disadvantages than benefits to states adopting such a policy. It has been employed on many occasions as a gesture of protest against the extinction of a previously existing state. The purpose of such a policy obviously was an attempt to harass the successor state and to prevent prescription from creating legal effects.

Collective Recognition. It has been asserted on numerous occasions that a state may be formally recognized through the collective action of a number of other states. This claim was made particularly in connection with efforts to prove the existence of a community of nations and of its collective admission of new members. Virtually every instance cited, however, could be shown to represent individual recognition of a new state, granted either simultaneously or within a very short interval of time by several other states. The frequently mentioned case of the recognition of Estonia represents an excellent illustration of the fact that admission into an international organization does *not* mean collective recognition by the members of the organization.

The establishment of the United Nations was followed by similar claims of collective recognition, but no change in the situation can be shown to have taken place. Admission of a state into the United Nations does not mean—nor could it mean, in view of the authority delegated to that body —that the other members of the Organization have to grant the new member access to their courts, exchange diplomatic representatives with it, or in any other manner deal with the new member as a recognized state *outside* of the United Nations. The latter "does not possess any authority to recognize either a new State or a new government of an existing State." [5]

Recognition by Treaty Adherence. The conclusion of the Nuclear Test Ban Treaty in 1963 revived an old controversy connected with recognition, namely, whether a hitherto unrecognized state or government

[5] Secretary-General Trygve Lie, March 8, 1950; see also Hans Aufricht, "Principles and Practices of Recognition by International Organizations," 43 *A.J.I.L.* (1949), pp. 679–704; and Whiteman, Vol. II, pp. 563–567.

would be accorded recognition by adhering to a multilateral treaty. To illustrate this question, let us examine briefly the instance which led to a re-examination of the problem. The German Democratic Republic (East Germany) has not been recognized, at the time of writing, by the government of the United States either as a state or as a government. The East German authorities did, however, subscribe (adhere) to the Test Ban Treaty. Did this act mean that the United States henceforth "recognized" the East German regime? The answer is clearly in the negative, for in international law the governing criterion in determining recognition or its absence is intent. It can be asserted, in fact, that there exists a well-established proposition of international law that participation with an unrecognized regime in a mutilateral treaty open for general adherence does not give rise to any implication of recognition.[6]

De Facto Recognition. At times an effort is made to achieve a compromise between the desirability of admitting that a community is in fact a state and continuing doubts as to whether a community, under prevailing conditions, is "legally" a state. The resolution of the conflict between these ideas often takes the form of *de facto* recognition, as opposed to acceptance of *de jure* statehood. In other words, a provisional recognition takes place.

From a logical as well as a practical point of view, *de facto* recognition is objectionable. The community in question either is or is not a state. The expressions "recognition of a *de facto* state," "recognition of a *de facto* government," and so on, are greatly to be preferred. As Whiteman pointed out, "In prevailing practice, when the United States extends recognition, it is recognition *per se*, not '*de facto*' recognition."[7]

In particular, recognition of a belligerent community would be more acceptable than *de facto* recognition of a rebel community (or authority). In fact, what would be involved would be recognition of a *de facto* community or authority.[8]

The recognition of belligerent communities has posed, in the past, many of the more perplexing problems connected with recognition. (See also Chapter 6.)

Traditionally, certain conditions must have been satisfied if recognition of any sort is to be extended to a rebel group or territory: (1) a government and military organization must have been established and must be operative in the rebel-controlled area; (2) the rebellion must have reached a stage beyond mere petty local revolt—that is, a condition of warfare

[6] See the relevant Opinion of the Legal Adviser to the Department of State, dated August 12, 1963, in 58 *A.J.I.L.* (1964), pp. 171–175; on the subject in general, consult Whiteman, Vol. II, pp. 53–59, 558–562.

[7] Whiteman, Vol. II, p. 3; see also Charles L. Cochran, "De Facto and De Jure Recognition: Is There A Difference?" 62 *A.J.I.L.* (1968), pp. 457–464, for an elaboration by Miss Whiteman of the point in question.

[8] See Cochran, *op. cit.*, and his "The Development of an Inter-American Policy for the Recognition of De Facto Governments," 62 *A.J.I.L.* (1968), pp. 460–464.

equivalent to conflicts between states must have developed; (3) the rebel government must in fact control a reasonable portion of the territory of the parent state (domestic revolt) or overseas territory (colonial revolt).

The determination of the degree to which these conditions have been met may be undertaken by the parent government or by outside states. If the conditions have been satisfied, then the recognition of the rebels as a belligerent community or insurgent group is lawful. When recognition takes place, then the rules of international law relative to warfare and neutrality come into force and, furthermore, the parent state is freed from all international responsibility for the acts of the rebels from the inception of the revolt. This last statement holds true, however, only if the parent government has made some attempt, implied in the second condition above, to assert its authority over the rebels.

Withdrawal of Recognition. Because recognition represents the acceptance of a fact, namely of the existence of a new state, it is not appropriate to withdraw such acceptance at a later date.[9] The only really proper occasion on which recognition can be cancelled is when the new state has become extinct or in some other manner has lost its independence, when, in other words, the fact recognized by recognition has ceased to be a fact.

Retroactive Effects of Recognition. It has been generally accepted that the recognition of a new state has retroactive effects to the moment of initial existence. This means that the state extending recognition accepts as valid all official acts of the government of the new state, from its inception. The recognizing state has a right to set a date as the official commencement of the life of the recognized state, and henceforth all acts of the latter that took place between the specified moment of birth and the date of recognition are held to be as valid as if recognition had been accorded at the time the new state came into being. Exceptions to the application of this principle have been made on occasion in various national courts, primarily when excessive hardships for individuals were shown to be involved in an unqualified application of the retroactive effects of recognition.

THE RECOGNITION OF GOVERNMENTS

Recognition of a government is a political act differing from the recognition of a state only in the nature of the entity being recognized. A government is merely an operative agency of a state, but it is that part of a state which undertakes the actions which, attributable to the state, are subject to regulation by the application of the principles and rules of international law.

Logically the recognition of a new state automatically involves recognition of the government of that state, for no one could envision recognition of the whole unit without inclusion of its operating agency, its govern-

[9] On this point, consult Whiteman, Vol. II, pp. 27-30, 45-46.

ment. It would, of course, be possible to recognize a provisional government as a *de facto* government while extending recognition to the state on a *de jure* basis, as was done in the American recognition of the state of Israel, but this would still represent a concurrent recognition of both entities.[10]

The real problems involved in the recognition of governments tend to appear when a change in the form of a government takes place—either because of a change in type or through an unconstitutional or otherwise irregular transfer of authority from one group to another group within the state in question. What is involved is the authority of a new group or a new person to act as the governing agency of a state and to represent it, to act as its agent, in its international relations.

It must be remembered that changes in the form of a *government* or in its personnel do not affect the continuing existence of the state involved.

In any event, even thorough transformations of the constitution of a state do not necessarily affect the latter's continuity of legal personality. The classic example commonly cited is that of France for the period from 1791 to 1875, during which time a succession of constitutional changes brought into being, after the monarchy, a republic, an empire, a return to monarchy, again an empire, and finally the Third Republic. But during these changes in the form of government, France remained the "state of France," the identical international legal person, with the same "rights" and immunities and with the same unchanged international obligations. These concepts were illustrated in the case of *The Sapphire:*

THE SAPPHIRE

United States, Supreme Court, 1871
11 Wallace 164

FACTS

The private American ship *Sapphire* and the French naval transport *Euryale* collided in the harbor of San Francisco on December 22, 1867. The *Euryale* suffered heavy damage. Two days later, a libel was filed in the District Court, in the name of Napoleon III, Emperor of the French, as owner of the *Euryale*, against the *Sapphire*.

The owners of the American ship filed an answer, alleging that the damage had been caused through the fault of the French vessel. The District Court decided in favor of the libelant (Napoleon III) and awarded him $15,000, representing the total amount claimed. The owners of the *Sapphire* appealed to the Circuit Court which, however, upheld the verdict of the lower court. They then appealed to

[10] Following the Israeli elections of October 24, 1948, and of January 25, 1949, the U.S. government extended *de jure* recognition to the government of Israel on January 31, 1949; see Denys P. Myers, "Recognition of States," pp. 703–720 in his "Contemporary Practice of the U.S. Relating to International Law," 55 *A.J.I.L.* (1961), pp. 697–733.

the Supreme Court of the United States in July, 1869. In the summer of 1870, Napoleon III was deposed as Emperor of the French. The case came to be argued on February 16, 1871.

QUESTIONS

(1) Did the Emperor of the French have a right to bring a suit in United States courts?

(2) If such a suit had been brought rightly, had it not become abated by the deposition of the Emperor Napoleon, or, in other words, did the French state, because of the change in its form of government, lose the identity which had permitted it to sue in a foreign court?

DECISION

The Supreme Court believed that the officers of the *Euryale* had also been at fault and that, both parties being at fault, the damages should be equally divided between them. It therefore reversed the decree of the Circuit Court and remitted the cause to that court with directions to enter a decree in conformity with the opinion of the Supreme Court.

REASONING

As regarded Question No. 1: There was no question in the minds of the Court as to the right of a recognized friendly foreign sovereign to sue in United States courts. "A foreign sovereign as well as any other foreign person, who has a demand of a civil nature against any person here, may prosecute it in our courts. To deny him this privilege would manifest a want of comity and friendly feeling."

As regarded Question No. 2: The suit brought originally in the name of Napoleon III had not become abated by the Emperor's deposition. "The reigning sovereign represents the national sovereignty, and that sovereignty is continuous and perpetual, residing in the proper successors of the sovereign for the time being. Napoleon was the owner of the *Euryale*, not as an individual, but as sovereign of France. . . . On his deposition the sovereignty does not change, but merely the person or persons in whom it resides. The foreign state is the true and real owner of its public vessels of war. The reigning Emperor, or National Assembly, or other actual person or party in power, is but the agent and representative of the national sovereignty. A change in such representative works no change in the national sovereignty of its rights. The next successor recognized by our government is competent to carry on a suit already commenced and receive the fruits of it. . . . The vessel has always belonged and still belongs to the French nation."

Similarly, the complete changes brought about in the Russian government through the two revolutions of 1917 did not affect the legal personality of the state of Russia, and even though the final government emerging from the internal upheavals of the nation was not recognized by other countries for a number of years, the State of Russia continued to exist as a member of the community of nations and as a legal person under international law.

PRINCIPLES OF THE RECOGNITION OF GOVERNMENTS

The normal transfer of power from one group or one individual to another in accordance with the constitutional provisions in force in a given country does not require the recognition of the new government by outside states. Strictly speaking, there is no "new" government at all, in view of the presumed direct and automatic transfer of authority involved. A political party in charge of a country's government may be replaced by another party as a result of an election, yet from an international legal point of view, the same government continues to function.

Even when minor constitutional irregularities have occurred in the transfer of authority, other states quite frequently find it convenient to overlook such infractions of domestic law and to view the government in question as a direct and continuing successor of the preceding one. This is particularly true when all available information indicates that stability is assured in the country in question and that the nation's international obligations will continue to be honored as in the past.

The question of recognition of a new government arises, on the other hand, when serious violations of a constitution are recorded or when the basic form of government is changed in a country. The "outsiders" then have to pass individual judgments on the competency of the new government to represent its state in its foreign relations. This judgment is obviously important, for a state can be held legally responsible only for the actions of its government recognized as such by other states.

Objective Tests. Traditionally the judgment of a government as to the competence of another, new, government is based on the answers to certain quite objective questions or tests. If (a) the new government exercises *de facto* control over the administrative machinery of its country; and if (b) there is an absence of resistance to the authority of the new government; and if (c) the latter appears to have the backing of a substantial segment of public opinion in its country—then it can be said that the so-called objective tests of its competence to act as the representative of the state have been met and that recognition should be extended, *provided* that political objections to recognition do not bar the latter.

Most writers on international law point out, in this connection, that no rule of the law has ever ascribed anything like a sacred character to the constitution of any country. No rule of the law can be held to deprive a people of its right to change its form of government, whether by ballot or by bullet, nor does any existing rule maintain that such a change must be the handiwork of a majority in any nation.

During the period from roughly 1913 to about 1929, the government of the United States did insist that a new government, in order to be recognized *de facto* or *de jure,* had to come into office by legal and constitutional means. This so-called Wilson Doctrine was applied against new governments in Mexico (General Huerta), El Salvador, Costa Rica, and Nicaragua. It denied to the peoples of those states the right to select their own governments by whatever means they chose to apply. It meant that the government of the United States claimed for itself the right to determine the legality of a foreign government, and assuredly this meant concern with a purely internal and sovereign sphere of another state. Commendably, the doctrine was abandoned when the Hoover administration came into office.[11]

In the absence of special political considerations, a new government was normally recognized quite promptly by other governments, once the objective tests relating to its *de facto* authority had been met satisfactorily. Examples abound in modern history: the establishment of a republic in France in 1870, the republican government of Brazil following the overthrow of the empire in 1889, the new Vargas government in Brazil in 1930, the government of Fidel Castro in Cuba in more recent years. The list of illustrations could be extended almost indefinitely; it would also include the Hitler government of Germany in 1933, which was recognized at once despite its revolutionary character and the highly dubious methods, from a constitutional point of view, through which it came to power.

Subjective Test. The second half of the nineteenth century, however, saw the emergence of a second test, applied by some states to a new government in connection with recognition. This second, subjective, test centered around the determination of the new government's willingness to carry out the international legal obligations of its state.

It might seem that such a test would be superfluous, for any government judged to represent its state might be expected to assume unquestioningly the legal obligations of that state. But practice increasingly favored the application of this second test. If a given new government came into power by unconstitutional, possibly even violent means, could this not indicate that it would perhaps adopt a rather cavalier attitude toward its international obligations, just as it had admittedly done toward its domestic constitution and laws? And if the new government made its appearance in a country chronically beset by internal change and unrest, could much reliance be placed on its willingness, or even its ability, to honor its international obligations?

Such considerations led to the application of the second test. It had to have, of necessity, a subjective character, for it had to do with the expected future behavior of a government and could not be exposed to the same factual investigation possible in the application of the traditional objective tests.

The emergence of ideologies regarded, rightly or wrongly, as inimical or subversive by many governments, coupled with the ability of followers of such movements to gain control of certain governments, usually by unconstitutional means, served to center additional attention on the subjective test for recognition. No doubt political motives played a part then, for if a given regime had indicated its subversive ambitions before the seizure of power, it would appear logical that the new regime would not subsequently honor any of its obligations that conflicted with those aims or impeded their achievement.

---

[11] See Philip M. Brown, "The Legal Effects of Recognition," 44 *A.J.I.L.* (1950), pp. 617–640, particularly pp. 621–623.

It is in this sphere that we find the reason for the refusal of monarchical governments to recognize French revolutionary governments between 1789 and 1793, as well as for the widespread hesitation to recognize the Russian government which emerged from the November 1917 revolution, and definitely for the current refusal on the part of the United States to recognize the Communist government of China. The nonrecognition of the U.S.S.R. was defended on March 21, 1923, by Secretary of State Charles Evans Hughes when he stated that

The fundamental question in the recognition of a government is whether it shows ability and a disposition to discharge international obligations. Stability is, of course, important; stability is essential. . . . What, however, would avail mere stability if it were stability in the prosecution of a policy of repudiation and confiscation? In the case of Russia we have a very easy test of a matter of fundamental importance, and that is of good faith in the discharge of international obligations. I say that good faith is a matter of essential importance because words are easily spoken. Of what avail is it to speak of assurances, if valid obligations and rights are repudiated and property is confiscated? [12]

In all instances cited, the new governments succeeded within a relatively short time in assuming virtually complete domestic authority, thereby satisfying the requirements laid down in the objective tests demanded for recognition. In the latter two instances, on the other hand, application of the second test was cited repeatedly as the basis for nonrecognition.

The government of the United States did not apply the subjective test to any extent until relatively late in the nineteenth century but has utilized it increasingly in the twentieth century. As far as the current nonrecognition of the government of the People's Republic of China is concerned, the major reasons advanced by official spokesmen include the wholesale expropriation of American private property in China without compensation; the forcible seizure of United States government properties, title to which rested on treaty rights; and the arrest without cause, coupled with brutal mistreatment, of individual American citizens, including consular personnel.[13]

It should be noted that the United States has dealt directly with the Chinese People's Republic since 1955 through the unusual arrangement known as "Ambassadorial Talks," held first in Geneva and, since 1958, in Warsaw.[14] During the past few years, the participants in these discussions

[12] See also 17 *A.J.I.L.* (1923), p. 296, and N. D. Houghton, "Policy of the United States and Other Nations with Respect to the Recognition of the Russian Soviet Government, 1917–1929," *International Conciliation* (No. 247, February, 1929), pp. 83–108.

[13] The entire problem of Chinese recognition is outlined in commendable fashion in Robert P. Newman, *Recognition of Communist China?* (New York: Macmillan, 1961); see particularly pp. 242–261 for a discussion of U.S. precedents and their legal implications. See also the appended list of Suggested Readings.

[14] Consult Kenneth T. Young, "American Dealings with Peking," 45 *Foreign Affairs* (1966), pp. 77–87, and his *Diplomacy and Power in Washington-Peking Dealings:*

were the Chinese and American ambassadors accredited to Poland. Thus far, only one agreement, covering the return of American prisoners of war held in China after the Korean War, resulted from the meetings, but at the very least some clarifications of respective national policies must have been achieved during the normally secret discussions. The U.S. government has indicated repeatedly that no intent to recognize the Chinese mainland government should be construed from the existence and continuation of these ambassadorial talks.

Political and Economic Factors. Both political and economic motives enter into the recognition picture when a question of concessions or debts granted or incurred by a previous government is involved. In Latin America, particularly, the practice developed on the part of governments to demand a formal pledge to honor *past* obligations as the price of recognizing a new government. Unfortunately such pledges were given very freely in many cases, for the new governments were anxious to be recognized; when they in turn were overthrown at a later date, the successor government, in many instances, refused to honor such pledges, regarding them as mere personal promises of an extinct regime. When major nations such as the United States then failed to recognize the latest and "uncooperative" government, such denial of recognition, it is said, was the direct cause of still another revolution, with the newest leaders willing to make the required pledge as the price of recognition. The power to grant or to withhold recognition thus came to represent an effective method of intervening in the internal affairs of another country without violating, technically at least, the duty of nonintervention.

Recognition of a new government represents, generally speaking, an individual political act on the part of the recognizing government, just as in the case of the recognition of new states. The question of collective recognition of a new government does not come into the picture at all, for it appears to be well established that admission to membership by an international organization does not constitute implied *de facto* and *de jure* recognition of the government in question by the individual member states of the organization. Whatever recognition does take place simply means recognition of the government by the organization *solely* for membership purposes.

On the other hand, it is possible for an international organization to *recommend* to its member states that a given government be recognized by them, individually, as the *de facto* or *de jure* government of a state. This was done, for instance, through a resolution dated December 12, 1948, by which the General Assembly of the United Nations declared the government of the Republic of Korea to be the only lawful government in Korea.

1953–1967 (Chicago: University of Chicago Center for Policy Study, 1967), as well as the documentary material in Whiteman, Vol. II, pp. 551–555.

Finally it should be mentioned that on occasion and for purely political or psychological reasons, a demand is heard to withdraw recognition of a given government viewed as unfriendly to the state in which such views are voiced. However, no measurable good, except a gesture of protest which would have little effect on the states concerned, could result from an adoption of nonrecognition. For example, withdrawal of recognition of Soviet satellite governments by the United States not only would deprive it of its diplomatic "listening posts" behind the Iron Curtain, but would make protection of American nationals and property behind that Curtain a much more difficult undertaking than it already represents.

THE CONSEQUENCES OF RECOGNITION

Relatively little has been written about the actual effects of the recognition of a new government. In general, such an act means that the recognizing government acknowledges the stability of the recognized government as well as its willingness to honor its obligations; that the recognizing government acknowledges its willingness to enter into normal international relations, including the exchange of diplomatic agents, with the recognized government; and that the recognizing state henceforth will hold the recognized government responsible for its international obligations as well as all official acts affecting them. As in the case of the recognition of states, the recognition of a new *de jure* government has retroactive effects, dating back to the inception of the life of the new government. Retroactivity of recognition thus validates acts of a *de facto* government which has subsequently become the new *de jure* government, but does *not* invalidate acts of the previous *de jure* government.[15]

Once recognition has been extended to a new government, the latter has access to the courts of the recognizing state:

REPUBLIC OF CHINA v. MERCHANTS' FIRE ASSURANCE CORPORATION OF NEW YORK

United States, Circuit Court of Appeals,
Ninth Circuit, 1929, 30 F. [2d] 278

FACTS

The Republic of China had insured certain of its public buildings with the defendant company, among them the building of the Chinese Government Telephone Administration at Wuchang. Fire damaged this particular structure. After the loss occurred, Wuchang was captured by the troops of the "National Government" from the lawful government of the Republic of China. Soon afterward, the National Government, by then controlling 15 of the 18 provinces of China, demanded payment for the loss from the insurance company. When the latter refused payment, the National

---

[15] See also *Oetjen* v. *Central Leather Co.*, United States, Supreme Court, 1918, 246 U.S. 297.

Government filed suit against the company in the [then] United States Court for China.

The insurance company claimed that the plaintiff was not the Republic of China but merely a revolutionary organization, not recognized as the government of the Republic of China, hence without any legal capacity to sue in United States courts. The company was sustained and the case was dismissed. The National Government appealed this dismissal.

ISSUE

Under what conditions, and when, may an unrecognized government originating through unconstitutional or revolutionary acts, sue in the courts of a foreign state?

DECISION

The Republic of China won its appeal. In view of certain events that had taken place since the dismissal of the suit in the lower court, the circuit court reversed that decision.

REASONING

1. The courts of a state cannot recognize the existence of a government which originated in revolution until it has first been recognized by the political department of the government under which such courts function. By this standard, the National Govern-

ment, unrecognized at the time it sought access to the United States Court for China, had no legal capacity to sue in that court.

2. However, on July 25, 1928, a commercial treaty was concluded between the American Minister to China and the Minister of Finance of the National Government of the Republic of China. This treaty, although not yet given consent for ratification by the Senate of the United States, constituted recognition by the Executive Department of the United States of both the National Government and of its accredited representative. In addition, a telegram from the U.S. Secretary of State to the circuit court stated that the minister of the National Government had been officially received by the President of the United States.

This, the Court held, conclusively settled the question of United States recognition of the National Government: implicit recognition had taken place through entering into negotiations, sending a diplomatic agent, receiving a diplomatic agent in formal audience.

Hence the changes that had taken place had to be recognized by the Court and the recognition extended to the National Government validated the suit already begun by it in the United States courts.

Following recognition, the new government acquires title to the assets of its predecessor, located in the territory of the recognizing state, including bank deposits, investments, embassy or legation buildings, the contents of consular offices, and so on. It also falls heir to all claims previously asserted by its predecessor government.[16]

PROVISIONAL RECOGNITION

On occasion it has appeared difficult to apply at once objective and subjective tests to a new revolutionary government. Under such circum-

[16] Whiteman, Vol. II, pp. 665–746.

stances, it has been the frequent practice of states to grant what is called provisional or *de facto* recognition to the new government.[17] This means that the foreign states in question indicate their willingness to deal with the new government purely on the basis and to the extent of its control of the administration of its country. This enables other states to continue commercial relations and to protect their nationals and their property in a country torn by civil strife, without the need for determining right away whether the new government is entitled to represent its state internationally.

Such provisional recognition is fraught with many problems as long as the *de facto* government is not in complete control of the territory of its state, that is, as long as the legitimate sovereign is still in office, even though limited in the extent of its own territorial jurisdiction. (See also Chapter 6.) Should the legitimate government ultimately win the civil war, the provisional recognition extended to its opponents by outsiders could result in logical hostility, for by any standard the recognition granted would have been premature and inimical to the sovereign status of the lawful government.

The Spanish Civil War, caused by the rising of a faction ultimately headed by General Francisco Franco, supplied a variety of interesting situations illustrative of the working of provisional recognition. When Mr. Clement Atlee asked Prime Minister Chamberlain in the House of Commons on November 4, 1937, what was the significance of the provisional recognition extended by Great Britain to the Franco regime, the Prime Minister replied, in part, that

. . . the protection of British nationals and British commercial interests throughout the whole of Spain including those large areas . . . of which General Franco's forces are now in effective occupation [made it] increasingly evident that the numerous questions affecting British interests in these areas cannot be satisfactorily dealt with by means of the occasional contacts which have hitherto existed. . . . His Majesty's Government have entered upon negotiations for the appointment of agents by them and by General Franco respectively for the discussion of questions affecting British nationals and commercial interests, but these agents will not be given any diplomatic status.[18]

On November 29, 1937, Viscount Cranborne, the Undersecretary of State for Foreign Affairs, explained in the House of Commons that while there were two authorities in existence in Spain, Great Britain recognized only one of them, and then went on to say that

At Barcelona, therefore, we have a Minister Plenipotentiary and in the other case [Franco Spain] we have commercial agents to protect our commercial

[17] *Ibid.*, pp. 119–133.
[18] Cited by Herbert W. Briggs, "Relations Officieuses and Intent to Recognize: British Recognition of Franco," 34 *A.J.I.L.* (1940), pp. 47–56, at p. 48.

interests. . . . Both the Minister and the agents . . . are subordinate to the Ambassador at Hendaye.[19]

On February 17 and again on May 28, 1938, the Foreign Office informed British courts that the government of the Spanish Republic was recognized as the *de jure* government of Spain, while the Nationalist government of General Franco was recognized as exercising *de facto* administrative control over the larger portion of Spanish territory.[20] In both cases the courts interpreted this information as meaning that the British government had granted *de facto* recognition to the Franco authorities. This interpretation was officially denied as late as February 13, 1939, when Prime Minister Chamberlain stated that no decision on the recognition of the Franco government had been taken.

Recognition normally involves an intention to recognize a new government (or state). It is, of course, possible for a state to have dealings (*relations officieuses*) with an unrecognized government or state without proceeding to recognition, provided that the absence of intention is made clear. Thus the United States maintained agents in several Latin American republics before recognizing their independence from Spain, as did Great Britain. During the War Between the States, Great Britain sent agents to the Confederate States. Many other governments have acted similarly in modern history. A recent notable example of "dealing" with an unrecognized government has been supplied by the negotiations conducted by the United States on a number of topics with the communist Chinese regime.

Such relations with unrecognized states or governments create vexatious problems for the courts of a state maintaining the unofficial contacts in question. The classic modern case, which had caused the first inquiry by a British court mentioned above in connection with the Spanish Civil War, was that of the *Arantzazu Mendi*.

GOVERNMENT OF THE REPUBLIC OF SPAIN v. S. S. ARANTZAZU MENDI AND OTHERS

Great Britain, House of Lords, February 23, 1939,
55 The Times Law Reports 454

FACTS

The *Arantzazu Mendi*, a privately owned Spanish vessel registered at the port of Bilbao, had been requisitioned by the Republic of Spain on June 28, 1937, under a decree issued that day; Bilbao was then in the hands of the Franco regime and the vessel was on the high seas. The ship had also been requisitioned by the Nationalist government by a similar decree dated March 2, 1938. At neither time was the vessel in Spanish waters. When

---

[19] *Ibid.*, p. 49.

[20] See Lawrence Preuss, "State Immunity and the Requisition of Ships during the Spanish Civil War: I. Before the British Courts," 35 *A.J.I.L.* (1941), pp. 263–281.

the *Arantzazu Mendi* arrived in England on August 11, 1937, her owners applied for a writ of possession, claiming the vessel as their property and asking that it be arrested and turned over to their representatives. The vessel was arrested by the Admiralty Marshal on August 24, 1937.

On April 5, 1938, the Franco agent in London notified the owners of the requisition of their property and the owners supplied him with notarized acceptances of the order of requisition, as did the master of the vessel. This resulted in the withdrawal of the owners' action to regain possession; the vessel, however, remained under arrest. The Spanish Republic then secured a writ on the same day (April 11, 1938) to obtain possession, and the Nationalist Government entered an appearance under protest, asking the court to set aside both the writ and the warrant of arrest, asserting that those instruments violated the position of the Franco government as a foreign sovereign state.

The court requested information from the Secretary of State for Foreign Affairs and was informed that the Republican government was recognized as the *de jure* government of Spain but that at the same time the Nationalist government was recognized as a government exercising *de facto* control over the larger part of Spain and that it "was not a government subordinate to any other government in Spain."

The court interpreted this to mean that, for purposes of the case, the Nationalist government was recognized as a foreign sovereign state. It ordered the writ to be set aside but continued the warrant of arrest in force to prevent the ship from leaving British jurisdiction pending the outcome of an expected appeal.

The Republic of Spain appealed at once, but the decision of the lower court was upheld. The appeal was then carried to the House of Lords, which affirmed.

ISSUE

[In court of original jurisdiction]

Whether the Nationalist government of Spain was recognized by His Majesty's government as a foreign sovereign state.

DECISION

[In court of original jurisdiction, upheld on appeal, affirmed by the House of Lords]

The Nationalist government had to be recognized as a foreign sovereign state in view of the reply received by the Court from the Secretary of State. Such a reply had to be treated by a British court as a statement of fact which could not be discussed by the court on grounds of law.

REASONING

[Based on the reply from the Secretary of State]

(1) The British government recognized Spain as a foreign sovereign state.

(2) The British government recognized the government of the Spanish Republic having its seat in Barcelona as the *de jure* government of Spain.

(3) No government other than that referred to above was recognized by the British government as the *de jure* government of Spain or any part thereof.

(4) The Nationalist government of Spain was a government in conflict with the government of the Spanish Republic established at Barcelona. It claimed to be the government of Spain and was seeking to overthrow the government of the Spanish Re-

public and to establish its authority over the whole of Spain.

(5) The British Government recognized the Nationalist government as a government which then exercised *de facto* administrative control over the larger portion of Spain.

(6) The British Government recognized that the Nationalist government exercised effective administrative control over all the Basque provinces of Spain.

(7) The British government had not accorded any other recognition to the Nationalist government.

(8) The Nationalist government was not a government subordinate to any other government in Spain.

(9) The question whether the Nationalist government was to be regarded as that of a foreign sovereign state appeared to be a question of law to be answered in the light of the preceding statements and having regard to the particular issue with respect to which the question was raised.

Briggs pointed out that the use of *de facto* or *de jure* to characterize a government means an assumption of ability to pass on the lawfulness of that government, even when an official document states specifically that no such judgment on the lawfulness of a government is passed when it is recognized as a *de facto* government.[21] In reality, the decision on the legality of a given government is not a question of international law but of the domestic constitutional law of the state in which that government functions. The continuing practice of many states, as reflected in the *Arantzazu Mendi* case, to designate a *de facto* government of a given state, is based not so much on legal principles as on political considerations, particularly on those related to expediency.

The proper manner of handling the knotty problem of recognition in the event of a civil war was represented in this writer's opinion, in the decision in the *Campuzano* case:

THE SPANISH [REPUBLICAN] GOVERNMENT
v. FELIPE CAMPUZANO

Norway, Supreme Court, November 2, 1938

FACTS

At the time of the outbreak of the Spanish Civil War in 1936, the Spanish Minister in Oslo was absent on vacation and the affairs of the Legation were in the hands of the Secretary of the Legation, Felipe Campuzano, as Chargé d'Affaires. On August 13, 1936, Mr. Campuzano notified the Norwegian Ministry of Foreign Affairs that he had resigned and was no longer a representative of the Spanish Republic, and when the Spanish Minister returned, he, too, sent a similar declaration to the Ministry. He left

---

[21] Herbert W. Briggs, "De Facto and De Jure Recognition: The Arantzazu Mendi," 33 *A.J.I.L.* (1939), pp. 689–699, at p. 689; his article reported in detail the arguments advanced by both sides at all three levels of judicial consideration.

Norway a few weeks later to join General Franco's Nationalist regime.

For several months, neither Spanish government had a representative in Norway. On December 10, the Norwegian Ministry of Foreign Affairs was notified by the Republican government of Spain that Dr. Joaquin Pastor had been appointed Secretary of the Legation and Chargé d'Affaires in Oslo; he arrived at his post at the end of 1936.

During the interval mentioned, the Spanish Legation had to be moved from its former accommodations and Mr. Campuzano assumed responsibility for this enterprise. He directed that portions of the movables be stored by the moving company but that others, including the Legation archives, be brought to his house. When Dr. Pastor arrived in Oslo, he claimed possession of all contents of the former Legation but Campuzano refused to surrender the archives and certain other articles in his possession, arguing that he held them on behalf of the Nationalist government as the true government of Spain.

Dr. Pastor, on behalf of the Spanish Republic, sued in a Norwegian court for possession of all Legation property. The case ultimately came before the Norwegian Supreme Court by appeal.

ISSUES

(1) The Spanish Republican government, claiming to be the only Spanish government recognized by Norway, asserted legal ownership of all property belonging to "Spain" or the "Spanish State." Should all such property be turned over to its representative, Dr. Pastor?

(2) Felipe Campuzano argued that the Nationalist government, as the lawful government of Spain, was immune from suit in Norwegian courts as a foreign sovereign state. Should this be denied, the articles in his custody belonged to "Spain"; "Spain," so ran his contention, was represented by General Franco's government which, in turn, was represented by Campuzano in Norway. Hence he sion of the articles removed from the should be permitted to retain posses- Legation premises by him.

DECISION

For Dr. Pastor, against Campuzano; all articles removed from the Legation were ordered to be returned under the control of Dr. Pastor.

REASONING

(1) The government of Norway recognized the Spanish Republican government as the only government of Spain or of the Spanish state.

(2) The properties in question belonged to the Spanish state.

(3) As long as the Republican government was the only Spanish government recognized by Norway, it was entitled, through its accredited representative in Norway (Pastor), to possession of all Spanish public property located in Norway.

On March 12, 1966, the French government evicted the staff of the Chinese Nationalist Embassy from the embassy building, having recognized the government of the People's Republic of China in 1964. The French government quite properly considered the embassy premises to be the property of the representatives of that government of China that had received recognition on the part of France.

CONSEQUENCES OF NONRECOGNITION: POSITION OF A
NONRECOGNIZED GOVERNMENT IN NATIONAL COURTS

Nonrecognition is, in some respects, a strange concept. It often assumes that through what at times is an act of moral disapproval, one nation may be able to let loose such disruptive forces in another that the government of the latter cannot long survive. Or, at times, it assumes that the status conveyed through recognition might place a government so honored in a position of such strength that it would last for a long time to come.[22] In most instances, history does not bear out the alleged truth of either assumption. Nevertheless, the failure of a government to be recognized by foreign governments produces definite legal consequences, well established through numerous court decisions. Those consequences represent one of the most interesting areas in international law.

Nonrecognized De Facto Government. It has been established beyond question that a nonrecognized government does not possess a right of access to the courts of such other states as deny it recognition, *i.e.*, an unrecognized government cannot sue in such courts. In one of the classic cases dealing with this principle, *R.S.F. Soviet Republic v. Cibrario,*[23] the court pointed out that it could not find any precedents for the concept that an unrecognized government could seek relief in United States courts, and then proceeded to cite with approval the British decision in:

A. M. LUTHER v. *JAMES SAGOR & CO.*

Great Britain, Court of Appeal, 1921
3 K.B. 532, 37 The Times Law
Reports 777–784

FACTS

The plaintiffs were a company incorporated in 1898 in the Empire of Russia. Their head-office was at Reval, where they had a factory for the manufacture of veneers and plywood, and another factory at Staraja Russa, where, in 1919, a large stock of boards marked with the name "Venesta" or "V.L.," the trademark of Venesta, Ltd., a British company, was stored.

In January, 1919, Russian authorities, acting under a decree of confis-

cation of June 20, 1918, took over the plaintiffs' factory at Staraja Russa.

On August 14, 1920, L. B. Krassin, a representative of the Russian Commercial Delegation in London, made a contract with James Sagor & Co., selling to this British firm a quantity of plywood including the wood seized at Staraja Russa. When James Sagor & Co. imported the wood into England, the plaintiffs claimed the goods seized in 1918 as their property and asked for an injunction restraining the defendants from selling the wood in

[22] See Whiteman, Vol. II, pp. 605–665, on this whole question.
[23] United States, Court of Appeals of New York, 1923, 235 N.Y. 255, 139 N.E. 259.

question. The defendants, in turn, claimed that the seizure of the wood and its subsequent sale to them were acts of state of the Soviet government and conferred a clear title to the purchasers.

When the injunction asked for was granted to the plaintiffs, the defendants appealed.

ISSUE

Had the Russian government been recognized by the British government so that its decrees and official acts would be recognized by British courts?

DECISION

The appeal was allowed and the decision of the lower court was reversed. Great Britain had recognized the Soviet government as the *de facto* government of Russia, hence the acts of that government had to be accepted as valid acts of state by British courts.

REASONING

(1) The Secretary of State for Foreign Affairs, in a letter dated July 28, 1920, had stated that L. B. Krassin was the authorized representative of the Soviet government and had been received by the British government for the purpose of carrying out certain negotiations, and was to be exempt from process in all British courts. This letter had not been accepted in the lower court as sufficient proof of recognition.

(2) A second letter from the Secretary of State, dated October 5, 1920, stated that "His Majesty's Government assent to the claim of the Delegation to represent in this country a State Government of Russia." This letter, too, had been termed insufficient proof of recognition in the lower court.

(3) Still another letter from the Secretary of State, dated November 27, 1920, had reaffirmed the contents of the earlier communications; it carried the additional comment that "I am to add that His Majesty's Government have never officially recognized the Soviet Government in any way." The lower court had held that this letter supplied proof of nonrecognition.

(4) On March 16, 1921, a trade agreement was concluded between the British Government and the government of the Russian Socialist Federal Soviet Republic. This fact came to light only after the decision had been handed down in the lower court. In consequence, an inquiry was made by the appellant's solicitors to the Under-Secretary of State for Foreign Affairs concerning the status of the Soviet Government and the reply, dated April 20, 1921, said that "I am to inform you that His Majesty's Government recognize the Soviet Government as the *de facto* Government of Russia." This changed the entire aspect of the case, and the appeal was sustained. An act of state of a recognized foreign government, going back to the latter's inception, could not be questioned in a British court.

NOTE: The French government protested, in a note dated May 25, 1921, against British recognition of the Soviet government as revealed in the above decision. The British government, replying in a note of June 14, 1921, rejected the French complaint.

Nonrecognized De Jure Government. The view that an unrecognized government does not have access to the courts of nonrecognizing states is not shared by all writers in international law. Thus the problem of the ships of the Baltic states annexed by the Soviet Union brought forth a strong dissent relative to the nonaccess theory by Herbert W. Briggs.[24] The occasion for his comments was the study of a rather perplexing question in the sphere of recognition: the status of the three republics of Estonia, Latvia, and Lithuania, annexed by the Soviet Union in 1940.

Subsequent to annexation, the three new Soviet republics were remade into the pattern of the U.S.S.R., including nationalization of all means of transportation. The formerly private shipping lines owned by Estonian, Latvian, and Lithuanian individuals or companies were transferred to various governmental agencies of the Soviet Union.

A number of vessels flying the flag of one of the three states happened to be outside their national territorial waters at the time of annexation and the captains in question refused to return them into the jurisdiction of the Soviet Union or its satellites. Subsequently the Soviet Union attempted to gain possession of individual ships or, in some instances, of insurance payable for the loss of Baltic ships sunk during World War II, by having recourse to national courts in several countries. These attempts were rebuffed since a number of states, including the United States, had refused to recognize the Soviet government as the *de jure* government of the three Baltic republics. (See also the relevant discussion of the Baltic Ship Cases in Chapter 9.) [25]

In accordance with its policy of recognizing the continued existence of the three republics, the United States has received diplomatic and consular representatives from them and has insisted that treaties concluded with these states are still in effect.[26]

Failure to recognize the Soviet government as sovereign in the three Baltic republics prevented the success of all claims to ownership of vessels or of insurance proceeds, because such claims in every case were grounded on some governmental act based on the unrecognized sovereignty of the U.S.S.R. in the three states.

Similarly, assets located in the United States and belonging to nationalized business enterprises in the three Baltic republics were not released to the agencies of the Soviet Union when such was requested.

Immunity of De Facto Government. An unrecognized government enjoys immunity in the courts of foreign states. Although this condition may appear paradoxical to some, it is based on logic.

[24] Herbert W. Briggs, "Non-Recognition in the Courts: The Ships of the Baltic Republics," 37 *A.J.I.L.* (1943), pp. 585–596, at pp. 595–596.

[25] See, among others, *Latvian State Cargo and Passenger S.S. Line* v. *McGrath*, United States, Court of Appeals, Dist. of Col., Feb. 23, 1951, 188 F. [2d] 1000, reported in 45 *A.J.I.L.* (1951), pp. 796–797.

[26] See *In re Estate of Kasendorf*, Supreme Court of Oregon, 1960, 353 Pac. 2d 531, reported in 55 *A.J.I.L.* (1961), p. 494, on treaties, and *In re Estate of Bielinis*, Surrogate's Court, New York County, N.Y., 1967, 284 N.Y.S. 2d 819, reported in 62 *A.J.I.L.* (1968), pp. 499–500, as well as Evald Roosaare, "Consular Relations Between the United States and the Baltic States," *Baltic Review* (No. 27, June, 1964), pp. 11–36, on U.S. relationships with the defunct Baltic republics.

In another classic case, *Wulfsohn* v. *Russian Socialist Federated Soviet Republic*,[27] the court pointed out that, even by admission of the plaintiff, the R.S.F. Soviet Republic was the existing *de facto* government of Russia, in control of the political and military power within its national territory, regardless of whether or not this government had been recognized by the government of the United States. The fact of existence of this Russian government meant that in its territory its jurisdiction was absolute and exclusive. Without its consent, such a government could not be brought before a foreign court. Judicial determination was prevented when an act was undertaken by a sovereign in his sovereign character, and only negotiation at the diplomatic level, or reprisals, or war, could be cited as methods of securing redress for injuries suffered as the result of such an act. Hence, once it was established as fact that an unrecognized government was actually in control in its national territory, it was immune from suit in other countries unless it waived such immunity.

Right of Access of Court of a Recognized Representative. Finally, the representative of a nonexisting government may undertake legal action in the courts of such other states as recognize him as the representative of his state. This apparent paradox results from the doctrine that the existence of a state as a legal person continues unimpaired despite *de facto* changes in forms of government or in executive personnel.

One of the governing cases on this point is the well-known *Lehigh Valley Railroad Company* v. *State of Russia*.[28] Originally the "State of Russia" had sued the Lehigh Valley Railroad Company in the U.S. District Court for breach of contract of carriage, arising out of the Black Tom explosion and fire on July 30, 1916, which had caused the loss of a large shipment of explosives and ammunition being sent to Russia. At the time of loss, the goods in question had been the property of the State of Russia.

Following the overthrow of the Imperial government, Boris Bakhemeteff was recognized on July 5, 1917, by the United States Department of State as the accredited representative of the successor government of Russia (the Provisional Russian Government). He continued to act as such representative until July 30, 1922, when he retired. Thereafter the Department of State recognized Mr. Ughet, the financial *attaché* of the Russian Embassy, as the custodian of all property of the Russian state for which Bakhemeteff had been responsible.

The United States government had not recognized the Soviet government which succeeded to power in Russia in November, 1917; therefore the Provisional Government had been the last Russian government recognized by the United States.

Bakhemeteff had started the suit against the Lehigh Valley Railroad Company, on July 23, 1918. Although by this time the government he represented had already ceased to exercise any authority in Russia, the

[27] United States, Court of Appeals of New York, 1923, 234 N.Y. 372, 138 N.E. 24.
[28] United States, Circuit Court of Appeals, Second Circuit, 1927, 21 F. [2d] 396.

United States recognized him as the representative of the State of Russia and as the custodian of all property and interests of that state in the United States.

The court held that the State of Russia survived; that Mr. Ughet, recognized by the Department of State as successor-custodian to the retired Bakhemeteff, could lawfully continue suits on behalf of the State of Russia, started by his predecessor; that

... The suit did not abate by the change in the form of government in Russia; the state is perpetual, and survives the form of its government. . . . The recognized government may carry on the suit, at least until the new government becomes accredited here by recognition.

RECOGNITION OF "ABSENTEE GOVERNMENTS"

Acts of territorial aggrandizement by states have led frequently to the establishment of governments-in-exile, or "absentee governments." [29] In most instances these bodies continued to be recognized for varying periods of time as the *de jure* governments of their nations by other states. Such practice affirmed effectively the continued existence of a state even though its territory was physically under the control of another state. Among more recent examples may be cited the absentee governments of Ethiopia, Poland, Czechoslovakia, Norway, the Netherlands, Belgium, Jugoslavia, Greece, and Luxembourg. In each instance the continued recognition of the absentee government represented a repudiation of the new *de facto* administration instituted by an aggressor state. As long as an absentee government continued to be recognized as representing its country, it could speak in virtually all respects in the name of that country. However, as soon as recognition was withdrawn by hitherto recognizing states, the personnel of the absentee government was deprived of all legal standing and could no longer claim to represent its country legally. Both of these principles were illustrated in the well-known case of

HAILE SELASSIE v. CABLE AND WIRELESS, LTD. NO. 2

Great Britain, Court of Appeal, 1939
[1939] Ch. 182

FACTS

Haile Selassie, as Emperor of Ethiopia, had entered into a contract with the defendant company for the construction of certain public service installations. Breach of contract was charged and the Emperor attempted to recover certain sums of money already paid to the defendants. Before

[29] See Whiteman, Vol. I, pp. 921–930, and Vol. II, pp. 467–486; consult also F. E. Oppenheimer's still valuable brief study, "Governments and Authorities in Exile," 36 *A.J.I.L.* (1942), pp. 568–595. On the subject of acts of state by governments in exile, see Whiteman, Vol. VI, pp. 66–76.

the Emperor's suit, Italy had invaded Ethiopia and the imperial government had evacuated the country and had assumed the status of a government-in-exile, continuing to be recognized by Great Britain as the *de jure* government of Ethiopia.

When the Emperor sought a writ in a British court, asking for an accounting of the contractual agreement in question and for payment of the sums claimed, the Italian government also filed a claim, as the *de facto* government (recognized as such by Great Britain).

The court of first instance ruled on January 4, 1937, in favor of Haile Selassie, holding that as head of the recognized *de jure* government of Ethiopia he possessed the right to sue for and to recover moneys due to the state in question. The defendant company appealed this verdict.

While the appeal was pending in the Court of Appeal, the Prime Minister announced in the House of Commons on November 3, 1938, that the British government intended to recognize the *de facto* sovereign of Ethiopia as the *de jure* sovereign of that country. The hearing of the appeal was suspended until such recognition should have been granted.

A little later, a certificate dated November 30, 1938, and signed by the Secretary of State for Foreign Affairs, was forwarded to the court. The document stated that the recognition of the *de facto* sovereign as the *de jure* sovereign of Ethiopia had been effected officially.

ISSUE

Who was entitled to sue in the British courts on behalf of the state of Ethiopia on the resumption of the hearing of the appeal?

DECISION

The Court of Appeal ruled in favor of the defendants, holding that Haile Selassie's claim had to be dismissed by virtue of his failure to be the recognized government of Ethiopia.

REASONING

The effect of the certificate supplied by the Secretary of State for Foreign Affairs was that

(1) the *de facto* sovereign of Ethiopia, now recognized as the *de jure* sovereign, was entitled by succession to the public property, including claims, of the state of Ethiopia; hence plaintiff's claim to such property and claims was no longer in existence;

(2) the right of succession dated back to the date of the *de facto* recognition of the King of Italy as sovereign of Ethiopia, *i.e.*, to the second half of December, 1936;

(3) since *de facto* recognition took place before the issue of the writ in the lower court (January 4, 1937), the plaintiff's claim failed and had to be dismissed.

It should be mentioned that, following the expulsion of Italian forces from Ethiopia, Haile Selassie resumed his position as emperor of that country and was recognized by Great Britain as the *de jure* and *de facto* government of the country. This writer does not know whether the Italian government had successfully pressed its own claim against the Cable and Wireless, Ltd.; if it had done so, then it would appear that Haile Selassie's government, following renewal of its recognition by Great Britain, had no further claim against the company; its only recourse would have been to add the sums in question to any reparation payments demanded from Italy at the end of World War II.

SUGGESTED READINGS

RECOGNITION OF STATES, GENERAL

T. Baty, "'De Facto' States: Sovereign Immunities," 45 *A.J.I.L.* (1951), pp. 166–170; Brierly, pp. 140–150; Briggs, pp. 105–117; Corbett, pp. 64–65; Charles De Visscher, *Theory and Reality in Public International Law* (Princeton, N.J.: Princeton University Press, 1957), pp. 228–238; Gould, pp. 213–240; Hyde, I, pp. 148–204; Lauterpacht's *Oppenheim*, Vol. I, pp. 125–133; Yuen-Li Liang, "Recognition by the United Nations of the Representatives of a Member State: Criteria and Procedure," 45 *A.J.I.L.* (1951), pp. 689–707; Denys P. Myers, "Contemporary Practice of the United States relating to International Law," 55 *A.J.I.L.* (1961), pp. 697–733, at pp. 703–720; Svarlien, pp. 96–98, 102–104, 106–109; and see the extensive collection of materials in Whiteman, Vol. II, pp. 133–242.

Cases

The Annette, Great Britain, Probate, Divorce, and Admiralty Division, 1919, Probate 105.
The Gagara, Great Britain, Court of Appeal, 1919, Probate 95.
Kennett et. al. v. *Chambers*, United States, Supreme Court, 1852, 14 How. (55 U.S.) 38.

RECOGNITION OF GOVERNMENTS IN GENERAL

K. E. Boulding et al., *The U.S. and Revolution* (Santa Barbara, Cal.: Center for the Study of Democratic Institutions, 1961); Charles G. Fenwick, "The Recognition of *De Facto* Governments: Is There a Basis for Inter-American Collective Action?" 58 *A.J.I.L.* (1964), pp. 109–113; Kaplan-Katzenbach, pp. 119–125; Lauterpacht's *Oppenheim*, Vol. I, pp. 133–152; Stanley Lubman, "The Unrecognized Government in American Courts: *Upright* v. *Mercury Business Machines*," 62 *Columbia Law Review* (1962), pp. 275–310; Svarlien, pp. 96–98, and see Whiteman, Vol. II, pp. 72–119, as well as the documentary materials found in that source at pp. 242–467.

Cases

Carl-Zeiss-Stiftung v. *Rayner and Keeler, Ltd.*, United Kingdom, 1966, 3 W.L.R. 125, analyzed in detail by Thomas W. Taylor in 8 *Harvard International Law Journal* (1967), pp. 373–388.
State of the Netherlands v. *Federal Reserve Bank of New York*, United States, District Court, S.D. N.Y., 1951, 99 F. Supp. 655, abstracted in 46 *A.J.I.L.* (1952), pp. 149–152, and appellate decision, Court of Appeals, 2nd Circuit, 1953, 201 F. (2d) 455, abstracted at length in 47 *A.J.I.L.* (1953), pp. 496–500.

Banco de Bilbao v. *Sancha*, Great Britain, Court of Appeal, 1938, 2 K.B. 176.

Dougherty v. *Equitable Life Assurance Society*, United States, Court of Appeals of New York, 1934, 266 N.Y. 71.

Guaranty Trust Co. v. *United States*, United States, Supreme Court, 1938, 304 U.S. 126.

The Rogdai, United States, District Court, N.D. of Cal., 1920, 278 Fed. 294.

The Tinoco Claims Arbitration (Great Britain–Costa Rica), 1923; see *A.J.I.L.* 18 (1924), pp. 147 ff.

United States v. *Pink, Superintendent of Insurance (N.Y.)*, United States, Supreme Court, 1942, 315 U.S. 203.

THE CHINA PROBLEM

For a reasoned criticism of the official United States attitude toward the Chinese Communist regime, consult Norman A. Graebner, "U.S. Foreign Policy toward China: A Critique," pp. 55–69, in *The Challenge of Communist China* (Proceedings of a Conference held at the University of Minnesota, April 4–5, 1960), Minneapolis: University of Minnesota Center for International Relations and Area Studies, 1960 (mimeo.). For defenses of the current U.S. policy on nonrecognition and on admission of Communist China into the United Nations, see Harold M. Vinacke, *United States Policy toward China* (Cincinnati, Ohio: Dept. of Political Science, University of Cincinnati, 1961); Josiah W. Bennett, "U.S. Foreign Policy toward China: A Reply," pp. 70–77 in *The Challenge of Communist China* [cited above]; U.S. Department of State, "Memorandum on Policy toward Communist China (August 11, 1958)," reprinted in 45 *U.S. News & World Report* (August 22, 1958), pp. 94–95; and the lengthy statement by the then Secretary of State, Dean Rusk, on March 16, 1966, before the Far East Subcommittee of the House Foreign Affairs Committee, reprinted in *The New York Times*, April 17, 1966, p. 34; see also the extensive collection of documentary material in Whiteman, Vol. II, pp. 90–110.

RECOGNITION OF BELLIGERENCY IN GENERAL

Ti-Chiang Chen, *The International Law of Recognition* (Foreword by J. L. Brierly) (London: Stevens, 1951), at pp. 303–407; Hackworth, Vol. VII, pp. 166–173; Hyde, Vol. I, p. 82; Lauterpacht, *Recognition in International Law*, pp. 175–238; Whiteman, Vol. II, pp. 486–523; Charles G. Fenwick, "Recognition of *De Facto* Governments: Old Guide Lines and New Obligations," 63 *A.J.I.L.* (1969), pp. 98–100.

Case

United States v. *Three Friends*, United States, Supreme Court, 1897, 166 U.S. 1.

8

Loss of International Personality
(State Extinction; State Succession)

STATE EXTINCTION

THE international personality of a state normally remains unaffected by increases or losses in territory, with corresponding gains or reductions in population, unless the changes in question are so profound that they change the central organization of the state or involve a loss to the state of the "core area" in which its governmental center is located.

A good example of a dramatic growth in size and population is the development of the United States of America from limited beginnings in the eighteenth century to the country's present extent. Despite an enormous expansion in area and population, the international legal personality of the United States has remained unchanged since 1783. Relevant increases in area of other nations, such as Romania after 1918, or Russia after 1938, did not affect their legal personality in any manner.

What about a shrinkage in the territory of a given state? The standard examples usually cited show that despite often drastic losses, states remained unaffected as far as their legal personality was concerned: Poland (partitions of 1772 and 1793) remained unchanged from a legal point of view, until 1795; Turkey, despite losses in 1856, 1878, 1911–13, and as a result of World War I, remained legally unaffected; and if the Confederacy had succeeded in its secession plans, the legal identity of the United States would have remained unchanged.

TOTAL EXTINCTION

Extinction by Voluntary Act. How may a state become extinct? On occasion the international personality of a state has been ended by a voluntary act. One instance would be the breakup of a federation into separate states: this was true in the case of the Republic of Colombia when it separated in 1828–30 into three separate states (Ecuador, Venezuela, New Granada). One of these, New Granada, reverted to the name of Colombia at a later date and *possibly* retained the legal personality of Colombia even after 1830.

Merger. Again, extinction may come about through merger with another state: the cases of Texas (union with the United States) and of Syria (merger with Egypt in the United Arab Republic) come to mind. In the latter example, incidentally, it would seem that both states lost their individual personalities and a new state came into being.

Extinction by Forcible Means. Forcible annexation or conquest has been a common method for the extinction of hitherto independent states. World history is filled with examples: the Transvaal in 1901 and Korea in 1910 are favorite illustrations with writers. Later annexations pose distinct problems in view of the existence of the League of Nations and subsequently of the United Nations, both of which "prohibited" conquest. Thus the annexations of Ethiopia (1936) and Albania (1939) by Italy, the disappearance of Poland into Russia and Germany (1939), and the partition of Czechoslovakia in the same year have been held by many writers not to have affected the continuity of the legal personality of each of the states in question. Considerable disagreement has centered on the absorption of the three Baltic republics of Estonia, Latvia, and Lithuania into the Soviet Union in 1940. In view of the fact that numerous states have refused to accept the Russian acts of state relating to the three republics, it appears that some vestige of international personality has remained in each of them. (See the "Baltic Ship Cases" in Chapter 7.)

Rights and Obligations of a Totally Extinct State. When the international personality of a state is extinguished, the international rights and obligations of the entity also come to an end. All treaties and other agreements concluded by the defunct state with other countries automatically become null and void, with the possible exception of an agreement creating a territorial servitude on the territory of the defunct state. That agreement apparently is considered to be still in effect and to bind the successor state. The rights of the defunct state cease to be enforceable in its name, and its obligations can no longer be brought against it as a legal person. If there is a successor state, then the rights of the extinct entity devolve upon it and the obligations of the entity *may* be assumed, if assumed at all, by the successor state.

PARTIAL EXTINCTION

Most text writers in international law hold that when a previously independent state changes to the status of a protectorate, its legal personality may be characterized as having suffered a "partial" extinction. The present writer does not share this view and believes that the correct description of the change involved would be that the capacity of the legal personality of the protectorate to act has been placed in a state of suspension, capable of reanimation and full operation on termination of protectorate status.

In other words, the legal personality of, for instance, Morocco was unable to function in the international sphere from the legal inception of the French protectorate in 1912 until Moroccan sovereignty was restored by the Joint Declaration of March 2, 1956 (and subsequent agreements ending the protectorate status of the Spanish portions).

If a given protectorate did not possess an international legal personality prior to the establishment of its relationship with the protecting power (such as the instances of British Bechuanaland and Swaziland), then there could not be, of course, any question of the existence of a suspended capacity to act internationally: there never had been such a capacity to start with. In such a case, termination of the protectorate system would result in the appearance of an entirely new state, with presumed consequent recognition by other states as an international person.

STATE SUCCESSION

Hugo Grotius developed the basic theory of state succession as a corollary of the principle in Roman civil law under which an heir succeeded to the assets, rights, and also obligations of a deceased individual, becoming, as it were, at least in law, the latter's substitute.

The nature of states as sovereign entities possessed of legal personality precluded, of course, a strict application of the Roman rule in international law. Many modern writers question the existence of true succession, even though most treatises still hold to the traditional terminology. Generally speaking, two major varieties of state succession are recognized: (1) universal succession, and (2) partial succession.

UNIVERSAL SUCCESSION

Universal succession is said to occur when one state absorbs, takes over completely, the international personality of another state. This event may be caused by forcible annexation or by the absorption of the extinct state into a federal structure. On the other hand, if a given state is somehow divided into a number of separate states, a case of universal succession also takes place, involving this time as many successor states as there would be new entities created.

Rights and Obligations of the Successor State. Under the more normal instance of the absorption of one state by another, the question arises at once as to the extent to which the successor state acquires the rights as well as the obligations of the defunct state. If third states have any claims against the latter, the settlement of such obligations is up to the successor state. The citizens of the defunct state have no right of appeal under international law against any actions taken by the annexing state, for their former country has lost its international personality, is no longer a subject of international law. Questions of any claims by or against such citizens involving their former government now become domestic questions of the annexing state.

The new sovereign also decides to what extent it will be bound by the obligations of the extinct state toward its citizens: any rights possessed by such individuals under the law of the extinct state avail them nothing, for normally those laws have been set aside, do not exist anymore.[1]

The extinction of the international personality of a state results in the abrogation of all political and military treaties previously concluded between the now extinct entity and other states. This is true, of course, only in the case of total extinction; if partial succession involves only a portion of the territory of the original owner, the latter is still bound by treaties with other countries, because the legal personality of such a state continues alive; only provisions of treaties relating to lost parts of the territory would no longer bind the former sovereign.[2]

Despite the absence of applicable rules of customary law, successor states (both in the case of universal and of partial succession, be it noted) have generally been willing to assume contractual obligations of the extinct, or partially extinct, state with respect to third states or the citizens of such states. This has been true in the case of contracts involving concessions such as mining rights, transportation facilities, and so on. On the other hand, no common practice can be discovered in relation to the debts contracted by the annexed state. Debts owed to the citizens of the latter become domestic questions of the annexing state; in the case of partial succession, particularly of the sort described below, the instrument transferring the areas in question may regulate such questions. Debts owed to third states or to their citizens may or may not be honored by the successor state. The Government of the United States took over the debts of its member states in 1790, but refused in 1845 to assume the obligations of the Republic of Texas, although arrangements were made for the payment of the sums in question out of the proceeds of the sale of public lands in the territory of Texas. In 1866, Prussia assumed the debts of certain annexed states while, in contrast, Great Britain later declined to be responsible for certain obligations of the Transvaal. (See the *West Rand Central Gold Mining* case, Chapter 3.)

PARTIAL SUCCESSION

Partial succession occurs when a state assumes sovereignty over portions of territory formerly belonging to another state; when a new international personality is created by secession of a territory from an existing state; or when a member state of a federation or confederation, or a protectorate, obtains full independence. Partial succession poses many and complicated problems centering on the distribution or division of the rights and obligations somehow attached to the territory involved in the succession.

Effects on Public and Private Property Rights. Normally only two par-

---

[1] Consult Robert Delson, "Comments on State Succession," *Proceedings* (1966), pp. 111–119.

[2] See the suggestive essays by Gerard V. La Forest, "Towards a Reformulation of the Law of State Succession," *Proceedings* (1966), pp. 103–111, and by G. P. Verbit, "State Succession in the New Nations," *ibid.*, pp. 119–124.

ties tend to be involved in such questions and, fortunately, experience has taught most states to specify rather precisely how the questions posed are to be settled between them. Such matters are usually incorporated in the instrument transferring title to the territory. On occasion, however, third parties are involved in partial succession, usually because of claims existing on their part, or on that of their citizens, and involving the transferred territory.

Under partial succession, the public property of the "grantor" state (the extitleholder to the transferred territory) passes to the successor state. Private property rights, however, normally are not affected immediately or automatically.[3] The new sovereign, in the absence of specific treaty provisions in the form of guarantees linked to the transfer of the territory, is not bound to respect private property rights in the ceded or otherwise acquired area. On the other hand, all political and legislative authority is transferred at once to the successor state.

Domestic and Foreign Debts. Debts of the transferred area may or may not be assumed by the new sovereign; writers commonly have asserted that at least such debts as have been intimately associated with the development of the transferred territory ought to be assumed by the successor state. But most successor states have in practice displayed understandable aversion to the assumption of such obligations.

On occasion, however, the public debt of the grantor state was apportioned between it and the ceded territory, and the successor state assumed this assigned domestic and/or foreign debt. Again, if it could be shown that a particular debt had been incurred solely for the benefit of the transferred area, some few successor states have actually assumed such debt.

An unusual feature of the 1919 peace settlement with Germany involved the acquisition of all German governmental property in ceded areas by the successor states and payment for such property by the successor states to the Allied Reparations Commission (except in the case of territories ceded to Poland). The successor state (except for France) also assumed portions of the German debt, both national and state, proportionate to the area involved in each transfer in question.

Private property rights in territory ceded by one state to another or annexed by another are not formally affected by the change, as was pointed out earlier. Titles to land, provided they were complete and perfect at the time of change, are usually protected by the successor state, unless the latter is of the socialist variety and supports the theory of nationalization of all land.

Effects on Treaties. One other aspect of state succession merits brief examination, in view of the number of controversies it has caused in international relations. If one party to an international agreement changes its form of government or expands or contracts its geographical boundaries,

[3] See *German Settlers in Poland*, Advisory Opinion, *P.C.I.J.*, 1923, Ser. B, No. 6, p. 36.

the provisions of the treaty in question are usually unaffected by such changes, even if the expansion of territory involves the inclusion of other, former, states in the one which is a party to the agreement. Unless the changes were of such a nature as to suggest the desirability of new treaties, the prior agreements have generally been considered as remaining in full force and effect.[4]

An adequate discussion of the interesting, and complex, problem of the continued applicability of treaties to seceding states or to former colonial territories exceeds, regrettably, the limits of a general text.[5]

SUGGESTED READINGS

LOSS OF PERSONALITY, GENERAL

Briggs, pp. 231–238; Gould, pp. 411–437; Josef L. Kunz, "Identity of States under International Law," 49 *A.J.I.L.* (1955), pp. 68–76; Lauterpacht's *Oppenheim*, Vol. I, pp. 153–169; Moore, Vol. I, pp. 385–414; D. P. O'Connell, *State Succession in Municipal Law and International Law*, Vol. II (Cambridge: Cambridge University Press, 1967); Lucius Caflisch, "The Law of State Succession: Theoretical Observations," 10 *Netherlands International Law Review* (1963), pp. 337–366.

Cases

Amaya et al. v. *Stanolind Oil & Gas Co.*, United States, Circuit Court of Appeals, Fifth Circuit, 1946, 158 F. [2d] 554.

D. D. Cement Co. v. *Commissioner of Income Tax*, India, Pepsu High Court, June 7, 1954, All India Rep. 1955 Pepsu 3, reported in 49 *A.J.I.L.* (1955), pp. 572–574.

United States v. *Prioleau*, Great Britain, High Court of Chancery, 1865, 71 Eng. Rep. 580 [1865].

Molefi v. *Principal Legal Adviser*, Lesotho, High Court, 1969, reproduced in 8 *International Legal Materials* (1969), pp. 581–587.

---

[4] See the complicated series of decisions that began with the original case of *Artukovic* v. *Boyle*, United States, District Court, S.D. Cal., 1952, 107 Fed. Supp. 11, reported in 47 *A.J.I.L.* (1953), pp. 319–321, and involved, in order, *Ivancevic* v. *Artukovic*, United States, Court of Appeals, 9th Circuit, 1954, 211 F. (2d) 565, the key decision, reported in 48 *A.J.I.L.* (1954), pp. 660–662; denial of *certiorari* by Supreme Court, 1954, 348 U.S. 818; *Artukovic* v. *Boyle*, United States, District Court, S.D. Cal., 1956, 140 Fed. Supp. 245; and the concluding *Karadzole* v. *Artukovic*, United States, Court of Appeals, 9th Circuit, 1957, 247 F. (2d) 198. See also the relevant study by Michael H. Cardozo, "When Extradition Fails, Is Abduction the Solution?" 55 *A.J.I.L.* (1961), pp. 127–135, at pp. 127–131; Hackworth, V, pp. 374–375; 13 *Department of State Bulletin* (1945), p. 1020, and *ibid.*, 14 (1946), p. 728; and Whiteman, Vol. II, pp. 771–778.

[5] Consult Kenneth J. Keith, "Succession to Bilateral Treaties by Seceding States," 61 *A.J.I.L.* (1967), pp. 521–546, and also Piet-Hein Houben, "Principles of International Law Concerning Friendly Relations and Co-operation Among States," *ibid.*, 61 (1967), pp. 703–736, especially n. 125, p. 726.

9
Rights and Privileges of International Persons

THE RIGHTS OF STATES

Traditional Theories. Until shortly before the end of the nineteenth century, jurists agreed almost unanimously that all states belonging to the community of nations enjoyed the possession of so-called fundamental rights, including a right of equality, of existence, of external independence, of self-defense, of territorial supremacy (sovereignty), of intercourse, and of respect.

These asserted rights were stated to be basic and absolute and were held to be essential to any community claiming to be a state. Their basis was found in the doctrine of natural law, despite the logical impossibility of proving that nature did possess a determinable will imposing duties and sanctioning rights on any organized human community. A newer version of the theory maintained that the rights in question represented legal principles on which all positive international law was built and which could be deduced from the nature of that law. That version ignored the obvious fact that legal principles could only be created by a legal order and could not be presupposed by it.

Still another school of thought held that the fundamental rights in question could be deduced from the personality of the state. Such a view presupposed, however, that the state existed as a personality, as a subject of rights, before it ever entered the community of nations and that it claimed retention of those rights upon its voluntary entrance into that community. This theory approached very closely to the old concept of the social contract, in this instance represented by the belief that the legal order of a worldwide community of states depended on mutual consent or agreement. Such a contract has never taken place, of course, and must be regarded as a fiction. As such it is a most convenient one by which to assert that the members of the community are bound by common duties and enjoying common rights. The fictional aspect of this theory is shown clearly by the fact that when a new state enters a legal order, it is bound by customary international law without any explicit act of acceptance of such law by the state in question. The law applies to it as soon as it is recognized as a state by the other members of the community.

As a result of recent dissatisfaction with the traditional theories concerning the rights of states, several writers have urged an abolition of the whole concept, maintaining that the rights of states under general international law always reflect the duties imposed by customary international law on other states.

There is an incontestable primacy of the duty over the right. The norms of general international law impose duties upon the states and by so doing they confer rights upon the others. If the duties are correctly formulated, the formulation of the corresponding rights is superfluous.[1]

If this view is correct, it will still be necessary to survey the claimed rights of states, even though they might be viewed as reflections of the more important duties of those states. At the same time it must be admitted that the majority of jurists do not yet share the same point of view and that many governments, particularly those of smaller countries, have time and again stressed the existence and importance of their fundamental rights: primarily, it must be assumed, in order to protect themselves against aggressive tendencies of stronger neighbors.

Recent Attempts to Define the Rights and Duties of States. Until recently it has been only within the regional inter-American community that repeated efforts have been made to proclaim a general and definitive declaration of the rights of states. Starting with the Declaration of the Rights and Duties of Nations of the American Institute of International Law in 1916,[2] a project called Fundamental Rights and Duties of American Republics was prepared for the meeting of the International Commission of Jurists at Rio de Janeiro in 1927. This one resulted in a draft treaty, States, Their Existence, Equality and Recognition, at the Havana Conference of 1928; the draft was not accepted because of the strong opposition of the United States to the absolute form of the nonintervention duty outlined in the draft.

Official action concerned with the rights and duties of states was then taken at the Montevideo Conference of 1933 through the adoption of a convention on the subject, followed by reiteration of most of the principles involved at the Buenos Aires Conference of 1936 and at the Lima Conference of 1938. In 1945, the Mexico City Conference passed a resolution calling for the preparation of a new declaration of rights and duties, a draft of which was submitted by the Pan American Union to the American republics for approval in July, 1946.

The most ambitious modern attempt to define the rights and duties of states resulted, however, from Resolution 178 (II) if the General Assembly

---

[1] Hans Kelsen, "The Draft Declaration of Rights and Duties of States—Critical Remarks," 44 *A.J.I.L.* (1950), pp. 259–276, at p. 264.

[2] See 10 *A.J.I.L.* (1916), p. 124, for the text, which emphasized the absolute character of the rights stated.

of the United Nations, adopted on November 21, 1947, asking the International Law Commission to prepare a draft declaration of such rights and duties.[3] This draft, delineating four rights (independence, territorial jurisdiction, equality in law, and self-defense) and ten duties, has been criticized on many counts, both during its formulation and afterward. Thus far no further progress on the project has been reported.

RIGHT OF EXISTENCE

The so-called right of existence has been held to be the fundamental condition for all other rights claimed by a state, for obviously an inability to continue its existence would lead to the extinction of the legal personality of any member of the community of nations. Governments have frequently insisted on this right but have styled it variously as the "right of self-defense" and the right of "self-preservation," depending on the issues confronting them at the time. As far as existence in the narrow meaning of the term is concerned, no such right can exist, for obviously existence represents an essential inherent characteristic of a state rather than a right.

Right to a Continued Existence. What is involved from a practical point of view in this "right" is a right to a *continued* existence, that is, the preservation of a state's corporate integrity through self-defense or some other mechanism.[4] This concept raises at once a number of interesting questions. Initially, it can be said that states have a duty to respect the existence of all other states; yet if this rule were to be inflexible, were to be regarded as an absolute right, then all states would have the duty to admit and endure every violation done to one another in self-preservation. But no state is obliged to do this and, instead, can defend itself and may do so lawfully in any case of true necessity. This matter of necessity, however, cannot be left to the determination of each individual state, in view of the well-known fact that states have committed aggression against other states under the plea and guise of necessary self-defense.

Limited Right of Existence. The question of the right of existence, as it related to recognition, came under the scrutiny of the International Law Commission in the preparation of the latter's draft declaration. A number of the members of the Commission proposed to include in the draft an article providing that "Each State has the right to have its existence recognized by other States." The argument in favor of such a right was that, even before its recognition by other states, a community had certain rights in international law. When another state concluded after investigation that a political entity had satisfied all requirements for statehood, it had then a *duty* to recognize that entity as a state.

---

[3] Text of declaration in 44 *A.J.I.L.* (1950), Supp., pp. 15–21.
[4] See Whiteman, Vol. V, pp. 87–88.

The majority of the Commission felt, however, that the proposal went beyond generally accepted rules of law when it was to be applied to newly created entities, and that it would serve no useful purpose when related to already existing states.

On the other hand, the emergence of a network of treaties (North Atlantic Treaty, Rio Treaty, Warsaw Pact, and so on) in the past two decades has led to a slight change in the practical aspects of the "right of existence." As Jacobini pointed out, although these agreements are basically alliances motivated by political considerations, they do represent guarantees for states against the encroachments of others.[5] To this extent, a limited right, both legal and political, of existence appears to have come into being.

RIGHTS OF INDEPENDENCE AND OF TERRITORIAL SUPREMACY

Domestic Independence. Oppenheim correctly held that the independence of a state as well as its territorial and personal supremacy (supreme authority in its territory and over its citizens, both at home and abroad) were not rights at all but were recognized and protected qualities or characteristics of states as international persons.[6] Independence means that a state is free to manage its affairs without interference (domestic independence), that is, that it can organize its government as it sees fit, adopt a constitution to suit its own needs, lay down rules and regulations for the property rights as well as the personal rights of its citizens and subjects, determine under what specific conditions foreigners will enter its territory, and so on. In other words, an independent state is "absolute master" in its own house, subject only to such limitations as are imposed on it either by the rules of general international law or by such treaty arrangements as it has made with other states. In essence, therefore, domestic independence means freedom from interference on the part of other states.

External Independence. A second aspect of independence relates to the right of a state to conduct its foreign relations to the best of its ability in such manner as it desires, again without supervisory control on the part of other states (external independence). The absence of such control is necessary if a given state is to act as a free agent and be able to fulfill such international obligations as it assumes in dealing with other states. This external independence is regarded as a basic test for the admission of new members into the community of nations, because states lacking this quality cannot qualify for admission. Yet this external independence, again, rests upon a duty of other states to refrain from interference and hence, essentially, belongs among the duties rather than among the rights of states.

[5] Jacobini, p. 74.

[6] Lauterpacht's *Oppenheim*, Vol. I, p. 286; for further details on the subject in general, consult this source at pp. 286–297 and Whiteman, Vol. V, pp. 88–124.

One of the most important aspects of this asserted "right" involves respect by each sovereign state for the independence of every other sovereign state. It is in consequence of this respect that the courts of one country will not sit in judgment on the acts of the government of another state, done within the latter's own territorial jurisdiction. Without such recognition of official actions (the well-known "Act of State" Doctrine) by outside judicial agencies, the right of independence would appear to mean very little.

Meaning of Internal and External Independence. It should be noted that internal and external independence are to be viewed only as relatively absolute: they mean freedom from control or interference on the part of another state but involve submission to such restrictions as have been accepted as binding on all states—the rules of general international law. In addition, specific treaty obligations assumed by a given state, provided they are lawful, represent limitations on the "absolute" independence, domestic or external, of that state. Thus no state in the world today can be said to be absolutely independent, in the meaning given to sovereignty by Jean Bodin in his classic definition: "Sovereignty is supreme power over citizens and subjects, unrestrained by laws." [7] Rather, every state has yielded some measure of its internal and external independence because of the existence of international law and because of the treaties entered into with other states, insofar as those agreements "invade" the absolute freedom of action of the state concerned.

Reserved Sphere of Domestic Questions. The problem which has not yet been resolved satisfactorily is this: where is the line to be found which separates purely domestic questions from the sphere of action subject to the authority of general international law? Normally every government will insist that certain activities are completely under its jurisdiction and are not subject to outside authority. It could be argued, of course, with some justification that the very fact of the existence of such reserved spheres indicates that there is a rule of international law which states that the spheres in question are indeed properly subject to national jurisdiction alone, and not to the rule of international law. Examples of such "domestic questions" abound in the history of international relations. To cite but a few as illustrations: it is generally accepted that regulation of immigration represents a sphere subject to exclusive national control; that the type and contents of a national constitution are not subject to outside authority; that large but unspecified areas, particularly when deemed to relate to "vital national interests" such as defense, are wholly exempt from regulation except with the specific consent of the state in question.

To be specific, it would be illuminating to examine the reservations attached by various members of the United Nations to their acceptance of the "optional clause" of the Statute of the International Court of Justice.

---

[7] Jean Bodin, *Six Books Concerning the Republic* (1576), Book I, Chapter VIII.

The reservation of the United States is particularly noteworthy as an example of the continuing jealous endeavor of states to maintain national control over questions judged by them to be purely domestic in character. (See Chapter 23.)

The Charter of the United Nations also contains, in Article 2, sec. 7, a clear recognition of the concept of a reserved sphere of domestic questions, exempt even from interference by a global political organization.

RIGHT OF EQUALITY

Meaning of Equality in Fact; Equality in Law. One of the oldest "rights" claimed for states has been the right of equality.[8] This principle has been asserted since the days of Hugo Grotius by an impressive array of jurists and has been affirmed in countless governmental proclamations, particularly among the American republics. It is, of course, quite obvious that in most aspects the states of the world are not at all equal, differing as they do in area, population, resources, access to oceans, armament, and, in general, in all the factors involved in the concept of national power and of power politics. Haiti and the United States are not equal in those respects, Great Britain and Lebanon are not equal, Communist China and Cambodia are not equal, nor are the United States and the Soviet Union equal. What is involved in the "right" to equality is, rather, an equality in law, or an equality before the law, of all members of the community of nations.

The Permanent Court of International Justice, in 1935, drew a distinction between equality in fact and equality in law in its opinion on the *Minority Schools in Albania:*

It is perhaps not easy to define the distinction between the notions of equality in fact and equality in law; nevertheless, it may be said that the former notion excludes the idea of merely formal equality. . . . Equality in law precludes discrimination of any kind; whereas equality in fact may involve the necessity of different treatment in order to attain a result which establishes an equilibrium between different situations.[9]

Ironically enough, Article 2 of the Charter of the United Nations contains, among other principles, the notion of the "sovereign equality of its Members," yet this concept is violated in Article 23 of the same instrument in which five major powers are granted permanent seats on the Security Council while the other ten members of the body are elected for two-year terms. The ten nonpermanent members of the Security Council suffer a further diminution of their "sovereign equality" through the provisions of Article 27, which spells out the voting procedure in the Security Council,

---

[8] Consult also Whiteman, Vol. V, pp. 134–154.

[9] *Minority Schools in Albania,* Advisory Opinion, *P.C.I.J.,* 1935, Ser. A/B, No. 64.

including the veto of the permanent members. On the other hand, Article 23 may be taken to represent a realistic appraisal of the rôle traditionally played in international relations by the Great Powers.

Meaning of Equality in Law. What, then, is meant by equality in law? It means that a state has one vote (unless it has agreed to the contrary) whenever a question has to be settled by consent among states; it means that, legally speaking, the vote of the smallest state carries as much weight as the vote of the largest and most powerful member of the community of nations; it means that no state may claim jurisdiction over another state and hence no state normally can be sued in the courts of another state or can be subjected to the taxing power of the latter without its own consent; and it means that for a variety of reasons each state accepts the validity of official acts of another state, insofar at least as those acts take effect in the territory of the latter.

There is still one other aspect of equality which must be mentioned here: it is the part which the doctrine plays in the adoption and applicability of new rules of international law. No state is bound by a new rule of law unless it expressly or by implication assents to that rule. This doctrine was expounded forcibly by Chief Justice John Marshall in the case of *The Antelope* when he held that the slave trade, then lawful under international law, could not be declared to be piracy by one state in order to limit the rights of other states:

No principle of general law is more universally acknowledged, than the perfect equality of nations. Russia and Geneva have equal rights. It results from this equality, that no one can rightfully impose a rule on another. Each legislates for itself, but its legislation can operate on itself alone. . . . As no nation can prescribe a rule for others, none can make a law of nations.[10]

No serious controversy has centered on this concept, according to which no state would be bound by rules to which it had not agreed in some manner. But what about the right of any state, great or small, to participate on an equal basis in the formulation of new rules of law? What would happen if a small state, of no military strength or economic importance, were to set itself against the will of the rest of the states? Was there any need at all for consulting such a state when new rules were drawn up? It has been pointed out that the Great Powers refused to accept the equality of states in this matter and proceeded to draw up rules among themselves which assumed, on numerous occasions, at the very least the character of particular international law: the Congress of Vienna (1815), the Congress of Paris (1856), the Congresses of Berlin (1878 and 1885), the Algeciras Conference of 1906, and so on.

[10] United States, Supreme Court, 1825, 10 Wheaton 66; see also *Le Louis*, 1817, 2 Dodson 210, and *The Scotia*, 1871, 14 Wallace 170, for similar statements in Supreme Court decisions.

The dramatic change occurred during the two Hague Peace Conferences of 1899 and 1907; attendance by delegations from many of the small nations and a strict observance of the principle of equality in voting procedures forced the Great Powers to pay attention to the views of smaller states, whose voice had not been heard previously in the drafting of new rules of law. States signed or failed to sign conventions, ratified agreements with reservations, and even failed to ratify conventions signed by their own delegations—all on a basis of absolute legal equality. The results of such procedures were conspicuously displayed in the defeat of a project for the creation of a Judicial Arbitration Court, a plan generally favored by all the Great Powers but defeated by the vigorous opposition of the smaller states to a court not constituted on a basis of complete equality of all independent states.

The Charter of the United Nations, restoring in part *inequality* among the members of the Organization, indicates the direction of recent thought on the question of equality in law.

In the first place, unanimity has been abandoned in all organs of the United Nations, whereas it was still the rule in the Council and Assembly (in the latter under certain conditions) of the League of Nations. Qualified majorities may be required under specific circumstances, but unanimity, formerly assumed to be an essential element in state equality, has been forsaken. On the other hand, equality of representation has been preserved in the General Assembly as well as in the Economic and Social Council; it has been abandoned in the Security Council and the Trusteeship Council. Only the Security Council possesses the ability to make its decisions binding on the member states of the United Nations; in all other true organs of the Organization, decisions represent recommendations rather than binding obligations. Thus, with the exception of the Security Council, the introduction of the principle of majority votes has not impaired the equality in law of the member states.[11]

Summary of the Concept of the Right to Equality in Law. Returning to the original concept: it must be emphasized that the right to equality in law is not really a right at all, but involves a *duty* on the part of all states to "apply the law in conformity with the law" to each entity in the community of nations, to behave, in other words, in conformity with the rules of international law. In a way the concept itself is rather superfluous, for without it there could be no international law in existence. Nor does equality in law mean that each state has to treat all other states alike. All that is required is that every state is assured the equal protection of the rules of the law, is not denied in judicial or arbitral procedures such rights as it may possess, on the grounds of its relative weakness,

[11] See Herbert Weinschel, "The Doctrine of the Equality of States and Its Recent Modifications," 45 *A.J.I.L.* (1951), pp. 417–442, and Richard A. Gardner, "United Nations Procedures and Power Realities: The International Apportionment Problem," *Proceedings* (1965), pp. 232–245.

form of government, size, and so on. Nothing more than this can really be claimed by any state as a *legal* right under the concept of the equality of states.

RIGHT OF SELF-DEFENSE

Determination of What Self-defense Constitutes. There can be no doubt that every legal system in the world recognizes and supports a right of self-defense.[12] What is in question are the conditions under which such a right might be invoked and the means which are to be employed in the exercise of the right. Many writers have asserted that the use of force by a given state could be justified, even though no armed attack on it had taken place as yet in the course of a dispute with another state.

Limitation on the Right of Self-defense. On the other hand, there appears to exist a commonly accepted and fairly recently developed limitation on the right of self-defense: force used to defend a state must be reasonably proportionate to the danger that is to be averted. And at the same time an increasingly widespread attitude holds that the question of whether the defensive actions taken by a given state were really necessary or whether they should be regarded as excessive, could be determined by independent outside judges, such as by an international court, arbitration tribunal, or even by an international political body (say, the Security Council) acting as a judicial agency.[13] It is, of course, obvious that any such determinations would assume an *ex post facto* character in view of the time element involved. Immediate danger of extinction through armed attack or successful fifth-column activities would not permit recourse to judicial investigations of means to be employed to repel the danger before the desired steps were taken.

It has been asserted by some authorities that refusal to submit to an impartial judicial (or even political) determination of the necessity of self-defense would be clear proof of guilt, that is, of a violation of another nation's right of existence.

Illustrative of the desire to submit the question of "lawful" self-defense to outside determination was the rather categorical statement by the International Military Tribunal at Nuremberg that

whether action taken under the claim of self-defense was in fact aggressive or defensive must ultimately be subject to investigation and adjudication if international law is ever to be enforced.[14]

[12] See Cheng, pp. 92–97, as well as Whiteman, Vol. V, pp. 966–1048.

[13] Consult Lauterpacht's *Oppenheim,* Vol. I, pp. 297–304 (especially at p. 299) on self-preservation; and see Cheng, pp. 29–31, and Stone, pp. 243–253, on the subject.

[14] *Trial of the Major War Criminals Before the International Military Tribunal, Nuremberg, 14 November 1945—1 October 1946,* Nuremberg, 1947–1949 (42 vols.), Vol. I, p. 208.

On most occasions, however, the time factor, as mentioned, would defeat the intentions of such an orderly procedure without necessarily implying "guilt" on the part of the attacked state.

U.N. Charter Provisions Relating to Self-defense. The Charter of the United Nations deals in two key provisions with the problem of self-defense. Article 2 (4) states that

All Members shall refrain in their international relations from the threat or use of force against the territorial integrity or political independence of any State, or in any other manner inconsistent with the purposes of the United Nations,

while the main provisions of Article 51 read

Nothing in the present Charter shall impair the inherent right of individual or collective self-defense if an armed attack occurs against a Member of the United Nations, until the Security Council has taken the measures necessary to maintain international peace and security.

It should be mentioned that if the veto is used to prevent the Council from taking the measures in question, the power to exercise judgment and control may be assumed by the General Assembly under the "Uniting for Peace" Resolution of 1950.

Under general international law a state has always been the sole judge as to whether a degree of emergency existed that justified the employment of force in self-defense. Article 51, at least in theory, imposes a limitation: a state acting on the basis of self-judgment does so at its own peril and its actions are, again in theory, subject to scrutiny by the Security Council.

It is not surprising, therefore, that what the provisions of the Charter imply with respect to the right of self-defense has been the subject of considerable controversy.[15] A minority of commentators subscribe to the view that any threat or use of force not corresponding to self-defense against an armed attack falls automatically under the prohibitions of Article 2 (4). A far greater number of writers, on the other hand, assert that the use of "inherent" in Article 51 clearly establishes a natural and existing right of states to utilize force in self-defense and that Article 51 does not imply an impairment of that right *until* the Security Council (or the General Assembly) has acted. Such a view, shared by the present writer, holds therefore that the right of self-defense is not at all based on the Charter but is a normal right of states under international law. What Article 51 does, in this view, is to impose limits to the exercise of the right in question. Support for the inherent right of self-defense is found in the statement of Committee I at the San Francisco Confer-

[15] Consult Brierly, pp. 416–420, on which much of the following discussion is based; see also Stone, pp. 244–246.

ence which declared unequivocally (in the preparatory stages) that "the use of arms in legitimate self-defense remains admitted and unimpaired." [16] Committee III/4 at the Conference appears to have introduced Article 51 into the Charter primarily to coordinate Security Council authority to maintain peace with the actions of regional agencies set up for defensive purposes. Brierly pointed out that there is no indication that the inclusion of "armed attack" in Article 51 was intended to prevent the use of force in meeting unlawful forceful acts not in the nature of an armed attack.[17] For instance, heavy and continuing troop concentrations along a border might lead to "anticipatory" use of force to meet the threat of attack before the latter actually materialized.[18] This doctrine would justify the "preventive attack" by Israel on its Egyptian and Arab neighbors in the case of the "Six-Day War" of 1967.

Logic and practice have combined to clarify the apparent restriction of Article 51 to cases of attack "against a Member of the United Nations." The wording could be taken to mean that collective self-defense could not be applied through the use of armed force if aggression had been committed against a nonmember state. The events of 1950, however, showed that the invasion of South Korea, a nonmember, resulted in the utilization of collective defense efforts by the United Nations.

General agreement on the subject of defense against armed attack can be said to exist only on two counts: resort to force in self-defense is lawful in the event of instant and overwhelming necessity; and acts taken in self-defense must be limited to defense itself and must not be transformed into reprisals or "punitive sanctions."

Nothing, moreover, is said in Article 51 concerning unfriendly actions aimed at one state by another state but lacking any aspects of an armed attack. Failing an application of Article 2 (4) under given circumstances, a virtually unlimited right of self-defense by means short of the threat or use of force would seem to be indicated.

Collective Self-defense. The concept of collective self-defense requires some explanation. Prior to the creation of the United Nations, collective self-defense, under different labels, was well known and formed, in effect, the core of all military alliances, even though, on many occasions, assistance given by one state or a group of states to a given country was limited to instances of "unprovoked" attacks on the latter.

The employment of the term *collective self-defense* is somewhat misleading, for what is actually meant is defense, by one state or a group of states, of another state against attack.[19] The concept does not refer to an

[16] *United Nations Conference on International Organisation* (U.N.C.I.O.), Vol. VI, p. 334.
[17] Brierly, p. 418; see also Stone, pp. 263–265.
[18] Stone, p. 244, n. 8. See also the opposing arguments quoted in Whiteman, Vol. V, at pp. 868–871.
[19] See also Whiteman, Vol. V, pp. 1049–1175, on this subject.

action in the name or under the authority of the United Nations as an organization. It is, in other words, *not* synonymous with what is termed *collective security*. It means, rather, an independent exercise of armed force by states on behalf of another state under the specific conditions outlined in Article 51 of the Charter. It therefore does not in any manner correspond to the punishment of an aggressor, to a police or enforcement action on the part of the United Nations, but merely to the assistance given to the repulsion of an illegal armed attack on a state.

This last statement raises another and very important question: when is self-defense lawful or legitimate, As is shown in Chapter 25, the claim of "self-defense" has been used on numerous occasions to mask aggressive designs. If any state has the right to invoke the concept at its discretion and solely on the basis of its own judgment, then the entire idea of prohibiting wars of aggression becomes a sham and a delusion, a farce. Any state, when its leaders have determined to go to war, tends to plead self-defense in order to rally domestic and foreign opinion to its cause. And this plea has been defended and justified again and again in modern history.

Now Article 51 limits the concept of self-defense in one important respect: it refers to the one case of armed attack on a member of the United Nations. By this is meant an aggression by military force. But unfortunately, there is no general agreement among the states of the world as to what is meant by aggression; the Security Council is supposed to supply such determination in any given case, under the provisions of Article 39 of the Charter.

The real problem, then, centers on the nature of the act against which the doctrine of individual or collective self-defense is invoked. At this point the provisions of the Charter fail woefully. It is difficult to envision a government, conscious of its defensive obligations toward its citizens, willing to comply with an ultralegalistic interpretation of the provisions of Article 51 at the risk of national extinction.

RIGHTS OF INTERNATIONAL ORGANIZATIONS

The subjects of international law include not only independent states but also certain international legal or juristic persons, that is, international organizations. Whatever may have been the legal status of such agencies prior to World War II, there can be no question that since 1945 a number of organizations, created by states through international conventions, have enjoyed the position of subjects of the law. The attributes of their international personality, however, are limited by the treaty creating each of these international agencies. It is this treaty alone that shapes their constitution and delegates authority to them. They therefore are not original subjects, such as states, of international law, but are what should be termed *derived*, or *derivative*, subjects of that law.

The primary document certifying to this relatively new development in international law is the Advisory Opinion of the International Court of Justice on *Reparations for Injuries Suffered in the Service of the United Nations*.[20] The Court stated that the United Nations

is a subject of international law and capable of possessing international rights and duties, and that it has capacity to maintain its rights by bringing international claims. . . . Throughout its history, the development of international life, and the progressive increase in the collective activities of States has already given rise to instances of action upon the international plane by certain entities which are not States. . . . Fifty States, representing the vast majority of the members of the international community, had the power, in conformity with international law, to bring into being an entity possessing objective international personality, and not personality recognized by them alone, together with capacity to bring international claims.[21]

Because states, both in their corporate capacity and in the person of the chief of state, possess certain privileges, the question arises as to the possession of similar privileges on the part of international organizations which have achieved international legal personality.[22]

History of Privileges. The history of the privileges enjoyed by international organizations shows that three distinct approaches were adopted successively by the community of nations. Initially, rather far-reaching privileges, designed to assure the complete independence of an organization, were granted. This was followed, during the period from 1919 to the end of World War II, by the extension of *diplomatic immunity* to the essentially nondiplomatic functionaries of international agencies. And since 1945, the grant of privileges and immunities, as phrased typically in Article 105 of the Charter, has covered everything "necessary for the fulfillment of its purposes." A reversion to the older style of diplomatic privileges should be observed, however, in the United Nations General Convention.[23]

[20] International Court of Justice, 1949, *I.C.J. Reports, 1949*, p. 174; see also Paul E. Anderson, "Legal Capacity of the United Nations—Assertion of Claim on Behalf of Its Agents," 48 *Michigan Law Review* (1950), pp. 496–505.

[21] *Ibid.*, pp. 174, 178, 179, 185; the opinion was reprinted in 43 *A.J.I.L.* (1949), pp. 590–600; see also Quincy Wright, "Responsibility for Injuries to United Nations Officials," 43 *A.J.I.L.* (1949), pp. 95–104, and his "The Jural Personality of the United Nations," *ibid.*, pp. 509–516. The most comprehensive analysis available of the legal status of the United Nations is Guenter Weinberg's *The International Status of the United Nations* (Dobbs Ferry, N.Y.: Oceana Publications, 1961).

[22] See in particular the monographic coverage of the historical background and more recent theoretical aspects of this subject in Josef L. Kunz, "Privileges and Immunities of International Organizations," 41 *A.J.I.L.* (1947), pp. 828–862, with much valuable material on the legal status of the League of Nations, and D. W. Bowett, *The Law of International Institutions* (New York: Praeger, 1965).

[23] The full text of the convention, as approved by the General Assembly on February 13, 1946, is found in 43 *A.J.I.L.* (1949), Supp., pp. 1–7; concerning immunity,

It should be kept in mind that the privileges and immunities of international organizations are a matter wholly separate and different from the privileges and immunities of officials or agents of those same organizations. The latter question will be discussed later, in connection with the coverage of similar rights enjoyed by the diplomatic agents of states. What matters here, however, is the status of the organizations themselves, with reference to immunity from suit, process, execution, and so on.

Method of Achieving Status of a Legal Person. In view of the fact that independent states are the "basic" subjects of international law, an international organization achieves the status of a legal person under that law only through an explicit or implied grant of such status by means of a multilateral agreement on the part of those states. Once the status of a legal person has been assured to an organization, its relationship to the other legal persons in the community of nations, its "legal capacity under municipal (domestic) law" has to be delineated clearly. This relates to immunity from local jurisdiction, to the ability to sue in national courts, and, in some instances, notably in the case of the United Nations, to conclude international treaties.

There can exist little doubt that several international organizations in the past did enjoy complete immunity from local jurisdiction—the European Danube Commission may be cited as a well-known example—and that a number of such agencies existing today have, or should have, similar independence from the domestic jurisdiction of all states, whether the latter are members or not. Such independence is particularly important in relation to the sovereign in whose territory the headquarters of an international entity are located.

Method of Achieving Immunity. The best method of achieving the immunity of an organization is through multilateral conventions, setting down specific and binding obligations for all member states, reinforced by a special instrument, concluded between the organization itself and its "host sovereign."

Legal Personality of the UN. As far as the United Nations Organization is concerned, Article 105 of the Charter states that the Organization shall enjoy such immunities as are necessary for the fulfillment of its purposes. It should be noted that there is no comparison drawn with

---

see Article IV, section 11, paragraphs f and g; Article V, section 18, paragraphs e and f; and section 19 of the convention. The same wording is also found in the constitution of the Food and Agriculture Organization (Art. XV, par. 2, and Art. VII, par. 4) and in Article 19 of the Statute of the International Court of Justice. On the other hand, the style found in Article 105 of the Charter is duplicated in the constitution of the ITO (Art. 74) and of the World Health Organization (Art. 67). Consult also the "Headquarters" *Agreement between the United States and the United Nations,* of June 26, 1947, and the *Interim Agreement* of December 18, 1947, between the same parties; both documents reprinted in 43 *A.J.I.L.* (January 1949), Supp., pp. 8–26.

state immunities; instead, a standard appropriate to the needs of the entity has been created. Ehrenfeld pointed out that the report of the drafting committee in 1945 mentioned immunity from suit as an example of necessary privileges under Article 105 and made it quite clear that that Article was to be regarded as self-executing.[24] Other provisions of the Charter supply additional evidence that the United Nations Organization is a legal person by stating its jural powers as well as responsibilities (Arts. 24, 26, 41, and 42), by authorizing it to conclude binding agreements with its members and with specialized international agencies (Arts. 43 and 63), and by stating explicitly that "The Organization shall enjoy in the territory of each of its Members such legal capacity as may be necessary for the exercise of its functions and the fulfillment of its purposes" (Art. 104).

International Public Corporations. Quite different in status, as far as international personality is concerned, are certain other international organizations which may be termed international public corporations. Such entities as the International Monetary Fund, the International Bank for Reconstruction and Development (World Bank), and the Atomic Energy Development Authority do not possess the status of persons under international law, hence are not subjects of that law. Instead, they are directly or indirectly under the control or supervision of some other international organization. While it is, of course, highly desirable that such agencies, created by international conventions, enjoy in every respect the status of a corporation under the domestic laws of every one of their member states, it does not appear logical or necessary to grant to such technical agencies the privileges and immunities pertaining to persons under international law.[25]

UN Charter and Domestic Legislation. One of the important aspects connected with the legal status of the United Nations, as well as with the subject of treaties (discussed subsequently), is whether the Charter, as a multipartite treaty, might be taken to supercede conflicting domestic legislation of member states. This issue came into prominence in the well known case of *Sei Fujii* v. *State of California.*[26] Fujii had sued in an attempt to have the California Alien Land Law set aside as being in violation of the Charter of the United Nations. The law prohibited ownership of land by an alien who was ineligible to citizenship—unless some contrary treaty right existed. The Supreme Court of California, in holding that the law was indeed invalid and basing its decision on a vio-

---

[24] Alice Ehrenfeld, "United Nations Immunity Distinguished from Sovereign Immunity," *Proceedings* (1958), pp. 88–94, at p. 88; see also Kuljit Ahluwalia, *The Legal Status, Privileges and Immunities of the Specialized Agencies of the United Nations and Certain Other International Organizations* (The Hague: Martinus Nijhoff, 1964), and especially Whiteman, Vol. 13, pp. 1–31.

[25] Much of this discussion is based on Kunz, *op. cit.* (n. 22, above), pp. 847–851.

[26] 242 Pac. [2d] 617, 1952, reprinted in full in 46 *A.J.I.L.* (1952), pp. 559–573.

lation of the Fourteenth Amendment to the Constitution of the United States, said in part:

The humane and enlightened objectives of the United Nations Charter are, of course, entitled to respectful consideration by the courts and Legislatures of every member nation, since that document expresses the universal desire of thinking men for peace and for equality of rights and opportunities. The Charter represents a moral commitment of foremost importance, and we must not permit the spirit of our pledge to be compromised or disparaged in either our domestic or foreign affairs. We are satisfied, however, that the Charter provisions relied on by plaintiff [UN Charter, Preamble and Arts. 1, 55, 56] were not intended to supersede existing domestic legislation, and we cannot hold that they operate to invalidate the alien land law.[27]

The California court did not deny that the Charter was a treaty and that the United States Constitution provided (Art. VI) that treaties made under the authority of the United States are part of the supreme law of the land. A treaty, however, did not automatically supersede local laws which were inconsistent with it, unless the treaty provisions were self-executing. In other words, when the terms of the treaty imputed the existence of a contract, when either party engaged to perform a particular act, then the treaty related to the political and not to the judicial department. The legislative branch then had to execute the contract before the treaty could become a rule for the courts. And in the case at hand, no such execution by the legislative branch had taken place.

Agencies Having Limited Legal Personality. Certain international organizations possess what may be termed limited international personality. Thus the European Coal and Steel Community (ECSC), the European Economic Community (EEC), and the European Atomic Energy Community (EURATOM) all possess the right, under their basic instruments, to conclude agreements with states and to deal with the representatives of such states. The United States, for instance, has concluded treaties with the ECSC and with EURATOM, and maintains a diplomatic mission accredited to the three agencies listed.

IMMUNITIES OF STATES

Independence from outside control represents not only an alleged right of each sovereign state but also an essential characteristic of each such entity. In the course of time, each independent state consented to waive the exercise of a portion of its presumably exclusive territorial jurisdiction when the government of another independent state intruded, under cer-

---

[27] See 26 *Department of State Bulletin* (May 12, 1952), p. 744. Although the California Supreme Court split 4-3 on the constitutional issues in the case, all seven justices agreed that the human rights provision of the United Nations Charter did not operate *by themselves* to invalidate the Alien Land Law.

tain conditions and in time of peace, into that jurisdiction. In other words, by comity or courtesy initially, later on the basis of customary international law, the foreign sovereign enjoyed immunity from suit and other aspects of territorial jurisdiction.

According to the classical, or absolute, theory of sovereign immunity, a foreign sovereign could not, without his consent, be made a defendant in the courts of another sovereign. But according to a newer and restrictive theory of sovereign immunity, such exemption has been recognized only with respect to sovereign or public acts of a state but not necessarily with respect to its so-called private acts.

Long ago, the principle of sovereign immunity embraced both the government of a foreign sovereign (state immunity) and the individual head of the state in question (personal immunity). Today the two forms of immunity are quite distinct and have to be discussed separately.

PERSONAL IMMUNITY OF A FOREIGN SOVEREIGN

Theory of Absolute Immunity. Little has changed in the theory of personal immunity of a foreign sovereign or head of state. Regardless of whether an individual is constitutionally the actual head of a state or only its nominal head, he or she enjoys complete immunity from suit in the territory of another state. This principle applies equally to crowned heads of state and elected heads of state. And whatever the sovereign may do in the territory of another state, he is immune from all prosecution, civil or criminal.

Examples of this immunity abound in the literature of international law, and some of the questions raised by personal immunity are fascinating indeed, even though the problems involved in state immunity are far more important today. The leading case, cited in virtually every collection, is *Mighell* v. *Sultan of Jahore*, decided in 1894.[28] Similarly, the Gaekwar of Baroda, named as corespondent in the divorce suit of *Statham* v. *Statham and the Gaekwar of Baroda*,[29] was declared by a British court to be immune from suit because of his position as sovereign of an independent state in India.

A foreign sovereign or head of state not only enjoys personal immunity from suit but also cannot be named as a party defendant to a suit brought against him in his official capacity as the representative of his state. This was brought out clearly in the well-known case of *De Haber* v. *Queen of Portugal*,[30] in which a British court dismissed on grounds of immunity a suit for money allegedly wrongfully paid to the government of Portugal.

If, on the other hand, the foreign sovereign submits to the jurisdiction of a court and later is cited as defendant in an appeal from an earlier decision, it may be held that any claim of immunity put forth against the

---

[28] See Chapter 6.
[29] Great Britain, Probate Court, 1912, [1912] P. 12.
[30] Great Britain, Court of Queen's Bench, 1851, 17 Q.B. 196.

second action should be denied. This point of view was stated elaborately in *Sultan of Johore* v. *Abubakar Tunku Aris Bendahar*.[31] The Sultan of Johore had brought a suit in a Japanese court in Singapore (during the Japanese occupation of Malaya in World War II) against his son and the Japanese Custodian of Alien Property to obtain title to two lots in Singapore. The Sultan won his case, but after the defeat of Japan, his son started a suit in the new Supreme Court of the Colony of Singapore to set aside the verdict of the Japanese occupation court. The Sultan promptly claimed personal sovereign immunity and, when this claim was denied, appealed to the Privy Council.

Although the Sultan and the British government were in agreement about his status as an independent sovereign, the denial of his claim to immunity was upheld, for the reason that the proceedings before the Supreme Court of Singapore represented an appeal from the judgment in a case brought by the sovereign, who by that initial act had waived his normal immunity. The Privy Council commented that there had not been established (in England) any absolute rule exempting a foreign sovereign from any and all jurisdiction of British courts.

It might be added that a change appears to have been under way for some dozen years or so in connection with the traditional rule that a state or its sovereign lost a right to immunity in the event of counterclaims brought against it (or him, in the case of a head of state) by the defendants in a case originally brought to the courts of another country.[32] Until quite recently, such counterclaims were generally barred by national courts, because it appeared well settled that sovereign immunity was not waived by commencement of an action in a foreign court.[33] In 1955, however, the decision of the Supreme Court in *National City Bank* v. *Republic of China*[34] indicated that if the counterclaims by the defendants arose out of the same action and the same matter as the original claim, domestic courts might deny immunity with respect to such counterclaims to the foreign state or sovereign.[35]

---

[31] British Commonwealth of Nations, Privy Council, April 22, 1952, reported in 47 *A.J.I.L.* (1953), pp. 153-155.

[32] See Robert B. Looper, "Counterclaims against a Foreign Sovereign Plaintiff," 50 *A.J.I.L.* (1956), pp. 647-653, and consult the decision in *Republic of China* v. *Pang-Tsu Mow*, United States, Circuit Court, Dist. of Col., 1952, 201 F. [2d] 195.

[33] Examples are numerous in American court annals: see, for instance, *Kingdom of Roumania* v. *Guaranty Trust Co.*, 1918, Circuit Court, 2nd Circuit, 250 F. 341; and *Republic of Haiti* v. *Plesch et al.*, 73 New York Supreme Court, Special Term, 1947, 73 N.Y.S. [2d] 645.

[34] United States, Supreme Court, 1955, 348 U.S. 356; see also K. R. Simmonds, "Implied Waiver of Immunity: Permissible Counterclaims Against a Sovereign Plaintiff," 9 *International and Comparative Law Quarterly* (1960), pp. 334-343.

[35] For another instance of such denial of immunity see *Kingdom of Norway* v. *Federal Sugar Refining Co.*, United States, District Court, S.D. of N.Y., 1923, 286 Fed. 188. Consult Hackworth, II, pp. 483-489; Harvard Research in International Law, *Competence of Courts in Regard to Foreign States* (Arts. 5 and 6) in 26 *A.J.I.L.* (1932), Supp., pp. 451, 508-526.

STATE IMMUNITY

The question of state immunity is a far more complicated and also more important subject than the somewhat archaic personal immunity of heads of states. As was pointed out earlier, the traditional absolute theory of immunity exempted a state in every way from the jurisdiction of other countries: its government could not be sued abroad without its consent; its public property could not be attached; its public vessels could not be arrested, boarded, or sued; nor could any property or real estate owned by the state be taxed or attached in whatever country it might be located.

Governmental Property Abroad. As far as governmental property abroad is concerned, only the title to such property could be questioned in the courts of another country; once sovereign claim to title was established, absolute immunity prevailed.[36]

One of the classical cases illustrating the traditional theory of state immunity was that of the *Schooner Exchange:*

THE SCHOONER EXCHANGE v. MAC FADDON

United States, Supreme Court, 1812
7 Cranch 116 (1812)

FACTS

The defendants, MacFaddon and Greetham, alleged that they were the sole owners of the *Exchange* when it sailed from Baltimore for San Sebastian, Spain, on October 27, 1809; that the schooner was seized on December 30, 1810, by persons acting under the decrees and orders of Napoleon, Emperor of France, in violation of international law; that the vessel, renamed the *Balaou,* was in Philadelphia in possession of a certain Dennis Begon, although no sentence of decree of condemnation had been pronounced against the ship by any court of competent jurisdiction; that they asked that the courts restore the vessel to their ownership. The U.S. District Attorney had appeared in the District Court and argued that since peace existed between France and the United States, public vessels of France could freely enter and leave the ports of the United States, and that the former *Exchange* was now a public vessel of France, hence immune from American jurisdiction. The District Court dismissed the suit of MacFaddon and Greetham; this decision was reversed by the Circuit Court and the case came, by appeal, before the Supreme Court of the United States.

ISSUE

Could an American citizen assert in an American court title to an armed public vessel of a foreign country, found within the waters of the United States?

---

[36] See *French Republic v. Board of Supervisors of Jefferson County*, United States, Court of Appeals of Kentucky, 1923, 200 Ky. 18, 252 S.W. 124; *Brownell v. City and County of San Francisco*, United States, California Court of Appeals, 1st Dist., Div. 1, 1954, 126 Cal. App. [2d] 102, 271 P. 2d. 974, and the valuable pioneer study by William W. Bishop, Jr., "Immunity from Taxation of Foreign State-Owned Property," 46 *A.J.I.L.* (1952), pp. 239–258.

DECISION

Sentence of Circuit Court reversed and decision of District Court affirmed: the suit was dismissed for want of jurisdiction.

REASONING

(1) The jurisdiction of a state within its own territory is necessarily exclusive and absolute. It is not subject to any limitation not imposed by the state upon itself. All exceptions to this complete and absolute jurisdiction must be traced to the consent of the nation itself. But the perfect equality and absolute independence of sovereigns have given rise to a class of cases in which every sovereign is understood to waive the exercise of parts of that complete exclusive territorial jurisdiction, and one of these applies to warships entering the ports of a friendly power. If a sovereign permits his ports to remain open to the public ships of friendly foreign states, the conclusion is that such ships enter by his assent. And "it seems, then, to the court, to be a principle of public law, that national ships of war, entering the port of a friendly power open for their reception, are to be considered as exempted by the consent of that power from its jurisdiction." The courts are not competent to enforce their decisions in cases of this description.

(2) The *Exchange* [captured by the French navy in pursuit of its blockade of England] had been transformed in the port of Bayonne by order of the French Government into a public armed vessel of France. The vessel must be presumed to have entered American waters and the port of Philadelphia under the implied promise that while behaving in a friendly manner, it would be exempted from the jurisdiction of the United States.

The basic principle underlying the *Exchange* case is that of the act of state, which may be phrased in its generally accepted form as "international law requires each State to respect the validity of foreign State acts, in the sense of refusing to permit its courts to sit in judgment on the legality or constitutionality of the foreign act under foreign law." [37]

In another classic case, a court ruled that a foreign sovereign cannot be deprived of his property by domestic tribunals:

VAVASSEUR v. KRUPP

Great Britain, Court of Appeal
1878, 9 Ch. Div. 351.

FACTS

Josiah Vavasseur had brought an action against Friedrich Krupp, of Essen, Germany, Alfred Longsden, his agent in England, and Ahrens & Co., described as agents of the government of Japan, claiming an injunction and damages for infringement of his patent for making shells and other projectiles. The shells in question had been brought to England in order to be placed aboard three warships being built there to the order of the Japanese government.

On January 18, 1878, an injunction

[37] Briggs, p. 404.

was granted by a British court, restraining the defendants and the owners of the wharf where the shells were stored, from selling or delivering the shells to the Japanese government or any of its agents.

On May 11, 1878, an application was made to the British court on behalf of the Emperor of Japan and his Envoy Extraordinary [to Great Britain] that, notwithstanding the injunction granted, the Emperor and his agents be permitted to remove the shells and proposing that, if and insofar as it might be necessary, the Emperor and his Envoy should be added to the list of defendants in this suit. The Emperor submitted to the jurisdiction of the British court, deposited £100 as security for costs, and his name was added to the list of defendants. A motion then was made to dissolve the injunction. The Master of the Rolls granted permission to remove the shells from the wharf. This decision was appealed.

ISSUE

Could British courts deprive a foreign sovereign of his public property or deny him the right to remove his property from British jurisdiction?

DECISION

Appeal against the order of the Master of the Rolls dismissed, injunction dissolved. English courts may not deprive a foreign sovereign of his public property.

REASONING

(1) The shells were bought by the Emperor of Japan for the purposes of his government. They are the lawful property of the Emperor of Japan, transported to England on their way to Japan. Even if the patent of Vavasseur had been infringed, this was not a question to be considered. The shells themselves were not affected by any alleged violation of the patent laws.

(2) The claim of Vavasseur that the Emperor of Japan, by having himself added to the list of defendants, submitted to the jurisdiction of the British courts is irrelevant. The Emperor submitted to British jurisdiction for the single purpose of having the injunction dissolved, and clearly never intended to waive immunity and have his public property submitted to the jurisdiction of a foreign court.[38]

(3) If Vavasseur had any claims against F. Krupp in Essen, those claims should be prosecuted against F. Krupp. The Emperor of Japan, having lawfully acquired public property in Germany, was in no way connected with the alleged violation of patent rights.

Need for Restricting State Immunity. Thus, for decade after decade, the immunity of foreign sovereigns was affirmed by the courts of all major countries. But the passage of time brought new problems connected with state immunity. The fact that extensive commercial activities of modern governments began to be carried on beyond their borders through government-owned corporations resulted in ever-increasing

[38] A similar interpretation may be found in *Ex Parte Republic of Peru* (*The Ucayali*), United States, Supreme Court, 1943, 318 U.S. 578. Consult also *Banque de France* v. *Equitable Trust Company*, United States, District Court, S.D. of New York, 1929, 33 F. 2d 202, and *Auer* v. *Costa*, United States, District Court, Mass., 1938, 23 F. Supp. 22.

numbers of pleas of sovereign immunity when such corporations, or, in some instances, vessels operated by them, were sued in foreign courts.

Consequently a steadily increasing need for classification of the status of such enterprises, for a distinction between public and private activities of sovereigns, together with a growing conviction that the private activities of a foreign sovereign ought not to give rise to state immunity in foreign courts, arose in the twentieth century.

Curtailment of the traditional automatic immunity of foreign sovereigns proceeded rather slowly, however, until 1924. Since that year, which marked the beginning of the recognition of the government of the Soviet Union by a large number of other countries, the process of restricting state immunity was hastened appreciably, in part because the Soviet Union had adopted state-conducted monopolies in foreign trade and shipping.

Attempts to Restrict State Immunity. Even before 1924, state immunity, though upheld generally, had been questioned in cases involving governmental ownership and operation of merchant vessels. In one of the earliest relevant cases, a British Court of Appeals reversed the judgment of the High Court of Admiralty in the case of the *Parlement Belge* (1880, L.R.S.P.D. 197) and decided that the vessel, owned and operated by the Belgian government as a mail packet, as well as for general commercial purposes, was immune from suit *in rem* in a case for damages resulting from a collision. The appeal court held that in such a suit the owner of the vessel was indirectly involved, and that such could not be done in the case of an independent sovereign.

The precedent set by the *Parlement Belge* decision caused a lot of trouble after World War I, when an increasing number of states began to engage in ordinary commercial transactions by means of public commercial vessels and claimed for these the same immunities traditionally attached to true public vessels (warships, for example).[39]

State immunity of vessels began to be denied on purely technical grounds, such as uncompleted requisition of a ship or failure to assert immunity through diplomatic channels. Then more serious misgivings, based on a sense of unfairness involved in the immunity claimed for merchant vessels owned by governments, resulted in the drafting of a Convention for the Unification of Certain Rules concerning the Immunities of Government Vessels (Brussels, April 10, 1926), which would have placed the ships in question in the same category as privately owned vessels. The convention was ratified by so few states, however, that it could be taken at most as an indication of a shifting in legal opinion

---

[39] Thus see the well-known American cases of *Berizzi Brothers Co. v. S.S. Pesaro*, United States, Supreme Court, 1926, 271 U.S. 562; *The Maipo* (D.C.) 252 F. 627, and 259 F. 367, as well as the British cases of *The Gagara*, L.R. [1919] P.D. 95, *The Porto Alexandre*, L.R. [1920] P.D. 30, and *The Jupiter*, L.R. [1924] P.D. 236.

rather than as a wholesale abandonment of the traditional doctrine of absolute state immunity.

Various national courts proceeded to attempt to differentiate between sovereign (immune acts, acts of state, acts in public capacity) activities of a state and nonsovereign (liable acts, acts of management, acts in private capacity) activities of states in an effort to develop an acceptable basis for a denial of immunity to certain activities of foreign sovereigns. Other national courts approached the problem from the organizational basis of the foreign sovereign activities involved: denying state immunity if the sovereign had organized separate corporations to carry on the activities in question before those courts.[40]

In recent decades, almost every major country has denied governmental immunity to corporations wholly or partly owned by a foreign state,[41] except in a few instances in which little evidence of the existence of the corporation apart from the government could be adduced.[42]

State Immunity Involving Title to Real Property. It should be pointed out in connection with these varying approaches to the problem of curtailing state immunity, that long before these new interpretations made their appearance, national courts in most states had denied state immunity in the case of actions that involved title to real property. The theory behind this view was that the overwhelming interest of the territorial sovereign in its own real estate outweighed all considerations of foreign policy: the state in which the foreign sovereign owned real estate considered this property within its own borders to be subject to suits in its national courts despite ownership by a foreign sovereign.

Theory of Restricted State Immunity (Tate Letter). A significant change in American policy with respect to state immunity occurred in 1952 when the then Acting Legal Adviser to the Department of State, Jack B. Tate, wrote a letter to the Acting Attorney-General, outlining acceptance of the restrictive theory of immunity by the Government of the United States.[43] Tate pointed out the expansion in adoption of the

---

[40] See *Ulen & Company, Appellant,* v. *Bank Gospodarstwa Krajowego (National Economic Bank), Respondent,* United States, New York Supreme Court (Appellate Div., 2nd Dept.), 1940, reported in detail in 36 *A.J.I.L.* (1942), pp. 695–701.

[41] For examples, see *The Uxmal,* United States, District Court, Mass., 1941, 40 F. Supp. 258, and *Mirabella* v. *Banco Industrial de la República Argentina,* United States, Sup. Ct., New York County, N.Y., 1963, 237 N.Y.S. 2d 499.

[42] *Mason* v. *Intercolonial Railway of Canada,* United States, 1908, 197 Mass. 349, 83 N.E. 876; *Dunlop* v. *Banco Central del Ecuador,* United States, Sup. Court, New York County, 1943, 41 N.Y.S. 2d 650; and *Baccus S.R.I.* v. *Servicio Nacional del Trigo,* Great Britain, 1957, 1 Q.B. 438 (C.A.).

[43] Text in 26 *Department of State Bulletin* (June 23, 1952), pp. 984–985; see the detailed analysis of the "Tate Letter" in William W. Bishop, Jr., "New United States Policy Limiting Sovereign Immunity," 47 *A.J.I.L.* (1953), pp. 93–106, which may be taken to be the most knowledgeable representation of subsequent American policy available, with full documentation. Consult also the instructions of the Department of State, dated September 15, 1961, emphasizing that the Department follows the restric-

restrictive theory by more and more states, justified the restrictions involved, and in effect laid down the view of the Department of State that henceforth "private" activities of foreign sovereigns would be denied immunity in American courts. Professor Bishop quoted with approval the definition of such nonsovereign, private activities proposed in 1932 by the Harvard Research in International Law:

A State may be made a respondent in a proceeding in a court of another State when, in the territory of such other State, it engages in an industrial, commercial, financial or other business enterprise in which private persons may there engage, or does an act there in connection with such an enterprise wherever conducted, and the proceeding is based upon the conduct of such enterprise or upon such act.[44]

If this definition were to be adopted without change by the states of the world, a degree of nonuniformity would admittedly still prevail in its application. As Claudy showed, "the British Railways would not be immune from suit in the United States, where a private entity may engage in railroading, but would be immune from suit in the Soviet Union, where an individual may not engage in railroading." [45] But this would not constitute an insuperable difficulty in achieving general adoption of a needed definition of the "private acts" of a foreign sovereign.

The "new" doctrine expounded in the Tate Letter first played a prominent part in the case of *New York and Cuba Mail S.S. Co.* v. *Republic of Korea* in 1955.[46] The case involved a collision between a ship owned by the plaintiff and a lighter belonging to the Republic of Korea, while unloading a cargo of rice belonging to the Republic. The suit asked for an attachment of funds on deposit in New York banks and the property of the defendant government. The Secretary of State asked the Department of Justice to file in the court a suggestion to the effect that the principle of the immunity of a foreign sovereign's property from attachment and seizure was not affected by the Tate Letter. The Department of State, however, while agreeing with the Korean government that the latter's property was not subject to attachment in the United States, did not request that a suggestion of immunity be filed in this particular case, for the acts out of which the cause of action arose were not shown to be of a purely governmental character. The court, in turn, held that the principle of international law governing immunity had to apply and vacated the attachment of the Korean government funds.

---

tive theory of state immunity and denies claims of such immunity made in connection with private or commercial activities of governments and their agencies: reproduced in part in 56 *A.J.I.L.* (1962), p. 533.

[44] Quoted by Bishop, *op cit.*, p. 106.

[45] Donald E. Claudy, "The Tate Letter and the *National City Bank Case: Implications*," *Proceedings* (1958), pp. 80–85, at p. 84.

[46] United States, District Court, S.D. of New York, 1955, 132 F. Supp. 684.

Much of the foregoing discussion may have tended to create an impression that the absolute immunity theory has been discarded and has been replaced by the doctrine of restricted immunity. No such thing would be further from the truth, however, for, up to this time, only a few countries have as yet developed a *substantial* number of judicial decisions favoring the restrictive theory, and while a number of other states may point to judicial *dicta* leaning in the direction of the restrictive theory, the vast majority of states still assert the validity of the older doctrine.

The United States, however, has apparently taken the lead in promoting the application of the restrictive theory of state immunity. Between early 1948 and 1958, fourteen treaties were negotiated with six European, four Latin American, and four other states, each containing a clause obligating each of the parties to the instrument to waive sovereign immunity for state-controlled enterprises engaged in commercial activities in the territory of the other party.[47]

On the other hand, the recent case of *Chemical Natural Resources, Inc. v. Republic of Venezuela* serves to illustrate the unwillingness of the U.S. Department of State to apply the doctrine of the Tate Letter on a consistent basis. In this instance, the Department, without giving reasons, abandoned its own rationale.

CHEMICAL NATURAL RESOURCES, INC. v. REPUBLIC OF VENEZUELA

*United States, Supreme Court of Pennsylvania,
1966, 420 Pa. 134; 215 At. 2d 864; certiorari
denied, 87 Sup. Court 50 (1966)* [48]

FACTS

Chemical Natural Resources, Inc. (hereinafter cited as Chemical), an American corporation, and its wholly owned Venezuelan subsidiary, Venezuelan Sulphur Corporation, C.A., sued Venezuela. Having purchased certain mineral rights in the republic, the plaintiffs contracted with the Venezuelan government for the construction of certain power generation installations, the power in turn to be bought by the Venezuelan government. Later that government cancelled all contracts in question and expropriated all installations involved, causing the plaintiffs an alleged loss of over $116,800,000. All efforts to obtain redress in Venezuelan courts failed.

In the fall of 1963, a vessel, the SS *Ciudad de Valencia*, operated by the Venezuelan government through a

[47] Vernon G. Setser, "The Immunity Waiver for State-Controlled Business Enterprises in United States Commercial Treaties," *Proceedings* (1961), pp. 89–105, at p. 89; and see Robert P. Borsody, "The American Law of Sovereign Immunity Since the Tate Letter," 4 *Virginia Journal of International Law* (1964), pp. 75–97.

[48] Based on the digest, containing lengthy excerpts and an interesting dissenting opinion, by John R. Stevenson in 60 *A.J.I.L.* (1966), pp. 838–851.

wholly owned company and engaged in purely commercial activities, arrived in the port of Philadelphia. Chemical attempted, through a writ of attachment, to seize the vessel as part payment of the damages claimed against Venezuela. The writ was issued and the local sheriff seized the vessel. Two days later, however, the attachment was dissolved at the request of Chemical's attorneys.

Venezuela challenged the jurisdiction of the original court (Court of Common Pleas), claiming that the courts of Venezuela were open to the plaintiffs, that the vessel was not the property of the Venezuelan government, and that under the doctrine of sovereign immunity, courts in the United States could not exercise jurisdiction. Chemical filed an answer denying all of Venezuela's assertions. Venezuela then appealed to the Supreme Court of Pennsylvania for a writ of mandamus or, alternatively, a writ of prohibition, or both.

Venezuela also secured the intervention of the U.S. Department of State which filed a "Suggestion of Immunity," including a request to dismiss plaintiff's action against Venezuela because of a certification of sovereign immunity which was recognized and allowed by the Department. The lower court denied the Department's request, stating that Venezuela was not entitled to immunity. Venezuela then filed its appeal to the Supreme Court of Pennsylvania.

ISSUES

(1) Did the lower court acquire jurisdiction through the serving of the writ of foreign attachment on the captain of the vessel?

(2) Did Venezuela enjoy sovereign immunity despite the doctrine laid down in the Tate Letter?

DECISION

Appeal of Venezuela quashed, but a writ of prohibition issued, dissolving attachment of the vessel and dismissing the complaint of the plaintiffs.

REASONING

Re Issue (1): The Supreme Court affirmed that the lower court did acquire jurisdiction through the service of the writ of attachment on the captain of the vessel.[49]

Re Issue (2): The Court examined in considerable detail the doctrines of absolute and restricted sovereign immunity. It pointed out that the established rule of law was that "foreign Sovereigns, which are duly recognized by appropriate action by the State Department, and their property are not amenable without their waiver or consent, to suit in the Courts of this Country." And, furthermore, that "a determination of Sovereign Immunity by the Executive branch . . . when conveyed to a Court through proper channels or officials, is—in the absence of waiver or consent—binding and conclusive . . . no matter how unwise or, in a particular case, how unfair or unjust the Department's determination appears to be (a) to injured American citizens and (b) to vast numbers of the American people and (c) to our Courts. . . ."

The meaning of the Tate letter was clear and unmistakable, according to the Court. It meant that the Department of State had abandoned the old principle of *absolute* governmental immunity and had adopted a new and

---

[49] Details not supplied here, in favor of Issue No. 2; for details, see 60 *A.J.I.L.* (1966), at pp. 840–841.

restrictive principle of immunity, that is, absolute immunity did not apply to governments when they were engaged in commercial activities.

But, the Court held, it appeared that the Department "has silently abandoned the 'revised and restricted policy' set forth in the Tate letter and has substituted a case-by-case foreign Sovereign Immunity policy, that is, the State Department will recognize and suggest, or fail to recognize or grant or suggest Sovereign Immunity *in each case* presented to it, depending (a) upon the foreign and diplomatic relations which our coun-

try has at that particular time with the other Country, and (b) the best interests of our Country at that particular time."

The Court therefore held (1) that Sovereign Immunity of foreign governments is a matter for determination in the first instance by the executive branch of the government, namely, the State Department; and (2) "if and when that Department's determination has been made and has been appropriately presented to the courts, the Department's determination is binding and conclusive" on the courts.[50]

Public Commercial Vessels. After 1926, the courts of several countries began to rule that the immunity of state-owned vessels under international law did not apply to vessels used for private trading purposes but only to such ships as were utilized for strictly traditional governmental purposes. In 1945, a slightly less restrictive but still notable view of public vessels engaged in commerce was enumerated by the Supreme Court of the United States when, in the case of *Republic of Mexico* v. *Hoffman* (1945, 324 U.S. 30), it decided that American courts could not allow immunity from jurisdiction *in rem* to a vessel owned by a foreign government but not in its possession and service where the political branch of the United States government had not recognized such immunity.[51]

The corresponding shift in foreign opinion, centering on any kind of public vessel engaged in commercial activities, was pointed out in detail in the Tate Letter. Indicative of the change in outlook was also Article 21 of the 1958 Geneva Convention on the Territorial Sea and the Contiguous Zone, which specified that government vessels operated for commercial purposes were to be under the same regulations as applied to "all ships" and to "merchant ships" (Subsections A and B of the convention).

Judging by these tendencies, it appears that in the not too distant future only warships and public vessels engaged in strictly noncommercial functions will be accorded immunity in foreign waters, and some authorities

[50] See also *Hellenic Lines Ltd.* v. *Embassy of South Viet Nam, Commercial Division*, United States, District Court, S.D. N.Y., 1967, 275 F. Supp. 860, reported in 62 *A.J.I.L.* (1968), p. 783, and *Victory Transport Inc.* v. *Comisaria General de Abastecimientos y Transportes*, United States, Court of Appeals, 2d Circuit, 1964, 336 F. 2d. 354, abstracted *ibid.*, 59 (1965), pp. 388–390.

[51] See 39 *A.J.I.L.* (1945), pp. 585–590, for text; consult also Philip C. Jessup, "Has the Supreme Court Abdicated One of Its Functions?", *ibid.*, 40 (1946), pp. 168–172, and Frederic R. Sanborn, "The Immunity of Government-Owned Merchant Vessels," *ibid.*, 39 (1945), pp. 794–796.

feel that such restricted immunity should be limited still further by a requirement of reciprocal treatment.

On the other hand, the abandonment of consistent application of the restricted governmental immunity doctrine by the U.S. Department of State in the *Chemical Natural Resources* case implies that the conclusion of a multilateral law-making treaty dealing with sovereign immunity would represent a highly desirable solution to a vexing and complicated aspect of international law.

Requisitioned Vessels. A related problem centers on the question of the status of vessels requisitioned by a government, legitimate or rebel, during a civil war. This question came into particular prominence during the Spanish Civil War. Although this conflict predated the recent drift toward a restrictive interpretation of the immunity of foreign public vessels, the more noteworthy cases presented most instructive analyses of the general problems involved. Thus, in the famous case of the *Navemar*, the Supreme Court of the United States supported the immunity of a vessel requisitioned for commercial purposes by the Spanish (Madrid) government and recognized the right of the Spanish ambassador to intervene on behalf of his government in a suit brought against the vessel by the original owners.[52] In all of the major cases connected with the conflict mentioned, the relevant courts decided in favor of the immunity of vessels requisitioned by a foreign sovereign engaged in a civil war. It is doubtful whether a similar verdict would be handed down today, in view of the changed attitude toward government vessels engaged in commercial activities.

Immunity After Severance of Diplomatic Relations. The political nature of recognition implies continued enjoyment of immunity after a severance of diplomatic relations between two states. On one occasion this general rule appeared to have fallen: in 1961, when the government of the United States severed diplomatic relations with the Cuban government and the latter attempted to intervene in an admiralty proceeding brought by a drydock company to enforce a maritime lien against a vessel in which the Cuban state had mortgage and possessory interests. The U.S. District Court held in a Memorandum Opinion that the plea of sovereign immunity was not available to the Cuban government until such time as diplomatic relations between the United States and Cuba had been resumed.[53]

---

[52] *Compañía Española de Navegación Marítima, S.A., Owner of the Spanish Steamship "Navemar" v. Spanish Steamship "Navemar,"* 1938, 303 U.S. 68; original decision in U.S. District Court, E.D. N.Y., 1937 (18 Fed. Supp. 153) has been reprinted in many case books; see also Charles C. Hyde, "Concerning the Navemar," 33 *A.J.I.L.* (1939), pp. 530–534, and Lawrence Preuss, "State Immunity and the Requisition of Ships during the Spanish Civil War: II. Before the Courts of the United States," 36 *A.J.I.L.* (1942), pp. 37–55. Consult also the case of the *Cristobal Colon*, decided in 1937 by the Bermuda Supreme Court, in 39 *A.J.I.L.* (1945), p. 839.

[53] *Dade Drydock Corporation* v. *M/T Mar Caribe,* United States, District Court, S. D. of Texas, 1961, 199 F. Supp. 871, reported in 55 *A.J.I.L.* (1961), p. 749.

On the other hand, political considerations since that time appear to have dictated a continuing affirmation of Cuban sovereign immunity on the part of the United States government. In the words of the Secretary of State, writing to the Attorney General, the claim to immunity was sustained ". . . to avoid further disturbance to our international relations. . . ."[54]

Status of Nonrecognized Foreign Governments. Nonrecognition of a foreign government normally results in its inability to assert immunity for its vessels in foreign ports or waters. On the other hand, the seizure, in 1940, by the U.S.S.R. of the three Baltic republics of Estonia, Latvia, and Lithuania, followed by the absorption of the three states in the Soviet Union, was not recognized as lawful by a considerable number of foreign states, including notably the United States, Great Britain, and Eire. These and other governments have refused to recognize the transfers of sovereignty involved in the absorption of the three Baltic republics.

At the time of the takeover by the U.S.S.R., a number of vessels belonging to private owners, particularly in Estonia and Latvia, happened to be on the high seas. Several of these ships in question came into ports of the Republic of Eire and at once became the objects of suits. The U.S.S.R. asserted that the vessels were state property, that as such they were immune from the jurisdiction of Eire Courts without the consent of their sovereign owner, and that this immunity existed, whether the ships were used for public purposes or for commerce and whether they were in the possession of the sovereign or not.

The plaintiffs in the cases, that is, the accredited representatives of the (now defunct) Baltic governments, sought to act as trustees, to prevent acquisition of control over the vessels by agencies of the U.S.S.R. These so-called Baltic Ships cases[55] reinforced by corresponding decisions in a number of other countries (including the United States), helped to establish the doctrine that nonrecognition of an alleged successor state or government resulted in a failure to create immunity claimed for vessels of that state or government, and that, furthermore, immunity for vessels not engaged in strictly governmental activities could be granted only if such vessels were owned by, or in the physical possession of, the sovereign claiming such immunity.

Problem of Execution. One of the most vexatious problems connected with state immunity is the question of execution against a foreign sov-

---

[54] Excerpt from letter dated August 19, 1961, 56 *A.J.I.L.* (1962), p. 527. See also *Rich* v. *Naviera Vacuba, S.A. and Republic of Cuba; Mayan Lines, S.A.* v. *Republic of Cuba and the M/V Bahia de Nipe; United Fruit Sugar Co.* v. *5,000 Tons of Sugar; Navarro and Others* v. *the M/V Bahia de Nipe,* United States Court of Appeals, Fourth Circuit, Sept. 7, 1961, 295 F. (2d) 24, *ibid.,* 56 (1962), pp. 550–562.

[55] See *Zarine* v. *Owners, etc., S.S. Ramava; McEvoy & Ors.* v. *Owners, etc., S.S. Otto; McEvoy and Veldi* v. *Owners, etc., S.S. Piret and S.S. Mall,* Eire High Court [April 29, 30, and May 1 and 16, 1941, 75 *Irish Law Times Reports,* 153] in 36 *A.J.I.L.* (1942), pp. 490–504. See also *Latvian State Cargo & Passenger S.S. Line* v. *McGrath,* United States, Circuit Court of Appeals, D.C., 1951, 188 F. 2 1000.

ereign. By this is meant the process of attaching, taking, or seizing property of a foreign government, or depriving it of control over such property, in pursuance of a judicial order or ruling obtained in a domestic court against that foreign sovereign.[56] In other words, is a judgment obtained in the courts of a given state against a foreign sovereign always capable of enforcement when it involves seizure of that sovereign's property located in the state in which the judgment was handed down? Usually the answer is negative, for in most countries, certainly in the United States and Great Britain, the doctrine prevails that consent to waiver of state immunity does not at all imply consent to have state property attached or seized in execution of a judgment obtained against the sovereign of that property.

It should be noted, however, that when a judgment is obtained against a foreign sovereign with respect to nonsovereign (private, commercial) activities, the doctrine of restricted state immunity is being *gradually* applied to execution against the sovereign's property.[57]

Question of State Immunity. The question of state immunity, that is, of whether or not a domestic court has jurisdiction over a foreign entity on whose behalf immunity has been claimed by a foreign sovereign, normally is decided in accordance with instructions or suggestions received by the court in question from the political department of its government. If such "political" recognition of immunity from domestic jurisdiction leaves any gaps, if any matters relating to the case at hand are not covered by the instructions from the political department concerned, then the court still retains authority to determine for itself such omitted matters or legal issues.[58] If the political department issues no suggestion of immunity, then the case in question is subject to judicial consideration, such absence of suggestion implying a denial of state immunity.[59]

[56] On this topic consult William L. Griffin, "Execution against the Foreign Sovereign's Property: The Current Scene," *Proceedings* (1961), pp. 105–113; Robert Delson, "Applicability of Restrictive Theory of Sovereign Immunity to Actions to Perfect Attachment," *ibid.*, pp. 121–130; see also Hackworth, Vol. II, pp. 394–398, as well as the long list of cases cited in Bishop, pp. 580–581.

[57] See Griffin, *op. cit.*, p. 112, with reference to the decisions in *République Arabe Unie v. Dame X*, Switzerland, Supreme Court, February 10, 1960, digested in 55 *A.J.I.L.* (1961), pp. 167–171. As Griffin pointed out (p. 113), the "Tate Letter" of 1952 did not refer to execution but only to jurisdiction.

[58] See *United States of Mexico et al. v. Schmuck et al.*, United States, Court of Appeals of New York, May 24, 1945, reported in detail in 40 *A.J.I.L.* (1946), pp. 205–210, and especially *National Institute of Agrarian Reform v. Kane*, United States, Circuit Court of Appeals, Fla. Dist., 1963, 153 So. 2d 40, reported briefly in 58 *A.J.I.L.* (1964), pp. 189–190.

[59] See *Et Ve Balik Kurumu v. B.N.S. International Sales Corporation*, United States, Sup. Court, New York County, 1960, 204 N.Y.S. [2d] 971, reported briefly in 55 *A.J.I.L.* (1961), p. 172, and *Chemical Natural Resources, Inc. v. Republic of Venezuela*, abstracted above, as well as Denys P. Myers' analysis of *Weilamann v. Chase Manhattan Bank*, United States, New York, District Court, Westchester County, 1959, in 54 *A.J.I.L.* (1960), pp. 640–644.

Privilege to Bring Suit. No discussion of state immunity can be concluded without mentioning the privilege of foreign sovereigns to bring suit in the courts of a friendly state. General agreement appears to prevail concerning the duty of such a sovereign (state) to adhere to the procedures established for and in the courts of the state in which the suit is being brought. By implication, the privilege to sue is accompanied by the consent to submit to the jurisdiction of the court in question with reference to any counterclaims arising out of the same suit. (This matter has been discussed earlier.)

The right of access to foreign courts, however, does not permit a state to bring suit for the enforcement of its own revenue or penal laws by the foreign court, at least not in the absence of some form of reciprocal agreement to enforce such laws of another jurisdiction. The classic instance illustrating this point is the well-known case of

H.M. THE QUEEN OF HOLLAND (MARRIED WOMAN) v. DRUKKER

Great Britain, Chancery Division, 1928,
L.R.[1928] 1 Ch. Div. 877

FACTS

The plaintiff (Queen of the Netherlands) sued in this action as a married woman, alleging that she was a creditor of the estate of David Visser, a Dutch subject, who had died in Amsterdam on December 27, 1926. The defendants were Moritz Drukker and others. Mr. Drukker was the executor of Visser's will; the other defendants were the heirs to Visser's estate in England, amounting (after all British dues and fees) to £1150 in value.

The plaintiff alleged that under Netherlands law the estate of Visser owed to the Netherlands government certain "succession" duties which, under the same law, enjoyed priority over all other debts not secured by mortgages or pledges. Under the Netherlands laws, the administrator of the estate was obliged to supply the Netherlands government with a comprehensive statement of the nature and value of the estate and was to pay the dues (duties, taxes) owed by the estate.

The plaintiff asked the British Court of Chancery to assume control over Visser's estate in England and to see to it that the "succession" duties claimed were paid to the Netherlands government.

ISSUE

May a foreign sovereign sue in the domestic courts of a friendly state to obtain enforcement of that sovereign's fiscal legislation?

DECISION

Domestic courts will not enforce the fiscal legislation of a foreign sovereign; action dismissed.

REASONING

(1) For over 200 years, English courts have refused to take judicial notice of the revenue laws of foreign states and have refused to collect the

gn states for the benefit
gns of those states.
gn state cannot, there-
glish courts to recover
to be paid under the
.aws of that state.

(3) Since the foreign sovereign

(Queen of Netherlands) has submitted to the jurisdiction of the English Court of Chancery in bringing this suit in the court, and since the sovereign has lost the suit by the dismissal ordered, the foreign sovereign is ordered to pay the costs of the action.

Act-of-State Doctrine. International law is said to require each state to respect the validity of the public acts of other states, in the sense that its courts will not pass judgment on the legality or the constitutionality of the acts of a foreign sovereign under his own laws. One of the classic statements of this so-called act-of-state doctrine is found in the *dictum* of Chief Justice Fuller in *Underhill* v. *Hernandez:*

Every sovereign state is bound to respect the independence of every other sovereign state, and the courts of one country will not sit in judgments on the acts of the government of another done within its own territory.[60]

Similarly, other decisions of the Supreme Court had appeared to indicate that the act-of-state doctrine formed a principle of international law. In fact, however, the practice of many states indicated that they did not regard such an interpretation as correct. The Supreme Court joined this point of view in 1964, when in *Banco Nacional de Cuba* v. *Sabbatino* (376 U.S. 398, 421) it held that the act-of-state doctrine was not a rule of international law and that its application was *not* required by that law.[61]

In the *Sabbatino* case, the Court stated that, instead of laying down or reaffirming an inflexible and all-inclusive rule, the judicial branch would not examine the validity of an act of expropriation within its own territory by a foreign sovereign government (existing and recognized by the United States at the time of suit) in the absence of a treaty or other controlling legal principles, even if the allegation was made that the taking violated customary international law.[62]

---

[60] United States, Supreme Court, 1897, 168 U.S. 250. See also the monographic treatment in Michael Zander, "The Act of State Doctrine," 53 *A.J.I.L.* (1959), pp. 826–852.

[61] See Whiteman, Vol. VI, pp. 2–4, for evidence on this point from other countries. The text of the original Cuban Nationalization Law of July 6, 1960, which led to the events precipitating the preceding case, was reprinted in translation in 55 *A.J.I.L.* (1961), pp. 822–824.

[62] United States, District Court, S.D.N.Y., 1961, 193 F. Supp. 375, digested in 55 *A.J.I.L.* (1961), pp. 741–745; affirmed on appeal, Court of Appeals, 2nd Circuit, 1962, 307 F. 2d. 845, reprinted in 56 *A.J.I.L.* (1962), pp. 1085–1107; reversed and remanded, Supreme Court, 1964, 376 U.S. 398, abstracted at length in 58 *A.J.I.L.* (1964), pp. 779–814 (including Justice White's lengthy dissent); U.S. District Court, S.D.N.Y., 1965, on remand, 243 F. Supp. 957, and Memorandum Opinion, November 15, 1965, 272 F. Supp. 836, digested in Whiteman, Vol. VI, pp. 31–36 and reproduced at length in 60

As a direct consequence of the *Sabbatino* case, Congress incorporated in 1964 a new paragraph into the Foreign Assistance Act of 1961. As amended in 1965, the paragraph [620(a)2] provided that courts *in* the United States were to decline on the ground of the federal act of state doctrine to make a determination on the merits giving effect to the principles of international law in a case in which a claim to property was asserted, based on confiscation after January 1, 1959, *by an act in violation of the principles of international law*. The Department of State strongly objected to this so-called Sabbatino or Hickenlooper or act-of-state amendment.[63]

Similar provisions have been included by Congress in the Sugar Act of 1948, as amended [7 U.S.C. 1158(c)] and the Food for Peace legislation [Sec. 410 of the Agricultural Trade Development and Assistance Act of 1954, as amended—P.L. 480, 7 U.S.C. 1736 (d)].

An interesting recent case demonstrated that the "Hickenlooper," or "Sabbatino," Amendment did not affect the determination of a foreign government's immunity from suit in the U.S. courts: *American Hawaiian Ventures* v. *M.V.J. Latuharhary*.[64]

In connection with the act-of-state doctrine a principle of reciprocity appears to have developed in the course of time, according to which the courts of one state will give to the decisions of courts in another state only the same credence (conclusive proof, admission as evidence, and so on) as the courts of the second state give to the decisions of the courts in the first one.[65] Insofar as foreign laws are concerned, certain groupings will not be enforced in the courts of other states, in addition to foreign penal and fiscal legislation: the laws (or acts) of unrecognized governments or states (unless the political department concerned holds enforcement to be in the interest of public policy); foreign "political" laws; foreign legislation considered by the courts to be in violation of customary or conventional international law;[66] and foreign laws con-

---

A.J.I.L. (1966), pp. 107–119; decision affirmed on appeal, Court of Appeals, 2nd Circuit, 1967, 383 F. 2d. 166; *certiorari* denied, 1968, 390 U.S. 956; rehearing denied, 1968, 390 U.S. 1037. The complicated series of decisions is analyzed carefully, with supporting documents, in Whiteman, Vol. VI, pp. 20–36.

[63] See Whiteman, Vol. VI, pp. 27–31, for details. The formal reference to the "Hickenlooper" amendment is Section 620(e)(2) of the Foreign Assistance Act of 1961, as Amended [22 U.S.C. 2370(e)(2)]; the section in question is reprinted in 57 *A.J.I.L.* (1967), pp. 749–750. Consult also Andreas F. Lowenfeld, "The Sabbatino Amendment—International Law Meets Civil Procedure," 59 *A.J.I.L.* (1965), pp. 899–908, and Howard S. Levie, "Sequel to Sabbatino," *ibid.*, 59 (1965), pp. 366–370.

[64] United States, District Court, N.J., 1966, 257 F. Supp. 622, reported in detail by Charles R. Matthews, Jr., in 8 *Harvard International Law Journal* (1967), pp. 357–363.

[65] See the reasoning of the court in *Hilton* v. *Guyot*, United States, Supreme Court, 1895, 159 U.S. 113.

[66] Lauterpacht's *Oppenheim*, Vol. I, pp. 267–268; this is a new suggestion, initiated by the late Professor Lauterpacht. It is supported strongly, on the basis of judicial decisions, by Zander, *op. cit.*, pp. 839–844.

sidered by the courts to be in opposition to the public policy of the state in which the courts operate.

Yet another cause of exclusion from the jurisdiction of the courts in a given state would be an alleged wrong approved explicitly or tacitly by the government of the state in which a suit referring to the alleged wrong was being brought by a foreign sovereign.

A number of the principles governing the right of a foreign sovereign to sue in the courts of another state were illustrated in the reasoning of the British High Court of Chancery in the old case of

EMPEROR OF AUSTRIA AND KING OF HUNGARY v. *DAY AND KOSSUTH*

Great Britain, High Court of Chancery, 1861
3 De Gex, Fisher & Jones 217

FACTS

This was an appeal from a decision of a lower court, ordering Day and Kossuth to refrain from issuing monetary notes purporting to be notes of the Hungarian State and ordering them to deliver to the plaintiff the notes already produced as well as the printing plates utilized in such production.

The plaintiff was King of Hungary. In that capacity he possessed the exclusive right of authorizing the issue of notes to be circulated in Hungary as money, as well as the exclusive right of authorizing the affixing of the royal coat of arms of Hungary to any document intended to be circulated in Hungary. Almost all the money circulating in his kingdom had been issued by the National Bank of Austria under the authority of the plaintiff acting as King of Hungary and Emperor of Austria.

Day and Sons, a printing company in England, had been employed by Kossuth to prepare plates for the printing of notes purporting to be notes of the state or nation of Hungary, of various denominations, intended to be circulated as money in Hungary. After the plates had been prepared, Day and Sons began printing such notes from the plates. The total face value of the notes prepared exceeded 100 million florins.

The plaintiff charged that if such notes were sent to Hungary, they would infringe on his exclusive right and would be used to promote revolution and disorders; that they had never been authorized by him; that he had never permitted the use of the royal arms on such notes; that Day and Sons knew of the lack of authority on the part of Kossuth to issue such notes and knew for what purposes they were to be used. The plaintiff requested that all the plates and all the notes in question be delivered to him and that an injunction be issued, restraining Day and Sons from printing or delivering any such notes to Kossuth.

The lower court upheld the claims of the plaintiff; Day and Kossuth appealed.

ISSUES

(1) Can a recognized foreign sovereign sue in English courts, and under what conditions?

(2) Does the infringement of the prerogatives of a foreign sovereign constitute a ground of suit in an English court?

(3) Can a foreign sovereign sue in an English court on behalf of his subjects?

DECISION

A recognized foreign sovereignty may, under certain conditions, sue in an English court; an English court cannot interfere with or deal with the prerogatives of a foreign sovereign; a foreign sovereign can bring a suit in an English court on behalf of his subjects. Decree of lower court affirmed, except for a modification excluding the lower court's prohibition against the use of the Hungarian coat of arms by Kossuth.

REASONING

Re Issue (1): The Lord Chancellor held that a foreign sovereign, recognized by the British government, could sue in an English court, *provided* that his suit did not involve the maintenance of his political power or involve an alleged wrong sanctioned or approved by the government of England. He therefore could sue if a wrong had been done to him by an English subject not authorized to do so by the government of England, with respect to property belonging to the foreign sovereign in his individual or corporate capacity.

However, insofar as Kossuth's use of the royal coat of arms of Hungary was concerned, no prohibition on such use should be sustained, because the coat of arms in question was a "property" of which any Hungarian subject could make use.

Re Issue (2): The plaintiff had argued that the sovereign prerogative to coin or issue money was acknowledged by all nations and by international law; that because international law was a part of the law of England, the English courts should interfere in favor of protecting that sovereign prerogative. The court felt, however, that the domestic courts of a state should not interfere, favorably or unfavorably, with the prerogatives of foreign sovereigns.

Re Issue (3): The court held that the injury claimed by the plaintiff affected the private rights, not the political rights, of the subjects of the plaintiff, that is, if the notes were sent to Hungary, the value of the Bank of Austria notes would be affected adversely and thereby an adverse effect would be created relative to the rights of all property owners in Hungary. This claim was upheld by the court which believed that the plaintiff could sue on behalf of his Hungarian subjects, representing their collective interest in the English court.

IMMUNITIES OF INTERNATIONAL ORGANIZATIONS

Immunities Act. The drafting of the General Convention on the Privileges and Immunities of the United Nations (February 13, 1946) left no doubt as to the need for an immunity from suit as well as from every other form of legal process without an explicit waiver.[67] On that occasion, in contrast to the initial drafting of the Charter, an analogy to the corresponding immunity enjoyed by states was included. It is significant that

[67] Text of the convention was reprinted in 43 *A.J.I.L.* (January 1949), Supp., pp. 1–7.

in the International Organizations Immunities Act (which, together with the Charter, governs the immunities enjoyed by the United Nations in the United States by virtue of nonratification of the convention on the part of the United States) it is also provided that United Nations immunity can be waived only expressly by contract or for the purpose of any proceeding.[68] The Immunities Act has been invoked only on rare occasions by the Organization.

Immunities Enjoyed by the UN. United Nations immunity under the provisions of the United Nations General Convention is practically complete. It includes immunity for United Nations assets, wherever located, from any legal process; immunity of all United Nations premises from search, requisition, expropriation, confiscation, and any other sort of interference; immunity of archives; complete freedom from all financial controls, moratoria, or other monetary regulations; freedom to hold funds in any desired currency or metal; freedom to transfer funds; an absolute exemption of all assets and revenue from all direct taxes; exemption from all customs duties as well as from any foreign trade prohibitions on goods needed for the official use of the Organization; a guarantee of most-favored diplomatic treatment as far as rates, priorities, and so on, connected with all media of communications are concerned; exemption from all forms of censorship; the right to use codes; and the privilege of transporting correspondence by courier or otherwise under the full complement of customary diplomatic immunities.

The status of the United Nations headquarters in the United States, on the other hand, depending on the "housekeeping" agreement of June 26, 1947, between the United Nations and its host, presents some rather interesting deviations from the virtually absolute immunity provided for in the General Convention.[69]

UN Zone. The United Nations Zone in New York City is quite definitely within the United States, with no attempt made to create or uphold any fictitious extraterritoriality. United States civil and criminal laws (federal, state, and local) apply in the Zone, which is merely granted "inviolability," unless the contrary is specified in the agreement. Inviolability means among other things, that although the Zone is United States territory, United States officials (federal, state, or local) may enter the Zone only with the consent of the Secretary-General; the latter must also grant specific approval if any service of legal process is contemplated by American authorities. Within the area in question, the United Nations may operate its own radio station, airport, and postal service. An arbitration tribunal of three members is to settle all disputes between

---

[68] The text of the Statute Extending Privileges, Exemptions, and Immunities to International Organizations and to the Officers and Employees Thereof may be found in 40 *A.J.I.L.* (April 1946), Supp., pp. 85–90; see also Chapter 21.

[69] See text of agreement and of related documents in 43 *A.J.I.L.* (1949), Supp., pp. 8–26, and consult Chapter 21, and also Whiteman, Vol. 13, pp. 32–188.

the host sovereign and the United Nations concerning the interpretation of the agreement.

United States–United Nations Relationship with Respect to Immunities. Because the relations between the United Nations and the United States, as far as immunities are involved, are governed not only by treaty but also by elaborate domestic legislation, it does not appear likely that any restrictive theory of state immunity developed on the part of the United States government will affect the operations or legal status of the United Nations. Such a view appears reasonable for a number of reasons, not the least of which is based on the belief that no single member of the United Nations should have even a moral right to interfere through its courts in the functions or the utilization of the funds of an organization whose operations are determined collectively and whose finances are contributed collectively by over 100 states.

The wording of Article 105 of the Charter appears to indicate clearly that the immunities of the Organization are not to be based conditionally on reciprocity but should be viewed as the unconditional grant by the member states of certain privileges and immunities.

Protection Against Possible Injustices. In order to provide remedies for possible injustices arising out of the immunity of the Organization, a number of specific arrangements have been worked out, basically under the provisions of Article 29 of the General Convention mentioned previously. Property damage, personal injury liability, and so on, are covered by insurance for accidents in the Headquarters District, with a waiver of immunity in the case of suits based on such claims. On the other hand, contract claims against the Organization are subject to arbitration, under appropriate provisions inserted in purchase agreements, leases, and similar instruments. Until now, only the International Labor Organization appears to have found it desirable to establish a special agency (Administrative Tribunal) for the handling of claims against the ILO. This function is additional to the normal handling by the Tribunal of claims by staff members against the Organization; the latter function corresponds to the present assignment of the United Nations Administrative Tribunal. It should be noted, too, that the Specialized Agencies of the United Nations also have clauses dealing with privileges and immunities in their respective constitutions or charters.

SUGGESTED READINGS

RIGHTS OF STATES

E. D. Dickinson, *The Equality of States in International Law* (Cambridge, Mass.: Harvard University Press, 1920); D. W. Bowett, *Self-Defense in International Law* (New York: Praeger, 1958); Philip M. Brown, "Reserved International Rights," 38 *A.J.I.L.* (1944), pp. 281–283; Jessup, pp. 26–36.

RIGHTS OF INTERNATIONAL ORGANIZATIONS

J. W. Schneider, S.J., *Treaty-Making Power of International Organizations* (Geneva: Librairie E. Droz; Paris: Librairie Minard, 1959).

Case

International Refugee Organization v. *Republic S.S. Corporation*, United States, Circuit Court of Appeals, 4th Circuit, 1951, 189 F. [2d] 858, digested in 46 *A.J.I.L.* (1952), pp. 146–147.

IMMUNITIES OF STATES

T. Baty, " 'De Facto' States: Sovereign Immunities," 45 *A.J.I.L.* (1951), pp. 166–170; Briggs, pp. 442–451; Louis L. Jaffe, "Suits against Governments and Officers: Sovereign Immunity," 77 *Harvard Law Review* (1963), pp. 1–39; Theodor Meron, "Sovereign Immunity of Foreign Public Corporations," *International and Comparative Law Quarterly*, 6 (1957), pp. 290–300; J. M. Sweeney, *The International Law of Sovereign Immunity* (Washington, D.C.: U.S. Department of State, 1963); T. K. Thommen, *Legal Status of Government Merchant Ships in International Law* (The Hague: Martinus Nijhoff, 1962); Sigmund Timberg, "Expropriation Measures and State Trading," *Proceedings* (1961), pp. 133–121.

THE SABBATINO CASE

See a listing of references in Whiteman, Vol. VI, p. 36, as well as Eugene F. Mooney, *Foreign Seizures: Sabbatino and the Act of State Doctrine* (Lexington: University of Kentucky Press, 1967); Milo G. Coerper, "The Act of State Doctrine in the Light of the Sabbatino Case," 56 *A.J.I.L.* (1962), pp. 143–148; Quincy Wright, "Reflections on the Sabbatino Case," *ibid.*, 59 (1965), pp. 304–315; Richard A. Falk, "The Complexity of Sabbatino," *ibid.*, 58 (1964), pp. 935–951; John R. Stevenson, "The State Department and Sabbatino—'Ev'n Victors Are by Victories Undone," *ibid.*, 58 (1964), pp. 707–711.

Cases

Dexter & Carpenter v. *Kunglig Jarnvagsstyrelsen*, United States, Circuit Court of Appeals, 2nd Circuit, 1930, 43 F. [2d] 705.

Sullivan v. *State of Sao Paulo; Sullivan* v. *State of Rio Grande do Sul*, United States, Circuit Court of Appeals, 2nd Circuit, August 4, 1941, 122 Fed. Rep. [2nd Ser.] 355, reported in detail in 36 *A.J.I.L.* (1942), pp. 131–138.

Republic of Iraq v. *First National City Bank, Administrator*, United States, District Court, S.D.N.Y., 1965, 241 F. Supp. 567; affirmed, Court of Appeals, 2nd Circuit, 1965, 353 F. 2d. 47; *certiorari* denied, Supreme Court, 1966, 382 U.S. 1027. Consult also the relevant Note by Mark T. Horlings, 7 *Harvard International Law Club Journal* (1966), pp. 316–327, and see Whiteman, Vol. VI, pp. 36–41, on this case, as well as pp. 54–66 on acts of state affecting property rights in the forum state.

N.Y. World's Fair 1964–1965 Corporation v. *Republic of Guinea,* United States, Supreme Court, N.Y., Special Term, Queens County, 1968, 159 N.Y. Law Jl. 15, reported in 63 *A.J.I.L.* (1969), p. 343.

Municipality of the City and County of St. John, Logan and Clayton v. *Fraser-Brace Overseas Corp. et al.,* Canada, Supreme Court, 1958, 13 D.L.R. (2d) 177, reported briefly in 53 *A.J.I.L.* (1959), p. 189.

S. T. Tringali Co. v. *Tug Pemex XV,* United States, District Court, S.D. Texas, 1967, 274 F. Supp. 227, digested in 62 *A.J.I.L.* (1968), pp. 508–509.

Thomas W. Kendall et al. v. *The Kingdom of Saudi Arabia et al.,* United States, District Court, S.D.N.Y., 1965: letter from Department of State to U.S. Attorney General (September 14, 1965), excerpted in 60 *A.J.I.L.* (1966), pp. 100–101.

The Rigmor, Sweden, Supreme Court, 1942. Text of Judgment in 37 *A.J.I.L.* (1943), pp. 141–151.

IMMUNITIES OF INTERNATIONAL ORGANIZATIONS

Wilfred Jenks, *International Immunities* (Dobbs Ferry, N.Y.: Oceana Publications; London: Stevens & Sons, 1961).

Case

Lutcher S.A. Celulose e Papel, Candoi, Parana, Brazil v. *Inter-American Development Bank,* United States, District Court, D.D.C. (1966) 253 F. Supp. 568, analyzed in detail by Winston R. Webster, 8 *Harvard International Law Journal* (Winter, 1967), pp. 168–176, and also found in 5 *International Legal Materials: Current Documents* (May, 1966), pp. 480–482.

10

Duties of States

I T WAS pointed out earlier that many of the alleged rights of states either reflected characteristics of those entities or, in certain instances, represented duties or obligations. Whether or not one admits the existence of a moral code prevailing in the relations among nations, the fact remains that practicing statesmen, Machiavellian or otherwise, have agreed that some sort of code does exist. Thus states, concluding treaties among themselves, expect that the agreements will be observed; whoever breaches the treaty will either deny that fact or defend it by elaborate arguments designed to show that the act was morally or legally just. It therefore becomes necessary now to investigate what may be included properly among the duties of states in their mutual relations.

The most modern, though incomplete, listing of the asserted duties of states may be found in the Draft Declaration on the Rights and Duties of States, prepared in 1949 by the International Law Commission in conformity with a resolution of the General Assembly of the United Nations.[1] The discussion which follows deals with all the duties mentioned by the Commission, as well as with several additional obligations generally recognized as binding by the members of the community of nations.

RENUNCIATION OF UNLAWFUL INTERVENTION

One of the oldest duties of states, enshrined both in customary international law and in numerous multilateral conventions, is the basic obligation of a state to abstain from intervention in the internal and external affairs of any other state or in the relations between other states. It should be noted, however, that the inclusion of "and external" as well as of the last phrase represent very recent additions to an old principle. History indicates that states, generally speaking, do not regard interference with the foreign affairs (read "policies") of another state as being unlawful or even reprehensible. In fact, many external policies of states appear to be directed at blocking the success of the external policies of another state, and no one appears to regard such a conflict as unlawful in nature. Again, interference by one state in the relations existing between other states may represent a quite lawful attempt to break up an alliance pre-

---

[1] Text reprinted in 44 *A.J.I.L.* (1950), Supp., pp. 15-18.

sumably aimed at the interfering state, or some other perfectly legal activity on the international scene. On the other hand, an attempt, say, by state X, to interfere in the relationship between state A and the latter's protectorate of B would have to be considered as a violation of the obligations resting on state X. So the statement of the duty, as given earlier, should be regarded as a rather sweeping generalization, with certain portions representing an obligation or duty only under certain conditions.

Definition of Intervention. Few terms in international law have led to more and divergent discussions than the prohibition of intervention. Not only is there a general lack of agreement on a definition of the practice, but many writers as well as statesmen have attempted to demonstrate that under specific conditions there existed not merely a right but a duty on the part of one state to intervene in the affairs of another state.

The majority of commentators agree that intervention under present-day international law means *dictatorial* interference by one state in the affairs of another state for the purpose of either maintaining or changing the existing order of things,[2] rather than mere interference *per se*. Such intervention could take place by right and also without the existence of a right, but in any case, it concerns the independence, territory, or supremacy of the state involved.

There cannot be any doubt that, as a rule, such intervention is prohibited by international law, for that law has been created, at least in part, to protect the international personality of the states of the world.[3] However, there are exceptions to this principle, as will be shown, for some interventions take place by right and are thus lawful; and there are some forms of intervention which lack a right yet must be accorded lawful status.[4]

---

[2] See Lauterpacht's *Oppenheim*, Vol. I, p. 305; Brierly, p. 402; Whiteman, Vol. V, pp. 452–453; C. G. Fenwick, "Intervention: Individual and Collective," 39 *A.J.I.L.* (1945), pp. 645–663; Sumner Welles, "Intervention and Interventions," 26 *Foreign Affairs* (1947), pp. 116–133.

[3] The General Assembly, its Sixth Committee, as well as a thirty-one-member Special Committee are still at work on the drafting of an acceptable draft code of legal principles governing friendly relations among states: see Whiteman, Vol. V, pp. 24–33, and the Declaration on the Inadmissibility of Intervention in the Domestic Affairs of States and the Protection of Their Independence and Sovereignty, adopted by the Assembly on December 19, 1966 (UN Doc. GA 2225-XXI-1966), following a similar Resolution passed in 1965 [UN Doc. GA 2131-XX-1965, reproduced in 60 *A.J.I.L.* (1966), p. 662]; see also the commentary in Piet-Hein Houben, "Principles of International Law Concerning Friendly Relations and Co-operation among States," 61 *A.J.I.L.* (1967), pp. 703–736, at pp. 716–718.

[4] See the stimulating realistic analysis by Richard R. Falk, "Revolutionary Nations and the Quality of International Legal Order," pp. 310–331 in Morton A. Kaplan, ed., *The Revolution in World Politics* (New York: Wiley, 1962); the realistic appraisal by Hans J. Morgenthau, "To Intervene or Not to Intervene," 45 *Foreign Affairs* (1967), pp. 425–436, as well as the sharply critical study by Manfred Halpern, *The Morality and Politics of Intervention* (New York: Council on Religion and International Affairs, 1963).

It is also possible to distinguish between subvarieties of intervention, such as local interventions (Hyderabad, Kashmir, Tibet), hegemonial interventions (Hungary in 1956, Czechoslovakia in 1968, Cuba in 1961, and so on), and what has been termed hegemonial veto of intervention (Suez in 1956).

INTERVENTION BY RIGHT

The fact that certain varieties of intervention have been justified by outstanding jurists reflects the growing perturbation on the part of writers in international law who would like to perpetuate a theoretical doctrine of absolute prohibition of intervention, yet who are drawn in the direction of approving *some* form of intervention because it strikes them as desirable from humanitarian considerations, from a political point of view, or, sometimes, because logic appears to dictate the correctness of a particular employment of intervention, despite the overall legal prohibition extant.

Intervention by Right. A right of intervention may come about in one of several ways:

(1) A protector-state may, by treaty, have been granted intervention rights in a protected state.

(2) If the foreign relations of one state are at the same time the external affairs of another state, the latter may intervene lawfully if the former state proceeds to act unilaterally. This would be true, say, in the case of vassal and suzerain communities.

(3) If a given state has been restricted by treaty either in its territorial supremacy or in its external independence and violates the restrictions imposed, the other party or parties to the agreement would possess a lawful right of intervention.

(4) If a state violates generally accepted rules of customary or conventional law, other states would have a right to intervene. Thus, if a belligerent proceeded to violate rights of neutral states during a conflict, the neutrals would have rights of intervention against the violating belligerent state.

(5) Again, and this is a subject of much discussion, if the citizens of a state are mistreated in another state, the former, it has been asserted possesses a lawful right to intervene on behalf of its citizens after all available peaceful remedies have been exhausted.

The most frequently cited instances are the interventions in Nicaraguan internal affairs on the part of the United States, beginning in 1909, on grounds of protecting American private interests and citizens in that republic, and the collective intervention in China in 1900 through the joint military and naval expedition sent there by Germany, France, Great Britain, Italy, Austria-Hungary, Russia, Japan, and the United States. The present writer cannot subscribe to the belief that such actions represent lawful intervention—they ought to be viewed as prohibited dictatorial interference in the affairs of other states.

(6) Lawful intervention (intervention by right) would occur in the case of collective action undertaken by an international organ on behalf of the community of nations or for the enforcement of the principles and rules of international law.[5]

This is undoubtedly true for both preventive and remedial action undertaken on behalf of or by the agencies of such bodies as the United Nations. However, even Lauterpacht admitted that such United Nations intervention had to stop short of "dictatorial interference," hence it was not true intervention as defined by him. He illustrated permissible action, in the sphere of human rights, by citing study, discussion, investigation, and recommendation—none of these, he believed, could be taken to constitute true intervention.

(7) Intervention appears to be by right when it takes place at the genuine and explicit invitation of the lawful government of a state. A striking example of this kind of intervention was supplied by the landing of American Marines in Lebanon in 1958,[6] and the sending of requested British troops to Jordan, following charges of United Arab Republic intervention in the internal affairs of Jordan. On January 25, 1964, British forces went into action in Tanganyika, Uganda, and Kenya, in each instance at the request of the respective government, in order to put down mutinies by African troops.[7]

On the other hand, in the case of "invitational intervention" as in the case of all other forms of such action, the particular circumstances of a given instance determine whether the intervention did possess any legal merit at all. Thus the invasion of Austria by armed forces of Germany in 1938 did take place at the request of an Austrian government, to be sure, but it was highly dubious whether the government in question could be regarded at the time as the lawful government of the Republic of Austria. In that particular case of intervention, the motives prompting the action adopted by the intervening state differed radically from the motives ascribable to the actions of the United States in the case of the Lebanese landings.

Comparable in many respects with the Austrian situation, the military

[5] See Lauterpacht's *Oppenheim*, Vol. I, p. 320, and Quincy Wright, "The Legality of Intervention under the United Nations Charter," *Proceedings* (1957), pp. 79–88.

[6] See Quincy Wright, "United States Intervention in the Lebanon," 53 *A.J.I.L.* (1959), pp. 112–125, particularly at pp. 119–122; consult Pittman B. Potter, "Legal Aspects of the Beirut Landing," *ibid.*, Vol. 52 (1958), pp. 727–730, as well as Halpern, *op cit.*, pp. 11–14; Whiteman, Vol. V, pp. 519–522, 845–848; and the eyewitness accounts of Robert McClintock (then U.S. ambassador to Lebanon), "The American Landing in Lebanon," 88 *U.S. Naval Institute Proceedings* (October, 1962), pp. 65–79, and of Col. H. A. Hadd (Commander of the landing forces), "Orders Firm but Flexible," *ibid.*, pp. 80–87.

[7] *The New York Times*, January 26, 1964, pp. 1, 3.

intervention by the Soviet Union in Hungary in 1956 represented, in American eyes, an illegal intervention, because the Kadar government which had asked for Soviet assistance under the terms of the Warsaw Pact did not represent a legitimate government in Hungary but rather a puppet regime established by the very state whose military aid and intervention were requested.[8]

Another example of invitational intervention was the temporary stationing of British Air Force units in the Republic of Zambia in early December, 1965.

Most important of all recent examples of this kind of intervention has been the involvement of the United States and other states in the Vietnamese conflict.

The present writer believes that the United States intervention in that conflict has been a lawful intervention.[9] Under generally accepted rules of international law, outside assistance cannot be requested by a government faced by a purely domestic civil war in which the outcome is in doubt, for such a government cannot truly speak for its country. But if a civil war is aided and promoted from the outside, by agencies of another state—if, in other words, subversive intervention has occurred—then the target government has a legal right to ask for assistance in its struggle to maintain itself. This appears to have been the situation in South Vietnam after the initial phases of the civil war which began as a domestic uprising against the government in Saigon in 1957. Infiltration from the North appears to have started in early 1958, even though Northern military *units* did not penetrate the demilitarized zone until after the Gulf of Tonkin episodes in early August, 1964.

Regrettably the scope of a general text prevents a detailed account of events and motivations involved, and the reader must be referred to the readings suggested at the end of this chapter. But the writer wishes to reiterate that he believes U.S. intervention in Vietnam to have been proper from legal, political, and moral points of view.

Under the conditions described—that is, a civil war supported, on the rebel side, from the outside—third parties may assist the incumbent government regardless of a possible diminution of the control exercised by it over its national territory.

---

[8] See Whiteman, Vol. V, pp. 667–702.

[9] This endorsement of the legality of U.S. intervention is shared by other writers as well as by the Department of State: see, *inter alia*, John N. Moore, "The Lawfulness of Military Assistance to the Republic of Viet-nam," 61 *A.J.I.L.* (1967), pp. 1–34; Leonard C. Meeker (Legal Adviser of the Department of State), "The Legality of United States Participation in the Defense of Viet-nam [Legal Memorandum submitted to the Senate Committee on Foreign Relations, March 8, 1966], *ibid.*, 60 (1966), pp. 565–585; and Roger H. Hulland and John C. Novogrod, *Law and Vietnam* (Dobbs Ferry, N.Y.: Oceana Publications, 1968). For other materials, representing many differing points of view, see list of Suggested Reading. See also pp. 71–72, concerning the two Vietnams and other divided states.

PERMISSIBLE INTERVENTION NOT BASED ON RIGHT

Permissible intervention not based on right centers on genuine instances of self-defense. In this case, the act of self-help involving intervention must be an action in self-preservation. Self-defense against armed attack is lawful and cannot normally be classified as illegal intervention, provided certain conditions are met, such as the existence of immediate danger of attack.[10]

Any other form of intervention of a *military* nature would have to be considered unlawful (Anglo-French intervention in Egypt, 1956).[11]

The initial stages of Egyptian intervention in Yemen, in the fall of 1962, although made at the invitation of the Yemen Arab Republic, must be regarded as of dubious legality, in view of the limited control exercised from its beginning by the allegedly lawful government. Eventually, however, acknowledged support of the royalist faction in the struggle by Saudi Arabia appears to have provided a legitimate basis for Egyptian assistance to the republican faction.[12]

On the other hand, the Russian *cum* Warsaw Pact forces invasion of Czechoslovakia in August, 1968, appears to have been wholly illegal, even though initially justified by the Soviet Union as an invitational intervention. Subsequently no evidence whatever of any invitation could be produced by the Soviet government. The so-called Brezhnev Doctrine, asserting a right on the part of the USSR to intervene in any socialist country if the existence of socialism were threatened in any manner, reflects, in essence, power politics on a hegemonial basis, not a legal right of any kind.

However, military intervention at the behest of the United Nations or of a regional defense organization under the Charter must be viewed as lawful, indeed as intervention by right, even though such action has, on occasion, also led to some rather debatable consequences: ONUC in the Congo may be cited as an example.

Humanitarian Intervention. What about so-called humanitarian intervention, claimed by such writers as Grotius, Vattel, and Westlake to be legally valid when a state treated its people "in such a way as to deny their fundamental human rights and to shock the conscience of mankind?" [13] Such interference in the affairs of others was defended by the argument that if certain practices or actions, revolting when judged by

[10] See the classic example in *The Caroline Case (Great Britain-United States)*, 1837, in Moore, II, pp. 409 ff.; consult also Cheng, pp. 84–87, and R. Y. Jennings, "The Caroline and McLeod Cases," 32 *A.J.I.L.* (1938), pp. 82–99.

[11] Consult Whiteman, Vol. V, pp. 629–658.

[12] See Kathryn B. Doherty, "Rhetoric and Reality: A Study of Contemporary Official Egyptian Attitudes toward the International Legal Order," 62 *A.J.I.L.* (1968), pp. 335–364, at pp. 353–354, and "War in the Desert," 55 *U.S. News & World Report* (July 15, 1963), pp. 62–63.

[13] Lauterpacht's *Oppenheim*, Vol. I, p. 312.

generally accepted standards of morality and decency, continued to take place in a given state despite protests and objections by its neighbors, then humanitarian considerations outweighed the prohibition on intervention and justified a decision to interfere.

Humanitarian intervention has been carried out by individual countries (Russia in Turkey on behalf of Bulgarian nationalists in 1877; the United States in Cuba in 1898) or on a collective basis (the Great Powers in Turkey on behalf of Greece, in 1827; France in Syria in 1860, on the basis of an agreement among the major powers; the European Great Powers plus Japan in China in 1900, during the Boxer Rebellion).

If a moral consensus can be shown to exist, if the "conscience of mankind" is outraged by a repetition of repulsive practices within a state, then conceivably a moral justification *may* exist for intervention on the part of other states. The question remaining would, of course, be the old one: does the end justify the means? In this instance, some justification might be admitted in favor of interference, provided an absence of selfish aims could be demonstrated. But such intervention cannot as yet be regarded as lawful, even though some writers assert that humanitarian intervention is now justified as a rule of law under the United Nations Charter, with its emphasis on human rights and freedoms.

In late November, 1964, rebel forces in the eastern Congo had captured or isolated hundreds of white residents, increasing numbers of which were killed. The United States government agreed, for humanitarian reasons, to supply air transport for Belgian paratroopers and for the evacuation of white refugees. Within four days, this operation had been completed and two days later all paratroopers had also been removed from the Congo.[14] This intervention resulted in widespread criticism from African members of the United Nations and an unsuccessful attempt was made by eighteen of them to have the Security Council condemn the rescue operation as "armed aggression." In retrospect, however, the episode presents one of the clearest modern instances of true humanitarian intervention and should be viewed as lawful in character, in view of the conditions then existing in the "target state" and of the total inability of the incumbent government to protect the refugees in question.

One of the most publicized recent instances of alleged humanitarian intervention was the landing of U.S. marines in the Dominican Republic on April 28, 1965. Initially this intervention was explained in terms of protecting American citizens residing in the Dominican Republic and said to be threatened by the outbreak of civil strife. Two days later, President Lyndon Johnson substituted self-defense (national security) as the reason, citing the threat of the establishment of Communism in the Republic. After two more days, justification for the continuation of the

[14] See *The New York Times*, November 29, 1964, p. E-1; 84 *Time* (December 25, 1964), pp. 19-20; and Whiteman, Vol. V, pp. 475-476.

presence of American forces was sought in terms of a stop-gap measure until the Organization of American States could act effectively. And at all times, humanitarian intervention considerations intruded on more mundane reasons advanced for the armed intervention.[15] Little was said, at the time, about the clear violation by the United States of a number of Western Hemisphere agreements which categorically prohibited armed as well as unarmed intervention.[16] Ultimately the United States forces were withdrawn and replaced by an Inter-American Peace Force (IAPF) established by the OAS.

Abatement Theory. Another reason advanced on occasion in justification of intervention is the "abatement" of an international nuisance—quite frequently characterized by the addition of the adjective *intolerable*. It could be argued that this was one of the reasons cited in the United States in 1898 in partial justification of armed action in Cuba. The argument was actually utilized by Japan in 1932 in defense of the invasion and conquest of Manchuria. It was also brought forward, in conjunction with the concept of *debellatio*, in 1939, in defense of Russian interference in the form of invasion followed by annexation when the Polish state had crumbled under German attack.[17] And still another example—American—may be found in the dispatch of military forces into Mexico in 1916–17, following civil disturbances in northern Mexico, the Villa raid on Brownsville, Texas, and the manifest inability of the Mexican government to restore order along the United States border.

The abatement theory holds that when conditions in the territory of a neighboring state border on anarchy, with concurrent inability of the constituted authorities (if they still exist at the time) to restore order and to prevent a spilling over of the disturbance into one's own territory, then one has a duty to intervene—quite likely by armed force—to restore order along one's frontiers and to end the chaos next door. If no selfish aims are involved in the intervention in question, if no territorial aggrandizement or other gain is contemplated or realized, then it is difficult, in many instances, to deny a moral right, based on self-defense or self-preservation, to violate the ban on intervention for the sake of abating the nuisance at one's doorstep.

Collective Intervention. Yet another variety of intervention has been defended on a number of occasions: collective intervention, sometimes

[15] See the heavily documented study by David S. Bogen, "The Law of Humanitarian Intervention: United States Policy in Cuba (1898) and in the Dominican Republic (1965)," 7 *Harvard International Law Club Journal* (1966), pp. 296–315, and the critical analysis by Theodore Draper, *The Dominican Revolt: A Case Study in American Policy* (New York: Commentary, 1968).

[16] See Quincy Wright, "Intervention and Cuba in 1961," *Proceedings* (1961), pp. 2–19, at pp. 13–14; Ernesto Dihigo, "Legality of Intervention under the Charter of the Organization of American States," *ibid.* (1957), pp. 91–100.

[17] See George Ginsburgs' instructive "A Case Study in the Soviet Use of International Law: Eastern Poland in 1939," 52 *A.J.I.L.* (1958), pp. 69–84.

referred to as universal sanction. The classic example of this variation took place in 1863 when joint intervention in Japanese affairs was agreed on by the governments of Great Britain, the Netherlands, France, Russia, and the United States in order to compel Japan to desist from attacking foreign vessels, particularly in the Strait of Shimonoseki. Incidentally, no American public vessels being in the neighborhood of Japan, the American consul proceeded to rent a small old ship, armed it, and ordered it to participate with the rest of the Western armada to bombard the Daimu forts along the Strait. Japan paid a somewhat excessive indemnity after the bombardment. Although this incident appears, on the surface, to be quite similar to the collective Western action in China mentioned earlier, there are basic differences between the two interventions.

On other occasions, Greece requested UN intervention in 1947 when armed bands allegedly invaded Greece from Albania, Bulgaria, and Jugoslavia,[18] Guatemala, in 1954, requested UN action to halt aggressive attacks launched from Honduras and Nicaragua with covert United States support.[19]

Some writers, notably Richard A. Falk, have advocated or justified international (*read*, United Nations) intervention in civil wars, asserting correctly that such conflicts may easily escalate into international, regional, or even global wars. Yet the fact remains that United Nations intervention of any consequence could only take place if agreement prevailed among the Great Powers. And if such agreement should exist, then a given civil war would not be likely to constitute a danger to world peace calling for international intervention.[20]

Preventive Intervention. Other varieties of prohibited intervention include the attempt by one state to prevent unlawful intervention by another state in a third country: what might be termed preventive intervention. An example of this type of action would be the United States protests against French intervention in Mexico in 1861, followed by eventual undercover assistance to Mexican rebels against the imperial government in Mexico and the French garrisons maintaining that government in power. Also, military intervention has been resorted to when all lawful and peaceful methods of collecting claims or debts from other states have failed. Illustrations of this type of action abound in modern history, particularly in the case of the United States which, on numerous occasions, justified intervention in such countries as Haiti and the Dominican Republic on the grounds that debts could not be collected in any other manner.

[18] Text of Greek note in 3 *World Report* (August 12, 1947), pp. 37–38; consult Whiteman, Vol. V, pp. 281–291, 383–384, 433–442.

[19] See the prophetic analysis by Martin B. Travis, Jr., "Collective Intervention by the Organization of American States," *Proceedings* (1957), pp. 100–110; Charles G. Fenwick, "Jurisdictional Questions Involved in the Guatemalan Revolution," 48 *A.J.I.L.* (1954), pp. 597–602; and Whiteman, Vol. V, pp. 426–428, 802–808.

[20] On collective intervention in general, consult Whiteman, Vol. V, pp. 544–564.

Summary. No matter how moral or desirable or plausible some of the foregoing justifications of intervention may have appeared in specific instances, the fact remains that intervention *per se* is an act in violation of rights which should be inviolable, represents a hostile act, and may be taken to be an "act rendered possible only because of the superior force of the intervening state." [21]

The past few years have witnessed other instances of armed intervention, surrounded in a number of cases by such a multitude of contributory and confusing issues that debate about them still continues at the time of writing. One of these instances was intervention in the Congo (Leopoldville) in 1960. That state obtained a somewhat premature independence on June 20, 1960, and promptly fell into a state of anarchy, primarily as the result of an army mutiny. Belgium intervened at once by bringing in paratroopers to protect its nationals. Within two days, the Security Council responded to a plea for assistance by the Congolese government and authorized the sending of international forces to the Congo. Belgium's unilateral intervention ceased by July 23, except in the province of Katanga.

On April 17, 1961, came the ill-fated attempt on the part of the United States to effect the overthrow of the Castro government in Cuba by assisting in the formation of a liberation force composed of Cuban exiles trained and equipped with the benevolent support of the United States. The attempt to establish a beachhead in the Bay of Pigs failed, in part because of a leakage of information concerning the landing plans, in part because of a denial of air and naval cover by the United States. A contributing factor to the disastrous results of the enterprise was the failure of an expected massive uprising of the Cuban civilian population to materialize. But without doubt, and by official admission, the Government of the United States had attempted to intervene in Cuban affairs through the utilization of "friendly" armed force.[22] The fact that this force consisted of Cuban rather than of United States citizens had nothing to do with the essential illegality of the entire operation since a state has a definite and generally acknowledged duty to prevent armed bands from leaving its territory for the purpose of attacking the government of a presumably friendly state.

The locale of the 1961 American intervention in the Western Hemisphere emphasized the illegal nature of the enterprise, in view of the existence of numerous regional arrangements prohibiting such intervention in the Americas. The Charter of the Organization of American States, the Saavedra Lamas Anti-War Treaty of 1933, the Montevideo Convention of 1933 on the Rights and Duties of States, the Buenos Aires

[21] Sumner Wells, "Intervention and Interventions," 26 *Foreign Affairs* (October, 1947), p. 116–133, at p. 117.

[22] See Richard A. Falk, "American Intervention in Cuba and the Rule of Law," *Ohio State Law Journal* (Summer, 1961), pp. 546–585.

Protocol on Non-Intervention of 1936, the Buenos Aires Convention of 1936 on the Fulfillment of the Existing Treaties between the American States, the Act of Chapultepec of 1945, and the Declaration on Intervention of the Caracas Conference of 1954—all these instruments, to which the United States is a party, condemn and prohibit the action which the United States promoted against Cuba in 1961. Yet, and here political considerations both domestic and foreign intrude, large numbers of American citizens were bitterly disappointed at the failure of the United States to support the Cuban invasion by sending along its own armed forces in order to crush the Cuban Castro government. In fact, a number of critics of the failure to adopt an invasion policy by the United States believed that American support for anti-Castro rebels was fully justified as a measure of retaliation for the seizure of American properties in Cuba and for violation by the Cuban government of its own obligations under the anti-Communist provisions of the Caracas and other American instruments.[23]

The duty to abstain from armed intervention clearly means also that no state may permit the use of its territory for the staging of hostile expeditions against another state. Thus the United States acted correctly in arresting, on January 2, 1967, a group of seventy-three armed men on a Florida key. The individuals in question were preparing to invade Haiti in an effort to overthrow the incumbent government with the expected help of indigenous malcontents. A year later, the leaders of the group were sentenced to prison in a U.S. District Court.[24]

On the other hand, Cuba violated its obligations when it not only set up training schools for leaders of subversive movements in Latin America but permitted such individuals as well as members of the Cuban armed forces to depart from Cuba for their respective target states. In one instance, in May, 1967, the personnel of such a group, including four Cuban army officers, was captured or killed while landing in Venezuela. (See also the exploits, until his capture and execution, of Ernesto Che Guevara in Bolivia in 1967–1968.)

Regrettably, a general text cannot enter into a detailed analysis of the concept of "national wars of liberation," a phenomenon whose meaning and actual implementation have already produced an extensive literature.[25]

---

[23] The sequel to the Cuban episode of 1961 was the appearance of Cuban-sponsored subversive activity in other Latin American states. The answer to this activity was sought at the Punta del Este Conference of 1962; see Charles G. Fenwick, "The Issues at Punta del Este: Non-Intervention v. Collective Security," 56 *A.J.I.L.* (1962), pp. 469–474; A. J. Thomas, Jr., "The Organization of American States and Subversive Intervention," *Proceedings* (1961), pp. 19–24; Victor Bernstein and Jesse Gordon, "The Press and the Bay of Pigs," 10 *Columbia University Forum* (Fall, 1967), pp. 4–13.

[24] See also the case of *Bush* v. *United States*, United States, Court of Appeals, 5th Circuit, 1968, 389 F. 2d 485, reported in 62 *A.J.I.L.* (1968), pp. 977–978.

[25] See Gerhard von Glahn, "The Case for Legal Control of 'Liberation' Propaganda," pp. 115–150 in Clark C. Havighurst, ed., *International Control of Propaganda*

UNARMED INTERVENTION

Thus far discussion of intervention has centered on the traditional interference in the internal affairs of another state by means of armed force. But obviously this does not represent the only form of intervention possible.

SUBVERSIVE INTERVENTION BY STATES

One of the most difficult problems in this sphere is that dealing with what Wright termed "subversive intervention."[26] In a world torn between a variety of rival ideologies, with authoritarian and sometimes totalitarian regimes in control of several states and with conditions quite out of consonance with elementary concepts of human dignity prevailing in a number of areas, the writer on international law questions is faced with a dilemma of no small proportions.

Legal Obligations to Abstain from Intervention. On the one hand, there is in existence an undoubted legal obligation, reiterated in the Charter of the United Nations, to abstain from intervention, to respect the territorial integrity and political independence of all other states. At the same time, there exists an equally legal obligation, enshrined in the same Charter, for the members of the United Nations to seek realization of principles of respect for human rights and for the self-determination of peoples. To be sure, the relative standing in law of these two sets of obligations—a phrase unorthodox enough to horrify a lawyer who cannot conceive that one legal obligation should prevail over another equally legal one—is not quite the same. By this is meant that the duty to abstain from intervention is firmly grounded in rules of customary law as well as in numerous multilateral treaties, whereas the obligations relating to human rights and self-determination lack as yet a true acceptance by the members of the community of nations. Thus far at least, no state has a right to proceed by some measure of intervention to force compliance by another state as far as human rights, and so on, are concerned.

On the other hand, it has been generally recognized that there does exist an obligation or duty to abstain from subversive intervention, that is to say, from engaging in propaganda, official statements, or legislative action of any kind, with the intention of promoting rebellion, sedition, or treason against the government of another state.[27]

(Dobbs Ferry, N.Y.: Oceana Publications, 1967), originally published in 31 *Law and Contemporary Problems* (Summer, 1966), pp. 553–588, and the literature cited therein.

[26] Quincy Wright, "Subversive Intervention," 54 *A.J.I.L.* (1960), pp. 521–534, a pioneer investigation of this subject from a legal point of view, frequently cited by subsequent writers.

[27] See Wright, *op. cit.* (n. 21), p. 523, for a valuable list of references on the responsibility of states for international propaganda, as well as Vernon Van Dyke,

The General Assembly of the United Nations unanimously adopted a resolution on November 3, 1947, condemning all forms of seditious propaganda, limiting itself, however, to propaganda likely to provoke threats to peace or an act of aggression.[28] On December 1, 1949, the Assembly urged all states to refrain from, among other things, any threats or acts aimed at fomenting civil war or subverting the will of the people in any other state, a request which was reiterated in tones of greater concern on November 17, 1950.

The United States and the Soviet Union have been foremost in condemning subversive intervention. The former has generally been highly critical of the subversive activities promoted by the Communist bloc states, labeling such efforts "indirect aggression"; several of its spokesmen have pointed out the comparatively greater danger of such disguised aggression when compared with the menace of an open expedition setting forth against a given state.

The Soviet Union and its friends, on the other hand, have continuously attacked every form of aid by non-Communist countries as a manifestation of imperialist intervention, have attacked with vigor such public media of information as the Voice of America and the privately supported but officially encouraged Radio Free Europe as illegal and subversive capitalist enterprises, and became particularly incensed when President Eisenhower issued a proclamation, setting aside the third week of July, 1959, as "Captive Nations Week."

The world would be a more peaceful place for all if mutual vilification and attempts to subvert the populations of other countries were to disappear from the scene. As President Eisenhower stated on April 16, 1953:

Any nation's right to a form of government and an economic system of its own choosing is *inalienable*. Any nation's attempt to dictate to other nations their form of government is indefensible.[29]

He might have added that the second enterprise mentioned by him was also clearly illegal.

Problems of Subversive Intervention. The trouble is, of course, that although the jurisdiction of any state is territorial and is limited to its own domain, many states have interests abroad or follow a foreign policy which involves other states, often to a most intimate extent. When such a foreign policy or such interests appear to demand that a more friendly, or a more amenable, or a more radical, or a more conservative government is needed in another state to serve better the interests of the first one,

---

"The Responsibility of States for International Propaganda," 34 *A.J.I.L.* (1940), pp. 58–73.

[28] See Quincy Wright's detailed analysis of the background and meaning of the 1947 resolution in his "The Crime of 'War-Mongering,'" 42 *A.J.I.L.* (1948), pp. 128–136.

[29] *The New York Times*, April 17, 1953.

then the temptation is indeed great to attempt to subvert the other state in such a manner that the desired results are achieved. The problem of coping with such subversive intervention is complicated incredibly by considerations of freedom of expression of opinions that may prevail in a given country, and by the technical problems involved in stopping propaganda across national frontiers.

Infiltration by Foreign Governments. Certain kinds of subversive intervention have long been known and have been prohibited by customary or conventional international law. A much more difficult assessment occurs in the case of infiltration by a foreign governmental organization, for quite commonly the interfering state makes use of nationals of the state being subverted, and the degree of reliance on the organization by the citizens in question is often difficult to establish. But if it can be demonstrated that the infiltrators are agents of a foreign power, then evidence of illegal interference has been secured—provided, of course, that the laws of the discovering state do not permit the degree of infiltration contemplated here. Any open action or propaganda on the part of one state calculated to incite aggression by its people against another state, or by a third state against the latter, is obviously illegal. If the provisions of the Nuremberg Charter are held to constitute new rules of general international law, then "warmongering" is a crime and forms a part of the matters prohibited under a duty to abstain from intervention. But, as Wright repeatedly and cogently emphasized in his discussion of subversive intervention, the yardstick to be applied to any practice when determining its relevance to intervention should be the existence or lack of "clear and present danger."

SUBVERSIVE INTERVENTION BY PRIVATE GROUPS

All discussion thus far has dealt with actions of governments promoting some form of subversive intervention. When similar acts are undertaken by private individuals or groups, governments have usually refused to accept responsibility of such acts. Obviously a state adversely affected by such propaganda emanating from private sources in a neighboring country will not only protest the act but will attempt to prevent the subversive propaganda from reaching its own citizens, by censorship, jamming of broadcasts and telecasts, and so on. In all fairness, no matter what its nature, such defensive measures appear to be the right of any government and cannot be termed illegal.

Yet, and here ethics enters the picture, does not the liberal or democratic state encourage subversion, and thus promote a kind of intervention, when it permits its citizens to engage in propaganda aimed at the undemocratic or any other kind of state across the border? And does not the authoritarian state, in the pursuit of its efforts to exclude the propaganda emanating in its neighbor's territory, practice self-defense as well as violate the rather vague obligations concerning freedom and the self-determination of peoples?

Libel and Slander Against Foreign Governments. Still another aspect of this problem has to do with libel and slander against foreign governments. If private individuals utter libelous statements, no responsibility devolves on their government. There are, however, a few democratic states which apparently are willing to prosecute their own citizens for libeling foreign governments or the heads of the same, provided that reciprocity in this matter existed, that is, if the libeled state provided for similar punishment of its own citizens for equivalent acts.

If, on the other hand, a public official engages in such pursuits, it appears to be a duty of his government to restrain him, to rebuke him, or even to punish him, if friendly relations with the government allegedly slandered or libeled are to be preserved. On the other hand, allegedly slanderous remarks issuing from local or state officials not connected with a national government do not give rise to any national responsibility, unless, of course, political considerations demand the tender of an apology to the offended government or head of state.

Similarly, private broadcasts and telecasts attacking or libeling foreign governments must not be regarded as creating state responsibility, unless the offensive statements emanated over a government-owned or controlled station or system. In the latter case, such as statements made through a station operated as part of the Voice of America network, government responsibility would have been created.

Problems of Controls. The problem of imposing reasonable controls over international propaganda activities is such a serious one that further investigation, followed by eventual action through the medium of multilateral conventions, appears to be highly desirable. Yet the obvious difficulties in the way of achieving such controls are of a nature calculated to make any international body hesitate at making even a modest beginning in this task. Despite the vast literature already available on the subject,[30] little has been achieved on the action level: although a number of agreements have been concluded, they have not produced even an approximation of regional law. As long as ideological divisions split the nations of the world into contending groups, little hope can be held out for any rational and workable control system. The most one can hope for at present is that in the non-Communist world a reciprocal obligation to control, or even to ban, subversive propaganda aimed at other members of this grouping may be worked out and accepted by the states concerned.

---

[30] See, *inter alia*, the valuable bibliographical material in John B. Whitton, "Radio Propaganda—A Modest Proposal," 52 *A.J.I.L.* (1958), pp. 739–745; the article also provides a convenient summary of past attempts at control. See also his "An International Right of Reply," *ibid.*, 44 (1950), pp. 141–145. A most valuable collection of recent materials is found in Whiteman, Vol. XIII, pp. 903–1068.

OTHER DUTIES OF STATES

A second duty of states, generally accepted in theory but all too often violated in practice, is the obligation to refrain from fomenting civil strife in the territory of another state and to prevent the organization within its own territory of activities calculated to produce such civil strife. This duty has already been discussed in connection with the duty of nonintervention, even though the Draft Convention on the Rights and Duties of States, of the International Law Commission, lists it as a separate item.

Thirdly, every state has a duty to make certain that conditions prevailing in its territory do not menace international peace. This duty developed by the International Law Commission from a portion of the Panamanian draft of the convention just mentioned, needs little comment. Several of its aspects were touched on in the discussion of intervention, such as the example of conditions in northern Mexico in 1915–17. It would appear to be a reasonable corollary to the concept of national sovereignty, with each state presumably possessed of exclusive authority in its territory, that such authority be wielded in an effective manner to prevent any danger to neighboring states. If a state fails to maintain a degree of control sufficient to prevent such danger to its neighbors, then it is obligated to assume responsibility for the consequences of its failure as a sovereign government.

A fourth duty, technically applicable only to the members of the United Nations under Article 2 (3) of the Charter, is an obligation to settle international disputes by peaceful means. Because the Charter as a treaty is not binding on nonmembers of the Organization, countries which do not belong to the United Nations appear to be entitled in law to adopt forcible measures to settle disputes among themselves, either *ab initio* or after a failure of peaceful methods. On the other hand, the record since 1945 shows that members of the United Nations too have resorted to force outside the permissible condition of self-defense.

Corollary to the fourth duty is an asserted fifth one, a duty to abstain from resort to war as an instrument of national policy and to refrain from the threat of the use of force against another state. This alleged duty depends obviously on the interpretation adopted of the status of war under current international law. Support of this fifth duty negates one of the traditional characteristics or rights of a sovereign state, the right to go to war when other methods of obtaining justice, of satisfying claims on another state, of achieving presumably essential or vital national goals have failed. In view of the debatable nature of this fifth duty of states, discussion of its validity will be found in Chapter 25.

A sixth duty, again applicable to all members of the United Nations, is to refrain from giving assistance to any state against which the United

Nations is taking preventive or enforcement action. This duty is merely a restatement of Article 2 (5) of the Charter. A highly interesting aspect of this obligation is its nonapplicability to states which are not members of the United Nations. If, for instance, the latter Organization had approved an enforcement action of a military nature against one of its members, a nonmember would still be free to come to the assistance of that member.

A seventh duty, apparently under Article 2 (4) of the Charter, only binding on the member states of the United Nations, is to abstain from recognizing any territorial acquisitions made by a state acting in violation of the provisions of the Charter. This appears to be a restatement of the old Stimson Doctrine. Unfortunately, this duty has not always been observed by the members of the Organization. Instances such as Indian aggression against Hyderabad and, in 1961, against Portuguese enclaves in India; Chinese acquisitions of Burmese and Indian territories as well as of Tibet; and India's seizure of portions of Kashmir, come to mind.[31]

Again, there exists a duty for all states to carry out in good faith the obligations arising out of treaties and other sources of international law, and no state may invoke provisions in its constitution or laws as an excuse for failure to carry out this duty.

As will be discussed later, one of the oldest principles of international law is the doctrine of *pacta sunt servanda* (treaties must be observed), even though differences of opinion exist as to the absolute nature of the rule and as to possible conditions under which it could be set aside lawfully. The duty of honoring obligations in good faith represents an essential and basic condition for a legal order and there can be no doubt as to the existence of such a duty, even though its scope may be the subject of varying interpretations.

A ninth duty, frequently asserted, of every state is that of conducting its relations with other countries in accordance with international law. This, like the preceding duty, represents a basic condition for the existence of a legal order. Although compliance in every case cannot be expected, the basic duty is undeniable and is a binding obligation or duty of every state.

A tenth duty, of quite modern origin, is an obligation on the part of a state to see to it that no acts are performed in its jurisdiction that in some manner pollute the waters or the air of a neighboring state. As yet little treaty law exists on this subject but "general principles of justice" would appear to indicate the existence of such a duty. This belief is bolstered

---

[31] See Quincy Wright, "The Goa Incident," 56 *A.J.I.L.* (1962), pp. 617–632, as well as Whiteman, Vol. II, pp. 1140–1145; Clyde Eagleton, "The Case of Hyderabad before the Security Council," 44 *A.J.I.L.* (1950), pp. 277–302; the pre-UN analysis by James W. Garner, "Non-Recognition of Illegal Territorial Annexation and Claims to Sovereignty," *ibid.*, 30 (1936), pp. 679–688; Herbert W. Briggs, "Non-Recognition of Title by Conquest and Limitations of the Doctrine," *Proceedings* (1940), pp. 72–89.

by the conclusion of a number of bilateral agreements going back to 1909 when a treaty between the United States and Great Britain, dealing with Canadian-American boundary waters, provided that neither country in question would permit the pollution of such waters to the injury of the health or property of the other. This agreement led to the submission, in 1928, to an International Joint Commission, of a claim on the part of the United States that damage was caused to the State of Washington by the fumes originating from a smelter located in British Columbia. When the United States refused to accept the decision of the Commission, the dispute was referred to arbitration under a 1935 treaty. The United States was then awarded the arbitral decision in March, 1941.[32] It is interesting to note that the Arbitration Tribunal asserted that under the principles of international law no state had the right to use or to permit the use of its territory in such a manner as to cause injury by fumes in or to the territory of another state or the property or persons therein, and also that the Dominion of Canada was responsible in international law for the conduct of the Trail Smelter.

Recent oil tanker wrecks (the *Torrey Canyon* off the English coast and the *Ocean Eagle* at the entrance to San Juan Harbor, Puerto Rico) that have caused heavy property losses indicate the need for further international regulation of pollution. Such agreements as the 1954 Convention for the Prevention of the Pollution of the Seas by Oil, even though amended in 1962, do not appear to go far enough to assure adequate protection against pollution.[33]

Related to the question of state responsibility for such "nuisance damage" caused by smoke, fumes, and water pollution is the problem of responsibility for the fall-out and other by-products of testing nuclear devices.

An eleventh obligation of states centers on a duty to prevent the counterfeiting, within their jurisdiction, of the coins, currencies, postage stamps, and securities of another state.[34] Even when given states have not adhered to international conventions prohibiting such practices, they tend to regard it as their obligation to prevent counterfeiting by passing ap-

[32] See Hackworth, Vol. II, pp. 344–346; the award of the tribunal in the *Trail Smelter Arbitration* (*U.S.–Canada*), of March 11, 1941, was reprinted in full in 35 *A.J.I.L.* (1941), pp. 684–736. Consult also A. P. Lester, "River Pollution in International Law," 51 *A.J.I.L.* (1963), pp. 828–853; Whiteman, Vol. VI, pp. 253–268, 276.

[33] See Abel Wolman, "Pollution as an International Issue," 47 *Foreign Affairs* (1968), pp. 164–175; Robert Rienow, "The Oil Around Us," *The New York Times Magazine* (June 4, 1967), pp. 24 ff.; Tung, p. 186; the extremely valuable *Comment* on "Oil Pollution of the Sea," 10 *Harvard International Law Jl.* (1969), pp. 316–359; and the collection of documents on pollution problems in 8 *International Legal Materials* (1969), pp. 453–477, 497–501, 627–628.

[34] See Whiteman, Vol. VI, pp. 268–275; Hackworth, Vol. II, pp. 350–354; and the two classic cases of *Emperor of Austria and King of Hungary* v. *Day and Kossuth*, 1861, abstracted in Chapter 9, above, and *United States* v. *Arjona*, United States, Supreme Court, 1887, 120 U.S. 479.

propriate domestic legislation. However, just as in the case of practically all other state duties, the advent of a state of war cancels the duty in question insofar as it applies toward enemy states. In World War II, Germany counterfeited British £5 notes, whereas Great Britain counterfeited German postage stamps in order to expedite the mailing of propaganda postcards addressed to random samplings of German citizens in cities bombed by the Royal Air Force. Excellent imitations of German official mailbags filled with such stamped and addressed cards were dropped from planes in the hope that German citizens, believing the bags to have been lost from mail trucks during the confusion of a bombing attack, would turn them in to the nearest post office for dispatch to the addressees.

Many writers, as well as the International Law Commission, have asserted that there exists a twelfth duty, requiring each state to treat all persons in its jurisdiction with respect for their human rights and fundamental freedoms, without distinction as to race, sex, language, or religion. This duty cannot, however, be admitted as yet to exist on a general basis, no matter how admirable it may be from a moral point of view. The undoubted drastic degree of intervention in essentially domestic affairs of states involved in the application of this duty gives rise to this doubt as to the existence of the duty itself. It may well be that at some future time it may be accepted by the majority of the members of the community of nations and may be implemented by appropriate domestic legislation. But even granting such internal compliance with the duty, the question of the enforcement of such implementation will have to be met affirmatively before it can be maintained seriously that this asserted duty is in effect and consequential in nature.

Hence one of the most controversial subjects in the general area of intervention is the assertion of illegal intervention (unarmed and nonsubversive) by the United Nations in the internal affairs of member and nonmember states.[35] It has been charged that a number of recent UN policies, particularly in the spheres of human rights and in the Rhodesian situation, represent violations of Article 2 (7) of the Charter.

In the case of Rhodesia, a unilateral declaration of independence (UDI), proclaimed in the colony on November 11, 1965, climaxed four years of growing dispute between the white minority of Rhodesia and the United Kingdom. The General Assembly condemned UDI and the British Government denounced it as treason and rebellion. The Security Council then also condemned UDI and called on all member states to deny recognition to the new government; after a few days, it urged all members to break off all economic relations with Rhodesia. Subsequent Security Council resolutions reaffirmed the policies previously adopted. These

---

[35] See R. Blanpain, "The Meaning of the Term 'Intervene' in Article 2, par. 7," 5 *Tijdschrift* (1958), pp. 348–365; Quincy Wright, "Domestic Jurisdiction as a Limit on National and Supra-National Action," 56 *Northwestern University Law Review* (March-April, 1961), pp. 11–40.

United Nations actions were justified by the charge that Rhodesia's uni-lateral acts constituted a threat to the peace.[36] In essence, of course, the measures adopted by the Security Council represented the view that racial discrimination in a given state represented a threat to the general peace of a continent or of the world—a doctrine with far-reaching im-plications for many countries and one of somewhat doubtful validity.[37]

Similarly, the Republic of South Africa has been condemned in resolu-tions adopted in the General Assembly and the Security Council (GA Res. 2202–XXI of December 16, 1966, and several others) for its racial policies,[38] and its prison system was subject to severe criticism by a study group of the United Nations Commission on Human Rights.[39]

Last but not least in this connection should be mentioned a series of General Assembly declarations dealing with the granting of independence to colonial peoples, such as the Declaration on the Granting of Independ-ence to Colonial Countries and Peoples (GA Res. 1514–XV–December 14, 1960) and subsequent reaffirmations of the contents of those docu-ments by the Assembly.

Laudable as all such policies on the part of the United Nations agencies undoubtedly appear from a moral as well as a humanitarian point of view, they all do raise serious questions about the lawfulness of the intervention in the domestic affairs of independent states implied in the very subject matter of those policies.

Finally, an obligation to permit foreign states to bring suit in one's own courts has been said to exist. This concept could, of course, be turned around and phrased as a "right" of a recognized state to bring suit in the courts of a friendly foreign power. In actuality, this obligation is not a duty at all but represents another instance of international comity or courtesy.

SUGGESTED READINGS

DUTIES OF STATES

Whiteman, Vol. V, pp. 321–332; Richard A. Falk, "The United States and the Doctrine of Non-Intervention in the Internal Affairs of Independent States,"

---

[36] See texts of relevant GA and SC resolutions in 60 *A.J.I.L.* (1966), Supp., pp. 91–926; *ibid.*, 61 (1967), Supp., pp. 652–655; *ibid.*, 62 (1968), Supp., pp. 965–969.

[37] Consult Myres S. McDougal and W. Michaël Reisman, "Rhodesia and the United Nations: The Lawfulness of International Concern," 62 *A.J.I.L.* (1968), pp. 1–19, Charles G. Fenwick, "When Is There a Threat to the Peace?—Rhodesia," *ibid.*, 61 (1967), pp. 753–755, for contrasting views on the subject.

[38] Consult John Carey, ed., *Race, Peace, Law, and South Africa* (Dobbs Ferry, N.Y.: Oceana Publications, 1968), as well as Whiteman, Vol. V, pp. 336–346, 364–377; see also 8 *International Legal Materials* (1969), pp. 441–443, for text of General As-sembly resolution 2426 (XXIII), of December 18, 1968, on withholding assistance to Portugal and South Africa.

[39] See *The New York Times*, January 21, 1968, p. 2, for details.

Howard Law Journal (June, 1959), pp. 163–189; Manuel R. García-Mora, *International Responsibility for Hostile Acts of Private Persons Against Foreign States* (The Hague: Martinus Nijhoff, 1962); L. John Martin, *International Propaganda: Its Legal and Diplomatic Control* (Minneapolis: University of Minnesota Press, 1958); Urban G. Whitaker, Jr., ed., *Propaganda and International Relations* (San Francisco: Howard Chandler, 1960); Louis Henkins, "Force, Intervention, and Neutrality in Contemporary International Law," *Proceedings* (1963), pp. 147–162; Quincy Wright, "Is Discussion Intervention?" 50 *A.J.I.L.* (1956), pp. 102–110; F. V. Garcia Amador, " 'Internal Violence' and the Inter-American System," *Proceedings* (1966), pp. 67–74.

THE CONFLICT IN VIETNAM

Consult, *inter alia*, Marvin E. Gettleman, ed., *Vietnam: History, Documents, and Opinions on a Major World Crisis* (Greenwich, Conn.: Fawcett Publications, 1965); Robert Shaplen, *The Lost Revolution* (New York: Harper & Row, 1965); the invaluable and thoroughly documented collection by Richard A. Falk, ed., *The Vietnam War and International Law* [Sponsored by the American Society of International Law] (Princeton, N.J.: Princeton University Press, 1968); Richard A. Falk, "The International Regulation of Internal Violence in the Developing Countries," *Proceedings* (1966), pp. 58–67; Quincy Wright, "Legal Aspects of the Viet-nam Situation," 60 *A.J.I.L.* (1966), pp. 750–769; Wolfgang Friedman, "Intervention, Civil War and the Rôle of International Law," *Proceedings* (1965), pp. 67–75; Dean Rusk, Address before the American Society of International Law, April 23, 1965, excerpted at length in 58 *U.S. News & World Report* (May 10, 1965), pp. 74–77; and the full-page advertisement of the "Lawyers Committee on American Policy Towards Vietnam," *The New York Times*, January 15, 1967, p. E-9.

INTERVENTION IN CIVIL STRIFE

Whiteman, Vol. V, pp. 250–257, 276–281; James N. Rosenau, ed., *International Aspects of Civil Strife* (Princeton, N.J.: Princeton University Press, 1964); Richard W. Cottam, *Competitive Interference and 20th Century Diplomacy* (Pittsburgh: University of Pittsburgh Press, 1967); Linda B. Miller, *World Order and Local Disorder: The United Nations and Internal Conflicts* (Princeton, N.J.: Princeton University Press, 1967); Quincy Wright, "International Law and Civil Strife," *Proceedings* (1953), pp. 145–153, and his "International Law and the American Civil War," *ibid.* (1967), pp. 50–58; William E. Kane, "American Involvement in Latin American Civil Strife," *ibid.*, pp. 58–69; Richard J. Barnet, "United States Involvement in Foreign Civil Strife since World War II," *ibid.*, pp. 69–75; Donald W. McNemar, "The Post-Independence War in the Congo," *ibid.* (1967), pp. 13–18, particularly concerning Soviet Union assistance to the Congolese government; and Whiteman, Vol. V, pp. 522–534.

INTERVENTION IN THE DOMINICAN REPUBLIC

John B. Martin, *Overtaken by Events: The Dominican Crisis from the Fall of Trujillo to the Civil War* (Garden City, N.Y.: Doubleday & Co., 1966); John

Carey, ed., *The Dominican Republic Crisis of 1965* (Dobbs Ferry, N.Y.: Oceana Publications, 1967); *Dominican Action—1965: Intervention or Cooperation?* (Washington, D.C.: Center for Strategic Studies, Georgetown University, 1966); Charles G. Fenwick, "The Dominican Republic: Intervention or Collective Self-Defense?" 60 *A.J.I.L.* (1966), pp. 64–67, and its critique by R. T. Bohan, "The Dominican Case: Unilateral Intervention," *ibid.*, pp. 809–812; John N. Plank, "The Caribbean: Intervention, When and How," 44 *Foreign Affairs* (1965), pp. 37–48; and *The New York Times*, May 2, 1965, pp. 1, 3, 4; May 9, 1965, p. E-3; December 5, 1965, p. 20; June 12, 1966, p. E-3.

Case

Flota Mercante Dominicana, C. por A., v. *American Manufacturers Mutual Insurance,* United States, District Court, S.D.N.Y., 1967, 272 F. Supp. 540, reported in 62 *A.J.I.L.* (1968), pp. 501–502.

SUBVERSIVE INTERVENTION

Clark C. Havighurst, ed., *International Control of Propaganda* (Dobbs Ferry, N.Y.: Oceana Publications, 1967), a reprint of the contents of 31 *Law and Contemporary Problems* (Summer, 1966); B. S. Murty, *Propaganda and World Public Order: The Legal Regulation of the Ideological Instrument of Coercion* (New Haven: Yale University Press, 1968); Whiteman, Vol. V, pp. 257–275, 455–459, 837–843; John B. Whitton and Arthur Larson, *Propaganda* (Dobbs Ferry, N.Y.: Oceana Publications, 1964); C. A. Siepmann, "Propaganda and Information in International Affairs," 55 *Yale Law Journal* (1946), pp. 1258–1280; and John B. Whitton, "Cold War Propaganda," 45 *A.J.I.L.* (1951), pp. 151–153.

RHODESIAN QUESTION

Charles B. Marshall, *Crisis over Rhodesia* (Baltimore: The Johns Hopkins Press, 1967); U.S. Regulations relating to trade with Rhodesia, in 63 *A.J.I.L.* (1969), pp. 128–131, and in 7 *International Legal Materials* (1968), pp. 1088–1098.

PART III
The Law and the Individual

II

Individuals Under the Law

THE INDIVIDUAL: FROM OBJECT TO SUBJECT

PRIOR to the twentieth century, a virtually universal belief prevailed, to the effect that the treatment of its citizenry by a state fell outside the province of international law since the individual, alone or collectively, was merely an object and not a subject of the law of nations.

Since World War I, however, the community of nations has become increasingly aware of the need to safeguard minimal rights of the individual. In consequence, human rights have become a subject of vital and at times acrimonious concern to the traditional subjects of international law, and the individual himself has begun to emerge, to some extent at least, as a subject of that law.

RESTRICTIONS ON THE JURISDICTION OF STATES
OVER THEIR NATIONALS

The end of the Thirty Years' War marked the appearance of treaty provisions stipulating the guarantee of certain privileges to minorities within the populations of given states. Originally these rights of minorities were limited to matters in the religious sphere, a practice traceable down to the latter part of the nineteenth century (Treaty of Berlin, 1878, and other agreements).

The numerous changes in territorial ownership occurring after World War I pointed up the need for an expansion of the rights guaranteed to minorities, particularly because of the growth of nationalistic sentiments and the very real danger of suppression and oppression faced by racial, ethnic, linguistic, as well as by religious minorities. In consequence, the Principal Allied and Associated Powers concluded a number of treaties with such countries as Czechoslovakia, Austria, Greece, Bulgaria, Hungary, Poland, Turkey, Romania, and Jugoslavia, in which those states promised just and equal treatment of their minority groups.[1]

Sometime later, similar guarantees were given by Albania, Estonia, Iraq, Latvia, and Lithuania, as conditions of their admission to the League of Nations. Unlike the earlier guarantees, however, these subsequent grants

---

[1] For details, consult Marek St. Korowicz, *Introduction to International Law* (The Hague: Martinus Nijhoff, 1959), pp. 533-534, 552-558.

of rights to minorities took the form of unilateral declarations on the part of the countries in question. In turn, legal obligation was created for those declarations by various resolutions adopted by the Council of the League.

Minorities Clauses. In order to insure observance of the various rights guaranteed to minorities, the affected sovereign states acknowledged the "minorities clauses" to constitute "fundamental laws" and agreed that the clauses were "placed under the guarantee of the League of Nations" and would not be altered without the consent of a majority of the Council of the League. The League, in turn, worked out a definitive procedure to be adopted in dealing with any questions arising under the clauses in question.

All this looked fine on paper, but trouble appeared as soon as implementation became an issue. Regardless of the motives which had inspired acquiescence in the guarantees extended to minorities, the governments in question all too soon shared a growing conviction that the guarantees represented intolerable intrusion into the domestic jurisdictions of sovereign states. The Permanent Court of International Justice had to point out again and again that mere laws were not enough, that the prohibitions laid down in the minorities clauses had to operate in fact, and that a law supposedly general in its effects but actually discriminating against minorities and their members constituted a violation of treaty obligations.[2]

During World War II the necessity of promoting and preserving human freedoms and rights was affirmed in such statements as the Atlantic Charter (August 14, 1941), the Declaration by the (wartime) United Nations (January 1, 1942), and the Teheran Declaration (December 1, 1943). After the war, no provision for the protection of minorities were included in the various peace treaties except, on a most limited basis, in the Italian Treaty (Annex N, par. 1) and in the Austrian State Treaty (Art. 7). On the other hand, such treaties, with the exception of the one concluded in 1951 with Japan, provided for the granting of *human rights and freedoms to individuals* by Bulgaria, Finland, Hungary, Italy, and Romania, and these requirements were also incorporated in the 1955 Austrian instrument.

UN EMPHASIS ON HUMAN RIGHTS [3]

UN Charter. The interest in the subject of human rights, arising sporadically in the United Nations beginning with the founding Conference

---

[2] See Advisory Opinion relating to *German Settlers in Poland*, Ser. B, No. 6; Advisory Opinion on the *Treatment of Polish Nationals in Danzig*, Ser. A/B, No. 44; Advisory Opinion on *Minority Schools in Albania*, Ser. A/B, No. 64.

[3] One of the best brief guides to the efforts on behalf of human rights since 1945 is William Korey's "The Key to Human Rights—Implementation," *International Conciliation*, No. 570 (November, 1968), pp. 5–70; consult also the suggestive and valuable Evan Luard, ed., *The International Protection of Human Rights* (New York: Praeger, 1967) and Asbjorn Eide and August Schou, eds., *International Protection of Human Rights* (New York: Wiley & Sons, 1968).

of San Francisco in 1945, has been characteristic of a modern disposition to enlarge the concept of what is legitimately of international interest or concern. The Charter of the United Nations asserts in the sweeping terms of its Preamble that the members are "determined . . . to reaffirm faith in fundamental human rights, in the dignity and worth of the human person, in the equal rights of men and women. . . ." Article 1 of the Charter lists, among the purposes of the Organization, the "promoting and encouraging [of] respect for human rights and for fundamental freedoms for all without distinction as to race, sex, language, or religion." Article 13 assigns to the General Assembly the task of initiating and making recommendations directed to the accomplishment of these purposes. Article 55(c) commits the United Nations to promote "universal respect for, and observance of, human rights and fundamental freedoms." Article 62 directs the Economic and Social Council to make recommendations in pursuance of Article 55(c), while Article 68 sets up a commission for the "promotion of human rights."

This multitude of provisions did not spell out, however, any bill of human rights, beyond mentioning discrimination, nor did it command members to enact and enforce appropriate domestic legislation. In fact, no sanctions or enforcement machinery was set up. Only Article 56 represented a pledge by all member states to take joint and separate action to achieve the purposes outlined in Article 55.

It should be remembered also that Article 2 (7) of the Charter denied authority to the United Nations "to intervene in matters which are essentially within the domestic jurisdiction of any state. . . ." This explicit prohibition appeared to limit rigorously the rights of the Organization to deal with alleged violations of human rights beyond *discussion* in the General Assembly and *recommendations* with regard to such violations. Furthermore, it appeared that if any member state heeded such recommendations and acted on them against a state accused of violating human rights, a charge of illegal intervention in the internal affairs of a sovereign state could be lodged properly. The General Assembly, it should be noted, did engage in such discussion on numerous occasions. (*Inter alia*: in 1949 and 1950, accusations against Bulgaria, Hungary and Romania; from 1952 to date, violations of human rights charged against South Africa; in 1959, discussion of Chinese actions in Tibet; and in recent years, discussion of South African actions in Namibia—formerly known as South-West Africa.) [4]

In order to achieve positive protection of human rights, the Economic and Social Council (hereinafter abbreviated as ECOSOC) proceeded as early as 1946 with an effort to produce multilateral conventions through

[4] Consult Thomas Buergenthal, "The United Nations and the Development of Rules Relative to Human Rights," *Proceedings* (1965), pp. 132–136; Myres S. McDougal and Gerhard Bebr, "Human Rights in the United Nations," 58 *A.J.I.L.* (1964), pp. 603–641.

a Commission on Human Rights as a drafting body. The obvious by-product of such an endeavor, if successful, would be the achievement of the shift of the individual into the position of a partial subject of inter-national law.

Ultimately, on December 10, 1948, the General Assembly approved the "Universal Declaration of Human Rights," with no opposition but with eight abstentions, (the Soviet bloc, Jugoslavia, Saudi Arabia, and South Africa).[5] This document of thirty articles, containing a detailed list of personal, civil, political, and social rights "as a common standard of achievement for all peoples and all nations," nevertheless had to be judged to be vague and even ambiguous in parts. Being merely a declara-tion, it possessed no legally binding force, being comparable in this re-spect to the hortatory clauses found in some of the older state constitu-tions in the United States. Legal obligations could be created only through the ratification by member states of some convention on human rights, not by a voting consensus of the General Assembly. Furthermore, Article 22 of the Declaration recognized the fact that the realization of the rights in question had to be in accordance with the organization and resources of each state.

On the other hand, the Declaration had to be considered as an exposi-tory interpretation of the very general human rights provisions of the Charter, and those provisions represented, at least in theory, *binding* obligations on all member states. The Declaration should, therefore, be viewed as marking a definite advance toward the ultimate realization of human rights on a global basis and as somewhat distinct from other declarations adopted by the General Assembly.[6]

The next step involved the creation of draft treaties (styled Human Rights Covenants) for eventual ratification by states. It is interesting, however, that a number of states proceeded at once to include selected portions of the Universal Declaration into their domestic law, and that certain international agreements incorporated all of the rights cited in the Declaration.[7]

The Commission on Human Rights proposed at first a single instru-ment, covering all aspects of such rights, but such an omnibus covenant encountered sufficient opposition in the General Assembly that several

[5] Text in *Yearbook of the United Nations, 1948–1949*, at pp. 535–537, and in many other readily available sources; consult also P. Hassan, "The Word 'Arbitrary' as Used in the Universal Declaration of Human Rights: 'Illegal' or 'Unjust'?" 10 *Har-vard International Law Jl.* (1969), pp. 225–262.

[6] See also Egon Schwelb, "The Influence of the Universal Declaration of Human Rights on International and National Law," *Proceedings* (1959), pp. 217–229.

[7] See Government of the French Republic—Algerian National Liberation Front, *Declarations Concerning Algeria*, Evian, March 19, 1962: "Declaration of Guaran-tees," Part II, Chapter II, Article 2, and Part III, Article 3 (a); and "Declaration of Principles Concerning Military Questions," Annex, Article 31. Texts to be found in 57 *A.J.I.L.* (1963), at pp. 723, 727, and 748.

instruments were produced subsequently: the International Covenant on Civil and Political Rights, the International Covenant on Economic, Social and Cultural Rights, and the Optional Protocol to the Covenant on Civil and Political Rights. Although initial drafts were completed in 1954, bitter disagreements about contents and enforcement provisions in both the General Assembly and its Third Committee resulted in delay and in considerable redrafting. Finally all three instruments were adopted unanimously by the General Assembly on December 16, 1966; they represented, in effect, the achievement of the "international bill of rights" contemplated by the Assembly when it adopted the Universal Declaration in 1948.[8]

Covenant on Civil and Political Rights. The Covenant on Civil and Political Rights guarantees freedom of religious expression, peaceful assemblage, and movement. It prohibits inhuman treatment as well as arbitrary arrest or detention, asserts a right to life and to a fair trial, and provides for the protection of all varieties of minorities. Under the provisions of the "Optional Protocol," individuals as well as groups are granted the right to appeal to a Human Rights Committee consisting of eighteen members. As of July 31, 1968, twenty-six states had signed the Covenant and fourteen had signed the Optional Protocol. No ratification or accession had been recorded, however, by that time.

Covenant on Economic, Social, and Cultural Rights. The Covenant on Economic, Social, and Cultural Rights embraces the right to work, education, medical care, and related economic and social benefits. By July 31, 1968, twenty-eight states had signed this covenant, but no ratifications or accessions were on record.

Both covenants, oddly enough, assert the right of self-determination and of national sovereignty over natural resources (Articles 1 and 2 in each instrument). Each agreement is to be binding, at once, on any state ratifying it. Neither agreement contains provisions for effective enforcement in the event of the violation of any of its guarantees. Only public opinion could therefore be envisaged as a sanction, as matters stand at the time of writing.

In commemoration of the twentieth anniversary of the Universal Declaration, the General Assembly had, in 1963, designated 1968 as "International Year for Human Rights." The focal point of the anniversary celebration was an International Conference on Human Rights, held at Teheran from April 22 to May 13, attended by delegates from eighty-four states as well as by representatives of the United Nations and intergovernmental as well as nongovernmental organizations.

The Conference adopted twenty-six resolutions dealing with aspects of human rights, but not a single resolution dealt wholly (or effectively, in the view of this writer) with machinery implementing the rights discussed or advocated. The one really farsighted document adopted at the

[8] Texts of the three instruments reprinted in 61 *A.J.I.L.* (1967), pp. 861–890.

meeting was Resolution XXIII ("Human Rights in Armed Conflicts"), requesting the General Assembly to invite the Secretary-General to study ways and means by which the legal rules governing warfare could be revised and adopted to take cognizance of new developments in the conduct of hostilities.

Other draft instruments in the sphere of human rights adopted by the General Assembly also tended to transform the individual into a partial subject of international law. Thus the International Convention on the Elimination of All Forms of Racial Discrimination, adopted unanimously in 1965, represented a detailed prohibition of most objectionable discriminatory practices, with nine articles devoted to implementation.[9] That instrument entered into force on January 4, 1969; as of April 21, 1969, thirty-four states (not including the U.S.) had ratified the convention.

In 1967 the General Assembly passsed overwhelmingly a resolution on measures for the speedy implementation of prohibitions of racial discrimination and urged early ratification and implementation of the Racial Discrimination instrument and related agreements.[10] At the same session, the Assembly also adopted a Declaration on the Elimination of Discrimination against Women[11] and a Declaration on Territorial Asylum.[12]

As to the former, a multitude of unsolved problems prevented the drafting of a really meaningful and inclusive convention; these problems centered in part on the existence of social attitudes difficult to eradicate by an international convention to be implemented by domestic legislation. (See p. 421 on executory and self-executing treaties.) As for the Declaration on Territorial Asylum, difficulties arose at once over a laudable effort on the part of the delegations to create some form of balance between the rights of an individual, on the one hand, and the sovereign rights of a state, on the other. Some of the objections voiced initially were overcome by a revised wording of the Declaration, such as by the exclusion from asylum of individuals charged with war crimes, crimes against humanity, and crimes against peace. (See Chapter 32.) A major step toward agreement was reached when the evaluation of the reasons for granting asylum was left with the granting state itself. But so many delicate issues remained either unstated or were laid down in ambiguous wording that a draft convention on the subject is not likely to come into being very soon.

Related instruments recently under consideration by the Third Committee of the General Assembly include a draft declaration and draft convention on the Elimination of All Forms of Religious Intolerance,

[9] GA Res. 2106 (XX), Dec. 21, 1965; see also S. Oda in *Manual*, at pp. 502–503, and *The New York Times*, Dec. 22, 1965, pp. 1, 13; text in 5 *International Legal Materials* (1966), p. 350.

[10] GA Res. 2332 (XXII), December 18, 1967.

[11] GA Res. 2263 (XXII), November 7, 1967.

[12] GA Res. 2312 (XXII), December 14, 1967.

and a draft convention on the Non-Applicability of Statutory Limitations on War Crimes and Crimes Against Humanity (see Chapter 32).

The major weakness of virtually all recent UN instruments dealing with human (and therefore individual) rights lies in the sphere of implementation. Most governments appear to view with mixed feelings the growth of the doctrine that, under certain explicit conditions, individuals may be, and should be, considered to be subjects of international law. Some, such as the Soviet Union, even insist that no individual may claim UN protection against his own state: it is asserted that United Nations jurisdiction in the sphere of human rights is limited to the prevention of danger to peace and that this means discrimination against an entire racial group, such as in the instance of South Africa's *apartheid*. Ratification of a human rights covenant is viewed by many states as somewhat dangerous even without the presence of effective implementation provisions. If the latter were to be provided, then reluctance might easily change to unwillingness to participate in the effort to promote human rights.[13] Some commentators have even expressed the view that the continued production of nonimplemented conventions on human rights has harmed the United Nations and ECOSOC.

Nevertheless, if and when human rights covenants, together with implementing provisions or protocols, have come into force through governmental ratification or adherence, the individual will have become, under specified conditions, a subject of international law, enjoying qualified but real rights under that law.[14]

Regional Agencies: Europe. Before leaving this subject, brief attention must be paid to regional efforts in the sphere of human rights and freedoms. Perhaps more important, in the short run, than the activities of the United Nations has been a relatively early European attempt to protect human rights: in 1953 there entered into force the European Convention for the Protection of Human Rights and Fundamental Freedoms, signed at Rome in 1950.[15] Fifteen states have now been obligated through their ratifications to submit designated types of human rights disputes among themselves to binding decisions of an international agency. And two

---

[13] See, *inter alia*, William Korey, "Human Rights Treaties: Why Is the U.S. Stalling?" 45 *Foreign Affairs* (1967), pp. 414-424; Clarence C. Ferguson, Jr., "The United Nations Human Rights Covenants: Problems of Ratification and Implementation," *Proceedings* (1968), pp. 83-96.

[14] A running account of the progress in the codification of human rights may be found in the past issues for September of each year of *International Conciliation*, devoted in each case to the issues before the next session of the General Assembly; see also 1 *The International Lawyer* (July, 1967), pp. 589-600, for texts of other UN Human Rights Conventions, such as those on slavery (1956), forced labor (1957), and on the political rights of women (1953).

[15] Text in 45 *A.J.I.L.* (1951), Supp., pp. 24-39; see also discussion of the convention in *Manual*, pp. 503-505; Gordon L. Weil, "The Evolution of the European Convention on Human Rights," *ibid.*, 57 (1963), pp. 804-827.

thirds of the states concerned have gone further and have granted to private associations as well as to individuals a right to file complaints.

Initially, complaints are received and investigated by a European Commission on Human Rights, consisting of one member from each of the ratifying states. If a complaint is found admissible, a subcommission hears the complaint, with a view of negotiating a friendly solution. To be sure, only a tiny fraction of all complaints have thus far been found admissible: a majority has had to be rejected because the state in question had not been among those permitting the filing of complaints by individuals or because local remedies had not been exhausted by complainants, among other reasons.

If the subcommission fails to achieve a satisfactory settlement, the full commission normally reviews the complaint for a finding of fact and an opinion on the merits, both of which are then sent to the Committee of Ministers of the Council of Europe which is empowered to hand down a binding decision by a two-thirds vote. For those states which have ratified an optional protocol conferring jurisdiction on the European Court of Human Rights, a binding decision will be issued by that court.[16] The latter consists of eighteen judges elected by the Assembly of the Council of Europe, one from each member state of the Council. Noncompliance with a decision of the Court entails at most adverse publicity, because no enforcement machinery has been provided in the basic convention or in the optional protocol. In the event of a refusal to carry out a human rights decision handed down by the Committee of Ministers, enforcement measures appear to be limited to publicity and possibly to expulsion from the Council of Europe under the provisions of Article 8 of its Statute.

It should be pointed out that the Convention on Human Rights has been, thus far, more effective than many jurists had anticipated. Several relatively significant cases were rendered innocuous when the states involved quickly changed relevant legislation in anticipation of an unfavorable decision by the Court. Individuals also have benefited by being given comprehensive procedural protection before the Court in such matters as the right to counsel, private hearings, and so on.

Regional Agencies: Latin America. The Eighth Conference of American States, meeting at Lima in 1938, approved a declaration (XXXVI) condemning persecution of individuals or groups for racial or religious motives, while at the same time denying (Resolution XXVII) the rightfulness of any racial or religious group to claim the status of a minority.[17]

By the spring of 1948, however, concern about human rights and their protection led to the adoption, at the Ninth Conference of American

[16] No individual may file a complaint directly with the Committee or with the Court; all complaints have to be channeled through the Commission on Human Rights.

[17] See texts in 34 *A.J.I.L.* (1940), Supp., at pp. 198–199.

States, of Resolution XXX, the American Declaration of the Duties of Man.[18] This document contained no enforcemer but listed in great detail the rights in question. Articles duties which, however, in a number of instances really represe. tional rights rather than duties *per se*.

In 1959, the Fifth Meeting of Consultation of Ministers of Foreign Affairs, at Santiago, Chile, created the Inter-American Commission on Human Rights, to promote respect for such rights.[19] The functions of this body were expanded in November, 1965, at the Second Special Inter-American Conference at Rio de Janeiro through Resolution XXII.[20] But this enlargement was limited in essence to setting up an information and reporting service for the Commission; again no true *enforcement* machinery had been created.

Concurrently, slow progress was recorded in the elaboration of a proposed Inter-American Convention on Human Rights. The draft under consideration at the time of writing, a rather lengthy document, appears to have been modeled on the European human rights instruments, particularly as far as the functions of a future Commission for the Protection of Human Rights are concerned.[21]

OTHER EFFORTS TO CHANGE THE STATUS OF THE INDIVIDUAL

Responsibility of the individual established by rules of general international law or by treaty exists today in many spheres: piracy, breach of blockade, violation of contraband regulations, illegal warfare, and under the provisions of instruments such as the International Convention for the Protection of Submarine Telegraph Cables of 1884 (Art. 2); the Treaty for the Suppression of the African Slave Trade (1862); the International Convention for the Suppression of the Circulation of and Traffic in Obscene Publications (1923); the International Convention for the Suppression of Counterfeiting Currency (1929); and the Convention on Genocide (1948).

SUMMARY

Summing up the preceding discussion, it must be emphasized that the problem of the status of the individual centers on the question of whether or not there exists a legal right of international representation about the treatment of an individual. If such a right does not exist—and this appears to be true in general—then domestic jurisdiction could be invoked by a state in rejecting suggestions or even reprimands from the outside.

---

[18] Text *ibid.*, 43 (1949), Supp., pp. 133–139.
[19] See Pan American Union, *Doc. 89* (English), Rev. 2, October 12, 1959, p. 10.
[20] Text in full in 60 *A.J.I.L.* (1966), Supp., pp. 458–460.
[21] For details, consult José A. Cabranes, "The Protection of Human Rights by the Organization of American States," *ibid.*, 62 (1968), pp. 889–908.

On the other hand, if such a right should be acknowledged, then the individual's status has been changed at last.

Again, most individuals, as yet, lack the ability to affirm or assert their rights before an international tribunal. As long as this situation prevails, it must be doubted that international law grants rights to individuals. Only their state can take up their cause, by bringing a suit or filing a protest or claim with another state. This means that today, as in the past, it is the state which possesses an international legal right, not the individual.

A recent full-scale study of the position of the individual relative to international law led to the following conclusions. In his capacity as an official or an organ of a state, the individual should be categorized as a subject of duties under international law. In his private capacity, an individual might be made the subject of duties, particularly in such areas as piracy or the carrying of contraband of war. On the other hand, an individual may be a subject of rights, in his capacity as an agent or official of a state. In his private capacity, the individual is already the subject of numerous rules applicable to his status as a refugee, worker, employer, and above all as the possessor of human rights.[22]

SUGGESTED READINGS

INDIVIDUALS UNDER THE LAW IN GENERAL

Whiteman, Vol. I, pp. 50–58; Pieter N. Drost, *Human Rights as Legal Rights* (Leyden: A. W. Sythoff, 1965); British Institute of International and Comparative Law, *British International Law Cases*, Vol. IV: *The Individual in International Law* (London: Stevens & Sons; Dobbs Ferry, N.Y.: Oceana Publications, 1966); Hersch Lauterpacht, *An International Bill of the Rights of Man* (New York: Columbia University Press, 1945); James Simsarian, "Human Rights among Diverse World Orders," *Proceedings* (1959), pp. 245–248.

THE UN AND HUMAN RIGHTS

Whiteman, Vol. 13, pp. 660–679; Commission to Study the Organization of Peace, *The United Nations and Human Rights* (Dobbs Ferry, N.Y.: Oceana Publications, 1968); Egon Schwelb, "The Influence of the Universal Declaration of Human Rights on International and Natural Law," *Proceedings* (1959), pp. 217–229, as well as his "International Conventions on Human Rights," 9 *International and Comparative Law Quarterly* (1960), pp. 654–675, and his "Civil and Political Rights: The International Measures of Implementation," 62 *A.J.I.L.* (1968), pp. 827–868; John P. Humphey, "The United Nations Sub-Commission on the Prevention of Discrimination and the Protection of Minorities," *ibid.*, pp. 869–888; Louis B. Sohn, "United Nations Machinery for Im-

---

[22] Carl A. Nørgaard, *The Position of the Individual in International Law* (Copenhagen: Ejnar Munksgaard, Ltd., 1962), *passim.*

plementing Human Rights," *ibid.*, pp. 909–912; Brunson MacChesney the United States Ratify the Covenants? A Question of Merits, N stitutional Law," *ibid.*, pp. 912–917; John Carey, "The U.N.'s Double on Human Rights Complaints," *ibid.*, 60 (1966), pp. 792–803; George Haight, "Human Rights Covenants," *Proceedings* (1968), pp. 96–103; and the realistic analysis by Morris B. Abram, "The U.N. and Human Rights," 47 *Foreign Affairs* (1969), pp. 363–374.

EUROPEAN HUMAN RIGHTS DEVELOPMENTS

A. H. Robertson, "The Contribution of the Council of Europe to the Development of International Law," *Proceedings* (1965), pp. 201–209; *Human Rights in National and International Law*, Proceedings of the 2nd Int. Conference on the European Convention on Human Rights, Vienna, 1965, edited by the same author (Manchester, England: University of Manchester; Dobbs Ferry, N.Y.: Oceana Publications, 1968), and his earlier *Human Rights in Europe* (*ibid.* 1963); J. E. S. Fawcett, *The Application of the European Convention on Human Rights* (New York: Oxford University Press, 1969).

Cases

The Lawless Case, European Court of Human Rights, 1960 (*Preliminary Objections and Questions of Procedure*) excerpted at length by Eleanor H. Finch in 56 *A.J.I.L.* (1962), pp. 171–210; see also the analysis of the case by Dennis Thompson in 11 *International and Comparative Law Quarterly* (1962), pp. 721–741.

Case Relating to Certain Aspects of the Laws on the Use of Languages in Education in Belgium (*Preliminary Objection*), European Court of Human Rights, 1967, reported in 61 *A.J.I.L.* (1967), pp. 1075–1077; *Judgment* (July 23, 1968) excerpted at length in 8 *International Legal Materials* (1969), pp. 825–849.

The Greek Case (*Denmark, Norway, Sweden, The Netherlands v. Greece*), European Commission of Human Rights, January 24, 1968, reported in 62 *A.J.I.L.* (1968), pp. 988–992; full text in 7 *International Legal Materials* (1968), pp. 818–83; and see also *ibid.*, 8 (1969), pp. 890–892; consult also Thomas Buergenthal, "Proceedings against Greece under the European Convention on Human Rights," 62 *A.J.I.L.* (1968), pp. 441–450.

The Neumeister Case, European Court of Human Rights, 1968; *Judgment* excerpted in 8 *International Legal Materials* (1969), pp. 547–563.

THE RIGHT TO PETITION INTERNATIONAL AUTHORITIES

W. Paul Gormley, *The Procedural Status of the Individual before International and Supranational Tribunals* (The Hague: Martinus Nijhoff, 1966); J. W. Bruegel, "The Right to Petition an International Authority," 2 *International and Comparative Law Quarterly* (1953), pp. 542–563; Ian Brownlie, "The Individual before Tribunals Exercising International Jurisdiction," *ibid.*, 11 (1962), pp. 701–720; and the excellent summary of the problem by S. Oda in *Manual*, pp. 511–514.

12

Jurisdiction Over Persons

NATIONALITY OF INDIVIDUALS

MEANING *of National; Nationality.* Each state is composed of a multitude of persons and, as part of its sovereign powers, exercises jurisdiction over those persons. Its primary concern is with those individuals who are its citizens, its true members. Legal writers as well as legislators in many countries employ two terms in this connection, and it should be kept in mind that the two may not always be synonymous: nationals and citizens. *National,* in popular usage, has a broader meaning than *citizen:* before the Philippines became independent, the inhabitants of the archipelago were nationals of the United States but not citizens thereof. On the other hand, a citizen of a country is also its national.

Because the domestic laws of states relating to citizenship vary greatly, the following discussion will make use of the terms *national* and *nationality* as lending themselves more adequately to an international law approach. The relationship between state and citizen represents a link through which an individual normally can and does enjoy the protection and benefits of international law. If an individual lacks a nationality tie to a state, he would be without protection if a wrong were done to him by any government, for without this tie no state would be willing to protect him or to take up his cause against the government which had committed the wrong.

In the United States, *national* means a person owing permanent allegiance to a state, and "national of the United States" means either a citizen of this country or a person who, though not a citizen of the United States, owes such permanent allegiance to the United States.[1]

Nationality, then, is the bond which unites a given person with a given state, which identifies him as a member of that entity, which enables him to claim its protection and also subjects him to the performance of such duties as his state may impose on him.[2]

---

[1] 66 Stat. L. 163 (1952), Title III, Section 308.

[2] The International Court of Justice held in the famous *Nottebohm Case* (*Liechtenstein* v. *Guatemala*) judgment of April 6, 1955, that there must exist a specific link, a genuine connection, between a state and its nationals. This doctrine has been

Right of the State to Confer Nationality. Each state is free to decide who shall be its nationals, under what conditions nationality shall be conferred, and who—and in what manner—shall be deprived of such status. The prevailing principle was stated in somewhat general terms in *Tomasicchio* v. *Acheson:*[3]

Citizenship depends, however, entirely on municipal law and is not regulated by international law. Acquisition of citizenship of the United States is governed solely by the Constitution and by Acts of Congress.

Modes of Acquiring Nationality. Nationality may be acquired through either of two modes: by birth or by naturalization. The bulk of the population of every state acquires its nationality by the former method, but there have been occasions when tens of thousands of persons, as well as individuals singly, received a new nationality by the second method.

Limitation on Right of the State to Confer Nationality. Despite the acknowledged fact that most of the details of nationality are governed by domestic law, a limited number of rules of international law (some general, some particular in scope) apply in this sphere and do regulate certain aspects of nationality. Thus the Permanent Court of International Justice held in the case of the *Nationality Decrees Issued in Tunis and Morocco,*[4] that the discretion relating to nationality which normally represents an exclusive prerogative of each state may under certain conditions be restricted by some form of international obligation, and that in such cases jurisdiction which in principle belongs solely to the state would be limited by rules of international law.

By general agreement, any individual born on the soil of a given state of parents who are nationals of that state is regarded as a national of the state in question. This has not always been true, however, as will be discussed later.

Law of the Soil (jus soli). Beyond this point, the United States, Great Britain, and most Latin American states follow the law of the soil (*jus soli*) according to which mere birth on the soil of a state is sufficient to create the bond of nationality, irrespective of the allegiance of the parents. There are exceptions to this rule, based on comity or courtesy rather than on international law: children of foreign heads of state, of foreign diplomats,[5] and, in a few cases, children of foreign consular of-

---

criticized strongly. See the special section on this case in the appended list of suggested readings for references to the *Nottebohm* decision.

[3] United States, District Court, Dist. of Columbia, 1951, 98 F. Supp. 166.

[4] Advisory Opinion, *P.C.I.J.*, 1924, Ser. B, No. 4.

[5] See *In re Thenault*, United States, District Court, Dist. of Columbia, 1942, 47 F. Supp. 952. In the United States, children born on U.S. territory to foreign diplomats *not* accredited to the American government would *normally* be regarded as U.S. citizens. See Department of State MS. File 130, December 14, 1937, concerning Marie de Hedry, reprinted in Urban G. Whitaker, Jr., *Politics and Power* (New York: Harper & Row, 1964), at pp. 376–377.

ficials, are not claimed as its nationals by the state on whose soil they happen to be born.

One other condition serves to void the usual application of the *jus soli* in the United States: a child born in a portion of the United States then under the occupation of enemy military forces does not acquire American nationality under the *jus soli.*[6] This position is quite logical, because during such occupation the authority of the legitimate sovereign is suspended and the enemy occupation forces exercise temporary control over the territory in question. A child born there would, therefore, not be a person "born in the United States and subject to the jurisdiction thereof."

The essentially Anglo-Saxon concept of *jus soli* was illustrated strikingly in the celebrated classic case of

UNITED STATES v. WONG KIM ARK
United States, Supreme Court, 1898, 169 U.S. 649

FACTS

Wong Kim Ark was born in San Francisco in 1873 of Chinese parents who were subjects of the Emperor of China but were permanently domiciled in the United States. As Chinese, the parents were then not eligible to United States citizenship by naturalization. Wong Kim Ark went to China in 1894 and on his return to the United States in 1895 was refused admission to this country by the collector of customs, on the ground that he was a Chinese laborer, not a citizen, and not within any of the priviliged classes named in the Chinese Exclusion Act then in force.

Wong Kim Ark sued for a writ of habeas corpus, claiming American nationality on the ground of birth. The case eventually came before the Supreme Court by appeal.

ISSUE

Would a child born in the United States of alien parents ineligible to citizenship become at birth a national

(citizen) of the United States by virtue of the first clause of the Fourteenth Amendment of the Constitution: "All persons born or naturalized in the United States, and subject to the jurisdiction thereof, are citizens of the United States and of the State wherein they reside."

DECISION

The Court decided in favor of Wong Kim Ark: under the Fourteenth Amendment, his birth on United States soil conferred citizenship on him at birth.

REASONING

(1) "It is the inherent right of every independent nation to determine for itself, and according to its own Constitution and laws, what classes of persons shall be entitled to its citizenship."

(2) "The Fourteenth Amendment affirms the rule of citizenship by birth within the territory, in the allegiance and under the protection of the country, including all children here born

[6] See *Inglis* v. *Sailor's Snug Harbour*, United States, Supreme Court, 1830, 3 Peters 99.

of resident aliens, with the exceptions or qualifications (as old as the rule itself) of children of foreign sovereigns or their ministers, or born on foreign public ships, or of enemies within and during a hostile occupation of our territory, and with the single additional exception of children of members of the Indian tribes owing direct allegiance to their several tribes. The amendment, in clear words and in manifest intent, includes the children born within the territory of the United States of all other persons, of whatever race or color, domiciled within the United States."

Law of the Blood (jus sanguinis). Most European states, on the other hand, adhere primarily to the civil law principle of the law of the blood (*jus sanguinis*), according to which the nationality of a child follows that of the parents, regardless of the place of its birth. Thus a child born to French parents in the United States would be a French national under the *jus sanguinis* as well as an American national under the *jus soli*. In the United States that individual would be an American citizen, in France a French citizen, and in Ghana a citizen of both France and the United States (dual nationality).

Complications of Determining Citizenship. To complicate matters, most states do not follow either of these principles slavishly but accept both, with varying emphasis on one or the other, coupled quite commonly to specific residence requirements.

Children born aboard vessels registered in the United States are not nationals of this country under *jus soli*. In the classic case of *Lam Mow* v. *Nagle*,[7] Lam Mow was refused admission to the United States in 1927 as an alien. He had been born aboard a merchant vessel registered in the United States, on the high seas. His parents, domiciled in the United States but nationals of China, were returning to this country from a visit to China. The plaintiff contended that birth aboard an American ship constituted birth in the United States. The Circuit Court ruled, however, that the words of the United States Constitution (Art. 14, sec. 1) applied only to the land areas and territorial waters of the United States: areas possessing both a fixed location and recognized boundaries. Because vessels lacked the element of fixed location, the Court held that persons born aboard American vessels on the high seas followed the nationality of their parents. Hence Lam Mow was declared to be a Chinese national and his application for admission was denied.[8] It should be noted that the British nationality laws equate birth on a vessel registered in the United Kingdom with birth on the soil of that country.

[7] United States, Court of Appeals, Ninth Circuit, 1928, 24 F. (2d) 316.

[8] It is interesting to note that in *Ching Lan Foo* v. *Brownell* (United States, District Court, Dist. of Columbia, 1957, 148 F. Supp. 420) the Court ruled that American ships on the high seas should be considered to be part of United States territory for purposes of an alien being "physically present in the United States" in the meaning of the Immigration and Nationality Act of 1952.

The development of air travel has added another problem area analogous to the question of birth aboard vessels. Broadly speaking, the situation is similar, for again an aircraft flying above the high seas lacks fixed location, and the nationality of children born aboard under such conditions would follow that of the parents. A slightly different situation arises when the aircraft in question happens to be in the national air of some state at the time of an infant's birth. Possibly a case of dual nationality might result under such circumstances.

Innumerable controversies concerning the nationality of individuals have arisen over the years, because each state stresses one of the two basic modes of nationality by birth and adheres to a lesser extent to the other. Generally speaking, when two states have a claim on the allegiance of an individual on the basis of birth, the state asserting its primary preference as to principle *and* exercising actual jurisdiction over the person of the individual is acknowledged by the other claimant to be sovereign of the person in question.

This has been particularly true in cases involving the satisfaction of compulsory military service obligations. As yet there exists no general convention regulating this problem, although in 1930 a Protocol relating to Military Obligations in Certain Cases of Double Nationality was signed at The Hague by a few states. That instrument, to which the United States is a party, sensibly provided that habitual residence in one of the two claimant states would excuse a person possessed of dual nationality from all military service in the other state.

Naturalization. A second major mode of acquiring nationality is through naturalization, that is, through a (generally) voluntary act by which the national of one state achieves membership in the body of nationals of another state. Although normally involving an individual, naturalization may also apply to whole groups through an executive or legislative act. It is in collective naturalization that the voluntary aspect of individual naturalization may be absent.

As far as individual change of nationality is concerned, each state is free to lay down such rules as it pleases, for it alone has the right to decide whom to admit and under what conditions. Such regulation, being purely domestic in character, is not subject to the application of international law.

Collective Naturalization. Collective naturalization, often also purely internal in nature,[9] may on occasion bear an indirect relationship to international law when it is based either on treaty provisions (cession of territory, followed by collective naturalization of the inhabitants by the acquiring state) or on conquest followed by annexation of the enemy territory. It should be noted that most instances of voluntary cession of

[9] Such as the actions of the United States government in the collective naturalization sphere dealing with the inhabitants of Hawaii, Puerto Rico, Alaska, the Virgin Islands, and Indians living in the United States as members of tribes.

territory have been accompanied by some form of option available to the inhabitants of the ceded area by which they could choose whether to acquire a new nationality or to retain their former allegiance. On some occasions, to be sure, the option consisted of leaving the ceded territory within a given period of time if exemption from collective naturalization was desired.

It should be pointed out that most of the changes in territorial sovereignty following World War II have *not* been accompanied by options for the populations in question.

DUAL NATIONALITY

It was noted earlier that individuals have at times possessed two nationalities concurrently. Thus a number of Japanese-descent American nationals present in Japan at the outbreak of war in 1941 were forced to enter the Japanese armed forces. According to American regulations, the individuals were nationals of the United States under *jus soli;* under prevailing Japanese laws, they were Japanese citizens under *jus sanguinis.*[10]

Doctrine of Indelible Allegiance. Another and formerly very common basis for the possession of dual nationality by an individual is the unwillingness of a state to grant to its nationals the right to expatriate themselves by being naturalized in another state. Such an attitude is founded in the "doctrine of indelible allegiance," originally formulated in Great Britain but abandoned later by that state. Under this theory, an individual cannot lose his nationality without the prior consent of his sovereign. Such consent was quite generally denied until well past the middle of the last century.

Many states have insisted, however, down to recent times, that recognition of naturalization should hinge on explicit approval by the recognizing state of each individual's naturalization abroad, that is, on a fairly strict adherence to the doctrine of indelible allegiance. Such a recalcitrant attitude on the part of states losing large numbers of their nationals through emigration has led, understandably enough, to countless disputes and has caused the continuation of the status of dual nationality for many individuals. Most commonly affected in recent years have been former citizens of France, Egypt, Greece, Iran, Poland, Romania, Syria, and Turkey, when they returned to their former homelands. Czechoslovakia, according to recent reports, does not yet recognize American-born children of Czech parents as U.S. citizens.[11]

The problem of dual nationality itself, irksome as it is to both states and individuals concerned, has not yet been settled by means of a general

---

[10] See *Kiyokuro Okimura* v. *Acheson*, United States, District Court, Hawaii, 1951, 99 F. Supp. 587, digested in 46 *A.J.I.L.* (1952), pp. 157–159, together with numerous relevant citations. Consult also Nissim Bar-Yaacov, *Dual Nationality* (New York: Praeger, 1961), which includes many case citations and an excellent bibliography.

[11] 85 *Time* (May 7, 1965), p. 84.

international convention. A Convention on Certain Questions relating to Conflict of Nationality Laws, signed at The Hague in 1930, represented a modest beginning.[12] This instrument, to which the United States did not become a party, attempted to deal with the question but accomplished very little. It stated that a person having two or more nationalities could be regarded as its national by each of the states whose nationality he possessed (Art. 3); that a state could not afford diplomatic protection to one of its nationals against a state whose nationality such person also possessed (Art. 4); that in a third state a person having dual nationality should be treated as if he had only one (Art. 5); and that a person possessing two nationalities acquired without any voluntary act on his part was entitled to renounce one of them but only with the permission of the state whose nationality he desired to surrender (Art. 6).

SPECIAL STATUS OF WOMEN AND CHILDREN

One of the most interesting aspects of nationality was the special status for women and children created by certain laws in the United States. Traditionally, both English and American law did not deprive a female citizen of her nationality when she married an alien. In the course of time, however, this old common law principle underwent considerable changes.

In 1855, an Act of Congress conferred United States citizenship on any alien woman who married an American citizen. Then, in 1907, another Act provided that "any American woman who marries a foreigner shall take the nationality of her husband" and went on to state that such a woman would resume her American citizenship when the marriage in question terminated; resumption of citizenship would then take place either by mere residence in the United States or by registering at any American consulate. Great Britain had enacted similar legislation, and by 1908 all major countries in Europe and the Americas had created a uniform rule on this subject, because European and Latin-American states had long followed policies virtually identical with those found in the 1907 law.

The new United States regulations soon produced some rather ridiculous situations, such as when an American woman married an engineer of British nationality and promptly lost her United States citizenship, even though the couple resided in Portland, Oregon.

Cable Act. At last the famous Cable Act of September 22, 1922 (42 *Statutes at Large* 1021), brought some order into the United States nationality picture while marking, at the same time, a break in American policy with the rules generally observed elsewhere. The Act, adopted in order to put married women on a basis of independence, provided that an alien woman would not acquire United States nationality by marriage to an American citizen or through the naturalization of her husband, but

---

[12] Consult Jessup, pp. 74–76, and Corbett, pp. 167–169.

had to be naturalized personally in accordance with prevailing regulations. Furthermore, the Cable Act reversed the Act of 1907 and stated that a woman citizen of the United States would not lose her nationality by marriage to an alien unless she formally renounced her citizenship or married an alien ineligible for United States citizenship. Finally, the Act provided for a speedy process of renaturalization for women who had lost their citizenship under the 1907 law, unless the alien husbands were ineligible for citizenship.

Convention on the Nationality of Women. Soon the emancipation of women and the grant of female suffrage in more and more countries led to a demand abroad that the old principle of "family unity," as applied to nationality, be brought up to date in accordance with the new United States rules. Thus a League of Nations Committee of Experts prepared a draft convention on the status of married women as early as 1926; the Conference on the Codification of International Law at The Hague in 1930 accepted that draft, with expansions; and at the Conference of American States in Montevideo (1933), a Convention on the Nationality of Women was adopted which prohibited distinctions based on sex as regarded nationality. The 1933 instrument was ratified, however, only by the United States and a limited number of the Latin American states, so that at present it is only of "partial regional" application.[13]

Status of Children. Other and complicated questions have arisen with respect to the nationality of children, particularly of illegitimate offspring and of foundlings. A number of international conventions have been developed in attempts to deal with such questions, but limited ratification has caused the problems to continue.

One particular question appears to be of major interest in this connection: the status of children removed from the country of their birth by their parents when those parents subsequently become citizens of another state.

Under current United States legislation, a native-born United States citizen taken abroad by his parents while under the age of twenty-one years loses his American nationality through the foreign naturalization of the parents unless the citizen in question returns to the United States to establish a permanent residence prior to his twenty-fifth birthday.[14] Most other countries now hold that minor children follow the nationality of their parents and when the latter changes through naturalization, the nationality of the minor child changes accordingly.

States have declined, on occasion, to permit minor children, nationals

[13] See the case of *U.S.A. ex rel. Florence Strunsky Mergé* v. *Italian Republic,* Italo-American Conciliation Commission, 1955, digested in 50 *A.J.I.L.* (1956), pp. 154–156.

[14] Immigration and Nationality Act of 1952, sec. 349(a), par. 1. See also the famous decision in *Marie Elizabeth Elg* v. *Frances Perkins, Secretary of Labor et al.,* United States, Supreme Court, 1939, 307 U.S. 325.

under *jus soli*, to accompany departing parents abroad when it appeared likely that such departure would jeopardize retention of nationality on the part of the children.

LOSS OF NATIONALITY

The question of denaturalization as well as that of expatriation is intimately connected with both naturalization and dual nationality. Each country establishes its own rules and determines the acts or omissions which would cause loss of its nationality to native-born citizens, to naturalized citizens, or to both.[15]

Causes of Loss of Nationality. The acts which cause expatriation or denaturalization vary from country to country and no complete list can be drawn up in short order. They include, *inter alia*, voting in foreign elections, service in the armed forces of another country (especially when an oath of allegiance forms a prerequisite for such service), acceptance of an office abroad which is reserved under the relevant laws to citizens of the foreign state in question, desertion in time of war, "disloyalty," treason, as well as formal renunciation of nationality either through naturalization abroad or through an official declaration filed with an embassy, legation, or consul of one's country.[16]

STATELESSNESS

Statelessness—that is, the lack of nationality—used to occur but rarely before World War I; the relatively few recorded instances usually related to accidental loss of nationality without corresponding acquisition of a new one, frequently in connection with illegitimate children. The second quarter of the twentieth century, however, saw increasingly large numbers of people without nationality, in part owing to denaturalization acts of the National Socialist government of Germany, in part owing to Russian denationalization measures adopted on and after August 21, 1921. Ultimately hundreds of thousands of individuals belonged in the category of stateless persons.[17]

Problems of Stateless Persons. The problems faced by a stateless person may assume almost incredible complexity, particularly in relation to such matters as identity of documents, travel permits, work cards, marriage

[15] The following cases are useful for illustrative purposes: *Terada* v. *Dulles*, United States, District Court, Hawaii, 1945, 121 F. Supp. 6, reported in 48 *A.J.I.L.* (1954), pp. 663–664; *Trop* v. *Dulles*, United States, Supreme Court, 1958, 356 U.S. 86; and *Mitsugi Nishikawa* v. *Dulles*, United States, Supreme Court, 1958, 356 U.S. 129.

[16] Consult Leonard B. Boudin, "Involuntary Loss of American Nationality," 73 *Harvard Law Review* (1960), pp. 1510–1531.

[17] See particularly Jane P. C. Carey, "Some Aspects of Statelessness since World War I," 40 *A.P.S.R.* (1946), pp. 113–123 and the literature cited therein; consult also Paul Weiss, "The International Protection of Refugees," 48 *A.J.I.L.* (1954), pp. 193–221, and George Ginsburgs, "The Soviet Union and the Problem of Refugees and Displaced Persons 1917–1956," *ibid.*, 51 (1957), pp. 325–361, especially at pp. 329–333.

licenses, and other examples of the mass of papers commonly carried by the inhabitants of most states. Yet, despite some highly commendable activity on the part of the International Law Commission, only an innocuous draft convention dealing with *future* statelessness has been produced thus far.[18]

It is easy to see why no really effective instrument has been adopted: it would involve far-reaching intervention in and regulation of what virtually every state in the world considers to be matters of domestic jurisdiction.

One of the more striking cases involving statelessness was decided in 1947:

U.S. EX REL. STEINVORTH v. WATKINS

United States, Circuit Court of Appeals, 2nd Circuit, 1947
159 F. (2d) 50

FACTS

Steinvorth was born in Costa Rica of German parents who took him to Germany in 1901. During World War I he served in the German army and then returned to Costa Rica as a permanent resident in 1920. In 1941 he chose Costa Rican citizenship after the German consul there had informed him that this act would cancel his German citizenship.

On September 23, 1944, the President of Costa Rica caused a resolution to be published which stated that Steinvorth had lost his Costa Rican citizenship. The next day Steinvorth was arrested by Costa Rican authorities and taken to the United States by American officials, in cooperation with the Costa Rican authorities. In the United States, he was interned as an enemy alien. He petitioned for *habeas corpus* but this petition was denied by the District Court, Southern District of New York. He then appealed to the Circuit Court.

ISSUE

Was Steinvorth an enemy alien, a status which would have made lawful his internment?

DECISION

The order of the District Court was reversed and the appellant was discharged from custody and internment, because he was not an enemy alien but a stateless person.

REASONING

Under German law, Steinvorth terminated his German citizenship by opting for Costa Rican citizenship in

[18] See International Law Commission, "Report on . . . the Sixth Session (June 3–July 28, 1954)," 49 *A.J.I.L.* (1955), Supp., pp. 1–45, at pp. 3–16; Ivan S. Kerno, "The Draft Conventions on Statelessness of the International Law Commission," *Proceedings* (1956), pp. 155–159, followed by discussion and commentary, pp. 159–186; Paul Weiss, "The Convention relating to the Status of Stateless Persons," 10 *International and Comparative Law Quarterly* (1961), pp. 255–264, and his "The United Nations Convention on the Reduction of Statelessness, 1961," *ibid.*, 11 (1962), pp. 1073–1096.

1941. The 1944 cancellation of his Costa Rican nationality could not be judged by an American court. It was an act of state done in a foreign jurisdiction, and an American court had to accept it as canceling Steinvorth's citizenship in Costa Rica.

But the termination of his Costa Rican citizenship did not restore his German nationality: that could have been done only by Germany itself, and there was no evidence submitted that anything that happened since September 23, 1944, had made him a German citizen again. After that date, Steinvorth was a stateless person. The government of the United States could hold Steinvorth only if he was a native, a citizen, or a subject of a hostile country. Because he was none of these but was a stateless person, he had to be released.

Attempts to Improve the Status of Stateless Persons. The situation of many stateless persons has been improved, from a legal point of view, by the fact that a very large proportion of the individuals in question are refugees and thus enjoy the protection of the 1951 Geneva Convention on the Status of Refugees. That instrument has been ratified by sixteen countries. In addition, the 1954 United Nations Conference on the Status of Stateless Persons drew up a Convention relating to the Status of Stateless Persons, but this agreement, although signed by twenty-two states, has not yet come into force. A Protocol Relating to the Status of Refugees, developed at the United Nations in January, 1967, entered into force for the United States on November 1, 1968, subject to two reservations.[19] (See also Chapter 14 on refugees and territorial asylum.)

NATIONALITY OF BUSINESS ENTERPRISES

Corporations. Corporations enjoy the status of legal or juristic persons and therefore can be said to be endowed with nationality similar to the manner in which a natural, human being possesses nationality.

The traditional Anglo-American determinant of the nationality of a corporation was domicile or, more specifically, the place of incorporation. In the case of unincorporated associations, nationality was determined on the basis of the state in which they were constituted or in which their governing body normally met or was located.

Among most European states, on the other hand, strong preference was expressed for a long time for the concept that the nationality of a corporation was determined either by the location of its home office (*siège social*) or—a minority view—by the place in which the principal business operations were carried on.

Partnerships. In the case of business enterprises without legal personality, such as partnerships, no nationality can be assigned to the firm as such. The interests involved are those of the partners, and the nationality

[19] See text of Secretary of State Rusk's letter to the President in 63 *A.J.I.L.* (1969), pp. 123–128; text of protocol in 63 *A.J.I.L.* (1969), Supp., pp. 385–389; text of the convention, *ibid.*, pp. 389–407.

of the latter determines which state is entitled to represent the interests of the firm. It does not matter, for purposes of determining the "nationality" in question, where the operating establishment of the partnership is located: the nationality of the partners is the decisive factor.

Tests of Domicile and of Control. The events of World War I, particularly the development of economic warfare, led to a change in the definition of nationality, away from the test of domicile and in the direction of the test of control. In other words, regardless of the nominal seat of headquarters or of the place of incorporation, a company began to be viewed as invested with the status of an enemy national if the persons in control of the enterprise resided in an enemy country or were found to be acting under the control or instructions of enemy nations (shareholders, silent partners, directors, etc.).[20]

On the whole, the "control test" appears to be a more precise device through which the national character of a business enterprise may be determined. Nevertheless, the older test of domicile is still utilized side by side with the newer test. Such concurrent use is not as capricious as it might appear at first glance: availability of two devices or tests enables states to employ whichever appears most suitable at a given time when the question of protecting a business enterprise located in a foreign jurisdiction arises. Also, in time of war, either test may be applied to determine the enemy or neutral or friendly character of a given firm and may, it must be admitted, result in some rather dubious but highly profitable seizures of alleged enemy firms.

It should be mentioned that there exist few generally accepted rules in general international law as to the diplomatic protection of corporate entities as such. The nationality of the corporation does not appear, by itself, sufficient to generate a claim to protection abroad. State practice indicates that states normally will not afford diplomatic protection to corporations that are their own nationals, if a majority of the stockholders are citizens of another state. On the other hand, states normally are willing to grant such protection on behalf of those stockholders who are their own nationals, even if the corporation is in fact a foreign national.[21]

---

[20] See the classic but disputed case of *Daimler Co., Ltd., v. Continental Tyre & Rubber Co., Ltd.*, Great Britain, House of Lords, 1916, [1916] 2 A.C. 307. For American cases, consult *Clark v. Uebersee Finanz-Korporation, A.G.*, United States, Supreme Court, 1947, 332 U.S. 480, as well as *Uebersee Finanz-Korporation, A.G. v. McGrath*, United States, Supreme Court, 1952, 343 U.S. 205. The famous and controversial *Interhandel Case* involving a Swiss company assertedly controlled by German interests and in turn controlling the General Aniline and Film Corporation complex in the United States is so complicated that its discussion is beyond the scope of a general text; the interested reader is referred to the sources listed in the relevant special section of the Suggested Readings relating to this chapter.

[21] See Josef L. Kunz's review of Giovanni Battaglini, *La Protezione Diplomatica delle Società* (Padua: Cedam, 1957), in 53 *A.J.I.L.* (1959), pp. 211–212, on this important subject.

JURISDICTION OVER NATIONALS ABROAD

Right of Jurisdiction. Assertion of the continuing bond existing between a state and each of its nationals occurs most frequently in connection with the commission of crimes or other offenses by those nationals beyond the territorial jurisdiction of their state. Some countries assert a right to punish their nationals for offenses committed, regardless of the location of the offense. Other states, notably Great Britain and the United States, traditionally have restricted their criminal jurisdiction to acts committed within their territory. But even in the latter countries, a significant change in attitude has taken place during recent decades.

In the classic decision upholding the traditional Anglo-American view, *American Banana Co.* v. *United Fruit Co.*[22] the Supreme Court of the United States refused to enforce the provisions of the Sherman Anti-Trust Act against the United Fruit Company for activities undertaken in Panama and Costa Rica (where such acts were not in violation of local law), saying in part that "A conspiracy to do acts in another jurisdiction does not draw to itself those acts and make them unlawful, if they are permitted by the local law." The Court thus ruled that violations of American law committed abroad by United States nationals did not constitute grounds for trial in the United States if the acts in question did not violate the laws of the foreign state in which the acts had taken place. If, on the other hand, a crime was committed abroad by one national against another national and the culprit returned home, then his government could try him for the crime.

Again, if a national commits an offense abroad which has its effects in his own state, he may be tried for the offense when he returns to his country; a corporation may be tried at once in the United States.[23]

Taxation. A state may lawfully tax its nationals for income earned abroad. In order to avoid the easily occurring double taxation of an

---

[22] United States, Supreme Court, 1909, 213 U.S. 347; but see the more recent study by G. W. Haight, "International Law and Extraterritorial Application of the Antitrust Laws," 63 *Yale Law Journal* (1954), pp. 639–654. Consult also I. H. W. Verzijl, "The Controversy regarding the So-Called Extraterritorial Effect of the American Antitrust Laws," 8 *Tijdschrift* (1961), pp. 3–30; and the following illustrative cases (Supreme Court of the United States): *United States* v. *Sisal Sales Corp.*, 1927, 274 U.S. 268; *Steele* v. *Bulova Watch Co.*, 1952, 344 U.S. 280.

[23] *Sachs* v. *Government of the Canal Zone*, United States, Circuit Court of Appeals, Fifth Circuit, 1949, 176 F. (2d) 292, a case involving a United States citizen who composed libelous articles in the Republic of Panama for publication and circulation in the Canal Zone. See especially *United States* v. *Aluminum Company of America*, United States, Court of Appeals, 2nd Circuit, 1945, 148 F. 2d 416; Walter S. G. Kohn, "A New Look at the Jurisdiction in ALCOA," 61 *A.J.I.L.* (1967), pp. 547–570; Stanley D. Metzger, "The 'Effects' Doctrine of Jurisdiction," *ibid.*, pp. 1015–1018; and consult Whiteman, Vol. VI, pp. 118–160, citing numerous relevant cases.

individual or corporation, the United States and other governments have concluded in recent years numerous agreements.

Right of the State to Summon Nationals Home. A state may also call on its nationals abroad to assist in the prosecution of crimes. The well-known case of *Blackmer* v. *United States* [24] illustrated this point: Blackmer refused to return from France to testify in a criminal trial. After two subpoenas served on him by a U.S. consul failed to induce Blackmer to return home, the Supreme Court upheld a judgment that Blackmer was in contempt of the Supreme Court of the District of Columbia, for which he was in each instance fined $30,000 and costs.

The general principle has been phrased most cogently by W. Hall:

Its [the state's] laws travel with them [its nationals] wherever they go, both in places within and without the jurisdiction of other powers. A state cannot enforce its laws within the territory of another state, but its subjects remain under an obligation not to disregard them . . . and it preserves the power of compelling observance by punishment if a person who has broken them returns within its jurisdiction.[25]

Treasonable Acts. Since World War II, a new and fascinating sphere of jurisdiction over nationals has received much publicity: the right of a state to punish "treasonable" acts done outside its territorial jurisdiction either by its own nationals or by such aliens as could be held to owe allegiance to the state in question either because of the protection given to them as residents of that state or because they traveled abroad under its passports.

The best-known United States case in this special category is *Chandler* v. *United States*.[26] Chandler, indicted for treason to the United States committed while residing in Germany, asserted that the constitutional definition of treason did not cover adherence to an enemy by one residing in enemy territory. This interpretation was denied by the District Court which said, in part:

Treasonable acts endanger the sovereignty of the United States. It has never been doubted that Congress has the power to punish an act committed beyond the territorial jurisdiction of the United States which is directly injurious to the Government of the United States. . . . An alien domiciled in a foreign country as the defendant Chandler admittedly was during the period alleged

---

[24] United States, Supreme Court, 1932, 284 U.S. 421.

[25] W. E. Hall, *A Treatise on International Law*, 8th ed., A. Pearce Higgins, ed. (New York: Oxford University Press, 1924), pp. 56–57.

[26] *United States* v. *Chandler*, United States, District Court, Mass., 1947, 72 F. Supp. 230, reported in 42 *A.J.I.L.* (1948), p. 223; *Chandler* v. *United States*, Circuit Court of Appeals, 1st Circuit, 1948, 171 F. (2d) 921, digested in 43 *A.J.I.L.* (1949), pp. 804–805; *certiorari* denied by Supreme Court in 1949: 336 U.S. 918.

in the indictment was bound to obey all the laws of the German Reich as long as he remained in it, not immediately relating to citizenship, during his sojourn in it. All strangers are under the protection of a sovereign state while they are within its territory, and owe a local temporary allegiance in return for that protection. . . .

At the same time a citizen of the United States owes to his government full, complete, and true allegiance. He may renounce and abandon it at any time. This is a natural and inherent right. When he goes abroad on a visit or for travel, he must, while abroad, obey the laws of the foreign country, where he is temporarily. In this sense and to this extent only he owes a sort of allegiance to such government, but to no extent and in no sense does this impair or qualify his allegiance or obligation to his own country or to his own government.

This statement, particularly the portions dealing with a limited allegiance owed to a foreign host government, may be taken to represent the generally accepted view. A citizen of state X, traveling in state Y, must obey the traffic and sanitation regulations imposed by local law: to that extent, as an example, he owes a limited and temporary allegiance to state Y. But in his allegiance he is, and must remain until he renounces it, a citizen and subject of state X.

In another celebrated case, *Gillars* v. *United States*,[27] the Court of Appeals, in affirming the conviction of a United States national for treason (voluntary broadcasting in Germany on behalf of the German government during World War II), emphatically insisted that

. . . obedience to the law of the country of domicile or residence—local allegiance—is permissible but this kind of allegiance does not call for adherence to the enemy and the giving of aid and comfort to it with disloyal intent.

The Court rejected the defendant's argument that her duties to the United States had ceased before the start of her broadcasts in Germany because an American consular officer had revoked her United States passport. Said the Court: "The revocation of a passport . . . does not cause a loss of citizenship or dissolve the obligation of allegiance arising from citizenship."

The case now considered to be governing in the case of treason committed by aliens regarded as owing allegiance to a host state or traveling, in some manner, on its passports is that of "Lord Haw Haw" or, more properly, of William Joyce.[28]

[27] United States, Circuit Court of Appeals, District of Columbia, 1950, 182 F. (2d) 962, digested briefly in 45 *A.J.I.L.* (1951), pp. 372–373.

[28] *Rex* v. *Joyce*, Great Britain, Court of Criminal Appeal, 1945, 62 Times Law Reports 57. Dismissal of Joyce's appeal brought the case ultimately to the House of Lords.

JOYCE v. DIRECTOR OF PUBLIC PROSECUTIONS

Great Britain, House of Lords, 1946
62 Times Law Reports 208

FACTS

Joyce was born in the United States in 1906. When he was about three years old, he was brought to Ireland, where he stayed until 1921 when he came to England. He remained in England until 1939. "He was, therefore, brought up, educated, and settled within the King's dominions." On July 4, 1933, he applied for a British passport, describing himself as a British subject by birth, claiming to have been born in Galway. The passport was requested for the purpose of holiday touring on the Continent. Joyce received the passport, valid for a period of five years. On September 26, 1938, he applied for a renewal of the passport for one year, declaring himself to be a British subject by birth.

On August 24, 1939, he applied once more for a one-year renewal of the passport, again describing himself as a British subject by birth. He then left for Germany. When he was arrested later in that country, he possessed a document showing that he had been hired by the German Radio Corporation of Berlin—Charlottenburg as of September 18, 1939, as an announcer of English news. In this document, his "work book," Joyce's nationality was given as "Great Britain." Up to August 24, 1939, at least, Joyce owed allegiance as an alien resident, living in England under the protection of the British crown, to the British government.

Between the beginning of his employment in Germany and until at least July 2, 1940, Joyce broadcast propaganda on behalf of the enemies of Great Britain, under the name of "Lord Haw-Haw."

He was found in Germany at the end of World War II, arrested, and brought to trial in London on charges of treason. The court of first instance found him guilty and from that verdict an appeal was taken to the Court of Criminal Appeal. On affirmation of the original verdict, the case was brought by appeal to the House of Lords.

ISSUES

[Major issues only are listed.]

(1) Could a British court assume jurisdiction to try an alien for an offense against British law committed in a foreign country?

(2) Did Joyce owe any allegiance to Great Britain between September 18, 1939, and July 2, 1940?

(3) Since the renewal of Joyce's passport did not give him any British protection and he had no intention of availing himself of such, did he still owe any allegiance to Great Britain during the period spent in Germany?

DECISION

Verdict of lower court upheld. All three [major] issues answered in the affirmative.

REASONING

(1) Allegiance was owed to the Crown by such aliens as resided within the King's realm. All who were brought within the King's protection were *ad fidem regis;* they owed him allegiance from the day they came into his realm. Now trea-

son was the betrayal of a trust. Joyce, having long resided in British jurisdiction and owing because of this stay allegiance to the Crown, applied for and received a passport, and then proceeded to adhere to the King's enemies.

(2) A passport served as a means of identification. The possession of a British passport by one who was not a British subject gave him rights and imposed on the sovereign obligations which would otherwise not have been given or imposed. Joyce maintained by his own act of obtaining the passport the bond which bound him to Great Britain when he resided there. As one owing allegiance to the King, he sought and obtained the protection of the King for himself while abroad. In other words, he extended the duty of allegiance beyond the moment he left English territory. As long as Joyce held the passport, he was, within the meaning of a statute of 1351 A.D., a person who, if he adhered to the King's enemies in the realm or elsewhere, committed an act of treason.

(3) Because of the foregoing conclusion, a British court possessed jurisdiction to try Joyce.

(4) Since the appellant had admittedly adhered to the King's enemies outside the realm, he had been rightly convicted of treason.

NOTE: William Joyce was subsequently executed by hanging.

JURISDICTION OVER ALIENS [29]

Rights of Exclusion and Deportation. The exercise of territorial jurisdiction over aliens represents one of the logical consequences of the possession of sovereignty or independence by states. Each country is free to exclude or to admit aliens; the determination of the principles to be applied in such connection is of purely domestic concern.

Concurrent with the right of exclusion goes an equally unfettered right of each state to expel not only any alien who has illegally gained entry into its territory but also any alien whose conduct, after legal entry, is deemed prejudicial to public order and security. Deportation of such unwanted aliens normally is made to their home state. The latter may refuse admission to such deportees: usual reasons encountered for such rejection center on the stateless character of some of the individuals in question or, even more commonly, on their criminal record.[30] It should be noted, however, that deportation without good reason or without due regard to the legal interests of the individual involved, such as expulsion before local judicial proceedings against the alien have been completed, may lead to protests on the part of the individual's own state.

Because deportation is not a criminal proceeding, at least not in the United States, the *ex post facto* doctrine fails of application. Congress has an unquestioned right to legislate retroactively in order to provide legal standing for the expulsion of aliens for the commission of offenses which

[29] See the materials in Whiteman, Vol. VIII, pp. 348–379, 427–539, 573–622, and 634–660.

[30] *Caranica* v. *Nagle*, United States, Circuit Court of Appeals, Ninth Circuit, 1928, 28 F. (2d) 955.

did not render them subject to deportation when the offenses were committed.[31]

Right of Trial and Punishment. Aliens legally admitted to the territorial jurisdiction of a state may, of course, be punished for any offenses committed by them on the territory of the host state or on ships or aircraft registered in that state. They may be tried and punished for having, anywhere, counterfeited its currency, postage stamps, or official documents. Any state may try and punish an alien in its territory for a crime, wherever it may have been committed, constituting piracy under the law of nations. A state may prosecute and punish aliens within its territory for a crime, regardless of its location, against its independence or security. This right is regarded as part of a nation's right of self-defense.[32]

The United States attitude, affirming the right of American courts to try aliens for crimes committed beyond American territorial jurisdiction, is illustrated very clearly in

UNITED STATES v. RODRIGUEZ
United States, District Court, S.D. Cal., 1960, 182 F. Supp. 479

FACTS

Rodriguez, a citizen of Portugal, was charged with making a false statement in an immigration application and obtaining an immigrant visa based on false claim. He represented that he was the husband of Kathleen Walker, an American citizen, and claimed that, by reason of that marriage, he was a nonquota immigrant. The government asserted that the marriage was a sham entered into in Mexico without intention of consummation, but for the purpose of enabling defendant to obtain a nonquota visa to which he was not entitled. Defendant had moved to dismiss the indictment.

ISSUE

Could an alien be tried in a United States court for an offense committed abroad?

DECISION

Motions to dismiss the indictment denied; Rodriguez was found guilty of the crime charged.

REASONING

The United States government, under what is termed the "protective principle of jurisdiction," may acquire jurisdiction over a crime by reference to the national interest injured by the offense. In certain cases, in which the laws of the United States are violated and in which the crime constitutes an offense directed at the government in its capacity as sovereign, the government has the power to punish those

[31] See *Lehmann v. United States ex rel. Carson*, United States, Supreme Court, 1957, 353 U.S. 685, and *Mulcahey v. Catalanotte, ibid.*, 1957, 353 U.S. 692.

[32] The Harvard Research in International Law "Draft Convention on Jurisdiction in Respect of Crime" included a very desirable reservation which would exclude from this right any act "committed in exercise of a liberty guaranteed the alien by the law of the place" of the commission of the act (such as the right of assembly or the right of free speech): see 29 *A.J.I.L.* (1935), Special Supp., pp. 543 and 557.

who have broken its laws, should those persons later be found in the United States.

Entry by an alien into the United States secured by means of false statements or documents is an attack directly on the sovereignty of the United States. The crimes with which the defendant was charged fit in that category of crimes which the law of nations recognizes as offenses against sovereignty and within the express power of Congress to fashion penal legislation concerning offenses "against the Law of Nations," Article I, Section 8, Clause 10. Also, Congress was expressly authorized in Article III, Section 2, Clause 3, to provide for the place of trial when the crime has not been "committed within any State." [33]

A growing number of states is viewing favorably a principle under which crimes committed by aliens abroad would fall within the jurisdiction of any state arresting the offender, provided that an offer of extradition had been made to the state in whose territory the crime had been committed and that this offer had not been acted on.

Legal Position of Alien. The legal position of the alien within the territorial jurisdiction of a state depends primarily on the judgment of the host government; it is the latter which decides what rights, other than protection of life and property, shall be conceded to him. Most states have been willing, in recent decades, to grant to the alien civil rights substantially the same as those enjoyed by the nationals of those states, while at the same time denying to aliens the political rights and privileges enjoyed by those nationals. Thus aliens normally have the right to hold, inherit, and transfer real estate, the right to make contracts, to practice professions and licensed occupations (subject to certain restrictions in various states), the right of religious worship (violated on occasion, however, in a considerable number of states), and most of the normal civil rights in existence in a given country.

Ownership of real estate, a subject of many contentious arguments between states, is frequently restricted on a geographical basis: no such alien ownership is permitted within a given distance measured from a frontier. In certain countries, aliens are banned from owning or operating specific types of industrial enterprises subject to grants of concessions by the national government, grants which by law are available only to citizens of the state in question. Ownership of media of mass communications is frequently forbidden to aliens.

One of the more controversial aspects of territorial jurisdiction over aliens involves their induction into the armed forces or labor services of the host state. For obvious security reasons, only friendly aliens—that is, neutral citizens or "enemy citizens" opposed ideologically or in some other manner to a hostile government—are conscripted in time of war. Many, but certainly not all, countries, such as the United States, reward

[33] See also Frank G. Reeder, "Jurisdiction over Aliens for Crimes Committed Abroad," *Michigan Law Review*, 60 (1961), pp. 109–112.

military service by citizenship, often through a greatly accelerated procedure of naturalization. Refusal to serve may cost the alien the chance to be naturalized at a later date and frequently leads to deportation at the earliest possible occasion. In a most interesting decision in the case of *McGrath v. Kristensen*,[34] the Supreme Court of the United States held that Kristensen, a Danish national who had come to the United States in August, 1939, and had been unable to leave as planned because of the outbreak of war, was "not residing in the United States" for purposes of liability for military service. His filing a claim for relief from the application of the Selective Service Act did not, therefore, make Kristensen ineligible to citizenship.

JURISDICTION OVER ARMED FORCES ABROAD

The jurisdiction of a state normally extends to its armed forces stationed beyond its territory. This authority is not as completely exclusive as might appear at first thought.[35] Even though such armed forces enter a given state with the tacit or express permission of the territorial sovereign, they may not always be immune from the jurisdiction of the latter, despite the statement of the court in the *Schwartzfiger Case*[36] that ". . . exemption from the local jurisdiction is recognized by all civilized nations; and is not considered a diminution of their sovereignty or independence."

The obvious remedy to be adopted if a multitude of irritating controversies is to be avoided is to conclude a special agreement with the host state, in which the latter stipulates precisely to what extent it is willing to waive any claims to jurisdiction over allied or friendly troops crossing its territory or stationed therein.

Until World War II, agreements along the lines mentioned continued to reserve far-reaching authority over visiting military forces to the host state. Thus Article IV of the Anglo-American agreement of March 27, 1941 (modified in 1950), governing the status of United States military personnel in British islands off the American coasts reserved British authority over all nonmilitary offenses committed by such personnel outside air and naval bases. A complete waiver of jurisdiction did not occur until after the United States entered the war.

Status of Forces Agreements. Since World War II, the lessons learned during that conflict have resulted in the conclusion of so-called Status of

[34] United States, Supreme Court, 1950, 340 U.S. 162; see also Whiteman, Vol. VIII, pp. 540–573; William W. Fitzhugh, Jr., and Charles C. Hyde, "The Drafting of Neutral Aliens by the United States," 36 *A.J.I.L.* (1942), pp. 369–382; John Houck, "Neutral Aliens Who Sought Relief from Military Service Barred from Becoming U.S. Citizens," 52 *Michigan Law Review* (1953), pp. 265–276.

[35] Consult Gould, pp. 463–464, concerning some unusual limitations in this sphere; see also Lauterpacht's *Oppenheim*, Vol. I, pp. 846–851, on this topic.

[36] Panama, Supreme Court, 1925: see Hackworth, Vol. II, p. 405, and 21 *A.J.I.L.* (1927), p. 182.

Forces Agreements through which the position of friendly armed forces has been regularized in considerable detail. At the time of writing, armed forces of the United States stationed in sixty-seven countries are subject to the provisions of such agreements.[37]

Thus the Status of Forces Agreement (N.A.T.O.) of June 19, 1951 (in effect as of August 23, 1953) provided in Article VII for concurrent jurisdiction by both the sending and "receiving" state over members of the visiting armed forces, over civilian component personnel, and over the dependents of both categories.[38]

The Soviet Union has concluded similar agreements with the various satellite countries in which Russian military units have been stationed.

Security treaties concluded by the United States with Japan and a number of other countries have authorized the making of administrative agreements for the disposition and immunities of United States armed forces stationed in the countries involved.[39] The operation of those postwar arrangements was illustrated in a striking manner in the much publicized case of *Girard* v. *Wilson et al.* (United States, Supreme Court, 1957, 35 U.S. 524).

JURISDICTION OVER ALIEN CORPORATIONS

A state may permit alien corporations to do business within its territorial jurisdiction, but such discretionary permission entails adherence by the enterprises concerned to all regulations issued for them by the state in question.

Even though a given enterprise may be incorporated under the laws of the state in which it operates, it may be classified and treated as an alien corporation if the test of control is applied by the state granting the charter (directly or through one of its political subdivisions).

The fact of alien ownership does not serve to protect an enterprise against nationalization, nor does such ownership, whether complete or

[37] Consult also the extensive materials found in Whiteman, Vol. VI, pp. 379–427.

[38] See 48 *A.J.I.L.* (1954), Supp., pp. 83 ff., for text. Consult also the study by Joseph H. Rouse and Gordon B. Baldwin, "The Exercise of Criminal Jurisdiction under the Nato Status of Forces Agreement," 51 *A.J.I.L.* (1957), pp. 29–62, which examines many of the difficulties encountered in such concurrent jurisdiction, as well as Richard R. Baxter, "Jurisdiction over Visiting Forces and the Development of International Law," *Proceedings* (1958), pp. 174–180, with the discussion of that paper, *ibid.*, pp. 181–199.

[39] Consult the Note "Criminal Jurisdiction over American Armed Forces Abroad," 70 *Harvard Law Review* (1957), pp. 1043–1066, and see *United States* v. *Ekenstam et al.*, United States, Court of Military Appeals, June 22, 1956, 7 U.S.M.C.A. 168, 21 C.M.R. 294, digested in 50 *A.J.I.L.* (1956), pp. 961–962. The American-Japanese Security Treaty of 1951 was replaced by a new Treaty of Mutual Cooperation and Security, signed on January 19, 1960. The new instrument regulates, *inter alia*, the status of U.S. Armed Forces in Japan. The text of the 1960 agreement was reprinted in 38 *Current History* (1960), pp. 293–308.

partial, private or public, guarantee prompt and equitable compensation. In every respect, alien holdings are on a basis of complete equality of treatment with the nationals of the expropriating state.

A HISTORICAL NOTE: CAPITULATIONS

The nineteenth century still saw in existence a great variety of legal systems, many of which differed materially from institutions and values prevailing in the principal Western states. In order to assure their citizens judicial procedures somewhat akin to those found at home and deemed superior to or fairer than those found in Asia or Africa, a number of the Western powers developed a system of "extraterritorial jurisdictions" which they imposed on other states through superior strength.

Beginning in Turkey, this system entitled the resident citizens of a number of countries to be subject to the laws of their own governments and to be tried, if accused of offenses, by diplomatic or consular courts operated by, and under the laws of, the Western states in question. This system was based in part on custom and in part on special bilateral treaties ("capitulations"), with the latter imposing unilateral obligations on the non-European state. In other words, a British citizen in Turkey would be tried by a British court under British law, but a Turkish citizen residing in Great Britain would be tried in a British, not a Turkish, court and under the laws of Great Britain.

The system spread from Turkey to Egypt, Japan, Thailand (Siam), China, and a number of other countries.[40] In time, each of the states affected by these "unequal treaties" managed either to abrogate unilaterally or, by agreement, abolish these encroachments on its territorial sovereignty, such as Japan in 1899, Thailand in 1920, Turkey in 1923 (except with the United States, which relinquished the privileged position of its citizens by a treaty signed in 1931), Iran in 1927, Egypt in 1937,[41] China in 1943, and Morocco in 1956.

SUGGESTED READINGS

NATIONALITY

Whiteman, Vol. VIII, pp. 1–22, 64–101, 105–113, 119–187; Gould, pp. 438–452; Jessup, pp. 78–80 and 82–84, on "right of emigration"; Helen Silving, "Na-

[40] See Hackworth, Vol. II, pp. 493–621; Moore, Vol. II, pp. 593–755; Whiteman, Vol. VI, pp. 278–354. Almost every textbook on international law published before, say, 1930, contained an extensive and instructive section on capitulations.

[41] See the case of *Protection of French Nationals and Protégés in Egypt* (*France v. Egypt*), instituted by France before the International Court of Justice on October 13, 1949, as reported by Manley O. Hudson in 44 *A.J.I.L.* (1950), pp. 22–29. The dispute centered on incidents occurring during a transition period of twelve years following the abolition of capitulations in Egypt by the Montreux Convention of 1937. The proceedings were discontinued on March 29, 1950, after Egypt revoked the measures to which France had objected.

tionality in Comparative Law," 5 *American Journal of Comparative Law* (1956), pp. 410–442; Ivan Sipkov, "Settlement of Dual Nationality in European Countries," 56 *A.J.I.L.* (1962), pp. 1010–1019.

Cases

(1) General:

Kaplan v. Tod, United States, Supreme Court, 1925, 267, U.S. 228.

Petition of Berini, United States, District Court, Eastern Dist., New York, 1953, 121 F. Supp. 481.

Moser v. United States, United States, Supreme Court, 1951, 341 U.S. 41.

Stoeck v. Public Trustee, Great Britain, Chancery Division, 1921, [1921] 2 Ch. 67.

United States v. Best, United States, District Court, Mass., 1948, 76 F. Supp. 138 and 857, and also *Best v. United States*, United States, Circuit Court of Appeals, First Circuit, 1950, 184 F. (2d) 131.

Weedin v. Chin Bow, United States, Supreme Court, 1927, 274 U.S. 657.

(2) Dual Nationality:

The Canevaro Case, Tribunal of the Permanent Court of Arbitration, 1912, in James B. Scott, *Hague Court Reports*, 1916, pp. 284 ff.

Kawakita v. United States, United States, Supreme Court, 1952, 343 U.S. 717.

(3) Loss of Citizenship:

Schurmann v. United States, United States, Circuit Court of Appeals, Ninth Circuit, 1920, 264 F. 917.

Kennedy, Attorney General, v. Mendoza-Martinez; Rusk, Secretary of State, v. Cort. United States, Supreme Court, 1963, 372 U.S. 144, noted in *A.J.I.L.* 57 (1963), pp. 666–669.

THE NOTTEBOHM CASE

The commentary on the *Nottebohm Case* is very extensive: see the literature cited in Josef L. Kunz, "The Nottebohm Judgment (Second Phase)," 54 *A.J.I.L.* (1960), pp. 536–571. Consult also the digests of the decision of November 18, 1953, by the Court on the Preliminary Objection, *I.C.J. Reports, 1953,* pp. 111 ff. in 48 *A.J.I.L.* (1954), pp. 327–332, and of the 1955 judgment in *The Nottebohm Case (Liechtenstein v. Guatemala)*, International Court of Justice, April 6, 1955, *I.C.J. Reports, 1955,* pp. 4 ff., in 49 *A.J.I.L.* (1955), pp. 396–403.

POSITION OF ALIENS

Cases

United States v. Rocha, United States, Court of Appeals, 2nd Circuit, 1961, 228 F. 2d 545, *certiorari* denied, 1961, 366 U.S. 942.

United States v. Pizzarusso, United States, Court of Appeals, 2nd Circuit, 1968, reported in 62 *A.J.I.L.* (1968), pp. 975–976.

F. Kalshoven, "Criminal Jurisdiction over Military Persons in the Territory of a Friendly Foreign Power," 5 *Tijdschrift* (1958), p. 165–194; Edwin G. Schuck, "Concurrent Jurisdiction under the NATO Status of Forces Agreement," 57 *Columbia Law Review* (1957), pp. 355–371; Murray L. Schwartz, "International Law and the NATO Status of Forces Agreement," *ibid.*, 53 (1953), pp. 1091–1113; James H. Doyle, Jr., and Horace B. Robertson, Jr., "Our Status of Forces Agreements," 84 *U.S. Naval Institute Proceedings*, No. 3 (1958), pp. 77–85; G. I. Draper, *Civilians and the NATO Status of Forces Agreement* (Leyden: A. W. Sijthoff, 1966); Departments of the Air Force, the Army, and the Navy, *Status of Forces Policies, Procedures, and Information* (Air Force Regulation No. 110–12; Army Regulation No. 27–50; SECNAV Instruction 5820.4C) (Washington, D.C.: 28 June 1967).

Case

Reid v. Covert; Kinsella v. Krueger (On Rehearing), United States, Supreme Court, 1957, 354 U.S. 1, excerpted at length in 51 *A.J.I.L.* (1957), pp. 783–794.

THE INTERHANDEL CASE

Herbert W. Briggs, "Towards the Rule of Law?" 51 *A.J.I.L.* (1957), pp. 517–530, and the reply by Sidney B. Jacoby, "Towards the Rule of Law?" *ibid.*, 52 (1958), pp. 107–113; Malcolm S. Mason, "The General Aniline and Film Co. Case," *Proceedings* (1958), pp. 114–125, and the commentary thereon by Rosalind Branning, *ibid.*, pp. 125–127, as well as Herbert W. Briggs, "The Interhandel Case," *ibid.*, pp. 127–129, and Wallace McClure, "The Interhandel Case," *ibid.*, pp. 129–132; Herbert W. Briggs, "Interhandel: The Court's Judgment of March 21, 1959, on the Preliminary Objections of the United States," 53 *A.J.I.L.* (1959), pp. 547–563; *Interhandel Case (Switzerland v. U.S.A.)*, (Request by the Swiss Government for the Indication of Interim Measures of Relief), *Order of the International Court of Justice, October 24, 1957*, in *I.C.J. Reports, 1957*, pp. 105 ff., digested in 52 *A.J.I.L.* (1958), pp. 320–326; and the text of the judgment itself, *I.C.J. Reports, 1959*, p. 6 or an excellent digest by William W. Bishop, Jr., in 53 *A.J.I.L.* (1959), pp. 671–687. Consult also K. R. Simmonds, "The Interhandel Case," 10 *International and Comparative Law Quarterly* (1961), pp. 495–547. For various stages in the lengthy litigation, consult 46 *A.J.I.L.* (1952), p. 554; *ibid.*, 51 (1957), p. 818; *ibid.*, 53 (1959), p. 177 and p. 671; *ibid.*, 59 (1965), pp. 97–98; *ibid.*, 61 (1967), pp. 615–616; and 65 *Newsweek* (March 22, 1965), pp. 71–72.

13
Responsibilities of States for the Protection of Resident Aliens

INTRODUCTION

F EW AREAS in the international law of peace have evoked more numerous and more controversial questions than that which involves the relations between a state and aliens residing in its territory. In its broader aspects this sphere of the law involves not only foreign citizens living in a given state but also contractual agreements concluded between a state and the citizens of foreign countries, as well as the property of aliens located in a given country.

Each state is the sole judge of the extent to which aliens enjoy civil privileges within its jurisdiction. But beyond those permissive grants, each alien, as a human being, may be said to be endowed with certain rights, both as to person and to property, which are his by virtue of his being. It is primarily in connection with those basic rights that a responsibility on the part of the host state arises. It is in this sphere that claims originate and, under certain conditions, may be advanced against the host state by the government to which the alien owes allegiance.[1]

Concept of Imputability. Traditional theory and practice insisted that only a state could incur direct or indirect international responsibility. The actual author or authors of the act or omission responsible for the injury suffered by an alien were not involved in any international claim because only the state could be charged with a duty or responsibility to make reparation for such injury. The technical name for this concept is *imputability*, which means the legal attribution of a particular act by a person or group of persons to a state or some other international person, whereby the act in question is henceforth considered to be the latter's own act and hence responsibility. This concept underlies the entire notion of state responsibility in international law, because many acts creating

---

[1] General note: See Hackworth, Vol. V, pp. 471–851; Moore, Vol. VI, pp. 605–1037; Hyde, Vol. II, pp. 871–1012; Jessup, pp. 94–122; Harvard Research in International Law, "Responsibility of States," 23 *A.J.I.L.* (1929), Special Supplement, pp. 131–239; see note 5 for the recent revision of the original Harvard Research draft articles; Whiteman, Vol. VIII, pp. 697–1291.

such responsibility are undertaken initially by natural persons or groups of such persons.

The situation is not quite as simple at the present time. It has become increasingly apparent that only tradition prevented a combination of state responsibility with that of the organs or individuals directly responsible for the act or omission in question.

In 1930 the Hague Codification Conference called by the League of Nations failed to achieve a generally acceptable code of this portion of international law. A year earlier the Harvard Research in International Law had completed a draft code but that private effort remained just that, despite a recent revision.[2]

Status of Aliens.[3] Under normal conditions an alien traveling through or residing in a given state enjoys no special privileges because of his alien status. He cannot claim any substantive rights greater than those of the citizens of his host state, and, indeed, lacks any special political or civil rights reserved to the latter by their own state.

In like manner, the alien normally has to make use of the same courts and the same legal procedures utilized by the local citizens in seeking redress for injuries or wrongs suffered by them. The laws of the host state protect the alien to the same degree as they protect the local citizen, subject to any existing legal limitations as to the alien's property and contract rights. Thus, if a given state should prohibit the ownership by aliens of uranium mines, a citizen of a foreign country, residing in the state in question, could not find judicial relief in the courts of the host state if he tried to acquire ownership of such a mine and was blocked in his endeavors.

Similarly, an alien does not enjoy a privileged status with reference to taxes. If, however, some form of discriminatory tax is imposed, the state is responsible and an international claim may be lodged against it. In the past such discrimination was excluded through specific provisions found in commercial and other treaties, but by now it can be asserted that a rule of customary international law protects the alien against discriminatory taxation, even though he is *not* protected against possible double taxation, by his host state and by his own government, in the absence of contrary agreements.[4]

Many states reserve certain occupations or professions to their own citizens. Such restrictions may originate for numerous reasons: certain occupations involve security considerations and hence, it is felt, ought to be staffed with loyal nationals; in some professions, national standards are deemed to require training in the schools or colleges of the particular state in question; and so on. As long as reasonable objectives or logical

---

[2] See note 5 for details.

[3] See also Chapter 12 concerning *jurisdiction* over aliens.

[4] See Hackworth, Vol. III, p. 575; a representative case illustrating the problem at hand is *Burnet* v. *Brooks*, United States, Supreme Court, 1933, 288 U.S. 378.

purposes are behind the restrictions and as long as the latter apply only to individuals desiring to enter the occupations in the future, no objections can be raised by other states. On the other hand, there are treaties in existence which specifically forbid such limitations and a violation of such an agreement could create state responsibility.

What if an alien is exposed to an openly oppressive or discriminatory law or encounters a clearly unfair administration of a law? Or, again, what if the alien, seeking justice in the courts of the host state, should be denied justice? Or, what if an alien being prosecuted for a violation of local law is singled out for disproportional punishment?

Denial of Justice. In all these instances, a denial of justice is said to have taken place and such denial may justify a claim on the part of the alien's own state, in his name and on his behalf, to secure justice for the alien in question. Such a claim would, if advanced properly, rest on a right of his state and would involve the application of principles of international law.[5]

"Denial of justice," a much disputed term, involves in general terms any failure on the part of the authorities of the host state to provide adequate means of redress to the alien when his substantive rights have suffered or, if the alien has violated the laws of the host state, to observe due process of law in the prosecution and punishment of the alien offender. A broad interpretation of the term would expand its meaning to include such matters as denial of access to the local courts, inefficiency in the performance of police and judicial processes, or an obviously unfair treatment or judicial decision. But a word of caution is necessary: the real question involved in a "denial of justice" has usually been whether or not a state was responsible internationally for some particular act or some specific omission of an act, which under international law (1) was wrongful, (2) was attributable, and (3) caused an injury to an alien. It has not been whether such act or omission could be called denial of justice. In the absence of agreement among authorities as to the meaning of the term, specific reference to its special circumstances has to be had in each case before it can be claimed that responsibility has arisen because of a denial of justice.

Minimum Standard of Justice. Now standards of justice and the treatment of citizens vary considerably from country to country. Many governments, proceeding from the assumption that an alien entered their jurisdiction voluntarily, have asserted that no special favors should be

[5] Consult the "Draft Convention on the International Responsibility of States for Injuries to Aliens," [A revision of the draft prepared in 1929 by the Harvard Research in International Law, reproduced in 23 *A.J.I.L.* (1929), Special Supplement, pp. 133–239; the revision was completed in 1961 by the Harvard Law School.] Articles 3–8, in Louis B. Sohn and R. R. Baxter, "Responsibilities of States for Injuries to the Economic Interests of Aliens," 55 *A.J.I.L.* (1961), pp. 545–584, at pp. 548–551; see also the related discussion in *Proceedings* (1960), pp. 102–120, which reproduces additional important draft articles.

granted to him, even if their treatment of their own citizens fell below the standards prevailing in the alien's own country. This attitude, more prevalent than might be supposed, raises the question of the so-called minimum standard of justice. Is there a minimum standard below which no civilized state would or should go?

The United States, Great Britain, and other countries have insisted for many decades that there is indeed such a minimum standard, a view shared by a number of international arbitration tribunals.[6] As Elihu Root, the distinguished American jurist, once stated,

If any country's system of law and administration does not conform to that standard, although the people of the country may be content and compelled to live under it, no other country can be compelled to accept it as furnishing a satisfactory measure of treatment to its citizens.[7]

In view of the absence of a governing general international treaty, the rights of aliens may be assumed to be based on customary law, as was pointed out in *Hines* v. *Davidowitz et al.* [United States, Supreme Court, 1941, 312 U.S. 52]:

. . . apart from treaty obligations, there has grown up in the field of international relations a body of customs defining with more or less certainty the duties owing by all nations to alien residents—duties which our State Department has often successfully insisted foreign nations must recognize as to our nationals abroad. In general, both treaties and international practices have been aimed at preventing injurious discrimination against aliens.

The nature of the claimed minimum standard is also in dispute. This writer believes that the closest approach to a definition of a minimum standard of justice has thus far been achieved in the adoption, on December 10, 1948, of the Universal Declaration of Human Rights by the General Assembly of the United Nations.[8] Significantly, the states of Latin America, opposed traditionally to the concept of a minimum standard and upholding the idea of equality of treatment as late as the Montevideo Conference of 1933 (Convention on the Rights and Duties of States, Article 9), approved in 1948 at the Ninth International Conference of American States at Bogotá an American Declaration of the Rights and Duties of Man closely related to the United Nations instrument.[9]

[6] See Foreign Claims Settlement Commission (U.S.), Decision No. W-16119, *In the Matter of the Claim of Hugo Schlessinger and Eugene Schlessinger* (December 7, 1966), excerpted in 61 *A.J.I.L.* (1967), pp. 823–824.

[7] Presidential Address, *Proceedings* (1910), pp. 20–21.

[8] See Chapter 11; Whiteman, Vol. VIII, pp. 707–769; Arthur H. Kuhn, "International Standards of Criminal Justice," 33 *A.J.I.L.* (1939), pp. 338–341; E. Borchard, "The 'Minimum Standard' of the Treatment of Aliens," 38 *Michigan Law Review* (1940), pp. 445–461.

[9] Text in 43 *A.J.I.L.* (1949), Supp., pp. 133–139.

Assuming—for this must be done in order to justify many instances in which state responsibility is created—that there does exist a minimum standard of justice, ill-defined though it may be as yet, then we have to examine the precise conditions under which a state becomes responsible for what befalls an alien within its jurisdiction.

In the first place, because every state is responsible for the preservation of law and order in all territories under its control, any state is, in an indirect manner, responsible when any violence or violation of the law takes place. But obviously no government can be expected to prevent all violence (though all would devoutly wish for such ability) and therefore the responsibility of a state ceases when it makes available to the injured party the necessary facilities or means of redress for the wrongs suffered. In other words, a state is not responsible for, say, an attack on an alien by some individual, but would be held responsible if it failed to provide the alien with proper means of redress.

The practice of states as well as the decisions of national and international courts, all in accordance with the philosophy of positive international law, have demonstrated that as soon as a state espouses a claim by one of its nationals, the whole character of the claim changes: it is henceforth a claim by a state against a state.

Now, to exercise diplomatic protection (which is involved, of course, in the very concept of asserting a claim of a national as a claim of the state) represents without question a discretionary right of a state.[10] The latter may refuse to exercise this right for political reasons, even if its nationals have suffered injury through a violation of international law. And, as will be seen in connection with the Calvo Clause, the state may exercise its right even if the injured nationals refuse to make a claim. Damages, if such are involved in the settlement of a claim, are paid by a state to a state. The claimant state, in effect, claims for a wrong, for an injury, done to it as a state in the person of its citizens.

Rule of Local Remedies. It may not be amiss to mention at this point an aspect of state responsibility applicable to any injury to aliens, regardless of the source of that injury: the rule of local remedies.

It is a rule of international law that the international responsibility of a state for an injury to an alien may not be invoked (say, in the form of an international claim) as long as local remedies, available to the injured alien under the laws of the host state and providing adequate means of redress, have not been exhausted.

The injured alien must have resort to these local remedies which, normally, are represented by the courts of the host state, if only to determine whether the alleged injury had occurred, whether a denial of

[10] An interesting criticism of the belief that such a right exists on the basis of international law may be found in S. N. Guha Roy, "Is the Law of Responsibility of States for Injuries to Aliens a Part of Universal International Law?" 55 *A.J.I.L.* (1961), pp. 863–891.

justice had taken place, whether a violation of international law was evident, or whether any degree of state responsibility had already been created. Until such resort to local remedies has taken place, no international claim should be lodged against the host state, unless there is a question as to whether local remedies were available to the alien, provided adequate means of redress, or had been exhausted *ab initio*.[11]

RESPONSIBILITY FOR THE ACTS OF OFFICIALS

Responsibility Determined by Status of Officials. States are responsible for the acts of public officials affecting alien persons or property, but although these officials in a general way are the agents of the state, they are not equally related to that same state. Obviously, heads of state and national legislatures are directly connected with the state, and their acts become a direct responsibility of the latter. This is also true, but on a less immediate basis, for the major administrative officials and the courts of a state. Because their relationship to the state is slightly more remote than is the case, say, for a president, the state may at its discretion disavow the acts of administrators and, still responsible for such acts to another country, rid itself of the charge of intentional wrongdoing.

When the lower echelons of public officials are concerned in the act or omission affecting an alien, then their relative remoteness from the authority of the state creates, usually and at most, an indirect responsibility of the latter. True responsibility arises only if the state fails to punish the offending lower official, sheriff, policeman, and so on.

Regardless of the status of a public official, full and complete state responsibility may, however, be created under certain conditions. Thus, if an official at any level commits an unauthorized act against an alien and his government subsequently approves his action and ratifies or endorses it, then the act not only creates full state responsibility but the official concerned is absolved of all liability.

If, on the other hand, the injury done to the alien was due to the proper exercise of authority by law-enforcement agencies or agents, no state responsibility is created.[12]

[11] See Herbert W. Briggs, "The Local Remedies Rule," 50 *A.J.I.L.* (1956), pp. 921–927, at p. 526; David R. Mummery, "The Content of the Duty to Exhaust Local Judicial Remedies," 58 *A.J.I.L.* (1964), pp. 389–414; Stephen M. Schwebel and J. Gillis Wetter, "Arbitration and the Exhaustion of Local Remedies," *ibid.*, 60 (1966), pp. 484–501; see also Cheng, pp. 177–183, Hackworth, V, pp. 501–526, and the recent useful study by Castor H. P. Law, *The Local Remedies Rule in International Law* (Geneva: Librairie E. Droz, 1961). Consult the interesting decision in the *Panevezys-Saldutiskis Railway Case (Estonia* v. *Lithuania)*, Permanent Court of International Justice, *P.C.I.J.*, 1939, Ser. A/B, No. 76, and *The Ambatielos Case (Greece* v. *United Kingdom)*, Arbitral Award of March 6, 1956, reported in 50 *A.J.I.L.* (1956), pp. 674–679, especially at pp. 677–678.

[12] See *In the Matter of the Death of James Pugh (Great Britain* v. *Panama)*, Arbitral Decision of July 6, 1933, reproduced in 36 *A.J.I.L.* (1942), pp. 708–722.

Lack of Due Diligence. Illustrations of how state responsibility for injuries suffered by aliens is created, abound in the literature of the law. The following examples, several of which represent classic cases, may serve to show how "denial of justice" is established on the basis of the facts in a given incident.

UNITED STATES (LAURA M. B. JANES CLAIM) v. UNITED MEXICAN STATES

United States–Mexico, General Claims Commission, 1926
(Opinions of Commissioners, 1927, p. 108)

FACTS

Byron E. Janes, American superintendent of the El Tigre Mine at El Tigre, Sonora, Mexico, was shot to death at that location on July 10, 1918, by Pedro Carbajal, a discharged employee of the El Tigre Mining Co. The killing occurred in view of many persons living near the company's office. The local police chief was informed of Janes' death within five minutes and came at once. He delayed, however, the assembling of his men and then a further delay was caused by his insistence on a mounted posse. An hour after the shooting, the posse left in pursuit of the murderer who had hurried away on foot.

No trace of Carbajal was found, even though he stayed at a ranch some six miles from El Tigre for a week and, so it was rumored, visited the village twice during that period. Later it was reported that the fugitive was at a mescal plant 75 miles south of El Tigre. When the Mexican civilian and military authorities were informed of this news, no steps were taken to capture Carbajal until the mining company offered a reward. Then a small military detachment was dispatched to the mescal plant, but Carbajal had left again before the soldiers arrived. No further steps were taken by Mexican authorities, beyond

the circulation among the judges of first instance in the State of Sonora of a request for the arrest of the fugitive killer.

Mrs. Laura Janes, on her own behalf and that of her children, lodged a claim against Mexico with the Department of State, charging lack of diligence on the part of the Sonora authorities in apprehending, trying, and punishing Pedro Carbajal. The Department agreed to press a claim against Mexico on Mrs. Janes' behalf.

ISSUE

Were the authorities of Sonora guilty of a lack of due diligence in the Janes case and thereby gave rise to an American claim against the United Mexican States?

DECISION

The Commission decided that there had been a proven case of lack of due diligence and awarded the United States, on behalf of Mrs. Janes and her children, the sum of $12,000.

REASONING

The Mexican government was liable for not having measured up to its duty of diligently pursuing and properly punishing the offender (in both cases through the authorities of the State of Sonora). The damage caused by the culprit was the damage caused to Janes' relatives by the death of the superintendent; the damage caused by the government's negligence was the damage resulting from the nonpunishment of the murderer. If the government had not failed in its duty, Janes' family "would have been spared indignant neglect and would have had an opportunity of subjecting the murderer to a civil suit."

The Commission admitted that the measure of the damage caused by the delinquency of the government was more difficult than that of the damage caused by the killing itself. Taking into account the grief suffered by Janes' death and the additional suffering caused by the apparent neglect of its duty on the part of the Mexican government, the Commission settled on the sum of $12,000 as satisfaction for the damage caused by the nonapprehension and nonpunishment of the murderer.

Exercise of Due Diligence. In contrast to the Janes Claim, in which lack of due diligence resulted in an assumption of responsibility by a state, the following case shows what happens when reasonable diligence is exercised:

UNITED STATES (L. F. H. NEER CLAIM) v. UNITED MEXICAN STATES

United States–Mexico, General Claims Commission, 1926
(Opinions of Commissioners, 1927, p. 71)

FACTS

Paul Neer, an American citizen, was superintendent of a mine near Guanaceví, State of Durango, Mexico. On November 16, 1924, about 8 P.M., when he and his wife were riding from the village to their nearby home, they were stopped by a group of armed men who, after exchanging a few words with Neer, engaged in a gunfight with him. The American was killed.

Mrs. Neer summoned help and the village authorities went to the scene of the killing on the night it took place; on the following morning the local judge examined some witnesses, including Mrs. Neer. Several days passed during which a number of suspects were arrested but released subsequently because of lack of evidence. Mrs. Neer was unable to supply a detailed description of the members of the group which had been involved in the affair.

Mrs. Neer filed a claim for $100,000, on behalf of herself and her daughter, with the Department of State against Mexico, charging that the Mexican authorities showed an unwarrantable lack of intelligent investigation in prosecuting the culprits involved in the death of her husband. The claim was placed before the United States–Mexico General Claims Commission.

ISSUE

Had there taken place a lack of due diligence on the part of the Durango authorities and was that lack of diligence of such a nature as to create state responsibility for Mexico?

DECISION

The Commission decided that there had been no sufficient lack of due diligence to justify state responsibility;

it therefore rejected the American claim.

REASONING

The Commission agreed that the Durango and local authorities might have acted in a more vigorous manner in seeking to apprehend the culprits in the slaying of Neer. However, the Commission also recognized that the local authorities were handicapped by the fact that Mrs. Neer, the only prosecution eyewitness to the murder, had not overheard the exchange of words between Neer and his killers and that she could not supply the authorities with any helpful information, such as the description of the individuals involved.

In view of the steps taken by the authorities, such as the investigations carried out and the examination of arrested suspects, the Commission held that whatever lack of vigor had been displayed did not constitute a lack of diligence serious enough to charge the Mexican government with an international delinquency. For this reason the claim of the United States was disallowed.

More Examples of Lack of Due Diligence. Other cases mostly dating to the same period as the Janes and Neer claims, serve to illustrate the lack of or the existence of due diligence. Thus in the well-known Youmans case,[13] an American claim for $50,000 was allowed to the extent of $20,000 for the death of an American citizen who, together with two other United States nationals, was the victim of a mob attack in Angangues, State of Michoacán, Mexico.

The three men were hiding in a house following a wage dispute between one of them and a Mexican citizen, involving the sum of twelve cents. The killings had been accomplished under rather unusual circumstances: when a mob attacked the house in question, the local mayor, failing to quiet the crowd, had ordered a lieutenant in the state troops to use his men to quell the riot. The soldiers, arriving at the scene of the disturbance, instead of dispersing the mob, opened fire on the house, killing one of the Americans. The two others, driven from their refuge when part of the mob entered it from the rear, were killed by the troops and members of the mob. Their bodies were dragged through the streets, mutilated, and left under a pile of rocks by the side of a road.

The next morning Mexican federal troops arrived and restored order. Court action was started against twenty-nine members of the mob, but only eighteen of these were arrested. Several of this number were then released on nominal bail and were never troubled again. Five persons were sentenced to death, but their sentences were commuted, with no real effect, however, for one had died in the meantime and the other four had left town before they were even arrested. Seven were acquitted, the cases against six others were discontinued, and the charges against the remaining eleven were still left open as late as 1887, seven years after

---

[13] *United States (T. H. Youmans Claim)* v. *United Mexican States*, United States-Mexico General Claims Commission, 1926 (*Opinions of Commissioners*, 1927, p. 150).

the riot had taken place, just in case they were apprehended and prosecution could be undertaken against them.

The Claims Commission decided that the Mexican government had to assume responsibility for failure to exercise due diligence to protect Youmans and failure to take proper steps for the apprehension and punishment of the guilty parties. The participation of troops of the State of Michoacán aggravated the responsibility laid on the government of Mexico.

Frequently a charge of denial of justice forms the basis of a claim against a state. This generally occurs when an alien is brought to court and later claims irregularity in proceedings, cruel treatment, or a clearly unjust sentence. The following case, despite its bizarre elements, may serve to illustrate some of the meanings of denial of justice:

UNITED STATES (B. E. CHATTIN CLAIM) v. UNITED MEXICAN STATES

United States–Mexico General Claims Commission, 1927
(Opinions of Commissioners, 1927, p. 422)

FACTS

Chattin, an American citizen, had worked since 1908 as a conductor for the *Ferrocarril Sud-Pacífico de México* (Southern Pacific Railroad of Mexico). He was arrested on July 9, 1910, at Mazatlán, State of Sinaloa, on a charge of embezzlement. It appeared that Chattin and a Mexican brakeman employed by the railroad had been engaged in the fraudulent sale of railroad tickets and had kept the proceeds of their enterprise for themselves. Chattin was kept in prison until January, 1911, pending trial; was tried in that month, convicted on February 6, 1911, and sentenced to two years' imprisonment. He was released from the jail in Mazatlán in May or June, 1911, when the revolutionary forces of General Madero entered the town and liberated all prisoners.

Chattin returned to the United States and filed a claim with the Department of State, alleging that the arrest, trial, and sentence had been illegal, that he had suffered inhuman treatment in jail, and that all this merited damages to the amount of $50,000.

ISSUE

Had a denial of justice taken place in the judicial proceedings and imprisonment involving Chattin? If such denial had occurred, did responsibility devolve on the government of Mexico?

DECISION

The Commission decided in favor of the United States and ordered Mexico to pay to the United States, on behalf of Chattin, the sum of $5,000 as damages for denial of justice sufficiently grave to create state responsibility for Mexico.

REASONING

[NOTE: There appears to have been no question as to Chattin's guilt on the charge of embezzlement: he and the brakeman had been guilty as charged.]

The Commission found that Chattin

had been legally arrested, although the procedure used differed from that normally employed in the United States. On the other hand, the evidence produced indicated grave irregularities in the court proceedings, such as lack of proper investigation, insufficient confrontation with witnesses and evidence, failure to acquaint the accused with all the charges brought against him, undue delay in starting judicial proceedings, rendering the hearings in open court a mere formality, and a proven intentional severity of the judgment (without, however, proof of unfriendliness on the part of the judge,

as claimed by Chattin). Mistreatment in the prison was not proven, in the opinion of the Commission.

In view of the foregoing and of the fact that Chattin had stayed in prison for eleven months instead of the two years, the Commission allowed damages on his behalf to the extent of $5,000.

NOTE: It should be mentioned that Chattin and his fellow embezzler had appealed the decision of the Mazatlán court up to the Supreme Court of Mexico, but had lost the appeals; so local remedies had been exhausted before the claim was submitted to the Department of State.

Enactments of national legislative bodies are considered to be acts of state. This means that direct responsibility is created by the acts themselves, and foreign states are held to be entitled to protest against legislation clearly injurious to their citizens or their property.

INTERNATIONAL RESPONSIBILITY FOR PRIVATE ACTS

Under normal conditions a state does not assume international responsibility for injuries suffered by aliens in their persons or property at the hands of the state's own private citizens. However, under certain circumstances such state responsibility may develop. For instance, if the state fails to provide local remedies capable of effective and adequate redress of the injury sustained at private hands, the basis of an international claim has been established.

Outbreaks of mob violence resulting in injury to alien persons or property also may create state responsibility. In this case, the lawfulness of a claim would center on the presence of preventive efforts as well as on the adequacy of redress. It was stated earlier that no state can be expected to prevent all outbreaks of violence: the mere occurrence of a riot or mob attack does not, therefore, automatically lay the foundation for a claim. What matters is whether the state used due diligence to prevent the outbreak and, later, to punish persons guilty of injuring alien persons or property. If an outbreak is aimed only at aliens, the basis for a claim is more solid than if both citizens and aliens are the objects of an attack.

No generally applicable definition of due diligence can be supplied, for the circumstances of each particular incident have to be utilized to determine whether or not such diligence was lacking.

Law of State Responsibility. Summarizing the law of state responsibility as covered thus far, it can be said that a state is internationally responsible for an act or omission which, under international law, is wrong, is attributable to that state, and causes an injury to the alien. The latter is entitled to present an international claim to his own government only after he has exhausted the local remedies provided by the state allegedly responsible for the injury suffered by the alien. The host state is not internationally responsible if an alien suffers injury through violation of the laws of that state or through resistance offered to law-enforcement officers engaged in their lawful duties. State responsibility is created through the acts of public officials but the degree of responsibility and the redress to be granted vary with the nature of the officials and the acts committed by them. Ratification of an unauthorized official act makes that act a responsibility of the state. And denial of justice, including failure to use due diligence to prevent injury to an alien or to punish those guilty or injuring him may, depending on circumstances, create an international responsibility for the delinquent state.

RESPONSIBILITY FOR ALIEN PROPERTY

Property owned by an alien is subject to the same laws and regulations as apply to the property of citizens. This general principle does not exclude the issuing of laws or regulations prohibiting ownership of certain kinds of property by aliens or the acquisition of certain kinds of property in specified geographic areas by aliens. It would, therefore, be lawful to prohibit an alien from owning real estate within, say, ten miles of an important naval or missile base. Security considerations would or might justify such a prohibition and as long as all aliens would be affected by it, no valid exception to it could be taken by any government.

On the other hand, deliberate destruction of or damage to alien property would have to be considered to be unlawful unless such action were based on the judgment of a competent domestic court, or perhaps, of sanitation or health authorities, did not violate on a discriminatory basis the laws of the host country, and did not violate a treaty.

Right of Expropriation of Alien Property. Lay opinion to the contrary, every government possesses a right of expropriation, of eminent domain. The law of nations demands respect for private property, but it recognizes the right of the state to derogate from this principle, when its superior interest so requires. Thus it allows expropriation for reasons of public utility in time of peace and requisition in war.[14] Expropriated property may be foreign or domestic: no distinction need be drawn by the seizing government, except in the case of foreign-owned public (state-

---

[14] Portuguese–German Arbitration (1919), *Award II* (1930), in United Nations, *Reports of International Awards*, II, p. 1039.

owned) property. This principle has been affirmed again and again by international tribunals.[15]

Such taking of property could involve either a forcible transfer of title or a mere deprivation of the owner of the use of the property. In either case, as long as the following conditions outlined hold true, the action of the state does not create an international responsibility. Much as some may decry the taking away of private property by any state, there can be no question but that every independent political entity has an undoubted and lawful right to exercise the power of eminent domain.

Expropriation of foreign private property must, generally speaking, satisfy all of the following conditions if the question of basic state responsibility is to be avoided:

1. The taking must be by a foreign sovereign government.

2. The property must be within the territorial jurisdiction of that government.

3. The government in question must be existing and be recognized by the state of which the affected owners are citizens.

4. The taking must not violate any treaty obligations.

5. Prompt, effective, and adequate compensation must be paid, taking into account the fact that capacity to pay and to effect transfer of funds has a legitimate place in determining promptness and effectiveness of compensation.

6. No discrimination must exist in the taking.

7. The taking in question should be based on reasons of public utility, security, or national interest of a nature sufficiently great to override purely individual or private interests.[16]

It should be mentioned that in April, 1949, by a "supervening expression of Executive Policy," the government of the United States suspended the act of state doctrine for U.S. courts as far as forcible transfers of property under the laws of the former National Socialist government of Germany were concerned.[17]

There have been cases, however, in which the taking of alien property

---

[15] See *Norwegian Claims against the United States of America*, Permanent Court of Arbitration, 1922, in James B. Scott, ed., *Hague Court Reports*, II, at pp. 40–44, 70, as well as *German Interests in Polish Upper Silesia (Germany v. Poland)*, *Merits*, *P.C.I.J.*, 1926, Ser. A, No. 7, especially p. 22.

[16] On the last point mentioned, see also paragraph 4 of the Resolution on Permanent Sovereignty over Natural Resources, adopted by the General Assembly of the United Nations on December 14, 1962 (GA Res. 1803–XVII), reproduced in 57 *A.J.I.L.* (1963), pp. 710–712.

[17] Department of State Release No. 296, April 27, 1949, "Jurisdiction of U.S. Courts re Suits for Identifiable Property Involved in Nazi Forced Transfers"; see also William J. Cheeseman, "Note on *Menzel v. List*" (United States, Supreme Court of New York, 1966, N.Y.S. 2nd 804) in 8 *Harvard International Law Journal* (1967), pp. 130–144.

has been held to be "wrongful" regardless of whether or not compensation was paid: such cases hinged on the fact that the act of the state involved in the seizure violated a valid treaty. In such circumstances, restitution or replacement in kind was held to constitute the acceptable remedy. The classic example in this category is the *Case concerning the Factory at Chorzów*,[18] in which the court held that restitution was the appropriate remedy. The German-Polish Convention concerning Upper Silesia, the treaty applicable to the dispute in question, had specifically authorized expropriation of certain kinds of property but had excluded categorically the taking, even against payment of compensation, of other properties.[19] It should be noted that the *Chorzów* case has been the latest case before an international tribunal in which restitution was ordered; there have been, however, similar decisions by national courts and international claims commissions.

Nationalization of Alien Properties. Confiscation without payment of compensation has frequently reached enormous proportions in terms of the monetary value of the seized alien properties. Noteworthy instances relate to Russia's nationalization of alien properties immediately after the November Revolution of 1917, the seizure of American oil properties in Mexico on March 18, 1938 (eventually agreement was reached on the payment of what must be termed token compensation), the confiscation of foreign properties by the Russian satellite bloc in eastern Europe following the end of World War II, and the wholesale expropriation of foreign properties by the Chinese Communist state after 1949.

From a legal point of view, the two outstanding instances of nationalization in recent years were the Iranian seizure of the Anglo-Iranian Oil Company in 1951 and the Egyptian taking of the Suez Canal in 1956. (See Chapter 15 concerning the Suez Canal.)

Following the granting of Imperial assent on May 1, 1951, to two laws concerning seizure of the Anglo-Iranian Oil Company passed by the Iranian Majlis and Senate, a dispute arose between Iran and Great Britain. The British government, owning 35 per cent of the stock of the company, took the side of the corporation and on May 26 filed an application with the International Court of Justice. The Court, after considering the complicated evidence introduced by Great Britain, evidence mostly relating to the interpretation of earlier treaties concluded between the two disputants, decided that it lacked jurisdiction. The decision rested on the finding that Iran had not consented to the jurisdiction of the Court.

---

[18] *P.C.I.J.*, 1928, Ser. A, No. 17.

[19] *Ibid.*, p. 556; see also Martin Domke's comprehensively annotated study, "Foreign Nationalizations: Some Aspects of Contemporary International Law," 55 *A.J.I.L.* (1961), pp. 585–616, at pp. 596–598, on the question of treaty obligations and confiscation, and his "Nationalization of Foreign-Owned Property and the Act of State Doctrine: The Present American Attitude towards Nationalization of Foreign-Owned Property," *Duke Law Journal*, Vol. 1963, No. 2 (Spring, 1963), pp. 281–290.

Subsequently an international oil consortium worked out a scheme whereby it operated the oil properties in Iran as an agent of the Iranian government and paid annual sums to the previous owners as installments compensating them for the seizure of the properties in question.[20]

The Iranian seizure of the British oil properties gave birth to several interesting cases in national courts, centering on the question of the recognition of foreign expropriation decrees. The Iranian government, deprived of the tankers necessary to transport its newly acquired oil to the world's markets when British oil and shipping companies collaborated in a "tanker boycott" of Iran, arranged for the sale of oil to foreign companies, which in turn used their own or chartered tankers to fetch the oil from Iran.

In *Anglo-Iranian Oil Co.* v. *Jaffrate et al.*,[21] the company sued to obtain possession of a cargo of Iranian oil from the master (Italian citizen) of a tanker, against the Honduran corporation owning the vessel (registered in Panama), and the Swiss charterer of the vessel. The last had purchased the cargo of 700 tons of oil from the National Iranian Oil Company, the new agency operating the company's oil properties in Iran. The Aden court ordered transfer of the oil to the plaintiffs because of the failure of the Iranian government to pay compensation for the expropriated oil properties of the British company.

A decision in conflict with that handed down in the Aden case resulted when the Anglo-Iranian Oil Company sought to establish its ownership rights in a cargo of Iranian oil brought to Italy by an Italian company which had purchased the oil from the Iranian government agency. In *Anglo-Iranian Oil Company* v. *Società Unione Petrolifera Orientale*,[22] the court rejected the defendants' assertion that Italian courts had no jurisdiction and then rejected the plaintiff's claim to the oil in question, pointing out that the Iranian Nationalization Law provided for compensation in principle and set forth a procedure for arriving at its amount, even though the plaintiffs had rejected that procedure.

[20] The initial order of the Court, of July 5, 1951, was reprinted in 45 *A.J.I.L.* (1951), pp. 789–794; the excerpted judgment in *Anglo-Iranian Oil Company Case (Jurisdiction), United Kingdom* v. *Iran,* International Court of Justice, July 22, 1952, *I.C.J. Reports, 1952,* p. 93, is found in 46 *A.J.I.L.* (1952), pp. 737–751. Consult also Bin Cheng, "The Anglo-Iranian Dispute," 5 *World Affairs* (1951), pp. 387–405; Brendan F. Brown, "The Juridical Implications of the Anglo-Iranian Oil Company Case," *Washington University Law Quarterly* (Vol. 1952, June), pp. 384–397; and the excellent background material in J. Frankel, "The Anglo-Iranian Dispute," pp. 56–74 in London Institute of World Affairs, *Year Book of World Affairs, 1952* (New York: Praeger, 1952). The current operating arrangement is described in a pamphlet published by the Standard Oil Company (New Jersey) in 1960 (?), entitled *The Iranian Oil Agreement.*

[21] Colony of Aden, Supreme Court, January 9, 1953, reported in 47 *A.J.I.L.* (1953), pp. 325–328.

[22] Italy, Civil Tribunal of Venice, March 11, 1953, summarized in 47 *A.J.I.L.* (1953), pp. 509–510.

Nationalization can take effect immediately within the territory of the taking state. As soon as properties located beyond its jurisdiction are to be included in any expropriation, possibilities of conflict with the state in whose jurisdiction such properties are located are bound to arise. The general rule is that confiscations will not be given effect by a court in a foreign country with respect to assets located in that country unless the act of seizure is in accordance with the public policy of that foreign state. On occasion, however, particular political agreements and considerations result in deviations from this general rule.[23]

Other Means of Depriving Aliens of Property. Thus far only the actual expropriation, that is the assumption of title, of alien property has been considered. But there exist other ways of depriving an alien of his property, and such methods deserve brief comment.

Governments have attempted, for instance, to limit an alien's control or use of his property. Entrances to a factory have been barred on grounds of preserving public order; wage legislation and labor courts have lifted the wages of the employees of an alien enterprise to prohibitively high levels; entrance visas have been denied to vitally needed foreign technical personnel; allocations of required foreign exchange have been curtailed or stopped entirely; importations of replacement parts for machinery have been prevented; portions of buildings have been prohibited for use by the alien enterprise; conservators, managers, or inspectors have been introduced by government order into an enterprise and then prevented free use and direction on the part of the nominal foreign owners; or, by a simple prohibition on the sale of the property, the value of the assets was sharply reduced.[24]

Such interference with the utilization of an alien's property could easily bring about a decision to sell the property to the government in question or, in extreme cases, to a closing or even abandonment of the property. In many instances, the depreciation resulting from such state harassment was so great that sale to the government on its own terms brought far less than fair compensation for expropriation would have brought at the outset of the whole process. As yet no generally accepted rule of law exists which deals with such deliberate harassment of foreign-owned or controlled properties.

Guarantees to Foreign Investors. In response to the increasing risks of nationalization facing American investors in foreign countries, the United States government inaugurated an unusual program of guarantees to such investors in countries willing to sign relevant agreements with the United States. Beginning with the Marshall Plan in 1948, the program initially only covered the problem of currency convertibility; subsequently, not only expropriation but losses caused by war were included in the guarantees.

[23] See especially the famous case of *United States* v. *Pink, Superintendent of Insurance*, United States, Supreme Court, 1942, 62 Sup. Ct. 522.
[24] The list has been adapted from Sohn and Baxter, *op. cit.,* p. 559.

By the end of April, 1962, such agreements had been concluded, on a bilateral basis, between the United States and fifty-five countries.[25]

Protection of Foreign Investment. The increasing frequency of expropriation of alien property and of disputes concerning foreign investments prompted the Executive Directors of the International Bank for Reconstruction and Development (World Bank) to submit to governments, in March, 1965, a "Convention on the Settlement of Investment Disputes Between States and Nationals of Other States." This instrument was signed by forty-six governments and had been ratified by twenty-one of them when it entered into force on October 14, 1966.[26] It established an International Center for Settlement of Investment Disputes, located in the Bank, which is available to settle, by conciliation or arbitration, investment disputes between private foreign investors and sovereign states in which investments have been made. The center maintains panels of qualified persons from which arbitrators and conciliators may be selected. Its services are available to a contracting state and its nationals only after that state has become a party to the convention. Once a contracting state and a foreign investor have agreed to arbitrate or settle by conciliation a dispute, that agreement becomes binding and neither party may lawfully withdraw from it unilaterally. The United States ratified the convention on June 1, 1966.

It is hoped that if the new Center is utilized as planned in the settlement of investment disputes, a decline in recourse to diplomatic intervention in such disputes will be recorded.[27]

CONTRACTS BETWEEN A STATE AND ALIENS

A common source of international claims is that part of the general obligation of a state to protect aliens that has do with alleged breaches of contracts made between a state and an alien. The problem posed is not really one of state responsibility as such, for the state itself is one of the parties to the agreement and thus is involved directly from the beginning. The issue in question is the right, or lack thereof, of the alien's own

[25] For further details and a list of reference materials on the program, consult Bishop, pp. 694–695, as well as A. A. Fatouros, *Government Guaranties to Foreign Investors* (New York: Columbia University Press, 1962). See also Seymour J. Rubin, "The Investment Guaranty Program of the United States," *Proceedings* (1962), pp. 77–81; Aron Broches, "International Investment Guaranties: Possibilities and Problems," *ibid.*, pp. 81–87; and William C. Brewer, Jr., "The Proposal for Investment Guarantees by an International Agency," 58 *A.J.I.L.* (1964), pp. 62–87; and Edwin M. Martin, Jr., "Multilateral Investment Insurance: the OECD Proposal," 8 *Harvard International Law Journal* (1967), pp. 280–338.

[26] Text in 60 *A.J.I.L.* (1966), pp. 892–911.

[27] See Andreas F. Lowenfeld, "Diplomatic Intervention in Investment Disputes," *Proceedings* (1967), pp. 96–102, and also Richard B. Lillich, *The Protection of Foreign Investment* (Syracuse, N.Y.: Syracuse University Press, 1965).

state to assume his claim for breach of contract and to present a claim on his behalf to the state alleged to have violated the agreement.[28]

Although some governments have been most willing to press such claims of their citizens, many more have been rather reluctant to do so. This hesitation was based in part on the idea that anyone entering into contractual relations with a foreign state could be presumed to do so with a clear conception of the risks involved. Because many such contracts provided exceedingly large returns to the alien, he was presumed to have weighed the profits expected against the risks taken by dealing with a sovereign state. So many claims based on contract violations have been presented, however, to make this sphere of state-alien relations one of the most contentious ones in the realm of international law.

A state which arbitrarily violates the terms of a contract or concession to which it and an alien are parties is clearly in the wrong, and has done a wrongful act. The opinion of most writers and international tribunals has been that the alien must then exhaust available local remedies. Only when this has been done and no adequate redress has been obtained does he have a right to present his claim to his own government with the expectation that the latter will press the claim against the delinquent state. It should be noted, however, that the local law of the state alleged to have violated the contract might be of such a nature as to deprive the alien, through judicial action supporting the violation of the contract, of property rights or actual property. In that case the alien's own government might conclude quite properly that a denial of justice had taken place, that arbitrary acts had injured the alien, and that an international claim might be lawfully pressed.[29]

The Calvo Clause. It was to be expected that governments would view with disfavor appeals by aliens to their own governments to institute international claims based on an alleged violation of contract terms. Hence it could have cause no great surprise when a number of Latin American states began to write into contracts made with aliens a provision called the "Calvo Clause." This clause stipulated that the alien agreed that any dispute arising out of the terms of the contract was to be settled by the national courts of the contracting state in accordance with the latter's national law and was not to cause the lodgment of any international claim by the alien's government. A number of such clauses contained the additional provision that, for purposes of the contract, the alien was to be considered as a national of the contracting state.[30]

The introduction of the Calvo Clause gave rise to strong protests on

[28] See F. A. Mann, "State Contracts and State Responsibility," 54 *A.J.I.L.* (1960), pp. 572–591, and particularly Whiteman, Vol. VIII, pp. 906–915.

[29] See again the invaluable Sohn and Baxter, *op. cit.,* pp. 569–575, on this point and related issues.

[30] Alwyn V. Freeman, "Recent Aspects of the Calvo Doctrine and the Challenge to International Law," 40 *A.J.I.L.* (1946), pp. 121–147, at pp. 130–142.

the part of other states because, taken literally, the clause not only attempted to deprive the alien of his right to appeal to his own government after exhausting available local remedies but, in fact, declared the new doctrine that an individual citizen could, on his own responsibility, deprive his state of protecting its interests abroad. No major state outside of Latin America, in particular the United States, could agree to such a private restriction on the undoubted right of every sovereign state to assume the protection of the rights of its citizens, even over the written objections to or waiver of such protection by those citizens. When the Calvo Clause appeared as a material ingredient of cases and claims before international courts and arbitration tribunals, some decisions accorded validity to the clause, but the majority of recorded opinions appears to have denied the validity of a contractual agreement to set aside a right of protection on the part of the alien's government.[31]

Generally speaking, it must be assumed today that most states will not agree to be bound by a restrictive covenant on the part of one of their citizens, such as is represented by the Calvo Clause, and would not hesitate to take proper steps to protect the rights of such a citizen, provided always that an exhaustion of local remedies could be shown to have taken place.

Public Bonds. The situation is somewhat different, however, in the case of a particular kind of contractual obligation: public bonds. A bond issued by a state is normally a bearer obligation, freely marketable and transferable; interest and amortization payments are made to the holder of record at a particular time, and that holder more often than not is different from the original purchaser of the bond. Hence governments, in general, have adopted the attitude that a public bond represents a much looser and more impersonal contract than one drawn up directly between an alien and a state. Also, because many individuals and institutions buy public bonds not for investment but for speculative purposes, with the degree of risk usually indicated by a rather high rate of interest, governments tend to agree that the old maxim of *caveat emptor* applies to all holders of such securities. As far as the U.S. Department of State is concerned, it has tended to negate the limited effect given to the Calvo Clause in the *North American Dredging* case; yet in its conduct of claims practice the same Department *has* on occasion seen fit to give limited effect to the Calvo Clause.

On the other hand, when default occurs in any obligation attached to a public bond, the holder of that instrument quite often finds himself

[31] See *United States (North American Dredging Co. of Texas) v. United Mexican States,* United States–Mexico General Claims Commission, 1926 (*Opinions of the Commissioners,* 1927, p. 21), in which the Claims Commission agreed that an alien might sign a contract containing the Calvo Clause, but that he could not deprive his own government of the right of "applying international remedies to violations of international law committed to his damage."

barred from all local remedies by the immunity from suit claimed and enforced by the state that had issued the bond in question. This regrettable situation leads the holder of the bond to seek the aid of his own government. Although most states will not intervene on behalf of the bondholder, for the reasons previously stated, the majority will do so if circumstances indicate that lack of good faith or discrimination on the part of the foreign debtor took place.

Other breaches of good faith likely to lead to international claims involve such practices as diverting revenues pledged for the interest and redemption payments of bonds to other purposes, thereby depriving the bondholders of the security behind the public obligations held by them; payment of sums, promised in gold or "gold-currency," in depreciated paper money;[32] and paying interest to selected groups of bondholders while defaulting with respect to all others. Any of these actions appear to constitute valid grounds for the appearance of international claims.

The Drago Doctrine. Failure to pay compensation to injured aliens or to meet legitimate obligations to foreign bondholders has led on occasion to the threat of and even to the application of the use of force by the governments of the injured aliens against delinquent states.

Dr. Luis Drago, the then foreign minister of Argentina, evolved the so-called Drago Doctrine when he wrote on December 29, 1902, to the Argentine Minister in Washington that "a public debt cannot give rise to the right of intervention, and much less to the occupation of the soil of any American nation by any European power." [33]

The Drago Doctrine was interpreted by its framer as a logical supplement to the Monroe Doctrine, and as such, as well as on its presumed own merits, attracted much support among Latin American states. Some years later the "Porter Convention" was adopted at the Second Hague Peace Conference in 1907. In this instrument the contracting states agreed that they would not use armed force to recover "contract debts" claimed by one government as owed to its nationals by another government. However, a rather debilitating condition inserted in the convention provided that such abstention from the use of force depended on an acceptance by the debtor state of an offer of arbitration; or, having

---

[32] Failure to honor the so-called gold clause has led to a number of important decisions by international tribunals. Noteworthy are the *Case of the Serbian Loans Issued in France (France v. Kingdom of the Serbs, Croats and Slovenes)*, P.C.I.J., 1929, Ser. A, No. 20, in which the Court held that the gold clause involved had to be honored by Jugoslavia; and the *Case of Certain Norwegian Loans*, instituted before the International Court of Justice by France against Norway in 1955, centering on the suspension, by the latter state, in 1931 of the convertibility of certain housing bonds issued between 1896 and 1905. The Court decided on July 6, 1957, that it lacked jurisdiction to adjudicate this dispute: see *I.C.J. Reports, 1957*, p. 9, digested in 51 *A.J.I.L.* (1957), pp. 777-783.

[33] Moore, Vol. VI, p. 592; the complete "text" of the Doctrine may be found in *U.S. Foreign Relations, 1903*, pp. 1-5.

accepted such an offer, failure to honor the award handed down would release the creditor state from its promise not to resort to force.

RESPONSIBILITY OF STATES FOR THE ACTIONS OF REBELS AND INSURGENT GOVERNMENTS

The discussion of international claims arising out of the treatment of aliens has centered thus far only on acts undertaken, directly or indirectly, by the lawful, recognized government of a state. Frequently, however, aliens suffer injuries in their persons or property at the hands of rebels or insurgent governments. The rules governing such injuries are fairly simple, yet numerous controversies have arisen between states as a result of incidents connected with civil wars and uprisings.

In the event of a rebellion, the assumption of state responsibility centers on the concept of the exercise of "due diligence." Almost by definition, every government is vitally concerned with using all available means to prevent an outbreak of rebellion and, if such occurs, to suppress it effectively and as quickly as possible, with subsequent punishment of the rebels. If it can be demonstrated that reasonable precautions were taken to prevent a rebellion and that, after an uprising came into being, prompt measures were taken to subdue the rebels and to punish them, then no international responsibility arises for the acts committed by rebels against aliens.

This principle was illustrated strikingly in the

HOME MISSIONARY SOCIETY CASE (*UNITED STATES* v. *GREAT BRITAIN*)

United States–Great Britain, Claims Arbitration, 1920
(Claims Arbitration under a Special Agreement of August 8, 1910—
Nielsen's Report, 421)

FACTS

The United States presented a claim for $78,068.15, together with interest thereon from May 30, 1898, against Great Britain on behalf of an American religious body known as the "Home Frontier and Foreign Missionary Society of the United Brethren in Christ." This claim was in respect of losses and damages sustained by that body and some of its members during a rebellion in 1898 in the British Protectorate of Sierra Leone.

The British Administration in Sierra Leone had imposed in 1898 a new tax known as the "hut tax," on the indigenous population of the Protectorate. On April 27, as a result of the levy, a serious revolt broke out in the Ronietta District, accompanied by indiscriminate attacks on the persons and properties of Europeans.

All of the missions of the Society in the District were attacked and either destroyed or damaged. Several of the missionaries were killed.

The British authorities summoned troops to the District and quickly and firmly suppressed the revolt. In September, October and November, as many of the natives guilty of attacks on white property and persons as could be located were arrested, tried, and on conviction punished by the British law-enforcement agencies in the Protectorate.

The United States government called, on February 21, 1899, the losses sustained by the Society to the attention of the British government. The latter, on October 14, 1899, repudiated all liability for the acts of the rebels, expressing only its regret that no funds were available from which compensation could be paid as an act of grace.

The United States government then submitted its claim to arbitration under a special agreement signed by the two countries on August 10, 1910, alleging lack of due diligence on the part of the British authorities in Sierra Leone.

ISSUE

Did state responsibility devolve on Great Britain, with consequent liability for compensation, as a result of lack of due diligence in suppressing the revolt in Sierra Leone?

DECISION

The Arbitration Tribunal found no evidence of lack of due diligence on the part of the British authorities in question and therefore rejected the American claim, in the absence of British state responsibility.

REASONING

The hut tax was a lawful exercise of British authority in the Protectorate and was a tax quite generally encountered at the time in African colonies and protectorates.

The widespread levy of the tax in other parts of Africa did not suggest that its imposition in Sierra Leone would lead to an indigenous uprising.

Investigation by a Royal Commissioner indicated clearly that the British authorities did everything in their power to protect lives and property as soon as the revolt took place. Despite heavy losses, the number of troops in the affected areas was increased continuously. Difficulties in communications and the simultaneous outbreak of risings in widely separated localities made it impossible to have troops available at all points where losses of life or property occurred.

Repression of the revolt proceeded with the greatest possible dispatch and the hunting down, trial, and punishment of as many persons guilty of crimes as could be found was prompt and adequate.

The Tribunal could not, therefore, uphold the contention advanced by the United States government that the British authorities had failed to act with due diligence.

The Calvo Doctrine. The Sierra Leone case dealt with a native uprising, quickly suppressed. What, on the other hand, would be the situation as related to alien claims when a revolt assumed such proportions that a civil war could be said to exist, that is, when a revolutionary government had come into being and had troops and other appurtenances of an organized civil society at its disposal?

Under such conditions, could the lawful government be held responsible for injuries suffered by aliens when the latter, together with segments of the local population, were actually removed from the authority of the legitimate government and were placed under the temporary authority of an insurgent or rebel government?

The general principle applicable under such circumstances is that the legitimate government of the state in question could be held responsible for injuries suffered by aliens at the hands of insurgents only if it could be demonstrated that the lawful government failed to exercise due diligence in preventing or suppressing the rebel movement. Latin American states have adopted a more restrictive view under the so-called Calvo Doctrine, named after the inventor of the Calvo Clause.

According to the Calvo Doctrine, no state could accept responsibility for losses suffered as a result of insurrection or civil war, because such acceptance would tend to menace the independence of weak states by virtually asking for intervention by stronger states whose citizens had suffered losses, and also because acceptance of such a responsibility would place aliens in a more favorable position than would be true for the citizens of the state beset by civil war. The Calvlo Doctrine, today, must be regarded as constituting at best a principal of regional international law.

Numerous commentators have pointed out that certain countries suffer perennially from an absence of governmental stability: they could be termed revolution-prone. In such a state, it has been argued, the legitimate government should bear responsibility for injuries to aliens, not so much because of an absence of due diligence but because of an inherent weakness or flaw in the very organization of the country's political institutions. Since the application of an objective test to such a situation would be difficult at best, the determination of responsibility for losses from civil war tends to be influenced all too often by political considerations.

Many cases, some of them very well known, illustrate under what conditions international responsibility may be imputed to a state for the acts of insurgents.[34] The classic decision cited most commonly is that in

UNITED STATES (ROSA GELBTRUNK CLAIM)
v. SALVADOR

Arbitral Tribunal, 1902
(U.S. Foreign Relations, 1902, p. 876)

FACTS

In 1898 Maurice Gelbtrunk & Co., a partnership firm owned by two United States citizens, carried on a mercantile business in the Republic of El Salvador. In November of that year, a revolution broke out in that

---

[34] Thus especially *Italy (Sambiaggio Claim)* v. *Venezuela*, Italy–Venezuela, Claims Arbitration, 1903, in Ralston, *Venezuelan Arbitrations of 1903*, p. 679; see also Hyde, Vol. II, pp. 979–984; Hackworth, Vol. V, pp. 666–681.

state and a revolutionary force occupied the city of Sensuntepeque, where a quantity of goods valued at $22,000 and belonging to the Gelbtrunk enterprise was stored. The soldiers of the rebel army looted the goods in question and sold, appropriated, or destroyed them. This action was not done under the orders of any officer or as an act of military necessity but was an act of lawless violence on the part of the soldiers in question.

The firm assigned its claim against El Salvador to Rosa Gelbtrunk, the wife of one of the two partners. She, in turn, appealed to the United States Government to intervene on her behalf in claiming indemnification for the lost property. The Government accepted her appeal but failed to arrive at a settlement through diplomatic negotiations. The claim was then submitted to an arbitration tribunal already handling other United States claims against El Salvador.

ISSUE

Did state responsibility devolve on the lawful government of El Salvador for losses suffered by aliens as a result of the activities of insurgents?

DECISIONS

The Tribunal rejected the American claim, holding that the government of El Salvador could not be held responsible for the actions of the insurgents in question.

REASONING

An alien moving into another state to engage there in business must be considered as "having cast in his lot with the subjects or citizens of the state in which he resides and carries on business. . . . The state to which he owes national allegiance has no right to claim for him as against the nation in which he is resident any other or different treatment in case of loss by war—either foreign or civil—revolution, insurrection, or other internal disturbance caused by organized military force or by soldiers, than that which the latter country metes out to its own subjects or citizens."

The Tribunal considered that in the case in question, the Gelbtrunk firm had not been treated any less favorably than the citizens of El Salvador themselves.

What if the rebel government wins control over the territory of the entire state and replaces the lawful government against which it rose in the first place? In that case, the new government may be held responsible by other states for whatever injuries were caused to aliens from the very beginning of the existence of the then insurgent group. Contrariwise, the new government would not assume responsibility for whatever injuries were suffered by aliens at the hands of the overthrown previous administration of the state during the course of the civil war.

In other words, a lawful government is usually not responsible internationally for the acts of unsuccessful rebels, provided due diligence in preventing or suppressing the revolt can be demonstrated. A successful insurgent group may be held responsible internationally for all acts undertaken under its authority from its inception; no responsibility can be imputed to the group for the acts of the vanished government as long as those acts were of a political or military nature, incidental to the civil war, and were undertaken for public ends.

DETERMINATION OF COMPENSATION FOR INJURIES DONE TO ALIENS

No international claim can be presented by one state against another if the state pressing such a claim cannot show that the claimant is entitled to its protection, that is, had already possessed its nationality at the time the injury occurred.[35]

In this connection we encounter again the problem of the place of the individual in international law. According to traditional practice and theory, only a state possessed the right to present claims for damages or injuries suffered by its citizens in the jurisdiction of another state. This exclusive right was based, of course, on the notion that an individual was not a subject of international law.

A government will normally refuse to support a claim by an individual who became its national only after the claim had accrued or by one who enjoyed its protection and then assumed foreign nationality after the claim had accrued.[36]

Assuming that the claimant possesses the required nationality and that state responsibility for injuries suffered by him has been established, how is the compensation due him through his government established?

The general practice appears to be that the measurement of damages is not based on the degree or kind of delinquency shown to have been exhibited by the state held to be responsible, but rather is based on the loss caused to the claimant by whatever injury was done to him.

Thus, in the *Janes* case, to cite an example, once state responsibility was established by the Claims Commission, the determination of damages for compensation purposes was switched back to the original injury sustained.[37]

[35] See especially Hackworth, Vol. V, pp. 802–851, and Sohn and Baxter, *op. cit.*, pp. 579–580; consult also Moore, Vol. VI, pp. 628–642. Concerning the requirement of the nationality of the claimant state at the time the injury occurred, see the valuable collection of facts and documents by Denys P. Myers, "Nationality of Claims," pp. 908–915 in his "Contemporary Practice of the United States Relating to International Law," 53 *A.J.I.L.* (1959), pp. 896–923. For cases illustrating the nationality aspect of the claimant, see *United States (Agency of Canadian Car & Foundry Co.) v. Germany*, United States–Germany, Mixed Claims Commission, 1939, digested in Hackworth, Vol. V, pp. 833 ff.; *United States (Romano–Americana Claim) v. Great Britain* in Hackworth, Vol. V, pp. 702–705, 840–844.

[36] See Articles 1 and 4 of the Resolution on the National Character of an International Claim Presented by a State for Injury Suffered by an Individual" (September 10, 1965), of the *Institut de Droit International*, in 60 *A.J.I.L.* (1966), pp. 521–523, and the commentary on the resolution by Herbert W. Briggs, *ibid.*, pp. 517–521, at pp. 519–521.

[37] See Sohn and Baxter, *op. cit.*, pp. 580–583, for the most recent approach (Harvard Law School draft) to the varieties of injuries possible and for the basic computation of compensation for such varieties. Typical cases in which the determination of damages played an important part include *United States (Isaac M. Brower Claim) v. Great Britain*, Claims Arbitration Tribunal, 1923, digested in 18 *A.J.I.L.* (1924),

An area of constant dispute about compensation is that arising out of the nationalization of alien property. It has already been mentioned that most claims originating in the taking of such property revolve around the inadequacy or total lack of compensation rather than any question about the right of a state to engage in the nationalization as such of alien property.

It should be noted, in passing, that when the debtor (delinquent) state does not pay compensation promptly, it may become liable for moratory interest, and that the "Hickenlooper Amendment" (see Chapter 9) requires suspension of aid to all nations in which United States property has been expropriated without "adequate compensation" if the expropriating state failed within six months to take steps to make quick and equitable payment to the former owners in convertible currency.

The damages awarded against states may be compensatory, which is the normal case, or punitive. The latter instance is rare but not unknown. It is based on the concept that a state may claim damages, say, for the death of one of its citizens, even if no damage to another individual could be proved—such as when the deceased had no relatives who could claim a loss.[38] It is even possible to obtain an award for what might be termed "indirect damages" against a state. The example commonly cited is that of the famous *Alabama Claims*, when the United States government collected sums for such reasons as "enhanced payment of insurance" and the "prolongation" of the Civil War, from Great Britain.

Finally it should be noted that when a state recovers moneys from another state through successful prosecution of a claim for a wrong done to it (really to one of its citizens), the claimant whose claim had been accepted by his government does *not* possess a legal right to the sums collected by the latter. In practice, of course, the sums in question will be paid to him or to his heirs, as the case may be, even though on occasion states have deducted the expenses incurred by them in prosecuting the claim. If a number of private claimants are involved in a given instance, their government is perfectly at liberty to arrange for a distribution of moneys collected on any basis it deems fair and appropriate.

SUGGESTED READINGS

RESPONSIBILITY OF STATES: GENERAL

Gould, pp. 507–533; Lauterpacht's *Oppenheim*, I, pp. 338–369; Svarlien, pp. 133–152; Richard B. Lillich, *International Claims: Their Adjudication by National Commissions* (Syracuse, N.Y.: Syracuse University Press, 1962); Haig

---

p. 832; the *Chorzów Factory Case*, P.C.I.J., 1928, Ser. A, No. 17, pp. 27–28; and *The Lusitania Case* (*United States–Germany*), Mixed Claims Commission, 1923 (*Report on Decisions*, 1925, p. 17).

[38] See Clyde Eagleton, "Measure of Damages in International Law," 39 *Yale Law Journal* (1929), pp. 52–76, at p. 61, on this point, as well as Cheng, pp. 233–240.

Silvanie, *Responsibility of States for Acts of Unsuccessful Insurgent Governments* (New York: Columbia University Press, 1939); C. F. Amerasinghe, *State Responsibility for Injuries to Aliens* (Oxford and New York: Oxford University Press, 1967); Virginia V. Meekison, "Treaty Provisions for the Inheritance of Personal Property," 44 *A.J.I.L.* (1950), pp. 313–332.

Cases

The Mavrommatis Palestine Concessions, Permanent Court of International Justice, *P.C.I.J.,* 1924, Ser. A, No. 2.

United States v. *Diekelman,* United States, Supreme Court, 1876, 92 U.S. 520.

In re Estate of Larkin, United States, California Supreme Court, 1966, 416 P. 2d 473, reported by John T. Connor, Jr. in 8 *Harvard International Law Journal* (1967), pp. 191–202; see earlier note on same case, by Patrick L. Kelley, 7 *Harvard International Law Club Journal* (1965), pp. 165–171.

CONTRACTS

C. F. Amerasinghe, "State Breaches of Contract with Aliens and International Law," 58 *A.J.I.L.* (1964), pp. 881–913.

Case

United States (El Triunfo Company Claim) v. *Salvador,* Arbitration, 1902, in *U.S. Foreign Relations, 1902,* p. 859.

LOCAL REMEDIES

Cases

The Ambatielos Case (Greece v. *United Kingdom),* International Court of Justice, 1952–53; *I.C.J. Reports, 1952,* p. 28, and *ibid., 1953,* p. 10; see also the relevant arbitral decision of March 6, 1956, in 50 *A.J.I.L.* (1956), pp. 674–679, also Manley O. Hudson, "The Thirty-Second Year of the World Court," *ibid.,* 48 (1954), pp. 1–22, at pp. 1–6.

The Panevevezys-Saldutiskis Railway Case (Estonia v. *Lithuania),* Permanent Court of International Justice, *P.C.I.J.,* 1939, Ser. A/B, No. 76, and its coverage by Manley O. Hudson in "The Eighteenth Year of the Permanent Court of International Justice, 34 *A.J.I.L.* (1940), pp. 1–22, at pp. 1–5.

EXPROPRIATION OF ALIEN PROPERTY

Consult, *inter alia,* E. D. Re, *Foreign Confiscations* (Dobbs Ferry, N.Y.: Oceana Publications, 1951); Gillian White, *Nationalisation of Foreign Property* (New York: Praeger, 1962); Richard S. Miller and Roland J. Stanger (eds.), *Essays on Expropriations* (Columbus: Ohio State University Press, 1967); C. F. Amerasinghe, "The Ceylon Oil Expropriations," 58 *A.J.I.L.,*

(1964), pp. 445–450; "The Taking of Property: Evaluation of Damages" [Papers by John G. Laylin and Burns H. Weston, plus discussion of same], in *Proceedings* (1968), pp. 35–57; Hans W. Baade, "The Validity of Foreign Confiscations: An *Addendum*," 56 *A.J.I.L.* (1962), pp. 504–507; Samuel L. Sharp, *Nationalization of Key Industries in Eastern Europe* (Washington, D.C.: Foundation for Foreign Affairs, 1946); Ivan Sipkov, "Postwar Nationalizations and Alien Property in Bulgaria," 52 *A.J.I.L.* (1958), pp. 469–494; and B. A. Wortley, "Observations on the Public and Private International Law Relating to Expropriation," 5 *American Journal of Comparative Law* (1956), pp. 577–594. See also the extensive and valuable list of additional materials in Bishop, pp. 691–694 (notes 51–58).

Cases

Present v. *United States Life Insurance Co.*, United States, New Jersey Supreme Court, 1967, 232 At.2d 863, reported in detail in 62 *A.J.I.L.* (1968), pp. 494–496.
F. *Palicio y Compania, S.A.* v. *Brush*, United States, District Court, S.D.N.Y., 1966, 256 F. Supp. 481, excerpted in 61 *A.J.I.L.* (1967), pp. 601–609.

14

Extradition

EXTRADITION AND INTERSTATE RELATIONS

T HE escape of an alleged fugitive from justice from the territory of the state in which his offense was claimed to have been committed into the jurisdiction of another state leads to a temporary halt of an effort to punish the individual in question. Under the prevailing doctrine of the independence of states, the pursuing state is stopped at the boundary of another state's sovereignty: its own authority has no effect within that foreign sovereignty. Because states are still very jealous of their territorial integrity, they will not normally consent to the intrusion of the authority of another entity. At times this strict construction may lead to rather extraordinary consequences, as was shown in a famous old case:

THE SAVARKAR CASE: FRANCE–GREAT BRITAIN
Tribunal of the Hague Permanent Court
of Arbitration, 1911

FACTS

Vinayak Damodar Savarkar, a British Indian, was in custody aboard the English mail steamer *Morea* on his way to India for trial in connection with a murder case. On July 8, 1910, while the vessel was in the port of Marseilles, Savarkar succeeded in making his way ashore. He was arrested shortly by a member of the French maritime *gendarmerie* (the British authorities had previously warned the French police that an escape attempt might be made at Marseilles) and returned to the ship. On

July 9, the *Morea* left Marseilles with Savarkar aboard. It developed later that the arresting policeman did not know the identity of the escapee and believed him to be a member of the ship's crew, escaping after committing some offense on the vessel.

The French government then demanded the return of Savarkar to France, alleging that he had been removed from French territory without authorization; this request was followed by a formal demand for Savarkar's extradition to France. When Great Britain rejected both demands, the French government brought the dispute in 1911 before an arbitral tribunal of the Hague Permanent Court of Arbitration.

ISSUE

Should Vinayak Savarkar be restored or not restored to France by the British government, in accordance with existing rules of international law?

DECISION

The arbitral tribunal decided that Great Britain was not required to return Savarkar to France.

REASONING

The evidence presented showed that the local (Marseilles) French police authorities had placed themselves at the disposal of the captain of the *Morea* and had placed an agent aboard to assist the officer in charge of the prisoner. The return of the fugitive to the ship was done in good faith and did not represent recourse to fraud or force in order to obtain possession of an individual who had taken refuge in a foreign country. The act of the officer who returned Savarkar to the ship was not disowned before the *Morea* left the port and this left the British police under the impression that the French officer had acted under instructions or that his action had received the approval of his superiors.

Although it had to be admitted that Savarkar's return to the ship had been somewhat irregular, there was no rule of international law imposing, under the circumstances cited, an obligation on Great Britain to restore Savarkar to France—merely because of a mistake committed by the agent of the maritime police.

Extradition. A common interest in preventing flight abroad from foiling the apprehension and punishment of a fugitive from justice has led states to cooperate with one another and has caused the development of procedures by which fugitives could be returned to the state in which the alleged crime was committed.[1] These methods, which always include a formal request for surrender of the persons wanted, together with certain well-defined conditions for surrender, are called extradition. Although most of them are based on bilateral agreements, in the absence of a generally accepted convention on the subject, there has come into being sufficient similarity in state practices to hazard the view that by now a series of customary rules has developed or that the rules are in the final stages of development.

Problem of the Fugitive. The problem of alleged fugitives is actually a very complicated aspect of interstate relations. In its totality, at least five major divisions could be analyzed, space permitting:

1. Recovery of fugitive criminals in violation of international law.
2. Capture of a fugitive criminal in the territory of the sheltering

---

[1] On the general subject of extradition, consult Whiteman, Vol. VI, pp. 727–1122; Hackworth, Vol. IV, pp. 1–241; Harvard Research in International Law, "Extradition," in 29 *A.J.I.L.* (1935), Special Supp., pp. 16–434; and Hyde, Vol. II, pp. 1012–1063.

state, with the connivance of its officials, by private citizens of the seeking state.

3. Capture of the fugitive in the sheltering state, without the knowledge of its officials, by private citizens of the seeking state (the case of Eichmann comes to mind as a recent celebrated example).

4. Irregular apprehension of a fugitive criminal by officials of the sheltering state before extradition takes place.

5. Wrongful (mistaken) surrender of a fugitive by officials of the sheltering state to the seeking state.

The limitations of a general text precludes a detailed analysis of all the preceding possibilities, and only those aspects which have figured prominently in the recent history of extradition can be covered.

EXTRADITION TREATIES

The surrender of wanted fugitives was not transformed into a legal duty until the members of the community of nations created a vast network of bilateral extradition treaties. The latter fall into either of two major categories: the older, traditional type, which contains a specific list of offenses for the commission of which a fugitive will be surrendered, and the newer type, of twentieth-century origin, which contains no such list but which provides for extradition in all cases where the offense in question is punishable in both countries involved in a given case. Thus, for an offense to give rise to extradition, it must either be included specifically in the treaty or must be regarded as a crime under the laws of the contracting parties or both.

It should be pointed out that, in modern times at least, international law knows no right to extradition apart from treaties. A state may voluntarily decide to surrender a fugitive from justice, but a legal right to demand such surrender and a correlative duty to acquiesce in such a demand can exist only where created by treaty.[2] In the United States, official opinion denies the existence of any authority to surrender a fugitive in the absence of a treaty. On a few occasions, the surrender of a fugitive from another country was achieved when no relevant treaty existed, but in such instances the United States explained carefully that this government could not reciprocate the favor.

Up to about the middle of the eighteenth century, these extradition treaties covered primarily the surrender of *political* fugitives. Gradually, ordinary crimes began to be included as reasons for the surrender of an alleged offender. By the second half of the last century, however, the revolution in transportation had made the speedy escape of criminals ever easier; hence extradition treaties became increasingly general in character. Interestingly enough, as the scope of these agreements ex-

---

[2] *Factor* v. *Laubenheimer*, United States, Supreme Court, 1933, 290 U.S. 276.

panded to include ever more numerous categories of criminal offenses, political offenses ceased to play a part and today such latter offenses no longer form a basis for the surrender of fugitives.

Formal Procedure for Extradition. Although extradition treaties vary considerably as regards the offenses listed in them as the basis of surrender, the actual procedure utilized in extradition has been standardized fairly well all over the world.

A request for the surrender of an alleged fugitive criminal must be presented to the foreign state through the diplomatic agent of the seeking government. When such a request is received, the foreign government institutes an investigation through its judicial agencies to determine. whether there is sufficient evidence, in accordance with the local law, to warrant an arrest of the fugitive. If sufficient evidence is submitted and accords with the local law requirements, the fugitive is held pending the arrival of law-enforcement agents of the seeking state. The agents then receive the person of the fugitive into their custody and return him to the state in which the crime was committed. Naturally, because a fugitive might decide to leave his current place of refuge at the first hint of the start of extradition proceedings, most treaties provide for his arrest after informal—say, telegraphic—request pending preparation and sending of a formal extradition request. Normally the agreements limit such temporary detention to a relatively brief period of time, such as forty days.

The return of a surrendered alleged fugitive to the seeking state through the territory or airspace of third countries requires permission for such transit. Normally no difficulties are encountered in securing such permission in the case of charges of homicide or other serious crimes. On the other hand, offenses in the sphere of fraud may lead to problems on the part of the seeking state. Many countries, particularly those following Roman Law systems, have varying definitions of fraud and quite often the arresting officers escorting the surrendered individual to the seeking state have to plan circuitous routes of travel to avoid the airspace of such countries.

Gerhart Eisler Case. The modern requirement that the offense allegedly committed must be punishable in both states concerned was illustrated strikingly in the case of Gerhart Eisler. That person, an alien Communist in the United States, fled illegally while at liberty on bail pending decision on his appeal from criminal convictions for perjury and for contempt of Congress. He arrived in Great Britain as a stowaway on the Polish liner *Batory*. The United States government requested the British government to arrest, detain, and extradite Eisler on the charge that he had been convicted of perjury in connection with his application to leave the United States. The British court (Bow Street Magistrate's Court in London) decided, however, on May 27, 1949, that the act charged against Eisler did not constitute perjury in English law, extradition was denied, and Eisler was released and left England for asylum behind the Iron Curtain.[3]

When the fugitive is surrendered and tried after his return, he *must* be tried only for the specific offense mentioned in the request for his extradition. This is an absolute restriction: he may not even be tried for a lesser offense. Illustrations of the operation of this rule abound in the history of the law, and the case of *United States* v. *Rauscher*[4] is considered to be a classic in this sphere. Rauscher had been surrendered by Great Britain on a charge of manslaughter; he was tried in the United States on the charge of inflicting cruel and unusual punishment.

In the *Case of Blackmer*,[5] the United States government had requested the extradition of Henry Blackmer on a charge of perjury in connection with certain income tax returns. The French court held that the penalty for the offense differed in the two countries and that the corrective penalty for the offense specified by French law had been barred through prescription (expiration of a time limit of three years prevailing under French law).

Samuel Insull Case. The greatest amount of publicity was received by the extraordinary *Samuel Insull Case* decision of the Greek Court of Appeals in 1933.[6] In that instance, the United States requested the extradition of the former Chicago banker Samuel Insull, Sr., on charges of embezzlement and larceny. The Greek court ruled twice that the evidence submitted by the United States was insufficient under Greek law to prove that the fugitive had deliberately intended to evade laws of the United States when he concealed or transferred certain assets. It ordered the release of the detained Insull. The government of the United States asserted that the Greek court had exceeded its proper functions and notified Greece of the termination of a brand-new extradition treaty concluded between the two states. Amusingly enough, Insull was incautious enough to leave his Greek sanctuary and to venture in a chartered Greek vessel into Turkey. The United States filed a request for his extradition with the Turkish government and the latter removed Insull from the ship and permitted his transportation to the United States. At the time in question, no extradition treaty was in force between the United States and Turkey.

It will have become obvious by now that serious obstacles to an orderly surrender of fugitive criminals exist. The Harvard Research in In-

[3] See George A. Finch, "The Eisler Extradition Case," 43 *A.J.I.L.* (1949), pp. 487–491; Philip E. Jacob, "International Extradition: Implications of the Eisler Case," 59 *Yale Law Journal* (1950), pp. 622–634.

[4] United States, Supreme Court, 1886, 119 U.S. 407; see also the interesting German case, decided by the Federal Constitutional Court, First Division, February 4, 1959 (1 BuR 193/57), discussed by M. Magdalena Schoch in 54 *A.J.I.L.* (1960), pp. 416–419.

[5] France, Court of Paris, Chambre des Mises en Accusation, 1928, in Hudson, pp. 514–515.

[6] See 28 *A.J.I.L.* (1934), p. 362.

ternational Law, in its Draft Convention on Extradition (1935), suggested that a uniform rule might be desirable, such as agreement to surrender a fugitive charged with any crime for which the law of the requesting state provided, on conviction, a penalty of death or of confinement for two years or more. But in the absence of a general convention regulating extradition, the past practices still prevail and on occasion there takes place what must be termed a miscarriage of justice through failure to surrender. To be sure, a European Convention on Extradition, of December 13, 1957, came into force in April, 1960, but that instrument has been ratified thus far by only six states. The convention restricted offenses giving grounds for extradition to those punishable by at least one year's imprisonment, with political, fiscal, and military offenses excluded from the scope of the agreement. Extradition of its own nationals could be refused by a party to the convention, but in such a case that party, if so requested by the other party, was to submit the case to its own courts for possible prosecution. In Latin America a second regional Convention on Extradition, adopted at the Seventh International Conference of American States in 1933, represents another effort to substitute uniformity in extradition practices through multilateral treaties for the prevailing diversity in practice based on bilateral agreements.

Doctrine of Reciprocity. Another complicating factor in the extradition picture is the manifest unwillingness of most states to surrender their own citizens to another state when those individuals have fled back into their country. Most states in continental Europe as well as in Latin America hold to the concept that a crime committed by one of their citizens anywhere in the world constitutes a violation of their own law just as much as the law of the state in which the offense took place.[7] These countries then proceed to reserve to themselves the trial and punishment of the offender when he comes within their jurisdiction, refusing to honor extradition requests for the person of the fugitive. By contrast, Anglo-American practice follows the principle that crimes must be tried where they have been committed; their criminal courts lack jurisdiction over crimes that took place outside the territory of the

[7] Useful illustrative cases include *Charlton* v. *Kelly*, United States, Supreme Court, 1913, 229 U.S. 447, 33 Sup. Ct. 945, and the more recent *Coumas* v. *Superior Court of San Joaquin County*, United States, Supreme Court of California, 31 Cal. 2d 682 (1948). See also *The New York Times*, January 31, 1952, and 47 A.J.I.L. (1953), pp. 150–151, for details of the fascinating case of *In re Lo Dolce* (United States, District Court, W.D. of New York, 1952, 106 F. Supp. 455), which involved an Italian demand for surrender by the United States of two U.S. nationals for the murder of another American (Major William V. Holohan) by poisoned soup and shooting, while all three were behind enemy lines, and the embezzlement of $100,000 in gold and currency. The murder had taken place in Italy in 1944, behind the German lines, while the three men were engaged in carrying the valuables in question to Italian partisans; see also Samuel M. Fink and Ralph J. Schwarz, Jr., "International Extradition: The Holohan Murder Case," 39 *American Bar Association Journal* (1953), pp. 297–300, 346–347.

state in question. This means that if, say, the United States refused to surrender an American citizen charged with the commission of a crime in France and who had fled to this country, he would not be tried and punished for what he did.

This paradoxical situation has led to the widespread adoption of the doctrine of reciprocity. If the requesting state is shown to be willing, by past performance, to surrender its own citizens for trial by the courts of another country, the "detaining" state normally will be willing to surrender its own citizens. But this system does not operate in certain countries in which the local constitution prohibits the extradition of nationals to other countries, such as in the case of the Federal Republic of Germany (Art. 16, par. 2, of the constitution).

Numerous extradition treaties provide specifically that neither of the contracting parties will surrender its own nationals to the other party. This is true, for instance, in several such treaties to which the United States is a party; these agreements supersede the principles laid down in a number of earlier court decisions, considered at one time to be of classic importance.[8]

Because the principle of reciprocity may lead to nonpunishment of guilty parties, efforts have been made by legal experts as well as by governments to add to the principle an obligation on the part of his own government to prosecute the accused person for the offense with which he was charged by the state denied surrender of his person. Thus the Montevideo Convention on Extradition (1933), a regional instrument, imposed in Article 2 this obligation on the parties to the agreement, subject to certain conditions surrounding the crime in question.[9] A similar provision was incorporated in the Harvard Draft Convention on Extradition. Article 7 of the document called for a legal duty to prosecute if a state, by reservation, indicated its unwillingness to surrender its own citizens to another state.

POLITICAL OFFENSES

The most interesting aspect of extradition from a general point of view and the one receiving the greatest amount of publicity in the press has to do with political offenders.[10]

It has been pointed out already that a virtually complete reversal in state policy took place during the nineteenth century, when political

[8] See the careful analysis by Alona E. Evans, "The New Extradition Treaties of the United States," 59 *A.J.I.L.* (1965), pp. 351–362, and the key case on the subject, *Valentine* v. *United States ex rel. Neidecker*, United States, Supreme Court, 1936, 299 U.S. 5.

[9] Text in 28 *A.J.I.L.* (1934), Supp., p. 65; the United States is a party to this agreement.

[10] See Manuel R. García-Mora, "The Nature of Political Offenses: A Knotty Problem of Extradition Law," 48 *Virginia Law Review* (1962), pp. 1226–1257.

offenses were removed from the list of crimes for which individuals might be extradited. Modern extradition treaties specifically exempt political offenses, most likely because liberal and democratic governments developed strong antipathy toward the idea of surrendering political offenders into the hands of despotic or dictatorial governments.

Extradition being asserted to be a matter of domestic jurisdiction, the nonextradition of political offenders is also a domestic practice and each state is free to determine the extent to which it will adhere to the practice. In the absence of a treaty, a state is therefore free to surrender a person accused of a political offense without violating any principle of international law. Even if a treaty does exist, a state may choose to surrender a political offender if such should be dictated by national policy. This relatively new interpretation, found originally in a few court decisions,[11] gained acceptance through the provisions of the European Convention on Extradition, signed on December 13, 1957.

Meaning of Political Offense. The question then arises: What is a political offense? In general terms, it is an act directed against the security of a state. Until recently, treaties as well as the decisions of courts tended to define such an offense in relatively narrow terms. In order to be political in nature, it was maintained, the action in question had to satisfy the following conditions:

1. It had to be an overt (open) act.
2. It had to be done in support of a political rising.
3. The rising had to be connected with a dispute or struggle between two groups or parties in a state as to which one was to control the government.

In other words, a political offense may be an act which, although it is in itself a common crime, acquires a predominantly political character because of the circumstances and motivations under and for which it was committed. The injury done is generally held to have to be proportionate with the results sought. By that is meant that the stakes at issue must be sufficiently important to justify, or at the very least to excuse, the impairment which the act in question has caused to private legal values.

On the other hand, it appears that war crimes (see Chapter 32) do not fall within the sphere of political offenses and therefore represent acts which give grounds for extradition.[12]

[11] See *Chandler* v. *United States,* United States, Circuit Court of Appeals, 1st Circuit, 1948, 171 F. 2d 921, *certiorari* denied by Supreme Court, 1949, 336 U.S. 918, in Chapter 12.

[12] See the relevant case of *In re Bohne,* Argentina, Supreme Court, 1966, *Jurisprudencia Argentina, 1966*—V, 339 (Sept.-Oct. 1966), digested in 62 *A.J.I.L.* (1968), pp. 784-785.

The classic case in which the characteristics of a political offense were fully developed is

IN RE CASTIONI

Great Britain, Queen's Bench Division, 1890
[1891] 1 Q.B. 149

FACTS

Angelo Castioni, a Swiss citizen, had participated on September 11, 1890, in an uprising in the Canton of Ticino. The revolt had been caused by the refusal of the cantonal government to revise the Ticino constitution or to hold a plebiscite on this question. A large group of citizens, including Castioni, seized the arsenal of the town of Bellinzona, disarmed the police, caught and bound several persons connected with the cantonal administration and forced them to march in front of the armed crowd to the municipal "palace." A number of government officials, including a M. Rossi, barred access to the building, whereupon the crowd forced the gates and rushed into the structure.

Castioni, armed with a revolver, was among the first to enter. Rossi was shot and died a little while later; witnesses later identified Castioni as the person who fired the fatal shot. The crowd captured the palace and organized a provisional government which functioned briefly until it was dispersed following the arrival of Swiss federal troops.

Castioni fled to Great Britain where he had lived for seventeen years, having returned to Ticino only one day before the uprising.

The Swiss government formally requested the arrest and extradition of Castioni on charges of having committed wilful murder. After his arrest, his legal representative asked for the issuance of a writ of habeas corpus and for the freeing of Castioni, claiming that he had been guilty only of a political offense.

ISSUE

Was Castioni's act in the nature of a political offense?

DECISION

The Court ruled in favor of Castioni; his extradition to Switzerland was therefore denied.

REASONING

The Court held that Castioni had done an overt act, that is, the shooting of Rossi was done in plain view, as part of an attack on the "palace"; that the act was connected with an uprising aimed at the cantonal government; and that the uprising was part of a struggle between two groups, one seeking to hold on to the control of the government, the other seeking to gain control. In view of these findings, Castioni (who had not known Rossi and hence held no personal feelings against him) was held to have shot Rossi in the promotion of a political uprising. His act constituted a political offense for which he could not be surrendered to the Swiss authorities.

A companion case, of equal interest to students of law as well as of political theory, dealt with the offenses committed by a certain Meunier:

IN RE MEUNIER

Great Britain, High Court of Justice,
Queen's Bench Division, 1894
(L.R. [1894], 2 Q.B. 415)

FACTS

Meunier, a French citizen, by political belief an anarchist, took it upon himself in March, 1892, to cause two explosions, one at the Café Véry in Paris, which caused the death of two persons, the other at the Lobau military barracks in the same city. Both outrages represented part of an anarchist effort to revenge the execution of the anarchist Ravachol.

After committing the two attacks, Meunier fled to Great Britain. A French court tried him *in absentia* and on convictions on charges of murder sentenced him to death. The French government made formal application for his arrest and extradition. Meunier was arrested on April 4, 1894, in the Victoria Station in London. He protested his arrest and pending deportation to France, and his counsel claimed that while the bombing of the barracks had been a reprehensible act, it was possessed of political character, citing the *Castioni* case. His counsel also asserted that insufficient evidence had been produced in the case of the attack on the Café Véry to lay the blame for the two deaths on Meunier.

ISSUE

Did Meunier's acts in Paris correspond to the accepted definition of a political offense?

DECISION

The Court rejected Meunier's contention that his acts constituted political offenses and ordered his continued detention until he could be surrendered to agents of the French government.

REASONING

The attacks on the Café Véry and on the military barracks did not constitute political offenses. There was no struggle between two parties in the French state, each seeking to impose the government of its choice on the state. The group with which Meunier identified himself was the enemy of all governments and desired to abolish them, rather than to control them. The terrorist acts of anarchists, furthermore, were not directed primarily at governments (which might have given them a semblance of political character) but were usually aimed at private citizens (the attack on the Café Véry was cited as an example by the Court).

"The party of anarchy is the enemy of all Governments. Their efforts are directed primarily against the general body of citizens. They may, secondarily and incidentally, commit offences against some particular Government; but anarchist offences are mainly directed against private citizens."

Under these circumstances, Meunier's acts did not represent political offenses within the meaning of the British Extradition Acts of 1870 and 1873.

NOTE: After Meunier had been taken back to France, the death sentence imposed on him in his absence was carried out.

The two preceding cases illustrate the attempt made in the nineteenth century to separate acts committed in the preparation or carrying out of revolutions or revolts (viewed as political acts) from individual acts of violence not in any manner conducive to a change in the political system and therefore logically denied recognition as political offenses. In the latter category belonged all terrorist acts perpetrated by any kind of radical as well as acts of violence characterized by their especially atrocious nature.

Lest the criteria mentioned previously and brought out so clearly in the *Castioni* case be taken to be universal standards, it should be pointed out that no generally accepted standards have yet been evolved, despite the fact that the concept of the political offense is directly related to the protection of human rights. The Universal Declaration of Human Rights (see Chapter 11) states (Art. 14) that

Everyone has the right to seek and to enjoy in other countries asylum from persecution. This right may not be invoked in the case of prosecutions genuinely arising from non-political crimes or from acts contrary to the purposes and principles of the United Nations.

Purely political offenses usually have been limited to three categories of acts: treason, sedition, and espionage. So-called relative political offenses involve political acts as well as "acts connected therewith." A relative political offense is, therefore, characterized by the existence of one or several common crimes intimately connected with a political act; the concept is illustrated strikingly by the *Castioni* case. Such offenses always pose a delicate problem for national courts: the desire to see a crime punished conflicts with the obligation not to surrender a political offender. The obvious but frequently difficult-to-achieve solution is to determine the degree of connection between the common crime and the political act. Here again, national determination and national standards come into play.[13]

Act-of-State Doctrine. A recent example of the act-of-state doctrine related to extradition was supplied by the case of Marcos Perez Jimenez. Venezuela instituted proceedings in the United States for the extradition of its former president to stand trial for financial offenses alleged committed while dictator of his country. After a finding of probable cause as to each offense charged against him, he was arrested and confined, pending action by the Secretary of State.

Jimenez contended in a habeas corpus proceeding that his acts in Venezuela constituted acts of state, that in consequence the acts were not subject to the jurisdiction of United States courts. The Court of

---

[13] See García-Mora, *op. cit.*, pp. 1240–1256, for a scholarly and fascinating analysis of national tests and standards; a relevant recent case of interest is *In re Gonzalez*, United States, District Court, S.D.N.Y., 1963, 217 F. Supp. 717, digested in 58 *A.J.I.L.* (1964), p. 191.

Appeals, in affirming the denial of the writ of habeas corpus, held that the acts in question (embezzlement, breach of trust, fraud, and receiving money and securities while knowing that they had been obtained illegally) were not acts of state but acts undertaken by Jimenez in his personal capacity and for his own private benefit. Hence the acts-of-state doctrine was not a bar to extradition proceedings. Jimenez was subsequently surrendered to agents of the Venezuelan government and returned to his country for trial, after the Supreme Court denied *certiorari*.[14]

Attentat Clause. During the second half of the nineteenth century, a number of attempts (several of them successful) were made on the persons of heads of states. Such attacks did not constitute part of organized uprisings or struggles for the control of governments, but had to be viewed as the acts of individuals or of small terrorist groups. Following an unsuccessful attempt to extradite Celestin Jacquin, who had tried to blow up a train carrying the French emperor Napoleon III, Belgium, in 1856, adopted into its extradition law the so-called *attentat* clause. This provision excluded from the category of political offenses the attempt (whether successful or not) to kill the head of another state or a member of his family. The United States, after the assassination of President Garfield, inserted the clause in its extradition treaty with Belgium (1882), and the 1933 Montevideo Convention included a similar provision. Many modern extradition treaties have been equipped with the restrictive clause and either by direct provision or by interpretation it extends not only to crowned heads of state but to any head of a government as well as to the members of his family.

Expansion in Meaning of Political Offense. The second quarter of the twentieth century saw an expansion in the meaning of "political offense," as a result of the ideological divisions of mankind and of the rise of radical and conservative dictatorships. The Harvard Draft Convention of 1935, reflecting existing world conditions, included under political offenses such acts as the commission of treason, sedition, and espionage, even if each of these was to be undertaken by only one person. It also included any offenses connected with the activities of an organized group directed against the security or governmental system of the requesting state.

The appearance of the Cold War expanded the meaning of political offense still further. In 1952, a Swiss court ruled that three Jugoslavs who had diverted a passenger plane from its destination in their own country and had caused it to be landed in Switzerland were guilty of a political offense and hence not subject to extradition.[15] A similar ruling was handed

[14] *Perez Jimenez* v. *Aristeguita*, United States, Circuit Court of Appeals, Fifth Circuit, 1962, 311 F. 2d 547; *certiorari* denied, Supreme Court, May 13, 1963. Jimenez was convicted on August 1, 1968, by the Supreme Court of Venezuela of embezzling $13 million of government funds. Because he had already spent more time in prison than his four-year sentence, he was released and permitted to depart for Spain.

[15] *In re Kavic, Bjelanovic and Arsenijevic*, reported in 1 *International Law Reports* (1952), p. 371.

down in 1954 by a British court in the case of seven members of the crew of a Polish trawler. The men, fearing that they were suspected by their government of harboring anti-Communist opinions and that they would be subject to trial on their return, subdued the captain and other members of the crew, wounded the political officer aboard the vessel, and brought the ship to a British port. They were held to be political refugees and were given asylum in Great Britain.[16]

Galvao Case. A most unusual case occurred in 1963, as a sequel to the *Santa Maria Case.* (See Chapter 18.) In December, 1963, Henrique Galvao, a Portuguese rebel and former colonial inspector in Angola, who had been in charge of the hijacking of the Portuguese liner *Santa Maria* in 1961, requested a hearing before the Trusteeship Committee of the UN General Assembly in New York, in order to testify on conditions in Portugal's African colonies. He was then living as a political refugee in Brazil.

Galvao was wanted in Portugal to serve a twenty-two-year sentence imposed there on him *in absentia* for his capture of the vessel.

The question arose whether Galvao, as a witness before a United Nations committee, would be immune from arrest and extradition to Portugal, should such be requested, when he entered the United States on his way to the United Nations. The Headquarters Agreement (see Chapter 9) provided that the UN District should not become a refuge for persons required by the U.S. government for extradition to another country. On the other hand, the same instrument also granted immunity from arrest to persons called to the District on United Nations business. (See Articles 11 and 15 of the Agreement.) Galvao had not been called, he had volunteered his testimony before the Trusteeship Committee.

The position of the U.S. government was that while Galvao traversed U.S. territory, he would be subject to arrest and extradition if Portugal asked for such. The Department of State issued a "limited purpose" visa to Galvao, entitling him to enter the country, go to the United Nations, and then depart again as soon as possible.[17] The visa contained no provisions about immunity from arrest. Brazil, for its part, granted Galvao an exit permit and assured him that he could return without jeopardizing his political asylum—and then, remarkably enough, supplied him a Brazilian passport.[18]

Galvao arrived in New York on December 9, coincidentally at the same time as the Portuguese Embassy submitted a formal request to the Department of State for his extradition on charges arising from the *Santa Maria* episode. Unofficial State Department spokesmen hinted, however, that the processing of the request would probably be delayed

---

[16] *In re Kolczynski et al.,* 1 Q.B. 540 (1954), 1 All E.L.R. 31 [1955], digested in 49 *A.J.I.L.* (1955), pp. 411–412; consult also García-Mora, *op. cit.,* pp. 1242–1244.

[17] *The New York Times,* December 8, 1963, pp. 1, 22.

[18] *Ibid.,* December 9, 1963, p. 30.

long enough to enable Galvao to leave the United States prior to any attempt at detention.[19]

After his appearance before the Trusteeship Committee, Galvao, on December 10, obtained a re-entry visa from the Brazilian consulate in New York and, after a stay totaling thirty-six hours, left the United States before the Portuguese request had been fully processed in the Department of State.[20]

TERRITORIAL ASYLUM

The question of the treatment of foreign political offenders leads logically to the more extensive problem of territorial asylum and the conditions under which it ought to be granted.[21] Asylum or refuge is granted without question when a particular state denies a request by another state for the extradition of an individual adjudged to have committed a political offense. This was, in most instances, the normal limit of a grant of asylum.

During the nineteenth century, a few occasions were marked by the appearance of considerable groups of refugees or exiles, usually the remnants of the supporters of lost revolutions, such as participants in the Paris Commune. Then the twentieth century became the era of the political escapee. At times the number of seekers of asylum ran into thousands or even tens of thousands—white Russian refugees, both civilian and military; Jewish persons escaping from Hitler's Germany and later from countries dominated by him; the remnants of the Spanish Republican armies; the remnants of Russian ethnic minorities; escapees from Chinese-occupied Tibet; and the countless voluntary exiles from Iron Curtain countries and from Castro's Cuba. Thus, in August, 1964, the United States Committee for Refugees could report that 7.9 million refugees and displaced persons were still recipients of governmental or private aid around the world.[22]

CONDITIONS FOR GRANTING ASYLUM

Which of such individuals or groups should be admitted by another country and granted a haven of refuge, that is, political asylum? Most democratic states in the West have been willing to grant asylum, provided

[19] *Ibid.*, December 10, 1963, pp. 1, 2.

[20] *Ibid.*, December 11, 1963, p. 10. See also the lengthy statement about the affair by the U.S. representative in the Fourth Committee, Ambassador Sidney R. Yates, on the American interpretation of Articles 11 and 15 of the Headquarters Agreement, in 58 *A.J.I.L.* (1964), pp. 457–459.

[21] See the extensively documented monographic study by Otto Kirchheimer, "Asylum," 53 *A.P.S.R.* (1959), pp. 985–1016, as well as Lauterpacht's *Oppenheim*, Vol. I, pp. 676–678.

[22] *The New York Times*, August 9, 1964, p. 12.

the individuals seeking a refuge satisfied the host authorities that they were indeed political or racial persecutees. And once asylum had been granted, demands for extradition from the refugee's government would be denied on grounds of the commission of political offenses. This modern attitude meant that the original concept of such offenses had been expanded greatly and now included anyone who, for reasons of political or racial persecution, had felt the need to escape from the authority of his own state.

This new interpretation of who could be accorded asylum has been defined quite adequately in Article 1-A (2) of the Geneva Convention of July 28, 1951, on the Status of Refugees, which stated that a refugee was a person who

. . . as a result of events occurring before January 1, 1951 and owing to well-founded fear of being persecuted for reasons of race, religion, nationality, membership of a particular social group or political opinion, is outside the country of his nationality and is unable or owing to such fear unwilling to avail himself of the protection of that country; or who, not having a nationality and being outside the country of his former habitual residence as a result of such events, is unable or, owing to such fear, unwilling to return to it.

The writer's only quarrel with this generous definition of a refugee presumably entitled to asylum in any country which is a party to the Convention of 1951 is that it establishes "events occurring before January 1, 1951" as a cutoff date for refugees. Groups such as the more than 100,000 Cuban refugees in the United States would not fall under the provisions quoted, because the date of Prime Minister Castro's assumption of power came subsequently to the date specified in the convention.

On the other hand, even if a refugee did not meet the conditions laid down in the Geneva instrument, he still would qualify in many states for political asylum, because general international law knows of no rule limiting political asylum to "political criminals." In fact, it is rather difficult to be precise in the terminology applicable to this special sphere of the rules governing extradition. As Evans pointed out,[23] "the terms 'political refugee,' 'political offender,' or 'political fugitive' are rather flexible in usage. United States statutes are not specific as to the meaning of 'political offender' or 'political offense.' The legislation on extradition does not define either term."

The lack of generally accepted rules governing the granting of territorial asylum prompted the General Assembly of the United Nations to request the International Law Commission on November 21, 1959, to undertake codification of the "principles and rules of international law relating to the right of asylum."

[23] Alona E. Evans, "Observations on the Practice of Territorial Asylum in the United States," 56 *A.J.I.L.* (1962), pp. 148–157, at p. 149.

Pending the completion of codification, the General Assembly adopted unanimously on December 14, 1967, a Declaration on Territorial Asylum, recommending guidelines for the granting of such asylum and excluding, incidentally, individuals suspected of war crimes, crimes against peace, or crimes against humanity.[24]

In addition, the Office of the UN High Commissioner for Refugees has attempted to relieve the lot of this group through the operation of UN-aided but government-operated settlement camps, many of them in Africa.[25]

DIPLOMATIC ASYLUM

The general subject of asylum includes a fascinating and well-publicized special form known as "diplomatic asylum."

On hundreds of occasions, individuals either guilty of political offenses or qualifying as political persecutees have chosen (or have been forced by a time element) to stay in their own country and to seek asylum in foreign embassies or legations.

The passage of time saw the growth of a conviction on the part of the receiving states that an unlimited grant of asylum on the part of foreign diplomatic missions represented, in essence, an unwarranted intervention in the internal affairs of the host state (receiving state). As a result, the sphere of diplomatic asylum was circumscribed little by little, and many states abandoned the practice entirely, normally by issuing suitable prohibitory instructions to their diplomatic agents. Today extensive practice of the grant of diplomatic asylum appears to be restricted to the Latin American republics and to Spain.

The policy of the government of the United States with respect to diplomatic asylum has been fairly consistent over many decades. Beginning in the nineteenth century, American diplomatic agents were instructed not to grant such asylum except temporarily to persons whose lives were threatened by mob violence. The American attitude is based on a belief that diplomatic asylum does not represent a valid principle of international law but merely a usage. At most, therefore, diplomatic asylum is viewed as a "permissive local custom," acceptable as a mere temporary measure.

It was therefore quite logical for the United States to enter a reservation to this effect when signing the 1928 Havana Convention on Asylum [26] and to refuse to sign a new interpretative convention agreed on by the Latin American delegations at the 1933 Montevideo Conference.

On the other hand, American practice has on occasion departed from stated policy, and United States diplomats have granted asylum in em-

[24] Text in 62 *A.J.I.L.* (1968), pp. 822–824.
[25] On the general subject of refugees and of territorial asylum, consult Whiteman, Vol. VIII, pp. 660–696.
[26] Text in 47 *A.J.I.L.* (1953), p. 446.

bassies and legations on various occasions not involving mob violence: to deposed presidents in Peru (1870), the Dominican Republic (1906), Haiti (1911), and Chile (1924), as well as alternately to rival politicians in Chile in 1891.[27] More recently, a notable departure from traditional abstention took place when asylum was granted in the U.S. Legation in Budapest to Jószef Cardinal Mindszenty, since the Hungarian uprising of 1956.

Latin America and Spain were mentioned as continuing adherents of the doctrine of diplomatic asylum; in fact, the practice has been employed so consistently there that it can be said to represent by now a principle of regional international law. General acceptance led, in turn, to efforts aimed at providing adequate regulation of the granting of such asylum. Beginning with a conference in Montevideo in 1889, a series of Latin American conventions have been devoted to the subject (Caracas, 1911; Havana, 1928; Montevideo, 1933 and 1939). In 1948 the Ninth Conference of American States, meeting at Bogotá, drafted an American Declaration of the Rights and Duties of Man, which provided, in Article 27, that

Every person has the right, in case of pursuit not resulting from ordinary crimes, to seek and receive asylum in foreign territory, in accordance with the laws of each country and with international agreements.[28]

This provision could be interpreted to include the "foreign territory" represented by foreign embassies and legations.

The most recent regional agreements on the subject are the resolution adopted on February 14, 1951, by the Organization of American States, which recognized the right of asylum as a "juridical principle of the Americas," [29] and the Convention on Diplomatic Asylum, signed at Caracas in 1954 but ratified since then by only six of the twenty signatory states.

At times the exercise of the doctrine of diplomatic asylum has produced striking results, either as to the number of individuals involved or as to the publicity received from the actions taken. During the early phases of the Spanish Civil War, some 12,000 opponents of the Republican government of Spain found shelter in various embassies and legations in Madrid.[30] And a great amount of bitter denunciation, culminating in two cases laid before the International Court of Justice, was caused by

[27] Alona E. Evans, "The Colombian-Peruvian Asylum Case: The Practice of Diplomatic Asylum," 46 *A.J.I.L.* (1952), pp. 142–157, at p. 144.

[28] Text in 43 *A.J.I.L.* (1949), Supp., pp. 133–139.

[29] Council of the Organization of American States, *Decisions Taken at the Meeting Held on February 14, 1951*, Washington, D.C.: OAS, 1951, at pp. 25–26.

[30] Norman J. Padelford, *International Law and Diplomacy in the Spanish Civil Strife* (New York: Macmillan, 1939), at pp. 157–168.

the granting of diplomatic asylum by the Colombian Embassy in Lima to Victor Raúl Haya de la Torre, the leader of the Peruvian Aprista Party.[31]

On rare occasions, governments have not honored their own safe-conducts, intended to enable a fugitive to move abroad from the place of his diplomatic asylum. The most notorious recent example of such delinquency occurred in Hungary in 1956. Prime Minister Nagy and several members of his government had fled to the Jugoslav embassy building in Budapest and had been granted asylum there. After a short time, the Communist government of Hungary granted safe-conducts, as well as a promise not to prosecute them, to the fugitives. As soon as the latter had left the embassy premises, however, they were arrested and spirited away. The Jugoslav government addressed strong protests about this action to both Hungary and the U.S.S.R. (as the "protector" of Hungary), asking at the same time about the location of the individuals in question. The Hungarian reply of December 1, 1956, rejected the Jugoslav protest and declared that whatever action had taken place was of a strictly domestic concern and nature. Jugoslavia protested against this interpretation on December 6, 1956, repeating its objections once more on June 23, 1958, after Nagy's execution had been announced officially by Hungary.

PROBLEMS OF EXTRADITION AND ASYLUM

Informal Extradition. A problem connected with both the process of extradition and the granting of asylum is posed by what could be termed "informal" extradition. This refers to any of a great variety of devices and practices utilized by states to secure the apprehension of civil, criminal, and political offenders who have managed to escape beyond the frontiers of the seeking state—all without the formality of the procedural details characteristic of normal state practice under the terms of an extradition treaty.

Modern history is filled with examples of informal extradition and it is regrettable that the scope of a general text precludes a detailed presen-

[31] For the decisions of the Court, see *I.C.J. Reports, 1950*, pp. 266 ff., and *ibid.*, 1951, pp. 71 ff., or the (excerpted at length) first decision of November 20, 1950, in 45 *A.J.I.L.* (1951), pp. 179–195 and the digested second decision of June 13, 1951, *ibid.*, pp. 781–788. For discussions of the cases, see Alona E. Evans, *op. cit.* (n. 27), at pp. 147–157, as well as her earlier study, "The Colombian-Peruvian Asylum Case: Termination of the Judicial Phase," 45 *A.J.I.L.* (1951), pp. 755–762; Herbert W. Briggs, "The Colombian–Peruvian Asylum Case and Proof of Customary International Law," *ibid.*, pp. 728–731; and J. L. F. van Essen, "Some Reflections on the Judgments in the Asylum and Haya de la Torre Cases," 1 *International and Comparative Law Quarterly* (1952), pp. 533–539.

tation of a most interesting subject.[32] From a legal point of view, a state willing to surrender a political offender to the seeking state by some informal method rather than through formal procedures does not commit a wrong: all it does is to abandon the assertions and claims it has made or invoked, openly or tacitly, in the *particular case* when it accepted the refugee and by doing so initially denied extradition. The existence of an extradition treaty between the two countries concerned in such a transaction might well lead to a substantial defense of the fugitive when tried before the courts of his own state—on the concept that a treaty by incorporation is the law of his land—but in practice such a defense, while valid in theory, might not produce much in the way of results. Even in the United States, citizens have been prosecuted successfully after they had been delivered without due process and in violation of extradition treaties, by countries in which they had sought refuge in order to escape what might be termed "politically motivated criminal prosecution" at home.[33]

Forcible Abduction. Insofar as fugitives abducted and returned against their will to their own country are concerned, the judicial attitude in the United States appears to be that "the power of a court to try a person for a crime is not impaired by the fact that he had been brought within the court's jurisdiction by reason of a 'forcible abduction,' whether from another state[34] or from another country."[35] This view represents, of course, only an aspect of national law and jurisdiction.

The defense of illegal entry into a court's jurisdiction is therefore rejected, generally on the plea that the supposed violation in question was not that of the individual's interests but of the interests of the state whose rights were violated. This principle is supported by the laws of the overwhelming number of all states: once a prisoner is under the authority of a given court and has been properly charged in accordance with the local law, he may be tried and, if convicted, sentenced by that court regardless of the mode by which he was brought originally under the authority of that court.

The whole question of abducting a fugitive from his refuge for trial elsewhere came into worldwide prominence through the seizure on May 11, 1960, of Adolf Eichmann by "private" Israeli citizens in Argen-

---

[32] See Manuel R. García-Mora, "Criminal Jurisdiction of a State over Fugitives Brought from a Foreign Country by Force or Fraud: A Comparative Study," 32 *Indiana Law Journal* (1957), pp. 427–449, emphasizing the purely legal approach to the problem.

[33] Kirchheimer, *op. cit.*, pp. 998–999; the following cases might be cited as representative illustrative specimens: *United States* v. *Sobell*, District Court, S.D. of N.Y., 1956, 142 F. Supp. 515; *Chandler* v. *United States*, 1948, 171 F. (2d) 921; *Frisbie* v. *Collins*, Supreme Court, 1952, 342 U.S. 519; and *Ker* v. *Illinois*, Supreme Court, 1886, 119 U.S. 437.

[34] Thus in *Frisbie* v. *Collins*, cited in previous note.

[35] *Ker* v. *Illinois*, cited in n. 33.

tina and his transportation to Israel on an Israeli aircraft to face trial as a Nazi war criminal. Eichmann had been removed in violation of international law, a fact emphasized formally by the UN Security Council to which Argentina brought a complaint about the incident.[36] After Israel tendered an official apology, Argentina waived further action on the abduction. The matter was declared closed in a joint *communiqué* issued by the two states on August 3, 1960.

The question of Israel's jurisdiction was settled, in the opinion of many writers, when all other states which had some interest in trying Eichmann waived their claims, thus leaving Israel in unchallenged possession of the accused and at liberty to conduct a trial in accordance with its own law.

Status of Prewar Extradition Treaties. One of the many problems connected with extradition of the more formal variety arises at the conclusion of a war. The question is: Did prewar extradition treaties concluded between opposing belligerents survive the war? It may be suggested, on the basis of numerous decisions, that such agreements are not terminated by war but are merely suspended. They come into effect again at the end of the conflict, as soon as relevant notifications have been exchanged between the former belligerents.[37] The essential feature around which any discussion of the survival of a treaty in the event of war centers appears to be the intentions of the parties concerned. And in relation to extradition, a common intention appears to be a survival of the relevant treaty on a suspended basis for the duration of the conflict.

SUGGESTED READINGS

EXTRADITION IN GENERAL

Charles Fairman, "Extradition to a Country under Control of the United States," 48 *A.J.I.L.* (1954), pp. 612–616; Paul O'Higgins, "European Convention on Extradition," *International and Comparative Law Quarterly,* 9 (1960), pp. 491–494; Frederick Honig, "Extradition by Multilateral Convention," *ibid.,*

---

[36] On the question of Eichmann's abduction, consult especially the valuable study by Helen Silving, "In Re Eichmann: A Dilemma of Law and Morality," 55 *A.J.I.L.* (1961), pp. 307–358, particularly pp. 314–331, with its exhaustive bibliographical and historical background notes. See also Michael H. Cardozo, "When Extradition Fails, Is Abduction the Solution?" *ibid.,* pp. 127–135.

[37] See *Argento* v. *Horn,* United States, Circuit Court of Appeals, Sixth Circuit, 1957, 241 F. 2d 258, digested at length in 51 *A.J.I.L.* (1957), pp. 634–637; for subsequent developments in that case, see *ibid.,* 54 (1960), pp. 409–410. Earlier cases dealing with the problem of treaties and war include *Society for the Propagation of the Gospel in Foreign Parts* v. *Town of New Haven,* United States, Supreme Court, 1823, 8 Wheaton 464; *Karnuth* v. *United States ex rel. Albro,* United States, Supreme Court, 1929, 279 U.S. 231; *Terlinden* v. *Ames,* United States, Supreme Court, 1902, 184 U.S. 270; and *Clark* v. *Allen,* United States, Supreme Court, 1947, 331 U.S. 503.

5 (1956), pp. 549–569; Lauterpacht's *Oppenheim*, Vol. I, pp. 696–710; C. Neale Ronning, *Diplomatic Asylum: Legal Norms and Political Reality in Latin American Relations* (The Hague: Martinus Nijhoff, 1965); Alona E. Evans, "In re Sneyd, a/k/a Ray," 63 *A.J.I.L.* (1969), pp. 111–114.

Cases

Rivard v. *United States*, United States, Court of Appeals, 5th Circuit, 1967, 375 F. 2d 882, reported in 61 *A.J.I.L.* (1967), pp. 1065–1066.
Stevenson v. *United States*, United States, Court of Appeals, 9th Circuit, 1967, 381 F. 2d 142, reported *ibid.*, 62 (1968), p. 500.

POLITICAL OFFENSES

L. C. Green, "Political Offences, War Crimes and Extradition," 11 *International and Comparative Law Quarterly* (1962), pp. 329–354; Manuel R. García-Mora, "Crimes against Humanity and the Principle of the Nonextradition of Political Offenders," 62 *Michigan Law Review* (1964), pp. 927–960; Alona E. Evans, "Political Refugees and the United States Immigration Law: A Case Note," 62 *A.J.I.L.* (1968), pp. 921–926.

Cases

In re Ezeta, United States, District Court, N.D.Cal., 1894, 62 Fed. 972.
In the Matter of Ktir, Switzerland, Supreme Federal Court, 1961, digested in 56 *A.J.I.L.* (1962), pp. 224–227.
Ornelas v. *Ruiz*, United States, Supreme Court, 1896, 161 U.S. 502.

EICHMANN CASE

Whiteman, Vol. VI, pp. 105–109; Gideon Hauser, *Justice in Jerusalem* (New York: Harper & Row, 1966); Yosal Rogat, *The Eichmann Trial and the Rule of Law* (Santa Barbara, Calif.: Center for the Study of Democratic Institutions, 1961), at p. 24; Hans W. Baade, "The Eichmann Trial: Some Legal Aspects," *Duke Law Journal* (Vol. 1961, Summer), pp. 400–420; Zad Leavy, "The Eichmann Trial and the Role of Law," 48 *American Bar Association Journal* (1962), pp. 820–825. Consult also D. Lasok, "The Eichmann Trial," 11 *International and Comparative Law Quarterly* (1962), pp. 355–374; Telford Taylor, "Large Questions in the Eichmann Case," *New York Times Magazine* (January 22, 1961), pp. 11, 22–23, 25; Robert K. Woetzel, "The Eichmann Case in International Law," *Criminal Law Review* (October, 1962), pp. 671–682; the exceptionally valuable opinion in *The Attorney-General of the Government of Israel* v. *Eichmann*, District Court of Jerusalem, December 11, 1961, excerpted at length in 56 *A.J.I.L.* (1962), pp. 805–845. The verdict of the court in the case was summarized in 4 *Israel Digest* (December 22, 1961), Supp., pp. i–viii; see *ibid.*, 5 (June 5, 1962), p. 1, for a brief summary of the dismissal (May 29, 1962) of Eichmann's appeal by the Supreme Court of Israel. Eichmann was executed by hanging on May 31, 1962.

PART IV
Territorial Questions

15
Title to Territory

A STATE has an unquestioned right to exercise sovereign authority throughout the extent of its territory. By virtue of this fact, territory became in the legal order "the point of departure in settling most questions that concern international relations."[1]

In the earliest stages of Western history, effective control of a territory, together with the ability to defend it, represented the title that counted; soon, however, additional title requirements of a more legal nature entered into the picture, such as treaties of cession, marriage settlements, and occasionally claims based on an asserted hereditary right to succession. In the course of time, then, a rather considerable number of titles to particular areas or territories received express or tacit recognition by the majority of states.[2]

Beginning with the Age of Discovery, a more systematic approach to the problem of title to territory became necessary in view of the some-times sweeping claims based on discovery and of the assertion by certain seafaring nations of jurisdiction over enormous expanses of the world's oceans.

METHODS OF ACQUIRING TITLE
TO TERRITORY TODAY

Title to territory has been obtained by states through the transfer of land from one owner to another or through the acquisition of land not belonging to any other state. In the former case a "derivative" title was obtained, whereas in the latter instance an "original" title resulted for the owner.

Generally speaking, seven methods of acquiring title to territory are recognized by states today: occupation, accretion, prescription, voluntary cession, assimilation, treaties of peace, and conquest (the last with reservations, to be sure).

[1] Judge Max Huber in the *Palmas Island Arbitration* (United States–Netherlands), 1928; see 22 *A.J.I.L.* (1928), p. 867.
[2] See Georg Schwarzenberger, "Title to Territory: Response to a Challenge," 51 *A.J.I.L.* (1957), p. 308–324. One of the best monographic treatments of the subject of titles and claims to territory is found in Norman Hill, *Claims to Territory in International Law and Relations* (New York: Oxford University Press, 1945), particularly on pp. 143–163.

Discovery represented the oldest and, historically, the most important method of acquiring title to territory. Up to the eighteenth century, discovery alone sufficed to establish a legal title, but since then such discovery has had to be followed by an effective occupation in order to be recognized as the basis of a title to territory. The history of Spanish exploration abounds (as an example) with the landing of explorers in new territories and the establishment of claims to title by a proclamation of annexation, coupled with performance of such symbolic acts as the burying of inscribed lead tablets, and so forth.

The doctrine of the sufficiency of mere discovery to establish a valid title was asserted as late as 1823 by Chief Justice John Marshal in *Johnson and Graham's Lessee v. M'Intosh* (Supreme Court of the United States, 1823, 8 Wheaton 543), but the learned judge did qualify his dictum by adding that the "title might be consummated by possession." In fact, during the next year, the United States government maintained in its negotiations with Russia concerning territorial questions that "dominion cannot be acquired but by a real occupation and possession, and an intention to establish it is by no means sufficient." [3]

Occupation. Occupation means the settlement by a state of a territory hitherto not belonging to any other state for the purpose of adding the land in question to the national territory. Such "vacant" land (*terra nullius*) existed even if it had already a native population—provided the latter consisted of nomads or of a people judged to possess a civilization inferior to that of the standard prevailing in Europe (the Aztec Empire in Mexico may be cited as an example). The actual settlement had to be made if the at best vague claim based on discovery was to be transformed into a legal, recognized, title. Such settlement must be made within a "reasonable" time after discovery and must assume a permanent character. Mere visits by fishermen, or the maintenance of seasonal fishing settlements would not be held to constitute occupation in the legal meaning of the term.

One of the most interesting modern cases dealing with title to territory on the basis of discovery and claimed occupation was the dispute between France and Great Britain relative to sovereignty over the tiny islands in the English Channel called the Minquiers and Ecrehos groups. By a special agreement of September 24, 1951, the disputants asked the International Court of Justice to determine who was the sovereign of the islets in question. [4] The Court decided in favor of the British claim, denying the validity of alleged French occupation and exercise of sov-

---

[3] Quoted in Hill, *op. cit.,* p. 147.

[4] *Minquiers and Ecrehos Case (France–United Kingdom)*, International Court of Justice, November 17, 1953, *I.C.J. Reports, 1953*, p. 47, digested by William W. Bishop, Jr., in 48 *A.J.I.L.* (1954), pp. 316–326; see also D. H. N. Johnson, "The Minquiers and Ecrehos Case," 3 *International and Comparative Law Quarterly* (1954), pp. 189–216.

ereign acts in the islands. What makes this decision especially interesting is not only the reasoning of the Court, but the examination of historical evidence going back to the Norman Conquest in the case of England and, in the case of the evidence submitted by France, to A.D. 933.

Title to territory based on occupation lapses when the territory is abandoned again by its owner. The classic example of the operation of this doctrine is supplied by the dispute still going on between Argentina and Great Britain concerning sovereignty over the Falkland (Malvinas) Islands.[5]

A number of other instances of territorial titles claimed on alleged or actual abandonment have been recorded in the past four hundred years, such as the island of Santa Lucia, the area around Delagoa Bay in Africa, and the Atlantic island of Ilha da Trinidade. With the exception of the Falkland Islands dispute, however, no modern disagreements of consequence in this field are on record.

In the relatively few cases in which the fact of occupation played a major part, the extent of settlement needed to assert a valid title became a crucial issue. Generally speaking, a single permanent settlement, even if located along the fringes of an unappropriated area, has been held to constitute sufficient evidence of occupation. Exceptions are on record, of course, and the interested reader might profitably investigate the problems connected with the Louisiana Purchase, the boundary questions incidental to the Anglo-American Oregon controversy, and several of the disagreements centering around European territorial claims along the western coasts of Africa. For modern disputes, the disagreement between Norway and Denmark over title to Eastern Greenland, won by Denmark through a ruling by the Permanent Court of International Justice in 1933,[6] and the French-Mexican dispute over Clipperton Island in the Pacific, might be cited.

At the present time, only one area represents a disputed true territorial claim of the United States: a group of three tiny islands, the Swan Islands, a hundred miles off the coast of Honduras. The latter country periodically renews its claim through the medium of diplomatic notes to the United States, most recently in 1957 and 1960. The Honduran claim is based on the original Spanish conquests of Central America in the sixteenth century, while the American claim is founded on a Spanish lack of occupation, with consequent lapse of any alleged Spanish claim, followed by permanent American occupation of the group.

[5] For recent and at times farcial developments in that dispute, consult *The New York Times*, September 6, 1964, p. 24; December 12, 1965, p. 23; October 2, 1966, p. E-2. Also see 88 *Time* (October 7, 1966), p. 48; 68 *Newsweek* (October 10, 1966), p. 60. In November, 1965, the United Nations General Assembly had voted in favor of a negotiated settlement, by the two parties in question, of the dispute. It does not appear, at the time of writing, that progress toward a solution has been achieved.

[6] *Eastern Greenland Case (Denmark–Norway)*, P.C.I.J., 1933, Ser. A/B, No. 53.

In order to prevent a recurrence of repeated "discoveries," with resultant claims, the major powers agreed in the Final Act of the Berlin Conference of 1885 (Art. 34), that any occupation of African territory should be followed by notification of all signatory states so that any other claims to the area in question could be voiced and settled before a dispute could arise. Silence on the part of any signatory would therefore mean approval of the claim asserted by the notifying state.

In this connection, the doctrine of the "Hinterland" should be mentioned, even if it, like discovery *cum* occupation, possesses only historical interest today. In view of the problems encountered in arriving at interior boundaries in the Americas, the major powers involved in the partition of Africa in the last quarter of the nineteenth century concluded a number of bilateral agreements delimiting the territorial zones contiguous to the initial settlements set up along the coasts. Such interior zones were termed the "Hinterland" (backcountry) and although not occupied in the sense of actual permanent settlement, they were recognized as constituting spheres of interest of the state based on the coastal settlement. In effect, however, the Hinterland soon assumed the character of colonial territory and when interior borders were determined at a later date, the Hinterland normally remained a part of the new colony.

Accretion. A second but minor mode of acquiring title to territory comes about through accretion, the gradual deposit of soil by a river flowing past a shore or by an ocean along its coasts. The rule governing accretion dates back to Roman days and is quite simple: a thing that is added follows the fate of the principal thing. Soil added to a river bank represents an addition to the territory of the riparian state; islands built up within a riverbed become a part of the territory of the state within whose boundary lines the flats or islands are formed.

In the case of mudflats or islands built up within the territorial waters of a state, they not only become the property of that state but also cause an outward extension of the maritime frontier from the new islands to a distance normally claimed along its shores by the state in question (the baseline of the territorial sea being determined by reference to the low-water mark). The classic case dealing with accretion is

THE ANNA
GREAT BRITAIN, HIGH COURT OF ADMIRALTY, *1805*
(*5 C. Robinson 373*)

FACTS

The *Anna*, a vessel flying the American flag (although some authors claim that the ship was actually a Spanish one), carried a cargo of logwood as well as $13,000 from Spanish ports in the Caribbean to New Orleans. It was captured by the British privateer *Minerva* near the mouth of the Mississippi River, during the war then in progress between Great Britain and

Spain. The American minister filed a claim to the vessel and cargo, stating that the capture had taken place within the territorial waters of the United States.

The *Anna* had been taken outside of the three-mile limit if that limit was measured from the Balise, an ex-Spanish fort at the edge of the mainland, but within a three-mile limit if the latter was measured from a few small mud islands composed of earth and driftwood, formed by the Mississippi River. The islands were uninhabitable because of the consistency of their soft soil.

ISSUE

Could uninhabited mud islands formed by action of a river be claimed by the coastal state and serve to extend the latter's territorial sea limits?

DECISION

The Court ruled in favor of the United States; the ship and cargo were ordered released because of their capture within neutral American waters. The islands were a part of American territorial jurisdiction and extended the boundaries of the American territorial sea for three miles beyond the islands.

REASONING

The islands, formed by accretion, had to be taken to be "natural appendages of the coast on which they border. Their elements are derived immediately from the territory . . ." If they did not belong to the United States, any other state could occupy them, fortify them, and through them control all traffic to and from the mouth of the Mississippi. But they had been formed of American soil and American driftwood, since both shores of the Mississippi were in the United States, and hence were a part of American territory. As such, they formed the outermost land off their shore, and served to extend American territorial waters by three miles away from shore and into the ocean. Under these conditions, the *Anna* had been captured in American neutral waters. Such capture was a violation of neutral rights and was illegal.

Prescription. This is a legal term related to title to territory; it means continued occupation, over a long period of time, by one state of territory actually and originally belonging to another state. In essence, this corresponds to abandonment, but technically there is a difference. Abandonment implies a withdrawal, a kind of open retreat from a territory. Prescription means that a foreign state occupies a portion of territory claimed by a state, encounters no protests on the part of the "owner," and exercises rights of sovereignty over a long period of time. Eventually the original title lapses and the "squatter state" acquires legal title to the territory.

Most early writers on international law wrestled with the knotty problem of the actual length of time required to validate a title founded on prescription, and none of them could arrive at a generally acceptable number of actual years of occupation. Unlike the common law rules found in many states on this essential factor of continued adverse holding, there still exists no international standard which defines precisely just how long the occupant must hold on to an area before acquiring title. In one of the few arbitral decisions available on the subject, the *Island of Palmas Case*, a slight clue was supplied, however:

THE ISLAND OF PALMAS (MIANGAS) ARBITRATION

(United States–The Netherlands), Tribunal of the Permanent Court of Arbitration, 1928

FACTS

The treaty of peace ending the Spanish-American War included the cession by Spain of the Philippine Islands to the United States. The island of Palmas, also known as Miangas Island, was an isolated island located about midway between the southern tip of Mindanao in the Philippines and the northernmost island of the Nanoesa group in the (then) Netherland East Indies. The island, a small one (two miles by three-quarters of a mile) then had a population of about 750 and no economic resources to speak of.

The American governor of the Province of Moro visited the island on January 21, 1906, and was astonished to see the Dutch flag flying above Palmas. His maps, and the peace treaty of December 10, 1898, indicated that the island was located twenty miles inside the boundaries of the Philippine Islands as ceded by Spain to the United States.

A long diplomatic dispute then arose between the United States and the Netherlands about the status of Palmas. In 1925 the two governments agreed to submit the question of title to the island to arbitration, and a sole arbitrator, M. Max Huber, was selected.

ISSUE

Is a valid title to foreign territory obtained through exercise of acts of sovereignty when the lawful owner fails to protest such acts?

DECISION

The island was awarded to the Netherlands: despite original Spanish title to Palmas, the Dutch government had exercised sovereign rights for more than two hundred years and had obtained title by prescription.

REASONING

"The principle that continuous and peaceful display of the functions of State within a given region is a constituent element of territorial sovereignty" is a recognized principle of international law.

Spain could not cede in the 1898 treaty more rights than Spain possessed. If the original Spanish title to the island of Palmas was valid in 1898, then that title had been transferred by the peace treaty to the United States. But the Netherlands government submitted undeniable evidence to the effect that since 1700 the island had formed a part of successive native states on the Island of Sangi, which native states, since 1677, had been connected with the Netherlands East India Company. The vassal states or the Netherlands government had occasionally exercised "acts characteristic of State authority" on the island of Palmas, not only between 1700 and 1898, but also between 1898 and 1906. The evidence was clear that at least since the middle of the nineteenth century, the Netherlands government had considered the island of Palmas as a part of its lawful possessions.

No Spanish protests concerning Dutch acts or claims had been forthcoming since the Spaniards, withdrawing from the Moluccas in 1666, had made express reservations as to the continuation of their sovereign rights. No other power had attempted any display of sovereignty until the United States claimed the island in 1906. Thus an uncontested exercise of Netherlands sovereignty was shown to extend from 1700 to 1906. The Netherlands' title, acquired by continuous and peaceful acts of state authority, over two hundred years, and uncontested by the original holders of title to the island, held good.[7]

A much shorter period of adverse and uninterrupted possession than the two hundred years cited in the *Island of Palmas* arbitration was specified in the interesting case centering on title to Palmyra Island: *United States v. Fullard-Leo, et al.*[8]

Voluntary Cession. Cession means the formal transfer of title (sovereignty) over territory from one state to another. Voluntary cession conveys a lawful title to the new owner. Normally cession is formulated through the provisions of a treaty of cession which specifies precisely (if such is possible at the time) the area to be transferred as well as the conditions under which the transfer is to be accomplished. All kinds of related provisions may be encountered in such instruments, relating to the nationality of the inhabitants of the territory, the adjustment of public debts connected with the area, the establishment or fate of servitudes therein, and so forth.

Cession may take one of a number of forms. A common and simple type, particularly popular in past centuries but not unknown in modern times, is a *treaty of sale.* This form of conveyance of title was utilized by the United States in such well-known acquisitions as the Louisiana Purchase (1803), the Florida Purchase (1819), the Gadsden Purchase (1853), the Alaska Purchase (1867), and the purchase of the Danish West Indies (Virgin Islands) in 1916.

Another form of voluntary cession is represented by the exchange of one piece of real estate for another, such as the transfer of the island of Heligoland by Great Britain to Germany in 1890 in exchange for areas adjacent to German East Africa.

Again, cession has been effected by means of a gift: in past centuries

[7] See also Philip C. Jessup, "The Palmas Island Arbitration," 22 *A.J.I.L.* (1928), pp. 735–752; and R. V. Jennings, *The Acquisition of Territory in International Law* (Manchester: Manchester University Press; Dobbs Ferry, N.Y.: Oceana Publications, 1963) which contains, additionally, the full text of the *Palmas* award.

[8] United States, Circuit Court of Appeals, Ninth Circuit, February 1, 1943, as amended March 4, 1943, 133 F. 2d 743; *certiorari* denied by the Supreme Court, May 10, 1943. See also 37 *A.J.I.L.* (1943), at pp. 526–534, for a well-reasoned dissenting opinion by Circuit Court Judge Healy.

as part, say, of a royal dowry or, in more modern times, as illustrated by the donation of a portion of a reef in Lake Erie by Great Britain to the United States (1850), subject to the condition that the latter would assume responsibility for the construction and maintenance of a lighthouse on the reef in question.

Finally, cession has on rare occasions been accomplished by a conveyance of title by devise, such as the transfer of title to the Congo Free State to Belgium (1908) from King Leopold who was sovereign of the Congo in his personal capacity in addition to being King of the Belgians.

Involuntary Cession by Conquest. Involuntary cession has been accomplished most commonly through military conquest. A country defeated in war would be subjugated, that is, its government and armed forces would cease to exist and its territory would be occupied by the victorious enemy; the latter would then achieve legal title to the territory of the defeated state by annexation. Or, portions of enemy territory would be occupied and then retained as part of the occupant's territory without formal confirmation of such annexation in any peace treaty. Title in the latter case was based on a sort of doctrine of abandonment by the former owners. Such practice had disappeared during the nineteenth century but was revived once more when Turkey "abandoned" two provinces in 1912 (Tripoli and Cyrenaica) and Italy annexed them subsequently. The peace treaty ending the Italo-Turkish War (Treaty of Lausanne, October 18, 1912) did not mention the cession of either province to Italy.

Subjugation reappeared during the twentieth century with the end of Ethiopia through annexation after conquest by Italy (1936), the conquest and annexation of Poland by the U.S.S.R. and Germany, and with the Allied subjugation (not followed, however, by the usual step of annexation) of Germany by the Western Allies and Russia in May, 1945.

Involuntary cession of territory through subjugation followed by annexation whether by wartime "abandonment" or whether by peace treaty, had always been regarded as conveying a lawful title to the new holders of the areas involved. The establishment of the League of Nations, followed by the Kellogg-Briand Treaty (Pact of Paris) of 1928, appeared to have changed the traditional pattern and to have eliminated conquest as a source of valid title to territory.

Article 10 of the Covenant of the League, it has been asserted, *implied* an obligation on the part of member states to deny recognition to the seizure of territories from other members. It does not appear to have possessed similar implications relating to territorial losses suffered by nonmembers, nor was the Article interpreted meaningfully (as related to nonrecognition of title to territory) in practice when the Assembly decided, in December, 1939, to expel the Soviet Union for its aggression against Finland. Previous instances of forceful acquisition of territory (Manchuria, Ethiopia, Austria, Czechoslovakia, Albania, and all portions of Poland) all failed to secure implementation of Article 10.

Neither the Covenant nor the Pact of Paris contained *express* provisions obligating states to deny recognition to the results of "unlawful acts of conquest." It is difficult to see how even the implication of an obligation not to validate the results of a *de facto* situation, however "illegal" in origin, could be found in the two instruments in question.[9] But such a view, shared by the present writer, has been strongly criticized in the past.[10]

On the other hand, the Japanese seizure of Manchuria in 1931–32 led the then American Secretary of State, Henry Stimson, to issue a series of pronouncements (subsequently endorsed by the Assembly of the League) expressing a denial of the validity of the acquisition of territory by the use of force. Latin American states in particular expressed strong condemnation of conquest as a lawful means of territorial aggrandizement, especially after the outbreak of the Chaco War between Bolivia and Paraguay, and again at the Inter-American Conferences in 1933, 1936, 1938, as well as at the Foreign Ministers' Conference in Havana in 1940.

It can therefore be maintained that the Stimson doctrine of nonrecognition represents a basic principle of regional inter-American law, but not of general international law.[11]

It should be noted, moreover, that individual or multilateral declarations concerning the invalidity of conquest as a source of territorial titles have been more than counterbalanced by the contrary practices of states when viewed on a global basis. In consequence of the numerous annexations carried out in the decades between the end of World War I and the founding of the United Nations, it must be concluded that neither the Covenant nor the Pact of Paris nor the Inter-American declarations created a new and generally applicable principle of international law with respect to the topic under consideration.

The coming into force of the United Nations Charter ended, in this writer's opinion, the legality of the acquisition of title to territory through conquest. The relevant provisions of the instrument (especially Art. 2, par. 4) make it abundantly clear that, from a *legal* point of view, the use or threat of the use of force, in violation of obligations assumed under the Charter, to obtain territory from another state is clearly prohibited

[9] Robert W. Tucker, "The Principle of Effectiveness in International Law," in Lipsky, pp. 31–48, at p. 45; consult also Corbett, pp. 100–104, for a similar position relative to the Pact of Paris.

[10] See Quincy Wright, "The Legal Foundations of the Stimson Doctrine," 8 *Pacific Affairs* (1935), pp. 439–446; see Whiteman, Vol. II, pp. 1145–1152, 1157–1161, on the Stimson Doctrine and its status in regional Western Hemisphere law, and see the specific coverage of the Doctrine, *ibid.*, Vol. V, pp. 874–888. See also Whiteman, Vol. II, pp. 1111–1162, on acquisition of title through conquest.

[11] Consult, *inter alia*, Robert Langer, *Seizure of Territory: The Stimson Doctrine and Related Principles in Legal Theory and Diplomatic Practice* (Princeton, N.J.: Princeton University Press, 1947).

to all member states of the organization.[12] But, as has been pointed out already in Chapter 10, those same member states have acquiesced on several occasions in the forcible seizure of territory by one of their number or by a nonmember, and by tacit acceptance or mere verbal protest have created situations in which continued possession of seized territory is quite likely to end in valid title for the current possessor. Instances such as the aggression committed by India against the princely state of Hyderabad and in 1961 against the Portuguese enclaves in India, the occupation of Burmese and Indian territories as well as the absorption of Tibet by Communist China, and the territorial seizures by Israel during the "Six-Day War" in 1967 come to mind in this connection.

To this day, states have persisted in regarding territory acquired through the use of force as part of their lawful national domain. Although a few instances of involuntary cession have not been recognized as lawful by certain countries, a multitude of other cases of such involuntary cession have been accepted quite generally and the territories in question are now regarded as parts of the national territories of the acquiring states.

Thus the facts of international life appear to demonstrate that the theory according to which the use of force will not create valid title to territory in the future represents at best a "pure law" proposition. In order to cover the gap between a legal "wrong" and a practical "right," recourse may be had to what has been termed the concept of consolidation. When a state has seized by force some portion of territory and cannot be driven out, "it may eventually come about that a title by consolidation is acquired through recognition or other forms of acknowledgment of the position expressive of the will of the international community."[13] On the other hand, the practice of states quite clearly leads to the conclusion that recognition of title acquired by force is not at all essential to perfect such a title to territory. It cannot as yet be demonstrated beyond serious doubt that title by conquest (involuntary cession) is in any way incomplete unless and until it is recognized by third parties. Only if a new customary or conventional rule of general law were developed could there be no doubt that external recognition constituted an essential element in the perfection of title to territory gained by the use of force.

Several writers have pointed out an interesting and paradoxical aspect of conquest as related to the Charter of the United Nations. Although individual recognition of the fruits of aggression appears to be forbidden by the Charter, the United Nations as an organization may, so it seems,

---

[12] See also Lauterpacht's *Oppenheim*, Vol. I, p. 574, on this point; Lauterpacht stressed (p. 574, n. 4) that this interpretation represented a personal opinion, as is true for this writer, in the absence of authoritative judicial pronouncements on the matter.

[13] Jennings, *op. cit.*, p. 67.

itself accept a situation considered by it to be beneficial, even if that situation had an illegal origin. This has been true, one must assume, in the case of Israel, which in 1948 occupied by military force territory considerably in excess of the areas allocated to it by the United Nations resolutions adopted in 1947.[14] Similarly the United Nations suffered without effective action the partitions of both Kashmir and Korea, even though a policy of unification by plebiscite had been formulated.

On the other hand, numerous American court decisions reflect the conviction held by the United States government that conquest alone does not confer valid title. Thus, in *Brunell* v. *United States*,[15] the court held that Brunell, an entertainer injured in an army vehicle while touring the island of Saipan, could not bring suit against the United States under the Federal Tort Claims Act which excluded any claims arising in a foreign country. The court cited a letter from the Legal Adviser of the Department of State to the Attorney General of the United States in which it was stated that the island was an area under military occupation by forces of the United States but was not American territory because no treaty of cession covering the island had been concluded with Japan nor had Congress enacted any legislation incorporating the island into the United States.

POLAR REGIONS

National claims to areas in the Arctic and Antarctic regions did not raise any considerable international problems until a few decades ago. Careful exploration, beginning with the nineteenth century, had been followed in many instances by claims based exclusively on discovery, but because of an assumed lack of resources and of difficulties in travel and transport, no crises of consequence developed from such asserted rights.

Only the coming of the long-distance aircraft and the belief that sizable deposits of valuable minerals and coal might be found under the Antarctic ice caused a sudden interest in polar claims.

ARCTIC CLAIMS

Exploration had determined the absence of land near the North Pole, and claims on subsurface ocean resources could at best be based on the somewhat vague claim of contiguity, *i.e.*, on an extension of some part of the continental tableland. Occupation took form only in the shape of numerous weather stations and air bases, particularly during and after World War II.

Arctic Sector Theory. Existing territorial claims in the Arctic were based on discovery, occupation, and especially on a variation of the

---

[14] Quincy Wright, "The Goa Incident," 56 *A.J.I.L.* (1962), pp. 617–632, at p. 631.
[15] United States, District Court, S.D. of New York, 1948, 77 F. Supp. 68.

doctrine of contiguity, expressed more fortuituously as the Arctic Sector Theory. A state whose territory lies close to the Arctic claims all land to be found between a line extending from its eastern extremity to the North Pole and another line extending from its western extremity to the Pole. The Russian government, originally relying on the older version of the doctrine—extensions of the continental tableland under the ocean surface—switched to the sector theory in 1926. Other northern nations have also adopted the sector theory (United States, Canada, Denmark, Norway).[16] The writer does not know whether the Danish claim has been reduced by the emergence of an Icelandic sector following the separation of Iceland from Denmark in 1944, but believes that such has been the case. Within the sector claimed by the Soviet Union lie Nansen Land, claimed by Norway, and Wrangel Island, sovereignty over which has been asserted repeatedly by the United States.

It is doubtful that the "sector theory" represents a rule of international law.[17] It should probably be characterized as an accommodation device elaborated by the states concerned.

The reasons for the sudden emergence of the polar regions into legal prominence are obvious: across this part of the world run the short-distance trans-Arctic commercial aviation routes, extensively utilized by the lines of several states; and across this region might travel the inter-continental ballistic missiles employed in a war between the United States and the Soviet Union.[18]

ANTARCTIC CLAIMS

The existence of a landmass in the Antarctic prompted a development of territorial claims quite unlike that experienced in the Arctic regions. Numerous and conflicting claims have been set forth over the decades by Great Britain, Argentina, Norway, Australia, New Zealand, France, Chile, and, at one time, by Germany. Most of these claims were based exclusively on discovery, but in the Palmer Peninsula region a degree of permanent settlement has been achieved through bases maintained by Great Britain, Argentina, and Chile over a number of years.[19]

[16] See 22 *Life* (January 20, 1947), pp. 55–62, for an instructive survey of the polar regions; especially note the map on p. 55 delineating the various national sectors claimed; Whiteman, Vol. II, pp. 1267–1270; and David W. Heron, "Antarctic Claims," 32 *Foreign Affairs* (1954), pp. 661–667.

[17] See also Oscar Svarlien, *The Eastern Greenland Case in Historical Perspective* (Gainesville, Fla.: University of Florida Press, 1964), on this point.

[18] Consult Robert D. Hayton, "Polar Problems and International Law," 52 *A.J.I.L.* (1958), pp. 746–765, at pp. 746–753.

[19] John Hanessian, Jr., "Antarctica: Current National Interests and Legal Realities," *Proceedings* (1958), pp. 145–164, at p. 161; see also Hayton, *op. cit.*, pp. 753–765, and his "The 'American' Antarctic," 50 *A.J.I.L.* (1956), pp. 583–610; Lt. Cmdr. and Mrs. Clarence O. Fiske, "Territorial Claims in the Antarctic," 85 *U.S. Naval Institute Proceedings* (1959), pp. 82–91; see also the extensive bibliography in Bishop, p. 356, n. 18; and consult Whiteman, Vol. II, pp. 1232–1267.

The United States has not asserted any official claims to territory in the Antarctic. This policy, first enunciated by Secretary of State Hughes in 1924, is based on the theory that no claims in Antarctica could be recognized until discovery had been followed by effective occupation or control, including settlement as well as development. This abstention from the announcement of definite territorial claims has not always met with the unqualified support of every element in the United States. As Hanessian pointed out,[20] the nineteen fifties saw the introduction of a number of resolutions in Congress declaring United States sovereignty over specified portions of Antarctica. None of these proposed declarations passed, however, and as yet no formal United States claims have been communicated to other states.

By contrast, other countries have not only asserted such claims but in several instances have recognized each other's claims as valid. Thus, when France laid claim to Adélie Land and to certain islands near Antarctica in 1927, placing them under the administration of the Governor-General of Madagascar, Great Britain specifically recognized those claims at the time it asserted sovereignty over the large sector assigned to Australia.[21]

On the other hand, overlapping territorial claims have at times caused considerable bitterness between rival claimants, leading even to firing by competing national groups on one another. The Chilean claim, based on the sector theory, overlaps a British claim and almost half of the Argentine claim. The latter in turn covers most of the Chilean-claimed area as well as most of the British sphere called the "Falkland Island Dependencies," including a substantial portion of the Antarctic continent itself. French Adélie Land is inserted between the two portions of the British (Australian) claim on Wilkes Land, and so on. Despite these confusing claims and counterclaims, the sector theory generally applies to the Antarctic as it does in the Arctic. But in the cases of Argentina, Australia, Great Britain, and Chile, claims have been advanced to a greater area than that bounded by the projection of the outer limits of mainland domains adjacent to the Antarctic. The application of the sector theory to the Antarctic should be regarded, moreover, primarily as a method of asserting territorial claims and not as conferring a "right" of acquisition or sovereignty in lieu of continuous settlement. The necessary proof, for a lawful title, must remain, under existing international law, the power and the disposition on the part of a claimant to maintain control of Antarctic areas, by continuous settlement. As the Norwegian government correctly stated in 1929 in reference to Roald Amundsen's "acquisition" of Antarctic territory in the name of the king of Norway: "the said discovery and annexation constitute a valid basis for a claim of priority to acquire

---

[20] Hanessian, *op. cit.*, pp. 161–162.
[21] See especially Hayton, "The 'American' Antarctic," *op. cit.*, pp. 584–597, for the bases of various national claims.

such territories whenever the requirements of international law as to effective occupation of a new territory shall have been fulfilled." [22]

The existence of conflicting national claims and of consequent rivalries and possibilities of conflict led the United States Department of State in 1948 to initiate discussions among the interested countries on the desirability of holding a conference on Antarctic problems. It was suggested at that time that possible internationalization of the entire region might be the best solution for all concerned.

Most of the nations queried were averse to the proposal, preferring to maintain their established claims; furthermore, the Soviet Union, hitherto not consulted on Antarctic questions, indicated that it would demand full participation in any Antarctic settlement. It remained for the lessons in cooperation taught during the International Geophysical Year—actually a period of eighteen months, ending with the close of 1958—to bring about a partial international settlement of Antarctic questions.

Antarctic Treaty. On May 2, 1958, the United States invited eleven other nations to a conference on Antarctica; the meeting was held from October 15 to December 1, 1959, in Washington. The participating countries, in addition to the United States, were Argentina, Australia, Belgium, Chile, France, Japan, New Zealand, Norway, the Union of South Africa, the U.S.S.R., and the United Kingdom. At the conclusion of the conference, a multilateral instrument, The Antarctic Treaty, was signed by the delegates of all participating states.[23]

The treaty provided that Antarctica was to be used exclusively for peaceful purposes: no military bases were to be established there and no military maneuvers or the testing of any type of weapons were to be carried out, but military personnel and equipment could be used for scientific research. Other provisions of the instrument called for free exchange of information regarding plans for scientific programs in Antarctica, for an exchange of scientific personnel, and for an unhindered sharing in scientific observations made in Antarctica. All nuclear tests in the region and the disposal of radioactive waste materials there were prohibited unless, with reference to such disposal, subsequent treaties were concluded. In the latter case, such treaties should also apply to Antarctica.

Each contracting party was given the right to appoint observers to carry out inspections under Articles VII and IX of the treaty; these provided for complete freedom of inspection, in all parts of Antarctica, of all

[22] Hackworth, Vol. I, pp. 453–454.

[23] See *The Conference on Antarctica* (Conference Documents, The Antarctic Treaty, and Related Papers), Department of State Publication 7060 (Washington, D.C.: Government Printing Office, 1960); texts of the Final Act and of the Treaty may also be found in 54 *A.J.I.L.* (1960), Supp., pp. 476–483. Consult also the monographic study by John Hanessian, Jr., "The Antarctic Treaty 1959," 9 *International and Comparative Law Quarterly* (1960), pp. 436–480, as well as Robert D. Hayton, "The Antarctic Settlement of 1959," 54 *A.J.I.L.* (1960), pp. 348–371.

installations and equipment, as well as of ships and aircraft at points of discharge of both cargoes and personnel in the region. Aerial observation was permitted at any time over any or all of Antarctica.

Disputes between contracting parties concerned the interpretation or application of the Antarctic Treaty were to be settled by peaceful means of their choice. If such disputes could not be resolved by normal methods, provision was made for submission to the international Court of Justice for settlement.

On the other hand, the agreement contained a specific statement to the effect that it could not be interpreted as a renunciation, by any contracting party, of previously asserted rights or claims to territorial sovereignty in Antarctica or as prejudicing the positions of any such party as regarded its recognition or nonrecognition of any other state's rights of, or claims or bases of claims to, territorial sovereignty in Antarctica. No activities taking place while the Antarctic Treaty was in force were to constitute a basis for asserting, supporting, or denying a claim to sovereignty in the regions in question or to create there any rights of sovereignty. No new claim, or enlargement of any existing claim, to territorial sovereignty in Antarctica was to be asserted while the treaty was in effect.

The entire system established by the treaty was to be subject to review after thirty years by a conference of all the parties to the agreement.

It should be noted that adherence by states not originally parties to the Antarctic Treaty depended either on membership in the United Nations or on invitation by the original signatories. Such invitation to adhere required unanimous consent of all signatory states.

LEASED TERRITORIES

Leases of territory, regardless of the length of time specified in the relevant agreements, do not confer title, do not create changes in sovereignty. Thus Chinese leases of Port Arthur and Dalny to Russia, of Kiao-chao to Germany, of Wei-hai-wei, Tientsin, and of the so-called New Territories on the mainland opposite the island of Hong Kong to Great Britain, and of Kwang-chao-wan to France, did not transfer legal title to areas involved from the lessor to the lessee.[24] The same doctrine applies to the lease of the Canal Zone granted by Panama to the United States.

On the other hand, the legal position of the lessor has never been very strong in any of the instances cited. Transfers of control over a leased territory have been made repeatedly without consulting or seeking the

[24] See *In re Ning Yi-Ching and Others*, Great Britain, Vacation Court, August 23, 1939, 56 Times L.R., No. 1, p. 3, reprinted in 34 *A.J.I.L.* (1940), pp. 347–349. On leased territories in general, refer to Whiteman, Vol. II, pp. 1216–1224; see also Chapter 17.

consent of the nominal territorial sovereign. Thus the Russian leases of Port Arthur and Dalny were assigned to Japan after the Russo-Japanese War of 1904–5 and the German rights in Kiao-chao were turned over to Japan by the treaty of Versailles without consultation with the Chinese government (in 1922 Japan agreed to the return of Kiao-chao to China).

Authorities and statesmen have been in agreement that the conclusion of a lease treaty only effects a transfer of jurisdictional rights but does not at all effect an alienation of territory. In other words, sovereign *rights* are exercised by the leasing state, but *title* to the territory remains indisputably with the state granting the lease. This is true even when the lease entails use of the territory as a naval or military base by the leasing state, such as Guantanamo Bay in Cuba, leased by but not ceded to the United States.[25]

The leases of air and naval bases in Bermuda and Newfoundland obtained by the United States from Great Britain under the executive agreements and other arrangements of 1940–41 have figured in a number of judicial decisions which in turn have given rise to considerable discussion in legal circles.

Thus in *Vermilya-Brown Co.* v. *Cornell et al.*,[26] the Supreme Court of the United States affirmed a judgment of the Circuit Court of Appeals by holding that for purposes of the Fair Labor Standards Act of 1938, the air base leased in Bermuda was a "possession" of the United States.

Such a decision did not appear to be in accordance with the international legal status of a leased territory, but the majority on the Supreme Court succeeded in distinguishing the Vermilya-Brown case from the legal situation presented in 1949 in *United States* v. *Spelar*,[27] when it held that the U.S. air base in Newfoundland, acquired under identical conditions as prevailed in the case of the Bermuda base, was a "foreign country" within the provisions of the Federal Tort Claims Act. The basis of the distinction on which the 1949 decision was based had to do with the language of the Claims Act as compared with that of the Labor Standards Act of 1938. It is, however, somewhat difficult to see how leases derived from similar instruments can constitute "possessions" and "foreign countries" at the same time.

The only other leased territories now in existence are the American-

---

[25] See Joseph Lazar, "International Legal Status of Guantanamo Bay," 62 *A.J.I.L.* (1968), pp. 730–740, and his " 'Cession in Lease' of the Guantanamo Bay Naval Station and Cuba's 'Ultimate Sovereignty'," *ibid.*, 63 (1969), pp. 116–118, as well as the critique by Gary L. Maris, "Guantanamo: No Rights of Occupancy," *ibid.*, pp. 114–116. It is interesting to note that nominal annual rent ($3,386.25) was paid for the base by the United States until 1960 when the Cuban government refused to accept further payments on the grounds that the base should not be allowed to remain in American hands: see *The New York Times*, February 4, 1964, p. 14.

[26] United States, Supreme Court, 1948, 69 Sup. Ct. 140.

[27] United States, Supreme Court, 1949, 338 U.S. 217.

controlled Panama Canal Zone, the British-controlled New Territories facing Hong Kong, and the minor American leases of Guantánamo and Bahia Honda from Cuba and of Great Corn and Little Corn Islands from Nicaragua.

SERVITUDES

The otherwise complete sovereignty of a state over the territory under its jurisdiction may be limited or impaired by the existence of a servitude. The latter represents a binding obligation on the part of a given state to permit specified uses to be made of all or parts of its territory by or in favor of another state or states.[28] A servitude may also involve an obligation not to undertake certain acts.

A servitude is tied directly to the territory in question; it remains as an obligation regardless of any change in the form of the government of the state concerned; and it remains intact even when a case of state succession takes place. In the latter instance, the successor state assuming sovereign rights over the territory affected by a servitude is bound by that servitude until a different arrangement has been worked out, by treaty or exchange of diplomatic notes, with the state or states benefitting from the servitude as established at the time succession took place.

In view of the fact that territorial sovereignty represents one of the basic characteristics of an independent state, a diminution of that sovereignty by the institution of servitudes may reach at length a point at which serious doubts as to the continued existence of territorial sovereignty may arise. There is no definite line of demarcation which could be applied generally.

Classification of Servitudes. Any attempt to classify servitudes by types involves two points of view:

Most common is a distinction between negative (passive) and affirmative (active) servitudes, depending on whether the state in question agrees to suspend the exercise of one or of several of its sovereign rights over territory, or whether a foreign sovereign is suffered (permitted) to enter the territory of the state and exercise what in essence must be termed sovereign rights therein. An example of a negative servitude would be the assumption of an obligation not to fortify specified areas of a state's terri-

---

[28] On both general and specific aspects of servitudes, consult the most comprehensive treatment available in English, Ferenc A. Váli, *Servitudes of International Law: A Study of Rights in Foreign Territory,* 2nd ed. (New York: Praeger, 1958). The very existence of servitudes represents a subject of controversy among legal writers, although a majority of them, buttressed by numerous decisions by national and international courts, upholds the validity of the concept. See Whiteman, Vol. II, pp. 1173–1216, particularly at pp. 1183–1184, for the text of an internal Department of State memorandum, "State Servitudes Under International Law" (August 11, 1956), supporting the existence of servitudes in the form explained above. See also p. 438 concerning third-party treaty rights.

tory, or to limit the strength of one's armed forces to a specified total number of effectives. Among affirmative servitudes could be cited fishing rights granted by one state in its coastal waters to the citizens of another state, or transit rights to citizens of another state, and so on.

A second distinction among servitudes can be based on the purpose of the obligation in question; in other words, a common separation entails military servitudes on the one hand and economic servitudes on the other. An example of the former would be an obligation to permit armed forces of another state to traverse one's own territory, or to permit the permanent stationing on such territory of armed forces of another state, or to demilitarize certain areas on a permanent basis. On the economic side, numerous examples in the spheres of transportation and communications come to mind.

In both classifications, modern practice favors the establishment of military over economic servitudes: the obligation of France, between 1713 and 1783, not to refortify the town of Dunkirk; the prohibition laid down in the Treaty of Paris (1814) against militarization of the port of Antwerp; the mutual obligation assumed by Russia and Japan in the Treaty of Portsmouth (1905) not to construct fortifications on their portions of the island of Sakhalin.

The foundation of the great majority of all kinds of servitudes is found in a bilateral or multilateral treaty, with only a few based on custom or tradition.

Methods of Terminating Servitudes. Servitudes can be terminated in a number of ways. First, and very common, is a treaty by which the beneficiary or beneficiaries of a servitude agree with the burdened state to end the special situation in question. As was pointed out above, this method would also normally be used to end a servitude assumed with territory in a case of state succession (universal or partial, as the case might be).

A second method for the termination of a servitude would be a unilateral declaration to that effect issued by the state or states benefitting from the obligation involved, without any participation in such a step by the burdened state itself. A third method would occur if the benefitting state acquired the obligated state, or vice versa; in either case, an end of the servitude would take place by domestic enactment. Finally, a servitude would end with the physical disappearance of either party to the agreement establishing the servitude.

Among the areas of territorial jurisdiction circumscribed, on occasion, by the existence of servitudes have been, or are, navigation on certain rivers,[29] navigation on oceans, and the flow and diversion of waters.[30]

---

[29] See Higgins–Colombos, pp. 166–189, on the international control of rivers. Consult also H. Fortuin, "The Regime of Waterways of International Concern and the Statute of Barcelona," 7 *Tijdschrift* (1960), pp. 125–143; Josef L. Kunz, "The Danube

It is generally asserted that customary international law, now reinforced by Article 14 of the 1958 Convention on the Territorial Sea and the Contiguous Zone, imposes a servitude on all states fronting on an ocean: the right of ships of all nations to innocent passage through territorial waters as well as their right to make use of such waters as a refuge in the case of storms or in the event of distress.

This very important servitude is subject to several modifications or limitations. The littoral state is entitled to issue regulations for the protection of navigation and for the enforcement of its domestic legislation in such areas as quarantine and customs, and under certain conditions, to bar innocent passage from specific portions of its waters for security reasons. The servitude may be constricted greatly in time of war, that is, when the littoral state assumes either neutral or belligerent status; this restriction is particularly notable as it relates to the passage and activities of belligerent warships in the territorial waters of any state.

Straits. Straits connecting territorial bays or seas with an ocean are subject to the same rules as the territorial bay or sea itself. The only major problems arising in this connection involve straits connecting two oceans or seas. Among the few examples available is the former privilege of Denmark to levy tolls on all traffic passing between the Baltic and the North seas, abolished in 1857 when Denmark agreed to waive this customary right in exchange for payment on the part of all interested maritime states of a sum large enough to capitalize Denmark's costs incurred in providing navigational safeguards in the Danish Sound.[31] Another example was supplied by the Argentine-Chilean agreement of 1881 for the perpetual neutralization of and guarantee of free navigation in the Straits of Magellan.

Other straits connecting seas have been regulated by multilateral international instruments, notably the Dardanelles and the Bosporus, connecting the Black Sea with the Mediterranean and bordered exclusively by Turkey. Beginning in 1809, regulation of travel through these straits was attempted, and after an almost unbelievably complicated series of conferences, each resulting in some form of agreement, a presumably final settlement was achieved in the Montreux Convention of 1936, by which all previously existing international supervision was terminated and recog-

---

Regime and the Belgrade Conference," 43 *A.J.I.L.* (1949), pp. 104-113; and John C. Campbell, "Diplomacy on the Danube," 27 *Foreign Affairs* (1949), pp. 315-327.

[30] Consult Abraham M. Hirsch, "Utilization of International Rivers in the Middle East—A Study of Conventional International Law," 50 *A.J.I.L.* (1956), pp. 81-100; see also Bishop, pp. 391-392, for key excerpts from a Department of State Memorandum dated April 21, 1958, by William L. Griffin, on "Legal Aspects of the Use of Systems of International Waters"; see also the very important summary of key principles in Brierly, pp. 231-232.

[31] See C. E. Hill, *The Danish Sound Dues and the Command of the Baltic* (Durham, N.C.: Duke University Press, 1926); on straits in general, see Whiteman, Vol. IV, pp. 417-480.

nition of exclusive Turkish sovereignty over the straits was granted, including a Turkish right to militarize the straits.

A fairly recent major international incident involving a strait took place in the Straits of Corfu in 1946. Following the end of World War II, the victorious powers (with the help of many vessels and crews recruited from among their defeated opponents) engaged in a large-scale attempt to remove anchored and floating mines around the coasts of Europe. British vessels cleared the Straits of Corfu, between the Greek island of Corfu and the mainland shores of Greece and Albania. Shortly afterward, two British destroyers struck mines while traversing the Straits. Great Britain then sent minesweepers into the Straits, in accordance with a decision of the International Mine Sweeping Commission, and this action was protested by Albania on the grounds of invasion of Albanian territorial sovereignty.

When the dispute, which also involved a British claim for compensation arising out of the destroyer incident, was brought before the Security Council of the United Nations, that body decided on March 25, 1947, that Albania must have been cognizant of the presence of mines, a decision which implied a degree of Albanian responsibility for the placement of the mines in the Straits. The majority vote of the Security Council was rendered ineffective, however, by a Soviet Union veto. The dispute was then brought before the International Court of Justice by Great Britain:

THE CORFU CHANNEL CASE
(GREAT BRITAIN–ALBANIA)

I. C. Reports, 1949, pp. 4, 244; Judgment [Merits], April 9, 1949; Assessment of Amount of Compensation, December 15 1949.[32]

FACTS

In October, 1944, the North Corfu Channel was swept by the British Navy and no mines were found; as a result of this operation, Great Britain announced in November, 1944, the existence of a safe route through the channel. In January and February, 1945, the channel was checked again, with negative resutls. In May, 1946, two British cruisers went through the channel and no mines were discovered, nor were special precautions taken.

On October 22, 1946, a squadron of British warships (the cruisers *Mauritius* and *Leander* as well as the destroyers *Saumarez* and *Volage*) left the port of Corfu and proceeded north through the channel. Outside the Bay of Saranda, *Saumarez* struck a mine and was heavily damaged; the second destroyer was ordered to render assistance and to take the damaged vessel in tow. While towing the *Saumarez*, *Volage* struck a mine and also was badly damaged. Both destroyers succeeded, however, in reaching the port of Corfu.

[32] For texts of relevant documents, consult 42 *A.J.I.L.* (1948), pp. 690–708 [Ruling on Preliminary Objection]; *ibid.*, 43 (1949), pp. 558–589 [Merits]; *ibid.*, 44 (1950), pp. 579–582 [Assessment of Compensation].

Three weeks later (November 13), British minesweepers swept the channel and cut the cables of twenty-two moored mines. Two of these were taken to Malta for examination and were found to be of the German GY type.

The damage to both destroyers occurred in Albanian territorial waters. Expert analysis of the damage sustained by the two vessels excluded all possibility of its having been caused by floating mines or by ground mines —both of which had been suggested by Albanian authorities as likely causes.

The Albanian government had also suggested that the minefield discovered on November 13 might have been laid after October 22, so that the damage sustained by the destroyers would not have been caused by the contents of the field. But no evidence supporting this suggestion was produced; instead, the experts at Malta concluded that the damage suffered had been caused by mines identical to those found in the minefield.

Great Britain demanded compensation for damage to its ships and for the loss of life on the latter. Albania rejected the claim and Great Britain instituted proceedings in the International Court of Justice on May 22, 1947, against the People's Republic of Albania. On December 9, 1947, the Court rejected the objection filed by Albania.

Great Britain claimed that the minefield had been laid by or with the connivance and knowledge of the Albanian government or, alternatively —that the Albanian government had known that the minefield was in its territorial waters and, in violation of the Eighth Hague Convention of 1907, had failed to warn other countries of the existence of the minefield. Furthermore, according to the British claim, Albanian authorities had observed the approach of the British naval units and had failed to warn them of the existence of the mines, and that the existence without notification of the minefield was a violation of the right of innocent passage by foreign vessels through an international waterway such as the Corfu Channel. In reparation, Great Britain asked for £825,000 to cover the repair of damages to the two destroyers and £50,000 for pensions and other expenses resulting from the loss of life and injuries suffered by the crews of the two vessels.

Albania contended that no proof had been submitted that the mines responsible for the damage to the British ships had been laid by Albania; that no proof had been submitted that the mines had been laid by a third party on behalf of Albania; that no proof had been submitted that the mines were laid with the help, acquiescence, or knowledge of Albania; that a coastal state was entitled, under exceptional circumstances, to regulate the passage of foreign warships through its territorial waters and that this rule applied to the Corfu Channel; that the required exceptional circumstances existed at the time in question, so that foreign warships should have obtained prior authorization to pass through Albanian territorial waters; that passage of the vessels on October 22, 1946, without previous authorization constituted a breach of international law; that the British passage in question was not an innocent passage; that the sweeping operations of November 12–13, 1946, had not been permissible in Albanian waters and constituted a breach of international law. For these reasons, Albania maintained, no compensation was owed to Great Britain, but instead the latter should give to the

Albanian government satisfaction for the breaches of law committed.

ISSUES

(1) Was Albania responsible under international law for the explosions which occurred on October 22, 1946, in Albanian waters and for the damage and loss of human life which resulted from them?

(2) Was there any duty on the part of Albania to pay compensation if such responsibility was established?

DECISION

The Court ruled that Albania was responsible under international law for the explosions and for the damage and loss of life resulting from them, and that Albania owed a duty to Great Britain to pay compensation.

REASONING

Based on all the evidence submitted, the Court found that the two ships had been mined in Albanian territorial waters in a previously swept and check-swept channel. As far as the laying of the mines was concerned, the Court noted the Albanian government's formal statement that it had not laid the mines and was in no position to have done so, as Albania possessed no navy. However, the British reply had indicated that on or about October 18, 1946, two Jugoslav warships carrying contact mines of the German GY type, had sailed south from Sibenik and had entered the Corfu Channel. The British contention was that Jugoslavia had laid the minefield with the knowledge and connivance of the Albanian government, that is, collusion between the two states. The Court, after examining testimony about the alleged Jugoslav minelaying operations, felt that proof of the British charge had not been shown.

The Court ruled, therefore, that the authors of the minelaying remained unknown. It then proceeded to examine whether Albania had had any knowledge of the existence of the minefield. It decided that the Albanian government constantly kept a close watch over the waters of the North Corfu Channel, a watch occasionally reinforced by the firing of shots at passing vessels. All evidence indicated that the minelaying had to have taken place during the time Albanian authorities kept a close watch over the channel and were insisting that their permission had to be obtained before a foreign vessel should proceed through the channel. The Court held, further, that the actions of the Albanian government during and after the sweeping operations in November, 1946, indicated its knowledge of the existence of the mines. Expert testimony insisted that if any close watch had been kept over the channel—and Albania insisted equally strongly that this had been the case— the coastal guards had to have noticed the minelaying operations.

The Court held that it had been a duty of the Albanian government to notify the world in general of the existence of the minefield and to warn the approaching British naval units of their imminent danger. This duty was not incumbent on Albania because of the provisions of the Eighth Hague Convention of 1907, which was applicable in war, but because of elementary considerations of humanity, because of the principle of the freedom of maritime communication, and because of the obligation, resting on every state not to allow knowingly its territory to be used for acts contrary to the rights of other states.

Because nothing had been done by the Albanian authorities to prevent the disaster, this omission gave rise to the international responsibility of Albania.

In the final submissions, Great Britain asked for damages amounting to £875,000, while Albania asserted that the Court had no jurisdiction to assess the amount of compensation.

On December 15, 1949, the Court set the damages to the destroyer *Saumarez* at £700,087 (its replacement cost); the damage to the destroyer *Volage* at £93,812 (the sum asked by the British government); and costs for pensions and other grants resulting from loss of life and injuries suffered on the part of the two crews at £50,048. The total amount of compensation due Great Britain from the People's Reublic of Albania was therefore set at £843,947.

NOTE: Albania ignored the award of compensation and no workable suggestion has come forth as to how the judgment could be satisfied.[33]

A more recent controversy about a strait and a gulf centered on the Straits of Tiran and the Gulf of Aqaba. The latter, from ten to thirty miles wide, is bordered by four states and is connected to the high seas by the straits in question. On May 22, 1967, the United Arab Republic announced a blockade of the gulf, an action denounced by Israel as an open violation of international law as well as an act of aggression. President Johnson of the United States, in a statement on May 24, reflected the views of the Department of State in holding the gulf and the straits to be international waters.[34] Still more recently, a mild controversy between the United States and the Soviet Union revolved around the right of the former to have two icebreakers pass through certain portions of the Northeast Passage.[35]

Canals: When a canal is located within the territory of a state and does not connect two seas or oceans, it is considered to be under the exclusive jurisdiction of the sovereign in question and no servitude of innocent passage exists. Normally, too, even when such a canal does serve as a connecting link between seas, it is not burdened with a servitude. The state in whose territory the canal is found may offer the use of the canal to the vessels of other states, provided fixed tolls and possibly other service charges are met by the users; but such offers represent purely voluntary action on the part of the sovereign involved (Corinth Canal in Greece, Kiel Canal in Germany until 1919).

[33] For an abortive attempt on the part of Great Britain to collect from Albania, see the *Case of the Monetary Gold Removed from Rome in 1943 (Italy v. France, United Kingdom, and the United States of America)—Preliminary Question,* International Court of Justice, 1954, *I.C.J. Reports, 1954,* p. 19, digested and excerpted in 48 *A.J.I.L.* (1954), pp. 649–655; the text of the arbitral award figuring in the case may be found in 49 *A.J.I.L.* (1955), pp. 403–405; see also Covey T. Oliver, "The Monetary Gold Decision in Perspective," *ibid.,* pp. 216–221.

[34] *The New York Times,* May 24, 25, 1967; see also Leo Gross, "The Geneva Conference on the Law of the Sea and the Right of Innocent Passage through the Gulf of Aqaba," 53 *A.J.I.L.* (1959), pp. 564–594, as well as Chapter 17.

[35] See Donat Pharand, "Soviet Union Warns United States against Use of Northeast Passage," 62 *A.J.I.L.* (1968), pp. 927–935.

Kiel Canal. The Treaty of Versailles provided that the Kiel Canal, linking the North Sea with the Baltic, should be open to the vessels (public and private) of all states at peace with Germany, and that complete equality with German nationals, vessels, and cargoes should be granted to the nationals, vessels, and cargoes of such other states.

A test of the nature of this servitude arose in connection with the attempt of the British vessel *S. S. Wimbledon* to traverse the waterway in 1921:

THE S. S. WIMBLEDON

Permanent Court of International Justice, 1923,
P.C.I.J., Ser. A, No. 1

FACTS

The *S. S. Wimbledon*, a British merchant vessel, had been chartered by a French armament firm to carry war materials from France to the port of Danzig. The cargo was destined for the Polish government, then at war with the Russian state. On March 21, 1921, the vessel arrived at the western entrance to the Kiel Canal and was refused access by the German authorities on the grounds that, under the terms of its neutrality regulations, Germany could not permit the ship with its cargo to proceed through the canal. To grant such permission would expose Germany to a charge of performing an unneutral service, according to the German statements issued at the time.

The British, French, Italian, and Japanese governments filed suit against the German government before the Permanent Court of International Justice, claiming that the German action violated obligations arising from Article 380 of the Treaty of Versailles, the section which had imposed the canal servitude on Germany.

ISSUE

Did a servitude such as applied to the Kiel Canal override domestic neutrality legislation of the state obligated by the existence of the servitude?

DECISION

Decision against Germany. Article 380 of the Treaty of Versailles prevented Germany from applying to the canal the Neutrality Order promulgated by the German government on July 25, 1920. The German government was ordered to compensate the charterers of the vessel for the losses sustained as a result of the German action in barring the vessel from traversing the Kiel Canal.

REASONING

Article 380 of the Treaty of Versailles read, "The Kiel Canal and its approaches shall be maintained free and open to the vessels of commerce and of war of all nations at peace with Germany on terms of entire equality." The terms of the Article were clear and categorical. The canal had ceased to be an internal and national navigable waterway, the use of which might have been left to the discretion of the riparian state. Instead, the canal had become an international waterway intended to provide under treaty guarantee easier access to the Baltic for the benefit of all nations of the world. The only condition applicable to any closing of the canal related to the requirement that all vessels permitted to use it had to belong to nations at peace with Germany. The *S. S. Wimbledon* was owned by English interests and was registered in Great Britain, a country at peace with Germany. The vessel had been chartered by a firm domiciled in France, a country at peace with Germany.

Hence the vessel could not be barred from access to the Kiel Canal.

The only limitation permitted under the servitude created by Article 380 related to the right of Germany to defend itself and to bar the use of the canal by enemy vessels.

Germany was perfectly free to declare and regulate her neutrality in the Russo-Polish war, but subject to the condition laid down in Article 380 of the Treaty of Versailles.

It is interesting to note that the Permanent Court of International Justice did *not* define the provisions of Article 380 as a servitude; only the (German) National Judge Schücking, in a separate opinion, argued that a servitude had been created.

The weight of legal opinion appears to have favored the view that Article 380 of the Versailles instrument did create a servitude for Germany and that, barring the advent of the Hitler era, Germany would quite likely have continued carrying out the obligation imposed by Article 380 even after the other provisions of the Treaty of Versailles had been set aside in one manner or another.

Panama Canal. One of the two major interoceanic canals, the Panama Canal, has become the subject of a self-imposed servitude on the part of the United States, an obligation which assures to the members of the "world community" a right of innocent passage through the waterway, subject to the payment of tolls and to certain formal conditions.

The current *international* status of the Panama Canal is based on the Hay-Pauncefoote Treaty (United States—Great Britain) of November 18, 1901, which superseded the Clayton-Bulwer agreement of 1850. The 1901 instrument replaced the formerly anticipated joint control of a canal through the Isthmus of Panama with a plan for the construction, regulation, and management of such a canal under the sole authority of the United States.

The canal was to be open to the use of vessels of commerce and of war of all states on a basis of equality, and the United States was to protect the canal against acts of hostility by belligerents in time of war and its use by belligerents for strategic purposes.

It has been assumed by the United States that no discrimination in tolls or charges is permissible against the vessels of any nation : this assumption may also be taken to represent a self-assumed servitude.

The major legal problem posed by the Panama Canal has centered on its use in time of war. The United States government adopted the logical position that the use of the canal by enemies of the United States did not represent a part of the self-imposed servitude and proceeded in 1912 to construct fortifications for the defense of the canal against possible use by countries with which the United States might be at war. During both World Wars, belligerent warships passed freely through the waterway as long as the United States claimed a neutral status. As soon as the United States entered officially into each of the conflicts, the canal was closed to enemy ships of every kind.

Suez Canal. The Suez Canal, connecting the Mediterranean and the Red Sea, figured prominently in the history of servitudes until it was seized by the Egyptian state in 1956. Space, however, does not permit an account of the checkered fortunes of this vital waterway.[36]

Right-of-Way Servitudes. On rare occasions special servitudes relating to rights of way for the transit of persons and goods have been granted by treaty to some foreign state on the territory of the state obligated by the servitude. The peace treaties ending World War I created a whole series of right-of-way servitudes, relating particularly to transit across Germany and Austria, but also, for the benefit of the latter, across territories formerly a part of the Austro-Hungarian empire and lying between Austria and the Adriatic. The free zones in the German ports of Stettin and Hamburg granted to Czechoslovakia should also be regarded as right-of-way servitudes.

More recently, such a servitude was the core of a case before the International Court of Justice: the *Case concerning Right of Passage over Indian Territory (Portugal v. India).*[37] The dispute centered on a claim by

[36] See the monographic treatments by Thomas J. F. Huang, "Some International and Legal Aspects of the Suez Canal Question," 51 *A.J.I.L.* (1957), pp. 277–307, and by Joseph A. Obieta, S.J., *The International Status of the Suez Canal* (The Hague: Martinus Nijhoff, 1960). Consult also the following brief accounts, each of which, however, is supplied with copious documentation valuable for further study: Robert Delson, "Nationalization of the Suez Canal Company: Issues of Public and Private International Law," 57 *Columbia Law Review* (1957), pp. 755–786; Halford L. Hoskins, "The Suez Canal as an International Waterway," 37 *A.J.I.L.* (1943), pp. 373–385; George A. Finch, "Navigation and Use of the Suez Canal," *Proceedings* (1957), pp. 42–49 (commentary on pp. 49–56); "Suez Canal: Heads of Agreement, Signed at Rome, April 29, 1959," 54 *A.J.I.L.* (1960), Supp., pp. 493–513. For the post-1956 U.A.R.-Israel dispute about Israeli use of the Canal, see "The Suez Canal and the Law of Nations," 2 *The Israel Digest* (No. 18, September 4, 1959), p. 8; consult also *The New York Times*, April 28, 1957, "Egypt's Canal," for a comparison of the six Security Council principles with the Egyptian Declaration of April 24, 1957. Consult also Simcha Dinitz, "The Legal Aspects of the Egyptian Blockade of the Suez Canal," 45 *Georgetown Law Journal* (Winter, 1956–57), pp. 169–199. The Canal has been closed to all shipping since the end of the "Six-Day War" of 1967.

[37] International Court of Justice, Judgment on Preliminary Objections, November 26, 1957, *I.C.J. Reports, 1957*, p. 125, digested in 52 *A.J.I.L.* (1958), pp. 326–337; Judgment, April 12, 1960, *I.C.J. Reports, 1960*, p. 6, digested at length in 54 *A.J.I.L.* (1960), pp. 673–691. See also the excellent study of this specialized subject by Frank E. Krenz, *International Enclaves and Rights of Passage* (Paris: Minard, 1961). After the Indian seizure of Portuguese enclaves, the remaining examples of this territorial paradox are Büsingen and Veronahof, Campione, and Llivia.

Portugal to possess a right of passage for its nationals across Indian territory between the enclaves of Dadra and Nagar-Aveli and between those enclaves and the coastal district of Damão (one of three Portuguese districts in India, the other two being Goa and Din, in addition to the two inland enclaves). The Court found that Portugal indeed possessed such a right of passage "to the extent necessary for the exercise of Portuguese sovereignty over the enclaves and subject to the regulation and control of India, in respect of private persons, civil officials and goods in general." On the other hand, according to the Court, Portugal did not, in 1954, "have a right of passage in respect of armed forces, armed police, and arms and ammunition." The Court also found that India had "not acted contrary to its obligations resulting from Portugal's right of passage in respect of private persons, civil officials and goods in general."

Most famous of all right-of-way servitudes is that based on a 1903 agreement between the United States and Panama, by which the former country was granted a perpetual monopoly to construct a canal across Panamanian territory. The agreement did take the form of a lease, to be sure, but this technicality had no effect on the legal character of the obligation created for Panama: it was a servitude.

The terminology of the 1903 instrument left much to be desired as far as the clarification of the question of sovereignty over the Canal Zone was concerned. The United States was empowered to act as "if it were sovereign" in the Zone "in perpetuity" and "to the entire exclusion of the exercise by the Republic of Panama of any such sovereign rights, power or authority." In return for the control in question, the United States promised an immediate payment of $10 million, plus annual rental payments of $250,000 beginning nine years after ratification of the agreement (1904). In the course of time, the payments of "rent" have been increased on several occasions and since 1955 the compensation to Panama has amounted to $1.9 million per year.

Nonlegal factors gradually led to anti-American demonstrations in Panama, climaxed by a riot marked by bloodshed on January 7, 1964. Panama severed diplomatic relations with the United States, demanded "complete revision" of the 1903 treaty, and brought charges of aggression before the United Nations Security Council and the Council of the Organization of American States, both of which met at once in emergency sessions. The Security Council called for an immediate ceasefire, while the Organization of American States appointed a special Peace Committee to attempt reconciliation.

In view of the provisions of the 1903 agreement, it appears as if that instrument could be set aside only if one of the parties failed to fulfill its obligations. Panama could not break its "contract," thus killing the agreement and forcing the United States into renegotiation, except by somehow getting the United States physically out of the Zone. This would be a manifest impossibility because of the relative strength of the two parties.

The United States, on the other hand, has kept its part of the formal agreement concerning the Zone, and the only real violation of its obligations would be a failure to pay the annual "rent" for the Zone.

Panamanian desires for a greater degree of control, or even only influence, in the running of the Canal and of the Zone cannot be gratified, however, without revision of the 1903 treaty.

Between the middle of 1965 and late 1967, the United States had succeeded in negotiating a draft treaty with Panama. This instrument would have abrogated the 1903 treaty, would have recognized in a more effective manner Panamanian sovereignty over the area of the Canal, and would have provided for joint operation and management of the Canal. The 1968 Panamanian presidential election, however, appears, at the time of writing, to have doomed the agreements worked out: the candidate supported by the Marco Robles administration, which had undertaken the negotiations with the United States, was defeated.[38]

SUGGESTED READINGS

TITLE TO TERRITORY: GENERAL

Gould, pp. 347–358; Whiteman, Vol. II, pp. 1028–1232; Yehuda Z. Blum, *Historic Titles in International Law* (The Hague: Martinus Nijhoff, 1965).

DENIAL OF TITLE BY MERE CONQUEST

Lauterpacht's *Oppenheim*, Vol. I, pp. 451–460, 544–581; Pitman B. Potter, "The Principal Legal and Political Problems Involved in the Kashmir Case," 44 *A.J.I.L.* (1950), pp. 361–363; Herbert W. Briggs, "Non-Recognition of Title by Conquest and Limitations on the Doctrine," *Proceedings* (1940), pp. 72–82.

POLAR REGIONS

Corbett, pp. 112–119; Hackworth, Vol. I, pp. 399–476; Hyde, Vol. I, pp. 347–355; August Miller, Jr., "Antarctica—White Continent of Promise," 88 *U.S. Naval Institute Proceedings* (August, 1962), pp. 45–57; Oscar Svarlien, "The Legal Status of the Arctic," *Proceedings* (1958), pp. 136–143; and James Simsarian, "Inspection Experience under the Antarctic Treaty and the International Atomic Energy Agency," 60 *A.J.I.L.* (1966), pp. 502–510.

Case

Martin v. *Commissioner of Internal Revenue*, United States, Tax Court of the U.S., 1968, 50 T.C. No. 9, reported in 63 *A.J.I.L.* (1969), pp. 141–142.

[38] Consult *The New York Times, passim.*, particularly for September-October, 1965; June 27, 1967, pp. 1, 2; and again for July, 1967, and July, 1968.

SERVITUDES

Higgins-Colombos, pp. 166–170; Lauterpacht's *Oppenheim*, Vol. I, pp. 480–485; R. R. Baxter, *The Law of International Waterways* (Cambridge, Mass.: Harvard University Press, 1964); Steven Gorove, "Internationalization of the Danube: A Lesson in History," 8 *Journal of Public Law* (1959), pp. 125–154; see also the *Indus Waters Treaty* (India-Pakistan, 1960), in 55 *A.J.I.L.* (1961), Supp., pp. 797–822.

Case

Ares v. *S/S Colon,* United States, District Court, Canal Zone, Cristobal Div., 1967, 269 F.Supp. 763, reported in *A.J.I.L.* (1968), pp. 509–511.

JAPANESE ISLANDS UNDER FOREIGN CONTROL

The New York Times, January 23, 1966, p. 9; February 13, 1966, p. 9; December 10, 1967, p. 16; 91 *Time* (April 5, 1968), pp. 39–40; and the *Note* in 55 *A.J.I.L.* (1961), pp. 153–160.

Case

Burna v. *United States,* United States, Court of Appeals, 4th Circuit, 1957, 240 F.2d 720.

16

Land Boundaries

THE extent of the territory subject to the jurisdiction of any state is determined by definite boundary lines, as in the case of domestic real property of any citizen.

Most of the existing boundaries on land have been fixed by international conventions, in particular by peace treaties. Such general settlements as the Treaty of Westphalia (1648), the various agreements reached at the Congress of Vienna (1815), the peace treaties of 1919 and 1947, have redrawn the frontiers of European states on a wholesale basis, whereas more limited agreements, both in Europe and elsewhere, have served to determine new or old but disputed boundary lines.

Other instances of determination, say, by prescription, abound in Europe, Africa, Asia, and the Americas, with no specific document available to certify as to the origin of a particular line of demarcation between two states.

Although much loose talk has been evinced in discussions of natural frontiers when topography alone was cited in violation of other "natural" frontiers based on race, language, culture, or religion, it is true that certain basic rules have been evolved in the practice of states to assist in the determination of land boundaries.

A common device is to fix a border at the water divide or watershed when a chain of hills or mountains forms an approximate boundary between states. Although a convention may prescribe such a line as the boundary in general terms, the exact location of the frontier would then have to be made by surveys through a designated body, such as a boundary commission. When the topography of the area is such that the water divide is not coincidental with the highest elevations in the hills or mountains in question, trouble is likely to ensue.

The Grotian Rule. Rivers frequently have been included as part of a boundary line between states, either because they served as a strategic natural barrier or because a broad waterway appeared to all concerned parties to represent an obvious dividing line between them. The exact determination of the boundary in the river originally followed the Grotian rule that the frontier should be located in the middle of the river. This long-standing principle posed, in the case of navigable streams, a number of unanticipated problems when the main channel of navigation wandered back and forth across the political frontier, so that a vessel proceeding along the course of the stream would be now in one country and now in the other.

The Rule of the Thalweg. In view of the customs problems involved, coupled with the difficulties of collecting tolls and preventing the escape of subjects intent on departing against the will of their sovereign, the old rule was modified early in the nineteenth century to read that in the case of navigable rivers the boundary would follow the middle of the principal channel or the path of the strongest downstream current, technically known as the *Thalweg.*

The major advantage of the change was that the border would henceforth coincide with the main route of river commerce, allowing each of the riparian states an equal share of this route within its own territory. The rule of the *Thalweg* has been accepted generally among nations for redetermination of river boundaries (in the case of navigable streams only) and has also become the principle applicable to possible domestic disputes between political subdivisions of a state.[1]

Should the *Thalweg* shift gradually either by erosion or accretion along the banks of the river, the boundary line shifts with the channel in question.[2] If, however, the shift is not gradual but sudden and extensive ("avulsion"), the boundary line remains unchanged from its previous location. Should one of the riparian states yield either a part of its river domain or even a part of its shore domain to the other riparian state under a form of prescription, the doctrine of the *Thalweg* would, of course, be superseded in time and could no longer be cited in support of riparian or shore claims by the deprived state.[3]

United States–Mexico Chamizal Tract Dispute. The United States had been involved with Mexico in a controversy centering on avulsion and title to the Chamizal Tract, a piece of land adjoining the Rio Grande between El Paso, Texas, and Juarez, Mexico. The dispute dated back to 1864, in which year the Rio Grande changed its course and thereby placed the Chamizal Tract on the United States side of the border. After decades of fruitless argument, a convention was signed on June 24, 1910, for the arbitration of the rival claims of the two governments.

In 1911 the arbitrators awarded the greater part of the Tract to Mexico. This holding was proper from a legal point of view, because the prevailing

---

[1] *New Jersey* v. *Delaware*, United States, Supreme Court, 1934, 291 U.S. 361, which contains a most valuable history of the doctrine of the *Thalweg; Arkansas* v. *Tennessee, ibid.,* 1940, 311 U.S. 1. Older cases show ample evidence of the domestic application of the Grotian rule.

[2] *Kansas* v. *Missouri*, United States, Supreme Court, 1944, 322 U.S. 213; see the opinion in some detail in 39 *A.J.I.L.* (1945), pp. 122–133.

[3] See, for instance, *Arkansas* v. *Tennessee*, cited above, and consult *Nebraska* v. *Iowa*, United States, Supreme Court, 1892, 143 U.S. 359, as well as the extensive materials and reference materials on the problem of the United States—Mexican border compiled in Bishop, pp. 385–388.

rule was then, as now, that if a boundary river deserts its original bed and creates a new channel for itself, the boundary remained in the middle (or, on occasion, in the middle of the former main channel) of the deserted riverbed. The United States, however, rejected the award, charging that the commissioners had exceeded their powers in making the award.[4] The original United States claim to the Tract had been based on the doctrine of prescription: undisturbed and unchallenged adverse possession. The commission, however, decided that the conditions required for the application of prescription had not been met.

The controversy concerning title to the Tract continued, on a latent basis, until it emerged into prominence again in 1962. At the end of the Mexican visit of President Kennedy in June of that year, a communiqué on his conversations with President Adolfo Mateos of Mexico stated that the two chiefs of state "agreed to instruct their executive agencies to recommend complete solution of this problem which, without prejudice to their juridical position, takes into account the entire history of the Tract."[5]

After weeks of negotiation, a Convention for the Solution of the Problem of the Chamizal was signed at Mexico City on August 29, 1963.[6]

The respective transfers of title to the disputed lands took place on October 28, 1967.[7] Mexico acquired 630.3 acres, the United States obtained the former Mexican enclave of Cordoba Island, covering 193.2 acres north of the Rio Grande. The two governments shared equally the cost of constructing a new river bed, along the middle of which the new frontier now runs.

After the settlement of the Chamizal dispute, the determination of sovereignty over only nine small tracts of land along the Rio Grande remained for negotiation between the two countries. Altogether, 220 cases of border shifts through avulsion have been recorded along the course of the river since it became an international frontier by the treaty of Guadeloupe Hidalgo (1848).

Principle of the Middle of a Bridge Boundary. Paradoxically, the emergence of the *Thalweg* doctrine has not changed universally the principle according to which the middle of a bridge represents the boundary line between two states, regardless of the location of the main channel of navigation in the river itself, or of the path of the strongest downstream current. The only logical reason for clinging to the middle of the bridge as a

---

[4] Text of the award may be found in 5 *A.J.I.L.* (1911), pp. 785 ff.; consult also Jackson H. Ralston, *International Arbitration from Athens to Locarno* (Stanford, Cal.: Stanford University Press, 1929), at pp. 205–206; Gould, pp. 355–356; Bishop, pp. 387–388.

[5] 53 *U.S. News & World Report* (July 16, 1962), p. 6.

[6] Text in 58 *A.J.I.L.* (1964), pp. 336–340. Consult also Gladys Gregory, "The Chamizal Settlement: A View from El Paso," 1 *Southwestern Studies* (No. 2, Summer, 1963), pp. 1–52.

[7] *The New York Times*, October 29, 1967, pp. 1, 47.

dividing line above the waters of a navigable stream would appear to be the common practice of riparian states to divide the cost of bridge construction on an equal basis between them. On the other hand, some practical problems of rather amusing aspect have developed, such as when a vessel, traveling in the water of one riparian state, would collide (with its mast, its stack, or its superstructure in general) with a part of a bridge located in the jurisdiction of the other riparian state. In such instances the cause of the damage would be found in one country while the actual consequences, namely injury to the structure of the bridge, took place in the other one.

Some states have adopted the *Thalweg* principle for the bridge boundary too, notably the United States and Mexico in their convention of 1884 for determining boundaries, should a bridge be built across the Rio Grande. In the latter case, however, it was provided that the boundary line on such a bridge, once fixed, would not be moved even though the main channel of the river should be subject to a gradual shift toward the territory of one or the other of the parties.

Problems in the Use of Water. A problem relating to both river boundaries and servitudes (see Chapter 15) is the question of the use of water of boundary rivers, international rivers, and international drainage basins.[8] A discussion of the many troublesome questions involved in this sphere exceeds the scope and purpose of a general text, but it should be pointed out that more than 100 treaties govern the use of water in international drainage basins all over the world. Problems posed and causing the conclusion of such agreements deal not only with the actual use of water by affected states but also the creation or removal of obstructions in waters flowing from boundary rivers, the variations in water levels in adjacent countries caused by such obstructions, the effect of water flow on hydroelectric installations, pollution of boundary rivers by citizens of a riparian state, and many more aspects of boundary rivers and of drainage basins. The major disputes in this area of international relations have centered on the vexatious problem of water diversion by one state, to the disadvantage of another state.

Lake Borders. Legal theory and state practice agree on the principle that if a lake or a landlocked sea is enclosed entirely by the territory of a given state, such body of water is a part of the territory of that state. On the other hand, if such bodies of water are surrounded by the territories of a number of states, no agreement prevails. The majority of writers and governments concur in the belief that under such circumstances the lake

---

[8] See particularly William L. Griffin, "The Use of Waters of International Drainage Basins under Customary International Law," 53 *A.J.I.L.* (1959), pp. 50–80. Consult also T. Richard Witmer (ed.), *Documents on the Use and Control of the Waters of Interstate and International Streams: Compacts, Treaties, Adjudications* (Washington, D.C.: Government Printing Office, 1956), a basic work for any serious research on the problems in question.

or sea forms part of the surrounding states and that international agreements are needed to delimit the specific portions of the lake or sea belonging to each of the bordering or littoral states.

Examples of the lakes in question include Lake Constance, Lake Geneva, and most of the Great Lakes in North America (Huron, Erie, Ontario, and Superior).[9] The Black Sea is an example of a landlocked sea, but is regarded as part of the open or high seas (except for territorial waters along its shores), under the Peace Treaty of Paris (1856) and subsequent agreements, the latest of which was the Montreux Convention of 1936. An example of a "national" landlocked sea is supplied by the Aral Sea in the U.S.S.R.

Nicaragua–Honduras Boundary Dispute.[10] Lay opinion to the contrary notwithstanding, land boundaries still cause frequent disputes between nations, some of the older ones invested by the passage of time with a high degree of bitterness on both sides.

Thus a fifty-four-year-old quarrel between Nicaragua and Honduras was finally settled in November, 1960, by a decision of the International Court of Justice. The area in dispute, called Mosquitia, was a wedge-shaped, sparsely populated region extending for about 150 miles along the Caribbean coast and 175 miles inland. A long dispute between the two countries concerning the location of boundaries in this region had been offered for arbitration by the late King Alfonso XIII of Spain, who in 1906 had recommended that the main course of the boundary should follow the river Segovia (also called the Coco River). But Nicaragua continued to lay claim to certain valleys and flatlands beyond the Segovia. According to numerous Honduran protests, increasing numbers of Nicaraguans had crossed the river line and had settled in the areas claimed by their country.

In April, 1957, according to a Honduran complaint to the Council of the OAS, a Nicaraguan military force invaded Honduran territory by crossing the Segovia. Nicaragua countered with claims of invasion on the part of Honduras. The Chairman of the Council appointed a Committee of Investigation, which prevailed on both disputants to stop hostilities, and eventually both agreed to submit their boundary quarrel to the International Court of Justice.

The basic question to be settled by the Court was the validity of the arbitral award of 1906, an award asserted by Nicaragua as early as 1912 to be null and void.[11] When the Court handed down its decision on November 17, 1960, it ruled in favor of Honduras and declared that Nicaragua

[9] For details on the latter four, consult Don C. Piper, *The International Law of the Great Lakes* (Durham, N.C.: Duke University Press, 1967).

[10] Recent unofficial compilations show that at least twenty-four border disputes remain unsettled (excluding those along the Rio Grande), and that, in addition, several acrimonious quarrels concerning water use (Bolivia-Chile, since 1962; Iran-Iraq since the 1930's, and so on) have acerbated relations between states.

[11] For details consult Charles G. Fenwick, "The Honduras–Nicaragua Boundary Dispute," 51 *A.J.I.L.* (1957), pp. 761–765.

was obligated to give effect to the 1906 award, declared to be valid and binding on both disputing countries.[12]

Guatemala–Great Britain and Other Boundary Disputes. A number of recent or current boundary disputes have been of more than usual interest to students of international law. Among them is the long disagreement between Great Britain and Guatemala over the area known as Belize, still unresolved today. The disputing states agreed to mediation of their differences by an American mediator, Methuel M. Webster, who, on April 26, 1968, proposed a draft treaty to both countries.[13]

The 120-year-old controversy between Belgium and the Netherlands concerning the sovereignty over thirty acres of land located like a small island inside Dutch territory was finally decided in favor of Belgium by the International Court of Justice on June 20, 1959.[14]

A recently settled boundary dispute between Argentina and Chile went back to an arbitral award made in 1902 by King Edward VII of Great Britain. One particular region, Palena/Río Encuentro, comprising 260 square miles, remained in contention after that award. After increasing bitterness developed between the disputants about this area, Chile invited, in 1964, the United Kingdom to arbitrate the location of the border remaining unsettled after a 1955 decision handed down by an Argentina-Chile Mixed Boundary Commission. Argentina agreed to the Chilean arbitration proposal, and on November 24, 1966, Queen Elizabeth II handed down her award.[15] The final boundary determination left about 71 per cent of the disputed area in Argentina, the rest being allotted to Chile.

The acrimonious dispute between Thailand and Cambodia concerning the national location of the Temple of Preah Vihear was settled in 1962 by the International Court of Justice in favor of Cambodia.[16]

---

[12] *Case concerning the Arbitral Award Made by the King of Spain on 23 December 1906 (Honduras v. Nicaragua)*, International Court of Justice, November 18, 1960, *I.C.J. Reports*, 1960, 192; Whiteman, Vol. III, pp. 633–648; see D. H. N. Johnson, "*Honduras v. Nicaragua*—Decision of the International Court of Justice," 10 *International and Comparative Law Quarterly* (1961), pp. 328–337, and the discussion of the decision in the *Duke Law Journal*, Vol. 1961 (Autumn, 1961), p. 548–553.

[13] Consult D. A. G. Waddell, "Developments in the Belize Questions 1946–1960," 55 *A.J.I.L.* (1961), pp. 459–469, with copious documentation; Josef L. Kunz, "*Guatemala v. Great Britain:* In re Belize," *ibid.*, 40 (1946), pp. 383–390; and R. A. Humphreys, "The Anglo-Guatemalan Dispute," *International Affairs*, 24 (1948), pp. 387–404; see the report of the mediator, including the text of the proposed treaty, in 7 *International Legal Materials* (1968), pp. 626–632.

[14] *Case concerning Sovereignty over Certain Frontier Lands (Belgium–Netherlands)*, *I.C.J. Reports, 1959*, p. 209, digested in some detail by William W. Bishop, Jr., in 53 *A.J.I.L.* (1959), pp. 937–943. See also Leo Gross, "The Jurisprudence of the World Court: Thirty-Eighth Year (1959)," 57 *A.J.I.L.* (1963), pp. 751–780, at pp. 771–778, and Whiteman, Vol. II, pp. 1090–1093, and Vol. III, pp. 626–633.

[15] Text of award, excerpted at length, in 61 *A.J.I.L.* (1967), pp. 1071–1075.

[16] *Case concerning the Temple of Preah Vihear (Cambodia v. Thailand)*, International Court of Justice: *Preliminary Objections*, Judgment of May 26, 1961, *I.C.J.*

No solution has as yet been achieved for the India-China border dispute which has led repeatedly, in recent years, to armed clashes between forces of the two states.[17]

The delimitation of the border dividing the "Neutral Zone" between Kuwait and Saudi Arabia, by an agreement of July 7, 1965, with an exchange of ratifications on July 25, 1966, ended one of the most complicated border problems of modern times, one which was complicated both by the question of the international status of Kuwait and by the nature of the Neutral Zone in question.[18]

SUGGESTED READINGS

GENERAL

L. J. Bouchez, "The Fixing of Boundaries in International Boundary Rivers," 12 *International and Comparative Law Quarterly* (1963), pp. 789–817; Hyde, Vol. I, pp. 439–450, 489–510; D. P. O'Connell, "International Law and Boundary Disputes," *Proceedings* (1960), pp. 77–84; A. O. Cukwarah, *The Settlement of Boundary Disputes in International Law* (Manchester: Manchester University Press; Dobbs Ferry, N.Y.: Oceana Publications, 1968); and Whiteman, Vol. III, pp. 1–871, Vol. IX, pp. 1132–1143.

SPECIFIC DISPUTES

Isaiah Bowman, "The Ecuador–Peru Boundary Dispute," 20 *Foreign Affairs* (1942), pp. 757–761; Ecuador–Peru, "Protocol of Peace, Friendship and Boundaries, of January 29, 1942," in 36 *A.J.I.L.* (1942), Supp., pp. 168–170; Georg Maier, "The Boundary Dispute between Ecuador and Peru," 63 *A.J.I.L.* (1969), pp. 28–46.

"The Chaco Arbitral Award (Bolivia–Paraguay, October 10, 1938)," in 33 *A.J.I.L.* (1939), pp. 180–182, and its abstract, with map, in 49 *Current History* (December, 1938), p. 52. The Panama–Costa Rica boundary settlement of 1938 is reported at length in *The New York Times*, August 16, 1938. See also *The Monastery of Saint-Naoum, Advisory Opinion*, P.C.I.J., 1924, Ser. B, No. 9.

Reports, 1961, p. 17, excerpted in 55 *A.J.I.L.* (1961), pp. 978–984; *Merits*, Judgment of June 15, 1962, *I.C.J. Reports*, 1962, p. 6, excerpted in 56 *A.J.I.L.* (1962), pp. 1033–1053. See also the discussion of certain aspects of this case in Whiteman, Vol. II, pp. 1093–1097, and Vol. III, pp. 648–661, as well as in Chapter 23.

[17] Consult the opposing critical views of Surya P. Sharma, "The India-China Border Dispute: An Indian Perspective," 59 *A.J.I.L.* (1965), pp. 16–47, and of Alfred P. Rubin, "A Matter of Fact," *ibid.*, pp. 586–590.

[18] See Sayed M. Hosni, "The Partition of the Neutral Zone," 60 *A.J.I.L.* (1966), pp. 735–749.

17

The Maritime Border

TERRITORIAL SEAS

THE early writers in international law realized that the boundary of a coastal state should extend beyond the low-tide mark along the shore. Such an extension appeared to be dictated by the logic of defense as well as by the obvious necessity of protecting in some reasonable manner the rights of the coastal state to fishery resources along its own shores.

It should be kept in mind that there exists a difference between a particular width of territorial sea which represents a portion of a nation's domain and over which *sovereignty* is asserted, and waters beyond such territorial sea, that is, adjacent portions of the high seas (contiguous zones, conservation or customs zones) over which *protective or preventive rights* are asserted. (The latter subject is covered in the next chapter.)

METHODS OF DETERMINING EXTENT OF TERRITORIAL SEA

Three-Mile Limit. The states concerned in determining the precise extent of their sovereignty over what is now called the territorial sea or territorial waters appear to have based their ultimate agreement on a compromise between two different views. Denmark, controlling, in the seventeenth and eighteenth centuries, Norway, Iceland, and the Faroe Islands, promoted the concept of a territorial sea of measured width. The Netherlands, on the other hand, maintained that control by the coastal state should extend to the distance commanded by artillery on the shore, that is, by cannon range. The resulting compromise was the principle that the territorial sea comprised an area of water to a line three miles from the low-tide mark.[1]

At the time in question, the approximate limit of the range of coastal cannon was said to have been three miles, and the governing concept adopted seems to have been that a state could claim ownership over such waters as it was able to command with its armament.[2]

---

[1] See H. S. K. Kent, "The Historical Origins of the Three-Mile Limit," 48 *A.J.I.L.* (1954), pp. 537–553; consult also Higgins–Colombos, pp. 70–76.

[2] See Bynkershoek, *De Domino Maris* (1702), in the *Classics of International Law* translation, p. 44; a convenient summary of the historical background may be found

It should be noted here, parenthetically, that the "miles" referred to in connection with territorial seas, contiguous zones, and so on, are nautical (or marine, or geographical) miles: one such mile equals approximately 1.15 common or statute miles.

In the course of time, the three-mile limit was accepted by the major maritime nations, in particular by Great Britain and the United States. Some states, however, claimed wider areas as their marginal sea or territorial waters: Russia, North and South Korea, Bulgaria, Israel, Egypt, Pakistan, Brazil, Ecuador, Panama, Colombia, and Guatemala claim twelve marine miles, Albania ten miles, Mexico nine miles, Portugal and Spain six miles, and Norway four miles. The Soviet Union, claiming a twelve-mile territorial sea adjacent to its Baltic coasts, has been involved since 1948 in controversy with Sweden and Denmark, both of which deny the validity of this extension of sovereignty. Prior to 1948, Russia had claimed (since 1909) a twelve-mile customs zone in the Baltic, but this was not asserted to be a claim of sovereignty. The twelve-mile territorial sea has been claimed formally, by statute, since 1960. Today more than half the world's coastal states assert a territorial sea limit ranging between six and twelve miles.[3] Although the traditional three-mile limit is still maintained by the major maritime states, they now constitute a definite minority of the family of nations.

Doctrine of National Sovereignty over Territorial Waters. Within the limits of the territorial waters of a state, the jurisdiction of the coastal (littoral) sovereign is as complete as it is over its territory on land. Any limitations existing, whether they refer to a "right of innocent passage" or to privileges and immunities granted to foreign vessels, represent voluntary concessions which do not touch the essential principle of complete sovereignty unless, in certain instances, applications of rules of international law are involved. It has been stated that Sweden, in 1758, was the first country to have asserted this modern doctrine of national sovereignty over the territorial sea.

PROBLEM OF THE WIDTH OF THE TERRITORIAL SEA

The problem of the width of the territorial sea came to the fore in the twentieth century when unilateral establishment of fishing and conservation zones called attention to the varying limits set by coastal states for their territorial waters. The first major attempt to arrive at a generally acceptable and uniform width of the territorial sea was made at The Hague in 1930. No agreement on the matter could be reached then, the differences in views being so pronounced that not a single proposal of a limit was even put to a vote.

---

in Arthur H. Dean, "The Second Geneva Conference on the Law of the Sea: The Fight for Freedom of the Seas," 54 *A.J.I.L.* (1960), pp. 751–789, at pp. 756–762, together with numerous references suitable for further investigation.

[3] See *Manual*, p. 338.

The International Law Commission of the United Nations, in discussing the problem after World War II, had decided that international law did not justify an extension of the territorial sea beyond twelve miles, justifying its stand by the opinion that any greater width jeopardized the principle of the freedom of the high seas. On the other hand, the Commission did not succeed in fixing the limit between three and twelve miles.

The problem came up next for discussion at the 1958 Geneva Conference on the Law of the Sea, but again no conclusive results were obtainable.[4] It was this particular failure to reach agreement which prompted the calling of the Second Geneva Conference on the Law of the Sea in 1960.

The second meeting soon bogged down in a welter of conflicting claims to both territorial waters and fishing zones. Admittedly, no unilateral extension of territorial sea claims by any state can be accepted as valid under international law unless and until it is recognized by other states. And such recognition must be by the tacit or expressed agreement by the overwhelming majority of the members of the family of nations. That means that acceptance of a unilateral extension must be by such a large number of states that the dissenters recede into insignificance compared with those who consent, openly or tacitly.[5]

At the 1958 Geneva Conference, the United States had sponsored a proposal for a six-mile fishing zone beyond a six-mile territorial sea limit. That startling reversal of a traditional American insistence on a three-mile territorial sea failed of adoption at the time. During the 1960 Conference, the Soviet Union proposed a "flexible" rule, permitting each state to select its own limit to the width of the territorial sea from three to twelve miles, plus an exclusive fishing zone twelve miles out beyond the limits of that sea. A little later a strikingly similar proposal, but not sponsored by the U.S.S.R., was promoted by a group of eighteen nations, mostly representing the "Afro-Asian" bloc. In turn there followed a joint compromise proposal offered by the United States and Canada, including substantial sacrifices in American fishing claims in an attempt to bring about general agreement to a six-mile territorial sea. But the American-Canadian proposal went down to defeat. After this, no further agreement was reached, and the conference eventually terminated without having fixed upon a general limit to the width of the territorial sea.

Since 1960, the United States appears not to have pressed the issue of

[4] See Arthur H. Dean, "The Geneva Conference on the Law of the Sea: What Was Accomplished," 52 *A.J.I.L.* (1958), pp. 607–628, at pp. 610–616, and particularly Myres S. McDougal and William T. Burke, "Crisis in the Law of the Sea: Community Perspectives versus National Egoism," 67 *Yale Law Journal* (1958), pp. 539–589.

[5] On this point, see the lucid analysis in Lauterpacht's *Oppenheim*, Vol. I, p. 17, which was cited by the Saudi Arabian delegation at the 1960 Geneva Conference in protesting against adoption of a convention by a mere two thirds of the participating country delegations.

a traditional three-mile limit when a foreign state has asserted a twelve-mile limit, such as has been the case with most socialist countries. (See, *inter alia*, the case of the U.S.S. Pueblo, Chapter 19.)

Straight Baseline System. It should not be overlooked, however, that the 1958 Geneva Conference produced a rather significant innovation related to the concept of the territorial sea: the straight baselines system for delimiting that sea.

Traditionally, the outer boundary of territorial waters had been determined by following the low-tide mark along the contours of the coast at whatever distance had been fixed for the width of the territorial waters. Eventually an increasingly large number of states claimed that the baseline from which the territorial sea was measured should not necessarily be the actual coastline, but might be a system of straight lines drawn from points on or near the shore over areas of water to some other points on or near the shore.

The first major dispute centering on this system of determining the extent of the territorial sea resulted in the well-known *Anglo-Norwegian Fisheries Case*, decided by the International Court of Justice in 1951.[6] Beginning in 1911, British fishing vessels operating in waters off the coast of Norway were seized and condemned by Norwegian authorities for violating regulations of the coastal state governing fishing in waters allegedly part of the Norwegian territorial sea. The dispute not being amenable to other methods of settlement, the British government instituted proceedings before the International Court of Justice in 1949, the main argument being that the seizures occurred more than four miles off the Norwegian coast (Norway's territorial waters extend to a distance of four miles from shore); hence they took place, illegally, on the high seas.

The Court decided by a vote of 10 to 2 in favor of Norway, approving the Norwegian practice of drawing an outer boundary for its territorial sea which was based on straight baselines following the general directions of the coast but not the indentations of that coast.

The Court's opinion had dwelled in great detail on the extraordinary geographic peculiarities of the Norwegian coastline and appeared to have sanctioned the straight baseline method for exceptional use rather than a principle of universal applicability.

When, therefore, the International Law Commission drafted a convention on the territorial sea, prior to the 1958 Geneva Conference, it at-

---

[6] *United Kingdom* v. *Norway* (*Norwegian Fisheries Case*), *I.C.J. Reports, 1951*, No. 1, reported in detail in 46 A.J.I.L. (1952), pp. 348–370. Consult also the detailed study by Jens Evensen, "The Anglo-Norwegian Fisheries Case and Its Legal Consequences," 46 *A.J.I.L.* (1952), p. 609–630; and D. H. N. Johnson, "Anglo-Scandinavian Agreements concerning the Territorial Sea and Fishing Limits," 10 *International and Comparative Law Quarterly* (1961), pp. 587–597. The text of the Anglo-Norwegian agreement of 1960 may be found in 57 *A.J.I.L.* (1963), pp. 490–492.

tempted to embody this method as an exceptional approach in determining the boundaries of the territorial waters of a state. The Conference accepted the Commission's proposals in virtually unchanged form, and Article 4 of the 1958 Convention on the Territorial Sea and the Contiguous Zone read:

1. In localities where the coast line is deeply indented and cut into, or if there is a fringe of islands along the coast in its immediate vicinity, the method of straight baselines joining appropriate points may be employed in drawing the baseline from which the breadth of the territorial sea is measured.

2. The drawing of such baselines must not depart to any appreciable extent from the general direction of the coast, and the sea areas lying within the lines must be sufficiently closely linked to the land domain to be subject to the regime of internal waters.

3. Baselines shall not be drawn to and from low-tide elevations, unless lighthouses or similar installations which are permanently above sea level have been built on them.

4. Where the method of straight baseline is applicable under the provisions of paragraph 1, account may be taken, in determining particular baselines, of economic interests peculiar to the region concerned, the reality and the importance of which are clearly evidenced by a long usage.

5. The system of straight baselines may not be applied by a State in such a manner as to cut off from the high seas the territorial sea of another State.

6. The coastal State must clearly indicate straight baselines on charts, to which due publicity must be given.

The utilization of the straight baseline method means that areas of water previously part of the high seas may be assimilated to the territorial waters of a coastal state and thus come under the exclusive jurisdiction of that state, subject to a right of innocent passage for foreign vessels. It should be noted that straight baselines are still applicable in exceptional circumstances only, so that states with only slightly irregular coastlines are bound by the traditional method of delimiting the outer boundaries of their territorial sea.

Archipelago Theory. A striking new method of determining a territorial sea has been developed unilaterally by the Philippines and Indonesia: the so-called archipelago theory. Each of the two states has claimed the right to draw a perimeter around its outermost islands and to term all waters within that perimeter as historic internal waters. Territorial waters would then extend outward from the straight baselines envisioned by the two states.[7] Indonesia proposed a twelve-mile limit for its terri-

[7] See Dean, *op. cit.* (n. 2), pp. 753 and 765–767, concerning the precise wording of these Philippine and Indonesian claims, particularly his notes 4, 53, and 54, which supply documentation for those claims and their discussion both at Geneva and in the General Assembly of the United Nations. Consult also the detailed analysis of the concept by Max Sørensen, "Territorial Sea of Archipelagos," 6 *Tijdschrift*, (July 1959, Special Issue), pp. 315–331, as well as Higgins–Colombos, pp. 90–91; as well as Frank B. Case, "Constriction of the Free Sea," 46 *Military Review* (March, 1966), pp. 3–12.

torial sea, whereas the Philippines put forth a varying limit, ranging from three miles at some points to more than twelve miles at others. A glance at a map reveals the immense extent of the internal seas claimed under the archipelago theory. Indonesia's perimeter extends over 3,000 miles from east to west and about 1,300 miles in a north-south direction, and the Philippines cover an area roughly 600 miles wide and 1,000 miles long, from north to south. If the archipelago theory were accepted by other states, the proclaimed internal-waters status of the seas enclosed within the perimeters in question would abolish all rights of free passage, rights of submarines to travel submerged, and all rights of foreign aircraft to fly over the waters involved, unless special treaty rights were granted to the citizens and craft of particular nations ("conditionally innocent passage").

While it had been claimed that no abridgment of the right of innocent passage by foreign vessels had been contemplated, Indonesia in June, 1960, issued regulations (effective two months later) prohibiting the taking on board or discharge of passengers and cargo by Dutch vessels in Indonesian internal waters.

The traditional doctrine, opposing the archipelago theory, was upheld in the interesting American case of *Civil Aeronautics Board* v. *Island Airlines, Inc.*,[8] in which it was held that the channels separating the Hawaiian Islands beyond the three-mile limit were international waters: the boundaries of Hawaii, therefore, were represented by a three-mile belt of territorial sea surrounding each individual island.

SPECIAL RULES FOR GULFS AND BAYS

Thus far the discussion of the maritime border, that is, of the seaward limit of the territorial sea, has dealt with the usual coastline. The border thus would follow the convolutions of the coast at some uniform distance from the low-tide mark along the coast. But the facts in the Gulf of Aqaba dispute, discussed below, indicate that special rules apply to gulfs and bays. As soon as such indentations occur along the coast of a state, the delimitation of the maritime frontier becomes more difficult. A strictly logical interpretation of the rules governing the territorial sea would have left all bays and gulfs within that sea inside of a line drawn from shore to shore at points six miles apart (assuming a three-mile limit of the sea).[9]

There are, however, certain bays that are considerably wider than six miles at the mouth or entrance, and some of these inlets run deep into the territory of the coastal state. It was not surprising, therefore, that the

---

[8] United States, District Court (U.S.), Hawaii, 1964, 235 F.Supp. 990, excerpted in 59 *A.J.I.L.* (1965), pp. 635–642, and noted with citation of much relevant literature by James A. Nafziger in 7 *Harvard International Law Club Journal* (Winter, 1965), pp. 143–152. The decision of the District Court was affirmed by the Court of Appeals, 9th Circuit, 1965, 352 F.2d 735.

[9] See Higgins-Colombos, pp. 131–146, for an extensive analysis of specific problems encountered in connection with bays and gulfs.

coastal state laid special claim to complete sovereignty over such bays or gulfs and many such claims have received the tacit approval of other maritime states. Some of the best-known examples of such a claim are the ones supported by the United States over the Delaware and Chesapeake bays, the former ten miles wide at its entrance, the other nine and one-half miles wide, and the Canadian claim to Conception Bay in Newfoundland. Unique is the situation of the Gulf of Fonseca, which was ruled, in 1917, by a decision of the Central American Court of Justice, to be a historic bay and a closed sea, part of the territories of El Salvador, Costa Rica, and Nicaragua, the three states constituting the coastal states fronting on the Gulf.

The 1958 Geneva Convention on the Territorial Sea and the Contiguous Zone changed the traditional rule governing sovereignty over bays by stating (Art. 7, par. 5) that where the distance between the low-water marks of the natural entrance points of a bay exceeded twenty-four miles, a straight baseline of twenty-four miles should be drawn within the bay in such a manner as to enclose the maximum area of water that was possible with a line of that length. Paragraph 1 of Article 7 of the convention read, "This article relates only to bays and coasts of which belong to a single state." As Bishop pointed out, the particular language used was adopted in order to avoid the necessity of taking a position on the Gulf of Aqaba and access to it through the Straits of Tiran.[10] This area has been the source of a bitter and continuing dispute between Israel on the one hand and the Arab states on the other, at least until the time of writing (see also Chapter 15 under Servitudes).[11]

GENERAL RULES

Where the coasts of two states are opposite or adjacent to each other, neither of the two states is entitled, failing agreement between them to the contrary, to extend its territorial sea beyond the median line every point of which is equidistant from the nearest points on the baselines from which the breadth of the territorial seas of each of the two states is measured (Art. 12, 1958 Geneva Convention on the Territorial Sea). This rule would not apply, of course, where by reason of historic title

[10] Bishop, p. 49, n. 84.

[11] Consult, *inter alia*, Leo Gross, "The Geneva Conference on the Law of the Sea and the Right of Innocent Passage through the Gulf of Aqaba," 53 *A.J.I.L.* (1959), pp. 564–594, with its extensive documentation; Israel Office of Information, *The Gulf of Aqaba: Free Navigation or Return to Piracy?* (New York January, 1957); Paul A. Porter, *The Gulf of Aqaba: An International Waterway* (Washington, D.C.: Public Affairs Press, 1957), Leo Gross, "Passage through the Suez Canal of Israel-Bound Cargo and Israel Ships," 51 *A.J.I.L.* (1957), pp. 530–568; Malcolm W. Cagle, "The Gulf of Aqaba—Trigger for Conflict," 85 *U.S. Naval Institute Proceedings* (January, 1959), pp. 75–81. On May 23, 1967, the U.A.R. closed the straits of Tiran and the Gulf to Israeli shipping, an act partly responsible for the outbreak of the subsequent "Six-Day War."

or some other special circumstance it is necessary to delimit the territorial waters of the two states in some other manner.

What are the rights of a coastal state in its territorial waters? Theoretically, because all waters on the landward side of the border of the territorial sea are internal waters of that state and are under its sovereignty, it might be held that unlimited authority could be exercised by the coastal state. This is not quite true, however, because international law, until recently based on customary rules limits the exercise of absolute sovereignty in the territorial sea.

Subject to restrictions outlined in Chapter 19 in connection with vessels, ships of all friendly states enjoy a right of innocent passage through the territorial waters, and equally enjoy the right to enter such waters when in distress or in danger from threatening weather. But beyond this special restriction the coastal state enjoys an authority which corresponds in kind as well as in extent to that enjoyed by it on land and in the air above that land.

These basic principles were illustrated in an interesting case:

THE PEOPLE v. STRALLA AND ADAMS

United States, Supreme Court of California, 1939
(98 California Decisions 440)

FACTS

Stralla and Adams operated the *Rex*, a gambling ship, anchored in Santa Monica Bay, four miles from the city of Santa Monica and six miles landward from a line drawn between the headlands of the bay. Those headlands were separated by a distance of twenty-five nautical miles or about twenty-nine statute miles. The depth of the bay from a line connecting the headlands was about ten miles.

The authorities of Los Angeles County raided the ship and arrested its owner-operators. The latter were convicted of operating a gambling ship, in violation of the laws of California. Conviction was appealed from the Superior Court of Los Angeles to the District Court of Appeal and in turn came before the Supreme Court of California.

ISSUE

Was Santa Monica Bay part of the territory of California or was the vessel anchored in the high seas and thus immune from seizure by California authorities?

DECISION

The Supreme Court affirmed the previous conviction. All of Santa Monica Bay was held to be within the jurisdiction of the State of California.

REASONING

Santa Monica is a "historic" bay, title to which has been claimed by California over a long period of time. The state constitution claims all bays and harbors along the coast. The bay was part of California territorial waters, the outer limits of which extended seaward at a distance of three miles parallel to a line drawn between the headlands of the bay. Within the bay, the State of California could exercise its jurisdiction for all lawful purposes, including the prosecution of violators of the penal law of the state.

THE CONTINENTAL SHELF

Beginning with a proclamation issued by the President of the United States on September 28, 1945, claims have been advanced by many states to what is termed the *continental shelf*.[12] That shelf is the gentle slope from the edge of the land down to a point where a sudden increase in the steepness takes place to ocean depth. The width of the shelf varies enormously, from less than one to eighty miles, with an average width of about thirty miles. Owing to such divergent widths, the International Law Commission of the United Nations limited, in 1956, the shelf to "a depth of 200 metres (approximately 100 fathoms), or, beyond that limit, to where the depth of the superjacent waters admit of the exploitation of the natural resources of the said areas." This language was adopted without change into the 1958 Geneva Convention on the Continental Shelf, ratified by December, 1968, by thirty-eight states (but not, *inter alia*, by Canada, Chile, Iceland, Indonesia, Iran, and Peru).[13]

In essence, the various national claims have asserted that the seabed and subsoil of the land under the sea which extends as a sort of appendage of the landmass were under national jurisdiction of the littoral (coastal) state for exploitive purposes. The waters and the air above the continental shelf, on the other hand, were not claimed beyond the limits of the territorial sea of each of the states concerned.

The history of the concept of the continental shelf goes back to 1898 when the expression was first used by a geographer. Then "it made a fleeting appearance on the legal stage in 1916: but passed over it with 'printless feet.' "[14] Although a 1942 treaty between Great Britain and Venezuela concerning spheres of influence in the Gulf of Paria could be said to have hinted at the concept of the continental shelf, the latter entered into the sphere of international law proper only with the Truman proclamation of 1945. That proclamation was implemented in turn, somewhat belatedly, by the passage of the Outer Continental Shelf Lands Act of August 7, 1953, which reserved for the United States all "political" and

[12] Text, with the related executive order, reprinted in 40 *A.J.I.L.* (1946), Supp., pp. 45–46.

[13] Text in 52 *A.J.I.L.* (1958), Supp., pp. 858–862. For the background of the convention, consult the reports of the Commission covering its fifth (1953), seventh (1955), and eighth (1956) sessions.

[14] Footnote by the umpire, Lord Asquith of Bishopstone, in the *Arbitration between Petroleum Development (Trucial Coast) Ltd. and Sheikh of Abu Dhabi*, Award of August 28, 1951, Paris, France [1 *International and Comparative Law Quarterly* (1952), p. 247], digested in 47 *A.J.I.L.* (1953), pp. 156–159, at p. 157. The award supplies amusing reading, in view of the many pithy comments by the umpire.

civil jurisdiction both in the subsoil and the seabed of the shelf beyond the seaward boundaries allowed to the states under the terms of the Submerged Lands Act of May 22, 1953.

The present writer believes that a new rule of international law dealing with national rights in the continental shelf evolved in an extremely short period of time as a result of the rapid issuance of claims, with twenty states, plus the United Kingdom on behalf of a dozen dependencies, asserting such claims in the space of seventeen years. Although this new rule may not have been general in application, it is taken to have constituted a part of particular international law. This view has been challenged vigorously, however, for the period antedating the 1958 Convention on the Continental Shelf.[15] The new treaty makes the whole argument somewhat academic, of course. All parties agree that since 1958, the position of the continental shelf in international law has been regularized.

1958 CONVENTION ON THE CONTINENTAL SHELF

The 1958 Convention recognized exclusive sovereign rights to the seabed and subsoil resources of any continental shelf to a depth of 200 meters, or, beyond that limit, to where the depth of the "superjacent" waters permitted the exploitation of the natural resources of the shelf. If a coastal state chose not to exploit such resources, its sovereign rights prevented any other state from undertaking such exploitation without the express consent of the coastal state. The treaty further provided that the rights of the coastal state over the shelf did not depend on occupation or on any express proclamation. The rights of the coastal state over the shelf did not in any manner affect the legal status of the superjacent waters as high seas or that of the airspace above those waters.

The coastal state was not permitted to impede the laying or maintenance of submarine cables or pipelines on the continental shelf, subject to its right to take reasonable measures for the exploration of the shelf and for the exploitation of its resources (Art. 4). These legitimate activities were not to result, however, in an unjustifiable interference with navigation, fishing, or the conservation of the living resources of the sea above the shelf (Art. 5).

Subject to these restrictions, the coastal state was entitled to construct and operate on the continental shelf installations of various sorts necessary for its exploration and the exploitation of its natural resources. Safety zones not to exceed a distance of 500 meters from such installations could be established by the coastal state. For obvious reasons, any installations constructed by the coastal state on the shelf were denied the status of islands. They thus lacked any territorial sea of their own and their existence could not affect the delimitation of the territorial waters of the

---

[15] See Josef L. Kunz, "Continental Shelf and International Law: Confusion and Abuse," 50 *A.J.I.L.* (1956), pp. 828–853, denying the development of the new rule prior to 1958.

coastal state. Such installations were forbidden altogether where their presence would interfere with the use of recognized sealanes utilized in international navigation.

If another state should wish to sponsor or undertake research on the continental shelf, the consent of the coastal state would be required (Art. 5.)

Where the continental shelf was adjacent to the territories of two or more states whose coasts were opposite each other, the boundary of the shelf belonging to such states had to be determined by agreement between them. Failing such agreement, the boundary line would normally be the median line, equidistant at every point from the nearest points of the base lines from which the breadth of the territorial sea of each state was measured. Where the shelf was adjacent to the territories of two adjacent states, the boundary of the shelf would be determined by agreement between the states in question. In the absence of such agreement, the boundary would be determined by the application of the principle of equidistance from the nearest points of the relevant baselines (Art. 6).

As a point of interest it should be mentioned that each coastal state had and has a perfect right to exploit the subsoil of the seabed by means of tunneling, regardless of the depth of water above the subsoil in question (Art. 7). [16]

It should be obvious that whenever the coastal state is mentioned in a discussion of the right to exploit the resources of a continental shelf, such coastal state may conduct the exploration and exploitation through its own governmental agencies or may, at its discretion, grant the necessary concessions for such undertakings to private individuals or corporations.

It remains to be seen whether the emphasis which the 1958 Convention on the Continental Shelf placed on the legal status of the superjacent waters as high seas will influence the attitudes of such states as have established conservation zones in those same waters, once those states have ratified the Convention.

A last comment needs to be added about the rights of the coastal state to exploit resources consisting of living organisms on the bottom, that is, atop the surface of the continental shelf. The desire of many states, particularly those with pearl fishery interests outside their territorial sea, to preserve exclusive control over such resources was met by the inclusion of "living organisms belonging to sedentary species" (Art. 2, par. 4) among the resources reserved by the 1958 Convention for the coastal state.[17]

[16] See Max Sørensen, "Law of the Sea," *International Conciliation* (No. 520, November, 1958), pp. 195–255, at pp. 226–231, on these points.

[17] On this point consult Richard Young, "Sedentary Fisheries and the Convention on the Continental Shelf," 55 *A.J.I.L.* (1951), pp. 359–373. Early in 1963, Brazil objected strongly to the French government against the continuing fishing for lobsters by French fishermen on the continental shelf off the Brazilian coast.

Before leaving the subject of the shelf altogether, it might be of value to report the details of the arbitration award cited earlier (note 14). In 1939, the Sheikh of Abu Dhabi, one of the "Trucial States" of southeastern Arabia (described in the proceedings as "a British-protected state" for "external relations," while "internally, the Sheikh is an absolute, feudal monarch,") had made a contract with Petroleum Development (Trucial Coast) Ltd., a British company. The concession granted in that instrument involved a right of the company to drill for oil, for a period of seventy-five years, in all the lands under the rule of the Sheikh and in "all the islands and the sea waters which belong to that area." In 1949, the Sheikh proclaimed sovereignty over the continental shelf along the coast of Abu Dhabi and granted an oil concession in such shelf areas to an American company. Because the 1939 concession provided for arbitration and the British company asserted that the subsoil of the shelf was a part of the 1939 concession, the dispute was brought to arbitration.

The umpire held that since the concept of the continental shelf was not known in 1939, the British concession included only the soil under the territorial waters of Abu Dhabi; that the subsoil of the continental shelf was freely available to the Sheikh for disposal through a second concession; that, therefore, the British company's claim to possess a concession to the continental shelf resources had to be rejected.

SUGGESTED READINGS

TERRITORIAL WATERS

Hackworth, Vol. I, pp. 642–645, 651–653; and, on bays, pp. 691–712; Hyde, Vol. I, pp. 451–489; Lauterpacht's *Oppenheim*, Vol. I, pp. 487–504; Whiteman, Vol. IV, pp. 1–480; A. L. Shalowitz, "Where Are Our Seaward Boundaries?" 83 *U.S. Naval Institute Proceedings* (June, 1957), pp. 616–627; S. Whittemore Boggs, "Delimitation of Seaward Areas under National Jurisdiction," 45 *A.J.I.L.* (1951), pp. 240–266; Robert D. Powers, Jr. and Leonard R. Hardy, "How Wide the Territorial Sea? I. The Background and the Vote—1960 Conference," 87 *U.S. Naval Institute Proceedings* (February, 1961), pp. 68–74; George A. Codding, Jr. and Alvin Z. Rubinstein, "II. The Problems Left by Discord—Current and Future," *ibid.*, pp. 74–77; Mitchell P. Strohl, *The International Law of Bays* (The Hague: Matinus Nijhoff, 1963); and Tao Cheng, "Communist China and the Law of the Sea," 63 *A.J.I.L.* (1969), pp. 47–73.

Consult also United States: "An Act Prohibiting Fishing by Foreign Vessels in the Territorial Waters of the United States and in Certain Other Areas," 1964, 78 Stat. 194, reprinted in 58 *A.J.I.L.* (1964), pp. 1090–1093.

RUSSIAN TERRITORIAL WATERS

William E. Butler, *The Law of Soviet Territorial Waters* (New York: Praeger, 1967), his "Soviet Concepts of Innocent Passage," 7 *Harvard International Law Club Journal* (Winter, 1965), pp. 113–130, and his "The Legal Regime of Russian Territorial Waters," 62 *A.J.I.L.* (1968), pp. 51–77; Gene Glenn, "The Swedish-Soviet Territorial Sea Controversy in the Baltic," 50 *A.J.I.L.* (1956), pp. 942–949; and Henry G. Morgan, Jr., "Soviet Policy in the Baltic," 86 *U.S. Naval Institute Proceedings* (April, 1960), pp. 82–89; L. B. Schapiro, "The Limits of Russian Territorial Waters in the Baltic," 27 *B.Y.I.L.* (1950), pp. 439–448 (see Hackworth, I, pp. 634–636, on the 1912 Tsarist claim to a 12-mile territorial sea limit).

THE CONTINENTAL SHELF

The best suggested reading on this subject is Whiteman, Vol. IV, pp. 740–931; other recommended sources include Barry B. L. Auguste, *The Continental Shelf: The Practice and Policy of the Latin American States with Special Reference to Chile, Ecuador and Peru; A Study in International Relations* (Geneva: Librairie E. Droz, 1960); Gould, pp. 380–387; and Svarlien, pp. 159–163. Consult 57 *A.J.I.L.* (1963), pp. 899–902, on Mexican extensions of territorial waters. See also the relevant case of *Guess* v. *Read*, United States, Circuit Court of Appeals, Fifth Circuit, 1961, 290 F. (2d) 622, digested in 56 *A.J.I.L.* (1962), pp. 211–212. Some special problems of the continental shelf concept are examined in Richard Young, "Offshore Claims and Problems in the North Sea," 59 *A.J.I.L.* (1965), pp. 505–522, to which is related the British "Continental Shelf Act 1964," reprinted *ibid.*, 58 (1964), pp. 1085–1090; consult also William E. Butler, "The Soviet Union and the Continental Shelf," *ibid.*, 63 (1969), pp. 103–107; Arvid Pardo, "Whose Is the Bed of the Sea?" *Proceedings* (1968), pp. 216–229; Richard Young, "The Limits of the Continental Shelf—and Beyond," *ibid.*, pp. 229–236.

Case

North Sea Continental Shelf Cases (Federal Republic of Germany v. Denmark; Federal Republic of Germany v. Netherlands), *I.C.J.* 1969; text of decision in 8 *International Legal Materials* (1969), pp. 340–433.

18

The High Seas

ORIGINS OF THE LAW OF THE SEA

THE term *high seas* refers to all areas of the world's oceans located outside the limits of national waters and the territorial or marginal seas of coastal states.[1]

The origins of the rules governing the high seas can be traced back to the early Middle Ages; some authorities maintain that portions of the Code of Justinian represent ancestors of the modern law of the sea, but such claims should be regarded as possessing dubious validity.

Beginning in the twelfth century, a number of compilations of rules applicable on the seas began to circulate in Europe. Several of these purely private compendia gained such widespread acceptance and authority that the rules laid down in them achieved in time the status of customary law. In the Mediterranean area, the earliest generally accepted rules were collected in the *Lex Rhodia*, the Rhodian Sea Law, whose various existing versions were probably collected in the seventh century.[2] It was followed by the much better known collection of rules known as the *Consolato del Mare* (the Consulate of the Sea). The title of the work is derived from its compilers, the official judges of the ports who were designated as *consuls*, and assorted captains and prominent merchants. The date of the *Consolato* is not certain, but it saw light probably in the late thirteenth or early fourteenth century. Written in the Catalan language, its original title was "The Laws of Barcelona," and although several authorities claim that the code originated in Marseilles, the oldest existing printed version, dated 1494, came from Barcelona. The change in title appeared only in the fifteenth century and is believed to have been caused by initial recognition of the principles written down by the consuls of the various maritime nations around the shores of the Mediterranean.

In the Atlantic area, the basic rules of the sea were collected in the

---

[1] See Reiff for a basic reference work on the rules governing activities on the oceans of the world. Other extremely useful works on the subject are William McFee, *The Law of the Sea* (Philadelphia: Lippincott, 1950), the highly informative study by Higgins–Colombos, and Myres S. McDougal and William T. Burke, *The Public Order of the Oceans* (New Haven: Yale University Press, 1962).

[2] Text in McFee, *op. cit.*, pp. 299–305; see ibid., pp. 37–46, for a discussion of the background of the Rhodian law and, at pp. 55–60, of its contents.

Rolles d'Oléron (the Rules of Oleron), a compilation probably set down in the twelfth century in Old French.[3] Oddly enough, the rules contained in this work do *not* represent the laws of the island of Oléron but those of a number of ports in western France. Many of the concepts embodied in this code are still found in modern French and English rules applicable to the seas.

In England, the ancient *Black Book of the Admiralty*, compiled during the reigns of Edward III, Richard II, and Henry IV, represented a collection of rules for use in the Admiral's Court. Originally written in Norman French, the regulations were translated into English during the reign of Charles II in the seventeenth century.

In northern Europe, the *Sea Code of Wisby* may be taken to have been the most important collection of generally accepted rules.[4] Its first portion was merely a Flemish translation of the twenty-four oldest articles of the *Rolles d'Oléron;* its second half, the *Ordinancie*, compiled probably in Amsterdam in 1407, added numerous principles adopted by the Hanseatic Cities. The first printed edition of the work (Copenhagen, 1505) was entitled *Gothlantic Sea Law* and, it is assumed, represents the handwritten compilation used officially by the Maritime Court at Wisby, on the island of Gothland.

Subsequent centuries witnessed the growth of conventional laws of the sea through the conclusion of many multilateral treaties, such as the London Convention of 1841 Concerning the Closing of the Dardanelles, modified in 1856 and again in 1871; the London Convention of 1841 for the Suppression of the Slave Trade; the Declaration of Paris (1856) Concerning War at Sea (and for the abolition of privateering); the numerous treaties governing the construction, use, and protection of submarine cables; and many conventions relating to maritime war, protection of fishing rights, and so on. The culmination of international efforts to arrive at a common law of the sea by convention came with the two Geneva Conferences on the Law of the Sea in 1958 and 1960.

In sharp contrast to the majority of national attitudes prevailing until the early part of the nineteenth century, legal authorities as well as governments are in agreement that the high seas are common property and open to the use of all states. All former national claims over large areas of the world's oceans have now been abandoned, even though controversy continues about contiguous zones and coastal fishery rights.[5]

This "freedom of the seas" is essentially an achievement of the nineteenth century, even though the roots of the doctrine reach back at least

[3] *Ibid.*, pp. 305–310.
[4] See McFee, *op. cit.*, pp. 75–77, for the Code of Wisby, and pp. 68–75, for the Amalfi Code.
[5] Consult Higgins–Colombos, pp. 39–55, for a summary of the old claims and of their gradual abandonment.

to 1604 and the appearance of Grotius' well-known *Mare Librum*.[6]
Though late in point of time, the general acceptance of the doctrine of
the free seas had its basis in a common recognition of the desirability of
preventing one state, or a group of states, from asserting a legal right to
bar other members of the community of nations from the use of any
portion of the high seas.

Because the two recent Geneva conferences and the convention resulting from them represent the latest consensus of opinion as to the nature
of the freedoms existing on the high seas, the discussion which follows is
based primarily on the instruments in question.

1958 CONVENTION ON THE HIGH SEAS

The 1958 United Nations Conference on the Law of the Sea (Geneva),
attended by representatives of eighty-six states, drafted, among other
instruments, a Convention on the High Seas.[7] The major provisions of this
agreement summarize the current status of the law of the high seas.[8]

RIGHTS OF NATIONS

The high seas being open to all nations, no state may validly assert
sovereignty over any part of them. Freedom of the high seas means, for
both coastal and noncoastal states, freedom of navigation, of fishing, to lay
submarine cables and pipelines, and to fly over the high seas.

States having no seacoast have a right of free access to the sea (Art.
2). To this end, states interposed between the sea and an inland state
should, by treaty, grant to the landlocked state (on a basis of reciprocity)
free transit through their territory and accord to vessels flying the flag
of the landlocked state treatment equal to that accorded to their own
ships.

This principle has been the underlying cause for a quarrel of long
standing between Bolivia and Chile which led to a severance of diplomatic
relations between the two countries in 1962 and to a great protest march
headed by the President of Bolivia, in March, 1964. Bolivia, landlocked
since a defeat in 1879 by Chile, has demanded repeatedly that the small
Chilean port of Mejillones, thirty-five miles north of Antofagasta, should
be ceded to Bolivia, together with a small enclave. Bolivia did not insist on

[6] Whiteman, IV, pp. 501–542; Edward W. Allen, "Freedom of the Sea," 60 *A.J.I.L.*
(1966), pp. 814–816.
[7] Text of the convention in 52 *A.J.I.L.* (1958), Supp., pp. 842–851. The convention
entered into force on September 30, 1962; by December, 1968, forty-one states had
ratified it or acceded to it.
[8] A convenient summary of the achievements and shortcomings of the 1958 Conference may be found in Max Sørensen, "Law of the Sea," *International Conciliation*
(No. 520, 1958), pp. 195–255; consult also the analysis in Reiff, pp. 327–334; and
Arthur H. Dean, "The Geneva Conference on the Law of the Sea: What Was
Accomplished," 52 *A.J.I.L.* (1958), pp. 607–628.

the acquisition of a corridor linking the port with its territory, being apparently content to use an existing railroad to transport goods from the coast inland. In return for the cession of the port and enclave, Bolivia offered to divert water from five small rivers in the upper Andes to assist in the irrigation of Chile's northern desert region.[9]

The right of access granted to landlocked states was reinforced by the signing, on July 8, 1965, of the Convention on Transit Trade of Landlocked Countries, negotiated at a UN conference on this subject in New York.[10] This instrument provides, besides duty-free access to the sea for the goods of landlocked countries—except for a small, nondiscriminatory service charge—for "free, uninterrupted and continuous traffic in transit." The treaty is to stay in force in time of war so far as "the rights and duties of belligerents and neutrals" permit. A maritime state is assured specifically the right to keep out such goods as arms, narcotics, diseased animals and plants, as well as "persons whose admission into its territories is forbidden, on grounds of public morals, public health or security."

POLICE ACTIVITIES ON THE HIGH SEAS

Right to Visit and Search. A warship encountering a foreign merchant vessel on the high seas may stop such a vessel for purposes of investigation if one of the following suspicions is harbored by the commander of the warship or if other causes for such a "visit and search" are authorized for him by special treaty arrangements: (1) that the ship is engaged in piracy; (2) that the ship is engaged in the slave trade; or (3) that the vessel, although flying a foreign flag or refusing to show its flag, is in reality of the same nationality as the warship.[11]

These suspicions represent a limitation on the normal rule that a merchant vessel on the high seas can be boarded only by members of the crew of a warship flying the same flag as the merchant ship.

Should the suspicions prove to be unfounded, the state to which the warship belongs must compensate the owners of the merchant ship for any delay (loss, damage, and so on) caused by the actions of the warship.

Rule of Hot Pursuit. One of the more spectacular of the rules govern-

[9] See Barnard L. Collier, "Bolivia, Chile, and the Sea," *The New York Times*, March 12, 1967, p. E-7; on access in general, see Whiteman, Vol. IX, pp. 1143–1163.

[10] *The New York Times*, July 9, 1965, p. 7; the convention was approved by 46 countries, with none opposed but with seven abstentions (France, Pakistan, Romania, South Africa, the former French Congo, Thailand, and South Vietnam). It entered into force for the United States on November 28, 1968; text in Whiteman, Vol. IX, pp. 1156–1161.

[11] Consult also Anna van Zwanenberg, "Interference with Ships on the High Seas," 10 *International and Comparative Law Journal* (1961), pp. 785–817, as well as Whiteman, Vol. IV, pp. 633–640, 667–677.

ing the high seas has to do with what is termed *hot pursuit*.[12] This means the pursuit into the high seas of a foreign vessel suspected of having committed an infringement of the laws or regulations of a coastal state. To be lawful, hot pursuit has to commence when the foreign vessel or one of its boats is within the national waters, territorial sea, or contiguous zone of the pursuing state. The pursuit may be continued outside the territorial sea or contiguous zone only if such pursuit has not been interrupted. Once pursuit has been broken off, it cannot be resumed. The beginning of the pursuit normally has to be preceded by the hoisting of a visual signal or by giving an audible command to stop for visit and search. The International Law Commission refused to approve orders given by radio, because these could be sent from any distance.

If the foreign vessel is within the contiguous zone at the time pursuit is begun, the latter is lawful only if there has been a violation of the rights for the protection of which the zone was established. In other words, alleged violation of customs regulations may not give rise to pursuit begun in a contiguous zone created to protect, say, fishing rights. Hot pursuit ceases as soon as the ship pursued enters the territorial waters of its own country or of a third state.

In order to prevent possible abuses, the right of hot pursuit may be exercised only by warships, military aircraft, or other ships or aircraft or government services specially authorized to engage in this activity. If an aircraft is utilized, it must pursue the fleeing vessel until it can effect an arrest itself or until a vessel of the coastal state, summoned by the aircraft, or another governmental aircraft summoned by the original one, can effect the arrest.

As in the case of visit and search, if the allegations of unlawful activity are found to be without foundation, the arresting state is obligated to compensate the vessel's owners for any loss or damage caused by the hot pursuit and arrest of the ship.

By application of the principle of "constructive presence," the doctrine of hot pursuit has been expanded to cover cases of vessels that remain or "hover" on the high seas—beyond territorial waters—but maintain contact with the shore through small craft. Such vessels, if charged with prohibited activities, may be pursued and arrested even though they never entered the territorial sea of the injured or offended state.

PIRACY

Piracy, an age-old occupation of certain enterprising individuals, has not yet disappeared completely from the oceans of the world. Generally speaking, piracy may be of two kinds, *statutory piracy* and *piracy jure gentium*. The former variety is piracy as it is defined in the statutes of

---

[12] See Hackworth, Vol. II, pp. 700–709; Higgins–Colombos, pp. 123–128; Glanville L. Williams, "The Juridicial Basis of Hot Pursuit," 16 *B.Y.I.L.* (1939), pp. 83–97; Whiteman, Vol. IV, pp. 677–687.

individual states and is of no concern to us here. The second variety is piracy under international law. The traditional definition of such piracy corresponds to that supplied by Oppenheim:

Piracy in its original and strict meaning, is every unauthorised act of violence committed by a private vessel on the open sea against another vessel with intent to plunder (*animo furandi*).[13]

Jacobini defined piracy in more modern and comprehensive terms as "the act of doing or attempting to do an unauthorized act of violence by persons aboard one private ship or aircraft to persons or property aboard another ship or aircraft (or to the ship itself) on the high seas with intent of depredation; piracy also includes successful mutiny." [14]

Definition of Piracy by the 1958 Geneva Convention. The 1958 Geneva Convention on the High Seas, which dealt with piracy in Articles 14 through 22, defined the matter as follows:

Piracy consists of any of the following acts: (1) any illegal act of violence, detention or any act of depredation, committed for private ends by the crew or the passengers of a private ship or a private aircraft, and directed: (a) on the high seas, against another ship or aircraft, or against persons or property on board such ship or aircraft; (b) against a ship, aircraft, persons or property in a place outside the jurisdiction of any state; (2) any act of voluntary participation in the operation of a ship or of an aircraft with knowledge of facts making it a pirate ship or aircraft; (3) any act of inciting or of intentionally facilitating an act described in subparagraph 1 or subparagraph 2 of this Article [Art. 15].

Article 16 of the convention stated that "The acts of piracy, as defined in Article 15, committed by a warship, government ship or government aircraft whose crew has mutinied and taken control of the ship or aircraft are assimilated to acts committed by a pirate ship," and Article 17 affirmed that a ship or aircraft was considered a pirate craft if it was intended by the persons in dominant control to be used for the purpose of committing an act of piracy. Also, the pirate character continued to apply to such a craft after it had been used to commit an act of piracy, as long as it remained under the control of the persons guilty of that act.

Modern interpretations of piracy differ also from the older definitions in that the intention to rob, mentioned in Oppenheim's definition of piracy, is no longer required. It is now recognized that acts of piracy may be prompted by feelings of hatred or revenge, and not merely by a desire for gain. But even today an act must be committed for private ends in order to be classified as piratical.

[13] Lauterpacht's *Oppenheim*, Vol. I, p. 608; see *ibid.*, pp. 608–617, Whiteman, Vol. IV, pp. 648–667, and Higgins–Colombos, pp. 329–334, for general discussions of piracy. Consult also Hersch Lauterpacht, *Recognition in International Law*, pp. 304–308.

[14] Jacobini, p. 118.

The new definitions simply affirm and elaborate one of the oldest sets of principles of customary international law, developed in the early medieval period. The pirate, as a menace to the commerce of all maritime states, caused one of the few recorded attempts to unite all individual navies in a continuing cooperative effort to stamp out that menace. In effect, therefore, the prohibition of piracy represents a directive to all states to punish a pirate, whenever caught, in their appropriate courts.

Right of Suppression of Piracy. In former times, even private individuals were tolerated as enforcers of the prohibition on piracy. Today any state may seize, on the high seas or in any other place outside the territorial waters of another state, a pirate ship or aircraft, or a ship taken in piracy and under the control of pirates, and arrest the persons and seize the property on board. Craft and prisoners are supposed to be taken to the nearest appropriate court of the arresting state and that court will decide on the penalties to be imposed and on the disposition of the craft and its contents. Although private craft are not to hunt down pirates today, should a merchant vessel overpower its attacker, the "arrest" of the pirate craft and crew by the merchant vessel would be lawful. But in such a case, too, there must be a trial and disposition of goods through an appropriate court of the state whose flag the merchant vessel flies; normally, the merchant vessel would summon a warship to its assistance and turn the captured craft and crew over to the custody of that warship. Essentially, the capture of pirate craft may today be undertaken only by warships or military aircraft, unless other ships or aircraft on government service have been authorized to undertake such capture.

If an individual is found guilty of piracy, the state of which he is a national or citizen has, under customary international law, no right to defend him or to represent him in further proceedings that may take place. If, on the other hand, the seizure of a ship, aircraft, or individuals on suspicion of piracy has been effected without adequate grounds, the state making the seizure is liable, to the state whose nationality is possessed by the craft or individuals in question, for any loss or damage caused by the seizure.[15]

Status of Submarines and Aircraft. The failure of many German submarines during World War I to observe certain laws of war led to charges of piracy against the new type of warship. Such accusations were ill-founded, considering the nature of the problems faced by the commanders of submarines and especially because of the absence of a "private end" on the part of the submarine commander and his crew.

On the other hand, the views held during World War I about submarines were echoed again in 1937 when an "Arrangement" was signed at Nyon, France, by a number of maritime states as the result of attacks

---

[15] See the celebrated case of *The Virginius*, in Moore, Vol. II, pp. 895–903, and, for comparison, the well-known case of *The Marianna Flora*, United States, Supreme Court, 1826, 11 Wheaton 1.

by submarines of "unknown" or undeclared nationality on Spanish and neutral vessels during the Spanish Civil War. The agreement provided for the treatment as pirates of the crew of any submarine attacking a vessel belonging to neither party in that conflict. The Mediterranean was divided into zones to be patrolled by the signatory states, with orders to their warships to attack with intent to destroy any submarine guilty of the actions in question (see also Chapter 29).

Such charges and agreements appear somewhat archaic today, in the light of the practices followed by the major maritime Powers in the submarine warfare connected with World War II; the fact remains that piracy by definition can be committed only by private craft and for private ends.

The mere fact that a ship sails without displaying a flag or an aircraft travels without identifying markings is not sufficient to give such craft the character of a pirate.

The old view tended to be that a vessel lost its national character by the act of committing piracy. This attitude does not prevail in modern times. A pirate craft, by its commission of piratical acts, is no longer subject to the rule that it is subject only to the authority of its flag state. It is still possessed of the nationality of the state in which it is registered, except in the case where the national laws of that state view piracy as a ground for the loss of nationality; in the latter case, the ship or aircraft in question would be regarded by all countries as being stateless or without nationality.

The trial of a seized ship or aircraft suspected of piracy must take place in the courts of the arresting state; this right to try accused pirates cannot be exercised at some place under the jurisdiction of another state.

Piracy in municipal law is determined by the statutes of each individual state. This fact assumed some importance when airlines and private owners of aircraft in the Western Hemisphere began to be plagued by an increasing incidence of hijacking of planes. Since 1960, dozens of passenger planes have been diverted to Cuba, with such incidents on occasion occurring as often as twice a day. Planes, crews, and passengers were always permitted to return to their scheduled routing, with the captor remaining in Cuba.[16]

In 1961 President Kennedy signed a bill declaring hijacking of aircraft an act of piracy, with penalties for the offense ranging up to death. The law also provided for a $1,000 fine for carrying concealed weapons aboard an aircraft and for sentences of up to five years in prison for giving false information on plane hijacking. Application of such legislation proved to be almost impossible, however, for in almost all instances the "pirates" remained in Cuba, beyond the jurisdiction of American courts. In a few

---

[16] A much publicized illegal aerial seizure not connected with Cuba took place on July 22, 1968, when armed Palestinian refugees captured an El Al (Israeli) aircraft bound from Rome to Tel Aviv and forced the pilot to land the plane in Algeria.

instances, on the other hand, hijackers were subdued before the aircraft left the United States or reached Cuba. In such cases, prosecution of the individuals in question took place.

International action on the problem of aerial hijacking began in a modest way when a Convention on Offences and Certain Other Acts Committed on Board Aircraft was signed—under the auspices of the I.C.A.O.—on September 14, 1963, in Tokyo, by representatives of sixteen countries, including the United States. Article 11 of the instrument deals with the unlawful seizure of aircraft. The convention does not, however, apply the label of piracy to such an act.

On February 14, 1969, the Mexican Foreign Ministry and the Cuban national radio system announced that Mexico and Cuba had reached preliminary agreement on a treaty obliging the Cuban government to return persons charged with the hijacking of Mexican-registered aircraft to Mexico for prosecution.[17]

Status of Vessels Under Control of Insurgents. One of the problems connected with the subject of piracy is the status of a vessel operating on behalf and under the control of insurgents. Because acts connected legitimately with insurgency or with a belligerent community are not considered to be piratical, such a vessel would be exempt from a charge of piracy.[18] In the classic case of the brigantine *The Ambrose Light*,[19] a vessel captured by a United States gunboat while flying a flag representing Colombian rebels and carrying rebel soldiers, the court ruled that the ship would have been condemned as a pirate, because at the time of capture no kind of recognition of the rebels had taken place on the part of the United States or of any other country, if the American government had not extended implied recognition of insurgency to the rebels—by coincidence on the very day of the ship's capture.

Santa Maria Case. January, 1961, saw an instance in which the concepts of insurgent, pirate, and criminal were interwoven almost inextricably: the famous incident of the *Santa Maria*. The vessel, a 21,000-ton Portuguese cruise ship sailing the Caribbean, was seized on January 24 at gunpoint by a band of "patriot pirates," led by Henrique Galvao, a former Portuguese army captain. Seventy heavily armed members of the band, after killing the third officer of the liner, ordered the vessel, with its crew of 370 and more than 600 passengers, to proceed eastward from Martinique. A widespread search by British and American warships and aircraft "failed to locate" the liner for a day, despite the fact that radio messages from both hijackers and passengers continued to be received in New York.

---

[17] *Minneapolis* (Minn.) *Tribune*, February 16, 1969, p. 4-A; *Duluth* (Minn.) *News-Tribune*, February 16, 1969, p. 19.

[18] See Hersch Lauterpacht, *Recognition in International Law* (Cambridge: Cambridge University Press, 1947), pp. 296–304, for an intensive discussion of the question, and consult Higgins–Colombos, pp. 334–341.

[19] United States, District Court, S.D.N.Y., 1885, 25 F. 408.

The avowed purpose of the seizure of the *Santa Maria* was to call attention to the dictatorial nature of the Portuguese government. At one time, the goal of the voyage was stated to be the Portuguese African colony of Angola, then in the throes of a native uprising. By January 28, with the liner heading for northern Brazil, United States Navy authorities arranged for a rendezvous with the ship in order to negotiate the release of the passengers. Ultimately the liner reached Brazil and the rebel crew was granted asylum there as political offenders.[20]

From a legal point of view, the brief capture of the *Santa Maria* posed interesting questions.[21] Captain Galvao denied that he was a pirate, and certainly the seizure of the vessel was not inspired by pirate ends. He insisted that he was an insurgent, engaged in an attempt to overthrow the government of Portugal on behalf of Dr. Salazar's chief enemy, General Humberto Delgado. Unfortunately for the claim of his insurgent status, Galvao did not control any territory from which he could have proceeded to the capture of the liner. His insurgent group had not been recognized as such by any state; hence he could not enjoy any privileges accruing to the leader and armed forces of a belligerent community. A private citizen, even when he has a relative handful of followers, does not qualify as head of an insurgent community, especially when the latter lacks a territorial base. Nor could Galvao be classified as a privateer, for that category of individual has been abolished since 1856.

Lacking status as an insurgent band and failing to correspond to that of a pirate crew owing to the absence of private gain or private ends sought, the Galvao group, legally speaking, had to be classified as ordinary criminals, having committed murder and seized private property as well as private persons against their will.

The Brazilian government, in granting political asylum to the group, acted in error, for although the basic motives of the band may have been political, their actions were wholly criminal. Without question, the finale of the *Santa Maria* incident represented an unjustified extension of the regional principle of political asylum as practiced among Latin American states. (See Chapter 14 for the 1963 sequel to this case.)

OTHER POLICE ACTIVITIES ON THE HIGH SEAS

In addition to the suppression of piracy on the high seas, a second area in which the public ships of one state may lawfully interfere with the normal freedom of the seas enjoyed by the vessels of other states is represented by offenses specified by treaty.

---

[20] *The New York Times*, January 24–31, 1961; see also 77 *Time* (February 3, 1961), pp. 19–20, for a detailed account of the events, including a useful map.

[21] Charles G. Fenwick, "'Piracy' in the Caribbean," 55 *A.J.I.L.* (1961), pp. 426–428; Benjamin Forman, "The International Law of Piracy and the Santa Maria Incident," 15 *JAG Journal* (October–November, 1961), pp. 143–148, 166, 168; Ferenc A. Váli, "The Santa Maria Case," 56 *Northwestern University Law Review* (March–April, 1961), pp. 168–175.

An arresting illustration of this category was the Convention concerning the Abolition of the Liquor Traffic Among the Fishermen of the North Sea, signed in 1887 by Great Britain, Belgium, Denmark, France, Germany, and the Netherlands. The purpose of that agreement was the prohibition of the sale of liquor to the crews of fishing vessels in the North Sea, as well as the licensing and regulation of the so-called bumboats which brought provisions to the fishing vessels. The treaty granted the right of visit and search, as well as of arrest, to the public vessels of all signatory states, in order to ease the burden of enforcing the prohibition in question.[22]

Treaties for the Suppression of Slavery. In another connection a desire to eliminate the traffic in slaves led to the conclusion of a number of treaties which procured a minimum of international cooperation and conferred, in some instances, specific reciprocal rights of visit and search. Great Britain, which had abolished slavery in its empire as early as 1807, had persuaded France to agree in the Treaty of Paris of 1814 to assist in the promotion of a scheme to eliminate the traffic in slaves entirely. Also, at the Congress of Vienna, in 1815, the British government had obtained from the assembled delegations a solemn condemnation of the slave trade. But such promises and resolutions were not enough, of course, to bring an actual end to the slave trade.

Hence the British government proceeded to conclude bilateral treaties with a considerable number of countries, each of which agreements provided for reciprocal rights of visit and search by public ships of private vessels flying the flag of the other party. In addition, a number of multilateral conventions were developed after 1840, culminating in the Convention of St. Germain (1919) which provided for the complete abolition of slavery and of traffic in slaves on land or by sea; and the Slavery Convention of 1926, ultimately ratified or adhered to by over forty states, essentially reaffirming in more emphatic terms, and for a greater number of countries, the contents of the St. Germain agreement.[23]

In 1956, a United Nations Anti-Slavery Convention was submitted to the members for ratification. Supplementing a 1926 agreement, the instrument met with slow response on its way to general acceptance. By the end of 1967, forty-two member states had not yet ratified the convention, which, unfortunately, did not include any realistic enforcement machinery.

By the time of the first Geneva Conference on the Law of the Sea, there could exist little doubt that, primarily as a result of conventional

---

[22] See Lauterpacht's *Oppenheim*, Vol. I, p. 620; Higgins–Colombos, p. 310; and Reiff, pp. 125–127.

[23] For all these agreements, consult Lauterpacht's *Oppenheim*, Vol. I, pp. 733–735, Whiteman, Vol. IV, pp. 645–648, as well as Howard H. Wilson, "Some Principal Aspects of British Efforts to Crush the African Slave Trade, 1807–1929," 44 *A.J.I.L.* (1950), pp. 505–526.

international law, buttressed by a host of domestic legislation, the traffic in slaves could be regarded as being virtually on the same level as piracy: as a crime against mankind.

The Convention of the High Seas of 1958 provided, in Article 13, that

Every state shall adopt effective measures to prevent and punish the transport of slaves in ships authorized to fly its flag, and to prevent the unlawful use of its flag, for that purpose. Any slave taking refuge on board any ship, whatever its flag, shall *ipso facto* be free.

And Article 22, paragraph 1-b, of the same convention reaffirmed the right of all public vessels to stop, visit, and search any foreign merchant ship on the high seas when there was reasonable ground for suspecting that the foreign ship was engaged in the slave trade.

CONTIGUOUS ZONES

A generally recognized rule of customary international law holds that a coastal state may exercise protective as well as preventive control over a strip or belt of the high seas contiguous (or adjacent) to its territorial waters.[24] One obvious reason for the development of this principle was a desire to avoid what other states would consider to be excessive claims by a coastal state to sovereign rights over a broad belt of the high seas.

The United States has on many occasions asserted jurisdiction for limited purposes over adjacent waters. Thus, since 1790, it has claimed jurisdiction for customs purposes up to a distance of twelve miles from shore. Under a number of special "liquor treaties" with Great Britain and other states during the prohibition era, the United States had the right to stop, board, search, and seize vessels of the contracting states within one hour's sailing distance from the shore. When the Eighteenth Amendment to the Constitution had been repealed, an Anti-Smuggling Act was adopted in 1935, which authorized the President to establish at need so-called customs-enforcement areas up to fifty nautical miles beyond the twelve-mile limit and 100 miles in each lateral direction from the "place of hovering."

The 1958 Geneva Conference on the Law of the Sea dealt with the question of contiguous zones in Article 24 of the Convention on the Territorial Sea and the Contiguous Zone.[25] The convention provided that a coastal state could exercise, in a zone of the high seas contiguous to its territorial sea, controls necessary to prevent infringement of its customs, fiscal, immigration, or sanitary regulations within its territory or terri-

---

[24] See Whiteman, Vol. IV, pp. 480–498.
[25] Text in 52 *A.J.I.L.* (1958), p. 840. The convention entered into force on September 10, 1964; by December, 1968, thirty-four states had ratified it or acceded to it.

torial sea, and that such coastal state had a right to punish violations of such regulations committed in the contiguous zone.

More important, the convention provided that a contiguous zone could not extend beyond a limit of twelve miles from the baselines from which the breadth of the territorial sea was measured. This provision presupposed, therefore, that the width of the territorial sea was fixed at a distance less than twelve miles.

The 1958 Conference thus reaffirmed the traditional customary law concept of the contiguous zone, but it also refused to accept the demand of a number of states for a grant of special and exclusive fishery rights in the contiguous zone and assigned to the coastal state.

The waters of the contiguous zone, beyond the outer limits of territorial waters, are considered to be integral parts of the high seas.

CONSERVATION ZONES

The principle of the freedom of the high seas implies, at least at first glance, a right for the citizens of every country to engage in the exploitation of the resources of those seas, particularly as far as fishing is concerned.

This traditional view began to be questioned seriously, however, toward the middle of this century when it appeared that overfishing constituted a growing menace to what was regarded as a resource common to all mankind.

U.S. Conservation Zones. The United States was the first major nation to indicate its concern in this matter. On September 28, 1945, President Truman proclaimed the establishment of conservation zones in the high seas contiguous to the coasts of this country.[26] In areas where only American nationals had been fishing, such zones were to be created and controlled by the United States on a unilateral basis; in areas where fishing had been shared with the nationals of other states, it was proposed to set up conservation zones by agreement between the governments concerned.

More recently, a 1966 act defined the zones more precisely as a strip "nine nautical miles beyond and adjacent to the present territorial waters of the United States." [27]

Numerous incidents in the spring of 1967, stemming from the violation of the conservation zone (most cases involved Soviet vessels) uniformly resulted in the conviction of the captains in question, with fines imposed averaging $10,000. Similar incidents began to multiply in February, 1969, off the coast of Virginia.

---

[26] The text of the proclamation may be found in Reiff, p. 381, and in 40 *A.J.I.L.* (1946), Supp., pp. 46–47. See also Whiteman, Vol. IV, pp. 932–1240.

[27] *An Act to Establish a Contiguous Fishery Zone Beyond the Territorial Sea of the United States,* 80 Stat. 908 (1966); see also the useful and extensively documented *Note* on this law by Lucien E. Moreau, in 8 *Harvard International Law Journal* (Winter, 1967), pp. 156–168.

The initial American step toward the conservation of the resources of the high seas was followed shortly by similar conservation measures proclaimed by other countries for specified areas of the high seas off their coasts. In a number of instances, no question of joint control or even consultation was involved, but in some other cases outright discrimination against foreign fishermen became established policy for the new conservation zones.[28]

"WAR OF THE FISHES"

The most publicized early dispute concerning offshore fishing rights was the "War of the Fishes" between Iceland and Great Britain.[29] The disagreement, which was accompanied by comic opera overtones reminiscent of the better efforts of Messrs. Gilbert and Sullivan, had its origin in a unilateral decision on the part of Iceland in June, 1958, to extend its *territorial* waters to a twelve-mile limit and to prohibit all fishing by foreigners within that area.

Great Britain indicated a willingness to let Iceland establish an exclusive fisheries zone for two miles beyond the earlier four-mile territorial sea limit, with additional concessions to be made in a few important fishing areas.

Iceland stood firm on its claim to a twelve-mile territorial sea but began to hint about withdrawal from the North Atlantic Treaty Organization. Clashes between British frigates and Icelandic coast guard vessels became more numerous, accompanied by attempted rammings and the firing of blank shells. Finally, in November, 1960, both governments announced the end of the feud. Great Britain accepted the Icelandic twelve-mile limit, and Iceland in turn granted British fishermen a three-year period during which, at specified times and in specified areas, they could continue to fish up to six miles off the Icelandic shores.[30]

Declaration of Santiago. One of the most extensive set of claims to exclusive control over rather large areas of the high seas was created by the Joint Declaration on Maritime Zones (Santiago, August 18, 1952) through which Chile, Ecuador, and Peru (Costa Rica later adhered to the Declaration) created conservation zones extending for 200 miles from their coasts; each of the three states proposed to maintain its own control over its claimed zone. It should be noted, incidentally, that Chile and Peru

[28] See the list of such conservation zone limits, as of June 1, 1966, in a letter from the Department of State to Senator W. G. Magnuson, in 60 *A.J.I.L.* (1966), pp. 831–833, at p. 832; see also U.N. Food and Agriculture Organization, *Fisheries Technical Paper No. 79* (Rome, Italy: FAO, December, 1968), reproduced in part in 8 *International Legal Materials* (1969), pp. 516–539.

[29] See *The New York Times*, June 5, 1958; "The Codfish War," 72 *Time* (September 15, 1958), pp. 23–24; and "War's End," *ibid.*, 77 (March 10, 1961), p. 32; and Frank Goldsworthy, "More Fun than Fury in the Fish War," 87 *U.S. Naval Institute Proceedings* (February, 1961), pp. 58–67.

[30] Text of agreement in 57 *A.J.I.L.* (1963), Supp., pp. 490–492.

individually had advanced claims to such conservation areas as early as 1947.

Foreign fishermen desirous of exploiting the resources of these zones were required to obtain permits from the relevant coastal state. Ecuador, for instance, forced captains to buy a license good for one trip only, at a cost of $16 for each registered ton of their ship's capacity, and Peru levied a tax of about $14 a ton on fish caught, for export, within 200 miles of its coast.

El Salvador included a provision in its 1950 constitution claiming a 200-mile conservation zone but declared at the second Geneva Conference on the Law of the Sea (1960) that freedom of fishing rights would be recognized in that zone if new rules of international law covering the subject were to be developed.

Argentina has claimed, since 1946, exclusive fishing rights in the *epicontinental sea,* or waters above its continental shelf extending some 200 miles into the Atlantic.

The issuance of the Declaration of Santiago in 1952 was followed almost immediately by the seizure and subsequent fining of American fishing vessels operating within 200 miles of the Peruvian and Ecuadorian coasts. The Conference on United States–Ecuadorian Fishery Relations, held at Quito from March 25 to April 14, 1953, dealt, *inter alia,* with the right of innocent passage claimed by such American vessels. But seizures of such ships by Ecuadorian and Peruvian authorities did not stop and, in 1954, actually increased in number.[31] The incidents in question culminated in the seizures in March, 1955, of the American ships *Santa Anna* and *Arctic Maid,* some fifteen and twenty-five miles, respectively, from the coast. The Ecuadorian patrol boat effecting the arrest caused serious injury, by gun fire, of an American seaman. After being brought into an Ecuadorian port, the captains of the two ships were fined in excess of $49,000 for fishing for tuna without licenses inside Ecuador's conservation zone. New incidents of a similar nature, involving eleven U.S. fishing vessels, occurred between February and the latter part of June, 1969, and contributed greatly to a deterioration of relations between the United States on the one hand and Peru and Ecuador on the other. On July 8, 1969, Peru, Chile and Ecuador agreed to meet with U.S. technical experts at the end of the month to discuss Pacific fishing problems.

U.S. Fisherman's Protective Act. In response to the frequent seizures of American fishing vessels and of the imposition of heavy fines on their captains or owners, the Congress of the United States passed on August 27, 1954, the Fisherman's Protective Act. This law provides that the United States government will reimburse fishermen for all fines imposed on them by foreign states for fishing within zones or territorial sea limits

---

[31] See *Case of Sauger et al.,* Peru, Port Officer of Paita, November 26, 1954, reported in 49 *A.J.I.L.* (1955), pp. 575–577; consult also 81 *Time* (June 7, 1963), pp. 25–26.

not recognized by the United States. The latter would then attempt to recover the sums in question from the foreign states involved. In addition, the United States has repeatedly assisted American shipowners in presenting their claims for losses and damages sustained in the seizures of fishing vessels.[32]

Restrictions on Foreign Fishing Interests. There were, and are in some instances, other parts of the high seas that have been closed off or severely restricted by coastal states against foreign fishing interests. In March, 1956, for example, the Soviet Union imposed rigid controls on Japanese salmon fishing in the Sea of Okhotsk, the western Bering Sea, and a large area east and south of the Kamchatka peninsula. South Korea surrounded itself in 1952 with a sixty-mile-wide conservation zone, barring all Japanese fishermen from the area. In the China Sea, no Japanese fishing vessels are legally permitted to come within 100 miles of the coast of Communist China. And a United States–Canada–Japan treaty of 1952 closed to Japanese fishing vessels a vast stretch of waters in the Pacific, from the northern tip of Alaska to south of Hawaii and thence to the southern tip of California.

Conservation Treaties. Excessive unilateral acts are at best of doubtful legality when measured against the rules of international law, particularly against the principle of the freedom of the high seas, limited as such may be in modern times. On the other hand, numerous treaties have been concluded between regional groupings of interested states for the purpose of conserving certain species of marine life or of all species in a particular part of the high seas. For instance, the Indo-Pacific Fisheries Council (1949), the General Fisheries Council for the Mediterranean (1952), the South Pacific Commission (1947), and the Caribbean Commission serve such purposes. A somewhat larger number of international agreements provide for the establishment of commissions, either of an advisory type or of an administrative nature. Examples of this group are the Northwest Atlantic Fisheries Convention (1949), the North Pacific High Seas Fisheries Convention (1952), and the Northern Pacific Halibut Fisheries Convention of 1953.

Two of the more recent regional conservation agreements were the 1964 Fisheries Convention (North-East Atlantic Area) adopted at the European Fisheries Conference,[33] and the U.S.–U.S.S.R. agreements of February 13, 1967, and December 13, 1968, relating to fishing problems in the Eastern Bering Sea and along the U.S. Pacific coast, in the first case and in the middle Atlantic in the second instance.[34]

[32] Consult the Department of State Memoranda on the *Valley Gold* and the *Valley Ace* (1962), two vessels fined by Mexico, in 57 *A.J.I.L.* (1963), pp. 899–902.
[33] Text, with relevant supplementary documents, in 58 *A.J.I.L.* (1964), pp. 1068–1080.
[34] See 56 *Department of State Bulletin* (1967), p. 331, and 8 *International Legal Materials* (1969), pp. 502–515, respectively.

International Whaling Commission. On a still broader basis, both in scope of activities and in areas of the seas involved, is the work of the International Whaling Commission, established by convention in 1946. This body not only sets quotas for whaling but also possesses the authority to end a particular season as soon as the quotas have been filled.[35]

NEW CONVENTION OF THE 1958 GENEVA CONFERENCE

The fact that the numerous earlier conventions did not represent a unified system despite the obvious relationships obtaining between their several subject matters led the delegates to the 1958 Geneva Conference to adopt a new Convention on Fishing and Conservation of the Living Resources of the High Seas.[36]

Special Rights and Interests. In brief summary: the new convention reaffirmed the freedom of citizens of all states to fish in and on the high seas, subject, however, to certain rights and interests of coastal states. A state whose nationals alone fished a certain stock in a certain area of the high seas could, at its discretion, adopt for its citizens any and all conservation measures deemed necessary. If the nationals of two or more states fished the same stock or stocks of fish or other living marine resource in a particular area of the high seas, the states concerned were, at the request of any of them, to enter into negotiations for the adoption of an agreement applying conservation regulations, each to their nationals. If, on the other hand, nationals of different states fished different stocks in the same area, the provisions calling for negotiation of an agreement among the states was not to apply.

If negotiations failed to result in an agreement called for under the convention, any of the states concerned could initiate proceedings terminating in a binding decision by an impartial body (the word *arbitration* was not used in the instrument). This body was to be a special commission of five members, appointed in accordance with the provisions of Article 9 of the convention.

The special rights and interests of the coastal states, mentioned above, merit brief comment. Under Article 7 of the convention, any coastal state was entitled to undertake unilateral conservation measures in any area of the high seas adjacent to its territorial sea, provided that negotiations with other states whose nationals were fishing there had not led to an agreement within six months. This provision was the result of extremely strong

---

[35] The text of the basic convention may be found in 40 *A.J.I.L.* (1945), Supp., pp. 174–185; see also Reiff, pp. 293–397.

[36] The text has been reprinted in 52 *A.J.I.L.* (1958), Supp., pp. 851–858; see also Sørensen, *op. cit.*, pp. 195–255, at pp. 220–225, and William W. Bishop, Jr., "International Law Commission Draft Articles on Fisheries," 50 *A.J.I.L.* (1956), pp. 627–636. The convention, in force since March 20, 1966, had been ratified or acceded to by twenty-five states by December, 1968 (not including, however, *inter alia*, Canada, France, Iceland, the Netherlands, and Portugal).

pressure exerted at the Geneva Conference by most delegations against the states whose citizens were engaged in large-scale fishing on the high seas.

The principle laid down in Article 7 represents a serious encroachment on the older and basic principle of the freedom of the high seas, but its very existence is proof of the fact that international law is not static but is changing, slowly but surely. The weakness of the article in question was that no details were supplied as to the lawful extent of conservation zones established by coastal states acting under the provisions of the convention, nor were there given any clear-cut indications as to enforcement rights of conservation regulations.

SECOND GENEVA CONFERENCE (1960)

Because of the failure of the 1958 Conference to solve a number of important problems connected with the high seas, the General Assembly called a second conference which met in Geneva from March 17 to April 27, 1960, with eighty-seven nations participating. The two major questions to be considered were the breadth of the territorial sea (see Chapter 17) and fishery limits. No one could deny the urgency of arriving at some agreement on these subjects, but the Second Geneva Conference failed to achieve this goal. Opposition on the part of many newly independent nations to a restriction of their proclaimed conservation zones as well as the system of voting adopted at the conference precluded any agreement on fishery rights.[37]

Prevention of Pollution. The laws of the sea were augmented in 1958 when Article 24 of the Geneva Convention on the High Seas stipulated that each state should draw up regulations to prevent pollution of the seas by the discharge of oil from ships or pipelines or resulting from the exploitation and exploration of the seabed and its subsoil, taking account of existing treaty provisions on this subject.[38] The major multilateral instrument already in effect in this sphere was the International Convention for the Prevention of Pollution of the Sea by Oil (London, 1954), effective on July 26, 1958. That treaty called on all ratifying states to forbid the discharge of oil from ships sailing under their flag within specified areas of the sea—normally extending fifty miles from land. Regrettably enough, the practical consequences of the 1954 agreement have been slight, owing

[37] See Arthur H. Dean, "The Second Geneva Conference on the Law of the Sea: The Fight for Freedom of the Seas," 54 *A.J.I.L.* (1960), pp. 751–789, as well as the critical reply of Alfonso García Robles, "The Second United Nations Conference on the Law of the Sea—A Reply," *ibid.*, 55 (1961), pp. 669–675, and the rebuttal, "Response of Arthur H. Dean," *ibid.*, pp. 675–680.

[38] In connection with repeated instances of widespread ocean (and coastal) pollution by wrecked tankers (such as the *Torrey Canyon*, off England in 1967), the Office of the Legal Adviser of the Department of State prepared an instructive commentary on a questionnaire prepared by the International Maritime Committee: see text in 62 *A.J.I.L.* (1968), pp. 949–954.

to the limited number of states which have seen fit to ratify the instrument: Canada, Mexico, and a few European nations, none of them classifiable among the major maritime states of the world.[39]

Nuclear Tests. The resumption of nuclear testing by the U.S.S.R and the United States in 1962, together with the growing problem of how to dispose of dangerous radioactive waste materials, pointed up the relevance of the inclusion of Article 25 in the 1958 Convention on the High Seas. The article provided that each state should take measures to prevent pollution of the seas from the dumping of radioactive waste, taking into account any standards and regulations that might be formulated by competent international organizations.

Article 25 also called for cooperation by all states with the relevant international agency in taking measures for the prevention of pollution of the seas or of the airspace above, resulting from any activities with radioactive materials or other harmful agents.

Both articles dealing with pollution omit reference to foreign ships operating on the high seas: by implication, each state could enforce preventive measures *on the high seas* only against vessels flying its own flag.

The reference in paragraph 2 of Article 25 to "activities with radioactive materials" appeared to refer clearly to the controversial subject of nuclear tests on the high seas. International lawyers differed rather sharply as to the legality of such tests. Some, such as M. S. McDougal, defended nuclear tests as a lawful security and defense measure in an unsettled world.[40] Others, such as E. Margolis, held that nuclear tests, being prejudicial to the free use of the high seas by other states and their citizens, represented a clear violation of the principle of the freedom of the seas.[41]

Finally, at the initiative of the Indian delegation, the Geneva Conference adopted a resolution which gave expression to a widespread apprehension on the part of many states that nuclear test explosions did constitute an infringement of the freedom of the seas and indicated the decision of the Conference to refer the whole matter to the General Assembly for appropriate action.

The question of nuclear tests, however, was partially settled outside the framework of international organization. After 425 announced test blasts, the United States, Great Britain, and the Soviet Union succeeded, in ten days of negotiation, in producing the Nuclear Test Ban Treaty (Moscow Treaty) of 1963. The instrument, signed on August 5, 1963, and in force October 10, 1963, represented an agreement among the three powers to "prohibit, to prevent and not to carry out any nuclear weapons test explosion or any other nuclear explosion" in the atmosphere, in outer

---

[39] Whiteman, Vol. IV, pp. 687–726.

[40] Egon Schwelb, "The Nuclear Test Ban Treaty and International Law," 58 *A.J.I.L.* (1964), pp. 642–670; Reiff, pp. 363–368; Whiteman, Vol. IV, pp. 542–631.

[41] Emanuel Margolis, "The Hydrogen Bomb Tests and International Law," 64 *Yale Law Journal* (1955), pp. 629–647.

space, or under water. Underground testing was excluded deliberately because of Russian insistence that adequate inspection of such tests would open the way to espionage.

The three parties also agreed in the treaty to refrain "from causing, encouraging or in any way participating in the carrying out of any nuclear weapons test whatever." This provision was quite obviously aimed at France and at Communist China.

The treaty, to be of indefinite duration, permitted unilateral denunciation by any signatory on three-months' advance notice at any time that "extraordinary events . . . have jeopardized the supreme interests of its country." It also invited other nations to become signatories, and in a matter of weeks over a hundred additional states had thus adhered to the agreement. Amendments to the treaty could be proposed by any such new subscriber, but the three original signers retained a veto power over such future proposals for changes in the instrument.[42]

Resources of the Seabed. The latest development concerning the high seas has been a pronounced increase in interest in the development of resources in the deep-sea floor—and the question of protecting such resources. Whereas exploitation of the known or suspected resources beneath the high seas is not likely to become an actuality in the immediate future, the technical means for such exploitation have been, or are being, developed at this time. Given the growing global demand for industrial raw materials, some of the resources beneath the sea are likely to become attractive enough to warrant actual exploitation in the foreseeable future.[43]

The General Assembly of the United Nations has already adopted a number of resolutions dealing with resources beneath the high seas and, at its 2nd Session in late 1968, resumed the study of the problem.[44]

In 1969, an American presidential commission has urged the establishment of manned exploration bases on the deep-sea floor, to prepare for the actual and inevitable exploitation of seabed resources by 2000 A.D.[45]

Concurrently, a number of interesting private proposals for conserv-

[42] See also James H. McBride, *The Test Ban Treaty* (New York: H. Regnery, 1967). The text of the actual agreement may be found in 57 *A.J.I.L.* (1963), pp. 1026–1028; at the time of writing, France and Communist China were the only major countries that had not signed and ratified the agreement, or adhered to it subsequently.

[43] See the penetrating and well-documented analysis by Richard Young, "The Legal Regime of the Deep Sea Floor," 62 *A.J.I.L.* (1968), pp. 641–653, as well as Robert A. Creamer, "Title to the Deep Seabed: Prospects for the Future," 9 *Harvard International Law Journal* (Spring, 1968), pp. 205–231.

[44] See GA Res. 2172 (XXI), December 8, 1966; GA Res. 2340 (XXII), December 18, 1967; and especially GA Res. 2467 A-C (XXIII), December 21, 1968, in 8 *International Legal Materials* (1969), pp. 201–208. Consult also the analysis by Arvid Pardo (author of the 'Maltese Proposition' before the General Assembly), "Who Will Control the Seabed?" 47 *Foreign Affairs* (1968), pp. 123–137, and the earlier E. W. S. Hull, "The Political Ocean," *ibid.*, 45 (1967), pp. 492–502.

[45] *Minneapolis* (Minn.) *Tribune*, January 12, 1969, pp. 1-A, 8-A.

ing—or administering, as the case may be—the resources of the seabed have attracted considerable interest.[46]

Because all the resources in question are located beyond the limits of the continental shelf, interesting and complicated legal questions are bound to arise and will have to be settled when current discussions reach the level of international negotiation and ultimately of treaty making.

Sea Cables and Pipelines. A more traditional segment of the law of the sea has to do with submarine cables and pipelines on the bed of the high seas. All states possess an undoubted right to lay such pipelines and cables. No coastal state may impede the laying or maintenance of such installations by a foreign state, subject to an obvious modern right to take reasonable measures for the exploration and exploitation of the continental shelf and its resources.[47] The Iranian delegation, in signing the 1958 Convention on the High Seas, added a reservation to this principle (which appeared in Article 26, paragraph 2, of the instrument), emphasizing that the laying of submarine cables and pipelines was to be subject to the authorization of the coastal state, insofar as the continental shelf area was concerned.

Whenever a state undertakes to lay undersea cables or pipelines, it must pay due attention to cables or pipeline installations already in position on the seabed.

SUGGESTED READINGS

THE HIGH SEAS: GENERAL

Briggs, pp. 304–316; Lauterpacht's *Oppenheim,* Vol. I, pp. 587–608; Svarlien, pp. 185–192, 197–205; D. W. Bowett, *The Law of the Sea* (Manchester: University of Manchester Press; Dobbs Ferry, N.Y.: Oceana Publications, 1967); Myres S. McDougal and William T. Burke, *The Public Order of the Oceans* (New Haven: Yale University Press, 1962); Whiteman, Vol. IV, 631–633 (on landlocked states); Myres S. McDougal and Norbert A. Schlei, "The Hydrogen Bomb Tests in Perspective: Lawful Measures for Security," 64 *Yale Law Journal* (1955), pp. 648–710; see also Myres S. McDougal, "The Hydrogen Bomb Tests and the International Law of the Sea," 49 *A.J.I.L.* (1955), pp. 356–361, Stanley V. Anderson, "A Critique of Professor Myres S. McDougal's Doctrine of Interpretation by Major Purpose," 57 *A.J.I.L.* (1963), pp. 378–383, and Reiff, pp. 363–368.

CONTIGUOUS ZONES

Briggs, pp. 372–377; Lewis M. Alexander, ed., *The Law of the Sea: Offshore Boundaries and Zones* (Columbus: Ohio State University Press, 1967); Lloyd

[46] See, *inter alia,* "Uses of the Sea," Report of the 33rd American Assembly, May 2–5, 1968; Elisabeth Mann Borgese, *The Ocean Regime* (Santa Barbara, Calif.: Fund for the Republic, 1968), a research paper of the Center for the Study of Democratic Institutions, containing a complete Draft Treaty, together with commentary, for an international authority outside the United Nations.

[47] See Whiteman, Vol. IV, pp. 727–739.

C. Fell, "Maritime Contiguous Zones," 62 *Michigan Law Review* (1964), pp. 848–864.

Cases

Cook v. *United States*, Supreme Court, 1933, 288 U.S. 102.
The Grace and Ruby, United States, District Court, Mass., 1922, 283 F. 475.

HOT PURSUIT

Cases

Church v. *Hubbart*, United States, Supreme Court, 1804, 2 Cranch (6 U.S.)
    187 ["Hovering" Vessels].
The I'm Alone, U.S. Department of State, *Arbitration Series*, No. 2 (1–7),
    1931–1935 [Hot Pursuit].
The Katina, Egypt, Mixed Court of Appeal of Alexandria, 1929, in 24 *A.J.I.L.*
    (1930), pp. 175–181 [Hot Pursuit].

POLICE ACTIVITIES AT SEA

"International Convention Relating to the Arrest of Sea-Going Ships" (Brussels, May 10, 1952; in force November 20, 1955), text in 53 *A.J.I.L.* (1959), pp. 539–545; Harvard Research in International Law, "Draft Convention and Commentary on Piracy," 26 *A.J.I.L.* (1932), Supp., pp. 739–785; Hyde, I, pp. 765–777.

Cases

In re Piracy Jure Gentium, Great Britain, Judicial Committee of the Privy
    Council, 1934, [1934] A.C. 586.
The Le Louis, Great Britain, High Court of Admiralty, 1817, 2 Dobson 210.
The Magellan Pirates, Great Britain, High Court of Admiralty, 1853, 1 Spinks
    81.
United States v. *Smith*, United States, Supreme Court, 1820, 5 Wheaton 153.

CONSERVATION ZONES

Douglas M. Johnston, *The International Law of Fisheries* (New Haven: Yale University Press, 1965); Guenter Weissberg, *Recent Developments in the Law of the Sea and the Japanese-Korean Fishery Dispute* (The Hague: Martinus Nijhoff, 1966); J. E. Carroz and A. G. Roche, "The Proposed International Commission for the Conservation of Atlantic Tuna," 61 *A.J.I.L.* (1967), pp. 673–702; "Convention Concerning the High Seas Fisheries of the Northwest Pacific Ocean (Japan–U.S.S.R.), Signed at Moscow, May 14, 1956," *ibid.*, 53 (1959), Supp., pp. 763–773.

DEEP-OCEAN-FLOOR RESOURCES

Edmund A. Gullion, ed., *Uses of the Sea—An American Assembly Book* (Englewood Cliffs, N.J.: Prentice-Hall, 1968); F. V. García Amador, *The Exploitation and Conservation of the Resources of the Sea* (Leiden: A. W. Sijthoff, 1959); William T. Burke, *Ocean Sciences, Technology, and the Future Law of the Sea* (Columbus: Ohio State University Press, 1966); Committee on Foreign Affairs, House of Representatives, 90th Congress, 1st Sess., *The United Nations and the Issue of Deep Ocean Resources* (Interim Report, together with Hearings) (Washington: U.S. Government Printing Office, 1967—H. Rep. 999).

19

Jurisdiction Over Vessels

JURISDICTION ON THE HIGH SEAS

UNDER certain conditions, a state may lawfully extend its effective jurisdiction beyond its normal territorial limits. For instance, the allegiance of a citizen to his state is a personal one and is preserved no matter how far the citizen may travel into the world. If and when he returns to the territory of his state, the latter may hold him responsible for what he did while abroad. If the citizen is aboard a vessel flying his country's flag, he is legally in the same position as if he were back home in the actual territory of his state; hence that state may apply its domestic law to him. It is in this sense that a national vessel and, incidentally, a national plane (registered in a particular country) may be thought of correctly as a kind of an extension of a nation's territory.

Every state has the right to sail ships under its flag on the high seas.[1] In the past, this privilege was reserved to coastal or island states.

This tradition was first set aside in the various peace treaties ending World War I, which provided for the international (maritime) recognition of the flag of the Allied and Associated Powers. Soon afterward, in 1922, the states participating in the Barcelona Conference agreed to extend recognition of national flags for maritime purposes to all countries adhering to the Declaration resulting from the deliberations of the conference. During World War II, the major belligerents agreed to recognize the flag of Switzerland on the oceans of the world, and the old jibe about a Swiss navy became obsolete. It might be mentioned, as a matter of minor interest, that by agreement among the opposing belligerents, a portion of the Italian port of Genoa was set aside as a Swiss port-of-entry and guaranteed immunity from attack. Sealed freight trains conspicuously displaying the Swiss white cross on the sides and roofs of cars carried goods between Switzerland and its Genoese terminal zone. Currently thirty-three vessels ply the oceans under the Swiss flag.

Each state determines for itself the conditions for the grant of its na-

---

[1] See Myres S. McDougal, William T. Burke, and Ivan A. Vlasic, "The Maintenance of Public Order at Sea and the Nationality of Ships," 54 *A.J.I.L.* (1960), pp. 25–116, at pp. 66–70.

tionality to vessels, for the registration of ships in its territory, and for the right of ships to fly its flag.[2]

Generally speaking, once a vessel has been registered in a given state, it is regarded by that state, as well as by other states, as constituting a legal person; it may be sued and it may sue. Its nationality determines, at least on the high seas, the national location of most acts taking place aboard it.

The concept that vessels flying the flag of a given state represented a sort of floating extension of the territory of that state was taken quite literally in former days. A very large number of decisions handed down, especially by British and American courts, affirmed this fiction of extra-territoriality. In the twentieth century, the view has been adopted that ships shall sail under the flag of one state and, save in exceptional cases expressly provided for in treaties, shall be subject to its exclusive jurisdiction on the high seas. This means that its laws and regulations apply to most acts undertaken aboard the vessel, but that the latter cannot be regarded as part of the territory of the flag state, *except* in the case of public warships.

As was pointed out, the exclusive jurisdiction in question here must be viewed with minor reservations: in time of peace, the public vessels of all maritime states have rights of visit and search when there are grounds for suspicion that a given ship may be engaged in piracy or in the slave trade. Furthermore, a state has an undoubted right, under self-defense, to seize a vessel flying a foreign flag when it is suspected that the flag is used fraudulently or that the vessel is used by rebels or insurgents in an attack on the arresting state. And, finally, in time of war, belligerent warships possess extensive powers of visit and search to enforce contraband and blockade regulations. (See Chapter 29.)

Flags of Convenience. The national right to register vessels has led several states, particularly Panama and Liberia, to enact rather liberal legislation enabling the registration of ships owned and operated by foreign companies. The tonnage now under the flags of these companies and of a number of small states (for the convenience of the shipowners, hence the origin of the term *flag of convenience*) has increased sharply in recent decades until today both Panama and Liberia rank ostensibly among the top eight maritime nations in the world.

The reasons for adopting a flag of convenience are numerous and may include such considerations as low taxes; legislation providing for lower wages to seamen that those prevailing in the country in which the owners of the vessels do business; absence of, or minimal, social security contributions by the owners of the vessel under the laws of the registering state; and possibly absence of, or weakness of, labor unions in that country. The registering states appear to lack the administrative machinery to enforce whatever legislation they may have enacted for vessels flying their

[2] See also Herman Meijers, *The Nationality of Ships* (The Hague: Martinus Nijhoff, 1967); Whiteman, Vol. IX, pp. 1–51.

flags, and, furthermore, most of the ships in question never call at the ports of their "home" state. In consequence, real or fancied abuses have led repeatedly to picketing of such vessels when they arrive in the ports of the country in which the owners are domiciled, and series of labor disputes have punctuated the maritime history of several Western nations, particularly the United States.

Despite the traditional rule about granting a vessel the right to fly the flag of the registering state, Article 5 of the 1958 Convention of the High Seas imposed a rather interesting limitation on the freedom of a state to grant nationality to a vessel:

. . . There must exist a genuine link between the state and the ship; in particular, the state must effectively exercise its jurisdiction and control in administrative, technical and social matters over ships flying its flag.

This wording might be interpreted to mean that in the absence of such a genuine link, another state might feel free to deny recognition to the asserted nationality of a vessel flying a flag of convenience, to treat it, in other words, as a stateless vessel and to bar it from its ports.

At the 1958 Geneva Conference, Article 5 had been opposed by Panama, Liberia, and the United States. The same three nations, as an alternative proposal, sought to deny the right of another state to consider a vessel as stateless if no genuine link to the country of registration could be shown to exist.

The inclusion of the limitation in the final version of the convention did not, of course, settle the problem. To date, no instance of a denial of recognition of nationality because of the absence of a genuine link has occurred, and until such takes place, the traditional right of a state to decide who shall be entitled to its nationality remains unchanged in practice. On the other hand, one major legal precedent centering on the "genuine link" has been recorded in another connection,[3] and may serve to assist in a future court decision about vessels flying a flag of convenience without a genuine link to the registering state.

Ships can sail under the flag of only one state, and on the high seas are under the jurisdiction of that state alone. No ship can change its flag during a voyage or while in a port of call, except in the event of a real trans-

---

[3] *Nottebohm Case (Liechtenstein v. Guatemala)*, International Court of Justice, 1955, *I.C.J. Reports, 1955*, p. 4. See in particular the detailed and annotated discussion both of the question of a "genuine link" and of the issues raised by "flags of convenience" in McDougal, Burke, and Vlasic, *op. cit.*, at pp. 28–40 and especially at pp. 104–111; consult also the appraisal of the problem by Ira Dye, "Flags of Convenience: Maritime Dilemma," 88 *United States Naval Institute Proceedings* (February, 1962), pp. 76–87, and Thomas J. Romans, "The American Merchant Marine: Flags of Convenience and International Law," 3 *Virginia Journal of International Law* (1963), pp. 121–152. The most extensive study of the problems of flags of convenience has been undertaken by Boleslaw Adam Boczek in his *Flags of Convenience: An International Legal Study* (Cambridge: Harvard University Press, 1962).

fer of ownership or a change in registry. Should a vessel sail under the flags of two or more states, using them as convenience dictates, it is treated as a stateless vessel. On the other hand, a ship may lawfully fly the flag of an international organization (Art. 7, 1958 Geneva Convention). If and when a vessel should be entitled to fly, say, the flag of the United Nations, the question of a "genuine link" in the meaning of the 1958 Convention would then arise again in totally new surroundings and beset by new aspects and interpretations thereof.

A vessel displaying a flag not attributable to a member of the family of nations would be regarded as a stateless vessel.[4] The mere fact that a ship has no right to fly a flag does not, however, assimilate it to a pirate vessel, unless it has engaged in piratical acts. Normally a stateless vessel would not be admitted to the ports of any state.

The law of the flag state governs matters relating to internal affairs aboard a vessel, including discipline. However, if the "shipping articles" signed by members of the crew stipulate the application of the law of a state other than the flag state, then such stipulated law would apply, say, in injury claims.[5]

As mentioned earlier, a vessel is subject to the laws of the flag state. It is true that while in foreign waters, a ship owes what might be termed a limited allegiance to the foreign state in question; that is, it must obey navigation and similar regulations of the host country. But once the vessel returns to the high seas, it is bound by the law of the state in which it is registered. This principle was illustrated convincingly in a classic case in 1860:

REGINA v. LESLIE

Great Britain, Court of Criminal Appeal, 1860, 8 Cox's Criminal Cases 269

FACTS

Leslie was captain of the British private merchant vessel *Louisa Braginton*. When the ship came to the Chilean port of Valparaiso, the Chilean government contacted Leslie and persuaded him to sign a contract whereby he undertook to transport several Chilean citizens to Liverpool. The individuals in question had been banished from Chile for political reasons. They were taken under military guard to the port and placed aboard the *Louisa Braginton*. Whenever that vessel then touched a port on the voyage around South America and on to Liverpool, the exiled Chileans de-

---

[4] See *Naim-Molvan* v. *Attorney General for Palestine*, Great Britain, Privy Council, 1948, reported in 42 *A.J.I.L.* (1948), p. 953.

[5] See the relevant American cases of *Tjonaman* v. *A.S. Elittre*, U.S. Court of Appeals, 2nd Circuit, 1965, 340 F. 2d 290; *Shahid* v. *A/S J. Ludwig Mowinckeles Rederi*, U.S. District Court, S.D.N.Y., 1964, 236 F. Supp. 751; and especially *Kontos* v. *S.S. Sophie C.*, U.S. District Court, E.D. Pa., 1964, 236 F. Supp. 664. See also Whiteman, Vol. IX, pp. 51–83.

manded to be set ashore, but Leslie insisted on the fulfillment of his contract and brought the entire group to Liverpool. There the Chileans sued Leslie on charges of false imprisonment. The lower court ruled in favor of the plaintiffs and Leslie appealed to the Court of Criminal Appeals.

ISSUE

Was Leslie liable to an indictment in Great Britain for fulfilling his contract concluded in Chile with the government of that country?

DECISION

The conviction of Leslie was affirmed: he had been under the rule of English law as soon as he quit Chilean territorial waters.

REASONING

The conviction could not be sustained for what Leslie had done in Chile. It had to be assumed that in Chile the action of the local government toward its citizens was lawful; in consequence, Leslie was correct in what he did in Chile as an agent of the Chilean government.

However, the conviction had to be sustained for what Leslie did outside of Chilean territorial waters. As soon as he left the latter, he and his ship were subject to the laws of England, as were all persons, English and foreign, aboard the vessel. His activities subsequent to the departure from Chilean jurisdiction amounted to false imprisonment, for he took the Chileans without their consent to England, denying them the right to depart when they desired to leave his ship in other states. A Chilean captain and vessel would have acted correctly under the circumstances, but Leslie had violated the law of England.

Status of Warships. Warships on the high seas enjoy complete immunity from the jurisdiction of any foreign state. In order to be included in this category, a vessel must belong to the naval forces of a state, bear the external markings distinguishing warships of its nationality, be under the command of an officer commissioned by the government of the flag state, and be manned by a crew under regular naval discipline. An equal unlimited immunity is enjoyed on the high seas by vessels owned or operated by a state, provided they are used only on government noncommercial service.

Regulations for Safety at Sea. Every state is obligated to adopt measures for ships under its flag to ensure safety at sea, such as the use of signals, the maintenance of communications, the prevention of collisions.

In the event of a collision on the high seas, no penal or disciplinary proceedings may be instituted against allegedly responsible individuals except before the judicial or administrative authorities either of the flag state or of the state of which such a person is a national. This doctrine, accepted generally in recent decades, stands in sharp contrast to the former classic decision in the *Lotus Case.*[6]

A diplomatic conference, meeting in Brussels in 1952, disagreed with the conclusions of the Permanent Court in the *Lotus* decision and in conse-

[6] *The Lotus,* P.C.I.J., 1927, Ser. A, No. 10.

quence drafted the International Convention for the Unification of Certain Rules relating to Penal Jurisdiction in Matters of Collision and Other Incidents of Navigation, signed at Brussels on May 10, 1952. That instrument contained the provisions concerning trial of alleged offenders in connection with collisions on the high seas now reiterated in the 1958 Geneva Convention on the High Seas.

Again, every state is obligated to require its vessels to render assistance at sea to other vessels and persons in distress, provided, of course, that such can be done without unduly endangering the rescue vessel, its passengers, and its crew.

JURISDICTION OVER FOREIGN MERCHANT VESSELS IN NATIONAL WATERS AND PORTS

A foreign merchant vessel leaving the high seas and entering the territorial waters (and ports) of another state creates automatically a conflict between the jurisdiction applying to the vessel by virtue of its nationality and the physical jurisdiction into which it has come. This conflict has been adjusted, on the whole, by custom and treaty law, so that side by side there now exist a continuing but limited jurisdiction by the flag state and a rather extensive but *not* unlimited jurisdiction by the state in whose territory the vessel has entered.[7]

Right of Innocent Passage. The foreign vessel, on entering the territorial sea of the coastal state, has a right of innocent passage. This right includes stopping and anchoring, but only insofar as the same are incidental to ordinary navigation or are rendered necessary by *force majeure* or by distress. Passage of a foreign fishing vessel is not considered innocent if it fails to observe the laws and regulations issued by the coastal state in order to prevent such a vessel from fishing in the territorial sea. If the national security of the coastal state is felt to justify it, that state may suspend temporarily in specified areas of its territorial sea the right to innocent passage of foreign ships, provided no discrimination is shown between vessels of different nationalities. Such a suspension of the right of innocent passage normally takes effect only after it has been publicized. However, a coastal state may not suspend the innocent passage of foreign vessels through straits which are used for international navigation between one part of the high seas and another part of the high seas or the territorial sea of a foreign state.[8] On their part, foreign ships exercising their right to innocent passage are bound to comply with the laws and regulations

[7] On the general subject, consult Higgins-Colombos, pp. 239–251 as well as Chapter 17.

[8] Article 16, par. 4, of the 1958 (Geneva) Convention on the Territorial Sea and the Contiguous Zone, 52 *A.J.I.L.* (1958), Supp., p. 838. The I.L.C., in its draft of this paragraph, had used the expression "normally used for navigation," based on the decision of the International Court of Justice in the *Corfu Channel Case:* see 51 *A.J.I.L.* (1957), Supp., pp. 196–197.

of the coastal state, in conformity with international law, particularly with such rules as relate to transport and navigation.

The passage of a foreign vessel through the territorial sea is not considered innocent if it is prejudicial to the peace, order, or security of the coastal state. This means in practice that the vessel must not violate the prohibitions laid down by the coastal state in such matters as customs, imports, exports, transit prohibitions, and public health.

Criminal Jurisdiction. Internal discipline aboard a foreign vessel passing through the territorial sea normally is subject to the laws and regulations of the flag state, unless the captain of the vessel or a consul of the flag state requests the assistance of the authorities of the coastal state.

The coastal state may not take any steps on board a foreign ship passing through the territorial sea to arrest any person or to conduct any investigation in connection with any crime committed before the ship entered the territorial sea, if the ship, proceeding from a foreign port, is only passing through the territorial sea without entering internal waters.

When a foreign vessel is passing through the territorial sea, the criminal jurisdiction of the coastal state *should not* be exercised on board that vessel, to arrest any person or to conduct any investigation in connection with any crime committed on board the ship during its passage, except if the consequences of the crime somehow extend to the coastal state, or if it is of a nature to disturb the peace of the country or the good order of the territorial sea, or if it is necessary for the suppression of illegal traffic in narcotic drugs (Art. 19, par. 1, 1958 Convention on the Territorial Sea).

The same Article (19) of the 1958 Convention also provides that the preceding provisions do not affect the right of a coastal state to take any steps authorized by its laws for the purpose of an arrest or investigation aboard a foreign ship passing through the territorial sea after leaving internal waters. This provision confers on a coastal state greater powers over ships passing through the territorial sea after leaving that state's internal waters than over ships merely passing through the territorial sea. The logical assumption behind this differential treatment appears to be that the interests of a coastal state are more directly affected by ships stationary in the territorial sea, or passing through it after departing from a port, than by those engaged in mere innocent passage through the sea.

Finally, according to Article 20, paragraph 1, of the 1958 Geneva Convention the coastal state *should not* stop or divert a foreign ship passing through the territorial sea for the purpose of exercising civil jurisdiction in relation to a *person* on board the ship. On the other hand, the *ship* itself may be arrested or seized as the result of events occurring in the waters of the coastal state during the voyage in question, as for example, a collision, a salvage operation, and so forth.

When a foreign merchant vessel enters a port of a coastal state, the

Anglo-American view has been that the host state possessed the right to enforce not only various safety and navigation regulations, but also its criminal laws when the tranquillity of its port was disturbed by events aboard ship. The European view, on the other hand, had affirmed that all matters and events *aboard* the vessel represented an exclusive concern of the flag state.

The Anglo-American interpretation of the authority of the coastal state was laid down in striking fashion in the following case.

MALI v. KEEPER OF THE COMMON JAIL
(WILDENHUS' CASE)
United States, Supreme Court, 1887, 120 U.S. 1

FACTS

The Belgian steamer *Noordland* was docked in the port of Jersey City, New Jersey. On October 6, 1886, a Belgian member of the crew, Joseph Wildenhus, fought below decks with another Belgian crew member, by the name of Fijeus, and stabbed him with a knife. Fijeus died as a result of the wound.

The police of Jersey City boarded the vessel and arrested Wildenhus, who was then committed by a police magistrate to the common jail of Hudson County, New Jersey, pending trial for murder. The Belgian consul (M. Charles Mali) for New York and New Jersey then asked for a writ of habeas corpus, claiming that by international law and under the provisions of the Belgian-United States Consular Convention of 1880, the offense with which Wildenhus had been charged was to be handled under the laws of Belgium and that the State of New Jersey lacked proper jurisdiction.

Article 11 of the convention invoked stated, *inter alia*, that.

The local authorities shall not interfere [with the internal order of merchant vessels], except when the disorder that has arisen is of such a nature as to disturb tranquillity and public order on shore or in the port, or when a person of the country, or not belonging to the crew, shall be concerned therein.

The Belgian case rested on the assertion that no outside persons had been involved, that slayer and victim, both Belgian citizens, had been members of the crew of the *Noordland,* and that the commission of the issue, aboard ship and below deck, had not disturbed the tranquillity of the port and public order.

The Circuit Court of the U.S. for the District of New Jersey refused to deliver the arrested individuals (Wildenhus and two witnesses, both members of the ship's crew) to the consul. The consul then appealed that decision.

ISSUE

Does murder aboard a foreign vessel in port, affecting only members of the foreign crew, constitute a disturbance of the tranquillity of the port and thereby justify assertion of jurisdiction by the local law enforcement agencies?

DECISION

For the Keeper of the Common Jail, Judgment of the Circuit Court affirmed.

REASONING

The crime of murder, by its commission, disturbed tranquillity and public order on shore or in a port so that it had to be regarded as falling within the exceptions provided for in the treaty of 1880, in which the local authorities had a right to interfere.

The Eighteenth Amendment to the Constitution of the United States, together with its supplementary enforcement law, the Volstead Act, posed some new problems in the relations between local authorities and foreign ships in territorial waters and in ports. It will be remembered that the "prohibition" Amendment held that the "manufacture, sale, or transportation of intoxicating liquors within, the importation thereof into, or the exportation thereof from the United States and all territory subject to the jurisdiction thereof for beverage purposes is hereby prohibited." Trouble ensued as soon as the enforcement legislation began to be applied to alien ships. A number of foreign steamship lines sued for an injunction to prevent seizure of liquor supplies carried aboard their vessels and destined only for the consumption of passengers and crew.

The Supreme Court of the United States, in *Cunard Steamship Company* v. *Mellon*,[9] upheld the right of law-enforcement authorities to seize liquor supplies aboard foreign ships, under the concept that the jurisdiction of any state in its territory was exclusive and absolute and that any exceptions to be granted had to be granted by the state in question. As far as the United States government was concerned, only liquor in transit through the Panama Canal or by the Panama Railroad had been granted exemption from seizure.

Following a number of shipboard seizures during the next year, Great Britain and the United States concluded a treaty under which the United States granted exemption for seizure to liquor stores aboard British vessels in exchange for British obligation to keep such stores under lock and key as long as the vessel concerned was in American territorial waters and for agreement to American capture, within an hour's run from shore, of vessels flying the British flag and engaged in violating the Volstead Act and its governing Amendment.

A foreign merchant vessel in port may be subject to civil suit by a citizen of the host state, and its officers and crew may be sued individually, just as they are subject to criminal prosecution if they violate the laws of the host state.

An act committed on board a ship may on occasion be subject to the concurrent jurisdiction of several states: of the state in which the vessel is registered, the state in whose territory the ship happens to be at the time, and the state or states of which the individuals concerned are citizens or subjects. Naturally, only one of those concurrent jurisdictions can be exercised at a given time.

[9] United States, Supreme Court, 1923, 262 U.S. 100.

One of the classic cases illustrative of this problem of concurrent jurisdiction is the following.

REGINA v. ANDERSON

Great Britain, Court of Criminal Appeal, 1868
11 Cox's Criminal Cases, p. 198

FACTS

James Anderson, an American citizen, was indicted for murder on board a vessel belonging to the port of Yarmouth, Nova Scotia, and registered in Great Britain. At the time the offense was committed, the ship was moving up the river Garonne, on its way to the French city of Bordeaux, some ninety miles from the coast. The vessel, at the time, was therefore on the internal waters of the French Empire.

The accused was detained on the ship until it returned to England and was charged with murder in the Central Criminal Court in London. He was convicted of manslaughter, despite his plea that the court lacked jurisdiction to try him, since the offense had been committed in French territory, aboard a colonial vessel, by an American citizen. The judgment of the Criminal Court was appealed.

ISSUE

Which country had jurisdiction to try the accused under the conditions described?

DECISION

Conviction affirmed; British courts had jurisdiction to try offenses committed aboard British ships.

REASONING

The Court of Criminal Appeal found that the accused was subject to American jurisprudence as an American citizen, to French jurisprudence for having committed an offense in the territory of France, and to British jurisprudence, for the jurisdiction of British law and of British courts extended to the protection of British vessels, no matter where those vessels might be at a given time. The Court held that the French authorities could have enforced French law by arresting Anderson and placing him on trial for his offense. France had not asserted its undoubted right to prosecute Anderson for disturbing the tranquillity of a port and public order. Great Britain, in control of the vessel, then exercised its authority and prosecuted Anderson. This procedure was wholly approved by the Court of Criminal Appeal.

A more recent case, *Regina* v. *Governor of Brixton Prison, ex parte Minervini* [10] illustrates the modern application of the principle involved above. Minervini, an Italian seaman, was accused of having murdered a fellow crew member aboard a Norwegian merchant vessel. The Norwegian government instituted extradition proceedings when Minervini was located in England, and the accused was arrested and, after a hearing

[10] W.L.R. 559 Queen's Bench Div. Court, October 7, 1958.

before the Metropolitan Magistrate, committed to prison to await execution of an extradition order issued by the British Secretary of State for Foreign Affairs. Minervini then applied for a writ of *habeas corpus*, claiming that since the location of his ship at the time his alleged offense was said to have been committed had not been determined, the Anglo-Norwegian extradition treaty of 1873 was inapplicable, since it referred only to crimes committed on Norwegian territory. The court ruled that the term *territory* had to be construed as the equivalent of *jurisdiction*, and because the alleged offense had been committed on board a Norwegian vessel, that is, under Norwegian jurisdiction, the treaty applied. Hence Minervini's application was denied.

Granting of Asylum. Before leaving the subject of "normal" foreign merchant vessels in the territory of a coastal state, it must be pointed out that such ships cannot serve as places of asylum, either for alleged fugitives from criminal justice or for political refugees. There is no question but that the local authorities have a legal right to board foreign merchant vessels in the ports of the coastal state and remove from them such fugitives or refugees. It also appears that the commander of such a vessel can be tried in the courts of the host state for violations of the rule prohibiting the granting of asylum on merchant vessels.

It is not settled, on the other hand, whether the authorities of a coastal state possess the right to remove from a foreign merchant vessel coming into their port a passenger who, as a political refugee from the authorities of the coastal state, had boarded the vessel in question in a third state. Inconclusive evidence appears to support the view that such a right does exist, on the assumption that the refugee voluntarily reentered the jurisdiction of the country whose authorities were attempting to apprehend him. However, not all extant cases confirm this interpretation.

JURISDICTION OVER FOREIGN PUBLIC VESSELS

The position of foreign public vessels in the ports and waters of a coastal state is quite different, in most respects, from that occupied by merchant vessels, essentially because there does exist a close and immediate relationship between a state and its public ships.

In the first place, a foreign warship entering the territorial sea of another state is expected to comply not only with all applicable rules of international law, but also with all regulations of the coastal state insofar as navigation is concerned. Should such a foreign warship fail to follow those regulations, the coastal state may require the warship to leave the territorial sea.

Right of Innocent Passage. Although the right of innocent passage through territorial waters encompasses public vessels as well as private craft, a number of states have recorded reservations to the 1958 Geneva Convention on the Territorial Sea. The U.S.S.R., Bulgaria, the Byelorussian S.S.R., Hungary, Romania, the Ukrainian S.S.R., all require prior authorization or consent by the coastal state before passage of a foreign warship is permitted through the territorial sea. The republic of Colombia made a declaration amounting to a corresponding reservation because of a provision in the Colombian constitution. Other countries do not require such prior authorization, and all proposals to include state consent in the convention were rejected during the relevant meetings. Only the requirement that submarines which are warships must show their flag and proceed at the surface was accepted as a reasonable requirement on the part of the coastal state for passage through territorial waters.

Beyond these reasonable and proper limitations, the foreign public vessel, regarded as a floating portion of the territory of its flag state, is completely exempt from all jurisdiction of the coastal state. (See also Chapter 17.)

The status of a foreign warship in the territorial sea attracted worldwide attention in 1968 through the North Korean seizure of the *U.S.S. Pueblo*, an intelligence vessel operating off the coasts of North Korea. Being a part of the U.S. Navy, the *Pueblo* was entitled to the immunities recognized by Article 8 of the 1958 Geneva Convention on the High Seas. Even though North Korea was not a party to that agreement, the immunity of a foreign warship has long been a part of customary international law. Under Article 23 of the convention, the only authority possessed by North Korea, had it been a party to the treaty, would have been an order to the vessel to leave the territorial sea.

The United States government claimed to have no official knowledge of the width of the North Korean territorial sea but assumed that a claim of twelve miles, corresponding to that of other socialist states, was in effect. It maintained that the *Pueblo* was captured fifteen miles off shore.[11] On the other hand, if the ship did penetrate North Korean territorial waters, then two factors should be taken into consideration in judging the action of the North Korean authorities in seizing the vessel (but not excusing the apparently barbaric treatment of the crew until it was released in December, 1968): the nature of the activities reportedly carried on by the *Pueblo* ("intelligence gathering") and the fact that the 1953 armistice did not end the Korean war, insofar as its legal status as a war was concerned (see Chapter 27), so that, in effect, the *Pueblo* could have been classified as an enemy warship by North Korea.

A public vessel in a foreign port is immune from civil suits *in rem*, at least as far as warships and naval auxiliary vessels are concerned.[12]

---

[11] See copy of telegram dispatched by the U.S. Department of State to all U.S. diplomatic posts on February 8, 1968, in 62 *A.J.I.L.* (1968), pp. 756–757. See also the U.S. "admission" of espionage signed to obtain the release of the crew, and related documents, 8 *International Legal Materials* (1969), pp. 198–199.

[12] The classic case, still governing today, is *Schooner Exchange* v. *McFaddon*, United States, Supreme Court, 1812, 7 Cranch 116.

The "fiction" of the extraterritorial character of public vessels has been challenged repeatedly in modern times. One of the most vigorous denunciations of the doctrine was developed in the judgment in the following British case.

CHUNG CHI CHEUNG v. THE KING
Great Britain, Judicial Committee of the House of Lords, Dec. 2, 1938.
[*1939*] *A. C. 160*

FACTS

Chung, a British subject, was cabin boy on the Chinese maritime customs cruiser *Cheung Keng* when that vessel was in Hong Kong territorial waters. On January 11, 1937, he shot and killed Douglas Lorne Campbell, the captain of the cruiser and a British national. Both men were, at the time, in the service of the Chinese government. After killing the captain, Chung wounded the acting chief officer of the vessel and then shot and wounded himself. The chief officer ordered the cruiser to proceed at once to Hong Kong and to hail a police launch. A few hours later a police launch was sighted and came alongside in answer to the cruiser's signal. The police took the wounded officer and Chung to a hospital in Hong Kong.

On February 5, 1937, the chairman of the provincial government of Kwangtung requisitioned the extradition of Chung to China on charges of murder and attempted murder on board the Chinese customs cruiser "within the jurisdiction of China while the said cruiser was approximately one mile off Futaumun (British waters)." It later developed that the shootings took place in British territorial waters. After several adjournments the magistrate in charge of extradition proceedings decided that the accused was a British subject and that the proceedings therefore failed.

Chung was promptly arrested again and charged with murder "in the waters of this Colony." At his trial, the chief officer of the cruiser and three of the crew were called as witnesses for the prosecution. Chung was convicted and sentenced to death.

By appeal the case came before the Judicial Committee of the Privy Council in London.

ISSUE

Did a British court have a right to try the accused Chung?

DECISION

The local British court in Hong Kong had jurisdiction to try the appellant. Appeal dismissed.

REASONING

(1) ". . . A public ship in foreign waters is not, and is not treated as, territory of her own nation. The domestic courts in accordance with principles of international law will accord to the ship and its crew and its contents certain immunities, some of which are well settled, though others are in dispute. In this view the immunities do not depend on an objective extraterritoriality, but on implication of the domestic law. They are conditional, and can in any case be waived by the nation to which the public ship belongs."

(2) "Their Lordships have no hesitation in rejecting the doctrine of extraterritoriality expressed in the words of Mr. Oppenheim, which regards the public ship 'as a floating portion of the flag-state.' However the doctrine of extraterritoriality is expressed, it is a fiction, and legal fictions have a tendency to pass beyond their appointed bounds and to harden into dangerous facts. . . . Immunities may well be given in respect of the conduct of members of the crew to one another on board ship. . . . But if a resident in the receiving state visited the public ship and committed theft, and returned to shore, is it conceivable that when he was arrested on shore . . . the local Courts would have no jurisdiction?"

(3) ". . . it appears to their Lordships as plain as possible that the Chinese Government, once the extradition proceedings were out of the way, consented to the British Court exercising jurisdiction. It is not only that, with full knowledge of the proceedings, they made no further claim, but at two different dates they permitted four members of their service to give evidence before the British court in aid of the prosecution."

The immunity granted to a foreign warship in the territorial waters of the host state extends also to the members of that vessel's crew when they are on shore on duty.[13] On the other hand, if a member of such a crew commits a violation of the host's laws while on shore and while off duty, the individual in question normally does not enjoy immunity from local jurisdiction.[14] (See Chapter 9 for the immunities possessed by publicly owned vessels engaged in commercial activities.)

Asylum Aboard Foreign Public Vessels. The question of asylum aboard foreign public vessels has arisen frequently in every part of the globe. Earlier centuries saw the granting of asylum to both ordinary criminals and political fugitives. This generous interpretation of the immunity of foreign public vessels has been curtailed decisively since the middle of the last century and today only a customary right of asylum for political offenders is recognized. The government of the United States, traditionally averse to a broad grant of asylum rights, has restricted the use of American public vessels to occasions on which the life of the political refugee is in immediate danger by mob violence.[15] Latin American states, on the other hand, have laid down by convention (1928) a rule by which asylum may be granted aboard public vessels to political offenders in "urgent cases."[16]

---

[13] *Georges Triandafilou* v. *Ministère Public,* Mixed Courts in Egypt, Court of Cassation, June 29, 1942, reprinted in translation in 39 *A.J.I.L.* (1945), pp. 345–347.

[14] *Malevo Manuel* v. *Ministère Public,* Mixed Courts in Egypt, Court of Cassation, March 8, 1943, reprinted in translation, *ibid.,* pp. 349–355.

[15] See Hackworth, Vol. II, pp. 639–642, and Whiteman, Vol. VI, pp. 498–502, for examples.

[16] Hackworth, *op. cit.,* Vol. II, pp. 646–649.

SUGGESTED READINGS

JURISDICTION OVER VESSELS: GENERAL

John N. Hazard, "State Trading in History and Theory," *Law and Contemporary Problems*, 24 (Duke University, Spring, 1959), pp. 243–255; Vernon G. Setsen, "The Immunities of the State and Government Economic Activities," *ibid.*, pp. 291–316; Whiteman, Vol. IX, pp. 1–308.

Cases

Cunard Steamship Co. v. Mellon, United States, Supreme Court, 1923, 262 U.S. 100.
Strathearn Steamship Co. v. Dillon, United States, Supreme Court, 1920, 252 U.S. 348.
United States v. Flores, United States, Supreme Court, 1933, 289 U.S. 137.

FLAGS OF CONVENIENCE

Case

McCulloch, Chairman, National Labor Relations Board, et al. v. Sociedad Nacional de Marineros de Honduras; McLeod, Regional Director, National Labor Relations Board, v. Empresa Hondurena de Vapores, S.A.; National Maritime Union of America, AFL-CIO, v. Empresa Hondurena de Vapores, S.A. United States, Supreme Court, 1963, 372 U.S. 10.

LAW APPLICABLE TO SHIPS

Luke T. Lee, "Jurisdiction over Foreign Merchant Ships in the Territorial Sea: An Analysis of the Geneva Convention on the Law of the Sea," 55 *A.J.I.L.* (1961), pp. 77–96.

Cases

United States v. Dixon, United States, District Court, E.D.N.Y., 1947, 73 F. Supp. 683, noted in 42 *A.J.I.L.* (1948), p. 493.
Lauritzen v. Larsen, United States, Supreme Court, 1953, 345 U.S. 571, reported in 47 *A.J.I.L.* (1953), pp. 711–712.

20

Jurisdiction Over the National Air and Outer Space

NATIONAL AIRSPACE

THE invention of the balloon and more especially of the airplane brought about a necessity of clarifying the rights possessed by a state in the air above its territory. Initially a number of theories came into being, according to which (1) there prevailed complete freedom in airspace, just as on the high seas; (2) a nation could claim territorial jurisdiction in airspace up to about one thousand feet above the ground, with the upper air again free as in the case of the high seas; (3) the entire airspace above a state, with no upper limit, represented national air, with a servitude of innocent passage granted to all aircraft registered in friendly foreign countries; and (4) a nation had absolute and unlimited sovereignty over national airspace, with no upper limit.[1]

The last-mentioned theory received general approval when the outbreak of World War I led all belligerent states to assert immediately full sovereignty over their national air. Neutrals, in turn, denied all right of passage to belligerent aircraft, thus aligning national airspace with the rules applying to the land surface rather than with those applicable to neutral territorial waters. In fact, both the Swiss and the Netherlands governments, zealously maintaining the integrity of their neutral airspaces, brought down a number of belligerent aircraft that had penetrated into the national airspaces in question. By the end of the conflict, national sovereignty over airspace was accepted and only the question of innocent passage remained to be settled, particularly with respect to the problem of whether such passage, if permitted, represented a right or a special grant under some form of treaty.

There can be no question today about the legal status of national air space: states possess complete and exclusive sovereignty over the air above

---

[1] "The United States Government has not recognized any top or upper limit to its sovereignty."—From a speech by the Legal Adviser to the Department of State, May 14, 1958, reported in 38 *Department of State Bulletin* (1958), p. 962. Consult also H. B. Jacobini, "International Aviation Law: A Theoretical and Historical Survey," 2 *Journal of Politics* (1953), pp. 314–332.

their territories (including the territorial sea, of course).[2] This statement is not only declarative of a rule of customary law but has been affirmed in numerous conventions.[3]

Right of Innocent Passage. The major problem traditionally involved in the enforcement of a claim of absolute sovereignty over national airspace is the innocent passage of foreign aircraft through such space. It is clearly permissible for any state to assign entry and exit lanes, if only for purposes of control induced by considerations of national defense, and to delineate routes or lanes over its territory through which planes in innocent passage may traverse the national airspace. Equally lawful would be a designation of specified areas as closed to foreign aircraft, again in the interest of national security. In fact, a requirement forcing all foreign planes in innocent passage to land at some point in national territory to have their registration checked should be considered a valid national right.[4]

No right of innocent passage through the national airspace can be asserted to exist; permission for such passage is granted, either unilaterally or, more commonly, through conventions, to foreign *civil* aircraft. Most countries insist, however, on such passage taking place through designated corridors and, frequently, only after notification, including flight plans and so on, has been supplied to the relevant air-defense authorities. Specific permission is normally required if foreign military aircraft are to be permitted to enter into the national air.

The right to penetrate national airspace and to land on national territory in the event of distress or of unfavorable weather conditions has been generally accepted and is based on analogous rights of vessels in distress. National regulations govern the rights of aircraft involved in this category of intrusion into the national airspace and lead, at times, to rather unfortunate consequences. Thus the case of *U.S.* v. *582.33 Carat,*[5] affirmed after appeal as *Lisser* v. *United States,*[6] involved the forfeiture of undeclared diamonds brought into the United States by a passenger on board an airliner enroute from Europe to Canada. The craft had to be diverted and landed in the United States because of unforeseen and unfavorable flying conditions. The individual in question had not intended

---

[2] See Whiteman, Vol. II, pp. 1270–1285; Hackworth, Vol. VII, pp. 550, 552, 555–556; and Vol. IX, pp. 309–312; see also the references supplied by Oliver J. Lissitzyn, "The Treatment of Aerial Intruders in Recent Practice and International Law," 47 *A.J.I.L.* (1953), pp. 559–588, at p. 567.

[3] See, *inter alia,* the Convention for the Regulation of Aerial Navigation (Paris, 1919) and the Convention on International Civil Aviation (Chicago, 1944).

[4] See J. I. Perdomo-Escobar, "Aeronautical Servitudes: A Comparative Study," 44 *Michigan Law Review* (1946), pp. 1013–1034; Robert D. Hayton, "Jurisdiction of the Littoral State in the 'Air Frontier'," 3 *Philippine International Law Journal* (1964), pp. 369–398.

[5] United States, District Court, Mass., 1955, 137 F. Supp. 527.

[6] United States, Court of Appeals, First Circuit, 1956, 234 F. 2d. 648.

to enter the United States and, upon arrival, made immediate arrangements to proceed at once to Canada. However, he did not declare the diamonds on his person to a customs officer, and the United States government confiscated the diamonds in accordance with domestic regulations concerning the importation of goods from abroad. The appellate court rejected the owner's claim that involuntary entry in distress by air absolved him from the duty of declaring the diamonds in his possession.

Air space above the high seas is controlled by no one and hence is free for the use of all states.

The "height" of the air subject to national sovereignty has been a topic of much concern to states interested in establishing a legal regime for outer space. Although no agreement has as yet been reached as to the exact boundary between national air and outer space, an air space height of thirty miles has been suggested.[7]

AERIAL INTRUSION

Penetration of national airspace by foreign aircraft has led to numerous disputes and claims between countries, to one case brought before the International Court of Justice, and, in at least one instance, to a serious international crisis and the cancellation of a proposed "summit" conference.

Basic Principles. Before discussing a number of the more spectacular or publicized incidents relating to aerial intrusion, the basic principles involved need to be examined.

Under the doctrine of exclusive sovereignty over the national airspace, the territorial sovereign may adopt one of several actions when a foreign aircraft intrudes without permission into that space: he may ignore the intruder; he may attempt (in the event of a landing) to exercise administrative and possibly judicial authority over the craft and its occupants; he may attempt to destroy the craft after intrusion has become a fact; or he may attempt to force the craft to leave his airspace, change course, or land in a designated area.[8]

United States-Jugoslavia Dispute. On the other hand, firing at the in-

---

[7] See Whiteman, Vol. II, pp. 1281–1288, as well as Leon Lipson and Nicholas deB. Katzenbach, *Report to the National Aeronautics and Space Administration on the Law of Outer Space* (Chicago: American Bar Association, 1961), pp. 15–18. For earlier approaches to the problem, consult Charles G. Fenwick, "How High Is the Sky?" 52 *A.J.I.L.* (1958), pp. 96–99; the highly valuable analysis by John C. Cooper, "Legal Problems of Upper Space," *Proceedings* (1956), pp. 85–93; *ibid.*, pp. 93–114, for varied and illuminating commentaries on Cooper's paper; Eugène Pépin, "Space Penetration," *Proceedings* (1958), pp. 230–243 (commentary on pp. 243–252); Leon Lipson, "An Argument on the Legality of Reconaissance Satellites," *ibid.*, 1961, pp. 174–176; and H. B. Jacobini, "Problems of High Altitude or Space Jurisdiction," 4 *Western Political Quarterly* (1953), pp. 680–688.

[8] See Lissitzyn, *op. cit.*, at p. 559.

truder in an effort either to drive the craft out of national airspace or to down it in national territory has become a frequent occurrence and has led to serious diplomatic disputes. The first major incident of this sort took place on August 9, 1946. An unarmed American military air transport (C-47 type), on a regular flight from Vienna to Udine, Italy, was attacked over Jugoslav territory by Jugoslav fighter planes and forced to crash-land. All occupants of the plane were detained by Jugoslav authorities and questioned repeatedly, but were finally released on August 22. The United States government charged that the pilot had been instructed to avoid Jugoslav national air but had been forced to intrude because of adverse weather conditions. This existence of bad weather was denied by the Jugoslav government. The United States also claimed that no internationally accepted signal to land had been given, that the attack had begun without recognizable warning and had been repeated as the plane descended for a landing.

Before the occupants of the plane involved in the August 9 incident were released, a second American plane, of similar type and category, was shot down by Jugoslav fighter planes on August 19th, with a total loss of the five-man crew. This time the Jugoslav government claimed that a short time before firing on his plane commenced, the American pilot had been "invited" to land, but he had ignored the request. The United States government, in reply, cast doubts on the extension of such a request, stating that at the time in question the pilot had reported himself as above the city of Klagenfurt, Austria. A partial denial was also made of a Jugoslav charge of 278 unauthorized American intrusions into Jugoslav airspace between July 16 and August 29, 1946. The American reply acknowledged only 43 instances during this period in which United States planes had been close enough to the frontiers of Jugoslavia to lead to possible violations of those frontiers. Finally, the United States argued that the shooting down of the two planes constituted a clear violation of international law.[9]

After several exchanges of notes, the Jugoslav government agreed that military aircraft had a right of innocent passage when forced to intrude by stress of weather, and expressed regrets about the loss of lives involved in the second of the two incidents. Ultimately, that government voluntarily paid $30,000 to each of the families of the crewmen who died on August 19, 1946. The conclusion from these episodes appears to be that the Jugoslav government still claimed a right to down by force any intruding aircraft in time of peace, but only after the intruder had been given a chance to land after being clearly ordered to do so.

In 1948, the Jugoslav government, in a note to the Secretary-General of the United Nations for circulation among the members of the Security

[9] See *The New York Times*, Sept. 4 and October 10, 1946; the detailed documents are in 15 *Department of State Bulletin* (1946), pp. 415–418, 502–504.

Council, again charged the United States with numerous American violations of Jugoslav airspace.

Israel-Bulgaria Dispute. The years 1950 to 1953 saw a number of incidents similar to the 1946 episodes over Jugoslavia, but this time taking place in Soviet or satellite airspace in Eastern Europe.[10] A major occurrence, however, and the one which led to submission of the dispute to the International Court of Justice, took place on July 27, 1955, when a commercial aircraft belonging to the El Al Israel Airlines Ltd., on a flight between Vienna and Lydda (Israel), intruded over Bulgarian territory and was shot down by Bulgarian military aircraft. All seven crew members and the fifty-one passengers were killed in the crash of the burning plane.[11] When diplomatic negotiations failed to satisfy the demands of the government of Israel for compensation for the loss of the plane, its crew, and its passengers, Israel submitted the dispute to the Court on October 16, 1957. The Court sustained Bulgarian objections to the jurisdiction of the tribunal, agreeing that the adherence of the Bulgarian state to the compulsory jurisdiction of the Permanent Court of International Justice had ceased to apply when that Court was dissolved on April 18, 1946, and that Bulgaria had never ratified the optional clause of the Statute of the new court.

Protracted negotiations between Israel and Bulgaria over payment of compensation to the heirs of passengers killed in the incident resulted in an agreement, announced on June 3, 1963. Bulgaria agreed to pay a total of $195,000, which sum, however, excluded compensation for the loss of the plane.

U-2 and RB-47 Incidents. The most publicized recent incidents of aerial intrusion centered on two United States planes over Russian territory: the U-2 and the RB-47 incidents. In the latter case, an American military patrol craft was shot down over Soviet territorial waters off the northern coast of the U.S.S.R. after it had "intruded deliberately" into Soviet airspace and had disobeyed an order to land. The only two members of the crew who survived the crash of the bomber-type craft were jailed by the Russian authorities, pending trial, until they were released and permitted to leave, in January, 1961. During the exchange of notes following this incident, as well as during subsequent debates in the UN Security Council, the main controversy centered on the location of the craft at the time it was attacked—the Soviet Union maintaining a location

---

[10] See Lissitzyn, *op. cit.*, pp. 573–585 for a very full account of typical incidents, with excerpts from several key documents.

[11] *Case concerning the Aerial Incident of July 27, 1955 (Israel v. Bulgaria)* [Preliminary Objections, Judgment of May 26, 1959], *I.C.J. Reports, 1959*, p. 127. Consult Leo Gross, "The Jurisprudence of the World Court: Thirty-Eighth Year (1959)," 57 *A.J.I.L.* (1963), pp. 751–780, at pp. 753–771, and Lucius C. Caflisch, "The Recent Judgment of the International Court of Justice in the Case Concerning the Aerial Incident of July 27, 1955, and the Interpretation of Article 36 (5) of the Statute of the Court," 54 *A.J.I.L.* (1960), pp. 855–868.

well over Russian territorial waters, the United States holding that the craft was at least thirty miles off the Russian shore.

The U-2 incident of May 1, 1960, was the most noteworthy of the postwar intrusion cases, from the point of view of both political results and legal arguments.

The U-2, a high-flying United States craft, was engaged in aerial reconnaissance work over Russian territory. On May 1, 1960, while flying from Pakistan to Norway, the U-2 was brought to earth (by still undisclosed means) in Soviet territory near Sverdlovsk. Its pilot, Francis G. Powers, was arrested.

The flight of the U-2 was then only the latest in a series of reconnaissance penetrations of Soviet airspace carried on, over a period of four years, under general orders of President Eisenhower and under the control of the Central Intelligence Agency.[12] The incident served as the Russian excuse for abandonment of the planned Paris Summit Conference between President Eisenhower and Premier Khrushchev.

From a legal point of view, Russian citations of the Paris (1919), Havana (1928), and Chicago (1944) conventions, to the last two of which the United States was a party, served to point up the still unchallenged principle that sovereignty over its national airspace is a right of each state under international law, a principle supported even more dramatically by the fact that the United States did not protest against the Russian downing of the U-2 and the trial and conviction of the pilot. Powers was released and permitted to return to the United States in 1962, under the terms of an exchange agreement under which a convicted Russian spy was permitted by the United States to return to the Soviet Union.

Summarizing the U-2 incident, and disregarding strategic and political factors, it must be held that in authorizing the craft's flights over U.S.S.R. territory the United States violated international law and that the Soviet Union was justified in forcing the aircraft down and instituting criminal proceedings against its American pilot.

In March, 1964, a U.S. RB-66 reconnaissance bomber was shot down by Soviet military forces over East Germany. This was the twentieth U.S. aircraft brought down since 1950 adjacent to or inside the Iron Curtain countries, in addition to some seventeen "incidents" involving U.S. military aircraft.[13]

---

[12] See Quincy Wright, "Legal Aspects of the U-2 Incident," 54 *A.J.I.L.* (1960), pp. 836–854; Oliver J. Lissitzyn, "Some Legal Implications of the U-2 and RB-47 Incidents," *ibid.*, 56 (1962), pp. 135–142, as well as the copious literature cited in those sources. For the aftermath of the incident, consult also David Wise and Thomas B. Ross, *The U-2 Affair* (New York: Random House, 1962). See also "Legal Aspects of Reconnaissance in Airspace and Outer Space," 61 *Columbia Law Review* (1961), pp. 1074–1102, and Roland J. Stanger (ed.), *Essays on Espionage and International Law* (Columbus, Ohio: Ohio State University Press, 1963).

[13] See *The New York Times*, March 15, 1964, p. 4-E; March 22, 1964, pp. 1, 14.

In April, 1966, Turkey prohibited the use of United States airbases on Turkish soil for reconnaissance flights by the U.S. Air Force, asserting that such flights endangered Turkey's security.[14]

Beginning around 1964, the airspace above mainland China began to be penetrated by pilotless American jet-powered reconnaissance aircraft. Most of these were launched from C-130 transports over the high seas, were under remote control during flight, and were afterward directed to a recovery zone where films exposed over China were removed.

OUTER SPACE

VIEWS OF LEGAL WRITERS

Basically, the arguments put forth by legal writers about high flights and missiles in foreign airspaces center on two concepts: the undoubted right of any state to engage in genuine self-defense, and the equally undoubted exclusiveness of national airspace.[15] One school of thought holds that the argument of self-defense cannot be maintained, in the relevant connection, in time of peace, and that therefore all aerial spying, whether by manned craft, drone planes, or camera-equipped satellites, is illegal in someone else's national airspace. An opposing point of view holds that in an age of nuclear weapons capable of devastating entire nations in a matter of minutes, any state capable of launching intruding reconnaissance craft is fully entitled to do so under a right of self-defense. Obviously, however, the nation suffering such intrusion of its national airspace could claim, equally on the basis of self-defense, a perfect right to shoot down any intruding (unauthorized) craft, particularly because its ground-based defensive units could not distinguish by radar, say, an unarmed surveillance or reconnaissance craft of some kind and a plane or missile or satellite carrying a nuclear weapon for delivery. In this connection there exists an interesting theory, promoted by numerous writers in the Soviet Union and in the United States, to the effect that an earth satellite does not in fact violate the airspace of any state by intrusion, for the satellite is assumed not to be flying in space over other states but the territories of those states, by the rotation of the earth pass, so to speak, underneath the orbit of movement of the satellite. In other words, the satellite's orbit is constant in relation to the earth and stars, and national territories of states come beneath the satellite and then move away from underneath it again. The satellite, orbiting at an altitude at which there is virtually no air, could not be termed an aircraft in the conventional and legal sense; hence the various conventions covering true aircraft, *i.e.*, craft sustained by air, would not apply to a satellite.

[14] *The New York Times*, April 3, 1966, p. 22.

[15] Consult Bin Cheng, "International Law and High Altitude Flights: Balloons, Rockets and Man-Made Satellites," 6 *International and Comparative Law Quarterly* (1957), pp. 487–505.

On occasion the lofting of satellites has introduced the world to problems likely to multiply in the space age. Thus, for example, the Atomic Energy Commission (U.S.) admitted in May, 1964, that 2.2 pounds of lethal Plutonium-238 were lost some weeks earlier when rocket failure prevented a navigational satellite from going into orbit. The payload came down, instead, into the earth atmosphere off the West Coast of Africa. There the payload burned up, but the radioactive material was dispersed in minute particles in the atmosphere at a height of about 120,000 feet.[16]

PROBLEMS OF OUTER SPACE

But the problems of the law of the air have not ended with the questions posed by the increasingly common penetration of the upper layers of the earth's atmosphere: outer space has become one of man's next targets for voyages of discovery. Already the legal implications of space travel have begun to make their appearance.[17]

UN Ad Hoc Committee. The initial step taken toward a serious study of the legal problems connected with outer space was the establishment, on December 13, 1958, by the General Assembly of the United Nations of an *Ad Hoc* Committee on the Peaceful Uses of Outer Space, composed of eighteen members. However, the U.S.S.R., Czechoslovakia, and Poland announced at once that they would not participate in the activities of the committee because of an alleged "pro-Western" majority, and the United Arab Republic and India, apparently fearful of becoming embroiled in another aspect of the power struggle between the United States and the U.S.S.R., soon also decided to stay away.

The *Ad Hoc* committee, in its rump form, began its meetings in early May, 1959, and formed a technical committee and a legal committee. The technical committee, after consulting with numerous UN agencies, recommended a worldwide rather than a national effort at space penetration, in part because of the excessively high costs of most endeavors connected with outer space exploration. The legal committee suggested that the provisions of the Charter and of the Statute of the International Court of Justice, not being limited in principle to the Earth, be applied to outer space insofar as such should prove to be possible. It was suggested, furthermore, that a broad principle of freedom of outer space for exploration and use be adopted.

Neither committee felt that the time had come to attempt a determination of the upper limits of national airspace (and hence the beginning of outer space), of possible national claims to sovereignty over asteroids or

[16] *The New York Times,* May 24, 1964, pp. 1, 44.

[17] A source of primary importance today is Philip C. Jessup and Howard J. Taubenfeld, *Controls for Outer Space and the Antarctic Analogy* (New York: Columbia University Press, 1959). See also the appended list of suggested readings for valuable shorter studies, and consult Whiteman, Vol. II, pp. 1285-1321.

planets and other celestial bodies, or of the exploration and exploitation of such bodies. Both committees, however, were in favor of ultimately confining the use of outer space to peaceful purposes.[18] The United States suggested as early as 1957 a demilitarization of outer space, coupled with an inspection system. In view of the failure to achieve such a system in relation to nuclear weapons, its likelihood for outer space appeared remote at the time.

United Nations Resolution (1961). Late in 1961, the General Assembly adopted a Resolution on Peaceful Uses of Outer Space, in which it was asserted that international law, including the Charter of the United Nations, applied to outer space as well as to celestial bodies, and that both such space and such bodies were to be regarded as free for exploration and use by all states.[19]

The General Assembly, perhaps wisely, did not venture beyond these two basic principles and attempt to define where national airspace ended and outer space began. The resolution did, however, provide for registration with an outer-space committee of all objects launched into orbit or beyond. This inventory began when the United States submitted the required initial information to the office of the Secretary-General.

By implication, the resolution barred any state from unilaterally carrying on activities in space which would hamper its use by other states, including interference with manned orbital flights, radio communications, and radio astronomy.

During 1962–65, much research and drafting work took place in the United Nations, but progress toward a draft convention in any way likely to be adopted was rather slow.[20]

Outer-Space Treaty. The key year in these efforts proved to be 1966. On May 7, President Lyndon Johnson announced that the United States would seek a UN agreement to prevent any state from claiming title to the moon and other celestial bodies.[21] The Legal Committee (on Outer Space) at Geneva quickly undertook the definitive drafting of such an agreement, adding obviously desirable sections on prohibition of weapons of mass destruction in outer space or on celestial bodies.

After a number of differences between the views of the United States and the U.S.S.R. had been reconciled, the draft treaty was approved

[18] The best single source on the deliberations of the UN Committee is its report of July 14, 1959 (Document A/4141), excerpted at length in Bishop, pp. 377–380.

[19] Res. 1721 (XVI), U. N. General Assembly, 16th Session, reprinted in 56 *A.J.I.L.* (1962), Supp., pp. 946–949; see also James Simsarian, "Outer Space Co-operation in the United Nations," 57 *A.J.I.L.* (1963), pp. 854–867.

[20] See Simsarian, *op. cit.* and his "Outer Space Co-operation in the U.N. in 1963," 58 *A.J.I.L.* (1964), pp. 717–723; *International Conciliation*, No. 559 (September, 1966), pp. 36–39.

[21] *The New York Times*, May 8, 1966, pp. 1, 66; see also 54 *Department of State Bulletin* (1966), p. 900, for additional documentation.

unanimously in the General Assembly on December 19, 1966.[22] The signing of the agreement took place on January 27, 1967, at an unusual ceremony, involving representatives of sixty nations, in the White House, and thereafter the treaty was open for ratification. The United States Senate gave its consent on April 25, and the United States then ratified the treaty which entered into force on October 10, 1967.[23]

The most recent development of some legal significance in the sphere of outer space was the completion of a draft treaty by the UN Committee on Outer Space, on the "Rescue and Return of Astronauts."[24] As soon as the General Assembly had approved the draft, the agreement was opened to signature and ratification. It came into effect on December 3, 1968.

RADIO COMMUNICATIONS

The invention of wireless telegraphy resulted, at the beginning of the century, in discussions similar to those later posed by the advent of aircraft, but in no case was the issue of sovereignty over the national air debated as bitterly as in the latter instance. In 1906, an International Wireless Telegraph Convention was signed at Berlin, superseded by the International Wireless Convention of London (1912). Both instruments dealt with technical aspects of radio communications, including distress calls by ships, linking of coastal radio stations with telegraph systems, and so forth.

In 1927, the International Radiotelegraph Conference of Washington resulted in the International Radio Convention, signed by representatives of seventy-eight governments. This instrument, besides duplicating earlier agreements, expanded control over telecommunications and required private radio stations to obtain governmental licenses. More important, the treaty provided for the use and allocation of radio frequencies and types of sending.

As telecommunications expanded in scope, a still more modern method of control became desirable. The Madrid Telecommunication Convention of 1932 created a new international agency, the International Telecommunication Union. This body was placed in control of all varieties of

---

[22] GA Res. 2222 (XXI), 19 December 1966, "Treaty Governing the Exploration and Use of Outer Space, including the Moon and Other Celestial Bodies."

[23] Consult also the analysis of the agreement by Ambassador A. J. Goldberg, in 56 *Department of State Bulletin* (1967), p. 78 [or see 61 *A.J.I.L.* (1967), pp. 586–592 for his views], and Thomas R. Adams, "The Outer Space Treaty: An Interpretation in Light of the No-Sovereignty Provision," 9 *Harvard International Law Journal* (1968), pp. 140–157.

[24] *The New York Times*, December 17, 1968, pp. 1, 66; for the text of the treaty, see *ibid.*, p. 66. Consult also R. C. Hall, "Rescue and Return of Astronauts on Earth and in Outer Space," 63 *A.J.I.L.* (1969), pp. 197–210.

telecommunications, hitherto governed by separate treaties. For each mode of communication, a separate set of regulations was drawn up, and a central office of the Union was established at Bern, supervised by the Swiss government. Subsequently the Union has convoked a number of conferences and in 1947 evolved a new Telecommunication Convention, at Atlantic City, superseding all earlier instruments. That new agreement came into force on January 1, 1949. Regional telecommunications conventions have also been evolved in the Americas (Havana, 1937; Rio de Janeiro, 1945), and in Asia (Asian Broadcasting Union, 1964).

One of the basic regulations adopted by the Telecommunication Union has been the requirement that all radio stations must be operated in such manner as to avoid interference with the communications services of all contracting governments or agencies authorized by them. This regulation has been violated on a wholesale basis by the governments of the Soviet bloc states, which have caused to be set up extensive systems of radio stations purposely designed to interfere with (jam) broadcasts from western Europe and from the United States.[25]

Around 1958 a new phenomenon in the communications sphere made its appearance and soon involved several aspects of international law: pirate broadcasting.

Privately owned radio stations, located on vessels anchored or sailing outside the territorial sea, or established on artificial islands beyond territorial jurisdictions, began to broadcast to states whose governments did not permit, or controlled rigorously, the transmission of commercial advertising.[26]

Under the rules of the Telecommunications Union, such commercial broadcasting from international waters was prohibited, but responsibility for enforcement rested on the country in which the vessel in question was registered.

In 1962, the "Voice of Slough" began operations off the English coast and was joined, in 1964, by Radio Caroline, a large-scale operation on a former ferry, staffed by two diskjockeys and a crew of ten. When the British government protested to the I.T.U., the flag state of the *Caroline*, Panama, was reminded by the I.T.U. of its responsibilities, for on previous occasions Panama had agreed to withdraw its registration from vessels housing illegal radio stations off the Dutch and Danish coasts. Meanwhile the owners of the Caroline acquired a second vessel which soon began to broadcast off the British coast near Liverpool.

Two other pirate stations (Radio Invicta, later renamed Radio 390, and Radio City) were established on abandoned World War II anti-aircraft towers (Marbelle Towers), resting on the seabed in the Thames

[25] See also Gerhard von Glahn, "The Case for Legal Control of 'Liberation' Propaganda," 31 *Law and Contemporary Problems* (Summer, 1966), pp. 553–588.

[26] Such as Radio Nord, outside Swedish jurisdiction; Radio Mercur, off Denmark; Radio Veronica, off the Dutch coast.

estuary, outside British territorial limits, and Radio London operated from a former U.S. minesweeper, anchored outside the three-mile limit.

Denmark took direct action in August, 1964, when Danish police boarded the vessel housing Radio Mercur and closed the station. Similarly, Netherlands police, in December of 1964, boarded and silenced "Radio & TV Noordzee," the only known pirate television station, operating from a platform affixed to the North Sea bed five miles off the Dutch coast.[27]

Interference by the coastal state with pirate stations operating beyond the maritime border has been justified, properly, under Article 24(1) of the 1958 Geneva Convention on the Territorial Sea and the Contiguous Zone, as falling into the permitted activities of a coastal state in a contiguous zone.[28]

On January 20, 1965, the Council of Europe opened to signature the European Agreement for the Prevention of Broadcasts Transmitted from Stations Outside National Territories.[29] And in 1967, the United Kingdom enacted the Marine and Broadcasting Offenses Act, making it a criminal offense to assist a pirate station in any manner, after an earlier (1964) Territorial Waters Order in Council, aimed at the stations located on fixed tower sites.[30]

Even in the Pacific, pirate broadcasting made its appearance: in 1968, the vessel Tiri II housed an illegal station operating off the coast of New Zealand.

SUGGESTED READINGS

NATIONAL AIR

Gould, pp. 387–392; Lauterpacht's *Oppenheim*, Vol. I, pp. 517–529; Whiteman, Vol. IX, pp. 312–441, 634–717; Svarlien, pp. 213–225; David H. N. Johnson, *Rights in Air Space* (Manchester: University of Manchester Press; Dobbs Ferry, N.Y.: Oceana Publications, 1965).

OUTER SPACE: GENERAL

Myres S. McDougal, H. D. Lasswell, and I. A. Vlasic, *Law and Public Order in Space* (New Haven and London: Yale University Press, 1963); Maxwell Cohen, ed., *Law and Politics in Space* (Montreal: McGill University Press, 1964); C. Wilfred Jenks, *Space Law* (New York: Praeger, 1965); Andrew G.

---

[27] *The New York Times*, January 3, 1965, p. 14; consult also the detailed study by H. F. van Panhuys and Menno J. van Emde Boas, "Legal Aspects of Pirate Broadcasting," 60 *A.J.I.L.* (1966), pp. 303–341.

[28] See van Panhuys and Boas, *op. cit.*, pp. 316–317.

[29] *Ibid.*, pp. 324–326; text of the treaty may be found in 59 *A.J.I.L.* (1965), p. 715.

[30] See *Regina* v. *Kent Justices, Ex Parte Lye et al.*, Great Britain, Queen's Bench, 1966, (1966) 2 W.L.R., reported in 61 *A.J.I.L.* (1967), pp. 1077–1080, and noted, with elaborate documentation, by James R. Watts in 9 *Harvard International Law Journal* (1968), pp. 317–324.

Haley, *Space Law and Government* (New York: Appleton-Century-Crofts, 1967); J. E. Fawcett, *International Law and the Uses of Outer Space* (Manchester University Press; Dobbs Ferry, N.Y.: Oceana Publications, 1968); Leon Lipson, "An Argument on the Legality of Reconnaissance Satellites," *Proceedings* (1961), pp. 174–176.

THE SOVIET UNION AND SPACE

Robert D. Crane, "Soviet Attitude toward International Space Law," 56 *A.J.I.L.* (1962), pp. 685–723, and his "The Beginnings of Marxist Space Jurisprudence," *ibid.*, 57 (1963), pp. 615–625, both studies equipped with extensive documentation useful for further investigation.

PIRATE RADIO OPERATIONS

77 *Time* (April 14, 1961), pp. 35–36, and *ibid.*, 88 (July 1, 1966), p. 33; *The London Sunday Times*, January 14, 1962, p. 4; *The New York Times*, March 29, 1964, p. 18, and *ibid.*, November 28, 1965, p. 23; John Tebbel, "Britain's Troubled Air," 50 *Saturday Review* (August 12, 1967), pp. 60–61; Whiteman, Vol. IX, pp. 789–809.

PART V
International Transactions

21

Agents of International Intercourse

DIPLOMATIC AGENTS

ackground. International relations between friendly states have been characterized from the beginning of recorded history by a need for special organs of communication. For millennia, however, these organs, called ambassadors (diplomatic agents), did not possess the character of permanent representatives, but instead were made use of only on occassion for the purpose of achieving certain tasks. In other words, an ambassador would be sent to a certain country to conclude an alliance, to make a trade agreement, to seek the hand of a princess for his king, to arrange for a marriage dowry, or to carry out whatever special purpose was at hand. Once he succeeded or failed in his mission, he returned home. Nevertheless, classical antiquity, particularly among the Greek city-states, witnessed the development of firm rules governing the sending of such agents, such as their inviolability, which still prevail today.

The appearance of permanent representatives at foreign capitals did not take place until the middle of the fifteenth century—the city of Milano being usually cited as the originator of the practice, *c.* A.D. 1450. After a while, the occasional placement of permanent agents aboard was supplanted slowly by a general acceptance of the system. Among the various obstacles to a rapid and universally applied system of permanent representation was a major one: the distrust with which courts viewed a foreign ambassador, for all too many of them saw in him nothing but a spy— noble of birth, to be sure—of the sending state. Thus Russia, until the reign of Peter the Great, resisted successfully all attempts to locate permanent foreign representatives in its capital. Western Europe, on the other hand, quickly realized the many advantages accruing from the permanent presence of representatives aboard and the custom quickly spread in that portion of the Continent. Some states persisted for quite a while in assuring each other the right to send ambassadors, by means of bilateral agreements, but the majority regarded such a right as an aspect of sovereign independence. After the Treaty of Westphalia (1648), the establishment of permanent diplomatic missions became the rule in Europe.

DIPLOMATIC RELATIONS

Right of Representation. The *right of diplomatic intercourse* is divided into an *active* and a *passive* right. The active right involves the authority to send diplomatic agents aboard. This aspect represents an unquestioned right of every independent member of the family of nations. The problem of *who* is to exercise this right of representation in any given state is an internal constitutional question. As a rule it is the monarch in a monarchy and the president in a republic (alone or in conjunction with some legislative body) who exercise the right. Semisovereign states (limited members) possess the right of representation if their suzerain approves it. In the case of a confederation, the individual states usually possess the right of representation, although a paramount member may be granted the right also, either on a sole or concurrent basis.

Corresponding to the right to send diplomatic agents is the passive right—the right to receive such agents. Normally an international person possessing the former right also exercises the latter. But in the case of some former protectorates, instances had occurred in which the protected state enjoyed only the passive right.

Generally speaking, however, the right of representation, being a common attribute of sovereign states, posed questions only in the relatively few instances when it had to be determined whether or not a given community was entitled to this right.

Codification of Rules. Before entering into the details of diplomatic relations between states, it will be necessary to examine the basis of the principles involved.

Until 1815, the rules governing diplomatic intercourse were based primarily on customary international law, supplemented by practices founded on courtesy among nations. The classification of diplomatic ranks achieved at the Congress of Vienna and amended in the Protocol of Aix-la-Chapelle (1818) did not add materially to the existing rules, and it was not until 1927 that the first serious consideration of a possible codification of those rules was undertaken. In that year, the League of Nations Committee of Experts for the Progressive Codification of International Law reported to the Council of the League that it regarded the subject of diplomatic privileges and immunities as "sufficiently ripe for international regulation." The Council, however, disagreed with the conclusion of the Committee of Experts and decided that the subject would be excluded from the agenda of the proposed 1930 Hague Conference for the Codification of International Law. On the other hand, the Sixth Conference of American States, held in Havana in 1928, adopted a Convention on Diplomatic Officers.[1] This instrument, subsequently ratified by twelve American states, was signed but not ratified by the United States, which objected to the inclusion of provisions approving the granting of diplomatic asylum.

[1] Text of the convention in 22 *A.J.I.L.* (1928), pp. 142–151.

The International Law Commission of the United Nations selected the subject of diplomatic intercourse and immunities as one of fourteen topics for codification but did not give it any priority standing at the time the list was drawn up (first session of the Commission in 1949). At its seventh session, in 1952, however, the General Assembly passed a resolution requesting the Commission to undertake the codification of the subject. At its sixth session, in 1954, the Commission initiated a study of diplomatic intercourse and immunities. Work on a proposed draft convention proceeded between that year and 1959 and the Commission succeeded in completing a final and excellent draft by the latter year.[2]

On December 7, 1959, the General Assembly, by Resolution 1450 (XIV), decided to convene an international conference to consider the question of diplomatic intercourse and immunities. This gathering, the United Nations Conference on Diplomatic Intercourse and Immunities, met at the Neue Hofburg, Vienna, from March 2 to April 14, 1961. It was attended by delegations from eighty-one states, and by observers from three Specialized Agencies, and also from the International Atomic Energy Agency, the League of Arab States, and the Asian–African Legal Consultative Committee.

The conference, in addition to adopting a number of resolutions, prepared the following instruments: (1) Vienna Convention of Diplomatic Relations; (2) Optional Protocol concerning Acquisition of Nationality; and (3) Optional Protocol concerning the Compulsory Settlement of Disputes.[3] Of these, the Convention on Diplomatic Relations, of April 14, 1961, is the most important.[4] Although it followed to a large extent the draft convention prepared by the International Law Commission, there are significant departures from and additions to that draft in several articles of the Vienna Convention.

On April 18, 1961, the representatives of seventy-five states signed the convention and the instrument entered into force on April 24, 1964; it had not been ratified by the United States at the time of writing.

Although the Vienna Convention does not show basic deviations from hitherto existing customary law, the fact that codification has at long last been achieved marks a definite advance in the development of international law. The subject matter of the Vienna meeting was not encumbered

[2] See especially the "Reports" of the Commission covering its ninth session (April 23–June 28, 1957) in 52 *A.J.I.L.* (1958), Supp., pp. 177–209, and its tenth session (April 28–July 4, 1958), in 53 *A.J.I.L.* (1959), Supp., pp. 230–300, at pp. 253–291, for the progressive development of the draft convention and the extremely valuable commentary on individual articles.

[3] The texts of the convention, the protocols, and the resolutions are reprinted in 55 *A.J.I.L.* (1961), Supp., pp. 1062–1082. Consult also the study by Ernest L. Kerley, "Some Aspects of the Vienna Conference on Diplomatic Intercourse and Immunities," 56 *A.J.I.L.* (1962), p. 88–129, as well as Philippe Cahier, "Vienna Convention on Diplomatic Relations," *International Conciliation*, No. 571 (January, 1969), pp. 5–40.

[4] The convention will be cited hereinafter as *Vienna Diplomatic Convention*.

with too many contentious matters: disputes at the conference arose out of questions of balance and emphasis rather than from conflicting national interests. The writer believes that in a few years the provisions of the Vienna Convention will be generally accepted components of conventional international law and has treated the contents of the convention accordingly in this chapter.

It is interesting to note, in passing, that the final paragraph of the Preamble to the convention declares that the signatory states affirm "that the rules of customary international law should continue to govern questions not expressly regulated by the provisions of the present Convention."

REPRESENTATION

From a legal point of view, each sovereign state is completely free to decide whether, and in which foreign states, it wishes to be represented by diplomatic agents. Should a state decide, for some reason, to deviate from what certainly has become a general custom and endeavor to live in solitude, such deviation would be regarded by other states, at the very least, as an international incivility. And if the state in question resolved also to bar all foreign diplomatic agents from its jurisdiction, it would remove itself from further membership in the community of nations.

On the other hand, few states maintain diplomatic representation at all capitals of the world. A given country might not be able to afford the relatively enormous sums needed for such an enterprise, or it might properly decide that it had so few interests in maintaining relations with a given foreign state that they would not warrant the expense of a diplomatic mission. Hence some states content themselves with being represented in certain capitals through the diplomatic mission of a friendly third state or maintaining an ambassador at a capital who acts as their accredited representative to a number of other states. Thus Western Samoa, independent since 1962, decided, for reasons of economy, not to join the United Nations and not to establish diplomatic missions abroad. Its limited foreign relations were entrusted by special agreement to the embassies maintained by New Zealand in various parts of the world.

Somewhat different is the right of a state to break off diplomatic relations with another state on a temporary basis, that is, to recall its diplomatic agent. Such an occurrence does not dissolve all relations between the states in question because normally both states will arrange to be represented through a third state which acts then as an intermediary for purposes of communication. This arrangement was adopted when the United States chose Switzerland as the party through which communication was to be maintained with Cuba.

It should be pointed out, moreover, that a breach of diplomatic relations at a time when no change in government has taken place in the "offending" state, does not mean withdrawal of recognition of the government in power in that state. After the rupture of diplomatic relations with the

Castro administration in Cuba, the government of the United States continued to accord to the Cuban government such rights as accrue to the government of a sovereign state under international law.

BEGINNING AND TERMINATION OF A DIPLOMATIC MISSION

Acceptance of an Agent. No state is required to accept every individual proposed as the agent of a foreign state. The agent must enjoy the confidence of the government of the receiving state. Should the latter decide that a given nominee, for any reason, is not suitable as the representative of his government, it may reject the appointment.

Hence it is the rule that the sending state, before the appointment of a diplomatic agent, inquiries of the receiving state whether the nominee is acceptable to it, that is, if he is *persona grata*. If such notification is not given, the receiving state normally would refuse to admit the nominee. Rejection of the nominee as *persona non grata* may or may not be accompanied by reasons for the decision. Traditionally no reason is given or expected. For a long time, nevertheless, the United States and Great Britain not only insisted on being given reasons for the rejection of one of their nominees but indeed asserted their right to approve or reject those reasons as valid. This attitude, however, has had to be abandoned by both the United States and Great Britain, for in practice any receiving state can simply refuse to accept an individual whom it has judged to be *persona non grata*.

When the United States appointed a Mr. Keiley as minister to Italy, in 1885, without previous inquiry, he was denied reception for the interesting reason that some fourteen years earlier he had protested at a meeting in the United States against the Italian absorption of the Papal States. The Secretary of State (Bayard) viewed this as a sufficient reason for Keiley's rejection. But then the same individual was appointed, without previous nomination, American minister to Austria-Hungary and was rejected again. This time, however, the reason given did not satisfy the United States government: "The position of a foreign envoy wedded to a Jewess by civil marriage would be untenable and even impossible in Vienna." [5] President Cleveland contradicted his Secretary of State, who had held that each state had a right to exercise its discretion in receiving or rejecting diplomatic agents, and in protest refused to make a new nomination, leaving the affairs of the United States Legation for two years in the hands of the Secretary of the Legation. It might be mentioned, in passing, that beginning with the appointment of the first United States ambassadors to foreign posts in 1893, the Department of State has been very careful to inquire about the acceptability of a proposed diplomatic agent before actual appointment took place. While prior notification and inquiry by the sending state is not required by law for subordinate staff members of

[5] Moore, Vol. IV, pp. 480–483.

a diplomatic mission, courtesy has prompted most states to apply the practice to such individuals.

On August 20, 1940, the Department of State announced a new United States rule governing the acceptability of certain foreign nominees to diplomatic or consular posts in this country: after that date, the United States would declare the nominees of non-American governments *persona non grata* if they had been found unacceptable by other American states. The ruling was occasioned by the assignment of Friedrich Ried to the German consulate in New York after being asked to leave Brazil, where he had been stationed as consul, because of alleged fifth-column activities.

The legal basis of each diplomatic office is the agreement of the receiving state to the admission of a foreign mission. The receiving state, therefore, lays down the rules governing the legal position and activities of foreign diplomats, but in each instance the state is bound by the valid and applicable principles of international law. In effect, the receiving state concedes to the foreign diplomat certain rights, privileges, and spheres of activity, subject to international law. Thus each diplomatic activity carried out by an agent of a state rests on a kind of double basis or title: the agreement (concession) of the receiving state and the instructions issued to him within the framework of that concession by the sending state.

The appointment of a diplomatic agent is a constitutional act of the sending state. His rights and duties begin formally with the handing over and acceptance of his credentials (*lettre de créance*) in the receiving state which, by its acceptance of that document, recognizes the position of the individual concerned as the agent of his government. The acceptance of the credentials takes place, depending on the rank of the agent, either by the chief of state or the minister of foreign affairs (in the United States, the Secretary of State) or through some specially designated protocol officer or functionary.

Termination of a Mission. Because the accrediting of a diplomatic agent is a personal act—from the sender to the receiver—it terminates when one of the two parties ceases to represent his state. Therefore, when a change in monarchs takes place, one or the other party has to accredit again the ambassadors and other diplomats. A renewal of the credentials is also called for by a change in rank of the diplomat in question and, normally, when a change in the form of government takes place in either state. There are, however, many exceptions to the last rule. For instance, the United States ambassador to Russia, David R. Francis, reported to the Department of State on March 17, 1917, that the imperial government of Russia had been overthrown by revolution. He requested authorization to recognize the new government, which he received two days later from Secretary of State Lansing. On March 22, Francis called on the new Council of Ministers and presented his new credentials as United States ambassador. When the Provisional government was in turn ousted on November 7, 1917, Ambassador Francis did not receive new credentials and presumably his diplomatic mission terminated with the overthrow of the Provisional government. He did remain in Russia, however, and until he left, on July 25, 1918, continued in his privileges and immunities.

On the other hand, a mere change in the person acting as chief of state in a republic or in the person acting as foreign minister does not require a renewal of the credentials of diplomats.

Formally, the office of a diplomat ceases whenever one of the preceding conditions requiring renewal of accreditation takes place. Other reasons for the termination of a diplomatic office follow:

In the case of a nonpermanent diplomatic mission, the completion (success or failure) of the task entrusted to the mission ends its existence.

The diplomatic agent may be recalled by the sending state. In this case the diplomat hands to the chief of state to whom he is accredited, his letter of recall (*lettre de rappel*); normally he is handed, in return, a *lettre de recréance,* which contains an acceptance of the letter of recall as well as some sort of tribute to the effective role played by the departing agent. More recently however, this procedure has been changed by most states. The replacement of the departing diplomat, in handing his own credentials to the head of the receiving state, also hands over the letter of recall of his predecessor. These formalities are not observed if the recall results either from a conflict between the receiving and sending states or between the receiving state and the diplomatic agent in question, such as when the agent has been insulted and has not obtained satisfaction.

The reasons for which diplomats are recalled are many and varied: they may be founded on interstate relations; they may rest on the relationships between the diplomat and the government of the receiving state; or they may be of purely domestic origin, such as when a diplomat is transferred to another post.

The diplomatic mission may also end with the dismissal of the agent. If a diplomat somehow offends the government of the receiving state, he may be declared to be *persona non grata* and his recall will be requested of the sending state.

On many recent occasions the dismissal of a diplomatic agent represented merely a retaliatory action, caused by a similar dismissal (usually for purely political reasons) of an agent by the sending state. Thus the United States declared the counselor of the Tanzanian embassy in Washington *persona non grata* after Tanzania had expelled two American diplomats on charges of subversive activities.[6]

If the sending state refuses to accede to a request for recall, say, by deciding that the reasons advanced for it constitute insufficient cause for the recall of the diplomatic person, the receiving state either decides not to deal with the individual concerned—which ends his usefulness to his own state—or to dismiss him altogether. One of the more unusual related instances in this connection took place in 1806. The Spanish minister in

---

[6] *The New York Times,* February 14, 1965, p. 23.

Washington, Yrujo, had indulged in rather irresponsible public statements concerning the policies of the United States government and the latter quite properly requested his recall. When the Spanish government refused to act on this demand, the United States decided to have no further dealings with Yrujo, but permitted him, nevertheless, to remain in the country instead of escorting him to a vessel for return to Spain.[7]

A diplomat who is no longer *persona grata* may or may not be given a time limit within which to leave the jurisdiction of the receiving state. Should he refuse to leave, he may be placed under detention and escorted to the frontier for expulsion.

Diplomatic missions also terminate with a rupture of diplomatic relations between the sending and receiving states. Thus both diplomatic and consular missions terminated when the Federal Republic of Germany broke off relations with the Cuban government on January 14, 1963. The action followed Cuba's establishment of diplomatic relations with the German Democratic Republic, termed "the regime ruling in the Soviet-Occupied Zone of Germany" in the West German note announcing its decision.

The outbreak of war between two states ends their direct diplomatic relations. In each of them the ambassador or minister transfers limited representation rights to the agents of a third (neutral) state through which are maintained, for the duration of the conflict, whatever diplomatic relations there remain between the belligerents.

Finally, a diplomatic mission ends with the disappearance of the sending or receiving state. An unusual exception to this normal and logical rule took place in the case of the diplomatic representatives of the Republic of Latvia following that country's absorption in the Soviet Union in 1940. Because most of the world's governments refused to recognize the annexation of Latvia, Estonia, and Lithuania by the U.S.S.R., the diplomatic agents of the three Baltic republics continued to occupy their posts in all nonrecognizing states. The Latvian envoy in London, as the senior diplomatic agent of Latvia abroad, assumed the emergency powers of his government.[8] Thus a diplomatic representative assumed the status of a government-in-exile and claimed sovereignty over all Latvian citizens living in Western countries. Such jurisdiction naturally was limited to states in which Latvian diplomatic agents were still accredited.

DIPLOMATIC RANK

As long as there existed no permanent representatives abroad, distinctions between diplomatic agents depended almost entirely on the relative strength and importance of the sending state. But as soon as permanent representation made its appearance, bitter quarrelling ensued between the representatives of various powers stationed at the same court. It was

[7] See Moore, Vol. IV, p. 508, for details of Yrujo's case.
[8] See *Mrs. J. W.* v. *Republic of Latvia*, Germany, Landgericht, Berlin, October 3, 1953, digested in 48 *A.J.I.L.* (1954), pp. 161–163.

generally accepted that the representatives of monarchs (*ambaxatores*) occupied the highest category in rank. Besides such "ambassadors" there came into being one other class of representatives—the ministers, or residents, entitled, since the middle of the seventeenth century, *envoyés* (envoys). After some time, this second group was divided into two classes—ordinary and extraordinary envoys—and the latter began to claim special privileges and higher rank than the former. More and more states named *envoyés extraordinaires* and insisted that these constituted a class distinct from ambassadors and residents, even when their duties and powers corresponded in every detail with those of the residents.

The protracted negotiations leading to the Peace Treaties of 1648, which ended the Thirty Years' War, serve as a classic illustration of the difficulties under which early modern diplomacy operated. The eight-year span of time required to settle the war was due primarily to a lack of rules governing diplomatic ceremonial and etiquette. Thus an offer by Venice to mediate was ignored completely because the offer addressed Queen Christina of Sweden as *Serenissime* without adding *Très-Puissante* to her official title. The Venetian ambassador in Paris apologized for this *faux pas*, to Hugo Grotius, then the Swedish ambassador to France, but the apology had no effect. A little later, Sweden refused to send delegates to any peace conference at which Sweden's good friend and ally, France, would have precedence over Swedish diplomats.

One was reminded of these rather picayune incidents when, in 1968–69, protracted maneuvering preceded the decision to use a round-table seating arrangement for the Paris talks designed to bring an end to the war in Vietnam.

Categories of Diplomatic Representatives. At the beginning of the eighteenth century, three basic classes were recognized: ambassadors, envoys extraordinary, and residents (soon called ministers resident). By the end of the century, a fourth category had made its appearance, chargés d'affaires, occupying the bottom rank among diplomatic agents.

Emergence of definite categories did not, however, end the disputes among diplomats, for within each class quarrels concerning precedence continued. The Congress of Vienna finally cleared up a totally confused state of affairs when it adopted, on March 19, 1815, the *Règlément sur le Rang entre les Agents Diplomatiques*, a basic document supplemented later by the *Protocol* of Aix-la-Chapelle of November 21, 1818. The categories set up by these two instruments still exist today, even though the third class of diplomats, added by the 1818 *Protocol*, has disappeared from the world scene and is not listed any more in the Vienna Diplomatic Convention of 1961 (Art. 14). There are, then, four classes, or categories, of diplomatic representatives:

1. Ambassadors (ambassadors extraordinary, ambassadors plenipotentiary, and papal nuncios),

2. Ministers (envoys extraordinary, ministers plenipotentiary, and papal internuncios),

3. Ministers resident,

4. Chargés d'affaires.

The first three categories are accredited by and to chiefs of state; the fourth is accredited by and to ministers of foreign affairs.

Customarily, states exchange diplomatic agents of the same rank, even though exceptions to this practice have been recorded. In the past, ambassadors were exchanged only between the Great Powers, but in the past thirty or so years this custom has been abandoned in many cases, notably on the part of the United States. The sending of an ambassador to a small country supposedly ranks the latter equal with a powerful nation—and, regardless of facts, appears to flatter sometimes very susceptible egos in the small country's government. Thus the United States, in pursuance of the "Good Neighbor" policy adopted under the presidency of Franklin Roosevelt, elevated its heads of missions in all Latin American states to the rank of ambassador.

The vexatious question of precedence within each class has been settled, since 1815, by ranking the various agents in accordance with the date of their accreditation in a particular capital—a kind of seniority system as it were.

Nuncios (papal ambassadors) by custom act as the deans (*doyens*) of the diplomats accredited to a given government: they act as their spokesmen, particularly on ceremonial occasions. Legates are not really diplomats but are sent to other countries by the Vatican as its representatives for internal church matters. In many cases, legates by courtesy enjoy diplomatic rights and privileges.

Ministers (diplomatic agents of the second class) are *not* technically representatives of the head of their state, even though their credentials are signed by the latter and presented to the head of the receiving state. This technical inferiority has been ignored, however, in the twentieth century and today a minister, as well as the second class of papal diplomat, the internuncio, is regarded equal to the ambassador in his ability to speak for the head of his state.

The chargé d'affaires is accredited by and to a minister of foreign affairs (in the United States, the Secretary of State). Whereas he was customarily sent only to small, backward, unimportant states (*ad hoc*), he is today primarily an assistant, with specified administrative functions, to an ambassador or minister. Normally he assumes, on an acting bases (*ad interim*), the functions of his superior during the latter's absence from the diplomatic mission or until a replacement is sent to the mission. In the days of capitulations in Oriental countries, the various Western consuls equipped with diplomatic powers had the assimilated rank of chargés d'affaires.

Below the ambassador or minister, a diplomatic mission may comprise hundreds of persons. On occasion, distinctions are drawn between the official and nonofficial personnel of such a mission. The official personnel include all persons employed by the sending state or by the chief of mission to whom they are subordinate. This group comprises all the various functionaries of the mission, including the affiliated military or technical attachés, as well as the clerical staff (typists, secretaries, file clerks, interpreters, code clerks, and so forth).

The family of the chief of mission is definitely part of his official retinue. The nonofficial personnel are the servants of the chief of mission and of the embassy (ambassador) or legation (minister), such as chauffeurs, gardeners, and so forth. The legal position of this unofficial personnel is the subject of much dispute. In most states, individuals in this category enjoy, by courtesy, diplomatic privileges and immunities as long as they are in the employ of the embassy or legation and are listed as such employees with the foreign office (Department of State) of the receiving state. In other states, such employees do not enjoy any special standing (U.S.S.R.).

FUNCTIONS OF DIPLOMATIC AGENTS

The functions of the diplomat may be classified under six main headings:[9]

1. *Negotiation.* The original reason for the rise of diplomats—the intention of having a representative in a foreign capital empowered to negotiate agreements with the receiving state, was to "deal" directly with the foreign government. This basic function has been downgraded considerably in the past half century or so, in part because of progress in communications, which makes the diplomat more of a spokesman than a true negotiator, in part because of a tendency to substitute foreign ministers' meetings or summit meetings for negotiation at the ambassadorial level.

2. *Representation.* The diplomatic agent is the representative of the government of his state. He not only acts as such on ceremonial occasions but files protests or inquiries with the receiving government. He presents the policies of his government to the host state.

3. *Information.* The basic duty of a diplomat is to report to his government on political events, policies, and other related matters. He is not a spy in the orthodox meaning of the term—even though a few heads of missions have been spies in the true sense of the word, and others have acted as paymasters to spies.

4. *Protection.* The diplomat has a duty to look after the interests, persons, and property of citizens of his own state in the receiving state. He

[9] See also the excellent study of the "new" functions developed, in recent decades, in the diplomatic field: The American Assembly, *The Representation of the United States Abroad* (New York: Columbia University, Graduate School of Business, 1956).

must be ready to assist them when they get into trouble abroad, may have to take charge of their bodies and effects if they happen to die on a trip, and in general acts as a "troubleshooter" for his fellow nationals in the receiving state.

5. *Public relations.* The diplomat is engaged continually in efforts to create good will for his own state and its policies. This propaganda/public relations function involves the giving and attending of parties and dinners, the delivery of lectures and other speeches, attendance at or participation in dedications of monuments, building, and (lately) foreign assistance projects, and so on. The effectiveness of such public relations activities is questionable, however, because it is difficult to measure. Only one thing is certain: if the diplomat refrains from participating in such activities, ill will is created.

6. *Administration.* The chief of a diplomatic mission is the administrative head of the group, even though, in a large mission, he may have a personnel office and department heads subordinate to himself. In the last resort, the ambassador or minister is the person responsible for the operation of embassy or legislation, and ultimate administrative responsibility is lodged in his hands.

DIPLOMATIC PRIVILEGES AND IMMUNITIES

A diplomatic person enjoys a considerable range of privileges and immunities based on customary as well as conventional international law. The obvious intent behind the grant of these privileges has been the desire to enable a diplomatic agent to exercise his duties and functions without impediment on the part of the authorities of the receiving state.

The extent of such diplomatic privileges has varied considerably during the past five centuries. Today the following are generally recognized as valid.

Personal Inviolability. The person of the diplomatic agent is inviolable. This, his oldest privilege, was mentioned in the earliest records extant. Originally the sacred character of a diplomatic agent was a question of practical necessity, because in many parts of the world of antiquity a foreigner possessed no rights whatsoever and, in many instances, the injury or even killing of an alien was not punished by the local authorities. But ambassadors were not ordinary foreigners; they were always regarded as the representatives of their state. Hence any attack on an ambassador was an attack on his state and as such could lead to war: therefore one had to surround the ambassador with privileges in order to give him special protection. As the position of the foreigner improved, in general, in the course of time, with the grant of civil rights and protection on the part of most governments, diplomatic inviolability began to have less importance than in the past. This fact had been pointed out by Bynkershoek; however, later writers, to the end of the nineteenth century, continued to place extraordinary emphasis on the element of inviolability. In more recent times this privilege has been viewed in proper perspective; diplomatic inviolability today means little more than that the diplomat enjoys a somewhat greater protection under criminal legislation than is the case for other aliens. This protection is guaranteed to him by the law of the receiving state; hence it is a question of domestic law, not of international law. The latter only obligates each state to promulgate and enforce the inviolability, that is, protection of the diplomat. As should be obvious, such inviolability is not absolute or unconditional. If a diplomat acts in such an illegal manner that measures of personal self-defense or police action are needed to restrain him, he cannot stand on his privilege of inviolability.

Extraterritoriality. A second privilege of diplomatic persons is characterized as *extraterritoriality*. This concept involves a number of exemptions from local jurisdiction to which the diplomat is entitled under international law. Literally, as was mentioned, extraterritoriality means that the person or thing in question has to be viewed as not being in a given territory or jurisdiction. Although this assumption is obviously a fiction, it is nevertheless a matter of daily observance in the conduct of states.

Many writers confuse the two terms *inviolability* and *extraterritoriality*, but even though both have the same historic source and serve the same purpose, that is, to make the diplomat independent of local jurisdiction, they are not identical. Extraterritoriality is a far more recent development than is inviolability; it was totally unknown in classical antiquity and only made its appearance about the time of Grotius. The "fiction" of being outside the jurisdiction of the receiving state was abandoned some decades ago by continental writers, even though it was defended vigorously until quite recently by Anglo-Saxon commentators on the law of nations. Today it is generally agreed that the diplomatic person is no longer considered to be *extra territorium;* instead he is subject to the application of the local law of the receiving state but enjoys immunity from the *enforcement* of that law as long as his privileged status lasts. This exemption from enforcement of the local law operates in a number of spheres:

Exemption from Local Jurisdiction. The person of a diplomat is virtually exempt from the jurisdiction of the receiving state. No civil or criminal action can be taken against him except as noted below. Furthermore, a diplomat cannot be required to appear as a witness in a court proceeding.

Waiver of Immunity. A diplomat may not himself waive his immunity; this may be done only by the sending state in the case of heads of missions; subordinate staff members may have their immunity waived, in specific instances, by their authorized superior. National regulation of the sending state, however, governs such waivers of immunity. Theoretically, a diplomat could be considered to have waived his immunity if he brought suit in a local court: it appears that nowadays a counterclaim can be filed against him under such circumstances.[10] It should be mentioned in passing that the immunity enjoyed by the diplomat in the receiving state does not extend to his own country: he never is exempt from the jurisdiction of his own sending state, as reaffirmed in the *Vienna Diplomatic Convention* (Art. 31, par 4.).

Common exceptions to the immunity from the civil and administrative jurisdiction of the receiving state include (1) a real action relating to private immovable property situated in the receiving state, unless the diplomatic agent holds it on behalf of the sending state for the purposes of the mission; (2) an action relating to succession in which the agent is involved as executor, administrator, heir or legatee as a private person and not on behalf of the sending state; and (3) any action relating to any professional or commercial activity exercised by the diplomatic agent in the receiving state outside his official functions (Art. 31, par. 1). As far as the third of these exemptions is concerned, the Vienna Convention prohibits such outside professional or commercial activity for personal profit (Art. 42).

If, in the case of civil or administrative proceedings, the receiving state obtains a waiver of immunity relative to a diplomatic agent, such waiver does not imply a waiver of immunity in respect to the execution of a judgment against the diplomatic agent. A separate waiver would be required to permit execution of such a judgment (Art. 32, par. 4).

Exemption from Taxes and Personal Services. The head of a mission is exempt from certain fiscal obligations normally payable in or to the receiving state. Thus he does not have to meet any direct national, regional, or municipal dues and taxes relating to the premises of the mission (Art. 23, par. 1). And all diplomatic agents are exempt from all dues and taxes, personal or real, in the receiving state, except for: indirect taxes normally included in the cost of goods or services; taxes on real estate in the receiving state owned privately by the agent; estate, succession, or inheritance duties on personal property (except in the event of the agent's death when his movable property is treated as tax-exempt); taxes on private income and on investments made in commercial enterprises in the receiving state; and certain fees and duties relating to real estate (Art. 34, and Art. 39, par. 4).

Minor immunities include exemption from all personal services and from such military obligations as those connected with requisitioning, military contributions, and billeting (Art. 35). Subject to local regulations and laws, the receiving state waives payment of customs duties and similar charges on all incoming articles for the official use of a mission and for articles brought in for the personal use of a diplomatic agent or his family (Art. 36, par. 1). The baggage of diplomats is normally exempt from inspection. However, if a strong presumption exists that it contains articles which by law cannot be imported or exported, as the case may be, the receiving state may insist upon inspection in the presence of the diplomatic agent or his authorized representative (Art. 36, par. 2).

[10] *Vienna Diplomatic Convention*, Article 52 (3).

Immunity of Embassy and Legation Buildings. The embassy or legation quarters, as well as the residence of a diplomatic agent, are inviolable. The agents of the receiving state may not enter them, except with the consent of the head of the diplomatic mission.

The fiction that the diplomatic quarters are actually located in the territory of the sending state has been abandoned in modern legal theory.[11] Any offense against local law committed in such quarters is committed in the receiving state.[12] But the latter cannot *enforce* its laws in connection with the offense committed. Immunity also applies to the contents of diplomatic quarters, including archives and correspondence files, and to the means of transportation owned by the diplomatic mission.

The much publicized case of *Rose* v. *The King* [13] indicates, however, that there may be a limit to the immunity of the contents of diplomatic archives. In dismissing an appeal from the conviction of a member of the Canadian Parliament for conspiracy to commit offenses against the Official Secrets Act of 1939, in connection with the supplying of information to Soviet agents in Canada, the Court had to deal at some length with the defendant's objection that documents taken from the Soviet Embassy by an embassy employee could not lawfully be used in evidence against him. The Court held that when the acts of accredited diplomats were contrary to the laws of the receiving state, there was no longer any immunity of the documents to be found in diplomatic quarters: if by some means such documents were turned over to a court for the prosecution of a crime committed by a citizen of the receiving state, the court could not give effect to immunity.

The Cuban government, in July, 1963, "expropriated" the U.S. embassy building in Havana, ordering the Swiss mission that had occupied the embassy for the United States since 1961 to vacate the premises. This act, undertaken assertedly in retaliation for the "freezing" of Cuban assets in the United States, could at best be described as a reprisal (see Chapter 24), because it was in violation of international law.[14]

Right of Protection. Part and parcel of the immunity of embassy and legation buildings is a special duty of protection on the part of the receiving state. When a German mob attacked the British Embassy in Ber-

[11] See 72 *Time* (July 21, 1958), pp. 20–21, for the lively tale of Sam Sary, Cambodian ambassador to Great Britain, who wrongly maintained that he had every right under Cambodian law to whip, with the assistance of his No. 1 wife, a concubine; Sary justified his action by asserting that his Embassy was "Cambodia in London." See also the *Asylum Case (Colombia–Peru), I.C.J. Reports, 1950,* p. 274.

[12] See *Fatemi* v. *United States,* United States, District Court, D.C., 1963, At. 2d 525, in which the Court stated correctly "(1) that a foreign embassy is not to be considered the territory of the sending state; and (2) that local police have the authority and responsibility to enter a foreign embassy if the privilege of diplomatic inviolability is not invoked when an offense is committed therein in violation of local law."

[13] Quebec, Court of King's Bank, Appeal Side, 1946 (1947, 3 D.L.R. 618), digested in 42 *A.J.I.L.* (1948), pp. 945–947.

[14] See 82 *Time* (August 2, 1963), pp. 26, 28.

lin after the outbreak of World War I, the German government formally expressed its regrets to the British government.

Inviolability of Means of Communication. Diplomats enjoy complete secrecy as far as their correspondence and other communications are concerned. Their correspondence is immune from seizure, search, and censorship on the part of the receiving state. A mission may employ codes and ciphers in its communications, but the installation and operation of radio transmitters may be undertaken only with the consent of the receiving state.[15] Diplomatic couriers, traveling on diplomatic passports, cannot be arrested or impeded and the contents of their pouch or baggage cannot be inspected or confiscated.

On the other hand, abuses of the inviolability of the diplomatic mailbags will lead to protests and, if the practices in question are continued, to retaliatory action. Thus the French ambassador in Washington tendered an official apology to the U.S. Secretary of State when a federal grand jury in New York City had made a presentment in 1939 that the mail pouch of the French Embassy had been used to smuggle motion picture films into the United States in contravention of American customs regulation.

The privileges and immunities of diplomatic agents apply also to the members of their families.

Nationality of Children. It is of interest that the exemption of a diplomat from the territorial jurisdiction of the receiving state also covers the nationality of any children born to him while holding his official position. Such children are regarded as born on the territory of the diplomatic person's home state, subject to it *jure soli*. This would be true even if the diplomat and his wife were in transit through the territory of a third state.

Staff of a Diplomatic Mission. Equally, the usual privileges and immunities apply to the staff of a diplomatic mission other than diplomatic agents. This exemption was somewhat general until fairly recently when a rather logical limitation appeared: many states assert a right to exercise jurisdiction in the case of private (nonofficial) acts of administrative functionaries attached to foreign embassies or legations, as long as the officials perform nondiplomatic duties for their own government.[16] Thus the Tribunal of Rome held on July 13, 1953, in *Soc. Arethusa Film* v. *Reist*[17] that the defendant, Chancellor at the U.S. Embassy in Rome, could be held subject to the civil jurisdiction of the Italian courts with regard to his unofficial acts. The Tribunal cited a number of international agreements which provided that administrative personnel of foreign diplomatic missions were subject to the jurisdiction of the receiving state.

---

[15] *Vienna Diplomatic Convention*, Article 27 (1); see also Kerley, *op. cit.* (n. 3, *supra*), pp. 111–116, for an illuminating account of the discussions at the Vienna Conference dealing with the operation of transmitters by diplomatic missions.

[16] *Vienna Diplomatic Convention*, Article 37 (2 and 3).

[17] Reported in 49 *A.J.I.L.* (1955), p. 102.

The service staff of a mission enjoys diplomatic privileges and immunities in the execution of official functions and duties. However, a basic requirement is that such service staff members are registered for such immunity with the Foreign Ministry (or corresponding agency) in the receiving state. When their service with the foreign mission ends, these individuals are usually granted a period of grace of about thirty days, during which they continue to enjoy immunity and are expected to settle their affairs before leaving the receiving country.

A slightly different situation arises when a national or resident of the receiving country obtains employment in a foreign embassy and legation. Many countries permit such persons to be listed on the roster of employees entitled to diplomatic immunity (the United States does so; the U.S.S.R. does not). On the other hand, such individuals do not enjoy a period of grace following termination of their employment. They then may be held responsible for any and all offenses committed while cloaked with diplomatic immunity. Thus the judge in the Police Court of the District Court of Columbia ruled in April, 1939, in *District of Columbia v. Vinard L. Paris* [18] that the defendant's immunity had lapsed as soon as his embassy employment had terminated.

On the other hand, in *Carrera v. Carrera*, [19] the court affirmed on grounds of immunity the District Court's dismissal of the suit for separate maintenance and for custody and support of a child, filed by a wife against her husband. Both parties were nationals of Ecuador permanently resident in the United States and employed as domestic servants in the Czechoslovakian Embassy in Washington. Mr. Carrera had moved to dismiss the complaint, claiming diplomatic immunity which the Czechoslovakian ambassador had requested for him in a letter to the Secretary of State. The Department of State informed the District Court that Mr. Carrera enjoyed diplomatic immunity. Thus the court felt required to dismiss the suit of the wife.

The 1961 Vienna Diplomatic Convention provides that the private servants of members of diplomatic missions, if such servants were not nationals of or permanently resident in the receiving state, are to be exempt from taxes on their salaries or wages. Any other grant of immunity depends on the generosity of the receiving state (Art. 37, par. 4); the Diplomatic Relations Act of 1967 of the United States (S.1577, 90th Congress, 1st Sess.) does not grant any immunity to such private servants.

Status of Diplomatic Persons in Transit. All rights and privileges pertaining to diplomatic persons lawfully apply to them only in the receiving state, because no legal relationship exists between a diplomat and a third state. However, as a matter of courtesy and because it is a question of

---

[18] Cases 448485 to 448494, Inclusive; opinion reprinted in 33 *A.J.I.L.* (1939), pp. 787–792.

[19] United States, Court of Appeals, D.C., Feb. 28, 1949, 174 F. (2d) 496, digested in 44 *A.J.I.L.* (1950), pp. 184–185.

interest and convenience to all states, diplomats traveling through third states usually are granted the same privileges as would be their due in the receiving state.

The classic modern case in this area of diplomatic immunities is *Bergman* v. *De Sieyes*.[20] The defendant had been served with process in a tort action in New York while on his way to Bolivia, to which country he had been accredited as the French minister. The District Court had dismissed the complaint, holding that while De Sieyes was not entitled to immunity under Title 22, section 252, of the U.S. Code, that section was declaratory of existing international law and hence, under that law, the French diplomat should be granted immunity—and was upheld by the Circuit Court. The latter reviewed previous New York state court decisions in point and concluded that as a result of changing concepts of diplomatic immunity and changing conditions of travel, "the courts of New York would today hold that a diplomat *in transitu* would be entitled to the same immunity as a diplomat *in situ*."

However, a diplomat apparently must be enroute on an official mission in order to enjoy immunity: the Guatemalan ambassador to Belgium and The Netherlands had flown to New York from Europe on a personal visit and had been arrested on a narcotics charge. His motion to dismiss because of diplomatic immunity was denied because of the nature of his trip, and the court noted that the Guatemalan Consulate General in New York had submitted an affidavit which, *inter alia*, stated that the President of Guatemala had deprived the ambassador of his diplomatic appointment after the arrest had taken place.[21]

On the other hand, the lack of clarity of the rules governing diplomats "in transit" is illustrated by the case of *Carbone* v. *Carbone*[22] in which a Panamanian diplomat accredited to Italy was ruled to be subject to the jurisdiction of New York state courts in connection with a divorce action.

Status of Alleged Diplomatic Persons. Determination of the diplomatic status of a given individual claiming immunities pertaining to diplomats normally is left to the executive branch of a government. Following inquiry by, say, a court, the reply defining the status of the alleged diplomatic person received from the Foreign Office or other appropriate department of the government is then regarded as binding on the court. In the classic case of *Engelke* v. *Musmann*,[23] an individual bearing the title of Consular Secretary but employed in the German Embassy in London was held to possess diplomatic immunity and not consular immunity. He had been appointed to the staff of the German ambassador and had been

---

[20] United States, Circuit Court of Appeals, 2nd Circuit, 1948, 170 F. (2d) 360, digested in 43 *A.J.I.L.* (1949), p. 373.

[21] *United States* v. *Rosal*, United States, District Court, S.D. N.Y., 1960, 191 F. Supp. 663.

[22] Sup. Ct., N.Y. County, 1924, 123 Misc. 656, 206 N.Y.S. 40.

[23] Great Britain, House of Lords, 1928 (A.C. 433).

listed by the latter as a person entitled to diplomatic immunity. Furthermore, his name had been placed on the Diplomatic List by the British Foreign Office.

Restraints on Diplomatic Agents. The primary prohibition laid by international law on all diplomatic agents is abstention from all interference —by word or deed—in the internal affairs of the receiving state. This prohibition is all-inclusive: the diplomat may not discuss pending legislation, may not comment on political controversies, may not endorse or criticize political parties and their platforms. He may not correspond with the press and other news media on any matter which is still a subject of communication between his own government and the host government. He may not make public a communication from his government to that of the receiving state before the latter has received it, nor publish any correspondence from the latter without obtaining prior authorization. Equally prohibited but difficult to prove is the use of an embassy or a legation as a center for the dissemination of propaganda on a matter on which the two governments concerned may be in disagreement, and to convert either diplomatic mission into a center of subversive or spy activities in favor of the ideological or national interests of the sending state.

A minor violation of these restraints on the activities of a diplomatic person may be overlooked or lead to a protest by the appropriate authorities of the receiving state. If the violation is repeated or is of a serious nature, the receiving state is fully in its rights if it requests the recall of the offender.

In 1871, the United States government requested the recall of the Russian minister, M. Catacazy, because he had seen fit to indulge in personal criticism of President Ulysses S. Grant. The American note in question asserted that Catacazy's behavior was of a nature as "materially to impair his usefulness to his own government and to render intercourse with him, for either business or social purposes, highly disagreeable." [24]

More striking was the American demand, on September 9, 1915, for the recall of the ambassador of Austria-Hungary, Count Dumba, for acting as virtual paymaster for agents of the Central Powers engaged in sabotage activities in the United States and for using an American citizen to carry secretly official dispatches through Allied lines to the ambassador's own country. Three months later, on December 4, 1915, the Department of State notified the German government that the German naval attaché Captain Boy-Ed, and military attaché, Captain von Papen, were considered to be *personae non gratae*, following the discovery of incriminating documents relating to German espionage and sabotage activities in the United States.

It might be assumed that diplomatic persons would automatically enjoy complete freedom of movement and travel in the receiving state, for such

[24] Moore, Vol. IV, p. 501.

freedom would appear to be essential to the performance of their duties. However, the receiving state may create by its law and regulations zones, entry into which is prohibited or regulated for reasons of national security. Recent years have seen travel restrictions imposed on diplomats as a reprisal (more correctly, perhaps, as retorsion; see Chapter 24) for delicts of their own government. From July, 1966, to August 5, 1967, the United States curbed travel by Russian diplomats in retaliation for a similar Russian action; [25] similar travel curbs on the Yemen ambassador were lifted in early May, 1967. Brazil imposed in 1961 a twenty-mile travel limit on the personnel of the Soviet Union embassy, and Great Britain limited, in August, 1967, the embassy personnel of the People's Republic of China to an area five miles from the center of London, prohibiting, at the same time, use of the embassy radio transmitter.[26] One of the most drastic travel limitations on record was imposed in January, 1952, when the Soviet government converted 80 per cent of the area of the U.S.S.R. into a forbidden zone, including, incidentally, the capitals of the Ukrainian and Byelorussian Republics—both member states of the United Nations—in the ban.[27]

SPECIAL CATEGORIES OF AGENTS

SPECIAL OFFICERS

Several countries, notably the United States, have on occasion utilized the services of special officers of various types, in addition to the generally recognized categories of diplomatic personnel. Almost invariably the sending states attempted to secure diplomatic status, with its attendant privileges and immunities, for such special officers, whereas receiving states, generally speaking, opposed such efforts. In essence, whatever status was granted to such officers depended on the decision of the receiving state, and none of the categories involved is covered either by customary or by conventional rules of law.

The United States Treasury Department has employed a group of officers attached to embassies and legations in Europe and styled, at different times, Special Commissioner, Customs Attaché, Customs Representative, and Treasury Attaché. Despite repeated efforts to have these individuals accorded diplomatic status, only France has accepted the Treasury Department's agents as full-fledged diplomats. Other countries have only been willing to grant to them an exemption from income taxes on their salaries.

[25] *The New York Times,* August 6, 1967, p. 3.

[26] *Ibid.,* August 27, 1967, p. 4.

[27] Yuen-Li Liang, "Diplomatic Intercourse and Immunities as a Subject for Codification," 47 *A.J.I.L.* (1953), pp. 439–448, at p. 443.

Other United States special officers abroad include assistant commercial attachés under the Secretary of Commerce, later under the Department of State, and agricultural attachés. The latter were accorded diplomatic status in a few states.

COMMISSIONERS AND SPECIAL ENVOYS

Gould mentions that the High Commissioners of the Allied Powers that had been at war with Turkey enjoyed special privileges equivalent to diplomatic status there after World War I, even though a succession of United States Commissioners in Turkey did not hold such status and in fact were told by the Department of State not to take any action that in any way would appear to indicate a resumption of diplomatic relations.[28] And as Lauterpacht pointed out, agents sent by a state to another to negotiate technical or administrative matters, such as arrangements regarding railroads, posts, telegraphs, navigation, and so forth, while not characterized by law as possessing diplomatic immunities, should have that status. In a number of instances, by tacit agreement, such individuals have been accorded the immunities from territorial jurisdiction necessary to accomplish their tasks. Certainly such persons (and their official papers) should be immune, as long as they are sent and received for official purposes.

Special envoys, on the other hand, are usually granted temporary diplomatic status, and in recent decades have been, in fact, equipped with a diplomatic rank. Thus heads of country delegations to international conferences commonly are styled ambassadors or envoys extraordinary. Similarly, members of arbitration tribunals and boundary commissions are on occasion granted diplomatic privileges and immunities.

The foregoing remarks are based on past practices of states. However, when the International Law Commission was engaged, at its tenth session, in working out the 1958 Draft of its proposed convention on diplomatic intercourse and immunities, it mentioned in its report that the convention dealt only with permanent diplomatic missions. The Commission then went on to point out that diplomatic relations also assume other forms that could be given the name of "*ad hoc* diplomacy," namely itinerant envoys, diplomatic conferences, and special missions sent to a state for restricted purposes. The Commission decided that these forms of diplomacy merited study in order to determine the rules of law governing them.

This special topic came under detailed survey at the Commission's twelfth session (1960). A set of Draft Articles on Special Missions (omitting international conferences from consideration because of certain technical problems involved) resulted, as a sort of preliminary survey of the subject.[29]

[28] *Gould,* p. 277.
[29] Text in 55 *A.J.I.L.* (1961), Supp., pp. 303–305.

The General Assembly referred the Draft Articles to the Vienna Conference of 1961, which decided that the topic of special missions should be referred back to the General Assembly with the recommendation that the Commission be requested to give the topic further study.

As far as the Draft Articles themselves were concerned, the Commission decided that "special missions" meant an official mission of state representatives sent by one state to another to carry out a special task, as well as an itinerant envoy who carried out special tasks in the states to which he proceeded (Art. 1). Eventually the Commission completed the final portions of a draft convention on special missions, comprising fifty articles, in 1967.[30] The General Assembly then forwarded the draft to the member states for examination and comment. It is expected that the draft articles will become a new convention in the relatively near future, following a conference to be scheduled for the purpose.

AGENTS OF INTERNATIONAL ORGANIZATIONS: PRIVILEGES AND IMMUNITIES

The development of international organizations has been accompanied by an increasing number of problems connected with the privileges and immunities of the officials and agents of the agencies in question.[31]

While there is no generally applicable body of rules, court decisions and increasingly uniform practice are creating a new sphere of international law, the law of international organizations as related to diplomats and agents.

League of Nations. Article 7(4) of the Covenant of the League of Nations conferred on the representatives of the member states and the agents of the League diplomatic privileges and immunities. In some respects, the paragraph in question included definite innovations compared with earlier practices. Thus, for instance, the representatives of the International Labor Organization were entitled to full diplomatic status even when they represented states that were not members of the League. And at the same time diplomatic privileges were given to delegates representing workers and employers at the General Conferences of the ILO. Switzerland, as host country to the League, granted diplomatic status, privileges, and immunities to the permanent delegates accredited to the League, even though the same individuals were not accredited to Switzerland.

United Nations. In contrast to Article 7 of the Covenant, the corresponding Article 105(2), of the United Nations Charter grants to the

[30] Text, with commentary by the Commission, in 62 *A.J.I.L.* (1968), Supp., pp. 252–296; for a later revised version, see 8 *International Legal Materials* (1969), pp. 73–82.

[31] On the general subject consult Hackworth, Vol. IV, pp. 419–423, particularly with reference to the experiences of the League of Nations. See also the "Draft Articles on Representatives of States to International Organizations," with commentary, prepared by the International Law Commission at its twentieth session, in 1968, in 8 *International Legal Materials* (1969), pp. 151–168.

representatives of the member states "such privileges and immunities as are necessary for the independent exercise of their functions in connection with the Organization." [32]

On February 13, 1946, the General Assembly adopted a General Convention on the Privileges and Immunities of the United Nations.[33] Because the headquarters of the new Organization were to be located in the United States, arrangement had to be worked out with the prospective host government. The initial step was passage by Congress on December 29, 1945, of the Statute Extending Privileges, Exemptions, and Immunities to International Organizations and to the Officers and Employees Thereof (International Organizations Immunities Act).[34] The negotiations between the Secretary-General and the United States resulted in the definitive "Headquarters of the United Nations: Agreement between the United States of America and the United Nations," of June 26, 1947 (in force November 21, 1947) and an interim agreement of December 18, 1947, applying relevant provisions of the June 26 agreement to the temporary headquarters of the United Nations at Lake Success, New York.[35]

Diplomatic Privileges and Immunities of Member States. Article 4 of the General Convention details the diplomatic privileges and immunities of representatives of member states. These rights apply to delegates to the principal and subsidiary organs of the United Nations and to conferences convened by that Organization, but only while such representatives exercise their functions and during their travel to and from the place of meeting. The privileges listed include immunity from arrest or detention and from seizure of personal luggage, immunity from legal process of every kind for all acts (and words spoken or written) in their capacity as representatives; inviolability of all papers and documents; the right to use codes and to receive correspondence and papers by courier or in sealed bags; exemption for representatives and their spouses from immigration restrictions or national service obligations enroute or while visiting in the exercise of their functions; and equality of treatment as respects currency or exchange restrictions with representatives of foreign governments on temporary official missions.

In acknowledgment of the theory of functional necessity, Section 14 of Article 4 states that

Privileges and immunities are accorded to representatives of Members not for the personal benefit of the individuals themselves, but in order to safeguard the independent exercise of their functions in connection with the United Nations. *Consequently a Member not only has the right but is under a duty to waive*

[32] On the general subject of the immunity of UN officials, consult the excellent and heavily documented summary in Bishop, pp. 614–620.

[33] Text in 43 *A.J.I.L.* (1949), Supp., pp. 1–7.

[34] Text in 40 *A.J.I.L.* (April, 1946), Supp., pp. 85–91.

[35] Texts of agreements, together with notes and the required joint Congressional resolution of August 4, 1947, in 43 *A.J.I.L.* (1949), Supp. pp. 8–26.

the immunity of its representative in any case where in the opinion of the Member the immunity would impede the course of justice, and it can be waived without prejudice to the purpose for which the immunity is accorded. [Italics added.]

Officials of the United Nations falling into categories to be specified by the Secretary-General are to enjoy substantially the same privileges and immunities as representatives of member states, under Article 5 of the convention. And experts performing missions for the United Nations are also to be accorded substantially the same privileges (Art. 6, sec. 22).

In order to facilitate travel by UN officials and experts the convention provides in Article 7 for the issue of travel documents termed *laissez-passer* to such officials.

The Headquarters Agreement with the United States outlines the rules governing the Headquarters District in New York City. (See also Chapter 9.) The federal, state, and local laws of the United States and the jurisdiction of the federal, state, and local laws of the United States apply within the District, except as specified in the General Convention or in the Agreement. Normally, however, the United Nations makes regulations for the District, and no federal, state, or local law of the United States conflicting with such regulations can be applied in the District (Art. 3, sec. 8).

The District is inviolable. Federal, state or local officers or officials of the United States, whether administrative, judicial, military, or police, cannot enter the District without the consent and under the conditions agreed to by the Secretary-General. On the other hand, the District may not become a place of asylum (Art. 3, sec. 9-b).

The various levels of United States authorities may not impede the travel to or from the District by representatives of members, by the families of such persons, by experts performing missions for the United Nations, by representatives of media of mass communications who have been accredited by the UN or one of its agencies at their discretion after consultation with the United States; and other persons summoned to or having official business with the UN and its Specialized Agencies (Art. 4, sec. 11).

The resident representatives to the United Nations, as specified in Article 5, section 15 of the Agreement, are entitled in the territory of the United States to the same privileges and immunities as are enjoyed by diplomatic envoys accredited to the United States. In the case of member states whose governments are not recognized by the United States, such privileges and immunities need be extended to such representatives only within the Headquarters District, at their residences or offices outside the District, in transit between the District and their residences or offices, and in transit on official business to and from foreign countries.[36]

---

[36] See Sam P. Brewer, "U.S. Curbs Irk Cuban Officials at U.N.," *The New York Times,* October 29, 1967, p. 29.

Insofar as diplomatic immunity in general is concerned, the Headquarters Agreement took from the International Organizations Immunities Act of 1945 four categories of governmental representatives and conferred diplomatic immunity on them—leaving, however, United Nations officials and employees within the narrower ambit of limited immunity granted by the Act of 1945.

Under Article 6, the appropriate American authorities are charged with protecting the District against unauthorized entry and, at the request of the Secretary-General, may be asked for police protection (against reimbursement) *within* the District.

UN Problems in Immunities. Almost as soon as the United Nations began its operations in the United States, cases revolving around the immunities of representatives, officials, and servants of both categories, began to be reported.[37]

In most recent decisions dealing with such immunities, the functional necessity theory influenced the holdings of the courts. This was particularly true in the Advisory Opinion of April 11, 1949, on *Reparations for Injuries Suffered in the Service of the United Nations*,[38] in which the International Court of Justice clearly based the inviolability of persons serving the United Nations on functional necessity.

Two special areas concerned with UN immunities have posed a number of problems of interpretation since 1946: the status under certain conditions of UN staff members of United States nationality, and spying activities of employees of the United Nations.

The first problem area developed in consequence of the passage of the United States Internal Security Act of 1950. Investigations pursued under that Act soon sought to ascertain whether United States citizens on the staff of the Secretariat were or had been members of the Communist Party or other organizations declared subversive under the Act, or whether such citizens had been or were engaged in other subversive activities.

A Commission of Jurists was asked by the Secretary-General to clarify the status of staff members of the Secretariat who were of United States nationality, as their employment related to the Internal Security Act. The report of the Commission was completed on November 29, 1952.[39] As a result of the recommendations of the Commission, the Secretary-General appointed on January 16, 1953, an advisory panel to assist him in dealing with specific cases involving American employees of the United Nations in relation to the Internal Security Act.

---

[37] See the detailed analysis of early instances in Lawrence Preuss, "Immunity of Officers and Employees of the United Nations for Official Acts: The Ranallo Case," 41 *A.J.I.L.* (1947), pp. 555–578. Consult also *People v. Von Otter*, 114 N.Y.S. (2d) 295 (City Court, New Rochelle, July 30, 1952), reported in 47 *A.J.I.L.* (1953), p. 151, n. 1; *Tsiang v. Tsiang* (1949), 194 Misc. 259, 86 N.Y.S. (2d) 556.

[38] *I.C.J. Reports, 1949*, p. 174.

[39] Text, together with Annex and a Corrigendum, in 47 *A.J.I.L.* (1953), Supp., pp. 87–117.

Soon afterward a case involving four American citizens employed by UNESCO attracted enormous interest and publicity. The four, who held appointments for specific terms, refused in 1953 and 1954 to answer questionnaires from, or to appear before, the International Organizations Employees Loyalty Board of the U.S. Civil Service. On July 6, 1954, the four persons were informed by the Director General of UNESCO that their appointments would not be renewed because of their conduct. When the employees brought their cases before the UNESCO Appeals Board, the latter held that the decision of the Director General should be reversed. When the Director General refused to rescind, the four Americans took their cases to the ILO Administrative Tribunal, whose jurisdiction over any disputes with staff members had been accepted by UNESCO. The Tribunal ruled in favor of the employees.

The Executive Board of UNESCO decided to challenge the judgment of the Tribunal and on November 25, 1955, asked the International Court of Justice for an Advisory Opinion. The Court handed down the opinion on October 23, 1956.[40] The Court held that the Administrative Tribunal had been competent to hear the complaints of the four employees against UNESCO and that the validity of the Tribunal's decision was not open to challenge.

The problem of spying on the part of UN employees and staff members has been a knotty one. Two cases in this sphere have attracted considerable attention and may serve to illustrate some of the questions involved. The earlier of the two, *United States* v. *Coplon and Gubitchev*,[41] had its beginning in 1949. Valentin A. Gubitchev, a Soviet national, was employed in the Headquarters Planning Office of the UN Secretariat. He was indicted for a number of violations of the United States espionage laws and made a motion to dismiss on the grounds of diplomatic immunity. This motion was dismissed. Gubitchev had come to the United States on a diplomatic passport. The court denied the immune status of the accused because he had not been accredited to the United States government and the International Organizations Immunities Act did not apply to him because it conferred immunity only for acts performed in an official capacity and falling within the functions of officers or employees of the United Nations. The offenses charged against the accused did not fall within such categories.

Gubitchev retained counsel of his own choice and the court granted reargument of the case. This time the Soviet Embassy sent an official

---

[40] *Judgments of the Administrative Tribunal of the I.L.O. Upon Complaints Made Against the United Nations Educational, Scientific and Cultural Organization*, Advisory Opinion, October 23, 1956, *I.C.J. Reports, 1956*, p. 77, digested at length in 51 *A.J.I.L.* (1957), pp. 410–417.

[41] United States, District Court, S.D. N.Y., 1950, 88 F. Supp. 915, digested in 44 *A.J.I.L.* (1950), pp. 586–590; the first hearing of the case, May 10, 1949 (84 F. Supp. 472), was digested in 43 *A.J.I.L.* (1949), pp. 810–812.

communication to the Court, testifying to the diplomatic rank of Gubitchev before his arrival in the United States and asserting that "The Soviet Government has not revoked the diplomatic status of Mr. Gubitchev V.A. and up to the present time he remains an officer of the Ministry of Foreign Affairs of the U.S.S.R., with the diplomatic rank of Third Secretary."

The court regarded the presentment of the affidavit as being without precedent and simply forwarded it to the Secretary of State. The court then found that Gubitchev was not a member of the Soviet Embassy, that his name had not been submitted by the Secretary-General for inclusion in a list of members of delegations entitled to diplomatic privileges under the Headquarters Agreement, and was notified by the Secretary of State that the latter rejected Gubitchev's claim of diplomatic immunity; his diplomatic visa had been issued as a matter of courtesy.

The court properly denied again the claim of the accused.

In 1960, the well-known case of *United States* v. *Melekh* [42] achieved considerable prominence. Igor Y. Melekh, a Russian national, had been attached since June 10, 1955, to the UN Secretariat as Chief of the Russian Language Section, Office of Conference Services. He resisted removal to Illinois to stand trial on three counts of espionage, asserting that he enjoyed diplomatic immunity and that such immunity applied also to the preliminary proceeding of removal.

The court found that although Melekh was a Second Secretary of the Ministry of Foreign Affairs in the U.S.S.R. and arrived in the United States with a Soviet diplomatic passport, he had not been granted a diplomatic visa by the United States. His work in the UN was of nondiplomatic character, he had never been attached to the Soviet Embassy, he had never been accredited as a diplomatic officer to any government, nor was he a member of the Soviet Delegation to the United Nations.

The court, after a careful analysis, held that Melekh was not entitled to diplomatic immunity. Hence Melekh was ordered to be removed to Illinois to stand trial. In the District Court (Northern District of Illinois), Melekh's attorneys lost when the court denied a whole series of motions in which the assertion of immunity was raised again, and he was ordered to stand trial.

One incident in this sphere may have the greatest repercussions of all in the future. In November, 1962, a group of agents of the Cuban government, reported to have planned terror acts and acts of sabotage in the New York–New Jersey area, was arrested by agents of the United States government. Among those detained was one Casanova, a resident member of Cuba's Permanent Mission to the United Nations, who was charged with conspiracy to commit sabotage and to violate the Foreign Agents Registration Act. He sought release from detention under *habeas corpus*,

[42] United States, District Court, S.D. N.Y., 1960, 190 F. Supp. 67, digested at length in 55 *A.J.I.L.* (1961), pp. 734–738.

claiming that he was either entitled to diplomatic immunity under the Charter, the Headquarters Agreement, and international law, or that the Supreme Court of the United States had exclusive and original jurisdiction to try his case. The court dismissed the writ of *habeas corpus*, holding that Article 105 of the Charter did not confer diplomatic immunity on the representatives of member states, and even if the Article were held to be self-executing with respect to the functional activities of such representatives, a conspiracy to commit sabotage against the United States could not be held to be a proper function of any such representative; that the government of the United States did not, by issuing a nonimmigrant visa and a landing permit, give its consent that Casanova was entitled to diplomatic immunity; that under international law Casanova was not entitled to diplomatic immunity from the time of his arrival pending determination of his status, because his position was not comparable to that of a diplomat awaiting acknowledgment by a government to which he was accredited (international law could only define the nature and scope of immunity once it had been determined that an individual was entitled to such immunity); and that Casanova was not an ambassador or other public minister of a foreign state accredited to the United States within the meaning of the Constitutional or statutory provisions vesting original and exclusive jurisdiction in the Supreme Court of the United States.[43]

Other International Agencies. The judges of the International Court of Justice enjoy diplomatic privileges and immunities when engaged in official business, under the provisions of Article 19 of the Statute of the Court. Lesser staff members and employees of the Court are treated in the same manner as the comparable ranks among the members of diplomatic missions at The Hague. Similar rights and privileges attach to members of the Permanent Court of Arbitration (under Article 46 of the 1907 Hague Convention for the Pacific Settlement of International Disputes) when such members are on official duty outside of their own country.

It was pointed out earlier that the European Economic Community (EEC) as well as the European Atomic Energy Community (EURATOM) possess the right to deal with the representatives of individual states. Such representatives enjoy the customary diplomatic privileges and immunities in the state in which the headquarters of the respective community are located (Article 19 of each Charter). By the middle of 1962, forty-eight states had opened diplomatic relations with the Communities and forty-one of them had already sent accredited diplomatic agents to them. A whole specialized system of ranking of such agents has evolved.

A functional type of diplomatic immunity similar to that provided

[43] *United States ex rel. Casanova* v. *Fitzpatrick*, United States, District Court, S.D. N.Y., 1963, 214 F. Supp. 425, reported in 57 *A.J.I.L.* (1963), pp. 920–921.

under Article 105 of the UN Chapter was made available under Article 40 of the Statute of the Council of Europe for that organization itself, as well as for the representatives of members and for the staff of the Council's Secretariat. The specific terms involved in such immunities were to be determined by a special agreement between the Council and France as well as by a general convention among the member states of the Organization.

Officials of the European Commission of Human Rights enjoy diplomatic immunity, for official acts, in the United Kingdom, under an Act and an Order-in-Council of 1950.[44]

CONSULAR AGENTS

Background. Classical antiquity had developed certain institutions resembling in a number of details the modern consul. In the Greek city-states could be found officials (*proxenai*) responsible for the welfare of resident aliens in a given state, while Rome developed the office of the *praetor peregrinus.* All of these officials, however, were citizens of the territorial sovereign and not of the states whose nationals were in their charge. The end of Greek independence, followed eventually by the collapse of the Roman Empire, meant the disappearance of these predecessors of the modern consul.

The latter had his true beginning in the medieval period, in the Mediterranean area. Alien merchants settling in a port received the permission of the host state to establish a sort of corporation with a limited right of self-government and jurisdiction over its members. The latter function soon ended up in the hands of judges which, beginning in the eleventh century, were chosen by the merchants from among their own number. The competence of such judges extended primarily into the sphere of commercial disputes. Their titles varied, with *consules mercatorium (consuls de commerce, juges consuls)* being the most common one in use. In the twelfth century these officials were increasingly not only regarded as the heads of the foreign merchants' guild but as officials (frequently appointed) of the territorial sovereign.

The usefulness of specialized agents to deal with commercial matters was so apparent after a short time that the consular institution began to spread from Italy into other parts of the Mediterranean world, particularly to the Near East and North Africa. As increasing numbers of merchants established branches there, the home government sent out agents (*consules missi*) to take charge of the interests of the settlers and to exercise both criminal and civil jurisdiction over them. Most historians of the consular institutions point out that a number of these consuls, now stationed abroad, were elected by the emigrant merchant (*consules*

[44] *Zoernsch* v. *Waldock and Another,* United Kingdom, Court of Appeals, 1964, 2 All E.R. 256.

electi) but that such personages had, in general, less authority than those sent abroad by governments.

In the thirteenth century the concept of *consules missi* was expanded to cover the ports of southwestern Europe and by the fifteenth century to western and northern Europe. The Western consuls in Africa and the Near East did enjoy considerably greater authority, in every respect, than did their colleagues elsewhere. As most authorities emphasize, the Eastern consuls received special privileges from the local (Mohammedan) sovereigns, privileges centering on judicial prerogatives and the right to try cases involving their own nationals under their own, Western, law. The fact that such extraterritorial privileges devolved on the consuls by treaty (Capitulations) or by local concession, that they were achieved in most instances by negotiation, and in a few cases by threats of force, is immaterial. The essential fact was that under Mohammedan law, Christians were not allowed to be subjects of that law, which was based on the Koran. Hence, regardless of method involved, the special rights granted to Westerners represented an act of grace to individuals who otherwise would have been "lesser breeds without the law." To the Mohammedan of the time, it did not matter where the infidel found his law—if he desired to apply his own law to himself and his fellows, no objection would be made. All vestige of such preferential treatment of aliens has disappeared and the multitude of treaties, which began with a Turkish-Genoese agreement of 1453, by which extraterritorial privileges were established have been abrogated in one way or another.

In Western states themselves, the expansion of the practice of stationing permanent diplomatic representatives in foreign capitals tended to minimize the institution of the consul until the growth of international commerce, noticeably around the early part of the eighteenth century when it became apparent to many governments that the presence of commercial representatives in other countries might indeed be advantageous. Soon scores of consuls appeared and began to fulfill important nonpolitical functions abroad. Since then, the institution has proliferated until today thousands of consuls of various ranks are scattered all over the world.

CONSULAR RELATIONS

Consuls are not *representatives* of their state. They are not accredited, in the diplomatic meaning of the term, to a foreign government. The only "normal" situation in which a consul would be automatically entitled to diplomatic privileges and immunities would be if he were accredited also as chargé d'affaires to the receiving state. This, however, would be a most unusual situation today. A consul is appointed by a state; he is recognized by the receiving state as an official *agent* of his government and as such, he is permitted to undertake certain functions which normally would be entrusted to the agents of the state in which the consul resides. Hence the institution of the consul has acquired a limited international status and is governed by definite and recognized rules.

The greater part of the functions—and rights—of a consul have been based up to now on special bipartite agreements (consular treaties) between the state whose agent he is and the state within which he performs his functions.[45]

A welter of political controversy surrounded the negotiation and then the consideration in the Senate of the newest consular convention between the United States and the Soviet Union. Signed in 1964, the agreement was not ratified immediately because of that year's American political campaign and, subsequently, because of intrusive factors such as the Vietnamese conflict. The U.S. Senate finally gave consent to ratification on March 16, 1967, and President Johnson signed the ratification on March 31, 1967. Ratification of the agreement by the U.S.S.R. took place on May 4, 1968, and, following exchange of ratifications, the treaty entered into force.[46] Among its important provisions could be noted Article 12, which grants a right of visitation of foreign nationals; an obligation to notify of the death, imprisonment, or detention of a foreign national; and greatly expanded consular immunities, almost equivalent to those enjoyed by diplomatic personnel.

Codification of Rules. The first attempt to bring about codification of the rules governing the rights and duties of consuls was made at Havana when the American states participating in the 1928 Inter-American Conference signed a Convention on Consular Agents. This instrument bound, of course, only the limited number of American states that became parties to the convention.

By 1932, the Harvard Research in International Law had completed a detailed and annotated draft convention on the subject, intended, like others of the Harvard studies, for general rather than regional application.

The International Law Commission of the United Nations, at its seventh session in 1955, decided to begin the study of consular relations and appointed a special rapporteur for it. After several delays his report was followed by the drawing up of a draft convention at the eleventh session (1959). After much discussion and reworking of the draft document, the Commission submitted it to the member states of the UN for comment (1960). The final version, Draft Convention on Consular Relations, was completed during the Commission's thirteenth session (1961) and submitted to the General Assembly with the recommendation that the As-

---

[45] See, as an example, the *Consular Convention (France–United States)*, signed on July 18, 1966 (in force January 7, 1968), reprinted in 62 *A.J.I.L.* (1968), Supp., pp. 551–565. Consult also C. B. Donaldson, Jr., "Soviet Consular Conventions: Post-Vienna," 10 *Harvard International Law Jl.* (1969), pp. 360–373.

[46] Text in 50 *Department of State Bulletin* (1964), pp. 979–985; see also *The New York Times*, August 29, 1965; March 17 and 19, 1967; April 1, 1967; May 5, 1968; and S. Houston Lay, "The United States-Soviet Consular Convention," 59 *A.J.I.L.* (1965), pp. 876–891.

sembly convene an international conference of plenipotentiaries to study the draft and to conclude one or more conventions on the subject.[47]

The General Assembly, on December 18, 1961, concurred in this recommendation and as a result the United Nations Conference on Consular Relations met at the Neue Hofburg in Vienna from March 4 to April 22, 1963. The conference was attended by representatives of ninety-two states and by observers from Bolivia, Guatemala, Paraguay, the International Labor Organization, the Food and Agriculture Organization, the International Atomic Energy Agency, and the Council of Europe.

The Conference, in addition to adopting a number of resolutions, prepared the following instruments: (1) Vienna Convention on Consular Relations; (2) Optional Protocol Concerning Acquisition of Nationality; and (3) Optional Protocol Concerning the Compulsory Settlement of Disputes.[48] Of these, the Convention on Consular Relations, of April 24, 1963, obviously was the most important.[49]

On April 24, 1963, the representatives of the participating states signed the convention; the treaty entered into force on the thirtieth day following the date of deposit of the twenty-second instrument of ratification with the Secretary-General of the United Nations.

The International Law Commission already had pointed out that consular intercourse, together with related privileges and immunities, had been governed partly by municipal law and partly by international law. The Commission had decided to base its Draft Articles not only on rules of customary international law but also on the material furnished by international conventions, especially on consular treaties. Hence the Draft Articles and more particularly the Vienna Convention on Consular Relations based on those Articles may be taken to represent the currently accepted body of rules governing consular relations.

The following discussion will, therefore, draw heavily from the Vienna Convention of 1963 as evidence of the rules applicable to consular matters.

The establishment of consular relations between states takes place by mutual consent. Normally the consent required for the establishment of diplomatic relations implies also consent to the establishment of consular relations. On the other hand, a severance of diplomatic relations does not, *ipso facto*, mean a breaking off of consular relations. It is also possible to establish consular relations between states that do not have diplomatic relations with one another. In this situation, the consular relations represent

---

[47] The text of the Draft Articles, final version, is found in "Report of the International Law Commission Covering the Work of Its Thirteenth Session, May 1–July 7, 1961," 56 *A.J.I.L.* (1962), Supp., at pp. 276–354.

[48] The texts of the convention and of the protocols are reprinted in 57 *A.J.I.L.* (1963), pp. 993–1025, and see Luke T. Lee, *The Vienna Convention on Consular Relations* (Leyden: A. W. Sijthoff; Durham, N.C.: Rule of Law Press, 1966), and his brief but useful "Vienna Convention on Consular Relations," *International Conciliation*, No. 571 (January, 1969), pp. 41–76.

[49] The convention will be cited hereinafter as *Vienna Consular Convention.*

the only official relations of permanent character between the states in question. In most instances of this sort, the consular relations constitute a preliminary to diplomatic relations.

Consular relations are normally exercised through consular posts (*Vienna Consular Convention*, Art. 3), but it is possible for them to be carried on through diplomatic missions. If members of such a mission are assigned to consular functions, they may continue to enjoy diplomatic privileges and immunities (Art. 15; see also Art. 3(2), of the 1961 Vienna Convention on Diplomatic Relations).

It is only logical that the location of consulates or branches thereof and the boundaries of the districts assigned to each of them are determined by mutual agreement between the sending state and the receiving state; subsequent changes in either sphere must receive the consent of the receiving state (*Vienna Consular Convention*, Art. 4).

FUNCTIONS OF CONSULAR AGENTS

The major functions exercised by consuls may be summarized as follows:

1. Protecting in the receiving state the interests of the sending state and its nationals within the limits set by international law

2. Promoting trade and also the development of economic, cultural, and scientific relations between the two states in question

3. Reporting to the government of the sending state on conditions and developments in the economic, cultural, and scientific life of the receiving state and also giving such information to interested persons and firms

4. Issuing passports and travel documents to nationals of the sending state and visas or similar documents to persons desiring to go to that state [50]

5. Helping and assisting in all legitimate ways the nationals of the sending state

6. Acting as notary and civil registrar and performing certain administrative functions, particularly in the safeguarding of the interests of nationals of the sending state in cases of succession (caused by death) in the territory of the receiving state

7. Representing nationals of the sending state before the courts and other authorities of the receiving state when, for some reason or other, those nationals are unable to assume the defense of their rights, so as to preserve, on a provisional basis, those rights in accordance with the law of the receiving state

8. Serving judicial documents or executing commissions to take evi-

---

[50] See *Licea-Gomez* v. *Pilliod*, United States, District Court, N. D. of Illinois, October 11, 1960, 193 F. Supp. 577, in which an excluded alien in this country on parole requested a review of the denial of an immigration visa by an American consul. The suit was dismissed.

dence for the courts of the sending state in accordance with existing treaties or, in their absence, in accordance with the laws of the receiving state

9. Exercising rights of supervision and inspection, under the laws and regulations of the receiving state, in respect of vessels having the nationality of the sending state, of aircraft registered in that state, and in respect of their crews; examining and stamping ships' papers, conducting investigations into any incidents which occurred during the voyage, and settling disputes between the master, the officers, and the seamen to the extent that such settlement is authorized by the laws of the sending state (*Vienna Consular Convention*, Art. 5).

It is possible, incidentally, for a sending state to entrust a consulate located in a particular state with the exercise of consular functions in a third state. However, this may only be done with the consent of both other states (Art. 7).

BEGINNING OF A CONSULAR COMMISSION

Acceptance of Heads of Consular Posts. Heads of consular posts are appointed by the sending state and are admitted to the exercise of their functions by the receiving state (Art. 10). The head in question is supplied by the sending state with a *commission*, or notice, setting out in detail his category and class, the consular district, and the seat of his consulate (Art. 11, par. 1). Vice-consuls and consular agents are furnished with a similar document, usually known as a *brevet*.

Acceptance of the commission is followed by the granting of an authorization by the receiving state. Until and unless the head of a consular post receives this document, known as an *exequatur*, he may not enter on his duties (Art. 12). In other words, the granting of the *exequatur* is the official act whereby the receiving state grants admission to the consul and confers on him the right to exercise his consular functions. Municipal law determines which organ of the state is competent to grant the *exequatur*; in most states, this is done by the Ministry of Foreign Affairs. It should be noted that the grant of an *exequatur* to be head of a consular post may automatically cover the members of the consular staff working under his orders and responsibility.

CLASSES OF CONSULS

State practice has settled fairly uniformly on four classes of heads of consular posts: (a) consuls-general; (b) consuls; (c) vice-consuls; and (d) consular agents (Art. 9). At present not all states follow this classification. No country would be obligated, of course, to adopt all four titles, and indeed the class of consular agent is seldom utilized today.

A few states still follow the formerly common practice of permitting their consular officials, especially those of the lower two ranks, to engage in business activities in the receiving state. It should be noted that when such is the case, the official in question does not enjoy any privileges or immunities for such activities, because the latter are completely outside his official functions. The *Vienna Consular Convention,* on the other hand, forbids career consular officers to carry on for personal profit any professional or commercial activity in the receiving state (Art. 57, par. 1).

Consular officials, as a rule, possess the nationality of the sending state. However, such officials may be appointed from among the nationals of the receiving state or of a third state, subject to the consent of the receiving state which may be withdrawn at any time (Art. 22). Unlike the practice in the sphere of diplomatic missions, quite a few small states still appoint heads of consular posts of the two lower ranks from among the nationals of the receiving state. In fact, there are actually more honorary consuls (nationals of the receiving state) functioning today than there are career consuls.

TERMINATION OF A CONSULAR COMMISSION

If the conduct of a consular official gives serious grounds for complaint, the receiving state may notify the sending state that the person in question is no longer acceptable. In that case, the sending state is bound either to recall the individual concerned or put an end to his connection with the consulate. If the sending state refuses to do so, or fails to carry out this obligation within a reasonable time, the receiving state has a right, as the case may be, either to withdraw the *exequatur* from the person in question or cease to regard him as a member of the consular staff. A person may, of course, also be declared unacceptable before he arrives in the territory of the receiving state. In such a case, the sending state must withdraw the appointment of the individual (Art. 23). As in the instance of a diplomat held to be *persona non grata,* the receiving state does not have to give any reasons for rejecting an appointee to a consular post.

Under all conditions, including a case of armed conflict, the receiving state must grant facilities in order to enable consular personnel (other than its own nationals) and the members of its families to leave the state with their property at the earliest possible moment (Art. 26).

If consular relations between two states are severed, the receiving state must, even in case of armed conflict, respect and protect consular premises and their contents. The sending state may entrust the premises and their contents to the care of a third state acceptable to the receiving state, just as it may entrust the protection of its interests and those of its nationals to a third state acceptable to the receiving state (Art. 27, par. 1).

PRIVILEGES AND IMMUNITIES

Inviolability of Consular Premises. Consular premises are inviolable, and the agents of the receiving state may not enter them except with the consent of the head of the consular post. The receiving state is under a special duty to take appropriate measures to protect the consular premises, which are immune from any search, requisition, attachment or execution (Art. 31). A few consular treaties and the municipal law of some states also recognize an inviolability of the residence of a consul, but this is an innovation that has not gained widespread acceptance.

Consular archives and documents, wherever they may happen to be, are inviolable (Art. 33).

Inviolability of Means of Communication. The receiving state permits free communication to a consulate for all official purposes. The consulate may employ diplomatic or consular couriers, the diplomatic or consular bag, and may send and receive messages in code or cipher. It may install and use a wireless transmitter only with the express consent of the receiving state. The official correspondence of a consulate is inviolable from all interference, including inspection and censorship (Art. 35).

Freedom of Communication. The nationals of the sending state are to be free to communicate with the consulates of their state, and in turn the consular officials of that state are to be free to communicate with the nationals of their state located in the receiving state. (Art. 36, par. 1-a). The competent authorities of the latter are to notify, without undue delay, the consulate of a sending state if in the relevant district a national of the sending state is committed to prison or to custody pending trial or is detained in any other manner. Equally, any communication from such nationals is to be forwarded to the relevant consulate without undue delay (Art. 36, par 1-b). Consular officials are to have the right to visit any national of the sending state who is in prison, custody or detention, for the purpose of gaining information about the case and of arranging for his legal representation (Art. 36, par. 1-c). Obviously, these rights would have to be exercised in accordance with the laws and regulations of the receiving state, provided that such laws or regulations do not nullify the rights of consular officials.

Tax Exemptions on Fees and Charges. The fees and charges collected by consulates in the performance of authorized functions are exempt from all dues and taxes in the receiving state (Art. 39). This rule is based on the concept that the moneys collected are the property of the sending state.

Right of Protection. As in the case of diplomatic agents, the receiving state is under a duty to accord special protection to consular officials by reason of their official position and to treat them with respect. It must take all appropriate steps to prevent attacks on their person, freedom and dignity (Art. 40). This applies as soon as a consular official enters the territorial jurisdiction of the receiving state.

Personal Inviolability and Immunity from Local Jurisdiction. Consular officials are not liable to arrest or detention pending trial, except in the case of a grave crime and in accordance with the decision of the competent judicial authorities. If, however, criminal proceedings are instituted against a consular official, he must appear before the competent authorities (Art. 41). The purpose of this provision is to settle the question of the personal immunity of consular officials.[51]

This question had been controversial, both in theory and in state practice, since many states had refused to recognize the personal inviolability of consular officials, certainly not for any acts not part of the official duties of such officials.

The relevant provisions in the bulk of consular treaties exclude from personal inviolability such consular officials as may be nationals of the receiving state; consular officials engaged in commercial activities insofar as such activities are concerned; and specify what ranks or categories of consular officials are to enjoy such inviolability: some grant it only to heads of posts, others to all consular officials, and still others generously extend inviolability to specified categories of consulate employees.

In all instances, however, members of a consulate enjoy immunity from the jurisdiction of the administrative and criminal authorities of the receiving state with respect to any act performed in the exercise of consular functions (Art. 43).

The classic instance illustrating the liability of a consular official for nonofficial acts is the celebrated case of

BIGELOW v. PRINCESS ZIZIANOFF

France, Court of Appeal of Paris, 1928
Gazette du Palais, March 4, 1928 (No. 125)

FACTS

Bigelow was director of the Passport Service at the American Consulate General in Paris. He appealed from the judgment of the Conventional Tribunal of the Seine of April 5, 1927, which asserted its competence in a prosecution of Bigelow for defamation.

The Princess Zizianoff, a White Russian resident in France, had requested a visa of her passport in order to travel to the United States. Bigelow had refused to grant her the visa. The Princess protested against his decision and Bigelow proceeded to furnish information about her at a press conference, apparently to justify his refusal of the visa.

On September 5, 1926, the *Boston Sunday Post* carried a story over the byline of Robert Johnson, in which the essential sentences read:

"Did Beauty Spy on U.S.? Princess Zizianoff is an international spy. She worked for the Germans in Russia during the World War and was deported to Siberia when she was caught. She was sent to America by Zinovieff last year to do espionage work among the American patriotic organizations, and her anti-Bolshevik activity is only a blind. In the past week she has twice secretly visited the Soviet embassy in Paris."

As a result of this publication, Princess Zizianoff filed a suit before the

---

[51] See Lee, *op. cit.* (n. 48, 1966), pp. 132–133, on the weakness of the provisions of Article 41 from a consul's point of view.

12th Correctional Tribunal of the Seine against Mr. Kahn, Paris representative of the newspaper, and Mr. Bigelow, the latter being named an accomplice, for having furnished the elements of the article, on grounds of abusive language and libel. [*Princess Zizianoff* v. *Kahn and Bigelow*, reprinted in 21 *A.J.I.L.* (1927), p. 811.] Bigelow denied the competence of the Tribunal, but was overruled by the Court which declared itself competent in respect to him.

Bigelow's contentions were first, that French tribunals had no jurisdiction over consuls of the United States, both by reason of the provisions of the Consular Convention of February 23, 1853, between France and the United States, and those of the Consular Convention of January 7, 1876, between France and Greece, applicable to American consuls by virtue of the "most-favored nation" clause in the former convention; and second, that under a general principle of international law, it was not permitted, even in the absence of a consular treaty, to cite a foreign consul before the courts of the receiving state for acts done in the performance of his duties, not even for misdeeds committed in the exercise of his functions.

ISSUE

Is a consul immune from the jurisdiction of the receiving state in respect of a libel committed by giving information as to his reasons for denying a visa, that is, for an act outside his official duties?

DECISION

The Court of Appeal rejected Bigelow's contentions and ruled that the French courts were competent to try him for his private act. The Court confirmed the judgment of the Cor-rectional Tribunal and ordered Bigelow to pay the costs of the appeal.

REASONING

Each state has the right to interpret international treaties and its interpretation is final for all courts under its jurisdiction. The French government had decided on earlier occasions [cited in the judgment] that its consular convention, where it dealt with the immunities of consular officials, meant that "the personal immunity granted to consuls by the convention does not exclude the competence of our courts in penal matters." Hence Bigelow's argument based on the convention was rejected.

His second contention, based on a presumed rule of international law, also had to be rejected. Now, Bigelow had been well within his functions when he explained the reasons which led him to refuse the visa requested by Princess Zizianoff. Even the issuing of a communiqué or the calling of a press conference for such a purpose was legitimate and within the scope of consular functions.

But the nature of the remarks made by Bigelow, as reproduced in the press, injured the private interests of Princess Zizianoff and were quite divorced from his administrative acts. His statements accusing the Princess of having acted as a German and later as a Russian spy, of having visited the Soviet Embassy in Paris, and so on, were unsubstantiated and did not constitute the performance of an official act. Hence Bigelow stepped outside of his functions in a manner which excluded the application of the immunity asserted by him under international law.

"Whereas, moreover, as the judgment below declares, the defendant is prosecuted, not for refusal of a passport, which would be an act in his consular capacity and would consequently be outside any jurisdiction of the courts, but only for having, in his communication of that decision of his country, delivered himself on the subject of said refusal of the above-described comments, which were not its necessary and indispensable corollary; and as in these comments, viewed as apart from or included in the official act itself, there is a serious wrong susceptible of injuring private interests and having a personal character; and this wrong, which is clearly unconnected with the duty performed by Bigelow and is not at all required in the examination of the said official act, would, if it is established, involve him in penal liability by reason of the criminal elements which it appears to contain."

One of the most instructive modern cases touching on the exercise of consular functions, immunity of consular premises, amenability of consuls to legal process, and other aspects of consular agents, was the famous *Kasenkina* case.[52]

Mrs. Oksana S. Kasenkina, a Soviet citizen employed in New York City as a teacher of the children of members of the Soviet delegation to the United Nations, had appealed, on July 31, 1948, for refuge to the editor of a Russian-language newspaper in New York. She had been told by her employers to return to the Soviet Union and was supposed to sail on the day in question. The editor arranged to have Mrs. Kasenkina go to Reed Farm, a rural retreat managed by the Tolstoy Foundation, Inc., a White Russian welfare group. All accounts agreed that Mrs. Kasenkina went to Reed Farm of her own free will. She then wrote a letter to Y. M. Lomakin, Soviet Consul-General in New York. On August 7, 1948, Mr. Lomakin went to Reed Farm and, after some discussion, took Mrs. Kasenkina back to New York and into the premises of the Consulate General. Two days later the Soviet ambassador lodged a strong protest with the State Department, accusing the Tolstoy Foundation of kidnapping Mrs. Kasenkina; the same charges were repeated on August 11, in a note handed in Moscow to the U.S. ambassador by the Soviet foreign minister.

Meanwhile the American press began to express suspicions that Mrs. Kasenkina was being held against her will in the Consulate. On August 11, Consul-General Lomakin was served with a writ of *habeas corpus*, requiring him to produce Mrs. Kasenkina in the New York Supreme Court on the next morning. Lomakin ignored the writ, and at 6 A.M. the next morning the Soviet ambassador protested to the State Department and denied that a writ such as the one in question could be served on a

---

[52] *Emmet v. Lomakin*, United States, Sup. Ct., Special Term, New York County, 1948, 84 N.Y.S. (2d) 562, reported in 43 *A.J.I.L.* (1949), p. 381. Consult also Lawrence Preuss, "Consular Immunities: The Kasenkina Case (U.S.–U.S.S.R.)," *ibid.*, pp. 37–56, and *The New York Times*, August 21, 1948, as well as 19 *Department of State Bulletin* (August 29, 1948), pp. 251–253.

Consul-General and that any court of a receiving state could impose upon a consular official an obligation to secure the appearance, in court, of a citizen of the country he represented.

The Legal Adviser of the Department of State, however, advised the New York court, on inquiry, that:

It is the view of the United States Government that there is no basis under international law or under any law of the United States for considering that Mrs. Kasenkina is in any manner subject to the control or authority of the Soviet Government so long as she remains in this country. The Department of State already has advised the Soviet Embassy that Mrs. Kasenkina will not be placed under the control of any person against her own will. The Department has also advised the Soviet Embassy that although it recognizes the right of the Soviet Government, through its officials abroad to extend all proper assistance and protection to Soviet nationals, this right does not include authority to take charge of Soviet citizens in this country irrespective of their wishes.

It should be mentioned that a warrant of attachment to enforce the original writ was never issued, in view of the events, and the writ was eventually dismissed.

While telegraphic exchanges took place on August 12 between the Legal Adviser and the governor of New York, and between the governor and the judge who had granted the writ, events assumed dramatic aspects at the Soviet consular premises. At 4:20 P.M., Mrs. Kasenkina leaped from a third-floor window, suffering serious injuries. Members of the consular staff ran from the premises, picked up the woman, and carried her into the building. They were not quick enough, however, to prevent the simultaneous entrance of members of the New York City police force, one of whom called an ambulance even though the staff refused him permission to use a telephone. Several additional policemen entered after the arrival of substantial reinforcements and insisted on inspecting Mrs. Kasenkina's room; there they seized a letter written by her to Lomakin (sealed and left in that condition) after a scuffle with members of the consular staff. The letter was returned later, unopened, to Lomakin.

Mrs. Kasenkina, apparently at her own request, was removed to a hospital where she was kept under the protection of a police guard. The Soviet Vice-Consul made several attempts to see her and objected strongly when, on being granted permission to talk with Mrs. Kasenkina, he had to do so in the presence of police officers. Mrs. Kasenkina told the Vice-Consul, as she had told the police earlier, that she had been kept as a prisoner in the Consulate General.

The next day the Soviet ambassador called at the Department of State and demanded that Lomakin be permitted to place a twenty-four-hour guard over Mrs. Kasenkina, that Lomakin be allowed to see her at will, that she be placed under the protection of the consular authorities, and that she be moved from the hospital to any place to be stipulated by the Consul General. Those demands were rejected, except for the right of Mrs. Kasenkina to see any Soviet officials whom she wished to see. A U.S. note of August 19 contained the opinion that ". . . Soviet citizens are, however, themselves entitled to the protection of the applicable laws of the United States and the Government of the United States cannot permit the exercise within the United States of the police power of any foreign government. . . ." The concluding paragraphs of that note stated that

the Consul General has himself made or issued statements to the press which, in view of all the evidence available, the Department of State can only conclude were deliberately designed to mislead the American public in regard to a serious charge involving the United States Government. The United States Government considers that Consul General Lomakin's conduct constituted an abuse of the prerogatives of his position and a gross violation of the internationally accepted standards governing the conduct of foreign officials.

The Department of State is therefore requesting the President to revoke the exequatur issued to Consul General Lomakin, and it is requested that he leave the United States within a reasonable time.

On August 25, 1948, President Truman signed the order revoking Lomakin's exequatur.

Members of a consulate may be called on to attend as witnesses in the course of judicial or administrative proceedings. If they decline to do so, however, no penalty can be applied to them. On the other hand, members of a consulate are not obliged to give any evidence concerned with matters connected with the exercise of their functions nor are they obligated to produce official documents and correspondence relating to such matters (Art. 44).

Waiver of Immunity. The sending state alone may, of course, waive the immunity of its consular officials, but such waiver must in all cases be express. If the sending state waives the immunity of such officials, for the purpose of civil or administrative proceedings, the waiver does not constitute a waiver of immunity from measures of execution resulting from a judicial decision; a separate waiver, again express in nature, would be required for such measures (Art. 45). A consular official who initiates proceedings in a matter where he might normally enjoy immunity, is precluded from invoking such immunity from local jurisdictions in respect of any counterclaim directly connected with the principal claim.

Special Exemptions. Members of the consulate, their families, and their private staff are exempt from regulations and laws of the receiving state in regard to the registration of aliens, residence permits, and work permits (Art. 46).

Exemptions from Taxes and Personal Services. Members of a consulate, with the following exceptions, and members of their families are exempt from all dues and taxes, personal or real, national, regional or municipal, *except*

1. Indirect taxes normally included in the price of goods and services.
2. Dues and taxes on private immovable property in the territory of the receiving state, unless held on behalf of the sending state for purposes of the consulate.
3. Estate, succession or inheritance taxes, but not in the case of those concerning the succession of a member of the consulate or of a member of his family.
4. Dues and taxes on private income having its source in the receiving state and capital taxes on investments made in commercial or financial enterprises in that state.
5. Charges levied for specific services rendered.
6. Registration, court or record fees, mortgage dues and stamp duties (Art. 49).[53]

Excluded from all these provisions are members of the consulate and members of their families who carry on a private gainful occupation, members of the consulate and members of their families who are nationals of the receiving state, honorary consular officials, and the service staff of the consulate (Art. 57).

Members of a consulate, except the service staff, and members of their families, are exempt from all personal services and military obligations such as those connected with requisitioning, military contributions, and billeting (Art. 52). Other common exemptions of this kind are based on customary international law and cover such matters as military service, service in a militia, the function of juryman or law judge, or personal labor service ordered by a local authority in connection with a public disaster.

Status of Consuls in Transit. It will be remembered that diplomatic agents enjoy considerable privileges and immunities while in transit through third states. In the case of consular officials, the picture had been somewhat clouded. There appeared to be no rule of customary international law specifying that a third state had to or should grant passage through its territorial jurisdiction to consular officials, employees, and their families. This privilege has now been established, however, in the *Vienna Consular Convention* (Art. 54).

---

[53] It should be noted that, pending general adherence to the Vienna Convention, most consular treaties do not exempt consular premises from real estate taxes. Applicable local law has hitherto determined the tax status of such premises. See *Republic of Argentina* v. *City of New York*, United States, New York Supreme Court, New York County, Part I, 1967, 283 N.Y.S. 2d 389, digested in 62 *A.J.I.L.* (1968), pp. 497–499.

Duties Toward Receiving State. It is a fundamental duty of all persons enjoying privileges and immunities as consular officials or members of their families or personal staffs to respect the laws and regulations of the receiving state, without prejudice to their privileges and immunities. Consular premises must not be used in any manner incompatible with consular functions as laid down by treaty or by rules of international law (Art. 55). Consular officials and others enjoying privileges and immunities are prohibited from interference in the internal affairs of the receiving state.

Honorary Consuls. Many portions (notably Arts. 58 to 68) of the *Vienna Consular Convention* refer in whole or in part to so-called honorary consuls. A discussion of this aspect of consular relations exceeds the limits set by the nature of a general text. Suffice it to say that in contrast to career consuls, who always are nationals of the sending state, honorary consuls are recruited from among the nationals of the receiving state. Most honorary consuls carry on a private gainful activity in addition to their consular functions, and indeed some states classify as honorary consul any consular official, regardless of nationality, who engages in such private activity. Generally speaking, honorary consuls enjoy the same privileges and immunities as career consuls, but differences do occur. The interested reader is referred to the relevant portions of the 1963 treaty.

Status in Time of War. The status of consular officials in time of war presents numerous special problems. The receiving or sending state may move consulates to different locations. An invading belligerent decides whether or not neutral consulates are to remain and operate in occupied enemy territory. If the consuls are allowed to remain, they would not require new *exequaturs* from the occupant's government. Any misconduct of a neutral consul subjects him to the same penalties as would be visited on the indigenous inhabitants by the occupant.[54] It was quite common until the middle of the nineteenth century to continue consular relations between belligerents. The development of economic warfare and more especially the concept that each citizen of one belligerent is the enemy of each citizen of the other belligerent has prompted the total abandonment of that custom. During the past hundred years, the outbreak of hostilities usually has not only meant the end of diplomatic relations but also of all consular relations between belligerents.

SUGGESTED READINGS

DIPLOMATIC AGENTS: GENERAL

Brierly, pp. 254–267; Gould, pp. 259–282; Lauterpacht's *Oppenheim*, Vol. I, pp. 769–828; Svarlien, pp. 229–254; C. Wilfred Jenks, *International Immunities*

[54] See von Glahn, pp. 88–90, for further details on the treatment of neutral consuls in occupied territory; cf. Hackworth, Vol. IV, pp. 683, 689–691, 713–714.

(London: Stevens & Sons, Ltd.; Dobbs Ferry, N.Y.: Oceana Publications, 1961); Clifton E. Wilson, *Diplomatic Privileges and Immunities* (Tucson, Ariz.: University of Arizona Press, 1967); Leo J. Harris, "Diplomatic Privileges and Immunities: A New Regime Is Soon to Be Adopted in the United States," 62 *A.J.I.L.* (1968), pp. 98–113.

Cases

Dickinson v. *Del Solar,* Great Britain, King's Bench Division, 1929 [1930] 1 K.B. 376.

Holbrook, Nelson & Co. v. *Henderson,* United States, Superior Court of the City of New York, 1839, 6 N.Y. Super. Court (4 Sandford 619).

The Magdalena Steam Navigation Company v. *Martin,* Great Britain, Court of Queen's Bench, 1859, 2 Ellis & Ellis, 94.

Regina v. *Madan,* Great Britain, Court of Criminal Appeal, 1961, 1 All E.R. 588, reported briefly in 55 *A.J.I.L.* (1961), pp. 991–992.

People v. *Roy,* United States, Court of Special Sessions, Herkimer County, N.Y., 1959, 21 Misc. 2d 303, 200 N.Y.S. 2d 612.

Hellenic Lines, Ltd. v. *Moore,* United States, Court of Appeals, D.C. Circuit, 1965, 345 F. 2d 978, reported in 59 *A.J.I.L.* (1965), pp. 927–930.

Shaffer v. *Singh,* United States, Court of Appeals, D.C. Circuit, 1965, 343 F.2d 324; see also the extensive Note on this case by William H. Levit, Jr., *Harvard International Law Club Journal* (Winter 1965), pp. 153–164.

United States v. *Egorov,* United States, District Court, E.D.N.Y., 1963, 222 F. Supp. 106, noted in 58 *A.J.I.L.* (1964), p. 513.

Anonymous v. *Anonymous,* United States, N.Y. Family Court, N.Y. County, 1964, 252 N.Y.S. 2d 913, noted, 59 *A.J.I.L.* (1965), p. 391.

United States v. *Butenko,* United States, Court of Appeals, 3rd Circuit, 1967, 384 F. 2d 554, reported in some detail in 62 *A.J.I.L.* (1968), pp. 777–778.

SPECIAL MISSIONS

Maurice Waters, *The Ad Hoc Diplomat: A Study in Municipal and International Law* (The Hague: Martinus Nijhoff, 1963); A. D. Watts, "Jurisdictional Immunities of Special Missions: The French Property Commission in Egypt," 12 *International and Comparative Law Quarterly* (1963), pp. 1383–1399. For coverage of a special recent problem, consult Michael H. Cardozo, *Diplomats in International Cooperation: Stepchildren of the Foreign Service* (Ithaca, N.Y.: Cornell University Press, 1962).

CONSULAR AGENTS: GENERAL

Brierly, pp. 264–267; Gould, pp. 282–288; Lauterpacht's *Oppenheim,* Vol. I, pp. 829–845; Herbert W. Briggs, "American Consular Rights in Communist China," 44 *A.J.I.L.* (1950), pp. 243–258; Evald Roosaare, "Consular Relations Between the United States and the Baltic States," *Baltic Review,* No. 27 (January, 1964), pp. 11–36.

Cases

Fenton Textile Association v. *Krassin*, Great Britain, 1921, 38 Times L.R. 259.

Rocca v. *Thompson*, United States, Supreme Court, 1912, 223 U.S. 317.

Santovincenzo v. *Egan*, United States, Supreme Court, 1931, 284 U.S. 30.

United States v. *Trumbull*, United States, District Court, S.D. of Cal., 1891, 48 Fed. 94.

Bliss v. *Nicolaeff*, United States, New York Appellate Division, 1948, 79 N.Y.S. (2d) 63, reported in 42 *A.J.I.L.* (1948), p. 944.

22

International Agreements

TYPES OF TREATIES

Background. Treaties and other forms of international agreements have been in evidence throughout recorded history. In modern times, beginning with the writings of Grotius, writers and statesmen have depended mostly on rules of law governing contractual relations between private individuals in developing the principles regulating contractual arrangements between states. Only in the last few decades have there been attempts to draw up international codes governing treaties and other interstate agreements. While such efforts are still in the stage of draft articles, the general principles applied by state in actual practice have achieved a degree of uniformity which augurs well for a codification of the law of treaties in the not too distant future.[1]

Bilateral Treaties. The functions served by international agreements can best be understood through an examination of the various types of such instruments utilized by states. One distinction commonly emphasized is that between bilateral and multilateral treaties. Bilateral agreements involve only two states or parties. They are closely related, at least by analogy, to contracts between individuals. Normally a bilateral treaty is concluded between two states desiring to promote or regulate interests or matters of particular interest to them alone.

Multilateral Treaties. In the second place, states conclude multilateral (multipartite) treaties, that is, agreements negotiated by and involving more than two parties. Some of these agreements do not create new principles or rules of international law but represent merely an expanded version of a bilateral (bipartite) treaty; examples are particularly numerous in the area of multilateral military or political alliances (North Atlantic Treaty, Warsaw Pact, etc.). Other spheres of state interests served by the conclusion of multilateral instruments not characterized as lawmaking are in the economic and social areas—there a common aspect of multilateral treaties is the establishment of some form of international ad-

---

[1] For the general subject of treaties, consult Hackworth, Vol. IV, pp. 1–433; Moore, Vol. V, pp. 155–870; Harvard Research in International Law, "Law of Treaties," 29 *A.J.I.L.* (1935), Special Supp. pp. 653–1226; Hyde, Vol. II, pp. 1369–1558.

ministrative agency to carry out the common interest agreed upon in the treaty. Others, however, must be regarded as law-making treaties in the true sense. These fall again into two major categories: true treaties and so-called declarations.

Declarations. Declarations are a peculiarly American type of law-making agreement, resulting from inter-American conferences and meetings of foreign ministers. They produce statements of legal principles applying, on a regional basis, in the Western Hemisphere. Thus, the Preamble of the Act of Chapultepec (Conference on Problems of War and Peace, Mexico City, 1945), states that, "The American States have been incorporating in their international law, since 1890, by means of conventions, resolutions and declarations, the following principles. . . ." The governments of the American states do not differentiate, as far as legal status or binding force are concerned, between rules laid down in formal treaties and those found in resolutions or declarations, regarding all as possessed of equal standing.

The "law-making" function described must be understood clearly if confusion is to be avoided. Essentially, the delegates to an international conference engage in the drafting of a "law-making" treaty act is a legislative capacity but do not possess the authority to establish binding force for the products of their labors. The states represented at the meeting have the formal say and are bound by the new "law" only by consenting to it specifically and individually. The treaty comes into force only when ratified after the end of the conference, and binds only those states choosing to ratify it.

Classification of Treaties. All writers, from Hugo Grotius onward, have pointed out that the names or titles of international agreements included under the general term *treaty* have little or no legal significance. Certain terms are, to be sure, useful but they furnish little more than mere description. A unilateral treaty is binding on one party only (even though two parties may have concluded the agreement); a bilateral treaty is binding on two parties; a multilateral treaty, on a number of parties. A so-called simple treaty refers to an absolute obligation involved; a conditional treaty to a qualified one. Finally, a rather important distinction exists between an executed treaty and an executory treaty. The former type (sometimes referred to as a dispositive instrument) deals with a single matter which, when performed or taken care of, is disposed of. Good examples are supplied by agreements delimiting a boundary between two states and also by the numerous treaties dealing with voluntary cession. Executory treaties, by contrast, provide for continuous or occasional subsequent action or performance or application: examples are usually found among instruments governing commercial relations between states, extradition treaties, agreements establishing administrative organization, treaties of alliance, and so on.

A treaty in the accepted sense of the term may be characterized in the words of Sir Gerald G. Fitzmaurice, the third rapporteur on the law of treaties for the UN International Law Commission, of March 14, 1956:

. . . a treaty is an international agreement embodied in a single formal instrument (whatever its name, title or designation) made between entities both or all of which are subjects of international law possessed of an international personality and treaty-making capacity, and intended to create rights and obligations, or to establish relationships, governed by international law.[2]

Oppenheim's definition is more to the point: "International treaties are agreements, of a contractual character, between States, or organisations of States, creating legal rights and obligations between the Parties."[3]

Nomenclature. The variety of names given to treaties (and portions of multilateral instruments) over the years is astounding. Besides common varieties such as *convention, agreement, protocol, treaty,* and the less frequent *final act, general act,* and *declaration,* a bewildering array of relatively rare terms confronts the student. Among them, to list but a few, are *arrangement, accord, code, compact, contract, regulation, concordats,* and *statutes.* Many writers have insisted that *convention* has become the "standard name of instruments produced by multilateral bodies, which in particular instances study specific phases of a general subject."[4] This, however appears to be a very recent tendency and does not appear to have reached universal acceptance.

Executive Agreements. Executive agreements represent a peculiarly American practice in conducting relations with other states. Unlike a treaty concluded by the President (or his agents, that is, the Secretary of State and his subordinates) with another country, which requires submission to the United States Senate for the Constitutional two-thirds "advice and consent" before ratification is possible, an executive agreement does not have to be sent to the upper house of Congress. It is a binding international obligation made by the executive branch on the basis of prior Congressional authorization and within the limits set by the latter, or, on occasion, without prior Congressional authority within the powers generally recognized as vested in the presidential office. On a few occasions, an executive agreement did not come into force until Congress gave its specific approval, such as in the case of the United States–Canada Fur Seal Agreement of 1942, approved on February 26, 1944. Because bills in Congress require a mere majority for passage, it has been asserted on many occasions that executive agreements represent a modern and streamlined approach to dealing with other states. Also, because such an

[2] Denys P. Myers, "The Names and Scope of Treaties," 51 *A.J.I.L.* (1957), pp. 574–605, at p. 575.
[3] Lauterpacht's *Oppenheim,* Vol. I, p. 877.
[4] Myers, *op. cit.,* p. 578.

agreement comes into force on signature, the delay involved in the process of making a Constitutional treaty may be reduced greatly.[5]

The proportion of executive agreements out of the annual total number of agreements concluded by the United States testifies to the continuing emphasis on this mode of arriving at international concords: in 1956, only five out of 260 international agreements concluded by the United States required the advice and consent of the Senate; in 1965, only six of 198 agreements were in the nature of orthodox treaties, and in 1967, only thirteen out of 288 agreements required action by the Senate.[6]

The Department of State has held that executive agreements ought to be subject to certain limitations: in its Circular No. 175, of December 13, 1955, the Department stated that

Executive agreements shall not be used when the subject matter should be covered by a treaty. The executive agreement form shall be used only for agreements which fall into one or more of the following categories:
a. Agreements which are made pursuant to or in accordance with existing legislation or a treaty;
b. Agreements which are made subject to Congressional approval or implementation; or
c. Agreements which are made under and in accordance with the President's Constitutional Power.[7]

If an executive agreement was not authorized by prior legislation or did not fall within the sphere of constitutional presidential authority, the agreement would be regarded as void. This would be particularly true if the agreement contravened the provisions of a federal statute dealing with the matter involved in the executive agreement.[8]

What is the duration of an executive agreement? The question would appear superfluous because such instruments constitute binding obligations of the United States and in many instances specify a definite duration, expressed in terms of years, such as the fifty-year minimum agreement of April 6, 1939, concluded with the United Kingdom for the joint control of Canton and Enderbury Islands. But while it appears that

[5] On the problem of the desirability of substituting the executive agreement for "formal" treaties, consult *inter alia* Edwin Borchard, "Shall the Executive Agreement Replace the Treaty?" 38 *A.J.I.L.* (1944), pp. 637–743; Myres S. McDougal and A. Lans, "Treaties and Congressional–Executive or Presidential Agreements: International Instruments of National Policy," 54 *Yale Law Journal* (1945), pp. 181–352, 543–615, and Borchard's rejoinder, "Treaties and Executive Agreements—A Reply," *ibid.*, pp. 616–664.

[6] *Proceedings* (1958), p. 13; *ibid.* (1966), p. 200; *ibid.* (1968), p. 283.

[7] 50 *A.J.I.L.* (1956), Supp., pp. 784–789, at p. 785.

[8] See *United States* v. *Guy W. Capps, Inc.*, United States, Circuit Court of Appeals, Fourth Circuit, 1953, 204 F. (2d) 655, digested in 48 *A.J.I.L.* (1954), pp. 153–155.

the United States has never denied binding effect to an executive agreement on the grounds of presidential succession, the issue came into prominence in 1960. On April 6 of that year, the then Secretary of State, Christian A. Herter, stated in a news conference that a President could bind the United States only for his own term of office, a position apparently shared then by President Eisenhower.[9] Such views have no foundation, however, in international law (under which an executive agreement is regarded as a form of treaty), in previous policy statements issued by the Department of State, or in the practice of the United States.[10]

The most famous and controversial modern executive agreement is the Far Eastern Agreement signed at Yalta on February 11, 1945. Pan demonstrated rather convincingly[11] that President Roosevelt regarded the document as an executive agreement, yet did not admit this in his actual verbal report to Congress on March 1, 1945. He also pointed out the unique and unprecedented features of the instrument, down to the use of titles of the signatories (or lack thereof) and the immense political implications which involved most unusual duties on the part of one party (United States) as regarded an Allied but nonsignatory power (China).

An interesting sidelight on the history of the Yalta Agreement was provided by the fact that President Roosevelt requested Congress to "concur in the general conclusions" reached at Yalta, yet Congress could take no such action because the actual text of the agreement was not released by the Department of State until February 1946. In the meantime, however, the United States government, through the executive branch, undertook to carry out the measures called for in the Agreement.

CODIFICATION OF THE LAW

The International Law Commission developed Draft Articles on the Law of Treaties at its fourteenth, fifteenth, sixteenth, and seventeenth sessions, culminating in January, 1966, in a draft convention, complete with an elaborate commentary.[12] That draft was discussed at the first session of the United Nations Diplomatic Conference on the Law of Treaties, held at Vienna from March 26 to May 24, 1968. Sixty-five of the original seventy-five articles in question were adopted (many with relatively minor changes) by the Committee of the Whole, action was deferred on nine articles, four new ones were added, and one (Art. 38) was deleted.

[9] *The New York Times,* March 31, 1960.

[10] O. J. Lissitzyn, "Duration of Executive Agreements," 54 *A.J.I.L.* (1960), pp. 869–873.

[11] Stephen C. Y. Pan, "Legal Aspects of the Yalta Agreement," 46 *A.J.I.L.* (1952), pp. 40–59, at pp. 48–49, and the essentially opposing views of Herbert W. Briggs "The Leaders' Agreement of Yalta," 40 *A.J.I.L.* (1946), pp. 376–383. Text of the agreement is reprinted in full in both sources.

[12] Text in 61 *A.J.I.L.* (1967), Supp., pp. 263–463.

The revised draft was discussed again, in its entirety, and then voted on, article by article, at the second session of the Conference, April 9 to May 22, 1969, at Vienna. Thus a convention was produced for submission to governments. That agreement, the Vienna Convention on the Law of Treaties (hereinafter referred to as the *Vienna Convention*) was adopted on May 22, 1969, by a vote of seventy-nine in favor, one against (France), with nineteen abstentions (including all members of the Soviet bloc).[13]

Pending ratification of this agreement, it may be taken to represent a consensus of a majority of all governments on the subject of treaties, and much of the following discussion is based on the provisions of the Vienna instrument.

FORMATION OF TREATIES

The treaty-making process generally involves four major stages, several of which may, however, occur concurrently:

1. Negotiation (including the drawing up and authentication of the text).
2. Provisional acceptance of the text, normally through the affixing of the signatures of the negotiators.
3. Final acceptance of the treaty, normally through ratification.
4. The entry into force of the treaty.

Additional subjects intimately connected with the formation of a treaty include the acceptance of treaties with reservations as well as the registration of treaties.[14]

NEGOTIATION

A treaty is normally drawn up by a process of negotiation which may be carried on by any duly authorized persons or agencies. Diplomatic or other official channels may be utilized, a meeting of representatives may be arranged, or an international conference may be called for the purpose. In the case of treaties negotiated under the auspices of an international organization, the text may be drawn up either in an organ of that agency or at a conference convened by the agency.

No basic general limitations exist as to the actual persons entitled to negotiate a treaty. On occasion a head of state may do so himself (Presi-

[13] See text of the *Vienna Convention* and relevant documents in 8 *International Legal Materials* (1969), pp. 679–768.

[14] On the procedure of treaty-making in general, consult Hackworth, Vol. V, pp. 25–101; Hyde, Vol. II, pp. 1419–1460; Harvard Research in International Law, "Law of Treaties," 29 *A.J.I.L.* (1935), Special Supplement, at pp. 722–778; the Harvard Research in International Law code is hereinafter referred to as *Harvard Code*.

dent Wilson at the Paris Peace Conference was an example); or the head of the government may undertake the task; or the minister of foreign affairs may do so; or some diplomatic officers.

Representatives negotiating a treaty must be duly authorized to carry on their tasks and normally are required to have available credentials to that effect. If their sole function is negotiation, they do not need authority to sign the treaty. If both functions are to be carried out, then the agents of the parties have to have what are termed "plenary" or "full" powers. In the past this literally meant an agent had authority to bind his state to whatever he negotiated and signed. Today, however, it merely means that the agent has been authorized to negotiate an agreement, subject to constitutional limitations, the usual requirement of ratification, and the instructions of the authority under whose *supervision* and on whose behalf he acts.

On the other hand, heads of states and of governments as well as foreign ministers and heads of diplomatic missions (in the case of bilateral treaties) are presumed to have *ex officio* capacity to negotiate and to sign; they do not need to exhibit credentials to that effect (*Vienna Convention*, Art. 7, par. 2). The principle involved in the case of foreign ministers was illustrated strikingly through the ruling of the Permanent Court of International Justice in the well-known *Eastern Greenland Case (Denmark–Norway)*[15] in which the Court ruled that a valid and binding international agreement resulted from an official conversation between a foreign minister and a diplomatic agent of another state: the undertaking made by the foreign minister in the conversation and while he acted in the scope of his normal official authority, was binding on his state.

ADOPTION AND AUTHENTICATION

Adoption. Once the text of a treaty has been drafted in formal form by the negotiation, it is adopted by the parties in one of several ways: in the case of bilateral agreements, by mutual consent of the two parties; in the case of treaties negotiated between a limited number of states, usually by unanimous consent; in the case of multilateral instruments negotiated by an international conference, by the voting rules adopted by that conference; and in the case of treaties drawn up in an international organization or at a conference convened by such an organization, according to the voting rules provided either by the constitution of the organization or by the decision of an organ or agency competent to issue such rules.

Authentication. Adoption of a final text by the negotiators is followed by authentication. This step may take place in a number of ways: the negotiators may simply initial the text on behalf of their states; the text may be incorporated in the Final Act of the conference at which it was drawn up; the text may be incorporated in a resolution adopted by an

[15] *P.C.I.J.*, 1933, Ser. A/B, No. 53.

organ of an international organization; or the negotiators may append their signatures to the text of the agreement. Any of these procedures confirm that the text of the treaty is in its final form (*Vienna Convention*, Art. 10; see also *Harvard Code*, Commentary, pp. 734–735). The obvious purpose of the process of authentication is to supply to all parties (states) a text which is settled, so that each will know definitely what commitments are faced in the event of ratification. On rare occasions in modern times, dwindling into insignificance today, treaties have become effective on signature, and in such a case the authentication of the text would assume vital importance to all parties concerned, for it marked not only agreement as to the wording but also an act of binding acceptance of that wording.

Who may sign a treaty? Obviously, only persons who either have capacity *ex officio* to do so—such as heads of states or of governments and ministers of foreign affairs—or representatives of states to whom full (plenary) powers to negotiate and sign have been issued.

The right to sign or to authenticate in some other manner is usually restricted to the states which negotiated the treaty in question. These parties may, of course, decide to admit other states to signature, but such a decision is entirely at their option. If, however, a multilateral treaty has been drawn up at a conference, then the usual rule appears to be that the right to sign or to authenticate is granted to all states invited to participate in the negotiations or to attend the conference. Unless the treaty text provides otherwise, it would appear, therefore, that a state invited to attend a meeting has a right to sign the resultant treaty even though it had declined to accept the invitation to the conference.

RATIFICATION

Processes of Ratification. The overwhelming bulk of modern international treaties becomes effective only on ratification. Virtually every state has developed detailed domestic regulations spelling out the process of treaty ratification. Although the constitutional provisions vary greatly from country to country, a certain amount of common agreement is in evidence. Thus ratification is generally held to be an executive act, undertaken by the head of the state or of the government, as the case may be, through which the formal acceptance of the treaty is proclaimed. Until such acceptance is forthcoming, a treaty does not create obligations for the state in question—except, of course, in the rare instance of an agreement that becomes effective and binding on signature alone. In other words, normally a treaty is "concluded" as soon as mutual agreement has been manifested by the act of signature on the part of the duly authorized agents of the parties, but the binding force of the instrument is suspended until ratification has been completed. This statement raises the interesting question whether ratification is *always* necessary in the case of treaties which do not provide for their coming into force at signature. In the case of the European peace treaties negotiated in 1947, Finland, Bulgaria, and Italy ratified their respective treaties, but Hungary and Romania did not do so. Yet everyone, including the governments of the two nonratifying states, appears to have agreed that all the peace treaties possessed validity! In essence, therefore, it is the intention of the parties which is decisive in determining whether a nonratified treaty is to be regarded as binding. In many states, executive ratification must be preceded by some action on the part of the legislative branch of the government—commonly an action expressing the granting of consent to ratification. For the United States, a treaty must receive the "advice and consent" of two thirds of a quorum of the Senate. This, normally, is followed by the ratification act on the part of the President.

Unconstitutional Ratification. The unconstitutional ratification of a treaty should not be regarded as voiding the international obligations and responsibilities of the ratifying states. The Permanent Court of International Justice observed in the case of the *Treatment of Polish Nationals in Danzig that* "a State cannot adduce as against another state its own Constitution with a view of evading obligations incumbent upon it under international law or treaties in force." [16] Such an interpretation appears most reasonable and fully in accord with the principles of international law, for receipt of a notice of ratification would lead a state to expect that an agreement would be honored in good faith; a subsequent attempt to disclaim obligations incurred through the agreement on a plea of unconstitutional ratification would look like a deliberate violation of the requirement of good faith basic to all international engagements.[17]

Another problem connected with ratification has to do with its possible retroactive effects. A traditional American view held that a treaty became effective on the date of signature, once it had been ratified—that is, the act of ratification was assumed to possess definite retroactive force. This point of view was not shared by other states and a gradual shift in opinion took place in the United States. Beginning with the decision of the Supreme Court of the United States in *Haver* v. *Yaker*,[18] in which the Court held that the rule of retroactivity did not apply when a treaty affected private rights, the retreat from the old position proceeded apace. Today the view of both publicists and government appears to be that a treaty does not become effective until ratification has taken place—unless the instrument itself provides otherwise (*Harvard Code*, Art. 11, and *Vienna Convention*, Arts. 12–17).

[16] *P.C.I.J.*, 1932, Ser. A/B, No. 44, at p. 24; see also Hyde, Vol. II, p. 1385.

[17] See the succinct correct analysis by José S. Camara, *The Ratification of International Treaties* (Toronto: Ontario Publishing Co., 1949), as well as the letter, dated March 15, 1963, from the Secretary of State to the Ambassador of Austria, in 57 *A.J.I.L.* (1963), pp. 894–895, and the case of *Lazarou* v. *Moraros*, United States, Supreme Court, New Hampshire, 1958, 143 A.2d 669, noted in 53 *A.J.I.L.* (1959), p. 193.

[18] 1869, 9 Wallace 32; for utilization of the old rule, see Moore, Vol. V, p. 244.

Nowadays, following the official acceptances of a treaty, ratifications are exchanged by the parties to the agreement and the latter is announced to be in effect.

Adherence. Related to both signature and ratification is the subject of *adherence.* This means the formal act of a third party, one which had not signed or ratified a treaty, by which that party assumes the obligations and possible privileges involved in a treaty and considers itself bound by its provisions. Normally the permission of the original parties to the treaty is required before nonsignatories may join in the agreement, and commonly adherence is involved only in the case of originally multipartite agreements.[19]

REJECTION OF TREATIES

Except in the case of treaties effective on signature, a state is not bound by a treaty until ratification has taken place. It is, therefore, quite possible for a prospective party to an agreement to refuse consent to ratification, in accordance with its constitutional requirements. Thus the United States Senate is free to deny its consent to a treaty negotiated by the executive branch and while such an action might generate ill-feeling among the other parties to the agreement, it falls within the proper sphere of authority of the Senate. Under such conditions, the treaty could not be ratified by the President and hence would remain inoperative as far as the United States was concerned. Among the major treaties rejected by the Senate could be listed the agreements with Great Britain and Colombia of 1824 (suppression of slave trade); Texas, 1844 (annexation of Texas); Belgium, 1853 (extradition); Denmark, 1867 (acquisition of St. Thomas and St. Johns); Colombia, 1869 and 1870 (canal); Great Britain, 1869 (Alabama claims); Dominican Republic, 1870 (proposed purchase of country by the United States); Great Britain, 1889, and France, 1892 (extradition); the seven Kasson treaties of 1902 (commerce); and the somewhat different type of rejection involving the Versailles Treaty.

UNDERSTANDINGS

"Understandings" are statements attached to the ratification of a treaty by means of which a party to the agreement specifies its own interpretation of certain provisions of the instrument.[20] This is a quite common practice by means of which states are enabled to place on the record what would be called advance interpretations, particularly with respect to intent involved. If and when these interpretations are found acceptable by

---

[19] Hyde, Vol. II, pp. 1447–1448; see also Hackworth, Vol. V, pp. 74–84; *Harvard Code*, pp. 812–843; for example, 100 states had signed the Limited Nuclear Test-Ban Treaty by September 26, 1963.

[20] See Hackworth, Vol. V, pp. 144–153, for an extensive commentary on this topic.

the other party or parties to the agreement, they may serve as highly useful commentaries in the event of subsequent disagreement as to the meaning of treaty provisions.

The term *understandings* has fallen into disuse recently and has been replaced by *interpretative reservations*. It has long been established that if no other party to an agreement expresses dissent, it is assumed that the party which made the interpretative reservations can consider them to be integral parts of the instrument.

RESERVATIONS

Meaning of Reservations. Reservations, on the other hand, represent changes or amendments inserted into a treaty by one party as an implied or specified condition of ratification.[21] A reservation must be accepted by the other parties to the agreement if the latter is to come into force and possess legal effect. Normally a reservation possesses limiting effects; the state making the reservation denies the applicability of a portion of the treaty to relations of that state with the other state or states which may be parties to the instrument. Occasionally reservations assume the character of "nullifying reservations," changing the text of the treaty itself. A famous example was provided by several of the reservations proposed in 1919 by the late Senator Lodge of Massachusetts, which would have affected the conditions under which the League of Nations would have operated.

Bilateral Agreements. If the treaty is a bilateral agreement, few problems arise over a reservation: the other party either ratifies the original agreement as altered by the reservation or refuses to ratify it and thus kills the agreement.

Multilateral Treaties. Multilateral treaties, however, pose grave problems in connection with reservations.[22] It is generally agreed that two schools of thought prevail among the nations of the world. In the Americas, the view is held that a treaty is in force on a strictly national basis: those countries which accept another state's reservation are bound by it while others may declare not to do so and are not bound by it as altered but only by its original form. The Governing Board of the Pan American Union expressed the inter-American view in this manner:

1. The treaty shall be in force, in the form in which it was signed, as between more countries which ratify it without reservations, in the terms in which it was originally drafted and signed.

---

[21] See Gould, pp. 311–319, on the subject in general, *Harvard Code*, pp. 843–912, and *Vienna Convention*, Arts. 19–23.

[22] See G. G. Fitzmaurice, "Reservations to Multilateral Conventions," 2 *International and Comparative Law Quarterly* (1953), p. 1–26; H. G. Schermers, "The Suitability of Reservations to Multilateral Treaties," 6 *Tijdschrift* (1959), pp. 350–361; and Hackworth, Vol. V, pp. 130–131 (one of the clearest statements on this point).

2. It shall be in force as between the governments which ratify it with reservations and the signatory States which accept the reservations in the form in which the treaty may be modified by said reservations.

3. It shall not be in force between a government which may have ratified with reservations and another which may have already ratified, and which does not accept such reservations.[23]

A different point of view is generally held among European states and has been shared by the Secretariats of both the League of Nations and the United Nations. It has been outlined as follows:

A State may make a reservation when signing, ratifying or acceding to a convention, prior to its entry into force, only with the consent of all States which have ratified or acceded thereto up to the date of entry into force; and may do so after the date of entry into force only with the consent of all States which have theretofore ratified or acceded.[24]

The interesting feature of this conflict of views is that the International Court of Justice has supported a theory essentially identical with the inter-American view, in the Advisory Opinion on *Reservations to the Convention on the Prevention and Punishment of the Crime of Genocide in 1951*.[25] On the other hand, the International Law Commission has tended to follow the League of Nations–United Nations point of view in its own recommendations.[26] Sensibly enough, however, the Commission then proceeded to recommend a practice already encountered frequently in the actual usages of states: it suggested that each treaty should contain its own specifications of the status to be granted to reservations made on the occasion of the various steps involved in the formation of the treaty (signature, ratification, accession—in the case of multilateral agreements).

Article 20 of the *Vienna Convention* provides that

1. A reservation expressly authorized by a treaty does not require any subsequent acceptance by the other contracting States unless the treaty so provides.

2. When it appears from the limited number of the negotiating States and the object and purpose of a treaty that the application of the treaty in its en-

---

[23] See 45 *A.J.I.L.* (1951), Supp., p. 111; refer also to Charles G. Fenwick, "Reservations to Multilateral Treaties," *ibid.*, 45 (1951), pp. 145–148, and the earlier William Sanders, "Reservations to Multilateral Treaties Made in the Act of Ratification or Adherence," *ibid.*, 33 (1939), pp. 488–499.

[24] 45 *A.J.I.L.* (1951), Supp., p. 110. See also *Harvard Code*, Arts. 14–16.

[25] *I.C.J. Reports, 1951* (Pleadings, Oral Arguments), May 28, 1951, in 45 *A.J.I.L.* (1951), pp. 579–590; see also Yuen-li Liang, "The Third Session of the International Law Commission: Review of its Work by the General Assembly—I," 46 *A.J.I.L.* (1952), pp. 483–503, for a detailed analysis of the opinion.

[26] See 45 *A.J.I.L.* (1951), Supp., pp. 106–107, and Yuen-li Liang, "The Practice of the United Nations with Respect to Reservations to Multipartite Instruments," *ibid.*, 44 (1950), pp. 117–128.

tirety between all the parties is an essential condition of the consent of each one to be bound by the treaty, a reservation requires acceptance by all the parties.

3. When a treaty is a constituent instrument of an international organization and unless it otherwise provides, a reservation requires the acceptance of the competent organ of that organization.

4. In cases not falling under the preceding paragraphs and unless the treaty otherwise provides:

   (a) acceptance by another contracting State of a reservation constitutes the reserving State a party to the treaty in relation to that other State if or when the treaty is in force for those States;

   (b) an objection by another contracting State to a reservation does not preclude the entry into force of the treaty as between the objecting and reserving States unless a contrary intention is definitely expressed by the objecting State;

   (c) an act expressing a State's consent to be bound by the treaty and containing a reservation is effective as soon as at least one other contracting State has accepted the reservation.

5. For the purposes of paragraphs 2 and 4 and unless the treaty otherwise provides, a reservation is considered to have been accepted by a State if it shall have raised no objection to the reservation by the end of a period of twelve months after it was notified of the reservation or by the date on which it expressed its consent to be bound by the treaty, whichever is later.

And Article 21 of the same treaty states that

1. A reservation established with regard to another party in accordance with articles 19, 20 and 23:

   (a) modifies for the reserving State in its relations with that other party the provisions of the treaty to which the reservation relates to the extent of the reservation; and

   (b) modifies those provisions to the same extent for that other party in its relations with the reserving State.

2. The reservation does not modify the provisions of the treaty for the other parties to the treaty *inter se*.

3. When a State objecting to a reservation has not opposed the entry into force of the treaty between itself and the reserving State, the provisions to which the reservation relates do not apply as between the two States to the extent of the reservation.

On January 12, 1952, the General Assembly of the United Nations adopted a set of recommendations dealing with reservations to multilateral treaties.[27] The first of the three points brought out was a recommendation

---

[27] Text reprinted in 46 *A.J.I.L.* (1952), Supp., p. 66.

that the organs of the United Nations, specialized agencies, and states should, in preparing multilateral agreements, consider the insertion of provisions declaring the admissibility or nonadmissibility of reservations and the effects to be given to such reservations if they were permitted.

The second recommendation, relating to the Convention on the Prevention and Punishment of the Crime of Genocide, was that states should be guided by the relevant Advisory Opinion of the International Court of Justice. In that Opinion the Court had failed to indicate who should decide whether a given reservation to the particular instrument in question was or was not compatible with its object and purpose.

Finally, the Assembly requested the Secretary-General, in registering treaties deposited with the Secretariat, to accept future documents containing reservations or objections, without passing on the legal effects of such documents.

PROCLAMATION OF TREATIES

The constitutional requirements of many countries demand some further step beyond ratification of a treaty or conclusion of an executive agreement in order to create binding force on natural and legal persons as domestic law. In Belgium, for instance, promulgation of a treaty is required; in Switzerland, a treaty must be published in the official government journal before it acquires domestic effects. In the United States, the President does not have to issue a proclamation in order to make a treaty valid.

In this connection, it must be emphasized that certain treaties require the passage of domestic legislation before those instruments have any effect on or apply to citizens in a given country. This requirement is always present in the case of nonself-executing treaties.[28]

The domestic nature of the actions mentioned (proclamation, promulgation, publication, legislation) means that failure to carry out the implementary acts subsequent to ratification of a treaty does *not* free a state from any responsibilities incurred through ratification. The treaty stands, as far as the ratifying government is concerned, and its obligations toward the other parties to the agreement continue in force despite the nonperformance of the domestic acts called for.

REGISTRATION

The registration of international treaties is not a new idea at all. The practice of states on the other hand, was governed to a large extent by the concept of secret diplomacy. The search for the causes of World War I, however, led to strong criticism of secret diplomacy, and Presi-

---

[28] See Alona E. Evans, "Self-Executing Treaties in the United States of America," 30 *B.Y.I.L.* (1953), pp. 178–205. Refer also to the decisions in the *Sei Fujii Case* in 1952 (Supreme Court of California, 242 P. 2d 617), as well as the excellent summary and reference notes in Gould, pp. 330–331.

dent Woodrow Wilson emerged as the leader of a segment of international public opinion favoring not only open diplomacy but also the registration of treaties as a means of ensuring publicity for their conclusion as well as for their contents.[29]

Although the expectation of open diplomacy and full public knowledge concerning the making and contents of all kinds of agreements among nations has proved to be somewhat illusory, the idea of registering treaties was actually implemented, largely as the result of Wilson's crusade.

League of Nations' Provisions for Registration. Article 18 of the League Covenant provided that, "Every treaty or international engagement entered into hereafter by any Member of the League shall be forthwith registered with the Secretariat and shall as soon as possible be published by it. No such treaty or international engagement shall be binding until so registered."

Although the meaning of the last sentence appeared to be quite clear, the Permanent Court of International Justice held in the *Pajzs, Csázky, and Esterházy Case*[30] that certain international agreements concluded on the basis of the Young Plan "came into effect on April 19, 1931, and were registered by the Secretariat of the League of Nations on August 20, 1931, in accordance with Article 18 of the Covenant." The Court appears to have intended to indicate that in the absence of inordinate delay in registration the agreements came into effect when the parties involved desired them to do so, rather than at the time of registration.

United Nations' Provisions for Registration. The Charter of the United Nations provides in Article 102 for the compulsory registration of international treaties and agreements:

(1) Every treaty and every international agreement entered into by any Member of the United Nations after the present Charter comes into force shall as soon as possible be registered with the Secretariat and published by it.
(2) No party to any such treaty or international agreement which has not been registered in accordance with the provisions of paragraph 1 of this Article may invoke that treaty or agreement before any organ of the United Nations.

The significant change in the Charter from the provisions of Article 18 of the Covenant is, of course, the avoidance of the principle that unregistered treaties would lack binding force for the parties in question. That principle was tested in an unusual challenge posed by Mexico in 1928 in the *Pablo Najera Case*. Mexico, then not yet a member of the League of Nations, asserted that the French–Mexican Claims Convention of Septem-

---

[29] Note the wording of the first of Wilson's "Fourteen Points": "Open covenants of peace, openly arrived at, after which there shall be no private international understandings of any kind, but diplomacy shall proceed always frankly and in the public view."

[30] *P.C.I.J.*, 1936, Ser. A/B, No. 68, at p. 46.

ber 25, 1924, was not binding on either party because France had failed to register the agreement with the League Secretariat. The Claims Commission, however, ruled that a nonmember could not invoke failure to register as a fact in its favor and that Article 18 barred the invocation of an unregistered agreement only before organs of the League or tribunals related to them, and that in any case the prohibition in question only applied to members of the League of Nations.

The wording of Article 102 (2) of the Charter is, of course, more specific in that it provides, that "no party" (member or nonmember) may invoke an unregistered agreement before organs of the United Nations. The regulations adopted by the General Assembly in 1946 for the registration of treaties under Article 102 of the Charter also take into account the new and vitally important field of agreements concluded by and among international organizations. Coverage of this subject exceeds, however, the scope of a general text on international law.[31]

EFFECTIVE DATE OF A TREATY

Modern treaties increasingly contain a provision specifying the date or the acts which will bring them into force. The best-known recent example is that of the Charter of the United Nations which provided in Article 110 (3) that it would come into force when ratified by the five permanent members of the Security Council and "by a majority of the other signatory states."

In the absence of specific internal provisions, an international treaty is generally regarded as coming into force (1) after ratification by the parties, and (2) after such ratifications have been exchanged or deposited, as the case may be. In the case of adhering states rather than original parties to an agreement, receipt by the depository agency of the notice of adherence is taken to be the effective date of the treaty for the adhering party, unless either the treaty specifies some other date or the notice or adherence itself contains a contrary date for the coming into force of the agreement. Executive agreements normally come into force as soon as they have been concluded—provided no further approval or ratification is required by constitutional provisions in either state involved.

THE INTERPRETATION OF TREATIES

Basic Principles. Once an international agreement comes into force, questions of the interpretation of its meaning may arise. In order to discover just what obligations or privileges are involved in such an instrument, writers on international law beginning with Hugo Grotius have attempted to formulate rules and principles of astounding variety. Until

---

[31] The interested reader will find suggestive materials in Philip C. Jessup, "Modernization of the Law of International Contractual Agreements," 41 *A.J.I.L.* (1947), pp. 378–407, on pp. 381–385; see also *Vienna Convention*, Articles 76–80.

the appearance of international tribunals possessed of obligatory jurisdiction, the chief value of such private endeavors has been their recognition by national courts in settling disputes.[32] The decisions and pronouncements of international courts, on the other hand, must be regarded as supplying more reliable and authoritative guides for the interpretation of treaties.

Most modern writers agree that two basic principles govern all commentaries in the interpretation of treaties: (1) the object of interpretation is to determine the real meaning of the parties accepting the instrument; and (2) unless there is evidence to the contrary, a treaty must be assumed not to be intended to be without effect or even to be absurd (see *Harvard Code*, pp. 937–940; *Vienna Convention*, Arts. 31–33).[33]

Wording of the Treaty. A fundamental objective of interpretation is, therefore, to discover just what the parties to a treaty understood the agreement to mean when they entered into it. In order to discover this, the actual wording of the treaty must be regarded as taking priority over all other considerations. If the terms of the instrument are clear and specific, no contrary intent can be asserted by either party to the agreement. A commonly cited example illustrates this principle in a striking manner. Article III, sec. 1, of the Hay–Pauncefote Treaty of 1901 provided that the Panama Canal should be "free and open to the vessels of commerce and war of all nations observing these Rules, on terms of entire equality." The United States asserted, however, that the term *all nations* did not include the United States, because that country had built the Canal and was the owner of the Canal and could not have had any intention to yield preferential treatment of its own ships, to wit, exemption from payment of tolls under the Panama Tolls Act. Elihu Root, one of the most prominent international lawyers in the United States, sided with the British government in its protest that the clear terms and intentions of the treaty had been violated by the exemptions in question. After much discussion in Congress, the exemptions were eventually repealed in 1914.

The words used in the agreement are interpreted in their usual, ordinary meaning unless, by some chance, such would produce absurd, contradictory, or impossible consequences. Because a treaty is expected to reflect

[32] The literature on the subject is very extensive and most diversified in its approach. Consult, *inter alia*, Lauterpacht's *Oppenheim*, Vol. I, pp. 950–958 (which, incidentally, lists an unusually large total of 16 rules to be applied to the interpretation of treaties); Jessup, *op. cit.* (n. 31), pp. 391–392; and the illuminating opinions of the Legal Adviser of the Department of State concerning the 1963 Nuclear Test Ban Treaty, reprinted in 58 *A.J.I.L.* (1964), pp. 175–179.

[33] The U.S. objected to the division of the matter on hand into two articles, with Article 32 styled as "supplementary means" of interpretation, as creating a hierarchy of canons of treaty interpretation. In particular, U.S. objections centered on the low place accorded in that hierarchy to the *travaux préparatoires*, reflecting the traditional American attitude toward the parallel of legislative history in the interpretation of statutes. Consult, on the subject of U.S. objections, 62 *A.J.I.L.* (1968), Supp., pp. 1021–1027.

the intentions of the parties involved, it may be necessary in interpretation to depart from the literal meaning of certain words, in order to avoid conclusions quite obviously contrary to the intent of the treaty.

Gould cited the interesting problem posed for Poland by the Leaders' Agreement at Yalta.[34] Winston Churchill told the House of Commons on Feb. 27, 1945, that the Yalta Agreement for an independent Poland obligated that country to be friendly to the Soviet Union: "The Poles will have their future in their own hands, with the single limitation that they must honestly follow, in harmony with their Allies, a policy friendly to Russia." Since independence would appear to imply a right to be unfriendly to anyone else at one's own discretion, the intentions of the Leaders at Yalta would appear to have been expressed poorly through the choice of the word *independence* with regard to Poland.

Rules for Interpretation of Multilingual Treaties. When a treaty is concluded in two or more languages, all texts being authentic, considerable difficulties in interpretation may arise. For instance, a given term may have a broad, liberal, wide meaning in one of the languages and its equivalent in another language may possess a restrictive, narrow, context. Under such conditions, the tendency has been to utilize the more narrow meaning in interpreting the treaty. As in the case of virtually all other rules applicable to the subject, limitations to this one may be found, the most commonly cited one being the decision of the Permanent Court of International Justice in the *Mavrommatis Palestine Concessions Case*.[35] A question about the narrower meaning of *contrôle public* and the more extensive meaning of *public control* was decided in favor of the meaning of the English term.

On occasion a term found in a treaty has different meaning in the countries which are parties to the agreement; one commonly employed solution is to apply the meaning prevalent in the country where the action contemplated by the treaty is to take place. If, of course, such action is is scheduled for, say, both parties to such an agreement, then the application of this rule might result in the rather odd—and perhaps unacceptable—spectacle of different procedures or actions being taken under the terms of the same instrument in two countries.

Logical Interpretation. If grammatical analysis should prove insufficient to interpret a treaty, logical interpretation may be called into play. In other words, a given term or provision in an international instrument may be given a meaning which is logical and in harmony with the other parts of the agreement.[36] Such interpretation seeks to construe dubious passages

---

[34] Gould, p. 335.

[35] *P.C.I.J.*, 1924, Ser. A, No. 2.

[36] See such pertinent opinions of the Permanent Court as the one on the *Interpretation of the Statute of Memel*, 1932, Ser. A/B, No. 49, on the *Minority Schools in Upper Silesia*, 1928, Ser. A, No. 15; the *Mosul Case*, 1925, Ser. B, No. 12; and the opinion on the *Postal Service in Danzig*, 1925, Ser. B, No. 11.

or terms in their context—a principle with which one can find little quarrel.

Historical Interpretation. Again, courts have applied a historical interpretation to certain treaties, although this method appears to require considerable caution in its application. As long as a court restricts itself, in this sphere, to an examination of records concerned with the negotiation of the agreement and related documents, the utilization of the historical approach to interpretation appears quite reasonable. Once a court undertakes to accept previous history (historical relations among the parties, for example), it begins to tread on highly questionable ground.[37]

Purposes and Functions. Still another approach to treaty interpretation —all others having failed—is to relate one's inquiry to the function intended to be served by the treaty. A court may attempt to interpret the instrument on the basis of its purposes.[38]

SPECIAL PROBLEMS

Effect on Third Parties. Certain special problems connected with the interpretation of international agreements should be mentioned at this point. One of these is the effect of such instruments on third parties. Although many treaties contain explicit statements as to whether or not they affect states which are not parties to the agreements in question, the differing views of writers indicate quite clearly that as yet no rule of customary law has been developed on the point.[39]

Many agreements, by their positive terminology, have been clearly intended to benefit third parties. This is particularly true when a treaty contains an adhesion or accession clause, enabling third states to become parties to the instrument and to acquire by such a step a variety of *legal* privileges which, otherwise, might or might not have been conceded to them on a voluntary basis by the original parties to the agreement. Despite some contrary views a third party does *not* acquire enforceable rights under a treaty without adhering or acceding to it.

By contrast, no treaty can impose binding obligations on any state which is not a party to the agreement in question.

Charters and Constitutions of International Organizations. Special problems of interpretation may arise in connection with the charters or con-

---

[37] See Hersch Lauterpacht, "Some Observations on the Preparatory Work in the Interpretation of Treaties," 48 *Harvard Law Review* (1935), pp. 549–591; also the Advisory Opinion of the Permanent Court of International Justice in *Jurisdiction of the European Advisory Commission of the Danube Between Galatz and Braila*, 1927, *P.C.I.J.*, Ser. B, No. 14, at p. 28.

[38] See Permanent Court of Justice advisory opinions on the *Acquisition of Polish Nationality*, 1923, Ser. B, No. 7; on the *Competence of the International Labour Organization to Regulate, Incidentally, the Personal Work of Employers*, 1923, Ser. B, No. 13; in the judgment on certain *German Interests in Polish Upper Silesia*, 1926, Ser. A, No. 7; and in the *Chorzów Factory Case*, 1928, Ser. A, No. 17.

[39] But see *Vienna Convention*, Arts. 34–38.

stitutions of international organizations. The majority of such instruments, certainly in the case of most contemporary specialized agencies of the United Nations, contain provisions specifying rather precisely how any disputes concerning interpretation are to be settled. But the Charter of the United Nations lacks such a precise formulation. Some writers have held that this omission should be taken as evidence of an effort to continue the old rule of international law that, in the absence of any agreement to the contrary, a treaty can be interpreted only by the unanimous judgment of all parties to the treaty—and if such unanimity cannot be achieved, each party would be free to interpret the treaty as it desired.

The Charter does contain, however, a number of hints as to various possible methods of interpretation. The absence of specific provisions might indicate that unilateral interpretation is permissible. Again, designation in Article 92 of the International Court of Justice as "the principal judicial organ of the United Nations" could lead to the logical conclusion that the Court should serve as the agency of interpretation. Finally, the provision of Article 10 which grants competence to the General Assembly to "discuss any questions or any matters . . . relating to the powers and function of any organs provided for in the present Charter" could be viewed as authority for the General Assembly to interpret at least certain aspects of the Charter.

The factual development of Charter interpretation in the United Nations appears to have emphasized interpretation on the part of the political organs of the UN, but on occasion not only the International Court of Justice but also the Secretary-General has handed down rulings as to the meaning of the applicability of the Charter. The relatively strong tradition of "antijudicialism," expressed in a very widespread unwillingness of members to resort to the International Court of Justice, may be taken as due in part to a conviction held by many new states that judicial interpretations or judicial decisions will represent essentially "a restatement of the legalities of the past." Although most impartial observers would not agree with such an interpretation, it appears to have prevailed thus far in the United Nations Organization itself.

VALIDITY OF TREATIES

One of the oldest principles in international law is one usually rendered as *pacta sunt servanda:* treaties must be observed.[40] But, as in the case of domestic contracts as well as of domestic legislation, circumstances or conditions may exist which will serve to invalidate either. Hence we

---

[40] See the excellent historical analysis of the maxim in Hans Wehberg, "Pacta Sunt Servanda," 53 *A.J.I.L.* (1959), pp. 775–786; as well as the heavily documented study by Josef L. Kunz, "The Meaning and the Range of the Norm *Pacta Sunt Servanda*," *ibid.*, 39 (1945), pp. 180–197, and *Vienna Convention*, Art. 26.

must examine not only the validity of the principle itself but also the conditions under which treaties are valid or invalid, as the case may be.

As far as the validity of treaties is concerned, the student faces a frustrating but understandable paradox: every writer on international law asserts (though sometimes with qualifications) the binding force of treaties, yet is essentially unable to prove the validity of the principle. It is a situation comparable to efforts to find proof for the well-known assertion that every human being is endowed with certain inalienable rights, among which are life, liberty, and the pursuit of happiness. Most of us today, failing to find proof of the origin of the idea, are content to respect it as a basic principle and try to live up to it and to see it respected by others. And so it is with the validity of *pacta sunt servanda*. Without attempting to prove its validity, we must rest content with the undeniable assertion that without it friendly and reasonable relations among nations would be impossible. Yet, on many occasions, the principle has been understood, rightly or wrongly, to represent a device for maintaining the *status quo*, thus damaging the idea of good faith among nations.

What determines the validity of a treaty? The answer is, the existence or lack of binding force on the parties to the agreement. Many considerations play a part in the answer to that question, any or all of which may operate to nullify an international agreement.[41]

1. Capacity to Contract. A treaty is invalid if one of the parties to a bilateral agreement lacks the capacity to contract. That capacity is among the characteristics commonly ascribed to international persons. It does not mean that every state has a right to join in any treaty arrangement made between other states, but it does mean that every fully sovereign entity (and many international legal persons) has a right and ability to conclude binding agreements with others of its kind. To be sure, a few states have been prevented in some manner from concluding specific kinds of agreements (neutralized states are unable to conclude treaties of alliance), but this would be no bar to the conclusion of other valid agreements.

But if one of the parties to a treaty lacks capacity to contract, the treaty is not valid. Thus, if a party is not a member of the family of nations—such as a nomadic tribe—no treaty recognized as such under international law could be concluded with that party. To bring the matter closer to home: each of the fifty states which comprise the United States of America lacks the capacity to contract internationally, to enter into valid agreements with foreign states, under the provisions of the United States Constitution (Art. I, sec. 10, par. 3), which properly re-

---

[41] Validity, invalidity and termination of treaties are dealt with in the *Vienna Convention*, Articles 26–75; consult also the authoritative study by Herbert W. Briggs, "Procedures for Establishing the Invalidity or Termination of Treaties under the International Law Commission's 1966 Draft Articles on the Law of Treaties," 61 *A.J.I.L.* (1967), pp. 976–989.

flect the situation as it ought to exist in a federal state. In a confederation, the member units may or may not possess the capacity to enter into treaties with foreign states, depending on domestic constitutional factors. In Switzerland, for example, the various cantons may conclude treaties with foreign states, but only with respect to "local matters."

In other words, capacity to contract depends either on the external characteristics of a given unit or on the internal constitutional limitations prevailing. A protectorate normally lacks capacity to contract because of the transfer of the foreign relations power to the protecting state. A vassal state, should one be found to exist, normally could not conclude a treaty with a foreign state or, perhaps, would only be able to do so with the express approval of its suzerain.

Certain international organizations possess the right to conclude valid international agreements with states and/or among themselves. This ability adds a new aspect to the problems of capacity to contract: in the case of such organizations, the governing statutes, charters, or constitutions may have to be checked carefully to determine whether a given organization has the capacity to undertake the conclusion of a certain agreement or to commit itself to specific obligations.

2. *Authority Granted to Agents.* The validity of an international agreement depends in part on the authority granted by their respective governments to the agents entrusted with its negotiation. As mentioned earlier, although binding agreements have on occasion resulted through the subsequent ratification of negotiations by unauthorized or improperly authorized agents, such occurrences are very rare. Normally, a treaty negotiated by an unauthorized agent is not to be considered to represent any obligation on the state on whose behalf he claimed to act. Also, if an agent exceeds the powers conferred on him, any agreement representing the use of such unauthorized excess authority could not be presumed to create any obligation for his state (*Vienna Convention*, Art. 47). In either case, no international responsibility would accrue to his government for a refusal to satisfy or to be bound by the actions of the agent.

On the other hand, a state would most likely be held responsible for any injury suffered by another state when the latter reasonably assumed that the negotiating agent or organ of the first state was indeed competent to conclude an agreement (see *Harvard Code*, Art. 21, p. 661, and discussion of same, pp. 992–1009).

3. *Duress or Coercion (on Party or Parties).* A treaty is not necessarily invalid if it is accepted by one or several parties under duress or coercion. This sounds like an unreasonable dogma, and its practical application may be the cause of untold difficulties. Obviously a treaty, to be valid, must receive the assent or acceptance of two or more parties—a unilateral declaration by one state is not binding (in the legal sense; although it may be so in the political sphere) on other states and does not create legal obligations. "Assent," or "acceptance," furthermore, is usually modified

by writers by the adjective "voluntary"—a necessary modification, they believe. Yet, and this is where the problem arises: Are there not many treaties which involve a lack of this voluntary aspect? Is not every peace treaty at the end of a war imposed by the victors on the vanquished on an involuntary basis, under duress? However, the same writers who stress the need of free assent also maintain that the *particular* duress involved in a peace treaty does not negate its validity, and thus place peace treaties into an essentially separate and unique category.[42]

4. *Personal Duress or Intimidation.* A treaty is invalid when personal duress has been brought to bear against the negotiators of one party. All writers on international law concur in this statement.[43] The classic example cited throughout the relevant literature is the threat of Napoleon I, in 1807, to have Ferdinand VII of Spain arraigned at a trial for treason unless he abdicated. Following Napoleon's defeat at the Battle of Leipzig, the invalidity of the agreement was confirmed. Another well-known instance in which pressure was brought to bear on the person of a sovereign was that of the King of Korea, in 1905, forced to accept an obviously invalid agreement under which Korea became a Japanese protectorate.

More recently, a striking instance of the use of intimidation, not so much against the person of a head of state but involving the threat of wholesale bombing, took place in 1939. On March 14 of that year, Chancellor Hitler summoned President Hacha of Czecho-Slovakia to Berlin. When Hacha and his foreign minister arrived at the Reich Chancellery at 1 A.M. on the 15th, Hitler and a group of advisors demanded the immediate surrender of Czecho-Slovakia. Hacha was informed that unless he signed an instrument of surrender by 5 A.M., 800 German bombers would attack Prague and other cities in Czecho-Slovakia without previous warning. At 4 A.M., President Hacha yielded and signed an agreement creating the Protectorate of Bohemia and Moravia. Technically, the instrument placed the Czechs under German protection, with assurances of "autonomous development of indigenous life in accordance with their character."[44]

Just as in the case of sovereigns and heads of state, intimidation or coercion of negotiators of an agreement renders the instrument invalid *ab initio.* The question of who should decide whether coercion had been utilized is a moot one; the *Harvard Code* (p. 1159) recommended the utilization of "a competent international tribunal or authority."

5. *Use of Fraud in Negotiation.* A treaty whose negotiation involved

---

[42] Brierly, p. 319. See *Vienna Convention*, Article 52, with its modern version: "A treaty is void if its conclusion has been procured by the threat or use of force in violation of the principles of international law embodied in the Charter of the United Nations."

[43] See *Harvard Code*, pp. 1148–1161, particularly at p. 1156, and *Vienna Convention*, Article 51.

[44] *The New York Times*, March 15 and 22, 1939.

fraud would be considered to be invalid. Modern history can show very few instances in which outright fraud was a part of treaty negotiation, but this does not preclude the possibility of such instances occurring in the future.[45] However, mere failure to disclose some facts during negotiation when such disclosure would weaken the case or argument of one of the negotiating parties should not be taken to be a case of fraud; and such failure is generally assumed to have no effects whatever on the validity of the agreement concluded. Only deliberate fraudulent misrepresentation during the course of negotiation such as the use of falsified maps or documents, or false statements as to facts, would have the effect of invalidating the resulting agreement.

6. *Substantial Error.* A treaty is voidable, or, in some instances, void *ab initio*, if it can be shown that the agreement was concluded as a result of substantial error concerning the facts. In other words, if in the course of negotiation and ratification an assumption were made by one of the parties which was not correct, then the treaty may be considered void, or the party in question may consider it to be "voidable"—or, at the very least, refuse to be bound by the agreement. An illustrative instance might be the use of an incorrect map—note, in this case it would be an erroneous map, not one deliberately falsified to defraud the other party (see *Harvard Code*, pp. 1126–1134, and *Vienna Convention*, Art. 48).

7. *Conformity to Other Agreements.* A treaty is not necessarily invalid if its provisions do not conform to earlier agreements concluded among the same parties. Some writers have asserted a need for conformity with such prior instruments; but this does not make much sense, for changing times may require changes in relations between two given states. In the event of inconsistency between a new treaty and earlier agreements between the same parties, the general principle that applies is, the latest agreement prevails.

If a new treaty violates the rights of a third state under an earlier agreement with one of the parties to the new instrument, the *obligations* of the older treaty take precedence over those involved in the newer treaty.[46] Most authorities appear to be agreed that under such circumstances the newer treaty is not necessarily invalid. Only obligations affecting a third party (*not* a party to the new agreement) prevail over the text of the new treaty. In other words, both treaties would seem to be in force; and if inconsistencies between the two result in loss or damage to

---

[45] The interested reader is referred to Gould, p. 321, n. 1, for two nineteenth-century instances of fraudulent practices. The Harvard Research group definitely felt that some form of fraud could take place some time, however, and therefore decided to discuss that possibility: see *Harvard Code*, pp. 1144–1148, *Vienna Convention*, Article 49, as well as Hackworth, Vol. V, pp. 159–160, and Cheng, pp. 158–160.

[46] *Harvard Code*, pp. 1024–1029, particularly Article 22(c) on p. 1024. See also Gould, pp. 325–326; Hackworth, Vol. V, pp. 161–162; and especially Lauterpacht's *Oppenheim*, Vol. I, pp. 894–895.

a party, appropriate remedies or damages ought to be provided for by the parties to the new agreement which, after all, is the cause of the inconsistency existing.

8. Inconsistency with Provisions of UN Charter. A treaty inconsistent with the provisions of the Charter of the United Nations has to yield to the Charter, provided that all parties to the agreement are members of the United Nations.[47]

9. Conflict Between UN Charter and Prior Agreement. What if an obligation assumed under the Charter is inconsistent with a prior treaty between a member of the United Nations and a nonmember? Here, as in the case of inconsistency with respect to obligations to a third party to an earlier agreement, a somewhat complicated problem exists. The most just way to settle this, it would seem, would be to require the member of the United Nations to make good whatever loss or injury was sustained by anyone as a result of the inconsistency. In other words, the party to the earlier agreement ought to be able to lodge a claim against the United Nations member, because both the prior agreement and the Charter of the United Nations would have to be viewed as valid, yet inconsistent, instruments.

10. Conflict with International Law. Is a treaty invalid if its provisions run contrary to principles of general customary or conventional international law? A majority of writers believe such is the case. Their attitude reflects a conviction that a combination of rules of customary law and the rules laid down in law-making treaties constitutes a body of principles to which treaties between states must conform, even if one of the parties to the agreement had not ratified or acceded to a specific law-making treaty touching on the subject matter of the agreement in question. A division of opinion still exists as to whether international law recognizes the existence within its legal order of rules from which the law does not permit any derogation (peremptory norms). The International Law Commission, holding that the law of the Charter prohibiting the use of force in reality presupposed the existence in international law of peremptory rules, concluded that a treaty would be void if it conflicted with a peremptory norm of general international law from which no derogation was permitted and which could be modified only by a subsequent norm of general international law having the same character (*Vienna Convention*, Art. 53).

Many international lawyers have expressed disagreement with the effort of the Commission, feeling that either a pointed definition of peremptory norms should have been supplied or that examples of such norms (also known as *jus cogens*) should have been inserted in Article 53 by the Com-

---

[47] See *Charter*, Art. 103; consult also Lauterpacht's *Oppenheim*, Vol. I, pp. 895–896; Gould, p. 326, felt that Article 103 of the Charter meant that the Charter would also take precedence over conflicting treaties concluded with nonmembers, "if only before United Nations organs."

mission. In fact, legal opinion is divided as to the very existence of peremptory norms of general international law; proponents of the concept usually cite the dissenting opinion of Judge Schücking in the *Oscar Chinn Case*.[48] Others reply that state practice as well as certain treaty provisions demonstrate convincingly that *jus cogens* does not exist. (The present writer inclines toward that view.) But even granting that existence, it must be held that as yet no genuine consensus exists as to what are and what are not rules of a *jus cogens*. It should be mentioned that Article 61 of the *Draft Code* provided that, "If a new peremptory norm of general international law of the kind referred to in Article 50 [Art. 53 of *Vienna Convention*] is established, any existing treaty which is in conflict with that norm becomes void and terminates."

11. Immoral Object. Is a treaty void or voidable because it has an immoral object as its substance? Lauterpacht has given a most persuasive affirmative answer.[49] But dissent must be registered: to grant validity to the position taken by Lauterpacht implies not only that whatever is immoral is *ipso facto* illegal but also that there exists a fairly general agreement among states as to what may be considered immoral. Certainly grave doubts must be admitted about both assumptions—as yet morality and legality have not been united in marriage, as far as states are concerned, and definitions of immorality may, and indeed do, differ greatly, not only among different civilizations in the world but even among the member states of the "Western" group.

12. Oral Agreement. An agreement is not invalid because it is an oral agreement rather than a written instrument.[50] An agreement reached verbally between agents of states who are capable of binding their respective governments is quite sufficient—provided, of course, that the individuals in question intend at the time to conclude a binding agreement. Nevertheless, a written instrument is preferable to a verbal agreement, if only to avoid subsequent disputes about the nature of the understanding reached.

13. Intention. Finally, a unilateral declaration, if conceived as being a treaty, represents as binding an international obligation as if it were a negotiated instrument. Thus the unilateral declarations made by certain European states to the League of Nations on their treatment of minority groups, or the declarations relating to the Optional Clause by which states accept in advance the jurisdiction of the International Court of Justice for certain categories of disputes, represent binding obligations of a treaty nature.

---

[48] *Oscar Chinn Case (Belgium v. Great Britain)*, Permanent Court of International Justice, *P.C.I.J.*, 1934, Ser. A/B, No. 63, p. 148.

[49] Lauterpacht's *Oppenheim*, Vol. I, pp. 896–897. See also Hyde, Vol. II, p. 1374, and especially Alfred von Verdross, "Forbidden Treaties in International Law," 31 *A.J.I.L.* (1937), pp. 571–577.

[50] See *Eastern Greenland Case (Denmark–Norway)*, *P.C.I.J.*, 1933, Ser. A/B, No. 53.

TEXTUAL ELEMENTS

There are no generally accepted regulations as to the actual format of a treaty; on the other hand, most treaties follow an established pattern insofar as their textual elements are concerned. Many agreements are prefaced by a preamble stating the reasons why the agreement was concluded and the results expected to arise from it. Other treaties incorporate such a statement of purpose in the opening paragraphs of the actual text of the agreement.

Normally, a list of the negotiators appears at the beginning of the main portion of an agreement, together with some statement to the effect that they have examined each other's credentials and found them to be satisfactory.

Next comes the substantive part of the agreement, containing the detailed provisions of the treaty. This is followed by a number of sections dealing with mechanical but quite important matters, such as details of the ratification process (or whether such is not required), the method by which the agreement is to enter into force, the duration of the treaty if it is not stated to possess indefinite duration, the method by which the treaty may be terminated, and, lately, provisions governing the registration and deposit of the instrument. In some bilateral and most multilateral treaties there also appears a provision in this concluding portion which specifies whether the agreement is to remain open for signature, how accession by states other than the signatories is to be handled (if such accession is to be permitted). This last part is quite often omitted from the actual treaty and is found in an ancillary protocol.

A highly desirable procedural provision which ought to be included in every modern treaty would be an article outlining whatever method or agency had been agreed upon by the parties for the interpretation of the agreement.

TERMINATION OF TREATIES

Most writers agree that there exist six basic ways in which termination of a treaty may be effected: (1) in accordance with the terms of the treaty itself; (2) by explicit or tacit agreement of the parties concerned; (3) through violation of the provisions of the agreement by one party; the second party then asserting, if it so desires, that it considers the treaty abrogated by the violation; (4) by one party on the grounds that fundamental conditions on which the treaty rested had changed; (5) through emergence of a new peremptory norm of general international law conflicting with the treaty; and (6) through the outbreak of hostilities between parties to the agreement (*Vienna Convention*, Arts. 54–64). A seventh, and obvious, cause of termination—particularly true in the case of bilateral agreements—would be the disappearance (extinction) of one of the parties, by annexation or possibly by a natural disaster: all of Ceylon might sink beneath the Indian Ocean and at once all bilateral treaties made by other states with Ceylon would have come to an abrupt end.

The fact that so many ways of termination are listed indicates quite clearly that it is most unrealistic indeed to believe that any treaty will last forever. Even if a given instrument provides in its text that its duration shall be "in perpetuity," such an agreement will come to an end, sooner or later.

Let us now examine the methods of termination.

Terms of the Treaty. A great many treaties contain in their next specific details about their termination. In general, such provisions envisage three fundamental causes for the end of the agreement: performance, arrival of an open fixed termination date, and denunciation of the agreement as outlined therein.

Executed treaties come to an end when the acts called for by the agreement have been performed by the parties involved. Examples are most numerous in the sphere of voluntary cession of territory by sale. When the purchasing state has transmitted the appropriate sums to the selling state, title to the affected area is transferred and the treaty is terminated. The actual documents remain, of course, as evidences of the transaction and may serve to assist in the settlement of any disputes about the performance of the acts involved.

Numerous treaties contain a specific expiration date; when that date occurs, the treaty is terminated unless there has also been a provision for extending the life of the agreement and the parties concerned have acted in accordance with that provision to extend the duration of their agreement.

Again, many treaties contain provisions permitting denunciation (sometimes termed *renunciation*) of the agreement. Usually such provisions provide for a minimum duration of the agreement; after the date on which this minimum life comes to an end, the treaty continues in force but may terminate when denounced by a party. Commonly termination, as far as the denouncing party is concerned, does not occur immediately but a time interval (six months or a year are periods frequently utilized) between the time notice of denunciation has been filed and the effective termination of the agreement for the denouncing party. Normally no reason has to be given for denouncing a treaty when the action is taken in accordance with the relevant provisions of the instrument.

Explicit or Tacit Agreement. Any agreement between states may end by agreement of the parties to the instrument. Such agreement may take the form of a written declaration by which the parties abrogate a treaty. This method is most often encountered when a new treaty between them contains a provision terminating prior accords between them—referring to such earlier instruments by title and other details and announcing the effective date of their termination.

Similarly, states may terminate a treaty by implication, that is, through the conclusion of a treaty which obviously supersedes prior agreements among the same parties without mentioning such agreements in the text of the new instrument. And, on occasion, it appears that a treaty has terminated by tacit agreement among the parties involved to let the treaty lapse through nonobservance. In other words, each in turn fails to comply with the terms of the treaty and no one protests such nonobservance, because all are in tacit agreement that they no longer wish to be bound by the provisions of the instrument.

Violation of Provisions. In the event of a violation of the provisions of a treaty by one of the states party to it, the treaty is not *ipso facto* invalid or void, but must be considered voidable at the discretion of the other party or parties to the agreement. Such voidance would occur most likely if the other parties considered the violation to have injured them or to have eliminated the bases of the entire agreement.

The *Harvard Code* contains a reasonable answer to the problem posed by unilateral violation of treaty provisions in Article 27 of the *Code:*

If a state fails to carry out in good faith its obligations under a treaty, any other party to the treaty, acting within a reasonable time after the failure, may seek from a competent international tribunal or authority a declaration to the effect that the treaty has ceased to be binding upon it in the sense of calling for further performance with respect to such state.[51]

The Charter of the United Nations contains a somewhat different and harsher-sounding approach to the question of unilateral violation. The relevant provision, Article 6, boldly states that

A Member of the United Nations which has persistently violated the Principles contained in the present Charter may be expelled from the Organization by the General Assembly upon the recommendation of the Security Council.

It might be mentioned, as a matter of some interest that the Charter (unlike the League Covenant) does not contain any provisions for the voluntary withdrawal of any member; thus the Charter (a treaty) lacks the denunciation feature found in so many international agreements.

Changed Circumstances. Is a treaty void or voidable because fundamental circumstances have altered since the inception of the agreement? This question represents one of the most irritating problems in the realm of international agreements. Unilateral denunciation of a treaty on grounds of changed circumstances has been justified, though often regretfully by almost all modern writers on international law.

Since Vattel's time, the correctness of the concept of *rebus sic stantibus* has been recognized quite generally, not only by writers,[52] but by the

[51] *Harvard Code*, p. 1077, and the research group's comments on pp. 1077–1094; see *Vienna Convention*, Arts. 60, 65–68.

[52] See *Harvard Code*, pp. 1096–1126, and *Vienna Convention*, Article 62. Consult Brierly, pp. 335–343; cf. Jessup, pp. 151–152, 250–254.

Secretary-General of the United Nations in commenting on the termination of European treaties protecting minorities (between 1939 and 1947) through basic changes in conditions.[53] Numerous modern court decisions also have referred to the doctrine,[54] so that it may now be invoked by states. It should be pointed out, however, that this opinion has been disputed vigorously by a number of modern publicists. Thus Briggs referred to the doctrine of *rebus sic stantibus* as an "alleged principle of international law." [55] Unfortunately, a number of attacks on the applicability of the doctrine departed from legal considerations and undertook to question the need for or the wisdom of the application of the doctrine in specific instances. Approaches like these vitiated much of the validity of the legal criticisms with which such considerations of expediency and policy were intermixed. The present writer believes, however, that more recent practices and studies support the assertion that the doctrine of *rebus sic stantibus* should be regarded as a valid principle of international law.

The real problem involved in the doctrine of *rebus sic stantibus* arises when such invocation is sought in actual practice. Few writers and fewer statesmen appear to be able to agree on *when* the doctrine could be justifiably invoked. Brierly observed that, "There seems to be no recorded case in which its application has been admitted by both parties to a controversy. . . .[56]

Interestingly enough, numerous governments opposed the inclusion of *rebus sic stantibus* in the final version of the *Draft Code* to go before the 1968 Vienna Conference (including such states as Colombia, Turkey, and the United States). The International Law Commission decided, however, to preserve the doctrine in the draft submitted to the Conference.

Article 62 of the *Vienna Convention* contains two conditions for the application of the doctrine: (1) the existence of the circumstances subsequently changed "must have constituted an essential basis of the consent of the parties to be bound by the treaty," and (2) the effect of the changes must have been such as to "radically to transform the extent of obligations still to be performed under the treaty."

The same article also states that a fundamental change of circumstances may not be invoked if (1) the treaty established a boundary, or (2) if the change was the "result of a breach by the party invoking it either of an obligation under the treaty or of any other international obligation owed to any other party to the treaty."

It is clear that unless the entire fabric of international treaties is to be

[53] U.N. Document E/CN. 4/367, pp. 36–38, 71, cited by Gould, p. 340.

[54] Thus the Permanent Court of International Justice, in *Nationality Decrees Issued in Tunis and Morocco*, 1927, Ser. B, No. 4, and particularly in the case of the *Free Zones of Upper Savoy and the District of Gex*, 1932, Ser. A/B, No. 46.

[55] Herbert W. Briggs, "The Attorney General Invokes Rebus Sic Stantibus," 36 *A.J.I.L.* (1942), pp. 89–96, at p. 93.

[56] Brierly, p. 335; see also Corbett, pp. 83–89.

doomed to disintegration at the whim of any state invoking the doctrine of *rebus sic stantibus* to avoid obligations presumably assumed in good faith, some limitation must be applied to the doctrine. Since neither party to a treaty susceptible to invocation of the clause should self-judge the evidence, the decision about the nature of the changes and about their effect on the treaty in question should be left to a competent international authority or tribunal (see also *Harvard Code*, Art. 28, p. 1096).

Impossibility of Performance. Is a treaty void because one of the parties finds itself unable to perform the obligations called for? The answer must be in the affirmative, for impossibility of performance renders meaningless any attempt to perpetuate the existence of the instrument in question (*Vienna Convention*, Article 61). A commonly cited illustration of this principle involves a state which has concluded defensive alliances with two other states; should those two then proceed to go to war against each other, the first state is obviously unable to honor its commitments, and its alliance treaties are void. In such circumstances it would be proper to assert not only a physical impossibility but also a legal impossibility of performance. Another condition under which impossibility could be advanced in defense of voidance would exist if a state faced grave danger to its continued existence if it carried out military, economic, or other obligations called for by a treaty: if, in other words, honoring the agreement would represent a real danger of self-destruction.

Extinction of One of the Parties. Finally, a bilateral treaty would terminate with the physical disappearance of one of the two parties. This requires no comment. On the other hand, what happens if several states merge into a new unit? A treaty concluded prior to union by one of the states with an outside state commonly remains in force and, by agreement, binds the new union. Thus the treaty of peace, amity, navigation, and commerce, signed in 1846, and the consular convention, signed in 1850, between the United States and New Granada, continued in effect despite the constitutional changes through which the Republic of New Granada became the Confederation Granadina, then the United States of Granada, and later the Republic of Colombia. Similarly, the treaties in force in 1918 between the United States and the Kingdom of Serbia did not terminate at the formation of the Kingdom of the Serbs, Croats, and Slovenes but were applicable to the new entity.

REVISION OF TREATIES

If unilateral denunciation of an international agreement, whether on grounds of changed conditions or for other reasons, is regarded as an undesirable practice because of the frequent intrusion of political considerations and because it undermines the principles of good faith and of *pacta sunt servanda*, there still remains a need to provide procedures for the peaceful revision of treaties.

The literature on "peaceful change," which was a common term in the legal literature of the thirties, is vast, yet much of it is permeated with purely political arguments.[57]

A fundamental assumption underlying any discussion of treaty revision is that whatever instrument is being considered came lawfully into existence and that all parties to it are in agreement that the treaty is valid under international law.

Once this assumption has been established, discussion of methods of revision procedures may ensue with some promise of success. The trouble that arises at this point is that the reasons advanced by a party desiring revision tend to be exclusively political in nature. This fact complicates revision, for while lack of validity can be traced to legal causes and can be remedied by legal means, the intrusion of political issues renders impossible a juridical solution to the demand for revision.

Recognition of these "facts of life," together with the realization that treaties (especially peace treaties) may require revision, led in 1919 to the incorporation of the problem of revision in Article XIX of the Covenant of the League of Nations. Unfortunately political considerations prevailed in the postwar period and the revision question was quietly shelved by the members of the League.

Proponents of the establishment of specific machinery to be utilized in treaty revision then turned their attention to judicial agencies. Some favored the Permanent Court of International Justice as the agency to hand down judgments *ex aequo et bono* when the legal situation appeared to be in conflict with the justice of a given case; others advocated the creation of an International Equity Tribunal to handle revision. None of the proposals that emerged promised any real solution to the problems posed by demands for treaty revision.

If international tribunals would not be regarded as an answer to the problem, then, asserted other publicists, supranational legislation might well be regarded as the method to provide for the revision of treaties. The consent to revision of all parties to an international agreement might be impossible to obtain, because usually at least one such party, the *beatus possidens,* would object and refuse such consent. Under such circumstances, would it not be logical to provide overriding supranational legislation in order to effect treaty revision? The only trouble with this ostensibly reasonable view is that supranational legislation can be envisaged only in terms of the actions of a supranational government, a superstate.

Failing the applicability of judicial agencies as well as of supranational legislature, what else could be suggested to effect peaceful revision of treaties? One obvious answer, illustrated by many modern instances, would be to incorporate revision clauses in international agreements. Such clauses would be increasingly effective as their procedural provisions in-

---

[57] See the excellent summary by Joseph L. Kunz, "The Problem of Revision in International Law ('Peaceful Change')" 33 *A.J.I.L.* (1939), pp. 33–55; see also Jessup, *op. cit.* (n. 31), pp. 395–403.

creased in detail as well as comprehensiveness. (For the effect of war on treaties, see Chapter 27.)

SUGGESTED READINGS

TREATIES: GENERAL

Brierly, pp. 317–345; Lauterpacht's *Oppenheim*, Vol. I, pp. 877–976; Charles De Visscher, *Theory and Reality in Public International Law* (Princeton, N.J.: Princeton University Press, 1957), pp. 246–268; Elbert M. Byrd, Jr., *Treaties and Executive Agreements in the United States: Their Separate Roles and Limitations* (The Hague: Martinus Nijhoff, 1960); Hungdah Chiu, *The Capacity of International Organizations to Conclude Treaties, and the Special Legal Aspect of the Treaties So Concluded* (The Hague: Martinus Nijhoff, 1966); International Law Association, Committee on State Succession to Treaties, *The Effect of Independence on Treaties* (Hackensack, N.J.: F. B. Rothman & Co., 1965); Jan Triska and R. M. Slussar, *The Theory, Law, and Policy of Soviet Treaties* (Stanford, Calif.: Stanford University Press, 1962); Quincy Wright, "The United States and International Agreements," *International Conciliation*, No. 411 (May, 1945), pp. 379–398; Joseph W. Bishop, Jr., "The 'Contractual Agreements' with the Federal Republic of Germany," 49 *A.J.I.L.* (1955), pp. 125–147; Hungdah Chiu, "Certain Legal Aspects of Communist China's Treaty Practice," *Proceedings* (1967), pp. 117–126; Douglas M. Johnston, "Treaty Analysis and Communist China: Preliminary Observations," *ibid.*, pp. 126–134.

Cases

(1) Power to Conclude Treaties:
   United States v. *Belmont*, United States, Supreme Court, 1937, 301 U.S. 324.
   United States (Claim of United States and Venezuelan Co.) v. *Venezuela*, 1909, in Hackworth, V, pp. 156–157.
(2) Effect of Treaties:
   Haver v. *Yaker*, United States, Supreme Court, 1869, 9 Wallace (76 U.S.) 32.
   Whitney v. *Robertson*, United States, Supreme Court, 1888, 124 U.S. 190.
   Jurisdiction of the Courts of Danzig, Advisory Opinion, P.C.I.J., 1928, Ser. B, No. 15.
   Asakura v. *City of Seattle*, United States, Supreme Court, 1924, 265 U.S. 332.
   NOTE: See also the extensive list of cases related to the effect of treaties on individuals in Bishop, p. 144.

TREATY INTERPRETATION

Myres S. McDougal, H. D. Lasswell, and J. C. Miller, *The Interpretation of Agreements and World Public Order* (New Haven: Yale University Press, 1967); I. M. Sinclair, "Principles of Treaty Interpretation and Their Application by the English Courts," 12 *International and Comparative Law Quarterly* (1963), pp. 508–551; Peter J. Liacouras, "The International Court of Justice and Development of Useful 'Rules of Interpretation' in the Process of Treaty Interpretation," *Proceedings* (1965), pp. 161–169; Edward Gordon, "The World Court and the Interpretation of Constitutive Treaties," 59 *A.J.I.L.* (1965), pp. 794–833; Kenneth S. Carlston, "Interpretation of Peace Treaties with Bulgaria, Hungary, and Rumania, Advisory Opinion of the International Court of Justice," *ibid.*, 44 (1950), pp. 728–737; Ervin P. Hexner, "Interpretation of Public International Organizations of their Basic Instruments," *ibid.*, 53 (1959), pp. 341–370; and the critical analysis by Myres S. McDougal, "The International Law Commission's Draft Articles upon Interpretation: Textuality *Redivivus*," *ibid.*, 61 (1967), pp. 992–1000.

Cases

Interpretation of the 1919 Convention Concerning Employment of Women during the Night, Advisory Opinion, P.C.I.J., 1932, Ser. A/B, No. 50.
Nielsen v. Johnson, United States, Supreme Court, 1929, 279 U.S. 47.
Case Concerning Rights of Nationals of the United States of America in Morocco (France v. United States), International Court of Justice, 1952, *I.C.J. Reports 1952*, p. 176; reported also, at length, in 47 *A.J.I.L.* (1953), pp. 136–145.
United States of America ex rel. Treves v. *Italian Republic*, U.S.–Italy Conciliation Commission, Case No. 95, September 24, 1956; digested by William W. Bishop, Jr., in 51 *A.J.I.L.* (1957), pp. 436–439.

VALIDITY AND INVALIDITY OF TREATIES

Bhek Pati Sinha, *Unilateral Denunciation of Treaty Because of Prior Violations by Other Party* (The Hague: Martinus Nijhoff, 1966); George Ginsburgs, "The Validity of Treaties in the Municipal Law of the 'Socialist' States," 59 *A.J.I.L.* (1965), pp. 523–544; Alfred Verdross, "Jus Dispositivuum and Jus Cogens in International Law," *ibid.*, 60 (1966), pp. 55–63; Egon Schwelb, "Some Aspects of International *Jus Cogens* as Formulated by the International Law Commission," *ibid.*, 61 (1967), pp. 946–975; Richard B. Bilder, "Breach of Treaty and Response Thereto," *Proceedings* (1967), pp. 193–204; and "Statement of the Albanian Government of August 15, 1963," in 1 *Global Digest* (Hong Kong) No. 1 (October 1963), pp. 64–71, containing Albania's charge that the signing by the U.S.S.R. of the Partial Nuclear Test Ban Treaty violated the Warsaw Pact, hence was "illegal" and void.

TERMINATION OF TREATIES

Quincy Wright, "The Termination and Suspension of Treaties," 61 *A.J.I.L.* (1967), pp. 1000–1005; Oliver J. Lissitzyn, "Treaties and Changed Circumstances," *ibid.*, pp. 895–922, one of the best brief studies of *rebus sic stantibus* known to the present writer.

Cases

Terlinden v. *Ames,* United States, Supreme Court, 1902, 184 U.S. 270.

Charlton v. *Kelly,* United States, Supreme Court, 1913, 229 U.S. 447.

Van der Weyde v. *Ocean Transport Co., Ltd.,* United States, Supreme Court, 1936, 297 U.S. 114.

23
Peaceful Settlement of Disputes

INTRODUCTION

ONE of the major purposes of law at any level is to deal with disputes: either to prevent them altogether or to settle them. This is certainly true of international law, and throughout its long history it has been concerned with disputes between states.

In the course of time, statesmen and legal writers both realized that disputes are not all of the same kind, and that, in consequence, different procedures had to be developed to deal most effectively with a given type of quarrel.

Classification of Disputes. The common classification of disputes divided them into two basic categories: political and legal, and in recent decades a third category made its appearance: technical disputes. Almost by definition, each subdivision of this new type of dispute tends to be settled or handled by a specialized agency conversant with the technical problems involved and providing the special rules required by those particular questions.

Writers on international law have long been concerned with attempts to draw some kind of boundary line by which political disputes might be distinguished from legal disputes. The former were commonly referred to as "nonjusticiable," the latter as "justiciable." This distinction became an accepted part of positivist legal thinking and was enshrined in the provisions of a number of arbitration treaties.

The basic difference, using this terminology, appears to be that "nonjusticiable" disputes are such in which nonlegal considerations (political—such as "vital national interests," economic, psychological, and so on) play such an important role that the application of legal rules would not settle the dispute. "Justiciable disputes," on the other hand, are such in which not only is there a question of law involved but the law is relevant to the dispute and can be utilized to settle it.

From a practical point of view, however, the distinction is all too often an academic one, for it is frequently very difficult to separate political and legal considerations. In any case, it is unquestioned that "nonjusticiable" disputes may be settled peacefully in a number of ways, such as by negotiation, by mediation, by action of an international agency, and even by judicial action, as will be demonstrated later.

Today most writers would tend to view the difference between "legal" and "political" disputes as dependent on the attitudes of the parties involved. If, regardless of subject matter, the parties seek only their *legal* rights, then the dispute would be classifiable as justiciable, as a "legal" dispute. If, however, one or both of the parties demand not only legal rights but the satisfaction of some special interest, even though such would require changes in the prevailing *legal* situation, then the dispute would be nonjusticiable, that is, a "political" dispute.[1] Needless to say, a distinction arrived at in such a manner merely reiterates the fundamental fact that in our existing world society, states at times view a decision based on law as a satisfactory device for settling international disagreements; at other times they do not choose to adopt such a view.

One approach to the whole problem recommended by a number of authorities is to leave the determination of the nature of the dispute to the appropriate United Nations organ or specialized agency for referral to the International Court of Justice. Then, if the question of the nature of the dispute is raised again before the Court, the latter could itself make a final decision on the matter, utilizing objective criteria.[2]

Two Basic Types of Law. The theory of jurisprudence makes a distinction between *substantive law* and *adjective,* or *procedural,* law. The substantive law outlines positively the various rights which the law will aid and protect by means of a variety of legal procedures. Once the possession of a right is established, the possessor then can turn to procedural law to discover by what methods that right can actually be made effective.

The use of force, whether in the form of coercive measures short of war or of war itself, has been a traditional method of settling international disputes, particularly those classified as "nonjusticiable." Failure to achieve a peaceful solution, together with an unwillingness to use force, may mean that a dispute will continue to disrupt normal relations between the nations concerned, creating mounting rancor and bitterness between them. The use of force, on the other hand, has been regarded increasingly as unavailable for the solution of disputes. The Charter of the United Nations prohibits the use of force except on a collective basis (Preamble), or, under certain conditions, in self-defense (Art. 51). The members of the organization have agreed to "refrain in their international relations from the threat or use of force against the territorial integrity or political independence of any state, or in any manner inconsistent with the purposes of the United Nations" (Art. 2, par. 4).

The only remaining method for adjusting conflicts without the danger of total extinction is, therefore, settlement of disputes by peaceful means.

---

[1] Based on the reasonable analysis of the question to be found in Brierly, pp. 367–368.

[2] This was done by the Court, for instance, in the *Advisory Opinion Concerning Conditions of Admission of a State to the United Nations, I.C.J. Reports, 1948,* at p. 61.

This is where procedural law enters into the picture, for there are several kinds of such means available to parties seeking to make their rights effective. They include diplomatic negotiations, good offices, mediation, commissions of inquiry and conciliation, judicial settlement (adjudication), as well as settlement in pursuance of the United Nations Charter or of regional arrangements. Parties to a dispute thus have available a wide range of procedures from which to select the one, or the one in turn, by which a peaceful settlement of a dispute may be achieved and rights can be made effective and secure.

DIPLOMATIC NEGOTIATIONS

The oldest and most common method of settling disputes and the least encumbered with procedural details is that of diplomatic negotiation. Classical antiquity already recognized a legal obligation to negotiate before resorting to the use of force. Thus the College of Fetials in Rome sent agents or heralds who presented the demands of their government to the other party in a dispute and asked for redress of Roman grievances, before a state of war ensued. It may be argued with some justice that this procedure was nothing more than a formality, but the important thing is that the technical obligation to negotiate was present. The medieval period produced elaborate and wearisome discussions by the canonists and theologians about the nature of a just war, and again the need for negotiation before the use of force was agreed on by everyone. Hugo Grotius and his followers continued this tradition and insisted most vigorously on the necessity of negotiation.

In later centuries, negotiation has been deemed to constitute one of the prior conditions necessary to grant any designation of justice to the use of force. Even if one and all could see that whatever negotiation was carried on had all the earmarks of pretense, that pretense had to be undertaken in order to satisfy the generally accepted standards. Resort to force without negotiation, attack without warning, continued to be condemned. But even when morality and justice were left out of the picture altogether, negotiation had one highly desirable feature: it was an inexpensive means by which a state might conceivably achieve its aims without going into the risks and expenses of a war. Hence it would have been foolish, so the thought would run, to resort to force at once before utilizing negotiation first.

In our own time, hardly a week passes without one or more agreements being reached through negotiations between foreign offices, particularly since the number of sovereign states has increased so sharply during the past few decades. Because most diplomatic negotiations are conducted on the old basis of secrecy or at least relative privacy, the general public is not likely to realize the extent of current diplomatic negotiations. The United States alone concludes about 200 formal agreements (treaties and executive agreements) a year, and the United Nations, the international depository of treaties, published between 1946 and 1959 over 300 volumes containing more than 5,000 international agreements. And in addition, many disputes are settled each year by negotiations that do not lead to a formal treaty. No one can tell how great this aspect of negotiation is today, but each major state settles annually scores or even hundreds of moot points with other states through letters and memoranda as part of its continuing diplomatic negotiations.

If additional evidence were needed to prove the importance of negotiation, one would only have to check on the provisions of some of the many international treaties for the peaceful settlement of disputes: almost every one of those instruments restricts its applicability of disputes which have not been possible to settle by diplomatic negotiation. The Permanent Court of International Justice discussed this principle in some detail in the *Mavrommatis Palestine Concessions (Jurisdiction) Case* [3] and stated that "before a dispute can be made the subject of an action at law, its subject matter should have been clearly defined by means of diplomatic negotiations." The Court admitted that it would have to decide in each case whether sufficient negotiation had preceded the submission of a dispute, but that it would not overlook the views of the states concerned "who are in the best position to judge as to political reasons which may prevent the settlement of a given dispute by diplomatic negotiation."

GOOD OFFICES

When the parties to a dispute find that it cannot be settled by diplomatic negotiation but that the conflict of rights or claims appears to be of sufficient importance, the technique of "good offices" may be invoked.

Some writers refer to this as a form of intervention, yet that term, possessing a specialized meaning in international law, does not appear appropriate in most instances. Only when armed force was used would "intervention" be the correct name for the process, such as when the Great Powers intervened in the Greco-Turkish quarrel over Crete in 1868. The normal meaning of *good offices* is more adequately represented by *intercession* (the act of interceding—by a third state, a group of states, or even an individual of such standing as the Secretary-General of the United Nations—in an effort to bring the disputants together and to induce them to start or resume negotiations).

Good offices may be exercised only with the agreement of both parties to a dispute. The third party, in other words, will then be allowed to attempt to bring the parties together so as to make it possible for them to reach an adequate solution between themselves. Normally, the profferer of good offices meets separately with each of the disputing parties; seldom, if ever, does the third party attend a joint meeting.

[3] *P.C.I.J.*, 1924, Ser. A, No. 2.

The practice is particularly important when the two disputing states have reached a point where they have broken off diplomatic relations. Then the third party (always with the consent of the disputants) may act as a go-between, transmitting messages and suggestions in an effort to soothe the feelings of the aggrieved states and to restore an atmosphere in which the parties would finally agree to negotiate together. Needless to say, a proffer of good offices should never be used to hide selfish motives; it is supposed to be a friendly act on the part of the third party, never for the benefit of either disputant or of the state offering its services.[4]

There is no obligation on any state to offer its services in this connection, nor are any of the parties to a dispute obliged to accept proffered good offices. On the other hand, modern history is full of disputes that were settled eventually through the application of the technique. For instance, the Security Council, in November, 1947, appointed a Good Offices Committee (Australia, Belgium, United States) as well as a Consular Commission (the consuls of the Security Council members stationed in Batavia), to assist in bringing about negotiations between the emerging Indonesian Republic and The Netherlands.

The good offices normally terminate as soon as the disputing parties have been persuaded or assisted to resume negotiations. There are instances on record, however, in which both parties have invited the third state whose proffer of good offices had been accepted or whose assistance for such purpose had been sought, to be present during the negotiations.

MEDIATION

Often confused with good offices, mediation as a procedure to achieve the peaceful settlement of a dispute goes further than the utilization of good offices: the mediator actively participates in the settlement itself. Mediation may be undertaken by a third state, by a group of states, by an individual, or by an agency of an international organization.

Regardless of the nature of the mediator, he is expected to offer concrete proposals for a settlement of substantive questions instead of contenting himself with making negotiation possible. He therefore assists the parties directly. The mediator may meet with the parties either jointly or separately. His functions come to an end when the dispute is settled or when one of the parties (or the mediator) decides that the proposals made by him are not acceptable. It should be noted that the proposals submitted by a mediator represent nothing more than advice; under no condition can they be taken to possess any binding force on either party to the dispute.

[4] Both Hague Conventions for the Pacific Settlement of Disputes (1899 and 1907) emphasized in Article III that the right to offer good offices "can never be regarded by either of the parties in dispute as an unfriendly act"; consult also Moore, Vol. VI, p. 239.

Modern examples of mediation are numerous. Frequently cited instances are the mediation by Pope Leo XIII of the German-Spanish dispute over the Caroline Islands group in the Pacific, in 1885; the mediation achieved by the United States in 1866 between Spain, on the one hand, and Bolivia, Chile, Ecuador, and Peru, on the other; the request for mediation addressed to five Latin American presidents by the president of Ecuador, then engaged in a dispute with Peru, in 1938; the mediation activities of Dr. Ralph Bunche at the negotiations ending the phase of active hostilities between Israel and its Arab neighbors in 1948; and, most recently, the mediation by the United Nations in the Kashmir dispute between India and Pakistan.[5]

On rare occasions, mediation of a civil war is offered by other states. A recent example of this practice, which must not be confused with intervention, occurred in August, 1947, when the twenty states represented at the Inter-American Defense Conference, meeting at Quitandinha, Brazil, adopted unanimously a proposal for joint mediation of the civil war then in progress in Paraguay. The plan, originated by Uruguay, envisaged the dispatch of messages to both sides in the conflict, asking for a quick end to the fighting. The 1936 Buenos Aires Conference drafted a new Treaty on Good Offices and Mediation, stressing those old techniques but in a modern setting and providing for a single mediator to be chosen from a panel of available citizens of the Western Hemisphere. An interesting aspect of that treaty was its provision for privacy and lack of publicity in the settlement of disputes, including even the absence of any report from the mediator and completely confidential proceedings.

As in the case of good offices, either or both parties to a dispute are free to reject an offer to mediate, as was done in 1898 when the United States rejected such offers on the part of the Pope, Austria, France, and Great Britain.

COMMISSIONS OF INQUIRY

A number of international disputes involved an inability or unwillingness of the parties concerned to agree on points of fact. In consequence a number of bilateral agreements were concluded during the late nineteenth century, under which *ad hoc* fact-finding commissions were appointed to report to the parties in question on the disputed facts. Such commissions proved to be of particular value in the determination of boundary lines.

Hague Conventions (1899; 1907). The Hague Peace Conference of 1899 established such commissions of inquiry as a formal institution

[5] See a full account of this subject in Michael Brecher, "Kashmir: A Case Study in United Nations Mediation," 26 *Pacific Affairs* (September, 1953), pp. 195–207.

through Convention I for the Pacific Settlement of International Disputes. That instrument provided for the maintenance of a permanent panel of names, from which five were to be selected for specific cases.[6] Each party to a dispute was entitled to select two commissioners, only one of which was to be taken from its own appointees to the panel; the fifth commissioner was to be named by the other four. The report of such a commission was to be limited to a finding of facts and had in no way the character of an award. It was not expected, therefore, that the report would include proposals for the settlement of the dispute in question. The Second Hague Conference of 1907 expanded the procedural details involved in the earlier convention by prescribing such matters as the place of meetings, languages, and the filling of vacancies on a commission. It also permitted the parties to a dispute to send special agents to represent them and to act as intermediaries between them and the commission, as well as providing for the summoning of witnesses, either by a party or by the commission itself. One of the most important innovations was a requirement that three neutrals had to sit as members of each commission of inquiry.[7]

Commissions of inquiry, despite the obvious advantages accruing to disputants from their utilization, have been employed very rarely in the twentieth century. The best-known instance of their utilization was the famous *Dogger Bank Case*.[8] This was a dispute between Great Britain and Russia, arising out of an attack, in 1904, by Russian warships on their way to the Far East, on British fishing vessels in the North Sea. The Russians had opened fire, on a foggy day, on the British ships under the misapprehension that the latter were Japanese torpedo boats. One fishing vessel was sunk and another was damaged seriously. Because the facts of the incident were in dispute between the two countries, the French government suggested utilization of a commission of inquiry. A commission consisting of admirals from the British, Russian, French, Austrian, and American navies was selected to investigate and, interestingly enough, to fix responsibility for the incident. The group therefore was empowered to sit more in the nature of an arbitration tribunal than a commission of inquiry, but it is nevertheless usually listed as an example of the latter. The commission met in Paris from December 22, 1904, until February 26, 1905, when it reported that no Japanese vessels had been anywhere in the North Sea and that the attack by the Russian fleet had been completely unjustified. The report was accepted by the parties to the dispute and Russia paid an indemnity of £65,000 to Great Britain. In the *Tubantia Case*, one of the two other cases investigated since 1899 by a Hague

[6] *Reports to the Hague Conferences of 1899 and 1907* (New York: Carnegie Endowment for International Peace, 1917), pp. 34–35, hereinafter referred to as *Reports;* consult also Norman L. Hill, "International Commissions of Inquiry and Conciliation," *International Conciliation*, No. 278 (March, 1932), especially at pp. 9–94.

[7] Hague Convention of 1907, Articles 9–36, in *Reports*, pp. 312–327.

[8] James B. Scott, ed., *The Hague Court Reports* (New York: Carnegie Endowment for International Peace, 1916), pp. 403–413.

Commission, the question of fact centered on the sinking of the Dutch vessel *Tubantia* on March 16, 1916. The steamer had sunk as a result of an explosion, which the Netherlands government blamed on a German torpedo. A commission of inquiry was appointed to determine the cause of the explosion and reported on February 27, 1922, that the *Tubantia* had been sunk by a torpedo fired by a German submarine. The commission was unable, however, to decide whether the sinking was caused by deliberate intent or by a mistake on the part of the submarine commander.[9]

Bryan Treaties. The government of the United States became very much interested in the possibilities inherent in the use of commissions of inquiry, mostly as the result of efforts made by William J. Bryan. Within a month after Bryan become Secretary of State on March 5, 1913, he undertook negotiations with thirty-six countries in order to provide for the factual investigation of disputes (Treaties for the Advancement of Peace). Finally twenty-two treaties came into being, most of them operative by the end of 1915; the one with Venezuela was not ratified until 1921, however, and the one with the Netherlands only as late as 1928. The "Bryan Treaties" provided only for investigation and report, not for the submission of recommendations. On the other hand, each of the treaties provided for the submission of "all disputes of every nature whatsoever" that could be settled otherwise to a standing Peace Commission. Neither party to a dispute was to go to war until the report of the Commission had been received, and such report had to be completed within a year. Thus the Bryan Treaties provided in effect a cooling-off period. The commission was to consist of a national and a nonnational selected by each party, and a fifth member, who could not be a citizen of either party, chosen by agreement. As far as this writer knows, none of the commissions of inquiry called for by the agreements has ever been called into the investigation of a dispute, even though ten commissions were actually created. Most of these disappeared again, however, when vacant positions were not filled again.

Unlike European states, the American republics concluded numerous treaties calling for inquiry into disputes; most of these instruments tended to emphasize conciliation more than the investigatory function. Among them may be listed the bipartite agreement of 1915 between Chile and Hungary; a tripartite treaty of the same year between Argentina, Brazil, and Chile; a six-country agreement concluded at the Conference on Central American Affairs (Washington, 1922–23); and the so-called Gondra Treaty, which was one of the results of the Pan-American Conference at Santiago in 1923 and which was enlarged at two meetings in 1928 and 1929 to include conciliatory provisions. The last-mentioned in-

---

[9] See 16 *A.J.I.L.* (1922), pp. 485–492, for the text of the report. The other utilization of Hague Commissions, the *Tavignano, Camouna, and Gaulois Cases* (France-Italy, 1913), produced no usable report because the commission could not reach conclusions for lack of evidence: see Scott, *op. cit.*, pp. 413–423.

strument was utilized successfully in an investigation of the facts in the Gran Chaco conflict between Bolivia and Paraguay. This conflict was settled eventually by means of an arbitral award handed down by a tribunal consisting of the presidents of Argentina, Brazil, Chile, Peru, the United States, and Uruguay.[10]

Before leaving the subject of commissions of inquiry, it should be mentioned that the League of Nations made use, on at least six occasions, of such fact-finding bodies.[11]

On December 18, 1967, the General Assembly of the United Nations adopted unanimously a resolution 2329 (XXII) 1967 urging member states to make more effective use of the existing methods of fact-finding, in accordance with Article 33 of the Charter. The General Assembly also requested the Secretary-General to prepare a register of experts whose services might be utilized for fact-finding purposes.

The relatively limited role played by the General Assembly with respect to fact-finding procedures is somewhat surprising because it is well known that most interstate disputes center on questions of fact rather than on legal questions. One might suspect, however, that political considerations might intrude unduly into fact-finding by the General Assembly, in view of the kind of world in which the United Nations is as yet forced to operate.

COMMISSIONS OF CONCILIATION

The procedure of peaceful settlement of disputes through conciliation means the submission of a given dispute to an already established commission or a single conciliator for the purpose of examining all facets of the dispute and suggesting a solution to the parties concerned. Either or both parties are, of course, free to accept or reject proposals of the conciliators (styled, in the case of an organized group, "commission of investigation and conciliation" or "commission of conciliation"). As in the case of mediation, conciliators may meet with the parties jointly or separately.

The decades since the end of World War I have seen the establishment, by bipartite or multipartite conventions, of scores of such bodies. Many of these treaties provide for the establishment of permanent commissions which, in some instances, are even authorized to offer their services to the parties in dispute without being requested to do so. Others of the instruments in question call for the establishment of *ad hoc* commissions only

[10] Text of award, with map of the boundary as determined by the award, in *The New York Times*, October 11, 1938.

[11] The commissions investigated disputes involving Sweden and Finland in 1920; Jugoslavia and Albania in 1921; the Allied Powers and Lithuania in 1923; Great Britain and Turkey in 1923; Greece and Bulgaria in 1925; and China and Japan (Manchuria crisis) in 1931.

after a dispute has come into existence.[12] More recently, a number of agreements, some of considerable importance, contained provisions for the creation of conciliation commissions, such as the Pact of Bogotá (1948), the Treaty of Brussels (March 17, 1948). And in recent years, disputes in respectable numbers have been submitted to the consideration of such bodies: in 1949 a dispute between Romania and Switzerland; in 1947, a boundary dispute between France and Thailand; in 1952 a Danish-Belgian dispute; in 1955 two disputes between France and Switzerland; and in 1956 a disagreement between Greece and Italy.

On the other hand, although such listings appear quite impressive, actual usage of conciliation procedures represents an extremely rare phenomenon on the international scene. It has been suggested, with sound logic, that other procedures for the settlement of disputes are preferred because they provide for the issuance of a binding award or judgment (arbitration, adjudication), rather than leave each party free to reject mere recommendation, as in the case of conciliation.

It would be quite possible to expand already existing machinery and to provide conciliation services on a global basis. Thus Clark and Sohn outlined a rather detailed plan for a revision of the United Nations Charter with a view to establishing a World Equity Tribunal and a World Conciliation Board.[13] The Tribunal, of fifteen members, would deal primarily with nonlegal disputes involving states, nonself-governing territories, and the United Nations and its specialized agencies. The Board, composed of five members, would specialize in mutually acceptable agreements between states involved in disputes or situations representing a danger to peace.

ARBITRATION

Early Development of Arbitration. The procedure known as arbitration is one of the oldest methods used by Western man to settle international disputes.[14] The Greek city-states had already evolved not only comprehensive procedural details for arbitration, used in the peaceful solution of many disagreements, but had concluded many treaties under which the parties agreed in advance to submit either all or specified cate-

---

[12] See also Institut de Droit International, "International Conciliation" (including Regulations on the Procedure of International Conciliation), 50th Session, Salzburg, 1961, in 56 *A.J.I.L.* (1962), pp. 739–743.

[13] See the stimulating but somewhat overly optimistic presentation in Grenville Clark and Louis B. Sohn, *World Peace Through World Law* (Cambridge, Mass.: Harvard University Press, 1958), at pp. 321–330. Contrast the Clark-Sohn proposal with the more realistic "Draft Regulations on the Procedure of International Conciliation," drawn up in 1961 at Salzburg by the *Institut de Droit International:* text in 56 *A.J.I.L.* (1962), pp. 739–743.

[14] Consult the standard historical treatment of the subject, Jackson H. Ralston, *International Arbitration from Athens to Locarno* (Stanford University, Calif.: Stanford University Press, 1929), and see Stone, pp. 73–106, for a modern analysis.

gories of disputes to arbitration. The medieval period witnessed occasional recourse to the procedure, usually in the form of a papal arbitration, and almost every one of the classical writers on international law, from Vitoria and Suarez through Grotius to Vattel, endorsed arbitration. Some of the writings in question, notably Grotius, even advocated arbitration of disputes by assemblies or conferences of the Christian powers.

But although arbitration began to be utilized increasingly as a civil procedure, particularly between merchants, it did not play a prominent part in modern international relations until the key year of 1794, when Jay's Treaty provided for the use of arbitration to settle disputes between the United States and Great Britain. One single arbitration under the provisions of treaty resulted in more than 500 awards to private claimants.

American interest in arbitration continued ever since that agreement. Thus the New York Society of Peace (founded in 1815) and the Massachusetts Peace Society carried on consistent propaganda campaigns, and in 1820 appealed to Congress to promote arbitration of disputes as a permanent aspect of American foreign policy. Their efforts bore some fruit: Article 21 of the Guadeloupe-Hidalgo treaty with Mexico (1848) provided for arbitration of all future disputes before either country had recourse to war. Another Anglo-American arbitral tribunal, operating under the provisions of the Treaty of London of 1853, settled more than 100 claims. On the other hand, an American-Mexican Commission established under a treaty concluded in 1868 handled more than 2,000 claims but dismissed about 1,700 of these. The single event which suddenly called attention to the usefulness of the procedure was the successful arbitration under the Washington Treaty of 1871 of the *Alabama* claims at Geneva in 1872, in which the United States won the award of $15,500,000 in compensation for the losses caused by Confederate cruisers illegally supplied to the South by British interests.

At once great interest in the procedure was manifested in many places. As early as 1875, the private Institute of International Law drafted a body of arbitral procedure rules. At the First International Conference of American States (Washington, 1889-90), a comprehensive Plan of Arbitration, calling for obligatory submission to arbitration of virtually all kinds of disputes, was elaborated. The plan was, however, not ratified, yet served as a model for a number of bilateral arbitration treaties concluded in the Western Hemisphere.

Hague Peace Conference (1899). The acceptance of arbitration on a large-scale basis came at the Hague Peace Conference of 1899.[15] The Convention for the Pacific Settlement of International Disputes (revised in 1907) established the Permanent Court of Arbitration. Actually this title is a misnomer, for the treaty did not create a tribunal in the orthodox sense of the term. Instead, the "Court" consisted of a panel, a list of four

[15] Consult the excellent study of Alvin DeA. Dans, *The United States and the First Hague Peace Conference* (Ithaca, N.Y.: Cornell University Press, 1962).

names of individuals submitted to a central office at The Hague by each signatory to the Convention. When a dispute was referred to the Court, each party unless they agreed to some other procedure) would select two arbitrators from the panel. Only one of the two could be a national of the state in question. The four arbitrators would then select an umpire. Thus, as Brierly pointed out, there was set up a permanent panel of arbitration, but the Court itself had to be constituted anew for each case.[16] In order to bring the Hague machinery into operation, however, a network of bipartite arbitration treaties to supplement the 1899 Convention was required.

The actual operations of the Court were somewhat as follows: The states in dispute had to sign a special agreement (*compromis*) which specified in detail the subject matter of the dispute, the method to be used in appointing the arbitrators, any special needed powers to be conferred on the tribunal, the language to be utilized, and any special conditions or limitations on which the parties might agree. The awards were deliberated in secret and when a final decision had been readied by majority vote it was final and subject to no appeal, unless the *compromis* contained the right of a party to request a revision of an award.

Despite the relative simplicity and inexpensiveness of the Hague procedure, only a very small number of disputes (such as fourteen awards between 1902 and 1914) have been settled by reference to it, notably the Newfoundland Fisheries dispute between the United States and Great Britain in 1910.[17]

Although the nations of the world bypassed the institution of the Hague Court, they nevertheless utilized its procedure, arbitration, to an increasing extent during the twentieth century, and hundreds of bipartite compulsory arbitration treaties came into existence.

The largest accumulation of claims (over 70,000) were handled by the more than forty Mixed Arbitral Tribunals established after World War I to cover claims by nationals of the Allied and Associated Powers against the three Central Powers.

Procedure of Arbitration. Before examining the more recent developments in the sphere of arbitration, we must examine briefly how the procedure actually operates in the settlement of disputes.

The first characteristic of arbitration is the free selection of arbitra-

---

[16] Brierly, p. 350.

[17] See the rather plaintive Circular Note of the Secretary General, Permanent Court of Arbitration, of March 3, 1960, in 54 *A.J.I.L.* (1960), Supp., pp. 933–941, which contains a plea for more extensive utilization of the facilities of the Court. Today the major "practical" function of the Permanent Court appears to occur whenever a vacancy exists on the International Court of Justice. The "national groups" of the Permanent Court nominate candidates from among whom the General Assembly and the Security Council of the United Nations elect new judges to the International Court of Justice.

tors—quite different from judicial settlement by a permanently established true court.

Secondly, arbitration treaties generally specify that the arbitrators must respect the rules of international law and must attempt to come as close as possible in their award to what would normally be regarded as a legal decision. Obviously, some disputes submitted to arbitration do not center on legal principles and issues but on facts. In that case, the arbitrators would come rather close to the functions of a commission of inquiry— except for the feature of an award involved in arbitration.

Because not all rules of international law are clear beyond a doubt, the parties to a dispute frequently stipulate in the agreement (*compromis*)— that is, the instrument under which a dispute is submitted to arbitration— that the award is to be made on the basis of either specified rules of law or under general principles of equity. On occasion, the *compromis* even lays down special rules which are to apply only to the case on hand.

Thirdly, the procedure of arbitration assumes, explicitly or implicitly, an agreement by both parties to accept the award of the arbitration tribunal and to carry out its provisions. Only if the arbitrators disregard the instructions laid down in the *compromis* by not following specified rules and principles or by exceeding the terms of the document may the party against which the award has gone, rightfully claim not to be bound by the latter. This, as most texts point out, was the case in the famous award in the Northeastern Boundary Dispute in 1831. Both parties, the United States and Great Britain, rejected the award on the grounds that the arbitrator, the King of Holland, had exceeded the instructions given to him in the *compromis*.

Except under such unusual circumstances, the awards of arbitral tribunals settle the dispute definitely and without a right of appeal. On the other hand, the arbitrators may revise and even reverse an award if new facts pertinent to the dispute are discovered or disclosed later.

An obvious difficulty inherent in the final nature of an arbitral award relates to the unwillingness of states to submit questions of fundamental importance to a body on which they are not represented by a majority and whose decision they agree in advance to accept.

Efforts to Make Arbitration a Binding Obligation. The creation of the League of Nations placed new emphasis on the procedure of arbitration, because the latter had been mentioned expressly and repeatedly in the Covenant (Arts. 13 and 15, in particular). Because states found "gaps" in the Covenant and desired to devise means whereby resort to peaceful methods would be a binding obligation even as a final settlement of a dispute, a number of international agreements appeared on the scene. In 1924, the Geneva Protocol, stillborn because of the failure of signatures to ratify it, was the first of such efforts. It was followed in 1925 by the Locarno Treaties, a series of bipartite agreements concluded between

Germany, on the one hand, and Belgium, Czechoslovakia, France, and Poland on the other, which called for the submission of appropriate disputes either to arbitration or to judicial settlement. Then, in 1928, the Assembly of the League adopted the well-known General Act. That instrument, submitted to all members for ratification, dealt in considerable detail with conciliation, judicial settlement, and arbitration as methods of peaceful settlement.[18]

Concurrently, a series of regional agreements for the peaceful settlement of disputes were concluded: the Gondra Treaty (Santiago Inter-American Conference of 1923); the General Convention of Inter-American Conciliation and the General Treaty of Inter-American Arbitration (Both at the Washington Conference of 1929); the Anti-War treaty of Non-Aggression and Conciliation (Saavedra Lamas Treaty, 1933)—which, incidentally, limited the scope of the conciliation procedure stressed in the Gondra Treaty—and the Buenos Aires treaties of 1936, which attempted to correlate earlier instruments, particularly through the Treaty to Coordinate Existing Treaties.

Another of the Buenos Aires agreements, the Treaty on the Prevention of Controversies, merits brief mention because of the novelty of the concept underlying it. Rather than to provide a method of settling a dispute, the instrument was designed to bring into being machinery for the avoidance of conflict. The treaty called for the establishment of permanent bilateral mixed commissions, to be convoked at the request of either party and to meet after such convocation alternately in the capitals of the two states. The commissions were to study the causes of future difficulties or controversies with the object of eliminating them as far as possible.

All these instruments, coupled with the extensive use made of arbitral procedures in many parts of the world during the past few decades, led many writers as well as statesmen to question whether the time had not arrived when an international code of arbitral procedures might be evolved in the interest of clarity and uniformity.[19]

UN Draft on Arbitral Procedure. The International Law Commission of the United Nations at its first meeting in 1949 had selected arbitral procedures as one of the topics of codification. After appointing a special rapporteur, the Commission adopted in 1952 a draft on arbitral procedure which was sent to the members of the United Nations through the Secretary-General with a request for comments.[20] A revised draft was considered by the General Assembly in 1955, and was the subject of con-

---

[18] Text in 25 *A.J.I.L.* (1931), pp. 204 ff.

[19] See the heavily documented monographic study by Kenneth S. Carlston, "Codification of International Arbitral Procedure," 47 *A.J.I.L.* (1953), pp. 203–250, which even includes a fairly detailed draft code.

[20] Text, with comments of the Commission, reprinted in 47 *A.J.I.L.* (1953), Supp., pp. 6–23.

siderable criticism. Much of the latter centered on the Commission's recommendation that a convention on arbitration should be concluded. Many states objected to this concept, holding that the Commission's draft disturbed traditional arbitration practices and transformed them into quasi-compulsory jurisdictional procedures, producing binding and final solutions, to be sure, but emphasizing the development of new law instead of codifying custom. The Commission went back to work on its draft and changed its approach by deciding to set out "simply a set of rules which might inspire states in the drawing up of provisions for inclusion in international treaties and special arbitration agreements." [21] It thus abandoned the idea of developing a full fledged code of Arbitral Procedure, the aim of its earlier endeavors. By early July, 1958, the revised effort had resulted in a rather elaborate set of Model Rules on Arbitral Procedure.[22] The Commission recommended that the General Assembly adopt its report by resolution.

Examination of the draft articles reveals no significant departure from customary principles governing arbitral procedure. To be sure, Article 1 did provide for utilization of the International Court of Justice, but only for a determination of whether a dispute existed and whether the dispute was wholly or in part subject to the obligation to go to arbitration. This provision had been criticized by a number of countries on the grounds that it set up the International Court of Justice as a kind of supertribunal not subordinate to the agreement of the parties in a dispute. The Commission did not share this suspicion, pointing out that any of the draft articles applied only in so far as states accepted them and made them a part of an arbitral agreement.

The reformulations of 1958 were subjected again to much criticism, and finally the General Assembly, on November 14, 1958, restricted itself to taking note of the Commission's report and brought the latest draft to the members' attention for their possible consideration and use.

A unique arbitral award without modern precedent or successor took place in 1932: The *Arbitration of the Aaroo Mountain*. The mountain in question is situated on the boundary line between the Kingdom of Saudi Arabia and Yemen. The armed forces of Yemen occupied the mountain, claiming that they had been invited to do so by the inhabitants of Aaroo. Negotiations failed to settle the question of territorial sovereignty over the mountain and the Imam (King) of Yemen finally telegraphed a request for settlement by arbitration to King Abdul Aziz (Ibn Saud), agreeing that the latter should be the sole arbitrator and that he would accept his decision as final. Ibn Saud accepted and decided against himself.[23]

[21] 53 *A.J.I.L.* (1959), Supp., p. 234.

[22] *Ibid.*, pp. 239–248; the Commission's commentary is found on pp. 248–252.

[23] For texts of telegrams and of the award, see Quincy Wright, "The Arbitration of the Aaroo Mountain," 33 *A.J.I.L.* (1939), pp. 356–359.

ADJUDICATION [24]

The first serious attempt to create an international court, in the true meaning of the term, for the settlement of international disputes through judicial processes (adjudication) took place in 1907. In accordance with the Treaty of Washington of that year, the five Central American states situated between Mexico and Panama created the Central American Court of Justice. This court, consisting of five judges, sat at the city of Cartago in Costa Rica. The functions of the Court fell into three major categories: it had jurisdiction over international questions submitted to it by means of a special agreement between any one of the five states and a foreign state; over cases between any of the contracting states and individuals if such a case was submitted to the Court by agreement between both parties; and over claims by nationals of one of the five states against one of the other states, provided local remedies had been exhausted and a denial of justice had been proved.

The Court lasted only a short time, for it was unable to enforce an award handed down against Nicaragua in a case dealing with the rights of other states bordering on Fonseca Bay. Subsequently the five states in question signed another agreement at Washington (1923), providing for the creation of an International Central-American Tribunal, but that agency was never established. (See suggested readings for the coverage of a new "court" established in 1962.)

INTERNATIONAL COURT OF JUSTICE: ITS STRUCTURE AND OPERATIONS

The desirability of having in existence a true international court to settle legal disputes between states was reflected in Article 14 of the Covenant of the League of Nations which called on the Council to "formulate and submit to the members of the League for adoption, plans for the establishment of a Permanent Court of International Justice." As a result of this provision, an Advisory Council of Jurists was appointed and met at The Hague in June, 1920, to draft the basic instrument (Statute) of such a tribunal. The result of the meeting, called a Draft Scheme, was submitted to Council and Assembly. After certain changes had been incorporated in the Scheme, it was approved by the Assembly on December 13, 1920; it was to be binding on states only if they signed and ratified a Protocol of Signature dated December 16, 1920. Certain amendments adopted in 1928–29 were submitted to member states for ratification in the form of a sec-

---

[24] Consult Stone, pp. 107–164, for an excellent general analysis of the judicial settlement of international disputes.

[25] The major documents relating to the Court are found in "Instruments relating to the Permanent Court of Justice" (with an introduction by Manley O. Hudson), *International Conciliation*, No. 388 (March, 1943), pp. 137–193.

ond Protocol in 1929.[25] By December, 1942, the original Protocol had been ratified by fifty-one states, including all major powers except the United States.

After the end of World War II the statute was revised still further. The remaining judges of the Permanent Court resigned in January, 1946, and the former Assembly of the League of Nations dissolved the Court. The new International Court of Justice then was established as the successor to the League agency. In most details the Statute of the new court duplicates that of the old one, but there are certain significant differences, one of which centers on the fact that all member states of the United Nations are automatically parties to the Statute of the new Court, while in the case of the 1920 Statute only those states were bound by it that ratified the 1920 Protocol of Signature.

Because the old Permanent Court has been abolished, the following discussion is based on the Statute and operations of the current Court, whose first regular session began on April 18, 1946.

Structure of the International Court. The Court consists of fifteen judges qualified for holding the highest judicial offices in their own country or recognized as experts in international law. Candidates are nominated, as mentioned previously, by the "national groups" of the Permanent Court of Arbitration. In recent years, these groups have been either national groups in the Permanent Court appointed in accordance with the provisions of the Hague Conventions of 1898 and 1907 for the Pacific Settlement of International Disputes or special groups appointed by governments which are not parties to those conventions. The special groups are selected under the conditions laid down in the conventions. Normally national and special groups consist of four individuals.[26] From the list thus obtained, judges are elected by the General Assembly and the Security Council, voting separately.

Judges are elected for a term of nine years (five every three years) and may be re-elected. They may be dismissed only when the other members of the Court are convinced that they have ceased to fulfill the required conditions of holding office as a judge. No two judges may be nationals of the same state.

In a given case in which a party to a dispute before the court does not have a national sitting on the Court, an appropriate *ad hoc* judge is appointed to sit with the regular Court. Nine judges, excluding such *ad hoc* national judges, constitute a quorum.

As in the case of the old Permanent Court, states that are not members of the United Nations may become parties to the Statute of the International Court of Justice. However, in each instance, conditions are laid down by the General Assembly, and the state in question may become a party to the Statute only on recommendation of the Security Council.

[26] R. R. Baxter, "The Procedures Employed in connection with the United States Nominations for the International Court in 1960," 55 *A.J.I.L.* (1961), pp. 445–446.

This has happened in a few cases: Switzerland in 1947, Liechtenstein in 1950, Japan and San Marino in 1954.

Operations of the International Court. The competence of the Court is outlined in Articles 34 through 38 of the Statute. Only states may be parties in cases before the Court. If, therefore, an individual desires to bring a case before the Court, he must depend on his own government to take up his case or claim before it can be heard by the Court. The Court may request of public international organizations information relevant to cases under consideration and may receive such information presented by such agencies on their own initiative. Also, and this has been extremely useful and important, the United Nations may request advisory opinions on legal questions, as may be done by other organs authorized to do so by the United Nations. The General Assembly has granted this privilege to all Specialized Agencies, except the Universal Postal Union. In the case of the United States, a provision of the 1947 Headquarters Agreement, which calls for arbitration of differences between the United States and the United Nations, also calls for an advisory opinion on the part of the Court, which is to be taken into consideration by the arbitral tribunal.

In connection with advisory opinions, the Permanent Court established a very important precedent in the *Eastern Carelia Case* [27] when it refused to give such an opinion because the League of Nations had not obtained the consent of the Soviet Union before requesting the advisory opinion. To be sure, the Soviet Union was not a member of the League at the time, but, on the other hand, was an interested party to the dispute. Because the *Eastern Carelia* quarrel was between Russia and Finland, and because an advisory opinion would have been, in view of the facts in question, a decision of the dispute, the acceptance of the latter by the Court would in effect have imposed the Court's jurisdiction on the Soviet Union.

On the other hand, in the instance of the International Court of Justice, it should be noted that if the option clause is inapplicable to both parties in a dispute, consent of *both* must be obtained if the dispute is to be submitted to the Court. Thus, on numerous occasions the United States sought to bring incidents involving U.S. aircraft and Soviet military forces before the Court. In each case the U.S.S.R. refused to grant prior consent to adjudication and the Court removed the application in question from its General List (agenda).[28]

The Court is open to all states which are parties to the Statute; it may also be open to other states, subject to special provisions contained in treaties in force, subject to conditions laid down by the Security Council.[29] When a state which is not a member of the United Nations is a party to a case, the Court will fix the amount which that state is to contribute

---

[27] *Legal Status of Eastern Carelia, P.C.I.J.*, 1923, Ser. B, No. 5.

[28] For details consult Dennys P. Myers, "Contemporary Practice of the U.S. Relating to International Law," 54 *A.J.I.L.* (1960), pp. 632–638.

[29] Conditions are reproduced in 41 *A.J.I.L.* (1947), pp. 8–9.

toward the expenses of the Court unless the state in question is doing so already.

The jurisdiction of the Court comprises all cases which the parties refer to it and all other matters especially provided for in the Charter or in treaties in force.

However, a dispute submitted must not only be capable of being settled by a court (justiciable dispute), but the dispute must have arisen between the parties in question. The South West Africa cases (see Chapter 6) involved a dispute, not between the applicants (Ethiopia and Liberia) and the respondent (South Africa), but between the respondent and the General Assembly. And the two member states could not appear before the Court as either representatives or agents of the General Assembly.

The states which are parties to the Statute may at any time declare that they recognize as compulsory *ipso facto* and without special agreement, in relation to any other state accepting the same obligation, the jurisdiction of the Court in all legal disputes concerning (1) the interpretations of a treaty; (2) any question of international law; (3) the existence of any fact which, if established, would constitute a breach of an international obligation; and (4) the nature or extent of the reparation to be made for the breach of an international obligation.

The declarations mentioned (adherence to the "optional clause") may be made unconditionally or on condition of reciprocity on the part of several or certain states, or for a specified length of time, and are to be deposited with the Secretary-General of the United Nations. Any declarations made under Article 36 of the Statute of the Permanent Court of International Justice and still in force in 1946 were deemed, as between the parties to the new Statute, to be acceptances of the compulsory jurisdiction of the International Court in accordance with their terms. The question of the "renewal" of an acceptance of compulsory jurisdiction made in accordance with the Statute of the Permanent Court and carried over under the Statute of the International Court came up in two cases before the latter tribunal. In the case of the *Aerial Incident of July 27th, 1955 (Israel v. Bulgaria)*[30] the Court found that Bulgaria's declaration of acceptance of compulsory jurisdiction, made in 1921, had lapsed in 1946 and that Bulgaria had taken no steps to indicate either its renewal of the declaration or its acceptance of the compulsory jurisdiction of the International Court. The Court therefore was forced to conclude that Bulgaria was not obligated to submit to its jurisdiction.

In the *Judgment on Preliminary Objections* in the *Case Concerning the Temple of Preah Vihear (Cambodia v. Thailand)*, May 26, 1961,[31] a dispute as to territorial sovereignty over the region of the Temple of Preah Vihear, Thailand asserted that because of the decision in *Israel v. Bulgaria*,

---

[30] *I.C.J. Reports, 1959*, p. 127, digested by Leo Gross in 57 *A.J.I.L.* (1963), pp. 753–766, with special emphasis on the optional clause.

[31] *I.C.J. Reports, 1961*, p. 17, digested in 55 *A.J.I.L.* (1962), pp. 978–983.

Thailand was no longer bound by its renewal of its declaration of acceptance of compulsory jurisdiction.

The government of Thailand had accepted that jurisdiction (then relating to the Permanent Court of International Justice) on September 20, 1929, for a period of ten years. This declaration was renewed in 1940 for a further period, scheduled to expire on May 6, 1950. Thailand, however, sent a new declaration of acceptance under date of May 20, 1950. In the case on hand, the Thai government contended that the Court's decision in *Israel* v. *Bulgaria* revealed that the assumptions on which the language of the Thai 1950 declaration was based were incorrect and that the declaration, in the light of the Court's decision, was meaningless. Thailand admitted that it had fully intended to accept the compulsory jurisdiction of the Court, but now asserted that her declaration of 1950 had been revealed as having been ineffectual to achieve Thailand's purpose.

The Court ruled against the Thailand objection, holding that the renewal of acceptance of jurisdiction of the Permanent Court had expired on May 6, 1950; that the new declaration of May 20, 1950, was a new and independent instrument; that the new declaration had, in fact, no relation to the defunct Permanent Court and only relation to the International Court whose compulsory jurisdiction had thereby been accepted. The Court also pointed out that the decision in *Israel* v. *Bulgaria* was only binding under Article 59 of the Court's Statute, on the parties in that dispute and could not have any effects on Thailand's 1950 declaration.

On June 15, 1962, the Court handed down its judgment in the case, awarding the contested territory to Cambodia.[32] The lengthy decision was based primarily on an analysis of the reports and maps produced by boundary commissions in the early twentieth century and on Thailand's prolonged failure to assert a claim to the area in dispute. Judge Alfaro, concurring in the award, added an extensive discussion of "preclusion," the doctrine that a state which is a party to an international litigation is bound by its previous acts or attitudes when they are in contradiction with its claims in the litigation. He concluded that failure of a state to assert its right when that right was openly challenged by another state meant abandonment of right in question.

A slightly different problem was raised by Guatemala in the *Nottebohm Case*. Liechtenstein had instituted by application proceedings against Guatemala. The latter, however, contended in 1953 that the time limit of five years provided for in its declaration (accepting compulsory jurisdiction of the International Court) of January 27, 1947, had expired at midnight on January 26, 1952, and that from that moment the International Court of Justice had no jurisdiction to treat or decide cases which would affect

---

[32] *Case concerning the Temple of Preah Vihear (Cambodia v. Thailand)*, *Merits*. I. C. Justice, June 15, 1962, *I.C.J. Reports, 1692*, p. 6; the opinion is reproduced at length in excerpted form (William W. Bishop, Jr.) in 56 *A.J.I.L.* (1962), Supp., pp. 1033–1053.

Guatemala, except if Guatemala extended the duration of its declaration, submitted a new declaration with the Secretary-General, or signed a special protocol of submission with any interested state.

The Court ruled, however, that when an application was filed at a time when the law in force between the parties entailed the compulsory jurisdiction of the Court, the latter had to deal with the claim. It had jurisdiction to deal with all of its aspects and the subsequent lapse of a declaration of one of the parties by reason of the expiration of a time limit or by denunciation could not deprive the Court of the jurisdiction already established.[33]

Whenever a treaty in force provides for reference of a matter to a tribunal instituted by the League of Nations or to the latter's Court, the matter, as between the parties to the new Statute, are referred to the new Court.

Connally Amendment. The question of the optional clause has agitated many governments as well as jurists. Most states which have ratified the clause have done so by attaching not only a time limit after which their acceptance of compulsory jurisdiction would expire, but have also included in their ratifications numerous reservations which can be referred to against the reserving state by the other party in a dispute. Most famous of all the reservations is that of the United States, the so-called Connally Amendment, according to which the United States excluded from its acceptance of the compulsory jurisdiction of the Court "Disputes with regard to matters which are essentially within the domestic jurisdiction of the United States of America *as determined by the United States of America.*" [Italics added; the italicized words are the portion referred to as the Connally amendment.][34]

---

[33] *Nottebohm Case (Liechtenstein v. Guatemala)*, *Preliminary Objection*, International Court of Jutice, November 18, 1953, *I.C.J. Reports, 1953*, p. 111; digested and excerpted in 48 *A.J.I.L.* (1954), pp. 327–332.

[34] Text of U.S. declaration of August 14, 1946, in 41 *A.J.I.L.* (1947), pp. 11–12; the literature on the Amendment is enormous; consult, *inter alia*, Herbert W. Briggs, "The United States and the International Court of Justice: A Re-Examination," 53 *A.J.I.L.* (1959), pp. 301–318 [con]; Vincent F. DeCain, "The Connally Amendment," 10 *National Review* (March 11, 1961), pp. 143–147 [pro]; Lawrence Preuss, "The International Court of Justice, the Senate, and Matters of Domestic Jurisdiction," 40 *A.J.I.L.* (1946), pp. 720–736. See also the monographic study of the entire subject by Herbert W. Briggs, "Reservations to the Acceptance of the Compulsory Jurisdiction of the International Court of Justice," 93 *Hague Academy Recueil des Cours* (1958, I), pp. 223–367; the extensive coverage of the Connally Amendment by seven writers in 46 *American Bar Association Journal* (1960), pp. 726–754; John H. Crabb, "On Judging the Connally Amendment," 50 *Georgetown Law Journal* (1962), pp. 529–545; E. Smythe Gambrell, "The United Nations, the World Court and the Connally Reservation," 47 *American Bar Association Journal* (1961), pp. 57–62; Frank B. Ober, "The Connally Reservation and National Security," *ibid.*, pp. 63–67; Andre Aversa, "As Determined by the United States of America," 10 *American University Law Review* (1961), pp. 146–178; Arthur Larson, "The Facts, the Law, and the Connally Amendment," *Duke Law Journal*, 1961 (Winter, 1961), pp. 74–119.

One of the major arguments advanced by critics of the Amendment is that it has discouraged utilization of the Court and thus has lessened its importance. It is true, of course, that the existence of the Amendment or of equivalent reservations has tended to keep disputes out of the Court, in part because of the principle of reciprocity. This principle applies not only in a general sense, in that a country that accepts the jurisdiction of the Court cannot be sued without its consent by a country that has not done so, but also specifically. Thus France, which earlier had filed a reservation very similar to the Connally Amendment, sued Norway in 1957 over the latter's refusal to pay off certain bonds in gold. Norway invoked France's own reservation against her, claimed the matter was "domestic," and that was the end of the matter.[35] And Bulgaria invoked the Connally Amendment against the United States in the case of the *Aerial Incident of 27 July 1955*. The case was withdrawn on May 30, 1960, as a result of the acceptance by the United States of Bulgaria's preliminary objection based on the Connally Amendment.[36] On the other hand, it would be utterly fanciful to claim that American repeal of the Amendment would lead to a sudden influx of "business" for the International Court of Justice. The American reservation is but one of a great number, many quite similar in tenor, and only a general abandonment of such restrictive reservations would tend to bring an appreciably greater number of disputes before the Court.

The real argument in favor of American repeal of the Amendment is a psychological one: the United States, having assumed a position of leadership in the Western world, should implement that position by acting as a leader of that world toward acceptance of the rule of law.

Of all the states that have accepted the jurisdiction of the Court, only five (Liberia, Mexico, Pakistan, Sudan, South Africa) aside from the United States have filed what may be termed a "self-judging reservation." India and France, both of which has asserted similar self-judging privileges, have abandoned them, India completely, in September, 1959, and France by replacing its original reservation in July, 1959, by a somewhat more circumscribed reservation exempting from the jurisdiction of the Court "disputes arising out of any war or international hostilities and disputes arising out of a crisis affecting the national security or out of any measure or action relating thereto." The wording indicates that France did not completely discard self-judgment.

Historical Note. When Great Britain ratified a ten-year adherence to the optional clause of the Statute of the Permanent Court of International Justice, three exceptions were specified: the jurisdiction of the Court would not apply to differences that the disputants would agree to settle

---

[35] *Certain Norwegian Loans (France v. Norway), I.C.J. Reports, 1957*, No. 9, p. 22.

[36] See Leo Gross, "Bulgaria Invokes the Connally Amendment," 56 *A.J.I.L.* (1962), pp. 357–382, and his subsequent analysis, *ibid.*, 57 (1963), pp. 767–771.

by other peaceful methods, disputes within the British Empire, and matters that fell exclusively within British jurisdiction. On March 11, 1940, the British government published a series of letters from the Foreign Secretary to M. Joseph Avenol, Secretary-General of the League of Nations, in which Great Britain added a fourth exception to the applicability of the optional clause: "Disputes arising out of events occurring at a time when His Majesty's Government in the United Kingdom are involved in hostilities." [37]

Major Procedural Questions. The major procedural questions meriting brief mention in connection with the International Court of Justice are these.

The Court has the power to indicate, if it considers that conditions warrant it, any provisional measures which ought to be taken to preserve the respective rights of either party.

A decision by the Court has no binding force except between the parties and in respect of the particular case in question (Art. 59). A judgment of the Court is final and without appeal. An application for the revision of a judgment can be made only when it is based on the discovery of some fact of such a nature as to be a decisive factor, which fact must have been unknown to the Court and to the party claiming revision, at the time when the judgment was given.

Article 38 of the Statute instructs the Court to apply (a) international conventions, both general and particular, (b) international custom, as evidence of a general practice accepted as law, (c) the general principles of law recognized by civilized nations, and (d) subject to Article 59, judicial decisions and the teachings of publicists, as subsidiary means for the determination of rules of law. Finally, if both parties to a dispute agree, the Court can also decide a case *ex aequo et bono.* That phrase, in Anglo-Saxon practice, means "equity," but in the case of the International Court apparently that the Court can use its own judgment, even if this means a disregard of existing rules of law, in order to arrive at a fair decision.[38]

On the whole, the two World Courts have contributed greatly to the advancement of the peaceful settlement of disputes through adjudication. Both have dealt effectively with many cases and have not only decided numerous disputed points of law but have promoted the development of international law as a whole.

NEED FOR INCREASING USE OF THE INTERNATIONAL COURT

Limited Use of the Court. All too often disputes centering on the application of customary law or on the meaning of a treaty provision really represent political disagreements rather than true "legal" disputes. Whenever this occurs, one of the parties to the dispute, and possibly both, does

[37] See *The New York Times,* March 12, 1940, p. 2.
[38] See Whiteman, Vol. I, pp. 98–103.

not really desire a settlement through the medium of an outside agency. What is behind the dispute is quite frequently a desire to have the rules of law changed in form or content. Such an attitude vitiates what should be a fundamental prerequisite to adjudication: agreement among the parties as to the rules to be applied by a court.

Many disputes which appear to be legal in nature actually are motivated by quite different causes. Some writers mention, as an illustration, the dispute between Iceland and Great Britain about the breadth of the territorial sea. On the surface, the arguments revolved around Iceland's desire to protect her local fishing industry from foreign competition. Great Britain, on the other hand, wanted to prevent an exclusion of British fishing interests from the fishing grounds surrounding Iceland. But below the surface, Great Britain was interested, as a country with global maritime interests, in preserving a narrow, three-mile limit to territorial waters, not just in the case of Iceland, but elsewhere in the world.

Again, many ostensibly legal disputes involve what either or both parties may consider to be vital national interests. In such circumstances, negotiation may be regarded as the best method of settling the dispute, better by far than to submit it to the relatively narrow framework of reference within which a court must operate. And either party may develop great reluctance to entrust its presumed vital interests to decision by a body on which it would have at most one national to represent those interests.

Another reason for the limited utilization of the Court may be found in the relatively primitive state of international law today. The Court, in dealing with rules of customary law, has adopted the rather logical view that states are free to take whatever action they deem desirable, as long as there is no definite rule of such law prohibiting that action. Nearly the same approach has been taken by the Court when it has been asked to interpret a treaty: it has been quite willing to permit either party to interpret its own obligations as long as no clear prohibitions were encountered and the interpretation appeared to be reasonable.

Expansion of Jurisdiction. Several suggestions have been put forward in different quarters to increase the use of the Court. One obvious answer would be the withdrawal of limiting reservations adopted by many countries. It has also been suggested that groups of states, bound together by special interests and ties (political, cultural, legal, economic, and possibly even ideological) could make a convention conferring on the Court jurisdiction over all disputes within a given group. If the latter represented a regional arrangement, then possibly regional chambers of the International Court could be set up to handle intraregional disputes.

Weaknesses of Enforcing Judgments. One major problem left for brief examination before leaving the subject under consideration is the question of the enforcement both of arbitral awards and of judicial decisions.

Most judgments of the Permanent Court of International Justice were executed without difficulty, because no major international problems were submitted to the Court. There were, as could be expected, a few exceptions to the rule of execution: In the *S.S. Wimbledon Case*,[39] the Court had decided in favor of France but the judgment was not executed. The Reparations Commission, of which France was a member, had ruled that damages should not be paid, despite the fact that Germany, against which the damages had been assessed, had asked to be allowed to pay as ordered by the Court. In the *Société Commerciale de Belgique Case*,[40] the Court decided that Greece had to honor awards made against that country in a 1936 arbitration; Greece, however, failed to carry out the awards.

After the establishment of the International Court of Justice, greater obstacles to the execution of judgments were encountered. Albania refused to pay the compensation awarded to Great Britain in the *Corfu Channel Case;* Iran failed to institute the interim measure of protection ordered in the *Anglo–Iranian Oil Company Case;* and the decisions in the *Asylum Case* and the *Haya de la Torre Case* required tedious and somewhat acrimonious negotiations before they were carried out eventually.

In the case of arbitration, very few instances are known in which a party has refused to accept an award and carry out its provisions. Among such examples are the *Pelletier Case* (United States–Haiti, 1885), the *Chamizal Tract Case* (United States–Mexico, 1911), and a few others, some of which did not involve the United States.

The principle that an arbitral award or a judicial decision is binding on the parties and must be carried out in good faith is accepted without dissent, as far as legal theory is concerned. In arbitration treaties, the *compromis* normally specified that the award is to be binding on both parties— a safeguard only, for it is a rule of customary law that the losing side shall honor the award in an arbitration. In the case of adjudication, there is no question but that the decisions of the International Court of Justice are binding on all members of the United Nations (Art 94 of the Charter). If nonmember states adhere to the Statute of the Court or become plaintiffs in a case before the Court, they are burdened with the same obligation to comply with decisions of the Court.

When a state objects to the carrying out of an award or a decision, it tends to advance the doctrines of nullity or of impossibility of performance. Usually three reasons are encountered as grounds of such nullity: (1) excess of power, (2) corruption of a member of the tribunal, or (3) a serious deviation from the rules of procedure involved in the making of the award or decision.

The most common assertion centers on an excess of power—that is, the charge that the arbitral tribunal or the court in question exceeded the powers granted to it. Coupled with this assertion, or, at times, found separately is an assertion of an impossibility to carry out the award or decision.

What may the "winning" party in a dispute do when the losing state

[39] *P.C.I.J.*, 1923, Ser. A, No. 1: see Chapter 15.

[40] *P.C.I.J.*, 1939, Ser. A/B, No. 78; see also *Socobel and the Belgian State v. Kingdom of the Hellenes*, Brussels Civil Tribunal, 1951; digested in 47 *A.J.I.L.* (1953), p. 508.

refuses to comply with an arbitral award or a judicial decision? This is where self-help short of war enters, which is discussed in the following chapter. In other words, having failed to see compliance on the part of the losing side, the winning state may decide to take matters into its own hands and obtain damages, redress, or whatever may be involved. Remedies that come to mind are diplomatic (and possibly economic) pressure; the attachment of property belonging to the defaulting state by a third state on behalf of the creditor state (an intriguing idea, possibly illegal, certainly difficult of execution); attempts to seek justice through the municipal courts of a third state (a procedure most likely to come to grief on the rocks of sovereign immunity of states); commencement of reprisals, embargos, and possibly a pacific blockade; and the obvious last resort—to go to war against the state refusing to comply with the award or decision.

Because self-help procedures, particularly those employing force short of war, are somewhat risky with respect to preserving peace, and because, as will be seen later, such measures may easily degenerate into armed conflict, attention has been focused for some time on international organizations as enforcement agencies.

The Covenant of the League of Nations provided in Article 13 (4) for the joint enforcement of awards and decisions. In the case of the United Nations, Article 94 (2) of the Charter represents the corresponding provision:

2. If any party to a case fails to perform the obligations incumbent upon it under a judgment rendered by the Court, the other party may have recourse to the Security Council, which may, if it deems necessary, make recommendations or decide upon measures to be taken to give effect to the judgment.

The notable difference between the provisions of Charter and Covenant is that the former only refers to judgments of the Court, whereas the latter referred to "awards or decisions," thus including arbitration in the enforcement text. Also, the Covenant forbade all members of the League to resort to war against a member which complied with awards and decisions, while the Charter omits such an express statement.

Again, Article 94 (2) does not specify what measures may be taken by the Security Council to enforce a judgment of the Court, nor do the records of the San Francisco Conference indicate that any restrictions were intended to be imposed on actions contemplated by the Council in seeking to give effect to a judgment. Although it may be doubted that the use of armed force would be suitable for the purpose on hand, utilization of the other devices normally available under the Charter, such as partial or complete severance of communications, a breaking-off of diplomatic relations, and economic sanctions, would appear to be appropriate on the part of the Security Council.

Thus far, Article 94 (2) has been invoked only once, in the "interim measures of protection" decision in the *Anglo-Iranian Oil Company Case*.

Great Britain brought the case before the Security Council on a contention that the Council had the right to take action to deal with interim measures ordered by the Court but not carried out by Iran. The Council, however, decided to postpone any action until the International Court of Justice had decided whether it was itself competent to handle the case and when the Court decided that it lacked jurisdiction, the order for the measures of protection lapsed and with it all question of enforcement on the part of the Council.

Conceivably, additional measures might be adopted to secure compliance with a judgment of the Court: a judgment creditor might try to secure a decision from the Security Council ordering member states of the United Nations to attach or seize assets in their territorial jurisdiction belonging to the delinquent state. If the Council should decide to issue such an order, it would be obligatory on all members under Article 25 of the Charter and would supersede customary rules of international law as well as conflicting treaty engagements.

Members of the United Nations are free to bring instances of noncompliance with judgments of the Court before the General Assembly, under the provisions of Article 10 of the Charter. The Assembly, however, appears to be limited to making recommendations—both to the delinquent state and to all other members.

One of the more promising methods of securing compliance with a judgment has been evolved by the framers of the treaty creating the European Coal and Steel Authority: a member state failing to carry out obligations of that treaty, including compliance with judgments of the Authority may be fined effectively by a suspension of payments due to it from the other member states.[41]

In conclusion, the basic weakness of enforcing judgments of international tribunals must be pointed out. In a national system of adjudication, the effectiveness of the courts in restraining the actions of citizens is derived, at least in part, from the hierarchy of courts established there. A decision of one judicial level can be appealed to a higher level, and ultimately a supreme court of some kind will state with authority what is the law in the case on hand. The decisions of the various courts, operating under the rule of *stare decisis*, may be expected to be inherently logical and consistent within the entire system.

But in the international sphere, a heterogeneous collection of courts, including the International Court of Justice (which in no way can be compared with a national supreme court), hands down judgments but does not manifest legal connections between the individual courts. The latter, established for specific kinds of disputes, or for particular parties,

---

[41] Article 88, Treaty Establishing the European Coal and Steel Authority, 261 *U.N. Treaty Series*, p. 221; the Court, open to litigants on March 7, 1953, was reconstituted as the Court of Justice of the European Communities on October 7, 1958.

or even for individual cases, do not form a hierarchy, nor are they bound by the rule of *stare decisis*. Hence not only do their decisions vary from court to court but there is no obligation whatever to achieve consistency, least of all with the judgments of the International Court of Justice. This decentralization, characteristic of much of international law as such, is reflected in the difficulties involved in the securing of compliance with judgments, particularly because the "clients" of international courts are, mainly, sovereign states.

INTERNATIONAL ORGANIZATIONS

Although it cannot be maintained seriously that international organizations *per se* can be treated as "methods" for the settlement of international disputes, a number of such agencies have developed procedures for the achievement of such settlements. Thus, Article 12 of the Covenant of the League of Nations provided in its original form that all members of the League would submit a dispute either to arbitration or to inquiry by the Council; judicial settlement was added later as an alternative method for arbitration. Article 13 held that all matters suitable for submission to arbitration should be so dealt with, and listed such suitable matters, although the list was somewhat vague and general (the interpretation of a treaty, questions of international law, questions of fact having a bearing on a breach of an international obligation, and the reparation to be made for such a violation). All members of the League obligated themselves not to resort to war until three months after the arbitral tribunal had made its award or the Council had reported on its inquiry.

The United Nations, as well as regional organizations such as the Organization of American States, has been active in providing such procedures, usually combining the functions of investigation and conciliation. Thus the General Assembly set up a Panel for Inquiry and Conciliation, in 1949, which consists of a list of names of qualified persons capable and willing to serve on commissions. The United Nations also has appointed numerous special commissions to deal with specific disputes and situations. It should be noted at this point, however, that, in general, international organizations attempting to provide settlements of disputes tend to emphasize procedures, such as conciliation, or limit themselves to nonobligatory recommendations. Thus they stand, on the whole, on the side of commissions and not on that of arbitral tribunals, for the latter types of agencies normally hand down binding awards or decisions.

THE UNITED NATIONS AND THE SETTLEMENT OF DISPUTES

The United Nations, on the other hand, appears to have adopted a rather novel approach to certain situations demanding peaceful solution. Faced with national intransigeance on repeated occasions, the organization has proceeded to evolve what Claude called, appropriately enough, "instances of not-quite-pacific settlement and pacific non-settlement."[42] A number of disputes have been resolved into what may be described as peaceful perpetuation: no real settlement has been achieved through investigation and conciliation procedures. Instead, provisional pacification measures have been extended indefinitely, with occasional attempts to discover whether an actual resolution of the dispute might be possible. A good example of this mode of handling quarrels by bringing about an end of actual violence and then maintaining a degree of supervision until reconciliation might be possible is the Kashmir dispute between India and Pakistan.

The Charter of the United Nations imposes on all members of the organization a duty to "settle their international disputes by peaceful means in such a manner that international peace and security, and justice, are not endangered" (Art. 2, par. 6). The Charter also states that one of the principal purposes of the United Nations is "to bring about by peaceful means, and in conformity with the principles of justice and international law, adjustment or settlement of international disputes or situations which might lead to a breach of the peace" (Art. 1, par. 1).[43] It thus appears that the *members* have an unconditional obligation to settle their disputes peacefully, whereas the *organization* has an obligation limited to the settlement of disputes or situations "which might lead to a breach of the peace." Chapter VI of the Charter, which has to do with the peaceful settlement of disputes, is expressly limited to disputes "the continuance of which is likely to endanger the maintenance of international peace and security" (Art. 33, par. 1). It is therefore quite clear that the obligations of the United Nations in this sphere are limited and do not encompass all disputes between states.

If a given dispute falls within the proper competence of an organ of the United Nations, that organ is not to deal with the merits involved, but is to decide which method of procedure or of settlement is best adapted to the dispute (Art. 33). When the parties have failed to achieve a settlement by methods of their own choice and then by the methods recommended by the organ of the United Nations in a dispute, the latter is to be referred to the United Nations again for additional recommendations; only then can the UN organ recommend actual terms of settlement. Further action on the part of the UN is contingent on a finding that the dispute is "in fact" likely to endanger peace.

On the other hand, if *all* parties to a dispute so request, the United Nations is authorized to make recommendations for a pacific settlement, regardless of the limitations of the other provisions of Chapter VI of the Charter (Art. 28).

The whole process has been designed deliberately to permit a gradual approach to each dispute and to draw a distinction between disputes in-

[42] See Claude, pp. 242–244, for an analysis of several actual examples.
[43] See Stone, pp. 186–237, for a detailed analysis.

volving "compulsory jurisdiction" on the part of the UN (disputes whose continuance are likely to endanger peace) and those involving "contingent jurisdiction" (minor disputes submitted for recommendation at the request of all parties involved).

The bulk of Charter provisions dealing with disputes or situations entailing dangers to peace confer jurisdiction over these matters on the Security Council, in accordance with the basic assumption that the Council has primary responsibility for the maintenance of international peace and security (Art. 24, par. 1). Because the Council is in permanent session, speedy action on such disputes and situations had been anticipated at the San Francisco Conference. As is only too well known, the Security Council has failed to meet that expectation.

The General Assembly, under Article 12(2), of the Charter, has unlimited jurisdiction over all questions not brought before the Security Council or no longer being handled by the Security Council. In such instances the General Assembly is free not only to discuss but also to make recommendations on the matter in question. Such recommendations may be addressed either to the parties involved, or to the Security Council, or to both at the same time (Art. 11, par. 2). The Assembly may call the attention of the Security Council to situations likely to endanger peace and security and is duty-bound ("shall") to refer to the Council any question on which action is necessary, (Art. 11, par. 2).

What happens if the Assembly requests the Security Council to take action if certain events take place, and the Council fails to take such action? This has happened, notably in the case of the Palestine question, and has been debated repeatedly, particularly in connection with the Uniting for Peace Resolution of November 3, 1950.[44] The issue at hand is a very important one: Can the General Assembly take action itself if the Security Council fails to act in accordance with its responsibilities? The late Secretary-General Dag Hammarskjöld, held, in 1957, that only the Security Council had authority to order the use of force. The General Assembly could recommend, investigate, and pronounce judgment, but it lacked the power to compel compliance with recommendations. He asserted unequivocally that the Uniting for Peace Resolution did *not* involve any transfer of power from the Security Council. The most that the General Assembly could do under Article 51 of the Charter was to recommend economic sanctions and military assistance to the victim of armed attack, but the decision to act on such recommendations rested exclusively with the governments of the individual member states.[45]

Such an interpretation appears to be fully in accord with the "intentions" of the framers of the Charter at San Francisco. Beyond doubt it is

[44] Text reprinted in 45 *A.J.I.L.* (1951), Supp., pp. 1–6; also in Stone, pp. 282–284.
[45] See Josef L. Kunz, "The Secretary-General on the Rôle of the United Nations," 52 *A.J.I.L.* (1958), pp. 300–304, at p. 303; cf. Juraj Andrassy, "Uniting for Peace," 50 *A.J.I.L.* (1956), pp. 563–582.

generally agreed among states that a recommendation, whether it issues from the Security Council or from the General Assembly, has no binding force on the parties to a dispute, unless such parties have concluded a prior agreement to regard recommendations as binding on themselves. On the other hand, certain recommendations of the General Assembly have been held to possess binding effects. The Secretary-General pointed out in his report on the Middle Eastern Question on February 11, 1957, that it appeared "appropriate to distinguish between recommendations which implement a Charter principle, which in itself is binding on Member States" and other recommendations.[46] In other words, if a recommendation of the General Assembly represents a reiteration in specific form of an obligation assumed by members under the Charter, then such a recommendation would possess binding effect on all members.

Still another avenue of reaching a peaceful settlement of a dispute through the United Nations is the adoption by the Security Council of a recommendation to refer a dispute to the International Court of Justice or to request an advisory opinion on a dispute or question. The fundamental restriction imposed here is that such disputes or questions must be "legal" in character. This limitation raises the question of what yardstick is to be employed in order to determine the "legal" character of a dispute or question.[47]

PEACEFUL SETTLEMENT OF DISPUTES THROUGH REGIONAL ORGANIZATIONS

Development of Regional Organizations. The peaceful solution of international disputes has been achieved not only through the employment of traditional procedures and through the utilization of "universal" international organizations, but also through a multitude of regional arrangements frequently cast in the form of permanent institutional frameworks.

The concept of regional organization is not a new one at all. Thucydides described what today would be termed "mutual security groupings" among the Greek city-states in his *History of the Peloponnesian Wars.* Beginning with the close of the medieval period, numerous peace projects supplied blueprints for a European community of states, complete with joint institutions and, in some cases, even collective security arrangements. Still later, regional agencies such as the Central Rhine Commission (1832) and the European Danube Commission (1856) were established. And in the Americas a slow but steady development was observed, from the forerunners of the Pan American movement through the Conferences of the American Republics into the Organization of American States (OAS)

[46] General Assembly, *Official Records, 11th Session,* Annexes, Agenda Item 66, p. 59.

[47] See Lincoln P. Bloomfield, "Law, Politics, and International Disputes," *International Conciliation,* No. 516 (January, 1958), pp. 257–316, on this vexatious problem.

created through the Bogotá Charter of 1948. It is, however, the period since 1945 that has witnessed an almost incredible growth in the number and scope of regional organizations.

One of the major reasons for this expansion has been a belief in common interests and aims on the part of the members of such a grouping. And, not much publicized but nevertheless quite evident, there has also been a strong desire to consolidate blocs and to discuss and settle disputes and policies within a group of states "belonging" together. The Soviet Union has evinced a definite inclination to remove or lessen tensions and strains in the Communist bloc by procedures involving only the members of that bloc. The United States has pursued a similar policy in Europe (NATO) and in Latin America (OAS). Such resort to intrabloc resolution of disputes does not necessarily represent a deliberate flouting of a world organization, such as the United Nations, but reflects, in effect, a commendable alternative method to bring about desired results without exposing the members of the bloc in question to interference on the part of members of other blocs.

UN Emphasis on Regional Agencies. The UN Charter itself places considerable emphasis on a resort to regional arrangements before a dispute is ultimately submitted to the United Nations. Article 33 (1) of the Charter states that, "The parties to any dispute, the continuance of which is likely to endanger the maintenance of international peace and security, shall, first of all, seek a solution by . . . resort to regional agencies or arrangements, or other peaceful means of their own choice." And paragraph 2 of the same article provides that, "The Security Council shall, when it deems necessary, call upon the parties to settle their dispute by such means." These obligations are detailed at length in Chapter VIII of the Charter ("Regional Arrangements," Arts. 52–54).

One of the unresolved problems in this sphere of pacific settlement of disputes is the relationship between the provisions cited and the rules governing the relevant powers of the Security Council. The Charter states that the provisions on regional arrangements shall not impair the applications of those portions of the Charter which deal with the submission of disputes and situations to the Security Council and with the latter's authority to investigate such disputes or situations (Art. 52, par. 4). The lack of clarity involved led to unexpected and considerable difficulties in the Guatemala Crisis of 1954. Lack of space regrettably prevents a detailed account of the confusion resulting from Security Council activities (complicated by a Russian veto) and concurrent efforts on the part of the O.A.S.[48]

---

[48] The interested reader may consult Charles G. Fenwick, "Jurisdictional Questions Involved in the Guatemalan Revolution," 48 *A.J.I.L.* (1954), p. 597–602; David M. Key, "The Organization of American States and the United Nations: Rivals or Partners?" 31 *Department of State Bulletin* (1954), pp. 115–118; and John W. Halderman, "Regional Enforcement Measures and the United Nations," 52 *Georgetown Law Journal* (Fall, 1962), p. 89–118.

Almost every regional pact and every regional organization has some provisions for the settlement of intragroup disputes, but only in the Americas and in Europe has machinery been set up. While detailed coverage of this subject lies beyond the proper limits of a general text, brief mention of key concepts appears to be desirable.

Inter-American Regional Arrangements. Disregarding the various inter-American instruments drawn up in the course of the nineteenth-century, the modern practice of creating regional arrangements in the Western Hemisphere began with the Treaty to Avoid or Prevent Conflicts Between the American States (Santiago, 1923, generally called the "Gondra Treaty"—commission of inquiry). This convention, eventually ratified by eighteen states, was followed by the General Treaty of Inter-American Arbitration (Washington, 1929) supplemented by the Protocol of Progressive Arbitration (arbitration of disputes of legal character); the General Convention of Inter-American Conciliation (Washington, 1929—conciliation commissions); the Anti-War Treaty of Non-Aggression and Conciliation (Rio de Janeiro, 1933, usually termed the Saavreda Lamas Treaty—conciliation commissions); and culminated in the Treaty on the Prevention of Controversies (Buenos Aires, 1936—bilateral mixed commissions).

Organization of American States (OAS). The Charter of the OAS, of April 30, 1948, contains only very general provisions relating to the settlement of disputes, with emphasis on listing and recommending peaceful procedures (Arts. 20–23), in a manner similar to Article 52 (3) of the UN Charter.[49] Significantly, Article 1 of the Charter declares that "within the United Nations, the Organization of American States is a regional agency." The separate American Treaty on Pacific Settlement (Pact of Bogotá), signed at the same time, established detailed procedures for the settlement of disputes between the American states.[50] The Pact of Bogotá had been intended to replace all eight of the earlier instruments listed previously. Because it has been ratified by only a minority of the American states, however, the older agreements may still be applied to disputes in the Western Hemisphere. The problem arising in the event of any dispute is, therefore, first to ascertain whether the parties are bound by any of the agreements in question; then it has to be determined in what order applicable treaties are to be utilized by the parties to the dispute.

This difficulty has been avoided on a number of occasions by referring to the provisions of still another agreement, the Inter-American Treaty of Reciprocal Assistance (Rio de Janeiro, 1947).[51] This agreement was

[49] The text of the Charter is reprinted in 46 *A.J.I.L.* (April, 1952), Supp., pp. 43–66. See also Josef L. Kunz, "The Bogotá Charter of the Organization of American States," 42 *A.J.I.L.* (1948), pp. 568–589; and consult the excellent study of Charles G. Fenwick, *The Organization of American States* (Washington, D.C.: Pan American Union, 1963), as well as Ann V. W. Thomas and A. J. Thomas, Jr., *The Organization of American States* (Dallas: Southern Methodist University Press, 1963).

[50] Text of the Pact of Bogotá in 30 *U.N. Treaty Series*, pp. 84 ff. (English text).

[51] Text in 43 *A.J.I.L.* (1949), Supp., pp. 53–58.

drafted in a form which relates it explicitly to Articles 52–54 of the Charter of the United Nations—the intentions of its framers were made quite obvious by the attendance of Trygve Lie, the then Secretary-General of the UN, at the Rio meeting (Inter-American Conference for the Maintenance of Continental Peace and Security). Article 5 of the instrument states that

The High Contracting Parties shall immediately send to the Security Council of the United Nations, in conformity with Articles 51 and 54 of the Charter of the United Nations, complete information concerning the activities undertaken or in contemplation in the exercise of the right of self-defense or for the purpose of maintaining inter-American peace and security.

Articles 7 and 8 of the treaty provide for procedures for the re-establishment and maintenance of peace in the hemisphere system, whereas Article 2 outlines the commitments of the contracting parties to settle local disputes—in a manner intentionally reminiscent of Article 52 (2) of the Charter.

One of the most common and useful procedures adopted by the American states has been consultation. This concept has been embodied in a series of treaties, beginning with the Convention for the Maintenance, Preservation and Reestablishment of Peace (Buenos Aires, 1936), and normally functions through consultative meetings of ministers of foreign affairs. Currently the procedure invoked when a dispute threatens follows this pattern: The Council of the OAS convokes a meeting of the Organ of Consultation, but does not actually hold such a meeting at all. The Council can, after such a call, operate itself as a provisional organ and is empowered to take such steps as may be necessary. If required, an Investigating Committee is dispatched to the scene of the dispute and the recommendations contained in the committee's report commonly represent the basis of the decisions made by the Council acting as a provisional organ of consultation. Most of the decisions have been accepted as binding by the parties to the dispute.

The most promising inter-American instrument for the peaceful settlement of disputes may yet be the Pact of Bogotá which codified all the various methods adopted in the Americas between the two World Wars. The parties to the treaty agree to settle their controversies by regional pacific procedures before referring them to the United Nations (Art. 2). Once such a procedure has been initiated, no other can be started until the earlier one has been concluded (Art. 4). Although none of the procedures supplied through the treaty can be applied to matters in the domestic jurisdiction of states, either party to a dispute may submit to the International Court of Justice the preliminary question, whether the controversy concerns a matter of domestic jurisdiction (Art. 4). Article 7 provides that the parties will not make diplomatic representations in order to protect their nations, or to refer a controversy to a court of international jurisdiction for that purpose, when the said nationals have had available the means to place their case before competent domestic courts of the respective State.

This provision was rejected by the United States by means of a reservation.

The treaty contains not only the expected detailed provisions for commissions of investigation and conciliation, but arbitration, and for judicial procedure, but also establishes a permanent panel of American conciliators. In the event of a dispute, each party is to select two members from that panel and the four conciliators are then to choose a fifth one (Art. 19). Arbitral tribunals are to be chosen from a list of twenty names chosen from the general panel of members of the Permanent Court of Arbitration at The Hague (Art. 40).

In the event conciliation fails to bring about a solution to a dispute and if the parties have not agreed on arbitration, the dispute is to go to the International Court of Justice at the referral of either party (Arts. 31-32). If the Court decides that it has no jurisdiction because the dispute is not of a legal nature, then the parties are required to resort to arbitration (Art. 35). In case a party fails to comply with a decision of the Court or with an arbitral award, the other party is entitled to request a Meeting of Consultation of the Ministers of Foreign Affairs, which is to decide on measures to assure compliance with the decision or award (Art. 50).

Regional Arrangements in Europe. Development of regional arrangements and organization in Europe has been even more extensive and also perhaps more important than it has been in the Americas.

The earliest important regional arrangement following World War II was the Treaty of Economic, Social and Cultural Collaboration and Collective Self-Defense (Brussels Treaty) of March 17, 1948.[52] The contracting parties agreed to settle all legal disputes between them by reference to the International Court of Justice, subject only to such reservations as had been made by them when each accepted the jurisdiction of that Court. All nonlegal disputes were to be subject to conciliation procedures. If a dispute between parties to the treaty involved both legal and nonlegal matters (a "mixed dispute"), either party was conceded the right to "insist that the judicial settlement of the legal questions shall precede conciliation" (Art. 8). The Brussels Treaty itself lacked detailed provisions as to the conciliation procedures to be employed; instead, all contracting parties were to observe the conciliation provisions of the Geneva General Act for the Pacific Settlement of Disputes (1928).[53] Two territorial disputes between parties to the Brussels

---

[52] Text in 19 *U.N. Treaty Series*, p. 51, and 43 *A.J.I.L.* (1949), Supp., pp. 59-63. Much of the discussion which follows is based on the excellent summary in Kaplan-Katzenbach.

[53] Text in Manley O. Hudson, *International Legislation*, Vol. IV, pp. 2529 ff.

Treaty have been submitted thus far to the jurisdiction of the International Court: the Franco-British dispute concerning title to the Minquiers and Ecrehos islets and the Belgian-Netherlands dispute over certain lands in the communes of Baerle-Duc and Baarle-Nassau. In both instances the parties in question complied with the judgments of the Court.

The Council of Europe did not have any provisions in its constitutional instruments for the settlement of disputes among its members. After much urging on the part of the Consultative Assembly of the organization, a European Convention for the Peaceful Settlement of Disputes was evolved and ultimately signed on April 29, 1957.[54] This instrument provides for reference of all legal disputes between the contracting parties to the International Court: nonlegal disputes are to be settled through conciliation and if this fails, by arbitration; the provisions for the settlement of mixed disputes are patterned after the corresponding portions of the Brussels Treaty. One of the provisions, relating to arbitration, is rather unusual: Article 26 provides that

If nothing is laid down in the special agreement or no special agreement [*compromis*] has been made, the Tribunal shall decide *ex aequo et bono*, having regard to the general principles of international law, while respecting the contractual obligations and the final decisions of international tribunals which are binding on the parties.

European Coal and Steel Community. The Treaty Establishing the European Coal and Steel Community (Paris, April 18, 1951), created a Court of Justice "to ensure the rule of law in the interpretation and application" of the convention and of the regulations issued for its execution.[55] This Court was granted jurisdiction over appeals by any of the six member states or by the Council of Ministers of the Community "for the annulment of decisions and recommendations of the High Authority on the grounds of lack of competence, major violations of procedure, violation of the Treaty or of any rule of law relating to its application, or abuse of power" (Art. 33). Interestingly enough, enterprises as well as producers' associations were also given a right of appeal. The Court has the authority to assess damages against the Community where injuries result from "an official fault" of the Community in violation of the Treaty (Art. 40), to assess damages against any official of the Community in cases where injury results from "a personal fault" in the performance of his duties, and against the Community if the injured party is unable to recover from the official (Art. 40). The Court has the right to decide disputes among member states concerning the application of the Treaty only when the dispute

---

[54] Text in *International Court of Justice, Yearbook*, 1958–59, pp. 228 ff; see also Kaplan–Katzenbach, pp. 329–330.

[55] Text in 46 *A.J.I.L.* (1952), p. 107–148; see Articles 31–45. See also Kaplan–Katzenbach, pp. 323–324.

cannot be settled by another procedure provided for in the treaty (Art. 89).

The Court of Justice has been quite busy with interpretative decisions and has also set aside a few decisions of the High Authority.

European Economic Community. More significant than the fact that the Court of Justice commenced operations on an apparently satisfactory basis is the extensive expansion of its jurisdictional responsibilities which took place in 1957. In that year the Treaty Establishing the European Economic Community (Rome, March 25, 1957)[56] and the Treaty Establishing the European Atomic Energy Community (Euratom), of the same date,[57] both incorporated the jurisdiction of the Court of Justice.

North Atlantic Treaty Organization. On the other hand, the North Atlantic Treaty (Washington, April 4, 1949)[58] does not contain specific provisions for the settlement of disputes among the contracting parties. All reference to the question is limited to a general obligation (Art. 1) to settle international disputes by peaceful means in such a manner that international peace and security are not endangered. In view of the lack of procedural details in the treaty, the North Atlantic Council decided in December, 1956, that disputes not settled directly [by negotiation] should be submitted to good-offices procedures within the NATO framework before member states resorted to any other international agency. In the case of legal disputes, submission to a judicial tribunal was recommended, while economic disputes might well be considered in the appropriate specialized economic organizations. The Secretary-General of NATO was authorized to offer his good offices to any members involved in a dispute and, with their consent, to initiate or facilitate procedures of inquiry, mediation, conciliation, or arbitration.

The North Atlantic Council itself has dealt directly with a number of disputes among the member states, and the Secretary-General of NATO offered his good offices in order to effect conciliation of the acrimonious dispute, over the island of Cyprus, between Greece, Turkey, and the United Kingdom. The Greek government felt itself unable to accept the offer, which therefore was abandoned; in 1958, however, a renewal of the offer was accepted by the three parties and with the assistance of both the Secretary-General and the Council of NATO a mutually satisfactory agreement was achieved in February, 1959. The resulting Cyprus settlement lasted without major crises until the outbreak of civil war in 1964 and the despatch of international peacekeeping forces under UN auspices.

It should be noted that the Pacific Security Treaty between Australia,

---

[56] See Kaplan–Katzenbach, pp. 324–327; the text of the treaty with related agreements, may be found in 51 *A.J.I.L.* (1957), Supp., pp. 865–954.

[57] Text, with related agreements, *ibid.*, pp. 955–1004; consult also Hugo J. Hahn, "Euratom: The Conception of an International Personality," 71 *Harvard Law Review* (1958), pp. 1001–1056; and Kaplan-Katzenbach, pp. 327–329.

[58] Text in 43 *A.J.I.L.* (1949), Supp., pp. 159–162.

New Zealand, and the United States (ANZUS Treaty) of 1951 [59] as well as the Southeast Asia Collective Defense Treaty (1954)[60] both follow, in essence, the provisions (or basic lack thereof) concerning the settlement of disputes found in the North Atlantic Treaty.

SUGGESTED READINGS

PEACEFUL SETTLEMENT: GENERAL

Brierly, pp. 346–396; Claude, pp. 197–222; Svarlien, 284–329. Arthur Lall, *Modern International Negotiation* (New York and London: Columbia University Press, 1966); Oran R. Young, *The Intermediaries: Third Parties in International Crises* (Princeton: Princeton University Press, 1967); Arthur Larson, *When Nations Disagree: A Handbook on Peace Through Law* (Baton Rouge: Louisiana State University Press, 1961); Arthur Lall, *The U.N. and the Middle East Crisis, 1967* (New York: Columbia University Press, 1968).

ARBITRATION

J. L. Simpson and Hazel Fox, *International Arbitration: Law and Practice* (New York: Praeger, 1959); Stephen M. Schwebel and J. Gillis Wetter, "Arbitration and the Exhaustion of Local Remedies," 60 *A.J.I.L.* (1966), pp. 484–501; Paul B. Larsen, "The United States–Italy Air Transport Arbitration: Problems of Treaty Interpretation and Enforcement," *ibid.*, 61 (1967), pp. 496–520.

ADJUDICATION

C. Wilfred Jenks, *The Prospects of International Adjudication* (London: Stevens & Sons, Ltd.; Dobbs Ferry, N.Y.: Oceana Publications, 1964); Milton Katz, *The Relevance of International Adjudication* (Cambridge: Harvard University Press, 1968); J. H. W. Verzijl, *The Jurisprudence of the World Court* (A Case by Case Commentary). (Leyden: A. W. Sijthoff, 1965, 2 vols.); Shabtai Rosenne, *The Law and Practice of the International Court* (Leyden: A. W. Sijthoff, 1965, 2 vols.); Ibrahim F. I. Shihata, *The Power of the International Court to Determine Its Own Jurisdiction: Compétence de la Compétence* (The Hague: Martinus Nijhoff, 1965); Salo Engel, "The New Charter of the Organization of Central American States," 58 *A.J.I.L.* (1964), pp. 127–134 (text of charter, pp. 134–138, with Arts. 14–16 dealing with a new Central American "court of justice"); Leo Gross, "Some Observations on the International Court of Justice," 56 *A.J.I.L.* (1962), pp. 33–62; Manley O. Hudson, "The Twenty-Fourth Year of the World Court," 40 *A.J.I.L.* (1946), pp. 1–52 [a comparison of the Statutes of the two World Courts], supplemented by his "The Succession of the International Court of Justice to the Permanent Court of International Justice," *ibid.*, 51 (1957), pp. 569–573; Leo Gross, "Limitations upon the Judicial Function" [Re: *Case Concerning the Northern Cameroons*

[59] Text in 46 *A.J.I.L.* (1952), Supp., p. 93.
[60] Text in 31 *Department of State Bulletin* (1954), pp. 393–396.

(*Cameroon* v. *United Kingdom*), *Preliminary Objections.* International Court of Justice, *I.C.J. Reports, 1963*, p. 15], 58 *A.J.I.L.* (1964), pp. 415–431; D. W. Greig, "The Advisory Jurisdiction of the International Court and the Settlement of Disputes between States," 15 *International and Comparative Law Quarterly* (1966), pp. 325–368.

ENFORCEMENT OF JUDGMENTS

E. K. Nantwi, *The Enforcement of International Judicial Decisions and Arbitral Awards in Public International Law* (Leyden: A. W. Sijthoff, 1966); W. M. Reisman, "The Enforcement of International Judgments," 63 *A.J.I.L.* (1969), pp. 1–27; Oscar Schachter, "The Enforcement of International Judicial and Arbitral Decisions," *ibid.,* 54 (1960), pp. 1–24.

COURT OF JUSTICE (EUROPEAN COMMUNITIES)

Werner Feld, *The Court of European Communities: New Dimensions in International Adjudication* (The Hague: Martinus Nijhoff, 1964); the interesting analysis of the early activities of the Court in Eric Stein, "The Court of Justice of the European Coal and Steel Community: 1954–1957," 51 *A.J.I.L.* (1957), pp. 821–829; D. G. Valentine, "The Government of the Netherlands v. The High Authority of the European Steel Community—Decision of the Court of Justice of the European Communities," 10 *International and Comparative Law Quarterly* (1961), pp. 337–338; Dennis Thompson, "The *Bosch* Case, Court of Justice, European Communities," *ibid.,* 11 (1962), pp. 721–741; Stefan A. Riesenfeld, "The Decisions of the Court of Justice of the European Communities," 56 *A.J.I.L.* (1962), pp. 724–728, a review of the six volumes of the Court's decisions from 1954 through 1960; A. M. Donner, "National Law and the Case Law of the Court of Justice of the European Communities," 1 *Common Market Law Review* (1963), pp. 8–16.

Cases

The Dogger Bank Case (Great Britain–Russia), Commission of Inquiry, 1905, in James B. Scott, *Hague Court Reports*, pp. 403 ff.

N.V. Algemene Transporten Expeditie Onderneming van Gend & Loos v. *Netherlands Fiscal Administration*, Court of Justice of the European Communities, 1963, Case No. 26/62, digested in 58 *A.J.I.L.* (1964), pp. 194–196, and see the extensively documented analysis of this decision by Stefan A. Riesenfeld and Richard M. Buxbaum, *ibid.,* pp. 152–159.

Case Concerning the Barcelona Traction, Light and Power Company, Ltd. (New Application, 1962; *Belgium* v. *Spain*). *Preliminary Objections. I.C.J. Reports, 1964*, p. 6; excerpted at length in 59 *A.J.I.L.* (1965), pp. 131–160.

Commission of the European Economic Community v. *Government of the Republic of Italy*, Court of Justice of the European Communities, December 19, 1961, digested in 57 *A.J.I.L.* (1963), pp. 431–433.

24
Coercive Self-help Short of War

THE absence of a central authority able and willing to assist a state in obtaining justice and a satisfaction of legitimate claims has meant that when peaceful methods of settling a dispute fail, the state will resort to self-help. This means that a universal need to rely on one's own efforts continues to exist. There is no doubt that each instance of self-help, whether it occurs in pursuit of legitimate goals, in the protection of legal rights, or as an accompaniment of aggression, creates tensions, confusion, and a depreciation of the effectiveness of both law and peaceful settlement. On the other hand, the presence of methods of self-help short of war, in the twentieth century, represents a characteristic reflection of the state of transition in which international law and the community of nations are today. Some day in the future may see the emergence of a supranational authority able to assure the settlement of disputes without coercion, but until that time comes, self-help may be expected to be a part of international relations.

Although the Charter of the United Nations would seem to condemn methods of self-help based on the use of force short of war, the fact remains that such methods are still in use, precisely because the condition stated in the opening sentence of this chapter continues to prevail. Most of the methods of self-help described below can be applied only by a stronger state against a weaker state; however, in most instances, the basic idea has been to relate, in some fashion, the degree of pressure or even force to the offense or wrong committed. Third states tend to be unaffected by the procedures in question and to assume the position of watchful bystanders unless or until their own particular interests are involved.

The employment of coercive self-help obviously represents an anomaly in view of the fact that since 1918 a number of multipartite treaties have called for the peaceful settlement of disputes, a trend climaxed by the explicit formulations found in the Charter of the United Nations. The basic reasons for the continued use of self-help techniques may be listed quite succinctly: (1) the failure of the leading powers to take seriously the commitments mentioned; (2) a paralysis, on too many occasions, of the League and, later, of the United Nations machinery for the peaceful resolution of international differences; and (3) an apparent conviction on the part of many states that at least minor disputes could be settled efficiently and in their favor by the employment of self-help measures. This last attitude appears to be based either on the belief that all possible peaceful measures had been exhausted without success or on the suspicion that the employment of such measures would have resulted in a decision or solution favoring the other party involved.

SELF-HELP TECHNIQUES

Rupture of Diplomatic Relations.[1] Breaking off diplomatic relations with another state, although not actually involving coercion or force, should be mentioned at this point, for it frequently precedes the utilization of some coercive technique in an effort to settle a dispute or to obtain justice. It therefore represents a warning by one state to another that matters had reached a point where normal relationships were no longer possible and beyond which harsher methods were likely to be applied. The ironic result of the step is, of course, that peaceful negotiation is made extremely difficult, unless outsiders proffer their good offices or indicate their willingness to mediate the dispute. In other words, at the very time when discussion and negotiation would appear to be most needed, a rupture of diplomatic relations makes such negotiations virtually impossible.

A brand-new version of the *genus* boycott (see p. 503) came into being on May 14, 1963, when the United States government inaugurated a "limited diplomatic boycott" of the Haitian government of President François Duvalier. In an effort to express disapproval of the unconstitutional extension of Duvalier's tenure of office, the "boycott" introduced a no-contact policy between the U.S. embassy officials in Port-au-Prince and Haitian officials. The gesture obviously and admittedly represented a temporary, halfway measure, falling short of a suspension of diplomatic relations between the two countries. The policy was abandoned again on June 3, 1963.

Retorsion. The traditional definition of retorsion represents it as the commission of an unfriendly but legal act, undertaken in response to a prior, equally unfriendly but legal act by the other party to the dispute. On the other hand, such a legal response to an *illegal* and unfriendly prior act would also be entitled to the label of retorsion. The latter, in effect, is a lawful act undertaken in answer to an act in the legislative, administrative, or judicial sphere to which another state objects. Because retorsion involves no illegal action, both parties have to see to it that the activities in question violate neither general international law nor their respective treaty obligations.

The actual steps comprising retorsion vary from case to case; their severity normally depends on the initial act to which exception was taken.

[1] Consult Whiteman, Vol. II, pp. 30–34.

Among the causes of retorsion frequently cited in the literature of international law are discriminatory tariff rates, discriminatory treatment of aliens, and similar acts not governed by treaties. Generally, retorsion consists of retaliation in kind—if state A withdraws nontreaty concessions or privileges from nationals of state B, the latter will proceed to duplicate this action against nationals of state A living in the territory of B. A good example of retorsion was supplied by the United States at the beginning of 1955, when, in response to travel restrictions imposed by the U.S.S.R. on foreign diplomats, the United States government barred Russian diplomats from travel in large portions of the United States, except for certain "open cities" in otherwise closed areas.

Reprisals. The following is a definition of *modern* reprisals: "Illegal acts undertaken in retaliation against a state to compel it to agree to a satisfactory settlement of a dispute originating in an earlier illegal act done by it." In earlier centuries, going back to the Middle Ages, private citizens (usually merchants) who had suffered injury or loss at the hands of aliens compensated themselves by seizing the property of foreigners who were fellow nationals of the offender. When this practice led in time to grave abuses, the governments of many states intervened and regularized this form of self-help by issuing letters of marque and reprisal. Armed with such instruments of authority, the injured parties could then lawfully prey on the nationals of the state whose citizens had caused the original injury in order to make good the losses suffered by seizure of goods and ships. The obvious consequence was, of course, that the owners of the seized items would secure similar authority from their own government—and the process could go on almost indefinitely. The process of seizing private alien property under government authority was termed "special reprisals," but in essence was a modern resumption of the medieval practice of private warfare.

Special reprisals were abolished, initially on an individual country basis, then by all the states that signed the Treaty of Paris in 1856. Since that year, reprisals by private individuals have been illegal and only states may have recourse to this method of self-help. Such action must then be taken either on behalf of the state itself, if it believes itself to have been injured illegally, or by the state on behalf of its injured citizens.

It may appear astonishing that such remedies still exist, but their great and overriding advantage lies in the fact that immediate redress is afforded. The hostilities that sometimes ensue are usually carefully characterized as reprisal and most states have been rather reluctant to create a state of hostilities incommensurate with the original wrong claimed. The major limitations commonly associated with the acts of reprisal are that such acts are not to be started unless and until efforts at a peaceful settlement of the dispute have failed, that reprisals are to cease as soon as the offending state has made reparations for its illegal act (or has ceased its practice, as the case may be), that reprisals may not be instituted against reprisals, that they must not be employed when their application would injure third parties, and that the acts of reprisal are not out of proportion to the original injury suffered.

Modern reprisals have taken many forms. On occasion they have involved nonperformance of treaty obligations, invasion of the other party's territory, capture of some of the offending party's nationals, freezing the other party's assets, and seizure of any property belonging to the offending state. At times even the bombardment of the other party's territory and towns has been undertaken in reprisal, such as the Italian bombardment and subsequent temporary occupation of the island of Corfu in 1923 when Greece refused to admit responsibility and to pay compensation for the death of an Italian general serving on a boundary commission.[2]

The classic case of reprisal, modern style, complete with explanations of the limitations surrounding the concept, was the Naulilaa incident of 1914:

NAULILAA INCIDENT ARBITRATION

Portugal-Germany, Arbitral Decision of July 31, 1928, concerning the
Responsibility of Germany for Damage Caused in the Portuguese
Colonies of South Africa. (2 U.N. Reports of International
Arbitral Awards [*1949*], *pp. 1011 ff.*)

FACTS

In October, 1914, when Portugal was still a neutral, a German official and two German officers of South-West Africa were killed and two others interned by members of the Portuguese frontier garrison at Naulilaa in Portuguese Angola. The governor of the German colony ordered reprisals to be undertaken and sent German military forces into Angola. In the course of a short period of fighting, the fort of Cuangar and four minor posts along the Angola border were attacked and destroyed. The invaders also compelled the Portuguese garrison to evacuate Naulilaa. The indirect result of the Portuguese reverses was a minor native uprising, accompanied by a considerable amount of looting and pillaging. The German forces re-treated into South-West Africa as soon as the Portuguese frontier garrisons had been defeated.

Subsequent investigation showed that the original incident had been caused by the inability of the German officials and officers to understand Portuguese. The commander of the Naulilaa post, receiving no acceptable reply from the group, believed himself to be in danger of attack and ordered his men to open fire.

After some acrimonious exchanges, Germany and Portugal agreed to submit the question of responsibility to arbitration. The length of the war and other factors delayed the arbitral decision until July 31, 1928.

ISSUE

Was the German governor correct in ordering an invasion of Angola in the

---

[2] Consult James Barros, *The Corfu Incident of 1923: Mussolini and the League of Nations* (Princeton, N.J.: Princeton University Press, 1965), in which it is pointed out that the Commission of Jurists appointed by the Council of the League did not commit itself unequivocally on the legality, under the League Covenant, of reprisals involving the use of force, a legality asserted by the Italian Government.

name of reprisal? If not, was Germany responsible for damages?

The (three-man) tribunal found Germany responsible for all damages done by way of reprisal.

REASONING

1. Reprisals "are an act of appropriate justice of the injured state, in retaliation for an unredressed act of the offending state contrary to international law. They have for an object to suspend temporarily, in the relations between the two states, the observance of such or such a rule of international law. . . . They will be illegal unless a previous act in violation of international law has furnished the justification. They tend to impose on the offending state reparation for the offense or a return to legality and avoidance of new offenses."

2. The arbitrators held that since the death of the German officials was not the consequence of an act contrary to international law by the Portuguese authorities, the justification for reprisals was lacking.

The disarming and interning of German officials was a lawful right— and, indeed, a duty of the neutral Portuguese, because the Germans were "belligerents under arms" who had intruded into neutral territory.

The German authorities in South-West Africa had not attempted to secure a peaceful settlement before resorting to reprisals—this made the reprisals illegal.

The accidental death of the German officials was disproportionately smaller to a military campaign of almost three weeks, with the destruction of six Portuguese posts involved. In other words, the German authorities had violated the necessity of a proportionality between the reprisal and the offense alleged to have been committed. Although "international law does not require such proportionality . . . reprisals out of all proportion to the act which has motivated them" had to be considered as excessive, consequently as illegal.

According to compilations of the United States Department of State, some forty-eight instances of the use of military force in peacetime reprisals were recorded between 1811 and 1911. The United States thus utilized this form of self-help on numerous occasions.

On one celebrated occasion, American marines were landed in the Mexican port of Veracruz in 1914, after General Huerta had refused to apologize for the arrest of several American sailors. In this instance, Congress had passed a joint resolution authorizing the utilization of military force. Mexican charges that the occupation of Veracruz was an act of war were denied by the Department of State which insisted that no state of war existed and that, instead, a temporary occupation represented an act of redress, a reprisal.

A more recent celebrated case of reprisals occurred in 1937 during the Spanish Civil War. On the morning of Saturday, May 29, Spanish government aircraft sighted the German pocket battleship *Deutschland* engaged in international "neutrality patrol" duties, lying off the island of Iviza in the Mediterranean. Angry at German aid to the Franco forces, the crews of the aircraft appear to have been unable to resist the temptation to attack the warship. They proceeded to bomb it without warning and succeeded in killing a number of ship's officers then eating breakfast.

On Monday morning, May 31, the sister ship of the damaged craft, the pocket battleship *Admiral Scheer*, and four destroyers bombarded the Spanish (government-controlled) seaport of Almeria at dawn. Almeria was a fortified port and its coastal batteries returned the fire of the German ships, which withdrew about three-quarters of an hour after the attack began. Germany notified the International Non-Intervention Committee in London on the same day that the action had been taken in reprisal for the attack on the *Deutschland*.[3]

More recently, eight British fighter aircraft destroyed, on March 28, 1964, with rockets and shells a fort of the Republic of Yemen, across the frontier from the then South Arabian Federation. This action was taken in reprisal against repeated Yemeni air attacks on the territory of the Federation. The latter had invoked its mutual defense treaty with Great Britain after attacks by Yemeni and Egyptian planes had extended over a period of over two weeks.[4]

Another recent instance of reprisals involving the use of force related to the continuing "informal hostilities" between Israel and its Arab neighbors, following the "Six-Day War" of 1967. Terrorism, sabotage, artillery duels and air strikes on an escalating scale created mounting tensions in the Middle East since July, 1967. In many instances, retaliation appeared to be out of proportion to the initial offense charged, but on occasion either side maintained that its retaliatory act was in response to a number of prior acts of the other side. The most publicized reprisal by the time of writing was an attack by Israeli forces on the airport at Beirut, Lebanon, with an estimated damage to Lebanese aircraft of $100 million, in reprisal for an Arab terrorist attack on an Israeli passenger plane at Athens and several bombing attacks in Israel itself.[5]

The current legal status of peacetime reprisals is not too clear.[6] The Covenant of the League of Nations did not prohibit coercive measures of self-help short of war. On the other hand, the Charter of the United Nations requires the members of the organization to settle their disputes by peaceful means and to refrain from the threat or use of force.

---

[3] *The New York Times*, June 1, 1937, pp. 1, 2. Although the German "reprisal" did take place during a war, its nature appears closer to orthodox reprisals than to wartime reprisals undertaken by "official" belligerents.

[4] *The New York Times*, March 29, 1964, p. 15.

[5] See *The New York Times*, December 29, 1968, *et seq.*; 93 *Time* (January 3, 1969), pp. 26–27, and *ibid.* (January 10, 1969), pp. 27–28. Concerning the Israel-Arab conflict in general, consult the excellent summary by Robert H. Forward, Jr., *et al.*, "The Arab-Israeli War and International Law," 9 *Harvard International Law Journal* (1968), pp. 232–276. See also Security Council resolution 262 (1968), of December 31, 1968, in 8 *International Legal Materials* (1969), p. 445.

[6] See Ignaz Seidl-Hohenveldern, "Reprisals and the Taking of Private Property," 9 *Tijdschrift* (Special Issue, October, 1962), pp. 470–479.

The question which remains to be settled is whether reprisals undertaken by one member against another member do fall under the Charter prohibition *if* force in the military sense is not utilized. Presumably reprisals involving force could be said to be legal only if undertaken under the authority of some organ of the United Nations, such as by the Security Council under Articles 41 and 42 of the Charter. Here we see one of the paradoxes of modern international law. Under general international law, states have the unquestioned right to use military force as sanctions in the case of a delict, either in the form of war or of military reprisals, in addition to the equally unquestioned right to use such military force in self-protection by way of self-help. And, on the other hand, nonmilitary reprisals could be thought of as sanctions, because they presuppose a delict on the part of the "offending" state—even if the existence of that delict or delinquency was determined by the state carrying out the reprisals in a given case. The Charter prohibits resort to force except on a temporary basis in self-defense, in the event of an armed attack, a prohibition extending, at the time of writing, to 126 states. But force has been employed by member states in the exercise of reprisals. The least that can be said about such acts is that they violate the spirit, if not the letter, of Article 2 (3–4) of the Charter. Expediency appears to prevail, in this case, over the letter of the law, and states, generally speaking, utilize reprisals in disregard of the Charter.

Reprisals not involving force would appear to be legitimate as long as they do not threaten the peace. And it should be kept in mind that reprisals involving force are normally carefully stipulated not to correspond to a state of war, and are (normally) ended as soon as the objective in question has been achieved—namely, the ending of the delict (and sometimes reparation for the injury or damage caused by such delict).

The writer believes that, in the case of serious delicts, peacetime reprisals, even if they involve the utilization of force, are legitimate, provided they meet the three basic conditions laid down in the *Naulilaa Incident Arbitration* award: (1) the act of the offending state must have been illegal; (2) retaliatory "illegal" action must have been preceded by "a request for redress which has been unavailing"; and (3) a reasonable degree of proportionality must be shown to exist between initial offense and retaliatory action.[7] The problem which has plagued international lawyers in connection with many instances of reprisals, such as the Arab-Israeli incidents mentioned earlier, has been that the second of the three conditions has been lacking: reprisal has followed almost automatically the commission of the initial illegal act. Although the justification of peacetime reprisals employing force may appear to many as unorthodox, this writer believes that the members of the United Nations have, in practice (consen-

---

[7] See A. V. W. Thomas and A. J. Thomas, Jr., *Non-Intervention: The Law and Its Import in the Americas* (Dallas: Southern Methodist University Press, 1956), at pp. 136–138, and Hackworth, Vol. VI, pp. 152–153.

sus by action) suspended the application of the Charter to reprisals meeting, in essence, the previously listed conditions.

Embargo. An embargo represented at one time a specialized form of reprisal. Its early form, following the disappearance of the special reprisal, consisted of the detention in port of vessels flying the flag of the offending state in order to coerce the latter into remedying the wrong done. Seldom did such detention represent the prelude to confiscation, but the latter did take place on occasion when the offending state refused to grant redress for the wrongs done. The best-known American example of this type of embargo was established by Congress in the Act of December, 1807. That measure applied to all vessels, foreign as well as domestic, found in American ports; however, an exemption was granted to any foreign vessel willing to leave in ballast only.

Some states went further in the application of the older version of the embargo. In certain instances, vessels flying the flag of a particular foreign state were detained in port when the outbreak of war with that state was foreseen: detention made the subsequent arrest and condemnation as prizes of war much easier and assured the detaining state of a ready supply of every ship available for seizure. The legality of such a maneuver is highly questionable, however, and it cannot be said to fall into the category of self-help.

On the other hand, certain states were not content to detain vessels of an offending state in their ports but sent their warships out on the high seas to hunt down, arrest, and bring home for detention vessels flying the flag of the offending state. Many sources make use of such action by Great Britain in 1839 as a classic example. In that year, Great Britain, then involved in a quarrel over alleged violations of treaty rights and obligations by the Kingdom of the Two Sicilies, placed an embargo on all vessels of that state found in ports under British authority and, in addition, ordered the British navy to seize all Neapolitan and Sicilian ships found in their own national waters or on the high seas and bring them into British-controlled ports for detention. When the Two Sicilies settled the dispute in a manner satisfactory to Great Britain, all seized ships were returned to the control of their rightful owners. Because an embargo, when used in reprisal, does not normally endanger the peace nor constitute direct utilization of force against a state, the device would appear to be lawful even under the terms of the UN Charter, *provided* the conditions associated with other forms of reprisal are met. (See Chapter 30 for a discussion of wartime embargoes.)

The twentieth century saw the birth of new forms of the embargo, either as an action by a single state or as a collective act of a number of states, to prevent an alleged or potential aggressor from increasing its stockpiles of essential war materials and supplies.

This means that, on the outbreak of a conflict, individual neutral states may prohibit the export of war materials to either or both belligerents by placing an embargo on such exports. Similarly, embargos have been used to prevent the shipments of arms, ammunitions, and so forth, to countries involved in a civil war. Examples of these modern versions of the embargo are numerous: in 1912 the United States prohibited the export of arms and munitions to Mexico, and in 1951 the General Assembly of the United Nations recommended by a vote of 47–0, with thirteen abstentions, to all member states the establishment of an embargo on arms, implements of war, and on a list of strategic materials to all areas under control of Communist China and the government of North Korea.[8]

More recently, embargoes in the form of export prohibitions have been undertaken, individually or collectively, to force countries to cease assertedly illegal or undesirable activities or to prevent them from utilizing certain categories of goods, mostly war materials, for purposes objected to by the states instigating the embargoes. For purposes of illustration, one can cite the provisions of the 1921 Geneva Narcotics Convention which called for a joint prohibition of exports of narcotics to a country or area found to be amassing excessive quantities of narcotics, and, secondly, the recommendations of the Co-ordinating Committee of the League of Nations in 1935. The group, acting in accordance with Article 16 of the Covenant, recommended a wide variety of measures of nonintercourse aimed at Italy, including a prohibition of arms shipments to Italy, of the floating abroad of Italian public and private loans, of an extension of credit to Italian agencies or corporations, a prohibition on the importation of goods from territory under Italian control, and an embargo on the exports of specified goods, mostly in the category of war materials.

Still another variety of embargo was undertaken by the United States when all sales (public and private) of military equipment to the Republic of South Africa were halted by January 1, 1964, pending an end to that country's racial segregation policies. This step was taken after the United States government had earlier (1962) forbidden the sale to the South African government of all arms and military equipment which could be used by that government to enforce segregation either in South Africa proper or in Southwest Africa.

In May, 1951, the General Assembly approved a "strategic" embargo against mainland China and North Korea, involving arms, ammunition, atomic energy materials, petroleum, and any other commodity usable in the production of arms. Each member state was to determine which of its exports to China fell into the proscribed categories and then was to place an embargo on shipment. The main reason behind the embargo was increasing Chinese participation in the Korean War.[9] More recently, in November, 1962, the General Assembly voted an embargo—later commonly styled a boycott—on trade with the Republic of South Africa and

[8] See 57 *Time* (May 28, 1951), p. 28, for a good analysis of the loopholes in the measure as passed.

[9] 57 *Time* (May 28, 1951), p. 28.

a denial of harbor and airport facilities to that country's ships and aircraft. Also, the thirteen-member Arab League established a Boycott Office to correlate a ban on trade with Israel and on any foreign companies (such as Ford, RCA, and so on) investing, or granting franchises to concerns, in Israel.[10]

Other examples of embargoes of recent years include, among others, the O.A.S. measures adopted against Cuba on July 25, 1964,[11] and the economic sanctions applied first by Great Britain and then by the United Nations (including the United States) against Rhodesia.[12] In December, 1966, the United States embargoed more than 80 per cent of American imports from Rhodesia, following the decision, taken on December 16, of the Security Council to impose mandatory selective economic sanctions on twelve key Rhodesian export commodities.[13]

One interesting, and as yet unresolved, consequence of this Security Council action was a formal request, on February 3, 1967, by Portugal to the Secretary-General, for an indemnity amounting to $28 million for losses resulting from the imposition of sanctions against Rhodesia. The Portuguese request asserted that the economy of the province of Mozambique had suffered grave financial and economic effects as the result of the sanctions, particularly with respect to ports, railroads, and a pipeline, and that compensation should be arranged through discussions between Portugal and the Security Council.[14]

Subsequently the Security Council voted (15 to 0) on May 29, 1968, in favor of an almost total economic embargo against Rhodesian exports (to replace the selective measure of 1966). This action was coupled with a call for an embargo on virtually all exports from member states to Rhodesia. In addition, the Council voted in favor of an imposition of restrictions on travel (a ban on the honoring of Rhodesian passports and a prohibition on linking railroads and airlines of the member states to such facilities of Rhodesia) and on financial transactions, including a ban on the transmission of funds to Rhodesia.

Boycott. A modern form of retaliatory action involving the suspension of business and trade relations on the part of nationals of the injured state with the citizens of the offending state. As long as this concerted action is truly voluntary and does not involve any pressure or persuasion from the government, or any official act in its support, the boycott does not involve state responsibility and is, indeed, outside the purview of international law. If, on the other hand, the government of the injured state

---

[10] See, *inter alia*, 88 *Time* (December 2, 1966), pp. 93–94.

[11] *The New York Times*, July 26, 1964, pp. 1, 15.

[12] *Ibid.*, December 17, 1966, *et seq.*; see also the critical views of the action in 62 *U.S. News & World Report* (January 2, 1967), pp. 28–29, and *ibid.*, 64 (June 3, 1968), p. 10. See also Chapter 5, *supra*.

[13] *The New York Times*, December 18, 1966, p. 17.

[14] *Ibid.*, February 12, 1967, p. 5.

is involved in any manner in the boycott, the involvement creates state responsibility and represents a method of self-help. If the state at which a boycott is aimed has not committed any offensive act involving the boycotting state, the action in question would have to be considered as an unfriendly one and would give rise to legitimate protests on the part of the state whose nationals were affected by the action.

The most famous example of the modern boycott was the widespread suspension by Chinese citizens of trade and business relations with Japan in 1931. The Japanese government protested the action as a violation of international law, but the Chinese government took the official attitude that prior acts undertaken by Japanese authorities constituted far more serious violations of that law. The Committee of Nineteen, appointed by the League of Nations to investigate the findings of the Lytton Commission (which had inquired into the facts of the Manchurian invasion by Japan) decided that the Chinese boycott represented a lawful reprisal. The Chinese government officially supported the boycott and repeatedly urged states friendly to China to apply similar economic measures against Japan. Such appeals created much discussion abroad, particularly in the United States. The United States government took no official action in favor of a boycott, despite considerable pressure from certain Senators and many private groups. In consequence, numerous citizens' organizations undertook their own boycotts of Japanese, and later German, goods.

Occupation of Foreign Territory. Occupation of foreign territory is another method of self-help short of war; it frequently follows a naval demonstration off the coasts of a delinquent state. A show of military force has been adopted on a few modern occasions, such as the combined naval demonstration by fleet units of the Great Powers against Turkey in 1880, by the Allied Powers against Greece on September 1, 1916, and by the Netherlands against Venezuela in 1908.

Occupation by military force has also played a part in modern history. In 1895, Great Britain landed naval personnel at the port of Corinto in Nicaragua and took control of the local customs house until the government of the Republic agreed to pay indemnities for injuries suffered by British nationals residing in Nicaragua. In 1901, a French force occupied the then Turkish island of Mytilene in order to force Turkey to pay sums owed to two French nationals and to fulfill its treaty obligations concerning the Constantinople dues. In 1914, the United States undertook the military occupation of Veracruz in Mexico.[15] In 1923, Italy bombarded and then occupied the Greek island of Corfu, justifying this action, however, as a reprisal.

Blockade. There are two traditional types of blockade: pacific blockade

[15] Consult the excellent study by Robert E. Quirk, *An Affair of Honor: Woodrow Wilson & the Occupation of Veracruz* (Louisville: University of Kentucky Press, 1962).

and hostile blockade. A pacific blockade represents a highly effective method for the settlement of a dispute by coercive measures short of war, provided it is applied by a strong state against a weaker state. This procedure made its first appearance in 1827 when France, Great Britain, and Russia established a joint blockade of certain sections off the coasts of Greece in order to induce Turkey to grant independence to Greece. The blockade, originally intended to be pacific, did not remain so, however, for the fleets of Great Britain and Egypt fought a battle at Navarino, ending in a decisive allied victory. Since 1827, a considerable number of pacific blockades have been recorded, some engineered by individual states, others undertaken as a joint action. Most publicized were the British-French blockade of the Netherlands in 1832 in an effort to secure Dutch recognition of Belgian independence; the British blockade of Greek ports in 1850 to secure compensation for the burning, in the course of an Easter riot, of the house of Don Pacifico, a native of Gibraltar and a British subject; the blockade of Greece by a combined fleet of the Great Powers to prevent Greece from going to war against Turkey; and a similar action by the Powers in 1897 when they blockaded the coasts of Crete in order to prevent the inhabitants of the island from joining with Greece by self-annexation.

Later, during the First Balkan War, the Powers blockaded the port of Antivari in order to prevent a Montenegran annexation of the city of Scutari, which the Powers had intended to make a part of Albanian territory.

The best-known early pacific blockade in the Western Hemisphere was the joint effort in 1902 by Great Britain, Germany, and Italy against Venezuela in an attempt to force that country to honor a long list of claims filed against it by citizens of the three Powers. In view of the existence of the Monroe Doctrine, the claimant states first sought the consent of the United States for their joint action. That consent was granted, subject to certain conditions and limitations. Because no state of war existed, other states did not feel obligated to declare their neutrality. The United States, however, eventually protested vigorously after the allied fleet undertook to exercise the traditional practices of a hostile blockade and stopped the vessels of third parties. The American contention that such acts were illegal in the absence of a state of war was ultimately met by the allied assertion that such a state did actually exist—but then the stoppage of the vessels of third parties ceased and the blockade resumed the characteristics of a pacific blockade.

A pacific blockade differs from a hostile one in two important respects: in the former situation a formal state of war does not exist, and (in modern times) the pacific blockade is applied only to the ships of the blockaded state. Third states are not effected by the blockade, and because no formal war exists, do not achieve the status of neutrals. The United States in particular has insisted again and again that a pacific blockade can affect only the vessels of the blockaded (and, obviously, of the blockading) state; this point of view has prevailed in the community of nations.

EVOLUTION OF A NEW TYPE OF BLOCKADE

The reported arrival in Cuba, in the summer of 1962, of Soviet military equipment accompanied by large numbers of technicians and other, apparently military, groups led to a widespread demand in the United States for the establishment of a unilateral pacific blockade of Cuba. Even then it was interesting to note that many proponents of this step advocated application of the blockade to Russian and other foreign vessels, in view of the fact that Cuba itself had almost no merchant marine of its own. This position ignored the restriction characteristic of a pacific blockade: it did not apply to vessels of third parties. Because application of the second traditional type of blockade, the belligerent or hostile variety, would enable the United States to bar access to Cuba to all ships, adoption of this type was also considered, but under the rules of traditional international law, such a blockade was lawful only in time of war.

A two-day conference of the American foreign ministers (October 2–3, 1962) at Washington reached agreement that further economic and security measures were required in order to cope with the Cuban armament buildup, and an invitation was drafted to non-Communist states, asking them to tighten controls over ships flying their flags and carrying Soviet goods to Cuba. The United States, for its part, adopted three initial steps: it closed its ports to all ships carrying arms to Cuba; it closed its ports to ships sailing between a Communist-bloc port and Cuba; and it prohibited all vessels registered in the United States from engaging in any manner in the Cuban trade.

Missile Crisis. Discovery through United States aerial reconnaissance of the installation of medium-range (1,000 nautical miles) ballistic missiles and of the construction of sites for intermediate range (about 2,000 nautical miles) missiles of Cuba brought the whole matter to a high-crisis level. President Kennedy initiated, on the evening of October 22, 1962, seven steps:

1. A strict "quarantine" on all offensive military equipment bound for Cuba; all ships so bound, from whatever nation or port, were to be turned back by the United States Navy if found to be carrying offensive weapons.

2. A continued and increased aerial surveillance of Cuba, in line with the communiqué of the meeting of American foreign ministers which had rejected secrecy in such matters for the Hemisphere.

3. Proclamation of a United States policy that regarded "any nuclear missile launched from Cuba against any nation in the Western Hemisphere

as an attack by the Soviet Union on the United States requiring a full retaliatory response upon the Soviet Union."

4. Reinforcement of the garrison of the U.S. Naval base at Guantanamo, Cuba, from which United States dependents had been evacuated.

5. A call for an immediate meeting of the Organ of Consultation under the OAS to consider the Cuban situation and to invoke Articles 6 and 8 of the Rio de Janeiro Treaty.

6. A request for an emergency meeting of the United Nations Security Council "to take action against this latest Soviet threat to world peace."

7. A call to Soviet Premier Nikita Khrushchev to "halt and eliminate this clandestine, reckless and provocative threat."

On October 23, the OAS voted to take all measures held to be necessary to end the threat to the peace and security of the Western Hemisphere resulting from the military buildup in Cuba. This decision was communicated at once to the United Nations. Virtually at the same time, the President issued his Quarantine Proclamation. On October 24, the quarantine went into effect, at first implemented by Naval and Air Force units of the United States only.

The ensuing events are now history: the avoidance of trouble when components of the United States Navy actually stopped Russian ships; the diversion of Soviet-bloc vessels from the Cuba run; the attempt of Acting Secretary-General U Thant to prevail on the United States to suspend the blockade of Cuba and on Khrushchev to halt shipments to the island; the rejected Russian proposal of October 27 to withdraw offensive weapons from Cuba in exchange for American withdrawal of rockets from Turkey; and the Russian agreement on October 28 to dismantle the Cuban missile sites and to transport the missiles back to the Soviet Union.[16]

The United States (and Secretary-General U Thant) failed, however, to secure UN inspection of the dismantling of the sites, and supervision of the removal of missiles was instead undertaken by the blockading United States naval vessels through "visual inspection" not involving a boarding of the Russian ships.

Aerial surveillance of Cuba continued after the blockade was lifted and disclosed the continuing presence on the island of large quantities of Russian conventional weapons as well as of great numbers of Soviet technical and some military personnel (estimated at 17,000 as of February 6, 1963).

Before discussing the novel features of the 1962 "quarantine" of Cuba,

---

[16] A selection of all major published documents (Sept. 2–Oct. 28, 1962) is conveniently available in Foreign Policy Association, *The Cuban Crisis: A Documentary Record* (Headline Series, No. 157 [New York: Foreign Policy Association, 1963]; see also the appended list of suggested readings.

it might not be amiss to consider the three alternatives facing the United States during the crisis, for all involve aspects of international law.

Discovery of the Russian missile installations on Cuba left three basic courses of action open to the United States. It could

1. Institute a quarantine or blockade of Cuba, at the risk of becoming involved in a limited or unlimited war with the Soviet Union.

2. Bomb Cuban installations and follow this initial action with an invasion of the island to destroy remaining missile sites and to oust the Castro government. This action might have succeeded but posed two major dangers: virtual certainty of a conflict with the Soviet Union if its technical and military personnel were somehow entangled in the hostilities, and the strong possibility that some of the missiles already in place would have been launched at the United States, with heavy losses as a result.

3. Turn to the United Nations, request the establishment of a UN naval and air patrol, and thereafter solve the crisis through negotiations, either through the United Nations or through the Organization of American States.[17]

Initiation of the New Type of Blockade. The second and third alternatives were discarded in favor of the first policy, which then was tied in with both the UN and the OAS.

The legal position of the United States in instituting the Cuban blockade was somewhat dubious by traditional standards of international law. Yet the legal experts of the Department of State, advising the President and Secretary of State, succeeded in erecting a quite logical defense of the policies adopted. To be sure, no one would deny that by applying restrictions to vessels of a third party (Russia) the United States was committing, under traditional international law, an act of war. But it should be remembered that such an act would be regarded as an act of war *only* if both sides to the controversy would choose to do so, to view it as a hostile or belligerent act.

The term *quarantine* used initially to describe the action adopted indicated the realization that this was a new method of blockade. Analysis reveals that it falls somewhere between the two traditional types of blockade. It was a pacific blockade in that neither the element of intent for war nor a "state of war" did exist; at the same time, it was a hostile blockade in that the quarantine was to be applied against vessels of a third state.

SUMMARY OF THE "LEGAL CASE" OF THE UNITED STATES

The "legal case" of the United States may be summarized as follows:

1. The Rio Treaty of 1947 provided for regional collective action not

[17] See Quincy Wright, "Power Politics or a Rule of Law?" 147 *New Republic* (December 29, 1962), pp. 11–12.

only in the case of armed attack (Art. 3) but also in the case of any aggression, not an armed attack, affecting the territory or sovereignty of any American state (Art. 6).

Article 8 of the agreement specified the measures to be taken at the invocation of Article 6, and included the use of armed force.

On October 23, 1962, the Council of the OAS met and constituted itself as the Provisional Organ of Consultation. This body then studied the evidence submitted by the United States on the presence of Russian strategic missiles in Cuba and concluded logically that a situation existed that could endanger hemisphere peace in the meaning of Article 6. The Organ then adopted a resolution which recommended that the member states, collectively and individually, take measures, including the use of armed force, to prevent further receipt by Cuba of military material and supplies capable of endangering Hemisphere peace.

The issuance of the presidential proclamation of the defensive quarantine, which took place at once, was based on the action of the Consultative Organ. To be sure, the American announcement of intent to establish the quarantine preceded the action of the OAS; but the actual establishment of the quarantine followed that action.

2. Although the United States did not invoke the doctrine of self-defense, the OAS action was in conformity with Article 52 (1) of the Charter of the United Nations (regional defense arrangements) and the Consultative Organ directed that the contents of its October 23 resolution should be communicated at once to the Security Council, in accordance with Article 54 of the Charter.

It might be argued that the sequence of events violated the provisions of Article 53 (1) of the Charter, which state that no enforcement action is to be taken under regional arrangements without the authorization of the Security Council.[18] However, in view of the repeated paralysis of the Security Council insofar as swift action has been concerned, it is reasonable to regard Article 53 (1) as somewhat of a dead letter. But more important: the United States did place the Cuban situation before the Security Council, following President Kennedy's address of October 22. The Council met before the Consultative Organ and adopted its resolution, yet took no action on the quarantine that had been proposed by the United States. It could be argued, therefore, that tacit authorization for the quarantine had been obtained.

In any case, neither President Kennedy nor the OAS in the resolution of October 23 invoked Article 51 of the UN Charter (self-defense), even though quite obviously the problems posed by the Cuban missile armament bore a close and vital relationship to United States and hemisphere self-defense questions.

Regardless of this fact, however, it would seem that the quarantine

[18] See Joseph B. McDevitt, "The UN Charter and the Cuban Quarantine," 17 *JAG Journal* (April–May, 1963), pp. 71–80.

action was legitimate under the regional arrangements created to preserve peace and security in the Western Hemisphere.

The order instituting the blockade of Cuba, signed on October 23, 1962, is rather interesting in view of the new aspects of the blockade in question. The document, entitled "Interdiction of the Delivery of Offensive Weapons to Cuba," listed these weapons as offensive: surface-to-surface missiles; bombers, bombs, air-to-surface rockets and guided missiles; warheads for such weapons; mechanical or electronic support equipment; and any other weapons designated at a later time "for the purpose of effectuating this proclamation." [19]

It is interesting to note that amidst the enormous discussion of the blockade of Cuba almost nothing was said about the aerial reconnaissance of the island which the United States had instituted sometime before the missiles and sites were discovered. Clearly, here was a repetition of the sort of activity, on a much more extensive and intensive scale, that had produced the U-2 crisis of 1960 between the Soviet Union and the United States. Again the national airspace of an independent state had been violated, on a daily basis, by both high-level and low-level flights accompanied by photography of almost every square mile of Cuba's territory.

The only defense made in 1962 was by President Kennedy, who simply stated that the overflights of Cuba were justified because the security of the United States was at stake.

Under traditional principles of law, such overflights (aerial intrusions) had to be viewed as illegal and justified Cuban military action to clear the Cuban national airspace of such intruders. To be sure, the Rio Treaty for Reciprocal Assistance (1947), to which Cuba was a party, had authorized the Organ of Consultation to agree by a two-thirds vote on measures for both the common defense and the maintenance of the peace and security of the hemisphere (Arts. 6, 8, 17). On January 31, 1962, the Organ of Consultation approved at Punta del Este a resolution which called on the member states to "strengthen their capacity to counteract threats or acts of aggression, subversion, or other dangers to peace and security resulting from the continued intervention in this hemisphere of Sino-Soviet powers." And on October 23, 1962, the Organ of Consultation of the OAS adopted a resolution in which it was asserted that it was "desirable to intensify individual and collective surveillance of the delivery of arms to Cuba." [20] Nevertheless, under existing rules, grave doubts must be maintained about the legality of the flights over Cuba.

LEGAL STATUS OF BLOCKADES AND FORCIBLE SELF-HELP

The legal status of a traditional pacific blockade has engendered a great deal of controversy among jurists. If, say, the League of Nations, acting

---

[19] The text of the proclamation may be found in 57 *A.J.I.L.* (1963), Supp., pp. 512–513.

[20] Wright, *op. cit.*, p. 548.

under Article 16 of the Covenant, had called on its members to institute a collective pacific blockade against a state held to have violated its obligations under the Covenant, such a joint effort would have proven to be quite ineffective if one of the major maritime states had refused to tolerate interference with its shipping bound for or coming from the blockaded state. Many writers, moreover, believe that even a supposedly pacific blockade approximates a state of war. When the Charter of the United Nations was written, Article 42 appeared to prohibit unilateral institution of a pacific blockade as an enforcement action.[21] Most writers concur that a pacific blockade would be legal today only under one of two conditions: (1) if it were adopted by the United Nations as a collective enforcement action; or (2) if it were instituted by a state not bound by the obligations of the Charter, that is, by a state which was not a member of the United Nations. The argument is not a mere academic one, for it revolves around the touchy subject of unilateral enforcement of both the Charter and the rules of international law.

Outside the two conditions mentioned, it is difficult to reconcile a pacific blockade of the traditional type with the applicable provisions of the Charter (Art. 2, pars. 3 and 4), nor can such a blockade be found among the resolutions for an international dispute listed in Article 33 of the instrument.

If one is to assume that the Charter's prohibition of the use of military force as a unilateral sanction is binding, then states against which violations of international law not representing an armed attack have been committed may be on occasion without a really adequate remedy. In addition to the absence of a workable but forcible method of self-help it is conceivable that the machinery of the United Nations might not be able to secure redress for injuries suffered, and the various methods of peaceful settlement might be rejected by the offending state.

The attitude found in certain states, namely that Article 2, par. 4 of the Charter does not prohibit unilateral action by the threat or the use of military force (and, by implication, of a blockade) to enforce international rights if their exercise is illegally denied, was directly responsible for the French-British attack on Egypt in 1956. The British and French governments defended that attack as legitimate and this position was emphasized by the vetos cast by the two states in the Security Council.

The Anglo-French position, maintained even after the failure of military operations owing to United Nations opinion and pressure from both the United States and the Soviet Union, has been condemned by both the Secretary-General of the United Nations and most writers on international law. But a staunch defense of a total prohibition of the unilateral threat or use of military force still appears, to this writer, to be not only an unrealistic but also a highly dangerous attitude. What the provisions

[21] See Josef L. Kunz, "Sanctions in International Law," 54 *A.J.I.L.* (1960), pp. 324–347, at p. 331 on this point.

of the Charter have done, in effect, is to deprive states of valuable tools of self-help and of enforcement of international rights without substituting a really workable method for achieving the same ends. It remains to be seen whether states will stand by the prohibition if and when interests or rights considered to be vital are affected and peaceful methods of settlement or of sanction fail.

Returning once more to the subject of a pacific blockade: such an action obviously remains "pacific" only as long as both parties involved choose to treat it as such. The blockaded state could, at its discretion, regard itself to be in a state of war, supply naval escorts to its vessels and attempt to "shoot its way" through the blockading fleet. And if the blockading state attempts to bar the vessels of third parties from reaching the blockaded ports, those parties could supply escorts for their ships and, if need be, attempt to force passage to the blockaded ports. This risk of conversion into a state of war is inherent in most measures of self-help by forcible means and has to be faced by any state contemplating the use of such measures in the assertion of its international rights.

Two eminent jurists have pointed out recently that if limited war, reprisals, or limited retaliation remain politically feasible and practically effective without collective retaliation, then the prohibitions presumably imposed by the Charter will either fade into unimportance or will have to be altered.[22] At the present time, the prohibitions are "on the books." But it appears that when a state comes to believe that a vital interest or survival (or at least self-defense) justifies forcible measures short of war and hopes to escape total war despite the utilization of such measures, they will be undertaken, despite the existence of the Charter.

SUGGESTED READINGS

SELF-HELP: GENERAL

Evelyn S. Colbert, *Retaliation in International Law* (New York: King's Crown Press [Columbia University Press], 1948), a survey covering the period from the thirteenth to the eighteenth centuries.

Cases

The Boedes Lust. Great Britain, High Court of Admiralty, 1804, 5 C. Robinson 233 [Embargo].

United States v. *Curtiss-Wright Export Corporation,* United States, Supreme Court, 1936, 299 U.S. 304 [Embargo].

Gray, Administrator v. *United States,* United States, Court of Claims, 1886, 21 Ct. Cl. 340 [Reprisals].

[22] Kaplan-Katzenback, p. 217.

THE CUBAN CRISIS OF 1962

David L. Larson, *The "Cuban Crisis" of 1962 (Selected Documents and Chronology)* (Boston: Houghton Mifflin, 1963); Leonard C. Meeker, "Defensive Quarantine and the Law," 57 *A.J.I.L.* (1963), pp. 515–524; Carl Q. Christol, "Maritime Quarantine: The Naval Interdiction of Offensive Weapons and Associated Matériel to Cuba, 1962," *ibid.*, pp. 524–545; Charles G. Fenwick, "The Quarantine against Cuba: Legal or Illegal?" *ibid.*, pp. 588–592; Brunson MacChesney, "Some Comments on the 'Quarantine' of Cuba," *ibid.*, pp. 592–597; Myres S. McDougal, "The Soviet-Cuban Quarantine and Self-defense," *ibid.*, pp. 597–604; and the generally dissenting views of Quincy Wright in his "The Cuban Quarantine," *ibid.*, p. 546–565. Additional valuable studies include W. T. Mallison, Jr., "Limited Naval Blockade or Quarantine—Interdiction and Collective Defense Claims Valid under International Law," 31 *George Washington Law Review* (1962), pp. 335–398; Andrew J. Valentine, "Rx: Naval Quarantine," 89 *United States Naval Institute Proceedings* (No. 5, May, 1963), pp. 38–50; Covey Oliver, "International Law and the Quarantine of Cuba: A Hopeful Prescription for Legal Writing," 57 *A.J.I.L.* (1963), pp. 373–377; Edward D. Re, "The Quarantine of Cuba in International Law," 6 *JAG Bulletin*, U.S. Air Force, No. 1 (January–February, 1964), pp. 3–14; Neill H. Alford, Jr., "The Cuban Quarantine of 1962: An Inquiry into Paradox and Persuasion," 4 *Virginia Journal of International Law* (1964), pp. 35–73.

PART VI
War

25

Legal Nature of War Today

ATTEMPTS TO RENOUNCE WAR

W AR in the traditional sense may be defined as a contention, through the use of armed force, between states, undertaken for the purpose of overpowering each other.[1] True, such a definition does not cover the modern development of what has been called the *status mixtus* nor the intermediacy concept discussed at the end of this chapter, but it may serve for purposes of the discussion to follow, provided it is kept in mind that hostile relations between states *may* assume forms different from that outlined in the definition given.

The right to go to war was regarded for hundreds of years by both writers and the heads or governments of states not only as a lawful course of action for a sovereign state but indeed as one of the characteristics of such an entity.[2] War served two basic purposes in international society: it provided an effective method of self-help to achieve the enforcement of rights in the absence of competent international tribunals and it also supplied states with a method, again of the self-help type, to change the rules of international law and to adopt them to basically changed conditions. The latter function, which by analogy could be compared with a domestic revolution carried on to change laws no longer considered tolerable, appeared to be particularly justified in the continuing absence of any agencies of international legislation.

International law did not prohibit war; rather, it viewed the institution as a quite normal function of sovereign states. The preceding rights did not have to possess legal or moral merits: it was regarded as sufficient that a sovereign state asserted rights; failing to enforce them by peaceful means, it was free to pursue its aims by recourse to force.

---

[1] See Lauterpacht's *Oppenheim,* Vol. II, pp. 201–210. There appear to be as many definitions as there are writers on the subject: see, *inter alia,* Hyde, Vol. III, p. 1686; Moore, Vol. VII, p. 154; Kelsen, *Principles of International Law,* pp. 26–28; the collection of many different ones in Clyde Eagleton, "The Attempt to Define War," *International Conciliation,* No. 291 (June, 1933), pp. 237–287, and Georg Schwarzenberger, "Jus Pacis ac Belli?" 37 *A.J.I.L.* (1943), pp. 460–479.

[2] "To declare war is one of the highest acts of sovereignty"—Secretary of State Lansing to President Woodrow Wilson, August 16, 1919; quoted in Lauterpacht, *Recognition in International Law* (1947), p. 5, n. 1.

Under such conditions, the functions of international law were conceived as dealing primarily with the relations of states in time of peace, with heavy emphasis on the independence of every member of the family of nations. However, once a state decided to go to war, it was considered to have been released from the obligations imposed by the law, except from such few as regulated the conduct of armed conflicts, and could proceed "lawfully" to impair or even to extinguish the same independence of its opponent which had been preserved so jealously in time of peace under the rules of the law.

EARLY ATTEMPTS

The arrival of the mass army as well as the continuing discoveries of ever more efficient weapons led in the late nineteenth century to the first serious attempts to bring about limitations of war as a legal instrument and as a legally accepted method for enforcing legal rights and changing the rules of law. The Hague Conference of 1899 represented the official realization of many privately conducted studies and draftings of conventions designed to surround the institution of war with legal restrictions. The Second Hague Conference, of 1907, served the same purpose, with greater effectiveness because of the lessons learned from the results of its predecessor. Thus the Hague Convention of 1907 respecting the Limitation of the Employment of Force for the Recovery of Contract Debts, while limited in its scope and purpose, illustrated the trend well under way by them to employ law-making treaties for a gradual limitation of hitherto virtually unlimited rights of sovereign states. Next came the American "Bryan Treaties" with their requirement of a cooling-off period —until the report of a conciliation commission had been drawn up— before disputing states could have recourse to war. Still later, and more important, the Covenant of the League of Nations provided in its Preamble an acceptance by the contracting parties of obligations not to resort to war, and denied them the right to go to war under certain conditions (Art. 12, par. 1; Art. 13; Art. 15, pars. 1 and 7; Art. 17).

All these attempts were made with the intent to limit the use of war as a tool of law; more spectacular, in some respects, were the efforts made to establish aggressive war as an illegal enterprise. As early as 1923, the Treaty of Mutual Assistance—which never came into force—attempted to identify wars of aggression as an international crime. The equally abortive Geneva Protocol of 1924 similarly labelled aggressive war as a crime (Preamble) and in its Article 2 imposed an obligation on all parties to the agreement to refrain from war except in the specific circumstances listed in the treaty. In 1927, the Assembly of the League passed a resolution under which all wars of aggression were said to be prohibited and only pacific means were to be employed to settle international disputes of every kind, an approach reflecting the provisions of the Treaty of Mutual Guarantee (Locarno Treaty) of 1925. And in 1928, the Sixth Pan-American

Conference adopted a resolution asserting that a "war of aggression constitutes a crime against the human species . . . all aggression is illicit and as such is declared prohibited."

Briand-Kellogg Pact (Pact of Paris). The culmination of these efforts to "outlaw" aggressive war—the adjective is necessary, for none of these proposals really prohibited every kind of war—was represented by the General Treaty for the Renunciation of War (Briand-Kellogg Pact, or Pact of Paris) signed in Paris on August 27, 1928, by representatives of fifteen states and ultimately ratified or adhered to by sixty-five nations. The text of this famous instrument reads as follows:

ART. 1. The High Contracting Parties solemnly declare in the names of their respective peoples that they condemn recourse to war for the solution of international controversies, and renounce it as an instrument of national policy in their relations with one another.

ART. 2. The High Contracting Parties agree that the settlement or solution of all disputes or conflicts of whatever nature or of whatever origin they may be, which may arise among them, shall never be sought except by pacific means.

ART. 3. The present treaty shall be ratified by the High Contracting Parties named in the Preamble in accordance with their respective constitutional requirements, and shall take effect as between them as soon as all their several instruments of ratification shall have been deposited at Washington.

This treaty shall, when it has come into effect as prescribed in the preceding paragraph, remain open as long as may be necessary for adherence by all the other Powers of the world. Every instrument evidencing the adherence of a power shall be deposited at Washington, and the treaty shall immediately upon such deposit become effective as between the power thus adhering and the other parties thereto.

It shall be the duty of the Government of the United States of America to furnish each Government named in the preamble and every Government subsequently adhering to this Treaty with a certified copy of the Treaty and of every instrument of ratification of adherence. It shall also be the duty of the Government of the United States of America telegraphically to notify such Governments immediately upon the deposit with it of each instrument of ratification or adherence.

In faith whereof the respective Plenipotentiaries have signed this Treaty in the French and English languages, both texts having equal force, and hereunto affix their seals.

Done at Paris the twenty-seventh day of August in the year one thousand nine hundred and twenty-eight.

The Preamble of the instrument contained a statement by the signatory states in which they affirmed that "all changes in their relations with one another should be sought by pacific means and be the result of a peaceful and orderly process, and that any Signatory Power which shall hereafter seek to promote its national interests by resort to war should be denied the benefits furnished by this Treaty."

Interestingly enough, the Pact contained no provision for denunciation and did not state a date of termination. It thus represented one of the extremely rare modern instances of a perpetual agreement. This latter fact alone may be taken as an indication of the optimistic and unrealistic aspects of the instrument.

The purpose of the agreement was obviously to renounce war both as a tool of self-help to right an international wrong and as a rightful act of national sovereignty to change existing rights.[3] It was *not* intended to abolish the institution of war as such, for under its terms resort to war was still permitted in legally permissible self-defense and as an instrument of collective action to restrain an aggressor. The treaty also did *not* abolish resort to war between a party to the agreement and a country not a party to the agreement. The latter point has been well illustrated by the Chaco War between Bolivia and Paraguay: when Paraguay declared war in 1933, no infraction of the Pact of Paris had taken place, because Bolivia was not a party to the agreement. The treaty, furthermore, did not prohibit the resort to war against a country which had violated the provisions of the treaty.

The Pact of Paris failed to provide means of enforcement and, even more important, did not provide any definition of the measures and methods through which changes in relations between states might be effected without resorting to force.[4] On the whole, down to the outbreak of World War II, there continued widespread and sometimes outright cynical skepticism about any legal value of the "formal renunciation of war."

To be sure, eminent jurists such as Justice Robert H. Jackson of the United States Supreme Court upheld the Pact, stating that it was not wholly sterile despite the absence of an express legal *duty* of enforcement. It had legal consequences more substantial than its political ones. It created substantive law of national conduct for its signatories and there resulted a *right* to enforce it by the general sanctions of international law.[5]

The sad truth was that the statesmen of the world had proceeded to ignore a fundamental principle underlying the whole system of positive international law: any rule, to be effective, must correspond to the needs of states and must equally correspond to the practice of states. De Visscher expressed this concept very well when he wrote that, "A normative (law-making) treaty the content of which is too far in advance of development in international relations is stillborn, just as a treaty that ceases to be exactly observed in the practice of governments is no longer valid

---

[3] For a dissenting view, see Kaplan–Katzenbach, p. 210.

[4] See Roland S. Morris, "The Pact of Paris for the Renunciation of War: Its Meaning and Effect in International Law," *Proceedings* (1929), pp. 88–91, and discussion of that paper, *ibid.*, pp. 91–109; consult also Quincy Wright, "The Meaning of the Pact of Paris," 27 *A.J.l.L.* (1933), pp. 39–61.

[5] 27 *American Bar Association Journal* (1941), p. 691.

in its formal expression." [6] Or, as the translator of De Visscher's book observed, "Law cannot be built upon a heedless sacrifice of reality." [7] As far as the failure of the signatories of the Pact to provide methods of enforcement was concerned, the words of Justice Oliver Wendell Holmes in the case of *The Western Maid* come to mind: "Legal obligations that exist but cannot be enforced are ghosts that are seen in the law but that are elusive to the grasp." [8]

The present writer does not believe that war, except in self-defense, was outlawed by the Pact of Paris. He believes, instead, that it represented nothing more than a moral preachment, despite the trappings of a treaty surrounding the document. The states which had signed it denied validity to the doctrine, and armed conflicts in the ensuing decade were both more numerous and more serious than they had been between 1919 and 1928.

As McLaughlin pointed out,[9] the renunciation of war was a "statement of principle" which provided no criteria for testing compliance with the concept. The use of the Pact by the Nuremberg (International) Tribunal to assert that acts initiating an aggressive war constituted a crime should be viewed as exceeding the original intention of those who drafted the Pact.

Wright came to believe that the proponents of the outlawry of war did not expect immediate effects from the Pact but rather were thinking in terms of generations.[10] This may have been true—and if true, it casts some interesting light on the Pact as a treaty in the normal meaning of that term—but those same proponents later criticized the violations of the Pact when wars occurred within a few years after its ratification. In any case, the "legal" effect claimed for the Pact was not in consonance with the practical interpretation placed on it by the parties to the agreement.

Treaty law (and including the Covenant and possibly the Pact of Paris) is particular international law based on general international law. When the particular treaty rules, created in derogation of general law, cease to be effective, they are replaced, automatically and instantly, by the relevant or corresponding rules of general international law. Hence the return of the community of nations to traditional notions of neutrality and of warfare appears to have been well founded, in this writer's view.

Typical of the attitude of national leaders was their failure to label many of the conflicts of the 1930's as wars. If such a label were omitted, so the reasoning appears to have been, then no war existed; hence no one

---

[6] Charles De Visscher, *Theory and Reality in Public International Law* (Princeton, N.J.: Princeton University Press, 1957), p. 133.

[7] Percy E. Corbett, *ibid.*, p. viii.

[8] United States, Supreme Court, 1922, 257 U.S. 419.

[9] Lennox A. Mills and Charles H. McLaughlin, *World Politics in Transition* (New York: Holt, Rinehart & Winston, 1956), at p. 351.

[10] Quincy Wright, "The Outlawry of War and the Law of War," 47 *A.J.I.L.* (1953), pp. 365–376, at p. 369.

could be blamed for breach of his promises under the Pact. Or, if a war had to be declared, it became at once a war in self-defense.

Even a war presumed to be illegal under the Pact of Paris would require the application of a body of rules to the hostilities involved; otherwise a return to barbarism would be the consequence of such a resort to force. And the body of rules to be applied in an "unlawful" war, to be applied to both aggressor state and to its victim, *during the conduct of hostilities* must be the customary and conventional laws of war.[11]

It must be mentioned, however, that the tribunal at Nuremberg asserted vigorously that the Pact of Paris meant that an aggressive war was henceforth illegal under general international law and that, therefore, those who planned and waged such a war committed a crime in so doing. "War for the solution of international controversies includes a war of aggression, and such a war is therefore outlawed by the Pact." [12]

The present writer does not agree with that interpretation of the Pact of Paris.[13]

In any case, the Pact of Paris did not prohibit all kinds of war by any means. States could fight in self-defense; they could go to war in order to enforce international obligations, this not being a conflict classifiable as an "instrument of national policy" if undertaken, say, under the Covenant of the League of Nations. Again, in the absence of enforcement machinery and even of an agency to determine whether a breach of the Pact had taken place, states could evade the prohibitions of the instrument; because only "war" was mentioned in the Pact and because a generally accepted definition of war was unavailable, states could sidestep the agreement by not styling their military actions a war; and, lastly, wars against nonsigners of the Pact as well as against violators of the agreement were permissible.

League of Nations. How was peace to be preserved and enforced under these early instruments? The Pact of Paris did not enter into this vital subject. On the other hand, Article 16 of the Covenant provided for the imposition of sanctions against a member of the League that had resorted to war in violation of its obligations under the Covenant. The Article was applied in only one of the five major instances in which such a violation did take place. When Japan invaded Manchuria in 1931, the Assembly concluded that "without any declaration of war, part of the Chinese territory has been forcibly seized and occupied by the Japanese troops." [14] Nevertheless, the Assembly decided, Japan had not resorted to war in violation of the Covenant and therefore Article 16 did not apply.

[11] Views similar to the one expressed by the present writer have been criticized by several commentators; their best and most reasonable defense may be found in Hersch Lauterpacht, "Rules of Warfare in an Unlawful War," in Lipsky, pp. 89–113.

[12] *Trial of the Major War Criminals Before the International Tribunal, Nuremberg, 14 November 1945–1 October 1946*, I (1947), at p. 220.

[13] See Stone, p. 302, for a similar view.

[14] League of Nations Assembly Report on the Sino-Japanese Dispute," 27 *A.J.I.L.* (1933), Supp., p. 146.

In 1934, in connection with the Chaco War between Bolivia and Paraguay (1932–35), many members of the League, each deciding that Paraguay had violated the Covenant, applied the arms embargo originally imposed on both belligerents to Paraguay alone. The Japanese invasion of China proper, in 1937, led to a decision by the Assembly that Japan had violated the Nine-Power Treaty of 1922 as well as the Pact of Paris and that, consequently, Article 16 of the Covenant now applied to the dispute. Each member state, however, was judged to be free to apply such individual enforcement action against Japan as it saw fit—and none of them took any action. When the Soviet Union attacked Finland in late 1939, the Assembly did act under Article 16(4), and expelled the U.S.S.R. from the organization. Expulsion was not implemented by collective enforcement action, however.

Only in the case of the Italian invasion of Ethiopia, in 1935, had the Assembly concluded that the invasion represented resort to war in violation of the Covenant and that Article 16(1), was applicable. Collective economic sanctions were, therefore, authorized against Italy. This was not enough, however, and failure to adopt the obviously effective measures of an embargo on oil shipments and a closing of the Suez Canal, led to Italy's successful defiance of the League and to the conquest of Ethiopia. It should be pointed out, in passing, that the closing of the Suez Canal, which was urged on the League by prominent private persons in many countries, would have constituted a clear violation of the 1888 Constantinople Convention.

LATER ATTEMPTS

The United Nations. The experience of World War II and the approaching abolition of the League of Nations combined to bring about a renewed attempt to circumscribe resort to force by the provisions incorporated in the Charter of the United Nations. Article 2 of that document contained the relevant key regulations:

3. All Members shall settle their international disputes by peaceful means in such a manner that international peace and security, and justice, are not endangered.
4. All Members shall refrain in their international relations from the threat or use of force against the territorial integrity or political independence of any state, or in any other manner inconsistent with the Purposes of the United Nations.

The Charter, therefore, went beyond the provisions of the Pact of Paris in that the members of the United Nations renounced not only their right to go to war—except in instances of individual or collective self-defense—but also their right to resort to the threat or the use of force. It is, in fact, interesting to note that the only reference to "war" in the Charter occurs in its Preamble (". . . determined to save succeeding generations from the scourge of war"). Elsewhere, "threat or use of force" and "threat to the peace, breach of the peace, or act of aggression" are used in reference to situations in which the new organization, through the Security Council, could take action under specified conditions.

Taking the provisions of the Charter at face value, it would appear as if at long last legal controls had been established over the right of states to resort to the use of force—just as, long ago, individual states laid down legal controls over private warfare and resort to violence on the part of their individual citizens.

Unfortunately, the cited portions of the Charter have not only been qualified extensively through other provisions of that instrument, but the operating mechanisms intended to make the legal controls work have broken down or have been violated on numerous occasions since 1945. And the United Nations itself has had recourse to force in the Congo for purposes which many governments, as well as individuals, have felt difficult to locate in the avowed purposes of the organization as outlined in the Charter.

This brings us back to the status of war under the Charter. As mentioned earlier, various qualifications surround the optimistic provisions of Article 2(3-4). In the first place, Article 51 guarantees to all members the inherent right of individual or collective self-defense in the event of an armed attack. In theory, the Security Council may assume responsibility for an attacked member state and defend it against the attacker— but this could be done only if the permanent members of the Council were in agreement, a situation not yet realized. Until such agreement is reached, a state may continue to use force in its own defense.

In the second place, the Security Council may make "decisions" (determination of the existence of a threat to the peace, breach of the peace, or of an act of aggression) of facts and of action to restore the peace only if the concurrence of the same permanent members is obtainable. Until such concurrence is achieved, wars involving member states may continue. In the third place, even if the Security Council acted in either of the preceding instances, it would not enforce its decisions or act as a defender of a member unless adequate military forces were made available through voluntary action on the part of the member states. Until such forces were placed at the disposal of the Council, the war could go on without check. And, lastly, the Charter cannot be truly said to have affected the right of a nonmember to go to war, because despite fine-spun theories to the contrary, the Charter is a treaty and binds only the member states of the United Nations.

As matters stand now, two categories of war may be said to exist: defensive war and aggressive war. The former is clearly permissible, for as Article 51 of the Charter declares:

Nothing in the present Charter shall impair the inherent right of individual or collective self-defense if an armed attack occurs against a Member of the

United Nations, until the Security Council has taken the measures necessary to maintain international peace and security. . . .[15]

Aggressive war, on the other hand, has been asserted to be illegal, a position reinforced in the judgment of the International War Crimes Tribunal at Nuremberg when the tribunal asserted that

To initiate a war of aggression, therefore, is not only an international crime; it is the supreme international crime differing only from other war crimes in that it contains within itself the accumulated evil of the whole.[16]

Unfortunately, the actual situation is not as clear-cut as such a statement appears to indicate. Not only have great numbers of states resorted to war and have always justified their action on grounds of self-defense, but grave problems of definition have arisen in connection with the attempts to define the term "aggression."[17] One major instant in this effort to define illegal resorts to force has been the attitude of the Soviet Union and of Russian writers on international law.[18] Thus on December 27, 1951, a Col. F. Khrustov, writing in *Red Star* (the Soviet army newspaper), asserted that "Bolsheviks admit the complete lawfulness of wars of oppressed classes against oppressors." A just war, according to the Russian writer, was one which liberated people from capitalism or imperialism, whereas an unjust war was one representing "imperialist aggression." He then proceeded to quote Josef Stalin: "The just, nonaggressive liberation war is aimed either at defending people from attack from without and attempts at enslaving it, or at freeing people from the slavery of capitalism, or finally at freeing colonial and dependent countries from the yoke of the imperialists. The unjust, aggressive war is aimed at seizing and enslaving other peoples."[19] Recent years have seen no material change in

[15] See also Josef L. Kunz, "Individual and Collective Self-Defense in Article 51 of the Charter of the United Nations," 41 *A.J.I.L.* (1947), pp. 872–879.

[16] "International Military Tribunal (Nuremberg) Judgment and Sentences," 43 *A.J.I.L.* (Jan. 1949), p. 168; consult also Quincy Wright, "The Prevention of Aggression," 50 *A.J.I.L.* (1956), pp. 514–532.

[17] The complicated problem of definition has been summarized very well in Gould, pp. 606–618, with special emphasis on the activities of war crimes tribunals. See also Quincy Wright, "The Outlawry of War and the Law of War," 47 *A.J.I.L.* (1953), pp. 365–376, which enters also into the persistency of the ancient concept of a just war (*bellum justum*). On the latter, see Robert W. Tucker, *The Just War: A Study in Contemporary American Doctrine* (Baltimore: Johns Hopkins University Press, 1960). See also Arthur Nussbaum, "Just War—A Legal Concept," 42 *Michigan Law Review* (1943), pp. 453–479, and the important study by Joachim von Elbe, "The Evolution of the Concept of the Just War in International Law," 33 *A.J.I.L.* (1939), pp. 665–688.

[18] See, for instance, E. A. Korovin, "The Second World War and International Law," 40 *A.J.I.L.* (1946), pp. 742–755, and the important discussion by W. W. Kulski, "Present Trends in Soviet International Law," *Proceedings* (1953), pp. 59–67.

[19] AP Dispatch, December 28, 1951. See also International Commission of Jurists, "Aggression in Hungary: A Soviet Definition Condemns Russia," 43 *American Bar Association Journal* (1957), pp. 928–929.

such a Communist outlook. On January 6, 1961, Chairman Nikita Khrushchev, addressing a global meeting of Communist leaders in Moscow, stated that there were four kinds of war, two of which Communists opposed and two of which they regarded as "sacred" and worthy of strong support. The four categories were world wars, local wars, liberation wars, and "popular uprisings." Khrushchev held that world wars (undertaken and started by "imperialists") and local wars were opposed by Communists. Local wars were regarded as evil because, with the use of nuclear weapons, they could expand easily into world wars. On the other hand, popular uprisings and national wars of liberation were supported. Said Khrushchev:

Now a word about national liberation wars. The armed struggle by the Vietnamese people or the war of the Algerian people, which is already in its seventh year, serve as the latest examples of such wars. These wars began as an uprising by the colonial peoples against their oppressors and changed into guerrilla warfare.

Liberation wars will continue to exist as long as imperialism exists, as long as colonialism exists. These are revolutionary wars. Such wars are not only admissible but inevitable, since the colonialists do not grant independence voluntarily. Therefore, the people can attain their freedom and independence only by struggle, including armed struggle.[20]

On October 6, 1960, General Fu Chung wrote in the Peiping *Peoples Daily* that

We Communists are opposed to all kinds of war that impede progress, but we are not opposed to righteous wars that promote progress. . . . Marxists hold that righteous revolutionary wars are an antitoxin, a midwife who assists in the birth of a new society, and a bridge to a new world.[21]

The most authoritative guide to Communist Chinese attitudes on the subject appears to be the major doctrinal article by Marshal Lin Piao, Chinese Minister of Defense, of September 3, 1965, supporting the concept of wars of liberation in great detail.[22]

It appears, therefore, that civil wars and other internal conflicts should be regarded, in the Communist view, as mere domestic affairs as long as they are started, influenced, or supported by Communist states and parties; if, on the other hand, such events are of non-Communist origin or inspiration, they ought to be viewed as aggression and illegal intervention.

---

[20] *The New York Times*, January 7, 1961; see the heavily documented study of Edward McWhinney, " 'Peaceful Co-Existence' and Soviet-Western International Law," 56 *A.J.I.L.* (1962), pp. 951–970, at pp. 956–958.

[21] Quoted in Deane and David Heller, *The Cold War* (Derby, Conn.: Monarch Books, 1962), at p. 69.

[22] *The New York Times*, September 4, 1965, p. 2; the *Times* devoted its entire second page to a reprint of substantial portions of Lin's pronouncement.

Harvard Code. The Harvard Research in International Law made a detailed study, complete with draft convention, of the problem of aggression before the outbreak of World War II; but because of the time lag involved in publication, the results of the investigation did not appear in print until after the beginning of hostilities.[23] The Harvard group sidestepped the knotty problem of the definition of "aggression" by restricting itself to describing it as "a resort to armed force by a State when such resort had been duly determined, by a means which that State is bound to accept, to constitute a violation of an obligation" (*Harvard Code,* Art. 1-c).

Draft Code of Offenses Against the Peace and Security of Mankind. Regrettably, no generally accepted definition of aggression has been evolved. Although many of the war crimes tribunals sitting after World War II concerned themselves with aspects of aggression, they did not arrive at an acceptable definition.[24] In view of general realization that aggression did constitute an illegal act but could not be punished unless it were known just which acts constituted an offense against international law, the General Assembly of the United Nations moved to settle the issue. On December 11, 1946, it requested the International Law Commission to incorporate the principles of the Charter of the Nuremberg Tribunal and of the latter's judgment in the draft of an international criminal code.

The Commission then drew up such an instrument, the Draft Code of Offenses Against the Peace and Security of Mankind. The latest (1954) version of this code listed the following nine offenses related to the issue of aggression:

1. Acts of aggression, including the use of armed force for purposes other than national or collective self-defense.

2. A threat by the authorities of one state to resort to aggression against another state.

3. Preparation for the use of armed force against another state for purposes other than national or collective self-defense.

4. The organization, encouragement, or toleration of armed bands operating against another state.

5. Undertaking or fomenting civil strife in another state.

[23] Harvard Research in International Law, "Rights and Duties of States in Case of Aggression," 33 *A.J.I.L.* (October, 1939), Supp., pp. 821–909 (hereinafter referred to as *Harvard Code*); the study is extremely valuable, especially the extensive bibliographical section on pp. 831–843.

[24] See Gould, pp. 610–618, and Stone, pp. 330–334, for brief but admirable accounts of the problem and its difficulties; see also Sheldon Glueck, "The Nuremberg Trial and Aggressive War," 59 *Harvard Law Review* (1946), pp. 396–456. Consult the *Harvard Code*, pp. 848–855, for the usage of the term "aggression" by 65 states in treaties or official declarations and statements.

6. The undertaking or encouragement of terrorist activities in another state.

7. Violations of the obligations of treaties restricting or limiting armaments, military training, fortifications, and so on.

8. The annexation of territory belonging to another state or of territory under an international regime by means contrary to international law.

9. Intervention in the internal or external affairs of another state by means of economic or political coercion in order to obtain advantages of any kind.[25]

Thus far, nothing has been done in the General Assembly to transform the Commission's draft code into a law-making treaty. One basic reason for this lack of activity has been a desultory debate in the General Assembly (and also among writers on international law) as to whether a precise definition of aggression is possible or even desirable. A sizeable body of opinion opposes such a definition on the reasonable grounds that it would enable potential aggressors to evade culpability by circumventing precisely detailed formulations. Also, no agreement has been achieved on the question of whether any definition of aggression ought not to include what might be termed *indirect aggression*, such as fifth columns, infiltration, foreign-organized conspiracies, and ideological propaganda. Some of these have been included in the acts listed by the International Law Commission, yet not all such activities constitute aggression which, at least in the meaning of the Charter, is basically limited to the threat or the use of armed force against another state.

Ultimately the General Assembly resumed its endeavor to establish a generally accepted definition of aggression when, on December 18, 1967, it authorized the appointment of a thirty-five-member "Special Committee on the Question of Defining Aggression."[26] It remains to be seen whether this new effort, initiated by the U.S.S.R., will be more productive than past attempts, particularly because several members have intimated that such a definition would not be binding on states opposed to its adoption.[27]

What about the legality of a so-called preventive war (pre-emptive attack), an example of which would be the opening of hostilities by

[25] "Report of the International Law Commission, 1954," 49 *A.J.I.L.* (1955), Supp., pp. 21–22. Consult also D. H. N. Johnson, "The Draft Code of Offenses against the Peace and Security of Mankind," 4 *International and Comparative Law Quarterly* (1955), pp. 445–468, as well as the stimulating but rather controversial views in Julius Stone, *Aggression and World Order—A Critique of United Nations Theories of Aggression* (Berkeley: University of California Press, 1958).

[26] GA Res. 2330 (XXII), 1967; see also 8 *International Legal Materials* (1969), pp. 661–666, for three 1969 proposals on defining aggression.

[27] See John N. Hazard, "Why Try Again to Define Aggression?" 62 *A.J.I.L.* (1968), pp. 701–710.

Israel in the "Six-Day War" of 1967? It may well be that what Secretary of State Daniel Webster admitted in 1842 in the *Caroline* incident to be "instant and overwhelming necessity" should justify counteraction prior to impending attack, in the name of justified self-defense.[28]

Such an interpretation might be applied to the Charter provisions prohibiting threats of the use of armed force and would justify striking the first blow at an enemy gathering forces for an impending attack, particularly if appeals to international organizations had failed to produce actions designed to remove the threats existing. Under traditional international law, a clear-cut case for self-defense could be made, even if no attack had been launched, when there was a definite threat of injury. "Under the Charter, alarming military preparations by a neighboring state would justify a resort to the Security Council, but would not justify resort to anticipatory force by the state which believed itself to be threatened."[29] Well and good, but what if it could be anticipated with good reason that the Security Council would not act or if the threat of attack was so imminent that a nation's survival could not be made dependent on discussion, debate, and possible Security Council action at some future date? In that case, it is submitted, a preventive use of force by the threatened state would be justified.[30]

At the same time, unlimited freedom to strike at another state in the name of self-defense would reduce to rubbish all attempts to prevent the outbreak of international violence. Hence the least that should be done, under the conditions outlined, would be to provide a way for third-party judgment as to the validity of the claim of self-defense for the preventive use of force, if such validity had not been completely evident from the beginning, to assess damages, or even to impose sanctions against the offending state.

INTERMEDIACY CONCEPT

Before ending this introductory chapter, two subjects merit brief inspection. The struggles carried on in the past between states usually were clearcut in the methods by which they were carried on. Two countries would be found either in a state of peace or in a state of war, as far as their mutual relations were concerned. In either case, known and accepted rules and principles applied to those relations.

The appearance of ideologies such as Communism and Fascism, and the coming of the global struggle commonly termed the Cold War, have

[28] On this point see Quincy Wright, "Power Politics or a Rule of Law?" 147 *New Republic*, No. 26 (December 29, 1962), pp. 11–12; see also Chapter 9, *supra*, under Right of Self-defense.

[29] Philip C. Jessup, "Force Under a Modern Law of Nations," 25 *Foreign Affairs* (1946), pp. 90–105, at p. 96.

[30] For a contrary point of view, consult Warren G. Corliss, "The Case Against Pre-Emptive Attack," 87 *U.S. Naval Institute Proceedings* (July, 1961), pp. 31–35.

confused the picture. Fifth columns, subversion, propaganda of new and insidious kinds, armed clashes involving parties most unwilling to admit the existence of a state of war, "limited war," and various other new elements of international conflict have produced situations in which the distinctions between war and peace have become vague and unreal. The world has found itself, with increasing frequency, in a state corresponding neither to war nor to peace in the accepted meanings of those terms. If force is utilized, but neither party in the conflict refers to it as war, refuses to declare war, and retains a diplomatic mission at each other's capital, should the laws of war apply or should one and all continue to act as if true peace prevailed?

Considerations such as these have led a number of students of the world scene to ask whether a clearly demarked intermediate status between peace and war should not be developed in theory and then in law, in order to enable one and all to see matters more clearly, a "state of intermediacy," to use the phrase of one of those writers.[31] The concept of intermediacy is an intriguing one—it possesses much merit as a device to illuminate the zone between peaceful relations and general (total, or all-out) war, and might serve extremely useful purposes in outlining the rules possible of application to the currently fashionable concept of limited war and to "limited friction." As a number of commentators have hastened to point out, intermediacy has no place in existing international law. But because the concept appears to exist in practice, perhaps here, too, the law ought to follow the current activities of its subjects and provide guidelines and regulations for those activities.

UNITED NATIONS ARMED FORCES

The subject of the status of war in the modern world cannot be concluded without a brief consideration of the emergence of international commands as parties to a conflict. Logically this might have been left to the chapter dealing with participants in a modern war, but the topic is so fundamental to the status of war itself that it will be handled at this point.

The question of the legal basis for United Nations armed 'forces poses immense and practical problems for the future work of the organization in its announced major sphere of keeping the peace.[32]

[31] Philip C. Jessup, "Should International Law Recognize an Intermediate Status between Peace and War?" 48 *A.J.I.L.* (1954), pp. 98–102. See also Myres S. McDougal and Florentino P. Feliciano, "International Coercion and World Public Order: The General Principles of the Law of War," 67 *Yale Law Journal* (1958), pp. 774–779; the position of the two authors is clarified at length in their heavily documented basic study, "The Initiation of Coercion: A Multi-Temporal Analysis," 52 *A.J.I.L.* (1958), pp. 241–259. Consult also Myres S. McDougal, "Peace and War: Factual Continuum with Multiple Legal Consequences," *ibid.*, 49 (1955), pp. 63–68.

[32] See especially John W. Halderman, "Legal Basis for United Nations Armed Forces," 56 *A.J.I.L.* (1962), pp. 971–996; Committee of Study of Legal Problems of the United Nations, "The Establishment of the United Nations Emergency Force," *Proceedings* (1957), pp. 206–229.

The United Nations has already authorized, on four occasions, armed forces to deal with a threat to the peace of the world. The action in repelling the North Korean invasion of South Korea in 1950 may have prevented a third world war; the formation of the UN Emergency Force (UNEF) played a key part in ending the fighting in the Near East in 1956 and in restoring an uneasy peace in the region; the establishment of the UN Force in the Congo (ONUC) in 1960 reunited the secessionist province of Katanga with the rest of the state; in 1964, peace-keeping forces were dispatched to Cyprus.

The authority of the United Nations for the creation of armed forces is found in the Charter in Articles 1 (1), 39, 41, and 42. The last of these is undoubtedly the most important one:

Should the Security Council consider that measures provided for in Article 41 would be inadequate or have proved to be inadequate, it may take such action by air, sea, or land forces as may be necessary to maintain or restore international peace and security. Such action may include demonstrations, blockade, and other operations by air, sea, or land forces of Members of the United Nations.

After the attack by North Korean forces on South Korea in June, 1950, the Security Council voted (in the absence of the Soviet Union) to create a "unified Command under the United States" and recommended that the members of the United Nations make military forces and other aid available to that command. Sixteen states supplied combat units and five others sent medical units.

Despite argument to the contrary, there can be no doubt that the Korean operation was a measure taken by the United Nations, and one taken in accordance with the provisions of the Charter. The Security Council had officially determined that a breach of the peace had taken place (June 25, 1950) and its resolution of July 27, 1950, recommended effective assistance to the Republic of Korea "to repel the armed attack and to restore international peace and security in the area."[33] Further proof of the official character of the steps taken in the Korean situation is found in the resolution of the General Assembly of May 18, 1951, recommending the application of an embargo of arms and strategic materials against both the North Korean and Communist Chinese regimes. The reader should note, however, that in the Korean instance the United Nations only created a "unified command." The term *United Nations Command* was introduced, it must be suspected, for propaganda purposes. It achieved wide usage, but did not correspond to the technical fact that

[33] See Halderman, *op. cit.*, pp. 974–975; consult also Josef L. Kunz, "Legality of the Security Council Resolutions of June 25 and 27, 1950," 45 *A.J.I.L.* (1951), pp. 137–142; A. Kenneth Pye, "The Legal Status of the Korean Hostilities," 45 *Georgetown Law Journal* (Feb., 1956), pp. 45–60, and see also Bishop, pp. 759–770 for a good selection of relevant documents.

only a unified command under the United States could be attributed juridically to the United Nations. The forces operating in Korea were not, legally speaking, a United Nations Expeditionary Force.

United Nations Emergency Force (UNEF). The establishment of UNEF took place in connection with the Suez Crisis of 1956 and represented action by the General Assembly rather than by the Security Council. The inability of the latter to act because of the veto brought into being the first application of the "Uniting for Peace" Resolution.

The actual force was created by a variety of devices: the Command was established by the General Assembly Resolution of November 5, 1956; the commanding officer and the initial group of officers were taken from the United Nations Truce Supervision Organization in Palestine; the remainder, some 5,000 men, were supplied by a group other than the permanent members of the Security Council. As far as the legal basis for these methods and for the establishment of UNEF itself was concerned, the General Assembly relied entirely on the provisions of the Charter as developed by the 1950 "Uniting for Peace" Resolution.[34]

All units of UNEF were withdrawn from Egyptian territory on May 19, 1967, at the request of the government of the United Arab Republic, and the entire Sinai Peninsula along the Israeli border was declared by the U.A.R. military command to be a "forbidden area" to foreign military personnel. A few days later the "Six-Day War" erupted.

United Nations Forces in the Congo (ONUC). The creation of ONUC was different, procedurally, from the earlier instances cited and has remained the subject of controversy among a variety of commentators. The initial step leading to the establishment of ONUC was a request from the Congolese government (July 12–13, 1960) to the Secretary-General. In accordance with a recommendation of the latter, the Security Council on July 14, 1960, authorized the Secretary-General to furnish military assistance to the Congo until its own security forces would be able to fulfill their tasks. The Secretary-General thereupon supervised the creation of ONUC, which consisted of troops supplied voluntarily by members and which served under United Nations Command.

Of key importance to the role played by ONUC in the Congo during 1961 and to the end of January, 1962, when the rebellious province of Katanga surrendered to the control of central Congolese authorities was the Security Council resolution of February 21, 1961. In that document the Council urged that the United Nations should take all appropriate measures to prevent the occurrence of civil war in the Congo, including,

---

[34] See Leland M. Goodrich and Barriella E. Rosner, "The United Nations Emergency Force," 11 *International Organization* (1957), pp. 413–430, and Bishop, pp. 773–776, for materials relating to the Suez crisis of 1956 and UNEF. Consult also Francis O. Wilcox, "International Confederation: The United Nations and State Sovereignty," pp. 29–66 in Plischke, at pp. 47–50. The text of the "Uniting for Peace" Resolution has been reprinted in 45 *A.J.I.L.* (1951), Supp., pp. 1–5, and in Bishop, pp. 770–771.

if necessary and in the last resort, the use of force. Findings of a threat to the peace were contained in a report by the Secretary-General, on February 27, 1961, and in a General Assembly resolution adopted on April 15, 1961.

However, because enforcement measures and collective measures, under the Charter, are generally held to be the same, ONUC's status as a collective measure had been doubted by many. Not a single theory advanced to explain the basis of ONUC in the Charter has been entirely satisfactory. The problem was complicated by the fact that both before and after the Security Council action authorizing ONUC to use force, if need be, to prevent civil war in the Congo, the Secretary-General specifically denied that the operation was under the provisions of Articles 41 and 42 of the Charter—which would have overridden the domestic jurisdiction limitations found in Article 2 (7).

On April 17, 1961, he stated to Committee V of the General Assembly that the operation of ONUC represented "the use of military personnel or contingents for essentially internal security functions in the territory of a Member State at the invitation of the Government of that State. . . . The measures themselves did not constitute "sanctions" or enforcement action directed against a State as contemplated by Articles 42 and 43 of the Charter." [35]

A study of the relevant documents establishes clearly that ONUC has to be viewed as a subsidiary organ of the United Nations whose personnel possessed an international status and were subject to Article 100 of the Charter, prohibiting the seeking or accepting of instructions of their governments with respect to duties in ONUC.[36]

Cyprus Peace-Keeping Force. The latest UN effort to keep the peace took place on the island of Cyprus. Following outbreaks of violence between the Greek and Turkish elements of the population, and appeals for UN action addressed to the Security Council, the latter recommended in March, 1964, that a United Nations Peace-Keeping Force (UN-FICYP) be established, initially for a three-month period. The mandate for the force of about 4,500 troops was extended periodically, and it still occupied its position, interposed between the two hostile communities, at the time of writing. The Cyprus force has been financed jointly by the states providing military contingents, the government of Cyprus, and voluntary contributions from various member states of the United Nations. A mediator and his small staff, appointed by the Security Council, has been paid from contributions assessed on the United Nations membership.

United Nations Field Service. The difficulties encountered in securing necessary military and financial support from the members of the United

[35] U.N. Doc. A/C.5/864, quoted in Halderman, *op. cit.*, pp. 988–989.

[36] See the excellent analysis of ONUC in E. M. Miller, "Legal Aspects of the United Nations Action in the Congo," 55 *A.J.I.L.* (1961), pp. 1–28, particularly at p. 11 on this point.

cited led inevitably to consideration of the possibility of establishing a Permanent United Nations Force.

Such a concept was first explored in the United Nations in 1948 during the Palestine crisis. After some study by a Special Committee of the General Assembly, the Secretary-General was authorized to establish a United Nations Field Service, composed of several hundred communications technicians and some guards (October, 1949). This unit now forms a part of the UN Secretariat. In 1950 and 1952, the Secretary-General again brought up proposals to establish a United Nations Legion or, at the very least, a UN Volunteer Reserve, but encountered only unfavorable reactions to the idea.

UN Financial Crisis. One of the more curious but all too human problems encountered with distressing results by the United Nations has been the apparent willingness of some members to support (or at least not to oppose) various programs of action, yet to be quite unwilling to pay for them. Nowhere did this phenomenon display itself more clearly than in the continuing wrangling over payments for the costs of peace-keeping operations in the Middle East and in the Congo.

The 1956 General Assembly resolution to assess members with the costs of UNEF had been approved by an affirmative vote of 64 to 0, with twelve abstentions; the Assembly resolution establishing assessments for ONUC in 1960 had been approved 70 to 0, with eleven abstentions. Despite such overwhelming support for the operations in question, it soon became apparent that many members were increasingly in arrears in paying their assessments. By the fall of 1962, only twenty-nine states had paid what they owed on the expenses of UNEF, twenty-five others had made partial payments but were still in arrears, and twenty-four had paid no assessments at all. In the case of the maintenance costs of ONUC, only twenty-seven members had met their assessments by September 1, 1962, ten were in arrears for part of their contributions, and sixty-three had failed to make any payments whatsoever.[37]

The whole matter had received widespread publicity when the Acting Secretary-General had told the Fifth Committee of the General Assembly on December 11, 1961, that imminent bankruptcy faced the United Nations, with an estimated deficit at the end of 1961 of $107 million and a probable deficit of $170 million by the end of June, 1962. Peace-keeping operations in the Middle East and the Congo had, by that time, reached the staggering cost of $140 million per year.

The General Assembly authorized the Secretary-General to issue $200 million worth of UN bonds, repayable at 2 per cent interest over a period of 25 years. The proceeds from the sale of the bonds were to be used to meet the current expenses of the United Nations.

[37] Statement on the Collection of Contributions as of August 31, 1962, UN Document St/ADM/SER.B/163/Rev.1, September 10, 1962.

The General Assembly also adopted a resolution, by a vote of 52 to 11, with thirty-two abstentions, requesting an advisory opinion from the International Court of Justice as to whether the expenses authorized in the assessment resolutions covering UNEF and ONUC were "expenses of the organization" within the meaning of Article 17 of the Charter. If such was the case, then Article 17 provided that such expenses "shall be borne by the Members as apportioned by the General Assembly."

The Court gave notice of the proceedings to all UN members and invited them to submit views in writing or in oral pleadings. The results were astonishing: on no previous occasion had so many states participated in the proceedings of the Court. Twenty countries submitted written views, and nine states (including the United States and, for the first time, the U.S.S.R.) pleaded orally before the Court.

Two months later, the International Court of Justice handed down its opinion, holding, by a vote of 9 to 5, that the expenses in question were indeed "expenses of the Organization" in the meaning of Article 17 of the Charter.[38]

Almost at once delinquent members began to make payments, and by July, 1963, $16 million in arrearages had been collected from forty-six countries. But several states, some large, some small, refused to comply with the assessment resolutions. By the end of 1963, accumulated arrearages of assessments totalled $150 million (in addition to the $151 million of bonds issued and not yet repaid at that time.

What were the reasons advanced for nonpayment? The Soviet Union and France both maintained that the Security Council alone possessed authority to establish peace-keeping forces, including their financing, that accordingly the General Assembly had exceeded its powers in passing the assessment resolutions for UNEF and ONUC, and that in consequence neither resolution bound member states. A number of Latin American countries asserted the view that 70 per cent of ONUC costs should be borne by the five permanent members of the Security Council, because it had been that body which had established ONUC. France, Belgium, Portugal, and the Republic of South Africa objected, for various but obvious reasons, to the whole concept of ONUC and argued that they should not be burdened with any portions of the costs of that enterprise.

[38] *Certain Expenses of the United Nations (Article 17, Paragraph 2, of the Charter)*, Advisory Opinion, International Court of Justice, 1962, *I.C.J. Reports, 1962*, p. 151, in 56 *A.J.I.L.* (1962), pp. 1053–1083. Consult also Leo Gross, "Expenses of the United Nations for Peace-Keeping Operations: The Advisory Opinion of the International Court of Justice," 17 *International Organization* (1963), pp. 1–35; Inis Claude, Jr., "The Political Framework of the United Nations' Financial Problems," *ibid.*, pp. 831–859; Abram Chayes, "The Rule of Law—Now," excerpted in 57 *A.J.I.L.* (1963), pp. 912–918; "Statement of United States Ambassador Philip M. Klutznick before Committee V of the UN General Assembly, December 3, 1962," 48 *Department of State Bulletin* (1963), pp. 30–35.

Most of the Arab states objected as a matter of principle to any contribution on their part to UNEF, in view of their announced attitudes toward the state of Israel.

The Soviet Union in particular has led the continuing opposition of members against payment of the peace-keeping assessments, and on at least two occasions (June 27, 1963, and March 21, 1964), the Soviet delegation at the United Nations issued statements of the views of its government, namely, refusal to contribute any funds to UNEF, ONUC, the Korea Unification Commission, and the UN Truce Supervision Organization in the Middle East.[39]

Article 19 of the Charter. The legally fascinating aspect of these continued refusals to meet certain assessed expenses is found in the possibility that Article 19 of the Charter might be applied against members in arrears. That article reads

A Member of the United Nations which is in arrears in the payment of its financial contributions to the Organization *shall have no vote in the General Assembly* if the amount of its arrears equals or exceeds the amount of the contributions due from it for the preceding two full years. The General Assembly may, nevertheless, permit such a Member to vote if it is satisfied that the failure to pay is due to conditions beyond the control of the Member [italics added].

By March, 1964, the Soviet Union owed the United Nations a total of $52.6 million. Six countries had owed more than two years' contributions when the seventeenth session of the General Assembly was about to meet, and ten states were in the same position just before the special session of the Assembly in the spring of 1963. In all but one case, sufficient payments were made in each instance at the last moment to avoid an invocation of Article 17.

Only Haiti was in arrears for more than the total of two years' contributions when the 1963 special session began. When the Assembly convened on May 14, the Secretary-General informed the Assembly President by letter that Haiti owed more than the amount specified in Article 19. At the opening plenary session, the Haitian delegate was absent. The President of the Assembly then replied to the letter of the Secretary-General, stating that

. . . I would have made an announcement drawing the attention of the Assembly to the loss of voting rights in the Assembly of the Member State . . . , under the first sentence of Article 19, had a formal count of vote taken place in the presence of a representative of that State at the opening plenary meeting.[40]

[39] See *The New York Times*, June 28, 1963, and March 22, 1964.
[40] Chayes, *op. cit.*, p. 916.

In 1964, the arrearages of the U.S.S.R. made the provisions of Article 19 of the Charter applicable to that country. It was not expected that inability to pay because of conditions beyond the control of the Soviet Union could be pleaded successfully. Because the General Assembly, by formal resolution on December 19, 1962, accepted the advisory opinion of the World Court and because the language of Article 19 appeared to impose an obligatory loss of voting rights on delinquent members, the Soviet Union appeared to stand a good chance of being deprived of its vote in the General Assembly, with members of the Soviet bloc of satellites likely candidates for similar treatment when their arrearages met the requirements of Article 19.

The distinct possibility of the invocation of Article 19 helped to explain the vehemence with which the peace-keeping assessments were denounced by the Soviet Union, both before the International Court of Justice and in the statements released by the head of the Soviet mission to the United Nations. It was asserted that any actions designed to deprive the Soviet Union of its voting privileges in the Assembly would be considered as "the actions of those who do not care for the United Nations and who do not take into account the prospectives of its breakup as a result of such actions." [41]

The United States made it clear on several occasions that it regarded the provisions of Article 19 not only as mandatory but also as automatic in their application. Prior to the issuance of the Russian statement of March 21, 1964, the United States and the United Kingdom delegations at the United Nations had worked out a compromise scheme. The plan envisaged the creation, by the Assembly, of a committee to be charged with the financing of all future peace-keeping operations. Each member state currently in arrears would be asked to pay enough to prevent invocation of Article 19, and the proposed committee would then work out a scale of new assessments for future operations. The plan apparently also recognized the validity of certain Russian and French arguments by stipulating that future peacekeeping efforts would be submitted initially to the Security Council. If the latter then failed to act, the General Assembly would handle the question. The Russian statement of March 21, 1964, doomed the compromise scheme, however.

The 1964–65 session of the General Assembly witnessed scenes worthy of the talents of the late Messrs. Gilbert and Sullivan. In order to avert the crisis over the prospective loss of the vote of the Soviet Union, the device of not taking any votes was adopted. After weeks of frustrating debate, punctuated by attempts on the part of Albania and others to force a vote and hence a showdown about Russian arrears, the Assembly adjourned. As one of its last acts, the session created, on February 18, 1965, without a vote a Special (thirty-three member) Committee to study the

[41] *The New York Times*, March 22, 1964.

subject of peace-keeping operations and the coverage of their costs. The committee met fourteen times, yet was unable to reconcile fundamentally opposing views on the payments crisis.

Finally, on August 16, 1965, the United States yielded and declared that it "recognizes, as it simply must, that the General Assembly is not prepared to apply Article 19 in the present situation, and that the consensus of the membership is that the Assembly should proceed normally. We will not seek to frustrate that consensus. . . ." [42] Consequently the Special Committee could agree that Article 19 would not be raised again relative to UNEF and ONUC and that the financial problems of the United Nations should be solved by means of voluntary contributions. Hence the twentieth Assembly was able to proceed normally about its business.

Thus far, however, no way has been found of paying outstanding obligations arising out of the UNEF and ONUC operations. Total unpaid debts for the Middle East forces amounted to $25 million, owed to eight states, and $13 million was still owed to a total of eighteen states for the Congo action. The largest creditors were the United States ($4.5 million), followed in order by Denmark, Norway and Sweden. All were notified by the Secretariat in September, 1968, that any payment on these debts had to be postponed indefinitely.

SUMMARY

In summary, some varieties of war have come to be regarded as illegal, even as criminal, whereas other varieties are still regarded as lawful, such as self-defense against attack. As von Elbe observed, "A profound change in the general attitude towards war has occurred; the law must follow it." [43] Unfortunately, the law has not done so yet, at least not in clear and unmistakable terms. Even if war has been outlawed—and serious questions might be raised about such a sweeping generalization—it has not been abolished in fact. Nations are still arming for defense and, it is suspected in some cases, for possible attacks. From the end of World War II to the fall of 1965, at least twenty-two conflicts involving two or more states have taken place (as well as at least twenty-four civil wars, some of which must be suspected of having involved outside instigation or help to one side or the other). [44] As Ross phrased an unhappy conclusion,

Hitherto all attempts at prohibiting war must be regarded as a failure. Before an effective organ of power has been developed among the community of nations which in the name of the law can counteract and overcome the out-

---

[42] UN Doc. A/AC.121/PV.15.

[43] von Elbe, *op. cit.*, p. 688.

[44] See, *inter alia*, the revealing essay "On War as a Permanent Condition," in 86 *Time* (September 24, 1965), pp. 30–31.

rages of individual States, it is too early to introduce legal prohibitions on war and intervention.[45]

Small wonder, than, that it appears eminently desirable—even necessary—to devote the remaining portion of this volume to an examination of the rules governing international conflicts. Regardless of whether such conflicts are "legal" or "illegal," their occurrence will demand the application of principles designed to mitigate man's cruelty to man. On the other hand, the UN Charter prohibitions on the use of force reflect more than mere dreams: they represent, instead, a growing community policy aimed at preventing total disaster and anarchy. This is the great hope which, in a small way, to be sure, is expressed in the new attitudes toward war.

Some writers, optimistic in their beliefs concerning the efficacy of peaceful methods in settling all disputes and confident that the United Nations would prevent future wars, except police actions in the event of atavistic aggression, have reduced their coverage of the materials dealing with war to a minimum. The present writer, neither optimistic nor confident concerning the abatement of international strife, believes that substantial space has to be devoted, without apology, to covering the laws governing wars, military occupation, the remnants of neutrality, and war crimes and their punishment. It may be that someday war will have disappeared from the earth and mankind may live in peace under a common law, but this millennial condition does not loom over the horizon; hence the law of war needs to be continued as a subject of instruction for students of international law.

SUGGESTED READINGS

LEGAL NATURE OF WAR: GENERAL

Georg Schwarzenberger, "Jus Pacis ac Belli?" 37 *A.J.I.L.* (1943), pp. 460–479; R. W. Tucker, "The Interpretation of War under Present International Law," 4 *International Law Quarterly* (1951), pp. 11–38; Elihu Lauterpacht, "The Legal Irrelevance of the 'State of War'," *Proceedings* (1968), pp. 58–68; R. R. Baxter, "The Legal Consequence of the Unlawful Use of Force under the Charter," *ibid.*, pp. 68–76.

UN PEACE-KEEPING FORCES

Ruth B. Russell, *United Nations Experience with Military Forces: Political and Legal Aspects* (Washington, D.C.: The Brookings Institution, 1964); D. W. Bowett, *United Nations Forces: A Legal Study* (New York: Praeger, 1965); Arthur L. Burns and Nina Heathcote, *Peace-Keeping by U.N. Forces*

---

[45] Alf Ross, *A Text-Book of International Law* (New York: Longman's, Green & Co., 1948), pp. 185–186.

(*From Suez to the Congo*) (Princeton, N.J.: Princeton University Press, 1963); Arthur M. Cox, *Prospects for Peacekeeping* (Washington, D.C.: The Brookings Institution, 1967); Lincoln P. Bloomfield, ed., *International Military Forces* (Boston: Little, Brown and Co., 1963); David W. Wainhouse et al., *International Peace Observation* (Baltimore: The Johns Hopkins Press, 1966); Arthur L. Burns, *Peacekeeping by U.N. Forces* (New York: Praeger, 1964); Ernest W. Lefever, *Uncertain Mandates Politics of the U.N. Congo Operation* (Baltimore: The Johns Hopkins Press, 1967), as well as his *Crisis in the Congo* (*A U.N. Force in Action*) (Washington, D.C.: The Brookings Institution, 1965); Linda B. Miller, *World Order and Local Disorder: The United Nations and Internal Conflict* (Princeton, N.J.: Princeton University Press, 1967); James A. Stegenga, *The United Nations Force in Cyprus* (Columbus: Ohio State University Press, 1968); Donald W. McNemar, "The Post-Independence War in the Congo," *Proceedings* (1967), pp. 13–18; Lincoln P. Bloomfield, "Peacekeeping and Peacemaking," 44 *Foreign Affairs* (1966), pp. 671–682; Louis B. Sohn, "The Rôle of the United Nations in Civil Wars," *Proceedings* (1963), pp. 208–215; Oscar Schachter, "Preventing the Internationalization of Internal Conflict: A Legal Analysis of the U.N. Congo Experience," *ibid.*, pp. 216–224; Richard N. Gardner, "The Development of the Peace-Keeping Capacity of the United Nations," *ibid.*, pp. 225–234; Whiteman, Vol. XIII, pp. 586–610.

Case

Nissan v. *Attorney-General*, Great Britain, Court of Appeal, Civil Division, 1967, [1967] 2 All E.R. 1238, reported in 62 *A.J.I.L.* (1968), pp. 511–513, and, more extensively, in 8 *International Legal Materials* (1969), pp. 588–597.

UN PAYMENTS CRISIS

John G. Stoessinger et al., *Financing the United Nations System* (Washington, D.C.: The Brookings Institution, 1964); Office of the Legal Adviser, Department of State, "Memorandum of Law: Article 19 of the Charter of the United Nations," 58 *A.J.I.L.* (1964), pp. 753–778; Whiteman, Vol. XIII, pp. 307–339; and the revealing collection of U.N. documents in 8 *International Legal Materials* (1969), pp. 434–440.

26

Laws of War

GENERAL DEVELOPMENT

INTERNATIONAL law has always concerned itself as much with the conduct of states engaged in war as it has with their relations in time of peace. Indeed, the authors of the classics in the law gave priority in space and attention to hostile relations among nations, a practice quite justified by the "normalcy" of such relations compared with the relative abnormality of peace among the states of Europe. The gradual development of a stable international order favored the growth of rules governing the rights and duties of states in time of peace, and in modern times the "law of peace" occupies the bulk of any treatise on international law.

Beginning with the Thirty Years War (1618–48), isolated instances of humane practice in the conduct of hostilities acquired in the course of time the status of usages and ultimately came to be regarded as customs, as binding legal obligations to be observed by states at war with one another. To some it may appear paradoxical, even ridiculous, that the killing of human beings, facilitated increasingly by the development of more effective instruments of death, should be regulated equally increasingly by rules designed to introduce a measure of humaneness into a bloody business. Unthinking men may indeed have wondered time and again why it should make any real difference *how* one soldier should dispose of another soldier—an enemy who, given a chance, would kill him; or, why it should be acceptable to drop a shell on a military installation in an enemy town, yet illegal to drop another shell on the nearby house of a civilian engaged, during working hours, in producing the weapons used by the men in that military installation.

The answer to such observations is that many people in many countries have achieved a measure of pride in the fact that they have achieved a degree of civilization in which it is possible to show some decency even to a mortal enemy. Also, leaving aside such cultural, as well as any moral or religious, considerations (even though the latter are extremely important at times in justifying restraint from barbarism), there are some real practical values involved in the regulation of warfare. Moderation and humaneness have, at times, not only prevented retaliation by the enemy but have led forces of the latter to surrender instead of fighting to the bitter end, thus dispensing with the heavy losses to both sides involved in such a suicidal course of action. And until the development of such modern tools of war as saturation bombing (with incendiary and/or normal bombs) and nuclear bombing, the application of rules to the conduct of warfare has on many occasions lessened materially the destruction of property.

"*The Laws of War.*" Lauterpacht pointed out that three basic principles have determined the growth of the "laws of war": the principle that a belligerent is justified to apply any amount and any kind of force considered necessary to achieve the goal of a conflict—the defeat of the enemy. In the second place, the principle that because of humanitarian considerations any violence not necessary for the achievement of that goal should be prohibited. And, thirdly, the principle that a certain amount of chivalry, of the spirit of fairness, should prevail in the conduct of hostilities, that certain practices smacking of fraud and deceit should be avoided.[1] Naturally, no rules would prevail in any conflict if human beings considered themselves free of the application of all human values, of all sense of decency, fairness, justice, just as they would not prevail if a given conflict came to be regarded as a holy crusade designed to exterminate everyone on the opposing side. Such atavisms have occurred, of course, even in very modern times, but it is to the credit of man that each such instance has resulted in deep shock and disgust on the part of the vast majority of human beings and in a determination to prevent a recurrence of such acts.

The "laws of war," as mentioned, took the initial form of rules of customary law, beginning even before the sixteenth century. Their modern development, however, has taken place through the application of conventional law, through the conclusion of a number of multilateral treaties.

Early Attempts to Develop the Laws of War. The middle of the nineteenth century witnessed the birth of this stage in the growth of the law. First among the major instruments dealing with modern war was probably the Declaration of Paris (1856), under which privateering was abolished, regulations were formulated concerning the status of noncontraband goods, and the principle laid down that a blockade had to be effective in order to possess legal binding force. There followed the Geneva Convention of 1864, concerned with the wounded in the field; the original treaty was replaced by a revision, signed at Geneva on July 6, 1906. In 1868, the Declaration of St. Petersburg prohibited the use of small (under 14 ounces in weight) explosive or incendiary projectiles.

Following the Franco-Prussian War of 1870–71, which had amply demonstrated the inadequacy of existing customary rules of law and had led to acrimonious reciprocal accusations concerning real or fancied violations of those rules, an international conference, called at the initiative of Russia, met at Brussels in 1874. Fifteen states sent representatives, including

[1] Lauterpacht's *Oppenheim*, Vol. II, p. 227.

eighteen military men and ten diplomats, but only four jurists. The purpose of the gathering was the drafting of a comprehensive set of rules governing hostilities. Unfortunately this goal was not achieved, in part because of lack of cooperation on the part of Great Britain, in part because of political troubles in the Near East which occurred at the time.

The Declaration of Brussels, the sole result of the conference, possessed no legally binding force because the participating states failed to ratify it, but it served as the basis of succeeding private meetings devoted to the laws of war.[2]

The Hague Conferences. In 1899, the First Peace Conference at The Hague resulted in the signing of the Convention with Respect to the Laws and Customs of War on Land, derived from the *Instructions for the Government of Armies of the United States in the Field,* issued during the Civil War (April 24, 1863) and based on a draft by Dr. Francis Lieber of Columbia.[3] The Second Peace Conference, which met in 1907 at The Hague, revised the earlier convention and the new version is known as Convention IV [Convention Respecting the Laws and Customs of War on Land, The Hague, October 18, 1907]. The drafters of the document realized full well that many aspects of the conduct of hostilities had not been covered fully, or had been omitted altogether from the document. Hence the Preamble of the convention included toward its end the significant statement that

According to the views of the High Contracting Parties, these provisions, the wording of which has been inspired by the desire to diminish the evils of war as far as military necessities permit, are intended to serve as a general rule of conduct for the belligerents in their mutual relations and in their relations with the inhabitants.

It has not, however, been found possible at present to concert Regulations covering all the circumstances which arise in practice.

On the other hand, the High Contracting Parties clearly do not intend that unforeseen cases should, in the absence of a written undertaking, be left to the arbitrary judgment of military Commanders.

Until a more complete code of the laws of war has been issued, the High Contracting Parties deem it expedient to declare that, in cases not included in the Regulations adopted by them, the inhabitants and the belligerents remain under the protection and the rule of the principles of the law of nations, as they result from the usages established among civilized peoples, from the laws of humanity, and the dictates of the public conscience.

It should be noted that both Hague Conventions declared or stated principles and rules which, in essence, represented then existing customary

[2] See Doris A. Graber, *The Development of the Law of Belligerent Occupation, 1863–1914* (New York: Columbia University Press, 1949), at pp. 20–30, 297–317, and James B. Scott, *Resolutions of the Institute of International Law Dealing with the Law of Nations* (New York: Oxford University Press, 1916), pp. 8–12.

[3] See von Glahn, pp. 8–16; see also suggested readings for this chapter for the general and detailed background of the laws of war, as well as Chapters 28 and 29.

international law. A basic weakness, found in both instruments, was the so-called general participation clause which provided that the Regulations annexed to each treaty would apply only as long as all parties to a conflict were also parties to the convention in question; if a noncontracting state was involved in a war, the Regulations were not to be binding. Much ink has been spilled in discussing these clauses, the one in the 1907 Convention having been invoked by Germany in 1914. But the argument was essentially academic in nature, because the two instruments were declaratory, for the most part, of customary rules of law which would have applied to all parties to a conflict irrespective of the applicability of a Hague Convention.

The 1907 Conference resulted also in a number of additional instruments relating to the conduct of hostilities: a declaration concerning expanding bullets (dumdum bullets, named after a British arsenal in India in which such bullets had first been produced on a quantity basis), a declaration dealing with projectiles and explosives dropped from balloons, a declaration concerning projectiles diffusing gases of various kinds, a convention adapting to maritime warfare the principles of the Geneva Convention as revised in 1907, and conventions dealing with the opening of hostilities, the status of merchant vessels at the outbreak of hostilities, the conversion of merchant vessels into warships, the laying of automatic contact mines, bombardment by naval forces in time of war, restrictions on the right of capture in maritime war, and on the rights and duties of neutral states and persons in land warfare and in naval warfare. The convention concerned with the relations between neutral and belligerent states in maritime war was intended to be supplemented by the Declaration of London of 1909, but failed to be ratified.

Attempts to Develop Laws of War After World Wars I and II. After World War I, a number of additional instruments were negotiated. The arrival of effective air warfare was intended to be covered by a new convention drafted by a representative group of jurists at The Hague in 1922, but this convention again failed of ratification; on the other hand, there came into existence in 1925 the Protocol on the use in war of poison gases as well as on bacteriological warfare, the 1929 Geneva Conventions on the treatment of the sick and wounded as well as of prisoners of war, and the London Protocol of 1936 concerning the use of submarines against merchant ships. On the regional level, the Sixth Conference of American States at Havana in 1928 adopted a Convention on Maritime Neutrality (ratified by the United States in 1932), and in 1938 a group of regulations termed the Scandinavian Rules of Neutrality were adopted by Sweden, Norway, Denmark, Finland, and Iceland.

World War II was followed by extensive efforts to enact new lawmaking treaties in order to benefit from the bitter lessons in lawlessness learned during that conflict and to fill at least some of the major gaps in the laws of war. Thus the Geneva Diplomatic Conference of 1949 succeeded in drafting four major conventions: Treatment of Prisoners of War; Amelioration of the Condition of the Wounded and Sick in Armed Forces in the Field; Amelioration of the Condition of Wounded, Sick and Shipwrecked Members of Armed Forces at Sea; and Protection of Civilian Persons in Time of War.[4] But even with these modern additions, the "laws of war" are still quite badly in need of improvement.[5]

Customary laws of war are binding on all belligerents. The Hague Conventions of 1899 and 1907 are binding on all belligerents to the extent that they represent customary law and are binding wholly in the event that all belligerents in a given war are signatories of the convention in question. The treaties concluded since 1907 are binding wholly only on signatory or adhering states. There is some question whether a binding rule may be disregarded in the case of reprisals adopted by one belligerent in retaliation against prior illegal acts committed by an opposing belligerent.[6]

One of the most bitter arguments connected with the laws of war has centered on the traditional German assertion, adopted by other states on occasion, that the laws of war may be set aside in the case of extreme necessity—such as when only a violation of the laws would enable a country or a military force to escape from deadly danger or to achieve the purpose of the war, the defeat of the enemy.

An unlimited doctrine of military necessity (*Kriegsraison*) cannot be supported today. Its acceptance without qualification would serve to reduce all the laws of war to mere dogmas of military convenience, to be observed when it was not dangerous to do so, and to be disregarded whenever such a course of action appeared to possess merit or when it would appear essential to adopt it. Each particular instance in which the doctrine is invoked must, therefore, be judged on its own merits. If honest conviction and corroborating factual evidence can be marshalled in support of a given application of the concept, well and good; but if it can be shown that dire urgency did not exist or that the violation undertaken did not materially and immediately contribute to military success, then any tribunal judging the case on hand would be bound to rule that a war crime had been committed.[7]

[4] See subsequent chapters for most of the key provisions of the 1949 Conventions; consult also the thoughtful early appraisal by Josef L. Kunz, "The Geneva Conventions of August 12, 1949," in Lipsky, pp. 279–316.

[5] See Josef L. Kunz, "The Chaotic Status of the Laws of War and the Urgent Necessity for their Revision," 45 *A.J.I.L.* (1951), pp. 37–61.

[6] See Lauterpacht's *Oppenheim*, Vol. II, p. 231, who asserts that such reprisals may violate the laws of war.

[7] See the illuminating study by N. C. W. Dunbar, "Military Necessity in War Crimes Trials," 29 *B.Y.I.L.* (1952), pp. 442–452, and his later "The Significance of Military Necessity in the Law of War," 67 *Juridical Review* (1955), pp. 201–212, as well as the appraisals of the problem by William G. Downey, Jr., "The Law of War and Military Necessity," 47 *A.J.I.L.* (1953), pp. 251–262, and in Lauterpacht's *Oppenheim*, Vol. II, pp. 231–233. The history of the concept has been well developed in Paul Weiden, "Necessity in International Law," 24 *TGS* (1939), pp. 105–132.

Laws of Humanity. In addition to the normal rules of international law, both customary and conventional so-called laws of humanity have been invoked at times in an effort to mitigate the evils of war. This term embraced a group of rules based on what might be termed public morality. In essence, the laws of humanity prescribed that belligerents had to eschew certain acts of coercion which, because of innate cruelty or breach of elementary good faith, would tend to wreck the bases of human relationship, would make it ultimately impossible to conclude any kind of peace between warring states. By such acts were meant annihilation of the enemy population, needless cruelty practiced in attempts to win a conflict, and so on. Unfortunately, the defenders of such humane rules foresaw neither the development of modern weapons capable of blotting out entire cities in seconds nor the atavistic return to savagery encountered in certain nations during World War II. In fact, one body of opinion asserted that preservation of humane rules was inhuman, for they tended to prolong a conflict, whereas the absence of any restriction might enable a belligerent to end a war quickly and thus reduce the period of general suffering and agony. It might be argued, in reply, that a war might end earlier, to be sure, if all were given a free hand to act as they desired, but the amount of suffering would not be reduced necessarily and might, indeed, be drastically increased through the use of poison gas, bacteriological warfare, or nuclear bombing. In fact, there might not be any population left on either side to undergo suffering—after all hands had zestfully launched their most effective tools for mass killing.

THE LAWS OF WAR AND INTERNATIONAL FORCES

The development of a global collective security system in the shape of the United Nations and of numerous regional defense arrangements has posed numerous new problems in the sphere of the laws of war. Those laws developed in the context of armed struggles between individual states. Because collective security systems were not known at the time the customary and conventional rules governing warfare were drawn up, no provisions governing international armed forces were included. Even the most modern coventions on the subject, the 1949 Geneva instruments, are concerned with national and not with international forces.

Thus far no real answer has been found to the question of the extent to which international commands are bound by the existing rules. The fact that such forces operated in Korea, in the Near East, in the Congo, and on Cyprus, and may be called into activity under such organizations as NATO and SEATO raises the question of the extent to which such forces are bound by the laws of war.[8]

The problem posed above has been aggravated greatly by the assump-

[8] See Hersch Lauterpacht, "Rules of Warfare in an Unlawful War," in Lipsky, at pp. 89–113; Jessup, at pp. 188–221; and W. J. Bivens, "Restatement of the Laws of War as Applied to the Armed Forces of Collective Security Arrangements," *A.J.I.L.*,

tion implied in the formation of international armed forces, on a global or regional basis, that one side in the conflict has violated solemn treaty obligations and, as an aggressor, is engaged in fighting an unlawful war. If the laws of war are to apply to such a conflict, should they apply to the aggressor alone or to both sides? If they are to apply to the aggressor only, should all laws of war apply to him, including those under which he would derive possible benefits, or should only those apply to him which would limit and restrict him?

The present writer is convinced that both customary and conventional laws of war apply equally and unrestrictedly to both sides in a modern war, regardless of the fact that the conflict involves an international command and that one of the opposing parties has been guilty of aggression.[9] Similarly, the tribunal in *U.S. v. List et al. (The Hostage Case)* pointed out that "international law makes no distinction between a lawful and an unlawful occupant in dealing with the respective duties of occupant and population in occupied territory. . . . Whether the invasion was lawful or criminal is not an important factor in the consideration of this subject."[10] Lauterpacht asserted that "a war is still a war in the eyes of International Law, even though it has been illegally commenced. . . ."[11] Not all commentators share the belief expressed here,[12] even though the Korean conflict proved quite definitely that both sides were regarded as being bound by the customary and conventional rules of war.[13] At the Forty-Ninth Session of the *Institut de Droit International*, held at Neufchâtel in 1959, the draft resolutions presented by the Committee on Reconsideration of the Principles of the Law of War started with the proposition that

For the duration of hostilities (*durante bello*) the rules of the law of war are to be applied without discrimination between the parties in conflict, as well as when the competent organ of the United Nations has designated the aggressor as when military action is undertaken by or under the auspices of the United Nations.[14]

---

48 (1954), pp. 140–145. Consult also the Report of the Committee of the American Society of International Law on the Study of Legal Problems of the United Nations, "Should the Laws of War Apply to United Nations Enforcement Action?" *Proceedings* (1952), pp. 216–220, and see International Committee of the Red Cross, *Annual Report, 1961* (Geneva: International Committee of the Red Cross, 1962), at pp. 47–49.

[9] See also Felice Morgenstern, "Validity of the Acts of the Belligerent Occupant," 28 *B.Y.I.L.* (1951), pp. 291–322, at p. 321, n. 1, and see Whiteman, Vol. X, pp. 43–50, 51–54, 63–64.

[10] *Trial of War Criminals Before the Nuremberg Military Tribunals* (1948), p. 1247, cited in Harold D. Cunningham, Jr. "Civil Affairs—A Suggested Legal Approach," *Military Law Review* (October, 1960), pp. 115–137, at p. 125, n. 29.

[11] Lauterpachts *Oppenheim*, Vol. II, p. 299.

[12] See Howard J. Taubenfeld, "International Armed Forces and the Rules of War," 45 *A.J.I.L.* (1951), pp. 671–679, and Stone, pp. 314–316.

[13] See Whiteman, Vol. X, pp. 58–63, for relevant documents.

[14] Herbert W. Briggs, "The Neufchâtel Session of the *Institut de Droit International*," 54 *A.J.I.L.* (1960), pp. 132–135, at p. 133.

Although the *Institut* session failed to adopt the resolution in question because of strong differences of opinion and decided to have one of its commissions make a further study of the subject, the text quoted did represent the thought of a committee composed of eminent jurists.

A sensible solution would be the general adoption of a treaty provision similar to Article 80 of the treaty intended to establish the European Defense Community. That article stated that the forces of the Community would respect all rules "embodied in conventions concerning the laws of war which bind one or more of its member states." A protocol also obliged the member states of the Community to facilitate the acceptance by the Community as such of general treaties relating to the laws of war.[15]

Some writers have suggested, on the other hand, that collective security forces (global as well as regional is the implication) should not be bound by existing laws of war but should be free to select such rules as appeared desirable at the time and to discard all the rest in the fight against an aggressor state. Such a concept appears to be most improper. The great bulk of the existing rules were designed to protect certain groups, including the civilian populations as well as prisoners of war, from the worst effects of a war. That basic purpose is not at all changed by the accidental factor that an international force engages in hostilities or that a given state is engaged in presumably illegal aggression.

THE LOCALE OF WAR

Definition of "Locale." The "locale" or "region" of war embraces those parts of the world in which belligerents may carry on hostile acts against one another. The locale differs from the "theater of war," for the latter is a more limited concept, comprising the portions of the earth in which actual operations are carried on. The locale, on the other hand, may be conceived as a much larger area—no place outside the locale may be converted into a theater of war, but not all parts of the locale may actually represent such a theater.

The locale normally would include the entire land area as well as the territorial sea and national air of belligerent states, in addition to the high seas and the air above the latter. It may, on occasion, also include overseas colonies of belligerents; in the case of condominiums, if one of the powers governing this type of entity goes to war against another state, the condominium would fall within the local of the conflict, even though this might cause grave difficulties for the co-ruling state if the latter were to remain neutral. Quite possibly the condominium would, under such conditions, be excluded from the theater of war while remaining in the locale.

Problems of the Status of War Zones. Any belligerent may choose to

---

[15] Richard R. Baxter, "Constitutional Forms and Some Legal Problems of International Military Command," 29 *B.Y.I.L.* (1952), p. 325-359, at pp. 355-356.

exclude certain territories or certain portions of the high seas from the locale of war, provided that strict neutrality is observed for the areas in question. (Crete and Egypt, in the Italo-Turkish War of 1911-12, represent good examples.) Special problems have been posed in this connection by the status of waterways. On occasion, all armed forces and warships of all belligerents were barred from such routes by mutual agreement among the belligerents (so-called negative neutralization), whereas on other occasions all belligerents were free to use such waterways, even for the shipment of troops and the travel of warships, but were forbidden to engage in any military or naval operations in the waterways (so-called positive neutralization).

It has been pointed out that, generally speaking, war at sea is carried out not only in the territorial waters of belligerents but also on the high seas. Because the latter are, however, free to neutral ships in war as in peace, belligerents have found it necessary to impose limitations of this traditional freedom of the seas in the interest of the exercise of belligerent rights connected with blockade and contraband of war, as well as unneutral service by neutrals.

One of the modern limitations on the freedom of the seas, the creation of defense zones and war zones, made its appearance just before the outbreak of the Russo-Japanese War of 1904. The Japanese government authorized its top naval authorities to designate certain areas adjacent to the Japanese islands as "defense sea areas," with special restrictions to be imposed on all egress and ingress. Twelve such zones were declared, extending in several instances as far as ten miles from shore.

Similarly, the United States, on entering World War I in April, 1917, established by presidential order so-called defensive sea areas, controlling incoming as well as outgoing navigation in those areas. As in the case of the Japanese example, the outward limits of several of the American areas extended up to ten miles off shore.

In contrast to those rather modest endeavors, certain European belligerents in World War I created vastly expanded "war zones." As early as November 3, 1914, the British government declared all of the North Sea to be a military area in which exceptional measures were to be taken in reprisal against indiscriminate laying of mines by Germany. On February 4, 1915, Germany proclaimed all waters around Great Britain, including the Channel, a war zone in which every ship was subject to destruction, irrespective of its nationality. In contrast with the British action, the German establishment of a war zone left no channels at all for neutral traffic. The German government gradually expanded the extent of its zone until, on January 31, 1917, all waters around Great Britain, France, and Italy, as well as the entire eastern Mediterranean, were included. The British retaliated against each expansion of the German zones by laying additional duly notified minefields.

During World War II, the same conditions occurred again. In November, 1939, Germany instituted a "blockade" of Great Britain by means of unmoored and uncharted mines and also announced that the Baltic would be closed to all shipments aiding Germany's enemies directly or indirectly. On November 21 of the same year, Great Britain retaliated by announcing that all exports of German origin or ownership would be seized, regardless of destination. This step resulted in a strong protest on the part of the United States, citing the rules of international law as they pertained to neutral freedom to deal in noncontraband items with belligerent states. On August 17, 1940, Germany in turn declared a "total blockade" of Great Britain and announced that all shipping, regardless of nationality, would be attacked in certain only vaguely defined "war zones" around the British Isles, extending westward to more than 375 miles beyond the Irish Coast.

It is possible that all or part of a neutral state is included in the locale of a war. This would be true in every instance in which such neutral areas represent one of the objects for which the war is waged (Korea in the Russo-Japanese War of 1904–5), and also when a belligerent proceeds to attack and invade a neutral state (Germany v. Denmark and the Netherlands in 1940). Equally, neutral territory is shifted into the locale of a war when a neutral state fails to prevent a belligerent from utilizing its territorial waters or even its territory as a base of military operations against an opposing belligerent.

Territories, territorial waters, or portions of the high seas may be excluded from the locale of war by permanent neutralization through international conventions.

PARTICIPANTS IN A WAR

Participation in a war is restricted, legally, to sovereign states. Semisovereign states and entities not included in the community of nations do not have the legal right to become belligerents. A colony, therefore, while included in the locale of a war and possibly in a theater of war, is regarded as a subdivision of a sovereign belligerent, not as a belligerent in its own right. A neutralized state such as Switzerland may become a lawful belligerent in view of its character as a sovereign state. If such a neutralized state participates in a war purely in defense against an attack aimed at it, it does not lose its character as a neutralized state; if, on the other hand, it enters a conflict by undertaking offensive operations against another state, it loses its status as a neutralized entity.

The foregoing remarks are, of course, based on purely legal reasoning. The fact that a given entity was not a fully sovereign state has not prevented it necessarily from becoming a belligerent if it possessed the necessary military forces and resources and evinced a desire to go to war. Thus such Turkish vassal states as Montenegro and Serbia went to war in 1877 against Turkey, their own suzerain; and another Turkish vassal state,

Romania, became allied with Russia and joined in the Russo-Turkish War of the same year.

Recognition of a Belligerent Community. It is this distinction between legal qualifications and actual ability to go to war which explains why rebels (insurgents) may become belligerents, equipped with certain rights as well as duties.[16] Once recognition as a belligerent community has been extended by other states to an insurgent group, in answer to the existence of certain factual elements, the community enjoys temporarily limited status as a belligerent. The facts which have to be proven before such recognition should be lawfully extended would include such considerations as the existence of a civil war beyond the scope of a mere local revolt (existence of a "state of general hostilities"); occupation of a substantial part of the national territory by the rebels, together with the existence of a degree of orderly and effective administration by that group in the areas under its control; observance of the rules of war by the rebel forces, acting under the command of some responsible and ascertainable authority.

If those conditions of fact do not prevail or cannot be ascertained, recognition of the insurgents as a belligerent community is to be regarded as premature and as an unlawful intervention in the internal affairs of the lawful and recognized government of the state in question.

Where an outside state recognizes a rebel group as a belligerent community, this essentially political act does not normally bind the parent state against which the rebels are fighting. Although writers differ widely on this question, it appears that the parent state *may* treat the rebels as traitors even after they have received foreign recognition as a belligerent community. The modern tendency, on the other hand, appears to be that once such recognition has been received, the members of the rebel armed forces *should* be treated, when captured, as prisoners of war, entitled to the usual protection and rights of the latter under the laws of war.[17]

PARTICIPANTS: PERSONS.

Combatants and Noncombatants of the Regular Armed Forces. The normal combatants in a war are the regular armed forces of the belligerents—their armies, navies, and air forces. The precise determination of who is included in those forces is a matter of domestic, not of international, law. In other words, the inclusion or exclusion of such forces as militia or volunteer groups in the armed forces is left to each country.

The bulk of a country's armed forces is represented by combatants, but there are also always some noncombatant units or individuals, such as

[16] See Whiteman, Vol. X, pp. 31–32 and especially pp. 150–172, on this question.

[17] See Lauterpacht's *Oppenheim*, Vol. II, pp. 252–254, for a discussion of the intricate problems posed by the recognition of subjects of an enemy state as "cobelligerents" or as "allied belligerents" by a state engaged in war against the parent state of the individuals in question.

medical units (including doctors, nurses, medical corpsmen, ambulance drivers, and attendants), veterinarians, and chaplains, in addition to correspondents and possibly foreign military attachés detailed to headquarters. The precise legal position of these noncombatants has been a subject of controversy among both writers and military commanders.[18] Generally speaking, they represent noncombatant elements of an armed force and are entitled to treatment as prisoners of war, provided they can identify themselves as connected officially with a recognized armed force. The sex of combatants as well as of noncombatants is immaterial as far as their legal status is concerned.

Irregular Forces. In addition to these recognized armed forces, any given war may see the utilization of what are termed irregular forces. Such groups may have been authorized by a belligerent, or they may have originated privately and be acting without special authority and on their own initiative. Until recently, the laws of war granted no legal status to the private variety of irregular forces; if captured, the members of such organizations were viewed as war criminals and commonly were executed without much ceremony. However, beginning with the Spanish guerrilla war against Napoleon, the irregular force became an increasingly important factor in modern war. Known under a variety of names—such as guerrillas, partisans, resistance groups, and "the underground"—these groups lacked the technical status of lawful combatants. During World War II, most of such irregular forces operated with the approval of their own government and received supplies and arms from it; in fact, in several countries, notably in the Soviet Union, they were on the payroll of their sovereign.[19]

Both The Hague Regulations of 1907 (Art. 1) and the Third Geneva Convention of 1949 (Treatment of Prisoners of War, Art. 4-A, par. 2), reflect the "modern" view that under specified conditions, irregular forces are to be entitled to the rights and privileges of normal armed forces. Unfortunately for the members of such groups, however, the specified conditions would be tantamount to suicide, if obeyed literally: the treaties in question require that irregular forces, in order to enjoy the status of legal combatants, have to (1) be under the command of a person responsible for his subordinates; (2) wear distinctive insignia recognizable at a distance; (3) carry weapons openly; and (4) conduct their operations in accordance with the laws and customs of war. Such requirements would

---

[18] Whiteman, Vol. X, pp. 27–30, 131–137.

[19] See the excellent historical study of L. Nurick and R. W. Barrett, "Legality of Guerrilla Forces Under the Laws of War," 40 *A.J.I.L.* (1946), pp. 563–583; R. R. Baxter, "The Privy Council on the Qualifications of Belligerents," 63 *A.J.I.L.* (1969), pp. 290–296; and Robert D. Powers, Jr., "Guerrillas and the Laws of War," 89 *United States Naval Institute Proceedings* (March, 1963), pp. 82–87. Consult also von Glahn, pp. 51–54, and see *ibid.*, Appendix 4, p. 298, for text of a Red Army leaflet of 1941, addressed to partisans and mentioning the element of government pay to such irregulars.

be extremely difficult to meet, as far as most irregular forces are concerned, and so-called part-time partisans would find it literally impossible to qualify under the regulations laid down.

The situation today, therefore, is that irregulars operating in groups may *possibly* meet the conditions under which they are granted combatant status; individuals operating as partisans, and "part-time" guerrillas, are still, for practical purposes beyond the law and may be shot as war criminals when captured by the opposing belligerent.

Private Enemy Citizens. Private citizens taking up arms against an invading enemy may, however, achieve combatant status and thus be entitled to treatment as prisoners of war if they happen to belong to a *levée en masse*. This means an armed mass rising of the private citizenry *in advance* of an invading army. Provided that such a rising does take place on the approach of the enemy, and *not* behind his lines, the participating private individuals are entitled to combatant status under both the 1907 Hague Regulations and the 1949 Prisoners of War Convention. But again, two limitations apply to such individuals: they must carry arms openly and must observe the laws and customs of war.

Troops Behind the Enemy's Lines. Enemy troops, whether they are members of commando units or paratroopers, operating behind the lines of a belligerent are entitled to treatment as prisoners of war, provided they are members of the organized military forces of their government and are in uniform. Their execution (undertaken by Germany in World War II) under such conditions is a war crime.

Savage Forces. The employment of so-called savage or barbarous forces in war was a favorite subject of arguments among legal writers in the past. While the topic may appear academic now, it is still conceivable that such forces might be utilized by a belligerent; for example, the Netherlands could have used such forces in the former Netherlands New Guinea against invading Indonesian forces. The rule applicable to such a situation would be quite clear: employment of such forces would be lawful and their members would have to be treated as prisoners of war, provided they obeyed the laws and customs of war.

Foreign Volunteers. A new development made its appearance in the Korean War of 1950–53: the recognized appearance of foreign volunteers. The Spanish Civil War had already seen the participation of organized groups of Russian and other left-wing sympathizers on one side and of German and Italian groups on the other. During World War II, Spanish and other volunteers fought against the Soviet Union on the side of the Axis Powers. But in the Korean War, large and organized bodies of Chinese "volunteers" took a most active part. The novelty involving those Chinese was their participation in the negotiations leading to the Armistice of July 27, 1953, which was concluded between "the Commander-in-Chief, United Nations Command, on the one hand, and the Supreme Commander of the Korean People's Army and the Commander of the

Chinese People's Volunteers, on the other hand." This marked the first time in modern history that ideological "volunteers" became officially recognized cobelligerents in a war.

The government of the United States adopted the view that these Chinese forces, despite their volunteer label, were official forces of the People's Republic of China. This was shown clearly in a note of October 11, 1955, dealing with the downing of a Russian plane on July 27, 1953, the date on which the Korean Armistice was signed.[20]

Crews of Merchant Vessels. Turning briefly to the maritime side of war, the crews of captured enemy merchant vessels are normally interned. If, however, the vessel in question defends itself when attacked, the crew may be treated as prisoners of war, just as if they were members of the armed forces of their country. On the other hand, if the merchant vessel assumes the initiative in attack, such as by attempting to ram an enemy warship, the crew are liable to be executed as war criminals.

Traitors. Finally, deserters from the armed forces who join the forces of their country's enemies cannot claim the privileges of lawful combatants. They are treated as criminals and normally will be executed if captured by their legal sovereign. The same holds true for private citizens who join the armed forces of the enemy of their own nation. Both categories of traitors may be seized even if they appear among the forces of their country under the presumed protection of a flag of truce.

CONCEPT OF ENEMY CHARACTER

The modern laws of war do not restrict the concept of enemy to the armed forces of an opposing belligerent. Rather, one of the consequences of a state of war between two countries is that every national of the one state becomes the enemy of every national of the other state. Citizens of neutral countries may acquire enemy character if they enlist in the armed forces of a belligerent or commit hostile acts against a belligerent. A logical result of such change in status in that a belligerent may apply the same measures against such ex-neutrals as he would apply against the nationals of an enemy state. The Fifth Hague Convention of 1907 (Art. 18-b) provided, however, that neutral citizens residing in enemy territory and furnishing services to the enemy government in such matters as police or administration would not lose their neutral status through the performance of such services.

Neutral Citizens Living in Enemy Territory. Many commentators have pointed out, however, that neutral citizens residing in enemy territory do not enjoy special status or privileges, as far as another and opposing belligerent is concerned. They will be treated in the same manner as the

---

[20] For partial text, see note by Denys P. Myers on "Armed Intervention," 54 *A.J.I.L.* (1960), pp. 656–658; consult also Ian Brownlie, "Volunteers and the Law of War and Neutrality," 5 *International and Comparative Law Quarterly* (1956), pp. 570–580.

indigenous enemy population, sharing their fate in every respect. To this extent, therefore, such neutrals are to be regarded as possessing enemy character, a view reinforced by the fact that such neutrals actually contribute indirectly to the enemy's war effort by their payment of taxes, and so on. Hence a belligerent has a perfect legal right to treat such neutrals in a manner identical to his treatment of the enemy population. Obviously, on the other hand, such neutrals cannot be classified as completely identical with the true nationals of an enemy. They still enjoy the protection of their own government against arbitrary and discriminatory treatment. However, if the enemy territory in which they reside is invaded by another belligerent, the neutrals are again subject to the same contributions, requisitions, and regulations as the rest of the local population.[21]

Until World War I, enemy citizens, residing in neutral countries, lost their enemy character by the fact of the identification with the neutral state expressed through their residence therein. This doctrine, defended particularly in Anglo-Saxon countries, was not, however, universally accepted. France and a number of other European countries asserted that enemy character was not lost through neutral residence.

The Anglo-American attitude was abandoned, on the whole, as World War I progressed. The British government, as early as 1915, forbade its nationals to trade with any person (physical or legal) in foreign countries whose enemy nationality or enemy association called for such prohibition. In order to make clear who was to be regarded as possessed of enemy aspects, "blacklists" were issued, listing individuals and firms in neutral countries. British nationals could, of course, continue trade with anyone not featured on such lists. The British Trading with the Enemy Act of 1939 similarly regulated commercial intercourse during World War II. Both Great Britain and France on that occasion departed from the concept that enemy nationality automatically gave enemy character to an individual. Residence of such a person in enemy territory would, of course, make him an enemy; but if the individual resided in a neutral state, then inclusion of his name on a blacklist was necessary to a finding of enemy character.

Status of Corporations. The status of legal persons, such as corporations, in time of war proved to be even more complex and confusing than was the case in the instance of physical persons. International law does not offer any general rules on the subject, and national practices have varied greatly. General agreement appears to have prevailed for many decades that a corporation chartered in an enemy state possessed enemy character. Some doubts existed as to the status of a firm not incorporated in an enemy country but carrying on business there; eventually, the general view prevailed that such activities conferred enemy character on the firm in ques-

---

[21] See von Glahn, pp. 87–93.

tion. The classic case dealing with this problem is the famous *Daimler Co., Ltd.* v. *Continental Tyre and Rubber (Great Britain) Co., Ltd.*[22] A more recent case illustrating the application was

THE UNITAS

Great Britain, Privy Council (In Prize), May 8, 1950,
2 All Eng. L. R. 219

FACTS

The *Unitas* was a whaling factory ship, registered in Germany and flying the German flag. The vessel was captured in a German port by British forces in June, 1945, after the German surrender. Two Dutch companies contested the seizure, asserting that they, through Dutch subsidiaries, were the only stockholders in a German company controlled from Rotterdam. The two companies owned considerable properties in Germany and, in order to transfer some of those assets from the Reich, had arranged in 1936 for the construction, in Germany, of a German whaling fleet. The *Unitas* was one of the components of that fleet, chartered (after completion) by the German subsidiary to still another German company in which the former had less than 50 per cent interest.

The outbreak of World War II caused no separation of the Dutch companies from their German subsidiaries, at least not as long as the Netherlands remained neutral. The Dutch companies asserted that the *Unitas* had been registered in Germany under duress, being constructed only because of pressures exerted by the German government and that the British prize court should look behind the façade of German ownership to the true, that is, Dutch, ownership of the vessel.

The British Court (Probate, Divorce and Admiralty Division, February 20, 1948, 1 All Eng. L. R. 421) ruled against the alleged Dutch owners and condemned the *Unitas* as a lawful prize taken from the enemy and possessed of enemy character. The basic reason behind the Court's decision was that the nationality (in this case the enemy character) of a ship was determined by its flag. In addition, the Court pointed out that the Dutch companies had "a house of trade" in enemy territory and had not severed their connections with it after the outbreak of the war. The Dutch companies appealed the condemnation of the vessel. The Privy Council handed down its decision on May 8, 1950.

ISSUE

Did Dutch ownership, as expressed through stock control, override the fact that the vessel was registered in Germany?

DECISION

The Privy Council rejected the appeal and affirmed the condemnation of the vessel as a lawful prize taken from an enemy.

REASONING

"The flying of an enemy flag alone is in this and in most cases sufficient to dispose of the matter at issue." The alleged economic pressure exerted on

[22] [1916], 2 A. C. 307.

the appellant companies by the German government was rejected as insufficient to overrule the conclusive evidence that the ship was registered in Germany and flew the German flag.

Lord Porter, the presiding judge, commented that the building of the whaling fleet and the registration of the latter in Germany was not involuntary, as alleged by the appellants. "In truth, it was not involuntary in the sense of being unintentional: it was a deliberate choice taken between two distasteful alternatives. . . . Their Lordships accept the view that there may be circumstances which make the flying of the enemy flag inconclusive as a reason for condemning a ship in Prize, but such circumstances must be very exceptional." The Court then cited the few instances of such inconclusiveness, one of the more unusual of which revolved around *The Palme*. That vessel had been a German ship, purchased by the Swiss Red Cross from German owners. Both the Swiss and French governments refused to permit the Red Cross to use their flags, hence the vessel continued to fly the German flag for want of a more legitimate insigne. When the *Palme* was stopped by the British Navy, the German flag was held, quite properly, not to constitute conclusive proof of the vessel's enemy character.

Similarly, it is generally agreed that a company incorporated or doing business in territory under enemy occupation should be regarded as possessed of enemy character.[23]

The United States adopted, until World War II, the view that a company not incorporated in an enemy country nor doing business there should not be regarded as possessing enemy character. This traditional American attitude was abandoned during World War II, when the United States government decided to follow the French practice which applied the test of registration as well as control: the United States henceforth regarded enemy control, even when exercised indirectly through some form of holding company, as creating enemy character for a corporation.

Status of Vessels in Time of War. The question of enemy character applies also to vessels in time of war. In time of peace, the nationality of a ship is determined by the flag it flies, that is, it possesses the nationality of the state in which it is registered. In time of war, this is still the test applied to any vessel displaying an enemy flag, even if the actual owners of the ship happen to be citizens of a neutral landlocked state without a maritime flag. Regardless of ownership, any vessel flying the flag of an enemy state is regarded as an enemy vessel and is subject to capture or destruction.

The situation is not as clear, however, as far as an enemy-owned vessel flying a neutral flag is concerned. Most writers agree that even before World War I the display of a neutral flag determined the neutral char-

---

[23] See *Sovfracht* v. *Van Uden's Scheepvaart en Agentur Maatschappij*, United Kingdom, House of Lords, 1942, 1 All E.R. 76 [1943], 59 Times L.R. 101 [1942], and *Part Cargo ex M. V. Glenroy*, Great Britain, Privy Council, 1945, 61 Times L.R. 303, reported in 39 *A.J.I.L.* (1945), pp. 599–609.

acter of a vessel only if the ship was actually entitled to fly such flag through registration in the neutral state in question. A genuinely neutral ship would still acquire enemy character by participating in hostilities, by being under the orders of an enemy agent aboard the vessel, by being utilized for the transportation of enemy troops, or by serving in some manner for the transmission of information on behalf of an enemy state. Again, any neutral vessel resisting the exercise of any belligerent's lawful right to visit and search would, by such resistance, acquire enemy character.

Since World War II, the "control test" of the nationality of business enterprises has been extended to vessels and aircraft, at least in Anglo-American practice, even though the old flag (or registration) test prevailed as late as 1941 in American naval instructions. This changed attitude is reflected in Section 501 of the current U.S. Navy manual:

. . . Any merchant vessel or aircraft owned or controlled by or for an enemy State, enemy persons, or any enemy corporation possesses enemy character, regardless of whether or not such a vessel or aircraft operates under a neutral flag or bears neutral markings. . . .[24]

SUGGESTED READINGS

G. B. Davis, "The Amelioration of the Rules of War on Land," 2 *A.J.I.L.* (1908), pp. 63–77, and his "Doctor Francis Lieber's Instructions for the Government of Armies in the Field," *ibid.*, 1 (1907), pp. 13–25; Josef L. Kunz, "The Laws of War," *ibid.*, 50 (1956), pp. 313–337; Hersch Lauterpacht, "The Problem of the Revision of the Law of War," 29 *B.Y.I.I.* (1952), pp. 361–382; Myres S. McDougal and F. P. Feliciano, "International Coercion and World Public Order," 67 *Yale Law Journal* (1958), pp. 771–845; Stone, pp. 353–363, on sanctions and reprisals in war; and Whiteman, Vol. X, pp. 1–27, 38–43, 44–46.

IRREGULAR FORCES

John A. Armstrong, ed., *Soviet Partisans in World War II* (Madison: University of Wisconsin Press, 1967); U.S. Dept. of the Army, *Special Forces Operation* (that is, "unconventional" and counterinsurgency warfare), *Training Manual* (TM) *31–21* (Washington, D.C., June 1965); Whiteman, Vol. X, pp. 32–38; W. J. Ford, "Resistance Movements in Occupied Territory," 3 *Tijdschrift* (1956), pp. 355–384.

[24] U.S. Dept. of the Navy, Chief of Naval Operations, NWIP 10-2, *Law of Naval Warfare* (September 1955, as amended July 1959): see Whiteman, Vol. X, pp. 685–686. For further details concerning vessels in time of war, see Chapter 29.

27

Modern War: Commencement, Effects, Termination

COMMENCEMENT OF WAR

Undeclared Wars. Wars have begun with a declaration of war, with pronouncements or announcements by a state to the effect that it considered itself to be at war with another state, or simply through the commission of hostile acts employing military forces by one state against another state. Beginning with Hugo Grotius, many writers on international law asserted that a declaration of war was required before the commencement of hostilities, but the practice of states proved beyond doubt that they did not accept this rule. Thus a British report in 1870 showed that between 1700 and 1870, a total of 107 conflicts were initiated without the formality of a declaration of war. The United States, too, has conducted wars without a declaration: an undeclared war with France from 1798 to 1801, the invasion of Florida in 1811 under Generals Jackson and Matthews, the brief Mexican invasion in 1916, the undeclared war with the Soviet Union in 1918–19, and, of course, the Vietnamese conflict still in progress at the time of writing. To this list might be added the Korean military operations from 1950 to 1953 and the Chinese invasion of India toward the end of 1962.

Virtually all writers agreed that a dispute had to precede hostilities, that an unprovoked attack by one state on another was illegal, that the outbreak of war had to be preceded by unsuccessful efforts to solve a quarrel between the parties to the conflict. Once such efforts had failed, however, a fairly general opinion sanctioned a commencement of hostilities without the issuance of a declaration of war or other formal notice of intent to resort to the use of force.

Third Hague Convention of 1907. The absence of any customary or conventional rules governing the commencement of a war was finally remedied by the adoption at the Second Hague Peace Conference of Convention No. III Relative to the Opening of Hostilities, on October 18, 1907. The immediate cause of the drafting of this instrument was the unannounced attack by Japanese torpedo boats on Russian warships at Port Arthur in 1904.

Article 1 of the convention provided that

The Contracting Powers recognize that hostilities between themselves must not commence without previous and explicit warning, in the form either of a reasoned declaration of war or of an ultimatum with conditional declaration of war.

Because the article did not specify any time interval between the declaration and the outbreak of hostilities, the former could immediately precede an attack and no violation of the convention would be involved: surprise attacks were, therefore, not eliminated from the legal practices of states. Also, because only a limited number of states ratified the instrument and its application was limited to conflicts among the contracting parties, any war between noncontracting states or between a contracting state and a noncontracting state did not require a declaration of war.

It is interesting to note the inclusion of the adjective *reasoned* in Article 1. The intention of the drafters of the instrument was that a declaration of war ought to indicate the motives which led to its issue. Experience since 1907 has demonstrated, however, that on most occasions the reasons advanced for the outbreak of war were not necessarily the true reasons that a given country resorted to the use of force. In fact, the continued influence of the medieval doctrine of the "just war," as well as the emphasis on "self-defense" created by the adoption of such instruments as the Pact of Paris of 1928, has colored declarations of war, and all of them tend to emphasize reasons, with the intent, it seems, to create a picture not only of righteousness of cause but also of mere self-defense against unprovoked and intolerable acts of another state.

A declaration of war, representing an expression of the sovereign will of a person under international law, can only be issued by a member of the family of nations recognized as capable of such sovereign action.

The "ultimatum" mentioned in Article 1 of the Third Hague Convention of 1907 means final demands, normally specifying a time limit, which one state makes on another. In order to satisfy the wording of Article 1, such an ultimatum must contain a conditional but definite threat that hostilities will begin when the time limit has expired and the demands in question have not been met.

Article 2 of the same convention required that the existence of a state of war had to be notified to neutral states without delay and was not to take effect with regard to them until after the receipt of a notification. Neutral states, nevertheless, would not be able to rely on the absence of such notification if it was clearly established that they had been in fact aware of the existence of a state of war. This article was to be binding only as between a belligerent state which was a party to the convention and neutral states which were also parties to the agreement. Because relatively few states (28) ratified or adhered to the convention, the effects of this article, too, were rather limited in scope, and most neutral nations of the world would not necessarily have had to be notified of the commencement of a conflict.

General agreement appeared to prevail among writers that if a war commenced with the outbreak of hostilities and the latter was followed by a declaration of war, the legal beginning of the conflict dated to the time at which such declaration was issued. This traditional attitude was reflected in a number of American court decisions centering on the beginning of war with Japan in 1941.[1] However, the famous case of *Louise C. Bennion v. New York Life Insurance Co.*[2] appears to have reversed the doctrine as far as the United States is concerned. Captain Bennion, the commander of the U.S.S. *West Virginia*, was killed in the Japanese attack on Pearl Harbor on December 7, 1941. The insurance company paid the principal of $10,000 due on his policy but refused to pay an additional sum of $10,000 asked for as double indemnity in case of death by accident. The refusal was based on a provision of the policy which excluded an accident that took place in "war or an act incident thereto." The District Court awarded its decision to Mrs. Bennion, but the Circuit Court of Appeals reversed that verdict, holding that the attack on Pearl Harbor commenced the war with Japan. The Supreme Court refused *certiorari* and also denied a petition for a rehearing.

The Circuit Court based its reversal in part on the text of the President's address to Congress, on December 8, 1941, requesting a declaration of war: "I ask that Congress declare that since the unprovoked and dastardly attack by Japan on Sunday, December 7, a state of war has existed between the United States and the Japanese Empire." In other words, the Court took the reasonable view that an attack by one sovereign state on another with intent to wage war and resistance by the attacked state created a state of war without any formal declaration.

The military operations in Korea under the United Nations Unified Command have been held to have been a war, in relation to insurance policies.[3] The status of war for the conflict was also asserted by General Douglas MacArthur in a statement made on December 2, 1950: "A state of undeclared war between the Chinese Communists and the United Nations forces now exists."[4]

The practice of states since 1907 has demonstrated amply that preference is still given to a commencement of hostilities without a declaration

---

[1] *Savage v. Sun Life Assurance Co. of Canada*, United States, District Court, 1944, W. D. of La., 57 F. Supp. 620; *Pang v. Sun Life Assurance Co.*, Circuit Court, 1st Jud. Circ., Terr. of Hawaii, 1944, appeal, 37 Hawaii 208 (1945); and *Rosenau v. Idaho Mutual Benefit Association*, 145 Pac. (2d) 227. See also Edwin Borchard, "When Did the War Begin?" 47 *Columbia Law Review* (1947), pp. 742–748.

[2] United States, Court of Appeal, 10th Circuit, 1946, 158 F. 2d 260, *certiorari* denied by Supreme Court, 1947, 331 U.S. 811. Text of Circuit Court opinion in 41 *A.J.I.L.* (1947), pp. 680–689.

[3] *Weissman v. Metropolitan Life Insurance Co.*, United States District Court S.D. Calif., 1953, 112 F. Supp. 420, digested in 48 *A.J.I.L.* (1954), pp. 155–157.

[4] UP Dispatch from Tokyo, December 2, 1950.

of war, even when the parties involved have ratified or adhered to the Third Hague Convention of 1907.[5] Apparently such a course of action represents the real will of governments; the convention, in the view of many writers, should by now be regarded as obsolete. This attitude is not shared, however, by the United States Department of the Army: in its Field Manual on *The Law of Land Warfare*,[6] the Department cites the Third Hague Convention as operative. This point of view was also emphasized by the International Military Tribunal at Nuremberg which cited the violation of Article 1 of the convention among the breaches of treaty obligations by Germany, in the indictment of major German war criminals.[7]

Several sources have raised the question of the applicability of the Third Hague Convention since the creation of the United Nations. If the Charter prohibition on the use of force and even on the threat of force is regarded as valid, then any and all provisions of the Hague Convention directly conflicting with the Charter are null and void. In the case of collective security measures involving the use of force on the part of the United Nations, the declaration of war is replaced by the warnings and resolutions preceding the application of such measures. Nonmembers are not affected, of course, by the provisions of the Charter: if any of these should decide to go to war and were parties to the 1907 agreement, they would be bound by the latter's provisions only.

The outbreak of hostilities between two states, without a declaration of war or a qualified ultimatum, would normally be regarded as a war in the legal sense, unless both parties indicated clearly that they did not recognize the existence of a state of war. A mere attack by the armed forces of one on the inhabitants or armed forces of the other has been held by some courts not to constitute war, unless the government of the attacked state accepted or recognized the existence of a state of war.[8]

On the other hand, some courts have asserted that, for purposes of time charters of vessels, military operations lacking a declaration of war may be regarded as constituting a war and thereby bring "war clauses" of a charter into effect.[9] The constant series of border clashes along the Russo-Manchurian frontier between units of the Soviet and Japanese land and air forces from 1937 to 1939 were never regarded as acts of war by the

[5] See Whiteman, Vol. X, pp. 66–85.

[6] FM 27-10, Washington, D.C., July 1956, p. 15.

[7] Consult also Lauterpacht's *Oppenheim*, Vol. II, pp. 293–296, on the continued application of the convention to the parties to the instrument.

[8] See *West v. Palmetto State Life Insurance Co.*, United States, Supreme Court, 1943, 202 Sup. Ct. 422; consult the valuable survey by Richard W. Young, "Meaning of 'War' in Insurance Policies," 52 *Michigan Law Review* (1954), pp. 884–893.

[9] See *Kawasaki Kisen Kabushiki Kaisha of Kobe v. Bantham S. S. Company, Ltd.*, Great Britain, Court of Appeal, 1939, [1939] 2 K. B. 544, reproduced in 34 *A.J.I.L.* (1940), pp. 533–536.

two governments concerned, nor did the Chinese government assert the existence of a state of war when Japanese forces began their comprehensive invasion of coastal China in 1937.

LEGAL EFFECTS OF WAR

The principles of natural law asserted that the outbreak of war extinguished all legal relations between belligerents and reduced the latter to an anarchical condition of complete lawlessness, of a *bellum omnium contra omnes*. That view assuredly does not correspond to current attitudes about conflict, or it would be useless even to contemplate the idea of a law of war. The employment of armed force by states, even in the nuclear age, cannot be said to be totally anarchical.

Although numerous deviations may be cited, it can be asserted that, in general, the commencement of a war between two states has the following effects.[10]

Diplomatic Relations. The outbreak of war causes at once the breaking off of such diplomatic relations between the belligerents as may still exist at that time. The diplomats of both sides are recalled and leave for home as soon as the necessary arrangements for their safe return can be made. If conditions appear to make it desirable, enemy diplomatic personnel may be safeguarded in some particular location to assure observance of its immunity and safety—such as was done in the case of Japanese diplomats in the United States in December, 1941. The embassy or legation building is entrusted to the protection of a neutral state and if archives are left behind, they are usually sealed. In rare cases, a member of the diplomatic mission has been left behind in charge of both building and archives, but this can be done, of course, only with the permission of the host government.

Similarly, consular relations between belligerents end with the commencement of war. Consular offices are left in the care of neutral consuls, although here again, rare instances are known of an employee of a major consular mission being permitted by the host state to remain behind to assume charge of facilities and records.

Effect of War on Treaties. Legal writers differ greatly in their views of the effect which the outbreak of war between parties to a treaty has on that instrument.[11] A general statement, on the subject would have to mention that certain treaties, such as those regulating the conduct of hostilities, actually come into full effect at the outbreak of war; that treaties of friendship or alliance, as well as all other agreements classifiable as political in nature, concluded between opposing belligerents prior to a war, come to an end at the beginning of the conflict; that nonpolitical

[10] See also Whiteman, Vol. X, pp. 95-101.
[11] See, *inter alia*, Hyde, Vol. II, pp. 1529-1535, and especially Stone, pp. 447-450.

agreements are suspended for the duration of the conflict; and that a certain few types of treaties involving matters such as private property rights and possibly also boundary agreements not related to frontiers involved in the conduct of hostilities remain in force during the war.[12] Similarly, agreements which by their very nature were final in character would not be affected at all by the outbreak of war. Thus the Anglo-American Treaty of 1783 by which the independence of the United States was acknowledged by Great Britain was not touched by the subsequent War of 1812. Treaties of cession also normally are beyond the effects caused by the coming of war, except that an ultimate peace settlement might reverse the transfer of territory accomplished by the earlier instrument. Even such a cursory survey as the preceding indicates at once one obvious problem: which treaties are to be considered political in nature? On occasion the text of an agreement shows clearly that it is political, although in many instances the subject or object of the agreement reveals its obviously nonpolitical character. In certain cases recourse may have to be had to the intentions of the parties at the time the agreement was concluded in order to determine whether it is or is not a political instrument.

Generally speaking, it can be said that treaty provisions, or even entire treaties, not incompatible with a state of war are not suspended or terminated by the outbreak of hostilities.[13]

Multilateral agreements pose far fewer problems than do bilateral treaties, as far as the effects of war are concerned. General agreement prevails that multilateral treaties continue in effect during a war, except between opposing belligerent parties (when the provisions of the agreement are incompatible with the existence of a state of war). So-called law-making treaties do not lose their validity or applicability at the onset of a conflict; if the opposite were true, the bulk of the modern rules of international law would be set aside. On the other hand, certain multilateral agreements, not law-making in character, may not survive the course of a war for the simple reason that the doctrine of *rebus sic stantibus* can be involved on grounds of sweeping material changes brought on by the conflict. It may even be necessary to suspend the operation of multilateral non-lawmaking treaties between nonbelligerents

---

[12] See *Argento* v. *North*, United States, District Court, N. District of Ohio, E. D., 1955, 131 Supp. 538, digested in 50 *A.J.I.L.* (1956), pp. 140–141 and see the subsequent and more authoritative *Argento* v. *Horn*, 241 F. 2d 258; other relevant cases include the well-known *Techt* v. *Hughes*, New York, Court of Appeals, 1920, 229 N.Y. 222. The classic case is *Society for the Propagation of the Gospel in Foreign Parts* v. *Town of New Haven*, United States, Supreme Court, 1823, 8 Wheaton 464; cf. *Karnuth* v. *United States ex rel. Albro*, United States, Supreme Court, 1929, 279 U.S. 231.

[13] See the important decision in *Clark* v. *Allen*, United States, Supreme Court, 1947, 331 U.S. 503, on this point.

if the conditions created by the war make such a step desirable or inevitable. Interestingly enough, publicists generally agree that there exists no need for special reactivation procedures in such cases. The rule appears to be that when a peace treaty does not refer to such suspended multilateral instruments, they enter into force again, automatically, the moment the peace treaty becomes effective.

Enemy Public Property. Enemy public property is subject to confiscation. Under normal circumstances, enemy embassy or legation buildings are not seized but are left under neutral control for the duration of the conflict. On a few occasions, this practice has been varied by confiscation of the buildings concerned: during World War I, a number of Austro-Hungarian embassies were taken over by the Allied states, and the German embassy building in Rome was confiscated by Italy.

National Borders. National borders have not changed during modern conflicts, in contrast to past practice when occupation of enemy territory was taken to be tantamount to annexation, complete with a change in the nationality of the enemy inhabitants in question. Any shifting of frontiers has to await the end of the conflict and whatever settlement may be arrived at either through a peace treaty or through subjugation of the enemy.

Enemy Private and Merchant Vessels. The question of enemy private vessels found in national waters was regulated, from the end of the seventeenth century until World War I, by the principle of "days of grace" (*délai de faveur*); after the outbreak of hostilities, such vessels were granted a limited period of time during which they were allowed to leave without hindrance. This concept, based on comity and not on international law, was applied during the Crimean War, the Austro-Prussian War of 1866, the Franco-Prussian War of 1870–71, the Spanish-American conflict of 1898, as well as the Russo-Japanese War of 1904–5. Some of the time limits were extremely generous: the English Order-in-Council of March 29, 1854, gave Russian merchant vessels six weeks to load and depart from ports under English control.

When World War I came, Germany proposed to the governments of France, Belgium, Great Britain, and Russia that both sides grant periods of grace to enemy merchant vessels. No agreement was reached, in part owing to a British unwillingness to grant days of grace to vessels larger than 6,000 tons. Consequently, no party on either side in the conflict granted such delays, but seized any and all enemy merchant vessels within reach, except for France which, on August 4, 1914, granted a period of seven days of grace to German ships found in French ports at 6:45 P.M. on that day or afterward arrived in such ports.

Relations Between Citizens of Hostile States. In the absence of customary and conventional law, domestic legislation and public policy in each country determined the ending or continuation of relations between citizens of countries at war with one another. The Anglo-American practice, maintained unchanged until today, has been that the outbreak of war severs all legal and commercial relations between citizens of hostile states.[14] This view was reflected in the peace settlement of Versailles at the end of World War I, which treated all legal and commercial relationships between citizens of opposing states as extinguished by the coming of war.

The Anglo-American attitude was complicated by the fact that it determined the legal status of a particular merchant or other person (in time of war) by his domicile, or residence, rather than by his nationality. Hence both Great Britain and the United States treated as illegal any trade between one of their citizens and a neutral citizen or any one else residing in enemy territory, while permitting such trade with an enemy national residing in a neutral state.

Continental states, on the other hand, long had upheld the idea that the outbreak of war had no automatic effects on the legal and other relations between citizens of opposing states; only if and when a belligerent government acted by the issuance of specific prohibitions would such relations be affected adversely by the existence of a state of war.

Insofar as contracts between the citizens of warring states were concerned, the Anglo-American judicial attitude has been that contracts concluded during a war were null and void *ab initio*, unless special permission for such agreements had been granted by appropriate authority. Contracts entered into before the outbreak of the war were equally void if the time element was essential and required execution of the contract after the commencement of the war; if execution could be delayed without impairing the contract, the latter was held to be suspended for the duration of the conflict.[15]

World War I witnessed significant changes in the traditional approaches to the problem of relations with enemy citizens. The British government not only adopted its former policy by forbidding trade with any person residing or doing business in the German Reich but followed this, on December 23, 1915, by a new regulation prohibiting all trade with persons of enemy nationality engaged in business in neutral countries. In order to make certain that all concerned would know the identities of such persons (national and legal), blacklists were elaborated, listing all individuals and firms with whom British individuals and firms could not conduct business relations. The United States, after protesting this British action while it was still officially a neutral, reversed its stand as soon as it became itself a belligerent and adopted both British policies as its own. During World War II, virtually all belligerents followed the practices

---

[14] *The Hoop*, Great Britain, 1799, 1 C. Rob. 196; *The Rapid*, United States, Supreme Court, 1814, 8 Cranch 155.

[15] See *New York Life Insurance Co.* v. *Statham*, United States, Supreme Court, 1876. 93 U.S. 24. Consult also S.A. Diamond, "The Effect of War on Pre-Existing Contracts Involving Enemy Nationals," 53 *Yale Law Journal* (1944), pp. 700–720.

evolved during the earlier conflict: enemy character was presumed to exist not only on the part of all persons and firms in enemy territory but also all such persons controlled by the enemy or incorporated under the laws of the enemy, as well as natural and legal enemy citizens in neutral countries.

Frozen Assets. The United States, in fact, went several steps further during its initial phase of nominal neutrality in World War II. By executive orders, the assets of neutral countries invaded by Germany, as well as those of Latvia, Estonia, and Lithuania, were "frozen." A little later, the assets in the United States of China, Japan, Italy, and Germany were included under similar orders. The purpose of these measures was rather obvious: the government of the United States wished to prevent the use of American financial facilities in a manner deemed to be detrimental to America's interests, the liquidation of certain assets suspected of having been looted by Axis conquests, and the misuse of such assets for subversive activities in the United States. On July 17, 1941, the President authorized the drawing up of blacklists of persons and firms deemed to act on behalf of Germany or Italy. When Japan went to war against the United States, the previous lists were supplemented with Japanese names and the names of other firms held to act in the interests of Japan.

Enemy Property. Property located in a belligerent state and belonging to private enemy citizens not residing in that state was generally held to be subject to confiscation by the state in which such property was found. As late as 1814, this doctrine was upheld by the Supreme Court of the United States in the well-known case of *Brown* v. *United States.*[16] But within a matter of years after that decision, state after state swung to the contrary view and maintained that such private enemy property could not be confiscated by the belligerent on whose territory it was located. As long as the "property" was that of natural persons—consisting of bank deposits, titles to real estate, and so on—no quarrel could be sought with this new and liberal attitude. But the coming of World War I showed that a significant development had taken place: private property owned by nonresident enemy citizens belonged to a large extent to corporations carrying on business in the belligerent state but controlled from abroad by boards of directors consisting entirely or largely of enemy citizens. Great Britain started a new trend by appointing a custodian of enemy property on November 27, 1914. This step did not mean confiscation, but a kind of receivership by court action in order to prevent hostile misuse of property located in Great Britain. The custodian was entitled to appoint controllers who were placed in actual charge of enemy-owned or enemy-controlled enterprises, the operation of which was considered necessary, however, by the British government. Soon the British innovation was copied by France and Germany, as well as by the United States

---

[16] 8 Cranch 110; see also Hyde, Vol. II, pp. 1726–1743.

(beginning with an Act of October 6, 1917) after the latter's entrance into the war. In the United States, the custodian was specifically authorized to sell any property entrusted to his custody, and, in fact, most of such property was disposed of to the highest bidders.[17]

On the other hand, modern states tend to refrain from seizing the property of enemy aliens residing in their territory, a trend which is in sharp contrast to the practices prevailing a few hundred years ago. In fact, it can be asserted that by development of a rule of customary law, confiscation of such property under normal circumstances would now be considered to be a violation of international law.

This does not mean that such property may not be placed under some form of government control for the duration of a conflict if it is suspected that it might otherwise be misused on behalf of the enemy. But it does mean that such enemy alien property, even if seized temporarily, ought to be returned at the conclusion of the war.[18]

Status of Enemy Aliens. The outbreak of war creates for any belligerent state a host of problems concerning enemy aliens found in its territory. Grotius believed that such aliens could be lawfully detained for the duration of the conflict, the idea being that their absence would weaken their own (enemy) state. He asserted, however, that such internees should be released as soon as the war had ended. Vattel, in 1758, took a more moderate view of the problem: it was his contention that the admission of aliens involved a tacit acknowledgment on the part of the receiving state that such foreigners could leave again in full freedom and safety. The great influence of Vattel on the legal thinking of the late eighteenth century gave much weight to this argument.

It therefore shocked many people when Napoleon, in 1803, ordered the arrest of all male English citizens of military age to be found in France, even though he justified this act by labeling it a reprisal for an alleged illegal capture by English warships of two French merchant vessels before the issuance of any declaration of war.

Napoleon's action was the last of its kind for the rest of the nineteenth century. It is now generally agreed that under customary international law, enemy alien residents must be granted a reasonable time and an opportunity to leave a belligerent's territory. This act of grace does not apply, however, to such enemy aliens as are actual or potential members of the enemy's armed forces (active or reserve officers and other reservists);

---

[17] For practices during World War II, consult Mitchell B. Carroll, "Legislation on Treatment of Enemy Property," 37 *A.J.I.L.* (1943), pp. 611–630, and E. J. Cohn, "German Enemy Property," 3 *International Law Quarterly* (1950), pp. 530–551.

[18] Philip C. Jessup, "Enemy Property," 49 *A.J.I.L.* (1955), pp. 57–62; and see the legal reasoning outlined in Phanor J. Eder, "Confiscation of Enemy Alien Property Held Unconstitutional by Colombian Supreme Court," 54 *A.J.I.L.* (1960), pp. 159–160, as well as Whiteman, Vol. X, pp. 101–118.

such individuals may be detained for the duration of the war as prisoners of war. (But see note 22.)

Naturally, any belligerent may permit enemy aliens to remain in its territory during the entire course of a war, and this has been the practice of most states during the past 150 years or more. On a few occasions during that period, however, wholesale expulsions of enemy aliens took place: France forced all German nationals to leave in 1870; the South African states expelled almost all British citizens in 1899; Russia required all Japanese to leave the Far Eastern provinces in 1904; and Turkey expelled most Italians from Turkish territory in 1911.

Once enemy aliens are permitted to remain in the territory of a given belligerent, the latter may then decide whether to intern all of them or only some of them, or whether to leave them at liberty in their normal place of residence, subject to registration and a varying amount of regulation and control. During World War I, France, Germany, and eventually Great Britain resorted to general internment of enemy aliens; the United States did not follow suit. The outbreak of World War II led again to wholesale internment, but after a relatively short time only a minimum number of enemy aliens was detained in this manner, at least in England. In the United States a short-lived internment of 113,000 or so aliens as well as of Americans of Japanese descent took place, following the Japanese attack on Pearl Harbor. The detainees were placed in relocation centers for the duration of their internment. After the war, Congress eventually appropriated funds to compensate such internees for losses suffered as the result of a rather ill-considered and undemocratic action.

The rules applied in Anglo-American courts, as well as in many other countries in modern wars, hold that any individual (or firm) of nonenemy nationality voluntarily resident or carrying on business in enemy territory is an alien enemy by the territorial test; on the other hand, an enemy citizen allowed to remain in a belligerent's territory, to register himself, and to carry on business there is not an enemy alien by the territorial test—even if he is interned as an enemy alien.

This may seem confusing: let us examine it briefly. During World War II, an American or Swiss citizen residing voluntarily in Germany or doing business there would have been regarded as an enemy alien in an American court; United States businessmen would not have been permitted to make contracts with such a person or to deal with him. A German national permitted to remain in the United States after the commencement of war between the two countries would not have been an enemy alien in the eyes of the courts. United States nationals could have done business with him, and he would have been able to sue or be sued in United States courts.[19]

[19] See Whiteman, Vol. X, pp. 118–127; Lauterpacht's *Oppenheim*, Vol. II, pp. 310–313; consult also Robert R. Wilson, "Recent Developments in the Treatment of

Logically enough, a belligerent state permitting the continued residence of "harmless" enemy aliens in its territory has a perfect right to surround such individuals with all kinds of necessary restrictions. The persons in question may be restricted in their freedom of movement; they may be forbidden to possess arms, radio transmitters, or carrier pigeons, or to use code in their written communications. They may be removed from restricted areas for reasons of military security. They may be barred from certain jobs or even from entire occupations relating to the national war effort.

Resident enemy aliens could not sue in English courts until 1698 when a court finally granted them this right in time of war. Since then, alien enemies have been permitted access to English courts. In the United States, the Supreme Court ruled in 1813 that "a lawful residence implies protection, and a capacity to sue and be sued. A contrary doctrine would be repugnant to sound policy, no less than to justice and humanity." [20] This policy has been reaffirmed many times since then.

Abuses of resident enemy aliens, many of whom were prevented from leaving the territory of a belligerent and thus were unable to escape persecution and at times outrageous mistreatment, resulted in the incorporation of many new safeguards in the 1949 Geneva Convention on the Protection of Civilian Persons in Time of War.[21]

This instrument, which has been in force for the United States since February 2, 1956, goes in many respects beyond the previously existing rules of customary law as regards enemy aliens in belligerent territory. The convention, however, does not protect the nationals of a state which is not a party (by ratification or adherence) to the agreement. A detailed analysis of the relevant portions of the convention exceeds the limits of a general text. Suffice it to state that one specific section of the agreement (Sec. II, Arts. 35–46) deals specifically with the treatment of enemy aliens in belligerent territory and assures such individuals, classified as one of several groups of "protected persons" under the convention, of extensive safeguards against arbitrary acts of their "hosts." Such topics as permissible departure (Arts. 35, 36),[22] ability to receive relief shipments (Art.

Civilian Alien Enemies," 38 *A.J.I.L.* (1944), pp. 397–406, and his earlier "Treatment of Civilian Alien Enemies," *ibid.*, 37 (1943), pp. 30–45; and see especially the interesting decision in the case of *Ex parte Kumezo Kawato,* United States, Supreme Court, 1942, 317 U.S. 69, 63 Sup. Ct., 115, reprinted in 37 *A.J.I.L.* (1943), p. 336–341.

[20] *Clarke* v. *Morey,* United States, Supreme Court, 1813, 10 John. 69.

[21] Text in 50 *A.J.I.L.* (1956), Supp., pp. 724–773; see also U.S. Department of the Army, *The Law of Land Warfare* (FM-27-10), 1956, *passim.*

[22] It should be noted, however, that Article 35 of the IVth (Civilian) Convention, while authorizing voluntary departure of enemy aliens at the outbreak of hostilities, permits the belligerent in whose territory they then happen to be, to prohibit their departure when it believes such to be "contrary to the national interest." This really voids the guarantee of departure and allows the belligerent in question to detain any and all enemy aliens if it so desires.

38), employment opportunities and categories of permissible as well as prohibited work (Arts. 39, 40), place of residence (Art. 41), internment (Arts. 42–44), transfer of such protected persons by a belligerent to the territory of another state (Art. 45), are dealt with from a humane and liberal point of view as a result of the lessons taught by the experiences of World War II. Additionally, Articles 27–33 of the same convention, which apply to persons both in occupied enemy territory and the territory of a belligerent, provide other safeguards for the enemy aliens, particularly as relates to their honor, person, religion, and so on.[23]

Finally, the Fourth Geneva Convention of 1949 contains detailed provisions for remedies available to the individuals in question, that is, recourse to the "Protecting Powers," to the International Committee of the Red Cross, and to the national Red Cross (Red Crescent) Societies (Arts. 30 and 142), as well as extremely detailed regulations for the treatment of internees (Arts. 79–141). If—and this is, of course, the big question—belligerent states in a future war, bound by this convention, carry out its provisions faithfully, the lot of enemy aliens, both in belligerent states and in occupied enemy territory, will be a far better one than that which such persons have experienced in earlier wars.

Temporary Suspension of Hostilities. Before leaving this section on the legal effects of war, it should be pointed out that, although the normal tenor of relations between opposing belligerent states is hostile, there are a limited number of nonhostile activities or relations that may be carried on between them even after the commencement of a war.

On occasion, hostilities may be suspended by action of opposing field commanders in order to accomplish specific purposes, such as to collect casualties, to bring in the dead, or to permit the crossing of the lines by negotiators of the opposing party. On some occasions, such a cessation of fighting has been arranged to permit diplomatic agents of a belligerent, accredited to a neutral state, to cross into the opponent's territory as the only route open to them in order to reach the neutral receiving state.

Other instances of nonhostile relations between belligerents involve passports, which allow enemy personnel to move in and out of occupied territory; safe conducts, normally granted to couriers or messengers going to territory controlled by an opposing belligerent; and safeguards, which are documents issued by military personnel for the protection of enemy persons or property against the operations of that officer's own forces. Other examples of such relationships include the very rare licenses to trade, granted by a belligerent to neutral or enemy citizens, permitting the carrying on of trade relationships which would normally not be permitted as soon as a war had started.

Finally, opposing belligerents occasionally reach a rather formal agreement known as a *cartel*. This type of arrangement commonly deals with a

---

[23] See Lauterpacht's *Oppenheim*, Vol. II, pp. 316–317, and von Glahn, at pp. 57–62.

return or exchange of prisoners of war during a conflict; there have even been *cartel ships*, specially designated and provided with immunity from attack, for the conveyance of prisoners covered by cartel agreements.

THE TERMINATION OF WAR

Ways of Ending Hostilities. A war may end in one of several ways: (1) by a simple cessation of hostilities; (2) by subjugation; and (3) by a treaty of peace.[24]

Termination of a conflict by simple cessation of hostilities is a rather uncommon occurrence. Because it poses a number of practical postwar problems, particularly such as center on the precise time at which the conflict came to an end, states generally prefer to avoid this method of ending a war. The best-known instance of such termination is the ending of the Franco-Mexican War of 1867, which came to an informal conclusion when the last French troops left Mexican territory to return to France. Other modern examples include the ending of the Polish-Swedish War of 1716, of the Spanish-French War of 1720, the Russo-Persian war in 1801, the Spanish attempt to reconquer the lost American colonies (begun in 1810, terminated in 1825), the end of the state of war between Prussia and Liechtenstein that had begun in 1866, and the end of the Spanish–Chilean "war" of 1865–68, which came when Spain abandoned its efforts to achieve fulfillment of its demands made on Chile. Courts have adopted varying views concerning the cessation of hostilities and the actual end of a conflict, asserting in a majority of instances recorded that something more formal than an end to fighting was required to end a war.

Thus, in an action to collect on an insurance policy on the life of a correspondent killed by Egyptian forces on November 10, 1956, during the "Suez Incident," an American court decided that the "war" ended when the ceasefire agreement took effect on November 6, 1956, stating that "the resolution of the United Nations is to be considered here as having the same effect of terminating the war and restoring peace as a traditional treaty of peace." The Court pointed out that, in *interpreting private contracts*, many courts have viewed the actual cessation of hostilities as synonymous with the cessation of war.[25] But if two states terminate hostilities and show no indication of desiring to proceed to a more formal ending of their conflict, cessation of hostilities must be regarded as the termination of the war in question: the intentions of the belligerents ought to be taken as decisive by any court or commentator.

Meaning of Subjugation. "Subjugation" means the firm military conquest of the enemy state following *debellatio*, the disintegration and eventual disappearance of its government, and the total absence of orga-

---

[24] Consult also Whiteman, Vol. X, pp. 85–95.

[25] *Shneiderman* v. *Metropolitan Casualty Co.*, United States, Sup. Court (N.Y.), App. Div., 1st Dept., November 9, 1961, 220 N.Y.S. 2d 947.

nized resistance by citizens and soldiers of the defeated state. As Lauter-pacht correctly emphasized,[26] subjugation and conquest are not neces-sarily identical, even though there can be no subjugation without con-quest. Partial occupation of an enemy state and even complete conquest of the same, may not be subjugation, as long as the enemy has forces in the field, either on its own territory or on that of allies. Even the total destruction of the enemy forces may not presage subjugation, for the con-queror may treat with the government of the defeated state and may re-turn to it all or part of its prewar territory. Subjugation takes place only when the conqueror in effect destroys, abolishes, annihilates the existence and legal personality of the defeated enemy state by annexation. Hence "subjugation . . . may be correctly defined as extermination in war of one belligerent by another through annexation of the former's territory after conquest, the enemy forces having been annihilated." [27]

Obviously subjugation as defined above means the termination of the war, as far as the two belligerents in question are concerned. The situa-tion of Germany from its defeat in May, 1945, to September 20, 1949—a subject of incredibly elaborate legal discussions—did not, however, rep-resent subjugation in the classic sense, since conquest was not followed by annexation.[28]

Unconditional Surrender. World War II saw the introduction of a new term relative to the end of a state of hostilities, *unconditional surrender*. The legal consequences of such a surrender might or might not be the termination of a war *ipso facto*, depending on the situation prevailing at the time and on the subsequent conduct and intentions of the victors.[29]

The conventional laws of war did not encompass the concept of un-conditional surrender. The closest they came to it was in the formulation of military "capitulations," as outlined in the Fourth Hague Convention of 1907. A capitulation is an agreement between commanders of belliger-ent forces for the surrender of troops, of a defended locality, or of a district of a theater of operations. A capitulation in this sense is quite def-initely a contractual agreement, and not one referring to the surrender of an entire enemy state.

Equally obviously, unconditional surrender had nothing in common with an armistice; instead, it corresponded to what Grotius termed "pure surrender," in the *Three Books on the Law of War and Peace*, illustrated by him through the account of the surrender of Carthage at the end of the Second Punic War. Grotius, like the leaders of the Allies in World

[26] Lauterpacht's *Oppenheim*, Vol. II, p. 600; the general subject of subjugation is covered in considerable detail by Lauterpacht on pp. 599–605.
[27] *Ibid.*, p. 600.
[28] See von Glahn, pp. 273–284; Lauterpacht's *Oppenheim*, Vol. II, pp. 602–605; and Gould, pp. 186–188.
[29] Consult especially Francis C. Balling, "Unconditional Surrender and a Unilateral Declaration of Peace," 39 *A.P.S.R.* (1945), pp. 474–480.

War II, believed that such a surrender granted to the victor full authority, legal and actual, to do as he pleased with the defeated.

The absence of true modern precedents for unconditional surrender prior to 1945 meant that no traditional formula for such an act could be found. It may be assumed that an instrument of unconditional surrender is not an agreement in the juridical sense, for nothing is promised by the victor, and even the party surrendering may or may not make any promises.[30]

There can be no doubt that an unconditional surrender does *not* result in a termination of a war unless the victor clearly indicates that such termination will accompany the submission of the defeated state.[31]

General Armistice. An armistice is a war convention, that is, an agreement or contract concluded between belligerents. Its primary and traditional purpose is to bring about a *temporary suspension* of active hostilities. A truce, to all intents and purposes, is identical with an armistice although in former days it usually had a shorter duration. Whereas particular armistices, more commonly termed "truces," call for cessation of hostilities in a portion of a theater of war, general armistices cause a general temporary cessation of hostilities between the belligerents concerned. The following discussion centers on such general instruments. From the days of Greece and Rome until today, writers, statesmen, and military men have been of the same opinion that neither type of agreement resulted in the termination of a state of war (*Law of Land Warfare*, par. 479). The courts of numerous states have affirmed equally that the conclusion of an armistice does not end a war.[32]

No customary rules prescribe what may be written into an armistice agreement, and several modern examples have been referred to as "capitulatory armistices," such as those which ended the active hostilities in World War I. The term was apt, for the agreements in question involved troop movements, evacuations, and surrender of defensive positions on the part of the Central Powers, notably Germany, which rendered a resumption of hostilities hopeless, if not impossible, and thus constituted a capitulation or surrender in fact, if not in name. Normally, armistices envisage a future resumption of hostilities, because they represent merely a suspension of the latter.

Hostilities in the Korean conflict ended, under the provisions of an armistice, on July 27, 1953. Since then no legal end of that conflict has been achieved. A Military Armistice Commission, composed of UN

---

[30] For the text of the unconditional surrender instruments signed in May, 1945, by Germany and Italy at Caserta and by German representatives at Rheims and Berlin, see 39 *A.J.I.L.* (1945), Sup., pp. 168–171. For the texts of the U.S. Proclamation and Joint Resolution terminating the state of war with Germany (October 19, 1951), see 46 *A.J.I.L.* (1952), Supp., pp. 12–13.

[31] See *Schiffahrt-Treuhand* v. *Procurator-General*, United Kingdom, Privy Council, 1953, 1 All Eng. L.R. 364, excerpted in 47 *A.J.I.L.* (1953), pp. 722–725.

[32] *Kahn* v. *Anderson, Warden*, United States, Supreme Court, 1921, 255 U.S. 1.

observers and U.S. and North Korean officers, has met to date over 270 times at Panmunjom, in the demilitarized zone created in 1953. Each side has charged the other with violations of the armistice: in fifteen years, only ninety-three violations out of 56,889 charged by North Korea have been admitted by the U.N. side, whereas only two out of 6,313 violations charged against North Korea have been admitted by the latter's representatives—none after 1953.[33]

What legal situation prevails during the life of an armistice agreement? The state of war continues, beyond question, and not only between the belligerents themselves, but also "between the belligerents and neutrals on all points beyond the mere cessation of hostilities."[34]

Problems commonly arise in connection with the interpretation of an armistice as to what may be permitted and what has been prohibited. Modern practice indicates that during a general armistice the belligerents must only abstain from undertaking those acts which have been expressly prohibited by the armistice agreement.[35]

The contents of a typical armistice agreement have been succinctly outlined in paragraphs 487 and 488 of the current American manual *The Law of Land Warfare*. An armistice instrument would include provisions as to the effective date and time, duration, lines of demarcation and possible neutral zones to be established, relations with the indigenous population, prohibited acts, status of prisoners of war during the armistice, and possibly provisions dealing with the establishment of consultative machinery and various political and even economic matters involved in the temporary suspension of hostilities.[36]

If one of the parties to an armistice agreement commits a "serious" violation of one of the provisions agreed upon, the other party appears to be free to denounce the agreement and to resume hostilities, but this recourse to hostile acts may not be commenced without notice unless a case of urgency exists (Art. 40 of the Hague Regulations of 1907). The obvious difficulty inherent in this principle is the definition of what constitutes a "serious" violation and a "case of urgency."

Naval Armistice. As far as war at sea is concerned, little is found in the literature, but the governing principles are quite clear. A naval armistice (or a general armistice, which, of course, would apply also to the naval segment of hostilities) would preclude a naval battle as well as naval bombardments. Most writers, however, are silent on the subject of how an armistice would affect a blockade and of the relations between a blockading belligerent and neutrals. It appears that the blockading party may

[33] See 92 *Time* (July 26, 1968), pp. 38–39.

[34] Lauterpacht's *Oppenheim*, Vol. II, p. 546.

[35] *Law of Land Warfare*, par. 487-e, and the fully documented study of Howard S. Levie, "The Nature and Scope of the Armistice Agreement," 50 *A.J.I.L.* (1956), pp. 880–906, at pp. 886–888, especially notes 40–41.

[36] For details of the individual topics, with historical examples, consult Levie, *op. cit.*, pp. 889–901.

continue its activities in this sphere during an armistice, including the capture of enemy vessels and the stoppage of neutral vessels and the carrying of contraband, unless the armistice agreement contains specific provisions to the contrary.[37]

Treaty of Peace. A treaty of peace is the normal and greatly preferred mode of terminating a war. It must be re-emphasized at the outset that a ceasefire, a truce, an armistice, or even preliminary peace negotiations do *not* represent the *legal* termination of a war, despite much lay misunderstanding on the point. Thus the Korean War is still legally in effect, because the relevant armistice agreement only ended hostilities but did not restore peace; the same is true of the Arab-Israeli conflicts of 1948, 1956, and 1967. The end of hostilities, by varieties of agreements such as those mentioned, does not end the legal status of war, nor do the parties involved appear to regard that status as terminated by the conclusion of preliminary agreements or the carrying on of negotiations.

A treaty of peace has the primary effect of restoring a condition of peace between the ex-belligerents. As soon as the treaty becomes effective, all normal peacetime rights and duties go back into effect between the parties to the agreement. Acts deemed legitimate in time of war cease to be lawful. Diplomatic and consular relations are resumed. Unless the treaty provides to the contrary, each ex-belligerent retains movable public property seized from the other belligerent. Unless otherwise provided for, occupied ex-enemy territory may be annexed; this old rule has been modified, however, in modern times, and such annexation normally is provided for (in the peace treaty itself) by means of specific provisions for cession of territory.

An important effect of a peace treaty has been, traditionally, the release of all prisoners of war by all parties to the agreement. Such release did not have to be immediate, but was to take place as soon as possible. However, Article 118 of the 1949 Geneva Convention on Prisoners of War changed the existing customary and conventional law by requiring the immediate release and repatriations of all prisoners of war as soon as active hostilities had ceased. As Lauterpacht pointed out,[38] this provision appears to relate to the end of hostilities brought about by total surrender or by an armistice couched in such terms as to make resumption of warfare impossible for the defeated party. It grew out of the continued detention of prisoners of war long after the actual end of hostilities in World War II. (See also Chapter 28.)

The repatriation provisions of the Geneva Convention became a major

---

[37] See Levie, *op. cit.*, pp. 904–906, with historical examples, including the interesting relevant provisions of the Korean armistice of July 27, 1953. As regards the latter instrument, consult also the complete texts in 35 *U.S. News & World Report* (August 7, 1953), pp. 85–91, and C. Turner Joy, "The Korean Truce," *ibid.*, 39 (October 28, 1955), pp. 131–162.

[38] Lauterpacht's *Oppenheim*, Vol. II, p. 613.

reason for the delay in United States ratification of all four Geneva conventions of 1949, as a consequence of the end of hostilities in Korea. (See also Chapter 28.) After a large number of North Korean and Chinese prisoners of war, as well as a handful of American prisoners, refused to be repatriated, an Agreement on Repatriation of Prisoners of War (signed on June 8, 1953) and a Supplementary Agreement on Prisoners of War had to be worked out between the representatives of North Korea and the United Nations Command.[39] This agreement, signed on July 27, 1953, provided that prisoners of war who requested not to be directly repatriated were to be transferred to special neutral zones. There responsibility for the individuals in question was assumed by a Neutral Nations Repatriation Committee, and order was maintained by units of the armed forces of India. Each side then sent "explaining representatives" to the prisoners in question in an attempt to persuade them to be repatriated. Eventually those prisoners deciding to go to neutral countries were assisted in doing so, and those not desiring to do so, yet declining to be repatriated, were relieved of their status as prisoners of war and returned to civilian status.

Status of Prewar Treaties. The resumption of the effectiveness or validity of prewar treaties between ex-belligerents after the end of a war is a much discussed question.

Normally peace treaties are utilized to reactivate economic and technical agreements suspended during the conflict, although it should be pointed out that particularly in the sphere of economic agreements (commercial treaties, tariff agreements, and so on) reactivation quite commonly includes changes from the prewar stipulations and in effect then amounts to renegotiation of the agreements. On a few occasions, however, a party to the conflict refuses to revive prewar agreements, as was done by Spain in 1898 when it declared that the war had ended all agreements between Spain and the United States. If the war ends with a decisive victory of one side over the other, then usually it is left to the determination of the victorious side as to which treaties are to be regarded as still valid. Such, for instance, was the case in the Allied peace treaty of 1947 with Italy.

If a peace treaty is silent on the question of treaty validity, then all agreements that had been abrogated by the outbreak of the war (alliances and other political agreements) would be dead (null and void) on the return of peace. On the other hand, under such conditions, treaties merely suspended by the coming of the war would have to be regarded as reviewed and in full force on the effective date of the peace treaty.

The 1947 peace treaties concluded with Italy and other European Axis countries each contained identical articles relating to prewar bilateral agreements. The provisions in question called for each of the victorious powers to give notice to the defeated state, within six months from the

[39] Texts of the two agreements may be found in 35 *U.S. News & World Report* (August 7, 1953), pp. 92–94.

coming into effect of the respective peace treaty, as to which of its pre-war bilateral treaties were to be maintained in effect or were to be reactivated. Such instruments were to be registered with the Secretariat of the United Nations. Any bilateral treaties not included on the lists to be sent to each defeated nation were to be considered as abrogated.[40]

The Japanese peace settlement of 1951 also contained in the treaty provisions, rather elaborate in this instance, relating to the reactivation of prewar treaties, both bilateral and multipartite, in addition to a Supplementary Declaration relating exclusively to the continuing effects of multilateral agreements.[41] (See p. 565 for the renewed applicability of multilateral treaties.)

Enemy Property. A final and knotty problem related to the restoration of peace has to do with the return or retention by states of seized enemy property. As was pointed out earlier, a rapid change in the applicable rules of law during the last fifty years has led to a general acceptance of the idea that a belligerent is entitled to seize enemy private property located in his own territory, provided the enemy owners are not resident in the belligerent's jurisdiction. As mentioned then, during World War II, the anti-Axis belligerents seized all such enemy properties and entrusted them to the care of officials usually styled Alien Property Custodians.

What should become of such properties at the termination of a war when a treaty of peace does not call for their return to the former owners? Because the properties were held by governments, the obvious answer would be that they could be retained or sold, and that in the latter case the sums realized might be treated as a kind of reparation for war damage suffered by the seizing state and its citizens.

Eighteen Allied states adopted this view in the Paris Agreement on German Reparation of January 24, 1946, deciding that

Each Signatory Government shall, under such procedures as it may choose, hold or dispose of German assets within its jurisdiction in manners designed to preclude their return to German ownership or control . . .[42]

The Bonn Convention of May 26, 1952, provided specifically that the Allies waived all claims for reparations from Germany, that the latter agreed never to contest the retention of seized assets by the Allies and agreed furthermore to compensate the former owners of the seized properties.[43] As far as the United States was concerned, the War Claims Act

[40] See also Elmer Plischke, "Reactivation of Prewar German Treaties," 48 *A.J.I.L.* (1954), pp. 245–264, especially pp. 251–261, on the intricate problems involved in reactivating treaties with a former enemy state in the absence of a peace treaty.

[41] See the text of the Japanese peace treaty in 46 *A.J.I.L.* (1952), Supp., pp. 71–76, and of the Declaration, *ibid.*, pp. 86–87.

[42] Text in 40 *A.J.I.L.* (1946), Supp., p. 117.

[43] Relevant textual excerpts in Robert B. Ely III, "Return of Enemy-Owned Property," *Proceedings* (1958), pp. 59–65, at p. 61, n. 5; see also Oscar Schisgall, *The Enemy Property Issue* (New York: Public Affairs Committee, 1957), at p. 4.

of 1948 provided for retention of seized enemy property, and if such were sold, the proceeds were to be used to settle war claims of American nationals, the net balance remaining to go into the Treasury of the United States.[44]

Many of the enemy properties seized in this country were sold in the course of time. The largest remaining vested enterprise, the General Aniline and Film Corporation, valued at $35,000,000 when seized, and worth $100,000,000 by 1956, became the object of the celebrated *Interhandel* case. (See suggested readings in Chapter 12 for sources on that case and on the ultimate disposal, by sale, of the properties in question.)

In 1956, a movement began in the United States to return all properties vested in the Custodian to the former, now ex-enemy, owners.[45]

Lack of space prohibits an analysis of the complicated arguments which evolved from the suggestion that the seized properties be returned. One point, however, must be stressed: legally the United States was correct in retaining property vested in the Custodian or the proceeds from its sale. Any reliance on alleged contrary rules of international law fails to take cognizance of the change in those rules which has taken place since 1918 and which has been reaffirmed in numerous treaties of undoubted validity.

SUGGESTED READINGS

GENERAL

United States, *Proclamations Regarding Alien Enemies* (Japan: No. 2525, December 7, 1941; Germany, No. 2526, and Italy, No. 2527, December 8, 1941; Hungary, Bulgaria, Romania, No. 2563, July 17, 1942), 36 *A.J.I.L.* (1942), Supp., pp. 236–243; William Grewe, *A Peace with Germany?* (*An Analysis*), Washington, D.C.: German Embassy, n.d. [1959?]—containing the full text of the draft peace treaty with Germany sent by the U.S.S.R. to twenty-eight governments on January 10, 1959.

Cases

Brown v. *United States*, United States, Supreme Court, 1814, 8 Cranch (12 U.S.) 110.

Commercial Cable Co. v. *Burleson*, United States, District Court, S.D. of New York, 1919, 255 Fed. 99.

[44] 62 *Stat.* 1240, sec. 12; text in Ely, *op. cit.*, p. 61, n. 4.
[45] See, *inter alia*, Schisgall, *op. cit.*, pp. 6–11; William H. Reeves, "Return of Enemy Property," *Proceedings* (1958), pp. 48–53; Kenneth S. Carston, "Return of Enemy Property," *ibid.*, pp. 53–59; Robert B. Ely III, *op. cit.*, *ibid.*, pp. 59–65; Victor C. Folsom, "Return of Enemy-Owned Property,' *ibid.*, pp. 65–70 (with extensive bibliographical notes on pp. 65–66), and the discussion of the preceding papers, *ibid.*, pp. 70–79. The Office of Alien Property closed on June 30, 1966, after handling properties of the most varied kind valued at about $900 million.

The Eliza Ann, Great Britain, High Court of Admiralty, 1813, 1 Dodson 244, 165 Eng. Rep. 1298.

Kaufman v. *Société Internationale,* United States, Supreme Court, 1952, 343 U.S. 156.

Porter v. *Freudenberg,* Great Britain, Court of Appeal, 1915, [1915] 1 K.B. 857.

Stoehr v. *Wallace,* United States, Supreme Court, 1921, 255 U.S. 239.

COMMENCEMENT OF WAR

Philip M. Brown, "Undeclared Wars," 33 *A.J.I.L.* (1939), pp. 538–541; Clyde Eagleton, "Acts of War," *ibid.,* 35 (1941), pp. 321–326; L. C. Green, "The Nature of the 'War' in Korea" 4 *International Law Quarterly* (1951), pp. 462–468; A. Kenneth Pye, "The Legal Status of the Korean Hostilities," 45 *Georgetown Law Journal* (Fall, 1956), pp. 45–60. See also Harrison E. Salisbury, "Russians to Mark '39 Mongolia War," *The New York Times,* May 24, 1964, p. 8, concerning the undeclared border conflict of 1937–39 involving the Soviet Union and Outer Mongolia against Japan, a "war" ended by an "unofficial armistice" after a serious Japanese defeat.

Cases

For additional references to insurance cases centering on the beginning of a war, consult Myres S. McDougal and Florentino P. Feliciano, "The Initiation of Coercion: A Multi-Temporal Analysis," 52 *A.J.I.L.* (1958), pp. 241–259, at n. 30. p. 251, and at n. 32, p. 252.

Navios Corporation v. *The Ulysses II,* United States, District Court, Maryland, 1958, 161 F. Supp. 932.

VIETNAM WAR

Francis D. Wormuth, *The Vietnam War: The President versus the Constitution* (Santa Barbara, Calif.: Fund for the Republic, 1968)—a defense of the need for a formal declaration of war; for defenses of the policy adopted by the U.S. [Gulf of Tonkin Resolution, etc.] see, *inter alia,* the analyses in 59 *U.S. News & World Report* (December 20, 1965), p. 33; *ibid.,* 62 (March 13, 1967), p. 43; and *ibid.,* 62 (May 22, 1967) pp. 31–33, the last item including the testimony of the then Secretary of Defense (McNamara) on the avoidance of a formal declaration of war by the United States.

TREATIES AND WAR

Lord McNair and A. D. Watts, *The Legal Effects of War,* 4th ed. (New York: Cambridge University Press, 1967); Stuart H. McIntyre, *The Legal Effect of World War II on Treaties of the United States* (The Hague: Martinus Nijhoff, 1958); J. G. Castel, "Effect of War on Bilateral Treaties," 51 *Michigan Law Review* (1953), pp. 566–573; Richard Rank, "Modern War and the Validity of Treaties," 38 *Cornell Law Quarterly* (1953), pp. 321–355, 511–540.

ENEMY ALIENS

U.S. War Department, *Final Report: Japanese Evacuation from the West Coast* (Washington, D.C.: U.S. Government Printing Office, 1943); Allan R. Bosworth, *America's Concentration Camps* (New York: Norton, 1967); Michael Brandon, "Legal Control over Resident Enemy Aliens in Time of War in the United States and in the United Kingdom," 44 *A.J.I.L.* (1950), pp. 382–387.

TERMINATION OF WAR

David Brook, *Preface to Peace: the United Nations and the Arab-Israel Armistice System* (Washington, D.C.: Public Affairs Press, 1964); texts of Hungarian and Romanian Peace Treaties: 42 *A.J.I.L.* (1948), Supp., pp. 255–277; documents relating to the Italian Armistice of 1943, *ibid.*, 40 (1946), Supp., pp. 1–21; Tashkent Declaration (India-Pakistan, 1966), in *The New York Times*, January 11, 1966, p. C-15; Sir Charles K. Webster, "Patterns of Peacemaking," 25 *Foreign Affairs* (1947), pp. 596–611; Josef L. Kunz, "Ending the War with Germany," 46 *A.J.I.L.* (1952), pp. 114–119.

28

Laws of War
on Land and in the Air

BACKGROUND

THE legality of war had been acknowledged by eminent writers on international law, beginning with Hugo Grotius. At the same time, both governments and military leaders recognized that a regularization of the conduct of hostilities was highly desirable, as were an avoidance of needless suffering and an unnecessary loss of property. It was therefore not surprising that a relatively elaborate set of customary rules concerning the behavior of states during war was evolved between the end of the Thirty Years' War and the middle of the nineteenth century.

The true beginning of present-day rules applicable to land warfare came in 1863 when Lieber's *Instructions for the Government of the Armies of the United States in the Field* were issued to the Union Army on April 24, 1863, as General Orders No. 100.[1] The thoroughness of Lieber's work impressed military men elsewhere and the *Instructions* became the model for numerous national manuals (Italy, 1896 and 1900; Russia, 1904; and France, 1901 and 1912).

Concurrently, private and governmental efforts at codifying the laws of war on land proceeded on the Continent. An international conference, held at Brussels in 1874 at the initiative of Russia and attended by representatives of fifteen states, resulted in a Draft Declaration.[2] Although the instrument was not ratified by the participating states, it did exert considerable influence on the thinking of legal experts and apparently induced a number of states to base new military manuals on the provisions of the draft declaration.

Two private attempts at codification merit brief mention: in 1880 the Institute of International Law prepared the so-called Oxford Manual (*Manuel de Lois de la Guerre Sur Terre*), and in 1894 the German writer Geffcken prepared a private code, anticipating in it several important aspects of the 1894 and 1907 conventions.

---

[1] See also Chapter 26 on this famous manual.

[2] Text in Doris Graber, *The Development of the Law of Belligerent Occupation, 1863–1914* (New York: Columbia University Press, 1949), at pp. 297–317; see also Dr. Graber's account of the conference at pp. 20–28 and the commentary on the draft, at pp. 28–30.

The *Oxford Manual* was such an excellent effort, considering the type of warfare then current, that it is still cited with approval by European writers.[3]

Far more important than those early attempts were the conventions and regulations produced at the two Hague Peace Conferences in 1899 and 1907. In particular, the Fourth Convention Respecting the Laws and Customs of War on Land (1907) and its annexed Regulations formulated the rules which have been accepted subsequently by most nations of the world and have been incorporated in almost all military manuals.[4]

Although both World Wars showed up the inadequacy of many of the 1907 rules as well as the great gaps existing in the body of law presumably governing war on land, repeated attempts to modernize the rules have failed (conferences at Madrid, Monaco, and Liège), except for the results of the 1949 Geneva Diplomatic Conference.

LAWS OF WAR ON LAND

The actual rules in force in 1914 were based in part on custom, in part on the conventions adopted in 1899 at The Hague, and in particular on the Regulations annexed to the Fourth Hague Convention of 1907.

In view of limitations of space, the relevant text of the Regulations is reproduced below, followed by brief comments on selected individual provisions.[5]

REGULATIONS RESPECTING THE LAWS AND CUSTOMS OF WAR ON LAND [6]

Section I. On Belligerents

Chapter I. The Qualifications of Belligerents

Article 1. The laws, rights, and duties of war apply not only to armies, but also to militia and volunteer corps fulfilling the following conditions:

---

[3] The text of the *Manual* may be found in excerpted form in Graber, *op. cit.*, pp. 297–317, and complete in James B. Scott, ed., *Resolutions of the Institute of International Law dealing with the Law of Nations* (New York: Oxford University Press, 1916), at pp. 26–42. F. H. Geffcken's code may be found in his "Règlement des Lois et Coutumes de la Guerre," 26 *Revue de Droit International* (1894), pp. 586–604.

[4] See also Chapter 26 and below. The Regulations are cited hereinafter as HR.

[5] Consult Chapter 31 on the subject of belligerent occupation.

[6] The following States were parties to The Hague Convention IV of 1907: Australia, Belgium, Bolivia, Brazil, Canada, China, Cuba, Denmark, Finland, France, Germany, Great Britain, Guatemala, Haiti, Hungary, India, Ireland, Japan, Liberia, Luxembourg, Mexico, Netherlands, New Zealand, Nicaragua, Norway, Panama, Poland, Portugal, Romania, Russia, Salvador, South Africa, Sweden, Switzerland, Thailand, United States. Austria and Ethiopia had also been parties.

States parties to The Hague Regulations as annexed to Convention II of 1899 but which were not parties to Convention IV of 1907 were: Argentina, Bulgaria, Chile, Colombia, Dominican Republic, Ecuador, Greece, Honduras, Italy, (Korea, 1903), Paraguay, Peru, Persia, Spain, Turkey, Uruguay, and Venezuela.

1. To be commanded by a person responsible for his subordinates;
2. To have a fixed distinctive emblem recognizable at a distance;
3. To carry arms openly; and
4. To conduct their operations in accordance with the laws and customs of war.

In countries where militia or volunteer corps constitute the army, or form part of it, they are included under the denomination "army."

Article 2. The inhabitants of a territory which has not been occupied, who, on the approach of the enemy, spontaneously take arms to resist the invading troops without having had time to organize themselves in accordance with Article 1, shall be regarded as belligerents if they carry arms openly and if they respect the laws and customs of war.

Article 3. The armed forces of the belligerent parties may consist of combatants and non-combatants. In the case of capture by the enemy, both have a right to be treated as prisoners of war.

Chapter II. Prisoners of War

[Articles 4 to 20 omitted.] [7]

Chapter III. The Sick and Wounded

Article 21. The obligations of belligerents with regard to the sick and wounded are governed by the Geneva Convention.[8]

Section II. Hostilities

Chapter I. Means of Injuring the Enemy, Sieges, and Bombardments

Article 22. The right of belligerents to adopt means of injuring the enemy is not unlimited.

Article 23. In addition to the prohibitions provided by special Conventions, it is especially forbidden—

(a) To employ poison or poisoned weapons;
(b) To kill or wound treacherously individuals belonging to the hostile nation or army;
(c) To kill or wound an enemy who, having laid down his arms, or having no longer means of defence, has surrendered at discretion;
(d) To declare that no quarter will be given;
(e) To employ arms, projectiles, or material calculated to cause unnecessary suffering;
(f) To make improper use of a flag of truce, of the national flag or of the

---

[7] Articles 4–20 have been replaced by the Geneva Convention of August 12, 1949, Relative to the Treatment of Prisoners of War.

[8] The reference is to the Geneva Convention of August 22, 1864, revised in 1906, 1929, and 1949.

military insignia and uniform of the enemy, as well as the distinctive badges of the Geneva Convention;

(g) To destroy or seize the enemy's property, unless such destruction or seizure be imperatively demanded by the necessities of war;

(h) To declare abolished, suspended, or inadmissable in a court of law the rights and actions of the nationals of the hostile party.

A belligerent is likewise forbidden to compel the nationals of the hostile party to take part in the operations of war directed against their own country, even if they were in the belligerent's service before the commencement of the war.

Article 24. Ruses of war and the employment of measures necessary for obtaining information about the enemy and the country are considered permissible.

Article 25. The attack or bombardment, by whatever means, of towns, villages, dwellings, or buildings which are undefeated is prohibited.

Article 26. The officer in command of an attacking force must, before commencing a bombardment, except in cases of assault, do all in his power to warn the authorities.

Article 27. In sieges and bombardments all necessary steps must be taken to spare, as far as possible, buildings dedicated to religion, art, science, or charitable purposes, historic monuments, hospitals, and places where the sick and wounded are collected, provided they are not being used at the time for military purposes.

It is the duty of the besieged to indicate the presence of such buildings or places by distinctive and visible signs, which shall be notified to the enemy beforehand.

Article 28. The pillage of a town or place, even when taken by assault, is prohibited.

Chapter II. Spies

Article 29. A person can only be considered a spy when, acting clandestinely or on false pretenses, he obtains or endeavors to obtain information in the zone of operations of a belligerent, with the intention of communicating it to the hostile party.

Thus, soldiers not wearing a disguise who have penetrated into the zone of operations of the hostile army, for the purpose of obtaining information, are not considered spies. Similarly, the following are not considered spies: Soldiers and civilians, carrying out their mission openly, intrusted with the delivery of despatches intended either for their own army or for the enemy's army. To this class belong likewise persons sent in balloons for the purpose of carrying despatches and, generally, of maintaining communications between the different parts of an army or a territory.

Article 30. A spy taken in the act shall not be punished without previous trial.

Article 31. A spy who, after rejoining the army to which he belongs, is subsequently captured by the enemy, is treated as a prisoner of war, and incurs no responsibility for his previous acts of espionage.

Chapter III. Flags of Truce

Article 32. A person is regarded as a parlementaire who has been authorized by one of the belligerents to enter into communication with the other, and who advances bearing a white flag. He has a right to inviolability, as well as the trumpeter, bugler or drummer, the flagbearer and interpreter who may accompany him.

Article 33. The commander to whom a parlementaire is sent is not in all cases obliged to receive him.

He may take all the necessary steps to prevent the parlementaire taking advantage of his mission to obtain information.

In case of abuse, he has the right to detain the parlementaire temporarily.

Article 34. The parlementaire loses his rights of inviolability if it is proved in a clear and incontestable manner that he has taken advantage of his privileged position to provoke or commit an act of treason.

[Chapters IV and V deal with Capitulations and Armistices.]

COMMENTS ON THE REGULATIONS

Killing Treacherously. The prohibition of killing treacherously (HR, Art. 23-b) means that it is illegal to assassinate, proscribe, or outlaw an enemy, or to place a price on his head, or to offer a reward for his delivery "dead or alive." It is believed that the prohibition was not aimed at "sneak attacks" on individual members of an opposing armed force.

Article 23, par. 2, of the Regulations is self-explanatory.[9]

Killing an Unarmed Enemy. The provisions of HR Article 23-c do not imply a prohibition on firing on descending parachutists bound on hostile missions. Despite the fact that such individuals are temporarily unable to defend themselves effectively, their opponents have a lawful right to try to kill them. If, however, the descending parachutist is not bound on a hostile mission (doctors, nurses, chaplains, members of the crew of a disabled aircraft), he or she may not be attacked. The practical difficulty lies in the problem of discerning the nature of the individual, particularly if the descent is made at night or in poor visibility.

Denial of Quarter. The prohibition on the denial of quarter (HR, Art. 23-d) has several recognized exceptions: no quarter need be granted to enemy troops which resume fighting after hoisting a white flag or other sign of surrender, and a denial of quarter would be legitimate in reprisal for a similar refusal by an opposing military force.

Use of Ruses. The provisions of Article 24, concerning the lawful use of ruses, apparently were left vague by intent: no general treaty could list all the ingenious devices used or yet to be invented to confound an enemy. On the other hand, certain practices are recognized as unlawful, either under Article 24 or under customary law. Thus it is forbidden to misuse a flag of truce or the emblem of the Red Cross (HR, Art. 23-f). The

---

[9] Cf. von Glahn, pp. 81–85, concerning the meaning of the prohibition in occupied enemy territory.

enemy's uniform must not be misused: it may be worn by his opponents but must be discarded before hostilities commence. Such an attitude is not very consistent: it means that an enemy can be lured into an unfavorable situation by a form of legal disguise, which would then suddenly become illegal at a moment when the enemy could no longer extricate himself from the situation.[10] Soldiers of most nations appear to be united in a silent compact which justifies their killing of any enemy misusing their own uniform—especially when that enemy, still in the opponent's uniform, appears behind the latter's lines: examples abounded in the Battle of the Bulge in 1944.

On the other hand, an American war crimes tribunal at Dachau, in September, 1947, acquitted Otto Skorzeny and seven aides of charges of war crimes: the accused had infiltrated American lines during the Battle of the Bulge wearing American uniforms. Although the accused had obviously violated the spirit of Article 23 (f), they had not been captured in the act of violation but had been arraigned years later. Such a contingency was not covered clearly in the Hague Regulations.[11]

Prohibition of Certain Weapons. In line with the prevailing concept that needless suffering should be avoided, pre-1914 laws of war specified certain prohibited categories of weapons which, by their nature, would aggravate the sufferings of the wounded. Thus HR Article 23-e, forbade the employment of arms, projectiles and other material calculated to cause unnecessary suffering. The prohibition was somewhat vague, leaving, in essence, each state free to decide whether or not to utilize a certain weapon because in its judgment it possessed or lacked the prohibited effect. State practice has sanctioned the use of explosives in artillery shells, mines, and hand grenades. On the other hand, such weapons as lances with barbed heads, irregularly shaped bullets, shells filled with glass, and the application of some substance to bullets, intended to inflame a wound, have been accepted as forbidden. Correctly prohibited have been dumdum bullets, that is, bullets whose surface has been scored or nicked.[12] During World War I, both sides accused each other of using such bullets but at most individual instances were substantiated and it must be concluded that any dumdum bullets employed had been altered to that form by their individual users, without order or authority from their commanders.

Certain unissued weapons, privately acquired and then utilized occasionally by U.S. military personnel in the Vietnamese conflict, appear

[10] Consult Valentine Jobst III, "Is the Wearing of the Enemy's Uniform a Violation of the Laws of War?" 35 *A.J.I.L.* (1941), pp. 435–442; cf. U.S. Department of the Army (FM 27-10), *Law of Land Warfare* (July, 1956), p. 23.

[11] See also Maximilian Koessler, "International Law on Use of Enemy Uniforms as a Strategem and the Acquittal in the Skorzeny Case," 24 *Missouri Law Review* (1959), pp. 16–43.

[12] *Law of Land Warfare*, p. 18.

to be at the very least of dubious legality, particularly so in the case of hatchets and shotguns.

In accordance with the Declaration of St. Petersburg of December 11, 1868, seventeen states had agreed to prohibit, for themselves and such other states as would adhere to the Declaration, the use of any projectile weighing less than 14 ounces (400 grams) which was charged with some inflammable substance or was explosive in nature. By contrast, the use of weapons employing fire (tracer ammunition, flamethrowers, napalm bombs or sprayers) is *not* prohibited by any rule or treaty.

Napalm, in particular, developed and used extensively in World War II, the Korean War, and then in the Vietnamese conflict, has been attacked frequently as an illegal weapon. This charge, based on the asserted great number of injured said to result from the use of napalm, has not been accepted in all medical circles nor in military circles. A commission of physicians, headed by Dr. Howard Rusk of *The New York Times*, toured Vietnamese hospitals and reported that the total of civilian casualties traceable to the utilization of napalm was negligible.[13]

Poison and Poisoned Weapons. Under the Hague Regulations (Art. 23-a), the use of poison or of poisoned weapons was outlawed. This did not mean that water supplies and waterworks could not be rendered unusable by diversion or destruction, as the case might be, nor that crops intended solely for the use of the armed forces of an enemy could be rendered unfit for use by some chemical or bacterial means. The problem in the last instance was, of course, a difficult one: how would one determine that a given crop *was* destined only for consumption by the armed forces of one's opponent?

Poison Gases and Related Weapons. The First Hague Conference (1899) had adopted a declaration signed (July 29, 1899) by sixteen states which provided that the parties in question would not make use of shells used for the distribution of asphyxiating gases. This prohibition was, obviously, fully in accord with the outlawing of the use of poison and with the humane endeavor to avoid causing unnecessary suffering. The United States delegation refused to sign this prohibition as inconsistent with already accepted methods of warfare and because, it was asserted, no one knew what the actual effects of such gas shells were.

When Germany used poison gas in World War I, the Allied forces attempted to retaliate in kind, justifying their action as a reprisal. Since then a number of international agreements have been drafted in efforts to outlaw not only the use of poison gases but also of all other related methods of warfare, including bacteriological warfare. The peace treaties at the end of World War I reiterated the prohibition on asphyxiating gases; Article 5 of the Treaty of Washington (February 6, 1922: the United States, Great Britain, France, Italy, Japan) prohibited "The use in war of asphyxiating, poisonous or other gases, and all analogous liquids, materials, or devices," but since the treaty was to become effective only

[13] See 89 *Time* (March 24, 1967), p. 63.

when all the signatory powers had ratified it, and when such ratification failed to take place, the agreement did not become effective. On June 17, 1925, the Geneva Gas Protocol for the prohibition of the use in war of asphyxiating, poisonous, or other gases, as well as of bacteriological methods of warfare, was signed by the United States delegate as well as by the representatives of many other states; the instrument did come into force on April 3, 1928.[14] The United States Senate did not give its consent to ratification, however, citing as late as 1952 what it considered to be the inadequacies of the agreement. Because more than forty states have either ratified the instrument or have adhered to it, most writers today are in agreement that the Geneva Protocol is binding on practically all states, through the development of a general rule of customary law springing from the provisions of the Protocol.[15] The United States, however, is *not* bound by such a rule, because the U.S. government objected to the latter, as framed, from the beginning of the development of the rule. In December, 1966, the United States "endorsed" a General Assembly resolution urging member states to abide by the Geneva Protocol, but it should be remembered that such resolutions possess no binding force and also that such substances as tear gas are not normally classified as poison gas.

It is believed that gas and bacteriological warfare methods were not utilized to any extent during World War II, even though both sides in that conflict were prepared for such an eventuality. The major reason for their commendable abstention from the use of such weapons probably may be found in an inability to protect military and civilians alike against retaliatory use of similar weapons by an enemy: hence a tacit agreement to refrain from the use of such methods of warfare appears to have taken place.

The 1957 New Delhi Conference of the International Red Cross attempted in vain to secure agreement for the adoption of a new and comprehensive set of rules governing the employment of certain methods of warfare. The proposed regulations would have prohibited any weapons

whose harmful effects—resulting in particular from the dissemination of incendiary, chemical, bacteriological, radioactive or other agents—could spread to an unforseen degree or escape, either in space or in time, from the control of those who employ them, thus endangering the civilian population.[16]

[14] Text in 25 *A.J.I.L.* (1931), p. 94. Consult also Stone, pp. 553–557, as well as William V. O'Brien, "Biological/Chemical Warfare and the International Law of War," 51 *Georgetown Law Journal* (Fall, 1962), pp. 1–63; Carl A. Larson, "Biological Warfare Model 1967," 46 *Military Review*, No. 5 (May, 1966), pp. 31–39, as well as the illuminating summary of current developments in 92 *Time* (September 6, 1968), pp. 92, 94.
[15] See Lauterpacht's *Oppenheim*, Vol. II, p. 344; see *ibid.*, p. 343, n. 2, for instances of war crimes trials conducted by the U.S.S.R. for alleged violations of the prohibitions found in the Protocol.
[16] *The New York Times*, October 27, 1957.

This effort was part of an elaborate plan to secure adoption of new Draft Rules for the Protection of the Civilian Population from the Dangers of Indiscriminate Warfare, drawn up under the International Committee as early as 1954–55 by a committee of fifteen experts. If adopted at the 1957 Delhi meeting, the Red Cross would have submitted its proposals to a new diplomatic conference.[17]

In February, 1967, Yemeni royalists charged that Egyptian forces aiding the Republic of Yemen in that country's civil war had bombed the village of Ketaf with poison gas, killing more than 120 people.[18] In May of that year, a second alleged poison gas attack, on the village of Gahar, was investigated by two members of the International Committee of the Red Cross, who reported that some seventy-five persons appeared to have been killed by a form of toxic gas.[19] A few days later, unconfirmed reports alleged that on two occasions, in January, 1967, Egyptian forces had used lethal nerve gas attacks on two royalist settlements. After efforts had been made at the United Nations by Saudi Arabia to have all of these real or alleged events investigated, the issue was not pressed further, apparently for the sake of Arab solidarity.[20]

On August 8, 1968, the British government submitted a draft treaty prohibiting the manufacture and use of bacteriological weapons to the seventeen-nation disarmament conference at Geneva, and toward the end of September of that year, Secretary-General Thant of the United Nations announced the appointment of a committee of experts to study the uses and effects of both chemical and bacteriological weapons.

Atomic Weapons. Most controversial, although undreamt of before 1914, has been the use of atomic weapons, whether by land, sea, or air forces. As yet there is no *specific* conventional rule outlawing or limiting the utilization of atomic or nuclear weapons.[21] Responsible authorities, notably the late Sir Hersch Lauterpacht, have inclined toward a belief that the use of any of such weapons ought to be prohibited if it could be demonstrated that the aftereffects of their use would place them in the sphere of "biological" warfare, while at the same time not objecting to their use against strictly military objectives.[22]

Lauterpacht expressed deep concern over the abandonment—insofar as bombing was concerned—of the traditional distinction between com-

[17] See Josef L. Kunz, "The Laws of War," 50 *A.J.I.L.* (1956), pp. 313–337, at pp. 324–325 for a summary of the Geneva proposals of 1955.

[18] 89 *Time* (February 17, 1967), pp. 36, 39.

[19] Texts of reports in 63 *U.S. News & World Report* (July 3, 1967), p. 60.

[20] *The New York Times,* July 30, 1967, p. 6.

[21] Thus the *United States Law of Naval Warfare* (1955 ed.) states in par. 613 that "There is at present no rule of international law expressly prohibiting states from the use of nuclear weapons in warfare. In the absence of express prohibition, the use of such weapons against enemy combatants and other military objectives is permitted." See also Chapter 18 concerning the Nuclear Test Ban Treaty.

[22] Lauterpacht's *Oppenheim,* Vol. II, pp. 348–349.

batants and noncombatants, writing that to admit the impossibility of preserving that distinction was "to admit that in modern conditions there is no longer room for one of the most fundamental aspects of the traditional law of war." [23] He then went on to express his belief that even with the use of atomic weapons the distinction invariably would be obliterated and his conviction that the use of such weapons could be limited to military objectives proper.

On the other hand, this writer believes that the aftereffects resulting from the employment of nuclear weapons create violations, directly or by analogy, of Articles 23-a and 23-e of the 1907 Hague Regulations and also of the 1925 Geneva Protocol.[24] The fact, however, that major powers have continued to produce the weapons in question means that such powers have accepted existing rules as obsolete, have regarded the law as inadequate to control the new tools of destruction, have come to the conclusion that nuclear weapons will be utilized only on a basis of reciprocity and would not be used if the other party to a conflict would not first use them. They may also have decided that nuclear weapons would be utilized only in the instance of direct military necessity. It would appear, from a practical point of view, then, that production of stockpiles of nuclear weapons, coupled with fruitless endeavors to secure legal (express) prohibition of the use of such weapons, implies a present legality for them.[25]

There can be no doubt that a *destruction* of existing nuclear weapons, together with a working system of inspection to make certain that no more such weapons were being manufactured on the sly, would represent a great advance in the march of civilization. Unfortunately, all attempts to reach such an agreement have failed thus far, and indeed the "nuclear club" has expanded in membership. What effect the possible spread of nuclear weaponry to nations less responsible than present possessors of such dangerous equipment presaged, worried not only major but also minor powers. Hence, beginning as early as 1946 (U.S. Atomic Energy Act and the "Baruch Plan"), increasing thought was given to the concept of a treaty to assure nonproliferation of nuclear weapons.

After years of negotiations concerning draft proposals laid before successive disarmament meetings at Geneva, a "Nuclear Non-Proliferation Treaty" was signed on July 1, 1968, at parallel ceremonies in Washington, London, and Moscow by more than sixty states; eight months later, signatures affixed to the agreement totalled eighty-seven.[26] The United States delayed formal ratification, however, because of Soviet intervention in Czechoslovakia; the Senate finally agreed to ratification on March 13,

---

[23] *Ibid.*, p. 350.

[24] See Georg Schwarzenberger, *The Legality of Nuclear Weapons* (London: Stevens & Sons, 1958) on this point.

[25] For a concurring view, see Stone, pp. 342–348.

[26] Text of treaty in 7 *International Legal Materials* (1968), pp. 809–817.

1969; by that date, ten countries had ratified the treaty which, however, had not yet entered into force by then.

The agreement specifies that the sponsoring powers will not give nuclear weapons—or control over such—to other states nor will they assist others to make such weapons. Parties to the treaty not now possessing nuclear weapons waived their rights, for twenty-five years, to acquire or manufacture such weapons for their own defense. One of the key articles (3) recognized the International Atomic Energy Agency as the authority exercising overall control over safeguards. The latter were to be applied to all fissionable material in all peaceful nuclear activities in any state party to the treaty, or under its jurisdiction, or carried out under its control anywhere. Inspections, therefore, were to be made by the Agency.

The nuclear powers pledged themselves to protect nonnuclear states and agreed to provide immediate assistance to any nonnuclear state facing nuclear aggression or threats of such aggression.

On March 18, 1969, the United States and the Soviet Union proposed to the Geneva Disarmament Conference a new treaty to ban the placement of nuclear weapons on the ocean floors.

On a regional basis, an agreement prohibiting the manufacture, use, storage, or acquisition of nuclear weapons was signed at Mexico City on February 14, 1967, by representatives of fourteen Latin American states. That convention, covering the Western Hemisphere south of the United States, requires, beside ratification by the twenty-one negotiating states and such states outside the zone involved but controlling territory within it, guarantees by the nuclear powers that they would not violate the agreement. All nuclear powers except Communist China have since indicated informally that they would "observe" the Mexico City agreement.

Undefended Towns and Buildings. Article 25 of the Hague Regulations of 1907 prohibited the attack or bombardment, by any means, of towns, villages, dwellings, or buildings that were undefended. This rule reflected the warfare of the nineteenth century, in which forts were used, in which cities or towns were surrounded by fortifications (if the latter were inseparable from the community, say by reason of proximity, bombardment of the town would have been legal under Article 25), and when it was possible to pinpoint the limited number of factories, military warehouses, communications facilities used by armed forces, and so on, so as to isolate an attack on these from a general attack on the community in which they were located.

The rise of modern mass armies, with their staggering demands for every conceivable kind of supplies, and the distribution of production facilities of the "nation in arms" throughout communities, rendered Article 25 virtually obsolete before the end of World War I. Although the rule still stands technically, it has had to be abandoned in practice and only finds modern application in instances of wanton destruction totally unconnected with an attempt to weaken the enemy's war potential. In the latter case, a more appropriate rule to be cited against the party committing the acts in question would be Article 23-g of the Hague Regulations, which prohibits the destruction of enemy property unless such destruction appeared to be imperatively demanded by the necessities of war.

German use of V-1 (*Vergeltungswaffe-1*—Retaliation Weapon No. 1) rocket bombs against London in 1944–45 raised a storm of protest concerning the illegality of the weapon under Article 25 of the Regulations. Most of the protests centered on the obvious inability of its makers to aim the V-1 at a specific target; instead, the fuel supply was doled out in such a manner and in accordance with wind and atmospheric conditions that the bomb, properly aimed, would run out of fuel and descend somewhere into the sprawling metropolitan area of London, or, on occasion, some other British city. The speed of the V-1 was not very great—its approach could be seen, it could be pursued by fighter planes, but when the motor cut out, the city dwellers in the prospective target area had approximately ten seconds in which to find some kind of shelter. Thus no adequate warning was possible, despite the slow speed of the bomb. Its successor, the V-2, traveling at supersonic speed, gave no warning at all of its approach; only after the great bomb had already hit and exploded was its presence known.

Forewarning of Bombardment. Again, Article 26 of the Hague Regulations required that "the officer in command of an attacking force must, before commencing a bombardment, except in cases of assault, do all in his power to warn the authorities" of the locality to be attacked. This rule, too, reflected the conditions of war in the nineteenth century and did not anticipate the aerial bombardments of modern war, carried out, on most occasions, against strong defenses from the ground. To be sure, modern armies still insist that their ground commanders honor the provisions of Article 26 before bombarding a locality known to or suspected of still containing remnants of its civilian population. But as far as commanders of air forces would be concerned, any warning of an impending air strike might completely vitiate the effort and might result in heavy losses to the attacking force.

Classified Buildings. The provisions of Article 27 of the Hague Regulations, concerning the sparing of certain types of buildings, have been increasingly difficult to enforce. Although World War I saw a limited destruction of such exempt edifices, except for a deliberate German destruction of church towers in France on the grounds that the French armies consistently misused such elevated structures as the hiding places of artillery spotters, World War II saw a comprehensive ignoring of the rule. Saturation and atomic bombing played no favorites and the nature of a given building was commonly ignored. In addition, authenticated reports indicate that Germany, in particular, tended to locate genuine military targets near or next to an exempt building, hoping obviously that the military installation would benefit from the immunity of its neighbor. On the other hand, with one small lapse, the hospital-city character of Marburg, announced by Germany to the Allied armies and watched over by neutral observers as well as a daily aerial inspection, was maintained scrupulously.

Capitulations. As far as capitulations are concerned, they, of course, mean something entirely different in the military field than they do in the case of extraterritorial privileges. In the military sense, they refer to surrenders. Most armed forces authorize their commanders to surrender when continuation of battle has become impossible and when they cannot communicate with their superiors to receive other instructions. Capitulations extend only to the limits of the area under a commander's authority, and cannot normally bind other commanders or political authorities. On the other hand, capitulations may also be arranged by the respective political authorities without, at times, any reference to the commanders in the field. Such political capitulations tend to cover far more territory as well as nonmilitary subjects than do the similarly styled instruments through which individual commanders surrender.[27]

RULES OF WAR IN THE AIR

The use of balloons for the transport of mail and newspapers from besieged Paris during the Franco-Prussian War had led to considerable speculation toward the end of the nineteenth century as to the possibilities of aerial warfare. At the Hague Conference of 1899, a declaration, renewed at the Second Conference in 1907, prohibited until the end of a Third Peace Conference "the discharge of projectiles and explosives from balloons and by other new methods of a similar nature." Very few states signed the instrument in 1899; in 1907, France, Germany, Italy, Japan, and Russia refused to sign it, primarily, it appears, because these countries, impressed by the advance in aviation, desired to wait and see what promising and possibly legal use could be made of man's newfound ability to fly. Italy then became a pioneer, using balloons in the Italo-Turkish War of 1911–12 both for spotting enemy troops and for dropping explosives (bombs) on them.

Air Warfare in World War I. The outbreak of war in 1914 brought the airplane, and later the dirigible, into immediate prominence. Both sides not only fought one another in the air but proceeded to bomb enemy targets which all too soon appeared to be "undefended" cities. Both sides, too, piously insisted that their aviators received strict orders to attack only points of military importance and, in the case of cities, to bomb only genuine military targets. The usefulness of such instructions, even if willingness to carry them out could have been proven, was nil, for the speed of an airplane and the absence of bombsights or other aiming de-

---

[27] See *Law of Land Warfare*, pp. 170–171, for an extensive list of the subjects normally regulated by capitulations.

vices left the ultimate destination of a dropped bomb to chance and to the skill of the aviator. One did not have to be a cynic to be able to say before the end of the war that every inhabited enemy community had become a legitimate target, an attitude reinforced by the already mentioned concept of the "nation-in-arms." The distinction between undefended and defended communities had become meaningless, except in the rare cases of genuine "hospital towns," declared to be such and subject to neutral inspection.

Problems of Neutral Airspace. One of the new problems created by the extensive use of planes and dirigibles had to do with neutral airspace. Because each country's national air is included in its territorial jurisdiction, no military activities could be carried on in neutral national air and the state in question had a perfect right to protect its sovereignty by attempting to keep belligerent planes out of its national air. If violations of its airspace continued, it had the legal right to try to bring down belligerent planes and to intern the crews for the duration of the conflict.[28]

Regulation of Air Warfare—Post-World War I. The application of the rules of land warfare to the new weapon having failed to prevent indiscriminate bombing, thought was given after World War I to the possibility of developing a separate code of air warfare. Here, however, military considerations of the greatest magnitude intruded. The airplane, as perfected by 1918, had become the weapon of the future to many military staffs, and they successfully opposed any code promising to cripple this new item in the military hardware closet. The 1919 Aerial Navigation Convention left all parties to the treaty complete freedom of action in wartime (Art. 38). The Washington Conference of 1921–22 failed to provide a draft treaty on aerial war and had to be content to appoint a commission of legal experts to study the subject and to make recommendations. That commission succeeded in writing two sets of draft rules, of which Part II dealt with air war.[29] The code remained a paper project, however, and no action on it was taken by the powers. One basic reason for its failure was the stubborn attempt of the drafters of the code to fit the new method of warfare into the traditional (and already outmoded) patterns of war on land and at sea.

The failure of the Hague Rules of Air Warfare to achieve ratification left regulation of aerial conflict precisely where it had been at the end of World War I. The Spanish Civil War and the Japanese invasion of China showed, however, that some new rules governing aerial bombardment were needed most urgently. In 1938 the Prime Minister of Great

---

[28] See J. M. Spaight, *Air Power and War Rights* (3rd ed.) (London: Longmans, Green & Co., 1947), at pp. 420–460; C. P. Phillips, "Air Warfare and Law," 21 *George Washington Law Review* (1952–1953), pp. 311–315, 395–422; and Chapter 30.

[29] "General Report of the Commission of Jurists at The Hague, 1923," 17 *A.J.I.L.* (1923), Supp. pp. 242–260; see also the long "Letter to the Editor" from James W. Garner in *The New York Times*, October 3, 1937, which contains an account of the 1922–23 conference and its work. Consult Lauterpacht's *Oppenheim*, Vol. II, pp. 518–522.

Britain, in a statement made in the House of Commons, asserted that three principles ought to be observed by all participants in future wars: (1) a deliberate attack on civilian populations was a clear violation of international law; (2) "targets which are aimed at from the air must be legitimate military objectives and must be capable of identification"; and (3) "reasonable care must be taken in attacking these military objectives so that by carelessness a civilian population in the neighborhood is not bombed."[30] Later that year, the Assembly of the League of Nations unanimously adopted a resolution embodying the three principles.

World War II saw the manned plane in its heyday, with even greater bombing of enemy locations the order of the day, beginning with the German attack on Poland. Without going into details which would extend this section beyond reasonable limits, it can be stated that by 1945 it was generally accepted that strategic bombing from the air, without warning, was an accepted method of warfare and that those who attempted to punish captured perpetrators of those raids by execution would end up as war criminals themselves. Since then, the manned bomber at least seems to be on the way out and its replacement, the unmanned intermediate as well as intercontinental ballistic missile, together with its relatives aboard atomic-powered submarines, has appeared on the scene.

It should be pointed out, moreover, that May 11, 1940, may be regarded as the day on which virtually unrestricted air bombardment was "legitimized." It was on that date that the British Cabinet decided on strategic air attacks on the enemy's interior, a decision which resulted, on August 8, 1940, in the German "reprisal" raids against English nonmilitary targets, including the city of Coventry.

PRISONERS OF WAR

Prisoners had fared in many different ways during past centuries. In antiquity they were either killed or sold into slavery. After the coming of Christianity and until the sixteenth century, enslavement continued—St. Thomas Aquinas had justified this by treating the reduction of prisoners to slaves as punishment for cowardice in combat and as a judgment of God under the concept of the ordeal by battle in which the only just side would win and then was entitled to enslave surviving opponents. Noble prisoners, on the other hand, normally would be released on payment of a ransom depending, in amount, on their rank and resources. Still later special cartel arrangements for the treatment and return of prisoners were concluded, either at the outbreak of hostilities or soon thereafter.

Early Attempts to Protect Prisoners of War. The end of the Thirty Years' War saw also the end of enslavement, and gradually humane considerations began to govern the treatment of captive enemies. An Amer-

---

[30] Cited in Lauterpacht's *Oppenheim*, Vol. II, p. 523.

ican-Russian Treaty of Friendship, concluded in 1785, is now generally considered to contain the first stipulations of decent treatment of prisoners of war, prohibiting (Art. 24) confinement in convict prisons, the employment of irons, and guaranteeing facilities for exercise.

Hague Conferences of 1899 and 1907. By the nineteenth century, customary rules of law dictated treatment of prisoners of war at a standard comparable to that of the captor's own troops. In 1874, a conference held at Brussels drew up a draft convention relating to prisoners of war, but that instrument failed to be ratified. Thus no conventional rules on the subject existed until the Hague Conferences of 1899 and 1907.

The 1907 Hague Regulations (Arts. 4–20) provided in detail for the humane treatment of prisoners. Unfortunately the actual practices of belligerents during World War I illustrated the inadequacy of the rules and the many gaps that needed to be filled.

1929 Geneva Conventions. In July, 1929, the representatives of forty-seven states met in Geneva at the invitation of the Swiss government in order to improve the earlier conventional law. The conference succeeded in drawing up two instruments, one the Convention for the Amelioration of the Condition of the Wounded and Sick in Armies in the Field, the other a Convention on the Treatment of Prisoners of War consisting of ninety-four articles. Following widespread ratification, both conventions were in effect when World War II came. Only relations between Germany and the Soviet Union were not governed by those two instruments during the conflict in question. But again belligerent practices indicated the need for further conventional safeguards for prisoners of war.

1949 GENEVA CONVENTION

One of the most serious violations of customary and conventional rules was committed by the Soviet Union through its failure to repatriate prisoners of war at the end of the conflict. A report published at the beginning of July, 1952, by the Information Section of the North Atlantic Treaty Organization indicated that of the more than 7 million prisoners taken by the U.S.S.R., less than half had been repatriated by the middle of 1952; about 1 million were reported dead or still held in the Soviet Union; and some 2.5 million were completely unaccounted for, including about 370,000 members of the Japanese forces in Manchuria, captured at the very end of the war.[31] Hence the Geneva Conference of 1949, also called by the Swiss government, produced a new Convention relative to the Treatment of Prisoners of War, which incorporated, besides old material, many new provisions based on the experiences of the late war. This new instrument was ratified quickly by a considerable number of the major military powers and came into effect on October 21, 1950, replacing for its ratifiers all earlier instruments dealing with the treatment of prisoners of war.

[31] For further details from the report, see 60 *Time* (July 7, 1952), p. 33.

Owing to the extreme length of the 1949 Convention (143 articles) and the details incorporated in its provisions, an exhaustive analysis of the instrument would exceed the proper limits of a general text.[32] Hence only a few significant features can be mentioned here, together with some illustrative case materials.

COMMENTS ON THE 1949 CONVENTION

Application of the 1949 Convention to Conflicts. Under Article 2 of the convention, the instrument applies not only to all cases of declared war, but to all other armed conflicts which may arise between two or more of the contracting parties, even if the existence of a state of war is not recognized by one of them. The convention also applies to all cases of partial or total occupation of the territory of a contracting party, even if such occupation has not met with any armed resistance. Again, the convention applies in a war with a state which is not a party to the agreement, provided the latter accepts and applies the provisions of the instrument.

Prisoners of War. Persons entitled to the protection of the convention and hence to treatment as prisoners of war include regular armed forces personnel; members of militia forces; recognized or unrecognized volunteer corps (provided they satisfy the somewhat unrealistic requirements of the convention); officers and crews of civil aircraft and of the merchant marine of a belligerent; individuals who formed a part of a lawful *levée en masse;* authorized persons accompanying armed forces (war correspondents, contractors, and so on); under specified circumstances, former members of the armed forces of an occupied state; and high civil government personnel (Art. 4).

Prisoners of war are to be considered as in the custody of the capturing state and not of particular armies or military units. They are entitled to humane treatment. They are entitled to the same maintenance as troops of the same rank of the captor state. They are to be confined only to the extent that their detention is guaranteed and must not be punished except for acts committed by them after their capture.

On the other hand, Article 85 of the convention reads: "Prisoners of war prosecuted under the laws of the Detaining Power for acts committed prior to capture shall retain, even if convicted, the benefits of the present convention." The Soviet Union and its satellite states entered a reservation against Article 85 before and at the time of signature, to the effect that prisoners of war convicted by them of committing war crimes and crimes against humanity would be treated after such conviction like

---

[32] See *Law of Land Warfare*, pp. 25–82, and Lauterpacht's *Oppenheim*, Vol. II, pp. 369–396, for two exhaustive analyses of the provisions of the 1949 Convention. Consult also Jean S. Pictet, "The New Geneva Conventions for the Protection of War Victims," 45 *A.J.I.L.* (1951), pp. 462–475; Raymond T. Yingling and Robert A. Ginnane, "The Geneva Conventions," *ibid.,* 46 (1952), pp. 393–427; and the thorough study from a military point of view by Howard S. Levie, "Prisoners of War and the Protecting Power." 55 *A.J.I.L.* (1961), pp. 374–397.

other criminals. However, an Italian decision in 1952 asserted that Article 85 bore no relevance to war crimes.[33] Until United States ratification of the convention in 1956, the American official attitude had been that prisoners of war tried for war crimes were not entitled to the judicial safeguards of the 1929 Geneva Convention; this was brought out strikingly in *In re Yamashita*.[34] An unsuccessful attempt to escape may result only in disciplinary punishment; on the other hand, force may be employed against them to prevent an escape and it would be considered to be lawful even to shoot at, and kill, an escaping prisoner.

If, on the other hand, an escaping prisoner commits criminal offenses not directly connected with his escape, he may be punished for such acts. This rule has been illustrated clearly in the case of

REX V. BROSIG
Ontario Court of Appeal, March 1, 1945
2 D. L. R. 232

FACTS

Brosig was a German prisoner of war, moved to Canada for detention. On December 21, 1943, he hid in a prisoner-of-war mailbag which was placed in the mail car of a Canadian train, next to a radiator in the car. The prisoner finally cut open the bag from the inside and then opened another mailbag containing parcels. From these he took some cigarettes, some chewing gum, and a bottle of perfume. He smoked some of the cigarettes, used some of the gum and also some of the perfume. He was later captured and charged with theft from the mails. The magistrate's court trying the initial case dismissed the charge and the Crown appealed to the Court of Appeal.

QUESTION

Could an escaping prisoner of war be charged with the theft of goods stolen in the course of his escape and utilized by him?

DECISION

The appeal was allowed and a conviction of theft from the mails recorded. A jail sentence of two months' duration was imposed, after which Brosig was to be returned to his prisoner-of-war camp.

REASONING

The looting of the mailbag was not an act necessary for the escape of Brosig. It served no military purpose but represented an offense against civil authority for the personal advantage of the prisoner of war. The Court cited with approval the finding of the Magistrate's Court that

"With regard to the perfume, I have given him the benefit of the doubt and say that he used it in order to assist his escape by concealing the extreme odour of perspiration. With regard to the cigarettes and gum I am unable to see that they would assist his escape materially and I feel that he took them for his own comfort."

[33] The *Case of Kappler*, Italy, Supreme Military Tribunal, 1952, digested in 49 *A.J.I.L.* (1955), p. 96.

[34] United States, Supreme Court, 1946, 327 U.S. 1.

Enlisted personnel may be put to work not directly assisting the war effort of the captor state and are to be paid for such work. Officers cannot lawfully be forced to perform such work but may do so on a purely voluntary basis (Arts. 50–68). All prisoners are to be paid at the rate applicable to their rank at the time of capture, the actual terms of payment being outlined in the convention (Art. 60).[35]

Information required of prisoners must be restricted to their names, date of birth, rank, and serial number.

Communication with relatives is to be allowed at periodic intervals, and agents of a "protecting" neutral state as well as of the Committee of the Red Cross are to be permitted access to prisoners of war.

If a prisoner escapes and at a later date, after rejoining his own forces, becomes a prisoner of war again, he may not be punished for his escape. Disciplinary and judicial punishments for prisoners guilty of offenses after capture are delineated in the convention in considerable detail to protect them against arbitrary denial of justice (Arts. 89, 99–108).

Termination of Captivity. Particularly important are the new conventional rules governing the termination of captivity. Under the provisions of Article 118, prisoners of war are "to be released and repatriated without delay after the cessation of active hostilities," and elaborately detailed regulations now govern the earlier repatriation of sick prisoners of war (Arts. 109–117, 119).

The 1929 Geneva Convention had stipulated merely that the repatriation of healthy prisoners should be effected as soon as possible after the conclusion of peace. The importance of the new rule about immediate release when *hostilities* have ended stemmed from the problems encountered at the end of World War II. The Soviet Union, in particular, refused to repatriate German and other Axis prisoners on the grounds that Russia was not a party to prisoner-of-war conventions. Many unfortunates remained for years as prisoners in the U.S.S.R. and scores of thousands never returned home at all: in the case of the Japanese army captured in Manchuria, the Soviet Union disclaimed knowledge of the fate of the bulk of the forces in question and only a relatively small number returned to Japan, years after the war, heavily indoctrinated in favor of the Communist ideology.[36]

Repatriation Problem (Korea). The Korean conflict posed a different problem altogether. The experts at Geneva in 1949 had assumed that every prisoner of war wanted to go home as soon as possible. This somewhat erroneous impression should not have prevailed, in view of certain events that had taken place at the end of World War II. Then, thousands of Russian citizens who had joined General Vlassov's anti-Communist army on the side of Germany and who had fled westward as the Soviet armies

---

[35] Consult Howard S. Levie, "The Employment of Prisoners of War," 57 *A.J.I.L.* (1963), pp. 318–353.

[36] See the revealing analysis in 60 *Time* (July 7, 1952), p. 33.

advanced into Germany were captured by the Western Allies. Despite pleas not to be repatriated because of their well-founded fears of being tried for treason, these Russians were forcibly repatriated by the Western forces. In the case of Korea, thousands of North Koreans as well as Chinese "volunteers" refused to be returned to their countries because of ideological reasons. Concurrence in this request on the part of the United Nations Command created a dilemma which proved to be a key reason for the delay in United States ratification of the four Geneva Conventions of 1949 until 1956.[37] By then, those prisoners who were unwilling to return to North Korea or China had been screened and dispersed after release: by early 1954, slightly over 14,000 Chinese soldiers had already been transferred to Formosa.[38]

It should be noted that the four Geneva conventions of 1949 were not in force as regarded the opposing parties in the Korean conflict. Both sides, however, had stated that they would honor the principles laid down in those agreements.[39] On the other hand, fifteen U.S. airmen, members of the UN Command in Korea, were not released by the People's Republic of China until the middle of 1955. This action followed a denunciation of such detentions, as a violation of the Korean Armistice Agreement, in the General Assembly and a visit of the Secretary-General to Peking, as well as subsequent frequent communications to the Chinese government in an effort to secure the release of the detained airmen.

If, during captivity, a prisoner changes sides ideologically and desires to desert to the captor's side in the war, must he be held as a prisoner of war? The International Committee of the Red Cross has asserted repeatedly that such a prisoner should be released from his status as captive.[40]

SICK, WOUNDED, AND DEAD

Until 1864, only numerous bilateral agreements but no general conventional rules governed the care of captured sick or wounded members of an enemy's armed forces. In that year, however, the Geneva Conference

[37] See Chapter 27 for details concerning the arrangements finally worked out for the removal of the prisoners in question; see also Stone, pp. 680–683.

[38] See the illuminating study by Jaro Mayda, "The Korean Repatriation Problem," 47 *A.J.I.L.* (1953), pp. 414–438; Pitman B. Potter's note on "Repatriation of Prisoners," *ibid.*, 46 (1952), pp. 508–509; and the valuable analysis of the total problem in Jan P. Charmatz and Harold M. Wit, "Repatriation of Prisoners of War and the 1949 Geneva Convention," 62 *Yale Law Journal* (1953), pp. 391–415.

[39] See von Glahn, pp. 17–18; "Assurances to Respect Geneva Conventions," 9 *U.N. Bulletin* (1950), p. 101; "Report of the United Nations Command Operations in Korea, for the period of August 1–15, 1950," in 23 *Department of State Bulletin* (1950), p. 406; see *ibid.*, 23 (1950), pp. 287 and 333 for details concerning the North Korean "adherence" and its observance; and also consult *ibid.*, Vol. 33 (1955), at pp. 69–79.

[40] G.I.A. Draper, *The Red Cross Conventions* (New York: Praeger; London: Stevens and Sons, Ltd., 1958), at p. 53.

adopted the first treaty on the subject, providing for humane treatment of such prisoners.

In 1906, a revision of the Geneva Convention was undertaken at a conference called by the Swiss government in response to a request made to it at the First Hague Conference of 1899, and a new convention, signed by thirty-five states, resulted. The experiences of World War I convincingly demonstrated the need for further regulations, and the 1929 Geneva Conference accordingly formulated the 1929 Convention for the Amelioration of the Condition of the Wounded and Sick in Armies in the Field (Red Cross Convention). The 1949 Geneva Convention for the Amelioration of the Condition of the Wounded and Sick in Armed Forces in the Field somewhat belatedly brought the primitive rules of the nineteenth century up to date and incorporated lessons taught by World War II.

Space does not permit a detailed analysis of the regulations now in force.[41] However, in brief summary, medical treatment and humane care is to be given by the captor state to wounded or sick prisoners; enemy medical personnel are exempt from capture: if such personnel are detained, however, their members are to be used only for the care of the members of enemy armed forces. The personnel of relief agencies such as the Red Cross and Red Crescent societies are equally protected under the convention. Specified markings are to be applied to hospital facilities and areas; hospital zones are to be clearly designated, notified to the enemy, and are subject to inspection by protecting powers and/or private relief agencies. The enemy state is to be notified, through designated channels, of the wounded and the sick in the hands of the captor state.

As far as the war dead of military forces are concerned, each belligerent is to try to make proper identification and to bury bodies individually if such is at all possible under prevailing conditions. The dead are not to be robbed. The home state is to be notified, through designated channels, of the identity and disposal of the dead.

SUGGESTED READINGS

LAWS OF WAR ON LAND AND IN THE AIR: GENERAL

Morris Greenspan, *The Modern Law of Land Warfare* (Berkeley: University of California Press, 1960), pp. 95–153 (prisoners of war) and pp. 313–377 (methods and instruments of warfare); Josef L. Kunz, "The Chaotic Status of the Laws of War and the Urgent Necessity for their Revision," 45 *A.J.I.L.* (1951), pp. 37–61; Hersch Lauterpacht, "The Revision of the Laws of War," 29 *B.Y.I.L.* (1952), pp. 360–382; consult Quincy Wright et al., *Essays on Espionage and International Law* (Columbus: Ohio State University Press, 1962), on modern aerial and space espionage questions.

[41] See Lauterpacht's *Oppenheim*, Vol. II, pp. 353–355, for background information; consult the same source, pp. 355–364, for a summary of the relevant 1949 Convention, as well as *Law of Land Warfare*, pp. 84–97.

Case

Rex v. *Guenther Krebs*, Canada, Magistrate's Court, County of Renfrew, Ontario, October 7, 1943, reprinted in 38 *A.J.I.L.* (1944), pp. 505–508,

NUCLEAR WEAPONS

Y. Harkabi, *Nuclear War and Nuclear Peace* (New York: Donald Davey & Co., 1966); *Report* (to UN Secretary-General Thant) *of the Task Force on Nuclear Arms Escalation, 1967*, abstracted at length in 50 *Saturday Review* (December 9, 1967), pp. 16–19, 70–75; Mason Willrich, "Guarantees to Non-Nuclear Nations," 44 *Foreign Affairs* (1966), pp. 683–692, and his comprehensive study, *Non-Proliferation Treaty: Framework for Nuclear Arms Control* (Charlottesville, Va.: The Michie Co., 1968); Richard A. Falk, "The Shimoda Case: A Legal Appraisal of the Atomic Attacks Upon Hiroshima and Nagasaki," 59 *A.J.I.L.* (1965), pp. 759–793 [The *Shimoda Case* is, as yet, the only judicial attempt to assess the legality of atomic/nuclear weapons]; Lawrence Scheinman, "Nuclear Safeguards, the Peaceful Atom, and the IAEA," *International Conciliation* (No. 572, March, 1969).

29

Laws of War at Sea

ATTEMPTS TO FORMULATE RULES
FOR NAVAL WARFARE

THE rules governing warfare at sea appear to have survived the passage of two global wars to a far greater extent than was true in the case of the rules applicable to land warfare. This situation was caused primarily by the fact that the character of naval war did not undergo the profound changes which had taken place in land war. To be sure, the battleship had become obsolete and the air forces of belligerents began to play an ever more important part in hostilities. But, essentially, war at sea was at least similar in 1945 to the sort of conflict prevailing on the oceans of the world before 1914. At the same time, neutrals exerted far more pressure on belligerents as regarded the preservation of the rules governing naval war than was the case with the rules governing land warfare, if only because the conflicts on land affected neutrals less directly than did interference with commerce on the high seas. And since many neutrals were not only militarily strong but possessed supreme importance for belligerents from an economic point of view, their voice could make itself heard quite effectively in the case of naval warfare and its rules.

Declaration of Paris (1856). The first major international attempt to formulate rules for naval war took place in 1856 as a result of the experiences of the earlier Napoleonic conflicts and especially of the Crimean War. In 1856, the Allied Powers and Russia adopted the famous Declaration of Paris.[1] That instrument laid down four specific rules governing warfare at sea:

    1. Privateering was abolished.

    2. The neutral flag covered enemy's goods, with the exception of contraband of war.[2]

    3. Neutral goods, with the exception of contraband of war, were not liable to capture under the enemy's flag.

---

[1] Lauterpacht's *Oppenheim*, II, p. 460–464.

[2] In *The Dirigo*, Great Britain, Privy Council, 1919, 3 B. and C.P.C. 439, this rule was interpreted as representing a concept of general applicability, adopted not only for the benefit of the neutral vessel but also for that of the enemy owner.

4. A blockade, in order to be binding, had to be effective; that is to say, it had to be maintained by a force sufficient to prevent access to the coast of the enemy.

All maritime states, with the exception of Venezuela and the United States, soon adhered to the Declaration. Failure of American adherence was due to the refusal of the other countries to agree to an American proposal for the abolition of the right to capture any private property at sea. In practice, however, the United States saw fit to abide by the rules of the Declaration of Paris.

1868 Geneva Convention. The next step in the effort to secure a body of uniform rules governing naval war was taken at Geneva in 1868. There a conference met in order to extend the provisions of the 1864 Geneva Convention for the Amelioration of the Condition of Wounded Soldiers in Armies in the Field to war at sea, but the Project of Declaration resulting from the meeting was not ratified. On the other hand, many of the individual proposals found in the Project were gradually incorporated in the manuals issued by various states for the guidance of their navies.

1907 Hague Conference. The First Hague Peace Conference of 1899 adopted a convention which extended at last the provisions of the 1864 Geneva instrument to naval war (revised in 1906). The 1907 Hague Conference, however, concentrated heavily on naval questions and succeeded in drawing up several conventions dealing with maritime war, especially conventions No. VIII, IX, XI. The conference failed to develop a code of naval warfare, along lines similar to those on which the Hague Regulations concerning land warfare had been based. Hague Convention No. VII (Convention relating to the Conversion of Merchant Ships to Warships) was not signed by the United States.

Declaration of London (1909). The London Naval Conference of 1908 met from December 4, 1908, to February 26, 1909, when the Declaration of London was signed. This instrument "concerning the laws of naval warfare" contained fully seventy articles: blockade in time of war (1–21); contraband of war (22–44); unneutral service (45–47); destruction of neutral prizes (48–54); transfer to a neutral flag (55–56); enemy character (57–60); convoy (61–62); resistance to search (63); compensation (64); and final provisions (65–70). Two items intended to be included in the Declaration provoked such widely divergent points of view that no agreement was possible: the test of enemy character to be applied to goods— that is, domicile or nationality—and the conversion of merchant vessels into warships at sea. The Declaration was not ratified by Great Britain, with the House of Lords refusing to back the ratification of the House of Commons.

Significantly enough, the list of headings of the Declaration, given above, shows again a virtually complete absence of rules governing the behavior of hostile naval forces toward each other. Instead, the bulk of the seventy articles dealt with economic questions and the relations between belligerents and neutrals. Again no naval equivalent of the Hague Regulations on land warfare had been achieved.

RULES GOVERNING NAVAL WARFARE

Thus, when World War I came, naval warfare *per se* was governed primarily by the actual practices of the major belligerents rather than by a code of naval warfare adopted by international agreement. In fact, after the end of the war, the only phase of actual hostilities at sea "regulated" by treaty was the use of submarines against merchant vessels, by the abortive Treaty of Washington of 1922. The "rules" evolved from such national practices in the course of time may be summarized briefly as follows: [3]

1. Laws of Humanity. Considerations of humanity are to prevail in naval war as they are to prevail in war on land.

2. Attack and Seizure of Vessels (Enemy Character). The attack and seizure of enemy vessels is the most important means employed by a belligerent navy. With an enemy vessel, a belligerent seizes not only enemy individuals but also enemy goods, public and private.

This second principle raises the issue of enemy character as it is defined in war at sea. None of the early statements of rules (Declaration of Paris, Declaration of London) provided any clue as to what constituted an enemy. British prize courts have long followed the interpretation that domicile determined enemy character. An individual, whether of neutral or enemy nationality, residing in territory under enemy control is regarded as possessed of enemy character. Goods owned by him are, therefore, enemy goods, as far as the courts are concerned.[4] Domicile, in this connection, does not refer to the personal residence of an individual alone, but also the place where the latter's business is located. Thus, if countries A and B are at war and all others are neutral, a citizen and resident of C who conducts a business venture in country B would be viewed by the courts of A as possessing enemy character.[5]

Similarly, since territory under enemy occupation is regarded as enemy territory, property belonging to persons or corporations residing in such occupied areas is viewed as possessed of enemy character. Thus, during World War I, British prize courts correctly treated German-occupied

---

[3] For an extended treatment of the subject consult the excellent study by Robert W. Tucker, *The Law of War and Neutrality at Sea* (Naval War College, International Law Studies, Vol. XIX, 1955) (Washington, D.C.: U.S. Government Printing Office, 1957). Tucker's volume also contains, in an appendix, the official U.S. Navy Manual, *Law of Naval Warfare.* See Whiteman, Vol. X, pp. 614–618, 644–649, and *ibid.*, XI, pp. 1–77, 115–126.

[4] See *Part Cargo ex M. V. Glenroy*, Great Britain, Privy Council, 1945, 61 Times L.R. 303, reported in 39 *A.J.I.L.* (1945), pp. 599–609.

[5] See *The Kara Deniz*, Great Britain, Privy Council, 1922, 3 B. of C.P.C. 1070.

Belgium as enemy territory for the duration of the occupation. During the same war, Egyptian ports were treated as enemy ports with reference to Austrian and German vessels, since Great Britain at the time was a military occupant of Egypt.

During World War II, the same practice was adopted by the states opposing the Axis Powers. Thus, on July 30, 1940, Great Britain announced that all of France as well as Algeria, Tunisia, and French Morocco, were to be treated, for purposes of contraband and enemy export controls, as enemy-controlled territories. Earlier, the German occupation of hitherto neutral Denmark on April 10, 1940, changed the status of Danish citizens and ships, in the British view, to that of enemies. Logically enough, however, the enemy occupation must be an effective one. Mere temporary presence of an enemy in a given territory in the course of military operations, without the incidental creation of an effective belligerent occupation, is not sufficient to endow the territory with enemy character.

The enemy character of goods normally continues to be in effect as long as their owner is domiciled in enemy territory and the goods are in transit; if, however, ownership of the goods is transferred during their voyage from an enemy owner to a neutral owner, the goods lose their enemy character.[6]

Certain additional factors may play a part, on occasion, in the determination of enemy character: if the enemy country in which the owner of certain goods has his domicile, rises against an enemy state, it would still be regarded as an enemy country (and the individual's goods as enemy property) until the opposing belligerent has actually recognized the independence of the revolting territory or country. Although this well-established practice may wreak hardships on many persons and firms, it is sound, for a former enemy territory ought not to be treated as friendly or neutral until enemy control has been effectively and permanently removed during a conflict.

As far as the nationality of a vessel is concerned, it will be recalled that the customary rule of law holds that the flag which the vessel is authorized to display determines the nationality of the ship. Hence enemy ownership does not create enemy character for a vessel registered in and carrying the proper papers of a neutral state; on the other hand, neutral ownership does not offset the enemy character created for a vessel properly displaying an enemy flag.[7]

It remains to be noted that private individuals cannot lawfully effect a capture of a vessel or of its cargo as prize, unless they have received appropriate authorization or ratification from some government. The issue did, however, come up on at least one occasion in a memorably styled

[6] On this rather disputed point, see Higgins–Colombos, pp. 437–438; for the American interpretation cited, see *The Circassian*, United States, Supreme Court, 1864, 2 Wallace 135.

[7] See also Chapter 26 on enemy character in naval war.

case during World War II, the *Y. S. Ling et al.* v. *1,689 Tons of Coal Lying Aboard S.S. Wilhelmina.*[8]

3. Enemy Warships. All enemy warships and all other enemy public vessels met on the high seas or in the territorial waters of either belligerent may be attacked at once.

4. Enemy Merchant Ships. Enemy merchant ships may be attacked only if they refuse to submit to visit and search after they have been requested to do so. Naturally, such merchant vessels may refuse to honor the request and may choose to defend themselves. A merchant vessel of a belligerent attacking a public or private vessel of an opposing belligerent by taking the initiative would be regarded as a pirate and its crew would be considered as war criminals. Once an attack has been launched against it, however, a belligerent merchant vessel may pursue its attacker and even seize it, if this can be done.

5. Submarines. On the other hand, if a merchant vessel must expect an attack without warning by a "lawless" enemy, it does not have to wait to be attacked before it resorts itself to the commission of hostile acts. This rule would apply, for instance, in the case of an enemy whose submarines had received instructions to attack merchant vessels of opposing belligerents without warning. Application of the rule raises the whole issue of submarine warfare, a subject about which an incredibly extensive literature has already developed. Briefly, the problem posed has been this: a submarine by its construction is a rather fragile craft. If its commander abides by the rules applicable to normal warships and surfaces, signals to an enemy merchant vessel to stop for visit and search, he exposes his ship and crew not only to the danger of attack by the merchant vessel, by ramming or the use of "defensive" equipment such as artillery, but also by aircraft of the enemy to which a surfaced submarine represents a tempting and virtually defenseless target. Because the safety of his ship and crew is a primary responsibility of the commander in question, he will most likely solve his predicament by ignoring the conventional rules and sinking the merchant vessel, without warning, by means of a torpedo. By so doing, he commits, technically, a war crime.

A submarine could abide by the traditional rules governing encounters with enemy merchantmen, including visit and search, as long as those vessels were not armed, had not been instructed to ram submarines on sight, and as long as extended flights from shore or from carriers were not practicable. As soon as any of these three factors made its appearance, the submarine had to abandon adherence to customary procedures.[9]

---

[8] United States, District Court, W.D. of Washington, October 7, 1942, 78 F. Supp. 57, digested in 42 *A.J.I.L.* (1948), p. 940.

[9] See Lauterpacht's *Oppenheim*, Vol. II, pp. 468–471, Higgins–Colombos, pp. 384–388, and Stone, pp. 581–583, for brief accounts of the measures adopted by the different belligerents during the First World War in connection with submarine warfare; W. T. Mallison, Jr., *Studies in the Law of Naval Warfare: Submarines in*

Lauterpacht was legally correct when he asserted that "the novelty of a weapon does not by itself carry with it a legitimate claim to a change in the existing rules of war." But he became naive, from a practical point of view when, after admitting that international law must adapt itself to the changes required by the appearance of new weapons, he outlined how the rules might be changed to accommodate the peculiar problems connected with submarines.[10] To propose seriously that, in exchange for an abandonment of the arming of merchant vessels, submarines should be prohibited by treaty either from striking merchant vessels altogether or from sinking them anywhere except in certain areas close to shore was totally unrealistic. History has shown that almost every new weapon (the battle elephant, "Greek Fire," longbow, crossbow, siege gun, rifle, balloon, airplane, dirigible, submarine, and now nuclear weapons and ballistic missiles) has been initially greeted with outraged denunciation. If, however, the weapon proved effective and its users were able to defend themselves successfully against retaliatory use of the weapon in question, the use of the weapon would be regarded, sooner or later, as lawful.

The best-known incident involving the use of a submarine against an enemy merchant vessel was the sinking of the British liner *Lusitania*.

On May 1, 1915, the *Lusitania* sailed from New York for Liverpool, with 1,257 passengers and a crew of 702 aboard. On May 7, 1915, the vessel was torpedoed by a German submarine off the coast of Ireland and sank in eighteen minutes, with a loss of 1,198 lives. Contrary to German allegations, the British owners asserted that the *Lusitania* was not and had never been armed and had not carried any explosives aboard. It did carry eighteen fuse cases and 125 shrapnel cases (empty shells, without powder charges), 4,200 cases of safety cartridge, and 189 cases of infantry equipment, such as leather fitting, pouches, and so on.[11] The question of whether the ship was armed has never been settled, but the vessel was designed to carry guns. The question of whether explosives or munitions other than those mentioned were aboard has remained a subject of continuing debate. In 1962 a team of divers descended to the wreck and the pictures taken by them were shown in May of that year on television by the British Broadcasting Company. The leader of the team, an American (John Light), believed that the wreck had been tampered with since its loss in 1915. A section of steel deck appeared to have been cut away with torches

---

General and Limited Wars [U.S. Naval War College: International Law Studies 1966] (Washington, D.C.: U.S. Government Printing Office, 1968); consult Whiteman, Vol. X, pp. 650–666.

[10] Lauterpacht's *Oppenheim*, Vol. II, pp. 469–470.

[11] See *The Lusitania* (Petition of Cunard S.S. Co., Ltd.), United States, District Court, S.D. of New York, 1918, 251 F. 715; Thomas A. Bailey, "The Sinking of the *Lusitania*," 41 *American Historical Review* (1935), pp. 54–73. Consult also *The Lusitania Cases*, U.S.–German Mixed Claims Commission, 1923, in 18 *A.J.I.L.* (1924), pp. 361 ff., and the relevant collection of documents on the sinking in 2 *Current History* (1915), pp. 613–631.

and a mooring wire was found to be roughly shackled into the flying bridge of the ship. An earlier private expedition to the wreck, in 1935, had not used such mooring wire. Also, holes and bent steel doors on the vessel appeared to indicate an explosion on the side away from the strike of the German torpedo. One of the survivors of the sinking remembered having heard three explosions, whereas only one torpedo had been fired at the liner from the German submarine. The log of the latter stated that the detonation of the torpedo had been followed by a heavier, internal explosion.[12]

Light proceeded to purchase the wreck (for $2,800) from the British War Risks Commission that had acquired title to the *Lusitania*, in order to salvage the ship's propellers as well as 200 tons of copper and 400 tons of brass ingots in the hold. Although salvage operations had been scheduled to begin in the summer of 1968, no further information on the project was on hand at the time of writing.

Great Britain and the United States had proposed at the Washington Conference of 1919 that all submarines be scrapped. This concept was not accepted by the delegates, and the subject was brought up again at the Washington Naval Conference of 1922. At that meeting, a five-Power treaty (Washington Treaty of February 6, 1922) laid down a reiteration of the rules presumably governing submarine warfare:

1. No merchant vessels were to be sunk at sight; if such a ship had to be destroyed because of unavoidable circumstances, then the crew and any passengers aboard had to be placed in safety.

2. Submarines were subject to the same rules that governed surface vessels of war.

3. Any person in the service of a state adopting the "Washington rules" who violated any of the rules, whether or not under the superior orders of his government, was to be deemed to have violated the laws of war and was to "be liable to trial and punishment as if for an act of piracy," and could be "brought to trial before the civil or military authorities of any Power within whose jurisdiction" he might be found.

The 1922 Washington Treaty was not ratified, however. Subsequently, the London Naval Conference of 1930 resulted in a treaty signed by France, Great Britain, Italy, Japan, and the United States, which laid down, in Article 22, what were termed the "established rules of international law" governing submarines. These included the renewed assertion that the same principles applied to submarines as applied to surface craft and the prohibition on the sinking of merchant vessels except if the latter refused to stop when ordered to do so or actively resisted visit and search.

[12] *Duluth* (Minn.) *Herald–Tribune*, May 10, 1962, p. 7.

Article 22 was to be in effect without time limit. When, therefore, the treaty of 1930 expired on December 31, 1936, Article 22 still remained valid and bound its signatories. In order to grant this set of rules wider applicability, the original signatory states had signed on November 6, 1936, the London Protocol, embodying *verbatim* the provisions of Article 22 relating to submarines.[13] The Protocol included provision for the adherence of additional states, such adherence to be also without time limit, and by the outbreak of World War II, forty-eight states, including the Soviet Union as well as Germany, had formally indicated their adherence to the Protocol. In 1937 (September 14), the so-called Nyon Arrangement for "collective measures against piratical acts by submarines" in the Spanish Civil War had invoked the London Protocol of 1936 as "expressing rules of international law." The arrangement had been signed by Great Britain, Bulgaria, Egypt, France, Greece, Romania, Turkey, the U.S.S.R., and Jugoslavia. (See also Chapter 30.)

By the time World War II came, there thus existed what Corbett termed a broad consensus,[14] condemning as piratical and in violation of international law the destruction of merchant vessels by submarines when such acts were not accompanied by adequate protection of passengers as well as crews.

Yet World War II witnessed a repetition of the practices of 1914–18, with an early resumption of the sinking at sight of merchant vessels by submarines. As before, retaliatory measures were promptly adopted by the opposing belligerents, particularly when it became apparent that no regard was being paid to the safety of passengers and crews. In the Pacific area, in particular, United States as well as British submarines adopted unrestricted campaigns against Japanese merchant vessels. Unlike conditions in the Atlantic region, the operations in the Pacific led to a complete suspension of the Protocol of 1936.[15]

It should be mentioned that enemy merchant vessels sailing under convoy of warships or military aircraft may be attacked without warning, and that such practice is lawful today.

Self-defense has now become the justification for the abandonment by submarines of the traditional rules still governing surface vessels. This new point of view was emphasized in the Opinion and Judgment of the International Military Tribunal at Nuremberg in the trial of Admiral Doenitz (1947), in which the accused was absolved from guilt for his conduct of submarine warfare against British armed merchant ships. On the other hand, the German proclamation of operation zones and the sinking of

[13] See 31 *A.J.I.L.* (1937), Supp., pp. 137–138.

[14] Corbett, p. 224.

[15] To illustrate: on February 2, 1946, the U.S. Navy announced that it had sunk, through submarines, 1944 major Japanese merchant vessels during the Pacific campaigns, with a loss of 276,000 crewmen: *The New York Times*, February 3, 1946, p. 20.

neutral vessels entering those zones, without warning, were held to have constituted violations of the Protocol of 1936, and Admiral Doenitz was adjudged to have been guilty of war crimes in this connection.[16]

6. *Status of Armed Merchant Vessels Relating to Submarines.* Another aspect of submarine warfare, neglected by many modern commentators, has to do with the status of armed merchant vessels. During World War I, bitter disputes arose repeatedly between the opposing parties as to the legality of sinking, without warning, merchant ships armed for "defensive purposes only." It is somewhat difficult to see how a valid and precise differentiation can be made between "offensive" and defensive" armament, particularly when the enemy is in the vulnerable category of a submarine. Under international law, an armed enemy vessel may be sunk without warning if it carries offensive armament. The government of the United States, to cite a classic example, had proposed to the Allied governments on January 18, 1916, that all merchant vessels under belligerent flag should be prohibited from carrying any armament because "any armament... on a merchant vessel would seem to have the character of an offensive armament." Although the United States abandoned this position completely in March, 1918, and accepted the British assertion that "defensively" armed merchant vessels were not war vessels and therefore should be immune from attack without warning as well as from internment in neutral ports, the earlier position of the United States appears to have possessed much merit.[17] No change in this situation is foreseen for future conflicts. As long as submarines as well as aircraft attack merchant vessels without warning, the latter are entitled, to use Lauterpacht's phrase, to employ "all modes of attack by way of defence." [18]

On the other hand, it must also be recognized that one of the traditional assumptions on which the older rules were based, appears to be no longer present in modern war: the assumption that a clear distinction could be drawn between the naval forces of a belligerent and enemy merchant ships having no direct relation to that belligerent's military operations. Under modern conditions of warfare, merchant ships and their activities have tended increasingly to be integrated in the overall war effort, especially that part of it which takes place on the seas. The old rules must be held to apply today, to submarines as well as to merchant vessels, *provided* the latter are not incorporated into the military effort at sea. As soon as this condition fails to obtain—and increasingly this appears to be the case in modern war—a merchant vessel would seem to fall into a category permitting it to be attacked without warning, just as would be true if it tried

---

[16] See relevant portions of the judgment in Bishop, pp. 810–812.

[17] See Higgins–Colombos, pp. 397–403 for the background history of armed merchant vessels, and consult Stone, pp. 577–580, as well as Whiteman, Vol. X, pp. 656–657, 670–676.

[18] Lauterpacht's *Oppenheim*, Vol. II, p. 471.

to attack a submarine before any effort to halt and search the vessel had been made by the submarine.

The International War Crimes Tribunal at Nuremberg, in the *Doenitz Trial,* accepted as lawful German unrestricted submarine warfare in World War II, on the grounds that the British merchant marine had become an adjunct to, or an auxiliary of, the Royal Navy and hence, by assimilation, could be treated as if the vessels in question were in fact enemy public (war) vessels.[19]

7. *Mines.* The Russo-Japanese War of 1904–5 produced the first modern instance of the widespread utilization of mines. The resulting extensive damage to or loss of neutral ships quickly brought a realization that some form of regulation of this weapon was desirable. In consequence, Convention No. VIII Relative to the Laying of Automatic Submarine Contact Mines was adopted at The Hague in 1907. This instrument prohibited belligerents from laying unanchored automatic contact mines unless the latter embodied a mechanical feature rendering them harmless an hour after control over the mines was lost by those laying them. It also prohibited the laying of anchored automatic contact lines which would not be rendered harmless as soon as they broke from their anchoring devices. Article 2 of the convention forbade the laying of automatic contact mines off the ports and coasts of an enemy for the sole purpose of stopping commercial navigation—a rather unrealistic conception, because no one could assert conclusively that such mines had other than permitted objectives. Other provisions of the agreement covered such topics as notification by belligerents of danger zones to all governments and shipowners.

The instrument was disregarded by Germany during both World Wars, and during the second conflict extensive use of aircraft was made to deposit mines far off the shores of enemy states. In reprisal, the Allies in both wars resorted to the establishment of war zones and to the creation of permanent mine fields. World War II also saw the appearance of new forms of mines (acoustic and magnetic), capable of exploding without the necessity of an actual contact with the hull of a vessel. Because a considerable proportion of all mines laid during the recent conflict was not anchored, losses to neutral shipping from floating mines were very heavy. The end of both wars witnessed an immediate and strenuous effort to remove all floating and anchored mines from the sea-lanes of the world but, despite considerable success in this endeavor, losses from floating mines continued for many years after the termination of hostilities.[20]

8. *Enemy Ships Immune from Attack.*[21] Certain enemy vessels are immune from attack, under customary or conventional law. This category

[19] See Whiteman, Vol. X, p. 665, on this important point.

[20] See Reif, pp. 149–154. On mines in general, consult Whiteman, Vol. X, pp. 676–681.

[21] Consult Whiteman, Vol. X, pp. 624–643.

includes ships engaged in scientific exploration and research, under both customary law and Article 4 of Hague Convention No. XI of 1907, which latter instrument expanded the category to embrace vessels with a religious, scientific, or philanthropic mission. Naturally, as soon as such a ship abandons its normal functions and either engages in hostilities or serves the commercial interests of an enemy, its immunity comes to an end.

Small boats and fishing vessels engaged in local or coastal traffic were exempt from attack and seizure by one of the oldest rules of customary law and also, later, under Article 3 of Convention No. XI.[22] Germany was the first country to disregard this tradition during World War I, when a number of British coastal fishing vessels were sunk, and this practice was repeated during World War II, expanded, moreover, through the use of aircraft to bomb coastal vessels. At the same time the Allies, on discovering that numerous Japanese fishing vessels acted as observers and reporters for the Japanese Navy, proceeded to sink such vessels. It should be noted, too, that large vessels engaged in coastal trade and vessels devoted to deep-sea fishing have not been exempted from enemy attack by either customary or conventional international law.

Hospital ships did not enjoy immunity from attack under conventional law but under the customary rule dictating humane treatment of the enemy. During World War I, a number of Allied hospital ships were sunk at sight by German submarines, a practice repeated during the recent global conflict. Those sinkings were clearly illegal, particularly so because all vessels in question were clearly marked and identified in accordance with the requirements of the 1899 and 1907 Hague Conventions; in addition, the Allies (in both wars) had communicated the names of all such hospital ships to the opposing side.

The Geneva Convention of 1949 for the Amelioration of the Condition of Wounded, Sick, and Shipwrecked Members of Armed Forces at Sea, which greatly enlarged the earlier Hague Convention No. X of 1907, provided in Articles 22, 24, and 33 for the immunity of hospital ships of various categories from attack and seizure.[23]

In February, 1966, the U.S. government requested, through neutral diplomatic channels, the government of North Vietnam to respect the immunity of an American hospital ship operating in Vietnamese waters. No reply appears to have been received, because North Vietnam had consistently refused to recognize the applicability of Geneva conventions to the conflict on the grounds that no state of war had been declared.[24] The relevant 1949 agreement, however, specifies its applicability to both declared and undeclared wars in Article 2.

[22] See *The Paquete Habana; The Lola*, Chapter 3; consult also Higgins-Colombos, pp. 417–419.
[23] See Lauterpacht's *Oppenheim*, Vol. II, pp. 479–480 and especially pp. 502–505, including the valuable notes relating to incidents during World War II.
[24] *The New York Times*, February 13, 1966, p. 4.

9. Mail Ships. Mail ships enjoy no general immunity from attack under either customary or conventional law, but a number of states have agreed on their immunity by means of special bilateral agreements. Mailbags, on the other hand, were exempted from capture by Article 1 of Hague Convention No. XI (1907), provided the mail in question was not on its way to or from a blockaded port. It should be noted, too, that the immunity in question extends only to postal correspondence and *not* to parcel post. The latter is subject to confiscation when it contains contraband items, and even correspondence is now regarded as subject to censorship even when found on neutral ships entering belligerent waters. Neutral protests against such censorship have had no affect during both World Wars.[25]

10. Cartel Ships. So-called cartel ships, that is, vessels sailing under a safe-conduct issued by a belligerent and engaged in transporting prisoners back to their own country, are immune from attack or seizure both on their way to collect prisoners or to return them. Naturally, a cartel ship loses its immune status as soon as it engages in any activity not specifically connected with its special mission such as transmitting military data, engaging in the commission of hostile acts, or carrying any sort of cargo.

11. Position of Enemy Combatants.[26] The position of enemy individuals in warfare at sea is analogous to that of enemy combatants on land. Under customary law, only those may be killed or wounded who resist capture. Sick and wounded men, or those who surrender, must be granted quarter. The new 1949 Geneva Convention amplified the older rules governing the treatment of wounded and sick enemy combatants, based on lessons learned from the naval phases of World War II.

In former days, all enemy combatants as well as the officers and crews of captured enemy merchant ships could be made prisoners of war. Under the provisions of Hague Convention No. XI of 1907, crew members of merchant vessels who are subjects of neutral countries and neutral officers must not be made prisoners; in the case of such ship's officers, however, they are required to make formal written promise not to serve again on an enemy vessel during the rest of the war. Enemy citizens serving on enemy merchant vessels may not be made prisoners if they sign a declaration stating that they will not engage in any service connected with the operations of the war (Art. 6).

This convention was not in force during World War I because of the presence of a universal participation clause in the instrument.

The practice has been, since 1914, to intern the officers and crews (enemy nationals) of captured enemy merchant vessels. If, however, an enemy merchant vessel resists arrest or defends itself against capture, the ship may be sunk and the officers and crew, when taken, will be treated

[25] Higgins–Colombos, pp. 478–484; see also Whiteman, Vol. X, pp. 769–778.
[26] See Whiteman, Vol. X, pp. 618–624, 649.

as prisoners of war. As such they are protected by the Geneva Convention of 1949 as soon as they are landed by their captors. As long as they are still aboard the capturing vessel, they are protected, though less adequately, by the principle of customary law which asserts that prisoners must be treated humanely.

12. Position of Noncombatants. Noncombatant components of the crew of a belligerent warship, such as stokers, surgeons, chaplains, and so on, may not be attacked directly and killed or wounded. They may be taken prisoners of war, of course, unless they happen to be part of the medical, religious, or hospital staff, who are exempt under Articles 36 and 37 of the Geneva Convention of 1949 on the members of armed forces at sea.

13. Enemy Private Citizens. Enemy private citizens found aboard an attacked or captured enemy vessel may not be directly attacked or wounded if they are not members of the crew of the vessel or of the armed forces of the enemy—provided they do not take part in the fighting. Under certain conditions, such individuals may be made prisoners of war, on the same basis as would be permitted in the case of private persons in occupied enemy territory. This would also be true if the individuals were enemy officials of importance (heads of state, members of a cabinet, diplomats, and so on).

14. Position of Neutral "Combatants." If a neutral merchant vessel resists a belligerent attempt to visit and search, that is, if the vessel resists arrest or seeks to escape (even though otherwise innocent), its officers and crew become liable to detention as prisoners of war because of the illegal conduct of the ship which assimilates it to combatant or belligerent status. The vessel itself would be subject to capture and condemnation by a prize court.

15. Ruses. Ruses are permitted in warfare at sea, to the extent that such is allowed on land. Thus in World War I, the German cruiser *Emden*, easily recognizable by Allied warships at a great distance because of the small number of its smokestacks, was within its rights when it employed a canvas contraption resembling an additional stack which was hoisted on occasion to create the impression that the *Emden* was a French or British cruiser. The use of a neutral and even of an enemy flag by a belligerent warship has been endorsed as lawful by most writers whenever the ship in question is engaged in chasing an enemy ship, when trying to escape, or when attempting to lure an enemy vessel into action. On the other hand, universal agreement prevails that, immediately before an actual attack, the ship must display its own national ensign. Merchant vessels may use false colors at all times, although this ruse has given rise on many occasions to protests on the part of neutrals whose flag had been used by merchant vessels registered in belligerent states.

16. Naval Bombardment. The question of naval bombardment has been a highly controversial facet of warfare at sea. Under Article 3 of Hague Convention No. IX (1907), a naval force may bombard an undefended enemy community if the local authorities refused to deliver requested provisions or supplies for the immediate use of that naval force. The requisitions must be proportionate to the resources of the community; they must be requisioned by the commander of the naval force; and they are to be paid for in cash or, if sufficient money is lacking, a receipt must be issued to the supplying authorities.

Defended enemy coasts may be lawfully bombarded by naval forces, either acting on their own or in support of a besieging or landing force. Until 1907, however, no generally accepted answer had been found to the question whether undefended coastal places of the enemy could be lawfully bombarded. Hague Convention No. IX finally provided the rules applicable to this problem. Under Article 1 of that instrument, the bombardment of undefended ports, towns, and other communities or buildings by naval forces is unconditionally prohibited. Military works, depots of war materials or munitions, plants and other facilities usable for the enemy military forces, and warships in ports, all may be lawfully bombarded even when these targets are located in undefended localities.

A naval commander is supposed to give advance warning of such a bombardment to the local authorities to enable them to destroy the target facilities in question and thus to spare their community the damage incidental to a lawful naval bombardment. In the course of the latter, all efforts are to be made to spare buildings devoted to public worship, art, science, charitable purposes, as well as historical monuments, and hospitals and other facilities for the sick and wounded. In order to enable the protection of these places to be effected, they are to be clearly indicated by visible signs (large rectangular panels, divided diagonally into two triangular portions, the upper one black, the lower one white) (Art. 5).

The convention was technically inoperative during World War I, because not all belligerents were parties to the instrument. During World War II, the convention was ignored in the practices of virtually all belligerent naval powers, and naval bombardments of a most indiscriminatory nature took place.

17. Armistice. An armistice temporarily suspends hostilities and it might be thought that such suspension would, logically, also apply to belligerent seizures on the high seas. Such an interpretation was, in fact, specifically included in a number of armistice instruments during the nineteenth century (Franco-German armistice of January 28, 1871; Sino-Japanese armistice of March 30, 1895; Greco-Turkish armistice of June 4, 1897). A complete reversal was recorded, however, in World War I. Article 5 of the naval section of the Allied Armistice Convention with Austria-Hungary (November 3, 1918) and Article 26 of the Armistice Convention with Germany (November 11, 1918) both specified that seizures of enemy ships and cargoes encountered on the high seas would continue until peace had been concluded. Consequently a large number of such seizures were effected by the Allied navies and both ships and cargoes continued to be condemned by Allied prize courts.

Similarly, goods destined for Germany and seized after the 1918 armistice became effective were condemned on the grounds of intention to serve hostile purposes. British prize courts pointed out, correctly, that under the terms of Article 26 such procedures were lawful and also emphasized that, technically, an armistice does not preclude an ultimate resumption of hostilities. It would be wrong, therefore, for one party to the conflict to permit goods to be imported by an enemy when, on a later resumption of hostilities, such goods could be used to further that enemy's prosecution of the war.

Prize courts do not cease to exercise their functions even at the termination of a war. Their competence normally ends only when all matters and issues falling within their jurisdiction and arising during the conduct of hostilities have been disposed of by them. This explains why Allied prize courts continued to sit for many years after the end of World War I and were able to condemn ships and cargoes seized before the termination of that war. In fact, the last prize case arising out of the conflict was not decided until 1934! [27]

18. Submarine Cables. Some comment appears desirable on the subject of submarine cables in time of war. Part of the traditional principle of the freedom of the high seas involves the undoubted right of states to lay submarine cables for telegraphic, and lately telephonic, communications with other states. Cables frequently are encountered where the depth of the ocean is not very great, and hence are quite vulnerable to unintentional or intentional damage.

After much delay traceable to a variety of extraneous causes, a conference was held at Paris in 1882 which resulted in the International Convention for the Protection of Submarine Telegraph Cables, signed on March 14, 1884, by twenty-six states. The instrument (the Paris Convention) applied "outside territorial waters and to all legally established submarine cables landed on the territories, colonies or possessions of one or more of the High Contracting Parties."

The warships of the contracting states were granted the right to stop and check on the nationality of any merchant ships suspected of violating the regulations of the convention (Art. 10), but determination of any actual violation was to be handled exclusively by the courts of the state in which the infringing vessel was registered (Art. 8). Article 15 provided that the "stipulations of the present convention do not in any way restrict the freedom of action of belligerents."

---

[27] *The Bathori*, Great Britain, Privy Council, 1934, A.C. 91, cited in Higgins–Colombos, p. 436.

If there were no other body of regulations available, Article 15 would mean that any belligerent state would be free to do as it pleased about submarine cables. Article 54 of the Regulations on land warfare (Fourth Hague Convention of 1907, annex) provided, however, that

Submarine cables connecting an occupied territory with a neutral territory shall not be seized or destroyed except in case of absolute necessity; they must also be restored and the indemnities for them regulated at the peace.

This represents merely a minor limitation on the freedom of action of any belligerent because the Regulations only apply to that portion of any cable found in the territorial waters and on the adjacent land surface of an enemy state, and then only to the extent that the coastal stretch is occupied by an opposing party in the war.

Belligerents, therefore, have felt free to interrupt cable communications as they saw fit. Chile cut a British cable between its territory and Peru in its war against the latter country in 1883, but did pay full compensation to the owners. The United States, during the Spanish-American War in 1898, cut the cables connecting Cuba, Puerto Rico, and Manila with the rest of the world, despite the fact that the installations were all British property, that is, neutral. The severing of the Manila-Hong Kong cable interfered so greatly with commerce in South-East Asian waters that violent protests about the action ensued. When the United States refused to pay compensation to the owners of British cables, claims were eventually brought before an American-British Claims Arbitration Tribunal in 1923.[28] The tribunal held that the United States was under no obligation to pay compensation, asserting that every belligerent had a legal right to deprive its enemy of communication over the high seas while preserving it unimpeded for itself. The cutting of cables was not prohibited to a belligerent by any rule of law nor by any treaty. Furthermore, the tribunal stated the Manila-Hong Kong cable was under Spanish control to a degree that invested the installation with the character of a Spanish utility, despite British ownership. Basically, therefore, the rule was applied that a neutral whose business (cables in this instance) is located in belligerent territory cannot expect to receive compensation for losses sustained through belligerent operations which themselves are not prohibited by international law.

The outbreak of hostilities in 1914 was accompanied by an Allied severing of German-controlled submarine cables, portions of which were relaid later in order to provide additional lines of communication for Allied countries with neutrals and also among themselves. At the end of the war, the Treaty of Versailles provided for the transfer of German government-owned cables to the Allied Powers without compensation;

[28] *Great Britain* (Eastern Extension, Australasia and China Telegraph Co., Ltd.) v. *United States*, in *Nielsen's Reports*, p. 40.

the value of German privately owned cables, also taken from their pre-war owners, was credited (less depreciation) to Germany in the reparations accounts. (See also Chapter 31 on cables in occupied enemy territory.)

SUGGESTED READINGS

Josef L. Kunz, "British Prize Cases, 1939–1941," 36 *A.J.I.L.* (1942), pp. 204–228, containing many illustrative cases not available elsewhere; Stone, pp. 585–607; Whiteman, Vol. X, pp. 599–605, 610–614.

30
Neutrality

NATURE OF NEUTRALITY

Definition of Neutrality. Neutrality on the part of a state not a party to a war consists in refraining from all participation in the war and in preventing, tolerating, and regulating certain acts on its own part, by its nationals, and by the belligerents. It is the duty of all belligerents to respect the territory as well as the rights of neutral states.[1]

Concept of Nonbelligerency. Even though the current definition given omits the factor of impartiality, the latter must be assumed to have been part of the traditional concept of neutrality and ought to play a role today. The difficulty lies in the fact that modern practice indicates that numerous states somehow manage to remain outside of a conflict yet do not behave impartially toward belligerents. The term *nonbelligerency* has come into usage to describe such behavior. It does not as yet possess full standing in the vocabulary of the law, but it does describe the actual behavior of states and has achieved considerable employment. The term was apparently used for the first time in 1939 to describe the status of Italy before the latter state became a normal belligerent. The use of the term spread rapidly—R. R. Wilson cited its invocation by President Inönü on November 1, 1940, to characterize Turkey's position in World War II.[2]

A state behaving as a nonbelligerent will remain outside of a war as far as actual hostilities are concerned, will claim to be neutral, yet will not behave impartially but instead will favor one side or the other. In consequence of such action, it will not enjoy the full status or the full rights of a genuine neutral. Impartiality, just as much as abstention from participation in a conflict, are the characteristics of genuine neutrality; both must be present to support a claim of genuine neutrality, with full neutral

---

[1] Adapted from Department of the Army, FM 27-10, *The Law of Land Warfare* (Washington, D.C., July, 1956), p. 185. It is interesting to note that the 1940 edition of that manual included a phrase to the effect that a neutral state had to exercise "absolute impartiality" in the prevention, toleration, and regulation of certain acts.

[2] Robert R. Wilson, " 'Non-Belligerency' in Relation to the Terminology of Neutrality," 35 *A.J.I.L.* (1941), pp. 121–123, at p. 121.

rights.[3] Impartiality has been stressed in most major treaties applicable to neutrality—the Fifth Hague Convention of 1907 (Art. 9), the Thirteenth Hague Convention of 1907 (Preamble), and the Havana Convention on Maritime Neutrality of 1928 (Preamble)—as well as in the draft conventions drawn up by the International Law Association in 1920 (Art. 9) and in 1928 (Art. 9), and by Harvard Research itself (Art. 4).

It must be noted, however, that in the past there did exist on occasion a situation aptly described as "qualified" (imperfect) neutrality. This was the case when a given neutral rendered direct or indirect assistance to one of the belligerents in a conflict because of a treaty obligation contracted before the war, and not for that war in particular. Thus Great Britain, under a prewar treaty, prohibited, in 1848, the export of arms to Prussia but permitted such exports to Denmark. Similarly, Denmark, in pursuance of treaty obligations, supplied both warships and troops to Russia in 1788 during a war between Sweden and Russia; Sweden protested but eventually accepted Denmark's qualified neutrality.

Nevertheless, nonbelligerency was the status assumed during World War II by Spain and the United States (in the latter case until December 7, 1941). Needless to say, the continuing enjoyment of such status will depend almost entirely on the patience of belligerents against which the nonbelligerent practices its discrimination, and a declaration of war may eventually put an end to the anomalous status of the "neutral nonbelligerent."

Harvard Research Proposal. The traditional emphasis on impartiality as a neutral duty began to be challenged seriously as early as 1939. In that year the Harvard Research in International Law proposed that the concept in question be modified to read

A neutral State, for the purpose of better safeguarding its rights and interests as a neutral or of better fulfilling its duties as a neutral, may, during the course of a war, adopt new measures or alter the measures which it has previously adopted. . . .[4]

This proposal referred to the belief that changes in domestic neutrality legislation made in time of war would not necessarily violate the duty of impartiality. Such an interpretation, on the other hand, appears to contradict the traditional policies of states. For instance, when an embargo bill was introduced in Congress, in 1914, and Great Britain opposed such a step, deeming it to be an unneutral act, President Wilson and Secretary of State Lansing agreed with the British view. The German government continued, however, to urge the passage of embargo legislation, and the United States replied to these requests with a note, in 1915, which asserted

---

[3] Consult also Harvard Research in International Law, "Rights and Duties of Neutral States, in Naval and Aerial War," 33 *A.J.I.L.* (1939), Special Supplement, pp. 169–817, at pp. 232–235; the document is hereinafter referred to as *Harvard Draft.*
[4] *Harvard Draft*, p. 316.

that "Any change in its own [United States] laws of neutrality during the progress of a war which would affect unequally the relations of the United States with the nations at war would be an unjustifiable departure from the principle of strict neutrality." [5]

Controversy over United States Neutrality Legislation. The issue came fully into the open when the Congress of the United States revised American neutrality legislation in 1939 and President Roosevelt proposed repeal of the earlier mandatory arms embargo.[6] Many critics pointed out that the purpose of this basic change was to assist the enemies of Germany, hence constituted a violation of international law.[7]

The controversy over nonbelligerency flared up again with great vigor, accompanied by much publicity, after President Roosevelt announced to Congress on September 3, 1940, that the United States had received from Great Britain ninety-nine-year leases on eight naval bases in the Caribbean in exchange for supplying fifty overage destroyers.[8] This arrangement produced much disagreement among both members of Congress and jurists, even though the presidential message had been accompanied by a favorable opinion written by Attorney General Robert H. Jackson.[9]

That opinion maintained, *inter alia,* that the relevant Article 8 of Hague Convention XIII (1907) did not apply, because that Article only pertained to vessels "intended" originally to be used by a belligerent. Because the fifty destroyers had not been built with the intention of turning them over to Great Britain, the opinion held that neither Article 8 nor the Act of June 15, 1917 (40 *U.S. Stat.* 221) applied to the transfer of the vessels.

The present writer disagrees completely with the Attorney General's interpretation of the duties of a neutral: the Article cited referred to the prevention of certain acts on the part of private neutral citizens, and the pertinent reference should have been to the clear-cut prohibition imposed by Article 6 of Convention XIII: "The supply in any manner, directly or indirectly, by a neutral Power to a belligerent Power of war-

[5] Henry S. Fraser, technical adviser to George W. Wickersham on the League Committee for the codification of international law in 1926 and 1927, cited in an interview by the Associated Press, in *Knickerbocker News* [Albany, N.Y.], September 21, 1939; see also Higgins–Colombos, p. 500, in support of the view cited, and consult Charles H. McLaughlin, "Legislative Neutrality in the United States," 22 *Minnesota Law Review* (1937/1938), pp. 603–660.

[6] *The New York Times,* June 14, July 15, October 28, 1939.

[7] See letter by Charles C. Hyde and Philip C. Jessup, *The New York Times,* September 21, 1939, and the ensuing debate over the letter, *ibid.,* September 25, October 1, 5, 7, 14, and 15, 1939, as well as *The New York Herald Tribune,* October 25, 1939.

[8] See 34 *A.J.I.L.* (1940), Supp., p. 183. The text of the Agreement of March 27, 1941 (and of supplementary documents) for the American use of the bases was reprinted in 35 *A.J.I.L.* (1941), Supp., pp. 134–159.

[9] *The New York Times,* September 9, 1940, and 34 *A.J.I.L.* (1940), pp. 728–736. See also Edwin M. Borchard, "The Attorney General's Opinion on the Exchange of Destroyers for Naval Bases," 34 *A.J.I.L.* (1940), pp. 690–697.

ships, ammunition or war material of any kind whatever is forbidden." This prohibition had been acknowledged by the United States Department of State as early as October 15, 1917, when a department circular stated categorically that "for the Government of the United States itself to sell to a belligerent nation would be an unneutral act." [10]

The present writer also cannot accept the conclusion of Wright that United States and Latin American abandonment of the canons of impartiality were justified because German aggression violated international law as embodied in the Kellogg-Briand Pact and therefore exempted neutrals from the normal obligation of impartiality among belligerents.[11]

Attorney General Robert Jackson then added more fuel to the argument when he delivered a speech at Havana on March 27, 1941, in which he asserted that the United States was obliged as a matter of law to render to Great Britain all aid "short of war," while at the same time it was "the declared determination of the government to avoid entry into the war as a belligerent." [12]

The inescapable conclusion would seem to be that the United States abandoned its status as a neutral by the destroyer deal. It thereupon entered the status of a "nonbelligerent" or neoneutral.

Lend-Lease Bill. A second and major step in the shifting of the United States from traditional neutrality to an expanded version of nonbelligerency took place with the affixing of the presidential signature on March 11, 1941, to the Defense Act of 1941, introduced as House Resolution 1776 on January 10 of that year and popularly known as the Lend-Lease Bill.[13] This remarkable example of unilateral deviation from accepted norms of neutral behavior asserted that a nonbelligerent possessed the right to discriminate between belligerents and to favor one side against the other by means of supplying the former with military equipment through the medium of the nonbelligerent state.

The law itself authorized the President of the United States to grant various forms of aid to the "government of any country whose defense the President deems vital to the defense of the United States." Specifically, the Chief Executive was authorized to have manufactured in arsenals, factories, and shipyards any defense article for such governments, and to sell, transfer title to, exchange, lend, lease or otherwise dispose of, to any such government, any defense articles.[14]

[10] 33 *A.J.I.L.* (1939), Special Supp., p. 238.

[11] Quincy Wright, "Law and Politics in the World Community," in Lipsky, pp. 3–14, at p. 8.

[12] Cited by Edwin M. Borchard, "War, Neutrality and Non-Belligerency," 35 *A.J.I.L.* (1941), pp. 618–625, at p. 618.

[13] See Robert R. Wilson, *The International Law Standard in Treaties of the United States* (1953), at pp. 234–239.

[14] See text of the law in 35 *A.J.I.L.* (1941), Supp., pp. 76 ff. Consult also Warren F. Kimball, *The Most Unsordid Act: Lend-Lease, 1939–1941* (Baltimore, Md.: The Johns Hopkins Press, 1969).

Section 3 of the law authorized the President to inspect, prove, repair, outfit, recondition, or otherwise place in good working order any defense article for any such favored government or to procure any or all of such services by private contract. This, in turn, meant that henceforth belligerent warships, planes, and other matériel could be repaired or outfitted in American jurisdiction.

It was not surprising, then, that but a little later most of the remaining parts of the Neutrality Act of 1939 were scrapped when Congress, in November, 1941, authorized the defensive arming of American merchant vessels and their sailing into proclaimed war zones and belligerent ports.

HISTORICAL BACKGROUND

Early Development of Concept of Neutrality. The concept of neutrality has been connected intimately with the development of another idea, that of the society or family of nations. It, therefore, came into being only when such a society was developing. The word *neutrality*, in its modern meaning, first showed up in the fourteenth century.[15] By the end of the fifteenth century, the *Consolato del Mare* could record definite rules concerning neutral rights at sea, and in the sixteenth century, diplomatic correspondence cited international law on neutrality.

Hugo Grotius, dealing but briefly with neutrality, supported a theory based on the doctrine of the just war, under which a state might claim to be neutral. Yet such a state might proceed to judge the justice of a conflict and modify its conduct from impartiality toward not favoring the belligerent found fighting for an unjust cause:

It is the duty of those who have no part in the war to do nothing which may favor the party having an unjust cause, or which may hinder the action of one waging a just war and, in case of doubt, to treat both belligerents alike, in permitting transit, in furnishing provisions to the troops, in refraining from assisting the besieged [*Three Books on the Law of War and Peace*, Book III, Chap. 17].

Grotius thus came perilously close to the theory of nonbelligerency mentioned earlier.

The rapid growth of the importance of international trade led major neutral maritime states to resist ever more vigorously an increasing belligerent interference with neutral commerce. By the time Vattel's treatise was published in 1758, it was clearly and generally agreed that belligerent states were legally bound to honor the neutrality of any state choosing to remain outside a given conflict, and also that neutral status was characterized by a specific obligation of strict impartiality. Thus the basis of modern true neutrality was laid in the eighteenth century.

[15] See Lauterpacht's *Oppenheim*, Vol. II, pp. 624–642.

Concept of Due Diligence. Continuing belligerent interference with neutral persons and property led neutral states to resort to the use of force on numerous occasions since then. Among the best-known examples are the "Armed Neutrality" of 1780, led by Russia; the "Second Armed Neutrality" of 1800; and the unofficial belligerent acts on the part of the United States in 1798 in the Anglo-French War and from 1939 to December, 1941.[16] In the Declaration of Paris (1856), privateering was abolished, the law of blockade was laid down in fairly clear terms, and the rules of "free ships, free goods" and "free goods free even in enemy ships" were proclaimed. The American Civil War witnessed the basic neutrality of Great Britain (excluding isolated instances such as the affair of *The Alabama*) and led through the experiences of that country to a much better understanding on the part of all states of the rights and duties of a neutral. In addition, the Civil War contributed the rules of the Treaty of Washington of 1871, which asserted that a neutral must use "due diligence" to prevent evasion of its laws for the enforcement of its neutral duties.[17]

Concept of "Means at Its Disposal." It should be mentioned that the 1907 Hague Peace Conference modified the concept of "due diligence" to read that the neutral had to use "the means at its disposal" (Arts. 8 and 25 of Hague Convention XIII of 1907). The *Alabama* award had led to a recognition of the dangers inherent in permitting neutral private interests to outfit warships on neutral territory for the use of a belligerent state. Hence Article 8 of Hague Convention XIII of 1907:

A neutral Government is bound to employ the means at its disposal to prevent the fitting out or arming of any vessel within its jurisdiction which it has reason to believe is intended to cruise, or engage in hostile operations, against a Power with which that Government is at peace. It is also bound to display the same vigilance to prevent the departure from its jurisdiction of any vessel intended to cruise, or engage in hostile operations, which had been adapted entirely or partly within the said jurisdiction for use in war.

The substitution of "means at its disposal" for the "due diligence" contained in Rules 1 and 3 of the Washington Treaty of 1871 reflected much more accurately the duties of a neutral state. Thus, when the United States, before the outbreak of the war with Spain in 1898, purchased from Brazil two warships ordered by Brazil but still not completed in the yards of their British builders, the British government was correct in

[16] See Wilfred P. Deac, "America's Undeclared Naval War," 87 *U.S. Naval Institute Proceedings* (October, 1961), pp. 70–79.

[17] The phrase occurs in Article 6 of the Treaty of Washington. See *The Alabama Claims Award (United States–Great Britain)*, Arbitration under the Treaty of May 8, 1871. Consult also Wilson, *op. cit.*, pp. 191–223, for one of the best analyses available of the award and of the 1871 rules, as well as Lauterpacht's *Oppenheim*, Vol. II, pp. 714–716.

preventing both vessels from leaving British jurisdiction until the Spanish-American War had ended, and a similar policy was followed with regard to warships being built for Spain. The United States, for its part, had adopted at a much earlier date the policies later followed by Great Britain. The Act of 1795 had already prohibited, among other practices, the fitting out and arming of warships intended to be employed by a foreign belligerent, or the provision of increased armament by such vessels when already armed. The Supreme Court of the United States conscientiously applied these rules in all major cases.[18]

Rules Governing Neutral Rights and Duties. By the end of the nineteenth century, neutrality had been fully accepted as a legal status, but what were lacking as yet were clear and agreed-on definitions of both neutral rights and duties.

The major effort to fill this gap in international law was made at the Second Hague Conference in 1907. Two conventions on the subject were adopted, the Hague Convention V Respecting the Rights and Duties of Neutral Powers and Persons in Case of War on Land and the Hague Convention XIII Concerning the Rights and Duties of Neutral Powers in Naval War.

Failure of Convention XIII to lay down precise rules on hostile blockades and on the nature of contraband (forbidden) goods led a number of the major maritime states to hold the London Naval Conference of 1908. The draft agreements signed at that meeting (Declaration of London of 1909) were not ratified in time to be in effect at the outbreak of war in 1914; nevertheless, the instrument represented a "sense of the meeting" on many aspects of customary law.

Testing of Rules by World War I. World War I tested the new rules governing neutral status beyond any expectations. Despite early proclamations of neutrality by most states remaining outside the conflict, belligerents quite early began to undertake serious encroachments on neutral rights, particularly on the ancient doctrine of the freedom of the seas. Starting with the German invasion of Belgium, following that country's refusal to accede to a German demand for passage of troops through a neutral state, France and Great Britain proceeded to commit violations of neutral rights on their part when, in 1915 and 1916, they landed troops in Greece (Salonika and Corfu) and utilized Greek neutral territory as bases of military operations. The Germans, in turn, brought captured enemy vessels into United States and Chilean ports and attempted to keep them there in violation of the strict and detailed rules laid down at The Hague. By the late fall of 1916, neutrals had been harassed by both sides almost to the point of fighting to protect what remained of their rights.

Covenant of the League of Nations. The Covenant of the League of

---

[18] Such as *The Santissima Trinidad*, 1822, 7 Wheaton 283; *The Bolivar*, in *United States* v. *Quincy*, 1832, 6 Peters 445; and *The Meteor*, 1866, 3 Wharton's *Digest*, 561.

Nations modified the traditional right of any state to remain neutral. Under the provisions of Article 16, any member resorting to war in violation of its obligation to settle disputes by peaceful means was deemed to have committed an act of war against *all* other members and the latter were obligated to cut off all trade and financial relations with the aggressor.

On the other hand, it remained possible to be neutral, and neutrality continued to be practiced. The Covenant, after all, was only a treaty and, therefore, was binding only on the member states of the League or, as the British Foreign Office phrased it in 1929, "as between members of the League there can be no neutral rights because there can be no neutrals." [19] Outsiders were not bound by the provisions of the Covenant and were perfectly free to remain neutral in any conflict or dispute.

Pact of Paris of 1928. The adoption of the Pact of Paris of 1928 (Kellogg-Briand Pact) for the Renunciation of War did not accomplish any real change in the character of neutrality. The signatories of the Pact were expected to decline to observe toward a violator of the instrument such duties as international law prescribed for a neutral in relation to a belligerent, and were expected also to supply the attacked state with financial or material assistance, including munitions, and even to assist that state with armed forces.[20]

Reassessment of the Problem of Neutrality. Failure of the League system of collective security to prevent Japanese aggression in China and Italian conquest of Ethiopia led to a widespread reassessment of the problem of neutrality *vis-à-vis* the League. Many states decided that their own efforts had to be relied on for the protection of their neutrality, instead of entrusting the Geneva system with that task. Such examples as the Copenhagen Declaration of 1938 and extensive neutrality legislation passed in the Americas between 1935 and 1939 testified to a desire to ensure future neutrality, an attitude which culminated in the General Declaration of Panama in 1939.

As late as that year, the distinguished publicist Philip M. Brown could assert that legal neutrality could still be described in these terms:

A neutral nation will abstain from taking sides in the war. It will be strictly impartial in its treatment of belligerent nations. It will not adopt specific legislation or take any action calculated to affect either side unfavorably. . . . Belligerents must respect this attitude of strict neutrality and subject neutral

---

[19] Cited by Quincy Wright, "The Present Status of Neutrality," *op. cit.*, p. 391; cf. Higgins–Colombos, pp. 534–535, and see Howard Taubenfeld, "International Actions and Neutrality," 47 *A.J.I.L.* (1953), pp. 377–396, at pp. 378–383.

[20] International Law Association, "Budapest Articles of Interpretation (1934)," in 33 *A.J.I.L.* (1939), p. 825; see also Lauterpacht's *Oppenheim*, Vol. II, pp. 643–645, and Clyde Eagleton, "Neutrality and Neutral Rights Following the Pact of Paris for the Renunciation of War," *Proceedings* (1930), pp. 87–95.

nations to no infrigements on their independence or any molestation other than what may be required by the strict and unavoidable necessities of warfare. All violations of neutral rights require effective redress.[21]

World War II saw wholesale violations of neutral rights by belligerents on both sides in the conflict. Belgium, Luxembourg, the Netherlands, Denmark, and Norway were invaded despite their neutral status; Swiss national airspace was violated by both sides; vessels were attacked, sunk, or captured in neutral waters; and the United States became a nonbelligerent participant in the conflict long before it joined the Western Allies after the attack on Pearl Harbor.

UN Concept of Neutrality. The Charter of the United Nations did not cause the concept of neutrality to vanish. To be sure, Article 2, paragraph 5, states that

All Members shall give the United Nations every assistance in any action it takes in accordance with the present Charter, and shall refrain from giving assistance to any state against which the United Nations is taking preventive or enforcement action,

while the next paragraph of the same Article asserts the rather amazing doctrine that

The Organization shall ensure that states which are not Members of the United Nations act in accordance with these Principles so far as may be necessary for the maintenance of international peace and security.

These provisions of the Charter merit brief comment. As Gould pointed out,[22] the Cold War has led many leaders to wonder whether a given collective action under the flag of the United Nations (Korea and Katanga come to mind at once) did not really represent political and military action by one side in the great power struggle against the other side. If this were so, then members of the United Nations might easily come to believe that there did not exist a duty to participate in such action and to remain neutral, for obviously it could be argued quite cogently and convincingly that the actions in question were not undertaken in support of the principles of the Charter. Hence neutral status might be quite in order under certain conditions.[23]

---

[21] "Neutrality," 33 *A.J.I.L.* (1939), pp. 726–727, at p. 727.

[22] Gould, p. 624; see also Whiteman, Vol. XI, pp. 144–160, on neutrality and the Charter of the United Nations.

[23] Charles G. Fenwick has asserted for over thirty years that "the Covenant of the League of Nations put an end in principle to the traditional law of neutrality," (*International Law,* 2nd ed., 1934, p. 613; 3rd ed., 1948, p. 613; 4th ed., 1965, p. 719) and later that "the adoption of the Charter of the United Nations . . . finally marked the end of neutrality as a legal system," (*ibid.,* 3rd ed., p. 621; 4th ed., p. 727). Even more recently, Fenwick criticized Whiteman for suggesting, in the latter's Vol. XI, that something of neutrality was left: see his "Is Neutrality Still a Term of Present

The reality of such considerations were reflected not only in the slim support given to collective action in Korea, by the fact that the U.S.S.R. not only refused to participate on the side of the United Nations but gave assistance to the North Korean and Chinese aggressors, but also by the recently manifested unwillingness of large numbers of members of the Security Council, to contribute to the expenses of the Near East and Congo military expeditions under the UN flag.

As far as Article 2 (6), is concerned, any interpretation of the word "ensure" to mean coercion of nonmembers to abandon neutrality during United Nations collective actions would represent a gross negation of basic concepts of international law. At best, the paragraph can mean the use of "influence" on nonmembers. The present writer even believes that Gould erred when he suggested that *ensure* could mean *coerce* only if a nonmember actively and with prejudice assisted an aggressor.[24] Then, it is believed, a state of nonbelligerency could be claimed by a country assisting an aggressor; to interpret the Charter otherwise, it is felt, would grant legal rights to members that would not exist under international law as accepted today.

The failure to achieve the results planned for the Military Staff Committee under the Security Council produced a situation in the United Nations where a general "call to arms," with emphasis on binding obligations under Article 2, has been out of the question. Every one of the collective military actions carried out on the part of the United Nations has been on the basis of leaving actual participation to the free choice of the members. Only the payment for the total expenses incurred has been made a legal obligation under the terms of an advisory opinion of the International Court of Justice.

On the other hand, the existence of the United Nations does not eliminate the concept of neutrality altogether, or even in the bulk of likely conflicts. Article 2 (5), of the Charter only refers to action undertaken by the United Nations. Judging from the past record of the organization, a great number of conflicts "not endangering world peace" may occur without involving collective action. Under such conditions, every member of the organization would be free to remain neutral, and the rules governing neutral status would apply.

This has been true in the limited wars in the former French Indochina, in the Soviet reinvasion of Hungary in 1956, in the fighting preceding the grant of independence to Algeria, in the Indian conquest of Goa, and in

---

Law?" 63 *A.J.I.L.* (1969), pp. 100–102. The reality of the situation is that the *legal* basis for a position of neutrality may indeed have been weakened, if not abolished altogether, but that the practice of states, motivated by self-interest and political goals, has denied the *practical* basis on which neutrality can be abandoned universally. See also Howard J. Taubenfeld, "International Actions and Neutrality," 47 *A.J.I.L.* (1953), pp. 377–396, on this important point.

[24] Gould, p. 625.

the Chinese invasion of Tibet (1951) and of India (1962). If, therefore, collective action does not materialize, either because of a veto in the Security Council or because of an unwillingness on the part of the UN to intervene in a given dispute involving the use of force, then the traditional rules of law applicable to neutrality still apply.

Again, it must be remembered that even if the Security Council would call on the members for military action or assistance under the provisions of Articles 41, 43, 48, and 49 of the Charter, each member would lose its *right* to remain neutral but would actually lose its neutral status only to the extent to which it accepted and carried out the directions, orders, or suggestions issuing from the Security Council.

Status of Neutrality after Organization of the UN. Finally it is important to note that major law-making treaties concluded *after* the establishment of the United Nations still frequently refer to neutrality as a legal status. Thus the four Geneva Conventions of 1949 for the protection of war victims refer, in the sections on the treatment of prisoners of war and on the protection of civilians to "neutral state," "neutral power," and "neutral country," as well as, interestingly enough, to "neutral power or nonbelligerent."

Some commentators have insisted that neutrality is obsolete in view of the nature of modern war. Such a diagnosis ignores the vitally important distinction to be drawn between two different kinds of conflict.[25] A "dual" war, fought between two states, can be fought even with the most modern weapons under conditions allowing outsiders to assert their rights as neutrals. On the other hand, a major or global conflict would make prolonged maintenance of a neutral position difficult if not untenable.

Summing up the problem of nonbelligerency versus neutrality old style, it can be held that, although many states have followed in practice on some occasions a policy of nonbelligerency, the principle itself is not yet generally accepted as a rule of general international law. It is still quite ambiguous in its meaning as well as status, whereas traditional (impartial) neutrality is not.[26] Invocation of the Charter is not helpful on this point: it appears to be another instance in which the membership of the United Nations Organization has, by consensus, decided not to apply a principle of the Charter to the daily conduct of nations.

The discussion of neutrality which follows is centered mostly on the legal questions raised by naval warfare, because the bulk of all controversies involving belligerents and neutrals have occurred in that aspect of war. It should be kept in mind, too, that the so-called rights of neutrals have evolved by a long process of compromise between extreme demands by belligerents and equally extreme demands on the part of neutral states.

[25] See the commencement speech delivered by the late Secretary of State John Foster Dulles at the then Iowa State College at Ames on June 9, 1956, reprinted in full in 40 *U.S. News & World Report* (June 22, 1956), pp. 137–140.

[26] Consult also Whiteman, Vol. XI, pp. 163–174.

This may help to explain why many of these rules are somewhat vague and why others are afflicted with obvious weaknesses. There are many gaps in the law of neutrality, and here, usually, may be found evidence that no compromise could be achieved.

NEUTRAL RIGHTS AND DUTIES IN LAND WARFARE

Hague Convention V of 1907. The rights of a neutral state, formerly based on custom, were codified primarily in Hague Convention V of 1907. This instrument was, to a large extent, declaratory of the customary law of neutrality.

Basic Right of Inviolability of Neutral Territory. The basic right beyond any question is the inviolability of neutral territory (Art. 1), and most writers agree that all other neutral rights really represent mere corollaries to that fundamental principle governing territory. It is again affirmed in the Hague Convention dealing with neutrality in naval war.[27]

Other Neutral Rights. Corollary to the basic right, other neutral rights have been detailed in the Hague Conventions:

A neutral state may expect that belligerents will not erect on its territory radio or other facilities for the purpose of communicating with belligerent forces on land, on the seas, or in the air (Convention V, Art. 3-a); that belligerents will not make use of already existing facilities established by them before the war on now neutral territory for forbidden (military) purposes (V, Art. 3-b); that they will not open recruitment offices or form military courts on neutral territory (V, Art. 4). Most neutral states have been quick to close recruitment agencies or activities set up on their territory by a belligerent. The United States was therefore in accord with the already customary law when, in 1793, it ordered the French minister, Edmond C. Genêt, to cease issuing commissions on American soil. It is, indeed, the duty of a neutral to prevent the prohibited acts from being undertaken on its territory (V, Art. 5, par. 1). On the other hand, a neutral is not bound to prevent any of its citizens or residents from going abroad to offer their services to a belligerent (V, Art. 6). Thus the United States was not delinquent in its duties as a neutral when, in 1870, it permitted about 1,200 Frenchmen to leave on French vessels to join the armies of France against Prussia. Even though the ships carried considerable quantities of arms and ammunition aboard (96,000 rifles and 11,000,000 cartridges), the group involved did not represent an organized hostile expedition, hence no question of a violation of United States neutrality was involved. Similarly, Sweden

---

[27] Convention XIII, The Hague, 1907, Artcle 1: "Belligerents are bound to respect the sovereign rights of neutral Powers and to abstain, in neutral territory or neutral waters, from any act which would, if knowingly permitted by any Power, constitute a violation of neutrality." Article 1 of Convention V simply asserts "The territory of neutral Powers is inviolable."

was legally correct in permitting some 9,000 of her nationals to leave for service in the cause of Finland after that country was attacked by the Soviet Union on November 30, 1939. On the other hand, the Swedish government virtually became a nonbelligerent neutral for a brief time then, when it permitted recruitment of such volunteers on its territory and then went on to allow its citizens to leave for Finland fully armed and equipped. When fighting broke out again between the Soviet Union and Finland in June, 1941, several thousand Swedish volunteers crossed the frontier into Finland, but this time they received little official encouragement from their own government and most of them were back home by the middle of 1944.[28]

NEUTRAL TRADE

A neutral is not bound to prevent the export, on behalf of one or the other of the belligerents, of arms, munitions, or any other matériel of war by private persons (V, Art. 7), unless, of course, it wishes to prohibit such exports at its own discretion.

Restrictions on Neutral States. A neutral state as such is prohibited from furnishing a belligerent supplies or munitions. This rule has been of particular importance since 1917, that is, since the nationalization of all or numerous industries in certain states. In all cases where production or trade, or both, are in the hands of the state, in whole or in part, the governments in question are prohibited from supplying certain goods, notably arms, munitions, and implements of war in general, or loans, to countries at war. If they insist on an alleged right to do so, they lose their neutral status. Ships of such governments, except warships, are subject to the regulations applicable in the case of blockades, to the laws of contraband, and to other privileges exercised by belligerent states. Loans intended to be used for military purposes cannot be granted legally by a neutral government to a belligerent state. On the other hand, such loans when limited to strictly civilian or relief purposes are legally permitted, as was true in the case of the $10 million credit for civilian relief granted by the United States to Finland in late 1939.

Right of Private Persons to Trade with Belligerents. On the other hand, a neutral state may at its discretion permit private persons to make loans to either or both sides in a conflict, or to sell war materials to belligerents. This is true even in the case of rebellions. No state is bound to prevent its citizens from supplying war material to rebel groups—only the neutral government may not furnish such supplies. Thus Great Britain correctly refused to comply in 1817 with a Spanish demand to prohibit the export of arms and ammunition to the revolted Spanish colonies in Latin America. Sir Christopher Robinson admirably expressed the legal picture in his opinion given by Lord Castlereagh, when he wrote:

[28] Joachim Joesten, "Phases in Swedish Neutrality," 23 *Foreign Affairs* (1945), pp. 324–329, at pp. 325 and 327.

. . . there is no obligation to enforce such prohibition and the remedy against the supply of arms, as contraband of war, is ordinarily found in the vigilance of the injured Government and the penalities it has a right to inflict in the confiscation of such articles." [29]

Somewhat later, on October 15, 1914, the American Secretary of State, Robert Lansing, reiterated this classic approach to the problem of private neutral sales to belligerents:

It should be understood that, generally speaking, a citizen of the United States can sell to a belligerent government or its agents any article of commerce which he pleases. He is not prohibited from doing this by any rule of international law, by any treaty provisions, or by any statute of the United States. . . . Such sales by American citizens do not in the least affect the neutrality of the United States.[30]

In the case of civil wars, most governments tend to tolerate exports of any kind of goods, including munitions and other war materials, to the recognized government of the country afflicted with civil strife. To assist officially with such aid would also be correct, if done at the request of the recognized governments. Some states, however, desiring to preserve strict neutrality even in foreign civil wars, prohibit the export of war materials to either side in such a conflict. This was the policy adopted by the United States in the case of the Spanish Civil War. The Neutrality Act of 1937 was signed by President Roosevelt on May 1 of that year and was followed at once by two proclamations: one listing the commodities to be included under "arms, ammunition and implements of war" under the provisions of the Neutrality Act, and the second, prohibiting trade in such commodities with Spain.[31]

NEUTRAL RELATIONS WITH BELLIGERENT FORCES

Rights of States to Protect Their Neutrality. If any neutral rights are threatened by a belligerent and the neutral state has to resort to the use of force to preserve its lawful rights, such action cannot be regarded as a hostile act and as an abandonment of neutrality (Convention V, Art. 10).

On the other hand, if a neutral state either is unable, or fails for any reason at all, to prevent violation of its neutrality by the forces of one belligerent entering, or even passing through, its territory, then the other belligerent may be justified in attacking the enemy forces on the neutral territory. The degree to which such justification exists depends on the

---

[29] Quoted in Higgins–Colombos, p. 515.

[30] Quoted in T. J. Wertenbaker, "The Price of Neutrality," 157 *Atlantic Monthly* (January, 1936), pp. 100–108, at p. 102.

[31] Text of both proclamations in *The New York Times*, May 2, 1937.

circumstances of any particular instance; above all, the neutral is obliged only to make use of the means at its disposal. If those means are insufficient to prevent a belligerent incursion into neutral territory, no blame can be attached to the neutral—provided the available means have actually been utilized in an effort to block the incursion.

Duties of Neutral States. If a neutral state receives on its territory troops of any belligerent, it is obliged to intern them as far as possible from the theater of war. At the end of the war, the various states which had members of their forces interned in neutral countries have to repay the latter for the expenses incurred in caring for the interned forces (V, Art. 12).

Right of Granting Transit. A neutral is free to authorize the passage across its territory of the sick and wounded belonging to belligerent forces, provided that their means of transport (trains, trucks, and so on) do not carry healthy personnel or war material.

After Russia attacked Finland on November 30, 1939, the British and French governments approached the Norwegian and Swedish governments and announced their intention of sending an expeditionary force to Finland. They requested transit privileges and in return for such an unneutral concession promised to come to the aid of both countries if they were attacked by Russia in retaliation. The Swedish government refused the request at once, and the Norwegian government followed suit three days later.

Following their conquest of Norway in World War II, German forces stationed in that country encountered increasing difficulties in securing replacement personnel as well as supplies, owing to British naval supremacy in the North Sea. In consequence, Germany began to exert pressure on neutral Sweden to grant transit privileges to unarmed German troops and to military supplies so that a new route to Norway from the Baltic could be established. After much hesitation, Sweden acceded to this request, the alternative obviously being a German conquest of the country. The Western Allies appear to have been consulted by Sweden and to have agreed tacitly to the proposed transit agreement, which remained in effect from July 5, 1940, to August, 1943, when Sweden abrogated the agreement with German concurrence.[32]

A more basic violation of Swedish neutral duties took place in the summer of 1941, after the outbreak of hostilities between Germany and the Soviet Union. Sweden succumbed to extraordinary German pressure and permitted the passage of a fully armed and equipped German division from Norway to Finland. This event led to formal British and Russian protests; the Swedish government replied that this was a concession *ad hoc,* granted for that one division and never to be repeated again.

[32] See Bruce Hopper, "Sweden: A Case Study in Neutrality," 23 *Foreign Affairs* (1945), pp. 435-449.

NEUTRAL RIGHTS AND DUTIES IN WARFARE AT SEA

Declaration of Paris (1856). The Declaration of Paris (1856) contained certain provisions relating to warfare at sea: (1) it was established that a blockade had to be effective and not merely a "paper blockade" in order to be legally binding; (2) it was decided that a neutral flag covered an enemy's goods with the exception of contraband of war; and (3) it was asserted that neutral goods were immune from seizure on enemy ships.

CONVENTION XIII OF THE 1907 HAGUE CONFERENCE

The 1907 Hague Peace Conference produced a much more satisfactory document than did its predecessor, and a good deal of the modern law governing relations between belligerents and neutrals is based on Convention XIII Concerning the Rights and Duties of Neutral Powers in Naval War.[33] This instrument, like the convention on land warfare, was largely declaratory of existing customary rules of law. It was signed but not ratified by Great Britain, then the greatest naval power; however, the inclusion of numerous customary rules made the bulk of the instrument applicable to Great Britain.

Inviolability of Territorial Waters. Neutral territory, this time including neutral waters, was again declared to be inviolable (Art. 1). Accordingly, the commission of all hostile acts, including capture and the exercise of the right of search, undertaken by belligerent warships in neutral territorial waters was prohibited (Art. 2). If a vessel was captured in prohibited waters and was still within its jurisdiction, the neutral state had to employ all means at its disposal to release the prize and its crew and to intern the prize crew placed aboard the ship. If the captured vessel was no longer within neutral jurisdiction, the capture state had to release, on demand of the neutral in question, the prize and its crew (Art. 3).

Violations of Neutral Waters. The application of these principles, based on customary international law, may be illustrated through some well-known historical examples.

After a French privateer had captured the *Grange,* a British merchant vessel in Delaware Bay in 1793, the prize was released to its owners at the request of the United States government. In 1864, the Union warship *Wachusett* captured the *Florida,* a Confederate vessel, in the harbor of Bahia, Brazil. The offended neutral government protested against the illegal invasion of its territorial jurisdiction and the United States government ordered a court-martial of the captain of the *Wachusett,* and set the officers and crew of the *Florida* free. The vessel itself could not be restored because it sank after a collision in Hampton Roads, on its way to a Union port. The United States government then ordered an official

[33] Hereinafter referred to as Convention XIII.

salute to the Brazilian flag on the spot where the offense had originally taken place.

During the Russo-Japanese war of 1904–5, Korea and Manchuria, although technically neutral territories, were regarded by both belligerents as being combat zones. Japanese destroyers entered the Chinese port of Chefoo and there captured a Russian destroyer, the *Rieshitel'nyi*. This action was so widely condemned as a violation of Chinese neutrality that the Japanese government felt compelled to issue an elaborate justification of its act, based primarily on an alleged Chinese incapacity to perform the duties of a neutral.[34]

When the German cruiser *Dresden* sought refuge, in March, 1915, in Cumberland Bay, located within the territorial waters of Chile, the Chilean government ordered the vessel to leave within twenty-four hours. The captain of the *Dresden* refused, however, to accede to this request. Five days later a squadron of British warships entered the bay and ordered the German cruiser to surrender. The *Dresden* was thereupon scuttled by its crew.

The British government offered an apology but tempered it with observations which cast doubt on whether the *Dresden* had been interned properly as ordered by the government of Chile.

One of the most famous modern cases dealing with an alleged violation of neutral waters is that of the *Altmark* during World War II. This celebrated incident revolved around the somewhat obvious rule that the immunity of neutral waters holds only as long as belligerent vessels enter such waters only for what is called innocent passage. The *Altmark* was an auxiliary vessel in the service of the German Navy. It entered Norwegian neutral waters on February 14, 1940, with 326 British seamen aboard. Those men had been members of the crews of various British merchant vessels captured or sunk by the German battle cruiser *Admiral Graf von Spee*. The British seamen were being taken to a German port. Norway, as a neutral, had the right to exclude the *Altmark* from its waters but had not chosen to exercise this privilege. The German ship proceeded to sail along the coast of Norway, obviously attempting to evade capture by British warships. When news of this maneuver was received in Great Britain, the British destroyer *Cossack* drove the *Altmark* into Jössing Fjord and removed all British prisoners from the ship.

When the Norwegian government protested against this invasion of its territorial jurisdiction, Great Britain insisted that Norway had failed in its neutral duties as commonly understood in the meaning of Articles 1 and 2 of Convention XIII. The British notes emphasized that Norwegian authorities had ignored a request by the commander of nearby British naval forces that the *Altmark* be searched to make certain that the ship carried no prisoners aboard. Article 5 of Convention XIII also was in-

[34] S. Takahashi, *International Law Applied to the Russo–Japanese War* (1908), pp. 437–444.

voked, which states that "belligerents are forbidden to use neutral ports and waters as a base of naval operations against their adversaries."

The *Altmark* had passed through about 400 miles of Norwegian waters and had even been permitted to sail through the "Bergen Defended Area," forbidden to belligerent warships under the terms of the Norwegian neutrality legislation in force.[35]

Right of Neutral States to Bar Belligerent Warships. While Article 10 of Convention XIII specifically stated that the neutrality of a state was not violated [or, compromised: *n'est pas compromise*] by the mere passage of a belligerent warship and its prizes, every neutral state does have an undoubted and generally acknowledged right to prohibit the passage of belligerent warships (and, by implication, of naval auxiliaries) through its waters. Thus the Netherlands closed its waters to such ships in 1914, and Norway prohibited the passage of belligerent submarines in 1916. On the other hand, a neutral is not bound to issue such prohibitions, either for territorial waters or for ports, as long as neutral jurisdiction is not used for the conduct of hostilities or as a basis of attack against enemies on the high seas. This last possibility was illustrated strikingly in the famous old case of the *Twee Gebroeders:*

THE TWEE GEBROEDERS

British Prize Court, 1800,
3 C. Rob. 162

FACTS

The *Twee Gebroeders* was a Dutch merchant vessel captured by the British man-of-war *L'Espiègle* outside the neutral territorial waters of Prussia during a war between Great Britain and the Netherlands. The British warship was lying inside those neutral waters but sent boats beyond the three-mile limit to capture the *Twee*

Gebroeders, which was then sent to England under command of a prize crew. Prussia claimed in the British prize court that the vessel had been captured illegally and should be restored to its owners.

ISSUE

Was the *Twee Gebroeders* captured through a misuse of neutral territorial water for belligerent purposes?

---

[35] For further details, see Lauterpacht's *Oppenheim*, Vol. II, pp. 693–696; Higgins–Colombos, pp. 510–511, and C. H. Waldock, "The Release of the *Altmark's* Prisoners," 24 *B.Y.I.L.* (1947), pp. 216–238. Consult, on the other hand, Edwin M. Borchard, "Was Norway Delinquent in the Case of the *Altmark?*" 34 *A.J.I.L.* (1940), pp. 289–294, for a defense of the Norwegian position, based primarily on the "public vessel" character of the *Altmark* which was held to have precluded visit, search, or even inspection by Norwegian authorities. The Norwegian Government had adopted that attitude, stressing that the *Altmark* displayed the German Government Service flag, not a naval or merchant marine flag—hence was a "public" vessel and not a navy component in Norwegian eyes: see *Journal of Commerce*, February 20, 1940, pp. 3, 20; consult also Whiteman, Vol. XI, pp. 187–189, 193, 273–275, on the *Altmark* incident.

DECISION

The Court ruled in favor of Prussia and ordered restoration of the vessel, but refused costs and damages claimed because the violation of Prussian neutrality was asserted to have been unintentional and only by mistake.

REASONING

Sir William Scott, the judge, stated in part:

"I cannot but think that such an act as this, that a ship should station herself on neutral territory, and send out her boats (as was done in this case) on hostile enterprises, is an act of hostility much too immediate to be permitted. For, suppose that even a direct hostile use should be required to bring it within the prohibition of the law of nations, nobody will say that the very act of sending out boats to effect a capture is not itself an act directly hostile, not complete, indeed, but inchoate, and clothed with all the characters of hostility. If this could be defended, it might as well be said that a ship lying in a neutral station might fire shot on a vessel lying out of the neutral territory; the injury in the case would not be consummated, nor received on neutral ground; but no one would say that such an act would not be an hostile act, immediately commenced within the neutral territory. And what does it signify to the nature of the act, considered for the present purpose, whether I send out a cannonshot which shall compel the submission of a vessel lying at two miles distance, or whether I send out a boat armed and manned, to effect the very same thing at the same distance? It is in both cases the direct act of the vessel lying in neutral ground. The act of hostility actually begins, in the latter case, with the launching and manning and arming the boat that is sent out on such an errand of force."

In a relevant case arising out of the World War I capture of the German merchant vessel *Düsseldorf* in Norwegian neutral waters, the Privy Council decided[36] that a mistaken invasion of Norwegian waters had taken place. It ordered the return of the vessel to Norway, with suitable expressions of regret, and that the appellant, the Norwegian consul-general in London, was entitled to be paid such expenses of removing the vessel from British waters to Norwegian or other foreign waters as would fall on the government of Norway.

Panama Declaration of 1939. The controversies which had arisen during World War I about real or alleged misuses of Latin American territorial waters, together with the fear in 1939 that the new conflict would spread so close to the shores of South America as to represent a danger of involvement, caused the American republics to take swift action.

Acting in accordance with the provisions of the 1936 Buenos Aires Treaty and the 1938 Declaration of Lima, the foreign ministers of the republics met at the invitation of Panama at Panama City in September, 1939, and approved a number of resolutions designed to preserve the

[36] The *Düsseldorf*, 1920, A.C. 1034–1042.

neutral status of the participating countries.[37] The instruments of the greatest importance were Resolutions V, VII, XIV, and XV. Of these, Resolution V was a General Declaration of Neutrality, establishing for the duration of the war an Inter-American Neutrality Committee. Number VII dealt with contraband of war, and No. XIV, termed the Declaration of Panama, asserted that

As a measure of continental self-protection, the American Republics, so long as they maintain their neutrality, are as of inherent right entitled to have those waters adjacent to the American continent, which they regard as of primary concern and direct utility in their relations, free from the commission of any hostile act by any non-American belligerent nation, whether such hostile act be attempted or made from land, sea or air.

A zone averaging 300 miles around the American continents, except Canada, then was defined, and the governments agreed to "endeavor, through joint representation" to the belligerents, to secure their compliance with the Declaration, "without prejudice to the exercise of the individual rights of each state inherent in their sovereignty"; to "consult together to determine upon the measures which they may individually or collectively undertake" to secure the observance of the Declaration; and,

during the existence of a state of war in which they themselves are not involved, may undertake, whenever they may determine that the need therefor exists, to patrol, either individually or collectively, as may be agreed upon by common consent, and in so far as the means and resources of each may permit, the waters adjacent to their coast within the area above defined.

Reaction to the 300-Mile Zone. These instruments were interesting for several reasons: some of the resolutions mentioned included provisions claimed to represent rules of international law, yet constituting principles not yet generally accepted by the community of nations (transfer of flag, internment of merchant ships), and the establishment of the 300-mile zone created at best a new principle of regional international law and at the least represented an attempt by a group of states to legislate for the belligerent nations of Europe.

The second of these developments brought swift repercussions from countries at war: Great Britain, France, and Germany all refused to accept the validity of the Declaration of Panama. Legal opinion also was divided as to the merits of the "300-mile security zone" established at Panama, and although many of the initial criticisms were based on rather obvious misconceptions of the purposes of the Declaration, other critical observations remained unanswered by the defenders of the new regional concept.[38]

[37] Texts in 34 *A.J.I.L.* (1940), Supp., pp. 1–17.

[38] See Charles G. Fenwick, "The Declaration of Panama," 34 *A.J.I.L.* (1940), pp. 116–119; Philip M. Brown, "Protective Jurisdiction," *ibid.*, pp. 112–116; P. S. Wild,

Havana Declaration of 1940. Germany's violation of the neutrality of Belgium, Luxembourg, Norway, and the Netherlands in the spring of 1940 caused another meeting of the American foreign ministers to be held at Havana in July, 1940. The Declaration resulting from this assembly provided for reciprocal assistance and cooperation for the defense of the Americas in case of attack by a "non-American" nation and a convention signed provided for the provisional administration of European colonies and protectorates in the Americas; an emergency committee was created also to take any needed action pending ratification of the Act of Havana.[39]

Neutral Grant of Asylum to Belligerent Warships. Just as a neutral may bar access to its waters to belligerent warships, so it may grant a temporary asylum to such vessels, their auxiliaries, and to belligerent sea-planes, without being obliged to force them to disarm and to intern them. The reason for the grant of this privilege of asylum is that the ports of all states serve the interests of the traffic on the high seas and the grant of hospitality is necessary under many conditions peculiar to such traffic. Naturally, a belligerent warship enjoying a stay in neutral waters is obligated not to misuse such waters as a base of hostile operations against the enemy. If a neutral admits warships of one party in a conflict, then warships of the opposing party must also be admitted on a basis of complete equality (Article 9, Hague Convention XIII).

Problem of Belligerent Submarines. A major problem in connection with the neutral grant of asylum to belligerent warships arose during World War I in connection with submarines. The Allies had proposed to all neutrals in August, 1916, that no asylum should be granted to belligerent submarines of any sort. The neutrals would not agree on a joint course of action: the United States rejected the Allied proposal; Norway forbade its waters to all belligerent submarines except in the case of distress, a policy also followed by Sweden and the Netherlands; Spain closed her waters to all belligerent submarines regardless of prevailing circumstances.

Prior to entering World War II, the United States closed its waters to all belligerent submarines except in the case of *force majeure;* in the latter instance, a submarine had to travel on the surface as soon as it entered American jurisdiction. Virtually all other neutral states during World War II followed the United States example.

Detention of Warships. If a belligerent warship is granted temporary admission to neutral waters and then refuses to leave after being requested to do so, the neutral host may take all measures necessary to make the vessel incapable of putting to sea as long as the war lasts. An unusual inversion of this fairly common situation occurred in China in 1914. Two

Jr., "The 300-Mile Neutral Belt in International Law," 26 *American Bar Association Journal* (1940), pp. 237–238; and the "Recommendations" submitted by the Neutrality Committee to the participating governments on April 27, 1940, in 35 *A.J.I.L.* (1941), Supp., pp. 38–43, as well as Whiteman, Vol. XI, pp. 451–461.

[39] See Hackworth, Vol. V, pp. 465 ff., for texts and details.

German warships, the *Otter* and the *Vaterland*, happened to be in Chinese neutral waters at the outbreak of World War I. In order to avoid the choice between departure—which most likely would have resulted in the loss of the warships—and internment for the duration of the war, the German government sold both ships to a private company after the crews had dismantled the guns of each vessel and had rendered a major portion of the wireless equipment inoperable. The Chinese government, however, denied the German contention that these acts had converted the ships into merchant vessels and interned both, with their crews, until the end of the war.[40]

One of the spectacular illustrations provided by World War II in connection with the asylum aspect of neutrality was the fate of the German pocket battleship *Admiral Graf von Spee*. This ship, after a battle with three British cruisers in which the German warship suffered loss of its fire-control system among other damages sustained, found asylum in the harbor of Montevideo. The neutral Uruguayan government ordered the *Graf Spee* to leave when the seventy-two hours granted for its stay to make necessary repairs had expired. Because a British squadron had begun to assemble outside of Uruguayan waters to await the emergence of the *Graf Spee*, the captain of the latter vessel ordered the bulk of his crew to transfer to the German merchant vessel *Tacoma*. He then took the *Graf Spee* with a skeleton complement to a point about six miles off shore, but within water claimed by Uruguay to be in its territorial limits. There the German warship was scuttled. The captain committed suicide on the following day. The crew, on being landed, was interned by Uruguay but managed to reach Argentina individually, so that by the end of the war hardly any of the crew remained under Uruguayan control. The *Tacoma* was interned by Uruguay for rendering unneutral services from neutral territory. The hulk of the *Graf Spee* was sold by the German government to a Montevideo contractor for removal.

Neutral Asylum. Abuse of neutral asylum by a visiting belligerent warship is not restricted to the commission of hostile acts in neutral water but may occur through other acts entitling the neutral to end the asylum or to intern the vessel and its crew. Thus an abuse would take place if the vessel intentionally wintered in a neutral port to await reinforcements, if it undertook repairs calculated to increase its combat effectiveness (such as by repairing a damaged fire-control system), and if it remained in its shelter for an undue time in order to escape from attack by an opposing naval force or unit.

An ancient rule, now embodied in Convention XIII, prohibits the setting up of prize courts by belligerents in neutral territory.[41] This practice had been one of the offenses charged by the United States govern-

---

[40] Higgins–Colombos, p. 397.
[41] *The Betsey*, United States, Supreme Court, 1794, 3 Dallas 6, 19.

ment against the French Minister to the United States, Edmond C. Genêt, who, at the outbreak of the war between Great Britain and France in 1793, had attempted to set up prize courts connected with various French consulates in the United States.

REGULATIONS FOR NEUTRAL PORTS

Right of Neutral States to Regulate Their Ports. As mentioned earlier, any neutral state enjoys an absolute right to exclude all belligerent war ships from its ports. This was done by several neutrals during the Russo-Japanese War as well as during World War I. If such vessels are permitted the use of neutral ports, the neutral government also has the right to issue regulations for such visits.

Time Limits. If a neutral permits belligerent warships to enter its ports, the length of their stay must be limited. Under the provisions of Article 12 of Convention XIII, such vessels, in the absence of contrary domestic legislation of the neutral, are granted a maximum stay of twenty-four hours in neutral ports or waters. Article 14 exempts warships entering a neutral port in distress or because of adverse weather, as well as public vessels exclusively dedicated to religious, scientific, or philanthropic purposes.

If, at the outbreak of hostilities, a warship of one of the belligerents happens to be in a neutral port, it must be given notice to leave within twenty-four hours, or within the limit prescribed by domestic regulations of the neutral (Art. 13, Convention XIII). A well-known illustration of this situation was supplied by the Russian gunboat *Mandjur*, lying in the port of Shanghai at the outbreak of the Russo-Japanese War in 1904. The Chinese government ordered the vessel to leave within twenty-four hours, but the captain refused to carry out this lawful order because of the presence of a Japanese warship hovering outside the Chinese territorial waters. After some six weeks of discussion, the armament of the *Mandjur* was dismantled to the satisfaction of the Japanese authorities and the ship was allowed to remain in the port until after the war had terminated.[42]

Should warships of opposing belligerents happen to be in the same neutral port, the provisions of Article 16 of Convention XIII apply: a period of not less than twenty-four hours must elapse between the departure of the ship of one belligerent and that belonging to the other. The order of departure normally would be determined by the order of arrival in the port. If a merchant vessel of one belligerent and a warship of an opposing one happen to be in a neutral port, the warship would not be permitted to leave until twenty-four hours had elapsed after the departure of the merchant vessel.

Limit on Number of Warships in Port. Article 15 of the convention limits the number of belligerent warships in a neutral port, at any given

[42] Takahashi, *op. cit.*, pp. 418–435.

time, to three—in the absence of conflicting domestic regulations of the neutral state. Some neutrals have reduced this total to two, such as was done by the Netherlands for all ports in the then Netherlands East Indies during the Spanish-American War.

Permissible Repairs. One of the knotty problems posed by the visit of a belligerent warship to a neutral port has to do with the permissible repairs to be undertaken on such a vessel. Article 17 of the Hague Convention provides that only such repairs may be carried out as are absolutely necessary to render the vessel seaworthy; such repairs may not add in any manner whatever to the fighting capacity of the ship. The local neutral authorities are to decide what repairs are necessary, and the latter must be carried out as speedily as possible.

Recent wars, especially the Russo-Japanese conflict and World War I, have provided numerous additional examples of the visits of belligerent warships to neutral ports and of the resulting complications as far as the neutral was concerned. A mass problem arose in the case of the United States during World War I when a number of German warships (the *Prinz Eitel Friedrich*, the *Kronprinz Wilhelm*, and the *Geier*, together with the naval auxiliary *Locksun*) came to neutral American ports for repairs. Failing to achieve their avowed purpose in the relatively short time limit permitted them by the United States government, all the vessels were interned; on the entrance of the United States into the war as a belligerent, all ships in question were seized as government property.[43]

Reprovisioning and Refueling. As far as reprovisioning and refueling of belligerent warships in neutral ports and waters are concerned, the question of provisions is regulated by Article 19 of the Hague Convention: such reprovisioning is legal up to the peacetime standard of the vessel in question. The provisions of the same article (par. 2) dealing with refueling have, on the other hand, led to considerable controversy and caused Great Britain as well as Japan to reject them in 1907. The article stated that belligerent warships could only take on enough fuel to enable them to reach the nearest port of their own country. On the other hand, in neutral countries which had adopted the "bunker rule," a belligerent warship could take on enough fuel to fill its bunkers to capacity.[44]

Article 20 of the Hague Convention stated that belligerent warships that had refueled in a neutral port could not replenish their fuel supplies in a port belonging to the same neutral, within a period of three months.

Armed Merchant Vessels. None of the foregoing rules governing belligerent warships in neutral waters has any application to defensively armed merchant vessels of belligerent registration. Such ships are, proper-

---

[43] James W. Garner, *International Law and the World War* (New York: Longmans, Green & Co., 1920), II, at pp. 423–425.

[44] See the extensive commentary in the *Harvard Draft*, pp. 472–476, as well as Higgins–Colombos, pp. 525–528, for a British analysis of the controversy as well as of recent practice.

ly, regarded as falling into the category of private vessels, even if they are state property through some form of nationalization. It should be mentioned, however, that many neutrals during both World Wars laid down specific regulations as to what each considered to be purely defensive armament for merchant vessels. If a given ship exceeded the permitted maximum armament (caliber of guns, deck reinforcements, and so on), it was treated by the neutral in question as a warship and was subject to the rules applicable to that category.

Supplying Belligerent Warships at Sea. What about the question of supplying a belligerent warship at sea from neutral territory or waters? Thus far there exists no rule of international law governing this problem, although it appears obvious that a binding rule would be desirable. The British interpretation, dating back to 1870, is that as part of a neutral's duties of abstention, it is incumbent on him to prevent vessels flying its flag from serving as suppliers of belligerent warships at sea. Other countries have not generally followed this concept and thus it appeared lawful for German colliers to follow the Russian Baltic fleet on its epic and disastrous journey to the Far East during the Russo-Japanese War and to keep on supplying the Russians with food and especially fuel.

On a regional basis, the British view of the question was adopted in February, 1940, by the Inter-American Neutrality Committee through a recommendation that a neutral state must prevent merchant vessels in its waters from contacting belligerent warships for the purpose of assisting them with provisions and fuel. The recommendation was caused by the case of the *Tacoma*, a German merchant vessel in the service of the *Admiral Graf von Spee* in 1939, while the *Tacoma* was in neutral waters and the German warship on the high seas.[45]

Use of Neutral Ports for Captured Prizes. Articles 21–23 of Convention XIII regulate the use of neutral ports by prizes captured by belligerents. According to the very definite terms of the instrument, prizes may be brought into neutral ports only because of lack of seaworthiness, unfavorable weather conditions, or a shortage of fuel or provisions. The prize must leave the neutral port as soon as the conditions causing its entry have ceased or have been removed. Should the vessel not leave then, the neutral is obligated to order an immediate departure and, failing to secure compliance, must employ all means available to free the vessel and crew and release them, while interning the prize crew (Art. 21).

If a prize crew brings a prize into a neutral port for any reason not mentioned in Article 21, the neutral government is obligated to release the prize and intern the prize crew (Art. 22). On the other hand, under the provisions of Article 23, the neutral *may* permit prizes to enter its ports if they are brought there for sequestration (safekeeping) pending a decision of the prize courts of the captor belligerent. The United States, Great Britain, and Japan all opposed this Article at the 1907 Hague Con-

[45] See 34 *A.J.I.L.* (1940), Supp., p. 80, and Whiteman, Vol. XI, pp. 256–261.

ference and refused to accept it on signing Convention XIII. Despite the permissive wording of the Article, it quite obviously set aside, for practical purposes, the desirable prohibitions enshrined in Articles 21 and 22.

Articles 21 and 22 became well known through the case of the *Appam*.[46] This ship, a British passenger liner, had been captured by a German warship off Africa and had been brought across the Atlantic by a German prize crew. After the vessel arrived in the neutral American port of Newport News, the government of the United States set free the ship's crew and passengers, and interned the prize crew. The British owners then sued to obtain the release of the *Appam* itself. The U.S. District Court ruled that Articles 21 and 22 of Convention XIII, being declaratory of existing customary law, prohibited neutral ports from becoming places of asylum; that the *Appam* had been brought to the United States for reasons other than unseaworthiness, adverse weather, or lack of fuel or provisions; that in accordance with international law, the vessel should be released to its owners. When the case came before the Supreme Court by appeal, the decision of the court of first instance was affirmed.

TRANSFER OF REGISTRY

Test of the Lawful Flag. It appears appropriate at this point to insert a brief comment on the rules governing transfers of state registry in time of war.

Even before World War I, the flag of a neutral state was the decisive factor in determining the nationality of a vessel only if the flag was used legitimately. If it was found that a given vessel had no right, under the law of a neutral state, to display the flag of the latter, then further investigation had to be undertaken to determine the true nationality and hence enemy or neutral character of the vessel.

Article 57 of the Declaration of London made this test of the "lawful flag" conclusive except in the case of a transfer of registry. Both Great Britain and France initially adopted Article 57 as a guiding principle at the outbreak of World War I, but soon abandoned it again when it became evident that German interests were buying neutral vessels and sailing them under neutral flags in the interests of Germany. Both Great Britain and France then turned to the test of the nationality of the owner as conclusive of the nationality of a vessel.

Transfer of an Enemy Vessel to a Neutral Flag. The transfer of registry of a vessel from belligerent to neutral flag posed a quite different problem. This has been covered by Articles 55 and 56 of the Declaration of London which provided that: "The transfer of an enemy vessel to a neutral flag effected before the outbreak of hostilities is valid, unless it is proved that such transfer was made in order to evade the consequences to which an enemy vessel, as such, was exposed." There was, furthermore,

[46] United States Supreme Court, 1916, 243 U.S. 124; see also the comments of James Brown Scott in 10 *A.J.I.L.* (1916), pp. 809–831.

a presumption that if the "bill of sale is not on board a vessel which has lost her belligerent nationality less than sixty days before the outbreak of hostilities, that the transfer is void. This presumption may be rebutted"; and

When the transfer was effected more than thirty days before the outbreak of hostilities, there is an absolute presumption that it is valid if it is unconditional, complete, and in conformity with the laws of the countries concerned, and if its effect is such that neither the control nor the profits earned by the vessel remain in the same hands as before the transfer.

In November, 1939, it was reported that a number of German vessels including the liner *Bremen*, had been sold to the Soviet Union against deliveries of war materials and other products. The French government promptly announced that, in accordance with French practice dating back to July 26, 1776, and with Article 56 of the 1909 Declaration of London, any such vessel would be treated as an enemy vessel and its sale to Russia would not be accepted as valid.

Generally speaking, a prewar transfer of registry would also be regarded as void if the agreement in question contained provisions for repurchase by the former owners at the termination of the war.

In all instances in which a transfer of registry would be treated as void by a belligerent, the vessel would be considered to possess enemy character. Its loss or seizure and confiscation would not result in a valid claim against the captor state.

Transfer of Title to a Public Vessel. Transfer of title to a public vessel, particularly in the case of a warship of any kind, from enemy to neutral hands cannot be effected after the outbreak of a war. The classic instance of such an attempt occurred in 1914, when the German government sold the cruisers *Breslau* and *Goeben* to the then still neutral government of Turkey. The two ships, caught in the Mediterranean at the outbreak of the conflict, found refuge at Constantinople. Past Anglo-American prize court decisions indicated clearly that such a transfer could not be accepted as valid by belligerents and Great Britain was legally correct in holding, in 1914, that both cruisers were still enemy warships. The dispute in question became quite academic, of course, when Turkey entered the war as an ally of the Central Powers and the two cruisers, flying the Turkish flag, became a part of the fleets of Great Britain's enemies.[47]

It should be mentioned that, once a neutral vessel has acquired enemy status, all enemy goods aboard may be confiscated or destroyed, and neutral goods aboard such vessels will be presumed to be enemy goods unless and until the neutral owners can prove otherwise.

---

[47] See also the account, on a day-by-day basis, of the two vessels' trip to Turkey in Barbara W. Tuchman, *The Guns of August* (New York: Macmillan, 1962), at pp. 137–162.

CONTRABAND

Few areas in the sphere of international law have caused as many disputes to arise as the problem of what goods are to be regarded as contraband of war and therefore subject to seizure by a belligerent.[48]

Concept of Contraband. All authorities agree that the concept of contraband always involves two primary factors: the nature of the goods in question (their susceptibility of belligerent use) and an enemy destination. For several centuries statesmen and jurists also were in agreement that there existed three categories: (1) absolute contraband, (2) conditional contraband, and (3) noncontraband—even though these terms were not always used in practice.

Since the days of Hugo Grotius, a neutral supplying a belligerent with goods primarily useful for the prosecution of the war had to be regarded as being on that belligerent's side and such goods could be captured and condemned by an opposing belligerent: such goods, traditionally embracing arms and other war materials, were classified as *absolute contraband*. Goods useful in *both* peace and war and destined for a belligerent country were subject to seizure at an opposing belligerent's choice and could be included in the category of *conditional (occasional) contraband*. Goods obviously not contributing to a belligerent's war effort were considered to be *noncontraband* and could not be seized lawfully.

It became the practice of states to draw up lists of absolute and conditional contraband at the outbreak of hostilities. As war became more technological in character and as the "nation in arms" became increasingly a reality, more and more items were added to the list of conditional contraband goods while, at the same time, more and more items from that category were shifted to the absolute contraband lists. By the end of World War I almost every item conceivably of use to the enemy was on the absolute contraband lists of both sides: even rubber dolls were included, since that material could be converted into war materials. And World War II saw such an extension of the concept of absolute contraband that just about every commodity was subject to seizure and condemnation.

Doctrine of Continuous Voyage. In the determination of the lawfulness of such seizure, the doctrine of continuous voyage played a key role. This concept had its origin in the so-called "Rule of the War of 1756." In that conflict between Great Britain and France, the latter being cut off from direct trade with its colonies by British naval superiority, waived hitherto asserted monopolies and permitted neutral Netherlands vessels to carry on trade between the colonies and the mother country, under special licenses. Other neutrals were, however, still barred from such trade. The British prize courts correctly assumed that the Dutch vessels engaged in this trade

[48] Lauterpacht's *Oppenheim*, Vol. II, pp. 798–830. See Higgins–Colombos, pp. 541–563, for a brief but excellent discussion of the historical background, as well as Corbett, pp. 243–247, for the modern period.

had identified themselves with the French cause to an extent justifying seizure and condemnation of both vessels, and cargoes. When the French opened such colonial trade as well as their coastal trade to all neutrals in 1793, Great Britain extended the Rule of 1756 to all such neutral commerce.[49] The United States accepted and followed this expanded doctrine and, during the American Civil War, extended the concept of continuous voyage to contraband. Repeated decisions of the Supreme Court affirmed that if contraband goods, ostensibly destined for a neutral country, were eventually to be carried on to a belligerent country, that ultimate destination became the governing factor and the goods could be seized and condemned on their way to the neutral country.[50] Subsequent extensions of the doctrine applied it also to shipments which would go from the ostensible neutral destination to their ultimate belligerent destination by way of land transport.[51]

Major maritime powers happily seized on this new doctrine, and it found general application in the Boer War as well as in both World Wars. In all instances, however, seizure of goods under the doctrine of continuous voyage had to be undertaken on the high seas and not in neutral waters, for that would have violated neutral territorial jurisdiction.

The burden of proof of the forbidden nature or destination of goods aboard neutral vessels used to be based on the papers aboard the ship. This old-fashioned reliance disappeared, for obvious reasons, when the doctrine of continuous voyage in its expanded form was applied to such shipments, because in every instance the papers in question would give an innocent, neutral destination. Hence, one of the interesting aspects of the application of the doctrine during World War I had to do with the "rationing" of neutrals. The major belligerents in that conflict collected statistics on the average imports of certain commodities by selected neutral states over a period of years before 1914. When it could be shown that shipments of such goods greatly exceeded the average prewar imports, a presumption of ultimate enemy destination was asserted and the goods were seized and condemned.[52]

Navicert System. In modern war, therefore, the burden of proof is shifted to the captor government which has to prove to its own prize

---

[49] See T. Baty, "The History of Continuous Voyage," 90 *University of Pennsylvania Law Review* (1941), pp. 127–136.

[50] See *The Peterhoff*, United States, Supreme Court, 1866, 5 Wallace 28; *The Springbok*, 1866, 5 Wallace 1; *The Bermuda*, 1865, 3 Wallace 514.

[51] See Higgins–Colombos, p. 546, for the Italian prize court decision in the case of *The Doelwijk*. See also the illuminating decision in *In re Part Cargo ex S.S. Monte Contes (Conservas Cerqueira Limitada)* v. *H.M. Procurator General*, Great Britain, Judicial Committee of the Privy Council, 1943, 60 Times Law Reports 57, in 38 *A.J.I.L.* (1944), pp. 305–310.

[52] See the leading British cases on the subject: *The Kim*, 1915, P. 215; *The Antares*, 1915, I. B. & C. P. C. 261; *The Baron Stjernblad*, 1918, A.C. 173 (P. C.); The *Urna* affirmed 1920, A. C. 899.

courts that the seized cargo was indeed destined for an opposing belligerent and consisted of prohibited goods.

In order to permit an unhindered flow of legitimate trade between neutrals themselves as well as between them and belligerents, a number of devices have been developed during recent wars. First, during World War I, came a series of agreements concluded between the British government and merchants' associations in various neutral countries. Those instruments provided for a guarantee by the merchants that goods imported by them would not reach the enemies of Great Britain, while the latter in turn undertook not to interfere with shipments to the merchants' associations, subject to exceptional instances of suspected fraud. A little later the famous "navicert system" was evolved. This consisted originally of the granting by the British government of "letters of assurance" to neutral shipping companies after the cargoes of particular shipments had been investigated and approved. Beginning in March, 1916, American shippers began to utilize similar documents, called *navicerts*, issued to them by Allied diplomatic and consular agents in the United States. These documents allowed a vessel and its cargo to proceed without hindrance from the United States to its neutral destination—thus obviating the delay normally involved by enforced inspection in a British port. As the war went on, the navicert system was expanded greatly and was applied also to shipments from Latin America. Navicerts were reintroduced at the outbreak of World War II and expanded even beyond the scope the system had attained in the earlier conflict. A final expansion of the system took place in June, 1941, when mailcerts began to be issued by the British Ministry of Economic Warfare in order to pass packages and letters containing merchandise through the British contraband control.

Doctrine of Infection. What would be the effect on innocent goods carried aboard a neutral vessel if the latter were found to carry contraband commodities belonging to the same owner as did the innocent goods? Here enters a famous theory known as the *doctrine of infection.* For over 250 years, British prize courts, followed later by similar agencies in such countries as the United States and Japan and ultimately incorporated in the 1909 Declaration of London, have ruled that if innocent goods belonging to the same owner as contraband goods are found on a neutral vessel, the "innocent" goods are subject to seizure and condemnation.

Disposition of Captured Neutral Vessels. A captured neutral vessel is not supposed to be sunk or otherwise destroyed but is to be taken to the nearest port of the captor for action by a prize court. This is an old principle of customary law, reinforced by Article 48 of the Declaration of London. However, Article 49 of the same instrument provides that if such transfer to a belligerent port entails great danger to the captor, the vessel may be destroyed *provided* it is liable to condemnation by a prize court. During both World Wars the Allied Powers opposing Germany observed Article 47 fairly well, but German practice in World War I and Axis practice in the second conflict, was more often the destruction of captured vessels than attempts to bring such to a port of the captor state. In extenuation of these acts, particularly on the part of Germany, it should be pointed out that British naval superiority made it exceedingly difficult and dangerous for German prize crews to try to bring captured Allied or neutral merchant vessels into German ports for judicial action.

Finally, a modern development full of perplexing questions to the jurist has been the emergence of neutral governments as such dealing in contraband goods. A lawful belligerent attempt to stop such traffic is bound to lead to an immediate dispute between two states. This vexatious kind of neutral activity had its origin early in World War II.[53] As yet, the legal conclusions to be drawn from such obvious unneutral services have not been delineated clearly.

UNNEUTRAL SERVICE

Neutral ships are subject to capture and condemnation if they engage in unneutral services or hostile assistance, in the terminology of the Declaration of London. The latter instrument asserted the existence of two categories of unneutral services (Arts. 45, 46), but this distinction was dropped in practice at about the middle of World War I. Henceforth the traditional rule prevailed again: a neutral ship performing services for an enemy belligerent will be treated as an enemy ship.

What are unneutral services? The Declaration of London listed them and the list is quite instructive.

Proscribed Passengers. A neutral ship may not carry persons incorporated in the armed forces of a belligerent. If such individuals travel individually and not in uniform, then the direct knowledge of the ship's master or owner has to be proven before the vessel may be condemned. However, if such proscribed passengers are found aboard a neutral vessel, without the knowledge mentioned, they may be made prisoners of war and removed from the vessel even when the latter is not subject to capture.

Proscribed Services. A neutral vessel may not participate directly in hostilities; it may not be under the orders or control of an agent placed aboard by a belligerent government; it may not be in the exclusive service of such a government; it may not be exclusively engaged at the time in the transport of belligerent troops; it may not be engaged at the time in the transmission of intelligence in the interests of a belligerent government.

The classic case in the history of unneutral service was that of the British mail steamer *Trent*. In 1861 a Union cruiser stopped the *Trent*, then on its way from Havana to St. Thomas, and took from it by force two Confederate commissioners, Mason and Slidell, on their way to London and Paris, respectively. The Union government asserted that since dispatches constituted contraband, the bearers of such dispatches fell

[53] See Lester H. Woolsey, "Government Traffic in Contraband," 34 *A.J.I.L.* (1940), pp. 498–503.

"under the same condemnation." The British answer insisted that the office held by the two seized men did not in any manner make them contraband. The government of the United States released the two captives, however, in view of the fact that they had been removed from the *Trent;* it believed that the correct procedure should have been to bring the vessel for examination before a prize court.

Another famous case involving the concept of unneutral service was that of the *Manouba*.[54] This vessel, a French mail steamer, was stopped during the Italo-Turkish War in 1912 by an Italian warship and taken to the Italian port of Cagliari. Aboard the *Manouba* were twenty-nine Turkish citizens suspected of being incorporated in the Turkish armed forces. The Italian captain made no demand for the surrender of these enemy citizens until Cagliari was reached. There the Turks were removed from the *Manouba* and the vessel was released, having been in port one day. There was no evidence that the owners and the master of the ship had acted in bad faith. The French government protested against the taking of the *Manouba* to Italy, and the dispute eventually was submitted to the Permanent Court of Arbitration. The tribunal awarded damages to France because the arrest of the vessel should have been preceded by a demand for the surrender of the Turks, but emphasized that such a demand would have been lawful on suspicion of the character of the passengers in question.

Enemy Male Citizens of Military Age. More recent decisions, particularly during World War II, have shown that a belligerent nowadays appears to possess a right to remove male enemy citizens of military age and apparently good health from neutral vessels even if such individuals are not members of an enemy's armed forces.[55] The presumption justifying such capture is that the individuals in question, under generally prevailing conscription laws, will be incorporated in such forces when they reach their own country and must be considered to be on their way to swell the ranks of an enemy's military or naval forces.

Communications. Other aspects of unneutral service, much emphasized in the days before radio communications, centered on the carrying of enemy dispatches, an act universally considered to represent assistance to an enemy, hence leading to confiscation of the vessel engaged in such carriage. Such dispatches would nowadays involve communications between a belligerent government and its nonaccredited agents in neutral countries, as well as those addressed to persons in the military service of a belligerent.

[54] *The Manouba,* Permanent Court of Arbitration, May 16, 1913; English text in G. G. Wilson, *Hague Arbitration Cases* (1915), pp. 341–352.

[55] The traditional legal attitude was defended eloquently by Herbert W. Briggs, "Removal of Enemy Persons from Neutral Vessels on the High Seas," 34 *A.J.I.L.* (1940), pp. 249–259, caused by the incident of the *Asama Maru* on January 21, 1940; but see Lauterpacht's *Oppenheim,* Vol. II, pp. 845-846, for additional modern examples of the practice.

On the other hand, a neutral vessel may lawfully carry communications between a belligerent government and its accredited diplomatic and consular agents in neutral countries and may also carry such agents themselves without being guilty of an unneutral service. On rare occasions, diplomatic agents of enemy belligerents have been removed from neutral vessels, but in every major case, following strong protests, such personages have been released again. Higgins and Colombos cite the case of the Counsellor at the British Embassy in Moscow who was taken off an Estonian vessel by a German cruiser in December, 1939, while he was on his way to a new post in neutral Bolivia. Following a strong protest by the United States (it was protecting British interests in Germany at the time), the British diplomat was released by Germany.[56]

It should be mentioned, before leaving this subject, that if a neutral vessel is condemned for performance of an unneutral service, its cargo, regardless of ownership or nature, is normally condemned with the vessel.

HOSTILE BLOCKADE

Definition of Hostile Blockade. A hostile or wartime blockade has been defined as "the blocking by men-of-war of the approach to the enemy coast, or a part of it, for the purpose of preventing ingress and egress of vessels or aircraft of all nations." [57] Unlike the situation encountered in the instance of a pacific blockade, the hostile version applies to all merchant vessels and to all cargoes, irrespective of character or nationality, that attempt to enter or leave the area declared to be under blockade. Any violators may be captured, and their cargoes confiscated. This strict barring of all access is waived, occasionally, only as a matter of comity in the case of neutral warships, and on grounds of humanity in the case of neutral merchant vessels in distress [58] or engaged in a strictly philanthropic mission not contrary to the war aims of the blockading state.[59]

The modern concept of a hostile blockade had its origin in the sixteenth century when, in 1584, the revolting Dutch provinces declared all ports of Flanders, then still under Spanish control, to be blockaded. Since then, the institution has been developed to a point where it has become a major weapon in the effort to bring about victory on the part of a maritime power against a coastal state.

Thus, although the initial application of a blockade was aimed only at fortified towns and ports along an enemy coast, the concept was broadened and by the time of the Napoleonic wars the entire coast of an enemy

[56] Higgins–Colombos, p. 513.

[57] Lauterpacht's *Oppenheim*, Vol. II, p. 768; see also Chapter 26.

[58] Article 7, Declaration of London (1909), under which a vessel permitted to pass through a blockading force under the conditions mentioned could not load or discharge cargo in the blockaded area. See also *The Fortuna*, Great Britain, 1803, 5 C. Rob. 27, and *The Nuestra Señora de Regla*, United States, Supreme Court, 1872, 17 Wallace 29.

[59] See *The Rose in Bloom*, Great Britain, 1811, 1 Dodson 57.

state was declared to be under blockade. The United States viewed this development with disfavor and defended repeatedly, as late as 1859, the total abolition of commercial blockades; this attitude changed drastically, however, with the beginning of the American Civil War, and the Union government promptly and quite successfully blockaded the entire coastline of the Confederacy.

In order to be legal, a hostile blockade must meet certain well-established tests: (1) declaration, that is, notification of the blockading state to all neutrals of the establishment of the blockade; and (2) effectiveness of the blockade.

Declaration of a Blockade. Declaration of a blockade may only be made by a belligerent government or by its naval authorities on its behalf and under its explicit authority. The declaration must specify the date of the commencement of the blockade, the geographical limits of the blockaded area, and the period of grace normally permitted neutral vessels to come out of the blockaded area. As far as the third point is concerned, no particular period of time has been specified in conventional law. Customarily, fifteen days have been permitted during which neutral vessels in ballast or with cargoes bought and loaded before the beginning of a blockade have been allowed to leave unhindered. On the other hand, the United States granted thirty days for this purpose during the Spanish-American War, whereas certain blockades established during World War I permitted periods ranging from two to four days only.

Area of Blockade. The blockade is limited to the area of operation of the participating warships (and planes). In view of modern methods of naval warfare, involving aerial and surface operations as well as submarines and mines, a blockading squadron or naval force will tend to station its components at a considerable distance from a blockaded coast, so that the "area of operations" may assume rather extensive proportions.

Disposition of a Captured Neutral Vessel. A neutral vessel seized for an attempted breach of a blockade, either upon ingress or egress, is not to be destroyed; instead, it is to be taken to the nearest port of the captor state (or of one of its allies where a prize court of the captor state may have been established) in order that a proper trial before a prize court may be undertaken. Conviction on a charge of attempting to breach a blockade results in the condemnation of the vessel. The cargo is also condemned if it belongs to the owners of the vessel. If the owners are not the same, the cargo is released only if its owners can prove that at the time of the shipment they did not know, or could not have known, of the vessel's intention to breach the blockade.[60]

Lawful Blockades. Article 18 of the 1909 Declaration of London specifically prohibited the blockading of neutral ports and coasts. On the

___

[60] See the relevant English cases of *The Mercurius,* 1798, 1 C. Rob. 80, and *The Panaghia Rhomba,* 1857, 12 Moore P.C. 168; see the typical American cases of *The Springbok,* 1866, 5 Wallace 1, and *The Peterhoff,* 1866, 5 *ibid.,* 1; consult also Lauterpacht's *Oppenheim,* Vol. II, pp. 789–790.

other hand, no bar exists to a blockade of some of its own ports or coasts by a belligerent if such areas happen to be under enemy territory. Although such a situation, that is, enemy occupation of coastal stretches, has occurred frequently, few belligerents have actually established a blockade such as was done by France in 1870 with respect to the ports of Rouen, Dieppe, and Fécamp.

In view of the resulting advantages, it was not at all surprising that the major maritime powers quickly combined the doctrine of continuous voyage with the rules governing lawful hostile blockades. To be sure, Article 19 of the Declaration of London specifically prohibited application of the doctrine to a blockade, but World War I saw the end of that provision with the issuance of a number of British Orders-in-Council (1916) ordering the arrest of neutral vessels attempting to breach a blockade and suspected of carrying goods ultimately destined to arrive in enemy territory.

The United States discussed the application of continuous voyage concepts to blockade with Great Britain during World War I, and some rather strong diplomatic exchanges took place. But the entrance of the United States into the conflict changed the outlook of the United States government, and all hands appeared to agree that modern conditions of warfare made the old-style limited concept of blockade inappropriate except in the instances of a few island states such as Japan or Great Britain. Hence general agreement appears to prevail today that the old "close" blockade is no longer useful in most instances, that long-range blockades are the only really effective ones, and that the doctrine of continuous voyage may be coupled lawfully with the rules gverning blockades.[61]

Paper Blockade. The question of effectiveness must be discussed briefly at this point. Jurists and statesmen are in agreement that a blockade must be effective, must not be a "paper blockade," if it is to be lawful and binding on neutrals. A valid blockade requires not only naval supremacy on the seas on the part of the blockading state but the detachment of sufficient forces devoted to the maintenance of the blockade to make the latter effective.[62] But over and beyond the availability of blockading ships and planes, the effectiveness of a blockade is, and must be, a question of fact. Thus only a paper blockade came into being initially when President Lincoln declared, in 1861, a blockade of 3,000 miles of Confederate coastline when the Union had at its disposal only forty-two ships, of which only three were of the rating of a frigate. Similarly, effectiveness was lacking during the Crimean War when a single Allied warship claimed to blockade the Russian port of Riga while stationed 120 miles away from the only navigable channel leading to the port.[63]

[61] Lauterpacht's *Oppenheim*, Vol. II, pp. 791–797.

[62] See the case of *The Olinde Rodrigues*, United States, Supreme Court, 1899, 174 U.S. 510, on this point.

[63] See also L. H. Woolsey, "Closure of Ports by the Chinese Nationalist Government," 44 *A.J.I.L.* (1950), pp. 350–356.

Reprisals. Finally it should be mentioned that blockades in time of war have been utilized on many occasions as reprisals, that is, carried on in an illegal manner in order to force an enemy to desist from previously committed illegal acts. Thus Great Britain issued an Order-in-Council on February 16, 1917, in retaliation for the German War Zone proclamation of January 31, 1917. The British order classified all neutral vessels on their way to or from a neutral port affording access to enemy territory, without calling at a British or Allied port, as carrying goods with an enemy destination or of enemy origin, and provided for the arrest and examination, and prize court disposal, of such vessels.[64]

Belligerent institution of illegal interference with neutral commerce in the name of reprisals naturally places neutral states in a most unfortunate position. Because their interests are affected directly and adversely, it is their obligation to decide which one among the contending belligerents first broke the law so that neutral reprisals may be instituted against that belligerent or neutral complaints and claims properly lodged.

Civil Wars and the Blockade. Civil wars pose additional problems connected with the institution of the blockade. The United States and Great Britain have defended for a long time the concept that the *de jure* authorities of a country cannot close ports under the control of rebels by a mere decree, for this would constitute a paper blockade. If the lawful government has sufficient naval strength at its command so that it establishes an effective blockade, then indeed can the ports in question be considered to be closed.[65]

Can rebels lawfully bar entrance to the ports and coasts of the *de jure* government? This, like the previous topic, is the subject of much disagreement among legal experts. Many states refuse to recognize a rebel blockade and, on occasion, have used force to enable their merchant ships to go through such a blockade. Thus in 1893 and 1894, British and United States warships intervened to prevent the rebel Brazilian naval units in the port of Rio de Janeiro from enforcing a blockade against merchant vessels flying the flags of the intervening powers.

Most writers in more recent decades appear to favor, however, the view that if a rebel force has sufficient naval strength to prevent the egress or ingress of merchant vessels at a given port, they have a right to stop supplies from reaching the *de jure* enemy forces. Even Great Britain has accepted this interpretation when, in a given situation, it was clear that the necessary naval strength was present; for example, in Santiago, Chile, in 1891, Great Britain refused a naval convoy to a British ship attempting to breach the rebel blockade.

These considerations form in part the reason why it is so important for

---

[64] See Higgins–Colombos, pp. 603–606, for specific cases arising out of such reprisals.

[65] *Ibid.*, pp. 336–338; consult also Edwin D. Dickinson, "Closure of Ports in Control of Insurgents," 24 *A.J.I.L.* (1930), pp. 69–78.

a rebel group to receive recognition of a state of belligerency or of the status of a belligerent community. Such recognition removes the old suspicion of piracy from rebel vessels; it justifies the application of most rules governing naval war and neutrality to the civil war at hand. In this connection it should be emphasized that if a *de jure* government declares a blockade against any port or any part of its coasts in the control of rebels, such declaration is generally held to constitute a recognition of the group as a belligerent community (state of belligerency) by the parent government.

Recognition as a belligerent (insurgent) community grants to a rebel group the right to visit and search merchant ships on the high seas, to confiscate contraband goods, and to establish valid blockades. Such recognition does not mean, however, that the rebel authorities have been recognized as a successor government or as the government of an independent state.

The naval complications resulting from civil wars have been illustrated dramatically by two well-known examples. The Confederate cruiser *Shenandoah* continued its belligerent operations near Cape Horn for some time after the end of the American Civil War. Obviously, under normal conditions, such behavior would constitute a clear case of piracy. When the *Shenandoah* was seized by British authorities, it developed that her officers and crew were ignorant of the capitulation of the Confederacy. The English authorities, properly, released the officers and crew, clearing them of all charges of piracy, and turned the vessel over to the United States.

During the Spanish Civil War, the attacks made by Italian and German submarines on neutral merchant vessels had led to a very confused situation. Finally, a Conference of the Mediterranean Powers was held at Nyon in September, 1937, (September 14) resulting in an "Arrangement" signed by Belgium, Egypt, France, Great Britain, Greece, Romania, the Soviet Union, Turkey, and Jugoslavia, Italy subsequently indicated its willingness to abide by this pact. The instrument authorized the warships of the signatories, engaged on nonintervention patrol duty, to counterattack and, if need be, destroy any submarine found attacking a merchant vessel not belonging to either party in the Spanish Civil War. The patrol ships were also authorized to adopt the same course of action toward any submarine encountered so close to the scene of an earlier attack that no doubt of its guilt could be entertained reasonably. A supplementary agreement, signed by the same states on September 17, 1937, expanded the scope of the original instrument so as to make its rules applicable to surface vessels as well as to aircraft.

NEUTRAL RIGHTS AND DUTIES IN AIR WARFARE

The extensive utilization of aircraft for military purposes during World War I and the well-publicized failures of aircraft commanders to observe all regulations laid down at the 1907 Hague Conference led to a search for new rules applicable to the air age. The states participating in the 1922 Washington Conference on the Limitation of Armaments therefore appointed a Commission of Jurists to draft a Code of Air Warfare Rules, intended to be supplementary to the Air Navigation Convention of 1919. The code was completed in 1923 but failed of ratification. Nevertheless, several governments announced on subsequent occasions that they would abide by the 1923 Rules, which are generally termed the Hague Air Warfare Rules.

A number of articles of the Hague Air Rules referred to the position of neutrals in air warfare. Thus Article 30 specified the right of a belligerent to warn neutral aircraft off a particular area and to exclude them by force if need be. Article 35 dealt with the treatment of neutral aircraft over land and sea. Article 45 reaffirmed the then already established rule that a neutral state was not obligated to prevent the (private) export of aircraft to belligerents, and Article 46 stated that a neutral state was bound to use the means at its disposal

(1) to prevent the departure from its jurisdiction of any aircraft in a condition to make a hostile attack against a belligerent Power, or carrying or accompanied by appliances or materials the mounting or utilization of which would enable it to make a hostile attack, if there is reason to believe that such aircraft is destined for use against a belligerent Power; (2) to prevent the departure of any aircraft the personnel of which belongs to the combatant forces of a belligerent Power.

There is little doubt that today a few basic rules of customary law have been established with reference to aircraft: belligerent planes must not enter neutral airspace; if they do, then the neutral state is obligated to force them to land and, subsequently, to intern them and their crews for the duration of the conflict. In the case of aircraft carried aboard a warship, such craft may not leave their carriers as long as the latter are in neutral waters, and are treated as components of the vessel carrying them.[66]

In slight contrast to neutral practices during World War I, when personnel of belligerent aircraft rescued at sea by neutral merchant vessels were regarded as shipwrecked sailors and were not interned, Article 43 of the 1923 Rules provided that such military personnel, if rescued by neutral military aircraft and brought to neutral jurisdiction, were to be interned.

As far as a blockade is concerned, legal authorities are virtually unanimous in agreeing that there can be no such thing as an aerial blockade. On the other hand, planes do play a vital part in modern blockades as auxiliaries to naval forces; in addition, planes may be used effectively in preventing the entry or departure of other planes from a blockaded area.

---

[66] See Whiteman, Vol. XI, pp. 355–366.

RIGHT OF ANGARY AND DOCTRINE OF NECESSITY

Early Concept of the Right of Angary. In the Middle Ages, a practice known as *jus angariae*, the law of angary, developed when belligerents lacked sufficient vessels for their purposes. They claimed, under such circumstances, a right to seize neutral merchant ships in their ports and to force them and their crews to carry troops, provisions, and matériel to certain places on payment of freight charges in advance. This practice spread widely until in the seventeenth century, various states concluded bilateral agreements under which their vessels were exempted from the application of the law of angary. The original concept thereupon lapsed from the practice of states until the twentieth century when it reappeared in somewhat changed form.

Modern Concept of the Right of Angary. The modern right of angary consists of a right of belligerents to destroy, or use in case of need, neutral property on their own or on enemy territory and perhaps on the high seas. Unlike the original law, the modern concept applies only to property and does not permit the utilization of neutral crews of ships or trains seized under this right.

Every kind of neutral property is thus susceptible of belligerent seizure, provided it can be used for military purposes. However, in every case in which this right is applied, full compensation must be paid to the neutral owner. This rule is based on customary international law and should not be confused with the provisions for payment found in Article 53 of the Hague Regulations of 1907, which deals with compensation for means of transportation seized from the inhabitants of occupied enemy territory.[67] Examples of the exercise of the right of angary are not common until World War I. A celebrated example usually cited is the German sinking in 1871 of British coal-carriers at Duclair in order to prevent French warships from severing German military communications by moving up the river Seine. When Great Britain protested the act, the Prussian government denied a responsibility to pay compensation to the owners of the vessels, even though it agreed to do so. Some writers have held that this case did not represent an exercise of the right of angary, claiming that it was an example of requisitioning.[68] The present writer cannot agree with this interpretation and believes the German act to have been one based on the right of angary.[69]

Right of Angary During World War I. World War I witnessed the sudden rise to prominence of the doctrine underlying the right of angary. British prize courts frequently justified the seizure of neutral vessels and

[67] Hersch Lauterpacht, "Angary and Requisition of Neutral Property," 27 *B.Y.I.L.* (1950), pp. 455–459; Whiteman, Vol. XI, pp. 329–355; Cheng, pp. 42–43; W. I. Jennings, "The Right of Angary," 3 *Cambridge Law Journal* (1927–1929), pp. 49–57; and von Glahn, pp. 220–221.

[68] Higgins–Colombos, p. 445.

[69] See also a similar view in Lauterpacht's *Oppenheim*, Vol. II, p. 762, n. 5.

their cargoes under that right. Italy, then at war with Austria-Hungary but not yet with Germany, seized, in 1915, thirty-seven German ships in Italian ports and Germany did not protest this action. In February, 1916, Portugal seized seventy-two German vessels in Portuguese waters. In May, 1917, Brazil took over forty-two German ships that had found refuge in Brazilian ports. And in August, 1918, Spain seized ninety German ships found in its ports. All the seizing states were neutrals at the time the events in question took place. Subsequent to, and in consequence of, the ship seizures, Germany declared war on Portugal and Brazil on Germany. On March 20, 1918, the United States had seized seventy-seven Dutch ships then in American ports, promising full compensation to the owners. Within a few days Great Britain, France, and Italy undertook similar steps, all claiming a right to do so under the concept of angary. The Netherlands government protested vigorously but ineffectually against what it asserted to be "an ancient rule unearthed for the occasion and adapted to entirely new correlations in order to excuse seizure *en masse* by a belligerent of the merchant fleet of a neutral country." At the end of World War I, the United States paid in full for the use of the Dutch vessels and returned them reconditioned to their owners; two of the ships were sunk by German submarines and the United States paid for those two vessels in full.

Ships under construction may also be seized by a belligerent under the right of angary—Great Britain was legally correct in confiscating four warships being built in English yards to the order of the Turkish government, at a time when Turkey was still a neutral in World War I. The United States had also seized, in 1917, several incomplete Norwegian vessels and construction contracts. The compensation offered was rejected by Norway and the issue was settled by arbitration, the United States being required to pay $12,239,000 to Norway.

The action of Congress in passing on June 6, 1941, an act [70] enabling the President to purchase or seize, with just compensation, idle foreign ships in the waters under U.S. jurisdiction did not fall within the province of the normal right of angary, because this right usually is considered to be reserved for belligerents and, at the time, the United States was theoretically neutral though nonbelligerent. The action of the United States was followed, incidentally, by the other American republics in August-September, 1941.

Much greater publicity than the cases mentioned was given to the seizure of neutral vessels and cargoes by belligerents on the high seas. Most writers on the subject differ with Oppenheim when he asserted that belligerent states possessed such a right under angary, [71] and instead have asserted that the decision as to whether neutral property can be seized

---

[70] Text in 35 *A.J.I.L.* (1941), Supp., pp. 224–229; see also L. H. Woolsey "The Taking of Foreign Ships in American Ports," 35 *A.J.I.L.* (1941), pp. 497–506.

[71] Lauterpacht's *Oppenheim*, Vol. II, pp. 762; Sir Hersch Lauterpacht supported Oppenheim's view in every edition of Oppenheim's great work edited by him.

on the high seas is a matter for the courts, not for the executive branch, of a belligerent government.[72] The leading case on the subject, the well-known condemnation of the *Zamora*, illustrates this point clearly and points up the conditions under which the right of angary may be exercised on the high seas.

The *Zamora* was a Swedish vessel, on its way from New York to Stockholm with a cargo of copper and grain. On April 8, 1915, the ship was stopped by British cruisers between the Shetland and Faroe Islands, taken to Barrow-in-Furness, and placed before a prize court. On condemnation of the cargo, the case came by appeal before the Privy Council. In the absence of conclusive evidence that the cargo was urgently needed for the defense of the country, the Privy Council disallowed the requisition authorized by the prize court. In reviewing the decision of the prize court in this case, the Judicial Committee of the Privy Council asserted that three conditions had to be met: [73] (1) the neutral vessel or neutral goods had to be urgently required for the defense of the state, the prosecution of the war, or other matters of national security; (2) a real question had to be tried before the prize court so that it would be improper for the latter to order an immediate release of ship or goods; and (3) the applicability of the right of angary to the particular circumstances of each case had to be decided judicially by the prize court.

Basically, seizure of neutral ships or cargoes on the high seas revolves around the fundamental concept of military necessity. In fact, wherever such a seizure is legitimized by a prize court, military necessity has triumphed over the undoubted legal rights of neutrals, despite the inevitable payment of compensation for seized property.

Right of Angary and Land Warfare. One special aspect of the right of angary has to do with *land* warfare. Under the provisions of Article 19 of the Fifth Hague Convention of 1907, a belligerent may seize (or requisition) railroad material (regardless of ownership) coming into its territory from a neutral state, provided that absolute necessity requires this to be done; that such seized properties (rolling stock and motive power) be returned to the country of origin as soon as possible; and that compensation shall be paid for its use. The article in question also provides that a neutral state whose railroad rolling stock has been seized by a belligerent is lawfully entitled to seize and retain, to a corresponding extent, rolling stock and motive power coming from the territory of the belligerent in question. It might be added that these rules have been extended in practice to cover neutral rolling stock and motive power found by a belligerent in occupied enemy territory or coming into such territory in the normal course of any traffic still permitted by the belligerent occupant.

[72] Thus especially Higgins–Colombos, pp. 446–448; see also J. Eugene Harley, "The Law of Angary," 13 *A.J.I.L.* (1919), pp. 267–301.

[73] *The Zamora*, Great Britain, Judicial Committee of the Privy Council, 1916, 2 A.C. 77.

SUGGESTED READINGS

NEUTRALITY: GENERAL

The most comprehensive account of the history and practice of neutrality is to be found in *Neutrality: Its History, Economics and Law*, 4 vols.: I, *The Origins*, Philip C. Jessup and Francis Deák, 1935; II, *The Napoleonic Period*, W. Alison Phillips, 1936; III, *The World War Period*, Philip C. Jessup, 1936; IV, *Today and Tomorrow*, Philip C. Jessup, 1936 (New York: Columbia University Press); Whiteman, Vol. XI, pp. 139–475; Lauterpacht's *Oppenheim*, Vol. II, pp. 666–879; Stone, pp. 384–441, 478–544; Marion C. Siney, *The Allied Blockade of Germany*, *1914–1916* (Ann Arbor: University of Michigan Press, 1957); Gaddis Smith, *Britain's Clandestine Submarines*, *1914–1915* (New Haven: Yale University Press, 1964); Robert D. Powers, Jr., "Blockade: For Winning Without Killing," 84 *U.S. Naval Institute Proceedings* (1958), pp. 61–66; and Arthur K. Kuhn, "Aerial Flights . . . by Belligerents Over Neutral Territory," 34 *A.J.I.L.* (1940), pp. 104–107.

NONBELLIGERENCY

Clyde Eagleton, "The Duty of Impartiality on the Part of a Neutral," 34 *A.J.I.L.* (1940), pp. 99–104; Edwin M. Borchard, "War, Neutrality and Non-Belligerency," *ibid.*, 35 (1941), pp. 618–625; F. R. Coudert, "Non-Belligerency in International Law," 29 *Virginia Law Review* (1942), pp. 143–151.

DESTROYER-BASES EXCHANGE

Daniel S. Greenberg, "U.S. Destroyers for British Bases—Fifty Old Ships Go to War," 88 *U.S. Naval Institute Proceedings* (November, 1962), pp. 70–83; Quincy Wright, "The Transfer of Destroyers to Great Britain," 34 *A.J.I.L.* (1940), pp. 680–689, Herbert W. Briggs, "Neglected Aspects of the Destroyer Deal," *ibid.*, pp. 569–587, and Charles G. Fenwick, "Neutrality on the Defensive," *ibid.*, pp. 697–699.

Cases

The Adula, United States, Supreme Court, 1900, 176 U.S. 361.
The Kim, Great Britain, High Court of Justice, Probate, Divorce and Admirality Division, 1915, L.R. [1915] Probate 215.
The Peterhoff, United States, Supreme Court, 1866, 5 Wallace 28.
See also the incidents surrounding the *City of Flint*, in Charles C. Hyde, "The City of Flint," 34 *A.J.I.L.* (1940), pp. 89–95, Philip C. Jessup, "The Reality of International Law," 51 *Current History* (April, 1940), pp. 13–15, 61, and Theodore Taylor, "A Matter of Judgment," 84 *U.S. Naval Institute Proceedings* (1958), pp. 70–75.

31
Belligerent Occupation

BACKGROUND

T HE present rules governing the occupation of enemy territory in time of war (belligerent occupation, hostile occupation, military occupation) were drawn up after centuries during which no distinction was made between mere occupation and conquest. The general assumption guiding heads of states was that conquest of enemy territory created annexation to the conqueror's own realm. Hence no restrictions on the invader's action in the annexed territory were conceived of, for it was his by right and in law.

As late as 1808, after Russian occupation of Swedish-owned Finland, Czar Alexander I forced the Finnish inhabitants to take an oath of allegiance to him, even though the official cession of Finland by Sweden was not accomplished until September, 1809.[1] English practice as late as 1814 condoned annexation of enemy territory as soon as occupation had taken place.[2] The United States, on the other hand, swung to the modern view as early as 1828 when Chief Justice John Marshall held that "the usage of the world is, if a nation be not entirely subdued, to consider the holding of conquered territory as a mere military occupation, until its fate shall be determined at the treaty of peace." [3]

Army Manuals. A considerable portion of the older rules stipulating the rights and obligations of a military occupant in enemy territory dates back to 1863, to the manual *Instructions for the Government of the Armies of the United States in the Field*, drafted by Professor Francis Lieber and issued, after minor revisions, on April 24, 1863, as General Orders No. 100.[4] The manual remained in force until 1914 when a successor, *Rules of Land Warfare*, was compiled by the War Department.

[1] Lauterpacht's *Oppenheim*, Vol. II, p. 432, n. 2.

[2] *Ibid.,* II, *loc. cit.*: in the case of *The Foltina.*

[3] *American Insurance Company* v. *Peters,* United States, Supreme Court, 1828, 1 Peters 542.

[4] See Doris A. Graber, *The Development of the Law of Belligerent Occupation, 1863–1914* (New York: Columbia University Press, 1949), at pp. 14–20; the text of the *Instructions* may be found in Miss Graber's valuable work on pp. 297–317; consult also G. B. Davis, "Doctor Francis Lieber's Instructions for the Government of Armies in the Field," 1 *A.J.I.L.* (1907), pp. 13–25.

The military forces of other major nations, impressed by the *Instructions*, incorporated large sections of the American work in manuals issued by them to their own armed forces.[5]

Hague Conventions (1899, 1907). Following the drafting of a number of private law codes designed to outline rights and duties involved for both sides in hostile occupation, the basic rules of the relevant modern law were developed at the Hague Peace Conferences of 1899 and 1907. The 1899 Convention with respect to the Law and Customs of War on Land laid the basis for most of today's rules governing military occupation in wartime. The later (1907) Fourth Convention Respecting the Laws and Customs of War on Land and its appended Regulations, especially Articles 23g, 23h, and 42–56, detailed the rules adopted officially by the bulk of the states of the world into their military manuals.

Bellot Rules of War. After the experiences of World War I, the question of revising and expanding the provisions of the 1907 Hague Convention and its Regulations was brought up at several conferences (Madrid, Monaco, Liège), but no action resulted. The International Law Association, a private body, adopted in 1928 at Warsaw the so-called Bellot Rules of War in Occupied Territory. Dr. Hugh H. Bellot had based his liberal proposals on the Fourth and Fifth Hague Conventions of 1907, on the British and American military manuals, and on occupation practices and problems of World War I.

1949 Geneva Conventions. The second global conflict produced such gross violations of customary and conventional law applicable to occupation of enemy territory and resulted in such inhuman treatment of helpless enemy civilians caught in the hands of German, Japanese, and later Russian armies of occupation, that the need for a revision of the legal rules became undeniable.

The International Committee of the Red Cross emerged as the agency able to prod somewhat reluctant governments into action. After a number of preliminary meetings had been held, the Swiss government convened the Diplomatic Conference for the Establishment of International Conventions for the Protection of Victims of War. The conference met at Geneva from April 21 to August 12, 1949, was attended by representatives of sixty-three governments as well as by observers from many international organizations, and resulted in four conventions. The fourth of these, the Geneva Convention Relative to the Protection of Civilian Persons in Time of War, is the one related most intimately to the subject at hand.[6]

---

[5] Gerhard von Glahn, *The Occupation of Enemy Territory: A Commentary on the Law of Belligerent Occupation* (Minneapolis: University of Minnesota Press, 1957), at pp. 8, 12–14. This chapter is based in large part on the above study which is the latest general analysis of the subject. See also Stone, pp. 693–726, for a very good summary.

[6] See Jean Pictet, "The New Geneva Conventions for the Protection of War Victims," 45 *A.J.I.L.* (1951), pp. 462–468; Joyce A. C. Gutteridge, "The Geneva

Law of Land Warfare. After the United States had ratified the four conventions and they were in force with respect to this country (February 2, 1956),[7] the U.S. Department of the Army revised its rather outdated 1940 military manual and issued (July, 1956) a completely revised version, *The Law of Land Warfare*,[8] including the text of all four 1949 Geneva Conventions, with much valuable supplementary commentary.

Fourth Geneva Convention. The major provisions of the Fourth Geneva Convention have been incorporated in the rest of this chapter. Article 2, however, merits brief comment at this point; it stated that the convention would apply not only in declared wars but also in all other armed conflicts between two or more of the contracting parties, even if a state of war was not recognized by one of them. The convention would apply, furthermore, even if partial or total occupation of a party's territory met with no armed resistance. If, in a future conflict, one of the parties concerned were not a contracting party to the convention, it would still apply to all other parties in their mutual relations. And if the noncontracting party to a war should accept and apply the provisions of the convention, all contracting parties were bound to apply the instrument to the noncontracting party in question.

Despite its many valuable additions to the hitherto existing rules governing military occupation, the Fourth Convention left untouched many important facets of the occupation of enemy territory, particularly in the economic sphere. Such gaps will be mentioned below, but full treatment of the "missing rules" must by necessity be left to specialized treatments of the subject.

RIGHTS AND OBLIGATIONS OF THE OCCUPANT

Lawful Occupation. Territory is considered occupied when it is actually placed under the authority of the hostile army, according to Article 42 of the 1907 Regulations. Invasion, therefore, precedes but does not correspond to occupation; the latter comes into being when the enemy government has been rendered incapable of exercising its authority in a

---

Conventions of 1949, 26 *B.Y.I.L.* (1949), pp. 294–326; and Raymond T. Yingling and Robert Ginnane, "The Geneva Conventions of 1949," 46 *A.J.I.L.* (1952), pp. 393–427. The complete text of the Fourth Convention was reprinted in 50 *A.J.I.L.* (1956), Supp., pp. 724–783.

[7] See von Glahn, pp. 18–19, for some of the reasons involved in the delay in American ratification.

[8] Department of the Army, Field Manual FM 27–10, *The Law of Land Warfare* (Washington, D.C.: Government Printing Office, 1956); hereinafter referred to as *Law of Land Warfare*. It should be noted that, on June 9, 1959, it was announced that the U.S. Department of the Army had authorized the deletion of the term "military government": henceforth the term "civil affairs" has been utilized exclusively; see also Harold D. Cunningham, Jr., "Civil Affairs—A Suggested Legal Approach," *Military Law Review* (October, 1960), pp. 115–137.

given area. The invader (occupant) then substitutes his own authority for that of the legitimate sovereign. So-called fictitious occupations, created by the dispatch of flying columns into enemy territory, are not lawful occupations.

Three Systems of Law. The result of belligerent occupation, then, is that three distinct systems of law apply in territory under an enemy occupant: the indigenous law of the legitimate sovereign, to the extent that it has not been necessary to suspend it; the laws (legislation, orders, decrees, proclamations, regulations) of the occupant, as such are gradually introduced; and the applicable rules of customary and conventional international law.

Maintenance of Occupation. Once occupation has been established on a *de facto* basis, it has to be maintained in order to continue in existence. If the invader is expelled by the forces of the invaded state or of the latter's allies, occupation ceases. If the indigenous population, revolts successfully and evicts the occupant, the occupation also ceases and if, at a later date, it is restored, the native population should not be punished for its earlier and successful eviction of the occupant. (*Law of Land Warfare,* par. 360). If an invader fails to establish effective control over a portion of the enemy's territory, all orders issued by him are devoid of legal force.

Right of Administration. Legal writers are in general agreement that the legitimate government of an occupied territory retains its sovereignty but that the latter is suspended in the area for the duration of the belligerent occupation. The occupant, therefore, exercises a temporary right of administration on a sort of trusteeship basis until the occupation ceases in one way or another.[9] The occupant assumes international responsibility for the occupied territory and, as far as neutrals are concerned, his legitimate acts possess the same degree of validity as if they had been the acts of the lawful sovereign.

On the other hand, occupied territory is generally considered to be part of the occupant's realm as far as belligerent purposes (bombardment, contraband of war, etc.) are concerned. This common view was expressed long ago by the Supreme Court of the United States in the well-known case of *Thirty Hogsheads of Sugar* v. *Boyle* (1815, 9 Cranch 191), when it held that

Although acquisitions made during war are not considered as permanent until confirmed by treaty, yet to every commercial and belligerent purposes, they are considered as a part of the domain of the conqueror, so long as he retains the possession and government of them.

[9] On this point, see *Law of Land Warfare,* pars. 281–282 and 358, as well as *United States* v. *Rice,* United States, Supreme Court, 1819, 4 Wheaton 246. Consult also Whiteman, Vol. I, pp. 947–951; Georg Schwarzenberger, "The Law of Belligerent Occupation: Basic Issues," 30 *Nordisk Tidsskrift for International Ret* (1960), pp. 10–24; and the *Case of Solazzi and Pace,* Italy, Court of Cassation (Penal), 1953, 37 *Riv. di Dir. Int.* 387, noted in 49 *A.J.I.L.* (1955), p. 423.

Any attempt to supplant the legitimate sovereign by absorption of occupied territory during the course of a war must be considered as an unlawful premature annexation. Despite long juristic insistence on this point, numerous examples of the illegal practice exist in modern history, such as Italy's annexation on November 5, 1911, of two Turkish provinces, even though only five coastal towns had been occupied and the war was still going on. During World War II, Germany, on October 8, 1939, annexed districts in western Poland, and created, on January 29, 1940, another *Reichsgau, Wartheland*, out of Polish territory—despite the fact that a Polish government-in-exile functioned and Polish forces were being regrouped on other fronts against the Axis powers.

Legislation enacted by the legitimate sovereign was, traditionally, denied all validity in territory under enemy occupation. This blanket restriction has been modified in more recent times and today most, but certainly not yet all, writers appear to assert that the legitimate sovereign may legislate for an enemy-occupied portion of his territory *provided* that his laws do not conflict with the rights of the occupant as stipulated in conventional international law.

This liberalized interpretation lags behind judicial opinion, however. A number of decisions arising out of events during World War II lead to the conclusion that legislation by the lawful sovereign intended to interfere with the occupant's legitimate rule possesses no effective force in occupied territory but that if such legislation does not conflict with the legitimate rule of the occupying power, it should take effect in the territory under belligerent occupation.[10]

International law does not require the issuance of a formal proclamation of belligerent occupation, but recent practice has favored such announcement to the indigenous population.[11]

RIGHTS AND OBLIGATIONS OF THE INDIGENOUS POPULATION

Duty of Obedience. Most older texts in international law asserted the existence of a "duty of obedience" on the part of the local inhabitants toward a belligerent occupant, and thus favored the latter at the expense of the civilian population. Numerous justifications for such claimed obedience have been evolved, some of them highly ingenious indeed.[12]

---

[10] Refer, in particular, to *State of the Netherlands* v. *Federal Reserve Bank of New York*, United States, Circuit Court of Appeals, Second Circuit, January 21, 1953, 201 F. (2d) 455, abstracted in 47 *A.J.I.L.* (1953), pp. 496–500; see *ibid.*, 46 (1952), pp. 149–152, for the digest of the decision in the Court of first instance.

[11] See von Glahn, pp. 40–43, for the texts of a German and an Allied proclamation of occupation from World War II.

[12] See Richard R. Baxter, "The Duty of Obedience to the Belligerent Occupant," 27 *B.Y.I.L.* (1950), pp. 235–266, at pp. 240–244 for a list of such reasons.

More recently a change in point of view appears to have taken place, and it can be said that at most the inhabitants should give an obedience equal to that previously given to the laws of their legitimate sovereign and at the least that they should obey the occupant to the extent that such a result can be enforced through the latter's military supremacy. Articles 27, 64, and 65 of the Fourth Geneva Convention of 1949 appear at first glance to dictate a real *duty* of obedience for the native population. However, a careful perusal of the articles in question will show that, subject to certain conventional restrictions, it is the occupant who may actually dictate the limits of obedience expected by him. In any case, an occupant may not force the local population to act in a manner which can be construed as aimed at their legitimate sovereign.

The occupant must publish whatever penalties are to be attached to disobedience to his commands.[13]

Armed Resistance. Resistance on the part of the indigenous population to a belligerent occupant has given rise not only to a great body of literature but also to acts of great brutality and many diplomatic protests. As was mentioned earlier (Chapter 28) a *levée en masse*, that is, armed resistance by civilians, is lawful under Article 2 of the Hague Regulations, provided such resistance is offered to an invader from as yet unoccupied territory. On the other hand, an armed uprising *within* occupied territory is forbidden.[14] Individuals partaking in such a rising were always classified as war rebels and were subject to the death penalty. Unfortunately for the authors supporting such a view, few cases of a genuine *levée en masse* in occupied territory are on record, after the 1911 Italo-Turkish War.[15]

Compulsory Swearing of Oaths. Because a belligerent occupant does not acquire title to occupied enemy territory by mere occupation, it is forbidden to exact an oath of allegiance from the local citizenry, under Article 45 of the Hague Regulations. The occupant, may, however, force the indigenous population to take an oath of neutrality. In the case of native officials retained or hired to work under the occupant in the administration of the territory, a promise to serve faithfully may be required lawfully.

Right to Protection. The civilian inhabitants of an occupied territory possess a right to protection, especially as regards their personal rights. Initially and sketchingly detailed in Article 46 of the Hague Regulations, these personal rights are outlined in considerably expanded form in Article 27 of the Fourth Geneva Convention. Briefly, civilian inhabitants are guaranteed respect for their persons, honor, family rights, religious con-

---

[13] *Law of Land Warfare*, par. 435 (b), and Fourth Geneva Convention, Article 65.

[14] See von Glahn, p. 75, n. 24, for the basis of this statement, at least as far as the pre-1939 view was concerned.

[15] *Ibid.*, pp. 49–50, where alleged recent instances are cited.

victions and practices, and their manners and customs. Women are protected especially against any attack on their honor, in particular against rape, enforced prostitution, or any form of indecent assault.

Article 32 of the same treaty prohibits certain practices associated with Axis treatment of civilians, such as extermination, murder, torture, corporal punishment, mutilation, medical or scientific experiments not required by the medical treatment of an individual, and any other measures of brutality.

In connection with these guarantees to civilians, the extremely important Article 3 of the Fourth Convention must be noted. Prompted by the frequency of "normal" civil wars in certain parts of the globe and the intrusion of a new factor, subversive international movements, into world politics, the article in question provides for the protection of civilians, along the lines mentioned above, "in the case of armed conflict not of an international character occurring in the territory of one of the High Contracting Parties."

Nationality. The nationality of the inhabitants of an area under belligerent occupation normally does not change, as it would in the case of a shift in sovereignty. Under the laws of most states, therefore, children born in territory under enemy occupation possess the nationality of their parents. Under American law, however, children born on United States territory occupied by enemy forces do not acquire citizenship under *jus soli*, for the occupied territory is deemed—and correctly so—to be outside of the jurisdiction of the United States government at the time of their birth.

Arrest, Prosecution, or Conviction. Article 70 of the Fourth Geneva convention prohibits the arrest, prosecution, or conviction of members of the indigenous population for acts committed or opinions expressed before the occupation or during a temporary suspension thereof, except for breaches of the laws and customs of war. Also, nationals of the occupying state who, before the outbreak of the conflict, had sought refuge in the territory of the occupied state, may not be arrested, prosecuted, or deported from the occupied territory, *except* for offenses committed after the outbreak of hostilities or for offenses under common law committed before the outbreak of hostilities which, under the law of the occupied state, would have justified extradition in time of peace.

Religion. The religious convictions and practices of the native inhabitants are to be respected, in accordance with Article 48 of the Hague Regulations and Article 27 of the Fourth Geneva Convention. Logically, however, the pulpit must not be misused to discuss politics or to incite revolt or resistance among the population. Political meetings may not be disguised as religious assemblies.

Education. The control of education by a belligerent occupant has been the subject of a vast literature. During World War II, leading educators in the anti-Axis nations proposed that the youth of totalitarian countries should be educated away from Fascist doctrines and should be led on the road toward democratic traditions and practices.

Both customary and conventional international law rules prior to 1949 had nothing to say about the matter at hand. Writers had reached general agreement that the occupant could lawfully exercise supervision over the educational system in occupied areas but disagreed as to the precise limits of such control. Logically, any teaching promoting hostility toward the occupant and his cause could be stopped, as could be discussion of all political matters. Schools, it was agreed, could be closed temporarily if military necessity required this to be done.

Article 50 of the Fourth Geneva Convention provided that the occupant should facilitate the proper operation of educational institutions, with the cooperation of the native authorities in the territory, but several recent authors have contended that the article did not apply to institutions of higher learning.

Both World Wars saw wholesale interference in educational matters by belligerent occupants, contrary to the tolerant attitudes displayed by academic commentators. United States regulations for the control of occupied enemy territory had almost nothing to say on the subject of education, until the thirteenth proclamation of General Eisenhower (December 16, 1944) to the German people. That document announced the closing of all German educational institutions except orphanages and boarding schools, until Nazism had been eradicated.

When the Allied forces moved into Germany, this provision was carried out, and was followed by an intensive effort to eliminate National Socialist elements from all teaching staffs, to substitute democratically oriented texts for those produced in the Nazi period, and to lay the groundwork for a more democratic administration of the schools and universities.[16] In these endeavors the Allied education officers were still bound by whatever Hague Regulations could be deemed to apply to education, until Germany surrendered unconditionally. After that time, no restrictions appear to have applied.

Requisitioning of Services. One of the important rights of a belligerent occupant is that of requisitioning the services of the indigenous enemy population, providing such services are for the needs of the army of occupation. Under Article 52 of the Hague Regulations, requisitioned labor by the local inhabitants must not involve them in the operations of war against their own country. Anyone in the population is subject to such a call, either in his normal occupation or, in emergencies, as common laborer for the clearing of debris and the burying of corpses.

---

[16] See, *inter alia*, Harold Zink, *The United States in Germany, 1944-1955* (Princeton, N.J.: D. Van Nostrand Co., 1957), at pp. 193–214; and von Glahn, "Some Aspects of German Education in the U.S. Zone of Occupation," 33 *Science Education* (1949), pp. 7–13.

Axis abuse of this right caused the inclusion of comprehensive safe-guards for the civilian population in Articles 51 and 52 of the Fourth Geneva Convention. The new rules set a minimum age limit of eighteen years for requisitioned labor, prohibit the transportation of labor from occupied enemy territory, require payment of fair wages, and call for application of the labor legislation prevailing in the occupied territory prior to the arrival of the invaders.[17]

Deportation. Although deportation of native inhabitants is prohibited under the preceding provisions as well as more specifically by Article 49 of the Fourth Geneva Convention, it is still lawful to evacuate given areas in occupied enemy territory. The motive for such action must center on the security of the civilians involved or on imperative military reasons.

It should be noted, before leaving this section, that the indigenous population is not permitted to renounce the rights granted to it under the provisions of the Fourth Geneva Convention (Art. 8). This holds true even when the belligerent occupant introduces changes in existing institutions, when the occupant concludes contrary agreements with local authorities (German agreements with the Vichy régime in World War II), or when the occupant undertakes premature annexation (German absorption of Alsace-Lorraine, in the same conflict).

Position of Neutral Diplomats. The Hague Conventions of 1899 and 1907 totally ignored a vexatious problem of belligerent occupation: the position of neutrals found by an occupant in enemy territory under his control. Neutral diplomats remaining in occupied territory commonly had their privileges limited to the extent dictated by military necessities of the occupant. On the other hand, when such neutrals desired to leave after the commencement of an occupation, they were usually granted all necessary facilities and safe-conducts. If the occupant so desired, the neutral diplomatic agents were asked to leave the territory and no umbrage resulted from such requests: they were promptly carried out.

The status of neutral consuls in occupied territory was even more debatable than that of diplomats. If they were permitted to stay, which was the normal practice of many occupants, they were free to exercise most of their normal functions, and did not require the issue of new *exequaturs* from the occupant.

Modern practice appears to be that the occupant revokes the *exequaturs* of all neutral consuls found in the area under his control and requests them to leave the territory (Germany in Belgium in 1914, Germany in western Poland in 1939, Germany in Belgium, Luxembourg, Norway, and the Netherlands in 1940). As in time of peace, any business enterprises of consuls, together with their properties, are subject to the authority of the prevailing government: in occupied territory, this would be the military

---

[17] See von Glahn, pp. 69–73, concerning deportation practices by belligerents in both World Wars and other details relating to requisitioned labor.

government of the occupant. Such properties are not exempt from requisitions and contributions levied by the occupant.

Position of Private Neutral Citizens. Private neutral citizens in territory under belligerent occupation cannot claim privileged status by virtue of their nationality. They are subject to all rules and regulations affecting the indigenous population. They lack, furthermore, the status of protected persons under the terms of Article 4 of the Fourth Geneva Convention of 1949 as long as their own government maintains diplomatic relations with the occupant's government. If such relations have not existed, or are broken off, the private neutral citizen acquires protected status and benefits from the provisions of Article 48 of the Fourth Geneva Convention, which guarantees, essentially, their right to leave the occupied territory.

ADMINISTRATION OF THE LAW

Article 43 of the 1907 Hague Regulations provides that an occupant

. . . shall take all measures in his power to restore and insure, as far as possible, public order and safety, while respecting, unless absolutely prevented, the laws in force in the [occupied] country.

Normally, an occupant would honor this rule because administration of enemy territory would be greatly facilitated by the utilization of existing and known local laws and regulations. Naturally, certain laws might have to be suspended in the interest of the occupant's administration. In no case could the occupant substitute his own domestic laws for those of the enemy—at least not until the legitimate sovereign had disappeared or the territory had been ceded; in the latter case, occupation would have been replaced by sovereign jurisdiction. It would, of course, be possible to introduce domestic law through the back door by having lawful regulations issued by the occupant and having those regulations duplicate his own laws.

Suspension of Laws. Suspension of laws injurious to the interests of the occupant or to his war aims would be legitimate. Laws providing for discrimination could be suspended because they did not promote the public order for which the occupant is held responsible. Conscription laws, travel regulations, the right to bear arms, suffrage legislation, and local rights of free speech and of assembly would represent other categories of legislation subject to immediate suspension, for obvious reasons.

Internal Administration. The occupant may not change the internal administration of occupied enemy territory—he may not introduce a new indigenous governmental structure or change internal boundaries, except, in the latter case, on a purely temporary basis, for the benefit of the local population and for an easier administration of the area.

Local Law. Although the local law should be retained in force to the greatest possible extent, the occupant is, of course, free to legislate in the occupied territory, as long as his ordinances are in accordance with conventional international law. It should be noted that if native law conflicts with such legitimate legislation on the part of the occupant, the local law must yield to the occupant's rules.

Civil Law. Most authorities agree that civil law in the narrow sense is normally immune from interference on the part of the occupant: such laws as govern family life, property, debts, most contracts, inheritance, commercial activities, and so on, would appear to fall into this group. The writer has long questioned the validity of this assertion, in view of the increasingly total nature of war, yet the weight of legal commentary supports the principle cited.

Criminal Legislation. Criminal legislation in occupied enemy territory is subject to extensive temporary alteration by an occupant. Many acts, lawful under peacetime conditions, would constitute grave dangers to the occupying forces; other acts, already prohibited by the lawful sovereign, would be punished more severely by an occupant when undertaken against members of his forces or against his property than they would be when committed against civilian inhabitants.

In addition to his admitted legal right to effect existing legislation in the occupied territory, the occupant is apparently quite free to suspend or alter ordinances (as distinct from laws), decrees, and administrative regulations issued by the legitimate sovereign before the occupation.

JUDICIAL SYSTEM

Suspension of Indigenous Courts. The Hague Regulations had little to say about the varieties and operations of courts in occupied territory. Customarily, indigenous courts continue to function with the same personnel, jurisdiction, and under the same laws (unless suspended or supplemented by the occupant) as before the commencement of the occupation. The occupant has a right to dismiss judges, just as they have a right to resign if unwilling to serve under the invader. If a given judicial organ interferes through its functioning with the war aims of the occupant, such organ may be suspended. Thus the Allies invading Germany in World War II were legally correct when they suspended the *Volksgerichtshöfe* (People's Courts) and other special judicial agencies, such as the *Sondergerichte* (Special Tribunals) peculiar to the National Socialist government of the Reich.

In fact, an occupant may close down all indigenous courts under conditions of real need.[18]

Jurisdiction of Indigenous Courts. Under Article 23 of the Hague Regulations of 1907, an occupant may not bar the native inhabitants from access to their own courts of law in order to assert or to protect their civil

---

[18] See *Law of Land Warfare*, par. 373, for conditions involved.

rights.[19] On the other hand, the same inhabitants may not use their own courts to bring suit against the occupant, even when a claim arising out of a contract entered into with the occupant or his agents is involved. The occupant is not subject to the courts or to the laws of the occupied enemy state, and indigenous courts do not normally possess jurisdiction over members of the occupying forces; this traditional rule had only one exception: an occupant could consent to be sued in indigenous courts or to have such courts exercise jurisdiction over members of his forces.

Indigenous courts of an occupied territory generally have asserted their duty to enforce orders and regulations of a belligerent occupant as long as they were in accord with the Hague Regulations. Although few native courts escaped criticism for enforcing such lawful orders, the bulk of the latter was upheld even after liberation, in the case of World War II.

No clear-cut answer can be given, on the other hand, as to the capacity of native courts to review the acts and orders of a belligerent occupant. It may be argued with a good deal of logic that such review would be appropriate if the acts or orders were clearly illegal under conventional international law. But even if such a right were granted, the local courts would have no way in which they could enforce an adverse judgment on the actions of an occupant.

Establishment of Tribunals. Modern belligerent occupants, even if they have permitted some or all of the native courts to function, have tended to establish their own tribunals in occupied enemy territory. This practice is based on customary law and the practice of states and has now been made a part of conventional law through the provisions of Articles 66–76 of the Fourth Geneva Convention of 1949. Space does not permit a detailed examination of the new rules. It should be pointed out, however, that an occupant may create his own tribunals when the local judicial system has disintegrated or has had to be suspended for good reasons. He may also establish his own court to try offenses committed by local inhabitants against occupation personnel. And he may set up his courts to deal with all native violations of his orders, regulations, and occupation statutes. Naturally, he may also create his tribunals to try offenses committed by his own armed forces or civil occupation administration. Such a court would not be called an occupation court, however, for its basis would be found in the occupant's own domestic law and not in international law.[20]

If a military government (occupation) court handles civil cases not connected with the occupant or his forces—a situation quite possible in the absence of functionary indigenous courts—the law applied by such a

[19] See *Porter* v. *Freudenberg*, Great Britain, Court of Appeal, 1915, cited in Hackworth, VI, p. 368, and digested at length in Llewellyn Pfankuchen, *A Documentary Textbook of International Law* (New York: Farrar & Rinehart, 1940), at pp. 718–724).

[20] The literature on occupation courts as well as on military courts set up by occupants to deal with their own personnel is very extensive; see von Glahn, pp. 111–113, and the citations to sources supplied in the relevant footnotes on pp. 129–130.

court in the cases mentioned would be the law of the occupied territory, unless suspended by the occupant.

Extraordinary Courts. There has been some question as to the legality of the creation of so-called extraordinary courts by a belligerent occupant. Such courts, established in various occupied states by Germany during World War II, dealt with certain matters normally coming under the jurisdiction of the regular indigenous courts, which were still operating during the existence of the new type of organ. Returning legitimate sovereigns repeatedly denied validity to the judgments of those German courts, and where definite proof of misuse of the courts to promote the German cause and to cow the local population with dramonic punishments could be shown, the guilty judges and prosecutors were tried as war criminals.[21]

Conventional Law Based on Anglo-Saxon Jurisprudence. Finally it should be mentioned that the new conventional law governing occupation courts (Articles 66–76 of the Fourth Geneva Convention of 1949) has borrowed heavily from the procedures and judicial safeguards commonly encountered in Anglo-Saxon jurisprudence. This fact represents a most fascinating adaptation of a quite alien system of judicial procedure by the European states ratifying the Fourth Convention, states which, basically, follow a legal system based on Roman law and the Napoleonic Code, as adapted locally.

Death Penalty. One extremely controversial feature of the new rules is represented by the concluding sentence in paragraph 2, Article 68, of the Fourth Convention. The sentence in question states that the occupant may impose the death penalty only when the offense involved was punishable by the laws of the occupied country in force before the commencement of the occupation. Several states participating in the Geneva Diplomatic Conference of 1949 opposed this provision, including the United States. Opposition centered on two points: the new rule would deprive an occupant of a major deterrent to illegal acts, and the possibility that the legitimate sovereign, as the last act before his ouster from the area by an invading enemy, would abolish the death penalty in his jurisdiction. In consequence of this view, the United States, joined by Canada, Great Britain, the Netherlands, and New Zealand, signed and later ratified the Fourth Convention with a reservation against application of the death penalty clause in paragraph 2, Article 68.

Regional and Local Officials. Regional as well as local officials commonly are retained in office by an occupant, provided their government has not instructed them to the contrary and they are willing to continue to serve. Should they decline to serve or resign later, the occupant is now forbidden to apply coercion or punishment against them for their action, under Article 54 of the Fourth Convention. If native officials are retained, they may be lawfully required to give an oath or a promise of efficient and

---

[21] See A. V. Freeman, "War Crimes by Enemy National Administering Justice in Occupied Territory," 41 *A.J.I.L.* (1947), pp. 579–610.

unprejudiced service under the occupant. Salaries of such officials are met out of revenues collected either by the occupant or by remaining regional and local governmental organs in the occupied territory.

Occupation authorities possess an unquestioned right to dismiss indigenous officials, particularly in the case of police officials, subject to the relevant provisions of the Fourth Convention.

RESTRICTIONS ON ACTIVITIES OF THE NATIVE POPULATION

Communication Media. Many activities of the native population may be regulated or even forbidden by an occupant, even though the acts in question do not represent violations of the laws of war. Thus severe restrictions on or even the closing down of newspapers and periodicals is lawful; strict censorship of all permitted publications is authorized; censorship of the mails as well as of telephone calls, radio broadcasts, telegraphic communications, telecasts, and control of the use of carrier pigeons are legal. Virtually all military manuals prohibit the use of codes or ciphers by the indigenous population. Normally the belligerent occupant assumes immediate control of all surviving media of communication and, once their use is authorized, supervises all operations and programs.

Public Meetings. Public meetings, if not forbidden outright, are subject to permits issued by the organs of the occupant, and commonly advance copies of speeches to be delivered have to be submitted for censorship and approval. Religious assemblies and processions traditionally do not require permission by the occupant. This practice was abandoned, except for regular church services, by both sides during World War II.

Circulating and Traveling. For obvious reasons of security as well as of control, a belligerent occupant may restrict the circulation of civilians in occupied enemy territory; exceptions to this generally applied rule occur regularly in the case of medical personnel and members of fire-fighting agencies. Travel prohibitions, usually setting maximum distances from one's normal place of residence, are common, and special passes for travel beyond those limits are issued but seldom by occupation authorities.

Voting Privileges. Voting privileges of the indigenous population are normally suspended for the duration of the occupation, with a few exceptions recorded in the case of purely local elections.

National Anthem and Display of Flag. Modern practice sanctions a prohibition on the playing or singing of all songs disrespectful or hostile to the occupant, and the playing or singing of the native national anthem as well as the display of the flag of the lawful sovereign are usually forbidden.

Arms and Ammunition. Regardless of local laws pertaining to the ownership or use of firearms, occupants are permitted, for obvious reasons of security, to order the surrender of all arms and ammunition owned by the indigenous population.

Humanitarian Controls. Self-interest, combined with observance of his duty to restore public order and safety, grant to an occupant wide powers in such areas of public life as control over local hospitals, supplies of drugs and medicines, the sale of alcoholic beverages, prostitution and other forms of vice, and the creation of adequate safeguards to prevent the rise and spread of epidemics. Bitter experiences from German and Japanese interpretations of these humanitarian controls led to extensive codification of the necessary requirements, obligatory on future occupants, at Geneva in 1949. Articles 14 through 23 and 55 through 57 of the Fourth Convention of 1949 details required action in the spheres of hospitals, hygiene, and public health; Articles 24–26 and 50 are devoted to child welfare and related matters; Articles 59 through 63 as well as Article 143 deal with the various aspects of relief (collective and individual) and with Red Cross and other relief and welfare agencies.

In this connection, Articles 59 and 60 of the convention must be regarded as being of particular importance. Mindful of the faminelike conditions prevailing in many parts of the world occupied during World War II by the Axis powers, the drafters of the convention specified the conditions under which food and other outside relief was to be brought into territory under hostile occupation. One of the new aspects of these rules is the obligation of a belligerent occupant to agree to relief schemes on behalf of the indigenous population and to facilitate such programs by all the means at his disposal. Article 60 categorically affirms that an occupant is not relieved of his responsibilities for the welfare of the civilian population by his acceptance of relief shipments into the territory and also forbids all diversion of such shipments, except under rather unlikely conditions specified.

ECONOMIC SYSTEM

Rationing. Rationing may be lawfully instituted by an occupant and, under the conditions of modern war, is a normal feature of belligerent occupation. Recent practice shows that the actual administration of rationing tends to be delegated to remaining indigenous authorities, with direction and control vested in the agencies of the occupant.

Taxes and Customs Revenues. The occupant is entitled, under Article 48 of the Hague Regulations of 1907, to collect all taxes and customs revenues imposed by and for the benefit of the legitimate sovereign. Most military manuals and the writings of jurists are in agreement that all such revenues in excess of the sums needed to administer the occupied territory becomes the lawful spoils of the occupant and may be used by him for whatever purposes he sees fit. Administrative expenses thus represent a first charge against tax and revenue collections. Quite frequently, occupants have decided to entrust the collection of such national taxes (and possibly customs duties, if any foreign trade is permitted) to indigenous agencies.

An occupant is free to suspend the collection of certain "national" taxes if the remaining income from that source is sufficient to cover his administrative expenses and he should decide not to retain funds not needed for such purposes.

Taxes collected by local agencies for local needs are beyond the lawful reach of an occupant—except if the purposes in question could be held to be inimical to the interests of the occupant. Naturally, if local agencies had acted as tax collectors for their national government before the occupation, then any such sums collected by them after the commencement of the occupation would be treated by the occupant as subject to seizure and would have to be used primarily for the administrative expenses of the occupant. This conclusion would not apply, of course, if the sums formerly collected for the enemy government had been intended for eventual redistribution among local units of government. In that case, the occupant would act illegally if he treated the sums in question as "national" taxes of the enemy state and seized them.

An occupant is exempt from indigenous taxation of any kind, unless he takes the highly unlikely step of waiving his sovereign immunity. Practice shows that an early order is issued by the occupation authorities exempting the agencies, personnel, and property of the occupant from all direct taxes. The writer believes that indirect taxes, such as excise taxes or various indirect sales taxes, also would not apply to any instrumentality of a belligerent occupant.

Customs duties, which normally could be expected to bring in substantial amounts of revenue, appear to play little or no part in the financial aspect of modern belligerent occupations. Occupants tend to stop all normal exports and imports of the occupied enemy territory—a matter of little importance, because the conditions and destructiveness of modern warfare are not likely to leave much trade possible. Shipments of supplies and commodities from the occupant's own state into the occupied enemy territory will tend to be exclusively for the use of the occupation forces or for relief, hence would be exempt from the application of customs duties by the surviving authorities of the occupied territory.

Debts. One of the more confusing aspects of belligerent occupation is the status of enemy debts in occupied territory. An occupant may lawfully prevent all payments from the area to the enemy government. In accordance with one interpretation of Article 53 of the 1907 Hague Regulations, he may collect debts owed to the legitimate (enemy) sovereign, but the writer stands with a majority of the legal commentators on the meaning of the relevant provision and does not believe that an occupant is entitled to collect debts owed to the legitimate sovereign and falling due during the period of hostile occupation.

General agreement appears to prevail among jurists that an occupant may not contract new debts on behalf of an occupied portion of enemy territory. Some authorities disagree with this conclusion and make the reasonable point that such debts would be lawful if the occupant could submit conclusive proof that the indebtedness was not only required by the welfare of the indigenous population but constituted a reasonable and fair transaction. On the other hand, any occupant appears to be entitled to undertake a consolidation of already existing public debts of the occupied territory in the interest of an efficient administration—provided that the total debt and the related interest charges of the territory would not be increased by such a step.

Levying of Money Contributions. An occupant, requiring additional sums for the expenses of his occupation forces or for the administration of the territory, may levy money contributions on the indigenous population, under the provisions of Article 49 of the Hague Regulations of 1907. If such contributions are imposed, the conventional law requires that receipts be issued. These rules mean that the collection of money would be illegal if it were for the general war effort of the occupant, or for the purpose of buying supplies abroad for the occupation forces, or for the expense of belligerent operations outside the occupied enemy territory in which the contribution was imposed.

Actual payment of monetary contributions is usually organized through the local native authorities after their quota has been set by the agencies of the occupant. The actual individual assessment of payments is therefore left to the local officials who simply transfer the total sum collected by them to the occupant. It should be mentioned, too, that, under Article 50 of the 1907 Regulations, no general penalty, pecuniary or otherwise, may be inflicted on the indigenous population on account of the acts of individuals for which they cannot be regarded as jointly and severally responsible. Thus collective punishment for hostile acts against the occupant may not take the form of monetary contributions levied on a community or an entire territory—a rule violated conspicuously by Germany on many occasions during World War II.

Requisitions in Kind. Levies on the local population in terms of commodities of every description—called *requisitions in kind*—may take the place of monetary contributions and have been esteemed highly by many modern occupants. Under the terms of Article 52 of the 1907 Regulations, requisitions in kind (as well as of services of inhabitants) are not to be demanded from municipalities or individuals except for the needs of the army of occupation. Such requisitions are to be in proportion to the resources of the country. Requisitions in kind are to be paid for in cash, as far as possible; if this is not done, a receipt must be given and payment is to be made as soon as possible.[22]

---

[22] See the important case of *Bataafsche Petroleum Maatschappli & Ors.* v. *The War Damage Commission*, Singapore, Court of Appeal, April 13, 1956, 22 *Malayan Law Journal* (1956), pp. 155, opinion reprinted in 51 *A.J.I.L.* (1957), pp. 802–815, for a clear explanation of the rights and duties of an occupant as regards the seizure of private property without formal requisitioning being undertaken.

Both World Wars witnessed extensive violations of these regulations, particularly with relation to the removal of requisitioned commodities from occupied enemy territory to the home country of the occupant for the use of the latter's armed forces or even civilian population. Also, military occupation commanders conveniently overlooked the proviso that contributions (requisitions) in kind were to be proportionate to the resources of the country, and especially in the matter of food requisitions some extremely crass violations are on record. In this connection it must be emphasized that an occupant does not have to consider the resources of an individual in levying contributions in kind. As Feilchenfeld phrased it pithily, an occupant "may take a farmer's last cow and piece of bread as long as by doing so he does not unduly exhaust the cattle and bread supply of the whole country." [23]

Food Supply and Other Necessities. The vital matter of the food supply of an occupied territory is dealt with at some length in Article 55 of the Fourth Geneva Convention. There it is stated that the occupant, to the fullest extent of the means available to him, has a duty of ensuring the food and medical supplies of the population; he should, in particular, bring in the necessary food, medical stores, and other necessities if the resources of the occupied territory are inadequate. As far as requisitioning is concerned, Article 55 specifies that such levies can be exacted for the use of the occupation forces and administrative personnel only after the requirements of the civilian population have been taken into account.

The receipts mentioned in the Hague Regulations in connection with monetary contributions and requisitions in kind were intended as evidence that money, goods, or services had been furnished, and constituted a kind of deferred payment voucher. The writer does not believe that they constituted a promise on the part of the occupant to pay for whatever was supplied to him. Because Articles 52–54 of the Hague Regulations as well as Article 19 of the Fifth Hague Convention of 1907 and Article 55 of the Fourth Geneva Convention provide for payment for requisitioned goods, there must be someone intended to make that payment. Conventional law does not directly lay this responsibility on the occupant (but does so by implication); the modern practice seems to be to make the lawful sovereign of the occupied territory the one who is expected to make payment after the termination of the belligerent occupation.

State-Owned Immovable Property. Immovable public property of the lawful sovereign may not be appropriated by a belligerent occupant. Rather the latter is in the position of an administrator and usufructuary of such property under Article 55 of the 1907 Hague Regulations. As a mere usufructuary, the occupant is bound to preserve the substance of the property in question but is entitled to seize as his own the product or proceeds arising out of the property. He may not sell land which is enemy

[23] Ernst A. Feilchenfeld, *The International Economic Law of Belligerent Occupation* (Washington, D.C.: Carnegie Endowment for International Peace, 1942), at p. 37.

public domain, but is entitled to the crops raised on that land. Thus an occupant may use, for the duration of his stay, public buildings, real estate, forests, farmlands, docks, barracks, and all other immovable property of the enemy state.

World War II, which saw widespread violations of Article 55, also witnessed a development totally unforeseen by the drafters of the Regulations: the seizure of state-owned business enterprises by a belligerent occupant. This new problem arose in particular in the case of the Soviet Union. Under the terms of the Russian constitution of 1936, three kinds of property were recognized in the U.S.S.R.: personal property (Arts. 9 and 10), socialized property (Art. 5), and cooperative property, which included cooperative farms. Personal property presumably was safeguarded by the various protective clauses of the Hague Regulations, but the other two types posed the problem when the occupation authorities undertook to seize them.

A strict interpretation of the Hague Regulations would have placed all Russian state-owned enterprises into the category of immovable public property—and this would then have covered *all* enterprises of any kind in the Soviet Union. The German authorities denied the validity of such a view and proceeded to abolish most of the collective farms officially. Because implementation of the order would have ruined agricultural production in occupied territory, Germany actually permitted most of the farms to function as before, under German control. Later, many collective farms were broken up and the land was sold to German settlers, just as many state-owned factories were sold to German companies, in some cases simply turned over to German nationals, and in many instances shipped bodily into Germany.

Charges of illegality arising out of such practices were met with references to the fact that the 1907 Hague Regulations did not define what is meant by state property or explain how a test of state ownership is to be applied. Modern practice in other states appears to indicate that the general attitude is this: if there is doubt about the nature of the ownership of a given property, it is assumed to be public property until (or unless) private ownership can be proven. In the instance of "semistate" property, that is, property in which the enemy state has an interest but is not the absolute owner, modern practice favors treatment of it as public property. A fairer approach, so it seems to the writer, would be to consider the location of the assumption of risk connected with the enterprise or property. If the economic risk in question is assumed by the enemy state, then the property would be public in nature; if the risk were privately borne, then the property ought to be regarded as private in character.

State-Owned Movable Property. Public movable property of the enemy state, including cash and realizable securities owned by that state, may be lawfully appropriated by the belligerent occupant under Article 53 of the Hague Regulations of 1907. The only limitation laid down is that all such property must be usable for military operations—a restriction without much meaning today when virtually every commodity under the sun can somehow be fitted into the category of permitted seizure.

An occupant, on the other hand, may not seize funds on deposit in banks when such funds are not normally at the disposal of the enemy state.

Seized enemy movable public property may be used up, shipped from the occupied territory, or be utilized in any manner deemed necessary by the belligerent occupant. The writer does not agree with certain jurists who justify even the sale of such property, for Article 53 of the Regulations specifies that such property must be for military use. It should be noted here that illegal seizures of public property were held to constitute punishable war crimes under Article 6-b of the Charter of the Nuremberg War Crimes Tribunal.

Public Records and State Archives. Public records and state archives, although undoubtedly movable, have been held to be immune from seizure. The traditional interpretation was that the occupant might use the records during the occupation but had to restore them to their normal place of deposit. The one exception to this rule was the permitted seizure and retention of all materials directly relating to the war in progress. This widely accepted interpretation has been altered rather strikingly in recent times. In view of the extensive use of archival materials possibly for propaganda purposes during a war and for the arraignment of war criminals at a subsequent date, the modern occupant is now quite generally conceded to have a right to seize and retain any and all enemy archives and records, with no requirement for an ultimate return laid down.

Cultural Properties. International law prohibits the confiscation, destruction, or damage of historical monuments, works of art, and institutions devoted to the arts and sciences, under the provisions of Article 56 of the 1907 Hague Regulations and of the Hague Convention Relative to the Protection of Cultural Properties in Case of an Armed Conflict, of May 14, 1954. Regardless of ownership, such properties are to be treated as private property and as such beyond the reach of the occupant—yet, in practice, the looting of art objects as well as of historical movements on an official basis from occupied territory has assumed staggering proportions in modern wars.

On the other hand, the buildings of institutions presumably exempt under Article 56 of the Regulations may be utilized by an occupant, under necessity, for strictly military purposes.

Private Enemy Property. In former centuries, belligerent states could seize and confiscate all private enemy property encountered on the soil of occupied enemy territory. Since the early years of the nineteenth century, however, the exempt character of private enemy property has emerged slowly but definitely, and by 1899 the immunity of private property was generally acknowledged.

It was therefore not at all surprising that Articles 46 and 47 of the

Hague Regulations met with no opposition at either the 1899 or the 1907 conference. Article 46 stated that "private property . . . must be respected. Private property cannot be confiscated," and Article 47 prohibited pillage (looting).

Not all private property enjoys immunity, however. An occupant is entitled under Article 53, par. 2, of the Regulations to seize any war materials or goods, including transport, suitable for war purposes with, however, an obligation to restore such items after the war and to pay compensation. Article 52 allows him to requisition private property required for the needs of the occupation forces, and monetary contributions may be levied in accordance with Article 49. Again, an occupant's right to quarter troops (and animals) in the homes (and stables) of the civilian population represents an infringement on private property rights. Lastly, the duty of the occupant to maintain public order and safety would appear to entitle him to expropriate both public and private property for the benefit of the indigenous population (see also *Law of Land Warfare*, par. 431, on this point).

Military necessity, too, may allow temporary use by an occupant of privately owned land and buildings. But such property may not be sold later, even if the intention were to turn the proceeds over to the private owners at the end of the war.

Although most jurists are in full agreement that an occupant may not seize privately owned property and move it out of the occupied territory, both world wars were the occasions for wholesale violations of this principle. Military necessity was the basic defense advanced whenever justification was felt to be necessary, yet such actions had to be classified as war crimes under Article 6-b of the Nuremberg Charter.

During World War II, a development in the sphere of private property relations under occupation took place in many parts of Europe then under German occupation. In thousands of reported cases, title to private properties (business enterprises or real estate or both) changed hands from indigenous owners to either the government or nationals of the occupying state. Few of the instances in question represented a voluntary relinquishment of title: pressures of various sorts or, in a few cases, outright force influenced the decisions made. A number of states allied against the Axis powers issued a joint declaration on January 5, 1943, reserving their individual right to declare any and all of such transfers invalid after regaining control of the occupied areas.[24]

BANKS, CURRENCY, AND BUSINESS OPERATIONS

A major gap in the legal rules governing belligerent occupation occurs in the general subject area embracing central banks, currency, exchange reserves, and business operations in general. Conventional law is virtually

---

[24] See relevant textual excerpt in von Glahn, p. 189, and discussion of the transfer of title abroad, *ibid.*, pp. 193-196.

silent on these topics, despite their enormous importance both for the occupant and for his enemy. During both World Wars, occupants interfered on many occasions with the operations of central banks located in occupied enemy territory, with Germany even replacing banks of issue with new institutions serving primarily her own needs and the exploitation of the occupied territory.[25] An occupant may, of course, create new banks of issue, in the absence of restrictive rules, provided they do not serve to accomplish forbidden ends.

Regulation of Commercial Banks. Practice has sanctioned the regulation of commercial banks despite contrary views asserted by many legal commentators. In fact, one of the common initial steps taken during belligerent occupation is to close all banks and other financial institutions and to seal all vaults and safe deposit boxes. This measure usually accompanies an order instituting a general moratorium on all business payments. The reason behind these financial moves are quite obvious: financial institutions must be safeguarded, records must be preserved, and funds subject to lawful seizure by the occupant must be protected until inventories of accounts can be taken in order to identify moneys that may be acquired under conventional or customary law. Most moratoria on payments were lifted relatively early after their institution, and banks were permitted to reopen for business on a limited basis, but a common practice limited the amount of withdrawals by any depositor. The steps described have been applied to such a general extent during modern occupations that the present writer hazards the supposition that they represent permissible controls granted to an occupant through a rapidly developed group of new rules of customary law.

On the other hand, utilization of commercial banks in occupied territory for the purpose of acquiring indigenous enterprise on behalf of nationals or of the government of the occupant must be regarded as unlawful.

Currency. Practice as well as legal opinion have granted the occupant far-reaching authority over the monetary system of occupied enemy territory. Quite commonly a dual currency structure developed when an occupant paid his forces (and for requisitioned commodities) either in his own currency or in special occupation money.[26] Because in almost all cases the original native currency was permitted to circulate as before, two currencies existed side by side, and the occupant had the right to determine the rate of exchange between the two. As long as abuses designed for the ultimate enrichment of the occupant are not introduced

[25] See H. H. Bell, "Monetary Problems of Military Occupation," 6 *Military Affairs* (1942), pp. 77–88, and especially Stone, pp. 727–732, on the relationship between *laissez-faire* economic doctrines and the 1907 Regulations.

[26] See *Aboitiz & Co.* v. *Price*, United States, District Court, Utah, 1951, 99 F. Supp. 602, digested in 46 *A.J.I.L.* (1952), pp. 152–154, on the legality of issuing occupation currency.

into such a situation, no fault can be found, from a legal point of view, with the creation of such a dual currency system in occupied territory.[27]

Business Enterprises. The absence of rules of conventional law has enabled modern belligerent occupants to exercise sweeping powers over business enterprises (nonbanking) in occupied enemy territory. Supervision and regulation in any manner considered to be desirable from a military interest point of view or in the interests of the native population are sanctioned by custom as well as by military manuals (thus *Law of Land Warfare*, par. 376), the occupant may force a business enterprise to stay open and continue in operation or he may close it if it appears that its operations are against his interests or those of the indigenous population. If a given enterprise appears of sufficient importance for his needs or those of the civilian population, the occupant may place the business in question under his own direct control and management.

Needless to say, none of the steps mentioned may result in expropriation of the enterprise involved—regardless of the amount of control exercised by the occupant, title to the business must remain with its private owners if illegal procedures are to be avoided. If the control of an indigenous private enterprise results in a profit for the occupant, it would seem that the owners would have to be reimbursed to the extent of the sums involved, otherwise a confiscation of private property in violation of the Hague Regulations could be asserted to have taken place.

Most military manuals, a majority of jurists, and certainly the practices of all major occupants in modern wars have approved the right of a belligerent occupant to regulate prices in areas under his control. Conditions prevailing in such territories will promote a rapid rise in price levels unless regulatory measures are adopted from the outset. Although not all modern occupants have succeeded in stemming inflationary tendencies in areas controlled by them, and black markets have been inevitable accompaniment of recent occupations, price controls have always been attempted, on a few occasions with notable success.

AGRICULTURE, TRADE, COMMUNICATION, AND TRANSPORTATION

Regulation of Agriculture. Agriculture represents another aspect of the economic sphere in which customary as well as conventional law have placed no restrictions on an occupant, except in the most general way through the obligation to look after public order, public safety, and the general interests of the indigenous inhabitants. The normal but certainly not universal practice of modern occupants has been to leave intact, to the greatest possible extent, the regulations dealing with agriculture issued

---

[27] Consult *Law of Land Warfare*, par. 430; Ralphaël Lemkin, *Axis Rule in Occupied Europe* (Washington, D.C.: Carnegie Endowment for International Peace, 1944), at pp. 51–63; and *Hearings on Occupation Currency Transactions before Committees on Appropriations, Armed Services and Banking and Currency* (U.S. Senate, 80th Congress, 1st Session, 1947), pp. 72–84.

by the legitimate sovereign prior to the occupation. In some instances, notably in the practices of the Axis Powers during World War II, regulation of agriculture was manipulated in such a way as to create a maximum benefit for the occupying state instead of for the local population. Such practices obviously violated the *intent* of Articles 52, 53, and 55 of the Hague Regulations of 1907.

Foreign Trade. Little need be said about foreign trade under occupation. Conditions following entry into and conquest of enemy territory tend to render the existence of exportable surpluses highly doubtful, and means of payment for imports normally would not be available to the population. An occupant possesses an undoubted customary right to stop all trade across the borders of the occupied territory, and this is normally done as soon as effective occupation has been realized. This would be true especially of movements of gold, precious metals, jewels, and securities. In many modern occupations, an eventual revival of foreign trade was deliberately limited by an occupant to trade relations between his own country and the occupied territory. No legal rule appears to forbid such temporary reorientation of the trade relations of the occupied territory. Contrary to the views of some commentators, the present writer believes that all commercial treaties involving occupied enemy territory are suspended in their effects for the territory as long as the occupation lasts.

Communications. Means of communication are subject to seizure, control, and operation by an occupant if he wishes to exercise those powers. At the termination of the occupation, all such seized facilities must be restored to their owners. Even if communication media are left in native hands—a highly unlikely situation, especially during the early phases of a belligerent occupation—they are subject to rigid control and censorship by the occupant. Special provisions govern submarine cables terminating in occupied territory. If such cables connect the territory with a neutral country, they must not be seized or destroyed except in the case of absolute necessity; if seizure or destruction is undertaken, the properties must be returned at the end of the occupation and compensation for losses or damages will be fixed at that time.

An occupant may lawfully assume control, and even operation, of the postal service in occupied enemy territory. Former postal employees may be required to resume their duties, and the occupant appears to have the right to determine the charges for postal services, for these charges are not taxes but rather fees for services performed. Modern practice indicates that existing stocks of postage stamps, issued by the lawful sovereign, either will be overprinted or will be replaced with new issues for the occupied territory. Postal service with the outside world normally has been prohibited altogether, except for the admission of relief shipments, but the latter usually have been channeled through international bodies and not through normal postal channels. The Fourth Geneva Convention of 1949 (Arts. 23, 25–26, 38, 61–62, 98, 106–112, 128) now requires parties to the treaty to open or maintain certain types of postal communication between the occupied area and the outside world on behalf of the indigenous population and of internees.

Transportation. Railroads may be seized and operated by a belligerent occupant, but again all equipment and facilities have to be returned at the end of the war, at which time compensation is to be decided on.[28] Means of land transportation other than railroads (trucks, cars, busses, trolley cars, carts, etc.) may be seized by an occupant even when they are private property. Again restoration at the end of the war is called for by the Hague Regulations, and again compensation is to be fixed then.

In all instances cited, the conventional law does not state *who* is to be held responsible for losses and damages and, therefore, ought to pay the compensation mentioned. The obvious answer would seem to be that the occupant—who, after all, was the seizing state—ought to pay. But modern practice frequently shows that if the occupant turned out to be the victor in the conflict, he required the losing state to assume the financial burden of paying its own citizens for communication and transportation losses or damage suffered at the hands of the occupant.

The case of public and private vessels found in enemy territory by an occupant is quite different from the situation affecting means of land transport. Prize courts established by occupants have succeeded, in modern times, in expanding the lawful capture of property at sea to include the territorial waters and navigable rivers of occupied enemy territory, and vessels have been seized in dry dock, in port, and in rivers.[29]

THE QUESTION OF MILITARY NECESSITY

One of the more controversial aspects of belligerent occupation is the question of military necessity as it applies to this phase of warfare. The rules governing such occupation are founded on two basic assumptions: war is essentially a conflict between states, and the rules of law possess equal binding force for occupant and lawful sovereign. The first consideration governing the behavior of the occupant is the successful conclusion of the conflict. Now, if this primary purpose requires that certain measures be undertaken, then the occupant may desire to carry them out, even if this would mean that customary or conventional restrictions on his freedom of action have to be set aside in the process.

These considerations played an important part in the drafting of the

---

[28] Hague Regulations of 1907, Article 53; see von Glahn, pp. 217–220, on the complicated problems connected with public and private railroads in territory under belligerent occupation.

[29] See also *Law of Land Warfare*, par. 410 (a), detailing the now lawful seizure of various types of vessels, and *Schiffahrt-Treuhand* v. *Procurator-General*, United Kingdom, Privy Council, January 12, 1953, 1. All Eng. L.R. 364, digested in 47 *A.J.I.L.* (1953), pp. 722–725.

1907 Hague Convention on the Laws of War, and the Preamble to that instrument declared that "military necessity has been taken into account in framing the regulations, and has not been left outside to control and limit their application." Nevertheless, several of the individual Hague Regulations specifically permit the setting aside of certain prohibitions in case of military necessity. Thus a number of the conventional restrictions must be considered to be conditional in character, a fact that has been ignored on numerous occasions when an occupant legitimately invoked military necessity as justification for his acts.[30]

Thus Article 23 (g) of the 1907 Regulations provides that, "It is especially forbidden . . . to destroy or seize the enemy's property, unless such destruction or seizure be imperatively demanded by the necessities of war." If such urgent need does exist, the occupant has an undoubted right to destroy both public and private property in occupied territory. If the condition of imperative necessity is met, then the injured party has no legal claim against the occupant or against the legitimate sovereign, just as if the destruction had taken place in the actual conduct of hostilities. If, on the other hand, no such necessity can be shown to have existed, or if the destruction exceeded the demands of a necessity, then a violation of the laws of war has been committed by the occupant. Interestingly enough, the so-called scorched earth policy found in recent wars does not *always* fall under the prohibition of destruction, as has been shown in several war crimes trials.

THE TERMINATION OF BELLIGERENT OCCUPATION

Ways of Terminating Occupation. The belligerent occupation of enemy territory may terminate in a number of different ways: the area may be set free by the forces of the legitimate sovereign or of his allies; it may be liberated by a successful uprising of the indigenous population; it may be returned to the control of its legitimate sovereign under the terms of a peace treaty; it may be annexed by the occupant under the provisions of such a treaty; and, lastly, it may be annexed by the occupant after the subjugation of the legitimate sovereign.

Laws and Ordinances. Most modern occupations have ended with the return of the occupied territory to its legitimate sovereign, but even this normal situation has been complicated by many vexing problems. Thus what laws and ordinances issued by the occupant will lose their validity after his administration ceases? No clear-cut answer can be given. If any of his decrees or laws violate customary or conventional international law, they will be null and void in the eyes of the returning legitimate sovereign; if they correspond to what the occupant could do legally in

---

[30] See Cunningham, *op. cit.*, pp. 134–137, for an excellent analysis centering on Paragraph 3(a) of the *Law of Land Warfare* and on the conflict between *military* and *civil* necessity.

the occupied territory, then the returning sovereign will decide whether or not to keep the occupant's legislation in force as his own.

Administrative Acts. Administrative acts undertaken by an occupant in accordance with the laws of war should be respected and upheld by the returning sovereign. The latter is, of course, free to set aside all such lawful acts; but such a course of action would tend to prompt future occupants to pay little attention to legal requirements and might injure the interests of many of the sovereign's own nationals who acted in accordance with the lawful steps taken by the occupant. The legitimate sovereign ought, instead, to be bound by lawful administrative acts of the occupant and by their material consequences, if any.

Decisions of Military Tribunals. A number of writers have held that decisions of the occupant's military tribunals lost their validity at the termination of the occupation, unless a contrary provision was included in the treaty of peace.[31] After considerable reflection and study of several relevant cases, the present writer has been forced to disassociate himself from this view formerly shared by him. It appears that a decision of a military government court, if made in a case falling within the jurisdiction lawfully granted to it by the occupant, ought to be treated by the returning sovereign like all other decisions of competent courts in the territory. Naturally, such an interpretation would not apply in the case of an individual who had violated the occupant's security regulations (lawful or illegal) and had been sentenced in an occupation court on criminal charges. In such circumstances the judgment of the occupant's court would be set aside by the returning sovereign and the individual would be set free, as a patriotic subject. For instance, a Greek court at Thebes ordered in 1951 that the record of conviction by a German military court in Athens be expunged. The reason given for this decision was that the judgment, even though valid when it was pronounced, automatically ceased to be so when the German occupation of Greece terminated.[32]

Normally, the returning legitimate sovereign regards the judgments and decisions of occupation courts as decisions of foreign courts, based on the power and authority exercised by the occupant. On occasion, a formal agreement between the latter and the legitimate sovereign determines the future validity of the decisions of the occupation courts. This was done in the Convention on the Settlement of Matters Arising Out of the War and the Occupation, signed at Bonn on May 26, 1952, and in force on May 5, 1955, between the United States, the United Kingdom, France, and the Federal Republic of Germany. Article 5(1), and Article 7(1), of that instrument provides that "all judgments and decisions in criminal

---

[31] See P. De Visscher, "Enemy Legislation and Judgments in Liberated Countries: Belgium," 29 *Journal of Comparative Legislation and International Law* (1947, Parts 3-4), pp. 46-53.

[32] *Case of A.B.,* 6 *Revue Hellénique de Droit International,* 278, cited in 49 *A.J.I.L.* (1955), p. 423.

and noncriminal matters heretofore or hereafter rendered in Germany by any tribunal or judicial authority of the Three Powers or any of them shall remain final and valid for all purposes under German law, shall be treated as such by German courts and authorities and shall, on the application of a party, be enforced by them in the same manner as judgments and decisions of German Courts and authorities." [33]

Decisions of Indigenous Courts. Decisions of indigenous courts, handed down during belligerent occupation, would normally be kept in force by the returning sovereign unless the judgment could be shown to have been influenced by the occupant's authorities or violated the laws of war.

Duration of Applicability of the Convention. Until recently, no guide existed as to the principles applicable in occupied enemy territory after the cessation of hostilities. This regrettable omission led to much confusion as to the status of Germany after its unconditional surrender in May, 1945.[34] Article 6 of the Fourth Geneva Convention of 1949 has clarified, to some extent, the answer to the original question by asserting that the Convention shall apply for one year after the general close of military operations and that certain of its basic provisions are to apply for the entire duration of the occupation.

SUGGESTED READINGS

BELLIGERENT OCCUPATION: GENERAL

Whiteman, Vol. I, pp. 315–319, 325–338, 911–916, 946–996; Svarlien, pp. 374–392. For a fairly comprehensive listing of the extensive literature available, consult the bibliography of approximately 700 titles in von Glahn, pp. 313–340. See also "Agreements Relating to Germany, 1952 and 1954," 49 *A.J.I.L.* (1955), Supp., pp. 55–148; G. I. A. Draper, *The Red Cross Conventions* (New York: Praeger; London: Stevens and Sons, Ltd., 1958); Joyce A. Gutteridge, "The Rights and Obligations of an Occupying Power," pp. 149–169 in London Institute of World Affairs, *Year Book of World Affairs 1952* (New York: Praeger, 1952); Morris G. Shanker, "The Law of Belligerent Occupation in the American Courts," 50 *Michigan Law Review* (1952), pp. 1066–1083; F. S. V. Donnison, *British Military Administration in the Far East 1943–46* (London: H.M. Stationery Office, 1957); George M. McCune, "The Occupation of Korea," 23 *Foreign Policy Reports* (1947), pp. 186–195; Beate R. von Oppen, ed., *Documents on Germany Under Occupation, 1945–54* (New York: Oxford University Press, 1955); Hans W. Baerwald, *The Purge of Japanese Leaders under the Occupation* (Berkeley: University of California Press, 1959); John Gimpel, *A German Community Under American Occu-*

---

[33] 49 *A.J.I.L.* (1955), Supp., pp. 73, 75; see also the digests of two German cases hinging on the provisions of Art. 7, par. 1, in 52 *A.J.I.L.* (1958), pp. 800–801, and *ibid.*, 53 (1959), pp. 459–460.

[34] See von Glahn, pp. 273–285, for an analysis of the major schools of thought on this particular problem.

pation (Stanford, Calif.: Stanford University Press, 1961) and his *The American Occupation of Germany: Politics and the Military, 1945–1949* (Stanford, Calif.: Stanford University Press, 1968); F. Roy Willis, *The French in Germany, 1945–1949* (Stanford, Calif.: Stanford University Press, 1961); Werner Warmbrunn, *The Dutch Under German Occupation* (Stanford, Calif.: Stanford University Press, 1963); Alexander Dallin, *German Rule in Russia, 1941–1945: A Study of Occupation Policies* (New York: St. Martin's Press, 1957); Philip W. Whitcomb, trans. & ed., *France During the German Occupation, 1940–1944* 3 vols. (Stanford, Calif.: Stanford University Press, 1959); Vladimir Petrov, *Money and Conquest: Allied Occupation Currencies in World War II* (Baltimore: The Johns Hopkins Press, 1967); Martin and Joan Kyre, *Military Occupation and National Security* (Washington, D.C.: Public Affairs Press, 1968).

Cases

Fleming & Marshall v. *Page*, United States, Supreme Court, 1850, 9 Howard 603.
State of the Netherlands v. *Federal Reserve Bank*, United States, Circuit Court of Appeals, Second Circuit, 1953, 201 F. (2d) 455.
État Français c. *Établissements Monmousseau*, France, Cour d'Appel d'Orléans, 1948, reported in 43 *A.J.I.L.* (1949), p. 819.
Haw Pia v. *China Banking Corporation*, Philippines, Supreme Court, 1948, G.R. No. L-554, reported in 43 *A.J.I.L.* (1949), pp. 821–823.
Agati v. *Soc. Elettrica Coloniale Italiano*, Tripoli, Tribunal of Tripoli, 1950, reported in 49 *A.J.I.L.* (1955), p. 261 (see also six other occupation cases, briefly noted, *ibid.*, p. 262).
Kent Jewelry Co. v. *Kiefer*, United States, N.Y. Supreme Court, New York County, 1952, 119 N.Y.S. (2d) 242, excerpted in 47 *A.J.I.L.* (1953), pp. 503–504.
Anton Schaffner v. *International Refugee Organization*, U.S. Court of Appeals, Allied High Commission for Germany, 1951, Civil Case No. 11, Opinion No. 665, reported in 46 *A.J.I.L.* (1952), pp. 575–576.
Japanese Government v. *Commercial Casualty Insurance Co.*, United States, District Court, S.D.N.Y., 1951, 101 F. Supp. 243, reported in 46 *A.J.I.L.* (1952), p. 557.

32

Crimes Under International Law

A N Y person, whether a civilian or a member of the armed forces of a state, who commits an act which constitutes a crime under international law is responsible for his act and is liable to punishment.

This statement, if written in 1914, would have represented merely a pious hope; in 1919, it would have caused derision; in 1970, it represents general but not yet universal agreement on an existing rule of international law.

A discussion of crimes under that law is greatly complicated by the fact that today three categories of such offenses are recognized, one of which is still a subject of much debate: (1) war crimes; (2) crimes against humanity; and (3) crimes against peace. The third of these centers, of course, on an interpretation of the Pact of Paris of 1928. The problem, discussed earlier, revolves around the question whether aggressive war itself is unlawful or whether its planning, preparation, and waging constitutes a crime.[1]

An orderly analysis of the multitude of questions posed by crimes under international law can be achieved by examining each major category in turn and then discovering what has been done to implement each of the three in recent decades.

WAR CRIMES

Generally speaking, a war crime is any act for which soldiers or other individuals may be punished by the enemy on capture of the offender. The category includes acts committed in violation of international law and of the laws of the criminal's own country as well as acts in violation of the laws of war and undertaken by order and in the interest of the criminal's own state.

It should be pointed out that current concepts about the nature of war crimes represent striking departures from traditional legal attitudes on the subject. Thus it was assumed for many decades that offenses against the

[1] See Lauterpacht's *Oppenheim*, Vol. II, p. 192, where the latter view is espoused with vigor and is buttressed with copious references; see particularly note 1 on page 193.

laws of war constituted crimes against the municipal law of belligerents.[2] The defenses of *act-of-state* and *superior orders* conditioned prosecution for war crimes. The asserted municipal character of penal offenses against the laws of war was based also on the orthodox belief that individuals were not subjects of international law. Again, none of the pre-1914 conventions dealing with war crimes designated the sanctions that would be applied to states or to individuals for violations of the rules governing warfare, with the exception of Article 3 of the Fourth Hague Convention of 1907, which called for payment of compensation by the belligerent state guilty of violating the treaty. Lastly, the absence of an international authority made it the duty of states to incorporate the provisions of the conventions in their national law and to enforce the latter against their own nationals or subjects.[3]

All of these notions have been abandoned since the early days of World War II. Evidence for this change is available in overwhelming abundance in national military manuals, in the four Geneva Conventions of 1949, and in the decisions of the international and national war crimes trials. Today responsibility for war crimes can be placed on individuals, including heads of states; the defense of superior orders has been circumscribed drastically; international tribunals are possible for the trial of the offending individuals; and national judicial agencies (civil or military) may try alien war criminals. A revolution, mostly to the good, thus has taken place in this specialized aspect of international law, and at least in this sphere, the individual has at last become a subject of the law.

MAJOR KINDS OF WAR CRIMES

Most authorities concur that four major kinds of war crimes are encountered: violations of the rules governing warfare; hostile armed acts committed by persons who are not members of a recognized armed forces; espionage, sabotage, and war treason; and all marauding acts.

Acts Constituting War Crimes. The following list, although not complete, embraces the major acts falling under the concept of violations of the laws of war: (1) making use of poisoned or otherwise forbidden arms or munitions; (2) treachery in asking for quarter or simulating sickness or wounds; (3) maltreatment of corpses; (4) firing on localities which are undefended and without military significance; (5) abuse of or firing on a flag of truce; (6) misuse of the Red Cross or similar emblems; (7) wearing of civilian clothes by troops to conceal their identity during the commission of combat acts; (8) improper utilization of privileged

---

[2] George Manner, "The Legal Nature and Punishment of Criminal Acts of Violence Contrary to the Laws of War," 37 *A.J.I.L.* (1943), pp. 407–435, at pp. 407, 414–415.

[3] *Ibid.*, pp. 408–409, citing Art. 1 of the Hague Conventions on Land Warfare of 1899 and 1907; Articles 27–29 of the Red Cross Conventions of 1929; and Articles 82, 84, and 85 of the 1929 Convention Relating to the Treatment of Prisoners of War.

(exempt, immune) buildings for military purposes; (9) poisoning of streams or wells; (10) pillage; (11) purposeless destruction; (12) compelling prisoners of war to engage in prohibited types of labor; (13) forcing civilians to perform prohibited labor; (14) violation of surrender terms; (15) killing or wounding military personnel who have laid down arms, surrendered, or are disabled by wounds or sickness; (16) assassination, and the hiring of assassins; (17) ill-treatment of prisoners of war, or of the wounded and sick—including despoiling them of possessions not classifiable as public property; (18) killing or attacking harmless civilians; (19) compelling the inhabitants of occupied enemy territory to furnish information about the armed forces of the enemy or his means of defense; (20) appropriation or destruction of the contents of privileged buildings; (21) bombardment from the air for the exclusive purpose of terrorizing or attacking civilian populations; (22) attack on enemy vessels which have indicated their surrender by lowering their flag; (23) attack or seizure of hospitals and all other violations of the Hague Convention for the Adaptation to Maritime Warfare of the Principles of the Geneva Convention; (24) unjustified destruction of enemy prizes; (25) use of enemy uniforms during combat and use of the enemy flag during attack by a belligerent vessel; (26) attack on individuals supplied with safe-conducts, and other violations of special safeguards provided; (27) breach of parole; (28) grave breaches of Article 50 of the Geneva Convention for the Amelioration of the Condition of the Wounded and Sick in Armed Forces in the Field, of 1949 and Article 51 of the Geneva Convention of 1949 Applicable to Armed Forces at Sea: "wilful killing, torture or inhuman treatment, including biological experiments, wilfully causing great suffering or serious injury to body or health, and extensive destruction and appropriation of property not justified by military necessity and carried out unlawfully and wantonly"; (29) grave breaches of the Geneva Convention Relative to the Treatment of Prisoners of War, of 1949, as listed in Article 130: "wilful killing, torture or inhuman treatment, including biological experiments, wilfully causing great suffering or serious injury to body or health, compelling a prisoner of war to serve in the forces of the hostile Power, or wilfully depriving a prisoner of war of the rights of fair and regular trial prescribed" in the Convention; [4] (30) grave breaches of the Fourth Geneva Convention of 1949, as detailed in Article 147: "wilful killing, torture or inhuman treatment, including biological experiments, wilfully causing great suffering or serious injury to body or health, unlawful deportation or transfer or unlawful confinement of a protected person, compelling a protected person to serve in the forces of a hostile Power, or wilfully depriving a protected person of the rights of fair and regular trial prescribed in the present Convention, taking of hostages and exten-

[4] Consult the fully documented study by Howard S. Levie, "Penal Sanctions for Maltreatment of Prisoners of War," 56 *A.J.I.L.* (1962), pp. 433–468, for a comprehensive analysis of all important issues involved in this area.

sive destruction and appropriation of property, not justified by military necessity and carried out unlawfully and wantonly." [5] In addition, conspiracy, direct incitement, and attempts to commit, as well as complicity in the commission of, crimes against the laws of war are punishable.

Treatment of Prisoners. Recent conflicts have witnessed widespread violations of the rules governing the treatment of prisoners of war. During World War II, some 15,000 Polish prisoners of war were executed by the Soviet Union, which was not a party to the 1929 Geneva Convention Relating to the Treatment of Prisoners of War, but was bound by customary law.[6] During the Korean War, numerous illegal executions of prisoners by the North Korean forces came to light. During the Vietnamese conflict, many authenticated instances of maltreatment of prisoners by both sides took place.[7] In October, 1965, the government of North Vietnam announced to the International Red Cross in Geneva that henceforth captured U.S. pilots would be tried as war criminals, a threat which was not carried out. North Vietnam had adhered to the Geneva Convention of 1949 in 1957, but had decided to ignore the prohibition on reprisals against prisoners of war. (See also Suggested Readings at the end of this chapter.)

The crew of the U.S. surveillance ship *U.S.S. Pueblo,* captured in January, 1968, by North Korea, was ill-treated during most of its captivity, until released in December of the same year.[8]

Defense of Superior Orders. Violation of one of the laws of war on the order of a belligerent state or of an individual commander of such a state does not remove the stigma of a war crime from the act in question. Hence the defense of *superior orders* no longer constitutes a valid defense for an individual accused of committing a war crime. Only if it can be shown that he did not know and could not reasonably have been expected to know that the act ordered was unlawful can such an accused person plead superior orders in his defense. However, most military manuals today hold that where the order is held not to constitute a defense, the fact that the accused acted in pursuance of orders may be considered as a mitigating factor in the assessment of punishment (*Law of Land Warfare,* par. 509-a).

[5] Based on *Law of Land Warfare,* pars. 502–504, and on Lauterpacht's *Oppenheim,* Vol. II, pp. 567–568, n. 2.

[6] Consult J. K. Zawodny, *Death in the Forest: The Story of the Katyn Forest Massacre* (South Bend, Ind.: Notre Dame University Press, 1962).

[7] Note the important qualification about such violations, by Richard A. Falk: "In reading these materials, however, it is important to refrain from arriving at *legal* conclusions. These reports on battlefield operations are unverified newspaper accounts. Any particular report may be unreliable."—Falk, "International Law and the Conduct of the Vietnam War," pp. 22–27, at p. 23, in Seymour Melman (Director of Research), *In the Name of America* (New York: Clergy and Laymen Concerned about Vietnam, 1968). See also "The Geneva Convention on Prisoners of War," *National Observer,* May 26, 1969, p. 7, and 66 *U.S. News & World Report* (June 23, 1969), pp. 47–49.

[8] For a summary, see 93 *Time* (January 3, 1969), pp. 18–19.

The Charter of the International Military Tribunal (Nuremberg) created in 1945 rejected, expressly, the plea of superior orders as an absolute defense but provided in Article 3 that superior orders might be considered in mitigation of punishment if the Tribunal determined that justice required this to be done.

The question of acts done pursuant to orders issued by a superior poses, of course, serious problems to members of armed forces. It is their duty to obey all lawful orders; they cannot, under conditions of war discipline, be expected to weigh with care the legal merits of every order issued to them; they may realize that certain laws of war are worded somewhat ambiguously or are controversial, and may not be able to determine, at the time, the status of the order received as it relates to the rule in question; and, very important from the point of view of violations of the rules, many acts normally classified as a war crime may be ordered as reprisals for prior acts committed by the enemy (*Law of Land Warfare*, par. 509-b).

Responsibility of Military Commanders. Military commanders may be responsible for war crimes committed by subordinates in their armed forces, or other persons under their control. This would always be true if such acts as massacres and atrocities against enemy civilians or prisoners of war were to be committed. Obviously, direct responsibility ensues for commanders when war crimes are committed under their orders. A commander would also be responsible if he had actual knowledge, or should have had knowledge through reports received by him or through other means, that troops or other persons subject to his control are about to commit, or have committed, a war crime and if he fails to take the necessary and reasonable steps to insure compliance with the laws of war or to punish the violators in question (*Law of Land Warfare*, par. 501).

Failure of a commander to take preventive steps or to punish acts already committed presumes approval of the act, or at least connivance on the part of the individual in question. This was a major part of the reasoning which led to the death sentence imposed by a United States Military Commission in Manila in 1946 on General Yamashita.[9]

Responsibility of Heads of State. If a war crime is committed or ordered by an individual who acted as head of a state or in the capacity of a responsible government official, he is nevertheless not relieved of responsibility and is liable to punishment. And the fact that his own domestic law does not penalize an act which, under international law, is a war crime does not relieve the individual who committed or ordered the act

---

[9] *In re Yamashita*, United States, Supreme Court, 1946, 327 U.S. 1; consult similar cases cited in Lauterpacht's *Oppenheim*, Vol. II, p. 573, n. 1, and see J. G. Feldhaus, "The Trial of Yamashita," 13 *Current Legal Thought* (1947), pp. 251–262. There was persuasive evidence in this case that General Yamashita was quite unable to control his disintegrating forces and that he did not order, permit voluntarily, or condone the conduct of which they were guilty. See also n. 36, below.

from responsibility and punishment (*Law of Land Warfare*, pars. 510–511).

Status of Private Individuals Who Commit Hostile Acts. Private individuals who assert a right to take up arms and commit hostile acts against an enemy do not enjoy the rights and privileges of members of armed forces. They may, therefore, be treated as war criminals by the enemy, except in the case of a genuine *levée en masse*, as outlined earlier. When such individuals organize in accordance with the Hague Convention of 1907, they vacate private status and must be treated in accordance with the laws of war, provided they, too, obey those laws. Thus the French Forces of the Interior were organized in June, 1944, as a force under the command of a high French military officer. They were then recognized by the Supreme Commander of the Allied Expeditionary Force as a component part of that force, and when German units refused to honor that status, acts committed against French Forces of the Interior were judged by the Allied command to be war crimes.

Espionage. Spying represents a legitimate practice on the part of a belligerent, yet when spies are captured behind enemy lines, they are regarded as having committed an act of illegitimate warfare, hence are subject to punishment. Under the provisions of Article 106 of the Hague Regulations of 1907, a person can only be considered a spy when, acting clandestinely or on false pretenses, he obtains or endeavors to obtain information in the zone of operations of a belligerent, with the intention of communicating it to the opposing hostile part. Thus, soldiers not wearing a disguise who have penetrated into the zone of operations of the enemy, for the purpose of obtaining information, are not considered spies.

Spies include persons of all classes, military or civilian, without regard to citizenship or sex. When they are punished, this is not done because they violated the laws of war—for spying is legal—but to make spying as dangerous, difficult, and ineffective as possible. It is, therefore, somewhat doubtful whether spying should be described as a war crime. When caught, a spy must be given a trial (Art. 30, Hague Regulations of 1907); on conviction, the normal penalty is death.

A spy who, after rejoining his own armed forces, is subsequently captured by the enemy must be treated as a prisoner of war and incurs no responsibility for his previous acts of espionage (Art. 31, Hague Regulations).[10]

Sabotage. Individuals who, without meeting the conditions laid down in conventional law for recognition as lawful combatants, commit hostile acts behind the lines of the enemy will not be treated as prisoners of war and may be sentenced to imprisonment or to execution. Such acts include sabotage and destruction of communications facilities. Actual commission

[10] On spies, see Whiteman, Vol. X, pp. 150–153, 166–167, 177–195, and Maximilian Koessler, "The International Law on the Punishment of Belligerent Spies: A Legal Paradox," 5 *Criminal Law Review* (1958), pp. 21–35.

of the acts in question is not necessary for imposition of punishment, for attempts as well as conspiracy to commit hostile acts are sufficient. Normally, states include acts of sabotage under the next topic, war treason, in their military manuals.

War Treason. Offenses included in this broad category include all acts committed within the lines of a belligerent and deemed injurious to him and intended as promoting the cause of his enemy. Excluded from the concept of war treason are espionage and armed hostilities carried on by civilians in occupied enemy territory. A list of the major varieties of war treason would include any of the following acts:

1. Information of any kind given to the enemy.
2. The voluntary giving of supplies of any kind to the enemy.
3. Voluntary assistance given to military operations of the enemy.
4. Attempts to induce soldiers to desert, surrender, or spy.
5. Attempt to bribe officials or soldiers in the interest of the enemy.
6. Liberation of enemy prisoners of war.
7. Entering into a conspiracy against the armed forces or against individual members of such forces.
8. Wrecking of military trains or convoys, of lines of communication, or of communication media in the interests of the enemy as well as destruction of any war material for the same purpose.
9. Intentional misguiding of troops by hired or voluntary guides.
10. Acting as a courier for the enemy.
11. Harboring or protecting enemy personnel.[11]

The usual penalty for persons convicted of war treason is the death sentence, although imprisonment has been substituted at times. Enemy soldiers accused of war treason may be punished only if they have committed one of the acts in question during their stay within a belligerent's lines in disguise. Thus when two Japanese officers, dressed in Chinese civilian clothes, were caught behind the Russian lines in the Russo-Japanese War of 1904, in an attempt to blow up a railroad bridge, they were properly sentenced to death.[12] As in the case of espionage, acts labeled as war treason are permitted to a belligerent under the laws of war. But they possess a twofold aspect, and a belligerent capturing enemy soldiers or enemy civilians guilty of committing these acts behind his lines has a perfect right to regard the acts as illegal warfare and to punish their perpetrators. Acts of war treason are not war crimes, however, in the strict meaning of that term.

THE PUNISHMENT OF WAR CRIMES

Article III of the Hague Convention of 1907 on War on Land provided that "A belligerent party which violates the provisions of the said regu-

---

[11] Based on Lauterpacht's *Oppenheim*, Vol. II, p. 575, n. 5, and on the *Law of Land Warfare*, paragraph 79 ("Aiding the Enemy").

[12] Cited in Lauterpacht's *Oppenheim*, Vol. II, p. 576, n. 1.

lations shall, if the case demands, be liable to pay compensation. It shall be responsible for all acts committed by persons forming part of its armed forces." This wording implied that violations of the Regulations would be satisfactorily remedied by payment of money, but nothing was said about trial and punishment of the offenders actually guilty of violating the laws of war.

PRE-1945 RULES OF LAW

Rules of Land Warfare (1940). On the other hand, even under the pre-1945 rules of law, offending members of armed forces were held to be answerable, on an individual basis, to the wronged state. Many national military manuals stipulated that commanders ordering acts violating the laws of war were punishable by the injured belligerent once they fell into his hands. The revised version of the American manual (*Rules of Land Warfare*, 1940 edition) went even further and spelled out in detail the remedies of an injured belligerent (par. 346):

In the event of clearly established violation of the laws of war, the injured party may legally resort to such remedial action as may be deemed appropriate and necessary within the following classes, to wit: a. Publication of the facts, with a view to influencing public opinion against the offending belligerents. b. Protest and demand for punishment of individual offenders, sent to the offending belligerent through neutral diplomatic channels, or by parlementaire direct to the commander of the offending forces. c. Punishment of captured individual offenders. d. Reprisals.

It can thus be said that criminal punishment of individuals represents a sanction of the laws of war.

Treaty of Versailles and the Commission of Fifteen. The first major attempt to punish offenders guilty of committing war crimes took place at the end of World War I. On January 25, 1919, the Preliminary Peace Conference created a Commission of Fifteen to investigate and report on violations of international law that could be charged against Germany and its allies.[13] The Commission, in its report, specifically denied immunity from responsibility to high officials of the Central Powers, including even chiefs of states.[14] It recommended the establishment of an International High Tribunal, to apply "the principles of the law of nations as they result from the usages established among civilized peoples, from the laws of humanity and from the dictates of public conscience"[15]—a wording taken from the Preamble to the Hague Conventions of 1899 and 1907. The American representatives on the Commission differed with their

---

[13] The report of the "Commission on the Responsibility of the Authors of the War and on the Enforcement of Penalties," may be found in 14 *A.J.I.L.* (1920), Supp., pp. 95–154.

[14] *Ibid.,* pp. 116, 121–122.

[15] *Ibid.,* p. 122.

Allied colleagues and wanted the law to be applied limited to the laws and customs of war only.[16]

Over the dissenting views of the United States and Japanese members, the view of the majority was adopted and Article 227 of the Treaty of Versailles provided for the creation of a tribunal of five judges to be appointed to try the ex-Emperor of Germany not for war crimes, but for "a supreme offense against international morality and the sanctity of treaties." Because the Kaiser had found asylum and the Netherlands refused to surrender him to the Allied and Associated Powers, the scheme came to naught.

The treaty contained, however, additional punitive provisions in the form of Articles 228–230. Under Article 228, the German government recognized "the right of the Allied and Associated Powers to bring before military tribunals persons accused of having committed acts in violation of the laws and customs of war. Such persons shall, if found guilty, be sentenced to punishments laid down by law." The German government was to hand over all such accused, which were to be specified, for trial. Article 229 provided meager details of the trial procedures, and Article 230 required Germany to supply all documents and information that might be considered necessary to ensure a "full knowledge of the incriminating acts, the discovery of offenders, and the just appreciation of responsibility."

War Crimes Trials (Post-World War I). The Allied Powers thereupon drew up a list of 896 names of persons accused of war crimes. Following strong German resistance to the surrender of those persons, a compromise was evolved on German suggestions and on May 7, 1920, a sample "abridged" list of forty-five names were sent to the German government. These individuals were to be tried before the German Supreme Court at Leipzig. The trial began on May 23, 1921. Only twelve of the forty-five persons named on the "test list" were actually tried, and only six of these were found guilty. The sentences imposed were nominal, ranging from six months' to a maximum of four years' imprisonment. The final bizarre touch of these regrettable proceedings was added by the escape from detention of Lt. Boldt, a former submarine commander, who had received the four-year sentence, and of another former submarine commander convicted of atrocities. The Allies then ceased all further attempts to have war crimes trials continued.[17]

---

[16] *Ibid.*, pp. 134, 135, 144, 145.

[17] For a more detailed account, told more in sorrow than in anger, consult Sheldon Glueck, *War Criminals, Their Prosecution & Punishment* (New York: Alfred A. Knopf, 1944), at pp. 19–34; see also James W. Garner, *Recent Developments in International Law* (Calcutta: University of Calcutta, 1925), at pp. 455–463; Corbett, pp. 228–229; George A. Finch, "Retribution for War Crimes," 37 *A.J.I.L.* (1943), pp. 81–88, at pp. 82–84; Albert G. D. Levy, "The Law and Procedure of War Crimes Trials," 37 *A.P.S.R.* (1943), pp. 1052–1081, at pp. 1056–1063; and Georg

INTERNATIONAL MILITARY TRIBUNAL (NUREMBERG)

Demands for Postwar Punishment of War Criminals. The almost unbelievable violations of the laws of war at the hands of the Axis Powers and their minor allies led early in World War II to demands for an effective postwar punishment of the guilty individuals.[18] The list of relevant statements and declarations is very long: the most important among them were the statements by President Roosevelt and Prime Minister Churchill of October 25, 1941, on Axis executions of hostages;[19] the resolutions adopted on January 13, 1942, by representatives of nine European governments-in-exile at St. James' Palace in London, on postwar punishment of war criminals, particularly as regarded the shooting of hostages;[20] President Roosevelt's warning to war criminals on August 21 and October 7, 1942, dealing with trial of criminals in the national courts of the states in which their offenses had been committed; the announcement by the Lord Chancellor in the House of Commons on October 7, 1942, of the formation of a United Nations Commission for the Investigation of War Crimes, together with a warning that named offenders were to be surrendered at the time of any armistice, and that their delivery would be requested from any neutral country to which they might have fled;[21] the Allied statement, delivered by the British Foreign Secretary on December 17, 1942, on retribution to be visited on war criminals; the Moscow Declaration of October 30, 1943;[22] statements by Roosevelt and Churchill of March 24, 1944; the proposal of a warning by the Provisional French Government on July 15, 1944, that Germany be told not to carry out any last-minute executions of French nationals; and the American-British-Russian Declaration of Potsdam, published on July 26, 1945, announcing (par. 10) that ". . . stern justice shall be meted out to all war criminals, including those who have visited cruelties upon our prisoners,"[23] a sentiment reiterated in Articles III (A 5) and VII of the Report on the Tripartite Conference in Berlin (Potsdam).[24]

Moscow Declaration and London Agreement. In implementation of the Moscow Declaration, the governments of the United States, the United

Schwarzenberger, *International Law and Totalitarian Lawlessness* (London: Jonathan Cape, 1943), at pp. 68–73, and especially at pp. 113–147 for copious excerpts from the decisions at the Leipzig trials.

[18] Consult Whiteman, Vol. XI, pp. 874–880.

[19] Text in Schwarzenberger, *op. cit.*, pp. 147–148.

[20] *The New York Times*, January 14, 1942. China and the Soviet Union had observers at the meeting. See also M. E. Bathurst, "The United Nations War Crimes Commission," 39 *A.J.I.L.* (1945), pp. 565–570.

[21] See F. L. Neumann, "Neutral States and the Extradition of War Criminals," 45 *A.J.I.L.* (1951), pp. 495–508, on the problems posed by the 1942 announcement.

[22] 9 *Department of State Bulletin* (1943), pp. 310–311.

[23] *Ibid.*, 13 (1945), pp. 137–138.

[24] *Ibid.*, pp. 155, 158.

Kingdom, France, and the Soviet Union concluded on August 8, 1945, in London an Agreement for the Prosecution and Punishment of the Major War Criminals of the European Axis.[25] This instrument provided the details for the establishment of an International Military Tribunal. This body was to consist of four judges, each appointed by a party to the agreement, together with four alternates similarly chosen. Among other provisions, such as those dealing with the defense of superior orders, the individual's responsibility irrespective of official position, and the safeguarding of a fair trial, the key article of the Charter of the Tribunal was No. 6 which defined the jurisdiction of the court:

The following acts, or any of them, are crimes coming within the jurisdiction of the Tribunal for which there shall be individual responsibility:

(a) Crimes against Peace: Namely, planning, preparation, initiation or waging of a war of aggression, or a war in violation of international treaties, agreements or assurances, or participation in a common plan or conspiracy for the accomplishment of any of the foregoing;

(b) War Crimes: Namely, violations of the laws or customs of war. Such violations shall include, but not be limited to, murder, ill-treatment or deportation to slave labor or from any other purpose of civilian population of or in occupied territory, murder or ill-treatment of prisoners of war or persons on the seas, killing of hostages, plunder of public or private property, wanton destruction of cities, towns or villages, or devastation not justified by military necessity;

(c) Crimes against Humanity: Namely, murder, extermination, enslavement, deportation, and other inhumane acts committed against any civilian population, before or during the war, or persecutions on political, racial or religious grounds in execution of or in connection with any crime within the jurisdiction of the Tribunal, whether or not in violation of the domestic law of the country where perpetrated.

Leaders, organizers, instigators, and accomplices participating in the formulation or execution of a common plan or conspiracy to commit any of the foregoing crimes are responsible for all acts performed by any persons in execution of such plan. . . .

In accordance with the provisions of the Moscow Declaration, the Nuremberg Tribunal was to deal with "German Criminals, whose offenses have no particular geographical localization" and who could be punished "by joint decision of the Allies."

The resulting trials conducted by the Tribunal are too well known to discuss in detail, and the literature dealing with them has swollen to enormous proportions. Suffice it to state here that the trials began on November 20, 1945, and the hearing of evidence and the speeches of counsel

[25] Consult *International Conference on Military Trials, London, 1945* (Washington, D.C.: U.S. Government Printing Office [Department of State Publication 3080]), for texts of all proposals at the meeting.

ended on August 31, 1946. The Tribunal gave its judgment on September 30, 1946.[26] Sentences were pronounced on October 1, 1946.

The London Agreement of 1945 was adhered to by nineteen states (in addition to the original four signers) before the Nuremberg trial began.

Criticisms of the Nuremberg Trial. The trial itself has been the subject of much criticism, on a variety of grounds.[27] Leaving aside, for the time being, charges that *ex post facto* punishment was exacted for crimes against peace, there is no question but that the convictions for traditional war crimes were legally correct, on the basis of customary and conventional international law.

More to the point was criticism aimed at certain procedural details, notably the absence of neutral judges on the Tribunal. This, in the opinion of several commentators, constituted a definite defect in the constitution of the court and if it had been avoided, would have tended to remove charges that justice was really a form of revenge. But would the inclusion of neutral judges really have made any difference? The present writer cannot see that such judges would have supplied a truly impartial element to the composition of the Tribunal. The offenses of the accused were so horrifying, so lacking in the minimum of human decency and of the aspects commonly associated with the Judaeo-Christian civilization, that neutral judges, listening to the evidence, could not have remained neutral. Furthermore, they would inevitably have had to consider that their own state might be the victim of similar events if the offenders of World War II had not been punished, so that they might easily have been influenced in favor of punishment as a deterrent.

Some of the criticisms leveled at the Tribunal were based on the absence of German judges on the court. Certainly the record of German justice at the Leipzig trials mentioned earlier would have cast doubts on the advisability of a second attempt to have nationals of a state help to judge their own citizens accused of war crimes.[28]

Criticisms centering on the procedures used in the Nuremberg trial tend to ignore the rather obvious fact that procedures held to be utterly fair and normal in one country would appear lacking in one or several aspects

---

[26] Text of Judgment and of the Sentences reprinted in 41 *A.J.I.L.* (1947), pp. 172–332; see also Whiteman, Vol. XI, pp. 880–934.

[27] See Lord Maurice Hankey, *Politics, Trials and Errors* (Chicago: Henry Regnery Co., 1950); F. J. P. Veale, *Advance to Barbarism* (Appleton, Wis.: C. C. Nelson, 1953); Wilbourne E. Benton and Georg Grimm, *Nuremberg: German Views of the War Trials* (Dallas: Southern Methodist University Press, 1955); Hans Ehard, "The Nuremberg Trial against the Major War Criminals and Int. Law," 43 *A.J.I.L.* (1949), pp. 223–245; and the views of the late Senator Robert A. Taft of Ohio as well as Supreme Court Justice William O. Douglas. See also the suggestive discussion in Corbett, pp. 230–237.

[28] See John A. Appleman, *Military Tribunals and International Crimes* (Indianapolis: Bobbs-Merrill Co., 1954), at pp. 358–359 on the failure of numerous German denazification tribunals to pass adequate sentences on their fellow citizens.

to a citizen of another state, in view of the differences in procedure utilized in the countries in question.[29] In the Nuremberg trial, Anglo-Saxon trial procedures tended to predominate, and the German defendants and their counsel encountered considerable difficulties in accustoming themselves to such practices as cross-examination, to them a totally unfamiliar procedure.

One major criticism, voiced principally in German sources but echoed by individual Allied citizens, was the failure of the victors in World War II to investigate war crimes attributed to members of their own armed forces. The Tribunal itself refused to undertake any such inquiry, and the terms of its Charter justified this view. Thus the trials, conducted only against the losing party, were one-sided, to be sure. But leaving aside this factor, the introduction of an effective prosecution and punishment of war crimes may be regarded as a salutory object lesson for future prospective offenders against the laws of war. A procedural and legal set of procedents has been established and may well act as a deterrent in future wars. If the lessons of Nuremberg had been assimilated fully by the states of the world, a permanent structural unit, an international criminal court, might already have seen the light of day. This, however, will be discussed later in this chapter.

INTERNATIONAL MILITARY TRIBUNAL FOR THE FAR EAST (TOKYO)

Closely related to the Nuremberg trials was the establishment of the International Military Tribunal for the Far East. In this instance, too, the Charter in question specified the categories of war crimes, crimes against peace, and crimes against humanity, together with a separate grouping of a crime of conspiracy to commit the foregoing crimes. The Tribunal, in this case, consisted of eleven judges, representing the states at war against Japan.[30] The trial began on June 4, 1946, and the judgment was given on November 4, 1948. The initial proclamation setting up the Tribunal was issued by General Douglas MacArthur as Supreme Commander for the Allied Powers in the Pacific. In 1948, in a very significant decision, the Supreme Court of the United States ruled that the Tribunal was not a court of the United States, and that in consequence the Supreme Court had no jurisdiction to review or to set aside judgments of the Tribunal.[31]

TRIALS BY "NATIONAL" TRIBUNALS

The publicity given to the proceedings of the two international military tribunals overshadowed the fact that the vast majority of accused war criminals of World War II were dealt with, as prescribed in the Moscow

---

[29] See especially Gould, pp. 669–670 on this important point.

[30] Text of Charter in 14 *Department of State Bulletin* (1946), pp. 361 ff.

[31] *Koki Hirato et al.* v. *Douglas MacArthur*, United States, Supreme Court, 1948, 338 U.S. 197, digested at some length in 43 *A.J.I.L.* (1949), pp. 170–172; consult also Whiteman, Vol. XI, pp. 965–1009, 1017–1019.

Agreement, either by military courts of individual occupants or were returned to the scenes of their offenses and there were tried and punished by local courts and under local laws.[32] In some countries, where domestic legislation required this, the accused offenders were tried in ordinary criminal courts for violating the local criminal laws; most of them, however, were brought before military courts of particular states for violation of the laws and customs of war.

By late November, 1948, a total of 7,109 defendants had been arrested for war crimes, including the "major cases" at Nuremberg and Tokyo. Of these, 3,686 had been convicted and 924 trials had resulted in acquittals. Of those convicted, death sentences were received by 1,019, and 33 defendants had committed suicide. Prison sentences were received by 2,667 and 2,499 cases were still pending.[33] Numerous files remained open, however, where war crimes had been committed but the culprits had disappeared. In the intervening years, many of these, particularly in France and in Germany, have been discovered by their own governments and have been tried for violations of the laws of war. Thus by early 1964 some 5,500 individuals had been tried in West Germany, with about 1,000 cases still pending.

Many of these "national" trials were divorced from the Moscow Declaration and were based on violations of the laws of war as such; this, for instance, was true in the famous Belsen trial, dealing with the Auschwitz and Belsen camps, which was conducted by British authorities in their zone of occupation under the authority of a Royal Warrant.[34] The basis of such trials was international customary and conventional law as it existed at the time the alleged offense was committed.

It may be mentioned as a matter of some interest that a military tribunal trying an alien accused of war crimes is not bound by procedural safeguards established in the tribunal's own country by constitution or law. This principle was brought out strikingly in the decision of the Supreme Court on an appeal by General Yamashita against a conviction (and death sentence) by a U.S. Military Commission appointed for war crimes trials by General MacArthur in the Philippines.[35] The Supreme Court, in re-

---

[32] See Maximilian Koessler, "American War Crimes Trials in Europe," 39 *Georgetown Law Journal* (1950), pp. 18–112; William B. Cowles, "Trials of War Criminals (Non-Nuremberg)," 42 *A.J.I.L.* (1948), pp. 299–319; and Stone, pp. 372–376. A strong criticism of the U.S. trials, conducted under Control Council Law No. 10, may be found in August von Knieriem, *The Nuremberg Trials* (Chicago: Henry Regnery Co., 1959); Whiteman, Vol. XI, pp. 934–965.

[33] 52 *Time* (November 29, 1948), p. 31.

[34] See *War Crimes Trials*, Vol. II, *The Belsen Trial* (London: William Hodge & Co., Ltd., 1949). American, British and French military courts sentenced a total of 5,025 individuals, of whom 806 were executed. The Soviet Union is believed to have sentenced about 10,000 persons on charges of war crimes.

[35] *In re Yamashita*, United States, Supreme Court, February 4, 1946, 327 U.S. 1, 66 Sup. Ct. 340; this very important decision has been reprinted in 40 *A.J.I.L.* (1946), pp. 432–480.

jecting the appeal from a conviction for failure of a commander to take appropriate measures to prevent violations of the laws of war by troops under his command, emphasized in a classic but much criticized opinion that military tribunals trying such cases are not bound by constitutional requirements for due process of law in the domestic sense of that term.[36]

CRIMES AGAINST HUMANITY

The Charter of the International Tribunal at Nuremberg listed in Article 6 (a) a "new" category of crimes under international law, termed *crimes against humanity*.

This concept led to considerable criticism on the grounds that traditional international law had not recognized such an offense and that trial of accused violators of such a new concept represented *ex post facto*, or retroactive, punishment.

Offenses Constituting Crimes Against Humanity. The wording of the section in question reveals a combination of two different sets of offenses. "Murder, extermination, enslavement, deportation, and other inhumane acts committed against any civilian population" represented, in time of war and applied to enemy citizens, crimes against the laws of war. Offenders guilty of such acts were war criminals beyond a doubt. The section of the article in question went further, however, and specified not only the criminal character of such acts when done in time of war, but also "before" a war, and then stipulated further "or persecution on political, racial, or religious grounds in execution of or in connection with any crime within the jurisdiction of the Tribunal, whether or not in violation of the domestic law of the country where perpetrated."

The "before the war" part and the concluding portion of the quoted text must be taken to be a reiteration of the existence of fundamental human rights, superior to the law of any state and protected by international sanctions.[37] The Tribunal itself decided that it could only deal with acts listed in Article 6 (c) that had taken place after the beginning of the war and thus deliberately avoided the thorny issue of human rights:

> To constitute Crimes against Humanity, the acts relied on before the outbreak of war must have been in execution of, or in connection with, any crime within the jurisdiction of the Tribunal. The Tribunal is of the opinion that revolting and horrifying as many of these crimes were, it has not been satisfactorily proved that they were done in execution of, or in connection with, any such crime. The Tribunal therefore cannot make a general declaration that the acts before 1939 were Crimes against Humanity within the meaning of the Charter. . . .[38]

[36] See also Quincy Wright, "Due Process and International Law," 40 *A.J.I.L.* (1946), pp. 398–406, on the Yamashita case.

[37] Lauterpacht's *Oppenheim*, Vol. II, p. 579, n. 5; see also E. Schwelb, "Crimes Against Humanity," 23 *B.Y.I.L.* (1946), pp. 178–226.

[38] Judgment, October 1, 1946, in 41 *A.J.I.L.* (1947), at p. 249.

Only two of the accused criminals were found guilty of crimes against humanity alone: one was sentenced to death, the other to imprisonment for twenty years (Julius Streicher, Gauleiter of Franconia, was sentenced to death; Baldur von Schirach, Leader of Youth Education, Gauleiter of Vienna, Reich Governor of Vienna, and Reich Defense Commissioner for Vienna, received the prison sentence). All other German leaders accused of crimes against humanity and found guilty by the Tribunal were also sentenced because of the commission of ordinary war crimes.

Expansion of the Jurisdiction of International Criminal Law. Basically, crimes against humanity, beyond the sphere of traditional war crimes, represented offenses committed against civilians, and not so much against individuals as against civilian populations. Obviously such a development meant an expansion in the scope of international criminal law.[39] The interesting and debatable aspect of this expansion centers on the fact that neither the Charter of the Nuremberg Tribunal nor the provisions of Control Council Law No. 10 limited the offenses in question to those committed against alien populations or permitted the local law of the states where offenses had taken place to serve as authority for the acts done. Even acts of Germans against their fellow citizens were deemed to fall within the purview of the authority of the Allies, despite the fact that German law would have sanctioned a number of acts involved.

Such an unprecedented innovation in the law of nations must remain somewhat questionable even today, particularly on the grounds that the interpretation given disregards a basic principle of the law: no state shall intervene in the territorial and personal sphere of validity of another national legal order.[40] The innovation assumes even greater importance when it is remembered that the Charter of the United Nations, drafted some months before the war crimes trials took place, provided in Article 2 (7), that intervention was prohibited "in matters which are essentially within the domestic jurisdiction of any state." On the other hand, certain aspects of "crimes against humanity" have achieved legal recognition through the advent of the convention on genocide, discussed later.

It may well be that an expansion of this new sphere in the law will come about in the not too distant future. But, as we shall see later, the prospects for such a development appear dim at present, in the light of what has happened to draft codes designed for such a purpose. On the other hand, as Gould pointed out,[41] it is reasonable to expect that the various states which enforced the London Charter rules on crimes against humanity by prosecutions by their war crimes tribunals must henceforth view themselves as bound by the rules they enforced. To that extent at least, some

[39] See Gould, pp. 656–657, on this point, and note the war crimes trial decision cited there.

[40] F. B. Schick, "The Nuremberg Trial and the International Law of the Future," 41 *A.J.I.L.* (1947), pp. 770–794, at p. 785; for an opposing view, see Stone, pp. 360–361.

[41] Gould, p. 659.

progress has been made in the evolution of a new and revolutionary segment of international law.

It is interesting to note that, on November 26, 1968, the General Assembly of the United Nations approved, by a 58 to 7 vote, a convention to outlaw statutes of limitations as applied to war crimes and crimes against humanity. The United States and the United Kingdom were among the states opposing the proposal.

CRIMES AGAINST PEACE

The category of "Crimes Against Peace" represented a second and perhaps even more debatable aspect of the Nuremberg and Tokyo trials. Today it can be asserted with some degree of validity, even though perhaps rather academically, that under the provisions of Article 39 of the Charter of the United Nations, the planning, preparation, and launching of a war not strictly in self-defense *may* be regarded as unlawful and as a threat to the peace, or breach of the peace, in the meaning of the Charter of the United Nations.

But it must be pointed out that at the time the German and Japanese defendants committed their alleged offenses, there was no rule of international law which forbade the citizens of a sovereign state to plan or to carry out acts which could be termed afterward an illegal war, or to use a more common appellation, an aggressive war, despite the existence of the Covenant and of the Pact of Paris.[42]

Many reasons could be cited to support the absence, then and now, of a crime against peace. The members of the community of nations have been unable to agree on a definition of aggression, as noted below. It would be difficult, to say the least, to determine whether a given act, when planned or carried out, would lead to an aggressive war, assuming that an accepted definition had been obtained. Peacetime national efforts to improve the military potential of a given state may represent a needed bolstering of defensive strength or preparation for an attack on a neighbor. Scientific research for new or more effective weapons may possess both offensive and defensive aspects.

Looking back at the Nuremberg and Tokyo charges of crimes against peace, they appear, to this writer, to have been based primarily on the body of post-1919 declarations, pacts, and resolutions asserting the illegality of aggression. Because this assortment of statements cannot be asserted to represent either customary law (*vide* state practices) or conventional law, and because no definition of aggression has been agreed on, it would seem that the charges of crimes against peace were based on rather shaky foundations at best. In the opinion of this writer, the ancient principle of

---

[42] See *The Case Against Hermann Roechling and Others*, General Tribunal of the Military Government of the French Zone of Occupation in Germany, June 30, 1948, digested in 43 *A.J.I.L.* (1949), pp. 191–193; consult also Stone, pp. 360–361.

nullum crimen sine lege (no crime without a law) should not have been set aside in the case of the alleged crimes against peace, and the rather cavalier dismissal of the principle by the Nuremberg Tribunal deserves strong criticism.

Did the principles enunciated in the Charters of the International Tribunals and enforced in the decisions of both, as well as of a multitude of national courts, affect the body on international law to an important extent? Did they create new rules of law, binding on the community of nations? This subject has to be examined.

DRAFT CODE OF OFFENSES AGAINST THE PEACE AND SECURITY OF MANKIND

International Law Commission. On December 11, 1946 the General Assembly of the United Nations unanimously adopted a resolution reaffirming the "principles of international law" recognized by the Charter of the Nuremberg Tribunal and the Judgment of the Tribunal.

By Resolution 177 (II) of November 21, 1947, the General Assembly directed the International Law Commission to undertake a study of the principles in question and also to prepare a "draft code of offenses against the peace and security of mankind," indicating clearly the place to be accorded in such draft to the Nuremberg principles.

The Commission began a preliminary study of this assignment at its first session in 1949 and at once encountered the question of the extent to which the principles embodied in the London Charter and in the judgments constituted principles of international law. The Nuremberg Tribunal, in its judgment, had asserted that the Charter (including, of course, the principles found therein) was "the expression of international law existing at the time of its creation, and to that extent is itself a contribution to international law." The Commission, however, refused to express its opinion on this assertion and decided that its assigned task was merely one of formulation.[43]

At its 1950 session, the Commission set to work on a report prepared for it by its special rapporteur, Professor Jean Spiropolous, who had been assigned to both tasks called for in the 1947 Resolution. The formulation of the Nuremberg principles was then discussed at length at the fifth session of the General Assembly, in the latter's Sixth Committee. On December 12, 1950, the Assembly, after extensive debate, adopted Resolution 488 (V), which invited the members to offer their observations on the work done by the ILC and directed the Commission to take account of such observations in the preparation of the draft code.

The Commission had already circularized the members of the United Nations in order to secure listings of additional offenses to be included in the draft code, and appointed a drafting committee. The resulting provisional text was referred to the special rapporteur, who submitted his sec-

---

[43] See United Nations, *Report of the I.L.C. Covering its Second Session, June 5–July 29, 1950,* in 44 *A.J.I.L.* (1950), Supp., pp. 105–148, at pp. 125–126.

ond report on the code to the Commission at its third session in 1951. At that time, the ILC adopted a draft code, which it submitted, in its report, to the General Assembly.

The Assembly postponed the question of the draft code to its seventh session in 1952, but, after comments on the draft had been solicited and received from fourteen members, discussion was again delayed on the understanding that the matter would continue to be studied by the ILC. The latter asked its rapporteur to prepare another draft of the code, and this was considered at length during the sixth session of the Commission in 1954.[44]

Since the International Law Commission reported this 1954 draft of the code to the General Assembly, nothing more has been done about the matter. At present little interest appears to exist among the member states of the United Nations to make the draft code operative. In particular, the question of penalties had been omitted from any draft, because the ILC believed that this topic could be considered more conveniently after it had been decided how the code itself would become a part of international law.

It appears reasonable to assume, however, that the code will not become operative until aggression has been defined in terms acceptable to the members of the United Nations, for a number of the offenses listed in the code specifically refer to acts of aggression.

DRAFT STATUTES FOR AN INTERNATIONAL CRIMINAL COURT

A second aftermath of the postwar trials has also been left in incomplete form: the question of an international criminal court. The General Assembly, by Resolution 260B (III) of December 9, 1948, had invited the International Law Commission to "study the desirability and possibility of establishing an international judicial organ for the trial of persons charged with genocide or other crimes over which jurisdiction will be conferred upon that organ by international conventions." It requested the Commission, in carrying out this assignment, to "pay attention to the possibility of establishing a Criminal Chamber of the International Court of Justice." [45]

The matter was taken up at the first session of the ILC and two special rapporteurs were appointed to submit one or several working papers to

[44] Text of the revised draft code with comments on the modifications made, in United Nations, *Report of the I.L.C. Covering the Work of Its Sixth Session, June 3–July 28, 1954,*" in 49 *A.J.I.L.* (1955), Supp., at pp. 19–23; see also Whiteman, Vol. XI, pp. 839–844.

[45] Yuen-li Liang, "Notes on Legal Questions Concerning the United Nations," 45 *A.J.I.L.* (1951), pp. 509–524, at p. 524; consult also Vespasian V. Pella, "Towards an International Criminal Court," 44 *A.J.I.L.* (1950), pp. 37–68, with its full documentation; John J. Parker, "An International Criminal Court: The Case for Its Adoption," 38 *American Bar Association Journal* (1952), pp. 641–643; George A. Finch, "The Case Against Its Adoption," *ibid.*, pp. 644–648; and Stone, pp. 377–379.

the second session of the Commission in 1950. The two rapporteurs, however, presented opposing points of view in their papers: Mr. R. J. Alfaro contended that it was possible and desirable to create such a judicial organ, whereas Mr. A. E. F. Sandström asserted that such a court would damage the actual organization of the international community to the extent that more harm than good would result. The Commission, by a vote of 8 to 2, upheld Mr. Alfaro's view that a court was desirable and by a vote of 7 to 2 that the creation of such a court was possible. The Commission also decided that despite the possibility of amending the Statute of the International Court of Justice to establish a criminal chamber of the Court, it did not recommend such action.

The conclusions of the Commission resulted in extensive discussions in the Sixth Committee of the General Assembly, with strong opposition to the establishment of an international criminal court on the part of the Soviet Union, Byelorussia, and Poland, as well as criticism on the part of the United Kingdom representative. The result of the debate was passage of a resolution proposing to set up a committee of seventeen states to meet in Geneva on August 1, 1951, to prepare a draft convention for the establishment of an international criminal court. This resolution was, in substance, adopted by the General Assembly on December 12, 1950 (Poland and the Soviet Union refused to be represented on the drafting committee).

1951 Draft Statute. The United Nations Committee on International Criminal Jurisdiction met in Geneva and produced a Draft Statute for an International Criminal Court.[46] This instrument provided for a permanent court of nine judges elected by the parties to the agreement (Arts. 5–11); the Court was to meet only when cases arose (Art. 3); its jurisdiction extended to the trial of "persons accused of crimes under international law, as may be provided in conventions or by special agreements, among States parties to the present Statute" (Art. 1); the Court was to apply "international law, including international criminal law, and, where appropriate national law" (Art. 2); the competence of the Court was limited to natural persons, including persons who had acted as Head of State or agent of a government (Art. 25); the Court could only exercise jurisdiction when such had been conferred "upon the Court by the State or States of which he [the accused person] is a national and by the State or States in which the crime is alleged to have been committed" (Art. 25); no jurisdiction could be conferred on the Court without the approval of the General Assembly (Art. 28); proceedings could be instituted only by the Assembly, or by any organization of States authorized to do so by the General Assembly, or by "a State party to the present Statute which has conferred jurisdiction upon the Court over such offences as are involved in those proceedings" (Art. 29); and rather elaborate safeguards to assure a fair trial were provided (Arts. 35–54).

[46] Text reprinted in 46 *A.J.I.L.* (1952), Supp., pp. 1–11.

The 1951 Committee which had drafted the preceding statute had recommended to the General Assembly that the proposed criminal court should be made operative through the medium of a convention drawn up at an international conference convened by the General Assembly.[47] The latter body, after study of the 1951 Draft Statute and of the comments thereon received from twelve governments, decided on the recommendation of its Sixth Committee on December 5, 1952, by Resolution 687 (VII) that a new committee should be created for further study and for a review of the 1951 draft.

1953 Revised Draft Statute. The new body (1953 Committee on International Criminal Jurisdiction) met in New York from July 27 to August 20, 1953, and produced a report including a Revised Draft Statute. After weighing various methods of establishing the proposed Court, the 1953 Committee reiterated the desirability of an international convention resulting from a diplomatic conference. It rewrote Article 1 of the 1951 Draft Statute to read: "There is established an International Criminal Court to try natural persons accused of crimes generally recognized under international law," and Article 25 to read: "The Court shall be competent to judge natural persons, whether they are constitutionally responsible rulers, public officials or private individuals." The original provisions relating to the conferring of jurisdiction (Art. 26, 1951 version) were altered in a restrictive way to enable states to attach conditions under which they accepted jurisdiction of the Court and to preserve domestic jurisdiction of states. The provisions of the original Article 28 were changed to abolish the presumably political review by the General Assembly of conferment of jurisdiction on the Court. A new article granting the right of a state to withdraw jurisdiction from the Court was added. An alternate text was provided for the original provisions governing access to the Court. The number of judges was raised from nine to fifteen, with a quorum of seven, and minor changes in instigation and prosecuting procedures were incorporated.

At the insistence of the United States representative, Article 37 was rewritten to enable the use of a jury whenever the instrument conferring jurisdiction on the Court had provided for such utilization. And certain changes in voting procedures of the Court and on the execution of sentences were made in the original 1951 draft provisions.

To the best of the writer's knowledge, nothing further has been done by the General Assembly to make the Revised Draft Statute operative; certainly no call has been issued for the meeting of a diplomatic conference to draft the required international convention. Thus no progress has been achieved beyond the 1953 draft for an international criminal court.[48]

---

[47] See Yuen-li Liang, "Notes on Legal Questions concerning the United Nations—The Establishment of an International Criminal Jurisdiction: The Second Phase," 47 *A.J.I.L.* (1953), pp. 638–657, for details of the events described.

[48] See Whiteman, Vol. XI, pp. 844–848, on the entire question.

GENOCIDE

In sharp contract to these as yet abortive attempts to establish an international criminal court and a related code of crimes under international law, the world community has succeeded in developing an instrument prohibiting one particularly horrifying practice in the category of crimes against humanity—genocide.

Genocide means, in essence, any act committed with intent to destroy, in whole or in part, a national, ethnical, racial, or religious group. The word itself was coined by Dr. Raphaël Lemkin in his now famous *Axis Rule in Occupied Europe.*[49]

The practices of the German government before and especially during World War II, relating to the attempt to eliminate entire groups of its own citizens and later of citizens of occupied states, led to the question of whether such acts of destruction could be regarded any longer as domestic acts or whether they did not constitute crimes against humanity.

The consensus of the civilized world—and not merely of the victors in World War II—appears to have been that prohibitions and punishments of such barbarous acts were needed, even if such a development entailed a curtailment of the traditional territorial sovereignty of independent states.

Genocide, in practice, went beyond the killing of people: it covered such related acts as the practice of abortion, sterilization, artificial infection, working people to death in special labor camps, and the separation of families or of sexes in order to depopulate specific areas. None of these activities were carried out with the approval of the individuals concerned, and in every sense of the term had to be regarded as criminal in intent as well as in execution, even under the laws of the German Reich.

THE GENOCIDE CONVENTION

The General Assembly of the United Nations unanimously adopted on December 13, 1946, Resolution 96 (I) in which it condemned genocide as a crime under international law. The Assembly also requested the Economic and Social Council to begin studies toward the eventual drawing up of a draft convention on genocide. The Council, in turn, asked the Secretary-General to prepare a first draft and to circulate it among the members for comment. In 1948, the Economic and Social Council appointed an *ad hoc* committee consisting of seven members to revise the original draft. When that project had been completed, the Council, after a general debate, decided on August 26, 1948, to send the draft to the General As-

---

[49] (Washington, D.C.: Carnegie Endowment for International Peace, 1944), at p. 79; the author's chapter IX (pp. 79–95) dealt with the subject in question in detail, particularly as to Axis practices; consult also his "Genocide as a Crime under International Law," 41 *A.J.I.L.* (1947), pp. 145–151.

sembly for study and action. After further study at Paris by the Legal Committee of the Assembly, action followed in the parent body. On December 9, 1948, the General Assembly adopted the Convention on the Prevention and Punishment of the Crime of Genocide.[50]

The convention affirms the criminality of genocide in time of peace as well as in time of war (Art. 1). The offense itself is defined in Article 2:

> In the present Convention, genocide means any of the following acts committed with intent to destroy, in whole or in part, a national, ethnical, racial or religious group, as such:
> (a) Killing members of the group;
> (b) Causing serious bodily or mental harm to members of the group;
> (c) Deliberately inflicting on the group conditions of life calculated to bring about its physical destruction in whole or in part;
> (d) Imposing measures intended to prevent births within the group;
> (e) Forcibly transferring children of the group to another group.

Article 3 provides that all of the following acts are punishable: genocide; conspiracy to commit genocide; direction and public incitement to commit genocide; attempts to commit genocide; and complicity in genocide.

Persons committing any of the acts listed in Article 3 are punishable, whether they are constitutionally responsible rulers, public officials, or private individuals (Art. 4).

The parties to the convention undertook to enact the necessary domestic legislation to give effect to the convention and, in particular, to provide effective penalties for persons guilty of the forbidden acts (Art. 5).

Persons charged with any of the enumerated acts are to be tried by a competent tribunal of the state in which the act was committed, or by such international penal tribunal as may have jurisdiction with respect to those contacting parties which had accepted its jurisdiction (Art. 5).

Under Article 7, genocide and all other acts prohibited by the convention are not to be considered as political crimes for the purpose of extradition, and the parties to the convention have pledged to grant extradition in accordance with their laws and treaties in effect.

Article 8 provides that any party to the instrument could call on the competent organs of the United Nations to take such action under the Charter as they would consider appropriate for the prevention and suppression of acts of genocide.

Under Article 9, any dispute between the parties relating to the convention was to be submitted to the International Court of Justice at the request of any of the parties to the dispute.

---

[50] Text reprinted in 45 *A.J.I.L.* (1951), Supp., pp. 7–10. Consult also Josef L. Kunz, "The United Nations Convention on Genocide," *ibid.*, 43 (1949), pp. 738–746, and see the materials in Whiteman, Vol. XI, pp. 848–874.

The effective duration of the convention was set at ten years from the date on which it came into force (Art. 14).

The Genocide Convention was signed by twenty-five states and came into force on January 12, 1950. By early 1967, sixty-nine ratifications or adherences had been received by the office of the Secretary-General. The United States has refrained thus far from ratification. American objections to the treaty appear to be based on domestic constitutional questions, such as the belief by some that by undertaking to "prevent and punish" acts of genocide (Art. 1 of the convention), the federal government might usurp functions constitutionally reserved to the individual states.[51] The government of the United States also objects to being compelled to either extradite or try offenders against international rules when the acts in question might not be clearly illegal under domestic law.

A number of states made reservations at the time they signed the convention and others, such as Bulgaria and the Philippines, entered reservations at the time of ratification. These reservations caused strong objections on the part of other members of the United Nations which were parties to the convention.

Advisory Opinion of the International Court of Justice. In order to clear up the legal meaning of such reservations of multilateral conventions, the Secretary-General placed the question before the Fifth Session of the General Assembly. On recommendation of the Sixth Committee, the Assembly then adopted a resolution on November 16, 1950, in which it requested the International Court of Justice to give an advisory opinion on the following questions:

1. *Requests* the International Court of Justice to give an advisory opinion on the following questions:
"In so far as concerns the Convention on the Prevention and Punishment of the Crime of Genocide in the event of a State ratifying or acceding to the Convention subject to a reservation made either on ratification or on accession, or on signature followed by ratification:
"I. Can the reserving State be regarded as being a party to the Convention while still maintaining its reservation if the reservation is objected to by one or more of the parties to the Convention but not by others?
"II. If the answer to question I is in the affirmative, what is the effect of the reservation as between the reserving State and:
  (a) The parties which object to the reservation?
  (b) Those which accept it?
"III. What would be the legal effect as regards the answer to question I if an objection to a reservation is made:
  (a) By a signatory which has not yet ratified?
  (b) By a State entitled to sign or accede but which has not yet done so?"

[51] See Bishop, p. 476, n. 54, for references to U.S. comments; see especially George A. Finch, "The Genocide Convention," 43 *A.J.I.L.* (1949), pp. 732–738, which discussed criticisms in American legal circles. Consult also Arthur K. Kuhn, "The Genocide Convention and State Rights," *ibid.*, pp. 498–501, on the relation of the instrument to territorial sovereignty.

It also invited the International Law Commission, in its work on the codification of treaties, to study the problem of reservation of multilateral
conventions.

The advisory opinion handed down by the Court on May 28, 1951,
supported the inter-American view on the question of such reservations.[52]
It asserted in answer to Question I, that a state that had made and maintained a reservation that had been objected to by one or more of the
parties to the convention but not by others, could be regarded as being
a party to the convention if the reservation was compatible with the object and purpose of the agreement; otherwise, that state could not be
regarded as being a party to the treaty. (This situation had prompted the
request for the Court's advisory opinion. The ratification of the convention by the U.S.S.R. had contained such extensive reservations that other
parties to the agreement refused to consider it a ratification compatible
with the purposes of the convention. This exclusion was therefore sup-
reported by the advisory opinion.) With respect to Question II (a), the
Court held that if a party to the convention objected to a reservation
which it regarded as incompatible with the object and purpose of the
agreement, it could in fact consider that the reserving state was not a party
to the Convention; as to Question II (b), the Court said that if a party
accepted a reservation as compatible with the object and purposes of the
agreement, it could in fact consider the reserving state to be a party to
the convention. On Question III (a), the Court, by a vote of 7 to 5, held
that an objection to a reservation made by a signatory state which had
not yet ratified the convention could have the legal effect indicated in
the reply to Question I only on ratification. Until that moment it merely
served as a notice to the other state of the eventual attitude of the signatory state. On Question III (b), by the same vote, the Court answered
that an objection to a reservation made by a state entitled to sign or
accede but which had not done so, was without any legal effect.[53]

Returning to the convention itself, history has seen instances of acts of
genocide after the drafting of the instrument and has thereby shown the
need for universal acceptance and enforcement of its provisions. In the
Korean War, an appalling number not only of war crimes but also of acts
of genocide took place.[54] And in 1956, the Soviet Union was accused in

[52] See Chapter 22; for the excerpted text of *Reservations to the Convention on
Genocide*, International Court of Justice, Advisory Opinion, 1951, *I.C.J. Reports,
1951*, p. 15, see 45 *A.J.I.L.* (1951), pp. 579-590.

[53] See Chapter 22 for the recommendations that emanated later from the International Law Commission; see also Gould, pp. 316-318, for a valuable summary of
the debates which ensued in the Sixth Committee after the handing down of the
Advisory Opinion of the International Court of Justice.

[54] Consult, *inter alia*, "Atrocities in Korea—How Bad?" 34 *U.S. News & World
Report* (May 1, 1953), pp. 16-17; "Red China: The Mask Comes Off," *ibid.*, 35 (November 6, 1953), p. 25, which summarized the report of the War Crimes Division
of the U.S. Army in Korea, of June 30, 1953; and see "Genocide Charged by South

the United Nations of having committed acts of genocide during the suppression of the anti-Communist revolt in Hungary.[55]

GENEVA CONVENTIONS OF 1949

The Geneva Diplomatic Conference of 1949 also concerned itself with the subject of crimes under international law and, since its four conventions are in force, contributed significantly to an expansion of the rules of law governing in this sphere. The participants in the conference carefully avoided the terms *war crimes* and *Nuremberg Principles*, but wrote into the conventions much relevant material.

All four instruments include this common article:

The High Contracting Parties undertake to enact any legislation necessary to provide effective penal sanctions for persons committing, or ordering to be committed, any of the grave breaches of the present Convention defined in the following Article.

Each High Contracting Party shall be under the obligation to search for persons alleged to have committed or to have ordered to be committed, such grave breaches, and shall bring such persons, regardless of their nationality, before its own courts. It may also, if it prefers, and in accordance with the provisions of its own legislation, hand such persons over for trial to another High Contracting Party concerned, provided such High Contracting Party has made out a *prima facie* case.

Each High Contracting Party shall take measures necessary for the suppression of all acts contrary to the provisions of the present Convention other than the grave breaches defined in the following Article.

In all circumstances, the accused persons shall benefit by safeguards of proper trial and defense, which shall not be less favourable than those provided by Article 105 and those following of the Geneva Convention relative to the Treatment of Prisoners of War of August 12, 1949.[56]

Article 85 of the 1949 Prisoners of War Convention provided that "Prisoners of War prosecuted under the laws of the Detaining Power for acts committed prior to capture shall retain, even if convicted, the benefits of the present Convention." All the Soviet-bloc states made reservations to this article, under which individuals convicted of war crimes and crimes against humanity could be subjected "to the conditions obtaining

Koreans," 4 *Presbyterian Life* (July 7, 1951), p. 21, as well as 11 *Voice of Korea* (January 14, 1954), p. 4, for a summary of the debate in the General Assembly and the text of the latter's Resolution of November 20, 1953.

[55] See 41 *U.S. News & World Report* (November 30, 1956), p. 67, for a brief mention of the remarks made by U.S. delegate Henry Cabot Lodge, Jr.

[56] Article 49, Convention on Sick and Wounded; Article 50, Convention on Sick and Wounded at Sea; Article 129, Convention on Prisoners of War; Article 146, Civilian Convention. See also Howard S. Levie, "Penal Sanctions for Maltreatment of Prisoners of War," 56 *A.J.I.L.* (1962), pp. 433–468, at pp. 454–457, particularly with reference to possible extradition problems under the Geneva instrument of 1949.

in the country in question for those who undergo their punishment." Although the United States Senate, in approving ratification of the convention, rejected these reservations, it should be pointed out that the U.S.S.R. at least indicated clearly that its reservation was applicable only to conditions of punishment *after* a prisoner of war had been convicted and sentenced for a precapture act. Hence the provisions of the convention would appear to have been accepted by the U.S.S.R. for the trial period of the prisoner in question, even though not for the punishment phase.[57]

In the Fourth (Civilian) Convention of 1949, Article 148 asserts that no party to the convention is permitted to absolve itself or any other contracting party of any liability incurred by itself or by another party in respect to the grave breaches enumerated in Article 147 of the treaty—and the breaches parallel to a considerable extent the definitions laid down in Article 6 (b and c) of the Charter of the Nuremberg Tribunal. In the Convention relative to the Treatment of Prisoners of War, of 1949, on the other hand, a limitation appears to have been created as far as international trials of certain criminals are concerned.

The provisions of Articles 85, 99, and 102 of the Prisoner Convention require that prisoners of war accused of war crimes must be tried in the same courts and in accordance with the same law as would apply to the armed forces of the captor state. Because the military law of few, if any, states permits, or is likely to permit, foreign officers to sit among the judges of military personnel, it may prove to be that countries will find it rather difficult to constitute tribunals of mixed nationality composition. In the case of an international command, "national military tribunals . . . which try war criminals cannot be described as international tribunals if they operate only with the authorization of the supreme commander, and deserve that name only if they are convened at his direction." [58] This last principle was illustrated strikingly in *Flick* v. *Johnson*,[59] in which a United States Court ruled that "Military Tribunal IV," composed of United States military personnel and convened at Nuremberg by General Lucius Clay, the Military Governor and Zone Commander, under Control Council Law No. 10, was not a tribunal of the United States. Hence its judgments could not be reviewed by United States Courts, even though the members of Tribunal IV were all United States citizens.

The Tribunal, being convened under an inter-Allied law, was not a court of the United States, but if General Clay, in his capacity as Zone Commander, had authorized a military court to act, it might have been viewed as a court of the United States. Tribunal No. IV was operating

---

[57] Levie, *op. cit.*, p. 457, n. 98; see also Richard R. Baxter, "The Geneva Conventions of 1949 before the United States Senate," 49 *A.J.I.L.* (1955), pp. 550–555, at p. 553.

[58] Richard R. Baxter, "Constitutional Forms and Some Legal Problems of International Military Command," 29 *B.Y.I.L.* (1952), pp. 325–359, at pp. 354–355.

[59] United States, Circuit Court of Appeals, Washington, D.C., 1949, 174 F. (2d) 983; digested at length in 44 *A.J.I.L.* (1950), pp. 187–189.

under the authority of the "supreme commander," in this case the Quadri-partite Control Council for Germany.

One final comment must be made in connection with the new trend of thought concerning crimes against international law. There can be no question that, at least in this restricted sphere, the individual has become a direct subject of the law. Three distinct schools of thought relate to this expansion of jurisdiction. The most radical view, represented by both the Genocide Convention and the Draft Code of Offenses against the Peace and Security of Mankind, envisages the individual as the only re-sponsible subject for the commission of such crimes. A second, more conservative view, asserts that in certain instances the state as such may be held responsible for the offenses and in other instances the individual may be held responsible. A third and rather uncommon point of view is that the individual should be the subject of criminal responsibility whereas the state should be held responsible for civil liability.[60] Which of these views will prevail in the practice of states remains to be seen.

SUGGESTED READINGS

CRIMES UNDER INTERNATIONAL LAW: GENERAL

Whiteman, Vol. XI, pp. 835–1021. See also the selections from three directives issued in 1967 and 1968 by the Headquarters, United States Military Assistance Command, Vietnam, dealing with war crimes, classification of detainees, and determination of eligibility to be treated as prisoners of war, in 62 *A.J.I.L.* (1968), pp. 765–775; Edmond Paris, *Genocide in Satellite Croatia, 1941–1945* (Chicago: American Institute for Balkan Affairs, 1961); Yosal Rogat, *The Eichmann Trial and the Rule of Law* (Santa Barbara, Calif.: Center for the Study of Democratic Institutions, 1961), particularly at pp. 32–43; Svarlien, pp. 396–415; Stone, pp. 368–371; Quincy Wright, "International Law and Guilt by Association," 43 *A.J.I.L.* (1949), pp. 746–755, and his "Legal Positivism and the Nuremberg Judgment," *ibid.*, 42 (1948), pp. 405–414.

DEFENSE OF SUPERIOR ORDERS

Yoram Dinstein, *The Defense of "Obedience to Superior Orders" in Interna-tional Law* (Leyden: A. W. Sijthoff, 1965); Guenter Lewy, "Superior Orders, Nuclear Warfare, and the Dictates of Conscience: The Dilemma of Military Obedience in the Atomic Age," 55 *A.P.S.R.* (1961), pp. 3–23; Jacob Berger, "The Legal Nature of War Crimes and the Problem of Superior Command," *ibid.*, 38 (1944), pp. 1203–1208; *Court-Martial Trial of Captain Howard Levy*, 1967, noted in 9 *Harvard International Law Journal* (1968), pp. 169–171. See also *The New York Times*, May 10–June 10, 1967; 89 *Time* (May 26, 1967), p. 20; Ira Glaser, "Justice and Captain Levy," 12 *Columbia Forum*, No. 1

---

[60] F. V. García-Amador, "State Responsibility in the Light of the New Trends of International Law," 49 *A.J.I.L.* (1955), pp. 339–346, at pp. 345–346.

(Spring, 1969), pp. 46–49; see also *The New York Times*, October 9, 1966, p. 24, relative to the new French Military Code of 1966 and its provisions relating to the problem of superior orders.

NUREMBERG WAR CRIMES TRIALS

Consult, *inter alia*, Robert H. Jackson, *The Case Against the Nazi War Criminals (And Other Documents)* (New York: Alfred A. Knopf, 1946); Quincy Wright, "The Law of the Nuremberg Trial," 41 *A.J.I.L.* (1947), pp. 38–72; George A. Finch, "The Nuremberg Trial and International Law," *ibid.*, pp. 20–37; Henry L. Stimson, "The Nuremberg Trial: Landmark in Law," 25 *Foreign Affairs* (1947), pp. 179–189; M. Radin, "Justice at Nuremberg," *ibid.*, 24 (1946), pp. 369–384; Leo Gross, "The Punishment of War Criminals: The Nuremberg Trial," 2 *Tijdschrift* (1955), pp. 356–374; Sheldon Glueck, *The Nuremberg Trial and Aggressive War* (New York: Alfred A. Knopf, 1946). See also the excellent bibliographical notes in Lauterpacht's *Oppenheim*, Vol. II, pp. 579–580 (n. 5), and in Bishop, pp. 859–860 (n. 182). The documentary material covering the trial is forbidding in scope: International Military Tribunal, Nuremberg, *Trial of the Major War Criminals before the International Military Tribunal, Nuremberg, 14 November 1945–1 October 1946*, Nuremberg: n. p. 1947–1949, 42 vols. Also see Robert K. Woetzel, *The Nuremberg Trials in International Law* (New York: Praeger, 1960); Eugene Davidson, *The Trial of the Germans* (New York: Macmillan, 1967); Quincy Wright, "War Criminals," 39 *A.J.I.L.* (1945), pp. 257–285; Robert M. W. Kempner, "The Nuremberg Trials as Sources of Recent German Political and Historical Materials," 44 *A.P.S.R.* (1950), pp. 447–459; and N. C. H. Dunbar, "The Maxim *Nullum Crimen sine Lege* in the Law of War," *Juridical Review*, Nos. 2 & 3, (1959), pp. 176–196.

Cases

The Case of Abetz, France, Cour de Cassation, 1950, Sirey, 1950, reported in 46 *A.J.I.L.* (1952), pp. 161–162.

The Peleus Trial [War Crimes Trials, Vol. I] (London: William Hodge & Co., 1949).

United States v. *Berrigan et al.*, United States, District Court, Maryland, 1968, 283 F.Supp. 336, reported in 63 *A.J.I.L.* (1969), pp. 147–148.

Stig Jägerskiöld, "A Swedish Case on the Jurisdiction of States over Foreigners: *Crown* v. *von Herder* [Supreme Court of Sweden]," 41 *A.J.I.L.* (1947), pp. 909–911.

PART VII
Conclusion

33

The Present Status of
International Law

A CASUAL observer may be misled quite easily about the present status of international law by the information obtained from newspapers and other media of mass communication. Aggressive attacks on weak neighbors, violations of solemn treaty obligations, derogatory charges that the law favors the strong at the expense of the weak, intervention in the internal affairs of others, all these impinge almost daily on the consciousness of the public. Thus a relatively widespread attitude of pessimism, or at best skepticism, has developed concerning the effectiveness of the rules of the law of nations, echoing the wartime despair of Sorokin, "Neither God, nor the moral imperative, nor juridical law, nor contracts longer possess any cogency. International relations are governed almost exclusively by rampant nihilism." [1]

The true picture, however, does not correspond to such dismal views of the law. Granting all that headlines proclaim, the fact still remains that the generally accepted rules of the law are observed consistently and routinely by the nations of the world and that the breaches of those rules form exceptions. Hundreds of treaties, dealing with every conceivable subject matter, are observed by the signatory states. Customary rules governing the privileges of diplomats are honored throughout the world. Thousands of claims for damages by one country against another have been handled by special tribunals and the awards made have been satisfied without question by the state found to have been derelict in its behavior. Many of the rules of international law have been incorporated in the domestic laws of various states and are enforced by the courts and governments of those states. And, finally, the law provides an imposing array of procedures for the settlement of disputes among states, procedures which have been and are being utilized on innumerable occasions.

On the other hand, international law not only is incomplete in its coverage of interstate relations but is also afflicted with a number of weaknesses which thus far have prevented the development of a true and effective legal order in world society. Many serious disputes are not strictly

[1] Pitirim A. Sorokin, *The Crisis of Our Age* (New York: E. P. Dutton, 1941), p. 202.

legal in nature and thus the majority of such disagreements do not lend themselves easily to solutions in legal terms. Many disputes arise when both parties involved act in accordance with rules of the law, and no legal solution to such disagreements can be discerned.[2] Again, each state is free to accept or to reject a legal determination of its rights, owing to the voluntary aspect of the jurisdiction of the law. This has led inevitably to a limitation of the scope of the law to relatively minor disputes and to an exemption of "vital interests" from the effective application of the law.

At the same time, the subjects of international law, the members of the community of nations, constitute the ultimate authority for interpreting the law, for deciding what each rule means to each of them, and for implementing the rule through domestic legislation, where such is called for, and through governmental action. Here again, vital national interests play a major role in deciding the course adopted by a major state.

Recent developments on the world scene have also shown a steady corrosion of the old ideal of a universal law applicable to a homogeneous group of states possessed of common values and relatively common interests. Gradually, so it appears to this writer, a system of regional legal orders is taking shape, at the expense of a system of law uniform in its essentials on a global basis.

The existence, in our time, of great and small revolutionary nations (the U.S.S.R., Communist China, the United Arab Republic, and Cuba come to mind) has led to an instability in the pattern of international relations which has obvious effects on the role played by law in those relations. As Falk pointed out, one central aspect resulting from the existence of the revolutionary spirit in our world is a "refusal to accept the limits of permissible behavior as developed by the established order, especially its legal limits."[3]

The community of nations has not evolved a method to legislate peaceful change into existence, despite the presence of the United Nations, in the absence of a world legislature. Unfortunately the leaders of most revolutionary societies will yield only to pressure, or perhaps only to force, and it appears that internal change in such societies can be produced only by the application of coercion from abroad—and such coercion is deemed to be unlawful among the members of the established order.

Equally troublesome are the messianic or evangelistic aspects associated with almost every revolutionary society—the common and urgent desire to spread a gospel to neighboring nations, usually by means characterized as unlawful intervention.

---

[2] See the highly suggestive study by Richard A. Falk, "Revolutionary Nations and the Quality of International Legal Order," pp. 310–331, in *The Revolution in World Politics*, Morton A. Kaplan, ed. (New York: John Wiley and Sons, Inc., 1962), at pp. 318–319.

[3] Falk, *op. cit.*, p. 311; see also John N. Hazard, "The Sixth Committee and New Law," 57 *A.J.I.L.* (1963), pp. 604–613.

The successful establishment of a revolutionary society in a given state usually is accompanied or followed by an attempt to evade or to set aside completely many of the rules of international law when such rules limit the freedom of a state to determine its internal form and shape. Thus, in the interest of social changes based on some particular interpretation of social justice, the revolutionary government tends to take over internal capital and means of production and to repudiate external commitments such as bonded debt and similar obligations. The demand for prompt and adequate compensation by the injured foreign interests is then viewed as inimical by the revolutionary leadership and the legal rules favoring the injured party will be seen by that leadership as hostile to its own existence and operations. Because those rules form a part of general international law, the latter is also looked upon with disfavor as a tool of the established order.

Experience has shown, on the other hand, that, in the course of time, revolutionary governments have come to appreciate at least some of the benefits accruing to the members of a community living under a stable and effective legal order.[4]

The appearance of ideological conflicts of global magnitude and the emergence of conditions approximating Jessup's state of "intermediacy" in the shape of the Cold War between the groups of states led by the United States and by the Soviet Union, respectively, has had a further result. The political and ideological rivalry characteristic of our time makes it very difficult to render impartial decisions in the case of important disputes between states. Each of the major parties to this rivalry tends to view an unfavorable decision (unfavorable, that is, to its own national interest as seen by it) as biased and prejudicial to its good and cause. Hence each such party hesitates and ultimately is not likely to be inclined to entrust the determination of decisions to any third party or to any procedure if these do not, somehow, embody or represent its own ideology.

The root cause of most of our troubles in the international sphere, and hence in the area of international law, too, is quite obviously the basic legal fiction underlying the current world scene and the current law: absolute state sovereignty.[5] As has been pointed out throughout this work, states have on numerous occasions yielded up certain spheres of authority to external legal regulation. But even though this procedure made possible the very existence of the rules of international law, it was always done in full recognition of the claim that each state, being fully sovereign, could yield as much or as little of its authority as it desired toward the creation

[4] See Falk, *op. cit.*, p. 315, and consult Roger Fisher, "Bringing Law to Bear on Governments," 74 *Harvard Law Review* (1961), pp. 1130–1140.

[5] See Hans Kelsen, "Sovereignty and International Law," 48 *Georgetown Law Journal* (1960), pp. 627–640, and especially Marek St. Korowicz, "Modern Doctrines of the Sovereignty of States," 5 *Tijdschrift* (1958), pp. 32–56, 150–164.

of legal principles to which it would submit only to the extent that it had yielded such authority.

There is no real indication at present that the states of the world are disposed to waive their claim to national sovereignty. Hence it cannot be a cause of astonishment to discover that the law binding these states is weak, incomplete, and filled with loopholes easily discoverable by a state desiring to evade some of the more onerous obligations theoretically binding on it.

Nevertheless, despite all the shortcomings, serious or minor as the case may be, of the law of nations, that law does exist and its rules and principles are utilized every day. The existing gaps should be viewed as a reflection of the realities of international life and of the relative immaturity of our present legal order. What matters is, first, that there is already on hand and in use a substantial body of rules representing agreement among the members of the world community, despite the many and formidable factors operating against a rule of law in an essentially anarchistic and atomistic world. And, second but no less important, that international law is not a static but a changing and, in the opinion of this writer, progressive force in the world.

There is a danger that current emphasis in scholarly as well as popular publications on "world law" may lead to undue optimism on the part of the uncritical and subsequently to disenchantment and perhaps even revulsion at the very concept of law among nations. World law is an attractive slogan but, as it is being portrayed in books and in the resolutions of such bodies as the International Law Association, it bears little resemblance to reality.

A number of well-informed and well-meaning individuals and groups in the United States and elsewhere have insisted that a full-fledged judicial system for the world is not only necessary—and who would deny that such would be necessary at some distant time in the future—but feasible now or in a very short time from now, an assertion exuding undue optimism. Common sense and a hard look at the world as it is appear to dictate the view that such conceptions are little more than lovely mirages.

The common ground of agreed first principles which is basic to all national legal systems is as yet (regrettably, to be sure) lacking—and some might say, even more lacking today than some decades ago—in the international sphere. And without that common ground, in the presence of national sovereignty, nationalism, revolutionary societies, a dearth of agreement on moral absolutes, and suspicion of one's opponents, it is, in this writer's view, utopian in the worst sense of that abused word to dream of an early realization of "world law."

The law of nations is today in a stage of transition and development, full of promise for more amicable and stable relations among the nations of the world. Its role is limited as yet, and quite likely will remain so for a long time to come. Its future importance and its place in international relations will be determined by the conduct of the society it is designed to regulate. And that society has grown enormously in the number of its members, all of which lay claim to having a share in the development of the law in the future, whereas but a few short decades ago it could be asserted legitimately that the rules of the law were being developed in a handful of states possessed of many common values and interests. When further processes of implementation are provided by the members of the community of nations, the role of the law will grow correspondingly, for no mere statements of barren norms of national conduct represent law, despite all casuistry expended on the subject: only when rules are supplied with a methodology for their application and enforcement may we presume the existence of a true law.

SUGGESTED READINGS

Oliver J. Lissitzyn, *International Law Today and Tomorrow* (Dobbs Ferry, N.Y.: Oceana Publications, 1965); Philip C. Jessup, *Transnational Law* (New Haven: Yale University Press, 1956); Josef L. Kunz, ed., *The Changing Law of Nations* (Columbus: Ohio State University Press, 1964); Milton Katz, *The Relevance of International Adjudication* (Cambridge, Mass.: Harvard University Press, 1968); K. W. Deutsch and S. Hoffman, eds., *The Relevance of International Law* (Cambridge, Mass.: Schenkman Publishing Co., 1968); Wolfgang Friedmann, "Some Reflections on the State of International Law in 'International Co-operation Year'," 59 *A.J.I.L.* (1965), pp. 857–871; Charles G. Fenwick, "International Law: The Old and the New," *ibid.*, 60 (1966), pp. 475–483; John P. Humphrey, "On the Foundations of International Law," *ibid.*, 39 (1945), pp. 231–242; H. L. Nieburg, "The Threat of Violence and Social Change," 56 A.P.S.R. (1962), pp. 865–873; Robert N. Williams, "World Rule of Law," 63 *West Virginia Law Review* (1961), pp. 118–129; and see the special issue, "Post-War Thinking on the Rule of Law," 50 *Michigan Law Review* (1961), pp. 483–613.

Table of Cases

Italic indicates cases abstracted in the text; roman indicates cases cited, discussed in court opinions, or contained in footnotes or suggested readings.

Aaroo Mountain Arbitration, 469
A.B., Case of, 689
Abetz, The Case of, 720
Aboitiz & Co. v. Price, 684
Admissibility of Hearings of
    Petitioners by the Committee
    on South-West Africa, 80
Admission of a State to the United
    Nations, Conditions of, 456
Adula, The, 662
Aerial Incident of July 27, 1955
    (Israel-Bulgaria), 364, 473,
    474, 476
Agati v. Soc. Elettrica Coloniale
    Italiano, 691
Alabama Claims, 247, 465, 626
Algemene Transporten Expeditie
    Onderneming van Gend & Loos
    v. Netherlands Fiscal
    Administration, 493
Amaya et al. v. Stanolind Oil &
    Gas Co., 122
Ambalietos Case (Greece v. United
    Kingdom), 227, 248
Ambrose Light, The, 330
American Banana Co. v. United
    Fruit Co., 210
American Hawaiian Ventures v.
    M.V.J. Latuharhary, 155
American Insurance Co. v. Peters, 663
Anglo-Iranian Oil Co. Case (United
    Kingdom v. Iran), 236, 479, 480
Anglo-Iranian Oil Co. v. Jaffrate, 236
Anglo-Iranian Oil Co. v. Società
    Unione Petrolifera Orientale, 236
Anglo-Norwegian Fisheries Case, 312
Anna, The, 276
Annette, The, 115
Anonymous v. Anonymous, 418

Antares, The, 649
Antelope, The, 129
Appam, The, 646
Ares v. S/S Colon, 301
Argentina-Chile Arbitration
    Award, 307
Argentina v. City of New York, 416
Argento v. Horn, 269, 564
Argento v. North, 564
Arkansas v. Tennessee, 303
Artukovic v. Boyle, 122
Asakura v. City of Seattle, 452
Asylum Case (Colombia v. Peru),
    389, 479
Attorney-General of Israel v.
    Eichmann, 270
Auer v. Costa, 143

Baccus S.R.I. v. Servicio Nacional
    del Trigo, 145
Banco de Bilboa v. Sancha, 116
Banco Nacional de Cuba v.
    Sabbatino et al., 154
Banque de France v. Equitable
    Trust Co., 143
Barcelona Traction, Light and
    Power Co. Case (Belgium v.
    Spain), 493
Baron Stjernblad, The, 649
Bataafsche Petroleum Maatsch. &
    Ors. v. The War Damage
    Commission, 679
Bathori, The, 618
Belsen Trial, The, 705
Bennion v. New York Life Insurance
    Co., 561
Bergman v. De Sieyes, 392
Berini, Petition of, 220
Berizzi Bros. Co. v. S.S. Pesaro, 144

Bermuda, The, 649
Best v. United States, 220
Betsey, The, 642
Bielinis, In re Estate of, 111
Bigelow v. *Princess Zizianoff, 411*
Blackmer, Case of, 254
Blackmer v. United States, 211
Bliss v. Nicolaeff, 419
Boedes Lust, The, 512
Bohne, In re, 257
Bolivar, The (see U.S. v. Quincy)
Brown v. United States, 567, 579
Brownell v. City and County of
    San Francisco, 141
Brunell v. United States, 283
Burna v. United States, 301
Burnet v. Brooks, 223
Bush v. United States, 172

Canevaro Case, The, 220
Caranica v. Nagle, 214
Carbone v. Carbone, 392
Carl-Zeiss-Stiftung v. Rayner and
    Keeler, Ltd., 115
Caroline Case (Great Britain v.
    United States), 167
Carrera v. Carrera, 391
Castioni, In re, 258
Cayuga Indians Claim (Great
    Britain—United States), 22
Certain Aspects of the Laws on the
    Use of Languages in Education
    in Belgium, 197
Chaco Award (Bolivia-Paraguay),
    308, 463
Chamizal Arbitration (Mexico-
    United States), 303, 479
Chandler v. United States, 211,
    257, 268
Charlton v. Kelly, 255, 454
Chemical Natural Resources, Inc. v.
    *Republic of Venezuela, 147,
    150, 152*
Ching Lan Foo v. Brownell, 201
Chorzów Factory Case, 235, 247,
    438
Chung Chi Cheung v. *The King,
    25, 357*
Church v. Hubbart, 343

Circassian, The, 607
Civil Aeronautics Board v. Island
    Airlines, Inc., 314
Clark v. Allen, 269, 564
Clark v. Uebersee Finanz-
    Korporation, 209
Clarke v. Morey, 570
Commercial Cable Co. v. Burleson,
    579
Commission of the European
    Economic Community v.
    Government of the Republic
    of Italy, 493
Competence of the I.L.O. to
    Regulate . . . Personal
    Work of Employers, 438
Cook v. United States, 30, 343
*Corfu Channel Case (Great Britain
    v. Albania), 292, 350, 479*
Coumas v. Superior Court of
    San Joaquin County, 255
Cristobal Colon, The, 150
Crown v. von Herder, 720
Cunard Steamship Co. v. Mellon,
    353, 359

Dade Drydock Corp. v. M/V Mar
    Caribe, 150
Daimler Co. v. Continental Tyre
    & Rubber Co., 209
D. D. Cement Co. v. Commissioner
    of Income Tax, 122
De Haber v. Queen of Portugal,
    139
Dexter & Carpenter v. Kunglig
    Jarnvagsstyrelsen, 160
Dickinson v. Del Solar, 416
Dirigo, The, 604
District of Columbia v. Vinard
    L. Paris, 391
Doelwijk, The, 649
Doenitz Trial, The, 611, 613
Dogger Bank Case (Great Britain
    v. Russia), 461, 493
Dougherty v. Equitable Life
    Assurance Society, 116
Dunlop v. Banco Central del
    Ecuador, 145
Düsseldorf, The, 639

Eastern Carelia, Legal Status of, 472

Eastern Greenland Case, 275, 426, 445

Eisler [Extradition] Case, 253

Elg v. Frances Perkins, Secretary of Labor, 205

Eliza Ann, The, 580

Emmet v. Lomakin, 413

Emperor of Austria and King of Hungary v. *Day and Kossuth, 156, 179*

Engelke v. Musmann, 392

État Français c. Établissements Monmousseau, 691

Et Ve Balik Kurumu v. B.N.S. International Sales Corp., 152

Ex parte Kumezo Kawato, 570

Ex parte Republic of Peru (The Ucayali), 143

Expenses of the United Nations (Art. 17, Par. 2, of the Charter), 535

Ezeta, In re, 270

Factor v. Laubenheimer, 252

Fatemi v. United States, 389

Fenton Textile Association v. Kressin, 419

Fleming & Marshall v. Page, 691

Flick v. Johnson, 718

Flota Mercante Dominicana v. American Manufacturers Mutual Insurance, 183

Foltina, The, 663

Fortuna, The, 653

Free Zones of Upper Savoy and the District of Gex (France-Switzerland), 22, 449

French Republic v. Board of Supervisors of Jefferson County, 141

Frisbie v. Collins, 268

Fujii v. State of California, 137, 433

Gagara, The, 115, 144

German Interests in Polish Upper Silesia, 33, 234, 438

German Settlers in Poland, 121, 188

Gillars v. United States, 212

Girard v. Wilson, 218

Gonzales, In re, 260

Grace and Ruby, The, 343

Gray, Administrator, v. United States, 512

Great Britain (Eastern Extension, Australasia & China Telegraph Co.) v. United States, 619

Greco-Bulgarian 'Communities', 33

Greek and Turkish Populations, Exchange of, 33

Greek Case, The, 197

Guaranty Trust Co. v. United States, 116

Guess v. Read, 321

Haile Selassie v. *Cable and Wireless Ltd. (No. 2), 113*

Haver v. Yaker, 428, 452

Haw Pia v. China Banking Corp., 691

Haya de la Torre Case, 267, 479

Helena, The, 89

Hellenic Lines, Ltd. v. Embassy of South Viet Nam, 149

Hellenic Lines, Ltd. v. Moore, 418

Hilton v. Guyot, 21, 31, 155

Hines v. Davidowitz, 225

Hirota v. Douglas MacArthur, 704

Holbrook, Nelson & Co. v. Henderson, 418

Home Missionary Society Case (United States—Great Britain), *242*

Honduras v. Nicaragua, 306

Hoop, The, 566

I'm Alone, The, 343

Indonesian Case, The, 89

Inglis v. Sailor's Snug Harbour, 200

Insull, Case of Samuel, 254

Interhandel Case (Switzerland-United States), 209, 221

International Refugee Organization v. Republic S.S. Corp., 160

Interpretation of the 1919 Convention concerning Employment of Women during the Night, 453

Interpretation of the Statute of Memel, 437

Ionian Ships, The, 75

Italy (Sambiaggio) v. Venezuela, 244
Ivancevic v. Artukovic, 122

Japanese Government v. Commercial
  Casualty Insurance Co., 691
Jimenez v. Aristeguita, 261
Johnson and Graham's Lessee
  v. M'Intosh, 274
Joyce v. *Director of Public
  Prosecutions, 213*
Judgments of the Administrative
  Tribunal of the I.L.O., 400
Jupiter, The, 144
Jurisdiction of the Courts of
  Danzig, 22, 452
Jurisdiction of the European Advisory
  Commission of the Danube, 438
J.W. v. Republic of Latvia, Mrs., 382

Kahn v. Anderson, Warden, 574
Kansas v. Missouri, 303
Kaplan v. Tod, 220
Kappler, Case of, 599
Kara Deniz, The, 606
Karadzole v. Artukovic, 122
Karnuth v. United States ex rel.
  Albro, 269, 564
Kasendorf, In re Estate of, 111
Kasenkina Case (see Emmet v.
  Lomakin)
Katina, The, 343
Kaufman v. Société Internationale,
  580
Kavic, Bjelanovic and Arsenijevic,
  In re, 261
Kawakita v. United States, 220
Kawasaki Kisen Kabushiki Kaisha
  of Kobe v. Bantham S.S. Co., 562
Kendall et al. v. Kingdom of Saudi
  Arabia et al., 161
Kennedy, Attorney General v.
  Mendoza, 220
Kennett et al. v. Chambers, 115
Kent Jewelry Co. v. Kiefer, 691
Ker v. Illinois, 268
Kim, The, 649, 662
Kingdom of Norway v. Federal
  Sugar Refining Co., 140

Kingdom of Roumania v.
  Guaranty Trust Co., 140
Kinsella v. Krueger (Rehearing), 221
Kolczynski, In re, 262
Kontos v. S.S. Sophia C., 348
Ktir, In the Matter of, 270

Lam Mow v. Nagle, 201
Larkin, In re Estate of, 248
Latvian State Cargo and Passenger
  S.S. Line v. McGrath, 111, 151
Lauritzen v. Larsen, 359
Lawless Case, The, 197
Lazarou v. Moraros, 428
Lehigh Valley Railroad Co. v.
  State of Russia, 112
Lehman v. United States ex rel.
  Carson, 215
Le Louis, The, 129, 343
Levy, Court Martial of Capt.
  Howard, 719
Licea-Gomez v. Pilliod, 407
Ling et al. v. 1689 Tons of Coal
  Lying Aboard S.S. Wilhelmina,
  608
Lisser v. United States, 361
Lo Dolce, In re, 255
Lotus, The, 349
Lusitania, The, 609
Lusitania Cases (United States–
  Germany), 247, 609
Lutcher S.A. Celulose e Papel v.
  Inter-American Development
  Bank, 161
Luther v. *Sagor, 109*

Magdalena Steam Navigation Co.
  v. Martin, 418
Magellan Pirates, The, 343
Maipo, The, 144
Mali v. *Keeper of the Common Jail*
  (Wildenhus' Case), *352*
Manouba, The, 652
Manuel v. Ministère Public, 358
Marianna Flora, The, 328
Martin v. Commissioner of Internal
  Revenue, 300
Mason v. Intercolonial Railway of
  Canada, 145

Mavrommatis Palestine Concessions, 248, 437, 458

Mayan Lines v. Republic of Cuba, etc., 151

McCulloch . . . et al. v. Soc. Nac. de Marineros de Honduras, 359

McEvoy & Ors v. Owners, etc., S.S. Otto, 151

McEvoy & Veldi v. Owners, etc., S.S. Piret and S.S. Mall, 151

McGrath v. Kristensen, 217

McLeod . . . v. Empresa Hondurena de Vapores, 359

Menzel v. List, 234

Mercurius, The, 654

Meteor, The, 627

Meunier, In re, 259

Mighell v. *Sultan of Johore*, 74, 139

Minority Schools in Albania, 128, 188

Minority Schools in Upper Silesia, 437

Minquiers and Ecrehos Case (France-United Kingdom), 274, 490

Mirabella v. Banco Industrial de la República Argentina, 145

Missouri v. *Holland, U.S. Game Warden*, 29

Molefi v. Principal Legal Adviser, 122

Monaco v. Mississippi, 89

Monastery of Saint-Naoum, The, 308

Monetary Gold Removed from Rome, Case of the, 295

Mortensen v. *Peters, 26*

Moser v. United States, 220

Mosul Case, The, 437

Mulcahey v. Catalanotte, 215

Municipality of the City and County of St. John, Logan and Clayton v. Fraser-Brace Overseas Corp. et al., 161

Murray v. The Charming Betsey, 30

Naim-Molvan v. Attorney-General for Palestine, 348

National City Bank v. Republic of China, 140

National Institute of Agrarian Reform v. Kane, 152

National Maritime Union v. Empresa Hondurena de Vapores, 359

Nationality Decrees Issued in Tunis and Morocco, 89, 199, 449

Naulilaa Incident Arbitration (Portugal-Germany), 497, 500

Navarro et al. v. M/V Bahia de Nipe, 151

Navemar, Case of the, 150

Navios Corporation v. The Ulysses II, 580

Nebraska v. Iowa, 303

Nereide, The, 28

Netherlands v. Federal Reserve Bank of New York, 115, 667, 691

Neumeister Case, 197

New Jersey v. Delaware, 22, 303

New York and Cuba Mail Steamship Co. v. Republic of Korea, 146

New York Life Insurance Co. v. Statham, 566

New York World's Fair 1964–1965 Corp. v. Republic of Guinea, 161

Nielsen v. Johnson, 453

Ning Yi-ching, In re, 287

Nishikawa v. Dulles, 206

Nissan v. Attorney-General, 540

North Sea Continental Shelf Cases, 321

Northern Cameroons, Case Concerning the, 89, 492

Norwegian Claims against the United States, 234

Norwegian Loans, Certain (France v. Norway), 241, 476

Nottebohm Case (Liechtenstein v. Guatemala), 198, 220, 347, 474, 475

Nuestra Señora de Regla, The, 653

Oetjen v. Central Leather Co., 102

Okimura v. Acheson, 203

Olinde Rodrigues, The, 655

Ornelas v. Ruiz, 270

Oscar Chinn Case, 445

Pablo Najera Case, 434

Pajzs, Csázky, and Esterházy Case, 434

Palicio y Compania v. Brush, 249

Palmas Island Arbitration (United States-Netherlands), 273, *278*

Palme, The, 557

Panaghia Rhomba, The, 654

Panevezys-Saldutiskis Railway Case, 227, 248

Pang v. Sun Life Assurance Co., 561

Paquette Habana; The Lola, 28, *30, 32,* 614

Parlement Belge, The, 144

Part Cargo ex M.V. Glenroy, 557, 606

Part Cargo ex S.S. Monte Contes v. Procurator General, 649

Pelletier Case (United States-Haiti), 479

People v. Roy, 418

People v. Stralla and Adams, 316

People v. Von Otter, 399

Pesaro, The (see Berizzi Bros. Co. v. S.S. Pesaro)

Peterhoff, The, 649, 654, 662

Petroleum Development (Trucial Coast) Ltd. v. Sheikh of Abu Dhabi, 317, 320

Piracy Jure Gentium, In re, 343

Polish Nationality, Acquisition of, 438

Polish Nationals in Danzig, Treatment of, 33, 188, 428

Porter v. Freudenberg, 580, 674

Porto Alexandre, The, 144

Portuguese-German Arbitration (1919, Award II), 233

Postal Services in Danzig, 437

Present v. U.S. Life Insurance Co., 249

Princess Zizianoff v. Kahn and Bigelow, 412

Protection of French Nationals and Protégés in Egypt, 219

Pugh, In the Matter of the Death of James, 227

Queen of Holland v. Drukker, 153

Rapid, The, 566

Regina v. Anderson, 354

Regina v. Governor of Brixton Prison ex parte Minervini, 354

Regina v. Kent Justices, 371

Regina v. Leslie, 348

Regina v. Madan, 418

Reid v. Covert (Rehearing), 221

Reparation for Injuries Suffered in the Service of the United Nations, 87, 135, 399

Republic of China v. Merchants' Fire Assurance Corp. of New York, 102

Republic of China v. Pang-tsu Mow, 140

Republic of Haiti v. Plesch et al., 140

Republic of Iraq v. First National City Bank, Administrator, 160

Republic of Mexico v. Hoffman, 149

Republic of Spain v. S.S. Arantzazu Mendi, 105

Republiek Maluku Selatan v. De Rechtsperson Nieuw-Guinea, 86

Republique Arabe Unie v. Dame X, 152

Reservations to the Convention on Genocide, 431, 716

Rex v. Brosig, 599

Rex v. Guenther Krebs, 603

Rex v. Jacobus Christian, 84

Rex v. Joyce, 212

Rex v. Ketter, 84

Rich v. Naviera Vacuba and Republic of Cuba, 151

Right of Passage over Indian Territory (Portugal-India), 298

Rights of Nationals of the U.S.A. in Morocco, 453

Rigmor, The, 161

Rivard v. United States, 270

Rocca v. Thompson, 419

Roechling and Others, Case against Hermann, 708

Rogdai, The, 116

Rose v. The King, 389

Rose in Bloom, The, 653

Rosenau v. Idaho Mutual Benefit Association, 561

R.S.F. Soviet Republic v. Cibrario, 109

Rusk, Secretary of State, v. Cort, 220

Sabbatino Case (see Banco Nacional de Cuba v. Sabbatino et al.)

Sachs v. Government of the Canal Zone, 210

Santa María, The, 262, 330, 331

Santissima Trinidad, The, 627

Santovincenzo v. Egan, 419

Sapphire, The, 96

Sauger, Case of, 336

Savage v. Sun Life Assurance Co. of Canada, 561

Savarkar Case (France-Great Britain), *250*

Schaffner v. International Refugee Organization, 691

Schiffahrt-Treuhand v. Procurator General, 574, 687

Schlessinger, Hugo, and Schlessinger, Eugene, In the Matter of the Claim of, 225

Schooner Exchange v. *MacFaddon, 141, 357*

Schurmann v. United States, 220

Schwartzfiger Case, The, 217

Scotia, The, 15, 28, 129

Serbian Loans Issued in France, 241

Shaffer v. Singh, 418

Shahid v. A/S J. Ludwig Mowinckeles Rederi, 348

Shimoda Case, The, 603

Shneiderman v. Metropolitan Casualty Co., 572

Skorzeny Case, The, 587

Soc. Arethusa Film v. Reist, 390

Société Commerciale de Belgique Case (Belgium-Greece), 479

Society for Propagation of the Gospel in Foreign Parts v. Town of New Haven, 269, 564

Socobel and the Belgian State v. Kingdom of the Hellenes, 479

Solazzi and Pace, Case of, 666

South-West Africa Cases, 81, 473

South-West Africa, Status of, 80

Sovereignty over Certain Frontier Lands (Belgium-Netherlands), 307, 490

Sovfracht v. Van Uden's Scheepvaart, 557

Spanish Government v. *Felipe Campuzano, 107*

Springbok, The, 649, 654

Statham v. Statham and the Gaekwar of Baroda, 89, 139

Steele v. Bulova Watch Co., 210

Stevenson v. United States, 270

Stoeck v. Public Trustee, 220

Stoehr v. Wallace, 580

Strathearn Steamship Co. v. Dillon, 359

Sullivan v. State of Rio Grande do Sul, 160

Sullivan v. State of Sao Paulo, 160

Sultan of Johore v. Abubakar Tunku Aris Bendahar, 140

Talbot v. Seeman, 30

Tavignano, Camouna and Gaulois Cases, 462

Techt v. Hughes, 564

Temple of Preah Vihear (Cambodia-Thailand, Preliminary Objections), 307, 473

Temple of Preah Vihear (Cambodia-Thailand, Merits), 308, 474

Terada v. Dulles, 206

Terlinden v. Ames, 269, 454

Thenault, In re, 199

Thirty Hogsheads of Sugar v. Boyle, 20, 666

Tinoco Claims Arbitration (Great Britain-Costa Rica), 116

Tjonaman v. A.S. Elittre, 348

Tomasicchio v. Acheson, 199

Trail Smelter Arbitration (United States-Canada), 179

Triandafilou v. Ministère Public, 358

Tringali Co. v. Tug Pemex XV, 161

Trop v. Dulles, 206

Tsiang v. Tsiang, 399

Tubantia Case, The, 461

Twee Gebroeders, The, 638

Uebersee Finanz-Korporation v. McGrath, 209
Ulen & Co. v. Bank Gospodarstva Krajowego, 145
Underhill v. Hernandez, 154
Unitas, The, 556
United Fruit Sugar Co. v. 5000 Tons of Sugar, 151
United States v. Aluminum Co. of America, 210
United States v. Arjona, 179
United States v. Belmont, 452
United States v. Berrigan, 720
United States v. Best, 220
United States v. Butenko, 418
United States v. Chandler, 211
United States v. Coplon and Gubitchev, 400
United States v. Curtiss-Wright Export Corp., 512
United States v. Diekelman, 248
United States v. Dixon, 359
United States v. Egorov, 418
United States v. Ekenstam, 218
United States v. 532.33 Carats (see Lisser v. United States)
United States v. Flores, 359
United States v. Fullard-Leo, 279
United States v. Guy W. Capps, Inc., 423
United States v. List et al. (The Hostage Case), 547
United States v. McCullagh, 29
United States v. Melekh, 401
United States v. Pink, 116, 237
United States v. Pizzarusso, 220
United States v. Prioleau, 122
United States v. Quincy (The Bolivar), 627
United States v. Rauscher, 254
United States v. Rice, 666
United States v. Rocha, 220
United States v. Rodriguez, 215
United States v. Rosal, 392
United States v. Schooner La Jeune Eugénie, 22
United States v. Shauver, 29
United States v. Sisal Sales Corporation, 210

United States v. Smith, 28, 343
United States v. Sobell, 268
United States v. Spelar, 288
United States v. Three Friends, 116
United States v. Trumbull, 419
United States v. Wong Kim Ark, 200
United States (Agency of Canadian Car & Foundry Co.) v. Germany, 246
United States (Brower) v. Great Britain, 248
United States (Chattin) v. Mexico, 231
United States (El Triunfo Co.) v. Salvador, 248
United States (Gelbtrunk) v. Salvador, 244
United States (Janes) v. Mexico, 228
United States (Neer) v. Mexico, 229
United States (North American Dredging Co. of Texas) v. Mexico, 240
United States (Romano-Americana) v. Great Britain, 246
United States (U.S. and Venezuelan Company) v. Venezuela, 452
United States (Youmans) v. Mexico, 230
United States ex rel. Casanova v. Fitzpatrick, 402
United States ex rel. Mergé v. Italian Republic, 205
United States ex. rel. Steinworth v. Watkins, 207
United States ex rel. Treves v. Italian Republic, 453
United States of Mexico v. Schmuck, 152
Urna, The, 649
Uxmal, The, 145

Van der Weyde v. Ocean Transport Company, 454
Vavasseur v. Krupp, 142
Vermilya-Brown Co. v. Connell, 288
Victory Transport, Inc. v. Comisaria General de Abastecimientos y Transportes, 149
Virginius, The, 328

War Criminals before the International Tribunal, Nuremberg, Trial of the, 131, 522, 525, 547, 702–04, 706–07, 720

Weedin v. Chin Bow, 220

Weilamann v. Chase Manhattan Bank, 152

Weissman v. Metropolitan Life Insurance Co., 561

West v. Palmetto State Life Insurance Co., 562

West Rand Central Gold Mining Co. v. *The King, 23,* 120

Western Maid, The, 521

Whitney v. Robertson, 452

Wildenhus' Case (see Mali v. Keeper of the Common Jail)

Wimbledon, The S.S., 296, 479

Wulfsohn v. Russian Socialist Federated Soviet Republic, 112

Yamashita, In re, 599, 696, 705

Zamora, The, 661

Zarine v. Owners, etc. S.S. Ramava, 151

Zoernsch v. Waldock and Another, 403

Index

Abdul Aziz (Ibn Saud), 469
Absentee governments, 113–15
Abu Dhabi, 320
Access to seas, 324–25
Accretion, title by, 276, 303
Act of state, 154–55, 260–61, 693
Adélie Land, 285
Ad hoc judges, 471
Adjudication, 470–82, 489
Administered provinces, 75–76
Admiral Graf von Spee, 637, 642, 645
Admiral Scheer, 499
Aerial reconnaissance, 364–66, 506, 507, 510
Agents, *see* International Organizations; Consular agents; Diplomatic agents; Special agents
Agreements, international, *see* Treaties
Aggression, 521, 522, 525, 526–29, 692, 708
Aircraft
  Convention on Offences on (1963), 330
  Crews of civilian, in war, 598
  piracy of, 329
Air pollution, 179, 340–41
Air space, territorial authority, 317, 360–66
  neutral, 595
Aix-La-Chapelle, Protocol of (1818), 376, 383
Alabama Claims, 247, 429, 465, 626
Alaska, 202n, 279, 337
Albania, 78n, 118, 170, 187, 280, 292, 295n, 310, 479, 505, 537
Alexander I (Russia), 663
Alfaro, Alejandro, 474, 711
Alfonso XIII (Spain), 306
Algeciras Conference (1906), 129
Algeria, 329n, 526, 607, 630
Alien Land Law (Calif.), 137–38
Aliens
  civil war, and, 242–45

Aliens (*cont.*)
  compensation to, 246–47
  contracts with, 238–42
  exclusion of, 214–15
  international responsibility for, 222–47
  jurisdiction over, 214–17, 218–19, 222–27
    see also War
  position of, 222–27, 242–45
  property of, 233–38
Allied and Associated Powers, 76, 187, 345, 504, 565, 612, 619, 641, 650, 700
  Mixed arbitral tribunals of, 466
  Reparations commission of, 121, 479
Allied armistice (Austria-Hungary), 617
Allied commissioners in Turkey, 395
Allied conference of ambassadors, 78n
Almeria, 499
Alsace-Lorraine, 671
Altmark, 637, 638
Alvarez, A., 48
American Declaration on Rights and Duties of Man (1948), 266
American Institute of International Law, 124
American–Mexican Claims Commission, 465
Amercan Republics, Fundamental Rights and Duties of (1927), 124
Amundsen, Roald, 285
Andorra, 77, 78
Angary, 659–61
Anglo-American treaty of 1783, 564
Anglo-Egyptian Sudan, 78
  see also Sudan
Anglo-French War (1793), 643
Anglo-French War (1798), 626
Anglo-Iranian Oil Company, 235–36
Angola, 331
Annexation, 178, 280–83, 285, 573
Antarctic, 284–87

Antarctic (*cont.*)
  Antarctic Treaty, 286–87
Anti-Smuggling Act (1935), 333
Antivari, blockade of, 505
Antwerp, 290
ANZUS Treaty, *see* Pacific Security
    Treaty
Aqaba, Gulf of, 295, 315
Aquinas, St. Thomas, 596
Arab League, 503
Arab states, 315, 320, 460, 536
Aral Sea, 306
Arbitration, 464–69, 472, 479, 482, 487,
    489, 490
  General Convention of Inter-American
    (1929), 468
  General Treaty of Inter-American
    (1929), 468, 487
  Model Rules on Procedure, 469
  Permanent Court of, *see* Permanent
    Court of Arbitration
  Protocol of Progressive (Washington,
    1929), 487
Archipelago theory, 313–14
Arctic, 283–84
Arctic Maid, 336
Argentina, 269, 275, 284, 285, 286, 307,
    336, 462, 463, 642
  Argentina-Chile Mixed Boundary Com-
    mission, 307
  Argentine Anti-War Treaty, *see*
    Saavedra Lamas Treaty
  Argentine-Chilean Treaty of 1881, 291
Armed forces abroad, jurisdiction over,
    217–18
Armed Neutrality (1780, 1800), 626
Armistices, 553, 554, 574–76, 617–18
Assent, requirement of, *see* Consent
Astronauts, Treaty on Rescue of, 369
Asylum
  Declaration on (1962), 192, 265
  diplomatic, 13, 265–67, 376
    conventions on, 266
  territorial, 192, 263–65, 267–69, 398, 637,
    641, 642
  vessels, on, 13, 355, 358
    Convention on (1928), 358
  see also Political offenses
Athens, 499
Atkin, Lord, 25
Atlantic Charter, 188
Atlantic Ocean, 336
Atlee, Clement, 104

Atomic Energy Act (1946), 591
Atomic Energy Commission (U.S.), 367
Atomic Energy Development Authority,
    137
Atomic weapons, *see* Nuclear weapons
Attentat clause, 261
Austin, John, 7
Australia, 77, 78, 284, 285, 286, 459, 491
Austria, 69, 70, 78n, 165, 281, 298, 460
  Peace Treaty (1955), 70, 188
Austria-Hungary, 67, 76, 164, 379, 393,
    565, 607, 660
Austro-Prussian War, 565
Avenol, Joseph, 477
Aviation
  Aerial Navigation, Convention on
    (1919), 361n, 365, 595, 658
  International Civil Aviation, Conven-
    tion on (1944), 12, 361n
Avulsion, 303, 304
Axis countries, 577, 650, 667, 677, 686, 701
Ayala, Balthasar, 37

Baarle-Nassau, 490
Baerle-Duc, 490
Bahia, 636
Bahia Honda, 289
Bakhemeteff, Boris, 112–13
Balkan War, First, 505
Baltic republics, 111, 118
Baltic Sea, 296, 310, 550, 635
Baltic ships, 111
Barcelona, 322
  Convention of (1921), 345
Baruch Plan, 591
Baselines, 312–14, 315, 319, 334
Bay of Pigs, 171
Bayard, Thomas F., 379
Bays, 314–15
Beirut, 499
Belgium, 32, 66, 69, 78n, 113, 168, 171, 261,
    280, 286, 307, 332, 392, 429, 433, 459,
    464, 468, 490, 505, 535, 565, 607, 627,
    629, 641, 657, 671
Belize (British Honduras), 307
Belli, Pierino, 37
Belligerency, recognition of, 84–86, 551
Belligerent community, *see* Insurgency
Bellot, Hugh H., 664
Bellot Rules, 664
Belsen trial (Auschwitz and Belsen
    camps), 705
Bentham, Jeremy, 36, 62

Bergen Defended Area, 638
Bering Sea, 337
Berlin
  Conference (1885), 129, 276
  Congress of (1878), 70, 129
  Treaty of (1878), 187
  Treaty of (1906, Telegraphy), 369
Bermuda, 288
Bern, 370
Betchuanaland, 119
Bidassoa River, 78
Bishop, William W., Jr., 146, 315
Black Book of the Admiralty, 323
Black Sea, 291, 306
Blockade, 504–12
  Cuban (1962), 506–10
  hostile, 346, 505, 508, 542, 575–76, 605, 626, 636, 653–57, 658
  pacific, 504–506, 508, 510, 511, 512
Boer War, 649
Bogotá
  American Declaration, Rights and Duties of Man (1948), 225
  Pact (Charter) of 1948, 464, 486, 487, 488
Bohemia-Moravia, 442
Bolivia, 172, 281, 306n, 324, 325, 392, 406, 460, 463, 520, 522, 653
Bonds, 240–42, 476
  United Nations, 534
Bonn Convention (1952), 578, 689–90
Bosnia-Herzegowina, 75
Bosporus, 291
Boundaries, 302–308, 309–20
  bays, 314–15
  continental shelf, 317–20
  lakes, 305–306
  land, 302–308, 565
  oceans, 309–17
  rivers, 302–305
  straits, 315–16
Boxer Rebellion, 168
Boycott, 503–504
Boy-Ed, Captain, 393
Brazil, 99, 262, 263, 310, 319n, 331, 380, 394, 460, 462, 463, 626, 636, 656, 660
Bremen, 647
Breslau, 647
Brezhnev Doctrine, 167
Bridges and river boundaries, 304–305
Brierly, James L., 52, 133, 449
Briggs, Herbert W., 107, 111, 449
British Columbia, 179

British Commonwealth, 66, 80
Brown, Philip M., 628
Brownsville (Texas), 169
Brussels
  Conference (1874), 582
    (1952), 349–50
  Convention (Navigation, 1952), 350
  Declaration (1874), 542–43, 582
  Treaty of (1948), 464, 489, 490
Bryan Conciliation Treaties (1914), 462, 518
Buenos Aires
  Conference (1936), 124, 281, 460
    Treaties from, 468, 488
  Convention on Existing Treaties (1936), 172, 468, 639
  Protocol on Nonintervention (1936), 171–72
  Treaty on Prevention of Controversies (1936), 468, 487
Bulgaria, 70, 74, 168, 170, 187, 188, 189, 310, 355, 364, 428, 473, 476, 611, 715
Bunche, Ralph, 460
Burma, 178, 282
Byelorussian Soviet Socialist Republic, 64, 68, 355, 394, 711
Bynkershoek, Cornelius van, 41, 43–44, 45

Cable Act (1922), 204–205
Cables, undersea, 318, 325, 342, 618–20
  Convention on (1884), 195, 618–19
Cagliari, 652
California, 337
Calvo Clause, 226, 239–40, 244
Calvo Doctrine, 243–44
Cambodia, 128, 307, 474
Canada, 68, 179, 284, 311, 315, 317, 337, 338n, 340, 361, 362, 389, 675
Canals, 295–98
Canal Zone (Panama), 287, 288
Cannon-shot rule, 44, 309
Canton Island, 78, 423
Capitulations, historical, 219
  military, 573, 594
Captive nations week, 174
Caracas
  Convention on Asylum (1911), 266
  Convention on Diplomatic Asylum (1954), 266
  Declaration on Intervention (1954), 172
Caribbean Commission, 337

Caroline Islands, 460
Cartels, 571–72, 596
  Cartel ships, 572, 615
Carthage, 573
Castlereagh, Lord, 633
Castro, Fidel, 99, 171, 264
Catacazy's case, 393
Central America, Republic of, 67
Central American Affairs, Conference on
    (1922–23), 462, 470
Central American Court of Justice, 315,
    470
  Tribunal, 470
Central Powers, 466, 574, 647, 699
Cessation of hostilities, 572
Cession, acquisition of title by, 279–80
Chaco War, 281, 463, 520, 523
Chamberlain, Neville, 104, 105
Chamizal Tract, 303–304
  Convention on (1963), 304
Chapultepec, Act of (1945), 172, 421
Charles II, 323
Charter, *see* United Nations Charter
Chefoo, 637
Chesapeake Bay, 315
Children, nationality of, 199, 205–206
Chile, 266, 284, 285, 286, 306n, 307, 317,
    324, 325, 335, 460, 462, 463, 619, 627,
    637, 656
China
  pre-1949, 63, 72, 164, 168, 170, 201, 219,
    287, 288, 424, 504, 523, 563, 567, 595,
    617, 628, 637, 641, 642, 643
  People's Republic of, 71, 108, 128, 178,
    189, 308, 337, 341, 366, 394, 502, 531,
    554, 559, 592, 601, 630, 631, 724
    nonrecognition of, 100, 105, 235, 282
  Republic of (Formosa), 71, 108
China Sea, 337
Christina, Queen (Sweden), 383
Churchill, Winston, 437, 701
Citizenship, *see* Nationality
Civil wars, *see* Insurgency *and also* spe-
    cific wars
Claims, international
  bonded debts, 240–42
  Calvo Clause, 226, 239–40, 244
  Calvo Doctrine, 243–44
  civil wars and, 242–45
  compensation, 246–47
  contracts, 238–42
  Drago Doctrine, 241–42
  local remedies, exhaustion of, 226–27

Claims (*cont.*)
  mob violence and, 232
  responsibility-creating conduct, 222–47
    see also Due diligence; Justice, de-
      nial of; Responsibility for acts of
      officials, *and* Responsibility for pri-
      vate acts
Clark, Grenville, 464
Claude, Inis, 482–83
Claudy, Donald E., 146
Clay, General Lucius, 718
Clayton-Bulwer Treaty (1850), 297
Cleveland, Grover, 379
Clipperton Island, 275
Cobelligerents, 551n, 554
Cold War, 529, 629, 725
Collisions, jurisdiction over, 349–50
Colombia, 117, 310, 330, 356, 429, 449, 450
Comity, 15
Commissioners, *see* Special agents
Commissions, *see* Conciliation; Inquiry
Community of nations, 61–88
Compromis, 467, 479
Compulsion short of war, *see* Self-help
    short of war
Conception Bay, 315
Conciliation, 463–64, 489, 490
  see also Saavedra Lamas Treaty
  Commissions of, 463–64
  Equity Tribunal, 464
  General Convention of Inter-American
    (1929), 487
  World Board, 464
Conditions, states admitted under, 70–71
Condominium, 78–79, 548
Confederate States, 117, 654, 655, 657
Confederation, 66–67
  Rhine, of the, 67
Congo, Democratic Republic of the, 167,
    168, 171, 524, 532, 546, 629
  Free State, 66, 69, 280
  Republic of the, 325n
Connally amendment, 475–77
Conquest, acquisition of title by, 280–83,
    573
Consent and international law, 42, 44, 46
Conservation
  fisheries, of, 319, 334–39
  resources of seabed, 341–42
  treaties, 337–39
  zones, 319, 334–37, 339
Consolato del Mare, 322, 625
Constance, Lake, 306

Constantinople, 647
  Convention of (1888), 523
Consular agents, 403–17
  appointment, 408
  functions, 407–408
  historical background, 403–404
  immunities of, 199–200, 409–16
  under occupation, 671–72
  ranks and types of, 408–409
  termination of commission, 409
  during war, 417
Consular Commission (Indonesia), 459
Consular relations, 404–407, 563
  Inter-American conventions on, 405
  Vienna Convention (1963), 406–17
    passim
Contiguous zones, 309, 333–42
  Contiguous Fishery Zone Act (1966),
    334–35
  Convention on the Territorial Sea and
    the Contiguous Zone (1958), 291,
    315, 350n, 351, 355, 371
  Declaration of Santiago on, 335
  War of the Fishes, 335
Continental shelf, 317–20, 336, 342
  Convention on the (1958), 317, 318–19
Continuous voyage, 648–49, 655
Contraband, 346, 627, 640, 648, 651
Contracts, breach of, 238–42
  in time of war, 566, 572
Control Council (Germany), 718
  Law No. 10, 707, 718
Control test, nationality of corporations,
  209, 557
Conventions, *see* Treaties
Copenhagen Declaration (1938), 544, 628
Corbett, Percy E., 611
Cordoba Island, 304
Corfu
  island, 292, 497, 504, 627
  Straits of, 292
Corinth Canal, 295
Corinto, occupation of, 504
Corporations, alien, jurisdiction over,
  218–19
  nationality of, 208–209
  during war, 555–57
Cossack, 637
Costa Rica, 98, 210, 315, 335
Counterfeiting, 179–80
  Convention on (1929), 195
Covenant, *see* League of Nations
Coventry, 596

Cranborne, Viscount, 104
Crete, 74, 458, 505, 549
Crimean War, 565, 604, 655
Crimes
  genocide, 21n, 195, 433, 707, 714–17
  humanity, against, 265, 598, 692, 702,
    706–708, 713
  against peace, 265, 692, 702, 708–10
  see also War crimes
Cuba, 99, 168, 169, 172, 288, 289, 329, 330,
    378, 379, 382, 389, 503, 619, 724
  blockade of (1962), 506–10
  invasion of (1961), 164, 171–72
  refugees from, 264
Cumberland Bay, 637
Custom, as source of international law,
  14–18
Customary law, 63–64, 316
Cyprus, 76, 491, 531, 533, 546
Cyrenaica, 280
Czechoslovakia, 70, 113, 118, 164, 167, 187,
    203, 281, 298, 367, 442, 468, 591

Daimu forts (Japan), 170
Dalny, 287, 288
Danish Sound, 291
Danish West Indies, 279
Danube, International Commission of the,
    485
Danzig, 76
Dardanelles, 291–92
  Convention Concerning the Closing of
    the (London, 1841, rev. 1856 and
    1871), 323
  Montreux Convention (1936), 291–92,
    306
Debellatio, 169, 572
Debts, public, and succession, 118, 119–
    20, 121
Declaration of the Rights and Duties of
    Nations (1916), 124
Defense Act of 1941, 624
Delagoa Bay, 275
Delaware Bay, 315, 636
Delgado, Humberto, 331
Denmark, 66, 67, 275, 284, 291, 310, 332,
    371, 429, 464, 538, 544, 550, 607, 622,
    629
Deutschland, 498–99
DeVisscher, Charles, 520, 521
Diplomatic agents, 375–94
  appointment of, 379–80
  Convention on (Havana, 1928), 376

Diplomatic agents *(cont.)*
functions, 385–86
historical background, 375–79
privileges and immunities of, 42, 199, 386–94
ranks of, 383–85
termination of mission of, 380–82
under occupation, 671
see also International organizations, agents of; Diplomatic intercourse; Special agents
Diplomatic asylum, 13, 265–67, 376
Diplomatic Intercourse and Immunities, Conference on (Vienna, 1961), 12, 377, 396
Convention on (1961), 12, 377, 378, 383–91 *passim*
Diplomatic protests, 54
Diplomatic relations
Diplomatic Relations Act (1967), 391
rupture of, 382, 495, 563
Diplomatic representation, 378–79
Discovery, acquisition of title by, 274–76
Discrimination, Convention on Elimination of Racial, 192
Disputes
pacific settlement of, 177, 455–92
Vienna Optional Protocol on (1961, 1963), 377, 406
Divided states, 71–72
Doenitz, Admiral, trial of, 611, 612, 613
"Domestic" jurisdiction, 180
Domicile test, 208–209
Dominican Republic, 168–69, 170, 266, 429
Drago doctrine, 241–42
Dresden, 637
Droit des gens, 36, 63
Dual Nationality, Protocol Relating to Military Obligations in, 202
Dualist theory, 5–6, 48
Due diligence, 228–32, 233, 242–45
Duguit, Léon, 47
Dumba, Count, 393
Dunkirk, 290
Duties of states, 162–81
Draft Convention on, 177
Duvalier, François, 495
Dwarf states, 77–78

East Prussia, 76
Eastern Bering Sea Fisheries Agreement (1967), 337
Eastern Greenland, 275

Eban, Abba, 3
Ecuador, 117, 310, 335, 336, 460
Edward III, 323
Edward VII, 307
Egypt, 67, 74, 78, 118, 133, 167, 203, 219, 310, 505, 549, 572, 590, 607, 611, 657
Suez Canal, and, 235, 298
see also United Arab Republic
Eichmann, Adolf, 268–69
Eighteenth amendment, 333, 353
Eisenhower, Dwight, 174, 670
Elbe, Joachim von, 538
Elizabeth II, 307
El Paso, 303
El Salvador, 67, 98, 315, 336
Embargo, 501–503, 523, 623
Embargo Act (1807), 501
Emden, 616
Enderbury Island, 78, 423
Enemies, *see* War
English Channel, 549
Epicontinental sea, 336
Equality, right of, 44, 128–31
Erie, Lake, 280, 306
Estonia, 93, 111, 118, 187, 382, 567
Ethiopia, 70, 81, 113, 114, 118, 280, 281, 473, 523, 628
Europe, Council of, 403, 406, 490
Agreement on Broadcasting, 371
assembly of, 194, 490
council of ministers of, 194
European Atomic Energy Community, 138, 402, 491
European Coal and Steel Community, 65, 138, 481, 490–91
European Communities, Court of Justice of, 491
European Convention for Peaceful Settlement of Disputes (1957), 490
European Defense Community Treaty, 548
European Economic Community, 87–88, 138, 402, 491
European Fisheries Conference (1964), 337
Evans, Alona E., 264
Ex aequo et bono, 451, 477
Execution against foreign sovereigns, 151–52
Executive agreements, 422–24
Exequaturs, *see* Consular agents
Exiled governments, 113–15
Existence, right of, 125–26

Expropriations, 154–55, 233–38
Extinction of states, 117–20
Extradition, 250–69, 429
  European Convention on (1957), 255, 257
  Latin American Convention on, 255, 358

Fair Labor Standards Act (1938), 288
Falk, Richard A., 170, 724
Falkland (Malvinas) Islands, 275, 285
Family of Nations, *see* Community of nations
Far Eastern Agreement (Yalta, 1945), 424, 437
Federal states, 67–68
Federal Tort Claims Act, 288
Feilchenfeld, Ernst A., 680
Ferdinand VII (Spain), 442
Fetial College, 457
Finland, 188, 281, 428, 472, 523, 544, 633, 635, 663
Fisheries
  continental shelf, 319n
  high seas, 334–39
Fisherman's Protective Act (1954), 336
Fishery Relations, Conference on United States-Ecuadorian, 336
Fishes, War of the, 335
Fishing and Conservation of the Living Resources of the High Seas, Convention on (1958), 338–39
Fishing zones, 311, 334–35, 339
Fitzmaurice, Sir Gerald G., 422
Flags of convenience, 346–48
Flanders, port of, 653
Florida, 559
  purchase of, 279
Florida, 636
Fonseca, Gulf of, 315, 470
Food and Agriculture Organization, 406
Food for Peace Act (1954), 155
Force
  self-defense, in, 177
  use of, 177
  see also Self-help
Foreign Assistance Act (1961), 155
Formosa, 601
France, 32, 66, 70, 78, 96, 99, 100, 108, 121, 164, 168, 170, 201, 203, 219n, 241n, 254, 274, 275, 284, 285, 286, 287, 290, 319n, 323, 325n, 332, 338n, 341, 383, 425, 429, 435, 460, 461, 464,

France (*cont.*)
  468, 479, 490, 504, 505, 511, 535, 537, 549, 555, 557, 559, 565, 567, 568, 569, 582, 588, 593, 594, 607, 610, 611, 627, 632, 635, 640, 643, 646, 647, 648, 649, 652, 655, 657, 659, 660, 689, 701, 702, 705
  Forces of the Interior, 697
  Suez Canal, and, 167
Francis, David R., 380
Franco, Francisco, 104, 105
Franco-Mexican Claims Convention, 434–35
Franco-Mexican War (1867), 572
Franco-Prussian War (1870–71), 542, 565, 594, 632
  armistice (1871), 617
Free cities, 76–77
Freedom of the seas, 323–24, 334, 339, 627
Fu Chung, 526
Fuller, Chief Justice, 154

Gadsden Purchase, 279
Galliani, Abbé, 37
Galvao, Henrique, 330–31
Garfield, James A., 261
Gas warfare, *see* War, chemicals, gases
Geffcken, Friedrich, 582
Geier, 644
General Aniline and Film Corporation, 209n, 579
  see also the *Interhandel Case* in Table of Cases
General Assembly, *see* United Nations
General Convention on the Privileges and Immunities of the United Nations (1947), 135
General (universal) participation clauses, 544
General principles of law (justice) and international law, 18–19, 178
Genêt, Edmond C., 632, 643
Geneva
  Accords (1954), 72
  ambassadorial talks, 100–101
  conferences
    (1906), 602
    (1929), 602
    (1964), 602
    Diplomatic (1949), 544, 583, 597, 664, 675, 717
    on disarmament, 590–92

Geneva (*cont.*)
  conferences (*cont.*)
    Law of the Sea (1958), 12, 311, 312, 313, 323, 324, 332, 333-34, 338, 339 (1960), 311, 323, 336, 339
    Laos (1962), 69
  Convention
    Armed Forces at Sea (1949), 545, 616, 694, 717
    Civilian Persons in Time of War (1949), 545, 570-71, 664, 668, 669, 670, 671, 672, 674, 675, 677, 680, 686, 690, 694, 717, 718
    Continental Shelf (1958), 317, 318-19
    High Seas (1958), 45, 324, 327, 333, 339, 340, 342, 347, 348, 356
    Narcotics (1921), 502
    Prisoners of War (1929), 597, 600, 695 (1949), 545, 552, 553, 576-77, 597-99, 600-601, 616, 694, 695, 717, 718, 719
    Red Cross (1864), 12, 542, 602, 605
    Territorial Sea and Contiguous Zone (1958), 149, 291, 313, 315, 333-34, 350n, 351, 355, 371
    Wounded and Sick (1868), 605 (1906), 542, 602, 605 (1929), 544, 597, 602 (1949), 545, 602, 614, 615, 694, 717
  Conventions (1949), general, 12, 45, 546, 577, 601, 631, 693, 717-19
  General Act (1928), 489
  Protocol (1924), 467, 518
  Protocol (Gas, 1925), 544, 589, 591
Geneva, Lake, 306
Genoa, 345
Genocide, 21n, 713-17
  Convention on (1948), 195, 433, 707, 714-17, 719
Gentilis, Albericus, 21, 39, 42
German Confederation, 67
German East Africa, 279
German Reparation, Agreement on (Paris, 1946), 578
Germany (1871-1952), 68, 76, 78n, 99, 118, 121, 164, 165, 169, 180, 206, 234, 279, 280, 284, 287, 295, 296, 297, 298, 332, 390, 460, 468, 479, 504, 505, 544, 545, 549, 550, 553, 565, 566, 567, 569, 573, 574, 578, 588, 593, 594, 596, 597, 600, 601, 606, 607, 611, 613, 614, 620, 622, 623, 627, 635, 640, 641, 642, 642,

Germany (*cont.*)
  646, 647, 650, 651, 653, 656, 659, 660, 664, 667, 670, 671, 673, 675, 679, 681, 683, 684, 689, 690, 699, 700, 701, 705, 707, 713, 719
  Armistice (1918), 617-18
  Democratic Republic of, 71, 94, 365, 382
  Federal Republic of, 64, 70, 71, 256, 382, 689, 690, 705
  status under occupation, 71
Ghana, 201
Goa, 299, 630
Goeben, 647
Gold clauses, 241
Gondra Treaty (1923), 462, 468, 487
Good faith, 178, 479
Good neighbor policy, 384
Good offices, 458-59
  Good Offices Committee (U.N.), 459
Gothlandic Sea Law, 323
Gould, Wesley L., 65, 395, 437, 629, 630, 707
Governments, recognition of, 95-115
Governments-in-exile, 113-15
Grace, days of, 565, 654
Gran Chaco, *see* Chaco War
Grange, 636
Grant, Ulysses S., 393
Great Britain (United Kingdom), 23, 25, 66, 70, 76, 77, 78, 104, 105, 114, 120, 128, 152, 164, 167, 170, 179, 180, 201, 203, 204, 210, 217, 219, 225, 235, 247, 253, 254, 262, 274, 275, 279, 280, 284, 285, 286, 287, 288, 292, 295n, 307, 310, 312, 317, 318, 323, 332, 333, 335, 341, 353, 354, 355, 370, 371, 379, 390, 394, 403, 423, 429, 436, 460, 461, 465, 466, 467, 476, 477, 479, 481, 490, 491, 499, 501, 503, 504, 505, 511, 537, 543, 549, 550, 555, 559, 564, 565, 566, 567, 569, 570, 588, 590, 595, 605, 607, 610, 611, 612, 622, 623, 624, 626, 627, 633, 635, 636, 637, 640, 643, 644, 645, 646, 647, 648, 649, 650, 655, 656, 657, 659, 660, 663, 675, 689, 701, 702, 708, 711
Great Corn Island, 289
Great Lakes, 306
Greece, 35, 113, 168, 170, 187, 203, 254, 292, 295, 375, 458, 464, 479, 485, 491, 497, 504, 505, 611, 627, 657, 689
  Greco-Turkish armistice (1897), 617
Grotius, Hugo, 21, 39-42, 43, 119, 128,

Grotius (*cont.*)
167, 324, 383, 421, 435, 457, 465, 559, 568, 573, 582, 625, 648
Grotian rule (rivers), 302–303
Grotians, 41, 44, 46
Guadeloupe-Hidalgo, Treaty of (1848), 304, 465
Guantanamo Bay, 288, 289
Guatemala, 170, 307, 310, 392, 406, 474, 475, 486
Guerrillas, *see* War, irregular forces
Guevara, Ernesto (Che), 172

Hacha, Chancellor (Czecho-Slovakia), 442
Hague
Conference
(1899), 130, 460, 465, 518, 543, 583, 588, 594, 602, 605, 664
(1907), 130, 241, 461, 518, 543, 559, 583, 594, 626, 627, 636, 664
Codification (1930), 376
Convention
Conversion of Merchant Ships (1907), 605
Cultural Properties in Armed Conflict (1954), 682
Force and Contract Debts (1907), 518
Opening of Hostilities (1907), 559–60, 562
Pacific Settlement of Disputes (1899 and 1907), 402, 459n, 461, 465, 471
Submarine Mines (1907), 613
Convention IV, Land Warfare, and Annexed Regulations (1907), 543, 552, 553, 573, 575, 583–94 *passim*, 597, 605, 619, 658, 659, 661, 664, 665, 668, 669, 670, 673, 674, 678, 679, 680, 681, 682, 683, 685, 686, 687, 688, 693, 697, 698–99
Convention V, Neutral Powers in War on Land (1907), 554, 622, 627, 632, 634, 635
Convention X, Wounded and Sick (1907), 602, 614
Convention XI, Naval War (1907), 32, 605ff, 614, 615, 694
Convention XIII, Neutral Powers in Naval War (1907), 622, 623–24, 626, 627, 632, 636, 637, 638, 641, 642, 643, 644, 645, 646
Conventions (1899 and 1907), 12, 38, 545, 582, 614, 671
Conventions, Land Warfare and Annexed Regulations (1907), 12, 543, 544, 664
Declaration on Gas Warfare (1899), 588
Rules on Air Warfare (1923), 544, 595, 658
Haile Selassie, 114
Haiti, 128, 170, 172, 266, 495, 536
Hamburg, 298
Hammarskjöld, Dag, 484
Hampton Roads, 636
Hanessian, John, Jr., 285
Hanover, 66
Hanseatic cities, 323
Harvard Research in International Law, 146, 405, 527
Draft Code, Law of Teaties, 425n
Draft Convention
Extradition, 255, 256, 261
Neutral states, 627
Havana, 651
Conference
(1928), 124, 281
(1940), 641
Convention
Asylum (1928), 265, 266
Diplomatic Officers (1928), 376
Maritime Neutrality (1928), 544, 622
Declaration (1940), 641
Draft Treaty, States, Their Existence, Equality and Recognition, 124
Hawaii, 202n, 314, 337
Hay-Pauncefoote Treaty (1901), 297, 436
Haya de la Torre, Victor, 267
Heligoland, 279
Henry IV, 323
Herter, Christian A., 424
Hickenlooper Amendment, 155, 247
High seas, 322–42
access to, 324–25
air above, 362
flag state, jurisdiction of, 345–49
Geneva Convention on (1958), 45, 324, 327, 333, 339, 340, 342, 347, 348, 356
jurisdiction of states other than flag states, 328, 331–33, 346
piracy on, 129, 326–30, 331, 608, 611
police activities on, 325–33, 346

High seas (*cont.*)
  safety regulations on, 349–50
  war and defense zones on, 625, 640, 656
Hinterland doctrine, 276
Hitler, Adolf, 442
Hobbes, Thomas, 41, 43
Holmes, Oliver W., 521
Holohan, William V., 255n
Hondouras, 67, 170, 275, 306
Hong Kong, 287, 289, 619
Hot pursuit, 325–26
Hovering rules, 326, 333
Huebner, Martin, 37
Huerta, General, 498
Hughes, Charles E., 100
Human rights, 70, 180, 187–96, 225
  American Declaration on Rights and
    Duties of Man, 266
  Commission (U.N.) on, 181, 190
  Committee (U.N.) on, 191
  Committee of Ministers, Council of
    Europe, 194
  convenants on, 190–91, 193
  European Commission on, 194, 403
  European Convention on (Rome, 1950),
    193–94
  European Court of (1959), 194
  Inter-American Commission on, 195
  Universal Declaration of, 190, 191, 225,
    260
Humanity
  crimes against, 265, 598, 692, 702, 706–
    708, 713
  Convention on Non-Applicability of
    Statutory Limitations on, 193, 708
  see also War crimes
Humanity, laws of, 546, 606
Hungary, 164, 166, 187, 188, 189, 267, 356
    428, 462, 630, 717
Huron, Lake, 306
Hyderabad, 164, 178, 282

Iceland, 67, 284, 317, 335, 338n, 544
Île des Faisans, 78
Ilha da Trinidade, 275
Immigration and Naturalization Act
    (1952), 201n, 205n
Immunities
  restrictive theory, 145–49
  sovereigns, 139–40, 199
  states, 141–52, 154–57, 233–34
  vessels
    state-owned, 146–51, 356–58

Immunities (*cont.*)
  vessels (*cont.*)
    Convention for the Unification of
      Rules Relating to Immunity of
      State-Owned Vessels (1926), 144
    see also Armed forces abroad; Consular
      agents; Diplomatic agents; Interna-
      tional organizations; United Na-
      tions
Impartiality, see Neutrality
Imputability, doctrine of, 222–23
Incorporation, doctrine of, 23–32
Independence, right of, 126–28
India, 178, 282, 299, 308, 367, 460, 476, 544,
    559, 577, 630, 631
Indians, American, 202n
Individuals as subjects of international
    law, 4–5, 187–96
  see also Human rights
Indochina, 630
  see also Vietnam
Indonesia, 313, 314, 317, 459, 553
Indo-Pacific Fisheries Council, 337
Infection, doctrine of, 650
Innocent passage
  aircraft, 361–66
  canals, 297
  territorial seas, 291, 310, 316, 336, 350–
    51
  warships, 291, 355–56
Inönü, President (Turkey), 621
Inquiry
  commissions of, 460–63, 489
  Panel for (U.N.), 482
Institut de Droit International, 465, 547,
    582
*Instructions for the Government of
    Armies of the United States in the
    Field*, 543, 582, 663, 664
Insurgency, 84–86, 242–45, 551, 634
  vessels in, 330, 346, 656–57
  see also Belligerent community; War:
    Irregular forces
Inter-American Defense Conference
    (1947), 460
Inter-American Neutrality Committee,
    640, 645
Inter-American Peace Force (IAPF), 169
Intermediacy, concept of, 517, 529–30
Internal Security Act (1950), 399
International agreements, see Treaties
International armed forces, see United
    Nations

International Atomic Energy Agency, 406

International Bank for Reconstruction and Development, 137, 238

International claims, *see* Claims

International Commission of Jurists, 124

International Court of Justice, 10, 20, 69, 80, 81–82, 87, 198n, 235, 241n, 266, 274, 292, 298, 306, 307, 312, 364, 400, 431, 433, 439, 466n, 469, 471–82, 485, 488, 489, 490, 535, 537, 710, 711, 714, 715–16

  advisory opinions, 472, 485, 630

  genocide convention, and, 431, 433

  immunities of, 402

  jurisdiction, 473–77, 485

  optional clause, 127–28, 445, 475–77

  procedure, 477

  Statute of, 367, 471ff

  utilization of, 479–82

International Criminal Court, *see* United Nations

International equity tribunal, 451, 464

International Geophysical Year, 286

International Labor Organization, 159, 396, 406

  Administrative Tribunal of, 400

International law

  application by U.S. courts, 20, 28, 30

  codification of, 13

  conventional law, 11–14

  custom as a source, 14–18, 45

  customary law, 63–64, 316

  definitions, 3–4

  expediency in, 53

  general principles as source of, 18–19

  historical development, 34–50

  individuals as subjects, 4–5, 187–96

    see also Human rights

  judicial decisions as sources, 19–20

  regional, 13, 640

  relation to municipal law, 23–32

  sanctions of, 52–57

  science, as a, 19n

  sources of, 10–21

  Soviet views of, 48–50

  treaties as source of, 11–13, 45

  writers as sources of, 21

International Law Association, 622, 664

International Law Commission, *see* United Nations

International Maritime Committee, 339n

International Mine Sweeping Commission, 292

International Monetary Fund, 137

International organizations

  agents of, 396–403

  personality of, 86–88

  regional, and disputes, 485–92

  rights and immunities of, 134–38, 157–59, 397, 399

  settlement of disputes by, 482–85

  see also League of Nations; United Nations

International Organizations Employees Loyalty Board, 400

International Organizations Immunities Act (1946), 158, 397, 399

International public corporations, 137

Intervention, 48, 163–76, 241–42, 551

  abatement theory, 169

  armed, 164–65, 166

  collective, 167–69ff

  humanitarian, 167–69

  illegal, 163, 167

  permissible, 164–66, 167, 168, 170

  preventive, 170

  subversive, 173–76

  unarmed, 173–76

Intolerance, Draft Declaration and Convention on Elimination of Religious, 192

Investment guaranties, 237–38

Ionian Islands, 69

Iran, 203, 219, 235–36, 317, 342, 479, 481

Iraq, 187

Ireland, 550

Israel, 269, 310, 315, 329n, 364, 460, 499, 500, 503, 536, 576

  Egypt, relations with, 133, 295

  recognition by U.S., 92, 96n

  "Six-Day" War, 133, 282, 499, 529, 532

Italy, 72, 76, 77, 78n, 80, 114, 115, 118, 164, 255n, 280, 379, 392, 428, 464, 497, 502, 504, 505, 523, 549, 565, 567, 582, 588, 594, 610, 621, 628, 660

  Peace Treaty (1947), 68, 188, 577

  war with Turkey (1911–12), 549, 594, 652, 667, 668

Iviza, 498

Jackson, Andrew, 559

Jackson, Robert H., 520, 623, 624

Jacobini, H. B., 327

Japan, 63, 80, 164, 168, 170, 203, 218, 219,

Japan (*cont.*)
281, 283, 286, 288, 290, 337, 442, 472, 504, 523, 549, 559, 561, 562, 563, 567, 569, 588, 594, 595, 597, 600, 610, 611, 614, 617, 628, 637, 643, 644, 645, 650, 655, 664, 700
  Manchuria and, 169, 522
  Peace Treaty (1951), 188, 578
Jay Treaty (1794), 465
Jenks, C. Wilfred, 8, 19
Jessup, Philip C., 3, 19, 81
Jimenez, Marcos P., 260–61
Johnson, Lyndon B., 168, 295, 368, 405
Jordan, Hashemite kingdom of, 165
Juarez (Mexico), 303
Judicial Arbitration Court, 130
Jugoslavia, 70, 76, 77, 113, 170, 187, 190, 241n, 267, 362, 363, 364, 450, 611, 657
Jurisdiction
  alien corporations, 218–19
  aliens, 214–17, 222–27
  armed forces abroad, 217–18
  business enterprises abroad, 210–11
  contiguous zones, 309, 333–42
  continental shelf, 317–20, 336, 342
  nationals, 198–214
  nationals abroad, 210–12, 217–18
  naturalization, 199, 202–203
  persons, 198–219
  territorial air, 317, 360–66
  territorial sea, 350–51
  vessels, 345–59
    flag state, 345–49, 351, 370
    host state, 348, 350–58
    immunities from, 356–58
    of other states on high seas, 346
Jurists, Advisory Council of, 470
Jurists, Commission of (Hague, 1923), 595, 658
Jus angariae, 659
Jus civile, 35–36
Jus gentium, 35–36, 38, 39, 40, 42
Jus inter gentes, 42
Jus sanguinis, 201, 203
Jus soli, 199–200, 201–203
Justice
  denial of, 224
  minimum standard of, 225
Justinian, Code of, 322

Kadar government (Hungary), 166
Kamchatka peninsula, 337

Karlstad, Treaty of, 67
Kashmir, 164, 178, 460
Kasson treaties (1902), 429
Katanga, 170, 532, 629
Keiley, A. M., 379
Kellogg-Briand Pact, *see* Pact of Paris
Kelsen, Hans, 47
Kennedy, John F., 304, 329, 506, 509, 510
Kenya, 165
Khrushchev, Nikita, 507, 526
Khrustov, F., 525
Kiao-chao, 287, 288
Kiel Canal, 295–97
Korea, 71, 72, 101, 118, 310, 337, 442, 550, 637
  armistice (1953), 553, 554, 574–75, 576, 601
  hostilities in, 101, 133, 502, 531, 546, 547, 553–54, 559, 561, 588, 600–601, 630, 695, 716
  North, 356, 502, 575, 577, 601, 630, 695
  prisoner repatriation, 101, 600–601
    Agreement on Repatriation of Prisoners of War (1953), 577
  South, 133
  Unification Commission, 536
  see also United Nations: Command (U.N.)
Krabbe, Hugo, 47
Kronprinz Wilhelm, 644
Kunz, Josef L., 47
Kuwait, 308
Kwang-chao-wan, 287

Lake boundaries, 305–306
Land boundaries, 302–308
Landlocked states, 324–25
Lansing, Robert, 380, 622, 634
Laos, 69
Lateran Treaty (1929), 72, 73
Latin American states, 13, 265, 266, 633
Latvia, 111, 118, 187, 382, 567
Lausanne, Treaty of (1912), 280
Lauterpacht, Sir Hersch, 165, 395, 445, 542, 547, 574, 576, 590, 609, 612
Law-making treaties, 11–14, 421, 631
Laws of Barcelona, 322
Leaders' Agreement (Yalta), 424, 437
League of Nations, 76, 78n, 118, 130, 187–88, 223, 280, 445, 463, 472, 510, 523
  agents of, 396
  Assembly, 93, 130, 280, 281, 468, 470, 471, 518, 522, 523, 596

League of Nations (*cont.*)
 Covenant, 12, 69, 79, 280, 281, 396, 434, 448, 451, 467, 470, 480, 482, 497n, 499, 502, 511, 518, 521, 522, 523, 627, 628, 708
 Committee of Nineteen (Manchuria), 504
 Coordinating Committee (1935), 502
 Council, 130, 187, 376, 470, 482, 497n
 General Act, 468
 legal status of, 87
 Lytton Commission, 504
 mandates, 79–84
 Secretariat, 431, 434, 435
 Secretary-General, 477
Leased territories, 287–89
Lebanon, 128, 165
Lehigh Valley Railroad, 112–13
Leipzig
 battle of, 442
 trials at, 700, 703
Lemkin, Raphaël, 21n, 713
Leo XIII (Pope), 460
Leopold II (Belgium), 280
Levée en masse, 553, 668, 697
Lex Rhodia, 322
Liberation, wars of, 49, 172, 526
Liberia, 81, 346, 347, 473, 476
Lie, Trygve H., 488
Lieber, Francis, 543, 582, 663
Liechtenstein, 64, 77, 472, 474, 572
Liège, Conference of, 583
Lima
 Conference (1938), 124, 194, 281
 Declaration of (1938), 194, 639
 Resolution of (1938), 194
Limited members, family of nations, 73–86
Lin Piao, 526
Lincoln, Abraham, 655
Liquor treaties, 332, 333
Lithuania, 111, 118, 187, 382, 567
Little Corn Island, 289
Locarno treaties (1925), 467–68, 518
Locksun, 644
Lodge, Henry C., 430
London
 Agreement (War Crimes, 1945), 702, 703, 709
 Conference, Naval
  (1908), 605, 627
  (1930), 610

London (*cont.*)
 Declaration (1909), 544, 605, 606, 627, 646–47, 650, 651, 653n, 654, 655
 Protocol
  Naval (1936), 611, 612
  Submarines (1936), 544
 Treaty of (1853), 465
 Treaty, Naval (1930), 611
Louisiana Purchase, 275, 279
Luxembourg, 66, 69, 113, 629, 641, 671
Lytton Commission, 504

MacArthur, Douglas, 561, 704, 705
McDougal, Myres S., 340
Machiavelli, Niccolò, 47
McLaughlin, Charles H., 521
Madagascar, 285
Madrid Conference, 583
Magellan, Straits of, 291
Mail, in war, 615
Maldive Islands, 77
Man, American Declaration of Rights and Duties of (1948), 195, 266
Manchuria, 93, 169, 280, 281, 522, 597, 600, 637
Mandates, 79–84
Manila, 619
Mandjur, 643
Marburg, 594
Margolis, Emanuel, 340
Maritime border, 308–20
Marque and reprisal, letters of, 496
Marshall, John, 20, 129, 274, 663
Martens, Georg von, 37
Martinique, 330
Massachusetts Peace Society, 465
Mateos, Adolfo, 304
Mediation, 459–60
 Treaty on Good Offices and (Buenos Aires, 1936), 460
Mediterranean, 291, 329, 549
 General Fisheries Council for the, 337
Mejillones, port of, 324
Memel, 78n
Mexico, 98, 169, 170, 177, 230–31, 235, 274, 275, 303, 304, 305, 310, 330, 340, 434, 465, 476, 498, 502, 504, 559
 French–Mexican Claims Convention, 434–35
Mexico City
 Conference (1945), 124
 Nuclear Weapons Pact (1967), 592
Micronesia, 84

Middle Atlantic Fisheries Agreement (U.S.-U.S.S.R., 1968), 337
Milano, 375
Mindszenty, Jószef Cardinal, 266
Minorities, 187–88, 445, 449
Minquiers and Ecrehos islands, 274, 490
Mob violence, 232
Moldavia, 74
Monaco, 64, 77
  Conference of, 583
Monist theory of law, 6–7
Monroe Doctrine, 241, 505
Montenegro, 70, 505, 550
Montevideo, 642
  Conference (1889), 266
  Conferences (1933 and 1939)
    Conventions on Diplomatic Asylum (1933 and 1939), 265, 266
    Extradition (1933 and 1939), 255, 256, 261, 281
    Rights and Duties of States (1933), 90, 124, 171, 225
    Status of Married Women (1933), 205
Montreux Convention (1936), 219n, 291–92, 306
Morocco, 78, 118–19, 219
  French, 607
Moscow Declaration (1943), 701, 702, 705
Moser, Johann Jakob, 45
Mosquitia, 306
Motor Vehicles, Convention on Circulation of (1909), 12
Mutual Assistance Treaty (1923), 518
Mytilene, occupation of, 504

Nagy, Imre, 267
Namibia, *see* South-West Africa
Nansen Land, 284
Napoleon I, 442, 552, 568
Napoleon III, 261
Napoleonic Code, 675
Nationality
  birth, 199–200, 201–203
  children, 199, 205–206
    by citizenship of parents, 201
  corporations, 208–209
  dual, 201, 202, 203, 204
  loss of, 206
  married women, 204–205
  meaning of, 198
  naturalization, 202–203, 205
  under occupation, 669

Nationality (*cont.*)
  partnerships, 208–209
  persons, 198–219
  statelessness, 206–208
  vessels, 345–49, 607
  Vienna Protocol on
    (1961), 377
    (1963), 406
Nationality Laws, Convention on Conflict of (1930), 204
Nationalization, *see* Expropriation
Nationals, jurisdiction over, 198–214
Natural law, 18–19, 36, 38, 39, 40, 41, 43, 45
  Naturalist school, 41, 45
  Social Naturalists, 47–48
Naturalization, 202–203, 204–205, 217
Naulilaa Incident, 497, 500
Nauru, 77
Navarino, battle of, 505
Navicerts, 649–50
Necessity, military, 543, 545, 671, 683, 687–88, 702
Negotiations, 457–58
Neopositivism, 47
Netherlands, 32, 66, 67, 78n, 113, 170, 307, 332, 338n, 360, 371, 392, 459, 462, 467, 490, 504, 505, 550, 553, 629, 638, 641, 644, 660, 671, 675, 700
  Netherlands East Indies, 644, 648
Neufchâtel, 547
Neutral Nations Repatriation Committee (Korea, 1953), 577
Neutral Zone (Kuwait), 308
Neutrality, 41, 44, 604, 621–61
  aerial war and, 595, 657–58
  angary, 659–61
  asylum, 641–42
  continuous voyage, 648–49, 655
  Destroyer–Naval Bases Agreement, 623–24
  due diligence in, 626–27
  embargoes, 501–502
  historical background, 625–32
  impartiality, duty of, 621–27
  infection, doctrine of, 650
  League of Nations and, 627–28
  legislation (U.S.), 625, 628, 634
  Lend-Lease Act, 624–25
  Maritime Neutrality, Convention on, 544
  Navicerts, 649–50
  nonbelligerency, 621–27, 629, 630, 631

Neutrality (*cont.*)
  qualified, 621–27
  relations with belligerent forces, 634–35
  rights and duties of neutral states, 627, 632–61
    air war, 595, 657–58
    land war, 632ff
    naval war, 636ff
    Scandinavian Rules of (1938), 544, 628
    United Nations and, 629–31
    unneutral acts and services, 622, 623–24, 651–53
    zones on the high seas, 640
    see also War, neutral citizens in
Neutralization, negative and positive, 549
Neutralized states, 68–69, 550
New Delhi Conference (1957), 589, 590
Newfoundland, 288, 315
  fisheries dispute, 466
New Granada (Confederation Granadina, U.S. of Granada), 117, 450
New Guinea, 84, 553
New Hebrides, 78
New Territories (Hong Kong), 287, 289
New York Society of Peace, 465
New Zealand, 77, 284, 286, 371, 378, 492, 675
Nicaragua, 67, 98, 164, 289, 306, 315, 470, 504
Nine-Power Treaty (1922), 523
Nonbelligerency, 621–27, 629, 630, 631
Non-Intervention Committee, International, 499
North Atlantic Treaty (1949), 492
North Atlantic Treaty Organization (NATO), 218, 335, 486, 491, 546, 597
North Pacific High Seas Fisheries Convention (1952), 337
North Sea, 296, 332, 549, 635
Northern Pacific Fisheries Convention (1953), 337
North-East Atlantic Fisheries Convention (1964), 337
Northeast Passage, 295
Northeastern Boundary Dispute (1831), 467
Northwest Atlantic Fisheries Convention (1949), 337
Northrup, F. S. C., 48
Norway, 67, 113, 241n, 275, 284, 285, 286, 310, 312, 354, 355, 476, 538, 544, 629,

Norway (*cont.*)
  635, 637, 638, 639, 641, 660, 671
Nuclear devices, 179, 340–41
Nuclear Non-Proliferation Treaty (1968), 591–92
Nuclear pollution, 340–41
Nuclear Test Ban Treaty (Moscow Treaty, 1963), 93–94, 340–41
Nuclear weapons, 590–92
Nuisance, abatement of a, 169
Nuncio, 383, 384
Nuremberg International Military Tribunal, 131, 702ff
  aggression and the, 521, 522, 525, 527
  Charter of, 175, 527, 682, 683, 696, 702, 703, 704, 706, 707, 709, 718
  crimes against humanity, 265, 598, 692, 702, 706–708, 708–710, 713
  crimes against peace, 265, 692, 702
  criticisms of, 703–704, 708
  establishment of, 701–702
  Judgment and Opinion, 562, 611, 613, 703, 706–707, 709
  war crimes, 702ff
Nyon Arrangement (1937), 328, 611, 657

Obscene Publications, Convention for the Suppression of (1923), 195
Occupation, belligerent, 200, 573, 606–607, 619, 661, 663–90
  "civil affairs," 665n
  economic system under, 665, 667–87
  effective, 665–66
  judicial system under, 673–65, 689–90
  laws under, 666, 667, 672–73, 688–89
  military necessity and, 671, 683, 687–88
  neutrals under, 671–72
  officials and, 675–76
  rights and duties, indigenous population, 663, 667–77
  sovereignty under, 663, 665–67
  termination of, 688–90
  territorial title through, 274–75, 285, 286, 573, 663
Ocean Eagle, 179
Offenses Against the Peace and Security of Mankind, Draft Code on, 527–28, 709–10
Offenses, political, 252, 256–63, 264
Officials, responsibility for acts of, 176, 227–33
Okhotsk, Sea of, 337
Oil tankers, 179

Ontario, Lake, 306
ONUC, 167, 171, 531, 532–33, 534, 535, 536, 538
Opium, International Convention on (1912), 12
Oppenheim, Lassa, 45, 327, 422, 660
Optional clause (I.C.J.), 127–28, 445, 475–77
Oregon controversy, 275
Organization of American States (OAS), 169, 299, 306, 482, 485, 486, 488, 503, 507, 508, 509, 510
  Charter of, 171, 487
Otter, 642
Ottoman empire, 63, 74, 75, 76
  see also Turkey
Outer Continental Shelf Lands Act (1953), 317–18
Outer space, 366–69
  Treaty (1967), 368–69
Outlawry of war, *see* Pact of Paris
Oxford Manual, 582, 583

Pacific Security Treaty (1951), 491–92
Pacific settlement of disputes, 177, 455–92
Pacifico, Don, 505
Pact of Paris (Briand-Kellogg Pact, 1928), 280, 281, 519–22, 523, 560, 624, 628, 692, 708
Pacta sunt servanda, 178, 439ff
Pakistan, 310, 325n, 460, 476
Palena/Río Encuentro, 307
Palestine, 484, 532, 534
  see also Israel
Palmer Peninsula, 284
Palmyra Island, 279
Pan, Stephen C. Y., 424
Panama, 210, 299–300, 310, 346, 347, 370, 392, 639
  Canal, 297–98, 353, 436
  Canal Zone, 287, 288, 299–300
  General Declaration of (1939), 628, 639–40
  Railroad, 353
  U.S.–Panama treaty (1903), 299, 300
Pan American Union, 124, 430
Panmunjon Agreement (1953), 574–75
Papen, Franz von, 393
Paraguay, 281, 406, 460, 463, 520, 522
Paria, Gulf of, 317
Paris, 594
  Agreement on German Reparation (1946), 578

Paris (*cont.*)
  Congress of (1856), 129
  Declaration (1856), 12, 323, 542, 604, 605, 606, 626, 636
  Pact of, *see* Pact of Paris
  Peace Conference (1919), 426
  Treaty of (1814), 290, 332
  Treaty of (1856), 63, 306, 496
  Vietnam peace talks, 383
Partnerships, nationality of, 208–209
Peace
  crimes against, 265, 692, 702, 708–710
  Draft Code of Offenses against the, 709–710, 719
  treaties, 572, 576ff
Peaceful change, 450–52
Pearl Harbor, attack on, 561, 569, 629
Peking (Peiping), 601
Permanent Court of Arbitration, 402, 465–66, 471, 489, 652
Permanent Court of International Justice, 128, 188, 275, 297, 426, 437, 451, 458, 470–71, 472, 473, 474, 476, 478–79
Persia, 63, *see also* Iran
Personal unions, 66
Persons, jurisdiction over, 198–219
Peru, 266, 267, 317, 335, 336, 460, 463, 619
Peter the Great, 375
Petroleum Development (Trucial Coast) Ltd., 320
Philippines, 68, 198, 313, 314, 715
Pipelines, underwater, 342
Piracy, 129, 326–330, 331, 608, 611, 657
Poland, 70, 76, 101, 113, 117, 118, 121, 169, 187, 203, 280, 367, 437, 468, 596, 667, 671, 695, 711
  Polish-Swedish War (1716), 572
Polar regions, 283–87
  Antarctic, 284–87
    Antarctic Treaty, 286–87
  Arctic, 283–84
  sector theory, 283–84, 285
Police activities on the high seas, 325–33, 346
Political offenses, 102, 263–65, 267–69, 358
Pollution of air or water, 178–79, 339–41
  Convention for the Prevention of Pollution of the Sea by Oil (1954), 179, 339
Port Arthur, 287, 288, 559
Porter Convention (1907), 241
Portsmouth, Treaty of (1905), 290

Portugal, 78n, 310, 338n, 503, 535, 660
    enclaves in India, 178, 282, 299, 630
Positivism, 41, 43, 45, 46, 48
Potsdam
    Conference (1945), 76, 701
    Declaration (1945), 701
Praetor peregrinus, 35, 36, 403
Preah Vihear, temple of, 307
Prescription, acquisition of title by, 277–79, 304
Preventive war, 133, 528–29
Prinz Eitel Friedrich, 644
Prisoners of war, *see* War
Private acts, responsibility for, 175–76, 232
Privateering, 496, 542, 604, 626
Prize courts, 618, 642–43, 650, 652, 654, 656, 659, 687
Protectorates, 74–75, 118–19
Prussia, 78n, 120, 572, 622, 632, 659
Pueblo, 356, 695
Puerto Rico, 65, 179, 202n, 619
Pufendorf, Samuel, 41, 43
Punic War, Second, 573
Punta del Este conference (1962), 172n, 510

Quarantine (Cuba, 1962), 506–10

Rachel, Samuel, 37
Radio communications, 176, 369–71
    pirate stations, 370–71
    Radio Free Europe, 174
Real unions, 67
Rebellion, *see* Insurgency
Rebus sic stantibus, 448ff, 564
Reciprocity doctrine, 255–56
Recognition, 90–115, 380
    absentee governments, 113–14
    belligerent communities, 94–95
    collective, 93, 101
    constitutive theory of, 91
    declarative theory of, 91
    de facto, 94–95, 98, 101
    de jure, 98, 101
    effects of recognition and nonrecognition, 95, 102–103, 109, 110, 111, 112
    governments, of, 95–115
    states, of, 90–95
Red Crescent societies, 571, 602
Red Cross, 600, 602, 677, 695
    Draft Rules, Civilian Population, 590
    International Committee of the, 571, 601, 664

Red Cross (*cont.*)
    New Delhi conference, 589, 590
Refugees, 206–208, 263–65
    Geneva Convention on (1951), 208, 264
    Palestinian, 329n
    UN Protocol on (1967), 208
Remedies, exhaustion of local, 226–27
Reparation for Injuries Suffered in the Service of the UN, 87
Reprisals, 496–501, 504, 545, 656
Reservations (treaties), 430–33, 715–16, 717–18
Resolutions as international agreements, 13–14
Resources
    high seas, 319, 334–39
    natural, 191
    seabed, 341–42
Responsibility
    acts of officials, 227–32
    private acts, 232–33
    states, *see* Claims, international
Retaliation, *see* Reprisals
Retorsion, 495–96
Rhine River (Central Rhine Commission), 485
Rhodian Sea Law, 322
Richard II, 323
Ried, Friedrich, 380
Rieshit'nyi, 637
Riga, 655
Right-of-way servitudes, 298–99
Rights of states, 123–34, 153–54, 156–57, 177
Rio de Janeiro, 656
    Conference (1947), 488
    Conference (1965), 195
    Treaty of Reciprocal Assistance (1947), 487, 508–509, 510
Rio Grande, 303, 304, 305, 306n
Rivers
    avulsion, 303
    boundaries, as, 302–305
Robinson, Sir Christopher, 633
Robles, Marco, 300
Rolles d'Oléron, 323
Roman law, 35–36, 119, 675
Romania, 70, 74, 117, 187, 188, 189, 203, 325n, 356, 428, 464, 551, 611, 657
Rome, 329n
Roosevelt, Franklin D., 384, 424, 623, 634, 701
Root, Elihu, 225, 436

Ross, Alf, 538
Rule of the War of 1756, 648, 649
Rules of warfare, *see* War
Rusk, Howard, 588
Russia (pre-Soviet), 112–13, 164, 168, 170, 274, 287, 288, 290, 375, 380, 393, 461, 505, 542, 551, 559, 565, 569, 582, 594, 604, 622, 626, 663
Russia (Soviet), *see* Soviet Union
Russo-Japanese War (1904–1905), 288, 549, 550, 565, 613, 637, 643, 644, 645, 698
Russo-Persian War (1801), 572
Russo-Turkish War (1877), 551

Saar, 78n
Saavedra Lamas Treaty (1933), 171, 468, 487
Sabatino amendment, 155
Sabotage, 697–98
St. Germain-en-Laye, Convention of (1919), 332
St. Petersburg Declaration (1868), 542, 588
St. Thomas, 651
Saipan Island, 283
Sakhalin Island, 290
Salazar, Antonio, 331
Salonika, 627
Samoa, 78n
Sanctions
  League of Nations, 502, 503
  United Nations, 503, 533
Sandström, A. E. F., 711
San Francisco Conference (1945), 132–33, 189, 480, 484
San Marino, 77, 472
Santa Anna, 336
Santa Lucia Island, 275
Santa Maria, 330–31
Santiago
  Declaration of (1952), 335, 336
  Pan American Conference (1923), 462, 468
Satellite peace treaties (1947), 68
Saudi Arabia, 167, 190, 308, 311n, 469, 590
Savages, 553
Scandinavian Rules of Neutrality (1938), 544
Schirach, Baldur von, 707
Schlesinger, Rudolph, 19
Schleswig-Holstein, 78n
Schücking, Walter, 297, 445

Scutari, 505
Seabed, resources of, 341–42
Seas, freedom of the, 323–24, 334, 339, 627
Sector theory, 283–84, 285
Segovia (Coco) River, 306
Self-defense, right of, 131–34, 177, 512, 522, 529, 560, 611
Self-determination, 191
Self-help short of war, coercive, 494–512
Serb-Croat-Slovene Kingdom, *see* Jugoslavia
Serbia, 70, 74, 450, 550
Servitudes, 289–300
Settlement of disputes, pacific, 177, 455–92
  Vienna Protocols on (1961 and 1963), 377, 406
Shanghai, 643
Shenandoah, 657
Shimonoseki, Strait of, 170
Siam, 63, 219
  see also Thailand
Sinai Peninsula, 532
Sino-Japanese armistice (1895), 617
Slave trade, 129, 332–33
  Convention for the Suppression of
    (London, 1841), 323
    (London, 1862), 195
    (London, 1890), 12
  Convention of 1926 on, 332
  UN Anti-Slavery Convention (1956), 332
Sohn, Louis B., 464
Somalia (Somaliland), 80
Sondergerichte, 673
Sorokin, Pitirim A., 723
South Africa, Republic of (formerly Union of), 80–84, 181, 189, 190, 193, 286, 325n, 473, 476, 502, 535
  South African (Boer) States, 569
South Arabian Federation, 499
Southeast Asia Collective Defense Treaty (SEATO Pact, 1954), 492, 546
Southern Rhodesia (Rhodesia), 55–56, 180–81, 503
South Pacific Commission, 337
South-West Africa, 79, 80–84, 189
Sovereign immunity
  heads of states, 139–40, 199
  states, 123–34, 138–39, 141–52, 154–57
Soviet Union, 66, 70, 71, 77, 97, 100, 111, 112, 116, 117, 118, 128, 146, 166, 167, 169, 174, 193, 206, 218, 235, 267, 280,

Soviet Union (*cont.*)
    281, 284, 286, 292, 295, 306, 310, 311,
    335, 337, 340, 341, 355, 364, 365, 366,
    367, 368, 381, 382, 385, 391, 394, 405,
    437, 472, 486, 496, 506, 507, 508, 510,
    511, 523, 525, 528, 535, 536, 537, 552,
    553, 559, 562, 591, 592, 597, 598, 600,
    611, 630, 633, 635, 647, 657, 664, 681,
    695, 701, 702, 705n, 711, 716, 718,
    724, 725
  bloc states, 717
  legal theory, 48–50
Spain, 13, 78, 105, 265, 266, 275, 310, 382,
    460, 552, 572, 577, 622, 627, 633, 634,
    641, 653, 660
Spanish–American War, 565, 577, 619,
    626, 627, 644, 654
  Spanish–Chilean War (1865–68), 572
  Spanish Civil War, 104–108, 266, 329,
    498–99, 553, 595, 611, 634, 657
  Spanish–French War (1720), 572
Special agents of states, 394–96
  Draft Articles on Special Missions, 395–
    96
Spies, 585, 586–87, 697
  UN agents as, 400–402
Spiropolous, Jean, 709
Stalin, Josef, 525
Statelessness, 206–208
  Convention Relating to Status of State-
    less Persons (1954), 208
  vessels, stateless, 348
States
  admission into community of nations
    under conditions, 70–71
  confederations, 66–67
  commercial acts of, 143–51
  continuity of, 111–13, 117–18
  debts of, 118–19, 120, 121
  definition of, 65–66
  dependent, 73–86
  divided, 71–72
  Draft Declaration on the Rights and
    Duties of (1949), 125, 162
  Draft Treaty on States (1928), 124
  duties of, 162–81
  dwarf, 77–78
  extinction of, 117–22
  federal, 67–68
  free cities as, 76–77
  immunities of, 123–34, 138–39, 141–52,
    154–57
  neutralized, 68–69

States (*cont.*)
  personal unions, 66–67
  property of, 141–51
  protectorates, 74–75, 118–19
  real unions, 67
  recognition of, 90–95
  responsibility of, *see* Claims, interna-
    tional
  rights of, 123–34, 153–54
  semisovereign, 73–86
  sovereign, 65–66
  unusual types of, 75–76, 78
  vassal states, 73–74
Status of Forces agreements, 217–18
Stettin, 298
Stimson, Henry, 281
Stimson Doctrine, 178, 281
Straits and servitudes, 291–95
Streicher, Julius, 707
Suárez, Francisco, 38–39, 61, 465
Subjugation, 280–83, 572–73
Submarines
  piracy, and, 328–29, 611, 657
  territorial sea, in the, 314, 638
  see also War, submarine
Submerged Lands Act (1953), 318
Succession, state, 118–22
  debts, 121
  property, 120–21
  treaties, 121–22
Sudan, 78, 476
  see also Anglo-Egyptian Sudan
Suez Canal, 298, 523
Suez Canal Crisis (1956), 164, 532, 572
Sugar Act of 1948, 155
Superior, Lake, 306
Superior orders, 693, 695–96
Suzerain, 73–74, 550
Swan Island, 275
Swaziland, 119
Sweden, 67, 310, 383, 538, 544, 622, 632,
    633, 635, 641, 663
Switzerland, 32, 64, 67, 69, 261, 345, 360,
    370, 378, 396, 433, 441, 464, 472, 550,
    597, 602, 629, 664
Syria, 67, 118, 168, 203

Tacoma, 642, 645
Tanganyika, 165
Tangier, 78
Tanzania, 381
Tate (Jack B.) Letter, 145–49 *passim*
Teheran

Teheran (*cont.*)
  Conference, 191–92
  Declaration, 188
Tel Aviv, 329n
Telecommunications Union, 369
  Convention on (1932), 369
  Convention on (1947), 370
  regional treaties on, 370
Television, 176, 371
Territorial asylum, 192, 263–65, 267–69,
    398, 637, 641, 642
  see also Political offenses
Territorial sea, 309–17
  aircraft above, 361
  bays and, 314–15
  Convention on (Geneva, 1958), 291,
    315, 350n, 351, 355, 371
  entry into in distress, 291, 316, 641
  extent of, 26n, 309–14, 334, 339, 356
  gulfs and, 314–15
  innocent passage through, 291, 316, 336,
    350–51, 637–38
  sovereignty over, 310, 316, 350–51, 355–
    58
  see also Neutrality; War
Territorial supremacy, right of, 126–28
Territory
  accretion, 276
  air space, 317, 360–66
  boundaries, 302–308, 309–20
  cession, 279–80
  conquest, 178, 280–83
  discovery, 274–76
  leases, 287–89
  occupation, title through, 274–75, 285,
    286
  prescription, 277–79, 304
  servitudes, 289–300
  title to, 178, 273–300, 573, 663
Texas, 118, 120, 429
Thailand, 219, 307, 325n, 464, 473, 474
Thalweg Rule, 303, 304, 305
Thant, U, 507, 590
Thirty Years' War, 63, 187, 383, 541, 582,
    596
Three-mile limit, 26n, 309–12, 314
Thucydides, 485
Tibet, 164, 178, 189, 282, 631
Tientsin, 287
Tiran, Straits of, 295, 315
Tokyo
  Convention on Offences on Board Air-
    craft (1963), 330

Tokyo (*cont.*)
  International Military Tribunal for the
    Far East, 68, 704, 705, 708, 709
Tonkin, Gulf of, 166
Torrey Canyon, 179, 339n
Trading with the Enemy Act (1939), 555
Trail Smelter, 179
Transit trade, convention on, 325
Transvaal, 118, 120
Treason, 211–14, 554
  war treason, 698
Treaties, 42, 420–452
  adoption, 426–27
  authentication, 427
  authority of agents, 441
  capacity to contract, 440–41
  changed circumstances, effect of, 448–
    50
  domestic law and, 28, 30
  duress, 441–42
  effect on third parties, 438–39
  effective date, 435
  executed treaties, 421
  executive agreements, 422–24
  executory treaties, 421
  extradition, 252–53, 269
  formation of, 425–45
  fraud or error in, 442–43
  International Law Commission drafts
    on, 424–25
  immoral, 445
  interpretation of, 435–38
  law-making, 11–14, 421, 631
  negotiation, 425–26
  oral, 445
  peace, 572, 576ff
  proclamation, 433
  ratification, 427–29
  registration, 433–35, 578
  rejection, 429
  relation to other agreements, 443–44
  reservations, 420–33, 715–16, 717–18
  revision, 450–52
  as sources of international law, 11–14,
    421
  state succession and, 118, 120, 121–22
  status of prewar, 577–78
  termination, 446–50
  textual elements, 446
  types of, 420–24
  understandings, 429–30
  unilateral, 445
  validity, 439ff

Treaties (*cont.*)
 violation of international law, 444–45
 and war, 563–65
Trent, 651, 652
Tribes, status of, 88
Trieste, 76–77
Tripoli, 280
Truce, *see* War
Trucial States, 320
Truman, Harry S, 92, 317, 334, 415
Trusteeship system, 79–84
Tunisia, 607
Turkey, 66, 74, 76, 79, 117, 168, 187, 203,
 219, 254, 280, 291–92, 366, 395, 449,
 458, 491, 504, 505, 507, 550, 569, 611,
 617, 621, 647, 657, 660, 667
 see also Ottoman empire
Two Sicilies, 501

U-2 incident (1960), 364, 365, 510
Uganda, 165
Ughet, Serge, 112
Ukrainian Soviet Socialist Republic, 64,
 68, 356, 394
Ulbricht, Walter, 71
UNEF, 531, 532, 534, 535, 536, 538
Union of South Africa, *see* South Africa,
 Republic of
Union of Soviet Socialist Republics, *see*
 Soviet Union
Unions, real and personal, 66, 67
United Arab Republic, 67, 118, 165, 295,
 367, 499, 511, 532, 724
 see also Egypt
United Kingdom, *see* Great Britain
United Nations, 65, 118, 165, 168, 177–78,
 193, 262, 282–83, 286, 325, 348, 458,
 460, 482, 503, 507, 508, 546, 572, 590,
 631, 717, 724
 Ad Hoc Committee on Outer Space,
  367
 Administrative Tribunal, 157
 agents, immunities of, 397–402
 Aggression, Special Committee on Defining, 528
 Anti-slavery Convention (1956), 332
 bonds, 534
 Charter, 12, 13, 84, 87, 128, 130, 132,
  135, 136, 137, 138, 173, 177, 178, 180,
  189, 281, 282, 367, 396, 434, 435, 439,
  448, 456, 457, 463, 464, 479, 480, 481,
  483–84, 486, 487, 488, 494, 499, 500,
  501, 509, 511, 512, 523, 524, 529, 531,

United Nations (*cont.*)
 Charter (*cont.*)
  533, 535, 536, 537, 539, 562, 629, 630,
   631, 707, 708, 714
 Command, UN (Korea), 531, 532, 553,
  561, 577, 601
 Commission on Human Rights, 181, 190
 Committee on Human Rights, 191
 Committees on International Criminal
  Jurisdiction, 711, 712
 Committee on Outer Space, 368, 369
 Congo, action in the, 171, 523, 531, 532–
  33, 629, 630
 Cyprus, action in, 491, 531, 533
 Economic and Social Council, 130, 189–
  90, 193, 713
 Educational, Scientific, and Cultural
  Organization, 400
 Emergency Force (UNEF), 531
 Field Service, 533–34
 financial crisis, 534–38
 forces, 530–34
 General Assembly, 13–14, 55, 101, 130,
  174, 180, 181, 189, 190, 191, 192, 225,
  264, 275n, 313n, 339, 341, 367, 368,
  369, 377, 396, 397, 405, 406, 432, 433,
  439, 463, 466n, 468, 469, 471, 472,
  473, 482, 484, 485, 502, 527 528, 531,
  532, 533, 534, 535, 536, 537, 538, 589,
  708, 709, 710, 711, 712, 713, 714, 715
  Declaration on Colonial Peoples
   (1960), 181
  President of, 536
  Resolution of November 3, 1947,
   174
  Resolution of November 21, 1947,
   124–25
  South-West Africa, and, 80–84
 General Convention on Privileges and
  Immunities of the UN (1947), 135,
  157–59, 397–98
 Genocide Convention, 21n
  see also War crimes
 Headquarters Agreement, 158, 262, 397–
  99, 472
 High Commissioner for Refugees, 265
 human rights, and, 188–93
 immunities, 135–38
 International Criminal Court, Draft
  Statutes of, 710–12
 International Law Commission, 10, 125,
  177, 180, 207, 264, 311, 312, 313, 317,
  326, 350n, 377, 395, 405, 406, 422,

United Nations (*cont.*)
  International Law Commission (*cont.*)
    424, 431, 444, 449, 468, 469, 527, 528,
    709, 710, 711
  intervention by, 167, 170, 180–81, 189,
    192
  Korea, action in, 531, 629, 630
    Unification Commission, 536
  legal status of, 86–87, 135–38
  Legion (UN), 534
  membership, 64, 69, 71, 77
  Military Staff Committee, 630
  Offenses against Peace and Security of
    Mankind, Draft Code on, 527–28,
    709–10
  ONUC (Congo), 167, 171, 523, 531,
    532–33, 534, 535, 536, 538
  outer space, and, 367–69
  recognition, and, 93
  Secretariat, 431, 434, 534, 538, 578
  Secretary-General, 77, 83, 158, 397, 398,
    399, 439, 449, 458, 463, 468, 473, 485,
    503, 507, 511, 532, 533, 534, 536, 590,
    601, 713, 715
  Security Council, 55–56, 76, 82, 83, 128,
    130, 132, 133, 168, 171, 180, 181, 292,
    299, 364, 459, 466n, 471, 472, 480, 481,
    484, 485, 486, 488, 500, 503, 509, 511,
    524, 525, 529, 531, 532, 533, 535, 630,
    631
  self-defense under, 132–34
  settlement of disputes through, 482–85
  Special Committee on Peacekeeping,
    537, 538
  specialized agencies of, 472
  spying by employees of, 400–402
  Truce Supervision Organization (Pal-
    estine), 532, 536
  Trusteeship Council, 130
  trusteeship system, 79–84, 262–63
  UNEF, 531, 532, 534, 535, 536, 538, 630
  Uniting for Peace Resolution (1950),
    132
  U.S. employees, and, 399–400
  veto in the, 292
  Volunteer Reserve, 534
  Zone (New York), 158–59
United Nations Declaration (1942), 188
United Nations War Crimes Commission
  (1942), 701
United States, 20, 28, 30, 66, 67, 68, 70, 77,
  78, 80, 92, 96n, 98, 100, 101, 102, 105,
  109, 111, 112, 117, 120, 124, 128, 138,
  145, 146, 147, 152, 154, 155, 158, 159,

United States (*cont.*)
  164, 165, 166, 168, 169, 170, 171, 172,
  174, 179, 198, 200, 201, 202, 203, 204,
  205, 209n, 210, 216, 217, 218, 219,
  225, 230, 234, 235, 237, 240, 247, 252,
  253, 254, 255n, 256, 260, 261, 262,
  263, 264, 265, 268, 274, 275, 279, 280,
  283, 284, 285, 286, 287, 288, 295, 297,
  299, 300, 303, 304, 305, 310, 311, 315,
  317, 325n, 330, 333, 334, 336, 337,
  340, 347, 353, 356, 358, 361, 362, 363,
  364, 365, 366, 367, 368, 369, 370, 376,
  377, 378, 379, 380, 381, 382, 384, 389,
  390, 391, 393, 394, 397, 398, 405, 422,
  423, 424, 428, 429, 433, 436, 440, 449,
  450, 457, 459, 460, 462, 463, 465, 466,
  467, 471, 475, 476, 479, 486, 489, 492,
  495, 496, 498, 502, 503, 504, 505, 506,
  507, 508, 509, 510, 511, 531, 532, 535,
  537, 538, 544, 549, 550, 554, 557, 558,
  559, 561, 562, 563, 564, 565, 566, 567,
  568, 569, 570, 577, 578, 579, 588, 589,
  591, 592, 599, 601, 605, 610, 611, 612,
  614, 619, 622, 623, 624, 626, 627, 629,
  632, 633, 634, 636, 641, 642, 643, 644,
  645, 649, 650, 651, 652, 653, 654, 655,
  656, 657, 660, 663, 665, 666, 668, 669,
  675, 689, 700, 701, 704, 708, 712, 715,
  718, 725, 726
  Civil War, 105, 247, 543, 626, 649, 651,
    652, 653, 655, 657
  domestic questions, and, 137–38
  trust territory, 84
United States–Canada Fur Seal Agreement (1942), 422
United States Commissioners in Turkey,
  395
United States Committee for Refugees,
  263
United States Military Commission (Philippines), 696, 705
United States–Panama Canal Treaty
  (1903), 299, 300
United States–Russia Treaty of Friend-
  ship (1785), 597
United States–U.S.S.R. Consular Conven-
  tion, 405
Uniting for Peace Resolution (UN,
  1950), 484, 532
Universal Declaration of Human Rights
  (UN, 1948), 190, 191, 225, 260
Universal Postal Union, 12, 73, 472
Upper Silesia, 235
Uruguay, 460, 463, 642

V-1 (and V-2) weapons, 593
Valley Ace, 337n
Valley Gold, 337n
Vassal states, 73–74, 550
Vaterland, 642
Vatican, 72–73
Vattel, Emmerich de, 21, 36, 37, 41, 167, 448, 465, 568, 625
Venezuela, 117, 172, 260, 261, 317, 462, 504, 505, 605
Venice, 383
Veracruz, occupation of, 498, 504
Verdross, Alfred von, 47
Versailles, Treaty of (1919), 76, 288, 297, 429, 566, 619, 699, 700
Vessels
  asylum on, 13, 355, 358
  births aboard, 201
  cartel ships, 572, 615
  crews of in war, 554, 598, 615
  crimes aboard, 351–55
  enemy, 607–13, 614
  immune, in war, 613–14, 615
  immunities from jurisdiction, 146–51, 356–58
  insurgent, 330, 656–57
  jurisdiction over, *see* Jurisdiction, vessels
  mail ships, 615
  nationality of, 345–49, 557–58, 607, 646–47
  nonrecognized states, of, 151
  public commercial, 146–51
  public noncommercial, 149–50
  requisitioned, 150–51
  war, *see* Warships
Veto (UN), 292, 631
Vichy government (France), 671
Vienna
  Conference
    Consular Privileges and Immunities (1963), 406
    Diplomatic Intercourse and Immunities (1961), 12, 377, 396
    Law of Treaties (1968), 424, 449 (1969), 425
  Congress of (1814), 12, 45, 129, 302, 332
    regulation of diplomatic ranks, 376, 383
  Convention
    Consular Relations (1963), 406–17 *passim*
    Diplomatic Relations (1961), 12, 377, 378, 383–91 *passim*

Vienna (*cont.*)
  Convention (*cont.*)
    Law of Treaties (1969), 424, 426–50 *passim*
  School, 47
Vietnam, 71, 72
  North, 71, 614
  South, 71, 325n
  Vietnam Peace Talks (Paris), 383
  war in, 166, 526, 559, 587, 588, 695
Villa, Pancho, 169
Virgin Islands, 202n, 279
Visit and search, 325, 332, 333, 346, 608, 610, 613, 616, 636
Vitoria, Francisco de, 38–39, 465
Vlassov, General, 600
Voice of America, 174, 176
Volksgerichtshöfe, 673
Volstead Act, 353
Voluntary law, 41
Volunteers, foreign, 553–54

Wachusett, 636
Wallachia, 74
War
  aerial, 594–96
  allied belligerents, 551n, 554
  angary in, 659–61
  armed merchant vessels, 612–13, 625, 644–45
  armistices, 553, 554, 574–76, 617–18
  belligerent occupation, 200, 573, 606–607, 619, 661, 663–90
  blockade, hostile, 346, 505, 508, 542, 575–76, 605, 626, 636, 653–57, 658
  bombardment
    aerial, 596
    land, 585, 592–94
    naval, 616–17
  capitulations, 573
  cartel ships, 572, 615
  cessation of, 572
  chemicals, gases, poisons, 588–90
    Geneva Gas Protocol (1925), 544
  civilians, 553, 568–71
    see also Occupation, belligerent
  cobelligerents, 551n, 554
  combatants, lawful and unlawful, 551–54, 615–16
  commencement, 559–63
  Communist views, 49, 172, 526
  continuous voyage, 648–49, 655
  contraband, 346, 627, 640, 648, 651
  corporations, 555–57

War (*cont.*)
crimes, 596, 598–99, 608, 692–719
declaration of, 559–63, 665
economic, *see* Neutrality; Occupation, belligerent
enemy aliens, status of, 568–71
enemy character, 554–58, 606–607
enemy property (land)
private, 567–68
public, 565, 567
enemy property custodians, 567–68, 578, 579
enemy vessels, 557–58, 607–13, 614, 615
forbidden methods and weapons, 584–94
hostages, 694, 701, 702
immune vessels, 613–14, 615
insurgency and, 656–57
intermediacy concept of, 517, 529–30
international forces, 530–34, 546–48
irregular forces, 552–53, 583–84, 598, 668, 697, 698
just war, 625
on land, 582–602
lawfulness of, 177, 517–39
laws of, 541–58, 582–602, 604–90
laws of humanity in, 546, 606
legal effects of, 563–72
levée en masse, 553, 598, 668
locale of, 548–50
maritime, 604–20
see also Neutrality
mines, 549, 550, 613
necessity, military, 543, 545, 671, 683, 687–88, 702
neutral citizens in, 554–57
noncombatants in, 616
nuclear weapons, 590–92
participants in, 550–54, 583–84, 598
preventive, 133, 528–29
prisoners of, 572, 576–77, 596–601, 616, 695, 701, 702, 717–18
private, 496, 542, 604, 626
prize courts, 618, 642–43, 650, 652, 654, 655, 659, 687
property
private, 565, 578–79, 679–80, 682–83
public, 565, 680–82
see also Angary
relations between citizens, 565–67
renunciation of, 517–29
reprisals in, 656
requisitions, 670–71, 679–83
ruses, 585, 616

War (*cont.*)
savages, 553
spies, 585, 586–87, 697
subjugation, 280–83, 572–73
submarine cables, 618–20
submarines, 608–13, 614, 638, 641, 657
superior orders, 693, 695–96
suspension of hostilities, 571–72, 574–76
termination of, 572–79
treason, 211–14, 554, 698
treaties, effect on, 563–65, 577–78
truce, 574
unconditional surrender, 573–74
vessels, enemy
crews, 554, 598, 615–16
immune, 613–14
mail ships, 615
nationality of, 557–58
private, 565, 607, 687
public, 608–13, 637–38, 656–57
visit and search, 608, 610, 613, 616, 636
volunteers, foreign, 553–54, 548–50, 601
war and defense zones, 625, 640, 656
wounded and sick, 542, 544, 545, 597, 600, 601–602, 614
see also Neutrality
War Claims Act (1948), 578–79
War crimes, 175, 553, 596, 598–99, 608, 692–719
aggression, 521, 522, 525, 527–28, 692
allied statements, World War II, 701–702
extradition for, 257, 265
Leipzig trials, 700, 703
military courts and, 704–706
national trials, 704–706
Non-Applicability of Statutory Limitations on, Convention on, 193, 708
punishment of, 598–99, 695–712
see also Nuremberg International Military Tribunal; Genocide; United Nations
responsibility of commanders, 696
responsibility of heads of states, 696–97, 702, 711, 712
War of 1812, 564
Warmongering, 175
Warsaw ambassadorial talks, 100
Warsaw Pact, 166, 167
Warships, 346, 349, 356–58, 608–13, 643ff
immunities of, 356–58
innocent passage of, 291, 355–56, 637–38
neutral waters, in, 643–44, 645

Wartheland, 667
Washington
  Conference
    (1919), 610
    (1929), 468, 487
    American States (1889–90), 465
    Naval (1922), 595, 610, 658
  State, 179
  Treaty
    (1871), 465, 626
    Central America (1907 and 1923), 470
    Naval (1922), 595, 610, 658
Waters, territorial, *see* Territorial sea
Watersheds, 302
Water use, 305, 306n
Webster, Daniel, 64, 529
Webster, Methuel M., 307
Wei-hai-wei, 287
Western Samoa, 64, 77, 378
Westlake, John, 167
Westphalia, Peace of (1648), 302, 375, 383
Whaling, International Commission, 338
Whiteman, Marjorie M., 94
Wilhelm II, proposed trial of, 700
Wilkes Land, 285
Wilson, Robert R., 621
Wilson, Woodrow, 426, 434, 622
Wilson Doctrine, 98
Wireless telegraphy, treaties on, 369
Wisby, Sea Code of, 323
Wolff, Christian, 37

Women
  Declaration on Elimination of Discrimination Against, 192
  nationality of, 204–205
  Convention on, 205
World War I, 79, 117, 298, 328, 345, 360, 390, 395, 433, 549, 555, 557, 565, 566, 567, 569, 574, 587, 588, 592, 594, 595, 597, 602, 606, 612, 613, 614, 616, 617, 619, 627, 639, 641, 642, 643, 644, 646, 648, 649, 650, 651, 654, 655, 657, 658, 659, 660, 664, 680, 684, 699
World War II, 76, 111, 115, 180, 188, 217, 292, 329, 345, 520, 523, 527, 538, 546, 549, 552, 553, 555, 557, 558, 566, 567, 569, 573, 576, 578, 588, 589, 593, 596, 597, 600, 602, 607, 611, 613, 614, 617, 621, 622, 629, 635, 637, 641, 642, 649, 650, 651, 652, 664, 667, 669, 671, 673, 674, 675, 676, 677, 679, 680, 681, 683, 684, 686, 693, 695, 701, 703, 704, 713
Wrangel Island, 284
Wright, Quincy, 173, 175, 521, 624
Writers as sources of international law, 21

Yalta (Far Eastern) Agreement (1945), 424, 437
Yemen, 167, 394, 469, 499, 590
Yrujo's case, 382

Zambia, 166
Zouche, Richard, 36, 41, 42–43